Ireland

Contents

PLAN YOUR TRIP

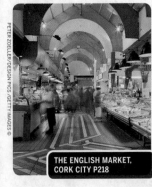

THE ENGLISH MARKET, CORK CITY P218

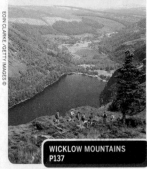

WICKLOW MOUNTAINS P137

ON THE ROAD

Contents

ON THE ROAD

Contents

SPECIAL FEATURES

Welcome to Ireland

A small country with a big reputation, helped along by a timeless, age-caressed landscape and a fascinating, friendly people, whose lyrical nature is expressed in the warmth of their welcome.

Ireland of the Postcard

Yes, it exists. Along the peninsulas of the southwest, the brooding loneliness of Connemara and the dramatic wildness of County Donegal. You'll also find it in the lakelands of Counties Leitrim and Roscommon and the undulating hills of the sunny southeast ('sunny' of course being a relative term). Ireland has modernised dramatically, but some things never change. Brave the raging Atlantic on a crossing to Skellig Michael or spend a summer's evening in the yard of a thatched-cottage pub and you'll experience an Ireland that has changed little in generations, and is likely the Ireland you most came to see.

Tread Carefully...

...for you tread on history. Ireland's history presents itself everywhere: from the breathtaking monuments of prehistoric Ireland at Brú na Bóinne to the fabulous ruins of Ireland's rich monastic past at Glendalough and Clonmacnoise. More recent history is visible in the *Titanic* museum in Cobh to the forbidding Kilmainham Gaol in Dublin. And there's history so young that it's still considered the present, best experienced on a black-taxi tour of West Belfast or an examination of Derry's astonishingly colourful political murals.

A Cultural Well

Throughout your travels you will be overwhelmed by the cultural choices on offer – a play by one of the theatrical greats in Dublin, a traditional music 'session' in a west-Ireland pub or a rock gig in a Limerick saloon. The Irish summer is awash with festivals celebrating everything from flowers in bloom to high literature.

Tá Fáilte Romhat

(Taw fall-cha row-at) – 'You're very welcome'. Or, more famously, *céad míle fáilte* – a hundred thousand welcomes. Irish friendliness is a tired cliché, an over-simplification of a character that is infinitely complex, but there's no denying that the Irish are warm and welcoming, if a little reserved at first. Wherever you meet them – the shop, the bar, the bank queue – there's a good chance a conversation will begin, pleasantries exchanged and, should you be a stranger in town, the offer of a helping hand extended. But, lest you think this is merely an act of unfettered altruism, rest assured that the comfort they seek is actually their own, for the Irish cannot be at ease in the company of those who aren't. A hundred thousand welcomes. It seems excessive, but in Ireland, excess is encouraged, so long as it's practised in moderation.

Why I Love Ireland

By Fionn Davenport, Author

There's an unvarnished informality about Ireland that I cherish, based on an implied assumption that life is a tangled, confusing struggle that all of us – irrespective of where we hail from, what our politics are and how we worship – have to negotiate to the best of our abilities. We're all in this together, come hell or high water, so we may as well be civil and share a moment when we can.

For more about our authors, see page 736

Above: Giant's Causeway, County Antrim

Ireland

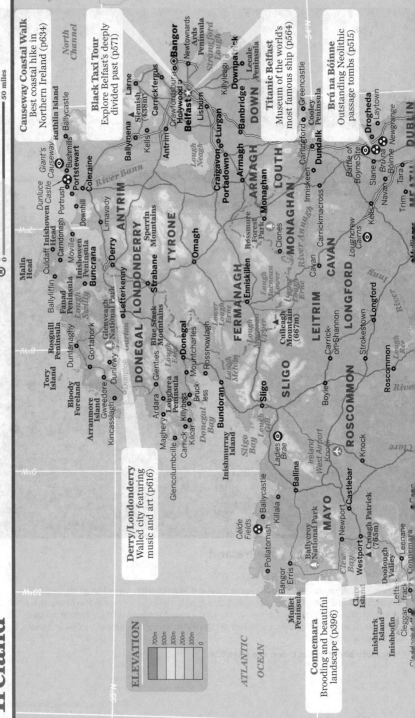

ELEVATION

700m
500m
300m
200m
100m
0

ATLANTIC OCEAN

North Channel

Causeway Coastal Walk
Best coastal hike in Northern Ireland (p634)

Black Taxi Tour
Explore Belfast's deeply divided past (p571)

Titanic Belfast
Museum of the world's most famous ship (p564)

Brú na Bóinne
Outstanding Neolithic passage tombs (p515)

Derry/Londonderry
Walled city featuring music and art (p616)

Connemara
Brooding and beautiful landscape (p396)

0 — 100 km
0 — 50 miles

Bangor
Newtownards
Ards Peninsula
Strangford Lough
Larne
Carrickfergus
kathlin Island
Ballycastle
Giant's Causeway
Bushmills
Portstewart
Dunluce Castle
Inishowen Castle
Culdaff
Carndonagh
Portrush
Downhill
Coleraine
Limavady
Crawfordsbur
Holywood
Belfast
Lisburn
Lurgan
Craigavon
Portadown
Banbridge
Downpatrick
Killyleagh
Lecale Peninsula
Greencastle
Carlingford
Cooley Peninsula
Dundalk
Drogheda
Laytown
Slane
Brú na Bóinne
Newgrange
Navan
Trim
Tara
DUBLIN

Malin Head
Moville
Inishowen Peninsula
Buncrana
Derry
Letterkenny
Strabane
Omagh
Sperrin Mountains
TYRONE
ANTRIM
LONDONDERRY
Ballymena
Kells
Antrim
Lough Neagh
ARMAGH
Armagh
Monaghan
MONAGHAN
Clones
Carrickmacross
Carrickmacross
LOUTH
Slemish (438m)

Rosguill Peninsula
Fanad Peninsula
Tory Island
Bloody Foreland
Gweedore
Dunlewy
Glenveagh National Park
Gortahork
Duntanaghy
Lough Swilly
Ardara
Glenties
Loughrea Peninsula
Maghery
DONEGAL
Blue Stack Mountains
Donegal
Mountcharles
Rossnowlagh
Bundoran
FERMANAGH
Enniskillen
Lower Lough Erne
Upper Lough Erne
Rossmore Forest Park
Cavan
CAVAN
Kells
Loughcrew Cairns
MEATH

Arranmore Island
Kincasslagh
Glencolumbcille
Carrick
Killybegs
Kilcar
Bruckless
Donegal Bay
Inishmurray Island
Sligo Bay
Ballysadare
Ladies Brae
Ballina
SLIGO
Sligo
Lough Gill
Carrick-on-Shannon
LEITRIM
Cuilcagh Mountain (667m)
Lough Macnean
Lough Melvin
Lough Allen
LONGFORD
Longford
Strokestown
ROSCOMMON
Roscommon
Lough Ree

Céide Fields
Pollatomish
Killala
Mullet Peninsula
Bangor Erris
Ballycroy National Park
MAYO
Newport
Castlebar
Westport
Croagh Patrick (765m)
Clew Bay
Doolough Valley
Leenane
Connemara
Letter
frack
Boyle
Knock
Ireland West Airport
Castlerea
CLARE
Clare Island
Inishturk Island
Inishbofin
Cleggan
ATLANTIC OCEAN

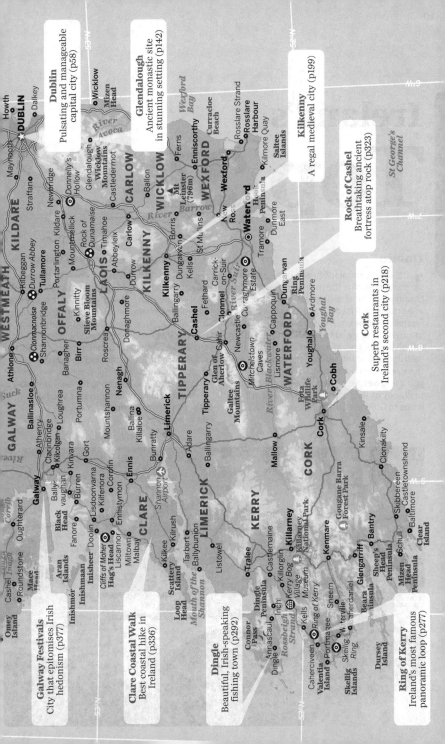

Dublin
Pulsating and manageable capital city (p58)

Glendalough
Ancient monastic site in stunning setting (p142)

Kilkenny
A regal medieval city (p199)

Rock of Cashel
Breathtaking ancient fortress atop rock (p323)

Cork
Superb restaurants in Ireland's second city (p218)

Ring of Kerry
Ireland's most famous panoramic loop (p277)

Dingle
Beautiful, Irish-speaking fishing town (p292)

Clare Coastal Walk
Best coastal hike in Ireland (p336)

Galway Festivals
City that epitomises Irish hedonism (p377)

Ireland's
Top 21

Dublin

1 Ireland's capital (p58) and largest city by some stretch is the main gateway into the country, but it has enough attractions to keep visitors mesmerised for at least a few days. From world-class museums and entertainment to superb dining and top-grade hotels, Dublin has all the baubles of a major international metropolis. But the real clinchers are Dubliners themselves, who are friendlier, more easy-going and welcoming than the burghers of virtually any other European capital. And it's the home of Guinness. O'Connell Bridge, Dublin

Connemara, County Galway

2 A filigreed coast of tiny coves and beaches is the Connemara Peninsula's (p396) beautiful border with the wild waters of the Atlantic. Wandering characterful roads brings you from one village to another, each with trad pubs and restaurants serving seafood chowder cooked from recipes that are family secrets. Inland, the scenic drama is even greater. In fantastically desolate valleys, green hills, yellow wildflowers and wild streams reflecting the blue sky provide elemental beauty. Rambles take you far from others, back to a simpler time. Mannin Bay, Connemara

HOLGER LEUE / GETTY IMAGES ©

The Pub

3 Every town and hamlet has at least one: no matter where you go, you'll find that the social heart of the country beats loudest in the pub, still the best place to discover what makes the country tick. In suitable surroundings – whether a quiet traditional pub with flagstone floors and a large peat fire or a more modern bar with flashing lights and music – take a moment or an evening to listen for that beating heart...and drink some decent beer in the process. Temple Bar, Dublin

Galway City

4 One word to describe Galway city? Craic! Ireland's liveliest city (p373) literally hums through the night at music-filled pubs where you can hear three old guys playing spoons and fiddles, or a hot, young band. Join the locals as they bounce from place to place, never knowing what fun lies ahead but certain of the possibility. Add in local bounty such as the famous oysters and nearby adventure in the Connemara Peninsula and the Aran Islands and the fun never ends. Quay Street, Galway

Glendalough, County Wicklow

5 St Kevin knew a thing or two about magical locations. When he chose a remote cave on a glacial lake nestled at the base of a forested valley as his monastic retreat, he inadvertently founded a settlement (p142) that would later prove to be one of Ireland's most dynamic universities and, in our time, one of the country's most beautiful ruined sites. The remains of the settlement (including an intact round tower), coupled with the stunning scenery, are unforgettable. Glendalough, County Wicklow

Dingle, County Kerry

6 Dingle is the name of both the picturesque peninsula (p290) jutting into the Atlantic from County Kerry, strewn with ancient ruins, and its delightful main town, the peninsula's beating heart. Fishing boats unload fish and shellfish that couldn't be any fresher if you caught it yourself, many pubs are untouched since their earlier incarnations as old-fashioned shops, artists sell their creations (including beautiful jewellery with Irish designs) at intriguing boutiques, and toe-tapping trad sessions take place around roaring pub fires. Harbour, Dingle

Traditional Music

7 Western Europe's most vibrant folk music is Irish traditional music (p684), which may have earned worldwide fame thanks to the likes of Riverdance but is best expressed in a more sedate setting, usually the pub. The west of Ireland is particularly musical: from Donegal down to Kerry there are centres of musical excellence, none more so than Doolin in County Clare, the unofficial capital of Irish music. It's unlikely you'll be asked to join in, but there's nothing stopping your foot from tapping and your hands from clapping. Kinnitty Castle bar

Walking & Hiking

8 Yes, you can visit the country easily enough by car, but Ireland is best explored on foot, whether you opt for a gentle afternoon stroll along a canal towpath or take on the challenge of any of the 31 way-marked long-distance routes. There are coastal walks and mountain hikes; you can explore towns and villages along the way or steer clear of civilisation by traipsing along lonely moorland and across barren bogs. All you'll need is a decent pair of boots and, inevitably, a rain jacket. Connemara

Brú na Bóinne, County Meath

9 Looking at once ancient and yet eerily futuristic, Newgrange's immense, round, white stone walls topped by a grass dome is one of the most extraordinary sights you'll ever see. Part of the vast Neolithic necropolis Brú na Bóinne (the Boyne Palace; p515), it contains Ireland's finest Stone Age passage tomb, predating the pyramids by some six centuries. Most extraordinary of all is the tomb's precise alignment with the sun at the time of the winter solstice. Newgrange

IIC / AXIOM / GETTY IMAGES ©

DORI OCONNELL / GETTY IMAGES ©

Rock of Cashel, County Tipperary

10 Soaring up from the green Tipperary pastures, this ancient fortress (p323) takes your breath away at first sight. The seat of kings and churchmen who ruled over the region for more than a thousand years, it rivalled Tara as a centre of power in Ireland for 400 years. Entered through the 15th-century Hall of the Vicars Choral, its impervious walls guard an awesome enclosure with a complete round tower, a 13th-century Gothic cathedral and the most magnificent 12th-century Romanesque chapel in Ireland.

Links Golf

11 If Scotland is the home of golf, then Ireland is where golf goes on holiday (p40). And the best vacation spots are along the sea, where the country's collection of seaside links are dotted in a steady string along virtually the entire Irish coastline, each more revealed than carved in the undulating, marram-grass-covered landscapes. Some of the world's best-known courses share spectacular scenery with lesser-known gems, and each offers the golfer the opportunity to test their skills against the raw materials provided by Mother Nature. Wicklow golf course

Cork City

12 The Republic's second city (p218) is second only in terms of size – in every other respect it will bear no competition. A tidy, compact city centre is home to an enticing collection of art galleries, museums and – most especially – places to eat. From cheap cafes to top-end gourmet restaurants, Cork City excels, although it's hardly a surprise given the county's exceptional foodie reputation. At the heart of it is the simply wonderful English Market, a covered produce market that is an attraction unto itself. Holy Trinity Church, Cork City

JÖRG GREUEL / GETTY IMAGES ©

Ring of Kerry

13 Driving around the Ring of Kerry (p277) is an unforgettable experience in itself, but you don't need to limit yourself to the main route. Along this 179km loop around the Iveragh Peninsula there are countless opportunities for detours. Near Killorglin, it's a short hop up to the beautiful, little-known Cromane Peninsula. Between Portmagee and Waterville, you can explore the Skellig Ring. The peninsula's interior offers mesmerising mountain views. And that's just for starters. Wherever your travels take you, remember to charge your camera battery! View from Valentia Island

Black Taxi Tour, Belfast

14 No trip to Northern Ireland is complete without visiting the Republican and Loyalist murals (p561) of Belfast's Falls and Shankhill districts. But for an outsider, the city's bitterly divided society can be hard to get your head around. Without a guide to provide some background and explanation, the murals can be just so much garish paint. Belfast's black taxi tours are justifiably famous because they provide that context, with drivers who are both insightful and darkly humorous without making light of a serious and often tragic situation. Falls Road murals

Kilkenny City

15 From its regal castle to its soaring medieval cathedral, Kilkenny (p197) exudes a permanence and culture that have made it an unmissable stop on journeys to the south and west. Its namesake county boasts scores of artisans and craftspeople and you can browse their wares at Kilkenny's classy shops and boutiques. Chefs eschew Dublin in order to be close to the source of Kilkenny's wonderful produce and you can enjoy the local brewery's namesake brew at scores of delightful pubs. St Canice's Cathedral and round tower, Kilkenny

Causeway Coastal Walk

16 Put on your walking boots and rucksack and set off along one of Ireland's finest coastal walks, stretching for 16 scenic kilometres between the swaying rope bridge of Carrick-a-Rede (p635) and the geological flourish of the Giant's Causeway (p631). This is coastal hiking at its best, offering an ever-changing vista of cliffs and islands, sandy beaches and ruined castles, framed by scenic, seabird-haunted Rathlin Island at one end and the cheering prospect of a dram or two at the Old Bushmills Distillery at the other. Carrick-a-Rede

Castles & Stately Homes

17 The Anglo-Normans left an indelible stamp on Ireland, best seen in the country's collection of handsome homes and impressive castles, built to reflect the power, glory and wealth of their respective owners. Although some have fallen into ruin, many have been meticulously maintained, including the superb country piles designed in the Georgian (or Palladian) style, found in pastoral settings around Dublin. Others have been converted from homes to luxury hotels and are memorable overnight experiences. Powerscourt Estate, County Wicklow

16

17

IIC/ AXIOM / GETTY IMAGES ©

Derry/ Londonderry

18 History runs deep in Northern Ireland's second city (p616). The symbols of the country's sectarian past are evident, from the 17th-century city walls, to the bipartite Republican/Loyalist name, Derry/Londonderry. But the new bridge that spans the River Foyle provides another symbol – an attempt to bridge that divide in a city filled with a restless creative energy. This is expressed in its powerful murals, vibrant music scene and numerous art works – it was the UK City of Culture 2013. Hands Across the Divide by Maurice Harron

A Gaelic Football or Hurling Match

19 It depends on whether you're in a football or hurling stronghold (some, like County Cork, are both) but attending a match of the county's chosen sport (p694) is not just a unique Irish experience but also a key to unlocking local passions and understanding one of the cultural pillars of Ireland. Whether you attend a club football match in County Galway or an intercounty hurling battle between old foes like Kilkenny and Tipperary, you cannot but be swept up in the emotion of it all. Women's hurling match

Titanic Belfast

20 The construction of the world's most famous ocean liner is celebrated in high-tech, multimedia glory at this wonderful new museum (p564). Not only can you explore virtually every detail of the *Titanic's* construction – including a simulated 'fly-through' of the ship from keel to bridge – but you can place yourself in the middle of the industrial bustle that were Belfast's shipyards at the turn of the 20th century. The experience is heightened by the use of photography, audio and – most poignantly – the only footage of the actual *Titanic* still in existence.

Clare Coast

21 Bathed in the golden glow of the late-afternoon sun, the iconic Cliffs of Moher (p358) are but one of the splendours of County Clare. From a boat bobbing below, the towering stone faces have a jaw-dropping dramatic beauty that's enlivened by scores of sea birds, including cute little puffins. Down south in Loop Head, pillars of rock towering above the sea have abandoned stone cottages whose very existence is inexplicable. All along the coast are cute little villages like trad-session-filled Ennistymon and the surfer mecca of Lahinch. Cliffs of Moher

ROBERT RIDDELL / GETTY IMAGES ©

Need to Know

For more information, see Survival Guide (p697)

Currency
Euro (€) Republic of Ireland
Pound Sterling (£) Northern Ireland

Language
English and Irish

Visas
Not required by most citizens of Europe, Australia, New Zealand, USA and Canada.

Money
Change bureaus and ATMs widely available, especially in cities and major towns. Credit cards accepted in all hotels, many B&Bs and most restaurants.

Mobile Phones
Phones from most other countries work in Ireland but attract roaming charges. Local SIM cards cost from €10; SIM and basic handset around €40.

Time
Western European Time (UTC/GMT November to March; plus one hour April to October).

When to Go

Warm to hot summers, mild winters

Belfast
GO May-Sep

Dublin
GO any time lots of indoor attractions

Galway
GO May-Sep

Kerry
GO May-Sep

Cork
GO May-Sep

High Season
(Jun–mid-Sep)

➡ Weather at its best.

➡ Accommodation rates at their highest (especially August).

➡ Tourist peak in Dublin, Kerry, southern and western coasts.

Shoulder
(Easter to end May, mid-Sep to end Oct)

➡ Weather often good, sun and rain in May. 'Indian summers' and often warm in September.

➡ Summer crowds and accommodation rates drop off.

Low Season
(Nov–Feb)

➡ Reduced opening hours from October to Easter; some destinations shut down.

➡ Cold and wet weather throughout the country; fog can reduce visibility.

➡ Big city attractions operate as normal.

Useful Websites

Entertainment Ireland (www.entertainment.ie) Countrywide listings for every kind of entertainment.

Failte Ireland (www.discoverireland.ie) Official tourist-board website – practical info and a huge accommodation database.

Lonely Planet (www.lonelyplanet.com/ireland) Destination information, hotel bookings, traveller forums and more.

Northern Ireland Tourist Board (www.nitb.com) Official tourist site.

Important Numbers

Include area codes only when dialling from outside the area or from a mobile phone. Drop the initial 0 when dialling from abroad.

Country code	☏353 Republic of Ireland +44 Northern Ireland
International access code	☏00
Emergency (police, fire, ambulance)	☏999

Exchange Rates

Australia	A$1	€0.67
Canada	C$1	€0.72
Japan	Y100	€0.77
New Zealand	NZ$1	€0.60
UK	£1	€1.17
USA	US$1	€0.75

For current exchange rates see www.xe.com

Daily Costs

Budget: Less than €60

➡ Dorm bed: €12–20

➡ Cheap meal in cafe or pub: €6–12

➡ Intercity bus travel (200km trip): €12–25

➡ Pint: €4.50–5

Midrange: €60–€120

➡ Double room in hotel or B&B (more expensive in Dublin): €40–100

➡ Main course in midrange restaurant: €10–18

➡ Car rental (per day): from €40

➡ Three-hour train journey: €65

Top End: More than €120

➡ Four-star hotel stay: from €150

➡ Three-course meal in good restaurant: around €50

➡ Top round of golf (midweek): from €80

Opening Hours

Banks 10am–4pm Monday to Friday (to 5pm Thursday)

Pubs 10.30am–11.30pm Monday to Thursday, 10.30am–12.30am Friday and Saturday, noon–11pm Sunday (30 minutes 'drinking up' time allowed); closed Christmas Day and Good Friday

Restaurants noon–10.30pm; many close one day of the week

Shops 9.30am–6pm Monday to Saturday (until 8pm Thursday in cities), noon–6pm Sunday

Arriving in Ireland

Dublin Airport (p131) Private coaches run every 10 to 15 minutes to the city centre (€7). Taxis take 30 to 45 minutes and cost €20 to €25.

Dun Laoghaire Ferry Port (p130) Public bus takes around 45 minutes to the centre of Dublin; DART (suburban rail) takes about 25 minutes.

Dublin Port Terminal (p130) Buses are timed to coincide with arrivals and departures; costs €2.50 to the city centre.

Getting Around

Transport in Ireland is efficient and reasonably priced to and from major urban centres; smaller towns and villages along those routes are well served. Service to destinations not on major routes is less frequent and often impractical.

Train A limited network links Dublin to all major urban centres, including Belfast in Northern Ireland. Expensive if you're on a budget.

Car The most convenient way to explore Ireland's every nook and cranny. Cars can be hired in every major town and city; drive on the left.

Bus An extensive network of public and private buses makes them the most cost-effective way to get around; there's service to and from most inhabited areas.

For much more on **getting around**, see p706

First Time Ireland

For more information, see Survival Guide (p697)

Checklist

➡ Make sure your passport is valid for at least six months past your arrival date

➡ Make all necessary bookings (accommodation, events and travel)

➡ Check the airline baggage restrictions

➡ Inform your debit/credit-card company

➡ Arrange appropriate travel insurance (p701)

➡ Check if you can use your mobile phone (p704)

What to Pack

➡ Good walking shoes, as Ireland is best appreciated on foot

➡ Raincoat – you will undoubtedly need it

➡ UK/Ireland electrical adapter

➡ Finely honed sense of humour

➡ A hollow leg – all that beer has to go somewhere

➡ Irish-themed MP3 playlist

Top Tips for Your Trip

➡ Quality rather than quantity should be your goal: instead of a hair-raising race to see everything, pick a handful of destinations and give yourself time to linger. The most memorable experiences in Ireland are often the ones where you're doing very little at all.

➡ If you're driving, get off the main roads when you can: some of Ireland's most stunning scenery is best enjoyed on secondary or tertiary roads that wind their narrow way through standout photo ops.

➡ Make the effort to greet the locals: the best experiences are to be had courtesy of the Irish themselves, whose helpfulness, friendliness and fun has not been overexaggerated.

What to Wear

You can wear pretty much whatever you want: smart casual is the most you'll need for fancy dinners, the theatre or the concert hall. Irish summers are warm but rarely hot, so you'll want something extra when the temperatures cool, especially in the evening. Ultimately, the ever-changeable weather will determine your outfits, but a light waterproof jacket should never be beyond reach for the almost inevitable rain.

Sleeping

From basic hostel to five-star hotel, you'll find every range of accommodation in Ireland. Advance bookings are generally recommended and an absolute necessity during the busy holiday period. See p698 for more information on accommodation.

➡ **Hotels** From chain hotels with comfortable digs to Norman castles with rainfall shower rooms and wi-fi – with prices to match.

➡ **B&Bs** From a bedroom in a private home to a luxurious Georgian townhouse, the ubiquitous B&B is the bedrock of Irish accommodation.

Money

ATMs are found pretty much everywhere. They're all linked to the main international money systems, allowing you to withdraw money with your own card – but be sure to check with your bank before you travel.

Credit and debit cards can be used almost everywhere except for some rural B&Bs that only accept cash. Make sure bars or restaurants will accept cards before you order. The most popular are Visa and MasterCard; American Express is only accepted by the major chains, and virtually no one will accept Diners or JCB. Chip-and-PIN is the norm for card transactions; only a few places will accept a signature.

If you don't want to rely on plastic, banks, post offices and some of the larger hotels will change cash and travellers cheques.

For more information, see p702.

Bargaining

Ireland doesn't do bargaining, at least not unless you're buying a horse.

Tipping

➡ **Hotels** €1/£1 per bag is standard; gratuity for cleaning staff at your discretion.

➡ **Pubs** Not expected unless table service is provided, then €1/£1 for a round of drinks.

➡ **Restaurants** For decent service 10%; up to 15% in more-expensive places.

➡ **Taxis** Tip 10% or round up fare to nearest euro/pound.

➡ **Toilet Attendants** Loose change; no more than 50c/50p.

Celebrating with pints of stout

Etiquette

Although largely informal in their everyday dealings, the Irish do observe some (unspoken) rules of etiquette.

➡ **Greetings** Shake hands with men, women and children when meeting for the first time and when saying goodbye. The Irish expect a firm handshake with eye contact. Female friends are greeted with a single (air) kiss.

➡ **Conversation** Generally friendly but often reserved, the Irish avoid conversations that might embarrass. They are deeply mistrustful of 'oversharers'.

➡ **Round System** The Irish generally take it in turns to buy a 'round' of drinks for the whole group and everyone is expected to take part. The next round should always be bought before the first round is drunk.

Eating

Booking ahead is recommended in cities and larger towns; same-day reservations are usually fine except for top-end restaurants – book those two weeks in advance.

➡ **Restaurants** From cheap cafe to Michelin-starred feast, covering every imaginable cuisine.

➡ **Cafes** Open during daytime (rarely at night), cafes are good for all-day breakfasts, sandwiches and basic dishes.

➡ **Pubs** Pub grub ranges from toasted sandwiches to carefully crafted dishes as good as any you'll find in a restaurant.

➡ **Hotels** All hotel restaurants take nonguests. They're a popular option in the countryside.

What's New

Remembering the Titanic

To mark the 2012 centenary of the world's most famous ocean liner, there's a brand-new multimedia museum in Belfast (p564), the city where it was built. The liner's last port of call before disappearing in the north Atlantic was Cobh in County Cork, which marked the anniversary by opening the Titanic Experience (p229) in the original office of the White Star company that owned the ship.

Croke Park Skyline, Dublin

The newest part of the Croke Park Experience is the Skyline, a guided tour around the stadium's roof that ends on a platform extending right over the pitch. (p98)

Medieval Museum, Waterford

The newest of Waterford's trio of museums devoted to exploring the city's 1000-year history is a fascinating exploration of Waterford during the Middle Ages. (p180)

Giant's Causeway Visitor Experience

New ecofriendly visitor centre with exhibits that explore in fun detail the geology and mythology of Northern Ireland's most famous natural attraction. (p634)

Crumlin Road Gaol, Belfast

Belfast's most notorious prison is now a brilliant museum where visitors experience first hand the conditions in which its myriad prisoners were kept. (p564)

Dingle Brewing Company

A new craft brewery in a converted creamery offers guided and self-guided tours, as well as the chance to drink a pint of its singular produce, Tom Crean's Fresh Irish Lager. (p292)

Jackie Clarke Collection, Ballina

One hundred thousand items spanning 400 years of Irish history: the superb efforts of one extraordinary collector are on display in a new museum housed in a converted 19th-century bank. (p430)

Athlone Castle Visitor Centre

An eclectic collection of exhibits ranging from displays on the Siege of Athlone to an old gramophone owned by local boy Count John McCormack make up the contents at this new visitor centre. (p508)

Forbidden Fruit, Dublin

Boutique festivals are the new megagig, and Forbidden Fruit, with its bespoke line-up of cool old bands and today's hipster favourites, is one of the best. (p93)

Restaurant 1826 Adare

An 1826-built thatched cottage is home to a new restaurant operated by Wade Murphy, one of Ireland's most respected chefs and purveyor of the very best of Irish cuisine. (p321)

For more recommendations and reviews, see lonelyplanet.com/ireland

If You Like...

Tracing Your Roots

Roughly 80 million people worldwide can claim to be part of, or descended from, the Irish diaspora, with about 41 million of those in the US alone. Most major towns have a heritage centre with a genealogical service.

Genealogy Advisory Service Based in the National Library in Dublin, this is the place to start your search for your Irish ancestors. (p70)

PRONI (Public Record Office of Northern Ireland) Belfast's purpose-built centre in the Titanic Quarter is the place to go to track down your Ulster family history. (p555)

Cobh, the Queenstown Story Cobh's superb heritage museum houses a genealogy centre. (p229)

Dún na Sí Heritage Centre A folk park 16km east of Athlone with an associated genealogical centre attached. (p508)

Ulster American Folk Park Ulster's rich links with the US explored in one of Northern Ireland's best museums. (p661)

Rothe House & Garden An excellent genealogical service is housed in this 16th-century merchant's house in Kilkenny City. (p199)

Literary Corners

Four Nobel laureates for literature are just the highlight of a rich literary tradition. Ireland is one of the English-speaking world's most notable heavyweights of the written word, a tradition that continues to thrive through contemporary writers and literary festivals.

Cape Clear Island International Storytelling Festival The storytelling tradition is kept alive by tales tall and long from all over the world. (p247)

Cúirt International Festival of Literature Galway attracts writers from far and wide to its April literary showcase. (p377)

Dublin Literary Tours No city of comparable size has been more written about or has produced as many great authors as the capital, so take one of its many literary tours to find out more. (p90)

Listowel Writers' Week The Irish literary festival, held in June in the home town of John B Keane. (p29)

Traditional Pubs

Everybody's got their favourite, so picking the best ones is a futile exercise. What can be done, however, is to select a handful that won't disappoint you, especially if you're looking for a traditional pub in the classic mould.

Blake's of the Hollow Ulster's best pint of Guinness in a Victorian classic. (p651)

John Benny's Stone slab floor, memorabilia on the walls and rocking trad sessions in this Dingle pub most nights. (p298)

McCarthy's A pub, restaurant and undertakers, all in one, in Fethard. (p334)

Morrissey's Half-pub, half-shop, this joint in Abbeyleix is one of the best drinking establishments on the whole island. (p487)

Séhán Ua Neáchtain In Galway, one of Ireland's best-known traditional pubs. (p383)

John Mulligan's The most famous of the capital's traditional pubs and a star of film and TV – where it usually plays itself. (p115)

Vaughan's Pub Superb bar in Kilfenora with outstanding reputation for traditional music. (p365)

Great Views

Irish scenery is among the most spectacular in Europe, with breathtaking views and stunning landscapes throughout the whole country. There are the famous spots, of course, but they're not alone.

Binevenagh Lake Spectacular views over Lough Foyle, Donegal and the Sperrin Mountains from the cliff top at the height of the Bishop's Road. (p629)

Clew Bay The 365 islands of this County Mayo bay are best viewed from the top of Croagh Patrick. (p419)

Kilkee Cliffs Jaw-dropping views of soaring cliffs that aren't the Cliffs of Moher. (p353)

Scarriff Inn Stunning views of Kenmare Bay and Bantry Bay from the windows of this Kerry restaurant. (p286)

Poisoned Glen The views down this Donegal valley are breathtaking; the final touch is the ruined church at the foot of the glen. (p467)

Priest's Leap A scenic cliff top on the north side of the Beara Peninsula with sensational views of Bantry Bay and the eponymous town. (p253)

Traditional Music

Western Europe's most vibrant folk music is kept alive by musicians who ply their craft (and are plied with drink) in impromptu and organised sessions in pubs and music houses throughout the country; even the 'strictly for tourists' stuff will feature excellent performances.

An Droichead Excellent music sessions at a Belfast arts centre dedicated to Irish culture. (p580)

Leo's Tavern Live nightly sessions in summer in a County Donegal pub owned by Enya's parents. (p466)

(Above) Cross of the Scriptures (p495), Clonmacnoise
(Below) Dún Aengus (p388), Aran Islands

Matt Molloy's The Chieftain's fife player owns this Westport pub where the live *céilidh* (session of traditional music and dancing) kicks off at 9pm nightly. (p423)

Miltown Malbay Every pub in this County Clare town features outstanding Irish trad sessions. (p355)

Tig Cóilí Galway's best trad sessions are held in a pub with a name that means 'house of music'. (p383)

Marine Bar Wonderful music nightly during summer months at this 200-year-old pub on the Ring Peninsula. (p189)

T&H Doolan's Wednesday evenings at this 300-year-old Waterford pub is informal jam night. (p183)

Live Music

A live gig in Ireland can be a transcendental experience as Irish music lovers go to great lengths to show their appreciation and love for their favourite musicians. There are venues in virtually every town, but some are truly special places to see a gig.

Whelan's The spiritual home of the singer-songwriter, this intimate Dublin venue allows fans to get up close and personal with their favourites. (p123)

Everyman Palace Theatre A respectful silence is the order of business when touring musicians take to the stage at this midsized venue in Cork City. (p225)

Róisín Dubh Galway loves live music, and this terrific pub venue is the place to hear emerging bands (and bands looking to hold on). (p383)

Sean's Bar A 100-year-old riverside bar in Athlone that has live music most nights in summer. (p509)

Peter Matthews The yard in this popular Drogheda pub has a great selection of live music most weekends. (p537)

Spirit Store Tiny harbourfront bar in Dundalk with a wonderful upstairs venue. (p540)

Family Days Out

There are family-friendly activities throughout the country, from heritage museums to ziplines across a forest canopy.

Dunlewey Lakeside Centre A combination craft shop, heritage museum, activity centre, concert venue and petting zoo in northwestern Donegal – the kids will especially enjoy the boat trips on the lake, complete with storyteller. (p466)

Lough Key Forest Park A 142-hectare adventure playland for the whole family, including a 300m-long canopy walk and an outdoor adventure playground, just outside Boyle in County Roscommon. (p500)

Great Western Greenway Flat and popular bike path from Westport to Achill with plenty of castles and sites to see along the way. Bikes for all ages available for rent as well as pick-up services for tired little (and big) legs. (p424)

Fota Wildlife Park Huge outdoor zoo just outside Cork City with ne'er a cage or fence in sight. The cheetah run is especially popular. (p228)

Tralee Bay Wetlands Centre When you're done learning about the habitats of this 300-hectare reserve, you can hop aboard a boat for the 15-minute safari ride. (p304)

Ancient Ruins

Thanks to the pre-Celts, Celts and early Christians, ancient and monastic sites are a feature of the Irish landscape. Thanks to the Vikings and Henry VIII, many of these are ruins, but no less impressive.

Askeaton The evocative 14th-century ruins of a castle, monastery and church. (p319)

Brú na Bóinne Europe's most impressive Neolithic burial site. (p515)

Carrowkeel Megalithic cemetery and majestic views. (p439)

Clonmacnoise Ireland's finest monastic site. (p495)

Devenish Island Ruins of an Augustinian monastery and near-perfect round tower on the biggest island in Lough Erne. (p656)

Dún Aengus Stunning Stone Age fort perched perilously on Inishmór's cliffs. (p388)

Glendalough Ruins of a once-powerful monastic city in stunning surroundings. (p142)

Month by Month

February

Bad weather makes February the perfect month for indoor activities. Some museums launch new exhibits, and it's a good time to visit the major towns and cities.

☆ Six Nations Rugby

Ireland, winners of the 2009 Grand Slam, play their three home matches at the Aviva Stadium in the Dublin suburb of Ballsbridge. The season runs from February to April.

Jameson Dublin International Film Festival

Most of Dublin's cinemas participate in the country's biggest film festival (www.jdiff.com), a two-week showcase for new films by Irish and international directors, which features local flicks, arty international films and advance releases of mainstream movies.

March

Spring is in the air, and the whole country is getting ready for arguably the world's most famous parade. Dublin's is the biggest, but every town in Ireland holds one.

St Patrick's Day

Ireland erupts into one giant celebration on 17 March (www.stpatricksday.ie), but Dublin throws a five-day party around the parade (attended by 600,000), with gigs and festivities that leave the city with a giant hangover.

April

The weather is getting better, the flowers are beginning to bloom and the festival season begins anew. Seasonal attractions start to open up around the middle of the month or at Easter.

☆ Circuit of Ireland International Rally

Northern Ireland's most prestigious rally race – known locally as the 'Circuit' (www.circuitofireland.net) – sees over 130 competitors throttle and turn through some 550km of Northern Ireland and parts of the Republic over two days at Easter.

☆ Irish Grand National

Ireland loves horse racing, and the race that's loved the most is the Grand National (www.fairyhouse.ie), the showcase of the national hunt season that takes place at Fairyhouse in County Meath on Easter Monday.

☆ World Irish Dancing Championships

There's far more to Irish dancing than Riverdance. Every April, some 4500 competitors from all over the world gather to test their steps and skills against the very best. The location varies from year to year; see www.irishdancing org.com for details.

May

The May Bank Holiday (on the first Monday) sees the first of the busy summer weekends as the Irish take to the roads to enjoy the budding good weather.

(Above) St Patrick's Day parade, Dublin
(Below) Oxegen, County Kildare

✿ Cork International Choral Festival

One of Europe's premier choral festivals (www.corkchoral.ie), with the winners going on to the Fleischmann International Trophy Competition; held over four days at the beginning of May.

✿ Cathedral Quarter Arts Festival

Belfast's Cathedral Quarter hosts a multidisciplinary arts festival (www.cqaf.com) including drama, music, poetry and street theatre over 10 days at the beginning of the month.

☆ North West 200

Ireland's most famous road race (www.northwest200.org) is also the country's biggest outdoor sporting event; 150,000-plus people line the triangular route to cheer on some of the biggest names in motorcycle racing. Held in mid-May.

✿ Fleadh Nua

The third week of May sees the cream of the traditional music crop come to Ennis, County Clare, for one of the country's most important festivals (www.fleadhnua.com).

✿ Listowel Writers' Week

Well-known writers engaged in readings, seminars and storytelling are the attraction at the country's premier festival (www.writersweek.ie) for bibliophiles, which runs over five days in the County Kerry town of Listowel at the end of the month. There's also poetry, music and drama.

June

The bank holiday at the beginning of the month sees the country spoilt for choice as to what to do. Weekend traffic gets busier as the weather gets better.

☆ The Cat Laughs Comedy Festival

Kilkenny gets very, very funny in early June with the country's premier comedy festival (www.thecat laughs.com), which draws comedians both known and unknown from the four corners of the globe.

☆ Irish Derby

Wallets are packed and fancy hats donned for the best flat-race festival in the country (www.curragh.ie), run during the first week of the month.

🎆 Bloomsday

Edwardian dress and breakfast of 'the inner organs of beast and fowl' are but two of the elements of the Dublin festival (p102) celebrating 16 June, the day on which Joyce's *Ulysses* takes place; the real highlight is retracing Leopold Bloom's steps.

🏃 Mourne International Walking Festival

The last weekend of the month plays host to a walking festival (www. mournewalking.co.uk) in the Mourne Mountains of County Down, designated an Area of Outstanding Natural Beauty.

July

There isn't a weekend in the month that a major festival doesn't take place, while visitors to Galway will find that the city is in full swing for the entire month.

☆ Willie Clancy Summer School

Inaugurated to celebrate the memory of a famed local piper, this exceptional festival of traditional music sees the world's best players show up for gigs, pub sessions and workshops over nine days in Miltown Malbay, County Clare (p355).

🎆 Galway Film Fleadh

Irish and international releases make up the program at one of the country's premier film festivals (www.galwayfilmfleadh. com), held in early July.

🎆 Galway Arts Festival

Music, drama and a host of artistic endeavours are on the menu at the most important arts festival (www. galwayartsfestival.com) in the country, which sees Galway go merriment mad for the last two weeks of the month.

🎆 Oxegen

Ireland's version of Glastonbury (albeit for a younger crowd) is a three-day supergig (www.oxegen.ie) in mid-July at Punchestown Racecourse in County Kildare, featuring some of the big names in dance music and pop.

🎆 Killarney Summerfest

From kayaking to street theatre to gigs by international artists, this week-long extravaganza (www. killarneysummerfest.com) in late July has something for everybody.

August

Schools are closed, the sun is shining (or not!) and Ireland is in holiday mood. Seaside towns and tourist centres are at their busiest as the country looks to make the most of its time off.

☆ Galway Race Week

The biggest horse-racing festival (www.galwayraces. com) west of the Shannon is not just about the horses, it's also a celebration of Irish culture, sporting gambles and elaborate hats.

🎆 Mary From Dungloe

Ireland's second-most important beauty pageant (www.maryfromdungloe. com) takes place in Dungloe, County Donegal, at the beginning of the month – although it's an excuse for a giant party, the young women really do want to be crowned the year's 'Mary'.

🎆 Féile An Phobail

The name translates simply as the 'people's festival' and it is just that: Europe's largest community arts festival (www.feilebelfast.com) takes place on the Falls Rd in West Belfast over two weeks.

Puck Fair

Ireland's oldest festival (www.puckfair.ie) is also its quirkiest: crown a goat king and celebrate for three days. Strange idea, brilliant festival that takes place in Killorglin, County Kerry in mid-August.

Rose of Tralee

The Irish beauty pageant (p304) sees wannabe Roses plucked from Irish communities throughout the world competing for the ultimate prize. For everyone else, it's a big party.

Fleadh Cheoil na hÉireann

The mother of all Irish music festivals (www.com haltas.ie), usually held at the end of the month, attracts in excess of 250,000 music lovers and revellers to whichever town is playing host – there's some great music amid the drinking.

September

Summer may be over, but September weather can be surprisingly good, so it's often the ideal time to enjoy the last vestiges of the sun as the crowds dwindle.

Dublin Fringe Festival

Upwards of 100 different performances take the stage, the street, the bar and the car in the fringe festival (www.fringefest. com) that is unquestionably more innovative than the main theatre festival that follows it.

All-Ireland Finals

The second and fourth Sundays of the month see the finals of the hurling and Gaelic football championships respectively, with 80,000-plus crowds thronging into Dublin's Croke Park for the biggest sporting days of the year.

Galway International Oyster Festival

Over the last weekend of the month Galway kicks off its oyster season with a festival (www.galwayoys terfest.com) celebrating the local catch. Music and beer have been the accompaniment since its inception in 1953.

October

The weather starts to turn cold, so it's time to move the fun indoors again. The calendar is still packed with activities and distractions, especially over the last weekend of the month.

Dublin Theatre Festival

The most prestigious theatre festival (www.dublin theatrefestival.com) in the country sees new work and new versions of old work staged in theatres and venues throughout the capital.

Belfast Festival at Queen's

Northern Ireland's top arts festival (www.belfastfesti val.com) attracts performers from all over the world for the second half of the month; on offer is everything from visual arts to dance.

Wexford Opera Festival

Opera fans gather in the Wexford Opera House, the country's only theatre built for opera, to enjoy Ireland's premier lyric festival (www. wexfordopera.com), which tends to eschew the big hits in favour of lesser-known works.

Guinness Cork Jazz Festival

Ireland's best-known jazz festival (www.guinness jazzfestival.com) sees Cork taken over by more than a thousand musicians and their multitude of fans during the last weekend of the month.

December

Christmas dominates the calendar as the country prepares for the feast with frenzied shopping and after-work drinks with friends and family arrived home from abroad. On Christmas Day nothing is open.

Christmas

This is a quiet affair in the countryside, though on 26 December (St Stephen's Day) the ancient custom of Wren Boys is re-enacted, most notably in Dingle, County Kerry, when groups of children dress up and go about singing hymns.

Christmas Dip

A traditional Christmas Day swim at the Forty Foot in the Dublin suburb of Sandycove sees a group of very brave swimmers go for a 20m swim to the rocks and back.

Itineraries

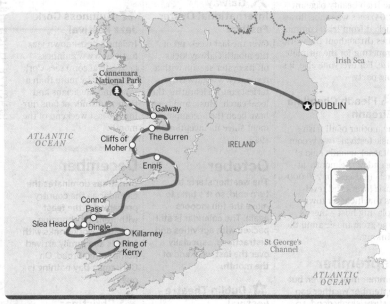

Ireland Highlights

This 300km-tourist trail takes you past some of Ireland's most famous attractions and through spectacular countryside. Start with a whistle-stop tour of **Dublin**, including visits to Trinity College and the Book of Kells as well as a sample of Guinness in its home town. The next day, head west to **Galway**, from where you should take a drive through stunning, brooding **Connemara** (which can be driven in a nice loop) before heading south through the moonlike landscape of **The Burren**. Take a detour to the **Cliffs of Moher**, then head to **Ennis**, a good spot to enjoy a bit of traditional Irish music. Keep going south through the **Connor Pass** into County Kerry, stopping for a half-day in **Dingle** before setting out to visit its peninsula, taking in the views and prehistoric monuments of **Slea Head**. Via the ferry, continue on to **Killarney**, the perfect base from which to explore the famous **Ring of Kerry**, a much-trafficked 179km loop around the Iveragh Peninsula.

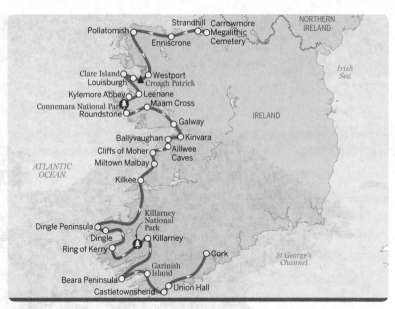

Best of the West

The west of Ireland is rightly at the top of most people's must-visit lists. Start in County Sligo, where prehistory and panorama combine to wonderful effect at **Carrowmore Megalithic Cemetery**. Wind your way south along the coast, stopping at some of Ireland's best surf beaches like **Strandhill** and **Enniscrone**, to the pretty village of **Pollatomish**. Continue south to the pub-packed heritage town of **Westport**. Southwest of here is magnificent **Croagh Patrick**, which is worth a climb if only to feast your eyes from a height on island-studded Clew Bay. Go west to **Louisburgh**, from where you can head offshore to craggy **Clare Island** (home of the pirate queen Grace O'Malley), before turning south along the beautiful Doolough Valley to **Leenane**, situated on Ireland's only fjord. This is the northern gateway to **Connemara**, which you can explore via the beautiful coastal route, passing **Kylemore Abbey**, venturing onto Clifden's scenic Sky Road and then winding your way around the coast through pretty **Roundstone**. Alternatively, you could savour the stunning wilderness of the inland route through **Maam Cross** to **Galway**, where you should devote at least a day to exploring its colourful streets and wonderful pubs.

South of Galway, the fishing villages of **Kinvara** and **Ballyvaughan** are at the edge of the strange karst landscape of The Burren, home to all manner of flora and fauna, as well as big-ticket attractions like the ancient **Aillwee Caves** and the **Cliffs of Moher**. Going south, be sure to sample some of Ireland's exquisite traditional music by attending a session in one of the pubs of **Miltown Malbay**; beach lovers should also opt for a stop in **Kilkee**, a favourite with surfers.

The easiest way to cross into County Kerry is via the ferry at Killimer. Take a day to explore the **Dingle Peninsula**, with its rich menu of ancient sites and stunning views, before overnighting in **Dingle** – one of the prettiest towns along the entire west coast. Take another day to explore the world-famous **Ring of Kerry**, ending in **Killarney National Park**, right on the edge of **Killarney** itself. Take the scenic route across the middle of the **Beara Peninsula** and make your way to the Italianate **Garinish Island**, with its exotic flowers. Then follow the coast through **Castletownshend** and the fishing village of **Union Hall** to the city of **Cork**.

DAVID EPPERSON / GETTY IMAGES ©

Top: Giant's Causeway, County Antrim

Bottom: Stone circle, Beara Peninsula

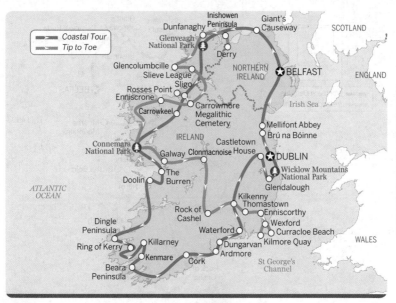

Coastal Tour
Tip to Toe

SCOTLAND
ENGLAND
Inishowen Peninsula
Dunfanaghy
Giant's Causeway
Glenveagh National Park
Derry
NORTHERN IRELAND
BELFAST
Glencolumbcille
Slieve League
Sligo
Rosses Point
Enniscrone
Carrowmore Megalithic Cemetery
Carrowkeel
Irish Sea
Mellifont Abbey
Brú na Bóinne
IRELAND
Connemara National Park
Galway
Castletown House
Clonmacnoise
DUBLIN
Wicklow Mountains National Park
The Burren
Doolin
Glendalough
ATLANTIC OCEAN
Rock of Cashel
Kilkenny
Thomastown
Enniscorthy
Wexford
Curracloe Beach
Dingle Peninsula
Waterford
Kilmore Quay
WALES
Ring of Kerry
Killarney
Dungarvan
Ardmore
Kenmare
Cork
St George's Channel
Beara Peninsula

Coastal Tour
3 WEEKS

Start in **Dublin**, then head north to the Neolithic necropolis at **Brú na Bóinne**. Continue on to **Mellifont Abbey** before crossing the border into Northern Ireland and heading to **Belfast**. Go northwest along the Antrim coast to the **Giant's Causeway**. Continue around the coastline of north Donegal, stopping at **Glenveagh National Park**. Head south into **Sligo** and climb the Stone Age passage grave at **Carrowkeel** for views of Lough Arrow. Make your way to the southwest via **Connemara**. Wonder at **The Burren** and check out traditional music in **Doolin** before crossing into County Kerry and exploring the **Dingle Peninsula**. Go through **Killarney** on your way round the **Ring of Kerry**. Camp in **Kenmare** and explore the **Beara Peninsula**, then Ireland's second city, **Cork**. Explore County Waterford from seaside **Ardmore**. Visit **Dungarvan** and its castle, and the Museum of Treasures in **Waterford**. Go north through Thomastown to St Canice's Cathedral in **Kilkenny** before exploring the city's medieval core. Visit **Castletown House** in County Kildare, then cut east to **Glendalough** in the **Wicklow Mountains National Park**. Head back to Dublin.

Tip to Toe
2 WEEKS

Begin in Northern Ireland's second city, **Derry**, walking the city walls and exploring the Bogside district. Then cross into County Donegal and explore the **Inishowen Peninsula** before overnighting in **Dunfanaghy**. Move down Donegal's coastline and check out the monastic ruins of **Glencolumbcille** and the sea cliffs at **Slieve League**. Cross into County Sligo and visit the **Carrowmore Megalithic Cemetery** before checking in to your **Sligo Town** hotel. The next day, treat yourself to a round of golf at the County Sligo Golf Course at **Rosses Point** or a seaweed bath in **Enniscrone**. You'll skirt the eastern edge of **Connemara** as you travel south to **Galway**, from where you should strike out for **Clonmacnoise**, a 6th-century monastic site. From here, move through the heart of the Midlands to another monastic gem, the **Rock of Cashel**. Medieval **Kilkenny** is only an hour away – visit its stunning castle before exploring nearby **Thomastown** and Jerpoint Abbey. Using **Wexford** as a base, explore **Curracloe Beach** and visit **Enniscorthy** and the excellent National 1798 Rebellion Centre. Or you could chill out and watch the fishermen draw in their lines in **Kilmore Quay**.

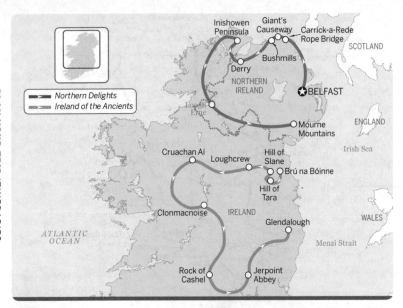

Northern Delights
Ireland of the Ancients

10 DAYS — Northern Delights

Start in **Belfast**, where you should take a black taxi tour and/or visit the docks on a boat trip, before heading north toward the Antrim coast and the **Carrick-a-Rede Rope Bridge**. Nearby is the Unesco World Heritage–listed **Giant's Causeway**, which shouldn't be missed by any visitor to Northern Ireland, and just beyond it the fascinating village of **Bushmills**, home to the famous distillery. **Derry** is worth a day – walk the city's walls and explore its more recent past in the Bogside district, and then cross the invisible border into the Republic by visiting the **Inishowen Peninsula** in County Donegal. Back in the North, go southeast to **Lough Erne**, taking in both White Island and the carved stones of Devenish Island before heading east to the famed **Mourne Mountains**, where you can hike along ancient smugglers' trails – or just admire the fabulous views before heading back to Belfast.

1 WEEK — Ireland of the Ancients

Begin at the stunning Neolithic tombs of Newgrange and Knowth in County Meath, in the heart of **Brú na Bóinne**. Nearby, stand at the top of the celebrated **Hill of Tara**, a site of immense folkloric significance and seat of the high kings of Ireland until the 11th century. Across the plain is the **Hill of Slane**, where St Patrick lit a fire in 433 to proclaim Christianity throughout the land. To the west is the Neolithic monument of **Loughcrew** – a quieter alternative to Brú na Bóinne. Keep going west to County Roscommon. Just outside Tulsk village is **Cruachan Aí**, the most important Celtic site in Europe. Head south to **Clonmacnoise**, the 6th-century monastic site in County Offaly, then continue through the heart of the country to the impressive **Rock of Cashel** in County Tipperary. Turn east and head through County Kilkenny, stopping at the Cistercian **Jerpoint Abbey**, at the pretty village of Thomastown. From here, travel northeast to Wicklow and magnificent **Glendalough**, where the substantial remains of a monastic settlement linger by two beautiful lakes.

Plan Your Trip
The Great Outdoors

It may not always have full cooperation from the weather, but Ireland is a country best appreciated out of doors. Whether you're a hiker, a cyclist, a surfer or an angler, it's merely a question of donning the right gear and going for it: there is something extraordinarily invigorating – never mind refreshing – about hiking in a summer storm or cycling into the teeth of a blowing gale. Then the clouds break and the sun appears, and you can while away an evening with a fishing pole by the banks of a river or catch a late wave when the rest of Europe has turned in for the evening.

Walking

There is simply no better way of experiencing this wildly beautiful country than on foot or on two wheels – and the rewards can be spectacular. From rolling hills of green to lush riparian woods, from rugged limestone escarpments to broad sandy beaches, and from dramatic sea cliffs to blankets of bog stretching as far as the eye can see, Ireland's landscapes will never disappoint.

There are, however, some issues that have made what should be some of the best walking in Europe a frustrating or even disappointing experience. Some trails run through kilometres of tedious forestry tracks and bitumen roads. The ways are marked with signposts showing the standard yellow arrow and hiker – in theory at least: waymarking is often variable and in some cases totally nonexistent. Ireland has a tradition of relatively free access to open country, but the growth in the number of walkers and the carelessness of a few have made some farmers less obliging. Unfortunately, it's not uncommon to find unofficial signs on gateways barring access

Best Outdoors

Best Long-Distance Routes
Wicklow Way (County Wicklow), Beara Way (County Cork), Dingle Way (County Derry), Kerry Way (County Kerry)

Best for Short Walks
Glendalough (County Wicklow), Connemara (County Galway), Lough Key (County Roscommon), Antrim Coast (County Antrim)

Best Surf Spots
Bundoran (County Donegal), Easkey (County Sligo), Mullaghmore (County Sligo), Rossnowlagh (County Donegal)

or physical barriers blocking ways. If you come across this problem, refer to the local tourist office.

The maintenance and development of the ways is administered in the Republic by the **National Trails Office** (☏01-860 8800; www.irishtrails.ie) and in the North by **Outdoor Recreation Northern Ireland** (☏9030 3930; www.outdoorrecreationni.com).

If you don't have a travelling companion you could consider joining an organised walking group. **South West Walks Ireland** (☏066-712 8733; www.southwestwalksireland. com; 6 Church St, Tralee, Co Kerry) provides a series of guided and self-guided walking programs around the southwest, north-west and Wicklow.

Where to Walk

For a small country, Ireland is packed with choice – from seaside ambles to long-distance treks in mountain ranges.

Day Walks

In just about any part of Ireland you can take a leisurely day hike.

➡ **Barrow Towpath** Along the River Barrow in Counties Carlow and Kilkenny, perfectly pleasant walks can be had along the towpath from Borris to Graiguenamanagh. (p157)

➡ **Glendalough** The wooded trails around this ancient monastic site in County Wicklow lure many a traveller from nearby Dublin for a few hours' rambling. (p142)

➡ **Lough Key Forest Park** The woods around this lake in County Roscommon have a wonderful canopied trail. (p500)

➡ **Sky Road** In County Galway, Clifden's Sky Road yields views of the Connemara coast; it's suitable for walking or cycling. (p402)

➡ **South Leinster Way** The prettiest section of this waymarked way is a 13km hike between the charming villages of Graiguenamanagh and Inistioge in County Kilkenny. (p213)

Coastal Walks

Ireland's coastlines are naturally conducive to long and reflective walks with or without shoes on. If that sounds like your particular nirvana, the coast of County Galway's Connemara and the pristine beaches of Counties Mayo and Sligo beckon. Some coastal walks, however, present unexpected challenges.

➡ **Causeway Coast Way** County Antrim is rife with rocky trails above the surf. Particularly spectacular is the final 16.5km of this waymarked way, starting from Carrick-a-Rede. (p631)

➡ **Wexford Coastal Walk** Following 221km of trails overlooking the bones of old shipwrecks.

Mountain Hikes

Ireland's mountain ranges aren't as magnificent as the Alps, but they do offer gratifying hill-walking opportunities, many of which can be done in a day.

➡ **Brandon Way** Not to be confused with Mt Brandon in County Kerry, the smaller Brandon Hill (516m) in County Kilkenny has a path that wends up to the summit from woodlands and moorlands along the River Barrow. (p213)

➡ **Killarney National Park** Superb and challenging routes for the walker. The top walk, of course, is up Mt Carrantuohil (1039m), the highest peak in all Ireland. (p270)

➡ **Mourne Mountains** You'll find Northern Ireland's best hill walking in the mountains of County Down. In this range, Northern Ireland's highest peak, Slieve Donard (853m),

---

WALKING GUIDES & MAPS

For comprehensive coverage of a selection of long and short walking routes, we (naturally) recommend Lonely Planet's very own *Hiking in Ireland*, which also covers places to stay and eat along the way. There are a host of other good walking guides for Ireland, including Michael Fewer's *Irish Long Distance Walks* and *Best Irish Walks* by Joss Lynam.

EastWest Mapping (☏053-937 7835; www.eastwestmapping.ie) has good maps of long-distance walks in the Republic and the North. Tim Robinson of **Folding Land-scapes** (☏095-35886; www.foldinglandscapes.com) produces superbly detailed maps of The Burren, the Aran Islands and Connemara. His and Joss Lynam's *The Mountains of Connemara: A Hill Walker's Guide* contains a useful detailed map.

Top: River, Killarney National Park (p270)

Bottom: Walking the Beara Way (p258)

EOIN CLARKE / GETTY IMAGES ©

is within reach on a day's walk from the town of Newcastle. (p601)

➡ **Mt Leinster** This County Wexford peak affords views of five counties from its 796m summit. (p178)

➡ **Mt Brandon** The highest peak (951m) on the Dingle Peninsula has spectacularly rugged trails that yield jaw-dropping views. (p302)

Waymarked Ways

The country's network of 31 long-distance 'waymarked ways' can keep a traveller walking for a week or longer. Though many of these run on for several hundred kilometres, you can jump in or jump out as you see fit.

➡ **Beara Way** A moderately easy loop of 196km that follows historic routes and tracks on a stunning peninsula in West Cork. (p258)

➡ **Burren Way** This 123km walk takes in County Clare's unique rocky landscape, the Cliffs of Moher and the musical town of Doolin. (p360)

➡ **Cavan Way** Impressive topographic variety packed into a short 26km route, taking in bogs, Stone Age monuments and the source of the River Shannon. (p543)

➡ **Dingle Way** A popular 168km route in County Kerry that loops around one of Ireland's most beautiful peninsulas. (p293)

➡ **East Munster Way** Starting in County Tipperary and ending up in County Waterford, a 70km walk through forest and open moorland, and along the towpath of the River Suir. (p334)

MORE WALKS IN IRELAND

➡ The Great Sugarloaf, County Wicklow (p151)

➡ Mt Seefin, County Cork (p253)

➡ Macgillycuddy's Reeks, County Kerry (p275)

➡ Tipperary Heritage Trail, County Tipperary (p328)

➡ Killary Harbour, County Galway (p407)

➡ Inisheer, County Galway (p393)

➡ Slieve Donard, County Down (p600)

➡ Fair Head, County Antrim (p631)

➡ The Cliffs of Magho, County Fermanagh (p658)

➡ **Kerry Way** A 214km route that takes in the spectacular Macgillycuddy's Reeks and the Ring of Kerry coast. (p268)

➡ **Ulster Way** A footpath totalling 900km, making a circuit around the six counties of Northern Ireland and Donegal. It can easily be broken down into smaller sections. (p656)

➡ **Wicklow Way** Ireland's most popular walking trail is this 132km route, which starts in southern Dublin and ends in Clonegal in County Carlow. (p198)

Golfing

With over 400 courses dotted around the island, golf is one of Ireland's most popular pastimes. There are plenty of parkland courses, but the more memorable golf experience is had on a seaside links – the Irish coastline is home to 30% of the world's links.

Most golf courses are privately owned, but all welcome nonmember bookings and walk-in green fees: to avoid disappointment, book the better-known courses in advance. For the top courses, expect to pay €80 to €100 per round; lesser-known courses charge as little as €25, depending on when you play. Some courses will insist that you have a registered handicap from your home country. Most courses will also rent clubs, but they're not usually very good.

Our favourite courses:

➡ Ballybunion Golf Club, County Kerry (p308)

➡ Royal Portrush Golf Club, County Londonderry (p630)

➡ County Sligo Golf Course, County Sligo (p437)

➡ Waterville Golf Links, County Kerry (p286)

➡ **Killeen Castle** (www.killeencastle.com; Dunsany, Co Meath; green fee €30-50)

For more information, check out **Golf Ireland** (www.golf.discoverireland.ie), a division of Fáilte Ireland, or the **Golfing Union of Ireland** (www.gui.ie), both of which offer booking services. There are specials and discounted green fees available throughout the year: a good online resource is www.teetimes.ie, where you can book heavily discounted green fees at dozens of courses throughout the country.

Cycling

Cyclists will have to share the road with the motorised bully, but they can find solace in scenic routes through sparsely populated countryside or along rugged coasts.

The tourist boards can supply you with a list of operators who organise cycling holidays. For group tours, try Irish Cycling Safaris (p708), which organises tours in the southwest, the southeast, Connemara and Counties Clare, Donegal and Antrim.

You can cycle the length and breadth of the country if you like, but you'll spend most of the time fighting off traffic and concrete views. There are, however, some stunning cycleways.

➜ **West Clare Cycleway** This 70km signposted cycleway stretches from Killimer on the Shannon Estuary (where you can get the Shannon Ferry to Tarbert in County Kerry) to Lahinch in County Clare. For more information, check out www. shannonregiontrails.ie.

➜ **Killarney National Park** The park has an adventurous 55km bike route that takes a scenic route via the lakes past Kate Kearney's Cottage to Lord Brandon's Cottage. (p271)

➜ **Kingfisher Trail** A waymarked, long-distance cycling trail stretching some 370km along the back roads of Counties Fermanagh, Leitrim, Cavan and Monaghan. (p650)

Horse Riding

Whether it's a gentle hack or a gallop across a wild beach, riding is one of Ireland's most beloved pastimes, and there's something for riders of every level. There are hundreds of centres throughout Ireland, offering possibilities ranging from a one-hour walk (from €25/15 per adult/child) to fully packaged, residential equestrian holidays.

Surprisingly, there is no legislation governing the set-up and conduct of horse yards, but the **Association of Irish Riding Establishments** (AIRE; ✆045-850 800; www. aire.ie; Beech House, Millennium Park, Naas, Co Kildare) has over 200 member schools and centres spread throughout the country. Being AIRE-approved means that the yard has qualified instructors, a resident first-aider, child-protection schemes and insurance certification – and, crucially, that all

---

TOP ADVENTURE CENTRES

Adventure centres can be found around Ireland, especially near the coast. These centres make it easy for travellers to indulge in such activities as canoeing, surfing, kayaking, orienteering, hiking, climbing and other sports. Some also provide accommodation. Here's a select list:

➜ Killary Adventure Centre (p407), County Galway

➜ Lilliput Adventure Centre (p511), County Westmeath

➜ Dunmore East Adventure Centre (p184), County Waterford

➜ Donegal Adventure Centre (p455), County Donegal

➜ Life Adventure Centre (p604), County Down

---

of the horses are maintained according to an acceptable standard of care. We recommend that you stick to AIRE-approved centres.

Water Sports

Ireland has 3100km of coastline and numerous rivers and lakes, so no matter where in the country you may be, you're never far from a place to surf, windsurf, scuba dive, paddle a canoe, swim or simply cast a line into a cool stream ribboned with salmon. Outfitters and information sources abound.

Surfing & Windsurfing

Surfing is all the rage on the coast, especially in the west. The most popular spots include the following:

➜ **County Donegal** The unofficial capital of Irish surfing, Bundoran (p454), hosts the Irish national championships in April. Along the coast there are at least half a dozen top-rated spots for beginners and advanced surfers to test their skills. Windsurfing and kitesurfing are equally popular around Port-na-Blagh (p470).

➜ **County Sligo** Easkey (p442) and Strandhill (p438) are famous for their year-round surf, and have facilities for travellers who seek room and board (with the room being optional).

Top: Hiker, Mourne
Mountains (p601)

Bottom: Surfer at
Bundoran (p454)

➡ **County Clare** Nice breaks at Kilkee (p352), Lahinch (p356) and Fanore (p367).

➡ **County Waterford** Tramore Beach (p470) is a coastal resort that's home to Ireland's largest surf school.

➡ **County Wexford** Surfing and windsurfing are popular in the shallow waters off Rosslare Strand (p169).

➡ **County Antrim** The beaches around Portrush (p632) afford good surfing and bodysurfing. The swells are highest and the water warmest in September and October.

Sailing

Ireland has over 120 yacht and sailing clubs. The southwestern coast – especially between Cork and Dingle – is popular, as is the coast of Antrim, the sheltered coasts north and south of Dublin, and some of the larger lakes like Loughs Derg, Erne and Gill. The **Irish Association for Sail Training** (☎01-605 1621; www.irishmarinefederation. com) watches over professional schools; the national governing body is the **Irish Sailing Association** (☎01-280 0239; www. sailing.ie).

Scuba Diving

Ireland's west coast has some of the best scuba diving in Europe. The best period for diving is roughly March to October. Visibility averages more than 12m, but can increase to 30m on good days. For more details about diving, contact Ireland's diving regulatory body, Comhairle Fó-Thuinn (CFT), also known as the **Irish Underwater Council** (☎01-284 4601; www.cft.ie); it publishes the dive magazine *SubSea* (available online).

Fishing

Fishing – either in the sea or a river – is a popular pastime. Ireland is justly famous for its (generally no-fee) coarse fishing, eg bream, pike, perch, roach, rudd, tench, carp and eel. The killing of pike over 6.6lb (3kg) in weight is prohibited, so anglers are limited to one pike; the killing of coarse fish is frowned upon and anglers are encouraged to return coarse fish to the water alive. Freshwater game fish available here include salmon, sea trout and brown trout. Some managed fisheries also stock rainbow trout.

The enormous Shannon and Erne river systems, stretching south from Counties Leitrim and Fermanagh, are prime angling spots, and Cavan, the 'Lake County', is a favourite with hard-core anglers. In the west, the great lakes of Corrib and Conn have plenty of lake-shore B&Bs, good sturdy boats and knowledgable boaters.

Rock Climbing

Ireland's mountain ranges aren't high – Mt Carrantuohil in Kerry's Macgillycuddy's Reeks is the tallest mountain in Ireland at only 1039m – but they're often beautiful and offer some excellent climbing possibilities. The highest mountains are in the southwest.

Adventure centres around the country run courses and organise climbing trips. For further information contact the **Mountaineering Council of Ireland** (☎01-625 1115; www.mountaineering.ie), which also publishes climbing guides and the quarterly magazine *Irish Mountain Log,* or check the forums on **Irish Climbing Online** (www. climbing.ie).

FISHING LICENCES

While no licence is needed for trout, pike and coarse fishing in the Republic of Ireland, a rod licence is required in Northern Ireland. You need a licence for salmon and sea-trout fishing in both jurisdictions.

Licences in the Republic are available from local tackle shops or direct from the **Central Fisheries Board** (☎01-884 2600; www.fisheriesireland.ie). In the North, rod licences for coarse and game fishing are obtainable from the **Foyle, Carlingford & Irish Lights Commission** (☎7134 2100; www.loughs-agency.org) for the Foyle and Carlingford areas, and from the **Fisheries Conservancy Board** (☎3833 4666; www.fcbni.com) for all other regions. You also require a permit from the owner, which is usually the Inland Waterways & Fisheries branch of the **Department of Culture, Arts & Leisure** (☎9025 8825; www.dcalni.gov.uk).

BIRDING RESOURCES
....

Some useful publications on birdwatching are Dominic Couzens' *Collins Birds of Britain and Ireland* and the slightly-out-of-date *Where to Watch Birds in Ireland* by Clive Hutchinson. More information can be obtained from the tourist boards and the following organisations:

Birds Ireland (☎01-830 7364; www.birdsireland.com)

BirdWatch Ireland (☎01-281 9878; www.birdwatchireland.ie) Runs birdwatching field courses, all of which take place on Cape Clear Island in County Cork.

National Parks & Wildlife Service (☎01-888 2000; www.npws.ie)

Royal Society for the Protection of Birds (RSPB; ☎9049 1547; www.rspb.org.uk; Belvoir Park Forest, Belfast)

Watching Wildlife

The country's forests, lakes, bogs, wetlands and coastal islands are rife with birds, furtive furry creatures and sea mammals. In many parts of the country your chance of spotting wildlife is quite high.

Land Mammals

Killarney National Park, in County Kerry, has been designated a Unesco Biosphere Reserve for its bounty of intriguing plant and animal species. It is home to the only wild herd of red deer, Ireland's most magnificent native mammal. Steely-nerved hares are commonly observed along many of Ireland's rural walkways.

Water Mammals

Aquatic mammals are commonly spotted around Ireland's periphery, as well in some of its streams. Whales, including fin whales, humpbacks and minke whales, are often spotted off the coast of West Cork during summer, when they come to feed offshore. Dolphins and porpoises are year-round residents of Irish waters, particularly favouring the natural harbours of Counties Kerry and Cork.

Seals live all around Ireland's perimeter. You can spot them around the island of Inishbofin off the coast of Galway; near Portaferry in County Down; on Rathlin Island off the Antrim coast; and around Greencastle in Donegal's Inishowen Penin-

sula. Shy river otters may be spotted along the streams of Connemara in County Galway. Some otters have been known to leave the water to search for food in boglands in the west of Ireland.

Birds

Ireland is a stopover for migrating birds, many of them from the Arctic, Africa and North America. Additionally, irregular winds frequently deliver exotic blowovers rarely seen in Western Europe. Birders on Ireland's coasts and islands are always on the lookout for breeding sea birds such as the gannet, kittiwake, cormorant and heron. The rare corncrake often appears along the west coast. Large colonies of puffins inhabit coastal cliffs, particularly on islands off Donegal and Northern Ireland. Peregrine falcons, long ago hunted out, were reintroduced to Donegal's Glenveagh National Park in 2001, and since then the species has shown signs it will re-establish itself in Ireland. The birding is good just about everywhere in Ireland. There are more than 70 reserves and sanctuaries in Ireland, many of them open to the public. Places to go include the following:

➡ **Inishowen Peninsula** In County Donegal. (p477)

➡ **Skellig Islands** Off the coast of County Kerry. (p284)

➡ **Cooley Birdwatching Trail** In County Louth. (p541)

➡ **Castle Espie** In County Down. (p594)

A full Irish breakfast

Plan Your Trip
Eat & Drink Like a Local

Ireland's recently acquired reputation as a gourmet destination is thoroughly deserved. A host of chefs and producers are leading a foodie revolution that is bringing to the table the kind of meals taken for granted on well-run Irish farms. Coupled with the growing sophistication of the Irish palate, it's relatively easy to eat well on all budgets. Needless to say, this has been a boon to the tourist industry.

Finding the Best of Irish Food & Drink

www.bestofbridgestone.com Extensive coverage of artisan producers and the best restaurants serving their produce.

www.bordbia.ie Irish Food Board website, with a few local producers listed, as well as a comprehensive list of farmers markets.

Good Food in Cork Excellent annual booklet detailing artisan producers in Cork, established by Myrtle Allen; pick it up from the Farmgate Café in Cork city.

www.irishcheese.ie The Association of Irish Farmhouse Cheesemakers, with every small dairy covered.

www.slowfoodireland.com Organisation supporting small producers, with social events across Ireland.

The Year in Food

January–March

The coldest time of the year is perfect for the fry – a cooked Irish breakfast.

April–June

The budding of spring sees freshly picked fruit and vegetables, such as asparagus and rhubarb, make an appearance. Food festivals include the following:

➡ **Waterford Festival of Food** (www. waterfordfestivaloffood.com) Three days of local produce and fine food in Dungarvan, including a seaside BBQ and a craft beer garden.

➡ **Só Sligo Festival** (www.sosligo.com) Professional chefs from around the globe compete in the World Irish Stew Championship in early May (there's also an amateur category).

➡ **Taste of Dublin** (www.tasteofdublin.ie) The capital's best restaurants combine to serve up sample platters of their best dishes amid music and other entertainment.

July–September

In July the first of the season's new potatoes appear, along with jams and berry pies with gooseberries, blackberries and loganberries. Culinary celebrations take place all over the country, and include the following:

➡ **Belfast Taste & Music Festival** (www. belfasttasteandmusicfest.com) Held in early August on the Great Lawn of the Botanic Gardens, this is Northern Ireland's top foodie event.

➡ **Carlingford Oyster Festival** (p541) Oysters come early in this County Louth town and the season is marked with a small festival.

➡ **Clarenbridge Oyster Festival** (p408) Long-running festival in the south Galway town.

➡ **Hillsborough Oyster Festival** (www. hillsboroughoysterfestival.com) Some 12,000 people from all over the world gather over the first weekend of September to sample the region's best and to take part in the World Oyster Eating Championships.

➡ **Taste of West Cork Food Festival** (p244) Skibbereen brings together its best producers to put on this weeklong festival.

➡ **Waterford Harvest Food Festival** (www. waterfordharvestfestival.ie) A 10-day festival in mid-September with food markets, tastings, celebrity-chef clinics and open-air picnics.

➡ **Midleton Food & Drink Festival** (www. midletonfoodfestival.ie) In mid-September this County Cork town hosts cookery demos, wine tastings and over 50 stalls featuring local produce.

➡ **Galway International Oyster Festival** (p377) Last weekend in September sees plenty of oysters, washed down with Guinness galore.

October–December

October is apple-picking month, and the main potato crop is dug up. The food-festival season goes out with a bang:

➡ **Kinsale Gourmet Festival** (www. kinsalerestaurants.com; ⊘early Oct) The unofficial gourmet capital of Ireland struts its culinary stuff over three days.

Food Experiences

Meals of a Lifetime

➡ **Restaurant Patrick Guilbaud** (p110), Dublin

➡ **Finn's Table** (p237), Kinsale, Country Cork

➡ **Castle Murray** (p456), Dunkineely, County Donegal

→ **Jacks Coastguard Restaurant** (p282), Cromane Peninsula, County Kerry

→ **Restaurant 1826 Adare** (p321), County Limerick

Dare to Try

Ironically, while the Irish palate has become more adventurous, it is the old-fashioned Irish menu that features some fairly challenging dishes. Dare to try the following:

→ **Black pudding** Made from congealed pork blood, suet and other fillings; a ubiquitous part of an Irish cooked breakfast.

→ **Boxty** A Northern Irish starchy potato cake made with a half-and-half mix of cooked mashed potatoes and grated, strained raw potato.

→ **Carrageen** Typical Irish seaweed found in dishes as diverse as salad and ice cream.

→ **Corned beef tongue** Usually accompanied by cabbage, this dish is still found on a traditional Irish menu.

→ **Lough Neagh eel** A speciality of Northern Ireland, typically eaten around Halloween; it's usually served in chunks with a white onion sauce.

→ **Poitín** Though it's rare to be offered a drop of the 'cratur', as illegally distilled whiskey (made from malted grain or potatoes) is called here, there are still pockets of the country with secret stills, in Donegal, Connemara and West Cork.

Local Specialities

To Eat

→ **Potatoes** It's a wonder the Irish retain their good humour amid the perpetual potato-baiting

TIM GRAHAM / GETTY IMAGES ©

Homemade soda bread

they endure. But, despite the stereotyping, and however much we'd like to disprove it, potatoes are still paramount here and you'll see lots of them on your travels. The mashed-potato dishes colcannon and champ (with cabbage and spring onion, respectively) are two of the tastiest recipes in the country.

→ **Meat and seafood** Irish meals are usually meat-based, with beef, lamb and pork common options. Seafood, long neglected, is finding a place on the table in Irish homes. It's widely available in restaurants and is often excellent, especially in the west. Oysters, trout and salmon are delicious, particularly if they're direct from the sea or a river rather than a fish farm. The famous Dublin Bay prawn isn't actually a prawn but a lobster. At its best, it's superlative, but it's priced accordingly. If you're going to splurge, do so here – but make sure you choose live Dublin Bay prawns because once these fellas die, they quickly lose their flavour.

→ **Soda bread** The most famous Irish bread, and one of the signature tastes of Ireland. Irish flour is soft and doesn't take well to yeast as a raising agent, so Irish bakers of the 19th century leavened their bread with bicarbonate of soda. Combined with buttermilk, it makes a superbly

---

THE BEST IRISH CHEESES

→ **Ardrahan** Flavoursome farm-house creation with a rich, nutty taste.

→ **Corleggy** Subtle, pasteurised goats cheese. (p545)

→ **Durrus** A creamy, fruity cheese, beloved of fine-food fans. (p251)

→ **Cashel Blue** Creamy blue cheese from Tipperary. (p327)

→ **Cooleeney** Award-winning Camembert-style cheese.

An Irish favourite – a cup of tea and biscuits

tasty bread, and is often on the breakfast menus at B&Bs.

➡ **The fry** Perhaps the most feared Irish speciality is the fry – the heart attack on a plate that is the second part of so many B&B deals. In spite of hysterical health fears, the fry is still one of the most common traditional meals in the country. Who can say no to a plate of fried bacon, sausages, black pudding, white pudding, eggs and tomatoes? For the famous Ulster fry, common throughout the North, simply add fadge (potato bread).

To Drink

➡ **Stout** While Guinness has become synonymous with stout the world over, few outside Ireland realise that there are two other major producers competing for the favour of the Irish drinker: Murphy's and Beamish & Crawford, both based in Cork city. To learn about pouring the perfect pint, see p120.

➡ **Tea** The Irish drink more tea, per capita, than any other nation in the world and you'll be offered a cup as soon as you cross the threshold of any Irish home. Taken with milk (and sugar, if you want) rather than lemon, preferred blends are very strong, and nothing like the namby-

pamby versions that pass for Irish breakfast tea elsewhere.

➡ **Whiskey** At last count, there were almost 100 different types of Irish whiskey, brewed by only three distilleries – Jameson's, Bushmills and Cooley's. A visit to Ireland reveals a depth of excellence that will make the connoisseur's palate spin while winning over many new friends to what the Irish call *uisce beatha* (water of life).

How to Eat & Drink

When to Eat

Irish eating habits have changed over the last couple of decades, and there are differences between urban and rural practices.

➡ **Breakfast** An important meal given the Irish tendency toward small lunches. Usually eaten before 9am (although hotels and B&Bs will serve until 11am Monday to Friday, to noon at weekends in urban areas), as most people rush off to work. Weekend brunch is popular in bigger

Where to Eat

➡ **Restaurants** From cheap 'n' cheerful to Michelin-starred, Ireland has something for every palate and budget.

➡ **Cafes** Ireland is awash with cafes of every description, many of which are perfect for a quick, tasty bite.

➡ **Hotels** Even if you're not a guest, most hotel restaurants cater to outside diners. Top hotels usually feature good restaurants with prices to match.

➡ **Pubs** Pub grub is ubiquitous, mostly of the toasted-sandwich variety. However, a large number also have full menu service, with some of them being as good as any top restaurant.

Dining Etiquette

The Irish aren't big on restrictive etiquette, preferring friendly informality to any kind of stuffy to-dos. Still, the following are a few tips to dining with the Irish:

➡ **Children** All restaurants welcome kids up to 7pm, but pubs and some smarter restaurants don't allow them in the evening. Family restaurants have children's menus, others have reduced portions of regular menu items.

➡ **Returning a dish** If the food is not to your satisfaction, it's best to politely explain what's wrong with it as soon as you can; any respectable restaurant will endeavour to replace the dish immediately.

Pulling pints of Guinness

towns and cities, although it pretty much copies traditional rural habits of eating a large, earthy breakfast late in the morning.

➡ **Lunch** Once the biggest meal of the day, lunch is now one of the more obvious rural/urban divides. Urban workers have succumbed to the eat-on-the-run restrictions of nine-to-five, with most eating a sandwich or a light meal between 12.30pm and 2pm (most restaurants don't begin to serve lunch until at least midday). At weekends, especially Sunday, the midday lunch is skipped in favour of a substantial mid-afternoon meal (called dinner), usually between 2pm and 4pm.

➡ **Tea** No, not the drink, but the evening meal – also confusingly called dinner. For urbanites, this is the main meal of the day, usually eaten around 6.30pm. Rural communities eat at the same time but with a more traditional tea of bread, cold cuts and, yes, tea. Restaurants follow international habits, with most diners not eating until at least 7.30pm.

➡ **Supper** A before-bed snack of tea and toast or sandwiches, still enjoyed by many Irish, although urbanites increasingly eschew it for health reasons. Not a practice in restaurants.

VEGETARIANS & VEGANS

Ireland has come a long, long way since the days when vegetarians were looked upon as odd creatures; nowadays, even the most militant vegan will barely cause a ruffle in all but the most basic of kitchens. Which isn't to say that travellers with plant-based diets are going to find the most imaginative range of options on menus outside the bigger towns and cities – or in the plethora of modern restaurants that have opened in the last few years – but you can rest assured that the overall quality of the home-grown vegetable is top-notch and most places will have at least one dish that you can tuck into comfortably.

OTHER IRISH BEERS

➡ **Beamish Red Ale** This traditional-style red ale, brewed in Cork city by Beamish & Crawford, is sweet and palatable.

➡ **Caffrey's Irish Ale** One of the most exciting additions to Ireland's beer map, this creamy ale has been around only since 1994. Brewed in County Antrim, it's a robust cross between a stout and an ale.

➡ **Kinsale Irish Lager** Brewed in the eponymous County Cork town, this golden-coloured lager has a slightly bitter taste that fades after a few sips.

➡ **McCardles Traditional Ale** This wholesome, dark, nutty ale is hard to come by but worthy of an exploration.

➡ **Smithwick's** A lovely, refreshing, full scoop with a charming history. It's brewed in Kilkenny, on the site of the 14th-century St Francis Abbey in what is Ireland's oldest working brewery.

➡ **Paying the bill** If you insist on paying the bill for everyone, be prepared for a first, second and even third refusal to countenance such an exorbitant act of generosity. But don't be fooled: the Irish will refuse something several times even if they're delighted with it. Insist gently but firmly and you'll get your way!

Regions at a Glance

Dublin

Museums
Entertainment
History

Cultural Exhibits

Dublin's small but impressive collection of museums includes some world-class institutions. The National Museum is home to the world's best collection of Celtic and pre-Celtic art, and the city's galleries range from the Renaissance to the contemporary with elegant ease.

Pubs & Nightlife

With a thousand-odd pubs to choose from, there is plenty of choice when deciding where to enjoy a pint of Dublin's most celebrated produce. But beyond Guinness and pub chatter there is theatre old and new, concerts fine and frenzied, and all manner of sporting distractions.

Story in Every Stone

Virtually every Dublin street is lined with monuments to its storied history, from the grounds of Trinity College to the bloodied walls of Kilmainham Gaol. Its finest buildings and most elegant streets belong to its golden Georgian age, when Dublin was the second city of the empire, but even the most unassuming house has a story to tell.

p58

Counties Wicklow & Kildare

Scenery
Monastic Ruins
Activities

Mountain Views

There are splendid views pretty much everywhere in the Wicklow Mountains, especially at the top of the passes that cut through the range; on a clear day you can see five counties in some spots. In Kildare, the fecund Bog of Allen offers another classic Irish landscape.

Ancient Monasteries

Not only are the ruins of Glendalough utterly absorbing, but their location, at the bottom of a glacial valley by two lakes, is absolutely enchanting and well worth the visit alone.

Walking Routes

Ireland's most popular walking trail, the Wicklow Way, cuts through the county north to south. Kildare is horse-breeding country, where the walking paths are a little bit gentler but no less enjoyable.

p136

Counties Wexford, Waterford, Carlow & Kilkenny

Scenery
History
Food

Seaside Vistas

Iconic emerald green fields above ragged ebony cliffs that end in a cerulean sea: you will never tire of the vista. Should you need a break, perfect pockets of sand dot the coast, while Wexford's beaches stretch beyond the horizon. Inland, rural Ireland includes wild rivers and bucolic farms.

Viking Trails

You half expect to encounter a Viking as you wander the streets of Waterford and Wexford, where traces of the Middle Ages are all around you. Kilkenny's medieval past is impossible to miss, from its soaring cathedral to its great castle.

Local Produce

Head to Dungarvan to enjoy Irish cooking at its best, and enjoy the region's wonderful produce in all towns, big and small.

p162

County Cork

Food
Scenery
History

Gourmet Treats

County Cork is the unofficial gourmet heartland of Ireland, from the fabulous eateries of Cork city to the wealth of local producers and foodie artisans of West Cork, where you can buy directly at the source and eat like a lord.

Peninsular Panoramas

The county's three western peninsulas – Mizen Head, Sheep's Head and Beara – have it all: mountain passes, lonely windswept hills, beautiful beaches and views that will stay with you long after you've left for home.

Story of Rebellion

The Rebel County wears its history with pride, even the sorrowful kind. You can explore it all, from famine memorials and scenes of 17th-century battles to the powerful tribute to its more recent fallen heroes.

p215

County Kerry

Scenery
Seafood
Traditional Music

An Irish Postcard

County Kerry is the very definition of scenic Ireland – the Connor Pass, the Dingle Peninsula and, particularly, the Ring of Kerry are the gold standard by which Irish landscapes are judged. Decide for yourself by picking up a postcard.

Fresh from the Sea

Kerry's intimate relationship with the sea means that the fresh catch of the day is exactly that: throughout the Dingle Peninsula you can eat fish fresh off the boat you've just watched land.

Traditional Sound

No Kerry town or village is complete without at least one pub featuring traditional music, played by musicians schooled in the respective styles of their region. It's the proper accompaniment to a visit to the county.

p263

Counties Limerick & Tipperary

Walking
History
Scenery

Heritage Trails

It's a long way to Tipperary, but keep going once you get there, tramping through the chequered Glen of Aherlow and along the more challenging Tipperary Heritage Trail, a 56km walk through beautiful river valleys dotted with ancient ruins.

Castles & Monasteries

From the mighty monastic city of Cashel in County Tipperary to the impressive fortifications of King John's Castle in Limerick city, the varied fortunes of the region's history are easily discernible throughout the two counties.

Atmospheric Ruins

At its broadest point, the mighty Shannon makes for some beautiful vistas, while the rolling hills and farmland of County Tipperary, peppered with ancient ruins, offer the kind of views for which Ireland is renowned.

p310

County Clare

Scenery
Music
Pubs

Dramatic Cliffs

Rising from the stormy Atlantic in all their sheer dramatic glory, the Cliffs of Moher are an arresting sight not to be missed. The rest of Clare's coast holds additional beauty, especially in the south where mysterious stone columns rise high above the waters. The Burren offers a landscape that's at once alien and beautiful.

Traditional Sessions

Clare plays Ireland's most traditional music, with few modern influences. At festivals, in pubs or even just around any corner, you can hear brilliant trad sessions by the county's surfeit of musicians.

Old-Style Drinking

There is *no* town in Clare that doesn't have at least one wonderful old pub where the Guinness is ready, the peat is lit and the craic never ends.

p336

County Galway

Scenery
Food
Culture

Islands & Mountains

Hundreds of years of ceaseless toil have brought green accents to the otherwise barren rocks of the Aran Islands. The results are gorgeous, and a walk around these windswept and intriguing islands is one of Ireland's highlights. In spring, when the gorse blooms in brilliant yellow, the Connemara Peninsula's beauty astounds.

Fresh Oysters

Even as you read this, millions of succulent oysters are growing to the perfect size out in the tidal waters of Galway Bay. Local chefs excel at creating taste treats with the water's bounty.

Gigs Everywhere

On any given night, Galway city's pubs and clubs hum with trad sessions, brilliant rock and tomorrow's next big band. It's a feast for the ears.

p371

Counties Mayo & Sligo

Islands
Megalithic Remains
Yeats Country

Scenery

There are reputed to be 365 islands in Clew Bay, including one once owned by John Lennon. There's also Craggy Island, which isn't the island of *Father Ted* fame but rather the home of the notorious pirate queen Grace O'Malley (or Granuaile).

Ancient Ruins

From the world's most extensive Stone Age monument at Céide Fields to the megalithic cemeteries at Carrowmore and Carrowkeel, the environs of Ballycastle are a step back into prehistory.

Poetic Inspiration

County Sligo is Yeats country: he's buried in the church at Drumcliff, in the shadow of Benbulben; and throughout the county you'll find tributes to him in museums and heritage centres, while the landscapes are reflected in his poetry.

p412

County Donegal

Wild Landscapes
Pristine Beaches
Surfing

Mountains & Cliffs

Untamed and almost impossibly wild, Donegal is the ultimate frontier country, from the wave- and wind-lashed cliffs and beaches of the coast to the mountainous interior, as brooding as it is beautiful.

Pristine Coastlines

The county with the second-longest coastline has the country's best beaches, including surf-friendly Rossnowlagh, unspoilt Tramore and the red-tinged sands of Malinbeg. The multitude of coves hides an astonishing number of sandy hideaways.

Sea Activities

In Donegal you can learn to surf as well as take on some of the world's toughest breaks – the county is arguably the best place in the country to ride the waves due to its great mix of beaches and abundance of surf centres.

p447

The Midlands

Traditional Pubs
Shannon Cruise
Ecclesiastical Remains

Authentic Atmosphere

Spread almost innocuously across the Midlands are some of the most atmospheric pubs in the country, including Morrissey's of Abbeyleix, perhaps the most perfect pub in Ireland.

The Mighty River

What better way to explore the length and breadth of the country's belly than by cruiser along Ireland's longest river? See the sights and stop off along the way to eat in the riverbank restaurants that have sprouted for that purpose.

Saints & Scholars

The top monastic site in Ireland is Clonmacnoise, perched on the edge of the Shannon in County Offaly. Within its walled enclosure you'll find early churches, high crosses, round towers and graves in astonishingly good condition.

p484

Counties Meath, Louth, Cavan & Monaghan

History
Fishing
Scenery

Chieftains & Conflict

Irish history was lived and written across these counties, at the Hill of Tara, the Neolithic monuments of Brú na Bóinne and Loughcrew, in the magnificent abbeys of Mellifont and Monasterboice, and in towns like Drogheda.

Angling & Coarse Fishing

County Cavan's myriad lakes are famed for coarse fishing. County Monaghan isn't far behind, and if you fancy a little sea angling, towns like Clogherhead and Carlingford in County Louth are the places to go.

Lakelands & Hills

These counties offer all kinds of scenery, from the lakelands of Cavan and Monaghan to the fecund hills of County Meath. There are beautiful seaside views too, along the Louth coast as far up as scenic Carlingford.

p514

Belfast

History
Pubs
Music

Troubled Past

There's nowhere in Europe where you can get as close to recent history as you can in West Belfast, which has turned the trauma of the Troubles into one of the most interesting tourist attractions in Ireland.

Victorian Gems

The Victorian pubs of the city centre are Belfast's most beloved treasure – the Crown might be the most famous, but equally beautiful are the John Hewitt and the Garrick, while older taverns like White's and Kelly's have even more atmosphere.

Banging Tunes

From DJs spinning tunes in the Eglantine to sellout gigs at the Odyssey, Belfast's music scene is top-notch. Best of the lot is probably the Belfast Empire, which features new bands and established acts nightly.

p551

Counties Down & Armagh

Activities
Wildlife
Food

Walking Festivals

With an impressive calendar of yearly events including birdwatching meets, walking festivals and more-strenuous activities like rock climbing and canoeing, there's enough to do here to keep you busy for every day of the year.

Birds & Seals

The bird-filled mudflats of Castle Espie in County Down are home to a wildfowl and wetlands centre that will entice even the most indifferent of ornithologists, while large colonies of grey seals are but the most obvious of visitors to Strangford Lough in County Armagh.

Gastro-Goodness

You'll find first-rate dining in the restaurants and gastropubs of Hillsborough, Bangor and Warrenpoint, all in County Down, plus wonderful spots in the unlikeliest of places, like the marvellous bistro at the back of Ireland's oldest pub in Donaghadee, on the Ards Peninsula.

p586

Counties Londonderry & Antrim

History
Scenery
Walking

A Walled City

Derry, Ireland's only walled city, has a rich historical past, poignantly told along the walls that withstood a siege in 1688–89, in its storied museums and, most tellingly, in the political murals of the Bogside district, where history was played out on its very streets.

Giant's Footsteps

Virtually the entire length of the Antrim coast is scenic gold, but the real stars are the southern section around Carnlough Bay and the North's most outstanding tourist attraction, the surreal geological formations of the Giant's Causeway.

On the Trail

The Causeway Coast Way stretches 53km from Portstewart to Ballycastle, but the most scenic section – the 16.5km between Carrick-a-Rede and the Giant's Causeway – can be done in a day and offers one of the finest coastal walks in Ireland.

p613

Counties Fermanagh & Tyrone

Activities
Scenery
History

Walking & Fishing

Need something to do? How about fishing in the waters of County Fermanagh, or taking part in the Ulster American Folk Park's annual Appalachian and Bluegrass Music Festival? Or, for something more spiritual, why not climb to the summit of Mullaghcarn along with other pilgrims?

From a Height

Whether you're boating on Lough Erne, staring out the windows at the top of the round tower on Devenish Island or hiking across the broad range of the Sperrin Mountains, the scenery is beguiling, especially if you have decent weather.

Conflict & Connections

The towns of Omagh and Enniskillen speak volumes about the atrocities of violence, but Northern Ireland's history isn't just one of conflict: the Ulster American Folk Park expertly tells the story of the province's strong links with the United States.

p647

On the
Road

Dublin

POP 1.27 MILLION / AREA 921 SQ KM

Best Places to Eat

➡ Chapter One (p113)

➡ Restaurant Patrick Guilbaud (p110)

➡ Musashi Noodles & Sushi Bar (p112)

➡ Fade Street Social (p105)

➡ Fumbally Cafe (p111)

Best Places to Stay

➡ Aberdeen Lodge (p100)

➡ Isaacs Hostel (p97)

➡ Merrion (p97)

➡ Radisson Blu Royal Hotel (p95)

➡ Pembroke Townhouse (p101)

Why Go?

Sultry rather than sexy, Dublin exudes personality as only those who've managed to turn careworn into carefree can. The halcyon days of the Celtic Tiger, when cash cascaded like a free-flowing waterfall, have long since disappeared and the city has once again been forced to grind out a living. But Dubliners still know how to enjoy life. They do so through their music, their art and their literature – things which Dubs often take for granted but, once reminded, generate immense pride.

There are world-class museums, superb restaurants and the best range of entertainment available anywhere in Ireland – and that's not including the pub, the ubiquitous centre of the city's social life and an absolute must for any visitor. And should you wish to get away from it all, the city has a handful of seaside towns at its edges that make for wonderful day trips.

When to Go

➡ March brings the marvellous mayhem of St Patrick's Festival, with 600,000 parade viewers.

➡ The world's most popular women's minimarathon is held in June, with over 40,000 participants.

➡ In August the Dun Laoghaire Festival of World Cultures brings musicians and artists from all over the world.

History

Dublin's been making noise since around 500 BC, when a bunch of intrepid Celts camped at a ford over the River Liffey, which is the provenance of the city's tough-to-pronounce Irish name, Baile Átha Cliath (*bawl-ya aw-ha klee-ya*; Town of the Hurdle Ford). The Celts went about their merry way for a thousand years or so, but it wasn't until the Vikings showed up that Dublin was urbanised in any significant way. By the 9th century raids from the north had become a fact of Irish life, and some of the fierce Danes chose to stay rather than simply rape, pillage and depart. They intermarried with the Irish and established a vigorous trading port at the point where the River Poddle joined the Liffey in a *dubh linn* (black pool). Today there's little trace of the Poddle, which has been channelled underground and flows under St Patrick's Cathedral to dribble into the Liffey by the Capel St (Grattan) Bridge.

Fast-forward another thousand years, past the arrival of the Normans in the 12th century and the slow process of subjugating Ireland to Anglo-Norman (then British) rule, during which Dublin generally played the role of bandleader. Stop at the beginning of the 18th century, when the squalid city packed with poor Catholics hardly reflected the imperial pretensions of its Anglophile burghers. The great and the good – aka the Protestant Ascendancy – wanted big improvements, and they set about transforming what was in essence still a medieval town into a modern, Anglo-Irish metropolis. Roads were widened, landscaped squares laid out and new town houses built, all in a proto-Palladian style that soon became known as Georgian after the kings then on the English throne. For a time, Dublin was the second-largest city in the British Empire and all was very, very good – unless you were part of the poor, mostly Catholic masses living in the city's ever-developing slums.

The Georgian boom came to a sudden and dramatic halt after the Act of Union (1801), when Ireland was formally united with Britain and its separate parliament closed down. Dublin went from being the belle of the imperial ball to the annoying cousin who just wouldn't take the hint, and slid quickly into economic turmoil and social unrest. During the Potato Famine (1845–51), the city's population was swollen by the arrival of tens of thousands of starving refugees from the west, who joined the ranks of an already downtrodden working class. As Dublin entered the 20th century, it was a dispirited place plagued by poverty, disease and more social problems than anyone cared to mention. It's hardly surprising that the majority of Dublin's citizenry were disgruntled and eager for change.

The first fusillade of transformation came during the Easter Rising of 1916, which caused considerable damage to the city centre. At first, Dubliners weren't too enamoured of the rebels, who caused more chaos and disruption than most locals were willing to put up with, but they soon changed their tune when the leaders were executed – Dubliners being natural defenders of the underdog.

As the whole country lurched radically towards full-scale war with Britain, Dublin was, surprisingly, not part of the main theatre of events. In fact, although there was an increased military presence, the odd shooting in the capital and the blowing up of some notable buildings (such as the Custom House in 1921) it was business as usual for much of the War of Independence.

A year later, Ireland – minus its northern bit – was independent, but it then tumbled into the Civil War, which led to the burning of more notable buildings, this time the Four Courts in 1922. Ironically, the war among the Irish was more brutal than the struggle for independence – O'Connell St became 'sniper row' and the violence left deep scars that took most of the 20th century to heal.

When the new state finally started doing business, Dublin was an exhausted capital. Despite slow and steady improvements, the city – like the rest of Ireland – continued to be plagued by rising unemployment, high emigration rates and a general stagnation that hung about like an impenetrable cloud. Dubliners made the most of the little they had, but times were tough.

A boom in the 1960s was followed by more recession in the 1970s and '80s; the mid-'90s brought prosperity courtesy of the Celtic Tiger, which transformed the city and its inhabitants into world-beating cosmopolitans before the crash of 2008 once again delivered the city (and the country) into recession.

◉ Sights

◉ Grafton Street & Around

Dublin's most celebrated shopping street is the elegant, pedestrianised spine of the

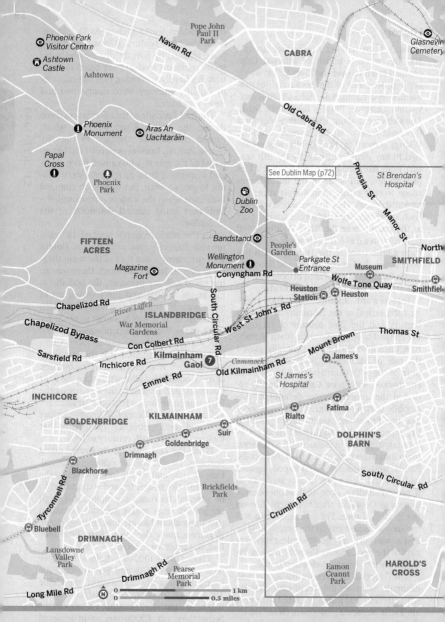

Dublin Highlights

1 Stroll the Elizabethan cobbled grounds of **Trinity College** (p62)

2 Pore over ancient books and other printed wonders from all around the world in the **Chester Beatty Library** (p66)

3 Explore your thespian side at one of Dublin's theatres, like the **Abbey** (p125) or the **Gate** (p125)

4 Get to grips with Ireland's historic treasures and ancient past with a visit to the **National Museum of Ireland – Archaeology** (p68)

5 Tap into your inner Victorian botanist (and watch the kids go 'wow') with a visit to the 'dead zoo', the **Museum of Natural History** (p69)

6 Enjoy Georgian gems surrounding landscaped **Merrion Square** (p71) and **St Stephen's Green** (p70)

7 See the past up close and personal at **Kilmainham Goal** (p77)

8 Quaff a pint or five in one of the many pubs – our favourite is **John Mulligan's** (p115)

southern city centre: at its northern end is Trinity College, the country's oldest and most beautiful university, which stretches its leafy self across a healthy chunk of south-city real estate. A few steps northwest is Temple Bar, where bacchanalia and bohemia scrap it out for supremacy – when the sun sets, Bacchus is king. Grafton St's southern end runs into the main entrance to St Stephen's Green, Dublin's perennially popular green lung; surrounding and beyond it is the capital's exquisite Georgian heritage, a collection of galleries, museums, and private and public buildings as handsome as any you'll see in Europe.

★ Trinity College   HISTORIC BUILDING
(Map p79; ☑ 01-896 1000; www.tcd.ie; ⊙ 8am-10pm; ▣ all city centre) FREE This calm and cordial retreat from the bustle of contemporary Dublin is not just Ireland's most prestigious university, but a throwback to those far-off days when a university education was the preserve of a very small elite who spoke passionately of the importance of philosophy and the need for empire. Today's alumni are an altogether different bunch, but Trinity still looks the part, and on a summer's evening, when the crowds thin and the chatter subsides, there are few more delightful places to be.

The college was established by Elizabeth I in 1592 on land confiscated from an Augustinian priory in an effort to stop the brain drain of young Protestant Dubliners, who were skipping across to Continental Europe for an education and were becoming 'infected with popery'. Trinity went on to become one of Europe's most outstanding universities, producing a host of notable graduates – how about Jonathan Swift, Oscar Wilde and Samuel Beckett at the same alumni dinner?

It remained completely Protestant until 1793, but even when the university relented and began to admit Catholics, the Church forbade it; until 1970, any Catholic who enrolled here could consider themselves excommunicated.

The campus is a masterpiece of architecture and landscaping beautifully preserved in Georgian aspic. Most of the buildings and statues date from the 18th and 19th centuries, each elegantly laid out on a cobbled or grassy square. The newer bits include the 1978 Arts & Social Science Building (Map p79), which backs on to Nassau St and forms the alternative entrance to the college. Like the Berkeley Library, it was designed by Paul

Koralek; it also houses the Douglas Hyde Gallery of Modern Art (Map p79; www.douglashydegallery.ie; ⊙ 11am-6pm Mon-Wed & Fri, to 7pm Thu, to 4.45pm Sat) FREE.

A great way to see the grounds is on a walking tour (Map p79; ☑ 01-896 1827; admission €5, incl Book of Kells €10; ⊙ tours every 40min 10.15am-3.40pm Mon-Sat, 10.15am-3pm Sun mid-May–Sep), which depart from the Regent House entrance on College Green.

➡ ★ Old Library
(Map p79; Library Sq; ▣ all city centre) To the south of Library Sq is the Old Library, built in a rather severe style by Thomas Burgh between 1712 and 1732. Despite Ireland's independence, the Library Act of 1801 still entitles Trinity College Library, along with four libraries in Britain, to a free copy of every book published in the UK. Housing this bounty requires nearly another 1km of shelving every year and the collection amounts to around 4.5 million books. Of course, these cannot all be kept at the college library, so there are now additional library storage facilities dotted around Dublin.

➡ Long Room
(Map p79; East Pavilion, Library Colonnades; adult/student/child €9/8/free; ⊙ 9.30am-5pm Mon-Sat year-round, noon-4.30pm Sun Oct-Apr, 9.30am-4.30pm Sun May-Sep; ▣ all city centre) Trinity's greatest treasures are kept in the Old Library's stunning 65m Long Room, which houses about 250,000 of the library's oldest volumes, including the breathtaking Book of Kells. Your entry ticket includes admission to temporary exhibitions on display in the East Pavilion. The ground-floor Colonnades was originally an open arcade, but was enclosed in 1892 to increase the storage area. Other displays include a rare copy of the Proclamation of the Irish Republic, which was read out by Pádraig Pearse at the beginning of the Easter Rising in 1916. Also here is the so-called harp of Brian Ború, which was definitely not in use when the army of this early Irish hero defeated the Danes at the Battle of Clontarf in 1014. It does, however, date from around 1400, making it one of the oldest harps in Ireland.

➡ Science Gallery
(Map p100; www.sciencegallery.ie; Pearse St; ⊙ exhibitions usually noon-8pm Tue-Fri, to 6pm Sat & Sun; ▣ all city centre) FREE Trinity's newest attraction opened in 2008, and since then has proven immensely popular with its refreshingly lively and informative explo-

ration of the relationship between science, art and the world we live in. Exhibits have touched on a range of fascinating topics including the science of desire and an exploration of the relationship between music and the human body. The ground-floor Flux Café (Pearse St; ☺8am-8pm Tue-Fri, noon-6pm Sat & Sun), bathed in floor-to-ceiling light, is a pretty good spot to take a load off.

Bank of Ireland   NOTABLE BUILDING
(Map p84; ☑01-671 1488; College Green; ☺10am-4pm Mon-Fri, to 5pm Thu; ☐all city centre) A sweeping Palladian pile occupying one side of College Green, this magnificent building was the Irish Parliament House until 1801 and is the first purpose-built parliament building in the world. The original building, the central colonnaded section that distinguishes the present-day structure, was designed by Sir Edward Lovett Pearce in 1729 and completed by James Gandon in 1733.

When the Parliament voted itself out of existence through the 1801 Act of Union, the building was sold under the condition that the interior would be altered to prevent it ever again being used as a debating chamber. It was a spiteful strike at Irish parliamentary aspirations, but while the central House of Commons was remodelled and offers little hint of its former role, the smaller House of Lords (admission free) chamber survived and is much more interesting. It has Irish oak woodwork, a mahogany longcase parliament clock and a late-18th-century Dublin crystal chandelier. Its design was copied for the construction of the original House of Representatives in Washington, DC, now the National Statuary Hall. There are tours of the House of Lords (10.30am, 11.30am and 1.45pm Tuesday) by Dublin historian and author Éamon MacThomás, which include a talk as much about Ireland and life in general as the building itself, the exterior of which was the inspiration for the British Museum in London.

Temple Bar   NEIGHBOURHOOD
(Map p84) Many weekend visitors will barely venture beyond the cobbled borders of Dublin's so-called 'cultural quarter', a maze of streets and alleys sandwiched between Dame St and the Liffey, running from Trinity College to Christ Church Cathedral.

If you visit during the day, the district's bohemian bent is on display. You can browse for vintage clothes, get your nipples pierced, nibble on Mongolian barbecue, buy organic food, pick up the latest musical releases and buy books on every conceivable subject. You can check out the latest art installations, watch an outdoor movie or join in a pulsating drum circle. By night – or at the weekend – it's a different story altogether, as the area's bars are packed to the rafters with revellers looking to tap into their inner Bacchus: it's loud, raucous and usually a lot of fun. Temple Bar is also Dublin's official 'cultural quarter', so you shouldn't ignore its more high-minded offerings.

Meeting House Square is one of the real success stories of Temple Bar. On one side is the excellent Gallery of Photography (Map p84; www.galleryofphotography.ie; ☺11am-6pm Mon-Sat; ☐all city centre) FREE, hosting temporary exhibitions of contemporary local and international photographers. Staying with the photography theme, the other side of the square is home to the National Photographic Archive (Map p84; ☺10am-4.45pm Mon-Sat, noon-4.45pm Sun; ☐all city centre) FREE, a magnificent resource for anyone interested in a photographic history of Ireland. On Saturdays it hosts a popular food market.

At the western end of Temple Bar, in the shadow of Christ Church Cathedral, is Fishamble St, the oldest street in Dublin. It dates back to Viking times – not that you'd know that to see it now.

On Parliament St, which runs south from the river to the City Hall and Dublin Castle, the Sunlight Chambers (Map p84; ☐all city centre) beside the river has a beautiful frieze around its facade. Sunlight was a brand of soap manufactured by the Lever Brothers, who were responsible for the late-19th-century building. The frieze shows the Lever Brothers' view of the world: men make clothes dirty, women wash them!

To the east, buildings on interesting Eustace Street include the 1715 Presbyterian Meeting House, now the Ark (p96), an excellent children's cultural centre. The Dublin branch of the Society of United Irishmen, who sought parliamentary reform and equality for Catholics, was first convened in 1791 in the Eagle Tavern, now the Friends' Meeting House (Map p84; Eustace St). (This shouldn't be confused with the other Eagle Tavern, which is on Cork St.)

Merchant's Arch leads to the Ha'penny Bridge (Map p114), named after the ha'penny (half-penny) toll once needed to cross. The

Trinity College, Dublin

STEP INTO THE PAST

Ireland's most prestigious university, founded on the order of Queen Elizabeth I in 1592, is an architectural masterpiece, a cordial retreat from the bustle of modern life in the middle of the city. Step through its main entrance and you step back in time, the cobbled stones transporting you to another era, when the elite discussed philosophy and argued passionately in favour of empire.

Standing in Front Square, the 30m-high **Campanile** 1 is directly in front of you with the **Dining Hall** 2 to your left. On the far side of the square is the Old Library building, the centrepiece of which is the magnificent **Long Room** 3, which was the inspiration for the computer-generated imagery of the Jedi Archive in *Star Wars Episode II: Attack of the Clones*. Here you'll find the university's greatest treasure, the **Book of Kells** 4. You'll probably have to queue to see this masterpiece, and then only for a brief visit, but it's very much worth it.

Just beyond the Old Library is the very modern **Berkeley Library** 5, which nevertheless fits perfectly into the campus' overall aesthetic: directly in front of it is the distinctive **Sphere Within a Sphere** 6, the most elegant of the university's sculptures.

Campanile
Trinity College's most iconic bit of masonry was designed in the mid-19th century by Sir Charles Lanyon; the attached sculptures were created by Thomas Kirk.

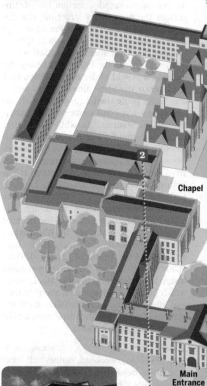

Chapel

Main Entrance

Dining Hall
Richard Cassels' original building was designed to mirror the Examination Hall directly opposite on Front Square: the hall collapsed twice and was rebuilt from scratch in 1761.

DON'T MISS

» Douglas Hyde Gallery, the campus' designated modern art museum.

» Cricket match on pitch, the most elegant of pastimes.

» Pint in the Pavilion Bar, preferably while watching the cricket.

» Visit to the Science Gallery, where science is made completely relevant.

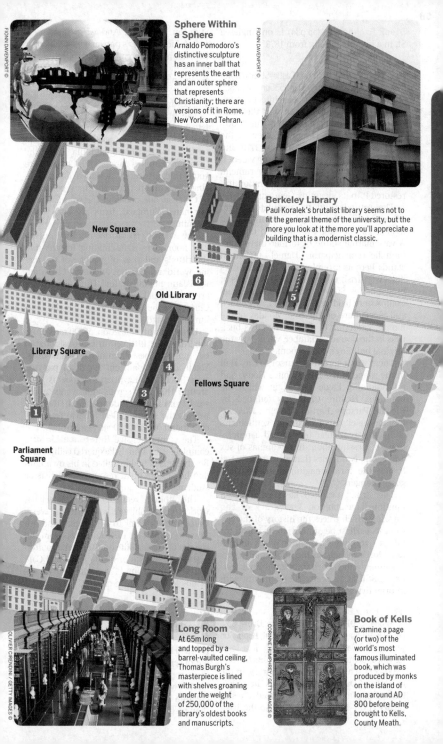

Sphere Within a Sphere
Arnaldo Pomodoro's distinctive sculpture has an inner ball that represents the earth and an outer sphere that represents Christianity; there are versions of it in Rome, New York and Tehran.

Berkeley Library
Paul Koralek's brutalist library seems not to fit the general theme of the university, but the more you look at it the more you'll appreciate a building that is a modernist classic.

New Square

Old Library

Library Square

Fellows Square

Parliament Square

Long Room
At 65m long and topped by a barrel-vaulted ceiling, Thomas Burgh's masterpiece is lined with shelves groaning under the weight of 250,000 of the library's oldest books and manuscripts.

Book of Kells
Examine a page (or two) of the world's most famous illuminated book, which was produced by monks on the island of Iona around AD 800 before being brought to Kells, County Meath.

Stock Exchange (Map p84) is on Anglesea St, in a building dating from 1878.

City Hall

MUSEUM

(Map p84; www.dublincity.ie; Castle St; adult/student €4/2/1.50; ⊘10am-5.15pm Mon-Sat; ⊒all city centre) One of the architectural triumphs of the Dublin boom was the magnificent restoration of City Hall (in 2000), originally built by Thomas Cooley as the Royal Exchange between 1769 and 1779, and botched in the mid-19th century when it became the offices of the local government. Thankfully, the more recent restoration has restored it to its gleaming Georgian best.

The rotunda and its ambulatory form a breathtaking interior, bathed in natural light from enormous windows to the east. A vast marble statue of former mayor and Catholic emancipator Daniel O'Connell stands here as a reminder of the building's links with Irish nationalism (the funerals of both Charles Stewart Parnell and Michael Collins were held here). Dublin City Council still meets here on the first Monday of the month, gathering to discuss the city's business in the Council Chamber, which was the original building's coffee room.

There was a sordid precursor to City Hall in the shape of the Lucas Coffee House and the adjoining Eagle Tavern, in which the notorious Hellfire Club was founded by Richard Parsons, Earl of Rosse, in 1735. Although the city abounded with gentlemen's clubs, this particular one gained a reputation for messing about in the arenas of sex and Satan, two topics that were guaranteed to fire the lurid imaginings of the city's gossipmongers.

The striking vaulted basement hosts a multimedia exhibition The Story of the Capital, which traces the history of the city from its earliest beginnings to its hoped-for future – with ne'er a mention of sex and Satan. More's the pity, as the info is quite overwhelming and the exhibits are a little textheavy. Still, it's a pretty slick museum with informative audiovisual displays.

★Chester Beatty Library

MUSEUM

(Map p84; ☑01-407 0750; www.cbl.ie; Dublin Castle; ⊘10am-5pm Tue-Fri, 11am-5pm Sat, 1-5pm Sun year-round, 10am-5pm Mon May-Sep, free tours 1pm Wed, 3pm & 4pm Sun; ⊒50, 51B, 77, 78A , 123) **FREE** This world-famous library, in the grounds of Dublin Castle, houses the collection of mining engineer Sir Alfred Chester Beatty (1875–1968), bequeathed to the Irish

State on his death. And we're immensely grateful for Chester's patronage: spread over two floors, the breathtaking collection includes more than 20,000 manuscripts, rare books, miniature paintings, clay tablets, costumes and other objects of artistic, historical and aesthetic importance.

The Artistic Traditions Gallery on the 1st floor begins with memorabilia from Beatty's life, before embarking on an exploration of the art of Mughal India, Persia, the Ottoman Empire, Japan and China. Here you'll find intricately designed little medicine boxes and perhaps the finest collection of Chinese jade books in the world. The illuminated European texts are also worth examining.

The Sacred Traditions Gallery on the 2nd floor gives a fascinating insight into the rituals and rites of passage of the major world religions – Judaism, Christianity, Islam, Buddhism and Hinduism. There are audiovisual explorations of the lives of Christ and the Buddha, as well as the Muslim pilgrimage to Mecca.

Head for the collection of Qu'rans from the 9th to the 19th centuries, considered to be among the best illuminated Islamic texts. You'll also find ancient Egyptian papyrus texts (including Egyptian love poems from around 1100 BC), scrolls and exquisite artwork from Burma, Indonesia and Tibet – as well as the second-oldest biblical fragment ever found (after the Dead Sea Scrolls).

The comprehensive Reference Library, complete with a finely lacquered ceiling that Beatty himself had installed in his own London home, is a great resource for artists or students.

The library regularly holds specialist workshops, exhibitions and talks on everything from origami to calligraphy, and admission is free. It's easy to escape from the rigours of Western life on the serene rooftop Japanese garden or at the Silk Road Café (p104) on the ground floor, which serves delicious Middle Eastern cuisine.

Dublin Castle

HISTORIC BUILDING

(Map p84; ☑01-677 7129; www.dublincastle.ie; Dame St; adult/child €4.50/2; ⊘10am-4.45pm Mon-Sat, noon-4.45pm Sun; ⊒50, 54, 56A 77, 77A) If you're looking for a turreted castle straight out of central casting you'll be disappointed; the stronghold of British power in Ireland for 700 years is principally an 18th-century creation that is more hotchpotch palace than medieval castle. Only the Record Tower (Map p84), completed in 1258, survives from the original Anglo-Norman fortress commissioned by King John in 1204.

It was officially handed over to Michael Collins on behalf of the Irish Free State in 1922, when the British viceroy is reported to have rebuked Collins on being seven min-

utes late. Collins replied, 'We've been waiting 700 years, you can wait seven minutes.' The castle is now used by the Irish government for meetings and functions, and can be visited only on a guided tour of the State Apartments and excavations of the former Powder Tower.

County Dublin

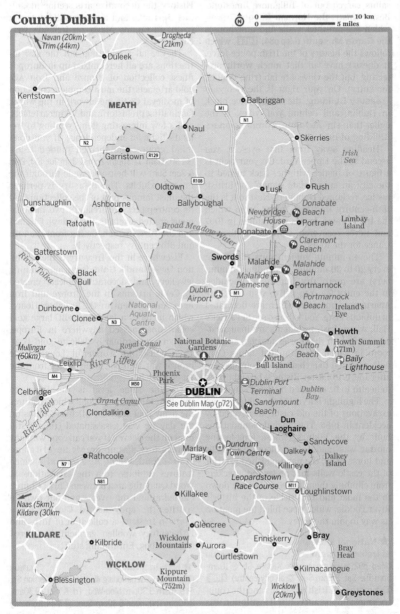

As you walk into the grounds from the main Dame St entrance, there's a good example of the evolution of Irish architecture. On your left is the Victorian Chapel Royal (occasionally part of the Dublin Castle tours), decorated with more than 90 heads of various Irish personages and saints carved out of Tullamore limestone. Beside this is the Norman Record Tower, which has 5m-thick walls and now houses the Garda Museum (Map p84) FREE, which follows the history of the Irish police force. It doesn't have all that much worth protecting, but the views are fab (ring the bell for entry). On your right is the Georgian Treasury Building, the oldest office block in Dublin, and behind you, yikes, is the uglier-than-sin Revenue Commissioners Building of 1960.

Heading away from that eyesore, you ascend to the Upper Yard. On your right is a figure of Justice with her back turned to the city, an appropriate symbol for British justice, reckoned Dubliners. Next to it is the 18th-century Bedford Tower, from which the Irish Crown Jewels were stolen in 1907 and never recovered. Opposite is the entrance for the tours.

The 45-minute guided tours (departing every 20 to 30 minutes, depending on numbers) are pretty dry, but they're included in the entry fee. You get to visit the State Apartments, many of which are decorated in dubious taste. You will also see St Patrick's Hall, where Irish presidents are inaugurated and foreign dignitaries toasted, and the room in which the wounded James Connolly was tied to a chair while convalescing after the 1916 Easter Rising – brought back to health to be executed by firing squad.

The highlight is a visit to the subterranean excavations of the old castle, discovered by accident in 1986. They include foundations built by the Vikings (whose long-lasting mortar was made of ox blood, egg shells and horse hair), the hand-polished exterior of the castle walls that prevented attackers from climbing them, the steps leading down to the moat and the trickle of the historic River Poddle, which once filled the moat on its way to join the Liffey.

⭐ **National Museum of Ireland – Archaeology**   MUSEUM
(Map p92; www.museum.ie; Kildare St; ⊙10am-5pm Tue-Sat, 2-5pm Sun; ⓐall city centre) FREE
The mother of Irish museums and the country's most important cultural institution was

established in 1977 as the primary repository of the nation's archaeological treasures. The collection is so big, however, that it has expanded beyond the walls of this superb, purpose-built building next to the Irish parliament into three other separate museums – the stuffed beasts of the Museum of Natural History, the decorative arts section at Collins Barracks and a country life museum (p431) in County Mayo, on Ireland's west coast.

They're all fascinating, but the star attractions are all here, mixed up in Europe's finest collection of Bronze and Iron Age gold artefacts, the most complete collection of medieval Celtic metalwork in the world, fascinating prehistoric and Viking artefacts, and a few interesting items relating to Ireland's fight for independence. If you don't mind groups, the themed guided tours (€1.50; 11am, 12.30pm, 2pm & 3pm Tue-Sat, 2pm & 3pm Sun) will help you wade through the myriad exhibits. The Treasury is perhaps the most famous part of the collection, and its centrepieces are Ireland's two most famous crafted artefacts, the Ardagh Chalice and the Tara Brooch, dating from the 12th and 8th century respectively.

Elsewhere in the Treasury is the exhibition Ór-Ireland's Gold, featuring stunning jewellery and decorative objects created by Celtic artisans in the Bronze and Iron Ages. Among them are the Broighter Hoard, which includes a 1st-century-BC large gold collar, unsurpassed anywhere in Europe, and an extraordinarily delicate gold boat. There's also the wonderful Loughnasade bronze war trumpet, which dates from the 1st century BC.

On the same level is the Road to Independence exhibition, which features the army coat worn by Michael Collins on the day he was assassinated (there's still mud on the sleeve). If you can cope with any more history, upstairs are Medieval Ireland 1150 – 1550, Viking Age Ireland – which features exhibits from the excavations at Wood Quay, the area between Christ Church Cathedral and the river – and our own favourite, the aptly named Clothes from Bogs in Ireland, a collection of 16th- and 17th-century woollen garments recovered from the bog. Enthralling stuff!

⭐ **National Gallery**   MUSEUM
(Map p92; www.nationalgallery.ie; West Merrion Sq; ⊙9.30am-5.30pm Mon-Wed, Fri & Sat, 9.30am-8.30pm Thu, noon-5.30pm Sun; ⓐ7, 44 from city

centre) FREE A magnificent Caravaggio and a breathtaking collection of works by Jack B Yeats – William Butler's younger brother – are the main reasons to visit the National Gallery, but not the only ones. Its excellent collection is strong in Irish art, but there are also high-quality collections of every major European school of painting. There are free tours at 3pm on Saturdays and at 2pm, 3pm and 4pm on Sundays.

Spread about its four wings you'll find works by Rembrandt and his circle; a Spanish collection with paintings by El Greco, Goya and Picasso; and a well-represented display of Italian works dating from the early Renaissance to the 18th century. Fra Angelico, Titian and Tintoretto are among the artists represented, but the highlight is undoubtedly Caravaggio's *Taking of Christ* (1602), which lay for over 60 years in a Jesuit house in Leeson St and was accidentally discovered by chief curator Sergio Benedetti.

The ground floor displays the gallery's fine Irish collection, plus a smaller British collection, with works by Reynolds, Hogarth, Gainsborough, Landseer and Turner. Absolutely unmissable is the Yeats Collection at the back of the gallery, displaying more than 30 works by Irish impressionist Jack B Yeats (1871–1957), Ireland's most important 20th-century painter.

With its light-filled, modern design, the Millennium Wing can also be entered from Clare St. It houses a small collection of 20th-century Irish art, high-profile visiting collections (for which there are admission charges), an art reference library, a lecture theatre, a good bookshop and Fitzer's Café.

Leinster House   NOTABLE BUILDING
(Oireachtas Éireann; Map p92; ☑ tour information 01-618 3271; www.oireachtas.ie; Kildare St; ☉ observation gallery 2.30-8.30pm Tue, 10.30am-8.30pm Wed, 10.30am-5.30pm Thu Nov-May, tours 10.30am, 11.30am, 2.30pm & 3.30pm Mon-Fri when Parliament is in session; ☐ all city centre) All the big decisions are made – or rubber-stamped – at Oireachtas Éireann (Irish Parliament). This magnificent Palladian mansion was built as a city residence for James Fitzgerald, the Duke of Leinster and Earl of Kildare, by Richard Cassels between 1745 and 1748 – hence the name by which it's still known. Its Kildare St facade looks like a townhouse (which inspired Irish architect James Hoban's designs for the US White House), whereas the Merrion Sq frontage was made to resemble a country mansion.

The first government of the Irish Free State moved in from 1922, and both the Dáil (lower house) and Seanad (senate) still meet here to discuss the affairs of the nation and gossip at the exclusive members bar. The 60-member Seanad meets for fairly low-key sessions in the north-wing saloon, while there are usually more sparks and tantrums when the 166-member Dáil bangs heads in a less-interesting room, formerly a lecture theatre, which was added to the original building in 1897. Parliament sits for 90 days a year. You get an entry ticket to the lower- or upper-house observation galleries from the Kildare St entrance on production of photo identification. Free, pre-arranged guided tours are available when Parliament is in session.

The obelisk in front of the building is dedicated to Arthur Griffith, Michael Collins and Kevin O'Higgins, the architects of independent Ireland.

★ Museum of Natural History   MUSEUM
(National Museum of Ireland – Natural History; Map p92; www.museum.ie; Merrion St; ☉ 10am-5pm Tue-Sat, 2-5pm Sun; ☐ 7, 44 from city centre) FREE Dusty, weird and utterly compelling, this window into Victorian times has barely changed since Scottish explorer Dr David Livingstone opened it in 1857 – before disappearing into the African jungle for a meeting with Henry Stanley. Compared to the multimedia-this and interactive-that of virtually every modern museum, this is a beautifully preserved example of Victorian charm and scientific wonderment. It is usually full of fascinated kids, but it's the adults who seem to make the most noise as they ricochet like pinballs between displays.

The Irish Room on the ground floor is filled with mammals, sea creatures, birds and some butterflies all found in Ireland at some point, including the skeletons of three 10,000-year-old Irish elk that greet you as you enter. The World Animals Collection, spread across three levels, has as its centrepiece the skeleton of a 20m-long fin whale found beached in County Sligo. Evolutionists will love the line-up of orangutan, chimpanzee, gorilla and human skeletons on the 1st floor. A new addition here is the Discovery Zone, where visitors can do some first-hand exploring of their own, handling taxidermy and opening drawers. Other notables include the Tasmanian tiger (an extinct Australian marsupial, mislabelled as a Tasmanian wolf), a giant panda from China, and several African and Asian rhinoceroses. The wonderful Blaschka Collection comprises finely detailed glass models of marine creatures whose zoological accuracy is incomparable.

National Library
HISTORIC BUILDING

(Map p92; www.nli.ie; Kildare St; ⊙ 9.30am-9pm Mon-Wed, 10am-5pm Thu & Fri, 10am-1pm Sat; 🖳 all city centre) FREE Suitably sedate and elegant, the National Library was built from 1884 to 1890 by Sir Thomas Newenham Deane, at the same time and to a similar design as the National Museum. Its extensive collection has many valuable early manuscripts, first editions and maps.

Parts of the library are open to the public, including the domed reading room where Stephen Dedalus expounded his views on Shakespeare in *Ulysses*. For those prints that are worth a thousand words, you'll have to head down to Temple Bar to the National Photographic Archive (p63) extension of the library. There's a Genealogy Advisory Service on the 2nd floor, where you can obtain free information on how best to trace your Irish roots.

★ St Stephen's Green
PARK

(Map p92; ⊙ dawn-dusk; 🖳 all city centre, 🖳 St Stephen's Green) FREE As you watch the assorted groups of friends, lovers and individuals splaying themselves across the nine elegantly landscaped hectares of St Stephen's Green, consider that those same hectares once formed a common for public whippings, burnings and hangings. These days, the harshest treatment you'll get is the warden chucking you off the green for playing football or Frisbee.

The buildings around the square date mainly from the mid-18th century, when the green was landscaped and became the centrepiece of Georgian Dublin. The northern side was known as the Beaux Walk and it's still one of Dublin's most esteemed stretches, home to Dublin's original society hotel, the Shelbourne (p97). Nearby is the tiny Huguenot Cemetery (Map p92), established in 1693 by French Protestant refugees.

Railings and locked gates were erected in 1814, when an annual fee of one guinea was charged to use the green. This private use continued until 1877 when Sir Arthur Edward Guinness pushed an act through Parliament opening the green to the public once again. He also financed the central park's gardens and ponds, which date from 1880.

The main entrance to the green today is beneath Fusiliers' Arch (Map p92), at the top of Grafton St. Modelled to look like a smaller version of the Arch of Titus in Rome, the arch commemorates the 212 soldiers of the Royal Dublin Fusiliers who were killed fighting for the British in the Boer War (1899–1902).

Across the road from the western side of the green is the 1863 Unitarian Church (Map p92; ⊙ worship 7am-5pm) and the early-19th-century Royal College of Surgeons (Map p92), which has one of the finest facades on St Stephen's Green. During the 1916 Easter Rising, the building was occupied by rebel forces led by Countess Markievicz (1868–1927). The columns are scarred from the bullet holes.

Spread across the green's lawns and walkways are some notable artworks; the most imposing of these is a monument to Wolfe Tone (Map p92), the leader of the abortive 1798 rebellion. Occupying the northeastern corner of the green, the vertical slabs serving as a backdrop to the statue have been dubbed 'Tonehenge'. At this entrance is a memorial (Map p92) to all those who died in the Famine.

On the eastern side of the green is a children's playground (Map p92) and to the south there's a fine old bandstand, erected to celebrate Queen Victoria's jubilee in 1887. Musical performances often take place here in summer. Near the bandstand is a bust of James Joyce (Map p92), facing Newman House (Map p92; 85-86 St Stephen's Green South; adult €5; ⊙ tours noon, 2pm, 3pm & 4pm Tue-Fri Jun-Aug; 🖳 10, 11, 13, 14, 15A, 🖳 St Stephen's Green), part of University College Dublin (UCD), where Joyce was once a student. On the same side as Newman House is Iveagh House. Originally designed by Richard Cassels in 1730 as two separate houses, they were bought by Benjamin Guinness in 1862 and combined to create the family's city residence. After independence the house was donated to the Irish State and is now home to the Department of Foreign Affairs.

Little Museum of Dublin
MUSEUM

(Map p92; ☑ 01-661 1000; www.littlemuseum.ie; 15 St Stephen's Green North; adult/student/child €6/5/4; ⊙ 10am-5pm Mon-Fri; 🖳 all city centre, 🖳 St Stephen's Green) The idea is ingeniously simple: a museum, spread across two rooms of an elegant Georgian building, devoted to the history of Dublin in the 20th century, made up of memorabilia contributed by the general public. You don't need to know anything about Irish history or Dublin to appreciate it: visits are by guided tour and everyone is presented with a handsome booklet on the history of the city.

Since opening in 2011, the contributions have been impressive – amid the nostalgic posters, time-worn bric-a-brac and wonderful photographs of personages and cityscapes of yesteryear are some extraordinary finds, including a lectern used by JFK on his 1963 visit to Ireland and an original copy of the fateful letter given to the Irish envoys to the treaty negotiations of 1921, whose contradictory instructions were at the heart of the split that resulted in the Civil War.

Merrion Square   PARK
(Map p92; ☉ dawn-dusk; 🚃 7, 44 from city centre) **FREE** St Stephen's Green may win the popularity contest, but elegant Merrion Sq snubs its nose at such easy praise and remains the most prestigious of Dublin's squares. Its well-kept lawns and beautifully tended flower beds are flanked on three sides by gorgeous Georgian houses with colourful doors, peacock fanlights, ornate door knockers and, occasionally, foot-scrapers, used to remove mud from shoes before venturing indoors.

The square, laid out in 1762, is bordered on its remaining side by the National Gallery and Leinster House – all of which, apparently, isn't enough for some. One former resident, WB Yeats (1865–1939), was less than impressed and described the architecture as 'grey 18th century'; there's just no pleasing some people.

Just inside the northwestern corner of the square is a flamboyant **statue of Oscar Wilde** (Map p92), who grew up across the street at No 1 (now used exclusively by the American University Dublin). Facing it just inside the square is a statue of Wilde, wearing his customary smoking jacket and reclining on a rock. Atop one of the plinths, daubed with witty one-liners and Wildean throwaways, is a small green statue of Oscar's pregnant mother.

Government Buildings   NOTABLE BUILDING
(Map p92; www.taoiseach.gov.ie; Upper Merrion St; ☉ tours 10.30am-1.30pm Sat; 🚃 7, 44 from city centre) **FREE** This gleaming Edwardian pile was the last building (almost) completed by the British before they were booted out; it opened as the Royal College of Science in 1911. When the college vacated in 1989, Taoiseach (Republic of Ireland Prime Minister) Charles Haughey and his government moved in and spent a fortune refurbishing the complex.

Free 40-minute guided **tours** take you through the taoiseach's office, the Cabinet Room, the ceremonial staircase with a stunning stained-glass window – designed by Evie Hone (1894–1955) for the 1939 New York Trade Fair – and many fine examples of modern Irish arts and crafts.

◉ The Liberties & Kilmainham

At the top of a small hill, just west of Dublin Castle, is the most impressive monument of medieval Dublin: Christ Church Cathedral. It stood firmly inside the city walls, whereas that other great place of worship, St Patrick's, lay just outside them: today there's nothing between them but a couple of buildings and the expanse of a garden. To the west of both is the Liberties, Dublin's oldest surviving neighbourhood. The western end of the Liberties has a curious aroma in the air: it is the smell of roasting hops, used in the production of Guinness – Dublin's black gold and, for many visitors, the epitome of all things Irish. Further along St James's St is Kilmainham, home to the old prison that was central to the struggle for Irish independence (now a city highlight) and an ancient soldiers' hospital, now the country's most important modern-art museum.

ⓘ DUBLIN BY APP

Smartphone users can get the city in their palm by downloading Visit Dublin's official **app** (www.visitdublin.com) **FREE**. The information – a quarterly update of the tourist office's own database – is cached, which means there are no roaming charges for its basic use, which includes comprehensive listings of sights, attractions, hotels and places to eat. It is also available from the Apple App Store.

For more in-depth information, reviews and recommendations at your fingertips, head to the Apple App Store to purchase Lonely Planet's *Dublin City Guide* iPhone app.

★ **Guinness Storehouse**   BREWERY, MUSEUM (Map p72; www.guinness-storehouse.com; St James's Gate, South Market St; adult/student/child €16.50/10.50/6.50, Conoisseur Experience €25, discounts apply for online bookings; ◷ 9.30am-7pm Jul-Aug, 9.30am-5pm Sep-Jun; ☐ 21A, 51B, 78, 78A, 123 from Fleet St, ☒ St James's) The most

popular visit in town is the beer-lover's Disneyland, a multimedia, bells-and-whistles homage to the country's most famous export and the city's most enduring symbol. The old grain storehouse, the only part of the massive, 26-hectare St James's Gate Brewery open to the public, is a suitable cathedral

Dublin

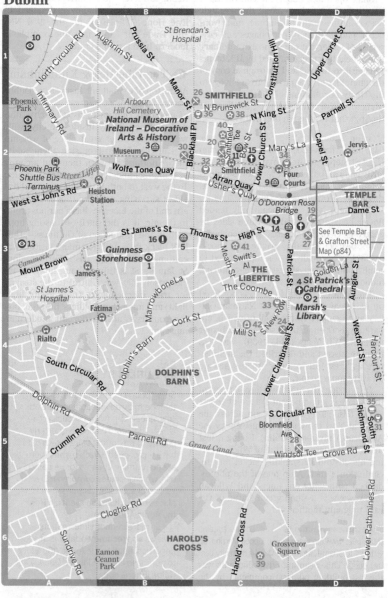

in which to worship the black gold; shaped like a giant pint of Guinness, it rises seven impressive storeys high around a stunning central atrium. At the top is the head, represented by the **Gravity Bar**, with a panoramic view of Dublin.

From the time Arthur Guinness (1725–1803) founded the brewery in 1759, the operation has expanded down to the Liffey and across both sides of the street; at one point, it had its own railway and there was a giant gate stretching across St James's St, hence the brewery's proper name. At its

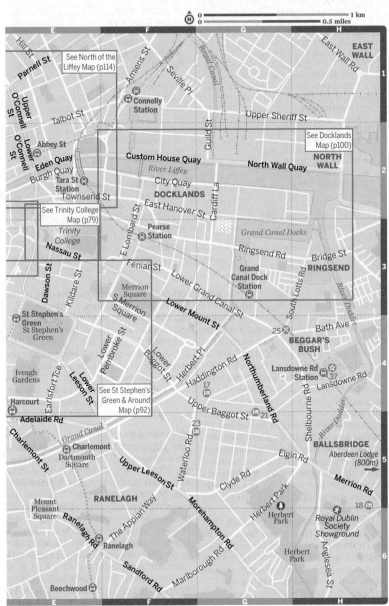

Dublin

apogee in the 1930s, it employed over 5000 workers, making it the largest employer in the city. Increased automation has reduced the workforce to around 600, but it still produces 2.5 million pints of stout *every day*.

You'll get to drink one of those pints at the end of your tour, but not before you have walked through the extravaganza that is the Guinness floor show, spread across 1.6 hectares and involving an array of audiovisual, interactive displays that cover pretty much all aspects of the brewery's history and the brewing process. It's slick and sophisticated, but you can't ignore the man behind the curtain: the extensive exhibit on the company's incredibly successful history of advertising is a reminder that for all the talk of mysticism and magic, it's all really about marketing and manipulation.

The point is made deliciously moot when you finally get a pint in your hand and let the cream pass your lips in the vertiginous heights of the Gravity Bar. It's the best pint of Guinness in the world, claim the cognoscenti, and die-hards can opt for the Conoisseur Experience, where a designated barkeep goes through the histories of the four variants of Guinness – Draught, Original, Foreign Extra Stout and Black Lager – and provides delicious samples of each.

Around the corner at **1 Thomas St** (Map p72; ⊙ closed to public) a plaque marks the house where Arthur Guinness lived. In a yard across the road stands **St Patrick's Tower** (Map p72; ⊙ closed to public), Europe's tallest smock windmill (with a revolving top), which was built around 1757.

★ **St Patrick's Cathedral** CHURCH
(Map p72; www.stpatrickscathedral.ie; St Patrick's Close; adult/child €5.50/free; ⊙ 9am-5pm Mon-Sat, 9-10.30am & 12.30-2.30pm Sun year-round, longer hours Mar-Oct; 🚌 50, 50A, 56A from Aston Quay, 54, 54A from Burgh Quay) It was at this cathedral, reputedly, that St Paddy himself dunked the Irish heathens into the waters of a well, so the church that bears his name stands on one of the earliest Christian sites in the city and a pretty sacred piece of turf. Although there's been a church here since the 5th century, the present building dates from 1190 or 1225 (opinions differ) and it has been altered several times, most notably in

1864 when the flying buttresses were added, thanks to the neo-Gothic craze that swept the nation. St Patrick's Park, the expanse of green beside the cathedral, was a crowded slum until it was cleared and its residents evicted in the early 20th century.

Like Christ Church Cathedral, the building has suffered a rather dramatic history of storm and fire damage. Oliver Cromwell, during his 1649 visit to Ireland, converted St Patrick's to a stable for his army's horses, an indignity to which he also subjected numerous other Irish churches. Jonathan Swift, author of *Gulliver's Travels,* was the dean of the cathedral from 1713 to 1745, but prior to its restoration it was very neglected. Also like Christ Church, St Patrick's is a Church of Ireland cathedral – which means that overwhelmingly Catholic Dublin has two Anglican cathedrals!

Entering the cathedral from the southwestern porch you come almost immediately, on your right, to the graves of Swift and his long-time companion Esther Johnson, aka Stella. On the wall nearby are Swift's own Latin epitaphs to the two of them, and a bust of Swift.

The huge, dusty Boyle Monument to the left was erected in 1632 by Richard Boyle, Earl of Cork, and is decorated with numerous painted figures of members of his family. The figure in the centre on the bottom level is the earl's five-year-old son Robert Boyle (1627–91), who grew up to become a noted scientist. His contributions to physics include Boyle's Law, which relates the pressure and volume of gases.

★Marsh's Library   LIBRARY
(Map p72; www.marshlibrary.ie; St Patrick's Close; adult/child €2.50/free; ⊘9.30am-1pm & 2-5pm Mon & Wed-Fri, 10am-1pm Sat; ▣ 50, 50A, 56A from Aston Quay, 54, 54A from Burgh Quay) This magnificently preserved scholars' library, virtually unchanged in three centuries, is one of Dublin's most beautiful open secrets, and an absolute highlight of any visit. Few think to scale its ancient stairs to see its beautiful, dark oak bookcases, each topped with elaborately carved and gilded gables, and crammed with books. Here you can savour the atmosphere of three centuries of learning, slow into synch with the tick-tocking of the 19th-century grandfather clock, listen to

DUBLIN SIGHTS

DUBLIN IN...

Two Days

If you've only got two days (whatever is taking you away better be worth it!), start with Trinity College (p62) and the Book of Kells before venturing into the Georgian heartland – amble through St Stephen's Green (p70) and Merrion Square (p71), but be sure to visit both the National Museum of Ireland – Archaeology (p68) and the National Gallery (p68). In the evening, try an authentic Dublin pub – Kehoe's (p115) off Grafton St will do nicely. The next day go west, stopping at the Chester Beatty Library (p66) on your way to the Guinness Storehouse (p72); if you still have legs for it, the Irish Museum of Modern Art (p77) and Kilmainham Gaol (p77) will round off your day perfectly. Take in a traditional Irish music session at the Cobblestone (p119).

Four Days

Follow the two-day itinerary, but stretch it out between refuelling stops at some of the city's better pubs. Visit Glasnevin Cemetery (p98) and the Dublin City Gallery – Hugh Lane (p78). Become a whiskey expert at the Old Jameson Distillery (p82) and a literary (or beer) one with a Dublin Literary Pub Crawl (p90). Explore the north side's blossoming foodie scene – L Mulligan Grocer (Map p72; 18 Stoneybatter; mains €14-21; ▣ 25, 25A, 66, 67 from city centre, ▣ Museum) for local grub or terrific Japanese at Musashi Noodles & Sushi Bar (p112). Oh, and don't forget Temple Bar (p63) – there are distractions there for every taste.

One Week

Follow the four day itinerary, but add a day for the seaside village of Howth (p133); be sure to eat in one of its fish restaurants along the pier); a visit to Phoenix Park (p83); and exploration of the Docklands (p82). There might even be someone you'd love to see performing at the Bord Gáis Energy Theatre (p123). Alternatively, attend a play at either the Abbey (p125) or the Gate (p125).

THE PAGE OF KELLS

More than half a million visitors stop in each year to see Trinity's top show-stopper, the world-famous **Book of Kells**. This illuminated manuscript, dating from around AD 800 and therefore one of the oldest books in the world, was probably produced by monks at St Colmcille's Monastery on the remote island of Iona, off the western coast of Scotland. Repeated looting by marauding Vikings forced the monks to flee to the temporary safety of Kells, County Meath, in AD 806, along with their masterpiece. Around 850 years later, the book was brought to the college for safekeeping and has remained here since.

The Book of Kells contains the four Gospels of the New Testament, written in Latin, as well as prefaces, summaries and other text. If it were merely words, the Book of Kells would simply be a very old book – it's the extensive and amazingly complex illustrations that make it so wonderful. The superbly decorated opening initials are only part of the story, for the book has smaller illustrations between the lines.

And here the problems begin. Of the 680 pages, only two are on display – one showing an illumination, the other showing text – which has led to it being dubbed the *page* of Kells. No getting around that one, though: you can hardly expect the right to thumb through a priceless treasure at random. No, the real problem is its immense popularity, which makes viewing it a rather unsatisfactory pleasure. Punters are herded through the specially constructed viewing room at near lightning pace, making for a there-you-see-it, there-you-don't kind of experience.

To really appreciate the book, you can buy your own reproduction copy for a mere €22,000. Failing that, the library bookshop stocks a plethora of souvenirs and other memorabilia, including Otto Simm's excellent *Exploring the Book of Kells* (€12.95), a thorough guide with attractive colour plates, and a popular DVD-ROM (€31.95) showing all 800 pages. Kids looking for something a little less stuffy might enjoy the animated *Secret of Kells* (2009), which is more fun than accurate in its portrayal of how the gospel was actually put together.

the squeaky boards and record the scent of leather and learning. It's amazing how many people visit St Patrick's Cathedral next door and overlook this gem – they're mad, they don't deserve a holiday.

Founded in 1701 by Archbishop Narcissus Marsh (1638–1713) and opened in 1707, the library was designed by Sir William Robinson, the man also responsible for the Royal Hospital Kilmainham (Map p72). It's the oldest public library in the country, and contains 25,000 books dating from the 16th to the early 18th century, as well as maps, manuscripts (including one in Latin dating back to 1400) and a collection of incunabula (books printed before 1500). In its one nod to the 21st century, the library's current 'keeper', Dr Muriel McCarthy, is the first woman to hold the post.

Christ Church Cathedral　　　CHURCH
(Church of the Holy Trinity; Map p72; www.cccdub.ie; Christ Church Pl; adult/child €6/2; ⊙9.30am-5pm Mon-Sat & 12.30-2.30pm Sun year-round, longer hours Jun-Aug; ⌨ 50, 50A, 56A from Aston Quay, 54, 54A from Burgh Quay) Its hilltop location and eye-catching flying buttresses make this the most photogenic by far of Dublin's three cathedrals as well as one of the capital's most recognisable symbols.

It was founded in 1030 on what was then the southern edge of Dublin's Viking settlement; the original wooden church was rebuilt by the Normans from 1172, mostly under the impetus of Richard de Clare, Earl of Pembroke (better known as Strongbow), the Anglo-Norman noble who invaded Ireland in 1170.

Throughout much of its history, Christ Church vied for supremacy with nearby St Patrick's Cathedral but it also fell on hard times in the 18th and 19th centuries – earlier, the nave had been used as a market and the crypt had housed taverns – and was virtually derelict by the time restoration took place. Today, both Church of Ireland cathedrals are outsiders in a largely Catholic nation.

From the southeastern entrance to the churchyard, walk past ruins of the chapter house, which dates from 1230. The entrance to the cathedral is at the southwestern corner and as you enter you face the northern wall. This survived the collapse of its southern counterpart but has also suffered from subsiding foundations.

The southern aisle has a monument to the legendary Strongbow. The armoured figure on the tomb is unlikely to be Strongbow (it's more probably the Earl of Drogheda), but his internal organs may have been buried here. A popular legend relates that the half figure beside the tomb is Strongbow's son, who was cut in two by his father when his bravery in battle was suspect.

The southern transept contains the superb baroque tomb of the 19th Earl of Kildare (died 1734). His grandson, Lord Edward Fitzgerald, was a member of the United Irishmen and died in the abortive 1798 Rising.

An entrance just by the southern transept descends to the unusually large arched crypt, which dates back to the original Viking church. Curiosities in the crypt include a glass display case housing a mummified cat chasing a mummified rat (known as Tom and Jerry), which were trapped inside an organ pipe in the 1860s! From the main entrance, a bridge, part of the 1871–78 restoration, leads to Dvblinia.

Dvblinia & the Viking World MUSEUM
(Map p72; ☑01-679 4611; www.dublinia.ie; adult/student/child €7.50/6.50/5; ☺10am-5pm Apr-Sep, 11am-4pm Mon-Sat & 10am-4.30pm Sun Oct-Mar; ☐50, 50A, 56A from Aston Quay, 54, 54A from Burgh Quay) A must for the kids, the old Synod Hall, added to Christ Church Cathedral during its late-19th-century restoration, is home to the seemingly perennial Dvblinia, a lively and kitschy attempt to bring medieval Dublin to life. Models, streetscapes and somewhat old-fashioned interactive displays do a fairly decent job of it, at least for kids. The model of a medieval quayside and a cobbler's shop are both excellent, as is the scale model of the medieval city. Up one floor is Viking World, which has a large selection of objects recovered from Wood Quay, the world's largest Viking archaeological site. Interactive exhibits tell the story of Dublin's 9th- and 10th-century Scandinavian invaders, but the real treat is exploring life aboard the re-created longboat. Finally, you can climb neighbouring St Michael's Tower (Map p84) and peek through its grubby windows for views over the city to the Dublin hills. There is also a pleasant cafe and the inevitable souvenir shop. Your ticket gets you into Christ Church Cathedral free, via the link bridge.

★**Kilmainham Gaol** MUSEUM
(www.heritageireland.com; Inchicore Rd; adult/child €6/2; ☺9.30am-6pm Apr-Sep, 9.30am-5.30pm Mon-Sat, 10am-6pm Sun Oct-Mar; ☐23, 25, 25A, 26, 68, 69 from city centre) If you have *any* desire to understand Irish history – especially the juicy bits about resistance to English rule – then a visit to this former prison is an absolute must. This threatening grey building, built between 1792 and 1795, has played a role in virtually every act of Ireland's painful path to independence.

The uprisings of 1798, 1803, 1848, 1867 and 1916 ended with the leaders' confinement here. Robert Emmet, Thomas Francis Meagher, Charles Stewart Parnell and the 1916 Easter Rising leaders were all visitors, but it was the executions in 1916 that most deeply etched the jail's name into the Irish consciousness. Of the 15 executions that took place between 3 May and 12 May after the revolt, 14 were conducted here. As a finale, prisoners from the Civil War were held here from 1922. The jail closed in 1924.

An excellent audiovisual introduction to the building is followed by a thought-provoking tour of the eerie prison, the largest unoccupied building of its kind in Europe. Sitting incongruously outside in the yard is the *Asgard,* the ship that successfully ran the British blockade to deliver arms to Nationalist forces in 1914. The tour finishes in the gloomy yard where the 1916 executions took place.

Irish Museum of Modern Art MUSEUM
(IMMA; Map p72; www.imma.ie; Military Rd; ☺10am-5.30pm Tue & Thu-Sat, 10.30am-5.30pm Wed, noon-5.30pm Sun, tours 2.30pm Tue-Fri & Sun, noon & 4pm Sat; ☐Heuston) **FREE** Ireland's most important collection of modern and contemporary Irish art is housed in the elegant, airy expanse of the Royal Hospital at Kilmainham, which in 1991 became a magnificent exhibition space and was almost completely refurbished in 2012–13.

The Royal Hospital Kilmainham was designed by William Robinson (who also designed Marsh's Library), and was built between 1680 and 1687 as a home for retired soldiers. It fulfilled this role until 1928, after which it languished for nearly 50 years until a 1980s restoration. At the time of its construction, it was one of the finest buildings in Ireland and there were mutterings that it was altogether too good a place for its residents.

The blend of old and new works wonderfully, and you'll find such contemporary Irish artists as Louis Le Brocquy, Sean Scully, Barry Flanagan, Kathy Prendergrass and Dorothy Cross featured here, as well as a film installation by Neil Jordan. The permanent exhibition also features paintings from heavy hitters Pablo Picasso and Joan Miró, and is topped up by regular temporary exhibitions. There's a good cafe and bookshop on the grounds.

There are free guided tours of the museum's exhibits throughout the year, but we strongly recommend the free seasonal heritage tours (50 min) of the building itself, which run from July to September.

St Audoen's Churches
CHURCH

(Map p72; ⊞ 50, 50A or 56A from Aston Quay, 54 or 54A from Burgh Quay) It was only right that the newly arrived Normans would name a church after their patron saint Audoen (the 7th-century bishop of Rouen, aka Ouen), but they didn't quite figure on two virtually adjacent churches bearing his name, just west of Christ Church Cathedral. The more interesting of the two is the Church of Ireland (Map p72; ⊘ 9.30am-4.45pm Jun-Sep) FREE, the only medieval parish church in the city that's still in use. It was built between 1181 and 1212, although a 9th-century burial slab in the porch suggests that it was built on top of an even older church. Its tower and door date from the 12th century and the aisle from the 15th century, but the church today is mainly a product of a 19th-century restoration.

As part of the tour you can explore the ruins as well as the present church, which has funerary monuments that were beheaded by Cromwell's purists. Through the heavily moulded Romanesque Norman door you can also touch the 9th-century 'lucky stone' that was believed to bring good luck to business.

St Anne's Chapel, the visitor centre, houses a number of tombstones of leading members of Dublin society from the 16th to the 18th centuries. At the top of the chapel is the tower, which holds the three oldest bells in Ireland, dating from 1423. Although the church's exhibits are hardly spectacular, the building itself is beautiful and a genuine slice of medieval Dublin.

The church is entered from the south off High St through St Audoen's Arch, which was built in 1240 and is the only surviving reminder of the city gates. The adjoining park is pretty but attracts many unsavoury characters, particularly at night.

Joined onto the Protestant church is the newer, bigger, 19th-century Catholic St Audoen's, an expansive church in which Father 'Flash' Kavanagh used to read Mass at high speed so that his large congregation could head off to more absorbing Sunday pursuits, such as football matches. In 2006 it was handed over to the Polish chaplaincy.

War Memorial Gardens
PARK

(www.heritageireland.ie; South Circular Rd, Islandbridge; ⊘ 8am-dusk Mon-Fri, from 10am Sat & Sun; ⊞ 25, 25A, 26, 68, 69 from city centre) FREE Hardly anyone ever ventures this far west, but they're missing a lovely bit of landscaping in the shape of the War Memorial Gardens – by our reckoning as pleasant a patch of greenery as any you'll find in the heart of the Georgian centre. Designed by Sir Edwin Lutyens, the memorial commemorates the 49,400 Irish soldiers who died during WWI – their names are inscribed in the two huge granite bookrooms that stand at one end. A beautiful spot and a bit of history to boot.

◉ North of the Liffey

Grittier than its more genteel southside counterpart, the neighbourhoods immediately north of the River Liffey offer a fascinating mix of 18th-century grandeur, traditional city life and the multicultural melting pot that is contemporary Dublin. Beyond its widest, most elegant boulevard you'll find art museums and whiskey museums, bustling markets and some of the best ethnic eateries in town.

Dublin City Gallery – The Hugh Lane
GALLERY

(Map p114; ⊘ 01-222 5550; www.hughlane.ie; 22 North Parnell Sq; ⊘ 10am-6pm Tue-Thu, 10am-5pm Fri & Sat, 11am-5pm Sun; ⊞ 3, 7, 10, 11, 13, 16, 19, 46A, 123) FREE Whatever reputation Dublin has as a repository of world-class art has a lot to do with the simply stunning collection at this exquisite gallery, housed in the equally impressive Charlemont House, designed by William Chambers in 1763. A modernist extension, which opened in 2006, has seen the addition of 13 bright galleries spread across three floors of the old National Ballroom.

The gallery owes its origins to one Sir Hugh Lane (1875–1915). Born in County Cork, Lane worked in London art galleries before setting up his own gallery in

Trinity College

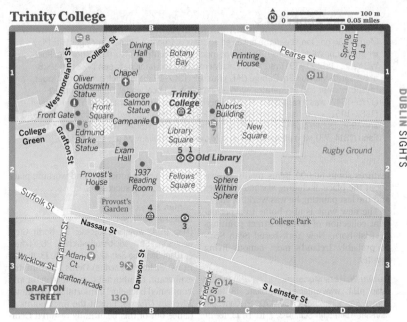

N 0 — 100 m
0 — 0.05 miles

Dublin in 1908. He had a connoisseur's eye and a good nose for the directions of the market, which enabled him to build up a superb collection, particularly strong in Impressionists.

Unfortunately for Ireland, neither his talents nor his collection were much appreciated. Irish rejection led him to rewrite his will and bequeath some of the finest works in his collection to the National Gallery in London. Later he relented and added a rider to his will leaving the collection to Dublin but failed to have it witnessed, thus causing a long legal squabble over which gallery had rightful ownership.

The collection (known as the Hugh Lane Bequest 1917) was split in a complicated 1959 settlement that sees some of the paintings moving back and forth. The conditions of the exchanges are in the midst of negotiation, but for now the gallery has Manet's *La Musique Aux Tuileries*, Degas' *Bains de Mer* and Monet's *Lavacourt under Snow*.

Impressionist masterpieces notwithstanding, the gallery's most popular exhibit is the Francis Bacon Studio, which was painstakingly moved, in all its shambolic mess, from 7 Reece Mews, South Kensington, London, where the Dublin-born artist (1909–92) lived for 31 years. The display

Trinity College

LITERARY ADDRESSES

Merrion Sq has long been the favoured address of Dublin's affluent intelligentsia. Playwright Oscar Wilde (1854–1900) spent much of his youth at 1 North Merrion Sq. Poet WB Yeats (1865–1939) lived at 52 East Merrion Sq and later, between 1922 and 1928, at 82 South Merrion Sq. George ('AE') Russell (1867–1935), the self-proclaimed 'poet, mystic, painter and cooperator', worked at No 84. Political leader Daniel O'Connell (1775–1847) was a resident of No 58 in his later years. The Austrian Erwin Schrödinger (1887–1961), co-winner of the 1933 Nobel Prize for Physics, lived at No 65 between 1940 and 1956. Dublin also seems to attract writers of horror stories: Joseph Sheridan Le Fanu (1814–73), who penned the vampire classic *Carmilla*, was a resident of No 70.

features some 80,000 items madly strewn about the place, including slashed canvases and the last painting he was working on.

The new wing is also home to a permanent collection of seven abstract paintings by Irish-born, New York–based Sean Scully, probably Ireland's most famous living painter.

Dublin Writers Museum   MUSEUM
(Map p114; www.writersmuseum.com; 18 North Parnell Sq; adult/child €7.50/4.70; ⊙10am-5pm Mon-Sat, 11am-5pm Sun; 🚌3, 7, 10, 11, 13, 16, 19, 46A, 123) Memorabilia aplenty and lots of literary ephemera line the walls and display cabinets of this elegant museum devoted to preserving the city's rich literary tradition up to 1970. A curious decision to omit living writers limits its appeal and no account at all is given to contemporary writers, who would arguably be more popular with today's readers.

Although the busts and portraits of the greats in the gallery upstairs are worth more than a cursory peek, the real draws are the ground-floor displays, which include Samuel Beckett's phone (with a button for excluding incoming calls, of course), a letter from the 'tenement aristocrat' Brendan Behan to his brother, and a first edition of Bram Stoker's *Dracula*.

The building, comprising two 18th-century houses, is worth exploring on its own. Dublin stuccodore Michael Stapleton decorated the upstairs gallery. The Gorham Library next door is worth a peek and there's also a calming Zen garden. The museum cafe is a pleasant place to linger, while the basement restaurant, Chapter One (p113), is one of the city's best.

While the museum focuses on the dearly departed, the Irish Writers Centre (Map p114; ☎01-872 1302; 19 North Parnell Sq) next

door provides a meeting and working place for their living successors.

James Joyce Cultural Centre   MUSEUM
(Map p114; www.jamesjoyce.ie; 35 North Great George's St; adult/student/child €5/4/free; ⊙10am-5pm Tue-Sat; 🚌3, 10, 11, 11A, 13, 16, 16A, 19, 19A, 22 from city centre) Denis Maginni, the exuberant, flamboyant dance instructor and 'confirmed bachelor' immortalised by James Joyce in *Ulysses*, taught the finer points of dance out of this beautifully restored Georgian house, now a centre devoted to promoting and preserving the Joycean heritage.

Inside are a handful of exhibits that will pique the interest of a Joyce enthusiast. These include some of the furniture from Joyce's Paris apartment; a life-size re-creation of a typical Edwardian bedroom (not Joyce's, but one similar to what James and Nora would have used); and the original door of 7 Eccles St, the home of Leopold and Molly Bloom in *Ulysses*, which was demolished in real life to make way for a private hospital.

It's not much, but the absence of period stuff is more than made up for by the superb interactive displays, which include three short documentary films on various aspects of Joyce's life and work, and – the highlight of the whole place – computers that allow you to explore the content of *Ulysses* episode by episode and trace Joyce's life year by year. It's enough to demolish the myth that Joyce's works are an impenetrable mystery and render him as he should be to the contemporary reader: a writer of enormous talent who sought to challenge and entertain his audience with his breathtaking wit and use of language.

While here, you can also admire the fine plastered ceilings, some of which are restored originals while others are meticulous reproductions of renowned plasterer Michael Stapleton's designs. The street has also been given a facelift and now boasts some of the finest Georgian doorways and fanlights in the city.

General Post Office
HISTORIC BUILDING

(Map p114; www.anpost.ie; O'Connell St; ⊘8am-8pm Mon-Sat; ⊒all city centre, ⊒Abbey) Not just the country's main post office, or an eye-catching neoclassical building: the General Post Office is at the heart of Ireland's struggle for independence as it served as command HQ for the rebels during the Easter Rising of 1916. As a result, it has become the focal point for all kinds of protests, parades and remembrances.

The building – a neoclassical masterpiece designed by Francis Johnston in 1818 – was burnt out in the siege that resulted from the rising, but that wasn't the end of it. There was bitter fighting in and around the building during the Civil War of 1922; you can still see the pockmarks of the struggle in the Doric columns. Since its reopening in 1929 it has lived through quieter times, although its role in Irish history is commemorated inside with a series of communist noble worker–style paintings depicting scenes from the Easter Rising.

St Mary's Pro-Cathedral
CHURCH

(Map p114; Marlborough St; ⊘8am-6.30pm; ⊒all city centre, ⊒Abbey) FREE Dublin's most important Catholic church is not quite the showcase you'd expect. It's in the wrong place for starters. The large neoclassical building, built between 1816 and 1825, was intended to stand where the GPO is, but Protestant objections resulted in its current location, on a cramped street that was then at the heart of Monto, the red-light district.

In fact, it's so cramped for space around here that you'd hardly notice the church's six Doric columns, which were modelled on the Temple of Theseus in Athens, much less be able to admire them. The interior is fairly functional, and its few highlights include a carved altar by Peter Turnerelli and the alto relief representation of the Ascension by John Smyth. The best time to visit is 11am on Sunday when the Latin Mass is sung by the Palestrina Choir, with whom Ireland's most celebrated tenor, John McCormack, began his career in 1904.

National Leprechaun Museum
MUSEUM

(Map p114; www.leprechaunmuseum.ie; Twilfit House, Jervis St; adult/child €12/8; ⊘9.30am-6.30pm Mon-Sat, from 10.30am Sun; ⊒all city centre; ⊒Jervis) Ostensibly designed as a child-friendly museum of Irish folklore, this is really a romper-room for kids sprinkled with bits of fairy tale. Which is no bad thing, even if the picture of the leprechaun painted here is more Lucky Charms and Walt Disney than sinister creature of pre-Celtic mythology.

There's the optical-illusion tunnel (which makes you appear smaller to those at the other end), the room full of oversized furniture, the wishing wells and, invariably, the pot of gold; all of which is strictly for the kids. But if Walt Disney himself went on a leprechaun hunt when visiting Ireland during the filming of *Darby O'Gill and the Little People* in 1948, what the hell do we know?

Four Courts
HISTORIC BUILDING

(Map p72; Inns Quay; ⊘9am-5pm Mon-Fri; ⊒25, 66, 67, 90 from city centre, ⊒Four Courts) FREE This masterpiece of James Gandon (1743–1823) is a mammoth complex stretching 130m along Inns Quay, as fine an example of Georgian public architecture as there is in Dublin. Despite the construction of a brand-new criminal courts building further west along the Liffey, the Four Courts is still the enduring symbol of Irish law going about its daily business.

The Corinthian-columned central block, connected to flanking wings with enclosed quadrangles, was begun in 1786 and not completed until 1802. The original four courts (Exchequer, Common Pleas, King's Bench and Chancery) all branch off of the central rotunda.

Visitors are allowed to wander through the building, but not to enter courts or other restricted areas. In the lobby of the central rotunda you'll see bewigged barristers conferring and police officers handcuffed to their charges.

St Michan's Church
CHURCH

(Map p72; Lower Church St; adult/student/child €5/4/3.50; ⊘10am-12.45pm & 2-4.45pm Mon-Fri, 10am-12.45pm Sat ; ⊒Smithfield) Macabre remains are the main attraction at this church, which was founded by the Danes in 1096 and named after one of their saints. Among the 'attractions' is an 800-year-old Norman crusader who was so tall that his feet were lopped off so he could fit in a coffin. Visits are by guided tour only.

The oldest architectural feature is the 15th-century battlement tower; otherwise the church was rebuilt in the late 17th century, considerably restored in the early 19th century and again after the Civil War. The interior of the church, which feels more like a courtroom, is worth a quick look as you wait for your guide. It contains an organ from 1724, which Handel may have played for the first-ever performance of his *Messiah*. The organ case is distinguished by the fine oak carving of 17 entwined musical instruments on its front. A skull on the floor on one side of the altar is said to represent Oliver Cromwell. On the opposite side is the Stool of Repentance, where 'open and notoriously naughty livers' did public penance.

The tours of the underground vaults are the real draw, however. The bodies within are aged between 400 and 800 years, and have been preserved by a combination of methane gas coming from rotting vegetation beneath the church, the magnesium limestone of the masonry (which absorbs moisture from the air), and the perfectly constant temperature. The corpses have been exposed because the coffins in the vaults were stacked on top of one another and some toppled over and opened when the wood rotted. The guide sounds like he's been delivering the same, albeit fascinating, spiel for too long, but you'll definitely be glad you're not alone down there.

Old Jameson Distillery MUSEUM
(Map p72; www.jamesonwhiskey.com; Bow St; adult/child €14/8; ☉9am-6pm Mon-Sat, 10am-6pm Sun; ⎯25, 66, 67, 90 from city centre, ⎯Smithfield) Smithfield's biggest draw is devoted to *uisce beatha* (*ish*-kuh ba-ha, 'the water of life'), the Irish for whiskey. To its more serious devotees, that is precisely what whiskey is, although they may be put off by the slickness of the museum (occupying part of the old distillery that stopped production in 1971), which shepherds visitors through a compulsory tour of the re-created factory (the tasting at the end is a lot of fun) and into the ubiquitous gift shop.

If you're buying whiskey, go for the stuff you can't buy at home, such as the excellent Red Breast or the superexclusive Midleton, a very limited reserve that is appropriately expensive.

★**National Museum of Ireland –
Decorative Arts & History** MUSEUM
(Map p72; www.museum.ie; Benburb St; ☉10am-5pm Tue-Sat, 2-5pm Sun; ⎯25, 66, 67, 90 from city centre, ⎯Smithfield) FREE Once the world's largest military barracks, this splendid early-neoclassical grey-stone building on the Liffey's northern banks is now home to the Decorative Arts & History collection of the National Museum of Ireland.

The building was completed in 1704 according to the design of Thomas Burgh, whose CV also includes the Old Library in Trinity College and St Michan's Church. Its central square held six entire regiments and is a truly awesome space, surrounded by arcaded colonnades and blocks linked by walking bridges. Following the handover to the new Irish government in 1922, the barracks was renamed to honour Michael Collins, a hero of the struggle for independence, who was killed that year in the Civil War; to this day most Dubliners refer to the museum as the **Collins Barracks**.

Inside the imposing exterior lies a treasure trove of artefacts ranging from silver, ceramics and glassware to weaponry, furniture and folk-life displays – and an exquisite exhibition dedicated to iconic Irish designer **Eileen Gray** (1878–1976). The fascinating **Way We Wore** exhibit displays Irish clothing and jewellery from the past 250 years. An intriguing sociocultural study, it highlights the symbolism jewellery and clothing had in bestowing messages of mourning, love and identity. An exhibition chronicling Ireland's **1916 Easter Rising** is on the ground floor. Visceral memorabilia, such as first-hand accounts of the violence of the Black & Tans and post-Rising hunger strikes, the handwritten death certificates of the Republican prisoners and their postcards from Holloway prison, bring to life this poignant period of Irish history. Some of the best pieces are gathered in the **Curator's Choice** exhibition, which is a collection of 25 objects hand-picked by different curators, and displayed alongside an account of why they were chosen.

◉ Docklands

It's a cardinal rule of any program of urban development: if your city is at the mouth of the sea, you cannot modernise without giving the docklands a revamp. And so it was with Dublin: the eastern banks north and south of the Liffey – aka 'Canary Dwarf' – have been given a major makeover and now sport an impressive array of contemporary office blocks, fancy apartments and snazzy public buildings, including Kevin Roche's angled, tubelike **National Convention**

Centre (Map p100) and Daniel Liebeskind's marvellous Grand Canal Theatre.

Custom House   MUSEUM
(Map p114; ⊘10am-5pm Mon-Fri, 2-5pm Sat & Sun; ▣all city centre) Georgian genius James Gandon (1743–1823) announced his arrival on the Dublin scene with this magnificent building (1781–91), constructed just past Eden Quay at a wide stretch in the River Liffey. It's a colossal, neoclassical pile that stretches for 114m topped by a copper dome, beneath which the Visitor Centre (Custom House Quay; admission €1; ⊘10am-12.30pm Mon-Fri, 2-5pm Sat & Sun mid-Mar–Oct, closed Mon & Tue & Sat Nov–mid-Mar) features a small museum on Gandon and the history of the building.

Best appreciated from the south side of the Liffey, its fine detail deserves closer inspection. Below the frieze are heads representing the gods of Ireland's 13 principal rivers, and the sole female head, above the main door, represents the River Liffey. The cattle heads honour Dublin's beef trade, and the statues behind the building represent Africa, America, Asia and Europe. Set into the dome are four clocks and, above that, a 5m-high statue of Hope.

Jeanie Johnston   MUSEUM
(Map p100; www.jeaniejohnston.ie; Custom House Quay; adult/child €8.50/4.50; ⊘tours 11am, noon & hourly 2-4pm; ▣all city centre) One of the city's most original tourist attractions is an exact working replica of a 19th-century coffin ship, as the sailing boats that transported starving emigrants away from Ireland during the Famine were gruesomely known. A small on-board museum details the harrowing plight of a typical journey, which usually took around 47 days.

This particular ship, a three-masted barque originally built in Quebec in 1847, made 16 transatlantic voyages, carrying more than 2500 people, and never suffered a single death. The ship also operates as a Sail Training vessel, with journeys taking place from May to September. If you are visiting during these times, check the website for details of when it will be in dock.

⊙ Phoenix Park

Measuring 709 glorious hectares, the Phoenix Park (www.phoenixpark.ie; ⊘24hr; ▣10 from O'Connell St, 25 or 26 from Middle Abbey St, then Phoenix Park Shuttle Bus from Parkgate St entrance.) FREE is Europe's largest city park: a green lung that is more than double the size of New York's Central Park (a paltry 337 hectares), and larger than all of London's major parks put together. Here you'll find gardens and lakes; pitches for all kinds of British sports from soccer to cricket to polo (the dry original one, with horses); the second-oldest zoo in Europe; a castle and visitor centre; the headquarters of the Garda Síochána (police); the Ordnance Survey offices; and the

---

O'CONNELL STREET STATUARY

O'Connell St is lined with statues of Irish history's good and great. The big daddy of them all is the 'Liberator' himself, Daniel O'Connell (Map p114), whose massive bronze bulk soars high above the street at the bridge end. The four winged figures at his feet represent O'Connell's supposed virtues: patriotism, courage, fidelity and eloquence.

O'Connell is rivalled for drama by the spread-armed figure of trade-union leader Jim Larkin (Map p114), just south of the General Post Office; you can almost hear the eloquent tirade.

Looking on with a bemused air from the corner of pedestrianised North Earl St is a small statue of James Joyce (Map p114), whom wagsters like to refer to as 'the Prick with the Stick'. Joyce would have loved the vulgar rhyme.

Further north is the statue of Father Theobald Mathew (Map p114), the 'Apostle of Temperance' – a hopeless role in Ireland. This quixotic task, however, also resulted in a Liffey bridge bearing his name. The northern end of the street is completed by the imposing statue of Charles Stewart Parnell (Map p114), Home Rule advocate and victim of Irish morality.

Finally, a word about the street's most dominant bit of decoration – the Spire (Map p114; O'Connell St; ▣all city centre, ▣Abbey). The brainchild of London-based architect Ian Ritchie, this 120m-high steel 'needle' is apparently the highest sculpture in the world; whatever the case it has become the city's most recognisable symbol since its erection in 2001.

homes of both the president of Ireland and the US ambassador, who live in two exquisite residences more or less opposite each other. There's even a herd of some 500 fallow deer.

The deer were first introduced by Lord Ormond in 1662, when lands once owned by the Knights of Jerusalem were turned into a royal hunting ground. In 1745 the viceroy Lord Chesterfield threw it open to the public and it has remained so ever since. (The name 'Phoenix' has nothing to do with the mythical bird; it is a corruption of the Irish *fionn uisce,* meaning 'clear water'.)

Temple Bar & Grafton Street

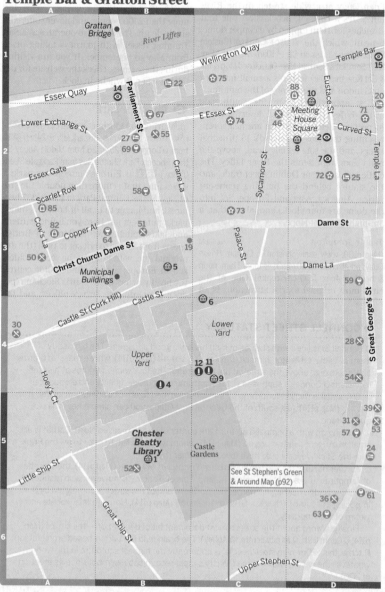

In 1882 the park played a crucial role in Irish history, when Lord Cavendish, the British chief secretary for Ireland, and his assistant were murdered outside what is now the Irish president's residence by an obscure Nationalist group called the Invincibles. Lord Cavendish's home is now called Deerfield

and is used as the official residence of the US ambassador.

Near the Parkgate St entrance to the park is the 63m-high Wellington Monument. This took from 1817 to 1861 to build, mainly because the Duke of Wellington fell from public favour during its construction.

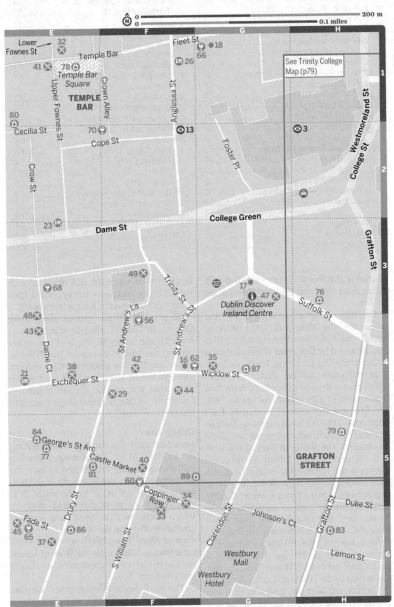

Temple Bar & Grafton Street

Nearby is the People's Garden (Map p72), dating from 1864, and the bandstand in the Hollow.

The large Victorian building behind the zoo, on the edge of the park, is the 19th-century Garda Síochána Headquarters (Map p72), designed by Benjamin Woodward (also author of the Old Library in Trinity College).

In the centre of the park, the Papal Cross marks the site where Pope John Paul II preached to 1.25 million people in 1979. The Phoenix Monument, erected by Lord Chesterfield in 1747, looks very un-phoenix-like and is often referred to as the Eagle Monument. The southern part of the park is a 200-acre stretch (about 81 hectares) known as the Fifteen Acres (don't ask, nobody knows), which is given over to a large number of football pitches – winter Sunday mornings are the time to come and watch. To the west, the rural-looking Glen Pond corner of the park is extremely attractive.

Back towards the Parkgate entrance is Magazine Fort on Thomas' Hill. Built at a snail's pace between 1734 and 1801, the fort has served as an occasional arms depot for the British and, later, the Irish armies. It was a target during the 1916 Easter Rising and

again in 1940, when the IRA made off with the entire ammunitions reserve of the Irish army (they retrieved it after a few weeks).

To get to Dublin's beloved playground, take bus 10 from O'Connell St or bus 25 or 26 from Middle Abbey St. The best way to get around the park is to hop on the Phoenix Park Shuttle Bus (adult/child €2/1; ☺hourly 7am-5pm Mon-Fri, 10am-5pm Sat & Sun), which goes from just outside the main gate on Parkgate St (Map p72) and loops around to the visitor centre.

Dublin Zoo ZOO
(www.dublinzoo.ie; Phoenix Park; adult/child/family €16/11.50/45.50; ☺9.30am-6pm Mar-Sep, 9.30am-dusk Oct-Feb) Established in 1831, the 28-hectare Dublin Zoo just north of the Hollow is one of the oldest in the world. It is well known for its lion-breeding program, which dates back to 1857, and includes among its offspring the lion that roars at the start of MGM films. You'll see these tough cats, from a distance, on the 'African Savanna', just one of several habitats created in the last few years.

The zoo is home to roughly 400 animals from 100 different species, and you can visit all of them across the eight different habitats that range from an Asian jungle to a family farm, where kids get to meet the inhabitants up close and milk a (model) cow. There are restaurants, cafes and even a train to get you round.

Áras an Uachtaráin HISTORIC BUILDING
(Phoenix Park; ⊙ guided tours hourly 10am-4pm Sat; ☐ 10 from O'Connell St, 25, 26 from Middle Abbey St) FREE The residence of the Irish president is a Palladian lodge that was built in 1751 and enlarged a couple of times since, most recently in 1816. It was home to the British viceroys from 1782 to 1922, and then to the governors general until Ireland cut ties with the British Crown and created the office of president in 1937. Queen Victoria stayed here during her visit in 1849, when she appeared not to even notice the Famine. The candle burning in the window is an old Irish tradition, to guide 'the Irish diaspora' home.

Tickets for the free one-hour tours can be collected from the **Phoenix Park Visitor Centre** (admission free; ⊙ 10am-5.45pm daily Mar-Sep, 9.30-5.30pm Wed-Sun Oct-Feb) FREE, the converted former stables of the papal nunciate, where you'll see a 10-minute introductory video before being shuttled to the Áras itself to inspect five state rooms and the president's study. If you can't make it on a Saturday, just become elected president of your own country or become a Nobel laureate or something, and then wrangle a personal invite.

Next door is the restored four-storey **Ashtown Castle**, a 17th-century tower house 'discovered' inside the 18th-century nuncio's mansion when the latter was demolished in 1986 due to dry rot. You can visit the castle only on a guided tour from the visitor centre.

🗗 Tours

A plethora of tours offer a range of exploring options; you can walk (or crawl, if you opt for a drinking tour), get a bus or hop aboard an amphibious vehicle. There are lots of themed tours too, while some companies will combine a city tour with trips further afield. You'll save a few euro booking online.

City Sightseeing BUS TOUR
(Map p114; www.citysightseeingdublin.ie; 14 Upper O'Connell St; adult/child €18/free; ⊙ tours every

1. Henry Street (p126)
Dublin's pedestrianised shopping street with its view of the iconic Spire.

2. St Stephen's Green (p70)
Elegantly landscaped parklands and ponds in the heart of Dublin.

3. Temple Bar (p63)
Street performers are a common sight in Dublin's entertainment district.

4. Ha'Penny Bridge over the Liffey (p63)
Named for the half-penny toll once charged to cross this bridge over the river.

WORTH A TRIP

SOUTH WALL WALK

One of the city's most rewarding walks is a stroll along the south wall to the Poolbeg Lighthouse (that red tower visible in the middle of Dublin Bay). To get there, you'll have to make your own way from Ringsend (which is reachable by buses 1, 2 or 3 from the city centre), past the power station to the start of the wall (it's about 1km). It's not an especially long walk – about 800m or so – but it will give you a stunning view of the bay and the city behind you, a view best enjoyed just before sunset.

8-15min 9am-6pm) A typical hop-on, hop-off tour should last around 1½ hours and lead you up and down O'Connell St, past Trinity College and St Stephen's Green, before heading up to the Guinness Storehouse and back around the north quays, via the main entrance to Phoenix Park.

Dublin Bus Tours　　　　　BUS TOUR
(Map p114; www.dublinbus.ie; 59 Upper O'Connell Street; tours €16-26) Offers a variety of daily tours, including the hop-on, hop-off Dublin City Tour, Ghost Bus Tour, Coast and Castles Tour, and South Coast and Gardens Tour.

Dublin by Bike　　　　　CYCLING TOUR
(Map p92; ☑01-280 1899; www.dublinbybike.com; Merrion Sq West; tours €28, twilight tours €15; ☺tours 10.30am, twilight tour 5.30pm) A great way to see the city, these three-hour tours start from the National Gallery and take in all the sights; the bikes are the small-wheeled kind, helmets are provided and the guides are fun and informative. It also runs a 90-minute twilight tour.

1916 Rebellion Walking Tour　　WALKING TOUR
(Map p84; ☑086 858 3847; www.1916rising.com; 23 Wicklow St; per person €12; ☺tours 11.30am Mon-Sat, 1pm Sun Mar-Oct) Superb two-hour tour starting in the International Bar, Wicklow St. Lots of information, humour and irreverence to boot. The guides – all Trinity graduates – are uniformly excellent and will not say no to the offer of a pint back in the International at tour's end.

Dublin Literary Pub Crawl　　WALKING TOUR
(Map p92; ☑01-670 5602; www.dublinpubcrawl.com; 9 Duke St; adult/student €12/10; ☺tours

daily 7.30pm Apr-Oct, 7.30pm Thu-Sun Nov-Mar) A tour of pubs associated with famous Dublin writers is a sure-fire recipe for success, and this 2½-hour tour/performance by two actors – which includes them acting out the funny bits – is a riotous laugh. There's plenty of drink taken, which makes it all the more popular. It leaves from the Duke on Duke St; get there by 7pm to reserve a spot for the evening tour.

Dublin Musical Pub Crawl　　WALKING TOUR
(Map p84; ☑01-478 0193; www.discoverdublin.ie; Oliver St John Gogarty's, 58-59 Fleet St; adult/student €12/10; ☺tours 7.30pm daily Apr-Oct, 7.30pm Thu-Sat Nov-Mar) The story of Irish traditional music and its influence on contemporary styles is explained and demonstrated by two expert musicians in a number of Temple Bar pubs over 2½ hours. Tours meet upstairs in the Oliver St John Gogarty's pub and are highly recommended.

James Joyce Walking Tour　　WALKING TOUR
(Map p114; ☑01-878 8547; James Joyce Cultural Centre, 35 North Great George's St; adult/student €10/8; ☺tours 2pm Tue, Thu & Sat) Joyce lived, schooled and lost his virginity on the north side – and he put it all down on paper with cartographical precision from his self-imposed continental exile. You can explore all of the north-side attractions associated with the bespectacled one on a 1¼-hour tour run by the James Joyce Cultural Centre (p80).

Pat Liddy Walking Tours　　WALKING TOUR
(Map p84; ☑01-831 1109; www.walkingtours.ie; Dublin Tourism Centre, St Andrew's Church, 2 Suffolk St; tours €10) Dublin's best-known tour guide is local historian Pat Liddy, who leads a varierty of guided walks including Dublin Highlights & Hidden Corners and The Best of Dublin – The Complete Heritage Walking Tour. He is also available for private guided walks. Check the website for timings. He also has a bunch of podcast walks (www.visitdublin.com/iwalks) available for download.

Sandeman's New Dublin Tour　　WALKING TOUR
(Map p84; ☑01-878 8547; www.newdublintours.com; City Hall; ☺tours 11am) **FREE** A high-energy and thoroughly enjoyable three-hour walking tour of the city's greatest hits for free: tip only if you enjoyed the tour. Spanish-language tours are also available.

River Liffey Cruises　　　　BOAT TOUR
(Map p114; ☑01-473 4082; www.liffeyvoyage.ie; Bachelor's Walk; adult/student/child €14/12/8;

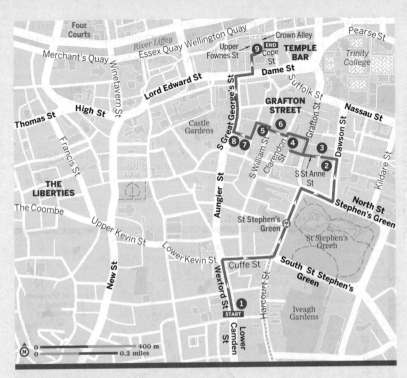

City Walk
Dublin Crawl

START LOWER CAMDEN ST
END CROWN ALLEY
LENGTH 2KM; ONE HOUR TO TWO DAYS

Dubliners of old would assure their 'bitter halves' that they were 'going to see a man about a dog' before retreating to the nearest watering hole. Visiting barflies need no excuse to enjoy the social and cultural education – ahem – of a tour of Dublin's finest, most charming and most hard-core bars.

Start in the always excellent ❶ **Anseo** (p116) on Lower Camden St, where hipsters rub shoulders with the hoi polloi and everyone toe-taps to the great bag of DJ tunes. Head deep into the city centre and become a character in Mad Men at the whiskey bar at the back of ❷ **37 Dawson St** (p116). Get even more old school by sinking a pint of plain in the snug at South St Anne St's ❸ **Kehoe's** (p115), one of the city centre's most atmospheric bars. Find a spot out front of ❹ **Bruxelles** (p117): the bronze statue of Thin Lizzy's Phil Lynott outside is testament to the bar's repu-

tation as a great spot for rock music, even if it's just on the stereo. Discuss the merits of that unwritten masterpiece with a clutch of frustrated writers and artists in ❺ **Grogan's Castle Lounge** (p117), a traditional haunt that admirably refuses to modernise. Directly across the street in the basement of the Powerscourt Townhouse Centre is ❻ **Pygmalion** (p117), which is all about now – it was the 'in' place with the cool kids for much of 2013. A couple of streets away, on Fade St, a couple of bars vie for hipster euros: the upstairs ❼ **No Name Bar** (p116) is elegant and discreet, while ❽ **Hogan's** (p117), at the corner with South Great George's St, has been one of the most popular watering holes in the city for longer than its clientele have been alive.

Finally, make your way into Temple Bar and ring the doorbell to access the ❾ **Vintage Cocktail Club**, upstairs behind a plain steel door on Crown Alley, where the beautiful people sip cocktails and eat delicious tidbits in a speakeasy atmosphere. If you've followed the tour correctly, it's unlikely that you'd now be referring to this guide. How many fingers?

⊙tours 9am-5.30pm Mar-Oct) Experience the city from the river aboard the (all-important) all-weather *Spirit of the Docklands*. The history of Dublin is told from a watery point of view, from the Vikings to the recent developments of the Docklands.

Viking Splash Tours   BUS/BOAT TOUR
(Map p92; ☑01-707 6000; www.vikingsplash.ie; North St Stephen's Green; adult/child €20/10; ⊙tours every 30-90min 10am-3pm) You stick a plastic Viking's helmet on your head and yell 'yay' at the urging of your guide, but the upshot is you'll get a 1¼-hour semiamphibious

tour that ends up in the Grand Canal Dock. 'Strictly for tourists' seems so...superfluous.

🎉 Festivals & Events

Temple Bar Trad Festival   MUSIC
(www.templebartrad.com; ⊙Jan) Traditional music festival in the bars of the cultural quarter over the last weekend in January.

**Jameson Dublin International
Film Festival**   FILM
(www.jdiff.com; ⊙mid-Feb) Local flicks, arty international films and advance releases of mainstream movies make up the menu of

St Stephen's Green & Around

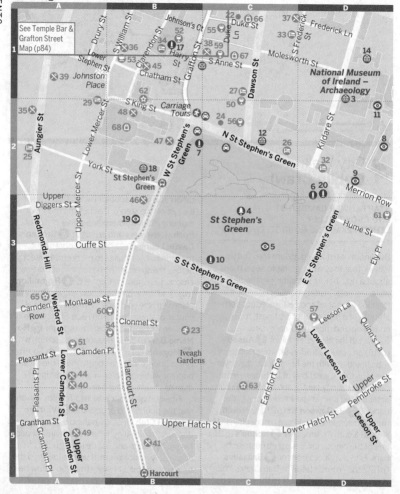

the city's film festival, which runs over two weeks in mid-February.

St Patrick's Festival   PARADE
(www.stpatricksfestival.ie; ☉17 Mar) The mother of all festivals; 600,000-odd gather to 'honour' St Patrick over four days around 17 March on city streets and in venues.

Dublin Writers Festival   LITERATURE
(www.dublinwritersfestival.com; ☉early Jun) Four-day literature festival in early June that attracts Irish and international writers to its readings, performances and talks.

Forbidden Fruit   MUSIC
(www.forbiddenfruit.ie; ☉Jun) A two-day alternative music festival over the first weekend in June in the grounds of the Irish Museum of Modern Art.

Taste of Dublin   FOOD
(Map p92; www.tasteofdublin.ie; Iveagh Gardens; ☉mid-June) The capital's best restaurants combine to serve up sample platters of their best dishes amid music and other entertainment over three food-filled days.

Longitude   MUSIC
(www.longitude.ie; Marlay Park; ☉Jul) A three-day alt music festival in mid-July featuring old and new acts, art installations and food stalls.

Street Performance World Championships   STREET CARNIVAL
(www.spwc.ie; ☉Jul) The world's best street performers – from jugglers to sword-swallowers – test their skills over two July weekends in Merrion Sq.

Dublin Fringe Festival   THEATRE
(www.fringefest.com; ☉Sep) Initially a festival for those shows too 'out-there' or insignificant to be considered for the main Dublin Theatre Festival, this is now a three-week extravaganza with more than 100 events and over 700 performances held in September.

Dublin Theatre Festival   THEATRE
(www.dublintheatrefestival.com; ☉Oct) For two weeks in October most of the city's theatres participate in this festival, originally founded in 1957 and today a glittering parade of quality productions and elaborate shows.

St Stephen's Green & Around

🛏 Sleeping

Hotel rooms in Dublin aren't as expensive as they were during the Celtic Tiger years, but demand is still high. Booking is highly recommended, especially if you want to stay in the city centre or within walking distance of it during the high season that runs roughly from May to September.

When it comes to price, location counts almost as much as quality. For instance, a large-roomed comfortable B&B in the northside suburbs may cost you as little as €50 per person, while the owners of a small, me-

diocre guesthouse within walking distance of Stephen's Green won't blink when asking €100 for a room the size of a shoebox. A quality guesthouse or midrange hotel can cost anything from €80 to €150, while rates at the city's top digs usually start at around €150 – even (and it bears repeating here) in this climate you'd be mad not to check around for deals or call the hotel directly and make polite enquiries along the lines of 'is that the best price you can offer me?' At the other end of the scale there's the ubiquitous hostel, the bedrock of cheap accommodation: their standards have uniformly gone up, but so have their prices and a bed will cost anything from €18 to as much as €34 (note that hostel rates don't include breakfast; exceptions are noted).

⌹ Grafton Street & Around

You can't get more central than the relatively small patch of real estate just south of the Liffey, which has a good mix of options ranging from backpacker hostels to the fanciest hotels. Bear in mind that the location comes with a price.

★ Trinity Lodge   GUESTHOUSE €
(Map p92; ☎ 01-617 0900; www.trinitylodge. com; 12 South Frederick St; s/d from €56/70; ☎; ⌺ all city centre, ⌺ St Stephen's Green) Martin Sheen's grin greets you upon entering this cosy, award-winning guesthouse, which he declared his favourite spot for an Irish stay. Marty's not the only one: this place is so popular that they've added a second townhouse across the road, which has also been kitted out to the highest standards. Room 2 of the original house has a lovely bay window.

Barnacles   HOSTEL €
(Map p84; ☎ 01-671 6277; www.barnacles.ie; 19 Lower Temple Lane; dm €19-22; ☎; ⌺ all city centre) If you're here for a good time and not a long time, then this Temple Bar hostel is the ideal spot to meet fellow revellers; tap up the helpful and knowledgeable staff for the best places to cause mischief; and sleep off the effects of said mischief whilst being totally oblivious to the noise outside, which is constant. Rooms are quieter at the back.

Avalon House   HOSTEL €
(Map p92; ☎ 01-475 0001; www.avalon-house. ie; 55 Aungier St; dm/s/d from €10/34/54; @ ☎; ⌺ all city centre, ⌺ St Stephen's Green) One of the city's most popular hostels, welcoming Avalon House has pine floors, high ceilings and large, open fireplaces that create the ambience for a good spot of meet-the-backpacker lounging. Some of the cleverly designed rooms have mezzanine levels, which are great for families. Book well in advance.

Kinlay House   HOSTEL €
(Map p72; ☎ 01-679 6644; www.kinlaydublin.ie; 2-12 Lord Edward St; dm/d €18/60; ☎; ⌺ all city centre) An institution among the city's hostels, this former boarding house for boys has massive, mixed 24-bed dorms, as well as smaller rooms. Its bustling location next to

Christ Church Cathedral and Dublin Castle is a bonus, but some rooms suffer from traffic noise. There are cooking facilities and a cafe, and breakfast is included. Not for the faint-hearted.

★ Radisson Blu Royal Hotel   HOTEL €€
(Map p72; ☎ 01-898 2900; www.radissonblu.ie/roy alhotel-dublin; Golden Lane; r €110-220; ❋ @ ☎; ⌺ all city centre, ⌺ St Stephen's Green) Our favourite hotel in this price range is an excellent example of how sleek lines and muted colours combine beautifully with luxury, ensuring a memorable night's stay. From hugely impressive public areas to sophisticated bedrooms (each with flat-screen digital TV embedded in the wall to go along with all the other little touches), this hotel will not disappoint.

Cliff Townhouse   GUESTHOUSE €€
(Map p92; ☎ 01-638 3939; www.theclifftownhouse. com; 22 St Stephen's Green North; r from €99; @ ☎; ⌺ all city centre, ⌺ St Stephen's Green) As pied-à-terres go, this is a doozy: there are 10 exquisitely appointed bedrooms spread across a wonderful Georgian property, the best of which overlook St Stephen's Green. Downstairs is Sean Smith's superb restaurant Cliff Townhouse (p111).

Grafton House   B&B €€
(Map p84; ☎ 01-648 0010; www.graftonguest house.com; 26-27 South Great George's St; s/d from €79/109; @ ☎; ⌺ all city centre, ⌺ St Stephen's Green) This slightly offbeat guesthouse in a Gothic-style building gets the nod in all three key categories: location, price and style. Just next to George's St Arcade, the Grafton offers the traditional friendly features of a B&B (including a terrific breakfast), coupled with a funky design – check out the psychedelic wallpaper. Hard to beat at this price.

DUBLIN FOR CHILDREN

Kid-friendly? You bet. Dublin loves the little 'uns, and will enthusiastically ooh and aah at the cuteness of your progeny. But alas such admiration hasn't fully translated into child services such as widespread and accessible baby-changing facilities.

Nevertheless, the city has plenty to keep kids entertained. If your kids are between three and 14, spend an afternoon at Ark Children's Cultural Centre (Map p84; www. ark.ie; 11a Eustace St; all city centre), which runs activities aimed at stimulating participants' interests in science, the environment and the arts – but be sure to book well in advance.

There are loads of ways to discover Dublin's Viking past, but Dvblinia (p77), the city's Viking and medieval museum, has interactive exhibits that are specifically designed to appeal to younger visitors. Kids of all ages will love a Viking Splash Tour (p92), where you board an amphibious vehicle, put on a plastic Viking hat and roar at passersby as you do a tour of the city before landing in the water at the Grand Canal basin.

A perennial favourite is Dublin Zoo (p86), while the National Leprechaun Museum (p81) lets the kids' imagination run wild amongst the optical illusions and oversized furniture. On the 2nd floor of the Powerscourt Townhouse Shopping Centre is the Dolls Store (Map p84; 10am-6pm Mon-Sat), which sells all kinds of dolls and doll houses; should your little one's doll or teddy get 'ill', this is also the home of Ireland's only doll and teddy-bear hospital.

All but a few hotels will provide cots and most top-range hotels have babysitting services (€8 to €15 per hour). Restaurants are generally accommodating until 7pm, after which things can get difficult, especially for babies: check while making a booking.

Central Hotel
HOTEL €€
(Map p84; 01-679 7302; www.centralhoteldublin. com; 1-5 Exchequer St; s/d from €75/89; all city centre, St Stephen's Green) The rooms are a modern – if miniaturised – version of Edwardian luxury. Heavy velvet curtains and custom-made Irish furnishings (including beds with draped backboards) fit a little too snugly into the space afforded them, but they lend a touch of class. Note that street-facing rooms can get a little noisy. Location-wise, the name says it all.

Paramount Hotel
HOTEL €€
(Map p84; 01-417 9900; www.paramounthotel.ie; cnr Parliament St & Essex Gate; s/d 69/120; all city centre) Behind the Victorian facade, the lobby is a faithful re-creation of a 1930s hotel, complete with dark-wood floors, deep-red leather chesterfield couches and heavy velvet drapes. The 70-odd rooms don't quite bring *The Maltese Falcon* to mind, but they're handsomely furnished and very comfortable. Downstairs is the Turk's Head (Map p84; 01-679 9701; 27-30 Parliament St; all city centre), one of the area's most popular bars.

Dublin Citi Hotel
HOTEL €€
(Map p84; 01-679 4455; www.dublincitihotel. com; 46-49 Dame St; r from €89; all city centre) An unusual turreted 19th-century building right next to the Central Bank is home to this midrange hotel. Rooms aren't huge but are simply furnished and have fresh white quilts. It's only a stagger (literally) from the heart of Temple Bar, hic.

La Stampa
HOTEL €€
(Map p92; 01-677 4444; www.lastampa.ie; 35 Dawson St; r from €120; all city centre, St Stephen's Green) La Stampa is an atmospheric boutique hotel on trendy Dawson St with 29 Asian-influenced, white rooms with rattan furniture and exotic velvet throws. Its Mandala Day Spa is a luxurious, all-frills ayurvedic spa, but to fully benefit from your restorative treatments, ask for a top-floor bedroom away from the noise of the bar below.

★ Number 31
GUESTHOUSE €€€
(Map p92; 01-676 5011; www.number31.ie; 31 Leeson Close; s/d/tr incl breakfast €180/260/300; all city centre) The city's most distinctive property is the former home of modernist architect Sam Stephenson, who successfully fused '60s style with 18th-century grace. Its 21 bedrooms are split between the retro coach house, with its fancy rooms, and the more elegant Georgian house, where rooms are individually furnished with tasteful French antiques and big comfortable beds.

Gourmet breakfasts with kippers, homemade breads and granola are served in the conservatory. Yeah, baby!

★ Merrion
HOTEL €€€

(Map p92; ☑ 01-603 0600; www.merrionhotel.com; Upper Merrion St; r/ste from €485/995; @ 🛜 🛋; 🖵 all city centre) This resplendent five-star hotel, in a terrace of beautifully restored Georgian townhouses, opened in 1988 but looks like it's been around a lot longer. Try to get a room in the old house (with the largest private art collection in the city), rather than the newer wing, to sample its truly elegant comforts.

Located opposite Government Buildings, its marble corridors are patronised by politicos, visiting dignitaries and the odd celeb. Even if you don't stay, come for the superb afternoon tea (€36), with endless cups of tea served out of silver pots by a raging fire.

Irish Landmark Trust
SELF-CATERING €€€

(Map p84; ☑ 01-670 4733; www.irishlandmark.com; 25 Eustace St; 2/3 nights for 7 people €600/875; 🖵 all city centre) This 18th-century heritage house has been gloriously restored to the highest standard by the Irish Landmark Trust. Furnished with tasteful antiques and authentic furniture and fittings (including a grand piano in the drawing room), it sleeps up to seven in its three bedrooms, which must be booked for a minimum of two nights.

Westbury Hotel
HOTEL €€€

(Map p92; ☑ 01-679 1122; www.doylecollection. com; Grafton St; r/ste from €199/299; @ 🛜; 🖵 all city centre) Visiting celebs looking for some quiet time have long favoured the Westbury's elegant suites, where they can watch TV from the Jacuzzi before retiring to a four-poster bed. Mere mortals tend to make do with the standard rooms, which are comfortable enough but lack the sophisticated grandeur promised by the luxurious public spaces – which are a great spot for an afternoon drink.

Westin Dublin
HOTEL €€€

(Map p79; ☑ 01-645 1000; www.thewestindublin. com; Westmoreland St; r from €179; @ 🛜; 🖵 all city centre) Formerly a grand branch of the Allied Irish Bank, this fine old building was gutted and reborn as a stylish upmarket hotel. The rooms, many of which overlook a beautiful atrium, are decorated in elegant mahogany and soft colours that are reminiscent of the USA's finest. You will sleep on 10 layers of the Westin's own trademark Heavenly Bed, which is damn comfortable indeed.

Shelbourne
HOTEL €€€

(Map p92; ☑ 01-676 6471; www.theshelbourne.ie; 27 St Stephen's Green North; r from €220; @ 🛜; 🖵 all city centre, 🚇 St Stephen's Green) Dublin's most iconic hotel, founded in 1824, was bought out by the Marriott group, which spent a ton of money restoring its rooms and public spaces to their former grandeur, a few years ago. The refurb was successful, but its management style has been criticised as being somewhat short of its five-star reputation.

Whatever your experiences, you're staying in a slice of history: it was here that the Irish Constitution was drafted in 1921, and this is the hotel in Elizabeth Bowen's eponymous novel. Afternoon tea in the refurbished Lord Mayor's Lounge remains one of the best experiences in town.

Clarence Hotel
HOTEL €€€

(Map p84; ☑ 01-407 0800; www.theclarence.ie; 6-8 Wellington Quay; r €109-259, ste €299-1499; @ 🛜; 🖵 all city centre) Bono and the Edge's discreet little bolt-hole is no longer the hottest bedroom in town, which is a good thing because the reality never lived up to the hype. Instead, what's left is a handsome boutique hotel designed to reflect the aesthetic of a 1930s gentlemen's club, complete with an excellent bar and a fine restaurant.

🛏 North of the Liffey

There are scattering of good midrange options between O'Connell St and Smithfield. Gardiner St, to the east of O'Connell St, is the traditional B&B district of town, but you're better off sticking to the southern end of the street where the properties are better and the street is safer.

★ Isaacs Hostel
HOSTEL €

(Map p114; ☑ 01-855 6215; www.isaacs.ie; 2-5 Frenchman's Lane; dm/tw from €14/54; @ 🛜; 🖵 all city centre, 🚇 Connolly) The north side's best hostel – hell, for atmosphere alone it's the best in town – is in a 200-year-old wine vault just around the corner from the main bus station. With summer barbecues, live music in the lounge, internet access and colourful dorms, this terrific place generates consistently good reviews from backpackers and other travellers.

WORTH A TRIP

BEYOND THE ROYAL CANAL

Beyond the Royal Canal lie the suburbs and an authentic slice of north-city life. There are also some beautiful gardens, the country's biggest stadium, a historic cemetery and one of the most interesting buildings in all of Dublin.

Croke Park Experience

The Gaelic Athletic Association (GAA) considers itself not just the governing body of a bunch of Irish games but also the stout defender of a cultural identity that is ingrained in Ireland's sense of self. To get an idea of just how important the GAA is, a visit to the Croke Park Experience (www.crokepark.ie; Clonliffe Rd, New Stand, Croke Park; adult/student/child museum €6/5/4, museum & tour €12/9/8; ⊘ 9.30am-5pm Mon-Sat, noon-5pm Sun Apr-Oct, 10am-5pm Tue-Sat, noon-4pm Sun Nov-Mar; ⊒ 3, 11, 11A, 16, 16A, 123 from O'Connell St) is a must – the interactive exhibits tell the compelling story of the games' symbiotic relationship with Irish culture and the struggle to establish its national identity. The twice-daily tours (except match days) of the impressive Croke Park stadium are excellent, and well worth the extra cost. The stadium's newest attraction is the Skyline (www.skylinecrokepark.ie; Croke Park; adults/student/child €25/20/15; ⊘ tours 11am & 2pm May-Sep, Fri-Sun only Oct-Apr), a guided tour around the stadium roof.

Glasnevin Cemetery

The tombstones at Ireland's largest and most historically important burial site (www.glasnevin-cemetery.ie; Finglas Rd; ⊘ 24hr; ⊒ 40, 40A, 40B from Parnell St) **FREE** read like a 'who's who' of Irish history, as most of the leading names of the last 150 years are buried here.

A modern replica of a round tower acts as a handy landmark for locating the tomb of Daniel O'Connell, who died in 1847. Charles Stewart Parnell's tomb is topped with a large granite rock, on which only his name is inscribed – a remarkably simple tribute to a figure of such historical importance. Other notable people buried here include Sir Roger Casement, Republican leader Michael Collins, docker and trade unionist Jim Larkin, and poet Gerard Manley Hopkins.

Jacob's Inn HOSTEL €
(Map p114; ☎ 01-855 5660; www.isaacs.ie; 21-28 Talbot Pl; dm/d from €12.50/74; ☎; ⊒ Connolly) Sister hostel to Isaacs (p97) around the corner, this clean and modern hostel offers spacious accommodation with private bathrooms and outstanding facilities, including some wheelchair-accessible rooms, a bureau de change, bike storage and a self-catering kitchen.

Globetrotters Tourist Hostel HOSTEL €
(Map p114; ☎ 01-878 8088; www.globetrottersdublin.com; 46-48 Lower Gardiner St; dm €16; ⊒ all city centre, ⊒ Connolly) This is a really friendly place with 94 beds in a variety of dorms, all with bathrooms and under-bed storage. The funky decor is due to the fact that it shares the same artistic ethos (and dining room) as the Townhouse Hotel next door. There's a little patio garden to the rear for that elusive sunny day.

Anchor Guesthouse B&B €€
(Map p114; ☎ 01-878 6913; www.anchorhousedublin.com; 49 Lower Gardiner St; r weekday/weekend from €71/143; ⊒ all city centre, ⊒ Connolly) This lovely Georgian guesthouse, with its delicious wholesome breakfasts, comes highly recommended by readers. They're dead right. While most B&Bs round these parts offer pretty much the same stuff – TV, half-decent shower, clean linen and tea- and coffee-making facilities – the Anchor does all of that, but it just has an elegance you won't find in many of the other B&Bs along this stretch.

Clifden Guesthouse GUESTHOUSE €€
(☎ 01-874 6364; www.clifdenhouse.com; 32 Gardiner Pl; s/d/tr from €70/90/110; ⊒ 36, 36A) The Clifden is a very nicely refurbished Georgian house with 14 tastefully decorated rooms. They all come with bathroom, are immaculately clean and extremely comfortable. A nice touch is the free parking, even after you've checked out!

Maldron Hotel Smithfield HOTEL €€
(Map p72; ☎ 01-485 0900; www.maldronhotels.com; Smithfield Village; r from €90; ☎; ⊒ 25, 25A, 25B, 66, 66A, 66B, 67, 90, 151 to Upper Ormond Quay, ⊒ Smithfield) With big bedrooms and plenty

The history of the cemetery is told in wonderful, award-winning detail in the museum (museum €6, museum & tour €12; ⊙10am-5pm Mon-Fri, 11am-6pm Sat & Sun), which tells the social and political story of Ireland through the lives of the people known and unknown that are buried here. The best way to visit the cemetery is to take one of the daily tours (11.30am, 12.30pm & 2.30pm).

National Botanic Gardens
Founded in 1795, the 19.5-hectare botanic gardens (Botanic Rd; ⊙9am-6pm Mon-Sat, 11am-6pm Sun Apr-Oct, 10am-4.30pm Mon-Sat, 11am-4.30pm Sun Nov-Mar; ☐13, 13A, 19 from O'Connell St, 34, 34A from Middle Abbey St) FREE are home to a series of curvilinear glasshouses, dating from 1843 to 1869, created by Richard Turner. Within these Victorian masterpieces you will find the latest in botanical technology, including a series of computer-controlled climates reproducing environments of different parts of the world. Among the pioneering botanical work conducted here was the first attempt to raise orchids from seed, back in 1844.

Casino At Marino
It's not the roulette-wheel kind of casino but the original Italian kind, the one that means 'summer home', and this particular casino (www.heritageireland.ie; Malahide Rd; adult/senior/child €3/2/1; ⊙10am-5pm May-Sep; ☐20A, 20B, 27, 27B, 42, 42C, 123 from city centre) is one of the most enchanting constructions in all of Ireland. It was built in the mid-18th century for the Earl of Charlemont, who returned from his grand tour of Europe with more art than he could store in his own home, Marino House. He also came home with a big love of the Palladian style – hence the architecture of this wonderful folly.

Entrance is by guided tour only. The exterior of the building, with a huge entrance doorway, and 12 Tuscan columns forming a templelike facade, creates the expectation that its interior will be a simple single open space. But instead it is an extravagant convoluted maze. A variety of statuary adorns the outside but it's the amusing fakes that are most enjoyable.

of earth tones to soften the contemporary edges, this functionally modern hotel is your best bet in this part of town. We love the floor-to-ceiling windows: great for checking out what's going on below in the square.

Morrison Hotel HOTEL €€€
(Map p114; ☎01-887 2400; www.morrisonhotel.ie; Ormond Quay; r from €199; @☎; ☐all city centre, ☐Jervis) A buy-out by Russian billionaire Elena Baturina has breathed new life into this quayside hotel, courtesy of a €7m refurbishment that has seen the rooms given a contemporary makeover and the already elegant public spaces a facelift. King-size beds (with Serta mattresses), 100cm (40in) LED TVs, free wi-fi and Crabtree & Evelyn toiletries are just some of the hotel's offerings.

It's now operated by Hilton Doubletree and you won't sleep in more luxurious surroundings anywhere on the north side.

Gresham Hotel HOTEL €€€
(Map p114; ☎01-874 6881; www.gresham-hotels.com; Upper O'Connell St; r from €200, ste €450-2500; ❋@☎; ☐all cross-city) This landmark

hotel shed its traditional granny's parlour look with a major overhaul some years ago. Despite its brighter, smarter, modern appearance and a fabulous open-plan foyer, its loyal clientele – elderly groups on shopping breaks to the capital and well-heeled Americans – continues to find it charming. Rooms are spacious and well serviced.

Townhouse Hotel INN €€€
(Map p114; ☎01-878 8808; www.townhouseofdublin.com; 47-48 Lower Gardiner St; s/d/tr €140/199/219; ☐36, 36A, ☐Connolly) The ghostly writing of Irish-Japanese author Lafcadio Hearn may have influenced the Gothic-style interior of his former home. A dark-walled, gilt-framed foyer with jingling chandelier leads into 82 individually designed, comfy (but cramped) rooms. It shares a dining room with the Globetrotters Tourist Hostel next door.

Docklands
You'll be relying on public transport or a taxi to get you in and out of town for things to do.

Docklands

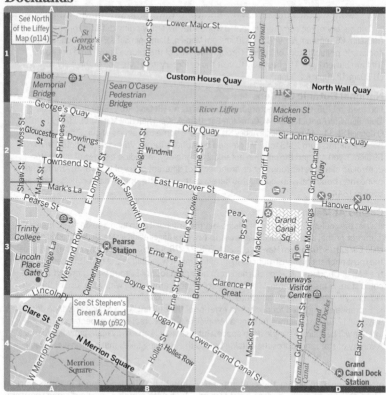

Gibson Hotel   HOTEL **€€**

(Map p100; ☑ 01-618 5000; www.thegibsonhotel.
ie; Point Village; r from €120; @ 🛜; 🚌151 from city
centre, 🚆 Grand Canal Dock) Built for business
travellers and out-of-towners taking in a
gig at the O2 next door, the Gibson is undoubtedly impressive: 250-odd ultramodern
rooms are decked out with snazzy Respa
beds, flat-screen TVs and internet worksta-
tions. The public areas are bright, big and
airy – lots of muted colours and floor-to-ceiling glass – and you might catch last night's
star act having breakfast the next morning.

The Marker   HOTEL **€€€**

(Map p100; ☑ 01-687 5100; www.themarkerhotel
dublin.com; Grand Canal Sq; r from €200; @ 🛜;
🚌56A, 77A, 🚆 Grand Canal Dock) Dublin's newest designer digs is impressive from the
outside – the shell is a stunning building
created by Manuel Aires Mateus. The recession put paid to it for a couple of years, but
it finally opened in 2013 with 187 ultraswish

contemporary bedrooms, a ground-floor
cocktail lounge and a decent restaurant. The
rooftop bar has great views.

🛏 Beyond the Grand Canal

You'll get more for your euro in the largely
stylish digs dotted throughout the suburb
of Ballsbridge, 3km south of the city centre.
You'll be rubbing shoulders with the jet set
and embassy crowd.

★ Aberdeen Lodge   GUESTHOUSE **€€**

(☑ 01-283 8155; www.aberdeen-lodge.com; 53-55
Park Ave; s/d €99/149; @ 🛜; 🚌2, 3, 🚆 DART Sydney Parade) Not only is this absolutely one of
Dublin's best guesthouses, but it's a carefully
guarded secret, known only to those who
dare stay a short train ride from the city
centre. Their reward is a luxurious house
with a level of personalised service as good
as you'd find in one of the city's top hotels.

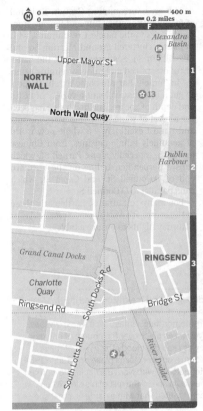

DUBLIN SLEEPING

Docklands

Sights
1 Jeanie Johnston A1
2 National Convention Centre...............D1
3 Science Gallery A3

Activities, Courses & Tours
4 Shelbourne Park Greyhound
    Stadium...F4

Sleeping
5 Gibson Hotel..F1
6 Home From Home Apartments.........D3
7 The Marker C2

Eating
8 Ely Bar & Brasserie.............................B1
9 Ely Gastro Pub......................................D2
10 Herbstreet..D2
11 Quay 16..C1

Entertainment
12 Bord Gáis Energy Theatre...................C3
13 O2...F1

pointed to reflect the best of contemporary design and style, right down to the modern art on the walls and the handy lift to the upper floors. May we borrow your designer?

Waterloo House   INN €€
(Map p72; ☑01-660 1888; www.waterloohouse.ie; 8-10 Waterloo Rd; s/d €129/145; ☎; ☐5, 7, 7A, 8, 18, 45 from city centre) Within walking distance of St Stephen's Green, this lovely guesthouse is spread over two ivy-clad Georgian houses off Baggot St. Rooms are tastefully decorated with high-quality furnishings in authentic Farrow & Ball Georgian colours, and all have cable TV and kettles. Home-cooked breakfast is included and served in the conservatory, or in the garden on sunny days.

Dylan   HOTEL €€€
(Map p72; ☑01-660 3001; www.dylan.ie; Eastmoreland Pl; r from €200; ✳@☎; ☐5, 7, 7A, 8, 18, 27X, 44 from city centre) The Dylan's baroque-meets-Scandinavian-sleek designer look has been a big hit, a reflection perhaps of a time when too much was barely enough for the glitterati who signed contracts over cocktails before retiring to crisp Frette linen sheets in the wonderfully appointed rooms upstairs.

Four Seasons   HOTEL €€€
(Map p72; ☑01-665 4000; www.fourseasons.com; Simmonscourt Rd; r from €225; @☎✳; ☐5, 7, 7A, 8, 18, 45 from city centre) You know you're

Most of the stunning rooms have either a four-poster, a half-tester or a brass bed to complement the authentic Edwardian furniture and tasteful art on the walls. The suites even have fully working Adams fireplaces. As there is one member of staff for every two rooms, the service is exceptional, not to mention totally hands-on and very courteous. The easiest way to get here is by DART from Pearse or Tara Sts – go southbound and get off at Sydney Parade, from where it's only a short walk.

★**Pembroke Townhouse**   INN €€
(Map p72; ☑01-660 0277; www.pembroketown house.ie; 90 Pembroke Rd; r from €99; ☎☝; ☐5, 7, 7A, 8, 18, 45 from city centre) This superluxurious townhouse is a perfect example of what happens when traditional and modern combine to great effect. A classical Georgian house has been transformed into a superb boutique hotel, with each room carefully crafted and ap-

in the presence of a diva when you step inside the grand lobby of this enormous hotel. To some, the effect is a little garish, but to others, the combination of marble, chandeliers and marvellous bedrooms scream luxury. It's in the grounds of the Royal Dublin Showgrounds.

 ## Eating

Most Dubliners will tell you that the foodie scene has never been better than it is right now – austerity notwithstanding. The last couple of years has seen a bunch of brilliant new eateries open their doors, offering more inventive menus and more competitive pricing. Leaner times have led restaurateurs and chefs to roll up their sleeves and reimagine virtually everything they do, and the result has been remarkable.

The area surrounding Grafton St is full of food joints of every hue and flavour, from funky cafes to the fanciest restaurants, with the latter clustered around Merrion Sq and Fitzwilliam Sq. Scattered among the panoply of overpriced and underwhelming eateries in Temple Bar are some excellent spots to get a bite that will suit a variety of tastes and depth of pocket. The north side has seen the arrival of some pretty fancy restaurants and – most excitingly – a whole new world of genuinely ethnic cuisines, from Chinese to Polish, especially along Parnell St, which runs a perpendicular line off the northern end of O'Connell St, and Capel St, which runs parallel to O'Connell St.

For many restaurants, particularly those in the centre, it's worth booking for Friday or Saturday nights to ensure a table.

BLOOMSDAY

It's 16 June. There's a bunch of weirdos wandering around the city dressed in Edwardian gear and talking nonsense in dramatic tones. They're not mad – at least not clinically; they're only Bloomsdayers committed to commemorating James Joyce's epic *Ulysses*, which anyone familiar with the book will tell you takes place over the course of one day (of course that doesn't necessarily mean they've *read* the bloody thing). What they mightn't be able to tell you is that Leopold Bloom's odyssey takes place on 16 June 1904 because it was on that day that Joyce first 'stepped out' with Nora Barnacle, the woman he had met six days earlier and with whom he would spend the rest of his life. (When James' father heard about this new love he commented that with a name like that she would surely stick to him.)

Although Ireland treated Joyce like a literary pornographer while he was alive, the country (and especially Dublin) can't get enough of him today. Bloomsday is a slightly gimmicky and touristy phenomenon that appeals almost exclusively to Joyce fanatics and tourists, but it's plenty of fun and a great way to lay the groundwork for actually reading what could be the second-hardest book written in the 20th century (the hardest, of course, being Joyce's follow-up blockbuster *Finnegan's Wake*, the greatest book *never* to be read).

In general, events are designed to follow Bloom's progress around town, and in recent years festivities have expanded to continue over four days around 16 June. On Bloomsday proper you can kick things off with breakfast at the James Joyce Cultural Centre (p80), where the 'inner organs of beast and fowl' come accompanied by celebratory readings.

In the morning, guided tours of Joycean sites usually leave from the General Post Office and the James Joyce Cultural Centre. Lunchtime activity focuses on Davy Byrne's (Map p92; 677 5217; www.davybyrnes.com; 21 Duke St; all city centre), Joyce's 'moral pub', where Bloom paused to dine on a glass of burgundy and a slice of gorgonzola. Street entertainers are likely to keep you amused through the afternoon as you take guided walks and watch animated readings from *Ulysses* and Joyce's other books; there's a reading at Ormond Quay Hotel (Map p114; Ormond Quay) at 4pm and Harrisons (Map p114; Westmoreland St) in the late afternoon.

Events also take place in the days leading up to and following Bloomsday. The best source of information about what's on in any particular year is likely to be the James Joyce Cultural Centre, close to the date.

✗ Grafton Street & Around

If you spent your whole time in this area you would eat pretty well; the south city centre is the hub of the best the city has to offer.

Honest to Goodness/Push 88   RESTAURANT €
(Map p84; www.honesttogoodness.ie; 12 Dame Court; mains €6-12; 🖵 all city centre) Downstairs, Honest to Goodness serves wholesome sandwiches, tasty soups and a near-legendary Sloppy Joe. Upstairs, Push 88 is Honest after dark, specialising in meatballs dished a whole variety of ways – with salad, sweet-potato mash or between two slices of homemade bread. Great food and great fun in a terrific atmosphere (helped along by the upstairs bar).

Fallon & Byrne   DELI €
(Map p84; www.fallonandbyrne.com; Exchequer St; mains €5-10; ⊙ 8am-9pm Mon-Wed, 8am-10pm Thu & Fri, 9am-9pm Sat, 11am-7pm Sun; 🖵 all city centre) Dublin's answer to the American Dean & DeLuca chain is this upmarket food hall and wine cellar, which is where discerning Dubliners come to buy their favourite cheeses and imported delicacies, as well as get a superb lunch-to-go from the deli counter. Sandwiches and a range of excellent dishes from lamb couscous to vegetarian lasagne have transformed desktop dining forever. Upstairs is an elegant **brasserie restaurant** (🕿 01-472 1000; mains €5-10; ⊙ lunch & dinner; 🖵 all city centre) that serves Irish-influenced Mediterranean cuisine.

Brioche   FRENCH €
(Map p92; www.brioche.ie; 65 Aungier St; dishes €4.50-8; ⊙ 8am-5pm Mon-Sat & 5.30pm-10pm Tue-Sat; 🖵 all city centre) By day, this is a regular cafe that serves excellent sandwiches and coffee. By night it is Brioche Ce Soir, where classically trained chef Gavin McDonagh engages the full range of his skills with a series of French tasting plates, all made with locally sourced ingredients and served in a wonderful brasserie atmosphere. A hidden treat.

Crave   SANDWICHES €
(Map p84; 79 South Great George's St; sandwiches €4.95-6.95; ⊙ 9am-5pm Mon-Wed, 10am-8pm Thu-Sat; 🛜; 🖵 all city centre) A new arrival on the scene, this lovely cafe opted for 'downtown baroque' decor and a menu that specialises in gourmet pitta sandwiches. Our favourite is the pittalicious (Parma ham and gorgonzola) served with a rocket and couscous salad. Linger a while and take advantage of the free wi-fi.

ⓘ BOOKING SERVICES

Your best bet for booking accommodation is using Dublin Tourism's computerised booking system. Alternatively, you can go it alone online using one of these competitive internet booking sites:

All Dublin Hotels (www.irelandhotels.com/hotels/dublin)

Dublin City Centre Hotels (http://dublin.city-centre-hotels.com)

Dublin Hotels (www.dublinhotels.com)

Go Ireland (www.goireland.com)

Hostel Dublin (www.hosteldublin.com)

For more options try www.lonelyplanet.com/hotels.

Green Nineteen   IRISH €
(Map p92; 🕿 01-478 9626; www.green19.ie; 19 Lower Camden St; mains €10-14; ⊙ 10am-11pm Mon-Sat, noon-6pm Sun; 🖵 all city centre) A firm favourite on Camden St's corridor of cool is this sleek restaurant that specialises in locally sourced, organic grub – without the fancy price tag. Braised lamb chump, corned beef, pot roast chicken and the ubiquitous burger are but the meaty part of the menu, which also includes salads and veggie options. We love it.

Neon   ASIAN €
(Map p92; 🕿 01-405 2222; www.neon17.ie; 17 Camden St; mains €10-12; ⊙ noon-11pm, delivery from 5pm; 🖵 all city centre) A brilliant new spot that specialises in authentic Asian street food from Thailand and Vietnam, served in takeaway boxes, which you can eat at home or in the canteen-style dining room. Hardened palates can jump right into the superspicy *pad ki mow* noodles (a stir-fried noodle dish also known as 'Drunken Noodles' because it was originally made with rice wine); more delicate tastebuds can live with a delicious massaman curry. It also delivers.

Bottega Toffoli   ITALIAN €
(Map p84; 34 Castle St; sandwiches & salads €9-12; ⊙ 8am-4pm Tue-Wed, 8am-9pm Thu &Fri, 11am-8pm Sat, 1-8pm Sun; 🖵 all city centre) Tucked away on a side street that runs alongside Dublin Castle is this superb Italian cafe, the loving creation of its Irish-Italian owners. Terrific sandwiches – beautifully cut prosciutto, baby tomatoes and rocket salad drizzled with imported olive oil on homemade *piadina* (a type of rustic

---

UNIVERSITY ACCOMMODATION

From mid-June to late September, you can stay in accommodation provided by the city's universities. Be sure to book well in advance.

Trinity College (Map p79; ☑ 01-896 1177; www.tcd.ie; Accommodations Office, Trinity College; s/d from €58/78; @ ☎; ☐ all cross-city) Comfortable rooms ranging from basic to those with private bathrooms in one of the most atmospheric settings in Dublin.

Mercer Court (Map p92; ☑ 01-478 2179; www.mercercourt.ie; Lower Mercer St; s/d 80/120; @ ☎) Owned and run by the Royal College of Surgeons, Mercer Court has modern rooms that are up to hotel standard.

---

bread – and its pizzas are as good as any you'd get out of a Neapolitan oven.

Lemon
PANCAKES €

(Map p84; 66 South William St; pancakes from €4.50; ☺ 9am-7pm Mon-Sat, 10am-6pm Sun; ☐ all city centre) Dublin's best pancake joint has branches on both sides of Grafton St, one on South William and the other on **Dawson St** (Map p79; 61 Dawson St). Each serves up a wide range of sweet and savoury crêpes – those paper-thin ones stuffed with a variety of goodies and smothered in toppings – along with super coffee in a buzzy atmosphere that is popular with literally everyone.

Simon's Place
CAFE €

(Map p84; George's St Arcade, South Great George's St; sandwiches €5; ☺ 9am-5.30pm Mon-Sat; ☑; ☐ all city centre) Simon hasn't had to change the menu of doorstep sandwiches and wholesome vegetarian soups since he first opened shop more than two decades ago – and why should he? His grub is as heartening and legendary as he is. It's a great place to sip a coffee and watch life go by in the old-fashioned arcade.

Listons
SANDWICHES €

(Map p92; www.listonsfoodstore.ie; 25 Camden St; lunch €5-12; ☺ 9am-6.30pm Mon-Fri, 10am-6pm Sat; ☐ all city centre) The lunchtime queues streaming out the door of this place are testament to its reputation as Dublin's best deli. Its sandwiches (with fresh and delicious fillings), roasted-vegetable quiches, rosemary potato cakes and sublime salads will have you coming back again and again – the only problem is there's too much choice! On fine days, take your gourmet picnic to the nearby Iveagh Gardens.

Queen of Tarts
CAFE €

(Map p84; 4 Cork Hill; snacks from €4; ☺ 7.30am-6pm Mon-Fri; ☐ all city centre) Diet dodgers rejoice, for this little cafe is to cakes what Wil-

lie Wonka was to chocolate, and you'll think you're in a dream when you see the displays of tarts, meringues, crumbles, cookies and brownies, never mind taste them. There are also great brekkies – such as potato-and-chive cake with mushroom and egg, plus the coffee is splendid and the service sweet. This is a treasure so popular that they opened a bigger version around the corner on **Cow's Lane** (Map p84; www.queenoftarts.ie; 3-4 Cow's Lane; mains €5-10; ☺ 8am-7pm Mon-Fri, 9am-7pm Sat, 10am-6pm Sun; ☐ all cross-city).

Zaytoon
MIDDLE EASTERN €

(Map p84; 14-15 Parliament St; meals €11; ☺ noon-4am; ☐ all city centre) If at the end of the night you need something to absorb the booze, then the Middle Eastern delights at this joint are the thing for you. Just don't expect anything more than what makes up a kebab. There's another branch on **Camden St** (Map p92; 44-55 Upper Camden St).

Gourmet Burger Kitchen
BURGERS €

(Map p92; www.gbk.ie; 5 South Anne St; burgers €9-13; ☺ noon-10pm Sun-Wed, to 11pm Thu-Sat; ☐ all city centre) With three city-centre branches – also at **South William St** (Map p84; 14 South William St; ☺ noon-10pm Sun-Wed, to 11pm Thu-Sat; ☐ all city centre) and **Temple Bar** (Map p84; ☑ 01-670 8343; Temple Bar Sq; burgers €9-13; ☺ noon-10pm Sun-Wed, to 11pm Thu-Sat; ☐ all city centre) – GBK's assault on the burger market is almost complete, as customers can't get enough of its various offerings. Try the Kiwiburger – a beef burger topped with beetroot, egg, pineapple, cheese, salad and relish. It also has decent veggie options.

Silk Road Café
MIDDLE EASTERN €

(Map p84; Chester Beatty Library, Dublin Castle; mains €11; ☺ 11am-4pm Mon-Fri; ☐ 50, 51B, 77, 78A, 123) Museum cafes don't often make you salivate, but this vaguely Middle Eastern–North African–Mediterranean gem on the ground floor of the Chester Beatty Library is the exception. Complementing the house specialities like Greek moussaka and spinach lasagne are daily specials like *djaj mehshi* (chicken stuffed with spices, rice, dried fruit, almonds and pine nuts). All dishes are halal and kosher.

★ **Fade Street Social**   MODERN IRISH €€
(Map p84; ☏ 01-604 0066; www.fadestreetsocial. com; Fade St; tapas €8-12, mains €19-29; ☺ lunch & dinner Mon-Fri, dinner Sat & Sun; ☒ all city centre) Two eateries in one, courtesy of renowned chef Dylan McGrath: at the front, the buzzy Gastro Bar, which serves up gourmet tapas from a beautiful open kitchen. At the back, the more muted Restaurant does Irish cuts of meat – from veal to rabbit – served with homegrown, organic vegetables. Designed to impress; it does. Reservations suggested.

Coppinger Row   MEDITERRANEAN €€
(www.coppingerrow.com; Coppinger Row; mains €18-25; ☺ noon-5.30pm & 6-11pm Mon-Sat, 12.30-4pm & 6-9pm Sun; ☒ all city centre) Virtually all of the Mediterranean basin is represented on the ever-changing, imaginative menu. Choices include the likes of pan-fried sea bass with roast baby fennel, tomato and olives; or rump of lamb with spiced aubergine and dried apricots. A nice touch are the filtered still and sparkling waters (€1), where 50% of the cost goes to cancer research.

Damson Diner   FUSION €€
(Map p92; www.damsondiner.com; 52 South William St; mains €12.50-25; ☺ noon-midnight; ☒ all city centre) Behind the glass-fronted entrance is a superb new eatery, where the menu offers up a mix of Asian dishes (fennel *bhaji, ssam* duck or pork) and American classics (Boston chowder, chilli con carne). Damson is also home to the best cheeseburger in town, where the beef is *stuffed* with cheese. Great food, great fun and superb music.

777   MEXICAN €€
(Map p84; www.777.ie; 7 Castle House, South Great George's St; mains €16-28; ☺ 5.30-10pm Mon-Wed, 5.30-11pm Thu, 5pm-midnight Fri & Sat, 2-10pm Sun; ☒ all city centre) You won't eat better, more authentic Mexican cuisine than here – the *tostados* (crispy corn tortillas with various toppings) and *taquitos* (filled, soft corn tortillas) are great nibbles, or the perfect accompaniment for a tequila fest (it serves 22 different types); the mains are all prepared on a wood-burning grill and include a sensational tuna steak and a mouthwatering Iberico pork flank.

Yamamori   JAPANESE €€
(Map p84; ☏ 01-475 5001; www.yamamorinoodles. ie; 71 South Great George's St; mains €16-25, lunch bento €9.95; ☺ 12.30-11pm; ☂; ☒ all city centre) Hip and inexpensive, Yamamori rarely disappoints with its bubbly service and vivacious cooking that swoops from sushi and sashimi to whopping great plates of noodles, with plenty in between. The lunch bento is one of the best deals in town and draws them in from offices throughout the area.

It's a great spot for a sociable group – including vegetarians – although you'll have to book at the weekend to be one of the happy campers. There's another branch north of the river.

Good World   CHINESE €€
(Map p84; 18 South Great George's St; dim sum €4-6, mains €12-19; ☺ 12.30pm-2.30am; ☒ all city centre) A hands-down winner of our best-Chinese-restaurant competition, the Good World has two menus, but to really get the most of this terrific spot, steer well clear of the Western menu and its unimaginative dishes. With listings in two languages, the Chinese menu is literally packed with dishes and delicacies that keep us coming back for more.

L'Gueuleton   FRENCH €€
(Map p84; www.lgueuleton.com; 1 Fade St; mains €19-26; ☺ 12.30-4pm & 6-10pm Mon-Sat, 1-4pm & 6-9pm Sun; ☒ all city centre) Dubliners have a devil of a time pronouncing the name (which means 'a gluttonous feast' in French) and have had their patience tested with the no-reservations-get-in-line-and-wait policy, but they just can't get enough of this restaurant's robust (read: meaty and filling) take on French rustic cuisine that makes twisted tongues and sore feet a small price to pay.

Dunne & Crescenzi   ITALIAN €€
(Map p92; www.dunneandcrescenzi.com; 14-16 South Frederick St; 3-course evening menus €30; ☺ 7.30am-10pm Mon-Sat, 9am-10pm Sun; ☒ all city centre) This exceptional Italian eatery delights its regulars with a basic menu of rustic pleasures, such as panini, a single pasta dish and a superb plate of mixed antipasto drizzled in olive oil. It's always full, and the tables are just that little bit too close to one another, but the coffee is perfect and the desserts are sinfully good.

Green Hen   FRENCH €€
(Map p84; ☏ 01-670 7238; www.greenhen.ie; 33 Exchequer St; mains €19-26; ☺ lunch & dinner Mon-

Continued on page 110

DUBLIN EATING

SASAR / GETTY IMAGES ©

Literary Dublin

Is there a city of comparable size anywhere in the world that can hold a candle to Dublin as a literary heavyweight? It's not just the Nobel Prize winners — it's the host of other scribes, writing in every conceivable genre, for every conceivable taste.

Marsh's Library

Dublin's oldest working library is an early 18th-century classic, packed with ancient books and manuscripts including some of the world's rarest.

Samuel Beckett

Like his great mentor Joyce, Beckett left Dublin for Paris, where he produced his finest work, including the watershed *Waiting For Godot,* a Modernist classic. A memorial bridge dedicated to Beckett, designed by architect Santiago Calatrava, was opened in Dublin in 2009.

James Joyce

Ireland's most famous literary export, Joyce devoted virtually his entire career to writing about one subject: Dublin. His book of short stories, *Dubliners,* remains one of the must-reads on the capital.

1. Memorial bridge dedicated to Samuel Beckett **2.** Marsh's Library **3.** James Joyce statue

BRUNO BARBIER / GETTY IMAGES ©

Dublin Writers Museum

A collection of memorabilia associated with Dublin's rich literary past, including Brendan Behan's union card and Samuel Beckett's phone.

Trinity College Library

Two super-highlights: the breathtaking 65m Long Room, the most beautiful library in Ireland, and the Book of Kells, the most famous illustrated Gospels in the world.

Oscar Wilde

Outstanding playwright, thoughtful poet, writer of children's literature and famous wit, Oscar Wilde is one of Dublin's most beloved literary progeny.

1. Trinity College Library **2.** Writers Gallery, Dublin Writers Museum **3.** Oscar Wilde statue, Merrion Square

Continued from page 105

Fri, brunch & dinner Sat & Sun; 🖳all city centre) New York's Soho meets Parisian brasserie at this stylish eatery, where elegance and economy live side by side. If you don't fancy gorging on oysters or tucking into a divine Irish Hereford rib-eye, you can opt for the plat du jour or avail of the early-bird menus; watch out for its killer cocktails. Reservations recommended for dinner.

Saba
FUSION €€

(Map p92; ✆01-679 2000; www.sabadublin.com; 26-28 Clarendon St; mains €13-23; ☉lunch & dinner; 🖳all city centre) The name means 'happy meeting place' and this Thai-Vietnamese fusion restaurant is just that, a very popular eatery with Dubliners who tuck into a wide selection of Southeast Asian dishes and test the limits of the cocktail menu. The atmosphere is all designer cool, the fare a tad shy of being genuinely authentic but it's a good night out.

Pichet
FRENCH €€

(Map p84; ✆01-677 1060; www.pichetrestaurant. ie; 14-15 Trinity St; mains €17-29; ☉lunch & dinner; 🖳all city centre) TV chef Nick Munier and Stephen Gibson (formerly of L'Ecrivain) deliver their version of modern French cuisine to this elongated dining room replete with blue leather chairs and lots of windows to stare out of. The result is pretty good indeed, the food excellent – we expected nothing less – and the service impeccable. Sit in the back for atmosphere.

Odessa
MEDITERRANEAN €€

(Map p84; ✆01-670 7634; www.odessa.ie; 13 Dame Ct; dinner mains €15-28; ☉lunch & dinner; 🖳all city centre) Odessa and the hangover brunch go hand in hand like Laurel and Hardy. But this stylish eatery's dining credentials have long been maintained by its excellent dinner menu, which combines solid favourites like the homemade burger with more adventurous dishes like roast fillet of hake served with chorizo, clams, white bean stew and serrano ham.

Nede
MODERN IRISH €€

(Map p84; ✆01-670 5372; www.nede.ie; Meeting House Sq; mains €16-28; ☉noon-2.30pm & 6-10.30pm Mon-Fri, noon-3pm & 6-11pm Sat & Sun; 🖳all city centre) A long-standing Temple Bar favourite, Nede serves up generous helpings of modern Irish cuisine in a stylish setting – it's designed to look like the interior of an (empty) pool. Beef, chicken, duck and venison all feature on the menu, but our favourite is weekend brunch, where you can linger with the papers and refills of coffee.

Brasserie Sixty6
FUSION €€

(Map p84; www.brasseriesixty6.com; 66 South Great George's St; mains €18-31; ☉8am-11.30pm Mon-Sat, from 11am Sun; 🖳all city centre) This New York–style brasserie's specialty is rotisserie chicken, done four different ways at any given time. Its meat-heavy menu also includes the likes of lamb shank and a particularly good bit of liver. For that special occasion, there's a whole roast pig (€300), but you need to order seven days in advance and be in a group of eight.

Avoca
CAFE €€

(Map p84; www.avoca.ie; 11-13 Suffolk St; mains €11-14; 🖳all city centre) The waiters are easy on the eye for a reason: the upstairs cafe of the city's best designer crafts store has long been the favourite spot of the Ladies Who Lunch. Designer bags can get very heavy, so there's nothing better to restore flagging energy than the simple, rustic delights on offer from the Avoca kitchen: organic shepherd's pie, roast lamb with couscous, or sumptuous salads. There's also a takeaway salad bar and hot-food counter in the basement.

Wagamama
JAPANESE €€

(Map p92; South King St; mains €11-17; ☉11am-11pm; 🖳all city centre) There's ne'er a trace of raw fish to be seen, but this popular chain dishes up some terrific Japanese food nonetheless. Production-line rice and noodle dishes served pronto at canteen-style tables mightn't seem like the most inviting way to dine, but boy this food is good, and the basement it's served up in is surprisingly light and airy – for a place with absolutely no natural light.

★Restaurant Patrick Guilbaud
FRENCH €€€

(Map p92; ✆01-676 4192; www.restaurantpatrick guilbaud.ie; 21 Upper Merrion St; 2-/3-course set lunch €40/50, dinner mains €38-56; ☉12.30-2.30pm & 7.30-10.30pm Tue-Sat; 🖳7, 44 from city centre) Its devotees have long proclaimed this exceptional restaurant the best in the country and Guillaume Lebrun's French haute cuisine the most exalted expression of the culinary arts, an opinion that has found favour with the good people at Michelin, who have put two stars in its crown. The lunch menu is an absolute steal, at least in this stratosphere.

The food is innovative without being fiddly, beautifully cooked and superbly presented. The room itself is all contemporary elegance and the service expertly formal yet surprisingly friendly – the staff are meticulously trained and are as skilled at answering queries and addressing individual requests as they are at making sure not one bread crumb lingers too long on the immaculate tablecloths. Owner Patrick Guilbaud himself usually does the rounds of the tables in the evening to salute regular customers and charm first-timers into returning. Reservations are absolutely necessary.

L'Ecrivain FRENCH €€€
(Map p92; ☑ 01-661 1919; www.lecrivain.com; 109A Lower Baggot St; 3-course lunch menus €35, 10-course tasting menus €90, mains €40-47; ☺ lunch Mon-Fri, dinner Mon-Sat; ☑ 38, 39 from city centre) A firm favourite with the bulk of the city's foodies, L'Ecrivain trundles along with just one Michelin star to its name, but the plaudits keep coming. Head chef Derry Clarke is considered a gourmet god for the exquisite simplicity of his creations, which put the emphasis on flavour and the use of the best local ingredients – all given the French once-over and turned into something that approaches divine dining.

Thornton's FRENCH €€€
(Map p92; ☑ 01-478 7000; www.thorntonsrestaurant.com; 128 West St Stephen's Green; midweek 3-course lunch €45, dinner tasting menus €76-120; ☺ 12.30-2pm & 7-10pm Tue-Sat; ☑ all city centre) Chef Kevin Thornton's culinary genius is to take new French cuisine and give it a theatrical, Irish revamp: the result is a Michelin-starred, wonderful mix of succulent seafood dishes and meatier fare like noisette of milk-fed Wicklow lamb. A nice touch is when Kevin himself comes out to greet his guests and explain his creations. Reservations are essential.

Shanahan's on the Green STEAKHOUSE €€€
(Map p92; ☑ 01-407 0939; www.shanahans.ie; 119 West St Stephen's Green; mains €46-49; ☺ from 6pm Mon-Thu, Sat & Sun, from noon Fri; ☑ all city centre) 'American-style steakhouse' hardly does justice to this elegant restaurant where JR Ewing and his cronies would happily have done business. Although the menu features seafood, this place is all about meat, notably the best cuts of impossibly juicy and tender Irish Angus beef you'll find anywhere. The mountainous onion rings are the perfect accompaniment, while the sommeliers are experts.

Cliff Townhouse IRISH €€€
(Map p92; ☑ 01-638 3939; www.theclifftownhouse.com; 22 North St Stephen's Green; mains €19-35; ☺ noon-2.30pm & 6-11pm Mon-Sat, noon-4pm & 6-10pm Sun; ☑ all city centre) Sean Smith's menu is a confident expression of the very best of Irish cuisine – Warrenpoint fish pie, organic fillet of pork and a loin of venison share the menu with a masterful fish and chips.

🍴 The Liberties & Kilmainham

Among the fast-food outlets and greasy-spoon diners you'll find one fabulous fine-dining restaurant, a superb cafe and Dublin's most famous fish-and-chip shop.

⭐ Fumbally Cafe CAFE €
(Map p72; Fumbally Lane; mains €5-8; ☺ 8am-5pm Mon-Sat; ☑ 49, 54A, 77X from city centre) Part of the new, trendy Fumbally Development is this terrific warehouse cafe. The superb menu has a range of pastries, homemade sandwiches, healthy breakfasts and daily lunch specials. The avocado sandwich is divine. A cut above the rest.

Leo Burdock's FISH & CHIPS €
(Map p72; 2 Werburgh St; cod & chips €9.50; ☺ noon-midnight Mon-Sat, 4pm-midnight Sun; ☑ all city centre) You will often hear that you haven't eaten in Dublin until you've queued in the cold for cod 'n' chips wrapped in paper from the city's most famous chipper. Total codswallop, of course, but there's something about sitting on the street, balancing the bag on your lap and trying to eat the chips quickly before they go cold that smacks of Dublin in a bygone age.

Lock's Brasserie MODERN IRISH €€€
(Map p72; ☑ 01-420 0555; www.locksbrasserie.com; 1 Windsor Tce; mains €25-32; ☺ lunch Thu-Sun, dinner daily; ☑ 128, 14, 142, 14A, 15, 15A, 15B, 15E, 15F, 65, 65B, 74, 74A, 83 from city centre) The most discreet of Dublin's Michelin-starred restaurants is this wonderful canalside brasserie, where head chef Sebastian Masi has wowed diners with his limited menu of old favourites. The six mains are evenly split between fish and meat, but each is a bit of culinary magic – the John Dory with squid ink and anchovy pappardelle, purple sprouting broccoli, broccoli puree and garlic foam is so good that you'll eat it especially slowly.

✖ North of the Liffey

Dublin's foodie revolution has done wonders for the north side's dining options, which now include a fine selection of cafes, mid-range restaurants and – especially – a broad range of ethnic cuisines.

Third Space
CAFE €

(Map p72; Unit 14, Block C, Smithfield Market; ⊗ 8am-7pm Mon-Tue & Fri, 8am-9.30pm Wed & Thu, 9.30am-5pm Sat; ⬚ Smithfield) One of the most welcoming cafes in town is this wonderful spot in Smithfield, which serves gorgeous sandwiches, wraps and baps, as well as a tart of the day (€5.95) and wines by the glass. Sit in the window, take out a book and just relax. The staff are fabulous.

Brother Hubbard
CAFE €

(Map p114; 153 Capel St; ⊗ 8am-5.30pm Mon-Fri, 10am-5pm Sat; ⬚ all city centre, ⬚ Jervis) When did the art of coffee become, well, an art? When the likes of this terrific little cafe began serving up its specialist beans (procured from coffee experts 3FE), turning each cappuccino into the perfect creation. For solid sustenance, the scones are excellent and the sandwiches as good as you'll find anywhere. The perfect hang-out spot.

Soup Dragon
FAST FOOD €

(Map p114; www.soupdragon.com; 168 Capel St; soups €5-10; ⊗ 8am-5pm Mon-Fri, 10am-4pm Sat; ⬚ all city centre, ⬚ Jervis) Queues are a regular feature outside this fabulous spot that specialises in soups-on-the-go, but it also does excellent curries, stews, pies and salads. The all-day breakfast options are excellent – we especially like the mini breakfast quiche of sausage, egg and bacon. Bowls come in three different sizes and prices include fresh bread and a piece of fruit.

Taste of Emilia
ITALIAN €

(Map p114; 28 Lower Liffey St; mains €4-10; ⊗ noon-10.30pm Wed-Sat, from 5pm Tue, from 3.30pm Sun; ⬚ all city centre) This warm, buzzing locale does a wonderful trade in cured meats and cheeses from all over Italy, paying particular attention to the produce of the true heartland of Italian cuisine, Emilia-Romagna. The sandwiches are made with homemade *piadina* bread or *tigelle* (a disc-shaped Italian bread similar to a muffin), and you can wash it down with a light sparkling wine from the north of Italy.

★ Musashi Noodles & Sushi Bar
JAPANESE €€

(Map p114; ☎ 01-532 8057; www.musashidublin.com; 15 Capel St; mains €15-25; ⊗ lunch & dinner; ⬚ all city centre, ⬚ Jervis) A lovely, low-lit room, this new spot is the most authentic Japanese restaurant in the city, serving up freshly crafted sushi to an ever-growing number of devotees. The lunch bento deals are a steal, and if you don't fancy raw fish it also does a wide range of other Japanese specialties. It's BYOB (corkage charged). Evening bookings recommended.

Wuff
INTERNATIONAL €€

(Map p72; 23 Benburb St; mains €14-24; ⊗ 7.30am-4pm Mon-Wed, 7.30am-10pm Thu & Fri, 10am-10pm Sat, 10am-4pm Sun; ⬚ 25, 25A, 66, 67 from city centre, ⬚ Museum) This neighbourhood bistro does excellent breakfasts and brunches – the truffle-infused poached eggs with gruyère on toast are divine – as well as fine mains that feature fish, duck, beef and a couple of veggie options.

HOME AWAY FROM HOME

Self-catering apartments are a good option for visitors staying a few days, for groups of friends, or families with kids. Apartments range from one-room studios to two-bedroom flats with lounge areas, and include bathrooms and kitchenettes. A decent two-bedroom apartment will cost about €100 to €150 per night. Good, central places include the following:

Home from Home Apartments (Map p100; ☎ 01-678 1100; www.yourhomefromhome.com; The Moorings, Fitzwilliam Quay; apt €110-180) Deluxe one- to three-bedroom apartments in the southside city centre.

Latchfords (Map p92; ☎ 01-676 0784; www.latchfords.ie; 99-100 Lower Baggot St; apt €100-160) Studios and two-bedroom flats in a Georgian town house.

Oliver St John Gogarty's Penthouse Apartments (Map p84; ☎ 01-671 1822; www.gogartys.ie; 18-21 Anglesea St; 2-bed apt €99-189) Perched high atop the pub of the same name, these one- to three-bedroom places have views of Temple Bar.

Yamamori Sushi   JAPANESE €€
(Map p114; www.yamamorinoodles.ie; 38-39 Lower Ormond Quay; sushi €3-3.50, mains €17-35; ⊙ lunch & dinner; 🚇 all city centre) A sibling of the long-established Yamamori on South Great George's St, this large restaurant – spread across two converted Georgian houses and including a bamboo garden – serves up all kinds of favourites from steaming bowls of ramen to a delicious *nami moriawase*. Like its sister restaurant, the lunchtime bento boxes are a popular choice.

Hot Stove   MODERN IRISH €€
(Map p114; www.thehotstoverestaurant.com; 38-39 Parnell Sq West; mains €17-22; ⊙ lunch & dinner Tue-Fri, dinner Sat; 🚌 3, 10, 11, 13, 16, 19, 22 from city centre) An elegant new restaurant that may one day vie for the northside's best, the Hot Stove serves locally sourced, beautifully prepared Irish dishes including pork belly, a changing selection of fish dishes and the ubiquitous steak. The pre-theatre menu (two/three courses €23/28) is a steal, the wine list is excellent and the service top-notch.

★ Chapter One   MODERN IRISH €€€
(Map p114; 📞 01-873 2266; www.chapteronerestaurant.com; 18 North Parnell Sq; 2-course lunch €29, 4-course dinner €65; ⊙ 12.30-2pm Tue-Fri, 6-11pm Tue-Sat; 🚌 3, 10, 11, 13, 16, 19, 22 from city centre) Michelin-starred and our choice for city's best eatery, it successfully combines flawless haute cuisine with a relaxed, welcoming atmosphere that is at the heart of Irish hospitality. The food is French-inspired contemporary Irish, the menus change regularly and the service is top-notch. The three-course pretheatre menu (€36.50) is a favourite with those heading to the Gate around the corner.

Winding Stair   MODERN IRISH €€€
(Map p114; 📞 01-873 7320; http://winding-stair.com; 40 Lower Ormond Quay; mains €23-27; ⊙ noon-5pm & 5.30-10.30pm; 🚇 all city centre) Housed within a beautiful Georgian building that was once home to the city's most beloved bookshop (the ground floor still is one), the Winding Stair's conversion to elegant restaurant has been faultless. The wonderful Irish menu – creamy fish pie, bacon and organic cabbage, steamed mussels, and Irish farmyard cheeses – coupled with an excellent wine list makes for a memorable meal.

Morrison Grill   INTERNATIONAL €€€
(Map p114; 📞 01-878 2999; www.morrisonhotel.ie; Morrison Hotel, Lower Ormond Quay; mains €18-30; ⊙ dinner; 🚇 all city centre) The main eatery of the newly refurbished Morrison Hotel is really a very fancy grill, the specialties of which are meats cooked in Ireland's only Josper indoor barbecue oven. If you don't fancy steaks, burgers or grilled fish, there's a selection of other main courses, but the real treat here is food cooked at over 500 degrees.

🍴 Docklands

Although the crash has put paid to some of the grander plans for restaurant openings in the Docklands, there are a couple of good options that reflect the best of new dining in the city.

Ely Bar & Brasserie   FUSION €€
(Map p100; www.elywinebar.ie; Custom House Quay; mains €13-21; ⊙ noon-3pm & 6-10pm Mon-Fri, 1-4pm & 6-10pm Sat; 🚇 Grand Canal Dock) ✈ Scrummy homemade burgers, bangers and mash, and wild smoked salmon salad is some of what you'll find in this converted tobacco warehouse in the heart of the International Financial Services Centre (IFSC). Dishes are prepared with organic and free-range produce from the owner's family farm in County Clare, so you can be assured of the quality. There's a large wine list to choose from, with over 70 sold by the glass.

Ely Gastro Pub   INTERNATIONAL €€
(Map p100; Grand Canal Quay; ⊙ lunch & dinner; 🚇 Grand Canal Dock) Amid the exposed brick, designer lampshades and comfortable seating is a terrific bar (30 craft beers on tap) that also doubles as an excellent restaurant, serving well-made classics (chicken, burger, steak and a particularly good fish-and-cheddar pie) that will more than satisfy if you're preparing for a gig at the Bord Gáis Energy Theatre or are just out for the night.

Herbstreet   FUSION €€
(Map p100; www.herbstreet.ie; Hanover Quay; mains €13-19; ⊙ lunch & dinner Mon-Fri, dinner Sat; 🚇 Grand Canal Dock) ✈ Low-power hand driers, one-watt LED bulbs, secondhand furniture and strictly European wines: this eatery is taking its green responsibilities seriously. The fish used here is farmed locally, and all of the other dishes – fine, delicious portions of sandwiches, burgers and salads – are sourced as close to the restaurant as possible.

Quay 16   FUSION €€€
(Map p100; 📞 01-817 8760; www.mvcillairne.com; MV Cill Airne, North Wall Quay; bar food €12-14, mains €23-30; ⊙ noon-3pm Mon-Fri, 6-10pm Mon-Sat)

DUBLIN EATING

North of the Liffey

DUBLIN EATING

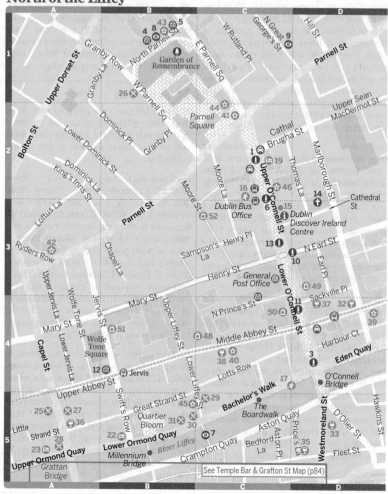

See Temple Bar & Grafton St Map (p84)

The MV *Cill Airne*, commissioned in 1961 as a passenger liner tender, is now permanently docked along the north quays, where it serves the public as a bar, bistro and fine restaurant. The food in this restaurant is surprisingly good – dishes such as Himalayan salt-aged fillet steak and pan-roasted sea bass are expertly prepared and are served alongside an excellent variety of wines.

✗ Beyond the Grand Canal

It's hardly surprising that the chichi southern suburbs would have their fair share of decent eateries – it's where the city's privileged classes can turn their collars up and unwind after a hard day of making money. If you're in Ranelagh or Ballsbridge, there's always somewhere to get a decent bite.

Paulie's Pizza   ITALIAN €€
(Map p72; www.juniors.ie; 58 Upper Grand Canal St; pizzas €12-17; ⊙ dinner; ⚙; ⊠3 from city centre, ⊠ Grand Canal Dock) In July 2010 the brothers who created Juniors (just around the corner) imported a traditional Neapolitan pizza oven and set about introducing Dubliners to proper, thin-crusted pizza from the city

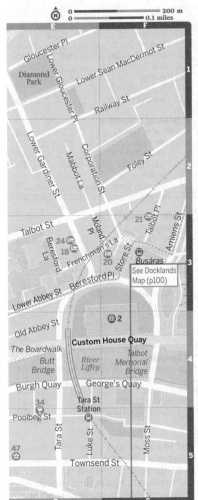

atmosphere always buzzing (it's often hard to get a table) and the ethos top-notch, which is down to the two brothers who run the place.

Drinking & Nightlife

If there's one constant about life in Dublin, it's that Dubliners will always take a drink. Come hell or high water, the city's pubs will never be short of customers, and we suspect that exploring a variety of Dublin's legendary pubs and bars ranks pretty high on the list of reasons you're here.

Last orders are at 11.30pm Monday to Thursday, 12.30am Friday and Saturday and 11pm on Sunday, with 30 minutes' drinking-up time each night. However, many central pubs have licences to serve until 1.30am or 2.30am.

Grafton Street & Around

John Mulligan's
PUB

(Map p114; 8 Poolbeg St; ☐all city centre) This brilliant old boozer was established in 1782 and has barely changed over the years. In fact, the last time it was renovated was when Christy Brown and his rowdy clan ran amok here in the film *My Left Foot*. It has one of the finest pints of Guinness in Dublin and a colourful crew of regulars. It's just off Fleet St, outside the eastern boundary of Temple Bar.

Kehoe's
PUB

(Map p92; 9 South Anne St; ☐all city centre) This is one of the most atmospheric pubs in the city centre and a favourite with all kinds of Dubliners. It has a beautiful Victorian bar, a wonderful snug, and plenty of other little nooks and crannies. Upstairs, drinks are served in what was once the publican's living room – and looks it!

Stag's Head
PUB

(Map p84; 1 Dame Ct; ☐all city centre) The Stag's Head was built in 1770, remodelled in 1895 and thankfully not changed a bit since then. It's a superb pub: so picturesque that it often appears in films and also featured in a postage-stamp series on Irish bars. A bloody great pub, no doubt.

Long Hall
PUB

(Map p84; 51 South Great George's St; ☐all city centre) Luxuriating in full Victorian splendour, this is one of the city's most beautiful and best-loved pubs. Check out the ornate carvings in the woodwork behind the bar and

of its birthplace. Margheritas, *biancas* (no tomato sauce), calzone and other Neapolitan specialities are the real treat, but there's also room for a classic New York slice as well as a few local creations.

Juniors
ITALIAN €€

(Map p72; ☏01-664 3648; www.juniors.ie; 2 Bath Ave; mains €16-24; ☺lunch & dinner; ☐3 from city centre, ☐Grand Canal Dock) Cramped and easily mistaken for any old cafe, Juniors is anything but ordinary: designed to imitate a New York deli, the food (Italian influenced, all locally sourced produce) is delicious, the

North of the Liffey

the elegant chandeliers. The bartenders are experts at their craft, an increasingly rare attribute in Dublin these days.

37 Dawson St
BAR

(Map p92; ☎ 01-672 8231; www.37dawsonstreet.ie; 37 Dawson St; ☐ all city centre) Antiques, eye-catching art and elegant bric-a-brac adorn this new bar that has quickly established itself as a favourite with the trendy crowd. At the back is the new Whiskey Bar, a '50s-style bar that Don Draper and Co would feel comfortable sipping a fine scotch at; upstairs is an elegant restaurant that serves a terrific brunch.

Anseo
BAR

(Map p92; 28 Lower Camden St; ☐ all city centre) Unpretentious, unaffected and incredibly popular, this cosy alternative bar – which is pronounced 'an-*shuh*', the Irish for 'here' – is a favourite with those who live by the credo that to try too hard is far worse than not trying at all. Wearing cool like a loose garment, the punters thrive on the mix of chat and terrific DJs, who dig into virtually every crate to provide the soundtrack, whether it be Peggy Lee or Lee Perry.

No Name Bar
BAR

(Map p84; 3 Fade St; ☐ all city centre) A low-key entrance just next to the trendy French restaurant L'Gueuleton leads upstairs to one of the nicest bar spaces in town, consisting of three huge rooms in a restored Victorian townhouse plus a sizeable heated patio area for smokers. There's no sign or a name – folks just refer to it as the No Name Bar or, if you're a real insider, Number 3.

Oliver St John Gogarty
PUB

(Map p84; 58-59 Fleet St; ☐ all city centre) You won't see too many Dubs ordering drinks in this bar, which is almost entirely given over to tourists who come for the carefully manufactured slice of authentic traditionalism... and the knee-slappin', toe-tappin' sessions that run throughout the day. The kitchen serves up dishes that most Irish cooks have consigned to the culinary dustbin.

Grogan's Castle Lounge PUB
(Map p84; 15 South William St) This place is known simply as Grogan's (after the original owner), and it is a city-centre institution. It has long been a favourite haunt of Dublin's writers and painters, as well as others from the alternative bohemian set, most of whom seem to be waiting for the 'inevitable' moment when they are finally recognised as geniuses.

Whelan's BAR
(Map p92; www.whelanslive.com; 25 Wexford St) The bar of one of the city's most beloved live-music venues is always full of earnest young things on a good night out. The bar is done up like a traditional pub, the crowd is fun and the music is all kinds of rock, folk and contemporary.

Dawson Lounge PUB
(Map p92; 25 Dawson St) To see *the* smallest bar in Dublin, go through a small doorway, down a narrow flight of steps and into two tiny rooms that always seem to be filled with a couple of bedraggled drunks who look like they're hiding. Psst, here's a secret: a certain sunglassed lead singer of a certain ginormous Irish band is said to love unwinding in here from time to time.

Pygmalion BAR
(Map p84; ☎01-674 6712; www.bodytonicmusic.com; Powerscourt Townhouse Shopping Centre, 59 South William St; 🚌all city centre) Currently one of the busiest bars in town, the 'Pyg' caters to a largely student crowd with its €10 pitchers, pounding music and labyrinthine nooks and crannies (perfect for a naughty hideaway). The owner thought it best to line the wall with carpet – perhaps they're worried that the action on the dance floor might get a little too crazy?

Hogan's BAR
(Map p84; 35 South Great George's St) Once an old-style traditional bar, Hogan's is now a gigantic boozer spread across two floors. Midweek it's a relaxing hang-out for young professionals and restaurant and bar workers on a night off. But come the weekend the sweat bin downstairs pulls them in for some serious music courtesy of the usually excellent DJs.

Bruxelles PUB
(Map p92; 7-8 Harry St) Although it has largely shed its heavy-metal and alternative skin, Bruxelles is still a raucous, fun place to hang out and there are different music areas. It's comparatively trendy on the ground floor, while downstairs is a great, loud and dingy rock bar with live music each weekend. Just outside, a bronze Phil Lynott (Map p92) is there to remind us of Bruxelles' impeccable rock credentials.

James Toner's PUB
(Map p92; 139 Lower Baggot St; 🚌7, 44 from city centre) Toner's, with its stone floors and an-

---

FARMERS & ORGANIC MARKETS

Dublin Food Co-op (Map p72; www.dublinfoodcoop.com; 12 Newmarket; ⊙2-8pm Thu, 9.30am-4.30pm Sat; 🚌49, 54A & 77X from city centre) A buzzing community market specialising in organic veg, homemade cheeses and organic wines; there's also a bakery and even baby-changing facilities.

Coppinger Row Market (Map p84; Coppinger Row; ⊙9am-7pm Thu) It's small – only a handful of stalls – but it packs a proper organic punch, attracting punters with the waft of freshly baked breads, delicious hummus and other goodies.

Harcourt St Food Market (Map p92; www.irishfarmersmarkets.ie; Park Pl, Station Bldgs, Upper Hatch St; ⊙10am-4pm Thu) Organic veggies, cheeses, olives and meats made into dishes from all over the world.

Temple Bar Farmers Market (Map p84; Meeting House Sq; ⊙9am-4.30pm Sat) This great little market is a fabulous place to while away a Saturday morning, sampling and munching on organic gourmet goodies bound by the market's only rule: local producers only. From cured meats to wildflowers, you could fill an entire pantry with their selection of delights.

For more info on local markets, check out www.irishfarmersmarkets.ie, www.irishvillagemarkets.com or local county council sites such as www.dlrcoco.ie/markets.

VEGGIE BITES

Vegetarians are having it increasingly easier in Dublin as the capital has veered away from the belief that food isn't food until your incisors have had to rip flesh from bone, and towards an understanding that healthy eating leads to, well, longer lives. There's a selection of general restaurants that cater to vegetarians beyond the token dish of mixed greens and pulses – places like **Nude** (Map p84; ☑ 01-675 5577; 21 Suffolk St; wraps €5-6; ☺ Mon-Sat; ☑; ☐ all city centre), Yamamori (p105) and **Chameleon** (Map p84; ☑ 01-671 0362; www.chameleonrestaurant.com; 1 Lower Fownes St; mains €16.50-19.50; ☺ dinner Tue-Sun; ☑; ☐ all city centre).

Solidly vegetarian places include **Blazing Salads** (Map p84; 42 Drury St; mains €4-9; ☺ 10am-6pm Mon-Sat, to 8pm Thu; ☑), with organic breads, Californian-style salads and pizza; **Cornucopia** (Map p84; www.cornucopia.ie; 19 Wicklow St; mains €10-13; ☺ 8.30am-9pm Mon & Tue, 8.30am-10.15pm Wed-Sat, noon-9pm Sun; ☑), Dublin's best-known vegetarian restaurant, serving wholesome salads, sandwiches and a selection of hot main courses; **Fresh** (Map p84; top fl, Powerscourt Townhouse Shopping Centre, 59 South William St; lunch €6-12; ☺ 9.30am-6pm Mon-Sat, 10am-5pm Sun; ☑), a long-standing restaurant serving a variety of salads, dairy- and gluten-free dishes, and filling, hot daily specials; and **Govinda's** (Map p92; www.govindas.ie; 4 Aungier St; mains €7-10; ☺ noon-9pm Mon-Sat; ☑), an authentic beans-and-pulses place run by the Hare Krishna.

tique snugs, has changed little over the years and is the closest thing you'll get to a country pub in the heart of the city. The shelves and drawers are reminders that it once doubled as a grocery shop.

Hartigan's
PUB

(Map p92; 100 Lower Leeson St; ☐ all city centre) This is about as spartan a bar as you'll find in the city, and is the daytime home to some serious drinkers, who appreciate the quiet, no-frills surroundings. In the evening it's popular with students from the medical faculty of University College Dublin (UCD).

O'Donoghue's
PUB

(Map p92; 15 Merrion Row; ☐ all city centre) Once the most renowned traditional music bar in all Dublin, this is where the world-famous folk group the Dubliners refined their raspish brand of trad in the 1960s. On summer evenings a young, international crowd spills out into the courtyard beside the pub. It's also a famous rugby pub and the Dublin HQ for many Irish and visiting fans.

International Bar
PUB

(Map p84; 23 Wicklow St; ☐ 7, 44 from city centre) This tiny pub with a huge personality is a top spot for an afternoon pint. It has a long bar, stained-glass windows, red-velour seating and a convivial atmosphere. Some of Ireland's most celebrated comedians stuttered through their first set in the Comedy Cellar, which is, of course, upstairs.

Porterhouse
BAR

(Map p84; 16-18 Parliament St; ☐ all city centre) The second-biggest brewery in Dublin, the Porterhouse looks like a cross between a Wild West bar and a Hieronymus Bosch painting – all wood and full of staircases. We love it, and although it inevitably gets crowded, this pub on the fringe of Temple Bar is for the discerning drinker and has lots of its own delicious brews, including its Plain Porter (some say it's the best stout in town) as well as unfamiliar imported beers.

Bernard Shaw
BAR

(Map p72; www.bodytonicmusic.com; 11-12 South Richmond St; ☐ 7, 44 from city centre) This deliberately ramshackle boozer is probably the coolest bar in town for its marvellous mix of music (courtesy of its owners, the Bodytonic production crew, which also runs Twisted Pepper, p120)) and diverse menu of events such as afternoon car-boot sales, storytelling nights and fun competitions like having a 'tag-off' between a bunch of graffiti artists. This place looks like a dump, but it works because it is the effortless embodiment of the DIY, low-cost fun that is very much the city's contemporary Zeitgeist.

Palace Bar
PUB

(Map p114; 21 Fleet St; ☐ all city centre) With its mirrors and wooden niches, the Palace (established in 1823) is one of Dublin's great Victorian pubs and a stubborn stalwart against the modernising influences of the last half century. Patrick Kavanagh and

Flann O'Brien were once regulars and it was for a long time the unofficial head office of the *Irish Times*.

Kilmainham & the Liberties

Fallon's
TRADITIONAL PUB

(Map p72; ☎ 01-454 2801; 129 The Coombe; ☒ 123, 206, 51B from city centre) Just west of the city centre, in the heart of medieval Dublin, this is a fabulously old-fashioned bar that has been serving a great pint of Guinness since the end of the 17th century. Prize fighter Dan Donnelly, the only boxer ever to be knighted, was head bartender here in 1818. It's a genuine Irish bar filled with Dubs.

Old Royal Oak
TRADITIONAL PUB

(11 Kilmainham Lane; ☒ 68, 69, 79 from city centre) Locals are fiercely protective of this gorgeous traditional pub, which opened in 1845 to serve the patrons and staff of the Royal Hospital (now the Irish Museum of Modern Art). The clientele has changed, but everything else has remained the same, which makes this one of the nicest pubs in the city to enjoy a few pints.

North of the Liffey

Cobblestone
PUB

(Map p72; North King St; ☒ Smithfield) This pub in the heart of Smithfield has a great atmosphere in its cosy upstairs bar, where there are superb nightly music sessions performed by traditional musicians (especially Thursday) and up-and-coming folk acts.

Walshe's
PUB

(Map p72; 6 Stoneybatter; ☒ 25, 25A, 66, 67 from city centre, ☒ Museum) If the snug is free, a drink in Walshe's is about as pure a traditional experience as you'll have in any pub in the city; if it isn't, you'll have to make do with the old-fashioned bar, where the friendly staff and brilliant clientele (a mix of locals and hipster imports) are a treat. A proper Dublin pub.

Grand Social
BAR

(Map p114; ☎ 01-874 0076; www.thegrandsocial.ie; 35 Lower Liffey St; ☒ all city centre, ☒ Jervis) This multipurpose venue hosts club nights, comedy and live-music gigs as well as being a decent bar for a drink. It's spread across three floors, each of which has a different theme: The Parlour downstairs is a cozy, old-fashioned bar; the midlevel Ballroom is where the dancing is; the upstairs Loft hosts a variety of events.

Dice Bar
BAR

(Map p72; ☎ 01-674 6710; 79 Queen St; ☒ 25, 25A, 66, 67 from city centre, ☒ Museum) Co-owned by Huey from the Fun Lovin' Criminals, the Dice Bar looks like something you might find on New York's Lower East Side. Its dodgy locale, black-and-red painted interior, dripping candles and stressed seating, combined with rocking DJs most nights, make it a magnet for Dublin hipsters. It has Guinness and local microbrews.

Hughes' Bar
PUB

(Map p72; 19 Chancery St; ☒ 25, 66, 67, 90 from city centre, ☒ Four Courts) Traditional purists love the nightly sessions at this pub, which by day caters to barristers, solicitors and their clients from the nearby Four Courts – all of whom probably need a pint, but for different reasons! Although the playing is very good, the atmosphere is a little lacking and the sessions can be a bit dead.

Flowing Tide
PUB

(Map p114; 9 Lower Abbey St; ☒ all city centre, ☒ Abbey) This beautiful, atmospheric old pub is directly opposite the Abbey and is popular with theatre-goers – it can get swamped around 11pm, after the curtain comes down. They blend in with some no-bullshit locals who give the place a vital edge, and make it a great place for a drink and a natter.

Sackville Lounge
PUB

(Map p114; Sackville Pl; ☒ all city centre, ☒ Abbey) This tiny, 19th-century, one-room, wood-panelled bar lies just off O'Connell St and is popular with actors from the nearby Abbey and Peacock theatres, as well as a disproportionate number of elderly drinkers. It's a good pub for a solitary pint.

Nightclubs

Dubliners like to throw down some dance-floor moves, but for the most part they do it in bars equipped with a late license, a decent sound system and a space on the floor. It's all changed from even a decade ago, when clubbing was all the rage: these days fewer people pay to simply go dancing, preferring instead the option of dancing in a bar they've been in most of the evening. DJs are an increasingly rare breed, but the ones that thrive usually play it pretty safe; the handful of more creative DJs (including occasional international guests) play in an increasingly restricted number of venues.

POURING THE PERFECT PINT

Like the Japanese tea ceremony, pouring a pint of Guinness is part ritual, part theatre and part logic. It's a six-step process that every decent Dublin bartender will use to serve the perfect pint.

The Glass

A dry, clean 20oz (568ml) tulip pint glass is used because the shape allows the nitrogen bubbles to flow down the side, and the contour 'bump' about halfway down pushes the bubbles into the centre of the pint on their way back up.

The Angle

The glass is held beneath the tap at a 45-degree angle – and the tap faucet shouldn't touch the sides of the glass.

The Pour

A smooth pour should fill the glass to about three-quarters full, after which it is put on the counter 'to settle'.

The Head

As the beer flows into the glass its passes through a restrictor plate at high speed that creates nitrogen bubbles. In the glass, the agitated bubbles flow down the sides of the glass and – thanks to the contour bump – back up through the middle, settling at the top in a nice, creamy head. This should take a couple of minutes to complete.

The Top-Off

Once the pint is 'settled', the bartender will top it off, creating a domed effect across the top of the glass with the head sitting comfortably just above the rim. Now it's the perfect pint.

Where to Find It?

Now that you know what you're looking for, it's time to find it. The pint in the Gravity Bar is good, but it's missing one key ingredient: atmosphere, the kind found only in a traditional pub:

➡ Kehoe's (p115) Stalwart popular with locals and tourists.

➡ John Mulligan's (p115) Perfect setting for a perfect pint.

➡ Grogan's Castle Lounge (p117) Great because the locals demand it!

➡ Fallon's (p119) Centuries of experience.

The busiest nights are Thursday to Saturday, and most clubs are free if you arrive before 11pm. After that, you'll pay between €5 and €10.

Mother CLUB
(Map p84; Copper Alley, Exchange St; admission €10; ⊙11pm-3.30am Sat; 🚇all city centre) The best club night in the city is ostensibly a gay night but does not discriminate: clubbers of every sexual orientation come for the sensational DJs who throw down a mixed bag of disco, modern synth-pop and other danceable styles.

Lost Society CLUB
(Map p84; ☎01-677 0014; www.lostsociety.ie; Powerscourt Town Centre, South William St; admission €6-10; 🚇all city centre) Part of the magnificent 18th-century Powerscourt complex, Lost Society offers two distinct nightlife experiences for the price of one ticket. Upstairs, spread across three levels and a host of rooms, the music is eclectic and the crowd beautifully self-aware. Downstairs is the Bassment, where the music is thumping and the dancing is hot and sweaty.

Twisted Pepper CLUB
(Map p114; ☎01-873 4800; www.bodytonicmusic.com/thetwistedpepper; 54 Middle Abbey St; ⊙bar 4pm-late, cafe 11am-6pm; 🚇all city centre, 🚊Abbey) Dublin's hippest venue comes in four parts: DJs spin great tunes in the Basement; the Stage is for live acts; the Mezzanine is a secluded bar area above the stage; and the Cafe is where you can get an Irish breakfast

all day. All run by the Bodytonic crew, one of the most exciting music and production crowds in town.

Copper Face Jacks   CLUB
(Map p92; www.copperfacejacks.ie; 29-30 Harcourt St, Jackson Court Hotel; admission free-€10; ⏱10.30pm-3am) In rural Ireland you don't go clubbing; you go to 'the disco', and Copper's is the capital's very own version of it, offering unvarnished mayhem to the throngs that want to spend the evening drinking, dancing to familiar tunes and – hopefully – going home accompanied. Purists may scoff, but it's a formula that works a treat judging by its popularity.

Andrew's Lane Theatre   CLUB
(ALT; Map p84; www.facebook.com/andrewslanetheatre; 9-17 St Andrews Lane; ⏱11pm-3am Thu-Sat) A full-on club venue that is popular with students and younger clubbers. The music is loud, fast and overwhelming.

Krystle   CLUB
(Map p92; ☎01-478 4066; www.krystlenightclub.com; Russell Court Hotel, 21-25 Harcourt St; ⏱Thu-Sat; 🚇all city centre, 🚇Harcourt/St Stephen's Green) The favourite venue of many a Celtic cub, Krystle (annoyingly pronounced 'cristal' by its snootiest devotees) is where you'll most likely find the current crop of celebrities and their hangers-on, although you'll have to wade your way through the huge main floor and gain access to the upstairs VIP lounge for maximum exposure. Chart hits and club classics are the mainstay here.

Lillie's Bordello   CLUB
(Map p79; ☎01-679 9204; www.lilliesbordello.ie; Adam Ct; admission €10-20; ⏱11pm-3am) The most upmarket club in town prides itself on being the venue of choice for whatever Cristal-swilling superstar is in town. Not that you'll rub shoulders with them, as they'll be safely ensconced in the ultra-VIP Jersey Lil's private members' bar. Take comfort though in having made it past the club's selective door policy. Bad music, bad attitude.

☆ Entertainment

Believe it or not, there is life beyond the pub or, more accurately, around it. There are comedy clubs and classical concerts, recitals and readings, marionettes and music – lots and lots of music, both live and recorded. The other great Dublin treat is the theatre, where you can enjoy a light-hearted musical alongside the more serious stuff by Beckett,

Yeats and O'Casey – not to mention a host of new talents.

Theatre, comedy and classical concerts are usually booked directly through the venue. Tickets for touring international bands and big-name local talent are either sold at the venue or through a booking agency like **Ticketmaster** (www.ticketmaster.ie), which sells tickets to every genre of big- and medium-sized show – but be aware that it charges between 9% and 12.5% service charge per ticket.

Friday's *Irish Times* has a pull-out entertainment section called the *Ticket*, which has comprehensive listings of clubs and gigs; the *Irish Independent's* version, also out on Friday, is called *Day & Night*. Online resources include the following:

➡ **Entertainment.ie** (www.entertainment.ie) For all events.

➡ **MCD** (www.mcd.ie) Biggest promoter in Ireland.

➡ **Nialler9** (www.nialler9.com) Excellent indie blog with listings.

➡ **Sweebe** (www.sweebe.com) Over 200 venues listed.

➡ **What's On In** (www.whatsonin.ie) From markets to gigs and club nights.

☆ Rock & Pop

Dublin's love affair with popular music has made it one of the preferred touring stops for all kinds of musicians, who seem to relish the unfettered manner in which audiences embrace their favourite artists.

CAFE CULTURE & BEST COFFEES

Dublin's coffee junkies are everywhere, looking for that perfect barista fix that will kill the hunger until the next one. You can top-up at any of the chains – including that one from Seattle – but we reckon your caffeine craving will get the best fix at individual locales such as **Clement & Pekoe** (Map p92; www.clementandpekoe.com; 50 South William St; ⏱8am-7pm Mon-Fri, 10am-6pm Sat, noon-6pm Sun; 🚇all city centre), Brother Hubbard (p112), **Wall and Keogh** (Map p72; www.wallandkeogh.ie; 45 Richmond St South; ⏱8.30am-8.30pm Mon-Fri, 11am-7pm Sat-Sun; 🚇all city centre) and Brioche (p103).

Workman's Club LIVE MUSIC
(Map p84; 01-670 6692; www.theworkmans
club.com; 10 Wellington Quay; all city centre) A
300-capacity venue and bar in the former
working men's club of Dublin. Keeps away
from the mainstream, which means a
broad range of performers, from singer-
songwriters to electronic cabaret.

Academy LIVE MUSIC
(Map p114; 01-877 9999; www.theacademydublin.
com; 57 Middle Abbey St; all city centre, Abbey)
A terrific midsized venue, the Academy's
stage has been graced by an impressive list
of performers, from Nick Cave's Bad Seeds
to '80s superstar Nik Kershaw. It's also the
place to hear those unknown names who

GAY & LESBIAN DUBLIN

Dublin's not a bad place to be gay. Most people in the city centre wouldn't bat an eyelid at cross-dressing or public displays of affection between same-sex couples, but discretion is advised in the suburbs.

Festivals & Events

International Dublin Gay Theatre Festival (www.gaytheatre.ie) The only event of its kind anywhere in the world, with more than 30 gay- and lesbian-themed productions over two weeks in May.

Gaze International Lesbian & Gay Film Festival (www.gaze.ie) An international film and documentary festival held at the Irish Film Institute in August.

Drinking

Dragon (Map p84; 64-65 South Great George's St) High-concept, high-octane and loaded with attitude, the Dragon is the slightly trendier alternative to the long-established George down the street (George and the Dragon; get it?). It's more popular with guys than gals, and even then with a certain type of guy – young, brash and unafraid to express themselves...on the dancefloor or in the arms of another.

George (Map p84; www.thegeorge.ie; 89 South Great George's St) The purple mother of Dublin's gay bars is a long-standing institution, having lived through the years when it was the only place in town where the gay crowd could, well, be gay. There are other places to go, but the George remains the best, if only for tradition's sake. Shirley's legendary Sunday-night bingo is as popular as ever.

Front Lounge (Map p84; 33 Parliament St; all city centre) The unofficially gay 'Flounge' is a sophisticated and friendly bar that is quieter and more demure than other gay joints, and popular with a mixed crowd. Sexual orientation here is secondary to having a drink and a laugh with friends, even though the 'Back Lounge' towards the back of the bar is traditionally predominantly gay.

Pantibar (Map p114; www.pantibar.com; 7-8 Capel St; all city centre) Pantibar is bold and brash, mostly because its owner, the eponymous Panti, is an outrageous entertainer who makes sure that a night in *her* bar is one to remember. The floor shows – both on and off the stage – are fabulous. It's open late Friday and Saturday.

Information

Gay & Lesbian Garda Liaison Officer (01-666 9000) If you encounter any sort of trouble on the streets, don't hesitate to call. (For sexual assaults, contact the Sexual Assault Unit.)

Gay Community News (www.gcn.ie) A useful, nationwide news- and issues-based monthly paper. The glossy *Q-Life* and *Free!* are entertainment guides that can be found in Temple Bar businesses and the Irish Film Institute.

Gay Switchboard Dublin (872 1055; www.gayswitchboard.ie) A friendly and useful voluntary service that provides information ranging from where to find accommodation to legal issues.

Sexual Assault Unit (01-666 6000) Call or visit the Garda Station on Pearse St.

stand a better-than-evens chance of making it somewhere.

Button Factory
LIVE MUSIC

(Map p84; 01-670 0533; Curved St; all city centre) This venue offers a wide selection of musical acts, from traditional Irish music to drum and bass (and all things in between), to a non-image-conscious crowd. One night you might be shaking your glow light to a thumping live set by a top DJ and the next you'll be shifting from foot to foot as an esoteric Finnish band drag their violin bows over their electric guitar strings.

Vicar Street
LIVE MUSIC

(Map p72; 01-454 5533; www.vicarstreet.com; 58-59 Thomas St; 13, 49, 54a, 56a from city centre) Smaller performances take place at this intimate venue near Christ Church Cathedral. It has a capacity of 1000, between its table-serviced group seating downstairs and theatre-style balcony. Vicar Street offers a varied program of performers, with a strong emphasis on soul, folk, jazz and foreign music.

O2
LIVE MUSIC

(Map p100; 01-819 8888; www.theo2.ie; East Link Bridge, North Wall Quay; Point Village) The premier indoor venue in the city has a capacity of around 10,000 and plays host to the very brightest stars in the firmament: Rihanna, Bryan Adams and the cast of Glee are just some of the acts that have brought their magic to its superb stage.

Whelan's
LIVE MUSIC

(Map p92; 01-478 0766; www.whelanslive.com; 25 Wexford St; bus 16, 122 from city centre) Perhaps the city's most beloved live venue is this midsized room attached to a traditional bar. This is the singer-songwriter's spiritual home: when they're done pouring out the contents of their hearts on stage, you can find them filling up in the bar along with their fans.

Ambassador Theatre
THEATRE

(Map p114; 1890 925 100; O'Connell St; all city centre) The Ambassador started life as a theatre and then became a cinema. Not much has changed inside, making it a cool retro place to see visiting and local rock acts perform.

Gaiety Theatre
THEATRE

(Map p92; 01-677 1717; www.gaietytheatre.com; South King St; to 4am; all city centre) This old Victorian theatre is an atmospheric

place to come and listen to late-night jazz, rock or blues on the weekend.

Olympia Theatre
THEATRE

(Map p84; 01-677 7744; 72 Dame St; all city centre) This beautiful Victorian theatre generally puts on light plays, musicals and pantomime, but also caters to a range of midlevel performers and fringe talents that are often far more interesting than the superstar acts – this is one of the best places for a more intimate gig.

Sugar Club
LIVE MUSIC

(Map p92; 01-678 7188; 8 Lower Leeson St; St Stephen's Green) There's live jazz, cabaret and soul music at weekends in this comfortable theatre-style venue on the corner of St Stephen's Green.

☆ Classical

Classical music concerts and opera take place in a number of city-centre venues. There are also occasional performances in churches; check the press for details.

Bord Gáis Energy Theatre
PERFORMING ARTS

(Map p100; 01-677 7999; www.grandcanalthea tre.ie; Grand Canal Sq; Grand Canal Dock) Forget the uninviting sponsored name: Daniel Liebeskind's masterful design is a three-tiered, 2000-capacity auditorium where you're as likely to be entertained by the Bolshoi or a touring state opera as you are to see Disney on Ice or Barbra Streisand. It's a magnificent venue – designed for classical, paid for by the classics.

National Concert Hall
CLASSICAL MUSIC

(Map p92; 01-417 0000; www.nch.ie; Earlsfort Tce; all city centre) Ireland's premier orchestral hall hosts a variety of concerts year-round, including a series of lunchtime concerts from 1.05pm to 2pm on Tuesdays, June to August.

Gaiety Theatre
CLASSICAL MUSIC

(01-677 1717; www.gaietytheatre.com; South King St; all city centre) This popular Dublin theatre hosts a program of classical concerts and opera.

Dublin City Gallery –
The Hugh Lane
CLASSICAL MUSIC

(Map p114; 01-874 1903; www.hughlane.ie; Charlemont House, Parnell Sq; 3, 7, 10, 11, 13, 16, 19, 46A, 123) At noon on Sunday, from September to June, the art gallery hosts up to 30 concerts of contemporary classical music.

DUBLIN BY SONG

Dublin is one of the most musical cities in Europe, so it stands to reason that there are a few worthwhile songs that sing its praises – and its faults. Here's our pick of tracks to download to your MP3 to enrich your Dublin saunter:

Running to Stand Still (U2) A poignant portrayal of the 1980s heroin epidemic; the 'seven towers' of the song refer to a (now demolished) notorious flat complex in the north-city suburb of Ballymun.

Old Town (Philip Lynott) If you want to see what Dublin looked like at the end of '80s, check out the video for this fabulous tune on YouTube.

Summer in Dublin (Bagatelle) A nostalgic, singalong pop tune that was the band's biggest hit and the city's favourite song about itself.

City of Screams (Paranoid Visions) Dublin in the 1980s, as imagined in all its anger and ugliness by the city's foremost '80s punk band.

Phil Lynott (Jape) Captures the essence of the city today – without naming any locations. The city's most famous folk band, the Dubliners, have a bunch of songs about the capital – these are our favourites:

Auld Triangle Taken from Brendan Behan's play *The Quare Fellow*, this poignant tune is about being imprisoned in Mountjoy Prison.

Raglan Road Patrick Kavanagh's poem given music, life and profound meaning by Luke Kelly.

Rocky Road to Dublin A traditional 19th-century tune about a difficult journey to Dublin.

Take Her Up to Monto A charming traditional ditty about taking a girl up to the city's one-time notorious red-light district.

☆ Cinemas

Ireland boasts the highest attendances in Europe of young filmgoers. Consequently it's best to book in advance by credit card, or be prepared to queue for up to half an hour for tickets at night-time screenings. Dublin's cinemas are more heavily concentrated on the northern side of the Liffey. Admission prices are generally €6 for early-afternoon shows and around €9 for the rest of the day.

Lighthouse Cinema
CINEMA
(Map p72; ☎01-879 7601; www.lighthousecinema. ie; Smithfield Plaza; ☐all city centre, ☐Smithfield) The most impressive cinema in town is this snazzy four-screener in a stylish building just off Smithfield Plaza. The menu is strictly art house, and the cafe-bar on the ground floor is perfect for discussing the merits of German Expressionism.

Irish Film Institute
CINEMA
(Map p84; ☎01-679 5744; www.ifi.ie; 6 Eustace St; ☐all city centre) The Irish Film Institute (IFI) has a couple of screens and shows classics and new art-house films, although we question some of their selections: weird and con-troversial can be a little tedious. The complex also has a bar, a cafe and a bookshop.

Weekly (€3) or annual (€25) membership is required for some uncertified films that can only be screened as part of a 'club' – the only way to get around the censor's red pen. A great cinema, if sometimes a little pretentious.

Savoy
CINEMA
(Map p114; ☎01-874 6000; Upper O'Connell St; ☉from 2pm; ☐all city centre) The Savoy is a five-screen, first-run cinema, and has late-night shows at weekends. Savoy Cinema 1 is the largest in the country and its enormous screen is the perfect way to view really spectacular blockbuster movies.

Screen
CINEMA
(Map p114; ☎01-671 4988; 2 Townsend St; ☉from 2pm; ☐all city centre) Between Trinity College and O'Connell Bridge, the Screen shows new independent and smaller commercial films on its three screens.

Cineworld Multiplex
CINEMA
(Map p114; ☎0818 304 204; www.cineworld.ie; Parnell Centre, Parnell St; ☐all city centre) This 17-screen cinema shows only commercial

releases. The seats are comfy, the concession stand is huge and the selection of pick 'n' mix could induce a sugar seizure. It lacks the style of the older-style cinema, but we like it anyway.

☆ Sport

Aviva Stadium   STADIUM
(Map p72; ☑01-647 3800; www.avivastadium.ie; 11-12 Lansdowne Rd) Gleaming, new, 50,000-capacity ground with an eye-catching curvilinear stand in the swanky neighbourhood of Donnybrook. Home to Irish rugby and football internationals.

Croke Park   SPECTATOR SPORTS
(☑01-836 3222; www.crokepark.ie; ☐19, 19A from city centre) Hurling and Gaelic football games are held from February to November at Europe's fourth-largest stadium (capacity around 82,000), north of the Royal Canal in Drumcondra; see www.gaa.ie for schedules.

Harold's Cross Park   GREYHOUND RACING
(Map p72; ☑01-497 1081; www.igb.ie; 151 Harold's Cross Rd; adult/child €10/6; ⊗6.30-10.30pm Mon, Tue & Fri; ☐16 or 16A from city centre) This greyhound track is close to the city centre and offers a great night out for a fraction of what it would cost to go to the horses.

Leopardstown Race Course   HORSE RACING
(☑01-289 3607; www.leopardstown.com; ☐special from Eden Quay) The Irish love of horse racing can be observed about 10km south of the city centre in Foxrock. Special buses depart from the city centre on race days; call the racecourse for details.

Shelbourne Park
Greyhound Stadium   GREYHOUND RACING
(Map p100; ☑01-668 3502, on race nights 01-202 6601; www.igb.ie; Bridge Town Rd, Ringsend; adult/ child €10/6; ⊗7-10.30pm Wed, Thu & Sat; ☐3, 7, 7A, 8, 45, 84 from city centre) A top-class dog track with terrific vantage points from the glassed-in restaurant, where you can eat, bet and watch without leaving your seat.

☆ Theatre

Dublin's theatre scene is small but busy. Theatre bookings can usually be made by quoting a credit-card number over the phone, then you can collect your tickets just before the performance. Expect to pay anything between €12 and €25 for most shows, with some costing as much as €30. Most plays begin between 8pm and 8.30pm. Check www.irishtheatreonline.com to see what's playing.

Gate Theatre   THEATRE
(Map p114; ☑01-874 4045; www.gatetheatre.ie; 1 Cavendish Row; ☐all city centre) The city's most elegant theatre, housed in a late-18th-century building, features a generally unflappable repertory of classic American and European plays. Orson Welles' first professional performance was here, and James Mason played here early in his career. Even today it is the only theatre in town where you might see established international movie stars work on their credibility with a theatre run.

Abbey Theatre   THEATRE
(Map p114; ☑01-878 7222; www.abbeytheatre.ie; Lower Abbey St; ☐all city centre, ☐Abbey) Ireland's renowned national theatre, founded by WB Yeats in 1904, has been reinvigorated in recent years by director Fiach MacConghaill, who has introduced lots of new blood to what was in danger of becoming a moribund corpse. The current programme has a mix of Irish classics (Synge, O'Casey etc), established international names (Shepard, Mamet) and new talent (O'Rowe, Carr et al).

DUBLIN ENTERTAINMENT

HANDEL WITH CARE

In 1742 the nearly broke GF Handel conducted the very first performance of his epic work *Messiah* in the since-demolished Dublin Music Hall, on the city's oldest street, Fishamble St. Jonathan Swift – author of *Gulliver's Travels* and dean of St Patrick's Cathedral – had suggested that his own and Christ Church's choirs take part, but revoked his invitation when he discovered that the sacred music would be performed in a common music hall rather than in the more appropriate setting of a church, and vowed to 'punish such vicars [who allowed their choristers to participate] for their rebellion, disobedience and perfidy'. The concert went ahead nonetheless, and the celebrated work is performed at the original spot in Dublin annually – now a hotel that bears the composer's name.

EVENSONG AT THE CATHEDRALS

In a rare coming together, the choirs of St Patrick's Cathedral and Christ Church Cathedral both participated in the first-ever performance of Handel's *Messiah* in nearby Fishamble St in 1742, conducted by the great composer himself. Both houses of worship carry on their proud choral traditions, and visits to the cathedrals during evensong will provide enchanting and atmospheric memories. The choir performs evensong in St Patrick's at 5.45pm Monday to Friday (not on Wednesday in July and August), while the Christ Church choir competes at 5.30pm on Sunday, 6pm on Wednesday and Thursday, and 5pm Saturday. If you're going to be in Dublin around Christmas, do not miss the carols at St Patrick's; call ahead for the hard-to-get tickets on ☑ 01-453 9472.

Work by up-and-coming writers and more experimental theatre is staged in the adjoining **Peacock Theatre** (Map p114; ☑ 01-878 7222; 🖳 all city centre, 🚇 Abbey).

Gaiety Theatre   THEATRE
(☑ 01-677 1717; www.gaietytheatre.com; South King St; 🖳 all city centre) The Gaiety's program of plays is strictly of the fun-for-all-the-family type: West End hits, musicals, Christmas pantos and classic Irish plays keep the more serious-minded away, but it leaves more room for those simply looking to be entertained.

International Bar   THEATRE
(Map p84; ☑ 01-677 9250; 23 Wicklow St; 🖳 all city centre) Early-evening plays in the upstairs space of this bar by nonestablished actors can offer up some worthwhile stuff; they're on early because they have to clear the room for the established comedy shows.

Olympia Theatre   THEATRE
(☑ 01-677 7744; 72 Dame St; 🖳 all city centre) This theatre specialises in light plays and, at Christmastime, pantomimes.

Players' Theatre   THEATRE
(Map p79; ☑ 01-677 2941, ext 1239; Regent House; 🖳 all city centre) The Trinity College Players' Theatre hosts student productions throughout the academic year, as well as the most prestigious plays from the Dublin Theatre Festival in October.

Project Arts Centre   THEATRE
(Map p84; ☑ 1850 260 027; www.project.ie; 39 East Essex St; 🖳 all city centre) This is the city's most interesting venue for challenging new work – be it drama, dance, live art or film. Three separate spaces, none with a restricting proscenium arch, allow for maximum versatility. You never know what to expect, which makes it all that more fun: we've seen some awful rubbish here, but we've also seen some of the best shows in town.

🛍 Shopping

If it's made in Ireland – or pretty much anywhere else – you can find it in Dublin. Grafton St is home to a range of largely British-owned high-street chain stores, but you'll find the best local boutiques in the surrounding streets, selling everything from cheese to Irish designer clothing and streetwear. On the north side, pedestrianised Henry St has international chain stores, as well as Dublin's best department store, Arnott's.

Traditional Irish products such as crystal and knitwear remain popular choices, and increasingly you can find innovative, modern takes on the classics. But steer clear of the mass-produced junk, the joke value of which isn't worth the hassle of carting it home on the plane: trust us, there's no such thing as a genuine *shillelagh* (Irish fighting stick) for sale anywhere in town.

Citizens of non-EU countries can reclaim the VAT paid on purchases made at stores that display a cash-back sticker; ask for details.

Most shops open 9.30am to 6pm Monday to Saturday, with later hours – usually 8pm – on Thursday. Many stores also open on Sunday, usually from noon to 6pm.

🛍 Grafton Street & Around

Avoca Handweavers   CRAFTS
(Map p84; ☑ 01-677 4215; www.avoca.ie; 11-13 Suffolk St; ☺ 9.30am-6pm Mon-Wed & Sat, 9.30am-7pm Thu & Fri, 11am-6pm Sun; 🖳 all city centre) Combining clothing, homewares, a basement food hall and an excellent top-floor cafe (p110), Avoca promotes a stylish but homey brand of modern Irish life – and is one of the best places to find an original present. Many of the garments are woven, knitted and naturally dyed at its Wicklow factory. The children's section, with unusual

knits, bee-covered gumboots and dinky toys, is fantastic.

Kilkenny Shop
CRAFTS

(Map p79; ☎01-677 7066; www.kilkennyshop.com; 6 Nassau St; ⊗ 8.30am-7pm Mon-Wed & Fri, 8.30am-8pm Thu, 8.30am-6pm Sat, 10am-6pm Sun; 🖳 all city centre) A large, long-running repository for contemporary, innovative Irish crafts, including multicoloured, modern Irish knits, designer clothing, Orla Kiely bags and lovely silver jewellery. The glassware and pottery is beautiful and sourced from workshops around the country. A great source for presents.

DESIGNYARD
IRISH CRAFTS

(Map p79; ☎01-474 1011; www.designyard.ie; 25 South Frederick St; ⊗10am-5.30pm Mon-Wed & Fri, to 8pm Thu, to 6pm Sat; 🖳all city centre) A high-end, craft-as-art shop where everything you see – glass, batik, sculpture, painting – is one-off and handmade in Ireland. It also showcases contemporary jewellery stock from young international designers. Perfect for that bespoke engagement ring or a very special present.

Cathach Books
BOOKS

(Map p92; ☎01-671 8676; www.rarebooks.ie; 10 Duke St; ⊗9.30am-5.45pm Mon-Sat; 🖳all city centre) Our favourite bookshop in the city stocks a rich and remarkable collection of Irish-interest books, with a particular emphasis on 20th-century literature and a large selection of first editions, including rare ones by the big guns: Joyce, Yeats, Beckett and Wilde.

Gutter Bookshop
BOOKS

(Map p84; ☎01-679 9206; www.gutterbookshop.com; Cow's Lane; ⊗10am-6.30pm Mon-Wed, Fri & Sat, 10am-7pm Thu, 11am-6pm Sun; 🖳all city centre) Taking its name from Oscar Wilde's famous line from *Lady Windermere's Fan*, 'we are all in the gutter, but some of us are looking at the stars', this fabulous bookshop is flying the flag for the downtrodden independent bookshop, stocking a mix of new novels, children's books, travel literature and other assorted titles.

Sheridan's Cheesemongers
FOOD

(Map p92; ☎01-679 3143; www.sheridanscheesemongers.com; 11 South Anne St; ⊗10am-6pm Mon-Fri, from 9.30am Sat; 🖳all city centre) If heaven were a cheese shop, this would be it. Wooden shelves are laden with rounds of farmhouse cheeses, sourced from around the country by Kevin and Seamus Sheridan, who have almost single-handedly revived cheesemaking in Ireland. You can taste any one of the 60 cheeses on display and pick up some wild Irish salmon, Italian pastas and olives while you're at it.

Brown Thomas
DEPARTMENT STORE

(Map p84; ☎01-605 6666; www.brownthomas.com; 92 Grafton St; ⊗9.30am-8pm Mon, Wed & Fri, 10am-8pm Tue, 9.30am-9pm Thu, 9am-8pm Sat, 11am-7pm Sun; 🖳all city centre) Soak up the Jo Malone–laden rarefied atmosphere of Dublin's most exclusive store, where presentation is virtually artistic. Here you'll find fantastic cosmetics, shoes to die for, exotic homewares and a host of Irish and international fashion labels such as Balenciaga, Stella McCartney, Lainey Keogh and Philip Treacy. The 3rd-floor Bottom Drawer outlet stocks the finest Irish linen you'll find anywhere.

Costume
CLOTHING

(Map p84; ☎01-679 5200; www.costumedublin.ie; 10 Castle Market; 🖳all city centre) Costume is

---

DUBLIN THEATRE TODAY

Here are five names to look out for in contemporary Irish theatre:

➡ **Marina Carr** Internationally recognised playwright – her latest play is *16 Possible Glimpses* (2011).

➡ **Marie Jones** Belfast-born playwright whose most recent play is *Fly Me to the Moon* (2012).

➡ **Conor McPherson** A well-respected talent whose most famous play is *The Seafarer* (2006).

➡ **Tom Murphy** One of Ireland's leading dramatists, his latest play was *The Last Days of the Reluctant Tyrant* (2009).

➡ **Mark O'Rowe** The writer of *Howie the Rookie* (1999) and *Made in China* (2001) works primarily in film these days but does get back to theatre from time to time.

SHOPPING CENTRES

Dublin offers a handful of 'under-the-one-roof' shopping experiences.

Powerscourt Townhouse Shopping Centre (Map p84; ☑ 01-679 4144; 59 South William St; ⊙ 10am-6pm Mon-Wed & Fri, 10am-8pm Thu, 9am-6pm Sat, noon-6pm Sun; ☐ all city centre) This absolutely gorgeous and stylish centre is in a carefully refurbished Georgian townhouse, built between 1741 and 1744. These days it's best known for its cafes and restaurants but it also does a top-end, selective trade in high fashion, art, exquisite handicrafts and other chichi sundries.

George's St Arcade (Map p84; www.georgesstreetarcade.ie; btwn South Great George's St & Drury St; ⊙ 9am-6.30pm Mon-Wed, Fri & Sat, 9am-8pm Thu, noon-6pm Sun; ☐ all city centre) Dublin's best nonfood market is sheltered within an elegant Victorian Gothic arcade. Apart from shops and stalls selling new and old clothes, secondhand books, hats, posters, jewellery and records, there's a fortune teller, some gourmet nibbles and a fish and chipper that does a roaring trade.

Jervis St Centre (Map p114; ☑ 01-878 1323; Jervis St; ☐ all city centre) This modern, domed mall is a veritable shrine to the British chain store. Boots, Topshop, Debenhams, Argos, Dixons, M&S and Miss Selfridge all get a look-in.

St Stephen's Green Shopping Centre (Map p92; ☑ 01-478 0888; West St Stephen's Green; ⊙ 9am-7pm Mon-Wed, Fri & Sat, 9am-9pm Thu, 11am-6pm Sun; ☐ all city centre) A 1980s version of a 19th-century shopping arcade, the dramatic, balconied interior and central courtyard are a bit too grand for the nondescript chain stores within. There's a Boots, Benetton and large Dunnes Store with supermarket though, as well as last-season designer warehouse TK Maxx.

Dundrum Town Centre (☑ 01-299 1700; www.dundrum.ie; Sandyford Rd; ⊙ 9am-9pm Mon-Fri, 8.30am-7pm Sat, 10am-7pm Sun; ☐ 17, 44C, 48A or 75 from city centre, ☐ Ballaly) Modern Ireland's grandest retail cathedral is this huge shopping and entertainment complex in the southern suburb of Dundrum. Over 100 retail outlets are represented.

considered a genuine pacesetter by Dublin's fashionistas; it has exclusive contracts with some of Europe's most innovative designers, such as Isabel Marant and Anna Sui. It also has the city's best range of Tempereley and American Retro.

Bow Boutique　　　　CLOTHING
(Map p84; ☑ 01-707 1763; Powerscourt Townhouse Shopping Centre, South William St; ⊙ 10am-6pm Mon-Wed & Fri, 10am-8pm Thu, 9am-6pm Sat, noon-6pm Sun; ☐ all city centre) The collective brainchild of four Irish designers (Eilis Boyle, Matthew Doody, Margaret O'Rourke and Wendy Crawford), this beautiful new boutique showcases original designs and made-to-measure items as well as promoting 'ecofashion' by stocking fairtrade labels from around the globe like People Tree and Camilla Nordback.

Hodges Figgis　　　　BOOKS
(Map p79; ☑ 01-677 4754; 56-58 Dawson St; ⊙ 9am-7pm Mon-Wed & Fri, 9am-8pm Thu, 9am-6pm Sat, noon-6pm Sun; ☐ all city centre) The mother of all Dublin bookshops has books

on every conceivable subject for every kind of reader spread across its three huge floors, including a substantial Irish section on the ground floor.

Jenny Vander　　　　CLOTHING
(Map p84; ☑ 01-677 0406; 50 Drury St; ☐ all city centre) This secondhand store oozes elegance and sophistication. Discerning fashionistas and film stylists snap up the exquisite beaded handbags, fur-trimmed coats, richly patterned dresses and costume jewellery priced as if it were the real thing.

Claddagh Records　　　　MUSIC
(Map p84; ☑ 01-677 0262; 2 Cecilia St; ☐ all city centre) An excellent collection of good-quality traditional and folk music is the mainstay at this centrally located record shop. The profoundly knowledgable staff should be able to locate even the most elusive recording for you.

Dubray Books　　　　BOOKS
(Map p84; ☑ 01-677 5568; 36 Grafton St; ⊙ 9am-7pm Mon-Wed & Sat, 9am-9pm Thu & Fri, 11am-6pm

Sun; 🖥 all city centre) Three roomy floors devoted to bestsellers, recent releases, coffeetable books and a huge travel section make this one of the better bookshops in town. It can't compete with its larger, British-owned rivals, but it holds its own with a helpful staff and a lovely atmosphere that encourages you to linger.

🔒 North of the Liffey

Arnott's   DEPARTMENT STORE
(Map p114; ☑ 01-805 0400; 12 Henry St; 🖥 all city centre) Occupying a huge block with entrances on Henry, Liffey and Abbey Sts, this is our favourite of Dublin's department stores. It stocks virtually everything, from garden furniture to high fashion, and it's all relatively affordable.

Eason's   BOOKS
(Map p114; ☑ 01-873 3811; www.easons.ie; 40 Lower O'Connell St; 🖥 all city centre) The biggest selection of magazines and foreign newspapers in the whole country can be found on the ground floor of this huge bookshop near the GPO, along with literally dozens of browsers leafing through mags with ne'er a thought of purchasing one.

Clery's & Co   DEPARTMENT STORE
(Map p114; ☑ 01-878 6000; O'Connell St; 🖥 all city centre) This elegant department store is Ireland's most famous retailer, and a real Dublin classic. Recently restored to its graceful best, Clery's has sought to shed its conservative reputation by filling its shelves with funkier labels to attract younger buyers.

BEST GUARANTEED IRISH

Avoca Handweavers (p126) Our favourite department store with myriad homemade gift ideas.

Barry Doyle Design Jewellers (Map p84; ☑ 01-671 2838; 30 George's St Arcade; ☺ 10am-6pm Mon-Wed, Fri & Sat, to 7pm Thu; 🖥 all city centre) Exquisite handcrafted jewellery with unique contemporary designs.

Cathach Books (p127) For that priceless first edition or a beautiful, leatherbound Joyce's *Dubliners*.

Louis Copeland (Map p84; ☑ 01-872 1600; www.louiscopeland.com; 18-19 Wicklow St; ☺ 9am-5.30pm Mon-Wed, Fri & Sat, to 7.30pm Thu; 🖥 all city centre) Dublin's very own top tailor.

ℹ Information

DANGERS & ANNOYANCES
Dublin is a safe city by any standards, except maybe those set by the Swiss. Basically, act as you would at home. However, certain parts of the city are pretty dodgy due to the presence of drug addicts and other questionable types, including north and northeast of Gardiner St and along parts of Dorset St, on the north side, and west along Thomas St, on the south side.

EMERGENCY
Drugs Advisory & Treatment Centre (☑ 01-677 1122; Trinity Ct, 30-31 Pearse St)
Police/Fire/Ambulance (☑ 01-999)
Rape Crisis Centre (☑ 01-661 4911, 1800 778 888; 70 Lower Leeson St)

DUBLIN MARKETS

In recent years Dublin has gone gaga for markets. Which is kind of ironic, considering the city's traditional markets, like Moore St, were ignored by those same folks who now can't get enough of the homemade hummus on sale at the new gourmet spots. It's all so...continental.

Best markets:

Book Fair (Map p84; Temple Bar Sq; ☺ 10am-5pm Sat; 🖥 all city centre) Rummage through secondhand books.

Cow's Lane Designer Mart (Map p84; Cow's Lane; ☺ 10am-5pm Sat; 🖥 all city centre) A real market for hipsters, bringing together over 60 of the best clothing, accessory and craft stalls.

Meeting House Square Market (Map p84; Meeting House Sq; ☺ 10am-5pm Sat; 🖥 all cross-city) The city's best open-air food market.

Moore Street Market (Map p114; Moore St; ☺ 8am-4pm Mon-Sat; 🖥 all city centre) Open-air, steadfastly 'Old Dublin' market, with fruit, fish and flowers.

INTERNET ACCESS

Wi-fi and 3G networks are making internet cafes largely redundant (except to gamers); the few that are left will charge around €6 per hour. Most accommodations have wi-fi service, either free or for a daily charge (up to €10 per day).

Global Internet Café (8 Lower O'Connell St; per hour €5; ⊙8am-11pm Mon-Fri, from 9am Sat, from 10am Sun)

Internet Exchange (3 Cecilia St, Temple Bar; per hour €5; ⊙8am-2am Mon-Fri, 10am-midnight Sat & Sun)

MEDICAL SERVICES

Should you experience an immediate health problem, contact the A&E (accident & emergency) department of the nearest public hospital; in an emergency, call an ambulance (999). There are no 24-hour pharmacies in Dublin; the latest any stay open is 10pm.

Baggot St Hospital (☑668 1577; 18 Upper Baggot St; ⊙7.30am-4.30pm Mon-Fri) Southside city centre.

Caredoc (☑1850 334 999; www.caredoc.ie; ⊙24hr) Doctors on call; available only out of regular surgery hours.

City Pharmacy (☑670 4523; 14 Dame St; ⊙9am-10pm)

Dental Hospital (☑01-612 7200; 20 Lincoln Pl; ⊙9am-5pm Mon-Fri, from 8am for prebooked appointments)

Grafton Medical Centre (☑671 2122; www.graftonmedical.ie; 34 Grafton St; ⊙8.30am-6.30pm Mon-Thu, to 6pm Fri) One-stop shop with male and female doctors and physiotherapists.

Health Service Executive (☑1800 520 520, 679 0700; www.hse.ie; Dr Steevens' Hospital, Steeven's Lane; ⊙9.30am-5.30pm Mon-Fri) Central health authority with Choice of Doctor Scheme, which can advise you on a suitable GP from 9am to 5pm Monday to Friday. Information services for those with physical and mental disabilities.

Mater Misericordiae Hospital (☑830 1122; Eccles St) Northside city centre.

St James's Hospital (☑01-410 3000; www.stjames.ie; James's St) Southside.

MONEY

Best exchange rates are at banks, although bureaux de change and other exchange facilities usually open for more hours. There are currency-exchange counters at Dublin airport in the baggage-collection area, and on the arrival and departure floors; they're open 5.30am to 11pm. There's a cluster of banks located around College Green opposite Trinity College and all have exchange facilities.

POST

The most convenient post offices in the city centre are the **General Post Office** (Map p114; ☑01-705 7000; O'Connell St; ⊙8am-8pm Mon-Sat) on the northside and **An Post** (Map p84; ☑01-705 8206; www.anpost.ie; St Andrew's St; ⊙8.30am-5pm Mon-Fri) on the southside.

TOURIST INFORMATION

You'll find everything you need to kick-start your visit at the **Dublin Discover Ireland Centre** (Map p84; www.visitdublin.com; St Andrew's Church, 2 Suffolk St; ⊙9am-5.30pm Mon-Sat, 10.30am-3pm Sun). Besides general visitor information on Dublin and Ireland, it also has a free accommodation booking service, a concert-booking agent, local and national bus information, rail information, and tour information and bookings. There are also branches at Dublin Airport and **O'Connell St** (Map p114; 14 O'Connell St; ⊙9am-5pm Mon-Sat).

USEFUL WEBSITES

Dublin City Council (www.dublincity.ie)

Dublin Tourism (www.visitdublin.com)

Entertainment.ie (www.entertainment.ie)

Overheard in Dublin (www.overheardindublin.com)

Totally Dublin (www.totallydublin.ie)

❶ Getting There & Away

AIR

Dublin Airport (☑01-814 1111; www.dublinairport.com), 13km north of the centre, is Ireland's major international gateway airport. It has two terminals: most international flights (including all US flights) use the new Terminal 2; Ryanair and select others use Terminal 1. Both terminals have the usual selection of pubs, restaurants, shops, ATMs and car-hire desks.

BOAT

Dublin has two ferry ports: the **Dun Laoghaire ferry terminal** (☑01-280 1905; Dun Laoghaire), 13km east of the city, serves Holyhead in Wales and can be reached by DART to Dun Laoghaire, or bus 7, 7A or 8 from Burgh Quay or bus 46A from Trinity College; and the **Dublin Port terminal** (☑01-855 2222; Alexandra Rd), 3km northeast of the city centre, serves Holyhead and Liverpool.

Buses from Busáras are timed to coincide with arrivals and departures: for the 9.45am ferry departure from Dublin Port, buses leave Busáras at 8.30am. For the 9.45pm departure, buses depart from Busáras at 8.30pm. For the 1am sailing to Liverpool, the bus departs from Busáras at 11.45pm. All bus trips cost adult/child €2.50/1.25.

BUS

Busáras (Map p114; 01-836 6111; www. buseireann.ie; Store St), the main bus station, is just north of the river behind Custom House, and serves as the main city stop for **Bus Éireann** (www.buseireann.ie), which has a countrywide network.

CAR & MOTORCYCLE

The main rental agencies, which also have offices at the airport, include the following:

Avis Rent-a-Car (01-605 7500, airport 01-605-7566; www.avis.ie; 35 Old Kilmainham Rd)

Budget Rent-a-Car (01-837 9611, airport 01-844 5150; www.budget.ie; 151 Lower Drumcondra Rd)

Europcar (01-648 5900, airport 01-844 4179; www.europcar.com; 1 Mark St)

Hertz Rent-a-Car (01-709 3060, airport 01-844 5466; www.hertz.com; 151 South Circular Rd)

Thrifty (01-844 1944, airport 01-840 0800; www.thrifty.ie; 26 Lombard St East)

TRAIN

Dublin has two main train stations: **Heuston Station** (01-836 5421), on the western side of town near the Liffey, which serves the southern half of the country; and **Connolly Station** (01-836 3333), a short walk northeast of Busáras, behind the Custom House, which covers the west and north. Heuston Station has left-luggage lockers of three sizes, costing €6 to €10 for 24 hours. At Connolly Station the facility costs €6.

Connolly Station is a stop on the DART line into town; the Luas Red Line serves both Connolly and Heuston stations.

ⓘ Getting Around

TO/FROM THE AIRPORT

There is no train service to/from the airport, but there are bus and taxi options.

Bus

Aircoach (www.aircoach.ie; one-way/return €7/12) Private coach service with two routes from the airport to 18 destinations throughout the city, including the main streets of the city centre. Coaches run every 10 to 15 minutes between 6am and midnight, then hourly from midnight until 6am.

Airlink Express Coach (01-873 4222; www.dublinbus.ie; adult/child €6/3) Bus 747 runs every 10 to 20 minutes from 5.45am to 11.30pm between the airport, the central bus station (Busáras) and the Dublin Bus office on Upper O'Connell St; bus 748 runs every 15 to 30 minutes from 6.50am to 10.05pm between the airport and Heuston and Connolly Stations.

Dublin Bus (Map p114; 01-873 4222; www. dublinbus.ie; 59 Upper O'Connell St; 9am-5.30pm Mon-Fri, to 2pm Sat) A number of buses serve the airport from various points in Dublin, including buses 16A (Rathfarnham), 746 (Dun Laoghaire) and 230 (Portmarnock); all cross the city centre on their way to the airport.

Taxi

There is a taxi rank directly outside the arrivals concourse. A taxi should cost about €20 from the airport to the city centre, including a supplementary charge of €2.50 (not applied going to the airport). Make sure the meter is switched on.

BICYCLE

Despite the intermittent presence of rust-red cycle lanes throughout the city centre, getting around by bike can be something of an obstacle course as cyclists have to share roads with buses and indifferent motorists. Bike theft is a major problem, so be sure to park on busier streets, preferably at one of the myriad U-shaped parking bars, and lock your bike securely. Never leave your bike on the street overnight or it may just be gone in the morning. **Dublin City Cycling** (www.dublincitycycling.ie) is an excellent online resource.

Bikes are only allowed on suburban trains (not the DART), either stowed in the guard's van or in a special compartment at the opposite end of the train from the engine. There's a flat €4 charge for transporting a bicycle up to 56km. Bicycle helmets are not compulsory.

Dublin by Bike

One of the most popular ways to get around the city is with the blue bikes of **Dublinbikes** (www. dublinbikes.ie), a pay-as-you-go service similar to the Parisian Vélib system: cyclists purchase a €10 Smart Card (as well as pay a credit-card deposit of €150) – either online or at any of the 40 stations throughout the city centre – before 'freeing' a bike for use, which is then free of charge for the first 30 minutes and €0.50 for each half-hour thereafter.

CAR & MOTORCYCLE

Traffic in Dublin is a nightmare and parking is an expensive headache. There are no free spots to park anywhere in the city centre during business hours (7am to 7pm Monday to Saturday), but there are plenty of parking meters, 'pay & display' spots (€2.50 to €5 per hour) and over a dozen sheltered and supervised car parks (around €5 per hour).

Clamping of illegally parked cars is thoroughly enforced, and there is an €80 charge for removal. Parking is free after 7pm Monday to Saturday, and all day Sunday, in most metered spots and on single yellow lines.

Car theft and break-ins are a problem, and the police advise visitors to park in a supervised car

FARE-SAVER PASSES

Fare-saver passes include the following:

Freedom Ticket (adult/child €28/12) Three-day unlimited travel on all bus services, including Airlink and Dublin Bus Hop-On, Hop-Off tours.

Adult (Bus & Rail) Short Hop (one/three days €12/24.50) Valid for unlimited travel on Dublin Bus, DART and suburban rail, but not Nitelink or Airlink.

Bus/Luas Pass (one/seven days €8.10/32.80) Unlimited travel on both bus and Luas.

Family One-Day Short Hop (€17.70) Valid for travel for one day for a family of two adults and two children aged under 16 on all bus and rail services except Nitelink, Airlink, ferry services and tours.

Rambler Pass (one/three/five days €6.90/15/25) Valid for unlimited travel on all Dublin Bus and Airlink services, except Nitelink.

10 Journey Travel 90 (adult €25) Valid for 10 90-minute journeys on all Dublin Bus and Airlink services, except Nitelink.

park. Cars with foreign number plates are prime targets; never leave your valuables behind. When you're booking accommodation, check on parking facilities.

The **Automobile Association of Ireland** (AA; ☑ 01-617 9999, breakdown 1800 667 788; www.aaireland.ie; 56 Drury St) is located in the city centre.

PUBLIC TRANSPORT
Bus

The office of **Dublin Bus** (Map p114; ☑ 01-872 0000; www.dublinbus.ie; 59 Upper O'Connell St; ☺9am-5.30pm Mon-Fri, to 2pm Sat) has free single-route timetables of all its services.

Buses run from around 6am (some start at 5.30am) to 11.30pm. Fares are calculated according to stages:

➡ one to three stages: €1.65
➡ four to seven stages: €2.15
➡ eight to 13 stages: €2.40
➡ 14 to 23 stages: €2.80
➡ more than 23 stages: €2.80 (inside Citizone; outer suburban journeys cost €4.40)

If you're travelling within the designated bus corridor zone (roughly between Parnell Sq to the north and St Stephen's Green to the south), you can use the €0.65 special City Centre fare. You must tender exact change when boarding; anything more and you will be given a receipt for reimbursement, only possible at the Dublin Bus main office. Avoid this by getting a **Leap Card** (www.leapcard.ie), a plastic smart card available in most newsagents. Once you register it online, you can top it up with whatever amount you need. When you board a bus, Luas or suburban train, just swipe your card and the fare – usually 20% less than a cash fare – is automatically deducted.

Luas

The **Luas** (www.luas.ie) light-rail system has two lines: the green line (running every five to 15 minutes) connects St Stephen's Green with Sandyford in south Dublin via Ranelagh and Dundrum; the red line (every 20 minutes) runs from Lower Abbey St to Tallaght via the north quays and Heuston Station. There are ticket machines at every stop or you can buy a ticket from newsagents in the city centre; a typical short-hop fare (around four stops) is €2. Services run from 5.30am to 12.30am Monday to Friday, from 6.30am to 12.30am Saturday and from 7am to 11.30pm Sunday. You can also use a Leap Card.

Nitelink

Nitelink late-night buses run from the College, Westmoreland and D'Olier Sts triangle. On Fridays and Saturdays, departures are at 12.30am, then every 20 minutes until 4.30am on the more popular routes, and until 3.30am on the less frequented ones; there are no services Sunday to Thursday. Fares are €5. See www.dublinbus.ie for route details.

Train

The **Dublin Area Rapid Transport** (DART; ☑ 01-836 6222; www.irishrail.ie) provides quick train access to the coast as far north as Howth (about 30 minutes) and as far south as Greystones in County Wicklow. Pearse Station is convenient for central Dublin south of the Liffey, and Connolly Station for north of the Liffey. There are services every 10 to 20 minutes, sometimes even more frequently, from around 6.30am to midnight Monday to Saturday; services are less frequent on Sunday. Dublin to Dun Laoghaire takes about 15 to 20 minutes. A one-way DART ticket from Dublin to Dun Laoghaire or Howth costs €2.30; to Bray it's €2.75.

There are also suburban rail services north as far as Dundalk, inland to Mullingar and south past Bray to Arklow.

TAXI

All taxi fares begin with a flag-fall fare of €4.10 (€4.45 from 10pm to 8am), followed by €1.03/km thereafter from 8am to 10pm (€1.35/km from 10pm to 8am). In addition to these there are a number of extra charges – €1 for each extra passenger and €2 for telephone bookings. There is no charge for luggage.

Taxis can be hailed on the street and found at taxi ranks around the city, including on the corner of Abbey and O'Connell Sts; **College Green** (Map p84), in front of Trinity College; and St Stephen's Green at the end of Grafton St. There are numerous taxi companies that will dispatch taxis by radio. Some options:

City Cabs (☑ 01-872 2688)

National Radio Cabs (☑ 01-677 2222; www. radiocabs.ie)

Phone the **Garda Carriage Office** (☑ 01-475 5888) if you have any complaints about taxis or queries regarding lost property.

AROUND DUBLIN

Without even the smallest hint of irony Dubliners will tell you that one of the city's best features is how easy it is to get out of it – and they do, whenever they can. But they don't go especially far: for many the destination

is one of the small seaside villages that surround the capital. To the north are the lovely villages of Howth and Malahide – slowly and reluctantly being sucked into the Dublin conglomeration – while to the south is Dalkey, which has long since given up the fight but has managed to retain that village vibe.

Howth

Tidily positioned at the foot of a bulbous peninsula, the pretty port village of Howth (the name rhymes with 'both') is a major fishing centre, yachting harbour and one of the most sought-after addresses in town, with the best properties discreetly spread atop the gorse-rich hill that dominates the peninsula – spectacular views of Dublin Bay are standard. Dubliners who can't afford to live here make do with a weekend excursion – there are beautiful walks around Howth Head and a popular farmers market at the seafront.

⊙ Sights

Howth Castle   CASTLE

Most of the town backs onto the extensive grounds of Howth Castle, built in 1564 but much changed over the years, most recently in 1910 when Sir Edwin Lutyens gave it a modernist makeover. Today the castle is divided into four very posh and private

---

WORTH A TRIP

SANDYCOVE & JAMES JOYCE MUSEUM

About 1km north of Dalkey is Sandycove, with a pretty little beach and a Martello tower – built by British forces to keep an eye out for a Napoleonic invasion – now housing the James Joyce Museum (☑ 01-280 9265; www.visitdublin.com; Joyce Tower; ☉ 10am-4pm) FREE. This is where the action begins in James Joyce's epic novel *Ulysses*. The museum was opened in 1962 by Sylvia Beach, the Paris-based publisher who first dared to put *Ulysses* into print, and has photographs, letters, documents, various editions of Joyce's work and two death masks of Joyce on display.

Below the Martello tower is the Forty Foot Pool, an open-air, seawater bathing pool that took its name from the army regiment, the Fortieth Foot, that was stationed at the tower until the regiment was disbanded in 1904. At the close of the first chapter of *Ulysses*, Buck Mulligan heads off to the Forty Foot Pool for a morning swim. A morning wake-up here is still a local tradition, winter or summer. In fact, a winter dip isn't much braver than a summer one since the water temperature varies by only about 5°C (9°F). Basically, it's always bloody cold.

Pressure from female bathers eventually opened this public stretch of water – originally nudist and for men only – to both sexes, despite strong opposition from the 'forty foot gentlemen'. They eventually compromised with the ruling that a 'Togs Must Be Worn' sign would apply after 9am. Prior to that time nudity prevails and swimmers are still predominantly male.

WORTH A TRIP

IRELAND'S EYE

A short distance offshore from Howth is **Ireland's Eye** (☏ 01-831 4200; return €12), a rocky seabird sanctuary with the ruins of a 6th-century monastery. There's a Martello tower at the northwestern end of the island, where boats from Howth land, while a spectacularly sheer rock face plummets into the sea at the eastern end. As well as the seabirds overhead, you can see young birds on the ground during the nesting season. Seals can also be spotted around the island.

Doyle & Sons (☏ 01-831 4200; return €14) takes boats out to the island from the East Pier of Howth Harbour during the summer, usually on weekend afternoons. Don't wear shorts if you're planning to visit the monastery ruins because they're surrounded by a thicket of stinging nettles. And please bring all your rubbish back with you – far too many island visitors don't.

Further north from Ireland's Eye is **Lambay Island**, an important seabird sanctuary that cannot be visited.

residences (although the grounds are open to the public). The original estate was acquired in 1177 by the Norman noble Sir Almeric Tristram, who changed his surname to St Lawrence after winning a battle at the behest (or so he believed) of his favourite saint. The family has owned the land ever since, though the unbroken chain of male succession came to an end in 1909.

On the grounds are the ruins of the 16th-century **Corr Castle** and an ancient dolmen (tomb chamber or portal tomb made of vertical stones topped by a huge capstone) known as **Aideen's Grave**. Legend has it that Aideen died of a broken heart after her husband was killed at the Battle of Gavra near Tara in AD 184, but the legend is rubbish because the dolmen is at least 300 years older than that.

The **castle gardens** (⊙24hr) **FREE** are worth visiting, as they're noted for their rhododendrons (which bloom in May and June), azaleas and a long, 10m-high beech hedge planted in 1710.

Also within the grounds are the ruins of **St Mary's Abbey** (Abbey St) **FREE**, originally founded in 1042 by the Viking King Sitric, who also founded the original church on the site of Christ Church Cathedral. The abbey was amalgamated with the monastery on Ireland's Eye in 1235. Some parts of the ruins date from that time, but most are from the 15th and 16th centuries. The tomb of Christopher St Lawrence (Lord Howth), in the southeastern corner, dates from around 1470. See the caretaker or read instructions on the gate for opening times.

Howth Summit VIEWPOINT

Howth is essentially a very large hill surrounded by cliffs, and Howth Summit (171m) has excellent views across Dublin Bay right down to County Wicklow. From the summit you can walk to the top of the Ben of Howth, a headland near the village, which has a cairn said to mark a 2000-year-old Celtic **royal grave**. The 1814 **Baily Lighthouse** at the southeastern corner is on the site of an old stone fort and can be reached by a dramatic clifftop walk. There was an earlier hilltop beacon here in 1670.

✕ Eating

Howth Fishermen's & Farmer's Market MARKET €

(☏ 01-611 5016; www.irishfarmersmarkets.ie; West Pier, Howth Harbour; ⊙10am-5pm Sun & bank holidays) One of the best in Dublin, this is the place to come not only for fresh fish (obviously) but also for organic meat, veg and homemade everything else, including jams, cakes and breads. A great option for Sunday lunch.

House IRISH €€

(☏ 01-839 6388; www.thehouse-howth.ie; 4 Main St; mains €16-23; ⊙9am-3pm Mon-Fri, 11.30am-3pm & 6-11pm Sat & Sun) Wonderful spot on the main street leading away from the harbour where you can feast on dishes like crunchy Bellingham blue-cheese polenta or wild Wicklow venison stew as well as a fine selection of fish.

Oar House SEAFOOD €€

(☏ 01-839 4562; www.oarhouse.ie; 8 West Pier; mains €16-24; ⊙12.30-10pm) A feast-o-fish is what the menu is all about at this newish restaurant – particularly the locally caught variety. Par for the course in a fishing village, but this place stands out both for the way the fish is prepared and because you can get everything on the menu in smaller, tapas-style portions as well as mains.

ℹ Getting There & Away

The easiest and quickest way to get to Howth from Dublin is on the DART, which whisks you there in just over 20 minutes for a fare of €2.50. For the same fare, buses 31 and 31A from Lower Abbey St in the city centre run as far as the summit, 5km to the southeast of Howth.

Counties Wicklow & Kildare

POP 345,000 / AREA 3718 SQ KM

Best Places to Eat

➡ Ballyknocken House (p152)

➡ Strawberry Tree (p155)

➡ Tinakilly Country House & Restaurant (p150)

➡ Grangecon Café (p151)

➡ Poppies Country Cooking (p141)

Best Places to Stay

➡ Brook Lodge & Wells Spa (p155)

➡ Rathsallagh House & Country Club (p151)

➡ Hunter's Hotel (p152)

Why Go?

Wicklow and Kildare may be neighbours and have a boundary with Dublin in common, but that's where the similarities end.

South of the capital is scenic, wild Wicklow. Its most imposing natural feature is a gorse-and-bracken mountain spine that is home to one of Ireland's most stunning landscapes, replete with dramatic glacial valleys, soaring mountain passes and important archaeological treasures – from breathtaking early-Christian sites to the elegant country homes of the wealthiest of Ireland's 18th-century nobility.

To the west, Kildare is far more sedate but one of the country's most prosperous farming counties. It is also where you'll find some of the most lucrative thoroughbred stud farms in the world, many with links to the horse-breeding centre of Kentucky in the US. Horse breeding is a big deal in Ireland, but in Kildare it's the very lifeblood of the county, generating many millions of tax-free euro.

When to Go

➡ Summer – June to September – is the best time to visit Wicklow, especially if you're going to walk the Wicklow Way or do a little green-thumb exploring.

➡ Running from Easter to late August is the Wicklow Gardens Festival.

➡ In May there's the Wicklow Arts Festival.

➡ In June there's the Irish Derby – the most prestigious flat race in the Irish racing calendar at the Curragh in County Kildare; but there are meets there right up to October.

COUNTY WICKLOW

Just south of Dublin, Wicklow (Cill Mhantáin) is the capital's favourite playground, a wild pleasure garden of coastline, woodland and a daunting mountain range through which runs the country's most popular walking trail.

Stretching 132km from Dublin's southern suburbs to the rolling fields of County Carlow, the Wicklow Way leads walkers along disused military supply lines, old bog roads and nature trails. Along the way you can explore monastic ruins, handsome gardens and some magnificent 18th-century mansions.

National Parks

Wicklow Mountains National Park covers just over 200 sq km of mountainous blanket bogs and woodland. Within the boundaries of the protected area are two nature reserves, owned and managed by the Heritage Service and legally protected by the Wildlife Act 1976. The larger reserve, west of the Glendalough Visitor Centre, conserves the extensive heath and bog of the Glendalough Valley plus the Upper Lake and valley slopes on either side. The second, Glendalough Wood Nature Reserve, conserves oak woods stretching from the Upper Lake as far as the Rathdrum road to the east.

Most of Ireland's native mammal species can be found within the confines of the park. Large herds of deer roam on the open hill areas, though these were introduced in the 20th century as the native red-deer population became extinct during the first half of the 18th century. The uplands are the preserve of foxes, badgers and hares. Red squirrels are usually found in the pine woodlands – look out for them around the Upper Lake.

The bird population of the park is plentiful. Birds of prey abound, the most common being peregrine falcons, marlins, kestrels, hawks and sparrowhawks. Hen harriers are a rarer sight, though they too live in the park. Moorland birds found in the area include meadow pipits and skylarks. Less common birds such as whinchats, ring ouzels and dippers can be spotted, as can red grouse, whose numbers are quickly disappearing in other parts of Ireland. For information, call in or contact the **National Park Information Point** (☏ 0404-45425; www.wicklownationalpark.ie; Miners' Rd, Bolger's Cottage, Upper Lake, Glendalough; ☺ 10am-6pm May-Sep, to dusk Sat & Sun Oct-Apr), off the Green Rd that runs by the Upper Lake, about 2km from the Glendalough Visitor Centre. There's usually someone on hand to help, but if you find it closed the staff may be out running guided walks. *Exploring the Glendalough Valley* (Heritage Service; €2) is a good booklet on the trails in the area.

❶ Getting There & Away

Wicklow is relatively easy to get around.

CAR

The main routes are the N11 (M11), which runs north–south through the county from Dublin to Wexford, and the N81, which runs down the western spine of the Wicklow Mountains through Blessington into County Carlow.

BUS

St Kevin's Bus runs twice daily from Dublin and Bray to Roundwood and Glendalough. Dublin Bus 65 runs regularly as far as Blessington.

TRAIN

The Dublin Area Rapid Transport (DART) suburban rail line runs southward from Dublin as far as Bray, and there are regular train and bus connections from the capital to Wicklow town and Arklow.

For more details, see the Getting There & Away section for each town.

Wicklow Mountains

As you leave Dublin and cross into Wicklow, the landscape changes dramatically. From Killakee, still in Dublin, the Military Rd begins a 30km southward journey across vast sweeps of gorse-, bracken- and heather-clad moors, bogs and mountains dotted with small corrie lakes.

The numbers and statistics aren't all that impressive. The highest peak in the range, Lugnaquilla (924m), is really more of a very large hill, but that hardly matters here. This vast granite intrusion, a welling-up of hot igneous rock that solidified some 400 million years ago, was shaped during the Ice Ages into the schist-capped mountains visible today. The peaks are marvellously desolate and as raw as only nature can be. Between the mountains are a number of deep glacial valleys, most notably Glenmacnass, Glenmalure and Glendalough – while corrie lakes such as Lough Bray Upper and Lower, gouged by ice at the head of the glaciers, complete the wild topography.

The narrow Military Rd winds its way through the most remote parts of the mountains, offering some extraordinary views of

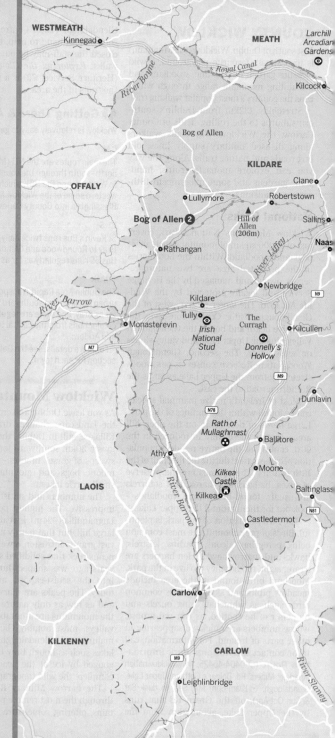

Counties Wicklow & Kildare Highlights

❶ Go back in time at the evocative ruins and the marvellous slopes and forests of gorgeous **Glendalough** (p142)

❷ Explore County Kildare's huge tracks of fecund land at the **Bog of Allen** (p158)

❸ Walk at least part of Ireland's most popular hiking trail, the **Wicklow Way** (p148)

❹ Examine the art and atmosphere of magnificent **Russborough House** (p150)

❺ Admire the gorgeous Italianate gardens and impressive waterfall at **Powerscourt Estate** (p140), near Enniskerry

❻ Take the tour at Ireland's most impressive Palladian mansion, **Castletown House** (p159), near Celbridge, once owned by the country's richest man

❼ Contemplate your spiritual health with an overnight stay in one of the **Glendalough Hermitages** (p148)

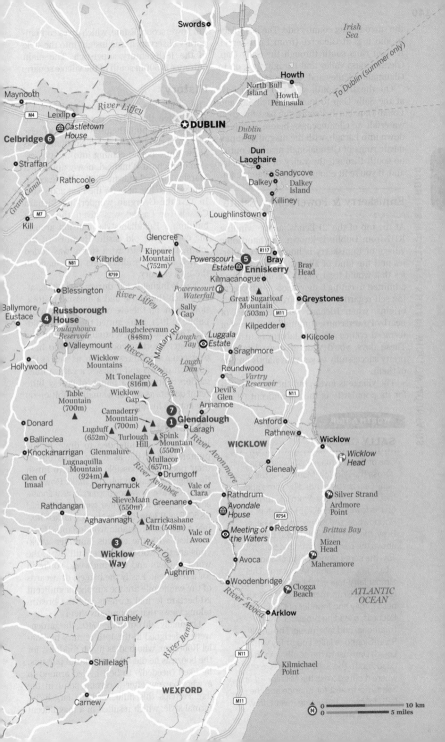

the surrounding countryside. The best place to join it is at Glencree (from Enniskerry). It then runs south through the Sally Gap, Glenmacnass Valley and Laragh, then on to Glenmalure Valley and Aghavannagh.

On the trip south you can divert east at the Sally Gap to look at Lough Tay and Lough Dan. Further south you pass the great waterfall at Glenmacnass before dropping down into Laragh, with the magnificent monastic ruins of Glendalough nearby. Continue south through the valley of Glenmalure and, if you're fit enough, climb Lugnaquilla.

Enniskerry & Powerscourt Estate
POP 2672

At the top of the '21 Bends', as the winding R117 from Dublin is known, the handsome village of Enniskerry is home to art galleries and the kind of all-organic gourmet cafes that would treat you as a criminal if you admitted to eating battery eggs. Such preening self-regard is a far cry from the village's origins, when Richard Wingfield, Earl of nearby Powerscourt, commissioned a row of terraced cottages for his labourers in 1760. These days, you'd want to have laboured pretty successfully to get your hands on one of them.

The village is lovely, but the main reason for its popularity is the magnificent 64-sq-

WORTH A TRIP

SALLY GAP
One of the two main east–west passes across the Wicklow Mountains, the Sally Gap is surrounded by some spectacular countryside. From the turn-off on the lower road (R755) between Roundwood and Kilmacanogue near Bray, the narrow road (R759) passes above the dark and dramatic Lough Tay, the scree slopes of which slide into Luggala (Fancy Mountain). This almost fairy-tale estate is owned by one Garech de Brún, member of the Guinness family and founder of Claddagh Records, a leading producer of Irish traditional and folk music. The small River Cloghoge links Lough Tay with Lough Dan just to the south. It then heads up to the Sally Gap crossroads, where it cuts across the Military Rd and heads northwest for Kilbride and the N81, following the young River Liffey, still only a stream.

km Powerscourt Estate, which gives contemporary observers a true insight into the style of the 18th-century super-rich. The main entrance is 500m south of the village square.

History

The estate has existed more or less since 1300, when the LePoer (later anglicised to Power) family built themselves a castle here. The property changed Anglo-Norman hands a few times before coming into the possession of Richard Wingfield, newly appointed Marshall of Ireland, in 1603. His descendants were to live here for the next 350 years. In 1731 the Georgian wunderkind Richard Cassels (or Castle) was given the job of building a Palladian-style mansion around the core of the old castle. He finished the job in 1743, but an extra storey was added in 1787 and other alterations were made in the 19th century.

The Wingfields left during the 1950s, after which the house had a massive restoration. Then, on the eve of its opening to the public in 1974, a fire gutted the whole building. The estate was eventually bought by the Slazenger sporting-goods family who have overseen a second restoration, as well as the addition of two golf courses, a cafe, a huge garden centre and a bunch of cutesy little retail outlets as well as a small exhibition on the house's history.

◉ Sights

Basically, it's all intended to draw in the punters and wring as many euros out of their pockets as possible in order to finish the huge restoration job and make Powerscourt Estate (www.powerscourt.ie; near Enniskerry; admission to house free, gardens adult/child €8.50/5; ⊙ 9.30am-5.30pm Mar-Oct, to dusk Nov-Feb) a kind of profitable wonderland. If you can deal with the crowds (summer weekends are the worst) or, better still, avoid the worst of them and visit midweek, you're in for a real treat. Easily the biggest drawcards of the whole pile are the simply magnificent 20-hectare formal gardens and the breathtaking views that accompany them.

Originally laid out in the 1740s, the gardens were redesigned in the 19th century by Daniel Robinson, who had as much fondness for the booze as he did for horticultural pursuits: he liked (needed?) to be wheeled around in a wheelbarrow after a certain point in the day. Perhaps this influenced his largely informal style, which resulted in a magnificent blend of landscaped gardens, sweeping terraces, statuary, ornamental lakes, secret hollows, rambling walks and walled enclosures replete with more than 200 types of trees and shrubs, all beneath the stunning natural backdrop of the Great Sugarloaf Mountain to the southeast. Tickets come with a map laying out 40-minute and hour-long tours of the gardens. Don't miss the exquisite Japanese Gardens or the Pepperpot Tower, modelled on a three-inch actual pepperpot owned by Lady Wingfield. Our own favourite, however, is the animal cemetery, final resting place of the Wingfield pets and even some of their favourite milking cows. Some of the epitaphs are astonishingly personal.

A 7km walk to a separate part of the estate takes you to the 130m **Powerscourt Waterfall** (adult/child €5/3.50; ⊙9.30am-7pm May-Aug, 10.30am-5.30pm Mar-Apr & Sep-Oct, to 4.30pm Nov-Jan). It's the highest waterfall in Britain and Ireland, and is most impressive after heavy rain. You can also get to the falls by road, following the signs from the estate. A nature trail has been laid out around the base of the waterfall, taking you past giant redwoods, ancient oaks, beech, birch and rowan trees. There are plenty of birds in the vicinity, including the chaffinch, cuckoo, chiffchaff, raven and willow warbler.

☞ Tours

All tours that take in Powerscourt start in Dublin.

Bus Éireann BUS TOUR
(☑01-836 6111; www.buseireann.ie; Busáras; adult/student/child €32.30/ 30.40 /23.75; ⊙tours 10am mid-Mar–Oct) A whole-day tour that takes in Powerscourt and Glendalough (all admissions included), departing from Dublin's Busáras (the main bus station).

Dublin Bus Tours BUS TOUR
(Map p84; ☑01-872 0000; www.dublinbus.ie; adult/child €24/12; ⊙tours 11am) A visit to Powerscourt is included in the four-hour South Coast & Gardens tour, which takes in the stretch of coastline between Dun Laoghaire and Killiney before turning inland to Wicklow and on to Enniskerry. Admission to the gardens is included.

Irish Sightseeing Tours BUS TOUR
(☑01-872 9010; www.irishcitytours.com; Suffolk St; adult/student/child €26/24/20; ⊙tours 10am Fri-Sun) Wicklow's big hits: Powerscourt, Glendalough and the lakes and a stop at Avoca,

then Dun Laoghaire and Dalkey (includes admission to Glendalough visitor centre and Powerscourt, but not coffee). Tours depart from the Discover Ireland Dublin Centre.

Alpine Coaches BUS TOUR
(☑01-286 2547; www.alpinecoaches.ie; Dublin Discover Ireland Centre, Suffolk St; ⊙tours 9.20am Tue, Wed & Fri-Sun) Full-day tour of Powerscourt Estate and the waterfall from various pick-up points in Dublin, returning to St Stephen's Green at 4.30pm.

🛏 Sleeping & Eating

Summerhill House Hotel HOTEL €€
(☑01-286 7928; www.summerhillhousehotel.com; r from €90; ☞⊛) A truly superb country mansion about 700m south of town just off the N11 is the best place around to lay your head, on soft cotton pillows surrounded by delicate antiques and pastoral views in oils. Everything about the place – including the top-notch breakfast – is memorable.

Coolakay House B&B €€
(☑01-286 2423; www.coolakayhouse.ie; Waterfall Rd, Coolakay; r €70-75; ☞) A modern working farm about 3km south of Enniskerry (it is signposted along the road), this is a great option for walkers along the Wicklow Way. The four bedrooms are all well appointed and comfortable, the views are terrific and the breakfast is sensational.

★Poppies Country Cooking CAFE €
(☑01-282 8869; the Square; mains €9; ⊙8.30am-6pm) If the service wasn't so slow and the organisation so frustratingly haphazard, this poky little cafe on the main square would be one of the best spots in Wicklow. The food – when you finally get a chance to eat it – is sensational: wholesome salads, filling sandwiches on doorstep-cut bread and award-winning ice cream will leave you plenty satisfied.

Emilia's Ristorante ITALIAN €€
(☑01-276 1834; Clock Tower, the Square; mains €12-16; ⊙5-10.45pm Mon-Sat, noon-9.30pm Sun) A lovely 1st-floor restaurant to satisfy even the most ardent craving for thin-crust pizzas. Emilia's does everything else just right too, from the organic soups to the perfect steaks down to the gorgeous meringue desserts.

Johnnie Fox SEAFOOD €€
(☑01-295 5647; www.jfp.ie; Glencullen; mains €12-20; ⊙noon-10pm) Busloads of tourists fill the

COUNTIES WICKLOW & KILDARE WICKLOW MOUNTAINS

place nightly throughout the summer, mostly for the knees-up, faux-Irish floor show of music and dancing. But there's nothing contrived about the seafood, which is so damn good we'd happily sit through yet another chorus of 'Danny Boy' and even consider joining in the jig. The pub is 3km northwest of Enniskerry in Glencullen.

ⓘ Getting There & Away

Enniskerry is 18km south of Dublin, just 3km west of the M11 along the R117. Getting to Powerscourt House under your own steam is not a problem (it's 500m from the town), but getting to the waterfall is tricky.

Dublin Bus (⌖ 01-873 4222, 01-872 0000; www.dublinbus.ie) Service 44 (€2.50, every 20 minutes) takes about 1¼ hours to get to Enniskerry from Hawkins St in Dublin.

Roundwood

POP 589

Unspectacular but useful to walkers along the Wicklow Way (which runs past the town 3km to the west), Roundwood is reputedly Ireland's highest village – although at 238m that's hardly too impressive. Still, it's a handy spot for a stopover and a decent meal.

🏃 Activities

Footfalls Walking Holidays   GUIDED TOUR
(⌖ 0404-45152; www.walkinghikingireland.com; Trooperstown, Roundwood) Guided or self-guided tours for up to eight days in Wicklow (and

WORTH A TRIP

GLENMACNASS

Desolate and utterly deserted, the Glenmacnass valley, a stretch of wild bogland between the Sally Gap crossroads and Laragh, is one of the most beautiful parts of the mountains, although the sense of isolation is quite dramatic.

The highest mountain to the west is Mt Mullaghcleevaun (848m), and River Glenmacnass flows south and tumbles over the edge of the mountain plateau in a great foaming cascade. There's a car park near the top of the waterfall. Be careful when walking on rocks near Glenmacnass Waterfall as a few people have slipped to their deaths. There are fine walks up Mt Mullaghcleevaun or in the hills to the east of the car park.

plenty of other spots in Ireland): an eight-day trek through the Wicklow Mountains complete with full bed and board will cost €549.

🛏 Sleeping & Eating

Roundwood Caravan & Camping Park   CAMPGROUND €
(⌖ 01-281 8163; www.dublinwicklowcamping.com; campsites per adult/child €8/4; ⊙ Apr-Sep; 🛜 📶) Top-notch facilities, including a kitchen, dining area and TV lounge, make this one of the best camping grounds in all of Wicklow. It is about 500m south of the village and is served by the daily St Kevin's Bus service between Dublin and Glendalough.

Roundwood Inn   INTERNATIONAL €€
(⌖ 01-281 8107; Main St; bar mains €12-17, restaurant mains €16-32; ⊙ bar noon-9pm, restaurant 7.30-9.30pm Fri & Sat, 1-3pm Sun) This 17th-century German-owned house has a gorgeous bar with a snug open fire, in front of which you can sample bar food with a difference: on the menu are dishes such as Hungarian goulash and Irish stew with a German twist. The more formal restaurant is the best in town with hearty cuisine. The menu favours meat dishes, including seasonal game, Wicklow rack of lamb and a particularly good roast suckling pig. Reservations are required.

ⓘ Getting There & Away

St Kevin's Bus (⌖ 01-281 8119; www.glendaloughbus.com) passes through Roundwood on its twice-daily jaunt between Dublin and Glendalough (one way/return €8/14, 1¼ hours).

Wicklow Gap

Between Mt Tonelagee (816m) to the north and Table Mountain (700m) to the southwest, the Wicklow Gap is the second major pass over the mountains. The eastern end of the road begins just to the north of Glendalough and climbs through some lovely scenery northwestwards up along the Glendassan Valley. It passes the remains of some old lead and zinc workings before meeting a side road that leads south and up Turlough Hill, the location of Ireland's only pumped-storage power station. You can walk up the hill for a look over the Upper Lake.

Glendalough

POP 280

If you've come to Wicklow, chances are that a visit to Glendalough (Gleann dá Loch, 'Valley of the Two Lakes') is one of your main reasons for being here. And you're not wrong, for this is one of the most beautiful corners of the whole country and the epitome of the kind of rugged, romantic Ireland that probably drew you to the island in the first place.

The substantial remains of this important monastic settlement are certainly impressive, but the real draw is the splendid setting: two dark and mysterious lakes tucked into a deep valley covered in forest. It is, despite its immense popularity, a deeply tranquil and spiritual place, and you will have little difficulty in understanding why those solitude-seeking monks came here in the first place.

History

In AD 498 a young monk named Kevin arrived in the valley looking for somewhere to kick back, meditate and be at one with nature. He set up camp in what had been a Bronze Age tomb on the southern side of the Upper Lake and for the next seven years slept on stones, wore animal skins, maintained a near-starvation diet and – according to the legend – became bosom buddies with the birds and animals. Kevin's eco-friendly lifestyle soon attracted a bunch of disciples, all seemingly unaware of the irony that they were flocking to hang out with a hermit who wanted to live as far away from other people as possible. Over the next couple of centuries his one-man operation mushroomed into a proper settlement and by the 9th century Glendalough rivalled Clonmacnoise as the island's premier monastic city. Thousands of students studied and lived in a thriving community that was spread over a considerable area.

Inevitably, Glendalough's success made it a key target for Viking raiders, who sacked the monastery at least four times between 775 and 1071. The final blow came in 1398, when English forces from Dublin almost destroyed it. Efforts were made to rebuild and some life lingered on here as late as the 17th century when, under renewed repression, the monastery finally died.

◉ Sights

UPPER LAKE

The original site of St Kevin's settlement, Teampall na Skellig is at the base of the cliffs towering over the southern side of the

Upper Lake and is accessible only by boat; unfortunately, there's no boat service to the site and you'll have to settle for looking at it across the lake. The terraced shelf has the reconstructed ruins of a church and early graveyard. Rough wattle huts once stood on the raised ground nearby. Scattered around are some early grave slabs and simple stone crosses.

Just east of here and 10m above the lake waters is the 2m-deep artificial cave called St Kevin's Bed, said to be where Kevin lived. The earliest human habitation of the cave was long before St Kevin's era – there's evidence that people lived in the valley for thousands of years before the monks arrived. In the green area just south of the car park is a large circular wall thought to be the remains of an early-Christian stone fort (caher).

Follow the lake-shore path southwest of the car park until you come to the considerable remains of Reefert Church above the tiny River Poulanass. It's a small, plain, 11th-century Romanesque nave-and-chancel church with some reassembled arches and walls. Traditionally, Reefert (literally 'Royal Burial Place') was the burial site of the chiefs of the local O'Toole family. The surrounding graveyard contains a number of rough stone crosses and slabs, most made of shiny mica schist.

Climb the steps at the back of the churchyard and follow the path to the west and you'll find, at the top of a rise overlooking the lake, the scant remains of St Kevin's Cell, a small beehive hut.

LOWER LAKE

While the Upper Lake has the best scenery, the most fascinating buildings lie in the lower part of the valley east of the Lower Lake, huddled together in the heart of the ancient monastic site.

Glendalough

WALKING TOUR

A visit to Glendalough is a trip through ancient history and a refreshing hike in the hills. The ancient monastic settlement founded by St Kevin in the 5th century grew to be quite powerful by the 9th century, but it started falling into ruin from 1398 onwards. Still, you won't find more evocative clumps of stones anywhere.

Start at the **Main Gateway 1** to the monastic city, where you will find a cluster of important ruins, including the (nearly perfect) 10th-century **Round Tower 2**, the **Cathedral 3** dedicated to **Sts Peter and Paul**, and **St Kevin's Kitchen 4**, which is really a church. Cross the stream past the famous **Deer Stone 5**, where Kevin was supposed to have milked a doe, and turn west along the path. It's a 1.5km walk to the **Upper Lake 6**. On the lake's southern shore is another cluster of sites, including the **Reefert Church 7**, a plain 11th-century Romanesque church where the powerful O'Toole family buried their kin, and **St Kevin's Cell 8**, the remains of a beehive hut where Kevin is said to have lived.

ST KEVIN

St Kevin came to the valley as a young monk in AD 498, in search of a peaceful retreat. He was reportedly led by an angel to a Bronze Age tomb now known as St Kevin's Bed. For seven years he slept on stones, wore animal skins, survived on nettles and herbs and – according to legend – developed an affinity with the birds and animals. One legend has it that, when Kevin needed milk for two orphaned babies, a doe stood waiting at the Deer Stone to be milked.

Kevin soon attracted a group of disciples and the monastic settlement grew, until by the 9th century Glendalough rivalled Clonmacnoise as Ireland's premier monastic city. According to legend, Kevin lived to the age of 120. He was canonised in 1903.

St Kevin's Cell
This beehive hut is reputedly where St Kevin would go for prayer and meditation; not to be confused with St Kevin's Bed, a cave where he used to sleep.

Deer Stone
The spot where St Kevin is said to have truly become one with the animals is really just a large mortar called a *bullaun*, used for grinding food and medicine.

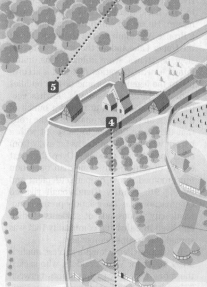

St Kevin's Kitchen
This small church is unusual in that it has a round tower sticking out of the roof – it looks like a chimney, hence the church's nickname.

Reefert Church
Its name derives from the Irish *righ fearta*, which means 'burial place of the kings'. Seven princes of the powerful O'Toole family are buried in this simple structure.

Upper Lake
The site of St Kevin's original settlement is on the banks of the Upper Lake, one of the two lakes that gives Glendalough its name – the 'Valley of the Lakes'.

Round Tower
Glendalough's most famous landmark is the 33m-high Round Tower, which is exactly as it was when it was built a thousand years ago except for the roof; this was replaced in 1876 after a lightning strike.

NORTH

Information
At the eastern end of the Upper Lake is the National Park Information Point, which has leaflets and maps on the site, local walks, etc. The grassy spot in front of the office is a popular picnic spot in summer.

Cathedral of Sts Peter & Paul
The largest of Glendalough's seven churches, the cathedral was built gradually between the 10th and 13th centuries. The earliest part is the nave, where you can still see the *antae* (slightly projecting column at the end of the wall) used for supporting a wooden roof.

Main Gateway
The only surviving entrance to the ecclesiastical settlement is a double-arch; notice that the inner arch rises higher than the outer one in order to compensate for the upward slope of the causeway.

FIONN DAVENPORT ©

Glendalough

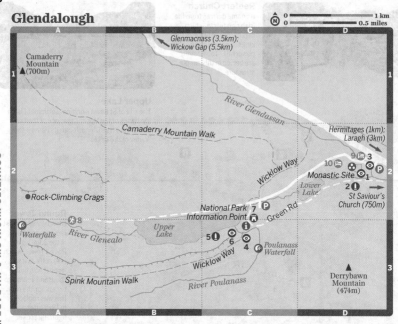

Just round the bend from the Glendalough Hotel is the stone arch of the monastery gatehouse, the only surviving example of a monastic entranceway in the country. Just inside the entrance is a large slab with an incised cross.

Beyond that lies a graveyard, which is still in use. The 10th-century round tower is 33m tall and 16m in circumference at the base. The upper storeys and conical roof were reconstructed in 1876. Near the tower, to the southeast, is the Cathedral of St Peter and St Paul with a 10th-century nave. The chancel and sacristy date from the 12th century.

At the centre of the graveyard to the south of the round tower is the Priest's House. This odd building dates from 1170 but has been heavily reconstructed. It may have been the location of shrines of St Kevin. Later, during penal times, it became a burial site for local priests – hence the name. The 10th-century St Mary's Church, 140m southwest of the round tower, probably originally stood outside the walls of the monastery and belonged to local nuns. It has a neatly western doorway. A little to the east are the scant remains of St Kieran's Church, the smallest at Glendalough.

Glendalough's trademark is St Kevin's Kitchen or Church at the southern edge of the enclosure. This church, with a miniature round towerlike belfry, protruding sacristy and steep stone roof, is a masterpiece. The oldest parts of the building date from the 11th century – the structure has been remodelled since but it's still a classic early Irish church.

At the junction with Green Rd as you cross the river just south of these two churches is the Deer Stone in the middle of a group of rocks. Legend claims that when St Kevin needed milk for two orphaned babies, a doe stood here waiting to be milked. The stone is actually a *bullaun* (a stone used as a mortar for grinding medicines or food). Many such stones are thought to be prehistoric, and they were widely regarded as having supernatural properties: women who bathed their faces with water from the hollow were supposed to keep their looks forever. The early churchmen brought the stones into their monasteries, perhaps hoping to inherit some of their powers.

The road east leads to St Saviour's Church, with its detailed Romanesque carvings. To the west, a nice woodland trail leads up the valley past the Lower Lake to the Upper Lake.

Activities

The Glendalough Valley is all about walking and clambering. There are nine marked ways in the valley, the longest of which is about 10km, or about four hours walking. Before you set off, drop by the National Park Information Point (p137) and pick up the relevant leaflet and trail map (all around €0.50) or, if you're solo, arrange for walking partners. It also has a number of excellent guides for sale – you won't go far wrong with Joss Lynam's *Easy Walks Near Dublin* (€8.99). A word of warning: don't be fooled by the relative gentleness of the surrounding countryside or the fact that the Wicklow Mountains are really no taller than big hills. The weather can be merciless here, so be sure to take the usual precautions, have the right equipment and tell someone where you're going and when you should be back. For Mountain Rescue call ☎ 999.

The easiest and most popular walk is the gentle hike along the northern shore of the Upper Lake to the lead and zinc mine workings, which date from 1800. The better route is along the lake shore rather than on the road (which runs 30m in from the shore), a distance of about 2.5km one way from the Glendalough Visitor Centre. Continue on up the head of the valley if you wish.

Alternatively, you can walk up the Spink (from the Irish for 'pointed hill'; 380m), the steep ridge with vertical cliffs running along the southern flanks of the Upper Lake. You can go part of the way and turn back, or complete a circuit of the Upper Lake by following the top of the cliff, eventually coming down by the mine workings and going back along the northern shore. The circuit is about 6km long and takes about three hours.

The third option is a hike up Camaderry Mountain (700m), hidden behind the hills that flank the northern side of the valley. The walk starts on the road just 50m back towards Glendalough from the entrance to the Upper Lake car park. Head straight up the steep hill to the north and you come out on open mountains with sweeping views in all directions. You can then continue up Camaderry to the northwest or just follow the ridge west looking over the Upper Lake. To the top of Camaderry and back is about 7.5km and takes about four hours.

Tours

A couple of bus tours depart Dublin if you don't want to explore Glendalough under your own steam:

Bus Éireann BUS TOUR
(☎ 01-836 6111; www.buseireann.ie; Busáras; adult/student/child €29/25/23; ☉ tours depart 10am mid-Mar–Oct) Includes admission to the visitor centre and a visit to Powerscourt Estate in this whole-day tour, which returns to Dublin at about 5.45pm. The guides are good but impersonal.

Wild Wicklow Tour BUS TOUR
(☎ 01-280 1899; www.wildwicklow.ie; adult/student & child €28/25; ☉ tours depart 9am) Award-winning tours of Glendalough, Avoca and the Sally Gap that never fail to generate rave reviews for atmosphere and all-round fun, but so much craic has made a casualty of informative depth. The first pick-up is at the Shelbourne hotel and then the tourist office, but there are a variety of pick-up points throughout Dublin; check the point nearest you when booking. The tour returns to Dublin about 5.30pm.

Sleeping & Eating

Most B&Bs are in or around Laragh, a village 3km east of Glendalough, or on the way there from Glendalough.

Glendalough International Hostel HOSTEL €
(☎ 0404-45342; www.anoige.ie; The Lodge; dm/d €14/48; @☎) Conveniently, this modern

COUNTIES WICKLOW & KILDARE WICKLOW MOUNTAINS

hostel is situated near the round tower, set within the deeply wooded glacial area that makes up the Glendalough Valley. All dorms have private bathrooms and there's a decent cafeteria on the premises.

Glendalough Hermitages BUNGALOW €
(☑ 0404-45571; www.glendaloughhermitage.ie; St Kevin's Parish Church, Glendalough; s/d €45/70)

Five hermitages (really just plain one- and two-bed bungalows) are rented out by St Kevin's Parish Church for anyone looking for a little spiritual R & R. Facilities are pretty basic but comfortable: besides the bedrooms there's a bathroom, a small kitchen area and an open fire supplemented by a storage heater. Visitors are welcome to join in morn-

---

WALK: THE WICKLOW WAY – GLENDALOUGH TO AUGHRIM

The Wicklow Way is one of Ireland's most popular long-distance walks because of its remarkable scenery and its relatively fluid and accessible starting and finishing points – there are plenty of half- and full day options along the way.

This section is 40km long and takes you through some of the more remote parts of the Wicklow Mountains and down into the southeastern foothills. There's relatively little road walking but the greater part of the day is through conifer plantations. The walk should take between 7½ and eight hours, with an ascent of 1035m.

From the National Park Information Point (p137) on the southern side of the Upper Lake, turn left and ascend beside Lugduff Brook and Poulanass Waterfall. Veer left when you meet a forest track, then left again at a junction and cross two bridges. The Way leads northeast for about 600m then, from a tight right bend, heads almost directly southwards (via a series of clearly marked junctions), up through the conifer plantations, across Lugduff Brook again and beside a tributary, to open ground on the saddle between Mullacor (657m) and Lugduff (652m; 1¾ hours from Glendalough). From here on a good day, massive Lugnaquilla sprawls across the view to the southwest; in the opposite direction is Camaderry's long ridge above Glendalough, framed against the bulk of Tonelagee. Follow the raised boardwalk down, contour above a plantation and drop into it where a steep muddy and rocky path descends to a forest road; turn left.

If you're planning to stay at Glenmalure Hostel, rather than go all the way down to the crossroads in Glenmalure, follow the Way from the left turn for about 1km southwards. At an oblique junction where the Way turns southeast, bear left in a westerly direction and descend steeply to the road in Glenmalure. The hostel is about 2km northwest.

To continue straight on along the Way from the left turn, follow forest roads south then southeast for 1.6km to a wide zigzag above open ground, then contour the steep slope, swing northeast and drop down to a minor road beside two bridges. Continue down to an intersection and Glenmalure; it's about 1¼ hours from the saddle.

The Way presses straight on (south) through the crossroads for 500m, across the River Avonbeg and past silent Drumgoff Barracks, built in 1803 but long since derelict, then right along a forest track. Keep left past a ruined cottage and start to gain height in two fairly long reaches; go through two left turns then it's down and across a stream. About 800m further on, turn right along a path to start the long ascent almost to the top of Slieve Maan (550m) via four track junctions, maintaining a southwesterly to south-southwesterly direction. Back on a forest track, the Way turns left (southeast) close to unforested ground to the west. With a few more convoluted turns, you're out of the trees and on a path between the plantation and the road (mapped as the Military Rd). The Way eventually meets the latter beside a small tributary of the River Aghavannagh (two hours from Glenmalure).

Walk down the road for about 250m, then turn off left along a forest track, shortly bearing left to gain height steadily on a wide path over Carrickashane Mountain (508m). Descend steeply to a wide forest road and continue down for about 1km. Bear right to reach a minor road and turn right. Leave the road 500m further on and drop down to another road – Iron Bridge is just to the right (an hour from Military Rd).

Walk 150m up to a road and turn left; follow this road down the valley of the River Ow for 7.5km to a junction – Aughrim is to the left, another 500m. Buses along the Dublin to Wexford line stop here.

ing and evening prayer, but the venture is not exclusively Catholic and all creeds and denominations are welcome. The church is 1km east of Glendalough on the R756 to Laragh.

Glendalough Hotel HOTEL €€
(☎ 0404-45135; www.glendaloughhotel.com; s/d from 90/140; @ 🖰 🗟) There's no mistaking Glendalough's best hotel, conveniently located next door to the visitor centre. There is no shortage of takers for its 44 fairly luxurious bedrooms.

Glendale B&B €€
(☎ 0404-45410; www.glendale-glendalough.com; Laragh East; r €72, cottage per week €355-755; 🗟) This is an immaculately modern and tidy B&B with large, comfortable rooms. Also available are five modern self-catering cottages that sleep six. Every cottage has all the mod cons, from TV and video to a fully equipped kitchen complete with microwave, dishwasher and washer-dryer. The owners will also drop you off in Glendalough if you don't fancy the walk.

Wicklow Heather INTERNATIONAL €€
(☎ 0404-45157; www.thewicklowheather.com; Main St, Laragh; mains €16-26; ⊗ noon-8.30pm) This is the best place for anything substantial. The menu offers Wicklow lamb, wild venison, Irish beef and fresh fish (the trout is excellent) – most of it sourced locally and all of it traceable from farm to fork. Next door is the owners' B&B, where there are five well-appointed rooms (single/double with bathroom €35/70).

❶ Information

Glendalough Visitor Centre (www.heritageireland.ie; adult/child €3/1; ⊗ 9.30am-6pm mid-Mar–mid-Oct, to 5pm mid-Oct–mid-Mar) At the valley entrance, before the Glendalough Hotel, has a high-quality 17-minute audiovisual presentation called *Ireland of the Monasteries*, which does exactly what it says on the tin.

❶ Getting There & Away

St Kevin's Bus (☎ 01-281 8119; www.glendaloughbus.com) departs from outside the Mansion House on Dawson St in Dublin at 11.30am and 6pm Monday to Saturday, and 11.30am and 7pm Sunday (one way/return €13/20, 1½ hours). It also stops at the Town Hall in Bray. Departures from Glendalough are at 7.15am and 4.30pm Monday to Saturday. During the week in July and August the later bus runs at 5.30pm, and there is an additional service at 9.45am.

Glenmalure

As you go deeper into the mountains southwest of Glendalough near the southern end of the Military Rd, everything gets a bit wilder and more remote. Beneath the western slopes of Wicklow's highest peak, Lugnaquilla, is Glenmalure, a dark and sombre blind valley flanked by scree slopes of loose boulders. After coming over the mountains into Glenmalure you turn northwest at the Drumgoff bridge. From there it's about 6km up the road beside the River Avonbeg to a car park where trails lead off in various directions.

Glenmalure figures prominently in the national tale of resistance against the British. The valley was a clan stronghold and in 1580 the redoubtable chieftain Fiach Mac Hugh O'Byrne (1544–97) and his band of merry men actually managed to defeat an army of 1000 English soldiers; the battle cost the lives of 800 men and drove Queen Elizabeth into an apoplectic rage. In 1597 the English avenged the disaster when they captured O'Byrne and impaled his head on the gates of Dublin Castle.

◉ Sights & Activities

Near Drumgoff is Dwyer's or **Cullen's Rock**, which commemorates both the Glenmalure battle and Michael Dwyer, a member of the United Irishmen who fought unsuccessfully against the English in the Rising of 1798 and holed up here. Men were hanged from the rock during the Rising.

You can walk up Lugnaquilla Mountain or head up the blind Fraughan Rock Glen east of the car park. Alternatively, you can go straight up Glenmalure Valley passing the small, seasonal An Óige Glenmalure Hostel, after which the trail divides: heading northeast, the trail takes you over the hills to Glendalough, while going northwest brings you into the Glen of Imaal.

The head of Glenmalure and parts of the neighbouring Glen of Imaal are off limits. It's military land, well posted with warning signs.

🛏 Sleeping

Glenmalure Hostel HOSTEL €
(☎ 01-830 4555; www.anoige.ie; Greenane; dm €15; ⊗ Jun-Aug, Sat only Sep-May) No telephone, no electricity (lighting is by gas), just a rustic two-storey former hunting lodge with 19 beds and running water. This place has a

couple of heavyweight literary links: it was the setting for JM Synge's play *Shadow of a Gunman* – at the time it was owned by Maud Gonne, the unrequited love of WB Yeats. It's isolated, but is beautifully situated beneath Lugnaquilla.

Glenmalure Log Cabin   LODGE €€

(☑01-269 6979; www.glenmalure.com; 11 Glenmalure Pines, Greenane; lodge €270; ☎⊕) In the heart of Glenmalure, this modern, Scandinavian-style lodge has two rooms with private bathrooms, a fully equipped kitchen and a living room kitted out with all kinds of electronic amusements, including a DVD library. Hopefully, though, you'll spend much of your time here enjoying the panorama from the sun deck.

Western Wicklow

As you go west through the county, the landscape gets less rugged and more rural, especially towards the borders of Kildare and Carlow. The wild terrain gives way to rich pastures; east of Blessington the countryside is dotted with private stud farms where some of the world's most expensive horses are trained in jealously guarded secrecy.

The main attraction in this part of Wicklow is the magnificent Palladian pile at Russborough House, just outside Blessington, but if it's more wild scenery you're after, you'll find it around Kilbride and the upper reaches of the River Liffey, as well as further south in the Glen of Imaal.

Blessington

POP 4018

Lined with pubs, shops, and 17th- and 18th-century town houses, Blessington makes a convenient exploring base for the surround-ing area. The main attraction is Russborough House.

The helpful **tourist office** (☑045-865 850; Unit 5, Blessington Craft Centre, Main St; ⊙9.30am-5pm Mon-Fri, also 10am-2pm Sat-Sun Jul-Aug) is across the road from the Downshire House Hotel.

◉ Sights

Russborough House   HISTORIC BUILDING

(☑045-865 239; www.russboroughhouse.ie; adult/child guided tour €10/6, 3D exhibition €6/4; ⊙10am-6pm daily May-Sep, Sun & bank holidays Apr & Oct) Magnificent Russborough House is one of Ireland's finest stately homes, a Palladian pleasure palace built for Joseph Leeson (1705–83), later the first earl of Milltown and, later still, lord Russborough. It was built between 1741 and 1751 to the design of Richard Cassels, who was at the height of his fame as an architect. Poor old Richard didn't live to see it finished, but the job was well executed by Francis Bindon.

The house remained in the Leeson family until 1931. In 1952 it was sold to Sir Alfred Beit, the eponymous nephew of the cofounder of the de Beers diamond-mining company. An avid art collector, he lined his walls with paintings by Velázquez, Vermeer, Goya and Rubens among others. In 1974 the IRA stole 16 of the paintings, all of which were later recovered. In 1984, Loyalist paramilitaries followed suit, hiring Dublin criminal Martin Cahill to mastermind the heist. Although most of that haul was also recovered, some were damaged beyond repair. In 1988 Beit donated the most valuable works to the National Gallery (p68), but that didn't stop two more break-ins in 2001 and 2002: one of the stolen paintings was a Gainsborough that had already been taken – and recovered – twice before. Thankfully, all of the paintings were recovered after both attempts.

WORTH A TRIP

TINAKILLY COUNTRY HOUSE & RESTAURANT

Wicklow has no shortage of fine country homes converted into luxury manor hotels, but **Tinakilly Country House & Restaurant** (☑0404-69274; www.tinakilly.ie; Rathnew; r €115-200, dinner mains €22-29), a magnificent Victorian Italianate house just outside Rathnew (about 5km west of Wicklow town), stands out for sheer elegance. The guest rooms are divided between the period rooms in the west wing, decked out in original antiques, four-poster and half-tester canopy beds, and the shockingly sumptuous suites in the east wing, which have gorgeous views of either the richly colourful garden or the Irish Sea, albeit somewhere in the distance. And then there's the restaurant, which takes country-house cuisine to a whole new level of sophistication.

The admission price includes a 45-minute tour of the house, decorated in typical Georgian style, and all the important paintings, which, given the history, is a monumental exercise in staying positive. A recent addition is the 3D exhibition on Sir Alfred's life and travels.

🛏 Sleeping & Eating

Haylands House   B&B €€
(☑ 045-865 183; haylands@eircom.net; Dublin Rd; s/d from €40/70) We highly recommend this modern bungalow for its lovely rooms (all with private bathrooms), warm welcome and excellent breakfast. It's only 500m out of town on the main Dublin road. As it's popular, book early if you can.

★ West Wing   APARTMENT €€€
(Russborough House; www.irishlandmark.com; Russborough House, Blessington; 3 nights Beit Residence €1200, 2 nights Garden Apartment €650) The Beit family lived in the west wing of Russborough House until 2005; their former digs have now been converted into two luxury self-catering apartments managed by the Irish Landmark Trust. The Garden Apartment is big – it sleeps seven comfortably across three bedrooms – but the Beit Residence is simply *huge*: eight people can live in the kind of luxury available usually only to the 1%.

★ Rathsallagh House & Country Club   HOTEL €€€
(☑ 045-403 112; www.rathsallagh.com; Dunlavin; mains €22-32; s/d from €150/210) About 20km south of Blessington, this fabulous country manor, converted from Queen Anne stables in 1798, is more than just a fancy hotel. Luxury is par for the course here, from the splendidly appointed rooms to the exquisite country-house dining (the food here is some of the best you'll eat anywhere in Ireland) and the highly rated golf course that surrounds the estate.

★ Grangecon Café   INTERNATIONAL €€
(☑ 045-857 892; Tullow Rd; mains €11-18; ☺ 10am-5pm Tue-Sat) Salads, home-baked dishes and a full menu of Irish cheeses are the staples at this tiny, terrific cafe in a converted schoolhouse. Everything here – from the pasta to the delicious apple juice – is made on the premises and many of the ingredients are organic. A short but solid menu represents the best of Irish cooking.

Russborough House hosts a monthly farmers market (☑ 087-611 5016; ☺ 10am-4pm, first Sun of the month) that goes indoors during the winter months.

ℹ Getting There & Away

Blessington is 35km southwest of Dublin on the N81. There are regular daily services by **Dublin Bus** (☑ 01-873 4222, 01-872 0000); catch bus 65 from Eden Quay in Dublin (€4.40, 1½ hours, every 1½ hours). **Bus Éireann** (☑ 01-836 6111; www.buseireann.ie) operates express bus 005 to and from Waterford, with stops in Blessington two or three times daily; from Dublin it's pick-up only and from Waterford drop-off only.

The Coast

Wicklow's coastline plays second fiddle to its mountains in terms of dramatic scenery, and its largely unassuming towns and small coastal resorts have a subtle charm that quickly disappears under a menacing sky. Highlights include the fine beaches at Brittas Bay, a wide lazy arc of coastline immediately south of Wicklow Town.

Kilmacanogue & the Great Sugarloaf

POP 839

At 503m, it's not even Wicklow's highest mountain, but the Great Sugarloaf is one of the most distinctive peaks in Ireland, its conical tip visible for many kilometres around. The mountain towers over the small village of Kilmacanogue, on the N11 about 4km south of Bray, which would barely merit a passing nod were it not for the presence of the mother of all Irish craft shops just across the road from the village.

Avoca Handweavers (☑ 01-286 7466; www.avoca.ie; Main St) is one hell of an operation, with seven branches nationwide and an even more widespread reputation for adding elegance and style to traditional rural handicrafts. Operational HQ is in a 19th-century arboretum, and its showroom will leave you in no doubt as to the company's incredible success. The attached restaurant (mains €12-18; ☺ 9.30am-5.30pm) is excellent and you can bring a little of it home with you by purchasing one (or all) of its cookbooks.

ℹ Getting There & Away

Dublin Bus (p709) operates bus 145 from D'Olier St in Dublin to Kilmacanogue (€4.40, 55 minutes, every 10 minutes). **Bus Éireann** (🖉 01-836 6111; www.buseireann.ie) bus ``133 from Dublin to Arklow stops in Kilmacanogue (one way/return €4.70/8.20, 45 minutes, 10 daily).

Greystones to Wicklow

The resort of Greystones, 8km south of Bray, was once a charming fishing village, and the seafront around the little harbour is idyllic. In summer the bay is dotted with dinghies and windsurfers. Sadly, the surrounding countryside is vanishing beneath housing developments.

⊙ Sights

Wicklow's nickname as the Garden of Ireland is justified by green idylls like the 8-hectare **Mt Usher Gardens** (🖉 0404-40116; www.mountushergardens.ie; adult/student/child €7.50/6.50/3.50; ⊙ 10.30am-6pm Mar-Oct), just outside the unremarkable town of Ashford, about 10km south of Greystones on the N11. Trees, shrubs and herbaceous plants from around the world are laid out in Robinsonian style – ie according to the naturalist principles of famous Irish gardener William Robinson (1838–1935) – rather than the formalist style of preceding gardens.

Another fine garden surrounds **Kilruddery House**, 6km north of Greystones just off the R761 coast road. A stunning mansion in the Elizabethan Revival style, Killruddery has been home to the Brabazon family (earls of Meath) since 1618 and has one of the oldest gardens in Ireland. The house, designed by trendy 19th-century architects Richard Morrisson and his son William in 1820, was reduced to its present-day huge proportions by the 14th earl in 1953; he was obviously looking for something a little more bijou. The house is impressive, but the prize-winner here is the magnificent orangery, built in 1852 and chock-full of statuary and plant life. If you like fancy glasshouses, this is the one for you.

🛏 Sleeping & Eating

★ Hunter's Hotel   HOTEL €€
(🖉 0404-40106; www.hunters.ie; Newrath Bridge, Rathnew; s/d €80/130; 🐾) This exquisite property just outside Rathnew on the R761 is an absolute find, with 16 stunning rooms, each decorated with unerringly good taste. The house, one of Ireland's oldest coaching inns, is surrounded by an award-winning garden that is part of the Wicklow Gardens Festival.

Three Q's   INTERNATIONAL €€
(🖉 01-287 5477; Church Rd; mains €17.95; ⊙ 9am-10pm Tue-Fri, to 3pm Sat & Sun) You'll find a smart menu at this elegant restaurant, with dishes like chargrilled spiced beef with sweetcorn salsa and lemon crème fraiche sharing the space with fish dishes like grilled fillet of hake with a confit cherry tomato orzo pasta and smoked paprika oil.

Hungry Monk   IRISH €€€
(🖉 01-287 5759; Church Rd; mains €17-29; ⊙ 7-11pm Wed-Sat, 12.30-9pm Sun; 👪) An excellent 1st-floor restaurant on Greystones' main street. The blackboard specials are the real treat, with dishes like suckling pig with prune and apricot stuffing to complement the fixed menu's classic choices – fresh seafood, Wicklow rack of lamb, bangers and mash and so forth. This is one of the better places to get a bite along the whole of the Wicklow coast.

❶ Getting There & Away

Bus Éireann (🖉 01-836 6111; www.buseireann.ie) operates bus 133 from Dublin to Wicklow

---

WORTH A TRIP

BALLYKNOCKEN HOUSE

As fine a country home as you could ever hope to find, **Ballyknocken House & Cookery School** (🖉 0404-44627; www.ballyknocken.com; s/d from €150/300; dinner mains €14-22) is a beautiful ivy-clad Victorian home, 5km south of Ashford on the R752 to Glenealy. Each of the bedrooms is carefully appointed with original furnishings and have private bathrooms, some with stencilled Victorian claw-foot tubs, which lends the whole place an air of timeless elegance that is becoming increasingly difficult to find. The old milking parlour on the farm grounds has been converted into a tidy two-bedroom loft that sleeps up to six people. Besides the home itself, the big draw is Catherine Fulvio's **cooking classes** (www.thecookeryschool.ie; €110), which run throughout the year; she also runs kids courses for junior chefs.

WICKLOW'S HISTORIC JAIL

Wicklow's infamous jail ([📞] 0404-61599; www.wicklowshistoricgaol.com; Kilmantin Hill; adult/student/child incl tour €7.30/6/4.50, adult-only tours €15; ⊙10.30am-4.30pm), opened in 1702 to deal with prisoners sentenced under the repressive Penal Laws, was renowned throughout Ireland for the brutality of its keepers and the harsh conditions suffered by its inmates. The smells, vicious beatings, shocking food and disease-ridden air have long since gone, but adults and children alike can experience a sanitised version of what the prison was like – and stimulate the secret sadist buried deep within – in the highly entertaining tour of the prison, now one of Wicklow's most popular tourist attractions. Actors play the roles of the various jailers and prisoners, adding to the sense of drama already heightened by the various exhibits on show, including a life-size treadmill that prisoners would have to turn for hours on end as punishment, and the gruesome dungeon.

On the 2nd floor is a model of HMS *Hercules*, a convict ship that was used to transport convicts to New South Wales under the captaincy of the psychotic Luckyn Betts: six months under his iron rule and most began to see death as a form of mercy. The top floor is devoted to the stories of the prisoners once they arrived in Australia. Tours are every 10 minutes except between 1pm and 2pm; on the last Friday of every month there are adult-only tours of the prison, complete with ghouls, finger food and a glass of wine.

Bus Éireann ([📞] 01-836 6111; www.buseireann.ie) bus 133 serves Wicklow Town (single/return €9.80/16.20, one hour, 10 daily) from Dublin on its way to Arklow.

COUNTIES WICKLOW & KILDARE SOUTHERN WICKLOW

town and Arklow with stops outside Ashford House, in Ashford (one way/return €7.60/12.50, one hour, 10 daily).

Southern Wicklow

Southern Wicklow is softer than its coastal northern half; the landscape is one of rolling hills and valleys cut through by rustling rivers and dotted with lovely little hamlets, including the especially beautiful Vale of Avoca, once favoured by both song and busloads of tourists.

Rathdrum

POP 2123

The quiet village of Rathdrum at the foot of the Vale of Clara comprises little more than a few old houses and shops, but in the late 19th century it had a healthy flannel industry and a poorhouse. It's not what's in the town that's of interest to visitors, however, but what's just outside it.

The small tourist office ([📞] 0404-46262; 29 Main St; ⊙9am-5.30pm Mon-Fri) has leaflets and information on the town and surrounding area, including the Wicklow Way.

⊙ Sights

Woe be to the man by whom the scandal cometh...It would be better for him that a millstone were tied about his neck and that he were cast into the depth of the

sea rather than he should scandalise one of these, my least little ones.
James Joyce, A Portrait of the Artist as a Young Man

Joyce's fictional dinner-table argument wasn't about a murderer or any criminal, but about Charles Stewart Parnell (1846–91), the 'uncrowned king of Ireland' and unquestionably one of the key figures in the Irish independence movement. Avondale House ([📞] 0404-46111; adult/student & child €5/4; ⊙11am-6pm May-Aug, Sat & Sun only Apr, by appointment rest of year), a fine Palladian mansion surrounded by a marvellous 209-hectare estate, was the birthplace and Irish headquarters of Charles Stewart Parnell. Designed by James Wyatt in 1779, the house's many highlights include a stunning vermilion-hued library (Parnell's favourite room) and beautiful dining room.

From 1880 to 1890 Avondale was synonymous with the fight for Home Rule, which was brilliantly led by Parnell until 1890, when a member of his own Irish Parliamentary Party, Captain William O'Shea, sued his wife Kitty for divorce and named Parnell as corespondent. Parnell's affair with Kitty O'Shea scandalised this 'priest-ridden' nation, and the ultraconservative clergy declared that Parnell was 'unfit to lead' – despite the fact that as soon as the divorce was granted the two lovers were quickly married. Parnell resigned as leader of the party and withdrew in despair to Avondale, where he died the following year.

ℹ WICKLOW GARDENS FESTIVAL

If you want unfettered access to more than 40 of Wicklow's famed public and private gardens, visit during the yearly Wicklow Gardens Festival (www.wicklowgardens.com) which runs from Easter roughly through to the end of August. The obvious advantage for green thumbs and other garden enthusiasts is access to beautiful gardens that would ordinarily be closed to the public. Some of the larger gardens are open throughout the festival, while other smaller ones open only at specific times; check the website for details of entrants, openings and special events, including all manner of horticultural courses.

Surrounding the house are 200 hectares of forest and parkland, where the first silvicultural experiments by the Irish Forestry Service (Coillte) were conceived, after the purchase of the house by the state in 1904. These plots, about half a hectare in size, are still visible today, flanking what many consider to be the best of Avondale's many walking trails, the Great Ride. You can visit the park during daylight hours year-round.

About 3km east of town (and 3km west of the N11) are the National Botanic Gardens (www.botanicgardens.ie) FREE at Kilmacurragh, a fine example of Robinsonian design that is emphasising the wild over the formal layout.

🛏 Sleeping & Eating

Old Presbytery Hostel HOSTEL €
(☑ 0404-46930; www.hostels-ireland.com; The Fairgreen; dm/d €15/48) This modern, centrally located IHH hostel looks more like campus accommodation. There is a mix of large, comfy dorms and well-appointed doubles with private bathrooms, as well as family rooms. A laundry and a TV room round off the facilities. You can also camp in the grounds.

Bates Inn PUB €€
(www.batesrestaurant.com; 3 Market Sq; mains €19-25; ⊙ 6-9.30pm Tue-Sat, 12.30-3pm & 6-9pm Sun) Housed in a coaching inn that first opened its doors in 1785 is this outstanding restaurant that puts a premium on exquisitely prepared meat dishes (the chargrilled beef options are particularly good). One of the better options in southern Wicklow. Bookings recommended for weekend evenings.

ℹ Getting There & Away

Bus Éireann (☑ 01-836 6111; www.buseireann.ie) Service 133 goes to Rathdrum from Dublin (one way/return €12.50/19.50, 1¾ hours, 10 daily) on its way to Arklow.

Iarnród Éireann (☑ 01-836 6222) Trains serve Rathdrum from Dublin on the main Dublin to Rosslare Harbour line (one way/return €15.50/20.50, 1½ hours, five daily).

Vale of Avoca

One of the most scenic spots in the county is the Vale of Avoca, a darkly wooded valley that begins where the Rivers Avonbeg and Avonmore come together to form the River Avoca. Bearing the literal name the Meeting of the Waters, this watery junction was made famous by Thomas Moore's 1808 poem of the same name.

Here you'll also find a pub called the Meetings (☑ 0402-35226; www.themeetingsavoca.com; ⊙ noon-9pm), which serves food (mains €11 to €17) and has music at weekends year-round. There are céilidh (traditional music and dancing sessions) between 4pm and 6pm Sunday, April to October. There's also a guesthouse attached with decent, clean rooms (single/double €40/72). Buses to Avoca from Dublin stop at the Meetings, or you could walk from Avoca, 3km south of here.

Avoca

POP 570

Tiny Avoca (Abhóca) is a pleasant enough village best-known as the birthplace of the superstar of all Irish cottage industries, Avoca Handweavers (☑ 0402-35105; www.avoca.ie; Main St, Old Mill; ⊙ 9am-6pm May-Sep, 9.30am-5.30pm Oct-Apr), housed in Ireland's oldest working mill. It's been turning out linens, wools and other fabrics since 1723, and a lot of Avoca's much-admired line is produced here. You are free to wander in and out of the weaving sheds.

Just in case you might want some local info, the tourist office (☑ 0402-35022; Old Courthouse; ⊙ 10am-5pm Mon-Sat) is in a small bungalow called The Courthouse.

🛏 Sleeping

★ Sheepwalk House & Cottages B&B €€
(☑ 0402-35189; www.sheepwalk.com; Arklow Rd; s/d €60/90, cottages per week €250-420; ☎) Built in 1727 for the Earl of Wicklow, this is one of our favourite places to stay

in Avoca (although it's 2km out of town). The main house is splendid, with beautifully appointed rooms, while the converted outbuildings – complete with beamed ceilings, fireplaces and flagstone floors – are a wonderful option for groups of four or six.

River Valley Park   CAMPGROUND €
(📋 0402-41647; www.rivervalleypark.com; family/adults-only campsites €13/24, microlodges from €55; 🏕️) With six different kinds of camping options, this is probably the best-equipped camping ground in the county. Besides the family campsites, there are self-catering chalets, mobile homes, glamping microlodges and an adults only section. It's about 1km south of the village of Redcross, 7km northeast of Avoca on the R754 country road.

🚌 Getting There & Away

Bus Éireann (📋 01-836 6111; www.buseireann.ie) 133 from Dublin serves Avoca (one way/return €13/21, two hours, 10 daily) on its way to Arklow.

COUNTY KILDARE

With some of the best farmland in Ireland, County Kildare (Cill Dara) has always been prime agricultural real estate, not least for the horse industry, with some of the country's most prestigious stud farms turning out one champion racehorse after another. In recent decades it has had to contend with the ever-expanding commuter belt that has swallowed up many of its towns and villages.

The county isn't especially stuffed with must-see attractions, but there are enough diversions to justify a day trip from the capital or a stop on your way out west.

Maynooth

POP 10,715

Bustling Maynooth (Maigh Nuad) is dominated by the local campus of National University of Ireland (NUIM), the students of which make up two-thirds of the inhabitants and bring a bit of life to this otherwise demure country town lined with stone-fronted houses and shops. Main St and Leinster St join and run east–west, while Parson St runs south to the canal and the train station (accessed via a couple of footbridges) and Straffan Rd runs south to the M4.

◉ Sights

St Patrick's College   UNIVERSITY
(📋 01-628 5222; www.maynoothcollege.ie; Main St) Turning out Catholic priests since 1795, St Patrick's College & Seminary is Ireland's second-oldest university (after Trinity College Dublin), founded so that aspiring priests didn't have to skip off to seminary school in France – and so get infected with strains of republicanism and revolution. In 1898 it was made a Pontifical College (which meant that its curriculum was determined and controlled by the Holy See) and in 1910 it became part of the recently established National University of Ireland. The college's student body remained exclusively clerical until 1966 when lay students were finally admitted, but even today, despite being part of the bigger university it remains largely autonomous and its 80-odd male seminarians are distinct from the university's 8500 other students.

COUNTIES WICKLOW & KILDARE MAYNOOTH

> **WORTH A TRIP**
>
> #### WILD LUXURY
>
> One of Wicklow's fanciest bolt-holes is the **Brook Lodge & Wells Spa** (📋 0402-36444; www.brooklodge.com; Macreddin; r/ste from €260/310; 🐾), 3km west of Rathdrum in the village of Macreddin. It has 86 beautifully appointed rooms spread about the main house and the annexes, ranging from standard bedroom to mezzanine suite that wouldn't seem out of place in a New York penthouse. The accommodation is pure luxury, but it's the outstanding spa that keeps guests coming back for more. Mud and flotation chambers, Finnish and aroma baths, *hammam* (Turkish bath) massages and a full range of Decléor and Carita treatments make this one of the top spas in the country. The **Strawberry Tree** (📋 0402-36444; www.brooklodge.com; Brook Lodge, Macreddin; dinner menu €65; ⊘ 7pm-midnight Tue-Sat) is one of the best restaurants in Wicklow.
>
> An **organic market** (Macreddin; ⊘ 10am-5pm Sun Apr-Oct) is held in Macreddin on the first Sunday of each month during summer.

The college buildings are impressive – Gothic architect Augustus Pugin had a hand in designing them – and well worth a ramble. You enter the college via Georgian Stoyte House, where the accommodation office (01-708 3576; 8.30am-5.30pm & 8-11pm Mon-Fri, 8.30am-12.30pm & 1.30-11pm Sat & Sun) sells booklets (€6) for guiding yourself. In summer there's also a visitor centre (11am-5pm Mon-Fri, 2-6pm Sat & Sun May-Sep) and a small science museum (admission by donation; 2-4pm Tue & Thu, to 6pm Sun May-Sep). The college grounds contain a number of lofty Georgian and neo-Gothic buildings, gardens and squares, but the highlight has to be the College Chapel. Pull open the squeaky door and you enter the world's largest choir chapel, with stalls for more than 450 choristers and some magnificent ornamentation.

Maynooth Castle   CASTLE

(01-628 6744; 10am-6pm Mon-Fri, 1-6pm Sat & Sun Jun-Sep, 1-5pm Sun Oct) FREE Near the entrance to St Patrick's College you can see the ruined gatehouse, keep and great hall of this 13th-century castle, home of the Fitzgerald family. The castle was dismantled in Cromwellian times, when the Fitzgeralds moved to Kilkea Castle (now closed). Entry is by a 45-minute guided tour only; there's a small exhibition on the castle's history in the keep.

Activities

Canoeing

Leixlip, on the River Liffey between Maynooth and Dublin, is an important canoeing centre and the starting point of the annual 28km International Liffey Descent Race (www.imnda.ie). Usually held in early September, the race attracts more than 1000 competitors.

Golf

On the edge of town, Carton House (01-651 7720; www.cartonhousegolf.com; green fees €60 Mon-Thu, €70 Fri-Sun), the former manor house of the earls of Kildare, is home to two outstanding 18-hole championship courses designed by Colin Montgomerie and Mark O'Meara respectively. See the Carton House sleeping review for details of the attached hotel.

Sleeping

NUI Maynooth   UNIVERSITY €€

(01-708 6200; www.maynoothcampus.com; s/d from €60/96;) The university campus can accommodate 1000 guests in seven types of room, ranging from a traditional college room to doubles in an apartment in the university village. Most are in the mid-1970s North Campus, but rooms are better in the South Campus. These are strewn around the courts and gardens of atmospheric St Patrick's College. Availability is best in the summer months.

Carton House   HOTEL €€€

(01-505 2000; www.cartonhouse.com; r from €110; @) Dating from 1739, the former country manor of the Fitzgeralds, the earls of Kildare (their city pile was Leinster House, now the Irish Parliament), is now an exquisite luxury hotel. The Palladian exterior (designed by Richard Cassels) belies the stylishly minimalist interior, the rooms of which are all equipped with the latest high-tech gadgetry. You can play golf on one of its two championship courses or just wander the 100 acre estate. To reach the hotel, follow the R148 east towards Leixlip along the Royal Canal.

Eating

Mohana   INDIAN €€

(01-505 4868; Main St; mains €13-17; noon-2.30pm & 5-11pm) Several cuts above the usual curry joint, Mohana has a wide range of excellent South Asian dishes. The dining room has a gracious air and it's a floor above the street. For a kick in the old masala, try the chicken chilli version.

Avenue   INTERNATIONAL €

(01-628 5003; www.avenuecafe.ie; Main St; meals €6-11; 8am-4pm Mon-Sat;) The menu at this cafe is designed for broadest appeal: steaks, bangers and mash and a particularly good fish and chips share space with a variety of salads and burgers to keep everyone happy.

Getting There & Away

Dublin Bus (01-873 4222; www.dublinbus.ie) runs a service to Maynooth (€2.80, one hour) leaving several times an hour from Pearse St in Dublin.

Maynooth is on the main Dublin–Sligo line, with regular trains in each direction: to Dublin (€3.50, 35 minutes, one to four per hour); to Sligo (€35, two hours 40 minutes, four per day).

Straffan

Teeny Straffan has a few small attractions for the young (or at least the young at heart), and another for the golfer.

The history of steam power and its role in the development of industry is told at the Steam Museum & Lodge Park Walled Garden ([☎]01-627 3155; www.steam-museum. com; adult/concession €7.50/5; ⊙2-6pm Wed-Sun Jun-Aug), located in an old church. The Power Hall has six 19th-century engines and holds regular demonstrations showing how they worked. Next door, the 18th-century walled garden has traditional fruits, flowers and formal plantings.

Just down the road at the Straffan Butterfly Farm ([☎]01-627 1109; www.straffan butterflyfarm.com; Ovidstown; adult/child €8/5; ⊙noon-5.30pm Mon-Fri, from 10am Sat-Sun Jun-Aug), you can wander through a tropical greenhouse full of enormous exotic butterflies, or commune with critters like Larry, the leopard gecko.

Two of Ireland's top golf courses can be found at the K Club (Kildare Hotel & Country Club; [☎]01-601 7200; www.kclub.ie; r from €415; [@][☎][☎]), a Georgian estate and golfers' paradise. Inside there are 92 well-appointed rooms and lots of public spaces for having a drink and lying about your exploits outside. Like everywhere else, the K Club is suffering the effects of the recession and has lowered its green fees from a prohibitive €250 to a more interesting €100. Not bad for the course where, in 2006, Europe won its third Ryder Cup in a row.

Bus Éireann ([☎]01-836 6111; www.buseir eann.ie) runs buses from Dublin (one way/ return €4/5.90, 30 minutes, every half-hour, six buses Sunday).

Along the Grand Canal

Heading west from Straffan, there are some interesting sites as you follow the banks of the Grand Canal, which flows gently from Dublin to tiny, tranquil Robertstown, just past Clane and well worth a detour. This picturesque village has remained largely untouched and is dominated by the now-dilapidated Grand Canal Hotel, built in 1801. It's a good place to start a canal walk.

Just southwest of Robertstown and at the centre of the Kildare flatlands, the Hill of Allen (206m) was a strategic spot through the centuries due to its 360-degree view. Today the top is marked by a 19th-century folly and the ruins of some Iron Age fortifications said to mark the home of Fionn McCumhaill.

Further west you'll find the wonderfully interpretive Bog of Allen Nature Centre ([☎]045-860 133; www.ipcc.ie; R414, Lullymore; adult/child €6/free; ⊙9.30am-5pm Mon-Fri), a fascinating institution run by the nonprofit Irish Peatland Conservation Council. The centre traces the history of bogs and peat production, and has the largest carnivorous plant collection in Ireland, including sundews, butterwort and other bog-native protein-eaters. A nearby boardwalk extends into the Bog of Allen.

A rather mangy rabbit mascot greets visitors to the cheerful Lullymore Heritage & Discovery Park ([☎]045-870 238; www.lullymoreheritagepark.com; Lullymore; adult/ family €9/28; ⊙10am-6pm Mon-Sat, from 11am Sun Easter-Oct, 11am-6pm Sat & Sun Nov-Easter), about 1km north of the Bog of Allen Nature Centre. Aimed right at kids, a woodland trail leads you past various dwellings (including Neolithic huts, a not-so-festive Famine-era house and an enchanting fairy village), and there's crazy golf and a road train. Should the unthinkable happen and it rains, the Funky Forest is a vast indoor playground.

Newbridge & the Curragh

POP 17,042

Unremarkable Newbridge (Droichead Nua), near the junction of the M7 and M9, is best known for its silverware and as the gateway to the Curragh, one of the country's largest

---

WALKING THE TOWPATH

The Grand Canal towpath is ideal for leisurely walkers and there are numerous access points, none better than Robertstown if you fancy a long-distance ramble. The village is the hub of the Kildare Way and River Barrow towpath trails, the latter stretching all the way to St Mullin's, 95km south in County Carlow. From there it's possible to connect with the South Leinster Way at Graiguenamanagh, or the southern end of the Wicklow Way at Clonegal, north of Mt Leinster.

A variety of leaflets detailing the paths can be picked up at most regional tourist offices. Waterways Ireland (www.waterwaysireland.org) is also a good source.

BOG OF ALLEN

Stretching like a brown, moist desert through nine counties, including Kildare, Laois and Offaly, the Bog of Allen is Ireland's best-known raised bog, and once covered much of the midlands. Unfortunately, in a pattern repeated across Ireland, the peat is rapidly being turned into potting compost and fuel. Once Ireland had almost 17% of its land covered in bogs; today it's less than 2%. Bogs are home to a wide range of plants and animals, including cranberries, insect-eating sundews, all manner of frogs and butterflies. For more information on ways to discover this rich land, enquire at the Bog of Allen Nature Centre found right along the Grand Canal.

pieces of unfenced fertile land and the centre of the Irish horse industry.

The Newbridge Silverware Visitor Centre (☑045-431 301; www.newbridgesilverware.com) is a purely commercial venture that trades on the area's metalwork heritage as it peddles vast quantities of silver-plated spoons, forks and whatnots. At the back of the showroom is the totally out-of-place Museum of Style Icons (☉9am-6pm Mon-Sat, 11am-6pm Sun) FREE, which displays an ever-changing range of star-studded memorabilia, including a jacket once worn by Michael Jackson; a dress that belonged to Princess Diana; and a gown worn by Bette Davis while starring as Elizabeth I.

Curragh renowned for its racecourse (☑045-441 205; www.curragh.ie; admission €15-60; ☉mid-Apr–Oct), the oldest and most prestigious in the country. Even if you're not a horsey type, it's well worth experiencing the passion, atmosphere and general craic of a day at the races, which can verge on mass hysteria. If you miss the chance to hear the hooves, you can still see some action: if you get up early or pass by in the late evening, you'll see the thoroughbreds exercising on the wide-open spaces surrounding the racecourse.

ⓘ Getting There & Away

The M7 runs through the Curragh (exit 12) and Newbridge from Dublin. There is frequent Bus Éireann service between Dublin's Busáras bus station and Newbridge (single/return

€9.80/16.20, 90 minutes). From Newbridge, buses continue to the Curragh racecourse (€1.90, 10 minutes) and Kildare town. There are extra buses on race days.

South Kildare Community Transport (☑045-871 916; www.skct.ie) runs a local bus service on two routes that serve Athy, Ballitore, Castledermot, Kildare town and Moone and Newbridge among others (five times daily).

The Dublin–Kildare **train** (☑01-836 6222) runs from Heuston train station and stops in Newbridge (€13.80, 30 minutes, hourly). Check the timetable for trains that stop at the racecourse.

Kildare Town

POP 7538

Built around a compact, triangular square fronting its impressive cathedral, Kildare is a busy enough place, even if there aren't a lot of attractions within the town itself. It is closely associated with Ireland's second-most important saint, Brigid.

⊙ Sights

St Brigid's Cathedral   CATHEDRAL
(☑045-521 229; Market Sq; admission by donation, round tower admission €6; ☉10am-1pm & 2-5pm Mon-Sat, 2-5pm Sun May-Sep) The solid presence of 13th-century St Brigid's Cathedral looms over Kildare Sq. Look out for a fine stained-glass window inside that depicts the three main saints of Ireland: Patrick, Brigid and Colmcille. The church also contains the restored tomb of Walter Wellesley, Bishop of Kildare, which disappeared soon after his death in 1539 and was only found again in 1971. One of its carved figures has been variously interpreted as an acrobat or a sheila-na-gig (a carved female figure with exaggerated genitalia).

The 10th-century round tower in the grounds is Ireland's second highest at 32.9m, and one of the few that you can climb, provided the guardian is around. Its original conical roof has been replaced with an unusual Norman battlement. Near the tower is a wishing stone – put your arm through the hole and touch your shoulder and your wish will be granted. On the north side of the cathedral are the heavily restored foundations of an ancient fire temple.

Irish National Stud & Gardens STUD, GARDENS
(☑045-521 617; www.irishnationalstud.ie; Tully; adult/student/child €12.50/9.50/7; ☉9am-6pm mid-Feb–Dec, last admission 5pm) With highlights like the 'Teasing Shed', the Irish Na-

tional Stud, about 3km south of town, is the big attraction in the locality – horse-mad Queen Elizabeth II dropped in during her historic 2011 visit. The stud was founded by Colonel Hall Walker (of Johnnie Walker whiskey fame) in 1900. He was remarkably successful with his horses, but his eccentric breeding technique relied heavily on astrology: the fate of a foal was decided by its horoscope and the roofs of the stallion boxes opened on auspicious occasions to reveal the heavens and duly influence the horses' fortunes. Today the immaculately kept centre is owned and managed by the Irish government. It breeds high-quality stallions to mate with mares from all over the world.

There are guided tours (many of the guides have a real palaver) of the stud every hour on the hour, with access to the intensive-care unit for newborn foals. If you visit between February and June, you might even see a foal being born. Alternatively, the foaling unit shows a 10-minute video with all the action. You can wander the stalls and go eye-to-eye with famous stallions. Given that most are now geldings, they probably have dim memories of their time in the aforementioned Teasing Shed, the place where stallions are stimulated for mating, while dozens look on. The cost: tens of thousands of euros for a top horse.

After the thrill of seeing such prized stallions up close, the revamped Irish Horse Museum is quite disappointing; its celebration of championship horses and the history of horse racing is one step above what you'd expect to see from a really good school project.

Also disappointing are the much-vaunted Japanese Gardens (part of the complex), considered to be the best of their kind in Europe – which doesn't say much for other contenders. Created between 1906 and 1910, they trace the journey from birth to death

COUNTIES WICKLOW & KILDARE KILDARE TOWN

WORTH A TRIP

CASTLETOWN HOUSE

The magnificent Castletown House (☑01-628 8252; www.castletownhouse.ie; Celbridge; adult/child €4.50/3.50; ☉10am-4.45pm Tue-Sun Easter-Oct) simply has no peer. It is Ireland's largest and most imposing Georgian estate, and a testament to the vast wealth enjoyed by the Anglo-Irish gentry during the 18th century.

The house was built between the years 1722 and 1732 for William Conolly (1662–1729), speaker of the Irish House of Commons and, at the time, Ireland's richest man. Born into relatively humble circumstances in Ballyshannon, County Donegal, Conolly made his fortune through land transactions in the uncertain aftermath of the Battle of the Boyne (1690).

The original '16th-century Italian palazzo' design of the house was by the Italian architect Alessandro Galilei (1691–1737) in 1718. In 1724 the project was entrusted to Sir Edward Lovett Pearce (1699–1733).

Inspired by the work of Andrea Palladio, Pearce enlarged the original design of the house and added the colonnades and the terminating pavilions. A highlight of the opulent interior is the Long Gallery, replete with family portraits and exquisite stuccowork by the Francini brothers. (In the US, Thomas Jefferson became a Palladian acolyte and much of official Washington DC is in this style.)

Conolly didn't live to see the completion of his wonder-palace. His widow, Katherine, continued to live at the unfinished house after his death in 1729, and instigated many improvements. Her main architectural contribution was the curious 42.6m obelisk, known locally as the Conolly Folly. Her other offering is the Heath Robinson-esque (or Rube Goldberg-esque, if you prefer) Wonderful Barn (☑01-624 5448; Leixlip; ☉closed to the public), six teetering storeys wrapped by an exterior spiral staircase, on private property just outside Leixlip.

Castletown House remained in the family's hands until 1965, when it was purchased by Desmond Guinness, who restored the house to its original splendour. His investment was continued from 1979 by the Castletown Foundation. In 1994 Castletown House was transferred to state care and today it is managed by the Heritage Service.

Buses 120 and 123 run from Dublin to Celbridge (€3.50, 30 minutes, every half-hour Monday to Friday, hourly Saturday, six buses Sunday).

through 20 landmarks, including the Tunnel of Ignorance, the Hill of Ambition and the Chair of Old Age. When in bloom the flowers are beautiful, but the gardens are too small and bitty to really impress.

St Fiachra's Garden is another bucolic feature, with a mixture of bog oak, gushing water, replica monastic cells and an underground crystal garden of dubious distinction. Both gardens are great for a relaxing stroll though.

The large visitor centre houses the obligatory cafe, shop and children's play area. A tour of the stud and gardens takes about two hours.

Lying outside the site, behind the museum, are the ruins of a 12th-century Black Abbey; and just off the road back to Kildare is St Brigid's Well, where five stones represent different aspects of Brigid's life.

🛏 Sleeping & Eating

Martinstown House   HOTEL €€
(☑ 045-441 269; www.martinstownhouse.com; The Curragh; s/d from €90/150; ⊘ mid-Jan–mid-Dec) This beautiful 18th-century country manor is built in the frilly Strawberry Hill Gothic style and set in a 170-acre estate and farm surrounded by trees. The house has four rooms filled with antiques; children are banned – darn. You can arrange for memorable dinners in advance (€55); ingredients are drawn from the kitchen garden.

Derby House Hotel   HOTEL €€
(☑ 045-522 144; www.derbyhousehotel.ie; s/d €40/70; 🛜🏠) This old hotel has 20 decent rooms right in the centre of town. It's an easy walk from here to bars, restaurants and all the St Brigid lore you could hope for.

Agape   CAFE €
(☑ 045-533 711; Station Rd; meals €6-12; ⊘ 9am-6pm Mon-Sat) Just off Market Sq, this trendy little cafe has a fine range of homemade food. There's a full coffee bar and a menu of salads, soups, sandwiches and tasty hot specials.

❶ Information

Tourist Office & Heritage Centre (☑ 045-521 240; www.kildare.ie; Market House, Market Sq; ⊘ 9.30am-1pm & 2-5.30pm Mon-Sat May-Sep) Has an exhibition (admission free) outlining Kildare's history. There's also local art for sale.

❶ Getting There & Away

There is frequent Bus Éireann service between Dublin's Busáras and Kildare (single/return €12.50/19.50, 1¾ hours). Some Dublin buses also service the Stud.

The Dublin–Kildare **train** (☑ 01-836 6222) runs from Heuston train station and stops in Kildare (€16.50, 35 minutes, one to four per hour). This is a major junction and trains continue to numerous places including Ballina, Galway, Limerick and Waterford.

Donnelly's Hollow to Castledermot

This 25km stretch south towards Carlow contains some interesting detours to tiny towns bypassed by the speedy but unlovely N9.

Donnelly's Hollow

Dan Donnelly (1788–1820) is revered as Ireland's greatest bare-knuckle fighter of the 19th century. He's also the stuff of legend – his arms were so long he could supposedly tie his shoelaces without having to bend down. This spot, 4km west of Kilcullen on the R413, was his favourite battleground, and the obelisk at the centre of the hollow details his glorious career.

Ballitore

POP 338
Low-key Ballitore is the only planned and permanent Quaker settlement in Ireland. It was founded by incomers from Yorkshire in the early 18th century. A small Quaker Museum (☑ 059-862 3344; Mary Leadbeater House, Main St; admission by donation; ⊘ noon-5pm Tue-Sat year-round, 2-6pm Sun Jun-Sep), in a tiny restored house, documents the lives of the community (including the namesake former owner who was known for her aversion to war). There's a Quaker cemetery and Meeting House, and a modern Shaker Store (☑ 059-862 3372; www.shakerstore.ie; Main St; ⊘ 10am-6pm Mon-Fri, from 2pm Sat & Sun), which sells delightfully humble wooden toys and furniture. It also has a tearoom.

About 2km west is Rath of Mullaghmast, an Iron Age hill fort and standing stone where Daniel O'Connell, champion of Catholic emancipation, held one of his 'monster rallies' in 1843.

Moone

POP 380

Just south of Ballitore, the unassuming village of Moone is home to one of Ireland's most magnificent high crosses. The unusually tall and slender Moone High Cross is an 8th- or 9th-century masterpiece, which displays its carved biblical scenes with the confidence and exuberance of a comic strip. The cross can be found 1km west of Moone village and the N9 in an atmospheric early Christian churchyard. Old stone ruins add to the mood of the drive.

The solid, stone 18th-century Moone High Cross Inn (☑ 059-862 4112; www. moonehighcrossinnonline.com; Bolton Hill; s/d from €50/80), 2km south of Moone, has five rooms decorated in quaint country-house style. The delightful bar downstairs serves good pub lunches and there's a proper restaurant (mains €12-19; ⊗ 6-8.30pm), which uses local and organic ingredients. The inn revolves around a Celtic theme, celebrating pagan festivals and hoarding healing stones, lucky charms and even a 'love stone' in the outside courtyards.

Castledermot

POP 1160

Castledermot was once home to a vast ecclesiastical settlement, but all that remains of St Diarmuid's 9th-century monastery is a 20m round tower topped with a medieval battlement. Nearby are two well-preserved, carved, 10th-century granite high crosses; a 12th-century Romanesque doorway; and a medieval Scandinavian 'hogback' gravestone, the only one in Ireland. Reach the ruins by entering the rusty gate on all-too-busy Main St (N9), then walking up the tree-lined avenue to St James' church. At the southern end of town, the ruins of an early-14th-century Franciscan friary can be seen alongside the road.

Counties Wexford, Waterford, Carlow & Kilkenny

POP 507,000 / AREA 7193 SQ KM

Includes ➡

Best Historic Buildings

➡ Hook Head Lighthouse (p172)

➡ Kilkenny Castle (p174)

➡ Reginald's Tower (p180)

➡ Jerpoint Abbey (p211)

➡ Kells Priory (p175)

➡ Tintern Abbey (p173)

Best Gardens

➡ Johnstown Castle & Gardens (p168)

➡ Duckett's Grove (p195)

➡ Altamont Gardens (p195)

➡ Delta Sensory Gardens (p195)

➡ Huntington Castle (p198)

Why Go?

Counties Wexford, Waterford, Carlow and Kilkenny are (along with the southern chunk of Tipperary) collectively referred to as the 'sunny southeast'. This being Ireland the term is, of course, relative. But it *is* the country's warmest, driest region. A golden tiara of wide sandy beaches graces the counties of Wexford and Waterford. There are plenty of eye-catching gems here as well, including picturesque fishing villages, elegant seaside towns and dramatic windswept peninsulas. If you're looking for real sparkle, check out the world-acclaimed Waterford crystal. Deeper inland, the meandering River Barrow separates the verdant counties of Carlow and Kilkenny. County Carlow offers farm-filled spaces, country lodgings and flowering estates. County Kilkenny's namesake city is the urban star with a castle, cathedral, medieval lanes and superb pubs and restaurants. The region's history is suitably swashbuckling with marauding Vikings, shadowy knights' sects and some of the country's most impressive fortresses and castles.

When to Go

➡ June to September is the best time for enjoying the superb beaches, seafront cafes and restaurants

➡ April to October is good for hiking and walking, although be sure to pack waterproof gear and warm clothing

➡ October to early November is great for music lovers with Wexford's world-acclaimed opera festival, while country and trad music fans should head for Kilkenny's *Celtic Festival* also held at this time of year

➡ Spring and autumn are the best months to visit if you are economising as prices (and tourists) dip when compared to mid-summer.

COUNTY WEXFORD

POP 145,273

County Wexford's navigable rivers and fertile land have long lured invaders and privateers. The Vikings founded Ireland's first major towns on the wide, easy-flowing River Slaney, which cuts through the middle of the county. The most enjoyable modern way for visitors to appreciate Wexford's swashbuckling maritime history is pausing in pretty waterfront villages and sampling catches from the surrounding waves.

Wexford Town

POP 19,913

At first glance, Wexford (Loch Garman) appears a sleepy port town with a silted estuary that sees considerably less traffic than Waterford and Rosslare Harbour. However, there are reminders of its glorious Viking and Norman past in the meandering lanes off Main St – as well as some medieval monuments. It's a pleasant pause if you're looking for an urban break from the coast.

History

The Vikings named it Waesfjord (meaning 'harbour of mud flats') and its handy location near the mouth of the Slaney encouraged landings as early as AD 850. The town was captured by the Normans in 1169; traces of their fort can still be seen in the grounds of the Irish National Heritage Park.

Cromwell included Wexford in his destructive Irish tour from 1649 to 1650. Around 1500 of the town's 2000 inhabitants were killed, including all the Franciscan friars. During the 1798 Rising, rebels made a determined, bloody stand before being defeated.

⊙ Sights

Wexford doesn't have any don't-miss museums, but you can sense its deep history on a two-hour stroll. The waterfront has been spiffed up and makes for lazy rambles past docked boats.

★ **St Iberius' Church**   CHURCH
(North Main St; ⊙10am-5pm May-Sep, to 3pm Oct-Apr) South of the Bull Ring, St Iberius' Church was built in 1760 on the site of several previous churches. Oscar Wilde's forebears were rectors here. The Renaissance-style frontage is worth a look, but the real treat is the Georgian interior with its finely crafted altar rails and set of 18th-century

monuments in the gallery. The church is also famed for its superb acoustics.

★ **Bull Ring**   HISTORIC SITE
Originally a beach where provisions were boated into the city, the Bull Ring became a centre for bull baiting in medieval times: the town's butchers gained their guild charter by providing a bull annually for the sport. The Lone Pikeman statue commemorates the participants in the 1798 Rising, who used the place as an open-air armaments factory. These days the Bull Ring is the site of the weekly Bull Ring Market (p168).

Westgate   LANDMARK
The only survivor of the six original town gates is the 14th-century Westgate. It was originally a tollgate, and the recesses used by the toll collectors are still intact, as is the lockup used to incarcerate 'runagates' – those who tried to avoid paying.

Selskar Abbey   RUIN
After Henry II murdered his former ally Thomas Becket, he did penance at Selskar Abbey, founded by Alexander de la Roche in 1190. Basilia, the sister of Robert FitzGilbert de Clare (better known as Strongbow), is thought to have married one of Henry II's lieutenants in the abbey. Its present ruinous state is a result of Cromwell's visit in 1649.

Franciscan Friary   HISTORIC BUILDING
(School St; ⊙10am-6pm) FREE In 1649 Cromwell's forces made a bonfire of the original 13th-century Franciscan Friary, so most of the present building dates from the 19th century. Only two original walls remain. The friary houses a relic and wax effigy of St Adjutor, a boy martyr slain by his own father in ancient Rome.

Keyser's Lane   HISTORIC SITE
Duck your head and dart down Keyser's Lane, a covered passage off North Main St that dates back to Norse times.

⊙ Tours

Walking tours (www.wexfordwalkingtours.com; tour €4; ⊙11am Mon-Sat Mar-Oct) of Wexford are the best way to understand its complicated past and confusing remains. The 90-minute walks depart from the tourist office.

🎊 Festivals & Events

Wexford Festival Opera   OPERA
(www.wexfordopera.com; tickets €20-30; ⊙late Oct-early Nov) An 18-day extravaganza held at

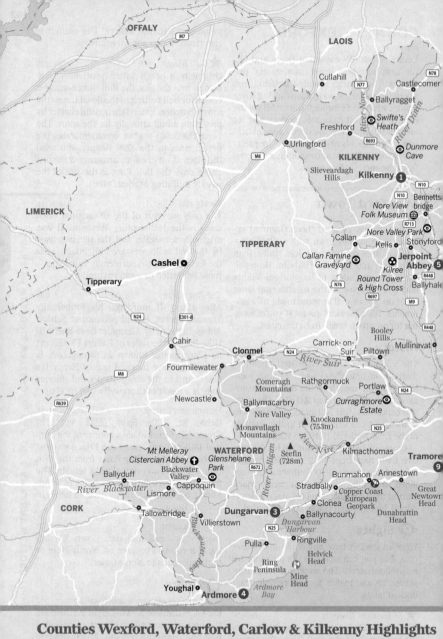

Counties Wexford, Waterford, Carlow & Kilkenny Highlights

❶ Revel in the urban pleasures of **Kilkenny** (p197), one of Ireland's most vibrant cities

❷ Learn about Ireland's poignant history aboard the **Dunbrody Famine Ship** (p174) in New Ross

❸ Savour a slice of foodie heaven at **Dungarvan** (p187), home of top chefs

❹ Immerse yourself in County Waterford's coastal beauty around historic **Ardmore** (p190)

❺ Get into monk mode at the evocative ruins of **Jerpoint**

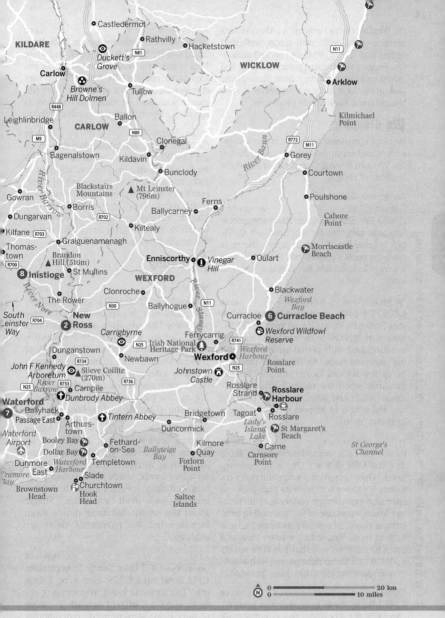

Abbey (p211) in County Kilkenny

6 Walk to the end of **Curracloe Beach** (p169) near Wexford, a seemingly endless vision of white powder

7 Relive the days of the Normans in the excellent museums of **Waterford** (p178)

8 Meander by the river in picturesque **Inistioge**

9 Brave the cold, don the wetsuit and catch some waves at **Tramore** (p185), the region's premier surfing spot

the Wexford Opera House, this is the country's premier opera event with rarely performed operas and shows playing to packed audiences. Fringe street theatre, poetry readings and exhibitions give the town a fiesta atmosphere, and many local bars run amateur singing competitions. Book tickets in advance.

🛏️ Sleeping

Wexford's proximity to Dublin attracts weekenders, and accommodation is scarce during the Wexford Festival Opera. Otherwise there is plenty of choice.

Ferrybank Camping & Caravan Park   CAMPGROUND €

(☑ 053-918 5256; www.wexfordswimmingpool.ie; Ferrybank; campsites per adult/child/tent €9.50/5/5; ⊙ Easter-Sep; ⊚) Right across the river from the centre, council-run Ferrybank is in a windy location but has fantastic views of town.

★ McMenamin's Townhouse   B&B €€

(☑ 053-914 6442; www.wexford-bedandbreakfast. com; Spawell Rd, 6 Glena Tce; s/d from €65/90; ⊚) Rooms at this red-brick late-Victorian B&B are furnished with period antiques including canopied beds (no Ikea pine numbers here). You are well looked after, not least at breakfast when the menu features homemade breads and jams, rum-laced porridge and the option of kippers or lamb kidneys in sherry (even).

Whites of Wexford   HOTEL €€

(☑ 053-912 2311; www.whitesofwexford.ie; Abbey St; r from €109; @⊚⊛) This is no ordinary hotel. White's is not only a contemporary colossus, it's super cool with its high-tech spa specialty: cryotherapy (extreme cold therapy). Warm up at one of the welcoming bars, enjoy a choice of restaurants or just retreat to your room. Request an estuary view and pay €10 more for one that has been slickly updated – all metal right-angles, tech touches and sparkling glass. Breakfast included.

Cuasnog   B&B €€

(☑ 053-912 3637; www.cuasnog.com; St John's Rd; r from €75; ⊚) Located a few minutes' walk from the centre in a sleepy residential street, hosts Caitriona and Theo not only extend a warm welcome – they treat you to smoked salmon on arrival as well. The compact rooms have a comfortable spare-room feel with rustic furniture and fireplaces. Breakfast includes homemade scones and local organic produce.

Abbey B&B   B&B €€

(☑ 053-912 4408; www.abbeyhouse.ie; 34-36 Abbey St; s/d €45/80; ⊚) This cute black-and-white B&B blazes with window boxes trailing red blooms in summer. Its seven rooms vary considerably in size, but all have private bathrooms with walk-in showers. Breakfast is served in a cheery floral-themed dining room.

Talbot Hotel   HOTEL €€

(☑ 053-912 2566; www.talbotwexford.ie; Trinity St; s/d €85/110; @⊚⊛) A landmark on Wexford's quay front, this hotel, established in 1905, has water views from many of its recently revamped rooms. Facilities include a steam room, sauna, gym and indoor pool. The stylish high-ceiling Ballast Bar dishes up traditional pub grub along with regular live music. Breakfast included.

🍴 Eating

★ Lotus House   ASIAN €

(70A South Main St; mains €10-12; ⊙ 12.30-10.30pm) The menu here is predominantly Chinese with some Thai favourites, such as Tom Yum soup. The stir fries here are renowned – choose from several options, including Tiger prawns, and select an accompanying sauce; the spicy satay comes warmly recommended. Decor is tasteful (ie no migraine-inducing moving pictures) and there's a handy adjoining off-licence for BYO booze.

Sky View Cafe   CAFE €

(Wexford Opera House, High St; snacks €6-12; ⊙ 10am-4pm Mon-Sat; ⊚) Whisk up to the 3rd floor of Wexford's snazzy opera house for salad bowls, sandwiches, baked potatoes and daily specials. Drink highlights include fresh fruit smoothies. Shame about the mildly utilitarian dining room furniture but the panoramic views are sublime.

Yard   MODERN IRISH €€

(www.theyard.ie; 3 Lower George St; lunch mains €9-12, dinner mains €17-25; ⊙ noon-3pm & 6pm-late) This intimate low-lit restaurant opens to an elegant courtyard beneath a canopy of fairy lights. Adventurous contemporary cuisine changes with the season, with an emphasis on fresh and unfussy; think wild-mushroom risotto, potato-and-herb fishcakes and similar.

★ Greenacres   DELI, BISTRO €€€

(www.greenacres.ie; 7 Selskar St; mains €20-30; ⊙ Deli 9am-6pm Mon-Sat, noon-6pm Sun; Bistro

Wexford Town

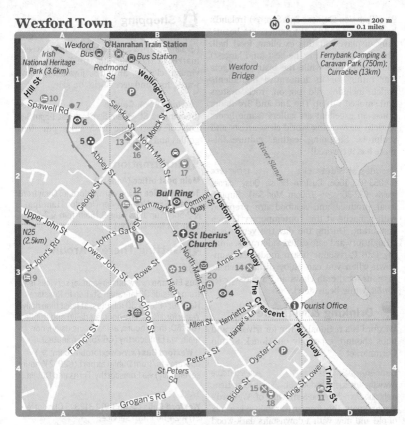

Wexford Town

◎ Top Sights
1 Bull Ring...B2
2 St Iberius' Church................................B3

◎ Sights
3 Franciscan Friary................................B3
4 Keyser's Lane......................................C3
   Lone Pikeman Statue......................(see 1)
5 Selskar Abbey.....................................A2
6 Westgate..A1

⊙ Activities, Courses & Tours
7 Walking Tours.....................................A1

⊟ Sleeping
8 Abbey B&B..B2
9 Cuasnog...A3
10 McMenamin's Townhouse..................A1
11 Talbot Hotel..D4
12 Whites of Wexford..............................B2

⊗ Eating
13 Greenacres...B2
14 Jacques at Sidetracks........................C3
15 Lotus House...C4
   Sky View Cafe...................................(see 19)
16 Yard..B2

⊙ Drinking & Nightlife
17 Centenary Stores................................B2
18 Sky & the Ground................................C4

⊗ Entertainment
19 Wexford Opera House.........................B3

⊟ Shopping
   Bull Ring Market..............................(see 1)
20 Wexford Book Centre.........................C3

9am-10pm Mon-Sat, noon-8pm Sun; 🖥) Ireland's best cheeses and local products are beautifully displayed at this excellent food hall. The wine selection is the best (and largest) south of Dublin while the bistro also gets star rating for its innovative ingredients which include wild pigeon, rock oysters and smoked rabbit. The 2nd and 3rd floors house an excellent art gallery (same hours as deli) showcasing world-class artists and sculptors. Shopping, eating, culture...this place has it covered!

Jacques at Sidetracks FRENCH €€€
(📞053-912 1666; Custom House Quay; dinner mains €22-30; ⊘6-9.30pm Mon-Sat) Superb local produce and seafood are prepared with panache at this contemporary French restaurant. During the day the venue is a straightforward cafe called Sidetracks, shifting into Parisienne bistro mode post sundown when you can enjoy dishes such as luscious local crab claws and a classic *cassoulet* (white-bean stew).

🍺 Drinking & Nightlife

Wexford is a regional centre for frivolity and pubs abound, especially on Monck St and Cornmarket.

Centenary Stores PUB, NIGHTCLUB
(www.thestores.ie; Charlotte St; ⊘pub 10am-11pm, nightclub 9pm-2am Thu-Sun) One of Wexford's livelier spots, this former warehouse is a mix of old and new with a downstairs dark-wood pub with basic food and a crusty local clientele, contrasted with a pulsating nightclub, the Backroom, that attracts a spirited youthful crowd at weekends. Enjoy the pub's Sunday lunchtime trad music sessions in summer.

Sky & the Ground PUB
(www.theskyandtheground.com; 112-113 South Main St; ⊘2-11.30pm Mon-Thu, 1pm-12.30am Fri-Sat, to 11pm Sun) A longstanding Wexford favourite, the Sky & the Ground's decor is classic, with enamel signage and a roaring fire. Trad music sessions often take place on weeknights and during the summer there's an upstairs outdoor deck.

☆ Entertainment

Wexford Opera House OPERA
(www.wexfordoperahouse.ie; High St; tickets €20-40) Opened in 2008, Wexford's gleaming opera house packs more architectural punch inside than out. In addition to opera, it stages theatre productions and concerts.

🛍 Shopping

Bull Ring Market CRAFTS
(⊘9am-2pm Fri & Sat) There is a lively weekly market at the Bull Ring (p163) with crafts, vintage clothes, antiques, jewellery, homewares, toys and accessories on sale.

Wexford Book Centre BOOKS
(5 South Main St; ⊘9am-6pm Mon-Sat, 1-5pm Sun) Lots of worthwhile Irish titles plus local guides and maps.

ℹ Information

Main post office (Anne St)

Tourist office (www.visitwexford.ie; Quayfront; ⊘9am-6pm Mon-Sat Apr-Oct plus 11am-1pm & 2-5pm Sun Jul & Aug, 9.15am-1pm & 2-5pm Mon-Sat Nov-Mar; 🖥)

ℹ Getting There & Around

BUS

Bus Éireann (www.buseireann.ie) services leave from outside O'Hanrahan Station to Rosslare Harbour (€5.50, 30 minutes, at least nine daily), Waterford (€10, one hour, six daily) and Dublin (€17.60, three hours, at least nine daily), normally via Enniscorthy (€6.75, 25 minutes).

Wexford Bus (www.wexfordbus.com; 🖥) operates to/from Dublin airport (€20, 2¾ hours, seven daily) via Enniscorthy, Ferns and Dublin.

TAXI

Wexford Cabs (📞053-912 3123; 3 Charlotte St) A 24-hour taxi service.

TRAIN

Irish Rail (www.irishrail.ie) has a service to Dublin Connolly (€17.60, 2½ hours) and Waterford (€10, 55 minutes) from **O'Hanrahan Station** (📞053-912 2522; Redmond Sq).

Around Wexford Town

◉ Sights

★ **Johnstown Castle & Gardens** MUSEUM, GARDENS
(combined ticket adult/child €8/4, gardens only €3/1; ⊘9am-4.30pm; 🖥♿) Parading peacocks guard this splendid 19th-century castellated house, the former home of the once-mighty Fitzgerald and Esmonde families. The empty castle overlooks a small lake and is surrounded by 20 hectares of beautiful wooded gardens complete with a sunken Italian garden, statues and waterfalls.

In the castle outbuildings, the Irish Agricultural Museum (www.irishagrimuseum.ie; combined ticket adult/child €8/4, gardens only €3/1; ⊙ gardens 9am-5.30pm daily, May-Sep, to 4.30 Oct-Apr; museum 9am-5pm Mon-Fri, 11am-5pm Sat & Sun; 9am-4pm Mon-Fri, noon-4pm Sat & Sun, Nov-Mar) has a bounty of items that will excite the tractor set, plus an exhibition about the Great Famine and quizzes and trails geared towards children. A cafe opens here in July and August.

The castle is 7km southwest of Wexford town.

Irish National Heritage Park   MUSEUM
(www.inhp.com; Ferrycarrig; adult/child €9/4.50; ⊙ 9.30am-6.30pm May-Aug, to 5.30pm Sep-Apr; 🔾) Over 9000 years of Irish history are squeezed together at this open-air museum. After a short audiovisual presentation, select a guided or audio self-guided tour, taking in a recreated Neolithic farmstead, stone circle, ring fort, monastery, *crannóg* (artificial island), Viking shipyard and Norman castle (on the site of original Norman fort remains). Activities include archery and an adventure playground. There is an excellent casual dining restaurant on site.

Wexford Wildfowl Reserve   NATURE RESERVE
(☑ 076-100 2660; www.wexfordwildfowlreserve.ie; North Slob; guided tours on request; ⊙ 9am-5pm) FREE Sitting below sea level and protected by Dutch-style dikes, this vast natural area protects a bird habitat and has an observation tower, assorted hides and a visitor centre with detailed exhibits. The name Slob may not sound inspiring (it derives from the Irish *slab*, meaning 'mud' or 'mire'), but the reserve inspires awe among birdwatchers. Each winter, it's home to one-third of the world's population of Greenland white-fronted geese – some 10,000 in total. Winter is also a good time to spot the Brent goose from the Canadian Arctic.

From Wexford, head north for 3km on the R741 towards Dublin and follow the signs.

Rosslare Strand
POP 1300

Surrounded by suburban-style homes, Rosslare (Ros Láir) town is rather soulless but opens onto a glorious Blue Flag beach. In summer the beach is the habitat of hordes of ice-cream-fuelled children. In winter the empty sands billow at the feet of the occasional solitary walker.

WORTH A TRIP

CURRACLOE BEACH

White powdery sand, gentle lapping surf and a lack of development are the most appealing aspects of the 11km-long, Blue Flag–rated Curracloe Beach. On sunny days when the temp cracks 20°C (68°F) families flock here, but due to the size you can easily find a half-acre to call your own. Walks on the strand and among the dunes go on and on. There are scattered parking sites and toilets.

Many of the birds found at the Wexford Wildfowl Reserve can also be seen at Curracloe's Raven Nature Reserve. It's signposted 13km northeast of Wexford (from Wexford, take the R741).

The long shallow bay is perfect for windsurfing. During the summer months, gear hire for a range of watersports is available at Rosslare Watersports Centre (www.rosslareholidayresort.ie).

🛏 Sleeping & Eating
B&Bs and pubs with fish and chips are as common as driftwood on the beach after a storm.

Killiane Castle   APARTMENTS €€
(☑ 053-915 8885; www.killianecastle.com; Drinagh; s/d from €75/100, 2-person apt from €75; 🔾🔾) Sleep in a castle... This farmhouse lodge is in a 17th-century house attached to a 13th-century Norman fort. Guests can climb the tower for panoramas of the surrounding countryside and coastline. Self-catering apartments are set in the leafy grounds, which also accommodate a golf range, tennis court, croquet lawn and nature trails. Head northeast of the N25 en route to Wexford.

★ Kelly's Resort Hotel   RESORT €€€
(☑ 053-913 2114; www.kellys.ie; Strand Rd; s/d from €90/180; @🔾🔾🔾) Established in 1895 and run by the fourth generation of the same family, this seaside family resort is an Irish institution. While the service remains delightfully old-fashioned and personal, the property is continually updated, with bright, contemporary rooms, jazzy art work and extensive facilities, including tennis, crazy golf, snooker, badminton, yoga, croquet, restaurants, bars and a state-of-the-art spa.

La Marine FRENCH €€

(📞 053-32114; Kelly's Resort Hotel; lunch mains €11-16, dinner mains €18-25; ⏱ noon-10pm; 📶 ♿) The wonderful Gallic bistro-bar at Kelly's has the most sophisticated menu south of Wexford city. Tasteful paintings line the walls in the rustic-style dining room with additional deck seating for those rare alfresco days. Local produce features in dishes such as St Helens crab linguine, plus there's a healthy children's menu.

ℹ Getting There & Away

Wexford Bus (📞 053-914 2742; www.wexford bus.com) runs four daily buses to Wexford (€4, 40 minutes).

On the main Dublin–Wexford–Rosslare Harbour line, **Irish Rail** (www.irishrail.ie) runs three trains per day to Rosslare Strand (from Dublin €23, three hours); from Wexford (€5, 20 minutes); and from Rosslare Europort (€5, 10 minutes).

Rosslare Harbour

POP 1475

Busy, functional Rosslare Harbour has connections to Wales and France from the Europort ferry terminal, home also to Rosslare Europort train station. A road leading uphill from the harbour becomes the N25. The main reason to stay here is if you have an early ferry out.

🛏 Sleeping & Eating

St Martin's Rd is lined with B&Bs that cater for ferry-catchers and there are plenty of pubs serving standard fare.

THIRST FOR KNOWLEDGE

During a hunting trip to the Slobs near Wexford in the 1950s, the Guinness Brewery's managing director, Sir Hugh Beaver, shot at but missed a golden plover. A spirited debate ensued among his hunting party over whether it, or the red grouse, was Europe's fastest game bird. Sir Hugh realised that similar debates regularly cropped up in pubs, and that publishing definitive answers could resolve them (over pints of Guinness, of course). He was right on that score (today the *Guinness Book of World Records* is a record-holder itself, as the biggest-selling copyrighted book in the world), but wrong about Europe's fastest game bird (it's the spur-wing goose).

★ **O'Leary's Farmhouse B&B** B&B €€

(📞 053-913 3134; www.olearysfarm.com; Killilane, Kilrane; s/d €45/70; 📶) Slightly out of town, the O'Leary family raises rare breeds of sheep and cattle at this working farm. There are four homey guest rooms, three with sea views, and the bathrooms sport smart black-and-white tiling (and similar) and powerful high-pressure showers. The delightful sitting room has a fireplace, piano and plenty of books. Breakfast includes vegan, vegetarian and coeliac options and the farm's produce, plus homemade bread.

To reach here follow the N25 until Kilrane and turn off between the two pubs – the Kilrane Inn and Culleton's – and follow the signs.

Harbour View Hotel HOTEL €€

(📞 053-916 1450; www.harbourviewhotel.ie; Cliff Rd; s/d from €45/90; 📶) Service at this buttercup-yellow hotel melts away the Europort's hulking presence, as do its sprightly, colourful rooms. The hotel's Mail Boat bar and bistro is popular with locals and good for a handful of sustaining dishes, ranging from sandwiches to stir-fries.

ℹ Getting There & Away

Buses and trains depart from the Rosslare Europort station, located at the ferry terminal.

BOAT

Rosslare ferries link Ireland to Wales and France.

Irish Ferries (www.irishferries.com) Sails to Pembroke in Wales (foot passenger €35, car and driver from €89, four hours, two daily). Also has ferries to Cherbourg, France (foot passenger €64, car and driver from €100, 19½ hours, up to three weekly mid-February to mid-December); and with similar fares to Roscoff, France.

Stena Line (www.stenaline.ie) Sails to Fishguard in Wales (foot passenger €35, car and driver from €99, one or two sailings per day). The crossing takes between two and 3½ hours.

BUS

Bus Éireann (📞 053-912 2522; www.buseir eann.ie) Services to numerous Irish towns and cities, including Dublin (€20, three hours, at least nine daily) via Wexford (€5.50, 30 minutes), and Cork (€25, four hours, three to five daily) via Waterford (€18, 1½ hours).

TRAIN

Irish Rail (www.irishrail.ie) run four trains daily on the Rosslare Europort–Dublin route: to Wexford (€5.60, 25 minutes) and to Dublin Connolly Station (€26, three hours).

South of Rosslare Harbour

The village of Carne has pretty, white-washed thatched cottages and a fine beach. It's lovely to ride or drive along these beachy backroads.

Lobster Pot (Carne; lunch mains €8-12, dinner mains €20-35; ⊙ restaurant dinner Tue-Sun, bar food noon-7.30pm Tue-Sun, closed Jan) packs in locals and visitors in summer but it's worth the squeeze to get at the fab fresh seafood. The chowder, brimming with cockles, mussels, prawns, salmon, crab and cod, is among the best anywhere.

Heading back up the road takes you past Lady's Island Lake containing Our Lady's Island, site of an early Augustinian priory and still a centre of devotion. Fervent pilgrims used to crawl round the island; people still walk it barefoot. When it's not water-logged, you can drive out to the castle on the island and walk a 2km circuit taking in the shrine.

St Margaret's Beach Caravan & Camping Park (☑053-913 1169; www.campingstmargarets.ie; St Margaret's Beach; camp sites per adult/child/tent €12/6/4, caravan rental per day from €50; ⊙ mid-Mar–Oct; 🐾) is a well-equipped campground 500m from the beach which also rents out small caravans.

Kilmore Quay

POP 417

Kilmore Quay is a small, working fishing village with thatched cottages and a harbour which is the jumping-off point for Ireland's largest bird sanctuary, the Saltee Islands. The cry of gulls and smell of the sea provide an appropriate atmosphere for sampling the local fish.

⊙ Sights & Activities

Sandy beaches stretch northwest and northeast from Forlorn Point (Crossfarnoge). There are some signposted walking trails behind the peaceful dunes, circled by serenading skylarks.

Wrecks such as the SS *Isolde* and SS *Ardmore,* both dating back to the 1940s, and extraordinary marine life keep divers enthralled. Contact Wexford Sub Aqua Club (www.divewexford.org) for info.

The local website, www.kilmorequayweb.com, has links to local activities such as fishing boat charters.

Ballycross Apple Farm   FARM
(☑053-913 5160; www.ballycross.com; Bridgetown; walking trails adult/child €2/1.50; ⊙ 11am-6pm Sat & Sun mid-May-Sep; 🐾) About 9km north of Kilmore Quay, Ballycross sells its apples, apple juices, chutneys and jams direct to the public. There are also delicious homemade waffles and several signposted walking trails that run via riverbanks, woodland and orchards throughout the farm.

🎊 Festivals & Events

Seafood Festival   FOOD
(www.kilmorequayseafoodfestival.com; ⊙ Jul) Mussel in on this four-day festival for music, dancing and fishy fare.

🛏 Sleeping & Eating

Mill Road Farm   B&B €€
(☑053-912 9633; www.millroadfarm.com; R739; s/d €45/70; ⊙ closed late Dec; 🐾) About 2km northeast of Kilmore Quay, this working dairy farm has four daintily decorated guest rooms with lots of floral fabrics (three with sea views beyond the paddock); the owner breeds horses for racing. The sitting room has plenty of games and books for wet days; breakfast includes homemade bread and free-range eggs.

Crazy Crab   SEAFOOD €€
(www.crazycrab.ie; Kilmore Quay; mains €14-20; ⊙ Thu 5-9pm, Fri-Sun noon-9pm) Nab a table on the sea-view patio at this simple place with its nautical themed blue-and-white frontage and porthole-style windows. All manner of fresh local seafood is on offer, ranging from classic fish and chips to classy pan-fried scallops.

Silver Fox Seafood Restaurant   SEAFOOD €€€
(www.thesilverfox.ie; Kilmore Quay; mains €16-32; ⊙ noon-10pm May-Sep, reduced hours other times; 🐾) The Silver Fox's fresh-from-the-ocean offerings include Kilmore Quay plaice, prawns and salmon, plus daily specials depending on what arrives at the docks. The dining room exudes white-table-clothed elegance – don't arrive in flip-flops. The restaurant also produces and sells a range of jams, chutneys, fish spreads, and similar items.

ℹ Getting There & Away

Wexford Bus (www.wexfordbus.com) Runs to/from Wexford up to four times daily (€7, 45 minutes).

Saltee Islands

Once the haunt of privateers, smugglers and 'dyvars pyrates', the Saltee Islands (www.salteeislands.info; ⊙visits 11.30am-4pm) now have a peaceful existence as one of Europe's most important bird sanctuaries. Over 375 recorded species make their home here, principally the gannet, guillemot, cormorant, kittiwake, puffin, auk and Manx shearwater. The best time to visit is the spring and early-summer nesting season. The birds leave once the chicks can fly, and by early August it's eerily quiet.

The two islands are privately owned. The 90-hectare Great Saltee and the 40-hectare Little Saltee (closed to visits) were inhabited as long ago as 3500 to 2000 BC. From the 13th century until the dissolution of the monasteries, they were the property of Tintern Abbey, after which various owners were granted the land.

Boats make the trip from Kilmore Quay harbour, but docking depends on the wind direction and is often impossible. Book through Declan Bates (☏087 252 9736, 053-912 9684; day trip €25). Note that there are no facilities on the island, including toilets.

Hook Peninsula & Around

The road shadowing the long, tapering finger of the Hook Peninsula is signposted as the Ring of Hook coastal drive. Around every other bend is a quiet beach, a crumbling fortress, a stately abbey or a seafood restaurant, and the world's oldest working lighthouse is flung out at its tip.

Strongbow (Robert FitzGilbert de Clare, Earl of Pembroke) landed here on his way to capture Waterford in 1170, reputedly instructing his men to land 'by Hook or by Crooke', the latter referring to the nearby settlement of Crooke in County Waterford across the harbour.

Fethard-on-Sea

POP 325

Fethard is one of the largest villages in the area. The short main drag has cafes and pubs and there are several B&Bs. The community run tourist office (☏051-397 502; www.hooktourism.com; Wheelhouse Cafe, Main St; ⊙10am-6pm May-Sep) covers the region

⊙ Sights & Activities

Fethard is home to the scant ruins of 9th-century St Mogue's and the unstable ruins of a 15th-century castle, which belonged to the bishop of Ferns. The small harbour is worth a visit for its views.

Southeast Ireland is popular with surfers and has many good dive sites, especially around Hook Head.

Freedom Surf School   SURFING
(☏086 391 4908; www.freedomsurfschool.com; Carnivan Beach; surfboard hire €15, surf lessons from €35; ⊙9am-7pm Jun-Sep, 10am-4pm Oct-May; ⊕) Located on the main surfing beach, this professionally run outfit has great facilities, including hot showers, changing rooms and complimentary tea and coffee.

Monkey's Rock Surf Shop   SURFING
(☏087 647 2068; Main St; ⊙11am-5pm Sat & Sun Jun-Sep; ⊕) Only open on summer weekends but with a good range of wetsuits, surfboards, bodyboards and boating accessories for hire.

Hook Head & Around

The journey from Fethard to Hook Head takes in a hypnotic stretch of horizon, with few houses between the flat, open fields on the tapering peninsula. Views extend across Waterford Harbour and, on a clear day, as far as the Comeragh and Galtee Mountains.

This is prime day-trip country from either Wexford or Waterford. Villages such as Slade, where the most activity is in the swirl of seagulls above the ruined castle and harbour, are beguiling. Beaches include the wonderfully secluded Dollar Bay and Booley Bay just beyond Templetown en route to Duncannon.

⊙ Sights

★Hook Head Lighthouse   LIGHTHOUSE
(www.hookheritage.ie; adult/child €6/3.50; ⊙9.30am-5pm; ⊕⊕) On its southern tip, Hook Head is capped by the world's oldest working lighthouse. It's said that monks first lit a beacon on the head in the 5th century and the first Viking invaders were so happy to have a guiding light that they left them alone. In the early 13th century William Marshal erected a more permanent structure, which is still standing today under its black-and-white exterior. Access is by half-hour guided tour, which includes a climb up the 115 steps for great views. The visitor cen-

DON'T MISS

TINTERN ABBEY

In better structural condition than its Welsh counterpart, from where its first monks hailed, Ireland's moody **Tintern Abbey** (Salt mills; adult/child €3/1; ◷10am-4pm) is secluded amid 40 hectares of woodland. William Marshal, Earl of Pembroke, founded the Cistercian abbey in the early 13th century after he nearly perished at sea and swore to establish a church if he made it ashore. You can still clearly see the cloister walls, nave crossing tower, chancel and south transept chapels.

The abbey sits amidst trails, lined with the twisted trunks of bay trees like the work of some mad sculptor. There are lakes and streams as well as crumbling ruins, including a small single-cell church. The highlight, though, is the beautiful 1-hectare **Colclough Walled Garden** (www.colcloughwalledgarden.com; Tintern Abbey), which has recently been replanted and restored to its former glory.

The grounds are always open and the visitor's centre and gift shop will have been rebuilt by the time by the time you read this, after a suspicious fire burned down the centre (along with the abbey's historic stables) in July 2012.

Tintern Abbey is signposted off the R734, around 5km north of Fethard.

tre has a small cafe while the grassy grounds and surrounding shore are popular for **picnics** and **walks**.

Loftus Hall HAUNTED TOURS
(☏051-397 728; www.loftushall.com; Hook Peninsula; adult/child €9/5; ◷11am-6pm ; 🅿) About 3.5km northeast of the Hook Head lighthouse, this ghostly manor house gazes across the estuary of The Three Sisters over to Dunmore East. Dating from the 1600s, Loftus Hall was re-built by the Marquis of Ely in the 1870s. Famed as being one of the most haunted houses in Ireland, it opened for tours at Halloween in 2012.

The first two tours of the day are historical, while subsequent tours are deemed "spooky" and comprise an hour long interactive visit when the guide will recount the ghostly history of the building, including spine-chilling accounts of its notorious visitor one stormy night 250 years ago. Check the website for special events.

🏃 Activities

There are brilliant, blustery **walks** on both sides of Hook Head. Poke around the tide pools while watching for surprise showers from blowholes on the western side of the peninsula. The rocks around the shore are Carboniferous limestone, rich in **fossils**. Search carefully and you may find 350-million-year-old shells and tiny disc-like pieces of crinoids, a type of starfish. A good place to hunt is **Patrick's Bay**, on the southeast of the peninsula.

At low tide, there's a good walk between **Grange** and **Carnivan beaches**, past caves, rock pools and **Baginbun Head**, which, surmounted by a 19th-century **Martello tower**, is where the Normans first landed (1169) for their conquest of Ireland. It's a good vantage point for **birdwatching**: over 200 species have been recorded passing through. You might even spot dolphins or whales, particularly between December and February.

🍴 Eating

Templars Inn SEAFOOD €€
(Templetown; mains €10-22; ◷noon-10pm) The inviting panoramic terrace here overlooks the ruins of a medieval church, fields of grazing cattle and the ocean beyond. Inside, the dark-timber interior resembles a wayfarers' tavern and is a cosy place for enjoying fresh seafood dishes.

Duncannon & Around

POP 328

The small, dusty holiday town of Duncannon slopes down to a sandy beach that's transformed into a surrealist canvas during August's **Duncannon International Sand Sculpting Festival**.

Just west of the village, star-shaped **Duncannon Fort** (www.duncannonfort.com; adult/child with tour €5/3; ◷tours 10am-5.30pm daily Jun–mid-Sep, site 10am-4.30pm Mon-Fri rest of year) was built in 1588 to stave off a feared attack by the Spanish Armada and later used by the Irish army as a WWI training base (most of its buildings date from this period). There's a small **military and maritime museum**, plus a cafe, a dry moat and an **art gallery**.

About 4km northwest of Duncannon is pretty Ballyhack, from where a car ferry travels to Passage East in County Waterford. It's dominated by the 15th-century Ballyhack Castle (www.heritageireland.ie; ⊘10am-6pm mid-Jun–late Aug) FREE, a Knights Hospitallers tower house, containing a small exhibition on the Crusades.

Beside the R733, some 9km north of Duncannon, the ruined Dunbrody Abbey (www.dunbrodyabbey.com; Campile; adult/child €3/1; ⊘11am-5pm May–mid-Sep) is a remarkably intact Cistercian abbey founded by Strongbow in 1170 and completed in 1220. A combined ticket (adult/child €6/3) includes a museum with a huge doll's house, minigolf, and an entertaining yew-hedge maze made up of over 1500 trees. There are tea rooms and a craft shop.

🛏 Sleeping & Eating

The Duncannon area is home to some magnificent country estates in addition to simple beachside B&Bs.

★ Glendine Country House   GUESTHOUSE €€
(✆051-389 500; www.glendinehouse.com; Arthurstown; s/d from €45/90; 🕸) Staying at this vine-covered 1830s-built former dower house is like staying with friends with impeccable taste. Bay windows overlook the estuary and grounds populated by deer, cattle and sheep; paintings by local artists adorn the walls. The rooms are all different but typically have hardwood floors, chandeliers and antiques. Request room 9 with its princely proportions and king-size bed. The welcoming Crosbie family lays on a vast, mostly organic, breakfast.

Aldridge Lodge Restaurant & Guesthouse   INN €€
(✆051-389 116; www.aldridgelodge.com; Duncannon; s/d from €55/100; ⊘restaurant 7pm-late Wed-Sun; 🕸) In a windblown spot on open fields above Duncannon, Aldridge takes a bit of finding, but it's worth it for the elegant, contemporary guest rooms and fresh local seafood like Hook Head crab claws or Kilmore cod (dinner €39). Two caveats: book your table in advance, and children under seven aren't allowed.

Dunbrody Country House
Hotel, Restaurant & Cookery
School   HOTEL, RESTAURANT €€€
(✆051-389 600; www.dunbrodyhouse.com; Arthurstown; s/d from €125/225; multicourse meals from €55;

🕸) Chef Kevin Dundon is a familiar face on Irish TV, the author of several cookbooks and even has his own line of cookware (www.kevindundonhome.com). His spa hotel, in a period-decorated 1830s Georgian manor on 120-hectare grounds, is the stuff of foodies' fantasies, with a gourmet restaurant and cookery school (one-day courses from €175).

Sqigl Restaurant &
Roche's Bar   MODERN IRISH €€
(✆051-389 188; www.sqiglrestaurant.com; Quay Rd, Duncannon; restaurant mains €19.50-23.50, bar mains €8-12; ⊘restaurant 6-9pm Wed-Sat; bar noon-9pm daily) Local produce is the mainstay of Sqigl, where dishes range from spring lamb to local seafood (bookings essential). Roche's Bar adjoins and has excellent bar food and an inviting atmosphere with vintage advertising posters and seamen's knots. Trad music sessions on Fridays.

ℹ Getting There & Away

There's limited public transport as far as Fethard, but none to Hook Head.

FERRY

If you're travelling directly to Waterford city, the Waterford–Wexford Ferry (www.passengerferry.ie; single/return €2/3, car €8/12; ⊘7am-10pm Mon-Sat, 9.30am-10pm Sun Apr-Sep, 7am-8pm Mon-Sat, 9.30am-8pm Oct-Mar) saves detouring via New Ross.

New Ross
POP 4552

The big attraction at New Ross (Rhos Mhic Triúin) is the opportunity to board a 19th-century Famine ship. But New Ross' historical links stretch back much further – to the 12th century, when it developed as a Norman port on the River Barrow. A group of rebels tried to seize the town during the 1798 Rising. They were repelled by the defending garrison, leaving 3000 dead and much of the place in tatters. Today its eastern bank retains some intriguing steep, narrow streets and the impressive ruins of a medieval abbey.

◎ Sights & Activities

★ Dunbrody Famine Ship   MUSEUM
(✆051-425 239; www.dunbrody.com; The Quay; adult/child €8.50/5; ⊘10am-6pm Apr-Sep, to 5pm Oct-Mar; 🖭) Called 'coffin ships' due to the fatality rate of their passengers, the leaky, smelly boats that hauled a generation

of Irish to America are recalled at this replica ship on the waterfront. The emigrants' sorrowful yet often inspiring stories (they paid an average of £7 for the voyage) are brought to life by docents during 45-minute tours. A 10-minute film provides historical background about Ireland at the time. The Hall of Fame cafe recently opened, serving snacks and meals.

Ros Tapestry MUSEUM
(www.rostapestry.com; Priory Court, The Quay; adult/child €6/4; ⊙10am-5pm Tue-Sun; 🐾) The Normans' influence on 13th-century Ireland (up to 400 boats with goods for trade would be in port at New Ross) is recalled via 15 tapestry panels created by more than 150 volunteer embroiderers. There are audioguides and a gift shop.

St Mary's Abbey CHURCH
(Church Lane) FREE One of the largest medieval churches in Ireland, St Mary's was founded by Isabella of Leinster and her husband William in the 13th century. Ask at the tourist office for access.

🛏 Sleeping & Eating

New Ross has an excellent farmers market (The Quay; ⊙9am-2pm Sat)

MacMurrough Farm Cottages COTTAGES €
(☑051-421 383; www.macmurrough.com; MacMurrough, New Ross; 2-person cottage €50; ⊙mid-Mar-Oct; 🐾) A strutting rooster serves as an alarm clock at Brian and Jenny's remote hilltop farm. The well-priced self-catering cottages are located in the former stables and pleasantly furnished with good facilities. Follow the hand-painted signs up a series of tracks 3.5km northeast of town. A cosy old pub and a market are close by.

Brandon House Hotel HOTEL €€
(☑051-421 703; www.brandonhousehotel.ie; New Ross; r from €80; @🐾🏊🐾) This 1865-built red-brick manor certainly lives up to its reputation as family friendly, with kids happily bounding around the place. Winning elements include river views, open log fires, a library bar and large rooms, as well as a spa. It's up a steep driveway 2km south of New Ross.

★Cafe Nutshell IRISH €€€
(8 South St; mains €10-16; ⊙9am-5.30pm Tue-Sat; 🐾) It's a shame that Cafe Nutshell closes in the evening, as New Ross' town centre is short on places of this calibre. Scones, breads and buns are all baked on the premises, hot lunch specials utilise local produce and

COUNTIES WEXFORD, WATERFORD, CARLOW & KILKENNY NEW ROSS

WORTH A TRIP

WEXFORD & THE KENNEDYS

In 1848 Patrick Kennedy left the horrible conditions in County Wexford aboard a boat like the Famine ship in New Ross. Hoping to find something better in America, he succeeded beyond his wildest dreams (a US president, senators and rum-runners are just some of his progeny). You can recall the family's Irish roots at two sites near New Ross.

Kennedy Homestead (☑051-388 264; www.kennedyhomestead.com; Dunganstown; adult/student €5/2.50; ⊙10am-5pm Jul & Aug, 11.30am-4.30pm Mon-Fri May, Jun & Sep, by appointment rest of year) The birthplace of Patrick Kennedy, great-grandfather of John F Kennedy, is a farm that still looks – and smells – much as it must have 160 years ago. When JFK visited the farm in 1963 and hugged the current owner's grandmother, it was his first public display of affection, according to his sister Jean. The outbuildings have been turned into a museum that examines the Irish-American dynasty's history on both sides of the Atlantic, plus an informative visitor centre that opened in 2013. The homestead is located about 7km south of New Ross along a very narrow but beautifully overgrown road.

John F Kennedy Arboretum (www.heritageireland.ie; adult/child €3/1; ⊙10am-8pm May-Aug, 10am-6.30pm Apr & Sep, 10am-5pm Oct-Mar; 🐾) On a sunny day, this place is so nice for families that it could be called Camelot. The park, 2km southeast of the Kennedy Homestead, has a small visitor centre, tearooms and a picnic area; a miniature train tootles around in the summer months. It has 4500 species of trees and shrubs in 252 hectares of woodlands and gardens. Slieve Coillte (270m), opposite the park entrance, has a viewing point from where you can see the arboretum and six counties on a clear day.

there's a great range of smoothies, juices and organic wines. Mains come with an array of fresh salads. The adjacent health-food shop and deli are perfect for picnic provisions.

ⓘ Information

Tourist office (www.newrosstourism.com; The Quay; ⊙9am-6pm Apr-Sep, to 5pm Oct-Mar) Located in the same building as the ticket office for the Dunbrody Famine Ship.

ⓘ Getting There & Away

Bus Éireann (www.buseireann.ie) Services depart from Dunbrody Inn on the Quay and travel to Waterford (€7, 30 minutes, seven to 11 daily), Wexford (€8, 40 minutes, three to four daily) and Dublin (€16, three hours, four daily).

Enniscorthy

POP 10,543

County Wexford's second-largest town, Enniscorthy (Inis Coirthaidh), has a warren of steep streets descending from Augustus Pugin's cathedral to the Norman castle and the River Slaney. Enniscorthy is inextricably linked to some of the fiercest fighting of the 1798 Rising, when rebels captured the town and set up camp at Vinegar Hill.

⊙ Sights

Enniscorthy Castle CASTLE
(www.enniscorthycastle.ie; Castle Hill; adult/child €4/2; ⊙10am-5pm; ⊞) During the 1798 Rising, rebels used this castle as a prison. The stout, four-towered keep was built by the Normans. Like much else in these parts, the castle was surrendered to Cromwell in 1649. It now houses a good local museum, which includes displays about the history of the town. There is also a rooftop deck with spectacular views.

National 1798 Rebellion Centre MUSEUM
(www.1798centre.ie; Mill Park Rd; adult/child €5.50/3; ⊙10am-5pm Mon-Fri, noon-5pm Sat & Sun Apr-Sep, 9.30am-4pm Mon-Fri Oct-Mar; ⊞) A visit here before climbing Vinegar Hill greatly enhances its impact. The centre's exhibits cover the French and American revolutions that sparked Wexford's abortive uprising against British rule in Ireland, before chronicling what was one of the most bloodthirsty battles of the 1798 Rebellion and a turning point in the struggle. Interactive displays include a giant chessboard with pieces representing key figures in the Rising, and a multiscreen recreation of the finale atop a virtual Vinegar Hill.

Vinegar Hill HISTORIC SITE
To visit the scene of the 1798 events, get a map from the tourist office and look for signs. It's a 2km drive or about a 45-minute walk from Templeshannon on the eastern side of the river. At the summit there's a memorial to the uprising, explanatory signs and sweeping views across the county.

St Aidan's Cathedral CATHEDRAL
(www.staidanscathedral.ie; Church St; ⊙8.30am-6pm) FREE Restored to its original glory (check out the star-spangled roof), the dazzling Roman Catholic cathedral (1846) was designed by Augustus Pugin, the architect behind the Houses of Parliament in London.

🏃 Activities

You can take an excellent 2km walk if you do a looping route on a visit to the rebellion centre that includes the promenade along the River Slaney. Including Vinegar Hill is best reserved for those with sturdy hill-climbing knees.

🎉 Festivals & Events

Strawberry Festival FOOD
(www.strawberryfest.ie; ⊙late Jun) During this weekend festival pubs extend their hours, bands are booked, and strawberries and cream is the sweet treat of choice.

🛏 Sleeping

The lush, rolling hills in this part of County Wexford shelter some truly lovely country houses.

Salville House B&B €€
(☑053-923 5252; www.salvillehouse.com; s/d from €60/100; 🅿) The views across the great lawn and through the birch trees to the River Slaney are reason enough to stay at this small country estate, with five bedrooms appropriately furnished with solid dark-wood furniture. Three of the rooms have their own bathrooms, the other two are in a self-contained apartment (price confirmed on booking). Dinner (€40) features four courses of seasonal, organic fare. It's about 2km south of town.

Riverside Park HOTEL €€
(☑053-923 7900; www.riversideparkhotel.com; The Promenade; r from €110) Enjoy strolls along the grassy banks of the river from this superbly positioned hotel. A circular lobby in contemporary purples and greys sets the scene with comfortable rooms furnished

with caramel-coloured carpets and neutral creams, browns and beige. Most have balconies and river views. This is a popular hotel for weddings so Saturdays may be booked up and/or noisy! Breakfast included.

Treacy's Hotel   HOTEL €€
(☑ 053-923 7798; www.treacyshotel.com; Templeshannon; r from €90; 📶) This handsome custard-coloured building has spruced-up rooms in earthy colours. Treacy's is a large hotel with two bars, two restaurants (one international, one Thai) and a nightclub. Entertainment includes live bands and Irish dancing, and guests can use the leisure centre opposite for free. Very central for the sights and shopping.

Woodbrook House   GUESTHOUSE €€€
(☑ 053-925 5114; www.woodbrookhouse.ie; Killanne; s/d from €95/150; ⊙ Easter-Sep; @ 📶 ⊠)
🏃 Damaged in the 1798 rebellion, this glorious country estate is now a three-room guesthouse. The entry features a gravity-defying spiral staircase that amazes now just as it did over 200 years ago. Green practices are used throughout and you can make arrangements for dinner (organic, of course). It is 13km west of Enniscorthy.

🍴 Eating & Drinking

Enniscorthy's farmers market (Abbey Sq; ⊙ 9am-2pm Sat) sells local and organic goods and prepared foods. Look for Carrigbyrne cheese. Pedestrianised Slaney St is a good place to start your pub crawl which, owing to its steepness, may literally be a crawl.

★ Cotton Tree Cafe   CAFE €
(☑ 053-923 4641; Slaney Place; mains €6-10; ⊙ 8.30am-5pm Mon-Sat, 11am-5pm Sun; 📶)
A pleasantly informal cafe charmingly adorned with homey (and historic) decorations and artwork. The menu includes gourmet sandwiches that feature roast Irish beef and hummus, as well as a choice of imaginative salads and a daily main.

Toffee & Thyme   CAFE €
(24 Rafter St; dishes €6-12; ⊙ 8am-5pm Mon-Sat) Handily located on this pedestrianised shopping street, this stylish cafe, with its rustic furniture and two small dining rooms, dishes up tasty light meals created from regional produce. Choose from sandwiches and salads, savoury soups and hot meals. If you're dropping in for a coffee, try the homemade scones.

Galo Chargrill Restaurant   PORTUGUESE €€
(19 Main St; mains €10-20; ⊙ noon-3pm & 7-10pm Tue-Sun) Spicy chargrilled dishes, such as double chicken fillets with chilli, are a burst of sunshine at this small Portuguese restaurant with a big reputation. On balmy days the front opens up like the lid on a can of anchovies.

Bailey   IRISH €€
(www.thebailey.ie; Barrack St; lunch mains €9-14, dinner mains €13-25; ⊙ 10am-10pm) The interior of this converted riverside grain store may look a tad dated with its leatherette banquettes, but Baileys remains one of the most popular summertime haunts in town with its regular live gigs, ranging from rock 'n' roll to blues. There's a spacious terrace out front and the pub grub is filling.

Antique Tavern   PUB
(14 Slaney St; ⊙ 5-11.30pm Mon-Fri, 11am-midnight Sat & Sun) Slanted on the side of a hill, across from the river, this creaky black-and-white pub dates from 1790 and is somewhere between twee and rustic. It attracts a rousing number of locals and has an upstairs glassed-in terrace for warm-weather tippling accompanied by great water views.

🛍 Shopping

Kiltrea Bridge Pottery   CERAMICS
(www.kiltreapottery.com; ⊙ 10am-1pm & 2-5.30pm Mon-Sat) The Enniscorthy area has been a centre of pottery since the 17th century. Continuing the tradition, Kiltrea creates hand-thrown terracotta pots including some stunning oversized conversation pieces. It's 6.5km west of Enniscorthy off the Kiltealy Rd (R702).

ℹ Information

Tourist office (☑ 053-923 4699; www.knight sandrebels.ie; Castle Hill; ⊙ 10am-5pm Mon-Fri, noon-5pm Sat & Sun Apr-Sep, 9.30am-4pm Mon-Fri Oct-Mar) Inside Enniscorthy castle.

ℹ Getting There & Away

BUS

Bus Éireann (www.buseireann.ie) runs nine daily buses to Dublin (€15.75, 2½ hours), and eight to Rosslare Harbour (€11, one hour) via Wexford (€6.75, 25 minutes).

TRAIN

The **train station** (Templeshannon) is on the eastern bank of the river. **Irish Rail** (www. irishrail.ie) runs to Dublin Connolly station (€10, 2¼ hours) and Wexford (€7, 25 minutes) three times daily.

COUNTIES WEXFORD, WATERFORD, CARLOW & KILKENNY ENNISCORTHY

Ferns

POP 1510

It's hard to believe that this workaday village was once the powerhouse of the kings of Leinster, in particular Dermot MacMurrough (1110–71), who is forever associated with bringing the Normans to Ireland. The Normans left behind a cathedral and a doughty castle, later smashed to pieces by Cromwell.

◎ Sights

Ferns Castle   RUIN

(www.heritageireland.ie; ⊙ visitor centre 10am-6pm Jun-Sep) The castle was built around 1220. A couple of walls and part of the moat survive ignominiously in the middle of town; you can climb to the top of the one complete tower. Parliamentarians destroyed the castle and executed most of the local population in 1649. The ruins are thought to stand on the site of Dermot MacMurrough's old fortress. The visitor centre holds regular informative exhibitions relating to the history of the town.

St Edan's Cathedral   CATHEDRAL

At the eastern end of the main street is the cathedral, built in early Gothic style in 1817. Its graveyard contains a ruined high cross, said to mark the resting place of Dermot MacMurrough.

Medieval Ruins   RUIN

Behind the cathedral are two medieval ruins sitting in lonely isolation surrounded by grass and grazing cattle: the Norman-built Ferns Cathedral and, with an unusual square-based round tower, St Mary's Abbey. Dermot MacMurrough founded the latter in 1158, inviting Augustinian monks to run a monastery here. An earlier Christian settlement founded in the same spot by St Aedan in 600 was destroyed by the Vikings.

St Peter's Church   CHURCH

Further out of town is St Peter's, which was built from stones taken, magpielike, from Ferns Cathedral and St Mary's Abbey.

❶ Getting There & Away

Ferns is an easy 12km drive northeast of Enniscorthy on the N11. Buses between Dublin and Wexford all stop here.

Mt Leinster

The highest peak in the Blackstairs Mountains, Mt Leinster (796m) has magnificent views of Counties Waterford, Carlow, Kilkenny and Wicklow from the top. It's home to some of Ireland's best hang-gliding: contact the Irish Hang Gliding & Paragliding Association (www.ihpa.ie) for further information.

The car park at the foot of the mountain is signposted from Bunclody, 16km northwest of Ferns. From here, it's a steep 1½-hour return walk.

COUNTY WATERFORD

POP 107,950

Diverse County Waterford harbours gorgeous seaside scenery, craggy beaches and villages like Dungarvan along its beautiful coast, a warren of walking trails in the beautiful Nire Valley, concealed by the Comeragh and Monavullagh Mountains, and lively Waterford city, with its winding medieval lanes and well-preserved Georgian architecture.

Waterford City

POP 49,200

Waterford is Ireland's oldest city and celebrated its 1100th anniversary in 2014. A busy port, it lies on the tidal reach of the River Suir, 16km from the coast. Some parts of the city still feel almost medieval, with narrow alleyways leading off larger streets; an ongoing revitalisation campaign is polishing up one block after another. New and existing museums tell the story of Ireland's Middle Ages better than any other city in the country.

History

King John extended the original Viking city walls in 1210 and Waterford became Ireland's most powerful city. In the 15th century it resisted the forces of two pretenders to the English Crown, Lambert Simnel and Perkin Warbeck and, in 1649, subsequently defied Cromwell. In 1650 his forces returned and Waterford surrendered. Although the city escaped the customary slaughter, Catholics were either exiled to the west or shipped as slaves to the Caribbean, and the population dramatically declined.

◎ Sights & Activities

The ancient streets northwest of the Mall (the so-called Viking Triangle) are getting a burnish with new museums and attractions that highlight the city's fascinating history.

Waterford

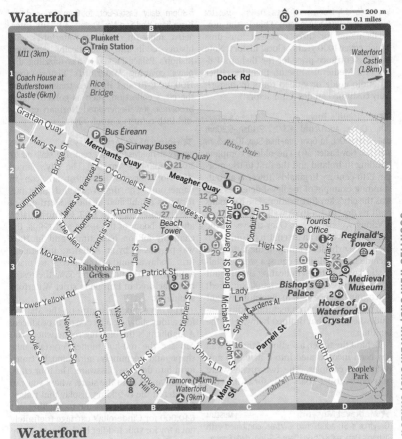

Waterford

Waterford Museum of Treasures   MUSEUM
(www.waterfordtreasures.com) This is the umbrella name for three excellent museums which cover 1000 years of local history. Note that the entrance price for the Bishop's Palace and Medieval Museum includes either an audio guide or guided tours by historically costumed guides (cum actors!).

★ **Reginald's Tower**   HISTORIC BUILDING
(The Quay; adult/child €3/1; ⊘ 10am-5.30pm daily Easter-Oct, to 6pm Jun–mid-Sep, 10am-5pm Wed-Sun Nov-Easter; ⊞) The oldest complete building in Ireland and the first to use mortar, 12th-century Reginald's Tower is an outstanding example of medieval defences and was the city's key fortification. The Normans built its 3m- to 4m-thick walls on the site of a Viking wooden tower. Over the years, the building served as an arsenal, a prison and a mint. The exhibits relating to the latter role include medieval silver coins, a wooden 'tally stick' with notches indicating the amount owed, a 12th-century piggy bank (smashed) and a coin balance used to determine weight and bullion value. Architectural oddities include the toilet that drained halfway up the building.

Behind the tower, a section of the old wall has been incorporated into a new pub and restaurant complex. The two arches were sally ports, to let boats 'sally forth' into the inlet.

★ **Medieval Museum**   MUSEUM
(Greyfriar's St; adult/child €7/free, combined with Bishop's Palace €8/2; ⊘ 10am-5.30pm daily Easter-Oct, to 6pm Jun–mid-Sep, 10am-5pm Wed-Sun Nov-Easter; ⊞) The latest museum of Waterford's illustrious trio, the exhibits here are expertly displayed with explanatory plaques throughout and several extraordinary highlights, including the original Great Parchment Book which documents in fascinating detail what medieval life was like, including cases of petty crime and the impact of the plague. There is also an entertaining (and suitable for kids) 12-minute audiovisual presentation about the history of the vestments which date from the 1450s and were discovered hidden under Christ Church Cathedral. The vestments, elaborately embroidered in gold thread and in surprisingly good condition, are also on view.

★ **Bishop's Palace**   MUSEUM
(The Mall, Bishop's Palace; adult/child €7/free, combined with Medieval Museum €8/2; ⊘ 10am-5.30pm daily Easter-Oct, to 6pm Jun–mid-Sep, 10am-5pm Wed-Sun Nov-Easter; ⊞) This interactive museum detailing Waterford's long history is in the aesthetically renovated Bishop's Palace (1741). It has dazzling displays covering Waterford's history from 1700 to 1970 and includes treasures from the city's collection, such as golden Viking brooches, jewel-encrusted Norman crosses and 18th-century church silver.

★ **House of Waterford Crystal**   GLASS
(www.waterfordvisitorcentre.com; The Mall; adult/student €12/4; ⊘ 9am-5pm) The city's famed Waterford Crystal is almost an icon in name only. The first Waterford glass factory was established at the western end of the riverside quays in 1783. Centuries later, after the boom of the 1980s and 1990s, the company fell on hard times and in 2009 was purchased by an American investment firm. Today around 60,000 pieces are made annually in Ireland, around 55%; the rest is manufactured in Europe to strict Waterford standards.

The large modern centre on the Mall offers a tour showing how crystal is produced. A highlight is the blowing room, where you can see the red-hot molten crystals take shape and seemingly miraculously transform into delicate glassware. The tour ends, understandably, in the store, where you can wonder at the twinkling display that ranges from a €30 bottle coaster to shelling out €40,000 for Cinderella's carriage (definitely not a toy for your toddler back home.). There is a cafe here, as well.

Edmund Rice International Heritage Centre   MUSEUM
(www.edmundrice.ie; Barrack St; adult/child €5/2; ⊘ 9am-5pm Mon-Fri, 10am-2pm Sat; ⊞) Edmund Ignatius Rice, founder of the Christian Brothers, established his first school at Mt Sion on Barrack St. A whiz-bang interactive museum recreates life in 18th-century Waterford. It incorporates a chapel, where Edmund Rice's tomb takes pride of place, awaiting the anticipated canonisation of its occupant.

Christ Church Cathedral   CATHEDRAL
(www.waterford-cathedral.com; Cathedral Sq; ⊘ 10am-6pm Mon-Fri, 10am-4pm Sat) FREE
Christ Church Cathedral is Europe's only neoclassical Georgian cathedral. Designed by local architect John Roberts, it was built on the site of an 11th-century Viking church,

also the site where the 12th-century marriage of Strongbow and Aoife took place. The rather grim highlight is the 15th-century tomb of James Rice, seven times Lord Mayor of Waterford: sculpted worms and frogs crawl out of the statue of his decaying body. On a jollier note, the cathedral also acts as a concert venue offering a diverse program and superb acoustics.

Holy Trinity Cathedral   CATHEDRAL
(Barronstrand St) FREE The sumptuous interior of this Catholic cathedral boasts a carved-oak baroque pulpit, painted pillars with Corinthian capitals and 10 Waterford Crystal chandeliers. It was built between 1792 and 1796 by John Roberts who, unusually, also designed the Protestant Christ Church Cathedral.

Historic Buildings   HISTORIC BUILDING
The Mall, a wide 18th-century street built on reclaimed land, was once a tidal inlet. From the river end, its stateliest buildings are John Roberts' City Hall (1788) and beautifully refurbished Theatre Royal (p183), arguably Ireland's most intact 18th-century theatre.

Crumbling fragments of the old city wall include Beach Tower at the top of Jenkin's Lane and Half Moon Tower (both are just off Patrick St). One impossible-to-miss building in Waterford is its landmark 1860s clock tower.

☞ Tours

★ Jack Burtchaell's
Guided Walking Tour   WALKING TOUR
(☑051-873 711; www.jackswalkingtours.com; tour adult/child €7/free; ⊙11.45am & 1.45pm; ⓓ) Jack's 'gift of the gab' brings Waterford's nooks and crannies alive, effortlessly squeezing 1000 years of history into one hour. Tours leave from near the tourist office (confirm the exact location there), picking up walkers from various hotels en route.

✲✲ Festivals & Events

Waterford International
Festival of Music   MUSIC
(www.waterfordintlmusicfestival.com; ⊙May) Now over 50 years old, the Waterford Music Festival focuses on light opera.

🛏 Sleeping

Waterford's centre has a surprisingly limited number of places to stay.

Mayor's Walk House   B&B €
(☑051-855 427; www.mayorswalk.com; 12 Mayor's Walk; s/d from €30/50) This respectable four-room B&B is in a period town building that dates from 1891. The two landing bathrooms are shared, but the midsized (if dated) rooms have high ceilings, central heating and washbasins.

★ Granville Hotel   HOTEL €€
(☑051-305 555; www.granville-hotel.ie; Meagher Quay; s/d from €80/100; ⓐ) The floodlit 18th-century building overlooking the waterfront is the Granville, one of Ireland's oldest hotels. Brocaded bedrooms maintain a touch of Georgian elegance, as do the public areas with their showstopping stained glass, historic prints and antiques. The restaurant and bar are popular with locals for their reasonable prices and touch of old world luxury. Star turns at breakfast are the organic porridge with Baileys and a perfect eggs Benedict.

Dooley's Hotel   HOTEL €€
(☑051-873 531; www.dooleys-hotel.ie; Mercant's Quay; r from €80; @ⓐ) Dooley's has grown from an eight-room modest guesthouse in the 1940s to a sleek spacious hotel with over 100 rooms. It's family-owned and run like clockwork. The rooms are large and repro Regency with brocade fabrics and a dark red-and-gold colour scheme. The breakfast is a belt-notch up from most hotel buffets and includes organic porridge, fresh fruit compote and cooked options. The onsite Thai Therapy Centre offers various treatments.

Coach House at
Butlerstown Castle   B&B €€
(☑051-384 656; www.butlerstowncastle.com; Butlerstown; r €80-150; ⊙Apr-Oct; ⓐ) A 10-minute drive away from town, this 19th-century stone B&B is as appealing inside as it is out, with deep, studded leather armchairs to sink into, toasty open fires to warm up by, canopied beds to drift off in, and pancakes to wake up to. It has 17 rooms and is 6km west of town off the N25.

Portree Guesthouse   B&B €€
(☑051-874 574; www.portreeguesthouse.ie; Mary St; s/d from €39/69; ⓐ) This large, 24-room Georgian B&B is on a quiet street – a bonus in noisy Waterford. It is well run by a couple of Londoners and the rooms are spick and span if not particularly memorable. There's a homey sitting room with plenty of tourist information and brochures, plus 24-hour coffee and tea on offer. Popular with groups.

★**Waterford Castle** LUXURY HOTEL €€€
(✆ 051-878 203; www.waterfordcastle.com; The Island, Ballinakill; r from €140, cottages from €130; @ 🗦) Getting away from it all is an understatement at this mid-19th-century turreted castle, located on its own 124-hectare island roamed by deer. A free, private car ferry signposted just east of the Waterford Regional Hospital provides round-the-clock access. All 19 castle rooms have clawfoot baths, and some have four-poster beds. There are also 48 contemporary self-catering cottages on the island. Both guests and nonguests can dine on organic fare in chef Michael Quinn's sublime oak-panelled restaurant (menus from €28), or play a round of golf (green fees €20). Breakfast included.

✖ Eating

Waterford has a great selection of restaurants and a lively food market on Saturday (10am to 4pm) in John Roberts Sq.

★**Merchant's Quay** MARKET, RESTAURANT €
(Merchants Quay; mains €8-12; ⊙ 10am-5pm Sat & Sun, to 10pm Fri; 🖫) Opened in early 2013, this former grain store dating from 1759 has been transformed into a three-floor space encompassing a farmers market, casual dining space with brazier-style grill and a top-floor venue for medieval-themed shows. Market stalls include an onsite bakery, organic produce, local ice cream, seafood, artisan cheeses and much more. Everything is sourced within a 50km radius. There are cookery demonstrations for children, as well as other activities planned.

Chocolate Cafe CAFE €
(Georges Court Shopping Centre; sandwiches from €3.50; ⊙ 8am-6.30pm Mon-Sat, 11am-6pm Sun; 🖫) The mint-chocolate colour scheme here is lip-smackingly apt for this shop and cafe selling not just Ireland's famous Lily O'Brien's chocolate (six chocs for €2), but such sweet treats as berry crumble, macaroons and slices of rich, dark carrot cake. Savoury snacks include gourmet sandwiches.

Berfranks CAFE, DELI €
(www.berfranks.ie; 86 The Quay; meals €6-10; ⊙ 8.30am-5pm Mon-Sat) Irish artisan foods line the shelves in the deli section while mouthwatering creations line the menu on the cafe side with its additional cosy back room with bookcases and sofas. This is an ideal place for a pit stop while you unravel Waterford's medieval past.

★**Harlequin** ITALIAN €€
(37 Stephen St; lunch mains €8-12, dinner mains €10-14; ⊙ 8.30am-8.30pm Mon-Wed, 8.30am-10.30pm Thu-Sat; 🗦) Italian run, this authentic little trattoria morphs throughout the day from a coffee and pastry stop to a busy dining spot to a candlelit wine bar. House speciality antipasti platters are laden with cheeses, marinated vegetables and/or finely sliced cured meats. No pizza.

Bodega! MODERN IRISH €€
(✆ 051-844 177; www.bodegawaterford.com; 54 John St; mains €7-25; ⊙ noon-midnight Mon-Sat) Although the ochre walls and Gaudi-style broken-tile floor seem Spanish, the latest Bodega reincarnation is contemporary Irish with an emphasis on local produce. The menu has a healthy mix of fish and meat dishes, as well as some lighter fare, such as goat's cheese tartlets and innovative salads. The dining room has a great atmosphere with its twinkling strings of red fairy lights and edgy artwork. Keeping it local is a long list of Irish craft brews.

L'Atmosphere FRENCH €€
(✆ 051-858 426; www.restaurant-latmosphere.com; 19 Henrietta St; mains €12-25; ⊙ 12.30-3pm Mon-Sat, 5.30-10pm Mon-Sun; 🗦) Always crowded, this stone-clad bistro has an energy most places in Paris wish they could import. Classic French dishes with modern Irish flair (and Waterford produce) are served with élan. The artwork is suitably provocative, the desserts sumptuously delicious, particularly the crème brûlée.

Munster Bar PUB €€
(www.themunsterbar.com; Bailey's New St; mains €8-16; ⊙ noon-9pm; 🖫) In a building dating from 1822, this historic pub and restaurant has a snug complete with roaring fire and a spacious bar in the former coachhouse. Enjoy upscale pub food, like beef-and-Guinness pie and melted-brie-and-chutney sandwiches. It's the perfect casual end to a long day touring.

La Bohème FRENCH €€€
(✆ 051-875 645; wwwlabohemerestaurant.ie; 2 George's St; mains €29-32; ⊙ 5.30pm-late Tue-Sat) This dress-for-dinner kind of place combines French flair with fresh Irish produce, resulting in mains such as mustard-and-honey rack of lamb or seaweed-encrusted scallops. A former kitchen of a Georgian townhouse, the dining rooms provide intimate spaces with barrel-vault roofs and

arches; the wine cellar is more extensive than most.

Drinking & Nightlife

There are superb pubs around town, and several places where you can hear live music.

★Henry Downes Bar   PUB
(Thomas St; ☺5pm-late) For a change from stout, drop into Downes, which has been blending its No 9 Irish whiskey for over two centuries. Have a dram in its series of character-filled rooms, or buy a bottle to take away (€32). This place is a real one-off – there's even a squash court out the back (€8 for 40 minutes).

T&H Doolan's   PUB
(www.thdoolans.com; 32 George's St; ☺10pm-11.30pm Mon-Thu, to 12.30pm Fri-Sat, noon-12.30pm Sun) Look for the eye-catching mock Tudor facade, home to this charming 300-year-old pub. Doolan's hosts traditional music every night of the week (from 9pm) and is one of the most popular bars in town. Wednesday is an informal jam session.

Geoff's   PUB
(9 John St; ☺11.30am-12.30pm) Hidden behind a wacky astro-turf frontage, Geoff's pub is full of character. Its moody cavernous bars have indigo-blue walls, heavy wooden furniture and lofty ceilings (head for the atmospheric so-called church bar out the back). Decent food also served.

Gingerman   PUB
(6/7 Arundel Lane; ☺10am-11.30pm Mon-Fri, to 12.30pm Sat, noon-11pm Sun) A dark-wood-clad pub on a narrow lane right in the centre, with plenty of blarney atmosphere and a good range of ales on tap, plus meals. Live trad music on Sunday (5pm).

☆ Entertainment

Garter Lane Arts Centre   THEATRE
(www.garterlane.ie; 22a O'Connell St) This excellent theatre stages art-house films, music, dance and plays in an atmospheric 18th-century building.

Theatre Royal   THEATRE
(www.theatreroyal.ie; The Mall) Beautifully refurbished, Waterford's flagship theatre stages plays, musicals and dance.

🔒 Shopping

The main shopping street runs directly south from the Suir.

★Kite Design Studios   ARTS & CRAFTS
(11 Henrietta St) Some of Waterford's best artists and craftspeople have space in this combination studio and shop. As well as the Irish Handmade Glass Company, master craftsman Sean Egan has a workshop here. In 2013 Sean was commissioned to create an engraved bowl depicting the Famine ship, which was presented to US President Barack Obama as part of the year-long commemorative events relating to the Gathering, which took place in 2013, aimed at celebrating Irish history, culture and genealogy.

Waterford Book Centre   BOOKS
(www.thebookcentre.ie; 25 John Roberts Sq; ☺9am-6pm Mon-Sat, 1-5pm Sun) Three floors of books – with an excellent selection of Irish classics – and a cafe.

ℹ Information

Tourist office (☐051-875 823; www.discoverwaterfordcity.ie; Parade Quay; ☺9am-6pm Mon-Sat, 11am-5pm Sun Jul & Aug, shorter hours rest of year) This large office is the best source of info and help in counties Waterford and Wexford. Note that it plans to move near Reginald's Tower but there was no definite date at research time.

ℹ Getting There & Away

AIR
Waterford Airport (WAT; ☐051-875 589; www.flywaterford.com) The airport is 9km south of the city centre at Killowen. Primarily has flights to London Luton, Manchester and Birmingham.

BUS
Bus Éireann (www.buseireann.ie; Merchant's Quay) Frequent services to Tramore (€3.25, 30 minutes), Dublin (€14.75, three hours) and Wexford (€10, one hour).

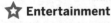

> ### ℹ FINDING WATERFORD'S ARTISANS
> Crystal aside, Waterford has a wealth of local craftspeople creating textiles, paintings, jewellery, pottery, papier mâché, candles, and furniture built from recycled materials. The website www.waterforddesignermakers.com maintains an updated list, including contact details to arrange appointments.

ℹ WATERFORD–WEXFORD FERRY

If you're going to travel between Counties Waterford and Wexford along the coast, you can cut out a long detour around Waterford Harbour and the River Barrow by taking the five-minute car ferry (www.passageferry.ie; ⊘ 7am-10pm Mon-Sat, 9.30am-10pm Sun Apr-Sep, 7am-8pm Mon-Sat, 9.30am-8pm Sun Oct-Mar) between Passage East and Ballyhack in County Wexford. Single/return tickets for pedestrians or cyclists cost €2/3 and for cars €8/12.

TRAIN

Plunkett Train Station (www.irishrail.ie) North of the river. Up to eight services to/from Dublin's Heuston Station (from €20, two to 2½ hours) and Kilkenny (from €10, 40 minutes).

ℹ Getting Around

There is no public transport to the airport. A **taxi** (☑ 051-77710, 051-858 585) costs around €15.

Curraghmore Estate

Lord and Lady Waterford dwell at the 1000-hectare Curraghmore Estate (www.curraghmorehouse.ie; Portlaw; house €10, shell house & gardens €5; ⊘ 10am-4pm Tue-Thu plus 1st & 3rd Sun of month Easter-Oct), which has belonged to the family since the 12th century. Located 14km northwest of Waterford, its lavish gardens incorporate the whimsical shell house built by Catherine Countess of Tyrone in 1754, who arranged for sea captains docking at Wexford's port to bring her shells from distant shores. The fine Georgian house (admission €15; ⊘ 9am-1pm Mon-Fri Feb & May-Jul, plus 1st & 3rd Sun of month May-Jul) is also open to visitors.

Southeast County Waterford

This hidden corner of the county makes an easy day trip from Waterford city. The waters are tidal and shift and change throughout the day, adding to the atmosphere.

Less than 14km east of Waterford is the estuary village of Passage East, from where car ferries yo-yo to Ballyhack in County Wexford. It's a pretty little fishing village with thatched cottages around the harbour.

A little-travelled 11km-long coast road wiggles south between Passage East and Dunmore East. At times single-vehicle-width and steep, it offers mesmerising views of the ocean and undulating fields. On a bike it is a thrill.

ℹ Getting There & Away

Suirway (www.suirway.com; adult/child €4/2, 30 minutes) buses connect Waterford with Passage East seven to eight times daily.

Dunmore East

POP 1795

Some 19km southeast of Waterford, Dunmore East (Dún Mór) is strung out along a coastline of red sandstone cliffs full of screaming kittiwakes and concealed coves. In the 19th century the town was a station for the steam packets that carried mail between England and the south of Ireland. Legacies include picturesque thatched cottages lining the main street and an unusual Doric lighthouse (1825) overlooking the working harbour. Information on the area is available at www.discoverdunmore.com.

◉ Sights & Activities

The area slumbers in winter but wakes up in summer when bathers head to a series of tiny cove beaches along the cliffs. Among them, Counsellor's Beach is near good pubs and cafes while Ladies Cove is close to a pretty park.

Heading west, the 16.5km scenic drive to the seaside frivolities of Tramore is packed with enough natural thrills (rolling green hills, soaring coastal vistas, herds of cattle crossing the road...) to more than match the resort's carnival appeal.

Dunmore East Adventure Centre ADVENTURE SPORTS (www.dunmoreadventure.com; Stoney Cove; 🚻) Hires out equipment for kayaking, surfing and snorkelling, and also runs sailing, kayaking, canoeing and windsurfing courses for children and adults, plus land-based activities including archery and rock climbing.

✹ Festivals & Events

Bluegrass Festival MUSIC (⊘ Aug) In mid-summer the air thrums with the beat of banjos.

🛏 Sleeping

Avon Lodge B&B   B&B **€**
(📳 051-385 775; www.avonlodgebandb.com; r from €60; 🐾) Although the exterior of this suburban-style house looks rather bland, it's in a great location near Ladies Beach. Run by traditional musician Richie Roberts, the homey rooms are clean, comfortable and brightened by punchy colour schemes with coordinated fabrics.

Haven Hotel   HOTEL **€€**
(📳 051-383 150; www.thehavenhotel.com; s/d from €45/90; ⊙ hotel & restaurant open Mar-Oct; 🐾) Built in the 1860s as a summer house for the Malcolmson family, whose coat of arms can still be seen on the fireplaces, the Haven is now run by the Kelly family and remains an elegant retreat with wood-panelled bathrooms and, in two rooms, four-poster beds. Local produce underpins dishes in the casual restaurant (⊙ 5.30-10pm Mon-Sat, 10am-3pm Sun; mains €12-20) and the low-lit crimson-toned bar.

🍴 Eating & Drinking

Bay Cafe   CAFE **€**
(Dock Rd; mains €7-11; ⊙ 9am-6pm) With harbour views so good there's a whale-watching guide stuck to the window, this artsy cafe serves interesting twists on casual cafe fare. The open-faced seafood sandwiches come highly recommended, while the guacamole-stuffed bagel is a novelty in these parts.

★ Lemon Tree Cafe   IRISH **€€**
(www.lemontreecatering.ie; mains €8-20; ⊙ 10am-6pm Tue-Sun, 7-10pm Fri & Sat Jun-Aug; 🖐) Come here for organic coffee, baked goods and a deli counter with takeaway dishes ranging from nut-and-lentil loaf to seafood pie. There's plenty of seating, inside and out, a menu of dishes with an emphasis on seafood, and a play section for children.

Spinnaker Bar   SEAFOOD **€€**
(www.thespinnakerbar.com; mains €14-25; ⊙ food noon-9pm) Eat at sidewalk tables watching beachgoers pass, inside amid nautical knick-knacks or out the back in the sheltered beer garden. Wherever you choose, you'll enjoy top-notch casual seafood fare. Chowders, fish and chips, salads and fresh specials are expertly prepared. There's live music on summer weekends.

Power's Bar   PUB
(Dock Rd; ⊙ noon-11.30pm Mon-Thu, to 12.30am Fri & Sat, 11.30am-11.30pm Sun) Toe-tapping trad sessions take place on Tuesday nights year-round at this butter-yellow corner pub. It's nicknamed 'the Butcher's' after its former incarnation as a meat and grocery store.

ℹ Getting There & Away

Suirway (www.suirway.com; adult/child €4/2) buses connect Waterford with Dunmore East around eight times daily (€4, 30 minutes).

Tramore
POP 10,328

In summer the seafront spread out below the steep town of Tramore (Trá Mhór in Irish, meaning 'big beach') is a whirl of fairground rides, amusement arcades and all the other tack of an old-style beach town. In winter, it's considerably quieter.

◎ Sights

Tramore Bay is hemmed in by Great Newtown Head to the southwest and Brownstown Head to the southeast. The 20m-high concrete pillars were erected by Lloyds of London in 1816 after a shipping tragedy: 363 lives were lost when the *Seahorse* mistook Tramore Bay for Waterford Harbour and was wrecked. Some of the best views of the heads extend from the delightful sheltered swimming spot, Guillamene Cove.

Atop Great Newtown Head is the inaccessible Metal Man, a 3.6m sailor made from iron in 1819. In white breeches and blue jacket, he points dramatically seawards as a warning to approaching ships. Legend has it that if a girl hops around the base of the statue three times on one leg, she will be married within a year (and no, it doesn't work in reverse for divorce!).

🏃 Activities

Tramore's wide, 5km-long beach is capped by 30m-high sand dunes at the eastern end and is a premier surfing spot suitable for all levels, including beginners, thanks to slow-forming waves. The town has year-round surf schools, which also offer eco-walks around the Back Strand, one of Europe's largest intertidal lagoons, and various other activities.

Surfing lessons cost around €45 for a group class and €90 for private tuition. Equipment hire is about €25 for two hours including wetsuits and (much-needed) boots, gloves and hoods during winter.

T-Bay Surf & Eco Centre SURFING
(☑ 051-391 297; www.tbaysurf.com; 🏄) Ireland's largest surf school organises a wide range of courses aimed at all levels, including summer surfing camps for children.

Oceanics SURFING
(☑ 051-390 944; www.oceanics.ie; Red Cottage, Riverstown; 🏄) Besides providing lessons and courses, Oceanics organises surf parties and summer camps for teens and younger children.

Freedom Surf School SURFING
(☑ 086 391 4908; www.freedomsurfschool.com; The Gap, Riverstown; 🏄) As well as surfing courses, this school runs lessons in 'blokarting' (sail-powered beach buggying).

Lake Tour Stable HORSE RIDING
(☑ 051-381 958; www.laketourstables.ie; treks from adult/child €25/20; 🏄) To saddle up, head here to Tramore's pony trekking and riding centre.

Tramore Golf Club GOLF
(☑ 051-386 170; www.tramoregolfclub.com; Newtown Hill; green fees €30-40) One of Ireland's oldest courses, established in 1894, with a new nine-hole (to add to the previous 18-hole) course. Home to several championships, including the Irish Close Championship on three occasions, scheduled here again in 2015.

🎊 Festivals & Events

Waterford & Tramore Racecourse HORSE RACING
(www.tramore-racecourse.com; Graun Hill) The first European horserace meeting of the year takes place on 1 January at Tramore Racecourse, and is one of many events throughout the year.

🛏 Sleeping

★ Beach Haven House B&B, HOSTEL €
(☑ 051-390 208; www.beachhavenhouse.com; Waterford Rd; B&B s/d from €30/60, dm from €15, 2-person apt from €50; ☺B&B and apts all year, hostel Mar-Nov; 🏄) American Avery and his Irish wife Niamh have all budgets covered with their B&B, hostel and apartments (two nights minimum stay). The B&B and apartments are tastefuly decorated with light wood and earth colours, while the hostel is predictably basic but has excellent facilities, including a comfortable communal sitting room. In true Californian fashion, Avery fires up the barbecue in the summer months.

O'Shea's Hotel HOTEL €€
(☑ 051-381 246; www.osheas-hotel.com; Strand St; s/d from €50/80; 🏄) O'Shea's rooms are not as classy as the flower-emblazoned, black-and-white exterior suggests. Still, this family-run hotel offers good value and a coveted location close to the beach; several rooms have sea views.

🍴 Eating & Drinking

If it's fried you'll find it on a Tramore menu. At weekends the pubs draw raucous crowds from the region, especially on long summer evenings.

Vee Bistro INTERNATIONAL €€
(1 Lower Main St; mains €10-28; ☺9am-late; 🏄) In a port-wine-coloured building with tribal art and abstract canvases on the walls, the Vee dishes up casual bistro-style fare such as chicken stir-fry and chorizo salad, plus some superb bakery goodies and daily specials.

Banyan THAI €€
(☑ 051-330 707; www.thebanyanthai.ie; Upper Branch Rd; mains €12-14; ☺6-9pm Tue-Thu, 5-10pm Fri & Sat, 4-9pm Sun) Come here for delicious Thai food in the elegant surroundings of this historic town house. Dishes include tom yum soup, massamam curry and satay chicken, delicately spiced with just enough heat. As usual the kitchen has to cater to Irish tastebuds with a choice of rice, noodles or chips to accompany the main dishes.

ℹ Getting There & Away

Bus Éireann (www.buseireann.ie) runs frequent buses daily between Waterford and Tramore (€3, 30 minutes).

The Copper Coast

Cerulean skies, azure waters, impossibly green hills and ebony cliff faces provide a vibrant palette of colour on the beautiful Copper Coast drive west of Tramore to Dungarvan. The R675 winds its way from one stunning vista to another.

Annestown has a couple of welcoming cafes and is a good place to stop after the boisterous charms of Tramore. At Dunabrattin Head watch for a small cove beach just west. It's wide and inviting with virtually no development.

At 25km west of Tramore, the rugged coastline of the Copper Coast European Geopark (www.coppercoastgeopark.com; ☺park office 9.30am-5pm Mon-Fri) takes its name from the 19th-century copper mines outside Bunmahon. Among the area's scalloped coves and beaches are geological formations dating back 460 million years, including quartz blocks, fossils and former volcanoes. Free one-hour guided walks are available in summer, or download a walking guide from the website.

To explore the Copper Coast's caves, coves and cliffs in sea kayaks, contact Sea Paddling (☑051-393 314; www.seapaddling.com; tours from €35; ☷). Tours last from a few hours to a few days and cover various parts of Waterford's coast. Also geared for children from 13 years.

Before you reach Dungarvan, on the north side of the harbour near Ballynacourty, is Clonea Strand, a beautiful stretch of pristine sand.

Dungarvan

POP 9427

Resembling a miniature version of Galway, pastel-shaded buildings ring Dungarvan's picturesque bay where the River Colligan meets the sea. St Garvan founded a monastery here in the 7th century, but most of the centre dates from the early 19th century when the Duke of Devonshire rebuilt the streets around Grattan Sq. Overlooking the bay are a dramatic ruined castle and an Augustinian abbey. Dungarvan is also renowned for its cuisine, with outstanding restaurants, a famous cooking school and the annual Waterford Festival of Food.

◉ Sights

Colourful 18th-century Davitt's Quay is the perfect place to grab a pint and watch the boats sail in. Grattan Square is a good anchor for exploring the surrounding atmospheric streets.

★ Dungarvan Castle   CASTLE
(www.heritageireland.ie; ◷10am-6pm Jun-Sep) FREE Renovation is restoring this stone fortress to its former Norman glory. Once inhabited by King John's constable Thomas Fitz Anthony, the oldest part of the castle is the unusual 12th-century shell keep, built to defend the mouth of the river. The 18th-century British army barracks house a visitor centre with various exhibits. Admission is by guided tour only.

Waterford County Museum   MUSEUM
(www.waterfordcountymuseum.org; St Augustine St; ◷10am-5pm Mon-Fri, 2-5pm Sat Jun-Sep) FREE This small well-presented museum covers maritime history (with relics from shipwrecks), Famine history, local personalities and various other titbits, all displayed in a former wine store.

St Augustine's Church   CHURCH
(St Augustine St; ◷varies) Overlooking Dungarvan Harbour, this solitary church, which is still in use, was built in 1832 and once had a thatched roof. There are features incorporated from the original 13th-century abbey, including a well-preserved tower and nave. The abbey was destroyed during the Cromwellian occupation of the town.

Old Market House Arts Centre   GALLERY
(Lower Main St; ◷11am-5pm Tue-Sat) FREE Housed in a handsome building dating from 1641, these light airy galleries showcase contemporary art by local artists.

🏃 Activities

★ Tannery Cookery School   COOKING COURSE
(☑058-45420; www.tannery.ie; 10 Quay St; courses €75-150; ☎) Looking like a futuristic kitchen showroom, this school run by bestselling author and chef Paul Flynn adjoins a fruit, vegetable and herb garden. Courses include foraging for ingredients, market gardening, traditional Italian cuisine and the popular 'How To Cook Better' option.

✵ Festivals & Events

★ Waterford Festival of Food   FOOD
(www.waterfordfestivaloffood.com; ◷mid-Apr) The area's abundant fresh produce is celebrated

---

TRIANGLE OF GOLF

There are three championship golf courses within five minutes' drive of Dungarven: West Waterford Golf & Country Club (www.westwaterfordgolf. com), Dungarvan Golf Club (www. dungarvangolfclub.com) and the Golf Coast Golf Club (www.goldcoastgolfclub.com). All three have participated in the Dungarvan Golf Triangle initiative whereby keen golfers can play at any three courses for the price of two. Check the website www.golftriangle. com for more information, including directions and maps.

at this hugely popular festival that features cooking workshops and demonstrations, talks by local producers and a food fair. A craft brew beer garden has suitably thirst-quenching appeal.

Féile na nDéise   MUSIC
(www.feilenandeise.com; ☉ May bank holiday weekend) Local pubs and hotels host a lively traditional music and dance festival that attracts around 200 musicians.

🛏 Sleeping

In keeping with Dungarvan's foodie street cred, breakfasts at B&Bs are often minor spectacles of intriguing dishes and prepared foods sourced from the owner's gardens.

Mountain View House   B&B €€
(☑ 058-42588; www.mountainviewhse.com; O'Connell St; s/d from €50/70; ☎) This Georgian house was built in 1815 and stands grandly above a more modern estate with sweeping views of the Comeragh Mountains. The rooms are comfortable although they lack the period features of the delightful breakfast room with its original fireplace and ceiling rose. It's a five-minute walk down O'Connell St from Grattan Sq.

Tannery Townhouse   GUESTHOUSE €€
(☑ 058-45420; www.tannery.ie; Church St; s/d €65/110; ☉ Feb-Dec; ☎) Just around the corner from the Tannery restaurant is this boutique guesthouse, which spans two buildings in the town centre. Its 14 rooms are modern and stylish, and have fridges stacked with juices, fruit and muffins so you can enjoy a continental breakfast on your own schedule. An honour bar and snacks ease the transition from afternoon to evening.

Cairbre House   B&B €€
(☑ 058-42338; www.cairbrehouse.com; Abbeyside; s/d from €40/80; ☉ closed mid-Dec–mid-Jan; ☎) Blazing with red flowers in summer, this four-room B&B is set on a half-hectare of riverside gardens. The gardens come into their own at breakfast, providing many of the ingredients, including fragrant herbs; a small terrace overlooks the water. The only downside is the 1km walk to town along busy roads but this is set to change, with a river path underway at the time of research.

Lawlor's Hotel   HOTEL €€
(☑ 058-41122; www.lawlorshotel.com; TF Meagher St; s/d from €60/90; ☎) Across the road from the tourist office, the landmark custard-yellow Lawlor's was praised by William Makepeace Thackeray in 1843 as a 'very neat and comfortable inn'. Its latest incarnation extends from its artfully lit restaurant and bar to the 94 contemporary, creamy-toned bedrooms, many of which have harbour views. The flip side is that some of the public areas are starting to look slightly scuffed.

🍴 Eating

As you'd expect, Dungarvan's **farmers market** (www.dungarvanfarmersmarket.com; Grattan Sq; ☉ 9am-2pm Thu) is a minor festival of breads, cheeses, chocolate, produce and hot food.

Meades   CAFE €
(☑ 087 411 6714; www.meadescafe.com; Grattan Sq; snacks from €4.50; ☉ 9am-5pm Mon-Sat, 11am-5pm Sun; ☎❄) Enjoying an ace position on the town's main square, this cafe has a buzzy cheerful vibe with a kids corner, papers to read and a menu of scrumptious baked goods, as well as savoury tartlets, homemade soups (and not just the ubiquitous vegetable), salads and cottage pie.

★**Nude Food**   MODERN IRISH €€
(www.nudefood.ie; 86 O'Connell St; mains €10-14; ☉ 9.15am-6pm Mon-Wed, to 9.30pm Thu-Sat; ☑❄) The only things bare naked here are the plates after diners finish. From carefully crafted coffees to a beautiful selection of deli items, this cafe stands out. Lunch and dinner menus feature top Waterford ingredients in sandwiches, salads, starters and hot mains that are hearty, honest and flavourful. Nude Food regularly hosts fringe events, such as poetry readings.

★**Tannery**   MODERN IRISH €€€
(☑ 058-45420; www.tannery.ie; 10 Quay St; mains €18-29; ☉ 12.30-2.30pm Fri & Sun, 6-9.30pm Tue-Sat, also Sun Jul & Aug) An old leather tannery houses this innovative and much-lauded restaurant, where Paul Flynn creates seasonally changing dishes that focus on just a few flavours and celebrates them through preparations that are at once comforting yet surprising. There's intimate seating downstairs or tables in the buzzing, loftlike room upstairs. Service is excellent. Book ahead.

🍷 Drinking & Nightlife

Look for Dungarvan Brewing's locally produced microbrews in the pubs here, including the crisp and hoppy Helvick Gold Blonde Ale.

Moorings
PUB

(www.mooringsdungarvan.com; Davitt's Quay;
⊙11am-midnight) Beautiful original timber
cabinetry and a snug are the main features
of the creaky original room at this waterfront bar. Outside there's a vast beer garden
where you can enjoy local beers on tap and a
DJ at weekends. Also offers solid traditional
food and accommodation (single/double
€35/70).

Kiely's
PUB

(O'Connell St; ⊙5-11.30pm Mon-Thu, to 12.30am
Fri & Sat, to 11pm Sun) A neighbourhood
pub in the centre, half-timbered Kiely's
has frequent trad sessions that pull in the
entire bar.

Bridie Dee's
PUB

(Mary St; ⊙6-11.30pm) Almost eternally burning peat fires, old codgers trading lies at the
bar and a little beer garden out back add
up to an unbeatable combination. Frequent
trad sessions.

ℹ Information

Tourist office (☑058-41741; www.dungarvan
tourism.com; Courthouse Bldg, TF Meagher St;
⊙9.30am-5pm Mon-Fri year-round, plus 10am-
5pm Sat May-Sep) A helpful tourist office with
stacks of informative brochures.

ℹ Getting There & Away

Bus Éireann (www.buseireann.ie) services pick
up and drop off on Davitt's Quay on the way to
and from Waterford (€12, one hour, 12 daily) and
Cork (€16, 1½ hours, 12 daily).

Ring Peninsula

POP 1689

Just 15 minutes' drive from Dungarvan,
the Ring Peninsula (An Rinn, meaning 'the
headland') is one of Ireland's best-known
Gaeltacht (Irish-speaking areas). En route,
views of the Comeragh Mountains, Dungarvan Bay and the Copper Coast drift away
to the northeast. You can easily spend a day
exploring quiet country lanes here, with the
promise of a hidden beach or fine old trad
pub around the next bend in the road.

Ex-Waterford Crystal worker Eamonn
Terry returned home to the peninsula to set
up his own workshop, **Criostal na Rinne**
(☑058-46174; www.criostal.com; ⊙by appointment), where you can buy deep-prismatic-
cut, full-lead crystal vases, bowls, clocks,
jewellery and even chandeliers.

🛏 Sleeping & Eating

Dún Ard
B&B €€

(☑058-46782; www.ringbedandbreakfast.ie; Ga-
otha, Dungarvan; s/d from €50/90; 🗑) Perched
high above Dungarvan Bay, the exterior of
this B&B on an (albeit upmarket) estate is
deceiving. Prices may seem high, but the
three rooms here really do equal the quality,
spaciousness and finish you find in a five-
star hotel. There is also a movie library and
projector screen for the use of guests.

Seaview
B&B €€

(☑058-41583; www.seaviewdungarvan.com; Pulla;
s/d from €45/70; 🗑) Handy for the wonderful
An Seanachaí and the Marine Bar, this light-
filled, pink-hued guesthouse has eight comfy
rooms and sweeping views of Dungarvan
and the Comeragh Mountains. Good walks
begin at the front door.

★ Marine Bar
PUB €€

(www.marinebar.com; Pulla; mains €10-20;
⊙kitchen noon-9pm) Sure, there's good traditional food at this two-century-old pub, but
the real reason to stop by is the craic. Year-
round, traditional sessions rock the place
on Monday and Saturday nights, while
locals contest the traditional Irish card
game '45' on Wednesday evenings (anyone
can join in). There's music most nights in
summer.

An Seanachaí
PUB €€

(☑058-46755; www.seanachai.ie; Pulla; mains
€12-20; ⊙kitchen 11am-9pm Mon-Sat, 12.30-
9pm Sun) The rough-hewn walls of the 'Old
Storyteller' could certainly tell a few stories
of their own. Parts of this thatched-roof
pub date back to the 14th century from its
earliest incarnation as a farm. It's an atmospheric spot for a pint, a meal (try the house-
speciality fish pie), regular live music or the
fortnightly Saturday storytelling sessions
(9pm). On the grounds, a dozen self-catering
cottages are available for weekly rental
(from €300).

ℹ Getting There & Around

Pubs, accommodation and shops are scattered
along the peninsula; you will need your own
wheels to get around.

Bus Éireann (www.buseireann.ie) stops in
Ring en route between Ardmore (30 minutes)
and Waterford (1¼ hours) via Dungarvan. But
frequency is seldom: once daily in summer, far
less at other times.

Ardmore

POP 410

The enticing seaside village of Ardmore may look quiet these days, but it's claimed that St Declan set up shop here between AD 350 and 420. This brought Christianity to southeast Ireland long before St Patrick arrived from Britain. Today's visitors come for its beautiful strand, water sports, ancient buildings and reliably good places to eat and sleep.

◉ Sights & Activities

Plan on spending a day strolling about the town, ancient sites, coast and countryside.

★ St Declan's Church
RUINS

In a striking position on a hill above town, the ruins of St Declan's Church stand on the site of St Declan's original monastery alongside an impressive cone-roofed, 29m-high, 12th-century round tower, one of the best examples of these structures in Ireland.

On the outer western gable wall of the 13th-century church are weathered 9th-century carvings set in unusual arched panels, while within are two Ogham stones featuring the earliest form of writing in Ireland, one with the longest such inscription in the country. Local lore claims St Declan was buried in the 8th-century oratory, which was modernised in 1716. Inside is an empty pit beneath a missing flagstone, the result of centuries of relic collection. The site was leased to Sir Walter Raleigh in 1591. In 1642 the building was occupied by Royalist troops, 117 of whom were hanged here.

St Declan's Well
HISTORIC SITE

Pilgrims once washed in these waters, which are located in front of the ruins of Dysert Church.

St Declan's Stone
LANDMARK

Different geologically from other rocks in the area, this stone steeped in lore is at the southern end of the beach. It was perhaps brought by glacier from the Comeragh Mountains but, according to legend, St Declan's bell, which he is often pictured holding, drifted across the sea from Wales on the stone after his servant forgot to pack it. He decreed that wherever the stone came to rest would be the place of his resurrection.

★ Ballyquin Beach
BEACH

(🚗) Tide pools, fascinating rocks and sheltered sand are just some of the appeals of this beautiful beach. It's 1km off the R673, 4km northeast of Ardmore. Look for the small sign.

Ardmore Pottery
GALLERY

(www.ardmorepottery.com; ☺10am-6pm Mon-Sat, 2-6pm Sun May-Oct) Near the start of the cliff walk, this cosy little house sells beautiful pottery, many in lovely shades of blue and cream. Other locally produced goods include warm hand-knitted socks. This is a good source of tourist information for the area.

Walks
WALKING

A 5km, cobweb-banishing cliff walk leads from St Declan's Well. On the one-hour round trip you'll pass the wreck of a crane ship that was blown ashore in 1987 on its way from Liverpool to Malta. The 94km St Declan's Way mostly traces an old pilgrimage route from Ardmore to the Rock of Cashel (County Tipperary) via Lismore. Catholic pilgrims walk along it on St Declan's Day (24 July).

Ardmore Adventures
ADVENTURE SPORTS

(www.ardmoreadventures.ie; Main St; 🚗) There's always something going on at this action-packed place: kayak tours of the coast (€45), surfing, climbing and more.

Phil's Walking Tours of Ardmore
WALKING TOURS

(📱087 952 6288; www.ardmorewalksandtours.com; walks from €5; ☺noon) Tours led by an archaeologist explore ruins in and around town.

🛏 Sleeping & Eating

Newtown Farm Guesthouse
B&B €€

(📱024-94143; www.newtownfarm.com; Grange; s/d from €45/72; 🚗) Fresh eggs, homemade scones, local cheeses and smoked salmon are on the breakfast menu at this stylish B&B on a working sheep farm with seamless sea views. Coming from Dungarvan on the N25, go past the Ardmore turn-off and take the next left 1km further on, from where it's 100m up the road.

Cliff House Hotel
LUXURY HOTEL €€€

(📱024-87800; www.thecliffhousehotel.com; r €225-450; @🚗🍽) Built into the cliff face, all guest rooms at this cutting-edge edifice overlook the bay, and most have balconies or terraces. Some suites even have two-person floor-to-ceiling glass showers (strategically frosted in places) so you don't miss those sea views. There are also sea views from the indoor swimming pool, outdoor jacuzzi and spa, the bar and the much-lauded modern Irish restaurant (menu from €68), which has a Michelin star to its name.

Ardmore Gallery & Tearoom CAFE €
(www.artmoregalleryandtearoom.ie; Main St; dishes €5-12; ⊙9.30am-6pm daily Apr-Sep, Sat & Sun Oct-Mar) Always a winning combination, the gallery displays local art, while the teashop sells delicious cakes, plus soup and savoury treats during the summer months. Jewellery, hand-painted silk scarves and knitware are also for sale.

White Horses SEAFOOD €€
(⊇024-94040; Main St; lunch mains €8-13, dinner mains €22-33; ⊙11am-11pm Tue-Sun May-Sep, Fri-Sun Oct-Apr) Energetically run by three sisters, this bistro concentrates on fresh seafood. Push the boat out and try the Dublin Bay king prawns (€33) on plates handmade in the village. Enjoy a drink on the bench out the front or a meal at a sunny lawn table at the back.

ⓘ Getting There & Away

Bus Éireann (www.buseireann.ie) operates one to three buses daily west to Cork (€15, 1¾ hours); connections east to Dungarvan and beyond range from one daily in summer to seldom at other times.

Cappoquin & Around

POP 760

Slinking up a steep hillside, the small market town of Cappoquin sits at the foot of the rounded, heathery Knockmealdown Mountains. To the west lies the picturesque Blackwater Valley, where traces of the earliest Irish people have been discovered, dating back more than 9000 years.

⊙ Sights & Activities

The Dromana Drive to Cappoquin from Villierstown (An Baile Nua) 6km south, traces the River Blackwater through the Dromana Forest. At the bridge over the River Finisk is a remarkable **Hindu-Gothic gate**, inspired by the Brighton Pavilion in England.

Mt Melleray Cistercian Abbey MONASTERY
(www.mountmellerayabbey.org; ⊙7am-7pm) **FREE** The beautiful Mt Melleray Cistercian Abbey is a fully functioning monastery with 28 Trappist monks, but welcomes visitors

wishing 'to take time for quiet contemplation'. The abbey was founded in 1832 by 64 monks who were expelled from a monastery near Melleray in Brittany, France. There are tearooms (closed Monday) and a heritage centre. It's signposted 6km north from Cappoquin in the Knockmealdown foothills. Turn right off the road to Mt Melleray for the forest walks and picnic spots at **Glenshelane Park**.

Cappoquin House and Gardens HISTORIC BUILDING
(www.cappoquinhouseandgardens.com; house/garden €5/5; ⊙house 9am-1pm Mon-Sat May-Jun, garden 10am-4pm year round) This is a magnificent 1779-built Georgian mansion and 2 hectares of formal gardens overlooking the River Blackwater. It's the private residence of the Keane family, who've lived here for 200 years. The entrance to the house is just north of the centre of Cappoquin; look for a set of huge black iron gates.

ⓘ Sleeping & Eating

Richmond House GUESTHOUSE €€
(⊇058-54278; www.richmondhouse.net; N72; s/d from €70/120; ⊙restaurant dinner nightly Apr-May, Tue-Sat Oct-Mar; ⓐ) Dating from 1704, Richmond House is set on 5.6 hectares of parkland. All the same, its nine guestrooms – furnished with countrified plaids, prints and mahogany – are cosy rather than imposing, and service is genuinely friendly. Nonguests are welcome at its **restaurant** (mains €25-40, 5-course menu €58), where local produce includes West Waterford lamb and Helvick monkfish.

Barron's Bakery BAKERY €
(www.barronsbakery.ie; The Square; dishes €3-8; ⊙8.30am-5.30pm Mon-Sat) This famous local bakery has used the same Scotch brick ovens since 1887. Sandwiches, light meals and a mouth-watering selection of cakes and buns baked on the premises are available in its Wedgewood-green-painted cafe, while the breads are famed throughout the area.

ⓘ Getting There & Away

Bus Éireann (www.buseireann.ie) services stop in Cappoquin en route to Lismore (€3.75, 10 minutes) and Dungarvan (€6, 20 minutes) on Sunday only.

Lismore

POP 1370

Lismore's enormous 19th-century castle seems out of proportion to this quiet, elegant town on the River Blackwater where most of the existing buildings date from the early 19th century. Over the centuries, statesmen and luminaries streamed through the town, where a great monastic university was founded in the 7th century on the site of the current castle.

◉ Sights

Between doses of history and legend at the castle and cathedral, you can picnic in the Millennium Gardens, beside the castle car park, or take a 20-minute riverside stroll along Lady Louisa's Walk.

Lismore Castle   CASTLE
(www.lismorecastlearts.ie; gardens adult/child €8/4; ⊙11am-4.45pm mid-Mar–Sep; ⓘ) From the Cappoquin road there are stunning glimpses of the riverside 'castle'. The original castle was erected by Prince John, Lord of Ireland, in 1185, although most of what you see now is from the early 19th century. While you can't get inside the four impressive walls of the main, crenulated building, you can visit the 3 hectares of ornate and manicured gardens. Thought to be the oldest in Ireland, they are divided into the walled Jacobean upper garden and less formal lower garden. There are brilliant herbaceous borders, magnolias and camellias, and a splendid yew walk where Edmund Spenser is said to have written *The Faerie Queen*. There are modern sculptures in the gardens and a contemporary art gallery in the west wing of the castle.

The castle stables and gardens are used as one of the venues during the annual Lismore Music Festival (www.lismoremusicfestival.com) in June. Mozart's *The Marriage of Figaro* was performed here in 2013.

St Carthage's Cathedral   CATHEDRAL
(⊙varies) FREE 'One of the neatest and prettiest edifices I have seen', commented William Thackeray in 1842 about the striking 1679 cathedral – and that was before the addition of the Edward Burne-Jones stained-glass window, which features all the Pre-Raphaelite hallmarks: an effeminate knight and a pensive maiden against a sensuous background of deep-blue velvet and intertwining flowers. Justice, with sword and scales, and Humility, holding a lamb, honour Francis Currey, who helped to relieve the suffering of the poor during the Famine. There are some noteworthy 16th-century tombs, including the elaborately carved MacGrath family crypt dating from 1557.

Lismore Heritage Centre   MUSEUM
(Main St; adult/child €5/3.50; ⊙9.30am-5.30pm Mon-Fri, 10am-5.30pm Sat, noon-5.30pm Sun mid-Mar–Christmas; ⓘ) A 30-minute audiovisual presentation takes you from the arrival of St Carthage in AD 636 to the present day via the discovery of the *Book of Lismore* behind a wall in the castle in 1814 and John F Kennedy's visit in 1947. There's also the Family Fun Experience, which is part nature trail, part treasure hunt and takes you around town. The information 'pack' costs €10; the kids will love it.

🍴 Sleeping & Eating

Lismore House Hotel   HOTEL €€
(☑058-72966; www.lismorehousehotel.com; Main St; s/d from €55/120; @🖨) Directly opposite the Heritage Centre, Ireland's oldest purpose-built hotel was built in 1797 by the Duke of Devonshire. He'd still recognise the exterior, but rooms within have had a contemporary makeover with sleek dark-timber furniture and cream-and-gold fabrics. Book online for deals.

★**Lismore Farmers Market**   MARKET €
(Castle Ave; ⊙10am-4pm Sun) The upscale surrounds attract a fab collection of vendors including Dungarvan's Naked Lunch, whose tasty sandwiches you can enjoy in the park or at tables set up on the gravel path.

Saffron   INDIAN €€
(☑058-53778; Main St; mains €10-14; ⊙5-11pm Wed-Mon) Saffron-coloured walls, muted lights and large gilt mirrors create an intimate atmosphere you don't usually find at your corner curry house back home. All the mainstream Indian favourites are here, plus some eye-watering curries that are even hotter than vindaloo.

Foley's   IRISH €€
(www.foleysonthemall.ie; Main St; mains €10-24; ⊙9am-9pm) This inviting trad pub serves good steaks, fish and bangers and mash in its interior replete with decorative wallpaper, leather-backed benches and an open fire. There's also a beer garden.

ℹ Information

Tourist office (www.discoverlismore.com; Main St; ⊘ 9.30am-5.30pm Mon-Fri, 10am-5.30pm Sat, noon-5.30pm Sun mid-Mar–Christmas) Inside the Lismore Heritage Centre; pick up the info-packed *Lismore Walking Tour Guide* (€3).

ℹ Getting There & Around

Bus Éireann (www.buseireann.ie) serves Cappoquin (€3.75,10 minutes) and Dungarvan (€6, 20 minutes) on Sunday only.
Lismore Cycling Holidays (✆ 087 935 6610; www.cyclingholidays.ie; bike hire per day from €18) Hires out bikes.

Northern County Waterford

Some of the most scenic parts of County Waterford are in the north around Ballymacarbry and in the Nire Valley, which runs between the Comeragh and Monavullagh Mountains. While not as rugged as the west of Ireland, this mountain scenery has a stark beauty and doesn't attract much tourist traffic, despite the abundance of megalithic remains. It's a place of long walks and country stays.

◉ Sights & Activities

The Comeragh Mountains, where there are ridges to trace and loughs to circle, are named after their many *coums* (valleys, often of glacial origin).

Stop for a pint and panini in Melody's Nire View (✆ 052-36169; Ballymacarbry), where the new owners have info on local walks and activities.

Otherwise make sure you're around for the Nire Valley Walking Festival (www.nirevalley.com), which takes place on the second weekend in October, with guided walks and traditional music in the pubs.

The East Munster Way walking trail covers some 70km between Carrick-on-Suir in County Tipperary and the northern slopes of the Knockmealdown Mountains. Access is at Fourmilewater, about 10km northwest of Ballymacarbry.

⌂ Sleeping

★ **Hanora's Cottage**   GUESTHOUSE €€
(✆ 052-36134; www.hanorascottage.com; Nire Valley, Ballymacarbry; full-board per person from €75, B&B s/d from €65/120; 🖤) This 19th-century ancestral home is in a breathtaking position,

between the bubbling River Nire and the picturesque church. The surrounding countryside is wonderful for walkers and the rooms are plush and luxurious with jacuzzi baths for that soothing post-hike soak. The full-board price is an excellent deal; everything in the gourmet restaurant (⊘ dinner Mon-Sat) is made on the premises. Take the road east from Ballymacarbry, opposite Melody's Nire View pub and follow signs.

Glasha Farmhouse B&B   B&B €€
(✆ 052-36108; www.glashafarmhouse.com; Ballymacarbry; s/d from €60/100; 🖤) Olive O'Gorman takes meticulous pride in maintaining the Regency-style bedrooms, with king-size beds, at her working dairy farm overlooking the Comeragh and Knockmealdown mountains. Some wonderful loop walks fan out around the farm (including one that takes in the local pub!); afterwards, reward yourself with dinner served by candlelight (€35 to €45) in a glass conservatory. The farm is signposted 2km northwest of Ballymacarbry.

ℹ Getting There & Away

Bus service is limited; this region is best seen by car, bike or on foot.

COUNTY CARLOW

POP 55,000

Strings of quietly picturesque villages wind through Carlow (Ceatharlach), Ireland's second-smallest county after Louth. The scenic Blackstairs Mountains dominate the southeast, while the region's most dramatic chunk of history is Europe's biggest dolmen, just outside quiet Carlow town. A ruined Gothic mansion and a reputedly haunted castle form the backdrop to two of the county's best flower-filled gardens.

Carlow Town

POP 13,623

The narrow streets and lanes of Carlow include a good museum and gallery. The town makes a good base for explorations of the county's real attractions: the countryside gardens.

◉ Sights

Carlow town's main sights are all within a compact central zone.

★ **Carlow County Museum** MUSEUM

(www.carlowcountymuseum.ie; cnr College & Tullow Sts; ◷10am-5pm Mon-Sat, plus 2-4.30pm Sun Jun-Aug; ▣) FREE This new incarnation of the local museum focuses on the lives of people in the county through the ages and is thoroughly engaging. Look for ancient treasures, which were often uncovered by Carlow's toiling farmers. There are also some real one-offs, including the country's only original gallows, dating from the early 1800s, and a 6m-high exquisitely-carved pulpit from Carlow Cathedral, which the Bishop apparently decided to replace with a more modern version (to the chagrin of many locals). The museum is housed in an atmospheric former convent with original stained-glass windows.

Visual Centre for Contemporary Art GALLERY

(www.visualcarlow.ie; Old Dublin Rd; ◷vary by exhibit; ☎) FREE This opaque-white cube-like space of this purpose-built centre is the county's cultural hub. British architect Terry Pawson is behind the factory-inspired industrial design of concrete, steel and glass which, some consider, sits in uneasy alliance with the historic cathedral across the way. The five separate galleries include the 'cathedral', the largest single exhibition space in Ireland. Rotating exhibits highlight local artists. It also houses the George Bernard Shaw Theatre.

Carlow Castle RUIN

(Castle Hill) Built by William de Marshall on the site of an earlier Norman motte-and-bailey fort, this soaring 13-century castle survived Cromwell's attentions. It later succumbed to the grand plans of a certain Dr Middleton, who decided to convert it into a lunatic asylum and blew up much of the castle in 1814 in order to 'remodel' it. The evocative portion that survives is a part of the keep flanked by two towers.

Cathedral of the Assumption CATHEDRAL

(College St; ◷varies) FREE Between the county museum and St Patrick's College is this elegant Regency Gothic cathedral dating from 1833. It was the brainchild of Bishop Doyle, a staunch supporter of Catholic emancipation. His statue includes a woman said to represent Ireland rising up against her oppressors. The church also has an elaborate pulpit and some fine stained-glass windows.

★ **Festivals & Events**

Éigse Carlow Arts Festival ARTS

(www.eigsecarlow.ie; ◷mid Jun) Musicians, writers, actors and street performers take over the town.

Garden Festival GARDENS

(www.carlowfloralfestival.com; ◷late Aug) Talks and tours by Irish gardening personalities.

🛏 **Sleeping**

Diminutive County Carlow has an abundance of charming countryside inns while the town's choices are somewhat limited.

Red Setter Guest House B&B €

(☎059-914 1848; www.redsetterguesthouse.ie; 14 Dublin St; s/d from €25/50; ☎) Great attention to detail, simply furnished but comfortable rooms and extra touches such as fresh flowers make this otherwise humble B&B the winning central-town choice.

Barrowville Townhouse B&B €€

(☎059-914 3324; www.barrowville.com; Kilkenny Rd; s/d from €45/80; ☎) This 18th-century town house has been meticulously converted into a classy B&B with elegant rooms. Enjoy local free-range eggs for breakfast in the airy conservatory overlooking the semiformal gardens.

✗ **Eating & Drinking**

The town is a nightlife hub with a squadron of large pubs at the east end of Tullow St. Look for local brew O'Hara, including a fine India Pale Ale.

★ **Farmers Market** MARKET €

(www.carlowfarmersmarket.com; ◷9am-2pm Sat) Fittingly held at the old Potato Market. Look out for Elizabeth Bradley's cheese, homemade pesto at the olive stall, plus handcrafted chocolates, organic vegetables, ready prepared meals, and more.

★ **Lennons** MODERN IRISH €€

(www.lennons.ie; Visual Centre for Contemporary Art; Old Dublin Rd; lunch mains €8-12, dinner mains €17-25; ◷lunch 10.30am-5pm Mon-Sat, noon-4pm Sun, dinner 6-9.30pm Thu-Sat; ☎) Carlow's best dining is found amid the artsy surrounds of the Visual Centre for Contemporary Art. It's a sleek and stylish space with a patio overlooking the college's grassy grounds. Lunch is popular with ladies-who-lunch and features creative sandwiches, salads and hot specials. Dinner is more refined with a seasonal menu that showcases local artisan produce.

Caffe Formenti CAFE €€
(20 Dublin St; mains €9-14; ☺8am-6pm) This buzzing cafe combines the talents of an Irish-Italian husband-and-wife team which equals a tempting combination of freshly made gelati, Italian pastries, and traditional scones so scrumptious they won the Best Scone of Ireland award in 2012. There are also daily lunch specials, including wholesome homemade soups.

Teach Dolmain PUB
(76 Tullow St; ☺9.30am-11.30pm Mon-Thu & Sun, to 1.30am Fri & Sat) One of an energetic strip of pubs, this earthy popular local has live trad music on Thursdays at 10pm while Sunday is more of a mix, ranging from jazz to blues (7pm). Food also served.

ℹ️ Information

Post Office (cnr Kennedy Ave & Dublin St)

Tourist Office (www.carlowtourism.com; cnr Tullow & College Sts; ☺9.30am-5.30pm Mon-Sat) A useful source of county-wide information located at the county museum.

ℹ️ Getting There & Around

BUS

Bus Éireann (www.buseireann.ie) goes to Dublin (€12, two hours, nine daily), Kilkenny (€8.75, 35 minutes, three daily) and Waterford (€11, 1½ hours, seven daily).

TAXI

Carlow Cabs (☎059-914 0000)

TRAIN

The **train station** (www.irishrail.ie; Station Rd) is to the northeast of town. Carlow is located on the Dublin Heuston (from €10, 70 minutes) to Waterford line (€16, 80 minutes) via Kilkenny. There are eight to 10 trains daily.

Around Carlow Town

Although the entire county is a day trip from Carlow, the following sights are very close.

◎ Sights

★ Delta Sensory Gardens GARDENS
(www.deltasensorygardens.com; Cannery Rd, Strawhall Estate; adult/child €5/free; ☺9am-5pm Mon-Fri, 11am-5pm Sat & Sun; 🚼) Some 16 interconnecting, themed gardens cover a hectare and span the five senses – from sculpture garden to a formal rose garden, water and woodland garden, willow garden and a musical garden with mechanical fountains. Admission proceeds benefit the adjoining Delta Centre, which provides services and respite for adults with learning disabilities. Find the gardens incongruously hidden in an industrial estate on the northern edge of Carlow.

★ Duckett's Grove GARDENS
(www.duckettsgrove.eu; ☺8am-8pm) FREE Adjoining a forebidding ruined Gothic mansion, the original high brick walls of this estate frame two sprawling, interconnected formal gardens. Filled with the scents of lavender and fruit blossom in spring and summer, they border a shaded woodland area, covering some 4.5 hectares. Check with Carlow's tourist office for the gardens' program of events. There's no public transport; the gardens are 12.5km northeast of Carlow off the R726.

Browne's Hill Dolmen HISTORIC SITE
This 5000-year-old granite monster is Europe's largest portal dolmen (tomb chamber) and one of Ireland's most famous. The capstone alone weighs well over 100 tonnes. It's signposted 3km east of Carlow on the R726.

Killeshin Church RUIN
Once the site of an important monastery with one of the finest round towers in the country, this medieval marvel was destroyed early in the 18th century by a philistine farmer worried that it might collapse and kill his cows. The ruins of a 12th-century church remain, including a remarkable Romanesque doorway dating from the 5th century. Look for the wonderful bearded face on the capstone. Killeshin is 5km west of Carlow on the R430.

Ballon
POP 684

Grand estates and gardens envelop the small village of Ballon. This is prime walking country.

◎ Sights

★ Altamont Gardens GARDENS
(www.heritageireland.ie; Kilbride, Ballon; ☺10am-7pm summer, to 5pm rest of year) FREE This is one of Ireland's most magnificent formal walled gardens, covering 16 hectares with

a design dating from Victorian times. Carefully selected plantings are arranged in naturalistic, idealised settings, surrounding a lake, streams and small waterfall. Peacocks, swans and wild hare add to the camera-clicking atmosphere. There is a small commercial nursery on site and a grand mansion which is, unfortunately, inhabited by squatters, hence its woebegone state. The gardens are 5km east of Ballon.

🛏 Sleeping & Eating

★**Sherwood Park House**   GUESTHOUSE €€
(☑ 059-915 9117; www.sherwoodparkhouse.ie; Kilbride, Ballon; s/d from €60/100) This greystone Georgian manor dates from 1730. The five guest rooms are huge with such period niceties as satin-and-velvet-adorned four-poster beds. You can make arrangements for dinner (€40 per person); breakfast is included. Altamont Gardens are just 600m south.

Forge Restaurant   IRISH €
(www.theforgekilbride.ie; Kilbride Cross, Ballon; dishes €5-10; ⊙ 9.30am-5pm Mon-Sat, 10am-5pm Sun; 🔊 📶) Mary Jordan cooks up delicious healthy soups and hot lunches using local produce at this former blacksmith's forge near Altamont Gardens. There are baked goods to take away plus deli items and crafts for sale.

Borris & Around

POP 650

This seemingly untouched Georgian village has a dramatic mountain backdrop and traditional main street with plenty of atmospheric bars hosting summertime trad music.

◉ Sights & Activities

Kilgraney House Herb Gardens   GARDENS
(www.kilgraneyhouse.com; Bagenalstown; admission €3; ⊙ 2-5pm Thu-Sun May-Sep) These delightful gardens are home to a heady cocktail of medicinal and kitchen plants. Herbs as you've never seen them grow in orderly profusion and are also used in the kitchens for the inn and restaurant here. The recreated medieval monastic herb garden is a favourite. Your admission includes a complimentary cup of herbal tea. The gardens are located off the R705 halfway between Borris and Bagenalstown.

Carlow Brewing Company   BREWERY
(☑ 059-913 4356; www.carlowbrewing.com; Royal Oak Rd, Bagenalstown; tours by reservation €11)

The popular microbrewery offers tours of its O'Hara's brand beers. Its award-winning Irish Stout bursts with flavour and certainly holds its own against that *other* Irish stout.

🛏 Sleeping & Eating

★**Step House Hotel**   HOTEL €€
(☑ 059-977 3209; www.stephousehotel.ie; 66 Main St, Borris; s/d from €75/130; 🔊) At the top end of town, this handsome hotel has rooms decorated in elegant shades of pastel green and gold. All have balconies with views framed by Mt Leinster and a comfortable feeling of opulence with expansive 'rainforest' showers. Tables in the Cellar Restaurant are tucked in romantic corners beneath vaulted ceilings while the rustic-style bar is the perfect place for a recuperative pint after a day striding out. Breakfast included.

Lorum Old Rectory   B&B €€
(☑ 059-977 5282; www.lorum.com; s/d from €85/150; ⊙ Mar-Nov; 🔊) Halfway between Borris and Bagenalstown off the R705, this historic manor house, dating from the 1800s, sits on a prominent knoll east of the road. The gardens provide peaceful views from each of the four rooms with their luxurious canopy beds. The largely organic cooking here is renowned; confirm your four-course dinner when you book (€45 per person).

Kilgraney Country House   GUESTHOUSE €€€
(☑ 059-977 5283; www.kilgraneyhouse.com; s/d from €120/170; ⊙ Mar-Nov; 🔊) The River Barrow burbles down the shallow valley from this six-room Georgian manor. The owners, veteran travellers, have created an exotic interior with artefacts collected from the Philippines and other far-away places. Unwind in the spa or the famous herb gardens, or over a six-course meal (from €50). It's off the R705 halfway between Borris and Bagenalstown.

M O'Shea   PUB
(Main St; mains €8-10; ⊙ noon-late) Surprises abound in this tidy warren of rooms that combines a general store, modern grocery store and old-fashioned pub where spare parts and bits of machinery still hang from the ceiling. Basic pub grub also served.

❶ Getting There & Away

Borris is on the east–west R702, which links the M9 with the N11 in County Wexford.

Eight to 10 daily trains run between Carlow town and Bagenalstown (€5.75, 15 minutes) en route to/from Kilkenny (€10, 35 minutes).

St Mullins

Tranquil little St Mullins sits 6km downstream from Graiguenamanagh, which is in County Kilkenny. The village is the maternal home of Michael Flatley of *Riverdance* fame. From the River Barrow towpath a trail winds uphill to the ruined hulk of an old monastery surrounded by the graves of 1798 rebels. A badly worn 9th-century Celtic cross still stands beside the monastery. Nearby, St Moling's Well is a holy well that seems to attract spare change.

Overlooking the weir at the river's edge, Martin and Emer O'Brien have eschewed corporate life to convert St Mullins' Old Grain Store (☑ 051-424 4440; www.oldgrainstorecottages.ie; cottages per week €380-480; ⊙ cafe 11am-6pm Tue-Sun summer, times vary rest of year) into a fabulous cafe serving a choice of homemade soups, cakes and breads. There are three small self-catering cottages for one to two people, set in the coach house, the forge and the stables. The interiors are stylish yet homey, with shelves of books and wood-burning stoves. Shorter stays are sometimes possible on request. Martin and Emer also lend guests bikes and kayaks.

COUNTY KILKENNY

POP 95,420

County Kilkenny's centrepiece is, of course, the namesake city. An enduring gift of the Normans, it mesmerises visitors with medieval alleys that wind past the castle, cathedral, ruined abbeys and dynamic modern-day and traditional pubs .

The county too is a delight; among its rolling hills, you'll soon run out of adjectives for green. Tiny roads navigate the valleys alongside swirling rivers, moss-covered stone walls and relics of centuries of Irish religious history. Characterful pubs and fine restaurants abound. Shamrock-cute Inistioge village may be star of many movies, but it's the real deal, as are towns such as Graiguenamanagh, Bennettsbridge and Thomastown. It's no surprise that so many artists and craftspeople have set up shop here.

Kilkenny City

POP 24,423

Kilkenny (Cill Chainnigh) is the Ireland of many visitors' imaginations. Its majestic

SCENIC WALKS & DRIVES

Borris is a starting point for the 13km Mt Leinster Scenic Drive (or walk) and is also on the South Leinster Way. To reach the mighty mountain from Borris, follow the Mt Leinster Scenic Drive signposts 13km towards Bunclody in County Wexford. The last few kilometres are on narrow, exposed roads with steep fall-offs. It takes a good two hours on foot or 20 minutes by car. On the northern slopes of Mt Leinster, the tiny village of Kildavin is the starting point of the South Leinster Way.

Alternatively, there's a lovely 10km walk along the River Barrow towpath to picturesque Graiguenamanagh (County Kilkenny) and on to St Mullins. Heading north from Borris, the R705 follows the scenic River Barrow Valley for 12km to Bagenalstown.

riverside castle, tangle of 17th-century passageways, rows of colourful, old-fashioned shopfronts and centuries-old pubs with traditional live music all have a timeless appeal, as does its splendid medieval cathedral. But Kilkenny is also famed for its contemporary restaurants and rich cultural life.

Kilkenny's architectural charm owes a huge debt to the Middle Ages, when the city was a seat of political power. It's also known as the 'marble city' after the local black limestone, which resembles a slate-coloured marble and is used on floors and in decorative trim throughout town.

To avoid the crowds and better appreciate the elegance and vibrancy of the town, visit on a weekday and avoid midsummer.

History

In the Middle Ages, Kilkenny was intermittently the unofficial capital of Ireland, with its own Anglo-Norman parliament. In 1366 the parliament passed the so-called Statutes of Kilkenny, aimed at preventing the assimilation of Anglo-Normans into Irish society. Anglo-Normans were prohibited from marrying the native Irish, taking part in Irish sports, speaking or dressing like the Irish or playing any Irish music. Although the laws remained theoretically for over 200 years, they were never enforced with any great effect and did little to halt the absorption of the Anglo-Normans into Irish culture.

WORTH A TRIP

CLONEGAL

The picturesque village of Clonegal has a tiny centre out of a nursery rhyme with an arched stone bridge over a river which, together with its banks, is home to an abundance of wildlife, including foxes and otters, as well as a rich birdlife with swans, kingfishers and moorhens.

It is the southern terminus of Ireland's inaugural long-distance walking trail, the Wicklow Way (www.wicklowway.com). Nonhikers can reach it by driving along a series of signposted winding local roads 5km east of Kildavin and the N80.

Huntington Castle (www.huntingtoncastle.com; Clonegal; castle & gardens tour adult/child €8/5, gardens only €5/3; ☉ house 2-6pm Jun-Aug, by appointment rest of year, gardens 10am-6pm May-Sep) is a spooky, dusty old keep built in 1625 by the Durdin-Robertson family, whose descendents still live here today. The family conduct 30- to 45-minute tours of the property, which, they claim, is haunted by two ghosts: Bishop Leslie (a former bishop of Limerick) and Ailish O'Flaherty (the granddaughter of Grace O'Malley, the Pirate Queen). Descending to the castle's basement brings you to the Temple of Isis, where the Fellowship of Isis, worshipping the ancient Egyptian goddess, was founded by the family in 1976.

The gardens combine the formal with rural fantasy and include a fabulous 500-year-old yew walk, rare trees and a 17th-century fish pond. Welcome new additions in 2013 include an adventure playground and a tearoom, plus gift shop.

Sha-Roe Bistro (☑ 053-937 5636; Main St; mains €18-25; ☉ lunch Sun, dinner Wed-Sat), tucked inside an 18th-century building, serves standout modern Irish cuisine that draws on the bounty of the region, including venison, pork and lamb. The menu lists local suppliers who provide ingredients fresh from the surrounding orchards and farms.

A traditional stop for Wicklow Way walkers, Osborne's pub (Main St) is slightly eerie thanks to its bar made from coffin lids.

During the 1640s Kilkenny sided with the Catholic royalists in the English Civil War. The 1641 Confederation of Kilkenny, an uneasy alliance of native Irish and Anglo-Normans, aimed to bring about the return of land and power to Catholics. After Charles I's execution, Cromwell besieged Kilkenny for five days, destroying much of the southern wall of the castle before the ruling Ormonde family surrendered. The defeat signalled a permanent end to Kilkenny's political influence over Irish affairs.

Today, tourism is Kilkenny's main economic focus, but it's also the regional centre for more traditional pursuits, such as agriculture – you'll see farmers on tractors stoically dodging tour buses.

◉ Sights

★ Kilkenny Castle   CASTLE
(www.kilkennycastle.ie; adult/child €6/2.50, audioguides €5, parkland admission free; ☉ 9.30am-5pm Mar-Sep, to 4.30pm Oct-Feb, parkland daylight hours) Rising above the Nore, Kilkenny Castle is one of Ireland's most visited heritage sites. The first structure on the strategic site was a wooden tower built in 1172 by Richard de

Clare, the Anglo-Norman conqueror of Ireland better known as Strongbow. In 1192, Strongbow's son-in-law, William Marshall, erected a stone castle with four towers, three of which survive. The castle was bought by the powerful Butler family in 1391 and their descendants continued to live there until 1935. Maintaining the structure became such a financial strain that most furnishings were sold at auction. The castle was handed over to the city in 1967 for the princely sum of £50.

One glance tells you that the castle has been modified through the centuries. First of all it's missing a wall – a key defensive deficiency. Second, there are all those windows – perfect targets for a catapult. Most of the changes date from the 19th century when the only real defensive worry was a peasant flinging a rotten potato.

During the winter months (November to January) there are 40-minute guided tours, which shift to self-guided tours from February to October. For most visitors the focal point of the visit is the Long Gallery, which showcases portraits of the Butler family members over the centuries and is an impressive hall with high ceilings vividly painted with Celtic and Pre-Raphaelite motifs.

The castle basement is also home to the Butler Gallery (www.butlergallery.com) FREE, featuring contemporary artwork in temporary exhibitions. Also in the basement, the castle kitchen houses a popular cafe. You can access the Butler Gallery and cafe without paying admission.

About 20 hectares of parkland are a refuge from the clamour of the city. The grounds echo with chirping birds and extend to the southeast, with a Celtic cross-shaped rose garden, a fountain to the northern end and a children's playground to the south. There are some great views of the river. The castle's former stables are now home to the Kilkenny Design Centre.

★ St Canice's Cathedral   CATHEDRAL
(www.stcanicescathedral.ie; St Canice's Pl; adult/child €4/free, round tower €3/free; ⊙9am-6pm Mon-Sat, 2-6pm Sun, round tower Apr-Oct) Soaring over the north end of the centre is Ireland's second-largest medieval cathedral (after St Patrick's in Dublin). This Gothic edifice with its iconic round tower has had a long and fascinating history. Legend has it that the first monastery was built here in the 6th century by St Canice, Kilkenny's patron saint. Records show that a wooden church on the site was burned down in 1087.

The existing structure was raised between 1202 and 1285, but then endured a series of catastrophes and resurrections. The first disaster, the collapse of the church tower in 1332, was the consequence of Dame Alice Kyteler's conviction for witchcraft. Her maid was also convicted, and her nephew, William Outlawe, was implicated. The unfortunate maid was burned at the stake, but Dame Alice escaped to London and William was spared when he offered to re-roof part of St Canice's Cathedral with lead tiles. His new roof proved too heavy, however, bringing the church tower down with it.

In 1650 Cromwell's forces defaced and damaged the church, using it to stable their horses. Repairs began in 1661; the beautiful roof in the nave was completed in 1863. Also worth a look is a model of Kilkenny as it was in 1642.

Inside, highly polished ancient grave slabs are set on the walls and the floor. On the northern wall, a slab inscribed in Norman French commemorates Jose de Keteller, who died in 1280; despite the difference in spelling he was probably the father of Alice Kyteler. The stone chair of St Kieran embedded in the wall dates from the 13th century.

The fine 1596 monument to Honorina Grace at the western end of the southern aisle is made of beautiful local black limestone. In the southern transept, a handsome black tomb has effigies of Piers Butler, who died in 1539, and his wife, Margaret Fitzgerald. Tombs and monuments (listed on a board in the southern aisle) to other notable Butlers crowd this corner of the church.

Outside the cathedral, a 30m-high round tower rises amid an odd array of ancient tombstones and is the oldest structure within the grounds. It was built sometime between AD 700 and 1000 on the site of an earlier Christian cemetery. Apart from missing its crown, the round tower is in excellent condition and those aged over 12 can admire a fine view from the top. It's a tight squeeze and you'll need both hands to climb the 100 steps up steep ladders.

Walking to the cathedral from Parliament St leads you over Irishtown Bridge and up St Canice's Steps, which date from 1614; the wall at the top contains fragmentary medieval carvings. The leaning tombstones scattered about the grounds prompt you to look at the very least for a black cat.

★ Rothe House & Garden   MUSEUM
(www.rothehouse.com; Parliament St; adult/child €5/4; ⊙10.30am-5pm Mon-Sat plus 2-5pm Sun Apr-Oct, 10.30am-4.30pm Mon-Sat Nov-Mar)

CRAFTY KILKENNY

At least 130 full-time craftspeople and artists work commercially in Kilkenny County – one of the highest concentrations in Ireland – thanks to its fine raw materials and inspirational scenery.

Among the best places to see their work are the following:

➡ **Bennettsbridge** Several craft studios are located in and around the village.

➡ **Graiguenamanagh** Wool and crystal studios operate near the centre.

➡ **Kilkenny city** Kilkenny Design Centre has works by more than a dozen local craftspeople.

➡ **Stonyford** A famous glass studio and a shop with locally produced foods.

Also, check www.kilkennytourism.ie/craft_trail for a comprehensive list of studios and shops.

1. Statue of Hermes
This lead statue in the grounds of Kilkenny Castle is based on the original in the Vatican Collection.

2. Gardens
Rolling lawns lead to the entrance of Kilkenny Castle.

3. Kilkenny Castle, Exterior
Visitors stroll around the imposing 12th-century Norman edifice.

4. Kilkenny Castle, Interior
Potraits of the Butler family – the castle's owners from 1391 to 1935 – line the walls of the impressive galleries.

Kilkenny

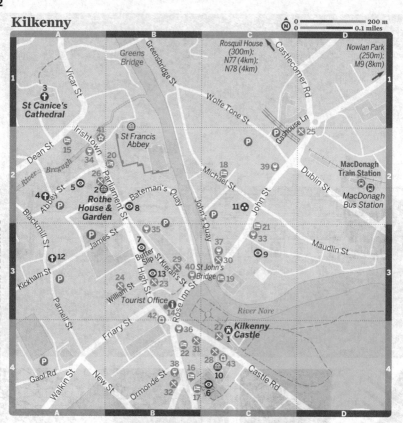

This is Ireland's best surviving example of a 16th-century merchant's house. Built around a series of courtyards, it now houses a **museum** with local artefacts including a well-used Viking sword found nearby and a grinning head sculpted from a stone by a Celtic artist. The king-post roof of the 2nd floor is a meticulous reconstruction. Recent changes include new exhibits about the Rothe family, as well as the delightful walled garden, divided into fruit, vegetable and herbs and a traditional orchard: the only aesthetic downside is the adjacent multistorey car park. There is also a genealogical service available (€30 to €90); enquire at the ticket office.

In the 1640s the wealthy Rothe family played a part in the Confederation of Kilkenny, and Peter Rothe, son of the original builder, had all his property confiscated. His sister was able to reclaim it, but just before the Battle of the Boyne (1690) the family

supported James II and so lost the house permanently. In 1850 a Confederation banner was discovered in the house; it's now in the National Museum in Dublin.

National Craft Gallery & Kilkenny Design Centre
GALLERY

(www.ccoi.ie; Castle Yard; ◎10am-5.30pm Tue-Sat; ⚑) Contemporary Irish crafts are showcased at these imaginative galleries in the former castle stables that also house the shops of the Kilkenny Design Centre. Ceramics dominate, but exhibits often feature furniture, jewellery and weaving from the members of the Crafts Council of Ireland. Family days are held on the second Saturday of every month with free hands-on workshops for children at 10am and 12.30pm. For additional workshops and events, check the website.

Behind the complex, look for the walkway that extends into the beautiful **Butler House gardens** with an unusual water feature constructed from remnants of the

Kilkenny

British-built Nelson Column, blown up by nationalists in Dublin around a century ago.

Black Abbey CHURCH
(Abbey St; ⊙ open daily for Mass) This Dominican abbey was founded in 1225 by William Marshall and takes its name from the monks' black habits. Much of what survives dates from the 18th and 19th centuries, but remnants of more ancient archways are still evident within the newer stonework. Look for the 13th-century coffins near the entrance.

Tholsel HISTORIC SITE
The Tholsel (City Hall) on High St was built in 1761 on the spot where Dame Alice Kyteler's maid, Petronella, was burned at the stake in 1324.

Butter Slip HISTORIC SITE
With its arched entry and stone steps, Butter Slip, a narrow and dark walkway connecting High St with St Kieran's St (previously called Low Lane) is the most picturesque of Kilkenny's many narrow medieval corridors. It

was built in 1616 and was once flanked with the stalls of butter vendors.

Black Freren Gate HISTORIC SITE
(Abbey St) This is the only gate from the old Norman city walls still standing, albeit with the help of metal bracing these days. Crumbling sections of the old walls remain throughout the centre.

Confederation Hall Monument HISTORIC SITE
On the corner of Parliament St and the road leading down to Bateman's Quay, this monument (really just a fragment) built into the Bank of Ireland marks the site where the national Parliament met from 1642 to 1649. Nearby is the carefully restored Grace's Castle, originally built in 1210, but lost to the family and converted into a prison in 1568, and then in 1794 into a courthouse, which it remains today. Rebels from the 1798 Rising were executed here.

St Mary's Cathedral CATHEDRAL
(Blackmill St; ⊙ varies) FREE The 19th-century cathedral is visible from most parts of town.

A plaque at the entrance notes: 'The construction of the cathedral began in 1843 and continued during the Famine years, the years of emigration, coffin ships, starvation, and even despair because of the many thousands of our people who died of hunger and disease', before going on to list yet more tribulations.

St John's Priory
RUIN

Across the river stand the ruins of this priory, which was founded in 1200 and was noted for its many beautiful windows until Cromwell's visit. Nearby Kilkenny College (John St) dates from 1666. Its students included Jonathan Swift, most famously, the author of Gulliver's Travels, but it now houses Kilkenny's county hall.

Tours

Kilkenny Cycling Tours
CYCLING TOUR

(☑086 895 4961; www.kilkennycyclingtours.com; adult/child from €17.50/10; 🖮) Explore the city and surrounds on a bike over a 2½-hour tour that can include a lunch option. Bikes delivered to your accommodation.

Tynan Tours
WALKING TOUR

(☑087 265 1745; €6; ⏱2-4 tours daily mid-Mar–Oct) Entertaining, informative hour-long walking tours that meander Kilkenny's narrow lanes, steps and pedestrian passageways. Meet at the tourist office.

Festivals & Events

Kilkenny hosts several world-class events throughout the year that attract revellers in the thousands.

Kilkenny Rhythm & Roots
MUSIC

(www.kilkennyroots.com; ⏱early May) Over 30 pubs and other venues participate in hosting this major music festival, with an emphasis on country and 'old-time' American roots music.

Cat Laughs Comedy Festival
COMEDY

(www.thecatlaughs.com; ⏱early Jun) Acclaimed gathering of world-class comedians in Kilkenny's hotels and pubs.

Kilkenny Arts Festival
ARTS

(www.kilkennyarts.ie) The city comes alive with theatre, cinema, music, literature, visual arts, children's events and street spectacles for 10 action-packed days.

Sleeping

If you're arriving in town with no room booked (an unwise move at weekends, in summer and during festivals), try the tourist office's efficient accommodation booking service (€4). Otherwise you'll find lodging at all prices throughout town.

Kilkenny Tourist Hostel
HOSTEL €

(☑056-776 3541; www.kilkennyhostel.ie; 35 Parliament St; dm/tw €17/42; @ 🛜) Inside an ivy-covered 1770s Georgian town house, this cosy, 60-bed IHH hostel has a sitting room warmed by an open fireplace, and a timber- and leadlight-panelled dining room adjoining the self-catering kitchen.

★Rosquil House
GUESTHOUSE €€

(☑056-772 1419; www.rosquilhouse.com; Castlecomer Rd; r from €70, 2-person apt from €60; 🛜) Phil and Rhoda are the delightful hosts at this immaculately maintained guesthouse. Rooms are decorated with dark-wood furniture and warm yellows with pretty paisley fabrics while the guest lounge is similarly tasteful with sink-into sofas, brass-framed mirrors and leafy plants. The breakfast is above average, with homemade granola and fluffy omelettes including spinach and feta. The apartment is well equipped and comfortable (minimum three days stay).

Butler House
BOUTIQUE HOTEL €€

(☑056-772 2828; www.butler.ie; 16 Patrick St; s/d from €77/135; @ 🛜) You can't stay in Kilkenny Castle, but this historic mansion is surely the next best thing. Once the home of the Earls of Ormonde, who built the castle, these days it houses a boutique hotel with aristocratic trappings including sweeping staircases, marble fireplaces, an art collection and impeccably trimmed gardens. The 13 generously sized rooms are individually decorated. Just to remind you you're staying in history, the floors creak.

Celtic House
B&B €€

(☑056-776 2249; www.celtic-house-bandb.com; 18 Michael St; s/d €35/70; @ 🛜) Artist and author Angela Byrne extends one of Ireland's warmest welcomes at her spick-and-span B&B. Some of the bright rooms have sky-lit bathrooms, others have views of the castle, and Angela's landscapes adorn many of the walls. Book ahead.

Butler Court
INN €€

(☑056-776 1178; www.butlercourt.com; Patrick St; r from €70; @ 🛜) Not to be confused with the grand Butler House a few doors uphill, this was originally the mail-coach yard for Kilkenny Castle. Wrapping around a flower-filled courtyard, contemporary rooms have Canadian-cherry parquet floors and eye-catching photography or Celtic art on the walls. A continental breakfast, including fresh fruit and filtered coffee, is stocked in your in-room fridge.

Bregagh House
B&B €€

(☑ 056-772 2315; www.bregaghhouse.com; Dean St; s/d from €45/70) If you want the cosiness that comes with staying in a family home, this B&B is a good bet for its convenient location near the cathedral, comfortable soundproof guest rooms and filling hot breakfasts (or continental). There's ample onsite parking and a conservatory overlooking a pretty back garden with its magnificent copper beech tree.

Langton House Hotel
HOTEL €€

(☑ 056-776 5133; www.langtons.ie; 67 John St; s/d from €65/99; @ 🎧) In the same family since the 1930s, but constantly evolving, this Kilkenny icon has 34 corporate-style rooms with parquet floors and dark wood and sombre-coloured furnishings. The mosaic-tiled bathrooms have superb high-power pressure showers. There's a fine restaurant and a popular pub. Breakfast included.

Pembroke Hotel
HOTEL €€€

(☑ 056-778 3500; www.pembrokekilkenny.com; Patrick St; r €109-160; @ 🎧) Wake up to castle views (from some of the 74 rooms) at this stylish, modern and central hotel. Deluxe rooms feature balconies, a rarity in Ireland, while the overall room decor is easy on the eye with a muted moss-green and soft-blue colour scheme. There's a leather-sofa-filled bar onsite and guests have the use of swimming and leisure facilities just around the corner. Breakfast included.

Kilkenny River Court
HOTEL €€€

(☑ 056-772 3388; www.rivercourthotel.com; John St; s/d €75/130; @ 🎧 🏊) When not unwinding in your spacious modern room, you can dine at the respected restaurant, swim laps in the award-winning health club's sunlit indoor pool, or sip a cocktail on the cobblestone terrace of the wraparound bar overlooking the bridge and castle. Staff are consistently helpful. Breakfast included.

✕ Eating

Kilkenny's restaurants are among the best in the southeast. See the range of local produce and prepared foods available at the farmers market (Mayors Walk, The Parade; ⊙9am-2pm Thu).

Café Mocha
CAFE €

(84 High St; meals €6-10; ⊙9am-6pm Mon-Thu, to 10pm Fri-Sat, 11am-6pm Sun; 🖶) All manner of juices, coffee, teas and drinks are served at this fashionable and friendly cafe. It is also a good spot for a light lunch, with Med-inspired salads and Irish smoked salmon. Dinners are similarly fresh and contemporary, featuring baked fresh fish (and similar) with sides such as fennel risotto. The decor is prettily feminine with cabinets displaying classic china for sale.

Lautrec's Tapas & Wine Bar
SPANISH €

(9 St Kieran's St; tapas €5-7; ⊙5-10pm Wed-Thu, 5pm-midnight Fri, 2pm-midnight Sat, noon-8pm Sun) Romantics can hold hands at the tiny tables in the tiny dining room and partake of the disproportionate wine selections at this seductive, rose-coloured tapas bar which spans continents with its Latino choice ranging from gazpacho to guacamole. Select an assortment for sharing.

Cafe Sol
MODERN IRISH €€

(☑ 056-776 4987; www.restaurantskilkenny.com; William St; mains lunch €11-13, dinner €17-25; ⊙noon-9.30pm Mon-Thu, 11am-10pm Fri & Sat, noon-9pm Sun; 🎧) Leisurely lunches stretch until 5pm at this much-loved restaurant. Local organic produce is featured in dishes that emphasise what's fresh each season. The flavours are frequently bold and have global influences. Service, albeit casual, is excellent and the whole place has recently had a revamp and exudes a modern Med-bistro look.

Rinuccini
ITALIAN €€

(☑ 056-776 1575; www.rinuccini.com; 1 The Parade; lunch mains €10-20, dinner mains €16-30; ⊙noon-10pm Mon-Sat, 5-9.30pm Sun) Follow a short flight of steps down to a candlelit basement to bliss out on Antonio Cavaliere's classical Italian cuisine, including his sublime *spaghetti al astice* (lobster tossed with pasta, shallots, cream, brandy and black truffle, doused with fresh parmesan, and served in the shell). There's a cute and romantic table at the front under an atrium. Service wins plaudits.

Zuni
CAFE, TAPAS €€

(www.zuni.ie; 26 Patrick St; dishes €7-15; ⊙9.30am-11pm; 🎧) Dark leather contrasting with lighter tables and walls at this one-time theatre provide a stylised backdrop for chef Maria Rafferty's inventive cooking. By day it's a swish cafe with a long breakfast and lunch

1. River Nore, County Kilkenny 2. Traditional pub, Kilkenny City
3. Local oysters

Kilkenny City

Whether it's strolling around Kilkenny's medieval quarters, lazing away the day on the banks of the River Nore or pub-hopping from one trad session to the next, you can't go out in this town and not find pleasure.

Traditional Pubs

You'll always find a pub with a song in its heart in Kilkenny. On boards battered by generations of drinkers, musicians perform impromptu trad sessions. Modern bands can be heard in one great setting after another on weekends.

Shopping

Shopping is greatly rewarding in Kilkenny, and not just for the shopkeeper. The county is loaded with artisans and craftspeople who sell their wares at shops and boutiques in the streets around the castle.

River Nore

Flowing through the centre of Kilkenny, the inky waters of the River Nore reflect the city's stone-built beauty. A walk along its banks or a pause on a bench are the perfect breaks from touring the surrounding streets.

St Canice's Cathedral

The soaring spire of St Canice's Cathedral looms large over much of the city and has since the 13th century. Despite the efforts of Cromwell and the forces of nature through the years, it still stands proud.

Kilkenny Kitchen

County Kilkenny offers a bounty of produce and local chefs are up to the task. From modern Irish creativity to classic seafood goodness, restaurants and cafes excel.

menu, by night there's a varied tapas menu with some more hearty seafood options. Linger over small plates of tasty morsels such as foie gras with chicken liver parfait and enjoy the fine wine selection.

Kilkenny Design Centre Cafe CAFE €€

(www.kilkennydesign.com; Castle Yard; dishes €8-13; ⊙10am-7pm; 🛜🖰) Upstairs from the craft shops, this arty, organic-oriented cafe serves home-baked breads and scones, a vast variety of salads, gourmet sandwiches, hot specials, and sumptuous desserts. It's cafeteria style so you can ponder your choices in detail.

Chez Pierre FRENCH €€

(17 Parliament St; mains €10-15; ⊙10am-3.30pm Mon-Fri, 7pm-10pm Sat) This sunny-sweet French spot does great *tartines* (open-faced sandwiches) with such belly-filling toppings as sausage and eggs, as well as soups, brioche and sweets, plus blackboard specials at lunch. Breakfast is served until noon; dinner menus start at €20.

Lemongrass THAI €€

(www.lemongrass.ie; 1 St John's Bridge; mains €8-12; ⊙noon-10pm Tue-Sun; 🖉) Sporting brick-and-bamboo decor and a menu of reliably authentic Thai dishes, this place is deservedly popular. Thursday is ladies night with a €22.50 two-course meal, including wine. There's also a vegetarian menu.

★ Campagne MODERN IRISH €€€

(📞056-777 2858; www.campagne.ie; 5 Gashouse Lane; 2-/3-course set lunch menu €24/29, dinner mains €25-30; ⊙12.30-2.30pm Fri-Sun, 6-10pm Tue-Sat) Chef Garrett Byrne, who gained fame and Michelin stars in Dublin, is the genius behind this bold, stylish restaurant in his native Kilkenny. He's passionate about supporting local and artisan producers and serves ever-changing, ever-memorable meals. There's a French accent to every culinary creation.

🍷 Drinking & Nightlife

John St is a hub of nightlife, along with Parliament St where there is another clutch of no-nonsense trad pubs.

★ Kyteler's Inn PUB

(27 St Kieran's St; ⊙11am-midnight Sun-Thu, to 2am Fri-Sat, live music 6.30pm Mar-Oct) Dame Alice Kyteler's old house was built back in 1224 and has seen its share of history: the Dame had four husbands, all of whom died in suspicious circumstances, and she was charged

with witchcraft in 1323. Today the rambling bar includes the orignal building, complete with vaulted ceiling and arches. There is a beer garden, courtyard and a large upstairs room for the live bands, ranging from trad to blues.

Left Bank BAR

(www.leftbank.ie; The Parade; ⊙noon-11.30pm Mon-Thu, to12.30am Fri & Sat) This former Bank of Ireland building has been resurrected as undoubtedly the most eye-catching bar in town. Dating from the 1870s, the interior is magnificent with original portico columns, carved wood detail, exposed brick walls and chandeliers. Snacks also served.

Tynan's Bridge House PUB

(St John's Bridge; ⊙11am-late) This historic 1703 Georgian pub flaunting a brilliant blue facade is the best traditional bar in town with its horseshoe bar, original tilework, regular clientele of crusty locals – and no TV! There is trad music on Monday to Thursday at 9pm

Bridie's General Store PUB, DELI

(John St; ⊙11am-10pm Sun-Wed, 6pm-2am Thu-Sat) Top design talent was employed by the Langton's empire to create the fictional trad grocery-cum-pub. But the results are worth it. The front is a beguiling retail potpourri of souvenirs, jokes, toys, preserves and deli items. Step through the swinging doors to arrive at a new/old pub with beautiful tiles, out the back is a fittingly classy beer garden.

O'Faolain's & Pegasus PUB, NIGHTCLUB

(John St, Kilford Arms Hotel; ⊙O'Faolains 10am-2pm, Pegasus 10pm-late Fri-Sat) Built on three levels around a 16th-century stone church that was brought over in crates from Wales and painstakingly rebuilt here, numbered stone by numbered stone, O'Faolain's is a lively night-time spot year-round. Between Easter and October, Pegasus (admission €10), in a strobe-lit space out the back, sees dancers getting sweaty on weekend nights.

John Cleere's PUB

(www.cleeres.com; 22 Parliament St; ⊙11.30am-11.30pm Mon-Thu, to 12.30am Fri & Sat, 1pm-11pm Sun) One of Kilkenny's finest venues for live music, theatre and comedy, this long bar has blues, jazz and rock, as well as trad music sessions on Monday and Wednesday. Recently introduced sandwiches and soups to the mix (five different soup choices daily).

Matt the Millers
BAR

(www.mattthemillers.com; 1 John St; ⊙9.30am-late; 🛜) Rose-coloured medieval mill with five bars over four floors, plus crowd-pleasing bands and DJs.

Morrison's Bar
NIGHTCLUB

(1 Ormonde St; ⊙10pm-late Thu-Sat; 🛜) Don the heels, spike the hair and head for the *belle époque* cellar of the Hibernian Hotel where DJs spin an eclectic mix for an upmarket crowd.

67 Club
NIGHTCLUB

(Langton House Hotel, 67 John St; cover varies; ⊙9pm-late Tue, Thu & Sat; 🛜) The pubs at Langton's morph into a lively club three nights a week. There's live music, DJs and occasional comedy.

☆ Entertainment

For information on local events, check out the weekly *Kilkenny People* newspaper (www.kilkennypeople.ie). Events are listed on the tourist office website, and on www.whazon.com.

Theatre

Watergate Theatre
THEATRE

(www.watergatetheatre.com; Parliament St) The top theatre venue hosts drama, comedy and musical performances. If you're wondering why intermission lasts 18 minutes, it's so patrons can nip into John Cleere's pub for a pint.

Sport

Nowlan Park
SPORTS

(www.kilkennygaa.ie; O'Loughlin Rd) One of the unique pleasures of a trip to Ireland is catching a game of hurling at the Kilkenny Cats' hallowed home stadium.

🛍 Shopping

An interesting mix of local stores concentrates on High St. The most-exclusive shops are found on the Parade and Patrick St. In parts of the old train station, the chain-store-filled shopping mall, MacDonagh Junction, is the largest in the region.

★ Kilkenny Design Centre
ARTS & CRAFTS

(☑056-772 2118; www.kilkennydesign.com; Castle Yard; ⊙10am-7pm) Top-end Irish crafts and artwork for sale include items by artisans county-wide. Look for John Hanly wool blankets, Cushendale woollen goods, Foxford scarves and Bunbury cutting boards.

Kilkenny Book Centre
BOOKSTORE

(10 High St; ⊙10am-5pm Mon-Sat) The largest bookshop in town, stocking plenty of Irish-interest fiction and nonfiction, periodicals and a good range of maps. There's a cafe upstairs.

❶ Information

Police (☑056-22222; Dominic St)

Tourist office (www.kilkennytourism.ie; Rose Inn St; ⊙9.15am-5pm Mon-Sat) Stocks excellent guides and walking maps. Located in Shee Alms House, dating from 1582 and built in local stone by benefactor Sir Richard Shee to help the poor.

❶ Getting There & Away

BUS

Bus Éireann (www.buseireann.ie) operates from a shelter adjacent to the train station. Services: Carlow (€8.75, 35 minutes, three daily), Cork (€18.50, three hours, two daily), Dublin (€12, 2¼ hours, five daily) and Waterford (€10.50, one hour, two daily).

JJ Kavanagh & Sons (www.jjkavanagh.ie; stop at Ormonde Rd) Dublin airport (€13, three hours, six daily).

TRAIN

Irish Rail (www.irishrail.ie) goes six times daily to/from Dublin's Heuston Station (from €10, 1¾ hours) and Waterford (from €10, 50 minutes) via the MacDonagh train station.

❶ Getting Around

There are large car parks off both sides of High St and numerous others throughout the city.

Kilkenny Cabs (☑056-775 2000)

Central Kilkenny

The area south – and notably southeast – of Kilkenny city is a patchwork of country roads and picturesque villages overlooking the rich, green Barrow and Nore Valleys. This is fine walking country and home to some of the county's most notable craftspeople, whose workshops can be visited.

Much of the area is easily visited on a day trip from the city, but you need your own wheels, as public transport is limited.

Kells & Around

Kells (not to be confused with Kells in County Meath) is a mere hamlet with a fine stone bridge on a tributary of the Nore. However, **Kells Priory** is one of Ireland's most evocative and romantic monastic sites. The village is 13km south of Kilkenny city on the R697.

Sights

★ Kells Priory
RUIN

This is the best sort of ruin, where visitors can amble about whenever they like, with no tour guides, tours, set hours or fees. At dusk with a clear sky the old priory is simply beautiful. Most days you stand a chance of exploring the site alone (apart from some nosy sheep).

The earliest remains of the monastic site date from the late 12th century, while the bulk of the present ruins are from the 15th century. In a sea of rich farmland, a carefully restored protective wall connects seven dwelling towers. Within the walls are the remains of an Augustinian abbey and the foundations of several chapels and houses. It's unusually well fortified for a monastery and the heavy curtain walls hint at a troubled history. Indeed, within a single century from 1250, the abbey was twice fought over and burned down by squabbling warlords. It slid into permanent decline, beginning when it was suppressed in 1540.

The ruins are 500m east of Kells on the Stonyford road. There are signposts for an excellent 3km walk around the ruins, river and village.

Kilree Round Tower & High Cross
HISTORIC SITE

About 2km south of Kells (signposted from the priory car park) there's a 29m-high round tower and a simple early high cross, said to mark the grave of a 9th-century Irish high king, Niall Caille. He apparently drowned in the King's River at Callan some time in the 840s while attempting to save a servant, and his body washed up near Kells. His final resting place lies beyond the church grounds because he wasn't a Christian.

Callan Famine Graveyard
HISTORIC SITE

West of Kilree, and signposted 2km off the R698 about 2km south of Callan, is a cemetery where the local victims of the Great Famine are buried. Park at the sign and then follow a farmers lane for 300m. It isn't much to look at, but the unmarked mass grave is a poignant reminder of the anonymity of starvation.

Sleeping

★ Lawcus Farm
GUESTHOUSE €€

(www.lawcusfarmguesthouse.com; Kells; r from €80; ☎) An extraordinary place to stay.

Bought as a thatched ruin dating from the 1700s, the farm has been aesthetically rebuilt and expanded by ebullient Englishman Mark Fisher and his Irish partner Anne Marie. The rooms are all different but typically have stone walls, rustic antiques and numerous quirky curiosities, plus modern amenities including kitchenettes and wi-fi. The 8-hectare farm is bordered by the River Barrow and home to pigs, sheep, cows, chickens and horses as well as wildlife, including otters, kingfishers, badgers and foxes. Breakfast features such treats as spinach and goat's cheese omelette and the farm's own eggs, sausages and ham.

Bennettsbridge & Around
POP 680

Just 7km south of Kilkenny city on the R700, Bennettsbridge is most famous for being home to the widely acclaimed Nicholas Mosse pottery.

Sights & Activities

Nore View Folk Museum
MUSEUM

(☑ 056-27749; Danesfort Rd; adult/child €5/2; ☉varies, generally 10am-6pm) On a small road above Nicholas Mosse, this is not your average museum. Seamus Lawlor is a passionate chronicler of Irish life and recounts fascinating facts about his private collection of local items, including farming tools, kitchen utensils and other wonderful old bric-a-brac.

Nore Valley Park
FARM

(www.norevalleypark.com; Annamult; day admission €6, campsites per adult/child/tent €8.50/4/4; ☉park 9am-6pm Mon-Sat Mar-Oct, campground Mar-Oct; ☎) A 73-hectare farm where you can also camp. Children can pet goats, cuddle rabbits, navigate a maze (in the former barn), play crazy golf and jump on a straw bounce. There's a tearoom and picnic area. If you're coming into Bennettsbridge from Kilkenny along the R700, turn right just before the bridge.

Shopping

Nicholas Mosse Irish Country Shop
CERAMICS

(www.nicholasmosse.com; ☉10am-6pm Mon-Sat, 1.30-5pm Sun) In a large mill by the river, west of town, this pottery shop specialises in handmade spongeware – creamy-brown pottery decorated with sponged patterns – which is exported worldwide to retail outlets such as Tiffany's. Short audiovisual displays explain the pottery process. The shop also sells linens and other handmade craft items (although some hail from lands of cheap labour far from Ireland). A seconds shop yields some 20% savings. Its cafe is the best choice locally for lunch, with a creative line-up of soups, sandwiches, hot dishes and its renowned scones.

Moth to a Flame   CANDLES
(www.mothtoaflamecandles.com; ⊗9am-6pm Mon-Sat year-round, plus noon-6pm Sun May-Dec) Located by the bridge, this longstanding place creates elaborate candles.

Thomastown

POP 1800

This small market town has a serenity it hasn't known in decades now that the M9 has diverted Dublin traffic away from the compact and attractive centre. Named after Welsh mercenary Thomas de Cantwell, Thomastown has some fragments of a medieval wall. Down by the bridge, Mullin's Castle is the sole survivor of the 14 castles once here.

Like the rest of Kilkenny, the area has a vibrant craft scene. Look out for Clay Creations (☑087-257 0735; Low St; ⊗10am-5.30pm Tue-Sat) displaying the quixotic ceramics and sculptures of local artist Brid Lyons.

Just 4km southwest of Thomastown, highfliers tee off at the Jack Nicklaus–blessed Mount Juliet (www.mountjuliet.ie; green fees from €100). Set over 600 wooded hectares, it also has its own equestrian centre, a gym and spa, two restaurants, wine masterclasses, and luxurious rooms (accommodation from €130) catering to every whim, right down to the pillow menu.

✕ Eating

★**Blackberry Cafe**   CAFE €
(www.theblackberrycafe.ie; Market St; dishes €4.50-7.50; ⊗9.30am-5.30pm Mon-Fri, 10am-5.30pm Sat; 🐾) Superb thick-cut sandwiches and warming soups are served with pumpkin-seed-speckled soda bread here. Much is organic and the tarts and cakes are baked daily. Between noon and 2pm, great-value multi-course hot lunches see the place squeezed to bursting. It's right in town.

Sol Bistro   MODERN IRISH €€
(Low St; mains €12-25; ⊗noon-4pm, 6-10pm; 🍴) Kilkenny's modern Irish cafe has a branch in Thomastown's centre. It's a small cafe in a tidy old storefront and combines the best local ingredients for Irish classics with an innovative twist.

❶ Getting There & Away

Trains on the Dublin-to-Waterford route via Kilkenny stop eight times daily in each direction in Thomastown. The station is 1km west of town.

Around Thomastown

STONYFORD

Only 6km west of Thomastown is the small village of Stonyford.

◉ Sights & Activities

Jerpoint Park   HISTORIC SITE
(☑086-172 8225; www.jerpointpark.com; Stonyford, Thomastown; admission €8, sheepdog trials €5; ⊗10am-7pm May-Sep) Jerpoint Park is a new attraction with an ancient history, the site of a 12th-century medieval town. Guided 90-minute tours over the tellingly bumpy terrain describe in detail exactly what once lay below (revealed by light detection and

COUNTIES WEXFORD, WATERFORD, CARLOW & KILKENNY CENTRAL KILKENNY

DON'T MISS

JERPOINT ABBEY

One of Ireland's finest Cistercian ruins, Jerpoint Abbey (☑056-772 4623; www.opw.ie; N9, Thomastown; adult/child €3/1; ⊗9am-5.30pm Mar-Oct, check hours Nov-Feb) is about 2.5km southwest of Thomastown. It was established in the 12th century and has been partially restored. The tower and cloister are late 14th or early 15th century. Look for the series of often amusing figures carved on the cloister pillars, including a knight. There are also stone carvings on the church walls and in the tombs of members of the Butler and Walshe families. Faint traces of a 15th- or 16th-century painting remain on the northern wall of the church. This chancel area also contains a tomb thought to belong to Felix O'Dulany, Jerpoint's first abbot and Bishop of Ossory, who died in 1202. The excellent 45-minute tours run throughout the day. Set yourself apart in the remains of the cloisters and see if you can hear the faint echo of a chant.

ranging imaging used to collect topographical data). The highlight is a visit to the ruined Church of St Nicholas where, according to local legend, St Nicholas (Santa Claus) is buried. The grave is marked by a broken slab decorated with a carving of a cleric. There are also sheepdog trials with geese and/or sheep and a tearoom (open July and August) famed for its homemade scones.

Jerpoint Glass Studio GLASS
(www.jerpointglass.com; ⊘ shop 10am-6pm Mon-Sat, noon-5pm Sun) The local highlight, the nationally renowned Jerpoint Glass Studio, is housed in an old stone-walled farm building where you can watch workers craft molten glass into exquisite artistic and practical items.

✕ Eating

Knockdrinna Farm Shop DELI
(www.knockdrinna.com; meals from €5; ⊘ 9am-6pm Tue-Fri, 10am-6pm Sat, noon-6pm Sun) Located right in town, this farm shop is a tiny tour de force of local foods. From the house-made cheese to cured meats, smoked fish, salads, coffees and much more, you can assemble a meal that may outclass your previous best picnic. Or settle in at the tables here.

KILFANE
The village of Kilfane, 3km north of Thomastown on the R448, has a small, ruined 13th-century church and Norman tower, 50m off the road and signposted. The church has a remarkable stone carving of Thomas de Cantwell called the Cantwell Fada or Long Cantwell. It depicts a tall, thin knight in detailed chain-mail armour brandishing a shield decorated with the Cantwell coat of arms.

Inistioge

POP 260
The little village of Inistioge (in-ish-teeg) is a picture. Its 18th-century, 10-arch stone bridge spans the River Nore and the central tranquil square is a delight. Somewhere so inviting could hardly hope to escape the attention of movie-location scouts: Inistioge's film credits include *Widow's Peak* (1993), *Circle of Friends* (1994) and *Where the Sun is King* (1996). After you have wandered through the tiny centre, take a river walk heading south from town.

With a scenic stretch of the South Leinster Way coursing through town, this is a good base for exploring the region. The R700 from Thomastown makes for a lovely scenic drive through the river valley, which features views of the ruined 13th-century Grennan Castle. Better yet, try the hiking trails that follow the river and side trails leading up into the hills.

Approximately 500m south, on Mt Alto, is the heavily forested Woodstock Gardens (www.woodstock.ie; parking in coins €4; ⊘ 9am-7pm Apr-Sep, 10am-4pm Oct-Mar), a beauty of a park with expansive 19th-century gardens, picnic areas and trails. The panorama of the valley and village below is spectacular. Coming from town, follow the signs for Woodstock Estate and enter the large gates then continue along the road for about 1km until you reach the car park. There are tearooms that open during the summer months.

🛏 Sleeping & Eating

There are one or two reasonable cafes in the centre and a decent sandwich bar at the Centra supermarket.

Woodstock Arms B&B, PUB €€
(📞 056-775 8440; www.woodstockarms.com; s/d/tr from €40/70/80; ⊘ noon-10pm) This picturesque pub has tables overlooking the square and seven simple rooms that are squeaky clean. The triples are particularly spacious. Breakfast is served in a pretty little room out back with wooden tables and traditional local china.

Graiguenamanagh

POP 1300
Graiguenamanagh (greg-*na*-muh-na; known locally simply as Graigue) is the kind of place where you could easily find yourself staying longer than planned. Spanning the Barrow, an ancient six-arch stone bridge is illuminated at night and connects the village with the smaller township of Tinnahinch on the County Carlow side of the river (look for the darker stones on the Carlow side – a legacy from being blown up during the 1798 rebellion).

◉ Sights & Activities

Some picturesque walks pass through and near town.

Duiske Abbey CHURCH
(⊘ 8am-6pm, Abbey Centre varies) This was once Ireland's largest Cistercian abbey. What you see today is the result of 800 years of addi-

WALKS: COUNTIES CARLOW & KILKENNY

The South Leinster Way slices through the hilly southern part of County Kilkenny, from Graiguenamanagh through Inistioge, down to Mullinavat and westward to Piltown. By far the prettiest part, a stretch of some 13km, begins on the River Barrow. It links Graiguenamanagh and Inistioge, two charming villages with amenities for travellers. In either village you can reward yourself with a top-notch meal.

Alternatively, along this path, you can branch off onto Brandon Way (4km south of Graiguenamanagh), which scales Brandon Hill (516m). The broad moorland summit is easily reached and affords a lovely view of the Blackstairs Mountains and Mt Leinster to the east. A return trip from Graigue is a fairly relaxed 12km walk.

The trail down River Barrow from Graiguenamanagh to St Mullins in County Carlow is equally beautiful, with a firm path wending past canals and through some wooded country and pleasant grassy picnic areas.

tions and changes and it is very much a working parish. In the grounds stand two early high crosses (7th century and 9th century), brought here for protection in the last century. The smaller Ballyogan Cross has panels on the eastern side depicting the crucifixion, Adam and Eve, Abraham's sacrifice of Isaac, and David playing the harp. The western side shows the massacre of the innocents.

Around the corner, the Abbey Centre houses a small exhibition of Christian art, plus pictures of the abbey in its unrestored state.

Waterside Bike & Hire CYCLING
(☑086-408 4008; www.watersideguesthouse. com; The Quay; pedal/electric bike per day €25/15; ⊙9am-6pm; 🚲) The owners of the Waterside hotel and restaurant have opened this handy bike-hire business specifically geared towards cycling the Barrow Towpath, a traffic-free grass track extending for several miles in either direction from Graiguenamanagh.

✦ Festivals & Events

Town of Books Festival LITERATURE
(www.booktownireland.com; ⊙mid-Sep) Graiguenamanagh's narrow streets spill over with booksellers, authors and bibliophiles during the three-day Town of Books Festival. Plans are under way for Graiguenamanagh to become a year-round 'book town' in the same vein as Wales' Hay-on-Wye. Meanwhile, there are a couple of good used and antiquarian bookshops.

🍽 Sleeping & Eating

Waterside GUESTHOUSE €€
(☑059-972 4246; www.watersideguesthouse.com; The Quay; s/d from €55/78; ⊙restaurant noon-3pm Sun year-round, 6-10pm Mon-Sat Apr-Sep, Fri &

Sat only Oct-Mar; 🚲) Down by the boats tied up along the river, this inviting guesthouse and restaurant occupies a converted solid granite 19th-century corn store. Its 10 renovated rooms have exposed timber beams. Hosts Brian and Brigid Roberts can point out the village's hidden nooks and crannies. The restaurant (mains €18-26) is well regarded for its interesting modern Irish menu and its regular 'After Dinner Live' music acts featuring anything from jazz to bluegrass.

Drinking

One of Graiguenamanagh's hidden treasures is its pair of unchanged-in-generations old pubs, Mick Doyle's (Main St) and Mick Ryan's (Main St). The former still has its sheep-dipping sign and sells a range of hardware; the latter has an equally untouched timber snug.

F J Murray PUB
On the corner of the Quay and Abbey St, this is another cosy, old-time pub. It's the life and soul of the village during its Sunday evening trad sessions; listen out for songs featuring local landmarks.

Shopping

★**Cushendale Woollen Mill** WOOL
(www.cushendale.ie; ⊙8.30am-12.30pm & 1.30-5.30pm Mon-Fri, 10am-1pm Sat) Produces knitting yarns, blankets, tweed and winter woollies; ask for an informal, behind-the-scenes peek at the mill's century-old machinery in action.

Duiske Glass GLASS
(www.duiskeglass.ie; ⊙9am-5pm Mon-Sat) This small studio creates contemporary and traditional crystal. It's in the village centre.

❶ Getting There & Away

Graiguenamanagh is 23km southeast of Kilkenny city on the R703. **Kilbride Coaches** (www.kilbridecoaches.com) runs two buses Monday to Saturday to/from Kilkenny bus station (€6, 55 minutes).

Northern Kilkenny

The rolling green hills of northern County Kilkenny are idyllic for leisurely drives along the back roads with the makings of a picnic stowed in the back of the car. There's not a whole lot going on in this part of the county; it's best enjoyed by simply taking in the scenery and discovering peaceful little villages.

Castlecomer & Around

POP 1500

Castlecomer is on the gentle River Dinin, some 18km north of Kilkenny. The town became a centre for anthracite mining after the fuel was discovered nearby in 1636; the mines closed for good in the mid-1960s. The anthracite, a very hard form of coal, contains very little sulphur and produces almost no smoke.

Coal-mining exhibits are set among lush woodlands at the Castlecomer Discovery Park (www.discoverypark.ie; Estate Yard; adult/child €8/5; ⊙9.30am-6pm May-Aug, 10am-5pm Sep-Oct & Mar-Apr, 10.30am-4.30pm Nov-Feb), including some ancient fossils predating dinosaurs found here.

About 10km southwest of Castlecomer is Swifte's Heath, home to Jonathan Swift during his school years in Kilkenny. The 'e' was evidently dropped from the name before

the satirist gained notoriety as the author of *Gulliver's Travels* and *A Modest Proposal*.

Bus Éireann (🗹056-64933) has five buses daily to Kilkenny (€5.50, 20 minutes).

Dunmore Cave

Striking calcite formations enliven Dunmore Cave (🗹056-776 7726; www.heritageireland.ie; Ballyfoyle; adult/child €3/1; ⊙9.30am-6.30pm Jun-Sep, 9.30am-5pm Mar-May & Sep-Oct, 9.30am-5pm Wed-Sun Nov-Mar), some 6km north of Kilkenny on the Castlecomer road (N78). In AD 928 marauding Vikings killed 1000 people at two ring forts near here. When survivors hid in the caverns, the Vikings tried to smoke them out by lighting fires at the entrance. It's thought that they then dragged off the men as slaves and left the women and children to suffocate. Excavations in 1973 uncovered the skeletons of at least 44 people, mostly women and children. They also found coins dating from the 10th century. One theory suggests that the coins were dropped by the Vikings (who often carried them under their arms, secured with wax) while engaged in the slaughter. However, there are few marks of violence on the skeletons, lending weight to the theory that suffocation was the cause of death.

Admission to the cave is via a compulsory but highly worthwhile guided tour. After a steep descent you enter caverns full of stalactites, stalagmites and columns, including the 7m Market Cross, Europe's largest free-standing stalagmite. Although well lit and spacious, it's damp and cold; bring warm clothes.

Contact the cave office for details of the bus service.

County Cork

POP 518,000 / AREA 7508 SQ KM

Best Places to Eat

➡ Finn's Table (p124)

➡ Manning's Emporium (p137)

➡ Josie's Lakeview House (p144)

➡ Glandore Inn (p129)

Best Places to Stay

➡ Garnish House (p109)

➡ Ballymaloe House (p119)

➡ Gilbert's (p117)

➡ Blair's Cove House (p135)

Why Go?

Everything good about Ireland can be found in County Cork. Surrounding the country's second city – a thriving metropolis made glorious by its location and its almost Rabelaisian devotion to the finer things of life – is a lush landscape dotted with villages that offer days of languor and idyll.

The city's understated confidence is grounded in its plethora of markets and ever-evolving cast of creative eateries, and its selection of pubs, entertainment and cultural pursuits.

Further afield, you'll pass inlets of eroded coasts and a multitude of perfectly charming old fishing towns and villages. The scenery is every bit as enchanting as the best bits of Ireland, particularly along the long Mizen, Sheep's Head and Beara peninsulas, where you can tackle mountain passes and touch Ireland's ancient past.

When to Go

Although the summer months promise the best weather, the shoulder seasons are festival times.

➡ Springtime is heralded in Baltimore with a fiddle fair, followed by a seafood and jazz festival in May.

➡ Autumn sees West Cork go food crazy, especially in Skibbereen, which hosts the Taste of West Cork Food Festival in September, and in the culinary capital of Kinsale, which has an excellent, long-established gourmet festival in October.

➡ Cork city's perennially popular jazz festival swings into town in late October.

County Cork Highlights

1 Revel in buzzing **Cork city**, with its brilliant selection of restaurants, pubs, music and theatres (p218)

2 Retrace the footsteps of the final passengers to board the fateful *Titanic* ocean liner at the **Titanic Experience Cobh** (p116)

3 Cycle along the windswept, wonderfully remote **Sheep's Head Peninsula** (p253)

4 Catch a culinary demonstration or take a class at the renowned **Ballymaloe Cookery School** (p119)

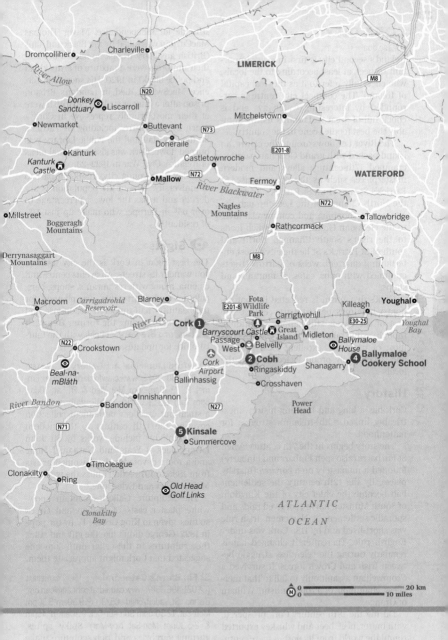

Dromcolliher • Charleville •

River Allow

LIMERICK

M8

Donkey
Sanctuary ◉ • Liscarroll
• Newmarket

N20

• Buttevant
Doneraile •

N73

Mitchelstown •

E201-8

• Kanturk
Kanturk
Castle ⌂

Castletownroche •

N72

• Mallow

N72

Fermoy •

River Blackwater

Nagles
Mountains

WATERFORD

• Tallowbridge

• Millstreet

Boggeragh
Mountains

• Rathcormack

Derrynasaggart
Mountains

M8

Blarney •

Carrigadrohid
Reservoir

Fota
Wildlife
Park

Killeagh • **Youghal** •

• Macroom

River Lee

E201-8

Carrigtwohill

E30-25

Youghal
Bay

Cork ❶

Barryscourt Castle ⌂ Great
Passage Island
West
❶ Belvelly

Midleton •
Ballymaloe ◉
House

Crookstown •

N22

Cork
Airport

❷ Cobh

Shanagarry •

❹ Ballymaloe
Cookery School

Beal-na-
mBláth ◉

Ballinhassig •

• Ringaskiddy

• Crosshaven

A T L A N T I C

River Bandon

• Bandon

• Innishannon

N27

Power
Head

N71

❺ Kinsale
• Summercove

O C E A N

Clonakilty •
• Ring

• Timoleague

Old Head ◉
Golf Links

Clonakilty
Bay

Ⓝ 0 ——————— 20 km
0 ——————— 10 miles

---

❺ Meander from the
medieval streets of **Kinsale**
(p233) along the shoreline to
mammoth Charles Fort, and
relax in Kinsale's seaside pubs

❻ Spot seals as you sail
to **Garinish Island** (p141),
a 10-minute ferry ride from
Glengarriff, before strolling its
flourishing tropical gardens

❼ Discover the unspoilt
fishing villages of **Union Hall**
and **Glandore** (p242)

CORK CITY

POP 120,000

Ireland's second city is first in every important respect, at least according to the locals, who cheerfully refer to it as the 'real capital of Ireland'. The compact city centre is surrounded by interesting waterways and is chock full of great restaurants fed by arguably the best foodie scene in the country.

The River Lee flows around the centre, an island packed with grand Georgian parades, cramped 17th-century alleys and modern masterpieces such as the opera house. St Patrick's St runs from St Patrick's Bridge on the North Channel of the Lee, through the city's main shopping and commercial area, to the Georgian Grand Parade, which leads to the river's South Channel. North and south of St Patrick's St lie the city's most entertaining quarters: webs of narrow streets crammed with pubs, cafes, restaurants and shops.

Cork's dynamism is reflected in contemporary buildings, bars and arts centres. The best of the city is still happily traditional, though – snug pubs with live-music sessions most of the week, excellent local produce and a genuinely proud welcome from the locals.

History

Cork has a long and bruising history, inextricably linked with Ireland's struggle for nationhood.

The story begins in the 7th century, when St Fin barre (also spelt Finbarr and Finbarre) founded a monastery on a *corcach* (marshy place). By the 12th century the settlement had become the chief city of the Kingdom of South Munster, having survived raids and sporadic settlement by Norsemen. Irish rule was short-lived and by 1185 Cork was under English rule. Thereafter it changed hands regularly during the relentless struggle between Irish and Crown forces. It survived a Cromwellian assault only to fall to that merciless champion of Protestantism, William of Orange.

During the 18th century Cork prospered, with butter, beef, beer and whiskey exported round the world from its port. A mere century later famine devastated both county and city, and robbed Cork of tens of thousands (and Ireland of millions) of its inhabitants through death or emigration.

The 'Rebel City's' deep-seated Irishness ensured that it played a key role in Ireland's struggle for independence. Mayor Thomas MacCurtain was killed by the Black and Tans (British auxilliary troops, so-named because their uniforms were a mixture of army khaki and police black) in 1920. His successor, Terence MacSwiney, died in London's Brixton prison after a hunger strike. The British were at their most brutally repressive in Cork – much of the centre, including St Patrick's St, the City Hall and the Public Library, was burned down. Cork was also a regional focus of Ireland's Civil War in 1922–23.

Today it's a young city, thanks in part to its university: 40% of the population is under 25 and it has the lowest percentage of over 65s in Europe, who make up just 11% of residents.

◉ Sights

The best sight in Cork is the city itself as you wander its streets. An events centre and cinema, along with restaurants, shops, bars, galleries and apartments, are planned for the beautiful half-timbered headhouse and complex surrounding the **former Beamish & Crawford Brewery** – check with the tourist office for updates.

Crawford Municipal Art Gallery GALLERY
(☑ 021-480 5042; www.crawfordartgallery.ie; Emmet Pl; ◷ 10am-5pm Mon-Wed & Fri-Sat, 10am-8pm Thu) FREE Cork's public gallery houses a small but excellent permanent collection covering the 17th century to the modern day. Highlights include works by Sir John Lavery, Jack B Yeats and Nathaniel Hone and a room devoted to Irish women artists from 1886 to 1978 – don't miss the works by Mainie Jellet and Evie Hone.

The Sculpture Galleries contain snow-white plaster casts of Roman and Greek statues, given to King George IV by the pope in 1822. George didn't like the gift and stuck the sculptures in the cellar until someone suggested that Cork might appreciate them.

St Fin Barre's Cathedral CATHEDRAL
(☑ 021-496 3387; www.cathedral.cork.anglican.org; Bishop St; adult/child €5/3; ◷ 9.30am-5.30pm Mon-Sat, 12.30-5pm Sun Apr-Oct, 9.30am-12.45pm & 2-5.30pm Mon-Sat Nov-Mar) Spiky spires, gurning gargoyles and rich sculpture make up the exterior of Cork's Protestant cathedral, an attention-grabbing mixture of French Gothic and medieval whimsy. Local legend says that the golden angel on the eastern side will blow its horn when the Apocalypse is due to start...

The grandeur continues inside, with marble floor mosaics, a colourful chancel ceiling and a huge pulpit and bishop's throne. Quirky items include a cannonball blasted into an earlier medieval spire during the Siege of Cork (1690).

Most of the ostentation is the result of an architectural competition held in 1863 and won by William Burges. Once victory was assured Burges promptly redrew his plans – with an extra choir bay and taller towers – and his £15,000 budget went out the window. Luckily, the bishop appreciated such perfectionism and spent the rest of his life fundraising for the project.

The cathedral sits about 500m south of the centre, on the spot where Cork's patron saint, Fin Barre, founded his monastery in the 7th century.

Lewis Glucksman Gallery   ART GALLERY

(☑021-490 1844; www.glucksman.org; University College Cork; suggested donation €5; ☺10am-5pm Tue-Sat, 2-5pm Sun) This award-winning gallery in the buzzing grounds of University College Cork (UCC) is a startling limestone, steel and timber construction displaying the best in both national and international contemporary art and installation. Don't miss the free fortnightly curatorial tours if you're in town. The onsite cafe is excellent.

Cork City Gaol   MUSEUM

(☑021-430 5022; www.corkcitygaol.com; Convent Ave, Sunday's Well; adult/child €8/4.50; ☺9.30am-5pm Apr-Oct, 10am-4pm Nov-Mar) This imposing former prison is well worth a visit, if only to get a sense of how crap life was for prisoners a century ago. An audio tour guides you around the restored cells, which feature models of suffering prisoners and sadistic-looking guards. It's very moving, bringing home the harshness of the 19th-century penal system. The most common crime was that of poverty; many of the inmates were sentenced to hard labour for stealing loaves of bread.

The prison closed in 1923, reopening in 1927 as a radio station, so the Governor's House has been converted into the Radio Museum Experience. Alongside collections of beautiful old radios you can hear the story of Guglielmo Marconi's conquest of the airwaves.

Atmospheric night tours take place on Thursday at 7pm (€10).

You can walk from the city centre, or take a bus from the bus station to the UCC – from there walk north across Fitzgerald Park, over Mardyke Bridge, along the Banks of the River Lee Walkway and follow the signs up the hill.

Shandon   NEIGHBOURHOOD

Perched on a hillside overlooking the city centre from the north, Shandon is a great spot for the views alone, but you'll also find galleries, antique shops and cafes along its old lanes and squares. Those tiny old row houses, where generations of workers raised huge families in very basic conditions, are now sought-after urban pieds-à-terre.

Shandon is dominated by the 1722 St Anne's Church (☑021-450 5906; www.shandonbells.ie; John Redmond St; tower including bells adult/child €5/2.50; ☺10am-5pm Mon-Sat, 11.30am-4.30pm Sun), aka the 'Four-Faced Liar', so called as each of the tower's four clocks used to tell a different time. Wannabe campanologists can ring the bells on the 1st floor of the 1750 Italianate tower and continue the 132 steps up to the top for 360° views of the city.

Cork has a long tradition of butter manufacturing (in the 1860s it was the world's largest butter market, exporting butter throughout the British Empire), and its history is told through displays and dioramas in the Cork Butter Museum (☑021-430 0600; www.corkbutter.museum; O'Connell Sq; adult/child €4/3; ☺10am-5pm Mar-Jun & Sep-Oct, 10am-6pm Jul & Aug). The square in front of the museum is dominated by the striking Firkin Crane, a round building central to the old butter market, which now houses a dance centre (p113).

☞ Tours

Cork City Tour   BUS TOUR

(☑021-430 9090; www.corkcitytour.com; adult/student/child €14/12/5; ☺10am-5.30pm Apr-Oct, last bus starts at 4pm) Hop-on-hop-off open-top bus linking the city's main areas of interest.

Cork Literary Tour   WALKING TOUR

FREE Free audio walking tour of Cork, downloadable from the Cork City Library (☑021-492 4900; www.corkcitylibraries.ie; 57-61 Grand Pde; ☺10am-5.30pm Mon-Sat).

WANT MORE?

Head to Lonely Planet (www.lonelyplanet.com/cork) for planning advice, author recommendations, traveller reviews and insider tips.

COUNTY CORK CORK CITY

COUNTY CORK CORK CITY

Cork City

Kent (100m);
Cobh (15.5km);
Midleton (20.5km)

Emerson House (250m)

Summer Hill

Lower Glanmire Rd

Ship St

Belgrave Pl

York St

Wellington Rd

Sidney Park

MacCurtain St

Bridge St

Devonshire St

Coburg St

Carroll's Quay

Upper John St

Bob & Joan's Walk

SHANDON

Dominick St

Old Butter Market

Pope's Quay

Shandon St

North Mall

Blarney St

Bachelor's Quay

Grattan St

Millerd St

Sheaves St

Woods St

Dyke Pde

Lancaster Quay

Grenville Pl

Banks of the River Lee Walkway

Cross St

Washington St

Hanover St

North Main St

South Main St

Castle St

St Paul's Ave

Paul La

Mutton Ln

Cornmarket St

Millennium Bridge

St Paul's Bridge

Emmet Pl

Academy St

French Church St

Carey's La

Oliver Plunkett St

English Market

Grand Pde

Princes St

Cork City Tourist Office

Sullivan's Quay

Bishop Lucey Park

Other Place

Tobin St

South Main St

Penrose's Quay

Anderson's Quay

Merchant's Quay

River Lee North Channel

St Patrick's Quay

Airccoach St Patrick's Quay Bus Stop

Cork Bus Station

Parnell Pl

Lavitt's Quay

St Patrick's Bridge

St Patrick's St

Winthrop St

Robert Morgan St

Caroline St

Pembroke St

Phoenix St

Maylor St

Cook St

South Mall

Morrison's Quay

Albert St

South City Link Rd

Albert Quay

Anglesea St

Albert Rd

Albert Quay

Albert St

Ringaskiddy (19km)

City Hall

River Lee South Channel

St Fin Barre's Cathedral (250m); Garnish House (250m); University College Cork (UCC; 960m)

Blarney Stone Guesthouse (110m); Garnish House (150m); Crawford House (300m); Hayfield Manor (1.5km)

0   200 m
0   0.1 miles

Cork City

Cork Walks   WALKING TOUR

FREE The council's two free self-guided tours cover the South Parish and Shandon. Pick up the guide and map at the tourist office.

Sunfish Explorer   KAYAKING
(☎087 947 4616; sunfishexplorer.com; Lapps Quay; per hr/4hr €30/100) Runs trips in motorised kayaks, combining the accessibility of kayaking with the comfort of boating.

★ Festivals & Events

Book well in advance, particularly for the jazz and film festivals.

Cork World Book Festival   LITERATURE
(www.corkcitylibraries.ie; ⊘ late Apr) A huge book festival with loads of authors; sponsored by the Cork City Library.

International Choral Festival   MUSIC
(www.corkchoral.ie; ⊘ early May) A major event held in the City Hall and other venues.

Cork Pride   GAY & LESBIAN
(www.corkpride.com; ⊘ Jul/Aug) Week-long gay pride celebrations.

Guinness Jazz Festival   JAZZ
(guinnessjazzfestival.com; ⊘ late Oct) Cork's biggest festival has an all-star line-up in venues across town.

Cork Film Festival   FILM
(www.corkfilmfest.org; ⊘ Nov) Eclectic, week-long program of international films.

🛏 Sleeping

🛏 City Centre

Whether you stay on the main island or to the north, across St Patrick's Bridge in Shandon or around MacCurtain St, you're right in the heart of the action.

THE BOOZE BUSTER

The imposing statue on St Patrick's St, just south of the River Lee North Channel, is of Father Theobald Mathew, the 'Apostle of Temperance', who crusaded against the ills of alcohol in the 1830s and 1840s with such success that a quarter of a million people took the 'pledge' and whiskey production was cut in half. The Holy Trinity Church (Fr Mathew Quay) was designed by the Pain brothers in 1834 in his honour.

Brú Bar & Hostel   HOSTEL €

(☑021-455 9667; www.bruhostel.com; 57 MacCurtain St; dm €15-20, d & tr €48-60; @🖘) This buzzing hostel has its own internet cafe, with free access for guests, and a fantastic bar, popular with backpackers and locals alike. The dorms (each with a bathroom) have four to six beds and are both clean and stylish – ask for one on the upper floors to avoid bar noise. Breakfast is free.

Sheila's Hostel   HOSTEL €

(☑021-450 5562; www.sheilashostel.ie; 4 Belgrave Pl, off Wellington Rd; dm €16-18, tw €44-50; @🖘) Sheila's heaves with young travellers, and it's no wonder given its excellent central location. Facilities include a sauna, lockers, laundry service, a pool table and barbecue. Cheaper twin rooms share bathrooms. Breakfast is €3 extra.

Kinlay House   HOSTEL €

(☑021-450 8966; www.kinlayhousecork.ie; Bob & Joan's Walk; dm €15-18, s €30-35, d €46-54; @🖘) This labyrinthine hostel near St Anne's Church in Shandon has a fun, laid-back atmosphere. Services include laundry and free breakfast. Guests can work out in the next-door gym at a discount.

★Imperial Hotel   HOTEL €€

(☑021-427 4040; www.flynnhotels.com; South Mall; d/ste from €109/450; @🖘) Recently celebrating its bicentenary, the Imperial knows how to age gracefully. Public spaces resonate with opulent period detail such as marble floors, elaborate floral bouquets and more. The 130 rooms are of four-star hotel standard and include writing desks, restrained decor and modern touches such as the Aveda spa and a digital music library – something unheard of when Charles Dickens stayed. Irish Free

State commander-in-chief Michael Collins spent his final night here; you can check into his suite.

Auburn House   B&B €€

(☑021-450 8555; www.auburnguesthouse.com; 3 Garfield Tce, Wellington Rd; s/d €58/80; 🖘) There's a warm family welcome at this neat B&B, which has smallish but well-kept rooms brightened by window boxes. Try to bag one of the back rooms, which have sweeping views over the city. Breakfast has vegetarian choices; the location near the fun of MacCurtain St is a plus.

Isaac's Hotel   HOTEL €€

(☑021-450 0011; www.isaacscork.com; 48 MacCurtain St; s/d/apt from €80/85/120; @🖘) Adjoining a cobbled laneway with a waterfall, location is the real selling point at this hotel housed in what once was a Victorian furniture warehouse (ask for a room away from the busy street). The decor is a faded salmon-rust scheme (including the apartments, which come with kitchen and washing machine). Rooms without a fan can get steamy on sunny days, no matter what you get up to...

🛏 Western Road & Around

Western Rd runs southwest from the city centre to the large UCC campus; it has the city's biggest choice of B&Bs. Take a bus from the central bus station, or walk, preferably along the less busy Dyke Parade.

★Garnish House   B&B €€

(☑021-427 5111; www.garnish.ie; Western Rd; s/d from €75/89; 🖘) Every attention is lavished upon guests at this award-winning B&B. The legendary breakfast menu (30 choices!) includes fresh fish and French toast. Typical of the touches here is the freshly cooked porridge, which comes with creamed honey and your choice of whiskey or Baileys. Enjoy it out on the garden terrace. The 14 rooms are very comfortable; reception is open 24 hours.

Blarney Stone Guesthouse   B&B €€

(☑021-427 0083; www.blarneystoneguesthouse. ie; Western Rd; s/d €59/89; @🖘) Although it's nowhere near Blarney Castle, the Blarney Stone will make you want to kiss something after you settle into one of its eight rooms. It standouts from this close-knit row of B&Bs with its brilliant white paint scheme on the front; inside, the decor is lavish in a way that harks back to the time when vinyl roofs were popular on cars; there are lots of frill and curlicues.

Crawford House B&B €€
(☑021-427 9000; www.crawfordhouse.ie; Western Rd; d €60-90; @🌐📶) Power showers and large spa baths feature in the 12 rooms of this B&B, along with king-size beds and restrained wooden furnishings. The standard is that of a contemporary hotel (24-hour reception); the atmosphere, that of a family home. Public areas (and four rooms) have wi-fi.

Hayfield Manor HOTEL €€€
(☑021-484 5900; www.hayfieldmanor.ie; Perrott Ave, College Rd; d €195-310; @🌐📶🏊) Roll out the red carpet and pour yourself a sherry, for *you have arrived*. Just 1.5km southwest of the city centre but with all the ambience of a country house, Hayfield combines the luxury and facilities of a big hotel with the informality and welcome of a small one. The 88 beautiful bedrooms (choose from traditional or contemporary styling) enjoy 24-hour room service, although you may want to idle the hours away in the library, luxurious spa and leisure centre or gourmet restaurants.

✖ Eating

Cork's food scene is reason enough to visit the city. The English Market (p111) is a local – no, make that national – treasure. The narrow, nearly lightless pedestrianised streets north of St Patrick's St throng with cafes and restaurants, and the place hops day and night.

Gourmet Burger Bistro BURGERS €
(☑021-4505 404; www.gourmetburgerbistro.ie; 8 Bridge St; mains €8-17; ⊙noon-10pm Mon-Sat, 2-9pm Sun; 📶🍴) At this chic, minimalist spot, organic burgers span the globe: from Indian (lamb kofta with mango) to Spanish (chicken, chorizo and manchego), American (with bacon, Monterey jack cheese and barbecue sauce), French (with brie) and, of course, the 'Full Irish' (bacon, Clonakilty black pudding and fried egg). Vegetarians aren't forgotten, with falafel and halloumi options. There are also salads and sandwiches (although that would be missing the point).

Idaho Café CAFE €
(☑021-427 6376; 19 Caroline St; mains €8.50-11.50; ⊙8.30am-5pm Mon-Thu,8.30am-6pm Fri-Sat; 🍴) It looks like a traditional old caf from the outside, but you'll find all sorts of creative

takes on Irish standards here. The tea selection includes scads of herbal numbers and there's a good per-glass wine menu. Tight seating means nothing is private.

★Electric MODERN IRISH €€
(www.electriccork.com; 41 South Mall; mains €15-27; ⊙noon-10pm; 📶) The market-sourced menu at this this transformed art deco bank spans from broccoli risotto with pear, blue cheese and walnut dressing to succulent steaks. From Thursday to Saturday there's a rustic Mediterranean-style fish bar too. But it's the big riverside deck and upstairs restaurant balcony with knock-out cathedral views that amp up the crowds – along with wines by the glass and over two dozen beers.

Nash 19 INTERNATIONAL €€
(☑021-427 0880; www.nash☺19.com; Princes St; mains €10.50-16; ⊙7.30am-5pm Mon-Fri, 8.30am-4pm Sat) 🖊 A sensational bistro with a small deli inside; local foods are honoured from breakfast to lunch and on to tea. Fresh scones draw in the crowds early; daily fresh specials (soups, salads, desserts etc), free-range chicken pie and platters of smoked fish from Frank Henderman (p229) keep them coming through the rest of the day.

Cafe Paradiso VEGETARIAN €€
(☑021-427 7939; www.cafeparadiso.ie; 16 Lancaster Quay; lunch mains €13-14, 2-/3-course dinner €33/40; ⊙noon-2.30pm Fri & Sat, 5.30-10pm Tue-Sat year-round, plus 5.50pm-10pm Mon Jun-late Aug; 🖊) 🖊 A contender for best restaurant in town in any genre, Paradiso serves contemporary vegetarian dishes, including vegan fare: how about sweet-chilli–glazed pan-fried tofu with Asian greens in coconut and lemongrass broth, or spring cabbage dolma of roast squash, caramelised onion and hazelnut, with cardamom yoghurt and saffron-crushed potatoes? Reservations are

TRACING YOUR ANCESTORS

Genealogy services covering the north and east of County Cork are available at the Mallow Heritage Centre (☑022-50302; mallowheritagecentre.com; 27/28 Bank Pl; ⊙by appointment) and the Cobh Heritage Centre (p116). For West Cork, contact the Skibbereen Heritage (p129) centre. There's no genealogy centre in Cork city, but the Cork City Library (p106) can give you advice.

COUNTY CORK CORK CITY

essential. Dinner, bed and breakfast rates staying in the funky upstairs rooms start from €100 per person.

Market Lane
IRISH, INTERNATIONAL €€

(✐ 021-427 4710; www.marketlane.ie; 5 Oliver Plunkett St; mains €11-25.50; ☺ noon-late Mon-Sat, 1-9pm Sun; 📶 ♿) It's always hopping at this bright corner bistro with an open kitchen and long wooden bar. The broad menu changes often to reflect what's fresh – look out for braised pork marinated in Cork dry gin, and steaks with awesome aioli. The €10 lunch menu is a steal. Lots of wines by the glass.

Star Anise
MODERN EUROPEAN €€

(✐ 021-455 1635; www.staranise.ie; 4 Bridge St; mains €19-25; ☺ noon-2.30pm & 6-10pm Mon-Sat) Fresh and creative cooking is the hallmark at this narrow, stylish little shopfront bistro. There are steaks for the masses but also treats such as maple-glazed duck breast, and slow-cooked lamb tajine. The wine list is both superb and affordable.

Uncle Pete's
PIZZA €€

(✐ 021-455 5888; http://unclepetes.ie; Paul St; pizza €6-18; ☺ noon-12.30am Sun-Thu, noon-1.30am Fri & Sat) Cork's best pizza, with over 25 varieties of gluten-free options.

Jacques Restaurant
MODERN IRISH €€€

(✐ 021-427 7387; www.jacquesrestaurant.ie; 23 Oliver Plunkett St; mains €20-28; ☺ 10am-4pm Mon, 10am-10pm Tue-Sat) Now in sleek new premises, Jacqueline and Eithne Barry continue to draw on the terrific network of local suppliers they've built up over nearly three decades to help them realise their culinary ambitions – the freshest Cork food cooked simply. The menu changes daily: quail with jewelled couscous, perhaps, or Castletown-bere scallops with pomegranate, raisin and caper salsa.

Les Gourmandises
FRENCH €€€

(✐ 021-425 1959; www.lesgourmandises.ie; 17 Cook St; 2-course menus €27.50-38.50, 3-course menus €29.50-45; ☺ 6-9.30pm Mon-Sat, 12.30-3pm Sun) Remember those beautiful fresh fish you saw in the English Market? Many of them end up at this cute little restaurant that reminds you of that perfect place you stumbled upon in Paris once... Meat and poultry also get their due, such as roast guinea fowl with foie gras and mushroom sauce. Service is gracious and calm.

Cornstore
MODERN EUROPEAN €€€

(✐ 021-427 4777; www.cornstorecork.com; 40A Cornmarket St; mains €17-34; ☺ noon-11pm) Buzzing day and night, this modern restaurant has a swish bar, where you can enjoy creative cocktails while waiting for a table. Some tables are minute, but if you're having the amazing house special of lobster hold out for a large one so your elbows and shells can fly. There's also excellent fresh fish, steaks and pasta and an aromatic truffle burger.

🍷 Drinking & Nightlife

In Cork pubs, drink Guinness at your own peril; even though Heineken now owns both of the local stout legends, Murphy's and Beamish (and closed down the latter's brewery). Cork's microbrewery, the Franciscan Well Brewery, makes quality beers, including Friar Weisse, popular in summer.

While pubs are Cork's best asset, there's a booming bar scene, too.

With such a big student population, the city's small selection of nightclubs does a thriving trade. Entry ranges from free to

---

DON'T MISS

THE ENGLISH MARKET

It could just as easily be called the Victorian Market for its ornate vaulted ceilings and columns, but the English Market (www.englishmarket.ie; Princes St; ☺ 9am-5.30pm Mon-Sat) is a true gem, no matter what you call it. Scores of vendors sell some of the very best local produce, meats, cheeses and takeaway food in the region. On decent days, take your lunch to nearby Bishop Lucey Park, a popular alfresco eating spot.

Looking down over the market from a mezzanine, Farmgate Café (www.farmgate. ie; Princes St; dishes €4.50-15; ☺ 8.30am-5pm Mon-Sat) is an unmissable experience. Like its sister restaurant in Midleton, this cafe has mastered the magic art of producing delicious meals without fuss or faddism. The food, from rock oysters to the lamb for Irish stew, is sourced from the market below. There are tables but the best seats are at the balcony counter, where you can ponder the passing parade of shoppers.

€15; most are open until 2am on Friday and Saturday. Also see Entertainment listings.

Sin É
PUB

(8 Coburg St) You could easily while away an entire day at this great old place, which is everything a craic-filled pub should be – long on atmosphere and short on pretension. There's music most nights, much of it traditional, but with the odd surprise.

Mutton Lane Inn
PUB

(Mutton Lane) Tucked down the tiniest of laneways off St Patrick's St, this inviting pub, lit by candles and fairy lights, is one of Cork's most intimate drinking holes. It's minuscule so try to get in early to bag the snug, or perch on beer kegs outside.

Long Valley
PUB

(10 Winthrop St) A Cork institution that dates from the mid-19th century and is still going strong. Some of the furnishings hail from White Star Line ocean liners that used to call at Cobh.

Suas Rooftop Bar
COCKTAIL BAR

(www.suasbar.com; 4-5 South Main St; 10am-11.30pm Mon-Thu, 10am-12.30am Fri-Sat, noon-11pm Sun summer, reduced hours in winter) You could easily walk along South Main St and never know that this sleek bar and heated roof terrace was right above you. Cocktails cover all the classics, proper caipirinhas with *cachaça* (fermented sugarcane) and fresh limes included. DJs hit the decks on Friday and Saturday nights.

Franciscan Well Brewery
PUB

(www.franciscanwellbrewery.com; 14 North Mall; ⊙3-11.30pm Mon-Thu, 3pm-12.30am Fri-Sat, 3-11pm Sun; ☎) The copper vats gleaming behind the bar give the game away: the Franciscan Well brews its own beer. The best place to enjoy it is in the enormous beer garden at the back. The pub holds regular beer festivals with other small (and often underappreciated) Irish breweries.

Abbot's Ale House
PUB

(17 Devonshire St) A low-key, 1st-floor pub, whose small size contrasts with a huge beer list. There are always several on tap and another 300 in bottles. Good for preclubbing.

Savoy
THEATRE, NIGHTCLUB

(☎021-422 3910; www.savoytheatre.ie; Patrick St; ⊙Thu-Sun) The city's best DJs (and a changing menu of visiting ones) show their skills on the Savoy's club nights.

GONE TO THE DOGS

If you tire of the pubs, the live music and the theatre, there's always the dogs. Greyhound racing is big in Ireland, particularly with families, and **Curraheen Greyhound Park** (☎021-454 3095; www.igb.ie/cork; Curraheen Park; adult/child €10/5; ⊙from 6.45pm, days vary) is one of the country's finest stadiums. There are 10 races a night, plus a restaurant, a bar and live music to keep you entertained in between. Curraheen is 5.5km from the centre; buses run here from Cork's bus station.

The Oliver Plunkett
LIVE MUSIC

(☎021-422 2779; www.theoliverplunkett.com; 116 Oliver Plunkett St; ⊙8am-late) Cork memorabilia (sporting, political and musical), a relaxed pub serving food, rockin' live music and club nights make this multipurpose venue a magnet for locals and visitors day and night.

☆ Entertainment

For listings of Cork's vibrant scene, pick up a copy of the free **WhazOn?** (www.whazon.com).

Theatre

Cork's cultural life is as fine as any in Ireland and attracts numerous internationally renowned performers.

Cork Arts Theatre
THEATRE

(☎021-450 5624; www.corkartstheatre.com; Camden Court, Carroll's Quay) An excellent theatre putting on thought-provoking drama and new works.

Cork Opera House
OPERA

(☎021-427 0022; www.corkoperahouse.ie; Emmet Pl; ⊙box office 10am-7pm Mon-Sat, from 6pm Sun performance nights, 10am-5.30pm Mon-Sat nonperformance nights) This leading venue has been entertaining the city for more than 150 years with everything from opera and ballet to stand-up and puppet shows.

Around the back, the **Half Moon Theatre** (☎021-427 0022; halfmoontheatre.ie; Emmet Place) presents contemporary theatre, dance, art and occasional club nights.

Everyman Palace Theatre
THEATRE

(☎021-450 1673; www.everymanpalace.com; 15 MacCurtain St; ⊙box office noon-7.30pm Mon-Fri, 2-7.30pm Sat, 4-7.30pm Sun performance nights, noon-5pm Mon-Fri, 2-5pm Sat nonperformance

GAY & LESBIAN CORK

➡ **Cork Pride** (www.corkpride.com; ⊙ Jul/Aug) Week-long festival in July/August, with events throughout the city.

➡ **Ruby Lounge** (☑ 021-4222 2860; www.facebook.com/MrRubyLounge; Washington St; ⊙ 9pm-late Wed-Sun) Cork's premier gay bar, Chambers, has been reborn as the Ruby Lounge.

➡ **Emerson House** (☑ 086 834 0891; www.emersonhousecork.com; 2 Clarence Tce, North Summer Hill; s/d from €60/80; 🖀) Gay and lesbian B&B in an elegant Georgian house. Host Cyril is a mine of information.

➡ **Gay Cork** (www.gaycork.com) What's-on listings and directory.

➡ **L.inC** (☑ 021-480 8600; www.linc.ie; 11A White St; ⊙ 11am-3pm Tue & Wed, 11am-8pm Thu) Excellent resource centre for lesbians and bisexual women.

➡ **Other Place** (☑ 021-427 8470; www.gayprojectcork.com; 8 South Main St; ⊙ cafe-bar 11am-7pm Tue-Fri, 1-7pm Sat) Affiliated with the **Southern Gay Health Project** (www.gayhealthproject.com); has a bookstore and a cafe-bar.

nights) Acclaimed musical and dramatic productions are the main bill here, but there's also the occasional comedy act and band (it's a great venue for gigs that require a little bit of respectful silence).

Firkin Crane THEATRE
(☑ 021-450 7487; www.firkincrane.ie; Shandon) One of Ireland's premier centres for modern dance.

Granary THEATRE
(☑ 021-490 4275; www.granary.ie; Dyke Pde) Contemporary and experimental works are staged by the UCC drama group and visiting companies.

Triskel Arts Centre ARTS CENTRE
(☑ 021-472 2022; www.triskelart.com; Tobin St; tickets around €15; ⊙ cafe 10am-5pm Mon-Sat) Expect a varied program of live music, installation art, photography and theatre at this intimate venue. There's also a cinema (from 6.30pm) and a great cafe.

Cinemas

Gate Multiplex CINEMA
(☑ 021-427 9595; www.corkcinemas.com; North Main St) Multiscreen cinema showing mainstream films.

Live Music

Cork's musical credentials are impeccable. Besides the pubs that feature live music, and theatres, there are also places that are either dedicated music venues or bars known particularly for their live events. For full listings, refer to *WhazOn?*, PLUGD Records and www.corkgigs.com.

Cyprus Avenue MUSIC VENUE
(☑ 021-427 6165; www.cyprusavenue.ie; Caroline St; ⊙ 7.30pm-late) A midsized venue that is probably the best spot in town to see all kinds of gigs, from heartfelt singer-songwriters to excellent bands on their way to fame (or on their way down from it).

Pavilion CAFE, LIVE MUSIC
(☑ 021-427 6230; www.pavilioncork.com; 13 Carey's Lane; ⊙ noon-late) By night this cafe has one of Cork's best mixes of bands, musicians and vocalists. Jazz, blues, rock, alternative and more are in the line-up.

Crane Lane Theatre THEATRE
(☑ 021-427 8487; www.cranelanetheatre.com; Phoenix St) Atmospheric venue for live music, decked out in 1920s to 1940s decor. Its courtyard beer garden is a central oasis.

🛍 Shopping

St Patrick's St is the retail heart of Cork, housing all the major department stores and malls. But pedestrianised Oliver Plunkett St is the retail spine; it and nearby narrow lanes are lined with interesting small shops.

O'Connaill CHOCOLATE
(☑ 021-437 3407; 16B French Church St) O'Connaill creates exquisite chocolates; don't leave Cork without sampling its Chocolatier's Hot Chocolate (€4).

P Cashell ANTIQUES
(☑ 021-427 5824; 13 Winthrop St; ⊙ 10am-5pm Tue-Sat) A timeless and jammed antique and curio shop that seems entirely out of place amid the glitz of central Cork. It's like a treasure hunt.

PLUGD Records MUSIC
(☑021-472 2022; www.plugdrecords.com; Tobin St; ☺noon-7pm Mon-Sat) Carries all kinds of music and is the place to keep up with the ever-changing club scene.

Pro Musica MUSICAL INSTRUMENTS
(☑021-427 1659; www.promusica.ie; Oliver Plunkett St; ☺9am-6pm Mon-Sat) The heart of Cork's world for musicians: sheet music, instruments and a notice board.

ℹ Information

Free wi-fi is available throughout the city centre's main streets and public spaces.

Cork City Tourist Office (☑021-425 5100; www.corkcity.ie; Grand Pde; ☺9am-6pm Mon-Sat, 10am-5pm Sun Jul & Aug, 9.15am-5pm Mon-Sat Sep-Jun) Souvenir shop and information desk. Sells Ordnance Survey maps; **Stena Line** ferries has a desk here.

General post office (☑021-485 1042; Oliver Plunkett St; ☺9am-5.30pm Mon-Sat)

Mercy University Hospital (☑021-427 1971; www.muh.ie; Grenville Pl) Accident and emergency services.

People's Republic of Cork (www.peoples republicofcork.com) Picking up on the popular nickname for this liberal-leaning city, this indie website has excellent info.

Webworkhouse.com (☑021-427 3090; www. webworkhouse.com; 8A Winthrop St; per hr €1.50-3; ☺24hr) Internet cafe; also offers low-cost international phone calls.

ℹ Getting There & Away

AIR

Cork Airport (ORT; ☑021-431 3131; www.cork -airport.com) is 8km south of the city on the N27. Facilities include ATMs and car-hire desks for all the main companies. Airlines servicing the airport include Aer Lingus, Ryanair and Jet2. com. There are flights to Dublin, London (Heathrow, Gatwick and Stansted) and a few other cities in Britain and across Europe.

BOAT

Brittany Ferries (☑021-427 7801; www.brittany ferries.ie; 42 Grand Pde) sails to Roscoff (France) weekly from the end of March to October. The crossing takes 14 hours; fares vary widely. The ferry terminal is at Ringaskiddy, 15 minutes by car southeast of the city centre along the N28. Taxis cost €28 to €35. Bus Éireann runs a service from Cork's bus station to link up with departures (adult/child €7.90/5.60, 40 minutes); confirm times. There's also a service to Rosslare Harbour (adult/child €26/17.50, four to five hours).

BUS

Aircoach (☑01-844 7118; www.aircoach.ie) serves Dublin Airport and Dublin city centre from St Patrick's Quay (€15; 4¼ hours; every two hours 1am to 11pm).

Bus Éireann (☑021-450 8188; www.buseir eann.ie) operates from the **bus station** (cnr Merchants Quay & Parnell Pl). You can get to most places in Ireland from Cork, including Dublin (€14.50, three hours, six daily), Killarney (€15.30, 1¾ hours, 14 daily), Kilkenny (€19, three hours, two daily) and Waterford (€21.20, 2¼ hours, 13 daily).

GoBus (☑091-564 600; www.gobus.ie; ☎) links Cork's bus station with Dublin (€12, three hours, nine daily).

Citylink (☑091-564 164; www.citylink.ie; ☎) operates services to Galway (three hours) and Limerick (1½ hours). Buses are frequent and fares are as low as €10.

TRAIN

Kent Train Station (☑021-450 4777) is north of the River Lee on Lower Glanmire Rd. Buses run into the centre (€1.80); a taxi costs from €9 to €10.

The train line goes through Mallow, where you can change for the Tralee line, and Limerick Junction, for the line to Ennis (and Galway), then on to Dublin (€38, three hours, 16 daily).

ℹ Getting Around

TO/FROM THE AIRPORT

Bus Éireann has frequent services between the bus station and Cork Airport between 6am and 11pm (€5, 30 minutes).

A taxi to/from town costs €20 to €25.

BUS

Most places are within easy walking distance of the centre. Single bus tickets costs €1.80 each; a day pass is €4.80. Buy all tickets on the bus.

CAR

Streetside parking requires scratch-card parking discs (€2 per hour), obtained from the tourist office and some newsagencies. Be warned – the traffic wardens are ferociously efficient and the cost of retrieving your vehicle is hefty. There are several signposted car parks around the central area, with charges of €2 per hour and €12 overnight.

TAXI

For taxi hire, try **Cork Taxi Co-op** (☑021-427 2222; www.corktaxi.ie) or **Shandon Cabs** (☑021-450 2255).

COUNTY CORK CORK CITY

AROUND CORK CITY

Blarney Castle

If you need proof of the power of a good yarn, then join the queue to get into this 15th-century castle (☑ 021-438 5252; www.blarneycastle.ie; adult/child €12/5; ⊙ 9am-7pm Mon-Sat, 9am-6pm Sun Jun-Aug, 9am-6.30pm Mon-Sat, 9am-6pm Sun May & Sep, 9am-6pm Mon-Sat, 9am-5pm Sun Oct-Apr), one of Ireland's most inexplicably popular tourist attractions.

People are here, of course, to plant their lips on the Blarney Stone, a cliché that has entered every lexicon and tour route. The object of their affections is perched at the top of a steep climb up slippery, spiral staircases. On the battlements you bend backwards over a long, long drop (with safety grill and attendant to prevent tragedy) to kiss the stone; as your shirt rides up, coachloads of onlookers stare up your nose. Try not to think of the local lore about the fluids other than saliva that drench the stone. Better yet, just don't do it.

The custom of kissing the stone (which supposedly gives one the gift of the gab – if not other things) is a relatively modern one, but Blarney's association with smooth talking goes back a long time. Queen Elizabeth I is said to have invented the term 'to talk blarney' out of exasperation with Lord Blarney's ability to talk endlessly without ever actually agreeing to her demands.

Be warned: this place gets mobbed. If it all gets too much, vanish into the Rock Close, part of the beautiful and often ignored gardens. And a hint: Barryscourt Castle (p118), east of Cork, is more impressive and much less crowded.

Blarney is 8km northwest of Cork. The castle itself is poorly signed – follow the signs for the Blarney Woollen Mills gift emporium and hotel complex. Buses run frequently from Cork bus station (adult/child €3.80/2, 30 minutes).

Fota

Kangaroos bound, cheetahs run and monkeys and gibbons leap and scream on wooded islands at Fota Wildlife Park (☑ 021-481 2678; www.fotawildlife.ie; Carrigtwohill; adult/child €14.30/9.20; ⊙ 10am-5pm Mon-Sat, 10.30am-5pm Sun), a huge outdoor zoo where animals roam without a cage or fence in sight. A tour train (on wheels, not tracks) runs a circuit

round the park every 15 minutes in high season (one way/return €1/2), but the 2km circular walk offers a more close-up experience.

From the wildlife park, you can take a stroll down to the Regency-style Fota House (☑ 021-481 5543; www.fotahouse.com; Carrigtwohill; house tour adult/child €8/3; ⊙ 10am-5pm Mon-Sat, 10am-4pm Sun Apr-Sep) The mostly barren interior contains a fine kitchen and ornate plasterwork ceilings; interactive displays bring the rooms to life. Attached to the house is the 150-year-old arboretum, which has a Victorian fernery, a magnolia walk and some beautiful trees, including giant redwoods and a Chinese ghost tree.

A car park (€3) is shared by the wildlife park and the house.

Three championship golf courses sprawl within the 315-hectare Fota Island Resort (☑ 021-488 3700; www.fotaisland.ie; Fota Island; s/d/ste from €164/179/249, green fees from €45; ◉ 🛜 🏊). The main hotel building's exterior resembles an airport terminal but inside it's filled with warm timbers and five-star elegance. In addition to a spa, there's an excellent restaurant and bar here but the most atmospheric place to drink and/or dine is the beautiful old stone clubhouse in a converted farmhouse overlooking the lake.

Fota is 10km east of Cork. The hourly Cork–Fota train (€2.45, 13 minutes) continues to Cobh.

Cobh

POP 6500

Cobh (pronounced 'cove') is a charming hill town on a glistening estuary, speckled with brightly coloured houses and overlooked by a splendid cathedral. It's popular with Corkonians looking for a spot of R&R, and with cruise liners (around 60 visit the port each year) as the second-largest natural harbour in the world (after Sydney Harbour in Australia).

It's a far cry from the harrowing Famine years when 2.5 million people left Ireland through the estuary in order to escape the ravages of starvation. Cobh was also the final port of call for the *Titanic*; a poignant museum opened in 2012 to commemorate the voyage's centenary.

Cobh is on the south side of Great Island, one of three islands that fill Cork Harbour. The other two (visible from the waterfront) are Haulbowline Island, once the base of the Irish Naval Service, and the greener, former prison Spike Island, which is now owned by Cork City Council and can be toured.

History

For many years Cobh was the port of Cork, and it has always had a strong connection with Atlantic crossings, including many fateful ones. In 1838 the *Sirius,* the first steamship to cross the Atlantic, sailed from Cobh. The *Titanic* made its last stop here before its disastrous crossing in 1912; and, when the *Lusitania* was torpedoed off the coast of Kinsale in 1915, it was here that many of the survivors were brought and the dead buried. Cobh was also the last glimpse of Ireland for millions who emigrated during the Famine.

In 1849 Cobh was renamed Queenstown after Queen Victoria paid a visit. The name lasted until Irish independence in 1921 when, unsurprisingly, the local council reverted to the Irish original.

The world's first yacht club, the Royal Cork Yacht Club, was founded here in 1720, but currently operates from Crosshaven on the other side of Cork Harbour. The beautiful Old Yacht Club now houses the tourist office and an arts centre.

◉ Sights

★ **Titanic Experience Cobh**   MUSEUM
(✆ 021-481 4412; www.titanicexperiencecobh.ie; 20 Casement Sq; adult/child €9.50/4.75; ⊙ 9am-6pm) The original White Star Line Offices, from where 123 passengers embarked (and one lucky soul absconded), now house this powerful insight into the ill-fated *Titanic.* Admission is by tour, which is partly guided and partly interactive, with holograms, audiovisual presentations and exhibits; allow at least an hour. The technical wizardry is impressive but what's most memorable is to stand where passengers were ferried to the waiting ship offshore, never to return.

★ **Cobh, The Queenstown Story**   MUSEUM
(✆ 021-481 3591; www.cobhheritage.com; Lower Rd; adult/child €7.50/4; ⊙ 9.30am-5.30pm Mon-Sat, 11am-5.30pm Sun, last admission 1hr before closing) The howl of storms almost blows your hair, there's a bit of fake vomit and the people in the pictures all look pretty miserable. That's just one room at **Cobh Heritage Centre**. Housed in the old train station (adjoining the current station), this interactive museum is far above average. The room described above deals with the mass Famine emigrations across the Atlantic: trips in which the people were green – and not with envy. There's also some shocking stuff on the fate of convicts shipped to Australia in transport 'so airless that candles could not burn'. Scenes of sea travel in the 1950s, however, might actually make you wistful for a more gracious way of transiting the world. There's a **genealogy centre** and a **cafe**.

St Colman's Cathedral   CATHEDRAL
(✆ 021-481 3222; Cathedral Pl; admission by donation; ⊙ tours 3.30pm Sun) Dramatically perched on a hillside terrace above Cobh, this massive French Gothic Cathedral is out of all proportion to the town. Its most exceptional feature is the 47-bell carillon, the largest in Ireland, with a range of four octaves. The biggest bell weighs a huge 3440kg – about as much as a full-grown elephant! You can hear carillon recitals at 4.30pm on Sundays between May and September.

The cathedral, designed by EW Pugin, was begun in 1868 but not completed until 1915. Much of the funding was raised by nostalgic Irish communities in Australia and the USA.

Cobh Museum   MUSEUM
(✆ 021-481 4240; www.cobhmuseum.com; High Rd; adult/child €2.50/1.50; ⊙ 11am-1pm & 2-5.30pm Mon-Sat, 2.30-5pm Sun Apr-Oct) Model ships,

COUNTY CORK COBH

LOCAL KNOWLEDGE

SMOKIN'

No trip to Cork is complete without a visit to an artisan food producer, and the effervescent Frank Hederman is more than happy to show you around **Belvelly** (✆ 021-481 1089; www.frankhederman.com), the oldest natural smoke house in Ireland – and indeed the only one. Seafood and cheese are smoked here – even butter – but the speciality is fish, in particular salmon. In a traditional process that takes 24 hours from start to finish, the fish is filleted and cured before being hung in the tiny smoke house to smoke over beech woodchips. The result is subtle and delectable. Phone or email to arrange a visit to the smoke house, located 12km out of Midleton on the R624 towards Cobh (look for the small lime-green sign). Or stop by Frank's booth at the Midleton farmers market (p118).

paintings, photographs and curious artefacts tracing Cobh's history fill this small but lively museum. It's housed in the 19th-century Scottish Presbyterian church overlooking the train station.

Tours

Michael Martin's
Walking Tours   WALKING TOURS
(021-481 5211; www.titanic.ie; adult €9.50-12.50, child €4.75-6.25, ghost walk €17.50/8.45; Titanic Trail 11am &, 2pm, Ghost Walk by arrangement) Michael Martin's 1¼-hour guided Titanic Trail walk leaves from the Commodore Hotel on Westbourne Pl, with a free sampling of stout at the end. Martin also runs a ghoulish Ghost Walk, and walking tours of Spike Island departing at 2pm from Kennedy Pier (subject to weather conditions and numbers), covering the history of this 7th-century monastic settlement later used as a smuggler haven, fortress and, as recently as 2004, a prison.

Sleeping & Eating

★ **Gilbert's**   BOUTIQUE HOTEL €€
(021-481 1300; www.gilbertsincobh.com; 11 Pearse Sq; s/d/penthouse €45/70/90;) The handful of rooms at this recent addition to Cobh's town centre are fresh and contemporary with handmade furniture, pure-wool blankets and rainshowers. Rates don't include breakfast, but the penthouse suite has a kitchenette. Downstairs, Cobh's best restaurant (mains €16-28; 9am-8.30pm Wed & Thu, 9am-9.30pm Fri & Sat, 10am-5.30pm Sun) serves dishes such as chicken liver parfait with saffron and apple chutney, prawn and mussel linguini.

Knockeven House   B&B €€
(021-481 1778; www.knockevenhouse.com; Rushbrooke; s/d €65/90) Knockeven is a splendid, relaxed Victorian house with huge bedrooms done out in period furniture and overlooking a magnificent garden full of magnolias and camellias. Breakfasts are great too – homemade breads and fresh fruit – and are served in the sumptuous dining room. The decor takes you back to 1st-class passage on a vintage liner. It is 1.5km north of Cobh.

Commodore Hotel   HOTEL €€
(021-481 1277; www.commodorehotel.ie; Westbourne Pl; s/d €60/110;) A classic seaside hotel with soaring chandeliered hallways and 42 well-appointed rooms (it's worth paying extra for one with a sea view).

The pool is indoors and a roof garden offers yet more views.

Farmers Market   MARKET €
(The Promenade; 10am-2pm Fri) Held on the seafront.

Titanic Bar & Grill   IRISH €€
(021-481 4585; 20 Casement Sq; mains €14-25; 10am-6pm Mon-Wed, 10am-11.30pm Thu, 10am-12.30am Fri & Sat, noon-11pm Sun;) Around the back of the Titanic Experience Cobh, with a huge deck overlooking the harbour, this is a stunning spot for a pint. The menu lives up to the stylish glossy timber surrounds with dishes such as assiette of pork (confit of pork belly, pan-fried pork medallion and homemade pork-and-leek sausages). Food is served all day.

Drinking & Nightlife

Roaring Donkey   PUB
(www.theroaringdonkey.com; Tiknock) It's a steep walk from the seafront but the pay-off is plenty of craic – and often live music – at the wonderfully named Roaring Donkey (allegedly so called because former patrons' donkeys made their presence known outside). It's 2.6km north of St Colman's Cathedral on Orilia Tce.

Kelly's   PUB
(Westbourne Pl;) Sociable punters fill Kelly's day and night. The pub's two rooms are decked out with pew-style seating, chunky wooden furniture, a wood-burning stove and, curiously, a stag's head.

Information

The website visitcobh.com has visitor info.
Tourist office (021-481 3301; cobhharbourchamber.ie; Westbourne Pl; 9.30am-5.30pm Mon-Fri, 11am-5pm Sat & Sun) In the Old Yacht Club.

Getting There & Away

Cobh is 15km southeast of Cork, off the main N25 Cork–Rosslare road; Great Island is linked to the mainland via a causeway. Hourly **trains** connect Cobh with Cork (€3.75, 25 minutes). Change in Glounthaune for Midleton.

No buses serve Cobh but you'll find taxis in Pearse Sq.

Barryscourt Castle

Immigrants from Wales in the 12th century, the Barry family quickly began intermarrying with important Irish families of the time. Soon they had huge tracts of land and real wealth. In order to protect their fortune, the clan began building a vast fortification in the 15th century.

Barryscourt Castle (☑ 021-488 3864; www.heritageireland.ie; Carrigtwohill; ⊙10am-6pm Jun-Sep) **FREE** survives in remarkably good condition (albeit with a lot of restoration). An authentic 16th-century kitchen and decorative gardens have been recreated.

The castle is just off the N25, 2km east of the turn-off to Cobh near Carrigtwohill.

Midleton & Around

POP 3700

Aficionados of a particularly fine Irish whiskey will recognise the name, and the main reason to linger in this bustling market town is to visit the old whiskey distillery. However, the surrounding region is full of pretty villages, craggy coastline and heavenly rural hotels such as Ballymaloe House (p119) – precisely why you should visit the town but stay elsewhere.

◉ Sights

Coachloads pour in to tour the restored 200-year-old building housing the **Jameson Experience** (☑021-461 3594; www.jameson whiskey.com; Old Distillery Walk; tours adult/child €13/7.70; ⊙shop 10am-6.30pm, tour times vary). Exhibits and tours explain the process of taking barley and creating whiskey (Jameson is today made in a modern factory in Cork). There's a well-stocked gift shop; the **Malt House Restaurant** (mains €9-11; ⊙noon-3pm) has live music on Sundays.

🛏 Sleeping & Eating

Loughcarrig House B&B €€
(☑021-463 1952; www.loughcarrig.com; Ballinacurra; s/d €50/80) Right on Cork Harbour, about 3km south of Midleton, this gracious old Georgian house's four rooms are ideal for those looking for a restful country retreat. Wi-fi is patchy at best but, in addition to walks and birdwatching on the beautiful land, the owners can also set you up for angling in the fish-filled waters. Breakfasts are suitably hearty.

Midleton Farmers Market MARKET €
(www.midletonfarmersmarket.com; ⊙9.30am-1pm Sat) 🌶 Midleton's farmers market is one of Cork's best, with bushels of local produce on

offer and producers who are happy to chat. It's behind the courthouse on Main St.

★**Farmgate Restaurant** IRISH, BAKERY €€
(☑021-463 2771; www.farmgate.ie; The Coolbawn, off Broderick St; lunch mains €12-15, dinner mains €18-30; ⊙coffee & snacks 9am-5.30pm, lunch noon-3.30pm Tue-Sat, dinner 6.30-9.30pm Thu-Sat) The original and sister establishment to Cork city's **Farmgate Café** (p224), the Midleton restaurant offers the same superb blend of traditional and modern Irish in its approach to cooking. Squeeze through its deli selling amazing baked goods and local produce, including organic fruit and vegetables, cheeses and preserves, to the farmhouse-style cafe-restaurant, where you'll eat as well as anywhere in Ireland.

ℹ Information

The **tourist office** (☑ 021-461 3702; www. eastcorktourism.com; ⊙ 9.30am-1pm & 2-5pm Mon-Fri May-Sep) is by the entrance gate to the Jameson Experience.

ℹ Getting There & Away

Midleton is 20km east of Cork. The **train station** (5 McSweeney Terrace) is 1.5km north of the Jameson Experience. From Monday to Friday, there are 21 services to Cork, with 17 on Saturday and nine on Sunday (€2.20, 20 minutes). Change in Glounthaune for Cobh.

There are less frequent buses to Cork bus station (€7.10, 25 minutes). You'll need a car to explore the surrounding area.

Youghal

POP 6900

The ancient seaport of Youghal (Eochaill; pronounced 'yawl'), at the mouth of the River Blackwater, has a rich history that may not be instantly apparent, especially if

---

ℹ **PASSAGE WEST FERRY**

From Ballynoe, 4km northwest of Cobh, the **Passage West Ferry** (☑021-481 1485; www.passagewestmonkstown.ie/ cross-river-ferry.asp; pedestrian/cyclist/car one way €1/1/5; ⊙7am-10pm) provides a handy shortcut to Passage West, 15km southeast of Cork City. The cross-river journey takes just five minutes. It's particularly useful if you're driving to or from the southern side of Cork (eg Kinsale) and want to skip the city traffic.

THE GOURMET HEARTLAND OF BALLYMALOE

Drawing up at wisteria-clad Ballymaloe House (☑021-465 2531; www.ballymaloe.ie; Shanagarry; s/d from €135/230; 🛜 🏊) you know you've arrived somewhere special. The Allen family bought the property in 1948 and has been running this superb hotel and restaurant in the old family home for decades. Myrtle Allen is a living legend, acclaimed internationally for her near single-handed creation of fine Irish cooking. Rooms are individually decorated with period furnishings and are a pleasing mass of different shapes and sizes. Amid the beautiful grounds, amenities, include a tennis court, a swimming pool, a shop and a cafe.

The menu at Ballymaloe House's celebrated restaurant (lunch mains €13-24, 4-course dinner menu €70; ⊙ 8-10.30am, 1-3pm & 7-9.30pm) changes daily to reflect the availability of produce from its extensive farms and other local sources, but might include local Ballycotton scallops and artichoke puree with garden herb relish, or spiced braised lamb with garden swede turnips. The hotel also runs wine and gardening weekends.

Just over 3km east on the R628, Myrtle's daughter-in-law, TV personality Darina Allen, runs Ballymaloe's famous cookery school (☑021-464 6785; www.cookingisfun.ie). Darina's own daughter-in-law, Rachel Allen, is also a high-profile TV chef and author who regularly teaches at the school. Demonstrations cost €70; lessons, from half-day sessions (€95 to €125) to 12-week certificate courses (€10,695), are often booked well in advance. There are pretty cottages amid the 40 hectares of grounds for overnight students.

you coast past on the N25. In fact, even if you stop, it may just seem like a humdrum Irish market town. But take a little time and you'll sniff out some of its once-walled past and enjoy views of the wide River Blackwater estuary.

The town was a hotbed of rebellion against the English in the 16th century, and Oliver Cromwell wintered here in 1649 as he sought to drum up support for his war in England and quell insurgence from the pesky Irish. Youghal was granted to Sir Walter Raleigh during the Elizabethan Plantation of Munster, and he spent brief spells living here in his house, Myrtle Grove.

◉ Sights & Activities

Youghal has two Blue Flag beaches, ideal for building sandcastles modelled after the Clock Gate. Claycastle (2km) and Front Strand (1km) are both within walking distance of town, off the N25.

Whale of a Time (☑086 328 3256; www. whaleofatime.ie; whale-watching trips €35; ⊙mid-Apr–Jan) runs 90-minute whale-watching trips. Seahunter (☑024-90437; www.seahunter. ie; fishing trips per adult/child from €25/12) organises fishing trips and can arrange rod hire as well as charters and wreck dives.

Dinky Fox's Lane Folk Museum (☑024-91145; www.tyntescastle.com/fox; North Cross Lane; adult/child €4/2; ⊙10am-1pm & 2-6pm Tue-

Sat Jul-Sep, by appointment rest of year) contains more than 600 household gadgets, dating from 1850 to 1950, and a Victorian kitchen.

🛏 Sleeping & Eating

Cafes and pubs congregate in the centre near the Clock Gate.

Aherne's INN €€
(☑024-92424; www.ahernes.net; 163 North Main St; d from €110; 🅿 🛜) The 12 rooms above the popular restaurant (bar food €10-18, dinner mains €24-33; ⊙bar food noon-10pm, dinner 6.30-9.30pm) are extremely well appointed; larger ones have small balconies, where you can breathe in the sea air. Rates include fabulous breakfasts (fresh-squeezed OJ, free-range eggs, locally caught fish) that will keep you going all day. Besides the upmarket seafood restaurant there's a stylish, cosy bar and a much larger one popular with locals.

La Petite Auberge B&B €€
(☑024-85906; www.lapetiteauberge.ie; 2 The Mall; s €50-60, d €70-80; 🛜) Wake up to sea views from every classically styled, uniquely furnished room at this charming 'little inn', built in the 1830s. The breakfast room also overlooks the water; choices include smoked kippers as well as fresh OJ and fruit and nuts in season.

Sage Cafe
CAFE €

(☏ 024-85844; 86 North Main St; dishes €5-9; ◷10am-6pm Mon-Sat; 🅿) 🍴 Everything at this luscious little cafe is homemade: lentil -and-nut loaf, quiche, cakes and more. Vegetarians in particular will be in heaven.

🍷 Drinking & Nightlife

Treacy's
PUB

(The Nook; www.findthenook.ie; 20 North Main St) For an end-of-day pint and traditional live music, nowhere beats Youghal's oldest boozer, Treacy's, aka the Nook. Enter via the adjacent laneway.

ℹ Information

Tourist office (☏ 024-20170; www.youghal.ie; Market Sq; ◷10am-3pm Mon-Sat) Housed in an attractive old market house on the waterfront, the Youghal Visitor Centre has tourist info, a small **heritage centre** and free town maps.

ℹ Getting There & Away

Bus Éireann (☏ 021-450 8188; www.buser eann.ie) runs services to Cork (€12.50, 50 minutes, 13 daily) and Waterford (€18.50, 1½ hours, 11 daily).

It's hoped that the train line from Midleton to Youghal may reopen.

KINSALE & WEST CORK

The Irish coast begins the slow build of beauty that culminates in counties further west and north, but what you find here in Cork is already lovely. It's perfect for aimless wandering as roads criss-cross the area like lace made by a deranged person.

Kinsale

POP 2200

Narrow, winding streets lined with artsy little shops, lively bars and superb restaurants, and a handsome harbour full of bobbing fishing boats and pleasure yachts make Kinsale (Cionn tSáile) one of Ireland's favourite midsized towns. Its sheltered bay is guarded by a huge and engrossing fort.

Most of Kinsale's hotels and restaurants are situated near the harbour and within easy walking distance of the town centre. The peninsula of Scilly is barely a 10-minute walk to the southeast, from where a path continues to Summercove and Charles Fort.

History

In September 1601 a Spanish fleet anchored at Kinsale was besieged by the English. An Irish army from the north, which had appealed to the Spanish king to help it against the English, marched the length of the country to liberate the ships, but was defeated

COUNTY CORK KINSALE

EXPLORING YOUGHAL'S HISTORY ON FOOT

Youghal's history is best understood through its landmarks. Heading through town from the south, the curious Clock Gate was built in 1777, and served as a clock tower and jail concurrently; several prisoners taken in the 1798 Rising were hanged from its windows.

The beautifully proportioned brick Red House, on North Main St, was designed in 1706 by the Dutch architect Leuventhen, and features some Dutch Renaissance details. Main St has an interesting curve that follows the original shore; many of the shopfronts are from the 19th century. A few doors further up the street are six almshouses built by Englishman Richard Boyle, who bought Raleigh's Irish estates and became the first Earl of Cork in 1616 in recognition of his work in creating 'a very excellent colony'.

Across the road is the 15th-century tower house Tynte's Castle (www.tyntescastle. com), which originally had a defensive riverfront position. When the River Blackwater silted up and changed course in the 17th and 18th centuries, the castle was left high and dry. It's currently under renovation.

Built in 1220, St Mary's Collegiate Church incorporates elements of an earlier Danish church dating back to the 11th century. The Earl of Desmond and his troops, rebelling against English rule, demolished the chancel roof in the 16th century. The churchyard is bounded by a fine stretch of the 13th-century town wall and one of the remaining turrets.

Beside the church, Myrtle Grove is the former home of Sir Walter Raleigh. His gardens, on the other side of St Mary's, have recently been restored and are accessible to the public.

in battle outside the town on Christmas Eve. For the Catholics, the immediate consequence was that they were banned from Kinsale; it would be another 100 years before they were allowed back in. Historians now cite 1601 as the beginning of the end of Gaelic Ireland.

After 1601 the town developed as a shipbuilding port. In the early 18th century, Alexander Selkirk left Kinsale Harbour on a voyage that left him stranded on a desert island, providing Daniel Defoe with the idea for *Robinson Crusoe*.

◉ Sights

Regional Museum   MUSEUM
(☑ 021-477 7930; Market Sq; adult/concession €3/1.50; ☺ 10am-5pm Sat, 2-5pm Sun) Based in the 17th-century courthouse that was used for the inquest into the sinking of the *Lusitania* in 1915, this nifty museum contains curiosities as diverse as Michael Collins' hurley and shoes belonging to the 2.4m-tall Kinsale Giant.

Desmond Castle   CASTLE, MUSEUM
(☑ 021-477 4855; www.heritageireland.ie; Cork St; adult/child €3/1; ☺ 10am-6pm Apr–mid-Sep) Kinsale's roots with the old wine trade are on display at this early-16th-century fortified house that was occupied by the Spanish in 1601. Since then it has served as a customs house, a prison for French and American captives and a workhouse during the Famine. There are lively exhibits detailing its history and a small wine museum that tells the story of the Irish wine-trading families, including Hennessy (of brandy fame), who fled to France because of British rule.

St Multose Church   CHURCH
(Church of Ireland Church; ☑ rectory 021-477 2220; Church St) This is one of Ireland's oldest Church of Ireland churches, built around 1190 by the Normans on the site of a 6th-century church. Not much of the interior is original but the exterior is preserved beautifully. Inside, a flat stone carved with a round-handled figure was traditionally rubbed by fishermen's wives to bring their husbands home safe from the sea. Several victims of the Lusitania sinking are buried in the graveyard.

★ Charles Fort   FORT
(☑ 021-477 2263; www.heritageireland.ie; adult/child €4/2; ☺ 10am-6pm mid-Mar–Oct, 10am-5pm Nov–mid-Dec, 10am-5pm Tue-Sun mid-Dec–mid-

Mar) One of the best-preserved, 17th-century, star-shaped forts in Europe, this wonderful fort 3km east of Kinsale would be worth a visit for its spectacular views alone. But there's much more here: ruins inside the vast site date from the 18th and 19th centuries and make for some fascinating wandering. Displays explain the typically tough lives led by the soldiers who served here and the comparatively comfortable lives of the officers. Built in the 1670s to guard Kinsale Harbour, the fort was in use until 1921, when much of it was destroyed as the British withdrew. It's a lovely walk around the bay.

🏃 Activities

For sailings to Charles Fort, James Cove and up the River Bandon, contact Kinsale Harbour Cruises (☑ 086 250 5456, 021-477 8946; www.kinsaleharbourcruises.com; adult/child €12.50/6). Departure times vary throughout the year and are weather dependent. Boats leave from near Vista Wine Bar on Pier Rd towards the marina.

Whale of a Time (☑ 086 328 3250; www.whaleofatime.ie) offers coastal cruises and whale-watching trips from €35 per person for 90 minutes on fast speedboats.

Anglers can rent fishing rods at Mylie Murphy's (☑ 021-477 2703; 14 Pearse St; ☺ 9.30am-6pm Mon-Sat year-round, plus noon-4pm Sun Jun-Sep) for €10 per day.

The tourist office has details of golf courses in the area, including the prestigious Old Head Golf Links (☑ 021-4778 444; oldhead.com; 18/36 holes €200/325), magnificently situated on a clifftop promontory 15km south of Kinsale via the R600 and R604. The remains of De Courcy castle frame the entrance; you'll see a ruined lighthouse from the 7th tee.

☞ Tours

Dermot Ryan's Heritage
Town Walks   WALKING TOUR
(☑ 021-477 2729; www.kinsaleheritage.com; 1hr tour adult/child €5/free; ☺ 10.30am & 3pm) Walks depart from the tourist office.

🎊 Festivals & Events

Gourmet Festival   FOOD
(www.kinsalerestaurants.com; ☺ early Oct) Tastings, meals and harbour cruises add to the town's foodie reputation.

Kinsale Jazz Festival   JAZZ
(www.kinsale.ie; ☺ late Oct) Chilled-out entertainment over the bank-holiday weekend.

Kinsale

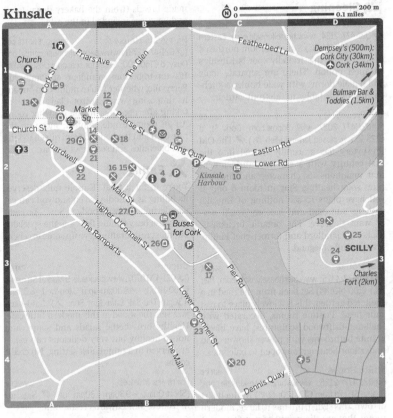

Kinsale

◎ Sights
1 Desmond Castle A1
2 Regional Museum A2
3 St Multose Church A2

◉ Activities, Courses & Tours
4 Dermot Ryan's Heritage Town
   Walks B2
5 Kinsale Harbour Cruises D4
6 Mylie Murphy's B2

⊜ Sleeping
7 Cloisters B&B A1
8 Old Bank House B2
9 Old Presbytery A1
10 Perryville House C2
11 Pier House B3
12 White House B1

⊗ Eating
13 Crackpots A1

14 Cucina A2
15 Farmers Market B2
16 Finn's Table B2
17 Fishy Fishy Cafe C3
18 Jim Edwards B2
19 Man Friday D3
20 Stolen Pizza C4

⊖ Drinking & Nightlife
21 An Seanachaí A2
22 Apéritif A2
23 Black Pig Wine Bar C4
24 Harbour Bar D3
25 Spaniard Bar & Restaurant D3

⊜ Shopping
26 Giles Norman Gallery B3
27 Granny's Bottom Drawer B2
28 Kinsale Chocolate Boutique A1
29 Kinsale Crystal A2

🛏 Sleeping

Dempsey's HOSTEL €

(☑021-477 2124; www.hostelkinsale.com; Eastern Rd; dm/d €18/44; 🛜) Situated 750m northeast of the centre, this friendly spot is Kinsale's cheapest option. There are separate male and female dorms with wide bunks, a kitchen, and picnic tables in the front garden.

Old Presbytery B&B €€

(☑021-477 2027; www.oldpres.com; Cork St; d €125-160; ☺closed Jan–mid-Feb; 🛜) 🏊 The Old Presbytery has gracefully moved into the 21st century with a careful refurbishment that maintains its character and incorporates solar heating. Stay in room 6 only if you have plans to see nothing of Kinsale: with its sunroom and balcony, you'll never want to leave. The organic breakfasts, cooked by landlord and former chef Phillip, are the stuff of legend.

Pier House B&B €€

(☑021-477 4475; www.pierhousekinsale.com; Pier Rd; r €100-140; 🛜) Set back from the road in a sheltered garden, this is a lovely place to rest your head. Pristine rooms, decorated with shell-and-driftwood sculptures, have black-granite bathrooms with power showers and underfloor heating; four open to balconies.

White House INN €€

(☑021-477 2125; www.whitehouse-kinsale.com; Pearse St; s/d from €75/120; @🛜) In the heart of town, this stylish inn has 10 large, modern rooms that are the height of comfort – not quite presidential, but fit for a cabinet secretary.

Cloisters B&B B&B €€

(☑021-470 0680; www.cloisterskinsale.com; Friars St; s/d from €55/100; 🛜) Little touches make the difference at this blue-shuttered B&B near Desmond Castle. Chocolates await your arrival, rooms are squeaky-clean and the orthopaedic mattresses are so comfy that only the creative breakfasts will tempt you out of bed.

Old Bank House HOTEL €€€

(☑021-477 4075; www.oldbankhousekinsale.com; 11 Pearse St; d €120-170; @🛜) Georgian elegance and style give a timeless quality to this top-of-the-range 18-room hotel. Beautiful objets d'art and paintings grace the walls, and the luxurious public rooms add a country-house ambience. Although rooms are lavish, they're subtle enough to avoid pretension. Superb breakfasts, with home-

made breads (from the bakery downstairs) and jams, are included in the rate.

Perryville House BOUTIQUE HOTEL €€€

(☑021-477 2731; www.perryvillehouse.com; Long Quay; d €160-300; ☺call for seasonal closures; 🛜) It's top-to-bottom grandeur at family-run Perryville, whether you're pulling up outside its imposing wrought-iron-clad facade or taking afternoon tea in the drawing room. All 26 rooms exude comfort; move up the rate card and the beds go from queen to king and balconies and sea views appear.

🍴 Eating

You're in for a treat. Kinsale fully deserves its billing as a foodie haven and you can eat wonderfully on every budget. Surf – brought in by the busy fishing fleet – is the specialty, but most restaurants serve up some excellent turf too.

Cucina CAFE €

(☑021-470 0707; www.cucina.ie; 9 Market St; mains €7.50-18.50; ☺8.30am-4pm Mon-Wed, 8.30am-9.30pm Thu-Sat, 9am-3pm Sun; 🏊) Laid-back jazz sets the mood at this modern little cafe. Healthy bruschetta, salads and soups, and not-so-healthy but very delicious cup cakes are served in a minimalist setting. No credit cards.

Farmers Market MARKET €

(Short Quay; ☺9.30am-1.30pm Tue) 🏊 Sets up in front of Jim Edwards restaurant.

Jim Edwards SEAFOOD €€

(☑021-477 2541; www.jimedwardskinsale.com; Market Quay; bar mains €13-19, restaurant mains €16-30; ☺bar food noon-10pm, restaurant 5.30-10pm) 🏊 Bar food at this unassuming pub is way above standard and the restaurant is exceptional. A very traditional ambience belies the high quality of the menu, which doffs a cap to meat-eaters but specialises in all kinds of locally caught fish.

Bulman Bar & Toddies SEAFOOD €€

(☑021-477 2131; www.thebulman.ie; Summercove; Bulman Bar mains €8.50-21.50, Toddies mains €21.50-29.50; ☺Bulman Bar food noon-5pm daily, Toddies 5.30-9.30pm Tue-Sun; 🛜) 🏊 Seaside eating at its best. Escape from central Kinsale to this gastro pub in an unspoilt harbourside venue, where salty informality is a style in its own right. Seafood excels here, whether swimming in chowder or laid out seductively on a platter. Ingredients are sourced locally – herbs are straight from the kitchen garden. The more formal restaurant Toddies serves an excellent range of beautifully prepared seafood – the lobster risotto is recommended. From Kinsale Harbour, take Lower Rd for 600m, turn left onto Scilly and follow it for 1.6km if you're travelling by car. On foot, take the path leading from Lower Rd all the way along the coast.

Stolen Pizza   ITALIAN €€
(021-470 0488; www.thestolenpizza.com; 18-19 Lower O'Connell St; mains €10-16; from 6pm) With double-height ceilings, exposed brick walls and a stunning chandelier, the Stolen Pizza's newer, bigger home brings a dash of metropolitan style to Kinsale. The food is equally adept: there's excellent pizza (including prawn) and, in a further nod to local tradition, fine crab ravioli.

Crackpots   MODERN IRISH €€
(021-477 2847; www.crackpots.ie; 3 Cork St; mains €13-28; 6-10pm) The title 'ceramic restaurant' over the front door refers to the fact that all the crockery in use here was made...here. Normally, when you combine art workshop and food something will give, but in this instance it's certainly not the grub, which relies on locally sourced meats, fresh catch from the sea and organically grown veg, resulting in dishes such as lemongrass-infused salmon or aubergine strudel.

★ Finn's Table   MODERN IRISH €€€
(021-470 9636; www.finnstable.com; 6 Main St; mains €24.50-33; from 5.30pm Thu-Mon) Opening a gourmet restaurant in Kinsale means plenty of competition but John and Julie Finn's new venture is more than up to the challenge. It pushes the culinary envelope with the likes of fillet steak and tobacco, and salt-and-pepper squid served with curried crab mayonnaise and herb oil. Seafood (including lobster in season) is from West Cork, while meat is from the Finn family's butchers.

Fishy Fishy Cafe   SEAFOOD €€€
(021-470 0415; www.fishyfishy.ie; Crowley's Quay; mains €19-34.50; noon-9pm Mar-Oct, noon-4pm Sun-Wed, noon-9pm Thu-Sat Nov-Feb) One of the most famous seafood restaurants in the country, Fishy Fishy has a wonderful setting, with stark white walls splashed with bright artwork and a terrific decked terrace at the front. It's pricey but all the fish is caught locally. Have the cold seafood platter – a concert of what's fresh.

Man Friday   INTERNATIONAL €€€
(021-477 2260; www.manfridaykinsale.ie; cnr River & High Rds, Scilly; mains €19.50-31; from 5pm Mon-Sat, 12.30-9.30pm Sun) Around the harbour in Scilly, this veteran restaurant has twinkling views back across the harbour to Kinsale. The menu might be global but the ambience evokes a tropical island, starting with the magical palm-covered walk down to the entrance. Book for a terrace table on balmy evenings.

🍷 Drinking & Entertainment

The line between eating and drinking venues is blurred in Kinsale; many places, such as Bulman Bar & Toddies, are equally good for both.

★ Black Pig Wine Bar   WINE BAR
(021-477 4101; 66 Lower O'Connell St; tapas €3-13; 5.30pm-midnight Thu-Sun) Along a gentrifying street, this sophisticated hideaway offers no less than 80 wines by the bottle and 40 by the glass including many organic varieties. There's a charming cobbled courtyard out the back, and a mouthwatering range of tapas and cheese boards sourced from artisan local suppliers. Tables are coveted – book so you don't miss out.

Spaniard Bar & Restaurant   PUB
(021-477 2436; www.thespaniard.ie; Scilly; bar mains €7.50-14.50; restaurant mains €16-24.50) The food is good, but the real appeal of this old pub (it feels as if it dates back to the Armada) lies in the quiet corners, where you can smell the peat fire and catch fragments of hushed conversations that could be about smuggling but are likely to be about sport.

Apéritif   WINE BAR
(021-477 2209; www.aperitifkinsale.com; Main St; tapas €6-10; from 5.30pm Thu-Sat, from 2pm Sun) Metallic-sheened furniture and walls make this wine bar a glitzy spot for a predinner tipple and tapas. Big picture windows let you see and be seen.

Harbour Bar   PUB
(Scilly; from 6pm) It might look permanently closed from the outside, but inside it's like being in someone's front room. Battered old sofas, a fire stoked in the hearth, characters in every corner and benches with water views in the garden are all part of the charm.

TRISH PUNCH / GETTY IMAGES ©

1. The English Market, Cork City 2. Baltimore, West Cork
3. Cottage window, Kinsale

County Cork

Scenic, beautiful and diverse, Ireland's largest county doesn't have the monopoly on marvellous landscapes, but it can lay claim to being the gourmet capital of Ireland, split between Cork city and the seaside towns and villages of West Cork.

Kinsale

The perfect Irish coastal town combines scenery, location and terrific restaurants in one tidy, alley-strewn package.

The English Market

A highlight of any visit to Cork is a walk through this covered Victorian market, home to a host of local producers and one of the best restaurants in town.

Clonakilty

Clonakilty is a bustling market town with good B&Bs, great restaurants and top-class pubs featuring great traditional music.

Baltimore

The West Cork village of Baltimore is a mariner's dream, with a cluster of colourful houses gathered around the busy fishing port and pleasure-sailing marina.

An Seanachai
PUB

(☑ 021-477 7077; 6 Market St) This cavernous, barnlike pub has traditional music sessions most nights.

🛍 Shopping

Kinsale Chocolate Boutique
CHOCOLATE

(6 Exchange Buildings, Market St; ☺ 10am-6pm May-Aug, 11am-5pm Wed & Thu, 10am-6pm Fri & Sat, 2-6pm Sun Sep-Apr) Handmade chocolates and pastel-shaded macaroons are among the enticing wares at this artisan chocolatier.

Giles Norman Gallery
PHOTOGRAPHY

(☑ 021-477 4373; www.gilesnorman.com; 45 Main St; ☺ 10am-6pm Mon-Sat, noon-6pm Sun) Evocative black-and-white imagery of Ireland from a master of the genre. Prints start at €25 (unframed) and €55 (framed).

Granny's Bottom Drawer
IRISH CRAFTS

(☑ 021-477 4839; 53 Main St; ☺ 10am-6pm) Beautiful Irish linen, damask and vintage-style homewares.

Kinsale Crystal
CRYSTAL

(☑ 021-477 4493; www.kinsalecrystal.ie; Market St; ☺ 9am-5.30pm Mon-Fri, 10am-6pm Sat, noon-6pm Sun) Exquisite work by an ex-Waterford craftsman who stands by the traditional 'deep-cutting, high-angle' style. A million tiny sparkles greet you as you enter.

❶ Information

Pearse St has a **post office** and banks with ATMs. **Tourist office** (☑ 021-477 2234; www.kinsale. ie; cnr Pier Rd & Emmet Pl; ☺ 9.15am-5pm Tue-Sat Nov-Mar, Mon Apr-Jun, Sep & Oct, 10am-5pm Sun Jul & Aug) Has a good map detailing walks in and around Kinsale.

❶ Getting There & Around

Bus Éireann (☑ 021-450 8188) services connect Kinsale with Cork (€8.50, 50 minutes, 14 daily Monday to Friday, 11 Saturday and four Sunday) via Cork airport. The **bus stop** is on Pier Rd, near the tourist office.

Kinsale Cabs (☑ 021-477 2642; www.kinsale cabs.com) also arranges golfing tours of West Cork.

Clonakilty

POP 4000

Cheerful, brightly coloured Clonakilty is a bustling market town that serves as a hub for the scores of beguiling little coastal towns that surround it. You'll find smart B&Bs, top restaurants and cosy pubs alive with music.

Little waterways coursing through add to the charm.

Clonakilty is famous for two things: it's the birthplace of Irish Free State commander-in-chief Michael Collins, embodied in a large statue on the corner of Emmet Sq; and it's the home of the most famous black pudding in the country.

Roads converge on Asna Sq, dominated by a 1798 Rising monument. Also in the square is the Kilty Stone, a piece of the original castle that gave Clonakilty (Clogh na Kylte in Irish, meaning 'castle of the woods') its name.

◉ Sights & Activities

For an insight into a pivotal chapter of Irish history, Michael Collins Centre (p128), 6km northeast of Clonakilty, is a must.

Wandering the centre is good for a couple of hours; Georgian Emmet Square attests to the area's traditional wealth. Spillers Lane has nifty little shops.

West Cork Model Railway Village

(☑ 023-883 3224; www.modelvillage.ie; Inchydoney Rd; adult/child €8/4.25; ☺ 11am-5pm Sep-Jun, 10am-5pm Jul & Aug) You can't help but smile at the West Cork Model Railway Village. It features a vast outdoor recreation of the West Cork Railway as it was during the 1940s and superb miniature models of the main towns in West Cork. A road train (adult/child incl admission to Railway Village €12/6.25; ☺ daily summer, weekends winter) leaves from the West Cork Model Railway Village on a 20-minute commentated circuit of Clonakilty. It's good if you like being cooped up and stared at.

Swimming
SWIMMING

The bay is good for swimming, albeit in a bracing sort of way. The sandy Blue Flag beach at Inchydoney Island, 4km from town, is good too, but watch out for the dangerous riptide; when lifeguards are on duty a red flag indicates danger.

Inchydoney Surf School
SURFING

(☑ 086 869 5396; www.westcorksurfing.com; 2hr beginner lesson adult/child €35/30) Learn to ride the waves at Inchydoney Island. The surf school also rents boards (from €20 for two hours) and wetsuits (€10 for two hours).

🛏 Sleeping

Emmet Hotel
HOTEL €€

(☑ 023-883 3394; www.emmethotel.com; Emmet Sq; d €89-129, mains €12-22; 🖥 🏠) This lovely

Georgian accommodation option on the elegant square successfully mixes period charm and old-world service with the perks of a modern hotel. The 20 rooms are large and plush; the onsite restaurant, bistro and bar all serve up tasty Irish food made from organic and local ingredients.

Bay View House B&B €€
(☑ 023-883 3539; www.bayviewclonakilty.com; Old Timoleague Rd; s/d €50/80; ☎) This frothy pink house offers immaculate B&B standards, a genial welcome and great breakfasts. Rooms 5 and 6 and the cosy landing lounge offer fantastic views over the fields that slope down to Clonakilty Bay. It is 300m east of the town centre, just off the main N71 roundabout into town.

Tudor Lodge B&B €€
(☑ 023-883 3046; www.tudorlodgecork.com; McCurtain Hill; s €40-50, d €60-80; ☎) Standards are kept up to scratch at this modern, mock-Tudor family home a short walk from the town centre.

O'Donovan's Hotel INN €€
(☑ 023-883 3250; www.odonovanshotel.com; Pearse St; s/d €45/90; ☎) Behind the vintage vivid-red exterior beats the heart of a classic old hotel. Rooms are straightforward but service is friendly and you can't beat the central location. A WWII plaque out the front will intrigue Americans in particular.

Inchydoney Island Lodge & Spa RESORT €€€
(☑ 023-883 3143; www.inchydoneyisland.com; s midweek/weekend €145/175, d €190/250, restaurant mains €18.50-34.50; ☺restaurant 6.30-9.45pm daily & 1-3pm Sun; @☎☒⌕) A superb sea-water spa is at the heart of this sprawling resort 5km south of Clonakilty, where the service is outstanding, the food at the French-inspired restaurant delicious, and recently redesigned rooms overlook the ocean from private balconies and terraces.

✕ Eating

Scannells MODERN IRISH €
(☑ 023-883 4116; www.scannellsbar.com; Connolly St; mains €6.50-11; ☺noon-3pm Mon-Fri, noon-4pm Sat) The sheltered, flower-filled garden at this gastropub is absolutely hopping, rain or shine, thanks to an ambitious menu that spans smoked mackerel or steak sandwiches with handcut chips to trad Irish stew and organic salads with beetroot, roasted hazelnuts, goat's cheese and quinoa.

Clonakilty Homemade Ice Cream ICE CREAM €
(☑ 023-883 3699; McCurtain Hill; ice cream €1.80-3.50; ☺11am-5.30pm Mon, Tue & Thu-Sat; ☎) Buy a cone or tub of lush ice cream made on these lemon-and-raspberry–painted premises or taste them in sundaes, milkshakes and smoothies. There's a sit-down area in the candy-striped interior.

Farmers Market MARKET €
(www.clonakiltymarket.com; ☺10am-2pm Fri) Clonakilty's farmers market sets up next to O'Donovan's Hotel.

★An Súgán MODERN IRISH €€
(☑ 023-883 3719; www.ansugan.com; 41 Wolfe Tone St; mains €12-22; ☺noon-10pm) A traditional bar with a national reputation for excellent seafood. You dine in a room crammed with knick-knacks – jugs dangle from the ceiling, patrons' business cards are stuffed beneath the rafters, and lanterns and even ancient fire-extinguishers dot the walls. But there's nothing idiosyncratic about the food – the seafood chowder and crab cakes are great, and there's a choice of around 10 different kinds of fish, depending on the daily catch.

Malt House Granary MODERN IRISH €€
(☑ 023-883 4355; 30 Ashe St; mains €16.50-25; ☺5-10pm Mon-Sat) You'll be able to check out the Clonakilty black pudding, Boilie goat's cheese, Gubbeen chorizo and Bantry Bay mussels among other ingredients on the menu at the Malt House, as everything on your plate originates from West Cork. The interior design is a hotchpotch of stylish and kitsch.

⚑ Drinking & Entertainment

★De Barra's PUB
(www.debarra.ie; 55 Pearse St) A marvellous atmosphere, walls splattered with photos, press cuttings, masks and musical instruments, plus the cream of live music, particularly folk, from around 9.30pm make this a busy pub.

An Teach Beag PUB
(5 Recorder's Alley) This intriguing pub, behind O'Donovan's Hotel, has all the atmosphere necessary for good traditional music sessions. You might even catch a *scríocht* (a session by storytellers and poets) in full flow. There's music nightly during July and August, and on weekends for the rest of the year.

DON'T MISS

THE BEST BLACK PUDDING

Clonakilty's most treasured export is its black pudding, the blood sausage that features on most local restaurant menus. The best place to buy it is from butcher Edward Twomey (☑ 023-883 3733; www.clonakiltyblackpudding.ie; 16 Pearse St; puddings from €2.75; ☺ 9am-6pm Mon-Sat), selling different varieties based on the original recipe that was formulated in the 1880s.

Shopping

Jellyfish Surf Co   SURF GEAR
(☑ 023-883 5890; www.jellyfishsurfco.com; Spillers Lane; ☺ 10am-6pm Mon-Sat) In addition to stocking the latest surfwear and boards, Jellyfish Surf Co can tell you where to hit the waves locally.

ℹ Information

Post office (Bridge St) In the old Presbyterian chapel.

Tourist office (☑ 023-883 3226; www.clonakilty.ie; Ashe St; ☺ 9.15am-5pm Mon-Sat)

ℹ Getting There & Away

There are seven daily buses to Cork (€14.20, 65 minutes) and Skibbereen (€9.80, 40 minutes). The **bus stop** is across from Harte's Spar shop on the bypass to Cork.

Note that the alternative route to Kinsale is on the R600.

ℹ Getting Around

MTM Cycles (☑ 023-883 3584; 33 Ashe St; ☺ 8.30am-6pm Mon-Sat) hires bikes per day/week for €10/50. A nice ride is to Duneen Beach, about 13km south of town.

Clonakilty to Skibbereen

Picturesque villages, a fine stone circle and calming coastal scenery mark the less-taken route from Clonakilty to Skibbereen. Rather than follow the main N71 all the way, at Rosscarbery turn left onto the R597 at the far end of the causeway (signposted Glandore); or, even better, take twice as long and freelance your way along narrow roads near the water the entire way.

A fun way for pirates (adults) to introduce buccaneers (under 16s) and scallywags (under threes) to golfing, the all-weather astroturf 18-hole course at Smugglers Cove Adventure Golf (☑ 023-884 8054; www.rosscarbergolf.com; Rosscarbery; adult/under 16/under 3yrs €7.50/5/free; ☺ 10am-8pm daily Mar-Sep, 10am-5pm Sat & Sun Oct-Feb) in Rosscarbery features wooden rafts and treasure chests.

Approximately 4km west of Rosscarbery, on an exposed hillside, with fields sweeping away towards the coast and bothered cattle braying in the distance, is the superbly atmospheric Dromberg Stone Circle. Its 17 uprights once guarded the cremated bones of an adolescent, discovered during a 1960s excavation. The 9m-diameter circle probably dates from the 5th century AD, representing a sophisticated Iron Age update of an earlier Bronze Age monument. Just beyond the stones are the remains of a hut and an Iron Age cooking pit, known as a *fulachta fiadh*. Experiments have shown that its heated rocks would boil water and keep it hot for nearly three hours – enough time to cook meat.

To get here, take the signposted left turn off the R597. From the car park, head left to follow the narrow walking path 120m to the stone circle.

Glandore & Union Hall
POP 250

The pretty waterside villages of Glandore (Cuan Dor) and Union Hall burst into life in summer when fleets of yachts tack into the shelter of the Glandore Harbour inlet. A tangle of back roads meanders across the area; you should, too.

Union Hall, 2.7km southwest of Glandore via a long, narrow causeway over the estuary, was named after the 1801 Act of Union, which abolished the separate Irish parliament. The 1994 film *War of the Buttons*, about two battling gangs of youngsters, was filmed here. There's an ATM, a post office and a general store here.

🏃 Activities

You can splash round the coast with Atlantic Sea Kayaking (☑ 028-21058; www.atlanticseakayaking.com; Union Hall; half-day trip €50; ☺ year-round), which offers many tours and classes, including night-time paddles.

Whale Watch West Cork (☑ 028-33357; www.whalewatchwestcork.com) and Whale Watch with Colin Barnes (☑ 086 327 3226; www.whalewatchwithcolinbarnes.com) both offer whale and dolphin tours year-round from Reen Pier, about 3km southwest of Union

Hall. Prices average €50/30 per adult/child for half-day cruises.

🛏 Sleeping & Eating

Meadow Camping Park CAMPGROUND €
(☎028-33280; meadowcamping@eircom.net; Rosscarbery Rd, Glandore; campsites €20; ☺Easter & May–mid-Sep) This small, idyllic site, in a garden filled with trees and flowers, is 2km east of Glandore on the R597 to Rosscarbery.

Bay View House B&B €€
(☎028-33115; Glandore; s/d €50/80) Bay View House has seriously spectacular views across the bay. Try to snag Room 1 for the best view of all. Bright citrus colours, tidy pine furniture and gleaming bathrooms add to the appeal. Local pubs are a stumble away.

Shearwater B&B B&B €€
(☎028-33178; www.shearwaterbandb.com; Union Hall; s/d €50/70; ☺Apr-Oct) On a low hill about 500m from the centre of Union Hall, rooms are comfy and there's a large terrace with killer views.

Fish Shop SEAFOOD €
(☎028-33818; Main St, Union Hall; ☺9am-5pm Mon-Fri, 9am-1pm Sat) Union Hall smoked salmon is renowned. You can buy it here at this factory outlet, along with fresh catches and live shellfish.

★Glandore Inn PUB €€
(☎028-33468; www.theglandoreinn.com; Main St, Glandore; mains €10-16; ☺from 10am summer, from noon winter; 🐾) 🍴 Front-row views over the harbour and a superlative menu make this one of Cork's finest places to dine. The menu spans homemade pork pies with fruit chutney; lambs liver and bacon on cabbage and mash; and Normandy chicken and cream, basil and mushroom sauce. Don't miss owner-chef David Wine's beer bread. The interior's rustic nautical charm has a contemporary edge; there are artisan beers too.

Hayes Bar PUB €€
(☎028-33214; The Square, Glandore; mains €8-20; ☺vary) Perfect portside pub with picnic tables outside.

ℹ Getting There & Away

Buses to/from Skibbereen (€3.80, 15 minutes) and Clonakilty (€7.10, 25 minutes) stop in nearby Leap (3km north), from where most B&B owners will pick you up if you arrange it in advance.

MICHAEL COLLINS – THE 'BIG FELLA'

Born on a farm just outside Clonakilty, Michael Collins is one of County Cork's most famous and beloved sons, the commander-in-chief of the army of the Irish Free State that won independence from Britain in 1922.

He became a key figure in Irish nationalism after the Easter Rising of 1916, revolutionising the way Irish rebels fought by organising them into guerrilla-style 'flying columns' that proved especially effective against the much larger but less mobile British forces. His political acumen landed him the job of main negotiator of the 1921 Anglo-Irish Treaty; forced to make major concessions, including the partition of the country, he signed reluctantly, famously declaring that he was signing his own death warrant.

He was tragically correct, as the Civil War broke out in the aftermath of the treaty and, during a tour of West Cork, Collins was ambushed and killed by anti-Treaty forces on 22 August 1922 at Beal-na-mBláth, near Macroom. Each year, a commemorative service is held on the anniversary of the killing. To visit the site, follow the N22 west from Cork for about 20km, then take the left turn (R590) to Crookstown. From there turn right onto the R585 to Beal-na-mBláth. The ambush site is on the left after 4km.

The useful map and leaflet *In Search of Michael Collins* (€4.50) is available at the Clonakilty tourist office, outlining places in the district associated with him. A visit to the Michael Collins Centre (☎023-884 6107; www.michaelcollinscentre.com; adult/child €5/3; ☺10.30am-5pm mid-Jun–Sep) is an excellent way to make sense of his life and that period of Ireland's history. A tour reveals photos, letters and a reconstruction of the 1920s country lane where Collins was killed, complete with armoured vehicle. The centre runs occasional tours of the crucial locations in Collins' life. It's signposted off the R600 between Timoleague and Clonakilty.

The Clonakilty Museum (☎023-883 3115; Western Rd; admission €2; ☺11am-4pm Tue-Fri Jun-Sep) has some more memorabilia, including Collins' weapons and uniform. The museum is run on a voluntary basis; contact the tourist office for current opening hours.

Castletownshend

POP 160

With its grand houses and higgledy-piggledy stone cottages dating back to the 17th and 18th centuries tumbling down the precipitously steep main street, Castletownshend is one of Ireland's most enigmatic villages. At the bottom of the hill is a small quayside and the castle (really a crenellated mansion) after which the village is named. Once you've seen these, you can just put your feet up and relax: you've ticked all the boxes.

On the waterfront, the castle ($\boxtimes$ 028-36100; www.castle-townshend.com; d from €70, self-catering apt & cottages per week from €150) is a rocky fantasy. Huge mullioned windows obviate any authenticity of the decorative defensive touches. The guest rooms range from one with an old four-poster to small but bright rooms, some with terraces and views. Nonguests can stroll the gardens (adult/child €5/free).

The only way here is by car down the R596 for 8km from Skibbereen. A taxi ($\boxtimes$ 028-21258) from Skibbereen costs about €15.

Skibbereen

POP 2500

Today, Skibbereen (Sciobairín) is a busy, workaday market town. During the Famine, however, Skib was hit perhaps harder than any other town in Ireland, with huge numbers of the local population emigrating or dying of starvation or disease. 'The accounts are not exaggerated – they cannot be exaggerated – nothing more frightful can be conceived.' So wrote Lord Dufferin and GF Boyle, who journeyed from Oxford to Skibbereen in February 1847 to see if reports of the Famine were true. Their eyewitness account makes horrific reading; Dufferin was so appalled by what he saw that he contributed £1000 (about €100,000 in today's money) to the relief effort.

The main landmark in town is a statue in the central square, dedicated to heroes of Irish rebellions against the British.

◉ Sights

Constructed on the site of the town's old gasworks, the passionately staffed Skibbereen Heritage ($\boxtimes$ 028-40900; www.skibbheritage.com; Upper Bridge St, Old Gasworks Bldg; adult/child €6/3; ⊙10am-6pm Mon-Sat mid-May–mid-Sep, 10am-6pm Tue-Sat mid-Mar–mid-May & mid-Sep–Oct, closed rest of year) centre houses a haunting exhibition about the Famine, with actors reading heartbreaking contemporary accounts. A visit here puts Irish history into harrowing perspective. There's also a smaller exhibition about nearby Lough Hyne, the first marine nature reserve in Ireland, plus a genealogical centre.

Guided evening historical walks (adult/child €5/2.50), lasting 1½ hours, leave from the heritage centre. Phone to confirm times.

The Abbeystrewery Cemetery is a 1km walk east of the centre, on the N71 to Schull, and holds the mass graves of 8000 to 10,000 local people who died during the Famine.

A beautiful and disused old railway bridge crosses the river near Ilen St. A cattle market on Fridays at the showgrounds is a frenetic, smelly glimpse of rural life.

✦ Festivals & Events

Taste of West Cork Food Festival   FOOD
(www.atasteofwestcork.com; ⊙mid-Sep) If you're in town in mid-September, don't miss the Taste of West Cork Food Festival, with a lively market and events at local restaurants.

⨁ Sleeping

★ Bridge House   B&B €€
($\boxtimes$ 028-21273; www.bridgehouseskibbereen.com; Bridge St; s/d €40/70; ☞) Mona Best has turned her entire house into a work of art, filling the rooms with fabulous Victorian tableaux and period memorabilia. The whole place bursts at the seams with cherished clutter, crazed carvings, dressed-up dummies and fragrant fresh flowers. Guests can request black satin sheets.

West Cork Hotel   HOTEL €€
($\boxtimes$ 028-21277; www.westcorkhotel.com; Ilen St; r €55-150; ☞) This stolid veteran has 30 comfortable, recently redone rooms next to the river and old railway bridge. Rooms at the back have pastoral views.

✗ Eating

Farmers Market   MARKET €
(⊙10am-1.30pm Sat year-round, plus 10am-1.30pm Wed Jul-Sep) ✐ Local producers set up on Old Market Sq.

Riverside Café & Restaurant   INTERNATIONAL €€
($\boxtimes$ 028-40090; www.riversideskibbereen.ie; North St; tapas €6-10.50, mains €10-24; ⊙noon-3.30pm Tue-Sat, 6-10pm Fri & Sat) Seafood casserole in lobster bisque, seaweed paella, and bang-

ers and mash with oxtail gravy are among the choices at this popular spot, along with cheese and smoked-fish boards. But the biggest drawcard is the riverside setting with alfresco seating in fine weather.

Kalbo's   INTERNATIONAL €€
(☑ 028-21515; 26 North St; dishes €4.50-12, dinner mains €14.50-26.50; ☺ 9am-6pm Mon-Thu, 9am-9pm Fri & Sat; ⊞) Locally sourced produce and a deft hand in the kitchen mean that vanilla pancakes in the morning and bacon sandwiches at lunch are tops. Dinner dishes such as crab linguine with coriander and lemon cream are creative.

❶ Information

Tourist office (☑ 028-21766; www.skibbereen. ie; North St; ☺ 9.15-5pm Tue-Sat) Can book accommodation in Baltimore and on Sherkin and Cape Clear Islands, advise on local walks and provide ferry timetables to the islands.

❶ Getting There & Away

Bus Éireann (☑ 021-450 8188; www.buseir eann.ie) runs buses to Cork seven times daily Monday to Saturday and five on Sunday (€18.50, 1¾ hours), and to Schull three times daily Monday to Saturday (€7.10, 30 minutes) from outside the former Eldon Hotel on Main St.

Baltimore

POP 400

Crusty old seadog Baltimore is a classic maritime village, its busy little port full of fishing trawlers and pleasure boats. Away from its central terrace overlooking the port are the multitude of holiday cottages that cater to the summer swell that brings sailing folk, anglers, divers and visitors to nearby Sherkin and Cape Clear islands.

On 20 June 1631 Barbary pirates attacked the village and made off with 108 townspeople, who were sold into slavery in North Africa; only three made it back to Ireland again.

◉ Sights & Activities

Besides the remains of the Dun na Sead (Fort of the Jewels; ☑ 028-20735; adult/child €3/ free; ☺ 11am-6pm Jun-Sep) castle, which overlooks the harbour, Baltimore is all about the sea.

Diving is excellent on the reefs around Fastnet Rock; the waters are warmed by the Gulf Stream and a number of shipwrecks

lie nearby. Aquaventures Dive Centre (☑ 028-20511; www.aquaventures.ie; Stonehouse B&B, Lifeboat Rd) charges €115 for a full day's diving including gear; a half-day snorkelling trip costs €40. It also offers diving and accommodation packages in the attached B&B; contact the centre for prices.

Baltimore Sailing School (☑ 028-20141; www.baltimoresailingschool.com) provides courses (five days for €290) from June to September for beginners and advanced sailors. For a shorter taste of the sea, set sail with Baltimore Yacht Charters (☑ 028-20160; www.bal timoreyachtcharters.com), which has a variety of cruises starting at €50. Also leaving from the harbour, Baltimore Sea Safari (☑ 028-20753; www.baltimoreseasafari.ie) has various sailing adventures starting at €25 for two hours.

Information about other diving, sailing and angling operators is posted by the harbour.

A white-painted landmark beacon (aka Lot's Wife) stands on the western headland of the peninsula and makes for a pleasant walk, especially at sunset.

Ten kilometres from Baltimore, on the R585 towards Skibbereen, there's good walking around Lough Hyne and the Knockamagh Wood Nature Reserve. Well-marked trails lead around the lake and up a steep hill through the forest. You're rewarded with stunning views at the top.

🎉 Festivals & Events

The town goes nuts in spring.

Fiddle Fair   MUSIC
(www.fiddlefair.com; ☺ 2nd weekend of May) Sessions from international and local musicians.

Walking Festival   WALKING
(www.westcork.ie; ☺ mid-May) Guided walks of Baltimore and the region.

Seafood Festival   FOOD
(www.baltimore.ie; ☺ last full weekend of May) Jazz bands perform and pubs bring out the mussels and prawns; wooden boats parade.

🛏 Sleeping & Eating

Rolf's Country House   GUESTHOUSE €€
(☑ 028-20289; www.rolfscountryhouse.com; Baltimore Hill; s/d €60/100, cottages per week from €500; ☺ Apr-Oct; @ 🛜) Upmarket Rolf's, in a much-restored old farmhouse in restful gardens on the outskirts of town, does the

COUNTY CORK BALTIMORE

lot: there are 14 smartly decorated private rooms, self-catering cottages, helpful staff and a charming **restaurant** (mains €22-29; ⌚6-9.30pm Jun-Sep).

Waterfront HOTEL €€
(☎028-20600; www.waterfronthotel.ie; The Quay; s/d €80/120; @📶) Smack in the middle of town is this 13-room hotel with small but tidy rooms. Ask for one with a view of the sea. Its restaurant, the **Lookout** (Chez Youen; mains €16-40; ⌚from 6.30pm Fri, Sat & public holidays Easter-Sep), also has sea views and luscious shellfish platters, containing lobster, prawns, brown crab, velvet crab, shrimps and oysters. Check annual schedules online.

Casey's of Baltimore HOTEL €€
(☎028-20197; www.caseysofbaltimore.com; Skibbereen Rd; s/d from €120/150; @📶) Ten of the 14 spiffy guestrooms here have estuary views and all have huge beds. The hotel is right at the entrance to town (should you be arriving by chopper, there's a helipad). Food comes with fantastic views, especially from the terrace. Seafood includes mussels fresh from the hotel's own shellfish farm in Roaringwater Bay, and the hotel specialty, crab claws in garlic butter.

Glebe Gardens & Café MODERN IRISH €€
(☎028-20232; www.glebegardens.com; dishes €6-10.50, 2-/3-course dinner menu €25/30; ⌚10am-6pm Wed-Sun & 7-10pm Wed-Sat Apr-Oct) 🍃 The beautiful gardens here are an attraction in themselves (garden entry per adult/child is €5/free). If you're dining, lavender and herbs add fragrant aromas that waft over the tables inside and out. Food is simple and fresh, sourced from the gardens and a list of local purveyors.

Drinking & Nightlife

Bushe's Bar PUB
(www.bushesbar.com; The Quay; sandwiches €6.50-11) Seafaring paraphernalia literally drips from the ceiling at this genuinely character-filled old bar. The benches outside on the main square are the best spots in town for a sundowner. Famous crab sandwiches are served when fresh crab has been caught.

Information

There's an information board at the harbour, or check out www.baltimore.ie. The nearest ATM is in Skibbereen.

Getting There & Away

Three daily buses Monday to Friday and two on Saturday link Skibbereen and Baltimore (€4.30, 20 minutes).

Sherkin Island

POP 100

Just a 10-minute ferry ride offshore from Baltimore, **Sherkin Island** (www.sherkinisland.eu) measures only 5km by 3km but until the Famine had a population of over 1000.

These days Sherkin is a magnet for artists, holidaymakers and foodies: the pirate-festooned **Jolly Roger** (☎028-20003; mains €12-20; ⌚10am-late, reduced hours in in winter) pub justifies a visit alone, with some of the best seafood chowder imaginable (the garlic mussels aren't bad either). Live music takes place daily in summer.

If you're not ready to head back to the mainland, you can gaze at it from your window at Sherkin's other pub, the **Islander's Rest** (☎028-20116; www.islandersrest.ie; s/d €80/120), which has 21 comfy rooms with private bathrooms.

Getting There & Away

Sherkin Island Ferry (☎087 911 7377; www.sherkinferry.com; adult/child return €10/4) sails to/from Baltimore up to nine times daily (seven on Saturday, five on Sunday, reduced services in winter).

Cape Clear Island

POP 150

With its lonely inlets, pebbly beaches, and gorse- and heather-covered cliffs, Cape Clear Island (Oileán Chléire) is an escapist's heaven – albeit one that is only 5km long and just over 1.5km wide at its broadest point. But that's just as well, as you'll want time to appreciate this small, rugged Gaeltacht (Irish-speaking area), the southernmost inhabited island in the country.

Facilities are few, but there are a couple of B&Bs, one shop and three pubs.

Sights

The small **heritage centre** (☎028-39119; www.capeclearmuseum.ie; admission €3; ⌚2.30-5pm May-Sep) has exhibits on the island's history and culture, and fine views north across the water to Mizen Head.

The ruins of 14th-century **Dunamore Castle**, the stronghold of the O'Driscoll clan, can be seen perched on a rock on the northwestern side of the island (follow the track from the harbour). The great hall lives up to its name and is sometimes open for tours (€3) when visitors turn up.

Activities

Cape Clear is one of the top birdwatching spots in Ireland, particularly known for sea birds, including Manx shearwater, gannet, fulmar and kittiwake. Guillemot breed on the island, but other birds head to and fro on hunting trips from the rocky outposts of the western peninsulas. Tens of thousands of birds can pass hourly, especially in the early morning and at dusk. The best time of year for twitching here is October. The white-fronted bird observatory is by the harbour (turn right at the end of the pier and it's 100m along).

There are marked walking trails all over the island.

Courses

Once you're this isolated, you might as well learn something, and Ed Harper at Chléire Goats (☑028-39126; www.oilean-chleire.ie/Goat Farm) farm west of the church can teach you everything you need to know about goat husbandry. He makes ice cream and hard goat's cheese, available for tastings, and runs half-day (€35) to five-day (€155) courses on goat keeping.

✯⚐ Festivals & Events

Cape Clear Island International Storytelling Festival STORYTELLING
(☑028-39157; www.capeclearstorytelling.com; ⊙early Sep) The Cape Clear Island International Storytelling Festival draws hundreds of people for storytelling, workshops and walks, as summer wanes.

🛏 Sleeping & Eating

Cape Clear Island Hostel HOSTEL €
(☑028-41968; www.capeclearhostel.com; Old Coastguard Station; dm/tw from €20/46; @🖲) A hostel in a large white building at the south harbour, amid lovely gardens. There's a spacious self-catering kitchen, a laundry and an amazing collection of model ships in bottles.

Chléire Haven CAMPGROUND €
(☑028-39119; www.yurt-holidays-ireland.com; campsite per person €10; ⊙Jun-Sep) 🌿 There are a limited number of campsites here and also yurts and tepees. The latter require

multiple-day stays (a good thing) and start at €240 for two nights in high season.

Ard Na Gaoithe B&B €€
(☑028-39160; www.ardnagaoithe.ie; The Glen; d from €70) Has restful rooms in a simple, sturdy house.

❶ Information

Tourist Information Post (☑028-39100; www.capeclearisland.ie; ⊙11.30am-4.30pm Mon-Sat, noon-5pm Sun May-Sep) Beyond the pier, next to the coffee shop.

❶ Getting There & Away

From Baltimore, the **Cailín Óir** (☑086 346 5110; www.cailinoir.com; adult/child return €16/8; ⊙10.30am-7pm) ferry takes 45 minutes to cover the 11km journey. There are four sailings daily.

The **Schull Ferry** (☑087 3899 711; www.schullferry.com; return €16) is now up-and-running; there are three sailings (45 minutes) daily except Monday and Thursday, when no services run.

MIZEN HEAD PENINSULA

From Skibbereen the N71 rolls west through Ballydehob, the gateway to the Mizen (rhymes with wizen). From here, the R592 continues to the pretty village of Schull. Travelling on the R592 and R591 into the undulating countryside takes you through ever-smaller settlements to the village of Goleen.

Even here the Mizen isn't done. Increasingly narrow roads head further west to spectacular Mizen Head itself and to the hidden delights of Barleycove Beach and Crookhaven. Without a decent map you may well reach the same crossroads several times.

Heading back from Goleen, you can bear north to join the scenic coast road that follows the edge of Dunmanus Bay for most of the way to Durrus. The R591 heads north through Durrus for Bantry while the L4704 turns west to Sheep's Head Peninsula.

Schull

POP 700

The boating and creative crowd (often the same folk) have turned the small fishing village of Schull (pronounced 'skull'; www.schull.ie) into a buzzing little spot, even if the regular townsfolk still go about their business as before, when the busy harbour was the main focus of their attentions. A cluster of vessels keeps the port alive, but there are also craft shops and art galleries to browse. Schull's popular Sunday Country Market (www.schullmarket.com; Pier Car Park; ⊙10am-2pm Sun mid-Mar–Sep) showcases the village's artists' and craftspeople's work, and draws producers and purveyors from around the region.

⊙ Sights & Activities

Founded by a German visitor who fell in love with Schull, the Republic's only planetarium (☑028-28315; www.schullcommunitycollege.com; Colla Rd; adult/child €5/3.50; ⊙Jun-Sep) is on the grounds of Schull Community College. During summer, there's a 45-minute star show. Call to confirm times. The planetarium is at the Goleen end of the village on Colla Rd. You can also reach it by walking along the foreshore path from the pier.

Walks in the area include a 13km return trip up Mt Gabriel (407m). It was once mined for copper, and there are Bronze Age remains and 19th-century mine shafts and chimneys. For a gentler stroll try the short 2km foreshore path from the pier out to Roaringwater Bay and a view of the nearby islands.

Divecology (☑086 837 2065; www.divecology.com; Cooradarrigan; diving courses/dives from €100/25) runs courses and dives to wreck and reef sites. Check around the dock for charter boats going out fishing.

🎣 Festivals & Events

Calves Week   SAILING
(www.shsc.ie) Sailing regatta usually held after the August bank holiday.

🛏 Sleeping & Eating

Grove House   B&B €€
(☑028-28067; www.grovehouseschull.com; Colla Rd; s/d from €50/80; 🛜) This beautifully restored ivy-covered mansion has lovely pine floors and is decorated in an easygoing antiques-and-homemade-rugs style. It also has a terrific restaurant (3-course menu €25; ⊙from 6pm Mon-Sat, 1-5pm Sun Mar-Sep) where Swedish influences combine with Irish staples.

Corthna-Lodge Guesthouse   B&B €€
(☑028-28517; www.corthna-lodge.net; s/d from €70/95; 🛜) There's an outdoor hot tub,

sauna house and gym at this rambling modern home just outside the centre, as well as seven sprightly rooms.

Newman's West   PUB €
(☑028-27776; www.tjnewmans.com; Main St; dishes €6.50-12.50; ⊙9am-11pm; 🛜) This sailor-filled wine bar (with many good choices by the glass) and art gallery serves soups, salads and enormous chunky sandwiches filled with local cheese and salami. Daily specials might include Bantry Bay mussels and chowder. The adjoining original pub, TJ Newman's, is a charmer.

Hackett's   MODERN IRISH €€
(☑028-28625; Main St; bar food €4-9; ⊙from noon Mon & Thu-Sun, from 5pm Tue & Wed) The town's social hub, Hackett's rises above the norm with a creative pub menu of organic dishes prepared from scratch. Black-and-white photos and tin signs adorn the pub's crooked walls and there's a mishmash of old kitchen tables and benches on the worn stone floor.

❶ Getting There & Away

There are two buses daily from Cork to Schull (€19.70, 2½ hours), via Clonakilty and Skibbereen.

❶ Getting Around

Betty Johnson's Bus Hire (☑086 265 6078, 028-28410) Bus and taxi service.

West of Schull to Mizen Head

If you're driving or cycling, take the undulating coastal route from Schull to Goleen. On a clear day there are great views out to Cape Clear Island and the Fastnet lighthouse. The landscape becomes wilder around the hamlet of Toormore. From Goleen, roads run out to thrilling Mizen Head and to the picturesque harbour village of Crookhaven.

Along the way, you'll spot old stone houses, many now derelict in fields. While there's obviously no shortage of materials, building these houses to withstand Atlantic gales required enormous amounts of labour on the part of locals, already challenged by the unreliable fertility of the land.

Goleen & Around

The largest settlement in these parts – with an impressive neo-Gothic church, along with four pubs, four shops and a petrol station – is the village of Goleen.

Sleeping & Eating

Heron's Cove B&B, RESTAURANT €€
(☑ 028-35225; www.heronscove.com; Goleen; s/d €60/80, mains €16-25; 🕿) 🍴 A delightful location, on the shores of the tidal inlet of Goleen Harbour, makes this fine restaurant and B&B a top choice. Rooms have been refurbished to a restful style and several have balconies overlooking the inlet. The small restaurant (3-course menu €27.50; ⊘ 7-9.30pm Apr-Oct, by reservation Oct-Mar) has an excellent menu of organic and local food.

Fortview House B&B €€
(☑ 028-35324; www.fortviewhouse.ie; Gurtyowen, Toormore; s/d €50/100; ⊘ Apr-Oct; 🕿 👪) On a working farm, this lovely house has three antique-filled, flower-themed bedrooms. Hostess Violet's breakfast is gourmet standard (hot potato cakes with crème fraiche and smoked salmon), with eggs from cheerfully clucking hens in the garden. From Goleen, head northeast along the R591 for 9km.

Getting There & Away

Bus Éireann has two buses a day from Skibbereen (€11.50, 70 minutes) via Schull. Goleen is the end of the line for bus service on the peninsula.

Crookhaven

Onwards from Goleen, the westerly outpost of Crookhaven feels so remote that you imagine it's more easily reached by boat than by road. And so it is for some people: in summer there's a big yachting presence. Outside summer, it's very quiet.

In its heyday Crookhaven's natural harbour was an important anchorage. Mail from America was collected here, and sailing ships and fishing vessels found ready shelter. On the opposite shore the gaunt remains of quarry buildings, closed in 1939, lie embedded in the hillside, and are the source of many dubious yarns from locals in response to curious questions from visitors.

Sleeping & Eating

Pints in the sunshine are the reward for venturing out on the crooked road to Crookhaven. (If it's raining, make that 'Pints by the fireplace...')

Galley Cove House B&B €€
(☑ 028-35137; www.galleycovehouse.com; s/d €55/ 90; 🕿) A cheerful welcome complements the secluded location of this modern home, 2km from Crookhaven, with terrific views across the ocean. It's handy for Barleycove Beach, and the pine-floored rooms are clean, airy and filled with light.

Crookhaven Inn PUB €€
(☑ 028-35309; www.crookhaveninn.com; mains €7-14; ⊘ 12.30-8pm Fri-Mon Apr-Sep) Set discreetly back from the water, this stone cottage of a pub also has a bulwark of picnic tables outside. The food here is an ambitious take on pub grub; seafood, of course, is supreme. In summer there are trad music sessions many nights.

O'Sullivan's Bar PUB €
(☑ 028-35319; mains €6-12.25; ⊘ kitchen noon-3pm) A timeless building right on the harbour. Several generations of picnic tables draw several generations of punters when there's even a hint of sun. Pub food such as seafood chowder and fried shrimp is popular – and good.

Shopping

Escallonia Jewellery JEWELLERY
(www.etsy.com/shop/escalloniajewellery; Main St; ⊘ 11am-5pm Thu-Tue) Crookhaven's ends-of-the-earth location fuels creative inspiration and Jorg Uschkamp makes exquisite gold and silver jewellery at his workshop-gallery on the harbourfront. Jorg also sells quirky sculptures, glassware and candles.

Brow Head

This is the southernmost point on the Irish mainland and is well worth the walk. As you leave Crookhaven, you'll notice a turn-off to the left marked 'Brow Head'. Park at the bottom of the hill – the track is very narrow and there's nowhere to pull over should you meet a tractor coming the other way. After 1km the road ends. Continue on a path to Brow Head where you'll see an observation tower, from which Guglielmo Marconi transmitted his first radio message (to Cornwall) that received a reply.

Barleycove

Vast sand dunes hemmed in by two long bluffs dissolve into the surf, forming West Cork's finest beach. Rarely crowded, it's a great place for youngsters, with gorgeous

COUNTY CORK WEST OF SCHULL TO MIZEN HEAD

stretches of golden sand and a safe bathing area where a stream flows down to the sea. Access is via a long boardwalk and pontoon, which protect the surrounding wetlands from the impact of visitors' feet. There's a car park at the edge of the beach, on the south side of the causeway on the road to Crookhaven.

Mizen Head Signal Station

Ireland's most southwesterly point is dominated by its Victorian-era signal station (☑028-35115; www.mizenhead.ie; Mizen Head; adult/child €6/3.50; ☉10am-6pm Jun-Aug, 10.30am-5pm mid-Mar–Apr & Oct, 11am-4pm Nov–mid-Mar), completed in 1909 to help warn ships off the rocks, which appear in the water around here like crushed ice in a cola.

From the visitors centre, it's a 10-minute walk via 99 steps out to the station, culminating in the crossing of a spectacular arched bridge that spans a vast gulf in the cliffs. The views are stunning, with spurting plumes of white water in every direction.

The station is beyond the bridge, at the far point of the outer rock island, and contains the keeper's quarters, engine room and radio room: you can see how the keepers lived and how the station worked (until its automation in 1993), but the real rush is the sense of so much Atlantic beneath vast skies.

Back at the visitors centre is Fastnet Hall, with plenty of information about local ecology, history and the namesake lighthouse. There's also a modest cafe.

To get to the area, follow the R591 southwest from Goleen to the end of the road.

Northside of the Peninsula

Although the landscape is less dramatic on this side of the peninsula, it's well worth driving along the coast road here for the great views out to Sheep's Head Peninsula and beyond to the magnificent Beara Peninsula.

Durrus

POP 900

The access point for both the Mizen Head and Sheep's Head peninsulas, this perky little crossroads at the head of Dunmanus Bay has become something of a gourmet hotspot in recent years, with some great places to

eat and artisan producers such as Durrus Farmhouse.

Travel a world of plants at Kilravock Garden (☑027-61111; Ahakista Rd; adult/child €6/3; ☉by appointment; ⚑), which has been transformed over two decades from a field of scrag and stone to a feast of exotic plants by a green-fingered couple.

🍽 Sleeping & Eating

⭐Blair's Cove House   B&B €€€
(☑027-61127; www.blairscove.ie; d €120-260, two- or three-course menu €46/58; ☉Mar-Jan) Set in 2 hectares of land overlooking the bay, this magnificent Georgian country house looks like it belongs in a style magazine. Superbly appointed rooms and a self-catering apartment centre around an exquisite courtyard. The restaurant (2-/3-course menu €46/58; ☉from 6pm Tue-Sat Mar-Oct) in a chandeliered hall, gives local produce international treatment. It's 1km south of Durrus on the R591.

Sheeps Head Inn   PUB €€
(☑027-62822; mains €10-23; ☉noon-3pm daily, from 7pm Fri & Sat; ⚑) In the heart of the village, this cosy black-and-white gastropub cooks up exceptional seafood such as pan-fried sea bass and salmon dressing, and crab claws in garlic and lemon.

Good Things Café   MODERN IRISH €€
(☑027-61426; www.thegoodthingscafe.com; Ahakista Rd; lunch mains €10-20, dinner mains €21-38; ☉varies) This foodie haven 600m west of town on Dunmanus Bay serves great contemporary dishes made with organic, locally sourced ingredients. Tables on a vast terrace have views of nervous sheep. Check for seasonal schedules.

Popular cooking courses include A Dozen Quickies in a Day (the 'culinary equivalent of speed dating', learning 12 mix-and-match dishes; €140) and a two-day Kitchen Miracle (€375) for those whose cooking skills stop after reading the microwave directions on a frozen meal.

Bantry

POP 3300

Framed by the craggy Caha Mountains, vast, magnificent Bantry Bay is one of the country's most attractive inlets and a worthwhile stop on any West Cork itinerary. Pride of place goes to Bantry House, the former home of one Richard White, who earned his place in history when in 1798 he warned authorities of the imminent landing of patriot Wolfe Tone and his French fleet in their effort to join the countrywide rebellion of the United Irishmen. In the end storms prevented the fleet from landing and the course of Irish history was definitively altered – all Wolfe Tone got for his troubles was a square and a statue bearing his name.

Bantry struggled through the 19th century due to famine, poverty and mass emigration but today its industry derives from the bay: you'll see Bantry oysters and mussels on menus throughout County Cork.

Sights

Bantry's narrow streets of old-fashioned, one-off shops and picturesque harbourfront make a pleasant stroll.

Bantry House   HISTORIC BUILDING
(☑ 027-50047; www.bantryhouse.com; Bantry Bay; adult/child €11/3; ☉10am-5pm Apr-Oct) With its melancholic air of faded gentility, 18th-century Bantry House makes for an intriguing visit. The house has belonged to the White family since 1729 and every room brims with treasures brought back from each generation's travels since then. The entrance is paved with mosaics from Pompeii, French and Flemish tapestries adorn the walls, and Japanese chests sit next to Russian shrines. Upstairs, worn bedrooms look out wanly over an astounding view of the bay – the 18th-century Whites had ringside seats to the French armada. Experienced pianists are invited to tinkle the ivories of the ancient piano in the library. It's possible to stay in the wings (p252).

Bantry House's gardens are its great glory. Lawns sweep down from the front of the house towards the sea, and the formal Italian garden has an enormous 'stairway to the sky', offering spectacular views.

In the former stables you'll find the 1796 French Armada Exhibition Centre, with its powerful account of the doomed French invasion of Ireland. The fleet was torn apart by storms; one frigate, *La Surveillante*, was scuttled by its own crew and today lies 30m down at the bottom of the bay.

Bantry House is 1km southwest of the town centre on the N71.

Festivals & Events

West Cork Chamber Music Festival   MUSIC
(www.westcorkmusic.ie; ☉Jun/Jul) Evening concerts held over a week at Bantry House, when the house closes to the public. The garden, craft shop and tearoom remain open.

Sleeping

Eagle Point Camping   CAMPGROUND €
(☑ 027-50630; www.eaglepointcamping.com; Glengarriff Rd, Ballylickey; campsites from €35; ☉mid-Apr–late Sep) An enviable location at the end of a filigreed promontory 6km north of Bantry makes this a popular site. Most of the 125 spots have sea views, and there's direct access to the pebbly beaches nearby.

Ballylickey House   B&B €€
(☑ 027-50071; www.ballylickeymanorhouse.com; Ballylickey; d €95-180; ☉Mar-Nov; 🗫🏊) Situated 5km north of Bantry in Ballylickey, this beautiful manor house with manicured lawns overlooks the bay. There are two choices for the night: rooms in the house or cute cottages set round a swimming pool. All are spacious and comfortably furnished.

Bantry Bay Hotel   HOTEL €€
(☑ 027-50062; www.bantrybayhotel.ie; Wolfe Tone Sq; s/d from €50/70; @🗫) Most of the 14 comfortable, if not exciting, rooms at this powder-blue hotel overlook the square, with glimpses of the bay. Rates include breakfast.

COUNTY CORK BANTRY

WORTH A TRIP

DURRUS CHEESE

Durrus has earned an international reputation for its marvellous cheese, thanks to the likes of Durrus Farmhouse (☑ 027-61100; www.durruscheese.com; Coomkeen, Durrus; ☉by appointment) whose produce is sold all over Ireland, the UK and even the US and Japan. You can't visit the production area, so you'll have to make do with an informal presentation but the setting is wonderfully rustic. You can also buy all the cheese you want. Head 900m out of Durrus along the Ahakista road, turn right at St James' Church and continue for 2.6km along the increasingly bumpy lane until you see a sign for the farm, from where it's a further 1km.

The bar's maritime theme may put you in the mood to hoist the mizzen-mast.

Sea View House Hotel HOTEL €€€
(☑ 027-50073; www.seaviewhousehotel.com; Ballylickey; s €95, d €140-170; ☜) You'll find everything you'd expect from a luxury hotel here: country-house ambience, tastefully decorated public rooms, expansive service and 25 cosy, smart bedrooms. The hotel is on the N71 in Ballylickey.

Bantry House MANOR HOUSE €€€
(☑ 027-50047; www.bantryhouse.com; Bantry Bay; d from €169; ☺ Apr-Oct; ☜) Bantry House's guest rooms, decorated in pale hues and a mixture of antiques and contemporary furnishings, are luxurious places to while away the hours – when you're not playing croquet, lawn tennis or billiards and lounging in the house's library once the doors are shut to the public (guests also receive free access to the house). Rooms 22 and 25 are double winners, with views of both the garden and the bay.

✖ Eating

★**Manning's Emporium** CAFE, DELI €
(www.manningsemporium.ie; Ballylickey; tasting plates €8; ☺ 9am-6pm Mon-Sat, 9am-5pm Sun)
🍴 It looks like a garden centre from the outside, with a profusion of pot plants and hanging baskets, but inside it's an Aladdin's cave of West Cork's best produce. Tasting plates are the best way to sample the local artisan produce and farmhouse cheeses on offer. Foodie events take place regularly. It's on the N71 in Ballylickey (on your right as you're coming from Bantry).

Bantry Market MARKET €
(Wolfe Tone Sq; ☺ 9.30am-1pm Fri) 🍴 Wolfe Tone Sq takes on a heady mix of aromas for the Friday Market, which draws in the masses – both vendors and shoppers – from a wide area. Fresh fruit, veg, bread, cheese and other local produce fill most stalls but there's clothing, bric-a-brac and farming tools too. The market morphs into an even bigger and busier affair on the first Friday of the month.

Fish Kitchen MODERN IRISH €€
(☑ 027-56651; www.thefishkitchen.ie; New St; lunch mains €6-11, dinner mains €15-28; ☺ noon-3.30pm & 5.30-9pm Tue-Sat) This outstanding little restaurant above a fish shop does seafood to perfection, from the live-tank local oysters (served with lemon and tabasco sauce) to Bantry Bay mussels in white wine. If you don't fancy sea fare, it does a juicy steak too. Friendly, unfussy and absolutely delicious.

O'Connors Seafood Restaurant SEAFOOD €€
(☑ 027-55664; www.oconnorseafood.com; Wolfe Tone Sq; mains €18.50-25.50; ☺ from noon) West Cork scallops with wild boar black pudding, Castletownbere cod pan roasted with crab and herb topping and Bantry Bay mussels done four ways are among the innovative preparations of the area's renowned seafood.

🍺 Drinking & Entertainment

Crowley's PUB
(Wolfe Tone Sq) One of the best bars for music, Crowley's has traditional bands on Wednesday nights.

Ma Murphy's PUB
(www.mamurphys.com; 7 New St) You can still buy cornflakes and sugar at this timewarp of a grocery pub, here since 1840. The regulars are always up for a chat.

Snug PUB
(Wolfe Tone Sq) Cosy local favourite on the waterfront.

❶ Information

Post office (William St)
Tourist office (☑ 027-50229; Wolfe Tone Sq; ☺ 9.15am-1pm & 2-5pm Mon-Sat Apr-Oct) In the old courthouse.

❶ Getting There & Away

Bus Éireann (www.buseireann.ie) has seven buses daily Monday to Saturday (four on Sunday) between Bantry and Cork (€19, two hours). There's five daily to Glengarriff (€4.70, 25 minutes). Heading north by bus to the Ring of Beara, Kenmare and Killarney requires backtracking through Cork.

Bantry Rural Transport (☑ 027-52727; www.ruraltransport.ie; 5 Main St) runs a useful series of circular routes to Dunmanway, Durrus, Goleen, Schull, Skibbereen and outlying villages. There's a set price of €4/6 one way/return. Service is not frequent; check the website for details.

❶ Getting Around

Bicycles can be hired at **Nigel's Bicycle Shop** (☑ 027-52657; Glengarriff Rd; per day/week €15/70; ☺ 10am-6pm Mon-Sat).

SHEEP'S HEAD PENINSULA

The least visited of Cork's three peninsulas, Sheep's Head has a charm all its own – and plenty of sheep. There are sweeping seascapes to appreciate from the loop road running along most of its length. A good link road with terrific views, called the Goat's Path Rd, runs between Gortnakilly and Kilcrohane (on the north and south coasts respectively), over the western flank of Mt Seefin (345m), which offers an exhilarating 1km stride to the summit.

Ahakista (Atha an Chiste) consists of a couple of pubs – including the charming, tin-roofed stone pub, the Ahakista Bar (Tin Pub; Ahakista; ⊙ Jun-Sep), aka the Tin Pub, set amid flowering gardens on the waterfront – and a few houses stretched out along the R591. Filled with colourful works of art and cute gifts, the Heron Gallery, Cafe & Gardens (📞 027-67278; www.herongallery.ie; Ahakista; snacks €2.50-5, mains €10; ⊙ 10.30am-5pm year-round, gardens Apr-Aug) is a charming place to pause; cakes are served year-round, and from around April to October its wholesome menu (including falafels, caramelised red onion and goat's cheese tart, and soups such as Thai-spiced parsnip) is excellent. Wildflowers bloom in the gardens.

An ancient stone circle is signposted at the southern end of Ahakista; access is via a short pathway.

The peninsula's other village is Kilcrohane, 6km to the southwest, beside a fine beach.

The peninsula's website (www.thesheeps head.com) has tourist info.

🏃 Activities

Walkers and cyclists will relish the chance to stretch their legs and enjoy the windswept moors, wild gorse, foxgloves and fuchsias in beautiful solitude. On the Goat's Path Rd, the steep Bantry–Kilcrohane section requires strong thighs; the Ahakista–Durrus stretch is more gentle. Bantry's tourist office can book accommodation along the Sheep's Head Way and has lots of info on the peninsula.

The Sheep's Head Way is an 88km-long walking route around the peninsula, on roads and tracks where possible. Use Ordnance Survey maps 85 and 88. There are no campsites on Sheep's Head Peninsula; camping along the route is allowed with permission from the landowner.

The 120km Sheep's Head Cycle Route runs anticlockwise from Ballylickey, round the coastline of Sheep's Head Peninsula, back onto the mainland and down to Ballydehob. There are opportunities to take short cuts or alternative routes (eg over the Goat's Path Rd, or along the coast from Ahakista to Durrus). The widely available brochure, *The Sheep's Head Cycle Route* (available from local tourist offices and bookshops) has full details.

ℹ Getting There & Away

Bantry Rural Transport (p138) buses run a circular route on various days via the Goat's Path Rd to Kilcrohane and Durrus (one way/return €4/6).

OFF THE BEATEN TRACK

PRIEST'S LEAP

If you're a faint-hearted driver, don't even think about heading up the vertiginous, single-car–width, poorly paved road to Priest's Leap, 17km northwest of Bantry. In fact, take this as a warning to watch out for errant GPS routing and avoid it. If you're feeling intrepid, however, this panoramic circuit rewards with monumental views across the mountains to Bantry and the bay beyond.

From Bantry, take the N71 north for 7.9km and turn right after the bridge in Ballylickey (signposted Kilgarvan/Coomhola) and continue for 1.7km. Turn left for 110m, then take your first right, from where the increasingly steep, grass-sprouting track continues for 7.8km to Priest's Leap, marked by a wind-buffeted crucifix. So the story goes, in 1601 Father James Archer was rallying Cork and Kerry's clans to continue resisting the English. English troops spotted him on the old road to Kerry and gave chase until he and his horse leapt from the cliff top and landed in Bantry.

The rest of the drive is a breeze by comparison: continue north for 2.85km, descending into a wooded valley. Turn left and continue for 2km, before turning left again and continuing for 400m, then left onto the N71, from where it's 17.3km east to Glengarriff, then 17.1km southeast back to Bantry.

1. Cheeses
Local produce from Kanturk in County Cork.

2. Traditional restaurant
Hospitality the County Cork way.

3. The English Market (p224)
Dining at this Victorian-era market is a don't-miss in Cork City.

4. Fresh bread
Artisan breads are a specialty of the region.

GOUGANE BARRA FOREST PARK

Gougane Barra (www.goganebarra.com) is a truly magical part of inland County Cork. It's almost alpine in feel, with spectacular vistas of craggy mountains, silver streams and pine forests sweeping down to a mountain lake, the source of the River Lee. St Fin Barre, the founder of Cork, established a monastery here in the 6th century. He had a hermitage on the island in Gougane Barra Lake (Lough an Ghugain), which is now approached by a short causeway. The small chapel on the island has fine stained-glass representations of obscure Celtic saints. A road runs through the park in a loop, but you're better off slowing down and walking the well-marked network of paths and nature trails through the forest.

The only place to air your hiking boots is the Gougane Barra Hotel (026-47069; www.goganebarrahotel.com; d from €110, 2-/4-course menu €21.45/27; restaurant 12.30-2.30pm & 6-8.30pm Mon-Sat, 12.45-2.30pm & 6-7pm Sun) There's an on-site restaurant, a cafe and a pub next door. The hotel runs a summer theatre festival.

Bus connections are limited; call the hotel for details and possible pick-up part way.

The park is signposted on the R584 after Ballingeary. Returning to the main road afterwards and continuing west, you'll travel over the Pass of Keimaneigh and emerge on the N71 at Ballylickey, midway between the Beara Peninsula and the Sheep's Head Peninsula

BEARA PENINSULA (RING OF BEARA)

After Kerry and Dingle, the Beara Peninsula is the third major 'ring' (circular road around a peninsula) in the west. A small part of the peninsula lies in Kerry, but is covered here for convenience.

You can easily drive the 137km around the coast in one day, but you would miss the spectacular Healy Pass Road (R574), which cuts across the peninsula from Cork to Kerry. In fact, if pressed for time, skip the rest and do the pass.

The south side, along Bantry Bay, is a series of working fishing villages. The north side, in contrast, is a stunner, with craggy roads in and out of the nooks and crannies of the peninsula. Many are off the tourist trail.

Other highlights include a thrillingly wobbly cable car at the tip of the peninsula out to tiny Dursey Island, and exhilarating hill walking requiring some skill and commitment, as well as proper clothing and navigational experience.

The 196km Beara Way is a signposted walk linking Glengarriff with Kenmare (in Kerry) via Castletownbere, Bere Island, Dursey Island and the north side of the peninsula. The 138km Beara Way Cycle Route takes a similar direction, passing through all the villages on Beara via small lanes.

The following section starts in Glengarriff and travels clockwise to Kenmare.

Glengarriff

POP 1100

Hidden deep in the wooded Bantry Bay area, Glengarriff (Gleann Garbh; www.glengarriff. ie) is an attractive village that snares plenty of passers-by in need of sweaters.

Nearby, the rough, rocky Caha Mountains make for good hill walking, and, if you're game, an exhilarating drive to Priest's Leap (p253). There are plenty of gentler strolls in and around town, too, in mature oak woodlands and through the coastal Blue Pool Amenity Area, where seals, perched on submerged rocks, appear to levitate on the water.

In the second half of the 19th century Glengarriff became a popular retreat for prosperous Victorians, who sailed from England, took the train to Bantry, then chugged over to the village in a paddle steamer. By 1850 the road to Kenmare had been blasted through the mountains and the link with Killarney was established. Today Glengarriff lies on the main Cork to Killarney road (N71).

◉ Sights

Wander down past the Blue Ferry pier and enjoy good nature walks along the coast. Signs with maps show you your options.

★ Garinish (Ilnacullin) Island   GARDENS
(027-63040; www.heritageireland.ie; adult/senior & child €4/2; 9.30am-6.30pm Mon-Sat, 11am-6pm Sun Jul & Aug, shorter hours in Apr-Jun & Sep-Oct, closed Nov-Mar, last admission 1hr before closing) Subtropical plants flourish in the

Beara Peninsula (Ring of Beara)

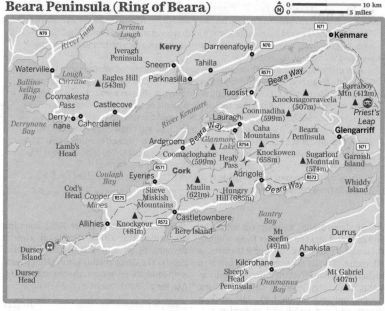

N 0 ——— 10 km
0 ——— 5 miles

Deriana Lough
N70
River Inny
Iveragh Peninsula
Kerry
Darreenafoyle N70
N71
•Kenmare
Waterville•
Lough Currane
Sneem •
Tahilla
Ballin-skelligs Bay
Eagles Hill ▲ (543m)
Parknasilla•
R571
Beara Way
Coomakesta Pass
Castlecove
Tuosist •
Knocknagorraveela (307m)
Barraboy Mtn (412m)
Derry-nane • Caherdaniel
River Kenmare
Lauragh •
Coomnadiha ▲ (599m)
Caha Mountains
Priest's Leap
Derrynane Bay
Beara Way
Glanmore Lake R754
Beara Peninsula
Glengarriff
Lamb's Head
Ardgroom •
Coomacloghane ▲ (599m)
Healy Pass
Knockowen (658m)
Sugarloaf Mountain ▲ (574m)
N71
Garnish Island
Coulagh Bay
Eyeries •
R571
Cork
Adrigole •
R572
Whiddy Island
Cod's Head
Copper Mines R575
Slieve Miskish Mountains
Maulin ▲ (621m)
Hungry Hill (685m)
Beara Way
Allihies •
Knockgour ▲ (481m)
R572
Castletownbere
Bantry Bay
Bere Island
Mt Seefin (491m)
Ahakista
Durrus •
Dursey Island
Dursey Head
Kilcrohane
Sheep's Head Peninsula
Dunmanus Bay
Mt Gabriel (407m)

rich soil and warm climate of the magical Italianate garden on Garinish Island, with camellias, magnolias and rhododendrons providing a seasonal blaze of colour. There are good views from a Grecian temple at the end of a cypress avenue, and a spectacular panorama from the top of the 19th-century Martello tower, built to watch out for a possible Napoleonic invasion.

This little miracle of a place was created in the early 20th century, when the island's owner, Annan Bryce, commissioned the English architect Harold Peto to design a garden on the then-barren outcrop.

The 10-minute boat trip to the island passes colonies of basking seals – try to time your trip for early morning when you're most likely to spot them. Ferry companies Blue Pool Ferry (☑027-63333; www.bluepool ferry.com), departing from a little cover near the Glengarriff village centre, and Harbour Queen Ferries (☑027-63116, 087 234 5861; www.harbourqueenferry.com), departing opposite Eccles Hotel, leave every 20 to 30 minutes when the garden is open. The return boat fare (adult/child €10/5) doesn't include entry to the gardens.

Bamboo Park GARDENS
(☑027-63007; www.bamboo-park.com; adult/child €6/free; ☺9am-7pm) Glengarriff's mild, frost-free climate allows this small 12-hectare park to flourish. It has a variety of exotic plants, including palm trees and tree ferns, as well as coastal woodland walks.

Glengarriff Woods Nature Reserve NATURE RESERVE
(☑027-63636; www.glengarriffnaturereserve.ie) **FREE** The 300-hectare ancient woodland lining Glengarriff's glacial valley was owned by the White family of Bantry House in the 18th century. The thick tree cover maintains humid conditions that allow ferns and mosses to flourish.

The woodlands and bogs are also home to Ireland's only arboreal ant and the rare and protected Kerry slug. If you're lucky, you'll see these spotty, cream-coloured gastropods on the lichen carpet munching after rainfall.

There are five marked trails through the reserve, separately covering woodland, mountain, river and meadow, ranging from 0.5km to 3km, which leave from the car park. Note there are no public toilets.

The entrance is about 1km from Glengarriff on the N71 towards Kenmare on your left.

Ewe Sculpture Gardens GARDENS
(☑027-63840; www.theewe.com; Toreen; adult/child €6.50/5; ☺10am-6pm Easter-Sep)

BEARA WAY

This moderately easy 196km walk forms a loop around the Beara Peninsula. The peninsula is relatively unused to mass tourism and makes a pleasant contrast with the Iveragh Peninsula to the north.

Part of the walk, between Castletownbere and Glengarriff, follows the route taken by Donal O'Sullivan and his band after the English took his castle following an 11-day siege in 1602. At Glengarriff, O'Sullivan met up with other families and set out on a journey north, hoping to reunite with other remaining pockets of Gaelic resistance. Of the 1000 or so men who set out that winter, only 30 completed the trek.

The Beara Way mostly follows old roads and tracks and rarely rises above 340m. There's no official start or finish point and the route can be walked in either direction. It could easily be reduced to seven days by skipping Bere and Dursey Islands and, if you start at Castletownbere, you could reach Kenmare in five days or less.

There's a good downloadable guide to the walk (and the peninsula itself) at Beara Tourism (www.bearatourism.com).

A giant sheep driving a vintage car marks the entrance and sets the tone for these whimsical sculpture gardens. Set over 2 hectares, a kilometre of trails takes you past sculptures including a bikini-wearing rhino, a handbag-toting emu, bicycle-riding fish and a pig blissing out in a bubble bath. The gardens incorporate a waterfall and magical mountain and sea views. The property is solar- and hydro-powered; the artist-owners also have a gallery and cafe on site.

The gardens are 4.5km northwest of Glengarriff on the N71 (on your right as you're coming from Glengarriff). Call ahead as opening times can vary.

🛌 Sleeping & Eating

Glengarriff Caravan & Camping Park   CAMPGROUND €
(📞 027-63154; glengarriffccp@gmail.com; Castletownbere Rd; campsites from €10; ⊙ Apr-Oct) This well-set-up park, 4km west of Glengarriff on the road to Castletownbere, enjoys a woodland setting. Amenities include a games room and a licensed bar staging traditional music most nights from June to August.

Murphy's Village Hostel   HOSTEL €
(📞 027-63555; www.murphyshostel.com; Main St; dm/d €15/40; ⊙ Jun-Sep) Right at the heart of Glengarriff, Murphy's is basic and convenient, with clean rooms furnished with wooden bunks. There's a small self-catering kitchen.

Eccles Hotel   HISTORIC HOTEL €€
(📞 027-63003; www.eccleshotel.com; Glengarriff Harbour; d from €100, bar food €4-12, restaurant mains €10-22; ⊙ bar food noon-4pm, restaurant 6-10pm; closed Nov-Mar; @) Just east of the centre, the grande-dame Eccles has a long and distinguished history (since 1745), counting the British War Office, Thackeray, George Bernard Shaw and WB Yeats as former guests. The decor retains some 19th-century grandeur; its 66 rooms are big and bright. Ask for a bayside room on the 4th floor.

Casey's Hotel   HOTEL €€
(📞 027-63010; www.caseyshotelglengarriff.ie; Main St; s €55-80, d €90-140; @ 🖥) Old-fashioned Casey's has been welcoming guests since 1884 (Éamon de Valera stayed here). The 19 rooms have been modernised a bit but are still small. It's got stacks of atmosphere, though, and the vast terrace is a treat. The bar (bar snacks €12-20; ⊙ noon-9.30pm) serves classics such as beef and Guinness pie; the restaurant (mains €14.50-26; ⊙ 6.30-9.30pm) ups the ante with crabmeat-stuffed salmon and honey-roasted half duck.

🍷 Drinking & Nightlife

P Harrington's   PUB
(Main St) This pub has a prime position at the junction of the N71 and the Beara Rd. Settle into one of the comfy outside benches with a pint.

❶ Getting There & Away

Bus Éireann has up to three buses daily to Bantry (€4.70, 25 minutes) and on to Cork (€19.70, 2½ hours).

Glengarriff to Castletownbere

The striations of the peninsula's underlying bedrock become evident as you drive west from Glengarriff towards Castletownbere. On the highest hills, Sugarloaf Mountain and Hungry Hill, rock walls known as 'benches' snake backwards and forwards across the slopes. They can make walking on these mountains quite challenging, and dangerous in fog. Take a map (Ordnance Survey Discovery series 84 and 85 cover the area) and compass if venturing into the hills, and seek local advice.

Adrigole is a scattered strip of houses. The West Cork Sailing Centre (☑027-60132; www.westcorksailing.com; The Boat House, Adrigole) organises skippered sailing boats, and also rents kayaks (per hour €12).

From Adrigole, a serpentine road travels 11km north across the other-worldly Healy Pass to Lauragh, offering spectacular views of the rocky inland scenery.

Castletownbere & Around

POP 900

Castletownbere (Baile Chais Bhéara) is a fishing town first and a pause in the road for tourists second. And that gives it great appeal for those looking for the 'real' Ireland. That's not to say it doesn't have its popular sights, particularly a world-famous pub: McCarthy's Bar.

On Main St and the Square, you'll find ATMs as well as cafes, pubs and grocery stores.

◉ Sights

On a lonely hill 2km from Castletownbere, the impressive Derreenataggart Stone Circle, consisting of 10 stones, can be found close to the roadside. It's signposted at a turn-off to the right at the western end of town. There are several other standing stones in the surrounding area.

Looming offshore, Bere Island makes Castletownbere seem like the big city. Only 12km by 7km, it has a couple of hundred permanent residents but attracts scores more to summer holiday homes. There are bits of old ruins and some craggy coves good for swimming. Bere Island Ferry (☑027-75009; www.bereislandferries.com; passenger/car return €8/25; ⊙every 90min Mon-Sat Jun-Aug, less often Sun & Sep-May) leaves from town but drops you in a remote part of the island. Alternatively, Murphy's Ferry Service (☑027-75014; www.murphysferry.com; pedestrian/car return from €8/25), departing from Pontoon pier, 5km east of Castletownbere, docks by the island's

main village, Rerrin, which has a shop, pub, cafe and accommodation.

🛏 Sleeping & Eating

Rodeen B&B   B&B €€
(☑027-70158; www.rodeencountryhouse.com; s/d €40/70; ⊙Apr-Nov) A delightful, six-room haven, tucked away above the eastern approach to town. The musical instrument–filled house has stunning sea views and is surrounded by gardens full of crumbling Delphic columns. Flowers from the garden grace the breakfast table, and there are home-baked scones with honey from landlady Ellen's bees.

Taste   DELI €
(☑027-71842; Main St; dishes €4-5; ⊙9am-5.30pm Mon-Wed, 9am-6pm Thu & Fri, 10am-2pm Sat) A wide range of local foods, including creamy Milleens cheese, is on offer, along with creative sandwiches to take away.

Olde Bakery   MODERN IRISH €€
(☑027-70869; Castletown House; mains €13-23; ⊙5.30-9.30pm daily year-round, plus noon-4.30pm Sun Apr-Sep) One of the best restaurants in town, the Olde Bakery serves top regional seafood. A few tables out the front are ideal on a long evening.

Jack Patrick's   INTERNATIONAL €€
(☑027-70319; Main St; mains €10-20; ⊙noon-9pm Jun-Sep, noon-7pm Oct-May) Run by one of the top local butchers – the shop is next door – this simple restaurant is the place for steaks, chops and other meaty mains such as bacon and cabbage.

🍺 Drinking & Nightlife

McCarthy's Bar   PUB
(Main St) If you're carrying an original copy of the late Pete McCarthy's bestseller, *McCarthy's Bar*, you'll be excited to see the front-cover photo in three dimensions. McCarthy's is a grocery as well as a pub, if you fancy a tin of peaches and a can of corn to go with your Beamish. There's frequent live music and a wee snug inside the door.

🛍 Shopping

Issie's Handmade Chocolate   CHOCOLATE
(www.issieshandmadechocolate.ie; Main St; ⊙noon-6pm) This cornflower-blue shop sells artisan chocolates as well as hot chocolate, homemade ice cream and a rainbow of old-fashioned sweets.

ℹ Information

Tourist office (☑027-70054; www.bearatour ism.com; Main St; ◎9am-5.30pm Mon-Fri) Just outside the Church of Ireland.

ℹ Getting There & Away

Bus Éireann (www.buseireann.ie) has up to two buses daily to Bantry (€12.50) and on to Cork (€19; 3¼ hours).

Dursey Island

POP 6

Tiny Dursey Island, at the end of the peninsula, is reached by Ireland's only cable car (☑028-21766; adult/child return €8/2; ◎9-11am, 2.30-5pm & 7-8pm Mon-Sat, 9-10.30am, 1-2.30pm & 7-8pm Sun plus 4-5pm Sun Jun-Aug), a rickety 1960s contraption which sways precariously 30m above Dursey Sound. The later times listed here are for returning only; bikes are not allowed.

The island, just 6.6km long by 1.5km wide, is a wild bird and whale sanctuary, and dolphins can sometimes be seen swimming in the surrounding waters. There's no accommodation, but camping is legal, as long as you respect the common rules and clean up after yourself.

The Beara Way loops round the island for 11km, and the signal tower is an obvious destination for a short walk.

Northside of the Beara

The entire north side is the scenic highlight of the Beara Peninsula. A series of roads, some of them single-lane tracks, snake around the ins and outs of the weathered, rugged coast. Boulder-strewn fields tumble dramatically towards the ocean and it's blissfully remote – your only company along some stretches are flocks of sheep and the odd sheepdog.

Allihies

The edge-of-the-world village of Allihies (Na hAilichí) has dramatic vistas, plenty of walks and a long history of mining.

Copper-ore deposits were first identified on the far Beara in 1810. While mining quickly brought wealth to the Puxley family who owned the land, it brought low wages and dangerous, unhealthy working conditions for the labour force, which at one time numbered 1300. Experienced Cornish min-

ers were brought into the area, and the dramatic ruins of engine houses replicate those of Cornwall's coastal tin mines. As late as the 1930s, more than 30,000 tonnes of pure copper were exported annually, but by 1962 the last mine was closed.

You'll see the most mine ruins along the R575 north of the village; signs mark the spots. In town the Allihies Copper Mine Museum (☑027-73218; www.acmm.ie; adult/child €5/2; ◎10am-4.30pm daily May-Sep, Sat & Sun Oct-Apr; ☞) is the result of years of work by the community and has engaging exhibits plus tourist information and a cafe.

🍴 Sleeping & Eating

Allihies Village Hostel HOSTEL €
(☑027-73107; www.allihieshostel.net; dm/d €18/50; 🖥) This bright, welcoming hostel has spotless wood-floored dorms and common areas, a courtyard and a barbecue area. Host Michael is a mine of information on the area and can advise on local walks and pony trekking.

Sea View Guesthouse GUESTHOUSE €€
(☑027-73004; www.seaviewallihies.com; Allihies; s/d €45/75) Clean, tidy and basic, the 10 rooms in this two-storey yellow building have an abundance of pine; some have views north over the waters. The spread at breakfast will help fuel your rambles.

O'Neill's PUB €€
(☑027-73008; mains €11-23; ◎pub food noon-8pm Mon-Thu, to 9pm Fri-Sun) The most appealing pub in town, with a tidy red and blue facade and some polished wooden benches and picnic tables out the front for enjoying the views. Pub standards intermingle with fresh local seafood.

Eyeries to Lauragh

Heading north and east from Allihies, the beautiful coastal road (R575), with hedges of fuchsias and rhododendrons, twists and turns for about 12km to Eyeries. This cluster of brightly coloured houses overlooking Coulagh Bay is often used as a film set. The town is also home to Milleens cheese (☑027-74079; www.milleenscheese.com; ◎by appointment), from pioneering producer Veronica Steele. She welcomes visitors to her farm; phone ahead.

From Eyeries, forsake the R571 for the even smaller coast roads (lanes really) to the north and east. This is the Beara at its most spectacular – and intimate. Tiny coves are like pearls in a sea of rocks and the views of the Ring of Kerry to the north are sublime.

Rejoin the R571 at the crossroads of **Ardgroom** (Ard Dhór). As you head east towards Lauragh, look for signs pointing to the Ardgroom **stone circle**, an unusual Bronze Age monument with nine tall, thin uprights. There's muddy parking at the end of a 500m-long narrow approach lane. The circle is visible about 200m away and a path leads to it across bogland. A crude sign says simply 'money' and a US dollar under a rock gives a hint.

Further along the R571, about 1km before Lauragh, is a road to **Glanmore Lake**, with the remains of an old hermitage on a tiny island in the middle. There are walking opportunities in the area, but gaining access can be problematic: ask locally for advice.

Lauragh (Laith Reach), situated northeast of Ardgroom, is in County Kerry. It's home to the **Derreen Gardens** (☑064-668 3588; adult/child €7/2; ◷10am-6pm), planted by the fifth Lord Lansdowne around the turn of the 20th century. Mossy paths weave through an abundance of interesting plants, including spectacular New Zealand tree ferns and red cedars, and you may see seals on the shore.

🛏 Sleeping & Eating

Glanmore Lake Hostel   HOSTEL €
(☑064-83181; www.uniqueirishhostels.com; Glanmore Lake; dm adult/child from €17/14; ◷end May–end Sep; 🐾) A rural atmosphere and an engaging location at the heart of Glanmore make this remote hostel an appealing place. It's in Glanmore's old schoolhouse, 5km from the R571.

★ **Josie's Lakeview House**   MODERN IRISH €€
(☑064-83155; www.josiesrestaurant.ie; Glanmore Lake; lunch mains €7-14, dinner mains €11-25; ◷from 10.30am) Captivating lake views accompany scrumptious, home-cooked food at Josie's, set on a hill overlooking forest-shrouded Glanmore Lake. Choose from salads and sandwiches for lunch, cakes at tea or heartier rack of lamb and local seafood specials at night; ask about B&B (double €70) or self-catering cottage accommodation to prolong the experience. Josie's is 4km from the R571; follow the signs.

❶ Getting There & Away

Bus Éireann (☑021-450 8188; www.buseireann.ie) has two buses a day between Kenmare and Castletownbere (€12.50, 40 minutes) via Lauragh (€7.10).

Lauragh to Kenmare

Leaving Lauragh, take the R573, which hugs the coast, rejoining the more no-nonsense R571 at Tuosist for the 16km run east to Kenmare in Kerry.

NORTHERN CORK

Northern Cork lacks the dramatic scenery and romantic appeal of the county's coastal regions, but the area's towns and villages have a refreshing rural integrity.

Mallow

Located in the Blackwater Valley on the main N20 highway, Mallow (Mala) is the county's largest town after Cork City. Visitors to its spa in the 19th century christened it the 'Bath of Ireland'. The comparison is far-fetched these days, though the architecture in the town centre hints at its former grandeur.

Up a flight of stairs in the town hall on the main street (opposite the **statue** of local politician JJ Fitzgerald), the **tourist office** (☑022-42222; www.visitmallow.ie; Thomas Davis St; ◷9.30am-1pm & 2-5.30pm Mon-Fri) can help with accommodation and activities.

You can spot white fallow deer around the imposing ruins of **Mallow Castle** (Bridge St), which dates back to 1585. Also look out for the distinctive **Clock House** (Bridge St), designed by an amateur architect after an alpine holiday – you'd never guess.

Around Mallow

Red deer scamper around the 60 hectares of landscaped gardens at **Doneraile Park** (◷8am-8pm Mon-Fri, 9am-8pm Sat & Sun, reduced hours in winter) **FREE**, 13km northeast of Mallow. There are woodland walkways, cascades and playgrounds to keep the kids happy.

At Buttevant, about 20km north of Mallow on the N20, are the ruins of a 13th-century **Franciscan abbey**.

In the small town of Liscarroll, on the R522 13km west of Buttevant, is the heartwarming **Donkey Sanctuary** (☑022-48398; www.thedonkeysanctuary.ie; Liscarroll; ◷9am-4.30pm Mon-Fri, 10am-5pm Sat & Sun) **FREE**, dedicated to rescuing Ireland's iconic beasts of burden. At this large, nonprofit farm, abandoned and abused donkeys are given a home for life. There are pastures, food, medical care and virtually no demands on them. There are some scenic ruins of a castle close by.

Between Mallow and Killarney, you might want to divert to see the well-preserved remains of 17th-century **Kanturk Castle**. Inhabited only by crows these days, the castle acted as both fortification and country house from the early 17th century to 1906.

County Kerry

POP 145,000 / AREA 4746 SQ KM

Best Places to Eat

➜ Jacks Coastguard
Restaurant (p282)

➜ Smuggler's Inn (p286)

➜ Out of the Blue (p298)

➜ Spillane's (p303)

Best Places to Stay

➜ Gormans Clifftop House
(p302)

➜ Aghadoe Heights Hotel
(p276)

➜ Teach de Broc (p309)

➜ Parknasilla Resort & Spa
(p287)

Why Go?

County Kerry contains some of Ireland's most iconic scenery: impossibly crenulated coastlines, endless green fields criss-crossed by tumbledown stone walls, and mist-shrouded mountain peaks and bogs.

With one of the country's finest national parks as its backyard, the lively tourism hub of Killarney spills over with colourful shops, restaurants and pubs with spirited trad sessions. Killarney is the jumping-off point for Kerry's two famed loop drives. The larger Ring of Kerry skirts the Iveragh Peninsula, fringed by islands scattered offshore. The compact Dingle Peninsula is like a condensed version of its southern neighbour, with ancient sites, sandy beaches and glimpses of a hard, unforgiving land.

Kerry's exquisite beauty makes it one of Ireland's most popular tourist destinations. But if you need to escape from the crowds, there's always a mountain pass, an isolated cove or an untrodden trail to discover.

When to Go?

Scads of festivals take place throughout the county during the warmer months, particularly June to August (when you'll need to book accommodation well ahead). These are some of the highlights on Kerry's annual calendar are:

➜ Listowel's Writers' Week is in June .

➜ Dingle town has races and a regatta in August.

➜ Killorglin's Puck Festival, which dates back at least as far as the 17th century is also held in August.

Even in the depths of winter, you'll find storytellers and musicians taking part in impromptu sessions in pubs throughout the county.

County Kerry Highlights

1 Row from Ross Castle across the Lower Lake to historic Inisfallen Island in **Killarney National Park** (p271)

2 Cycle through the dramatic **Gap of Dunloe** (p275)

3 Scuba-dive the crystal-clear waters around Castlegregory (p303)

4 Tour the Dingle Brewing Company and sample a pint before savouring seafood straight off the boats in charming **Dingle Town** (p292)

5 Tee off at the spectacularly sited **Waterville Golf Links** (p286), framed by the ocean on the Ring of Kerry

6 Clip-clop around **Killarney** (p265) in a horse-drawn jaunting car

7 Island-hop around the rocky **Skelligs** (p284) and evacuated **Blaskets** (p300)

8 Cruise through fresh and saltwater habitats on a safari at the **Tralee Bay Wetlands Centre** (p304)

KILLARNEY

POP 12,750

As a town that's been practising the tourism game for over 250 years, Killarney is a well-oiled machine in the middle of the sublime scenery of its namesake national park. Beyond the obvious proximity to lakes, waterfalls, woodland and moors dwarfed by 1000m-plus peaks, it has many charms of its own. Competition keeps standards high and, no matter your budget, you can expect to find good restaurants, fine pubs and plenty of accommodation.

Killarney and its surrounds have been inhabited probably since the Neolithic period and were certainly important Bronze Age settlements, based on the copper ore mined on Ross Island. Killarney changed hands between warring tribes, the most notable of which were the Fir Bolg ('bag men'), expert stonemasons who built forts and devised Ogham script. It wasn't until much later, in the 17th century, that Viscount Kenmare developed the town as an Irish version of England's Lake District. Among its many notable 19th-century tourists were Queen Victoria and the Romantic poet Percy Bysshe Shelley, who began *Queen Mab* here.

Mobbed in summer, Killarney is perhaps at its best in the late spring and early autumn when you can enjoy its outdoor pursuits and the crowds are manageable.

◉ Sights & Activities

Killarney's biggest attraction, in every sense, is Killarney National Park (p271). The town itself can easily be explored on foot in an hour or two.

St Mary's Cathedral   CATHEDRAL
(Cathedral Pl) Built between 1842 and 1855, St Mary's Cathedral is a superb example of neo-Gothic revival architecture. Designed by Augustus Pugin, the cruciform building was inspired by Ardfert Cathedral, near Tralee.

Franciscan Friary   FRIARY
(Fair Hill) This 1860s Franciscan friary displays an ornate Flemish-style altarpiece, some impressive tile work and, most notably, stained-glass windows by Harry Clarke. The Dublin artist's organic style was influenced by art nouveau, art deco and symbolism.

Fishing   FISHING
(www.fishinginireland.info) Fishing for brown trout in Killarney National Park's lakes is free. You can fish for trout and salmon in the Rivers Flesk and Laune (per day €25 to €35); a state salmon licence is required (€40 for three weeks). O'Neill's (☑ 064-6631 970; 6 Plunkett St; ⊙ 10am-9.30pm Mon-Fri, 10am-9pm Sat & Sun), which looks like a gift shop but is a long-established fishing centre, has information, permits and licences and rents equipment.

Killarney Golf & Fishing Club   GOLF, FISHING
(☑ 064-663 1034; www.killarney-golf.com; green fees from €75) Killarney Golf & Fishing Club, 3.4km west of town on the N72, has three championship golf courses: two alongside Lough Leane, one with artificial lakes, and all with mountain views.

✦ Festivals & Events

Rally of the Lakes   CAR RALLY
(www.rallyofthelakes.com; ⊙ late Apr/early May) Drivers take death-defying twists and turns around the lakes and mountains over the May bank holiday weekend. (Take care: cars often speed around Killarney's streets after the official stages.)

Killarney Summerfest   OUTDOOR ACTIVITIES
(www.killarneysummerfest.com; ⊙ late Jul/early Aug) Horse riding, canoeing, kayaking and walking are part of this family-oriented festival, in addition to art workshops and street performers.

⌕ Sleeping

You'll find numerous B&Bs just outside the centre on Rock, Lewis and Muckross Rds. The town also has scores of generic hotels aimed at tour groups. Many places offer bike hire (around €12 per day) and discounted tours. Book ahead everywhere in summer.

Railway Hostel   HOSTEL €
(☑ 064-663 5299; www.killarneyhostel.com; Fair Hill; dm €14-20, s/d from €45/52; @ �) Fronted by a terrace with picnic tables, this tucked-away place near the train station is about as inviting as hostels get, with bunks nestling in nooks, and maps and cycling itineraries on the walls. Private rooms have their

---

TRACING YOUR ANCESTORS

County Kerry currently has no genealogy centre, but some church records are available free of charge on the Irish Genealogy (www.irishgenealogy.ie) website.

KERRY FARMERS MARKETS

Farmers markets throughout County Kerry vary depending on the season. For updated details of towns hosting markets, visit www.kerryfarmersmarkets.com.

own bathrooms; prices include continental breakfast.

Killarney Flesk Caravan & Camping Park CAMPGROUND €
(☑064-663 1704; www.killarneyfleskcamping.com; Muckross Rd; campsites per campervan plus 2 persons €26, hiker €10; ⊙Jun-Sep; ☎⬛) About 1.3km south of town on the N71, this well-tended park is surrounded by woods and has majestic mountain views. Facilities include bike hire, a supermarket, cafe and bar.

Súgán Hostel HOSTEL €
(☑064-663 3104; www.killarneysuganhostel.com; Lewis Rd; dm €12-15, tw €38; ☎) Behind its pub-like front, 250-year-old Súgán is an amiably eccentric hostel with an open fire in the cosy common room, low, crazy-cornered ceilings and hardwood floors. Note that it's an alcohol-free zone, which is either a good thing or a bad thing, depending on your point of view.

Neptune's Killarney Town Hostel HOSTEL €
(☑064-663 5255; www.neptuneshostel.com; Bishop's Lane, New St; dm €16-20, s/d from €30/44; @☎) ✎ Neptune's dorms can sleep over 150, but this central hostel feels much smaller thanks to the roaring fire in reception and the staff's unfailing helpfulness. There's a laundry service; rates include breakfast.

★**Crystal Springs** B&B €€
(☑064-663 3272; www.crystalspringsbb.com; Ballycasheen Cross; s/d from €45/70; ☎⬛) You can cast a line from the timber deck of this wonderfully relaxing riverside B&B or just laze about on the adjacent lawn. Rooms are richly furnished, with patterned wallpapers and walnut timber; private bathrooms (most with spa baths) are huge. The glass-enclosed breakfast room also overlooks the rushing River Flesk. It's about a 15-minute stroll to town.

Murphy's of Killarney INN €€
(☑064-663 1294; www.murphysofkillarney.com; College St; d from €85; ☎) A great midrange option close to the action. Murphy's 20 rooms

have been stylishly refurbished – ask for one overlooking the street. If it's lashing rain, you won't have to leave as there's a highly respected restaurant and pub on site.

Fairview B&B €€
(☑064-663 4164; www.fairviewkillarney.com; Lewis Rd; d from €90; @☎) Done out in beautiful timbers, the individually decorated rooms (some with classical printed wallpaper, some with contemporary sofas and glass) at this boutique guesthouse offer better bang for your buck than bigger, less personal places around town. A veritable feast is laid on at breakfast; the elegant onsite restaurant is a winner come evening.

Killarney Haven APARTMENTS €€
(☑064-663 3570; www.killarney-selfcatering.com; High St; apt per week from €475; ⬛) Great central base. Contemporary apartments open onto balconies and have full kitchens.

Kingfisher Lodge B&B €€
(☑064-663 7131; www.kingfisherlodgekillarney.com; Lewis Rd; s/d €65/100; ⊙closed Jan; @☎) Lovely back gardens are a highlight at this immaculate B&B, whose 11 rooms are done out in vivid yellows, reds and pinks. Owner Donal Carroll is a certified walking guide with a wealth of knowledge on hiking in the area.

Chelmsford House B&B €€
(☑064-663 6402; www.chelmsfordguesthouse.com; Muckross View, Countess Grove; d from €60; @☎⬛) Overlooking the lake and the mountains, gardens frame the entrance of this friendly B&B. Rooms with private bathrooms are bright and airy, with timber floors and a minimum of frills. It's a 10-minute stroll into town.

Algret House B&B €€
(☑064-663 2337; www.algret.com; Countess Grove; s/d €40/80; ☎⬛) Knotted pine dominates the decor of this light, bright B&B a five-minute walk from the centre.

Killarney Plaza Hotel HOTEL €€€
(☑064-662 1100; www.killarneyplaza.com; Kenmare Pl; s/d from €115/160; @☎⬛⬛) Dominating the view of the south end of Main St, on the edge of Killarney National Park, this large, 198-room hotel is built in a brilliant white traditional style. Classically furnished guest rooms and public facilities are in keeping with its class; besides the marble lobby and lavishly tiled indoor pool, there's a sauna, steam room and spa, and three restaurants.

Killarney

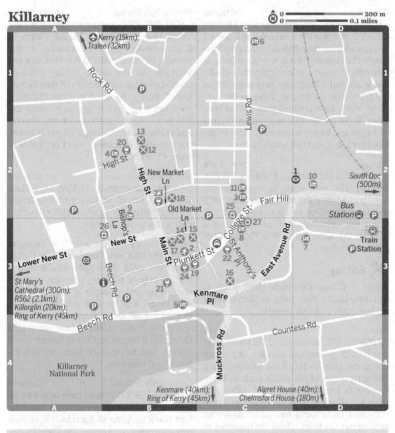

Killarney

Malton   HOTEL €€€

(☎064-663 8000; www.themalton.com; s/d from €120/180; @ 🛜 ⛵ 🅿) So commanding it doesn't need an address, the pillared, ivy-covered Malton in the centre of town is a throwback to Victorian elegance – at least from the outside. Inside it's had a thorough strip-and-refit; of the 172 rooms, the pick are those in the 1852 wing, which have retained their period opulence. There are several stunning restaurants and a spa and leisure centre with a 17m swimming pool, gym and two tennis courts.

Europe   LUXURY HOTEL €€€

(☎064-667 1300; Fossa; s/d from €240/260; @ 🛜 ⛵) The last word in contemporary five-star luxury, right on the lakeshore with indoor and outdoor swimming pools, a decadent spa, dedicated staff and discounted rates at the Killarney Golf & Fishing Club (p265) next door.

🍴 Eating

Many of Killarney's hotels have excellent restaurants. As elsewhere in Kerry, fresh seafood stars on many menus.

Jam   CAFE €

(☎064-663 7716; www.jam.ie; 77 Old Market Lane; mains €5-11; ⊙8am-6pm Mon-Sat; 🅿) Duck down the alley to this local hideout for a changing menu of hot meals such as Kerry shepherd's pie, deli items, and coffee and cake. It's all made with locally sourced produce and there are a few tables under an awning out the front. There are branches in Kenmare and Castleisland, and in Cork.

Lir Café   CAFE €

(☎064-663 3859; www.lircafe.com; Kenmare Pl; dishes €3-6; ⊙8am-9.30pm Mon-Sat, 8am-7pm Sun; 🛜) Food is limited to cakes, biscuits and the real treat, handmade chocolates, including Bailey's truffles. Great coffee, hip atmosphere.

Pay As You Please   INTERNATIONAL €

(☎087 190 2567; www.payasyouplease.ie; New Market Lane; ⊙12.30-4pm Thu-Sat, 7-10pm Fri & Sat, noon-4pm Sun) You guessed it, the premise at the casual PAYP is that you pay what you feel your meal is worth – although that's somewhat negated by the menu's 'suggested' prices (from €4 to €12). But it's a good bet for its crispy pizzas, crunchy salads and desserts, such as lemon, almond and polenta cake. Although it's not licensed, you can BYO; corkage costs €4 per bottle of wine, €1 per beer.

Murphy's Ice Cream   ICE CREAM €

(www.murphysicecream.ie; 37 Main St; ⊙11am-10.30pm) A branch of the superlative Dingle ice-cream maker, with wonderfully thick hot chocolates including chilli.

Smoke House   BISTRO €€

(☎064-662 0801; www.thesmokehouse.ie; High St; lunch mains €7-14, dinner mains €15-28; ⊙9am-late; 🅿) One of Killarney's busiest ventures since it opened a couple of years ago, this tiled bistro was the first establishment in Ireland to cook with a Josper (Spanish charcoal oven). Stylish salads include Norwegian king crab; its Kerry surf'n'turf burger – with prawns and house-made barbecue sauce – has a local following.

La Rambla Bistro   SPANISH €€

(☎064-663 9813; Old Market Lane; tapas €4-6.50, mains €15.50-22.50; ⊙4pm-midnight) The next best thing to flying to Barcelona is visiting this clattering, timber-floored Catalan restaurant. Tapas dishes including *tocino a la parrilla* (crispy pork belly) and deep-fried *manchego* (ewe's cheese) with tomato salsa, and mains such as *mejillones a la catalana* (mussels with spicy sausage and garlic) are as authentic as they come. Lots of Spanish wines by the glass and great sangria too.

KERRY WAY

The 214km **Kerry Way** (www.kerryway.com) is the Republic's longest way-marked footpath and is usually walked anticlockwise. Starting and ending in Killarney, it stays inland for the first three days, winding through the spectacular Macgillycuddy's Reeks and past 1039m Mt Carrantuohil, Ireland's highest mountain, before continuing around the Ring of Kerry coast through Cahirciveen, Waterville, Caherdaniel, Sneem and Kenmare.

You could complete the walk in about 10 days, provided you're up to a good 20km per day. With less time it's worth walking the first three days, as far as Glenbeigh, from where a bus or a lift could return you to Killarney.

Accommodation isn't a problem, but places to eat are few; consider carrying your own food. Ordnance Survey Discovery Series maps 78, 83 and 84 cover the walk.

Brícín
IRISH €€
(www.bricin.com; 26 High St; mains €19-26; ⊙6-9.30pm Tue-Sat) Decorated with fittings from a convent, an orphanage and a school, this Celtic deco restaurant doubles as the town museum, with Jonathan Fisher's 18th-century views of the national park taking pride of place. Try the house speciality, *boxty* (potato pancake).

Gaby's Seafood Restaurant
SEAFOOD €€€
(064-663 2519; www.gabysireland.com; 27 High St; mains €28-50; ⊙6-10pm Mon-Sat) Gaby's is a refined dining experience serving superb seafood served in a traditional manner. Peruse the menu by the fire before drifting past the wine cellar to the low-lit dining room to savour exquisite Gallic dishes such as lobster in cognac and cream. The wine list is long and the advice unerring.

🍷 Drinking & Entertainment
Most pubs put on live music, and nights are lively here. Plunkett and College Sts are lined with pubs.

★ O'Connor's
PUB
(High St) This tiny traditional pub with leaded glass doors is one of Killarney's most popular haunts. Live music plays every night; good bar food is served daily in summer. In warmer weather, the crowds spill out to the adjacent laneway.

Courtney's
PUB
(www.courtneysbar.com; Plunkett St) Inconspicuous on the outside, inside this timeless pub bursts at the seams with traditional music sessions many nights year-round. This is where locals come to see their old mates perform and to kick off a night on the town.

Hussy's
PUB
(High St) Escape the tourist mobs and muse over a pint in this small pub that retains a snug at the entrance.

Tatler Jack's
PUB
(www.tatlerjack.com; Plunkett St) Photos of proud local sports teams line the walls at this surprisingly large pub, which features pool tables, the comfiest stools in town and merciless craic.

McSorley's
BAR, NIGHTCLUB
(www.mcsorleyskillarney.com; College St) A local favourite for its big beer garden and nightclub with a decent-sized dance floor. Trad sessions take place from early evening to

10pm, with live bands from 11.30pm. Admission to the main bar is free.

Killarney Grand
BAR, NIGHTCLUB
(www.killarneygrand.com; Main St) There's traditional live music from 9pm to 11pm, bands from 11.30pm to 1.30am and a disco from 11pm at this Killarney institution. Entry is free before 11pm.

🛍 Shopping

Variety Sounds
MUSIC
(College St; ⊙10am-6pm Mon-Sat, noon-6pm Sun) Eclectic music shop with a good range of traditional music, instruments, sheet music and hard-to-find recordings.

O'Sullivan's Outdoor Store
OUTDOOR GEAR
(www.killarneyrentabike.com; New St; ⊙10am-6pm Mon-Sat, noon-6pm Sun) Crams a vast amount of activity gear into a small space.

Brícín
CRAFTS
(www.bricin.com; 26 High St; ⊙10am-9pm Mon-Sat) Interesting local craftwork, including jewellery and pottery, alongside touristy wares, plus a restaurant of the same name.

Dungeon Bookshop
BOOKS
(College St; ⊙8am-9pm) Excellent second-hand bookshop hidden above a newsagent (take the stairs at the back of the shop).

❶ Information
The website www.killarney.ie has lots of tourism links.

INTERNET ACCESS
Killarney Library (www.kerrylibrary.ie; Rock Rd; ⊙10am-5pm Mon, Wed, Fri & Sat, 10am-8pm Tue & Thu) Free internet access.

MEDICAL SERVICES
The closest accident and emergency unit is at Tralee General Hospital, 32km northwest of Killarney.
SouthDoc (☑1850-335 999; Upper Park Rd) Doctors outside surgery hours; 500m east of the centre.

MONEY
Banks with ATMs are prevalent; many have a bureau de change.

POST
Killarney post office (New St)

TOURIST INFORMATION
Tourist office (☑064-663 1633; www.kil larney.ie; Beech Rd; ⊙9am-6pm Mon-Sat year round, plus 9am-5pm Sun Jun-Aug. Can

FOOTBALL FEVER

Gaelic football clubs (see p694) are as common in Ireland as green fields and pub signs bearing the 'G' word. However, in Kerry, obsession with the sport reaches fever pitch.

If you'd like to watch a match and you're here during the season (February to September), head to the Fossa GAA (☑ 064-6636 636; http://fossagaaclub.com; Fossa) ground. To learn about the game from some lifelong pub commentators, have a drink at GAA bars such as Tatler Jack's (p269) .

handle almost any query, especially dealing with transport intricacies.

❶ Getting There & Away

AIR

Kerry Airport (KIR; ☑ 066-976 4644; www.kerryairport.ie; Farranfore) is at Farranfore, about 15km north of Killarney along the N22, then a further 1.5km along the N23. **Ryanair** (www.ryanair.com) rules the roost with daily flights to Dublin and London's Luton and Stansted airports, and less frequent services to Hahn, Germany, Faro, Portugal and Alicante, Spain.

The small airport has a restaurant, bar, bureau de change and ATM. Virtually all the major car-hire firms have desks at the airport.

BUS

Bus Éireann (☑ 064-663 0011; www.buseireann.ie) operates from the east end of the Killarney Outlet Centre, offering regular links to destinations including Cork (€19, two hours, 15 daily); Dublin (€28, six hours, six daily); Galway (€26, seven hours, seven daily) via Limerick (€20.20, 2¼ hours); Tralee (€8.70, 40 minutes, hourly); and Waterford (€26, 4½ hours, hourly).

TRAIN

Killarney's train station is behind the Malton Hotel, just east of the centre. **Irish Rail** (☑ 064-6631067; www.irishrail.ie) has up to nine direct trains a day to Tralee (€10.80, 45 minutes) and three trains a day via Mallow to Cork (€26.80, 1½ hours). There's one direct train daily to Dublin (from €33, 3½ hours), otherwise you'll have to change at Mallow.

❶ Getting Around

TO/FROM THE AIRPORT

Bus Éireann has six to seven services daily between Killarney and Kerry Airport (€5, 20 minutes); frustratingly, they're not coordinated with flight times.

Tralee-Killarney trains stop at Farranfore station, a 10-minute walk (at minimum) from the airport.

A taxi to Killarney costs about €35.

BICYCLE

Bicycles are ideal for exploring the scattered sights of the Killarney area, many of which are accessible only by bike or on foot.

O'Sullivan's Bike Hire (www.killarneyrentabike.com; per day/week €15/85) has branches on New St, opposite the cathedral, and on Beech Rd, opposite the tourist office. Road, mountain and children's bikes are available.

CAR

The centre of Killarney can be thick with traffic at times. **Budget** (☑ 064-663 4341; Kenmare Pl) is the only car-hire outfit with an office in town. Otherwise contact the companies at Kerry Airport.

JAUNTING CAR

Killarney's traditional transport is the horse-drawn **jaunting car** (☑ 064-663 3358; www.killarneyjauntingcars.ie), also known as a trap, which comes with a driver known as a jarvey. The **pick-up point**, nicknamed 'the Ha Ha' or 'the Block', is on Kenmare Pl. Trips around town cost €30 to €70, depending on distance; traps officially carry four people. Jaunting cars also congregate in the N71 car park for Muckross House and Abbey, and at the Gap of Dunloe.

TAXI

The town taxi rank is on College St. Taxi companies include **Killarney Taxi & Tours** (☑ 085-280 3333; www.killarneytaxi.com).

AROUND KILLARNEY

Castles, gardens and lake adventures are among the highlights of a visit to Killarney National Park, immediately south of the city. Just beyond, there's rugged scenery including the too-gorgeous-for-words Gap of Dunloe, with its rocky terrain, babbling brooks and alpine lakes.

Killarney National Park

You can escape Killarney for the surrounding wilderness surprisingly quickly. Buses rumble up to Ross Castle and Muckross House, but it's possible to find your own refuge in the 10,236 hectares of **Killarney National Park** (www.killarneynationalpark.ie) among Ireland's only wild herd of native red deer, the country's largest area of ancient oak woods and views of most of its major mountains.

Glacial **Lough Leane** (the Lower Lake or 'Lake of Learning'), **Muckross Lake** and the **Upper Lake** make up about a quarter of the park. Their peaty waters are as rich in wildlife as the surrounding soil: cormorants skim across the surface, deer swim out to graze on the islands, and salmon, trout and perch prosper in a pike-free environment. Lough Leane has vistas of reeds and swans.

The park was designated a Unesco Biosphere Reserve in 1982. Other wildlife includes the reintroduced white-tail eagles; in 2013, the first chicks hatched in Ireland in over 100 years.

Pedestrian entrances are located opposite St Mary's Cathedral in Killarney; there are other entrances for drivers off the N71.

Killarney's tourist office stocks walking guides and the map (Ordnance Survey Map Discovery Series No 78) for several mountains, including Carrantuohil (1039m), Ireland's highest peak, within the Macgillycuddy's Reeks range.

Knockreer House & Gardens

Near the St Mary's Cathedral entrance to the park stands Knockreer House, with gardens featuring a terraced lawn and a summerhouse. The original 1870s structure burned down; the present incarnation dates from 1958. The house isn't open to the public, but its **gardens** have magnificent views across the lakes to the mountains.

From the St Mary's Cathedral entrance, follow the path immediately to your right uphill for about 500m to reach the gardens.

Ross Castle

Restored by Dúchas, lakeside **Ross Castle** (☎064-663 5851; www.heritageireland.ie; Ross Rd; adult/child €4/2; ☉9am-5.45pm Mar-Oct) dates back to the 15th century, when it was a residence of the O'Donoghues. It was the last place in Munster to succumb to Cromwell's forces, thanks partly to its cunning spiral staircase, every step of which is a different height in order to break an attacker's stride.

The castle is a lovely 3km walk from the St Mary's Cathedral pedestrian park entrance; you may well see deer. If you're driving from Killarney, turn right opposite the petrol station at the start of Muckross Rd. Access is by guided tour only.

Inisfallen Island

The first monastery on Inisfallen Island (at nearly 9 hectares, the largest of the national park's 26 islands) is said to have been founded by St Finian the Leper in the 7th century. The island's fame dates from the early 13th century when the Annals of Inisfallen were written here. Now in the Bodleian Library at Oxford, they remain a vital source of information on early Munster history. On Inisfallen are the ruins of a 12th-century **oratory** with a carved Romanesque doorway and a **monastery** on the site of St Finian's original.

You can hire boats (around €5) from Ross Castle to row to the island.

Muckross Estate

The core of Killarney National Park is the Muckross Estate, donated to the state by Arthur Bourn Vincent in 1932. **Muckross House** (☎064-667 0144; www.muckross-house.ie; adult/child €7.50/4, combined ticket with farms €12.50/7; ☉9am-7pm Jul & Aug, to 5.30pm Sep-Jun) is a 19th-century mansion, restored to its former glory and packed with contemporaneous fittings. Entrance is by guided tour.

The beautiful **gardens** slope down, and a block behind the house is a restaurant, craft

THE KINGDOM OF KERRY

On your travels, you'll repeatedly hear Kerry referred to as 'the Kingdom'. The moniker's origins are as misty as the county's mountains – some believe it's simply because it's a land apart in terms of isolation and beauty (they have a point). But the most common theory is that it originates from Ciar, the son of Ulster King Fergus mac Róich and Connaught Queen Medb. Around AD 65, Ciar took possession of a large territory in Munster. It became known as Ciarraige ('Ciar's Kingdom'; his descendants were known as the Ciarraige, 'people of Ciar'), from which Kerry's Irish name, Ciarraí, derives.

272

1. Arctic char 2. Torc Waterfall 3. Red deer grazing
4. Rhododendrons, Killarney National Park

KEN WELSH / DESIGN PICS / GETTY IMAGES ©

Wildlife Watching in Killarney National Park

Although Killarney is one of southwestern Ireland's liveliest urban centres, a plethora of wildlife lives right on its doorstep, with pedestrian entrances to the national park right in the town centre.

The park's mountains, lakes and woodlands sprawl over 10,236 hectares. And while its proximity to Killarney and high visitor numbers are an ongoing risk, it's an important conservation area for many rare species. The park's upland areas are home to Ireland's only remaining wild herd of native red deer (around 700), which has lived here continuously for 12,000 years.

Fish in the park's waterways include brown trout and salmon, as well as rare Arctic char and Killarney shad.

Keep your eyes peeled too for the park's smallest residents, its insects, including the northern emerald dragonfly, which isn't normally found this far south in Europe and is believed to have been marooned here after the last ice age.

Birdlife abounds throughout the park. With a bit of luck, you might see white tailed sea eagles, whose 2.5m wingspan soars overhead. The eagles were reintroduced here in 2007 after more than 100 years of extinction in the area. There are now over 50 in the park and they're starting to settle around Ireland's rivers, lakes and coastal regions. And like Killarney itself, the park is also home to plenty of summer visitors, including migratory cuckoos, swallows and swifts.

Around Killarney

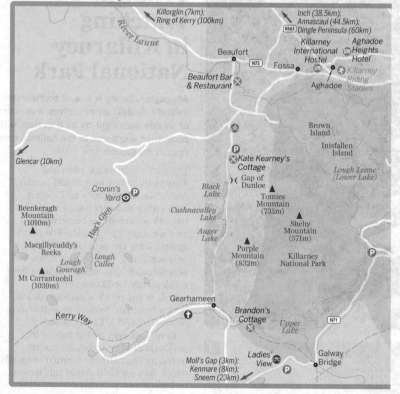

Killorglin (7km);
Ring of Kerry (100km)

Inch (38.5km);
Annascaul (44.5km);
R563 Dingle Peninsula (60km)

River Laune

Beaufort
N72
Fossa

Killarney
International
Hostel

Aghadoe
Heights
Hotel

Killarney
Riding
Stables

Beaufort Bar
& Restaurant

Aghadoe

Glencar (10km)

Brown
Island

Inisfallen
Island

Kate Kearney's
Cottage

Lough Leane
(Lower Lake)

Cronin's
Yard

Black
Lake

Gap of
Dunloe

Tomies
Mountain
(735m)

Beenkeragh
Mountain
(1010m)

Cushnavalley
Lake

Shehy
Mountain
(571m)

Hag's Glen

Macgillycuddy's
Reeks

Auger
Lake

Lough
Callee

Purple
Mountain
(832m)

Killarney
National Park

Lough
Gouragh

Mt Carrantuohil
(1039m)

Gearhameen

Brandon's
Cottage

Kerry Way

Upper
Lake

N71

Moll's Gap (3km);
Kenmare (8km);
Sneem (23km)

Ladies'
View

Galway
Bridge

COUNTY KERRY KILLARNEY NATIONAL PARK

shop and **studios** where you can see potters, weavers and bookbinders at work. Jaunting cars wait to run you through deer parks and woodland to Torc Waterfall and Muckross Abbey (about €20 each return; haggling can reap discounts). The visitor centre has an excellent **cafe**.

Immediately east of Muckross House are the **Muckross Traditional Farms** (☑ 064-663 1440; adult/child €7.50/4, combined ticket with Muckross House €12.50/7; ☺ 10am-6pm Jun-Aug, 1-6pm May & Sep, 1-6pm Sat, Sun & public holidays Apr & Oct). These reproductions of 1930s Kerry farms, complete with chickens, pigs, cattle and horses, show farming and living conditions when people had to live off the land.

Muckross House is 5km south of town, signposted from the N71. If you're walking or cycling, there's a cycle track alongside the Kenmare road for most of the first 2km. A path then turns right into Killarney National Park. Following this path, after 1km

you'll come to **Muckross Abbey**, which was founded in 1448 and burned by Cromwell's troops in 1652. William Thackeray called it 'the prettiest little bijou of a ruined abbey ever seen'. Muckross House is another 1.5km from the abbey ruins.

Cycling around Muckross Lake (Middle Lake) is easier and more scenic in an anti-clockwise direction.

Exploring the Gap of Dunloe

The best way to see the Gap is to hire a bike in Killarney and cycle to Ross Castle. Arrive before 11am to catch a boat up the lakes to Brandon's Cottage, then cycle through the Gap and back to Killarney via the N72 and a path through the golf course (bike hire and boat trip about €30).

The 1½-hour boat ride alone justifies the trip. It crosses all the lakes, passing islands and bridges and winding between the sec-

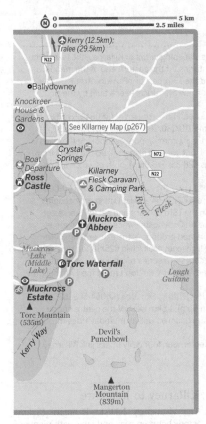

Gap of Dunloe

Geographically, the Gap of Dunloe is outside the Killarney National Park, but most people include it in their visit to the park. The land is ruggedly beautiful, and fast-changing weather conditions add drama.

In the winter, it's an awe-inspiring mountain pass, overshadowed by Purple Mountain and Macgillycuddy's Reeks. In high summer, though, it's a bottleneck for the tourist trade, with buses ferrying countless visitors for horse-and-trap rides through the Gap.

In the south, surrounded by lush, green pastures, Brandon's Cottage (dishes €3-6; breakfast & lunch Apr-Oct) is a simple old 19th-century hunting lodge with an open-air cafe and a dock for boats crossing the Upper Lake. From here a narrow road weaves up the hill to the Gap. Heading down towards the north the scenery is a fantasy of rocky bridges over clear mountain streams and lakes.

At the northern end is the 19th-century pub Kate Kearney's Cottage (064-664 4146; www.katekearneyscottage.com; mains €7.50-19.50; 10am-11.30pm Mon-Thu, 10am-12.30am Sat, 10am-11pm Sun;), where many drivers park in order to walk up to the Gap. You can also rent ponies and jaunting cars here (bring cash).

Continuing north to the N72, you'll reach a charming 1851 stone pub housing the Beaufort Bar & Restaurant (064-664 4032; www.beaufortbar.com; Beaufort; mains €13-20; 6.30-9.30pm Fri & Sat, 12.30-2.30pm Sun). Its gleaming timber dining room is refined, intimate and relaxed.

Macgillycuddy's Reeks

Ascending Macgillycuddy's Reeks and their neighbours (Purple, Tomies and Shehy mountains, between the Gap of Dunloe and Lough Leane, and Torc and Mangerton mountains, southeast of Muckross Lake) should never be attempted without a map and compass (and knowing how to use them). Weatherproof and waterproof footwear and clothing are essential at all times of the year. Seek advice locally before attempting mountain walks.

There are several ways up Carrantuohil, the country's highest peak, in the Macgillycuddy's Reeks range. Some require reasonable hill-walking ability, others are serious scrambling or rock-climbing routes. Get a

ond two lakes via Meeting of the Waters and the Long Range.

On land, walking, pony or four-person trap can be substituted for cycling. The Gap pony men charge €50 per hour or €80 for the two-hour trip between Brandon's Cottage and Kate Kearney's Cottage. Note that it's hard to do the Gap as part of a walking loop. From the south, you can get as far as Kate Kearney's, from where your best bet would be to call a cab, as it's a long slog back to Killarney on busy roads.

You *can* also drive through the Gap, but really only outside summer and even then walkers, cyclists and traps have the right of way (with nowhere to pull over), and the blind hairpin bends are nerve testing. Otherwise, to reach Brandon's Cottage by car you have to drive a long, scenic detour on the N71 to the R568 and then come back down a gorgeous rugged valley. It takes about 45 minutes.

> **WORTH A TRIP**
>
> ## AGHADOE
>
> On a hilltop just 5km west of town, Aghadoe's sweeping views of Killarney, the lakes and Inisfallen Island have made jaws drop for centuries. At the eastern end of the meadow are the ruins of a **Romanesque church** and the 13th-century **Parkavonear Castle**. Parkavonear's keep, still standing, is one of the few cylindrical keeps built by the Normans in Ireland.
>
> The ruins lie in front of the luxurious **Aghadoe Heights Hotel** (☎ 064-663 1766; www.aghadoeheights.com; Aghadoe; s/d/ste from €110/130/160, bar mains €15.50-18.50; ⊙ bar lunch & dinner; @ 🛜 ☒). A huge, glassed-in swimming pool overlooking the lakes is the centrepiece of this contemporary stunner, but you can also soak up the views from the bar and **Lake Room Restaurant** (mains €28-35; ⊙ 6-9pm), both of which are open to nonguests, as is the decadent spa.
>
> At the other end of the price spectrum, **Killarney International Hostel** (☎ 064-663 1240; www.anoige.ie; Aghadoe House, Fossa; dm €21, tw54; ⊙ Mar-Oct; @ 🛜) occupies the Headley barons' former residence, built in the 18th century and set in 75 acres of woodland. It's the regal quarters for a 137-bed An Óige hostel, whose common areas have open fires and a piano. In the hostel's forested grounds is the exhilarating **Killarney High Ropes** (☎ 064-663 1240; Aghadoe; high ropes adult/child €25/18, low ropes €10; ⊙ 11am-4pm daily Jun-Aug, Sat & Sun Sep-May) course - a series of zip lines, cargo nets and see-saws. There's a low ropes course for over fives who don't meet the 1.4m height requirement.
>
> Coming from Killarney, you'll pass **Killarney Riding Stables** (☎ 064-663 1686; www.killarney-riding-stables.com; Ballydowney; ⊙ 8am-6pm), 1.5km west of the centre on the N72, which offers short rides (from €35 for one hour) as well as multiday rides through the Iveragh Peninsula.
>
> Between Monday and Saturday, June to September, four daily buses link Killarney and Aghadoe. Some tours stop here.

taste of the Reeks at close quarters by walking up **Hag's Glen**, the beautiful approach valley that leads to the Callee and Gouragh lakes below the north face of Carrantuohill.

The best approach is from **Cronin's Yard** (☎ 064-662 4044; www.croninsyard.com; Mealis, Beaufort; camping pods per person €10), where there's a **tearoom**, showers and toilets, a public telephone and packed lunches available on request, as well as a handful of basic but nifty new **camping pods** resembling wooden igloos, sleeping three to five adults. It's at the road's end (OS ref 836873), reached from the N72 via Beaufort, west of Killarney. You may be asked to pay a small fee for using the car park. From here, the way lies alongside the River Gaddagh, with a new footbridge; still, care is required if it's in flood. It's just over 3km to the lakes.

The popular but hair-raising way to summit Carrantuohil from the lakes is via **Devil's Ladder**, a gruelling trudge up a badly eroded gully path, southwest of the lakes. The ground is loose in places, and in wet conditions the way becomes muddy. It takes six hours return from Cronin's Yard.

Killarney to Kenmare

The vista-crazy N71 to Kenmare (32km) winds between rock and lake, with plenty of lay-bys to stop and admire the views (and recover from the switchback bends). Watch out for the buses squeezing along the road.

About 2km south of the entrance to Muckross House, a path leads 200m to the pretty **Torc Waterfall**. After another 8km on the N71 you come to **Ladies' View**, where the fine views along Upper Lake were enjoyed by Queen Victoria's ladies-in-waiting.

A further 5km on **Moll's Gap** is worth a stop for great views and food. **Avoca Cafe** (☎ 064-663 4720; www.avoca.ie; mains €7.50-13.50; ⊙ 9.30am-5pm Mon-Fri, 10am-6pm Sat & Sun) has awesome panoramas and delicious fare such as smoked salmon salad, pistachio-studded pork terrine and decadent cakes.

Tours

Killarney Guided Walks WALKING TOUR
(☎ 087 639 4362; www.killarneyguidedwalks.com; adult/child €9/5) Guided two-hour national park walks leave at 11am daily from opposite

St Mary's Cathedral at the western end of New St. Tours meander through Knockreer gardens, then to spots where Charles de Gaulle holidayed, David Lean filmed *Ryan's Daughter* and Brother Cudda slept for 200 years. Trips are available at other times on request.

Ross Castle Open Boats BOAT TOUR
(☎ 087 689 9241) The open boats you can charter at Ross Castle offer appealing trips with boatmen who define 'character'. It costs €10 from Ross Castle to the Muckross (Middle) Lake and back; €15 for a tour of all three lakes.

Gap of Dunloe Tours BUS, BOAT TOURS
(☎ 064-663 0200; www.gapofdunloetours.com) This outfit runs Gap of Dunloe bus and boat tours (from €30), with the option of jaunting car (extra €20), or pony (extra €30) rides. Reserve ahead for bike-on-boat tours (bikes are transported for free).

Killarney Day Tour BOAT, WALKING TOURS
(☎ 064-663 1068; www.killarneydaytour.com) Bus and boat tours (€27) and boat-only tours (€13.50) from Ross Castle. It also arranges guided walks for all levels.

Corcoran's BUS TOUR
(☎ 064-663 6666; www.corcorantours.com) Runs Gap of Dunloe (€27), Ring of Kerry (€18) and Dingle and Slea Head (€22) tours, as well as tours around Killarney (€20).

Dero's Tours BUS TOUR
(☎ 064-663 1251; www.derostours.com) Gap of Dunloe (€27), Ring of Kerry (€19) and Dingle and Slea Head (€22) tours.

O'Connor Autotours BUS TOUR
(☎ 064-663 4833; www.oconnorautotours.ie; ☎) Ring of Kerry tours (from €24).

Outdoors Ireland ADVENTURE TOUR
(☎ 086 860 45 63; www.outdoorsireland.com) Kayaking (including three-hour sunset kayak trips, €50), walking and rock and mountain climbing.

Hidden Ireland Adventures WALKING TOUR
(☎ 087 221 4002; www.hiddenirelandadventures. com) Twice-weekly guided ascents of Macgillycuddy's Reeks (€75) and customised walks.

RING OF KERRY

The Ring of Kerry is the longest and the most diverse of Ireland's big circle drives, combining jaw-dropping coastal scenery with emerald pastures and villages.

The 179km circuit winds past pristine beaches, the island-dotted Atlantic, medieval ruins, mountains and loughs (lakes). The coastline is at its most rugged between Waterville and Caherdaniel in the southwest of the peninsula. It can get busy in summer, but even then the remote Skellig Ring can be uncrowded and serene – and starkly beautiful.

The Ring of Kerry can easily be done as a day trip, but if you want to stretch it out, places to stay are scattered along the route. Killorglin and Kenmare have the best concentration of dining options; elsewhere, with a couple of notable exceptions, basic pub fare is the norm.

❶ Getting Around

Although you can cover the Ring in one day by car or three days by bicycle, the more time you take, the more you'll enjoy it.

Tour buses travel the Ring in an anticlockwise direction. Getting stuck behind one is tedious, so consider driving clockwise; but be careful on blind corners. The road is extremely narrow and twisty in places, but surface upgrades are under way. There's little traffic on the **Ballaghbeama Gap**, which cuts across the peninsula's central highlands with some spectacular views: it's perfect for a shortcut by car or a long cycle, as is the longer **Ballaghisheen Pass** to Waterville.

The 214km Kerry Way (p268) starts and ends in Killarney.

Between late June and late August, **Bus Éireann** (☎ 064-663 0011; www.buseireann.ie) circumnavigates the Ring of Kerry daily (Killarney to Killarney €28.50, seven hours). Stops include Killorglin, Glenbeigh, Caherciveen, Waterville and Caherdaniel. Outside summer, transport on the Ring is not good.

A number of Killarney tour companies run daily bus trips around the Ring.

Killorglin

POP 4150

Travelling anticlockwise from Killarney, the first town on the Ring is Killorglin (Cill Orglan), 23km northwest. For most of the year, the town is quieter than the waters of the River Laune that lap against the 1885-built eight-arched bridge. In August, however, there's an explosion of time-honoured ceremonies at the famous pagan festival, the Puck Fair. A statue of King Puck (a goat) peers out from the Killarney side of the river. Author Blake Morrison documents his mother's childhood here in *Things My Mother Never Told Me*.

1. King Puck statue, Killorglin 2. Farmhouse, Skellig Ring
3. Traditional shopfront, Kenmare 4. Valentia Island

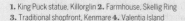

RICHARD CUMMINS / GETTY IMAGES ©

Ring of Kerry

Windswept beaches, Atlantic waves crashing against rugged cliffs and islands, medieval ruins, soaring mountains and glinting loughs are some of the stunning distractions along the twisting 179km Ring of Kerry circle drive around the Iveragh Peninsula.

Killorglin

Even if you're racing around the ring, don't miss its first town (heading anticlockwise). The riverside village of Killorglin is home to a salmon smokehouse, some standout restaurants and, in August, the historic Puck Fair Festival.

Kenmare

A fitting last (or first) stop on the ring, Kenmare sums up its greatest charms. A beautiful location on the bay (from where boat trips depart), colourful shops and gracious architecture are cornerstones of this classic Irish town.

Skellig Ring

A ring within the ring, this 18km loop off the main route offers an escape from the crowds. The wild, scenic drive links Portmagee and Waterville via a Gaeltacht (Irish-speaking) area centred on Ballinskelligs (Baile an Sceilg).

Valentia Island

Islands are a scenic highlight on the ring. Some are accessible by boat, but picturesque Valentia Island is even easier to reach, via a short bridge. There's also a summer car-ferry service departing just south of Cahersiveen.

Caherdaniel

The ring's scenery is at its most rugged around Caherdaniel. Highlights here include the Derrynane National Historic Park with its stately house and palm-filled gardens, horse riding, a Blue Flag beach and water sports galore.

Ring of Kerry

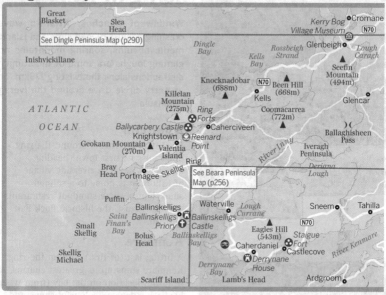

★ Festivals & Events

Puck Fair Festival HISTORIC
(Aonach an Phuic; www.puckfair.ie; ☉ mid-Aug)
First recorded in 1603, with hazy origins,
this lively festival is based around the custom of installing a billy goat (a poc, or puck),
the symbol of mountainous Kerry, on a ped-
estal in the town, its horns festooned with
ribbons. Other entertainment ranges from
a horse fair and bonny baby competition to
street theatre, concerts and fireworks; the
pubs stay open until 3am.

🛏 Sleeping & Eating

A bunch of old-boozer-style pubs line Upper
Bridge St.

Bianconi INN €€
(☎ 066-976 1146; www.bianconi.ie; Bridge St; s/d
from €70/110; mains €8.50-25.50; ☉ restaurant
8am-11.30pm Mon-Thu, 8-12.30am Fri & Sat, 6-11pm
Sun; ☎) Bang in the centre of town, this low-
lit inn has a classy ambience and Modern
Irish fare such as sage-stuffed roast chicken
with cranberry sauce. Its spectacular salads,
such as Cashel blue cheese, apple, toasted
almonds and chorizo, are a meal in themselves. Upstairs, newly refurbished guest
rooms have olive and truffle tones and luxurious bathrooms (try for a rolltop tub).

Coffey's River's Edge B&B €€
(☎ 066-976 1750; www.coffeysriversedge.com; the
Bridge; s/d €50/70; ☎) Next to the bridge,
you can sit out on the balcony overlooking
the river at this contemporary B&B, with
spotless spring-toned rooms and hardwood
floors.

Jack's Bakery BAKERY €
(Lower Bridge St) 🖉 Jack Healy bakes amazing
breads and also makes pâtés and beautiful
sandwiches at this cherry-red landmark.

KRD Fisheries SEAFOOD €
(☎ 066-976 1106; www.krdfisheries.com; Tralee
Rd; 200g smoked wild/farmed salmon €15/9.90;
☉ 9am-1pm & 2-5pm Mon-Fri, 9am-1pm Sat, 9-11am
Sun) Just across the bridge from Killorgan's
town centre, you can buy this 1782-estab-
lished smokery's salmon direct from the
premises.

Giovannelli ITALIAN €€
(☎ 087 123 1353; Lower Bridge St; mains €14-30;
☉ 6.30-9pm Mon-Sat) Northern Italian native
Daniele Giovannelli makes all of his pasta by
hand at this simple but intimate little restaurant. Highlights of the blackboard menu
might include seafood linguine with mussels in shells, and beef ravioli in sage butter.
Wonderful wines by the bottle and glass too.

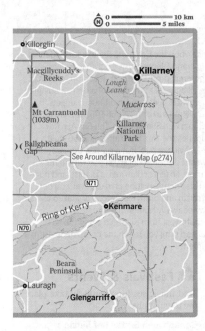

blacksmith, thatcher and labourer, as well as a dairy, and meet rare Kerry Bog ponies. The museum adjoins the sprawling Red Fox pub, which remains popular with locals for a sociable pint.

Rossbeigh Strand

This unusual beach, 1.6km west of Glenbeigh, is a tendril of sand protruding into Dingle Bay, with views of Inch Point and the Dingle Peninsula. On one side the sea is ruffled by Atlantic winds; on the other it's sheltered and calm.

Burke's Horse Trekking Centre (☑087 237 9110; http://beachtrek.ie; Rossbeigh; beach rides per hr from €25) offers horse trekking (beach rides per hour from €25).

Caherciveen

POP 1200

Caherciveen's population, over 30,000 in 1841, was decimated by the Great Famine and emigration to the New World. A sleepy outpost remains, overshadowed by the 688m peak of Knocknadobar. It's rather dour compared with the peninsula's other settlements, but in many ways this village does more to recall the tough 1930s in Ireland than any other you'll see in Kerry. Lately the community has undertaken a big spruce-up, dressing empty shop windows and cleaning, painting and gardening along the main streets to give the town a fresh lease of life.

◉ Sights

Paths along the river have information boards about the area's wildlife.

Ballycarbery Castle & Ring Forts   CASTLE, FORT

The atmospheric remains of 16th-century Ballycarbery Castle, 2.4km along the road to White Strand Beach from the barracks, are surrounded by green pastures inhabited by cows who like to get in the pictures.

Along the same road are two stone ring forts. Cahergall, the larger one, dates from the 10th century and has stairways on the inside walls, a *clochán* (beehive hut), and the remains of a house. The smaller, 9th-century Leacanabuile has the entrance to an underground passage. Their inner walls and chambers give a strong sense of what life was like in a ring fort. Leave your car

Sol Y Sombra   TAPAS €€

(☑066-976 2347; www.solysombra.ie; Lower Bridge St; tapas & raciones €5.50-13.50, mains €15-22; ⊙5-11pm Wed & Thu, 5pm-12.30am Fri & Sat, 1-8.30pm Sun) Set in a beautifully renovated 1816 church, Sol Y Sombra transports you to Mediterranean soil with its tapas and larger *raciones* dishes for sharing, such as grilled squid, marinated anchovy fillets and an array of tostadas. Bands often play.

❶ Information

Library (Library Pl; ⊙10am-5pm Tue-Sat) Free internet access.

Tourist office (☑066-976 1451; Library Pl; ⊙10am-4pm) Sells maps, walking guides, fishing licences and souvenirs. Opening times vary.

Kerry Bog Village Museum

On the N70 between Killorglin and Glenbeigh, the Kerry Bog Village Museum (www.kerrybogvillage.ie; admission €5; ⊙8.30am-6pm) recreates a 19th-century bog village, typical of the small communities that carved out a precarious living in the harsh environment of Ireland's ubiquitous peat bogs. You can see the thatched homes of the turfcutter,

OFF THE BEATEN TRACK

CROMANE PENINSULA

Unless you know it's here, you wouldn't chance upon the Cromane Peninsula, hidden off the N70. A five-minute drive from both Killorglin and Glenbeigh, it's home to Ireland's largest mussel bed, covering around 2050 hectares; production can reach up to 8000 tonnes a year. The peninsula's tiny namesake village sits at the base of a narrow shingle spit, with open fields giving way to spectacular water vistas and multihued sunsets.

Cromane's exceptional **Jacks Coastguard Restaurant** (☑066-976 9102; www. jackscromane.com; mains €16.50-35; ☺noon-9.30pm Wed-Sun May-Sep, Thu-Sun Apr, Nov & Dec, closed Jan & Feb) is a local secret and justifies the trip. Entering this 1866-built coastguard station feels like arriving at a low-key village pub. But a narrow doorway at the back of the bar leads to a striking, whitewashed contemporary space with lights glittering from midnight-blue ceiling panels, metallic fish sculptures, a pianist, and huge picture windows overlooking the water. Menu standouts include chicken liver and port parfait, followed by oven-roasted turbot with raisin and orange potatoes or glazed fillets of plaice stuffed with prawns, accompanied by heavenly homemade bread.

Cromane is 9km from Killorglin. Heading southwest from Killorglin along the N70, take the second right and continue straight ahead until you reach the crossroads. Turn right; Jacks Coastguard Restaurant is on your left.

in the parking area next to a stone wall and walk up the footpaths.

Barracks Heritage Centre
MUSEUM

(www.theoldbarracks.com; Bridge St; adult/student €4/2; ☺10am-5.30pm Mon-Sat, 1-5.30pm Sun May-Sep, other times by arrangement) The Old Barracks Heritage Centre is housed in a tower of the former Royal Irish Constabulary (RIC). The barracks were burnt down in 1922 by anti-Treaty forces. Today it looks over-restored, like an oddball confection.

Topped by a spiral staircase ascending to a lookout (best suited for those who don't care to see anything), the museum covers the Fenian Rising, Daniel O'Connell and Caherciveen's other great son, Gaelic football star Jack O'Shea. There are recreations of a local dwelling at the time of the Famine and of the barracks during the 1916 Easter Rising.

O'Connell's Birthplace
RUINS

The ruined cottage on the eastern bank of the Carhan River, on the left as you cross the bridge en route from Kells, is the humble birthplace of Daniel O'Connell, 'the Great Liberator'. On the opposite bank there's a stolid bust of O'Connell.

🏃 Activities

Local walks include the 5½-hour **Killelan Mountain circuit** and the less strenuous **foreshore walk** to the castle and ring forts. Ask at the tourist office for info on local guided walks and boat rides.

🎉 Festivals & Events

Trad music sessions regularly take place in the town's pubs.

Caherciveen Festival of Music & the Arts
MUSIC

(www.celticmusicfestival.com; ☺late Jul/early Aug) Celtic bands, busking competitions and set dancing star at this family-friendly festival held over the August bank holiday weekend.

🛏 Sleeping & Eating

Mannix Point Camping & Caravan Park
CAMPGROUND €

(☑066-947 2806; www.campinginkerry.com; Mannix Point; campsites per person €8.50; ☺Mar-Oct; 🛜🅿) Mortimer Moriarty's award-winning coastal site has an inviting kitchen, campers' sitting room with a peat fire (no TV but regular music sessions), a barbecue area and even a birdwatching platform.

Petit Delice
PATISSERIE €

(http://ringofkerrypatisserie.com; Main St; dishes €3.50-10; ☺9am-5.30pm Mon-Sat; 🛜) Scrumptious range of homemade chocolates, ice creams and sorbets, and a counter full of freshly baked cakes, patisseries and breads. Lunchtime dishes include quiches, soups and filled baguettes.

Thatch Restaurant
IRISH €€

(www.thethatchrestaurant.com; Strands End; mains €9.50-23; ☺1-3pm Mon-Fri, noon-4pm Sun, from 6pm Fri & Sat; 🅿) Inside a cute butter-coloured thatched cottage on the northern edge of town, you can tuck into hearty Irish standards over a pint. If there's a tour bus parked out the front (it's a popular coach stop), be aware that you might be waiting a while.

ℹ Information

Caherciveen has a **post office** and banks with **ATMs**.

The Barracks Heritage Centre is the best place for tourist information.

Valentia Island

POP 664

Crowned by Geokaun Mountain, Valentia Island (Oileán Dairbhre) is an altogether homier isle than the brooding Skelligs to the southwest. Like the Skellig Ring it leads to, Valentia is an essential, coach-free detour from the Ring of Kerry, with some lonely ruins worth exploring.

Valentia was chosen as the site for the first transatlantic telegraph cable. When the connection was made in 1858, it put Caherciveen in direct contact with New York, although without connection to Dublin. After the initial 27 days the link failed due to excessive voltage while trying to achieve faster operation. A second cable was laid in 1865 and completed in 1866, and continued functioning until 1966; the telegraph station also operated until 1966.

Measuring 11km by 3km, the island makes an ideal driving loop. Points of interest are listed on free maps available from the Skellig Experience heritage centre.

Tiny Knightstown, the only town, has pubs, food, walks, the ferry and the Skellig Island boats, as well as basic accommodation.

◉ Sights & Activities

Skellig Experience HERITAGE CENTRE
(☑066-947 6306; www.skelligexperience.com; adult/child €5/3, incl cruise €27.50/14.50; ◷10am-7pm Jul & Aug, to 6pm May, Jun & Sep, shorter hours rest of year) Immediately across the bridge from Portmagee, this distinctive building with turf-covered barrel roofs contains exhibitions on the life and times of the Skellig Michael monks, the history of the island's lighthouses and the wildlife. From April to September, it also runs two-hour cruises around the islands. If the weather's bad, there's often the option of a 90-minute minicruise in the harbour and channel.

In March, April, October and November the centre is open from 10am to 5pm five days a week, but the exact days change each year – check ahead.

St Brendan's Well HISTORIC SITE
Out in the boggy west, with its lonely vistas worthy of some lost world, look for signs for this ancient religious site that still attracts a smattering of pilgrims. Legend has it that St Brendan sailed here from Dingle, scaled the cliffs (in the 5th century), found a couple of dying pagans and anointed them.

ℹ Getting There & Away

A bridge links Valentia Island with Portmagee. From April to September, there's a **ferry service** (☑087 241 8973) to Knightstown on Valentia Island from Reenard Point, 5km southwest of Caherciveen. The five-minute crossing costs €6/9 one way/return for a car, €2/3 for a cyclist and €1.50/2 for a pedestrian. It departs every 10 minutes between 7.45am (9am Sunday) and 9.30pm (10pm in July and August).

Portmagee

POP 390

Portmagee overlooks the south side of Valentia Island from the mainland. Its single street is a rainbow of colourful houses and is much photographed. On summer mornings, the small pier comes to life with boats embarking on the choppy crossing to the Skellig Islands.

Portmagee holds set-dancing workshops (www.moorings.ie) over the May bank holiday weekend, with plenty of stomping practice sessions in the town's Bridge Bar (bar food €10-24.50), a friendly local gathering point, which itself is good for impromptu music by locals year-round and more formal sessions in summer.

The Bridge Bar neighbours the Moorings (☑066-947 7108; www.moorings.ie; s €70-100, d €100-140), with 16 rooms split between modern sea-view choices and simpler – and cheaper – options, most refreshingly white. The nautical-themed restaurant (mains €20-25; ◷dinner Tue-Sun Apr-Oct) specialises in seafood (including hot seafood platters) and its own pâté.

Perfect for hanging around waiting for the weather to clear for Skellig Islands trips or walks, Skellig Ring House (☑066-948 0018; www.skelligringhouse.com; tw without bathroom €30-36, d with/without bathroom €52/46; 🛜🖶) is a sociable, no-frills budget place with two self-catering kitchens and lots of pine furniture. Families are warmly welcomed.

COUNTY KERRY VALENTIA ISLAND

Skellig Islands

GANNET POP 50,000

The Skellig Islands (Oileáin na Scealaga) are impervious to the ever-pounding Atlantic. George Bernard Shaw said Skellig Michael was 'the most fantastic and impossible rock in the world'.

You'll need to do your best grisly sea-dog impression ('argh!') on the 12km crossing, which can be rough. There are no toilets or shelter on Skellig Michael, the only island that visitors are permitted to land on. Bring some food and drink and wear stout shoes and weatherproof clothing. Due to the steep (and often slippery) terrain and sudden wind gusts, it's not suitable for young children or people with limited mobility.

The Skelligs are a birdwatching paradise. During the boat trip you may spot diminutive storm petrels (also known as Mother Carey's chickens) darting above the water like swallows. Gannets are unmistakable with their savage beaks, imperious eyes, yellow caps and 1m-plus wing spans. Kittiwakes – small, dainty seabirds with black-tipped wings – are easy to see and hear around Skellig Michael's covered walkway as you step off the boat. They winter at sea then land in their thousands to breed between March and August.

Further up the rock you'll see stubby-winged fulmars, with distinctive bony 'nostrils' from which they eject an evil-smelling green liquid if you get too close. In May, puffins come ashore to lay a solitary egg at the far end of a burrow, and parent birds can be seen guarding their nests. Puffins stay only until the first weeks of August.

Skellig Michael

The jagged, 217m-high rock of Skellig Michael (Archangel Michael's Rock; like St Michael's Mount in Cornwall and Mont Saint Michel in Normandy) is the larger of the two islands and a Unesco World Heritage site. It looks like the last place on earth where anyone would try to land, let alone establish a community, yet early Christian monks survived here from the 6th until the 12th or 13th century. Influenced by the Coptic Church (founded by St Anthony in the deserts of Egypt and Libya), their determined quest for ultimate solitude led them to this remote, windblown edge of Europe.

The monastic buildings perch on a saddle in the rock, some 150m above sea level, reached by 600 steep steps cut into the rock face. The astounding 6th-century oratories and beehive cells vary in size; the floor of the largest cell is 4.5m by 3.6m. You can see the monks' south-facing vegetable garden and their cistern for collecting rainwater. The most impressive structural achievements are the settlement's foundations – platforms built on the steep slope using nothing more than earth and dry-stone walls.

Not much is known about the life of the monastery, but there are records of Viking raids in AD 812 and 823. Monks were kidnapped or killed, but the community recovered and carried on. In the 11th century a rectangular oratory was added to the site but, although it was expanded in the 12th century, the monks abandoned the rock around this time.

After the introduction of the Gregorian calendar in 1582, Skellig Michael became a popular spot for weddings. Marriages were forbidden during Lent but, since Skellig used the old Julian calendar, a trip to the islands allowed those unable to wait for Easter to tie the knot.

In the 1820s two lighthouses were built on Skellig Michael, together with the road that runs around the base.

Small Skellig

While Skellig Michael looks like two triangles linked by a spur, Small Skellig is longer, lower and much craggier. From a distance it looks as if someone battered it with a feather pillow that burst. Close up you realise you're looking at a colony of over 20,000 pairs of breeding gannets, the second-largest breeding colony in the world. Most boats circle the island so you can see the gannets and you may see basking seals as well. Small Skellig is a bird sanctuary; no landing is permitted.

❶ Getting There & Away

Skellig Michael's fragility places limits on the number of daily visitors. The 15 boats are licensed to carry no more than 12 passengers each, for a maximum of 180 people at any one time. It's wise to book ahead in July and August, bearing in mind that if the weather's bad the boats may not sail (about two days out of seven). Trips usually run from Easter until September, depending, again, on weather.

Boats leave around 10am and return at 3pm, and cost about €60 per person. You can depart from Portmagee, Ballinskelligs or Derrynane (and sometimes Knightstown). Boat owners generally restrict you to two hours on the island, which is the bare minimum to see the monastery, look at the birds and have a picnic. The crossing takes about 1½ hours from Portmagee, 35 minutes to one hour from Ballinskelligs and 1¾ hours from Derrynane.

If you just want to see the islands up close and avoid actually having to clamber out of the boat, consider a cruise with Skellig Experience on Valentia Island.

The Skellig Experience heritage centre, local pubs and B&Bs will point you in the direction of boat operators, including the following:

Ballinskelligs Boats (☑086 417 6612; http://bestskelligtrips.com; Ballinskelligs)

Casey's (☑066-947 2437; www.skelligislands.com; Portmagee)

John O'Shea (☑087 689 8431; www.skelligtours.com; Derrynane)

Seanie Murphy (☑066-947 6214; www.skelligsrock.com; Reenard Point, Valentia Island)

Skellig Ring

This fascinating and little-travelled 18km detour from the Ring of Kerry (N70) links Portmagee and Waterville via a Gaeltacht (Irish-speaking area) centred on Ballinskelligs (Baile an Sceilg). Ballinskelligs' name translates as 'town of the crag', which may elicit sniggers from fans of *Father Ted* and his Craggy Island pals. The area is as wild and beautiful as anything on Ted's fictional isle, with the ragged outline of Skellig Michael never far from view.

◎ Sights

Siopa Cill Rialaig   GALLERY
(☑066-947 9277; crsiopa@gmail.com; Dun Geagan; ☺11am-6pm Jul-Aug, by reservation rest of year) On the site of a village abandoned during the Famine, this contemporary art gallery displays work by local artists and talent from around Ireland and the world. It is the shop window of the Cill Rialaig Project, which provides a retreat for creative people who pay for their stay with art.

The gallery is by the R566 at the northeastern end of Ballinskelligs. You'll spot its circular thatched roofs and the sculpture that resembles a hallucinogenic mushroom. There's a cafe inside.

Ballinskelligs Priory & Bay   RUINS, BEACH
The sea and salty air are eating away at the atmospheric ruins of this medieval priory, a monastic settlement that was probably built by the Skellig Michael monks after

they fled their isolated outpost in the 12th century. To reach it, follow the sign to the pier at the western end of town and you will see it on the left.

Another sign points to the fine little blue flag beach. At the western end of the beach are the last remnants of the 16th-century castle stronghold of the McCarthys, built on the isthmus as a defence against pirates.

Skelligs Chocolate   CHOCOLATE FACTORY
(☑066-947 9119; www.skelligschocolate.com; St Finian's Bay) **FREE** You can get an overview of chocolate production at this chocolate-maker's whiz-bang new premises and taste it, too. Samples are free, and you can buy chocolates in boxes, bags and dishes plus hot chocolate at the onsite cafe.

🏃 Activities

St Finian's Bay is good for surfing. **Ballinskelligs Watersports** (☑086 389 4849; www.skelligsurf.com) hires out surfboards, kayaks and windsurfers, and gives lessons (€35/€45 per two hours for surfing/windsurfing).

🛏 Sleeping & Eating

Old School House   B&B **€€**
(☑066-947 9340; www.rascalstheoldschoolhouse.com; Cloon; s/d €49/70; ☜🅰) Colourful checked fabrics, rustic prints and painted architraves brighten the rooms of this charmer of a B&B. Pancakes with berries and cream are among the tempting breakfast choices.

Caifé Cois Trá   CAFE **€**
(☑066-947 9323; snacks €2.50-3.50; ☺9am-5pm; ☜) At the Ballinskelligs strand car park next to McCarthy's Castle, locals flock to this beach-hut cafe and craft shop for their morning caffeine jolt.

Waterville

POP 550

Waterville consists of a line of colourful houses strung on the N72 between Lough Currane and Ballinskelligs Bay. A statue of its most famous guest, Charlie Chaplin, beams out from the seafront. The Charlie Chaplin Comedy Film Festival (charliechaplincomedyfilmfestival.com) takes place in late August.

Sights in the town itself are few, but at the north end of Lough Currane, on Church Island there are ruins of a medieval church and beehive cell reputedly founded as a monastic settlement by St Finian in the 6th century.

Mór Active (☑086 389 0171; www.activityire land.ie) rents kayaks (€40 per half-day) and can also arrange abseiling and rock climbing.

Tiger Woods, Mark O'Meara and Payne Stewart are just some of the golfing greats who have teed off at **Waterville Golf Links** (☑066-947 4102; www.watervillegolflinks.ie; green fees 18 holes €144-163; ⊘by reservation), one of Ireland's most magnificently sited golf courses, with sweeping bay and mountain views.

Waterville Craft Market (☑066-947 4212; craftmarket@eircom.net; ⊘11am-6pm) has tourist information in addition to quality Irish jewellery, homewares, clothing and more.

🛏 Sleeping & Eating

Silver Sands HOSTEL €
(☑086 369 2283; silversandshostel@gmail.com; Main St; dm/d €19/36; @🛜) Backpackers should head to Silver Sands, a sociable spot on the seafront with musical instruments for jam sessions. Doubles have private bathrooms; avoid the dark downstairs room and go for one upstairs.

⭐**Smuggler's Inn** INN €€
(☑066-947 4330; www.the-smugglers-inn.com; Cliff Rd; d €90-130; 🛜) Across from the Waterville Golf Links at the water's edge, Smuggler's Inn is a diamond find (once you do: coming from the north it's hard to spot). Rooms are freshly renovated – try for room 15, with a glassed-in balcony overlooking

---

DON'T MISS

IRELAND'S FINEST VIEW

Midway between Waterville and Sneem, the **Scarriff Inn** (☑066-947 5132; http://scarriffinn.com; Caherdaniel; mains €16–25; ⊘9am-9pm, kitchen hours vary) claims to have 'Ireland's finest view'. And, even in such a scenic country, it might just be right. The Scarriff's wall-to-wall windows frame stupendous views across the rocky coastline and scattered islands to Kenmare Bay and Bantry Bay. You can wake up to them from one of its six basic but airy rooms with private bathrooms at its **B&B** (s/d €50/70) below the inn.

Ballinskelligs Bay. But the pièce de résistance is the gourmet **restaurant** (mains €14-29; ⊘restaurant 1-2.30pm & 6-9.30pm). Owner-chef Henry Hunt's creations not only span seafood (including sensational chowder) but also locally farmed poultry and meat, and elegant desserts. Breakfasts, including a catch of the day, are cooked to order.

Brookhaven House B&B €€
(☑066-947 4431; www.brookhavenhouse.com; New Line; d €80-120; 🛜🅿) The pick of Waterville's B&Bs is the contemporary Brookhaven House, run by a friendly family, with spick-and-span rooms, comfy beds, and a sunny sea-view breakfast room.

Dooley's Seafood & Steakhouse SEAFOOD, STEAKHOUSE €€
(☑066-947 8766; www.dooleyswaterville.com; opp Waterville Craft Market; mains €17-26; ⊘6-9.30pm; 🅿) Snazzy newcomer Dooley's serves what its name states, with finesse. Dry aged steaks are a speciality.

Caherdaniel

POP 350

Hiding between Derrynane Bay and the foothills of Eagles Hill, Caherdaniel barely qualifies as a tiny hamlet. Businesses are scattered about the undergrowth like smugglers – fitting since this was once a haven for the same.

This is the ancestral home of Daniel O'Connell, 'the Liberator', whose family made money smuggling from their base by the dunes. The area boasts a Blue Flag beach, plenty of activities, good hikes and some pubs where you may be tempted to break into pirate talk. Lines of wind-gnarled trees add to the wild air.

👁 Sights

Derrynane National Historic Park HISTORIC SITE
(☑066-947 5113; www.heritageireland.ie; Derrynane; adult/child €3/1; ⊘10.30am-6pm May-Sep, 10.30am-5pm Wed-Sun Oct-late Nov) **Derrynane House** is the family home of Daniel O'Connell, the campaigner for Catholic emancipation. His ancestors bought the house and surrounding parkland, having grown rich on smuggling with France and Spain. It's largely furnished with O'Connell memorabilia, including the restored trium-

phal chariot in which he did laps of Dublin after his release from prison in 1844.

The gardens, warmed by the Gulf Stream, have palms, 4m-high tree ferns, gunnera ('giant rhubarb') and other South American species. A walking track leads to wetlands, beaches and clifftops. You can spot wild pheasants and other birds, whose musical calls add a note of contrast to the dull roar of the surf. The chapel, which O'Connell added to Derrynane House in 1844, is a copy of the ruined one on Abbey Island, which can usually be reached on foot across the sand.

Look out for the Ogham stone on the left of the road to the house. With its carved notches representing the simple Ogham alphabet of the ancient Irish, the stone has several missing letters, but is thought to represent the name of a local chieftain.

🏃 Activities

Most of the activity here centres on the beach. The Kerry Way passes through and continues on to a megalithic tomb at the base of Farraniaragh Mountain, 248m above sea level.

Derrynane Sea Sports   WATER SPORTS
(✆087 908 1208; www.derrynaneseasports.com) Derrynane operates sailing, canoeing, windsurfing and waterskiing for all levels from the beach. In July and August ask about fun half-day kids camps for littlies and pirate camps for older children if you need a break from the kids (or they from you).

Sunfish Explorer   KAYAKING
(✆087 947 4616; http://sunfishexplorer.com; per hr/4hrs €30/100) This outfit runs trips in motorised kayaks, combining the accessibility and adventure of kayaking with the comfort of boating.

Eagle Rock Equestrian Centre   HORSE RIDING
(✆066-947 5145; www.eaglerockcentre.com) Beach, mountain and woodland treks for all levels from €30 per hour.

🛏 Sleeping & Eating

Wave Crest   CAMPGROUND €
(✆066-947 5188; www.wavecrestcamping.com; campsites from €19; @🖶) Just 1.6km southeast of Caherdaniel, this cliffside park has a superb setting and well-kept facilities. Book ahead during high season.

Olde Forge   B&B €€
(✆066-947 5140; www.theoldeforge.com; s/d €45/70; 🐾) Fantastic views of Kenmare Bay and the Beara Peninsula unfold from this B&B, which has six streamlined, comfortable rooms. If you want to base yourself here for some R&R, it also has two self-catering cottages (from €400 per week). It's 1.2km southeast of town on the N70.

Blind Piper   PUB €€
(✆066-947 5126; mains €11-23) This local institution with tables outside is a great family pub during the day, serving quality grub such as deep-fried monkfish. After dark, locals and visitors crowd inside, and music sessions strike up. Food served from noon.

Sneem

Halfway between Caherdaniel and Kenmare, Sneem (An tSnaidhm) is a good place to pause, especially if you're travelling anticlockwise, as for the remaining 27km to Kenmare the N70 drifts away from the water and coasts along under a canopy of trees.

The village's Gaeilge name translates as 'the knot', which is thought to refer to the River Sneem that swirls, knotlike, into nearby Kenmare Bay. Sneem is nicknamed 'the knot in the Ring of Kerry'. Other local puns include one about Charles de Gaulle, who holidayed here when Paris was burning in 1968. The statue commemorating this is called 'Le Gallstone'.

Take a gander at the town's two cute squares, then pop into the Blue Bull (South Square; mains €12-27; ⊘food served noon-2pm & 6-9.30pm), a perfect little old stone pub where you can probably learn more local puns.

The area is home to one of the finest castle hotels in the country, Parknasilla Resort & Spa (✆064-667 5600; www.parknasillahotel.ie; d/ste from €169/269; @🐾🏊), which has been wowing guests (including one George Bernard Shaw) since 1895 with its 200 hectares of pristine resort on the edge of the village of Sneem with the broad expanse of the Kenmare River separating it from the Beara Peninsula to the south (oh, the views!). From the modern, luxuriously appointed bedrooms to the top-grade spa (which includes a lap pool) and the elegant restaurant (bar snacks €12-16, 3-course menu €40; ⊘bar noon-8pm, restaurant 7-9pm Fri-Sun) everything here is done just right.

Kenmare

POP 2900

The copper-covered limestone spire of Holy Cross Church, drawing the eye to the wooded hills above town, may make you forget for a split second that Kenmare (pronounced 'ken-*mair*') is a seaside town. But with rivers named Finnihy, Roughty and Sheen emptying into Kenmare Bay, you couldn't be anywhere other than southwest Ireland.

In the 18th century, Kenmare was laid out on an X-plan, with a triangular market square in the centre. Today the inverted V to the south is the focus. Kenmare Bay stretches out to the southwest, and there are glorious views of the mountains.

◉ Sights

Kenmare Heritage Centre HERITAGE CENTRE
(☑064-664 1233; kenmaretio@eircom.net; the Square; ◌10.15am-5.30pm Apr-Oct) **FREE**
Reached through the tourist office, Kenmare's heritage centre tells the history of the town from its founding as Neidín by the swashbuckling Sir William Petty in 1670. The centre also relates the story of the Poor Clare Convent, founded in 1861, which is still standing behind Holy Cross Church.

Local women were taught needlepoint lace-making at the convent and their lacework garnered international fame. Upstairs from the Heritage Centre, the **Kenmare Lace and Design Centre** (www.kenmarelace. ie; ◌10.15am-5.30pm Apr-Oct) has displays including designs for 'the most important piece of lace ever made in Ireland' (in a 19th-century critic's opinion).

Stone Circle HISTORIC SITE
Signposted southwest of the Square is an early Bronze Age stone circle, one of the biggest in southwest Ireland. Fifteen stones ring a boulder dolmen, a burial monument rarely found outside this part of the country.

Holy Cross Church CHURCH
(Old Killarney Rd) Built in 1862, this church has a splendid wooden roof with 14 angel carvings. Intricate mosaics adorn the aisle arches and edges of the stained-glass window over the altar. The architect was Charles Hansom, collaborator and brother-in-law of Augustus Pugin (the architect of London's Houses of Parliament).

✵ Activities

The tourist office has details of walks around Kenmare Bay and into the hills, on sections of the Kerry Way and Beara Way .

Star Sailing WATER SPORTS
(☑064-664 1222; www.staroutdoors.ie; R571, Dauros) Star offers one-hour guided cruises (per adult/child €15/8) and other activities including sailing (per hour from €65 for up to six people; you'll need some prior experience), sea kayaking (single/double per hour €18/32) and hillwalking for all levels.

Seafari BOAT TOUR
(☑064-664 2059; www.seafariireland.com; Kenmare Pier; adult/child €20/12.50; ◌Apr-Oct)
Warm yourself on tea, coffee, rum and the captain's sea shanties on an entertaining two-hour spotting voyage to see Ireland's biggest seal colony and other marine life; binoculars (and lollipops!) are provided.

⌂ Sleeping

Virginia's Guesthouse B&B €€
(☑064-664 1021; www.virginias-kenmare.com; Henry St; s/d €60/90; ☐☐) You can't get more central than this award-winning B&B, whose creative breakfasts celebrate organic local produce (rhubarb and blueberries in season, for example, as well as fresh-squeezed OJ and porridge with whiskey). Its eight rooms are super comfy without being fussy.

Hawthorn House B&B €€
(☑064-664 1035; www.hawthornhousekenmare. com; Shelbourne St; d €80-90; ☐) This stylish house has eight spacious rooms, including a majestic family room, all named after local towns and decked out with fresh flowers. It's set back from busy Shelbourne St behind a low wall.

Whispering Pines B&B €€
(☑064-664 1194; www.whisperingpineskenmare. com; Glengarrif Rd; d from €70; ◌Easter-Nov; ☐)
In a quiet spot near the pier, this homey B&B has four immaculate rooms and a cheerful welcome. The location out here near the brine is fantastic; town is less than five minutes' stroll away.

Rose Cottage B&B €€
(☑064-664 1330; the Square; d €59-79; ☐☐) Opposite the park on the central square, amid beautiful gardens, this stone-fronted building has three rooms with private bathrooms. The Poor Clare nuns stayed here when they

arrived in Kenmare, then had to leave just as the apples were ripening in the orchard.

Sheen Falls Lodge BOUTIQUE HOTEL €€€
(☑064-664 1600; www.sheenfallslodge.ie; s/d from €160/220; restaurant 3-/4-course menu €45/65; ☺Feb-Dec; @🛜) The Marquis of Landsdowne's former summer residence still feels like an aristocrats' playground, with a fine-dining French restaurant, bar, a spa and 66 rooms with DVD players and Italian marble bathrooms, and views of the falls and across Kenmare Bay to Carrantuohil. Amenities are many (clay-pigeon shooting, anyone?).

✗ Eating

Bread Crumb BAKERY, CAFE €
(www.thebreadcrumb.com; New Rd; dishes €4-9; ☺8am-5pm Mon-Sat, 10am-5pm Sun) 🍴 Not only does this bakery have a tantalising selection of freshly baked breads, its vegetarian cafe has blackboard specials such as rice slices with roast pepper, spinach and blue cheese, and spelt pancakes with sun-dried tomatoes.

Truffle Pig DELI €
(dishes €6-13; ☺8.30am-6pm Mon-Sat) 🍴 Fine meats, farmhouse cheeses and a treasure trove of other deli items from the region.

Kenmare Ice Cream ICE CREAM €
(http://kenmareicecream.eu; Henry St; ice cream from €2.50; ☺9am-6pm Mon-Sat) Behind a candy-pink facade, this local ice-cream maker creates over 50 flavours – lemon meringue, caramel fudge, and orange and chocolate crisp among them.

Farmers Market MARKET €
(☺10am-5pm Wed) 🍴 On the Square.

★ Tom Crean Fish & Wine IRISH €€
(☑064-664 1589; www.tomcrean.ie; Main St; mains €17-25.50; ☺5-9.30pm; 🛜🍴) 🍴 Formerly known as D'Arcy's, this venerable restaurant has been renamed in honour of owner-chef Aileen d'Arcy's grandfather, Kerry's pioneering Antarctic explorer, Tom Crean. Local purveyors supply the best in organic produce, cheeses and fresh seafood, all served in modern, low-key surrounds. The raw oysters capture the scent of the bay; the homemade ravioli of prawn mousse and sesame-seed-crusted Atlantic salmon with lime and corriander are divine. Breakfast isn't included in room rates, but guests staying in its townhouse (d €60) get discounted evening meals.

Horseshoe PUB €€
(☑064-664 1553; www.thehorseshoekenmare.com; 3 Main St; mains €14-24.50; ☺kitchen 5-10pm Mon-Wed, noon-4pm & 5-10pm Thu-Sun) Ivy frames the entrance to this gastropub, which has a short but excellent menu that runs from Kenmare Bay mussels in creamy apple cider sauce to local lamb on mustard mash.

Mulcahys Restaurant IRISH €€
(☑064-664 2383; 36 Henry St; mains €19.50-28; ☺5.30-10pm Thu-Sun) Creative, often Asian-inspired twists on local seafood, such as salmon, prawn and cod sushi, are the pick of the menu here, but Mulcahys also serves meat-based classics such as beef Wellington.

🍷 Drinking & Entertainment

Crowley's TRADITIONAL PUB
(Henry St) This pub has good trad sessions.

PF McCarthy's LIVE MUSIC
(14 Main St) A wide range of acts perform here from Thursday to Saturday.

🛍 Shopping

Kenmare has many quality craft shops. On 15 August every year, marketers from throughout Ireland descend on the town with crafts, local produce, ponies, cattle, sheep and bric-a-brac for the Kenmare Fair.

★ Lorge Chocolatier CHOCOLATE
(☑064-667 9994; http://lorge.ie; Bonane; ☺10am-6pm Mon-Sat) Along the N21, 5km south of Kenmare, French native Benoit Lorge creates exquisite chocolates at his chocolaterie. Not only can you buy beautifully packaged chocolates here (and steaming hot chocolate too), you can also sign up for chocolate-making courses to create them yourself. A one-day beginners course (€150) covers tempering, moulding, dipping, truffle-making, chocolate mousse and more.

PFK Gold & Silversmith JEWELLERY
(www.pfk.ie; 18 Henry St; ☺10am-1pm & 2-6pm Tue-Sat) Minimalist jewellery by Paul Kelly and contemporary Irish designers. Kelly also takes commissions.

Soundz of Muzic MUSIC
(www.soundzofmuzic.ie; 9 Henry St; ☺10am-5.30pm Mon-Sat) Great selection of instruments and Irish and contemporary music.

ℹ Information

The website www.kenmare.com is good for tourist information. Banks and ATMs are common.

Post office (cnr Henry & Shelbourne Sts)
Tourist office (☑ 064-41233; The Square;
⊗9am-5pm Apr-Oct) Pick up free maps detailing a heritage trail around town and longer
walks of up to 13km.

🚌 Getting There & Away

The twisting, 32km-long drive on the N71 from
Killarney is surprisingly dramatic with tunnels
and stark mountain vistas. (Heading south,
it's 27km along the N71 and Beara Peninsula to
Glengarriff in County Cork.)

Twice-daily buses serve Killarney (€10.90, 50
minutes), with additional services in summer.
Buses stop outside Roughty Bar (Main St).
Finnegan's Coach & Cab (☑ 064-664 1491;
www.kenmarecoachandcab.com) Runs a variety of tours including the Ring of Kerry.

🚲 Getting Around

Finnegan's Cycle Centre (☑ 064-664 1083;
Shelbourne St; ⊗10am-6.30pm) Rents bikes
for €15/85 per day/week.

DINGLE PENINSULA

Unlike the Ring of Kerry, where the cliffs
tend to dominate the ocean, it's the ocean
that dominates the smaller Dingle Peninsula. The opal-blue waters surrounding the
promontory's green hills and golden sands
give rise to aquatic adventures and to fishing trawlers that haul in impossibly fresh
seafood, which appears on the menus of
some of the county's finest restaurants.

Dingle Peninsula culminates in Europe's
westernmost point, gazing across the sound
at the ghost town on Great Blasket Island.
Mt Brandon, the Connor Pass and other
mountainous areas add drama, as does a
high concentration of ring forts and other
ancient ruins. But it's where the land meets
the ocean, at whitewater-pounded rocks or
secluded coves, that Dingle's beauty is unforgettable.

Centred on charming Dingle town, there's
an alternative way of life here, lived by artisans and idiosyncratic characters and found
at trad sessions and folkloric festivals across
Dingle's tiny settlements.

The classic loop drive around Slea Head
from Dingle town is 50km, but allow a day to
take it all in. The main road to Dingle town
is the N86 via Tralee but the coast road is
far more beautiful and shouldn't be missed.

The following section follows a figure
eight, starting from the southwestern end
nearest Killarney and following the scenic
coast road to Dingle town, looping around
Slea Head and passing back through Dingle
town before traversing the Connor Pass to

Dingle Peninsula

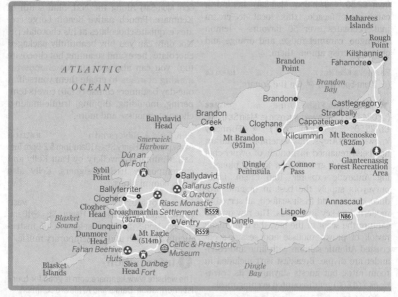

the northern side of the peninsula, from where you can rejoin the N86 to Tralee and Killarney.

☞ Tours

Several of Killarney companies also run daily day trips by bus around the Dingle Peninsula.

O'Connor's Slea Head Tours HISTORIC
(📱 087 248 0008; www.dingletourskerry.com; per person per hr €10; ☺ 11am & 2pm daily) Mainly covers the coast, with a focus on forts and other ancient sites. Tours last approximately three to four hours, departing from Dingle town's tourist office.

❶ Getting Around

Regular buses serve Dingle town from Killarney and Tralee, but service to the rest of the peninsula is limited to community buses running once or twice a week. Your own wheels (two or four) are the best way to explore the peninsula.

For drivers, the N86 from Tralee to Dingle town has little to recommend it other than being faster than the Connor Pass route. By bike it's less demanding.

On foot, the **Dingle Way** runs near the road for the first three days. The thicket of lanes on the north side of the Dingle Peninsula is matched only by the even thicker network of walking paths. Get the Ordnance Survey *Discovery series Map 70*, which shows every path on the peninsula in exhaustive detail.

Killarney to Dingle Town via Castlemaine

The quickest route from Killarney to Dingle passes through Killorglin and Castlemaine. At Castlemaine, head west on the R561. You'll soon meet the coast, then pass through the beachy seaside town of Inch before joining the N86 to Dingle.

Castlemaine is well connected with Tralee, Killorglin, and Limerick via Killarney, but there are no buses from Castlemaine to Annascaul via Inch.

Inch

Inch's expansive 5km-long sand spit was a location for both *Ryan's Daughter* and *Playboy of the Western World*. Sarah Miles, love interest in the former film, described her stay here as 'brief but bonny'.

The dunes are certainly bonny, scattered with the remains of shipwrecks and Stone Age and Iron Age settlements. The west-facing beach is also a hot surfing spot; waves average 1m to 3m. Learn to ride them with Offshore Surf School (📱 087 294 6519; http://offshoresurfschool.ie), which offers lessons starting from €25/20 per adult/child for a two-hour group class.

Cars are allowed on the beach, but don't end up providing others with nonstop laughs by getting stuck.

★ Sammy's (📱 066-915 8118; www.inch beach.ie; mains €14-20; ☺ 9.30am-10pm, reduced hours in winter; 🛜 ♿), at the entrance to the beach, is the nerve centre of the village. The beach-facing bar-restaurant serves a vast range of dishes from sandwiches to fresh oysters and mussels. There's a shop, tourist information and trad sessions during the summer.

Chic and contemporary, Inch Beach Guest House (📱 066-915 8333; www.inchbeach guesthouse.com; s/d €55/80; @ ♿) is more like a boutique hotel than a guesthouse: all skylights and sea views. Airy, neutral-toned rooms come with king-size beds. For longer stays, ask about its spectacularly sited self-catering cottages.

Annascaul

POP 271

The main reason to pause in the small village of Annascaul (Abhainn an Scáil), also spelled Anascaul, is to visit the South Pole Inn (☑066-915 7388; Main St; mains €10.50-18; ⊙lunch & dinner). Antarctic explorer Tom Crean ran this big blue pub in his retirement. Order hearty dishes worthy of an explorer as well as Dingle Brewing Company's Crean's lager on tap and in bottles. It's signposted from the coast road; buses stop here on the Dingle–Tralee run.

Dingle Town

POP 1500

Framed by its fishing port, the peninsula's charming little 'capital' is quaint without even trying. Dingle is one of Ireland's largest Gaeltacht towns; many pubs double as shops, so you can enjoy Guinness and a singalong among screws and nails, wellies and horseshoes. It has long drawn runaways from across the world, making it a cosmopolitan, creative place. In summer its hilly streets can be clogged with visitors; in other seasons its authentic charms are yours for the savouring.

Although this is Gaeltacht country, the locals have voted to retain the name Dingle rather than go by the officially sanctioned – and signposted – An Daingean.

◎ Sights

Dingle is one of those towns whose very fabric is its attraction. Wander up and down the streets, poke around back alleys, head off across the docks and amble into quality shops and pubs and see what you find.

Dingle Marine & Leisure (p300) runs boat trips to the Blasket Islands from the marina.

Dingle Oceanworld   AQUARIUM
(☑066-915 2111; www.dingle-oceanworld.ie; Dingle Harbour; adult/child/€13/7.50; ⊙10am-6pm Jul & Aug, 10am-5pm Sep-Jun; ♿) Dingle's aquarium is a lot of fun. Psychedelic fish glide through tanks that recreate such environments as Lake Malawi, the River Congo and the piranha-filled Amazon. Reef sharks and stingrays cruise the shark tank; water is pumped from the harbour for the spectacularly ugly wreck fish. There's a walk-through tunnel and a touch pool.

An Díseart   CULTURAL CENTRE
(☑066-915 2476; www.diseart.ie; Green St; adult/family €2/5; ⊙9-5pm Mon-Sat) In a magnificent neo-Gothic former convent, this Celtic culture centre has stained-glass windows by Harry Clarke depicting 12 scenes from the life of Christ. Admission includes a 15-minute guided tour.

Trinity Tree   SCULPTURE
(Green St) Close to St Mary's Church, the Trinity Tree sculpture, representing the Holy Trinity, is made from an unusual three-trunked sycamore. Its carved faces make it look like something out of a fairytale.

Dingle Brewing Company   BREWERY
(☑066-915 0743; http://dinglebrewingcompany. com; Spa Rd; admission €6; ⊙tours by reservation) 🍺 On the site of a 19th-century creamery, this terrific craft brewery was launched in 2011 on 20 July – not coincidently Tom Crean's birthday (its single brew, a crisp, hoppy lager, is named after the local Antarctic explorer). Admission includes a self-guided or guided brewery tour as well as a pint. If you're not doing the tour you can't stop in for a drink here, but you'll find it in bottled and draught form at numerous pubs throughout the peninsula and beyond.

🏃 Activities

In 1983 a bottlenose dolphin swam into Dingle Bay and local tourism hasn't been the same since. Showing an unnatural affinity for humans, he swam around with the local fishing fleet. Eventually somebody got the idea of charging tourists to go out in boats to see the friendly dolphin (nicknamed Fungie). Today up to 12 boats at a time and over 1000 tourists a day ply the waters with Dingle's mascot, the cornerstone of the local economy.

Fungie the Dolphin   BOAT TOUR
(☑066-915 2626; www.dingledolphin.com; the Pier; adult/child €16/8) Boats run by the Dingle Boatmen's Association cooperative leave the pier daily for one-hour dolphin-spotting trips of Dingle's most famous resident, Fungie. It's free if Fungie doesn't show, but he usually does.

In the warmer months, the association also runs a daily two-hour boat trip when you can swim with Fungie (☑066-915 1146; per person €25, wetsuit hire €20; ⊙8am or 9am Apr–mid-Sep). Advance bookings are essential.

Finn McCool's
SURFING

(☎066-915 0833; www.finnmccools.ie; Green St; surf lessons adult/child €30/20; ⊙shop 10am-6pm Mon-Sat year-round plus noon-4.30pm Sun Mar-Sep) McCool's offers surf lessons at Brandon Bay (transport included), and sells gear including its own groovy range of surfwear.

Irish Adventures
WATER SPORTS

(☎066-915 2400; www.irishadventures.net; Strand St; ⊙9.30am-5.30pm Mon-Fri, 9am-6pm Sat) The Mountain Man Outdoor Shop is a shopfront for Irish Adventures, which offers guided trips including rock climbing, mountain climbing, biking, and kayaking with Fungie (half-day or sunset trip €50).

Dingle Jaunting
CARRIAGE TOURS

(☎086 177 1117; www.dinglejaunting.com; adult/child €8/2) Horse-drawn jaunting cars depart on the hour from the harbour car park for a 40-minute trip around Dingle. At Christmas there are 'jingle jaunts'.

Dingle Hill Walking Club
WALKING

(www.dinglehillwalkingclub.com) Great local club that welcomes visitors for regular half-day guided hill walks (many of them free).

Dingle Music School
MUSIC LESSONS

(☎086 319 0438; www.dinglemusicschool.com; Dykegate Lane, Wren's Nest Cafe; per hr €30) John Ryan offers Bodhrán and tin-whistle workshops for everyone from beginners to experienced players – lessons can be arranged for early morning or evening. Instruments are supplied.

☆ Festivals & Events

Check upcoming events and gigs online at www.dingle-peninsula.ie/calendar.

Dingle Races
HORSE RACES

(www.dingleraces.ie; ⊙mid-Aug) Held every second weekend in August, Dingle's races bring crowds from far and wide. The racetrack is 1.6km east of town on the N86.

Dingle Regatta
BOAT RACES

(⊙late Aug) This harbour race in traditional Irish *currach* (or *naomhóg*) canoes is Kerry's largest event of its kind and inspired the trad song of the same name.

Dingle Food & Wine Festival
FOOD, WINE

(www.dinglefood.com; ⊙early Oct) Fabulous foodie fest featuring a 'taste trail' with cheap-as-chips sampling at over 40 locations around town, plus a market, cooking

DINGLE WAY

This 168km walk loops around the peninsula. It takes eight days to complete, beginning and ending in Tralee, with an average daily distance of 21km. The first three days offer the easiest walking but the first day, from Tralee to Camp, is the least interesting; it could be skipped by taking the bus to Camp. Ordnance Survey *Discovery Series map 70* covers the peninsula.

demonstrations, workshops, and a foraging walk.

🛏 Sleeping

This tourist town has loads of midrange B&Bs. A number of pubs also offer accommodation.

Hideout Hostel
HOSTEL €

(☎066-915 0559; www.thehideouthostel.com; Dykegate Lane; dm/d €18/50; @☎) Converted from a former guesthouse, this central hostel has inherited bathrooms in all rooms. Top-notch facilities include two lounges with groovy furnishings, bike storage and a well-equipped kitchen. Rates include light breakfast (tea, coffee, toast, cereal). Switched-on owner Mícheál is a fount of local info.

Dingle Harbour Lodge
HOTEL €€

(☎066-915 1577; www.dingleharbourlodge.com; the Wood; s/d from €50/75; ☎🖶) Recently transformed with an airy, timber-floored lobby filled with fresh flowers, neat rooms equipped with flat-screen TVs and ultra-efficient new managers, Dingle Harbour Lodge fills a niche for inexpensive contemporary accommodation. Although just five minutes' walk from the centre, its position above the harbour means no street noise and stunning views from upper-level rooms.

Pax House
B&B €€

(☎066-915 1518; www.pax-house.com; Upper John St; s/d from €100/115; ⊙closed mid-Nov–mid-Feb; @☎🖶) From its highly individual decor (including contemporary paintings) to the outstanding views over the estuary from room balconies and the terrace, Pax House is a treat. Choose from cheaper hill-facing accommodation, rooms that overlook the estuary, and two-room family suites opening to the terrace. Wi-fi is available in the lounge. It's 1km southeast of the town centre.

COUNTY KERRY DINGLE TOWN

Dingle Town

200 m
0.1 miles

Dingle Brewing Company (140m);
Connor Pass (8km);
Cloghane (15km);
Tralee (38km)

Pax House (450m)

Spa Rd

John St

Lower Main St

Upper Main St

The Mall

Goat St

Green St

Chapel Ln

Orchard Ln

Dykegate Ln

Grey's Ln

St Mary's Church

Bridge St

Strand St

Mountain Man Outdoor Shop

Dingle Boatmen's Association

Pier

Dingle Harbour

The Wood

Marina

Harbour Nights (250m);
Ventry (8km);
Dunquin (16km)

Dingle Skellig Hotel (500m);
N86 (2km);
Annascaul (11km);
Tralee (39km)

N86

Dingle Town

Harbour Nights　　　　　　　B&B €€
(☑ 066-915 2499; www.dinglebandb.com; the Wood; d €70-80; @ 🛜 🛦) All 14 rooms at this waterfront B&B have stunning views of Dingle's harbour, as does the upstairs sitting room, which opens to a terrace.

An Capall Dubh　　　　　　　B&B €€
(☑ 066-915 1105; www.ancapalldubh.com; Green St; s €60-65, d €80-90; 🛜 🛦) Entered via a 19th-century coach entrance to a cobbled courtyard, this airy B&B is furnished with light timbers and checked fabrics. Ask about its self-catering townhouses, which sleep up to six people.

Dingle Benner's Hotel　　　　HOTEL €€€
(☑ 066-915 1638; www.dinglebenners.com; Main St; s/d from €120/190; 🛜) A Dingle institution, melding old-world elegance, local touches and modern comforts in the quiet rooms, lounge, library and (refurbished, very popular) Mrs Benners Bar. Rooms in the 300-year-old wing have the most character; those in the new parts are quieter.

Dingle Skellig Hotel　　　　HOTEL €€€
(☑ 066-915 0200; www.dingleskellig.com; d €89-199; @ 🛜 🛦 🛦) An oceanlike swimming pool and a spa with an outdoor hot tub are the highlights of these luxurious digs down near the water, just off the N86. Rooms are rich in chocolate-box-like cream, caramel and hazelnut tones. There are interconnecting rooms for families, plus a crèche and kids club, as well as a restaurant and several bars.

🍴 Eating

In a county famed for its seafood, Dingle still stands out. There are some superb restaurants and cafes, as well as excellent pub fare, particularly at John Benny's (p298).

An Café Liteártha　　　　　　CAFE €
(Dykegate Lane; snacks €4-7.50; ⊙ 11am-4pm Mon-Sat) Curl up with a book, a cup of tea and a scone or a warming soup at this delightful cafe at the back of a bookshop specialising in Irish history, and soak up the spirit of literary Dingle.

Ti Koz　　　　　　　　　　　　CREPERIE €
(http://ti-koz.wix.com; 2 John St; crêpes €2-10; ⊙ noon-2pm & 5-9pm Mon-Sat) Behind its shamrock-green facade, this Breton crêperie is right at home here in Dingle. It's authentic down to its savoury *galettes* (made with buckwheat and including goat's cheese, walnut and honey), sweet crêpes such as salted caramel, and Breton cider.

Murphy's　　　　　　　　　　ICE CREAM €
(www.murphysicecream.ie; Strand St; cones from €3.80; ⊙ 11.30am-7pm; 🛜) Made in Dingle, with branches in Killarney and Dublin, amazing ice cream flavours include Guinness, Kilbeggan whiskey, brown bread, sea salt, honeycomb and cooling mint.

Farmers Market　　　　　　MARKET €
(cnr Bridge St & Dykegate Lane; ⊙ 9am-3pm Fri) 🍴 Fresh produce and homemade goodies galore.

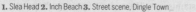

1. Slea Head 2. Inch Beach 3. Street scene, Dingle Town
4. Waterfall, Connor Pass

Dingle Peninsula

MICHAEL DIGGIN / ALAMY ©

The enchanting Dingle Peninsula distils County Kerry's best attractions into an eminently manageable day trip. But, like the many artisans who now call it home, the longer you spend here, the more likely it is you'll never want to leave – or at least return at the first opportunity.

Slea Head

The Dingle Peninsula's pièce de résistance is Slea Head, which has the greatest concentration of ancient sites in Kerry. In between them – and the camera-craving scenery – illuminating stops include the quirky Celtic & Prehistoric Museum.

Castlegregory

On the northern side of the Dingle Peninsula, Castlegregory is the gateway to its water sports playground. Diving is the number one attraction; there are also magical woodlands to wander.

Connor Pass

There are quicker routes across the Dingle Peninsula's interior, but none as scenic as Connor Pass. As Ireland's highest mountain pass, at 456m, it has captivating views across the peninsula.

Inch Beach

Perfect breakers, a wide, sandy shore and a brilliant pub/restaurant/cafe, Sammy's, make Inch Beach an essential stop. Sign up for surf lessons or take blustery walks along the 5km-long sand spit.

Dingle Town

The peninsula's namesake 'capital' fulfils every notion of an Irish seaside village: antique pubs still doubling as grocery stores, higgledy-piggledy streets, trad music sessions and a harbour unloading fresh seafood.

Global Village Restaurant   INTERNATIONAL €€
(☑066-915 2325; www.globalvillagedingle.com;
Upper Main St; mains €19-29; ⊙5.30-9.30pm
Wed-Sun Mar-Oct) 🍽 With the sophisticated
feel of a continental bistro, this restaurant
offers a fusion of global recipes gathered
by the well-travelled owner-chef, but uti-
lises sustainable local produce, such as
the Kerry mountain lamb. The wine list is
excellent.

Goat Street Cafe   CAFE €€
(☑066-915 2770; Goat St; mains €6-22.50;
⊙10am-4pm Mon-Sat) With its own photo
gallery, polished hardwood surfaces and sophisticated furnishings, this is one of Dingle's
most popular cafes for international fare –
from lamb tajines to Thai green curries, ginger stir-fries and Mediterranean casseroles.

★ **Out of the Blue**   SEAFOOD €€€
(☑066-915 0811; www.outoftheblue.ie; the Wood;
lunch €10-20, mains €22.50-29; ⊙5.30-9.30pm
daily, 12.30-3pm Sun) 'No chips', reads the
menu of this funky blue-and-yellow, fishing-
shack-style restaurant on the waterfront.
Despite its rustic surrounds, this is Dingle's
best restaurant, with an intense devotion
to fresh local seafood (and only seafood);
if they don't like the catch, they don't open.
Creative dishes change daily, but might include steamed crab claws in garlic butter and
pan-seared scallops flambéed in Calvados.
Who needs chips?

Doyle's   SEAFOOD €€€
(☑066-915 2674; www.doylesofdingle.ie; 4 John St;
mains €23.50-33; ⊙from 5pm, days vary seasonally) Scarlet-fronted Doyle's serves some of
the best seafood in the area (which in these
parts is really saying something). Starters
such as seafood risotto and seafood pie team
up with various mains including spicy Spanish fish stew, seafood linguine and lobster.

Half Door   SEAFOOD €€€
(☑066-915 1600; John St; mains €10-45;
⊙12.30-3pm & 5-10pm Mon-Sat; 🚼) Seafood is
superbly presented at this dignified, genteel
restaurant. Fish and shellfish are delivered
daily fresh from the docks; the local prawns
and larger crustaceans are especially good
here.

🍷 **Drinking & Entertainment**

Dingle has literally dozens of pubs, many
with entertainment.

★ **John Benny's**   PUB
(www.johnbennyspub.com; Strand St) A toasty
cast-iron woodstove, stone-slab floor, memorabilia, great staff and no intrusive TV make
this one of Dingle's most enjoyable pubs. Local musos pour in most nights for rockin' trad
sessions. Mains cost €12 to €22.50 and bar
food is available from noon till 9.30pm.

Dick Mack's   PUB
(http://dickmacks.homestead.com; Green St) Stars
in the pavement bear the names of Dick
Mack's celebrity customers. Ancient wood
and ancient snugs dominate the interior,
which is lit like the inside of a whiskey bottle. Out the back there's a warren of tables,
chairs and characters.

Shop Pubs   PUB
A number of Dingle's pubs are mongrel affairs that still have vestiges of their lives as
shops. Two untouched examples are **Foxy
John's** (Main St) and **Curran's** (Main St),
which respectively have old stock of hardware and outdoor clothing lying about.
Don't expect an exuberant welcome from
the flinty-eyed locals.

Small Bridge Bar   LIVE MUSIC
(An Droichead Beag; Lower Main St) Traditional
music kicks off at 9.30pm nightly at this
raucous pub by the bridge.

Blue Zone   JAZZ
(Green St; pizza €9.50-16; ⊙from 5.30pm) Great
late-night hangout that's part jazz venue,
part pizza restaurant and part wine bar,
with moody blue and red surrounds.

Phoenix Dingle   CINEMA
(www.phoenixdingle.net; Dykegate Lane) Cosy
family-run cinema screening first releases
and art-house films.

🛍 **Shopping**

Amid Fungie flotsam you'll find shops with
beautiful goods by local artisans.

Lisbeth Mulcahy   FASHION, HOMEWARES
(www.lisbethmulcahy.com; Green St; ⊙10am-6pm
Mon-Sat) Beautiful scarves, rugs and wall
hangings are created on a 150-year-old loom
by this long-established designer. Also sold
here are ceramics by her husband, who has
a workshop at Louis Mulcahy Pottery (p301),
west of Dingle.

An Gailearaí Beag   ARTS & CRAFTS
(www.angailearaibeag.com; Main St; ⊙11am-5pm
daily) Often staffed by the artists themselves,

this little gallery is a showcase for the work of the West Kerry Craft Guild, selling ceramics, paintings, wood carvings, photography, batik, jewellery, stained glass and more.

Brian de Staic   JEWELLERY
(www.briandestaic.com; Green St; ⊙9am-6pm Mon-Sat) This renowned local designer's exquisite modern Celtic work includes symbols such as the Hill of Tara, crosses and standing stones, as well as jewellery inscribed with Ogham script. All of de Staic's jewellery is individually handcrafted. De Staic's Dingle workshop (the Wood; ⊙9.30am-5.30pm Mon-Sat) also has a retail store.

Little Cheese Shop   CHEESE
(www.thelittlecheeseshop.net; Grey's Lane; ⊙11am-6pm Mon-Fri, 11am-5pm Sat) Swiss-trained cheesemaker Maja Binder's tiny shop overflows with aromatic cheeses including her own.

Dingle Record Shop   MUSIC
(www.dinglerecordshop.com; Green St; ⊙11am-5pm Mon-Sat) Tucked under jazz venue Blue Zone, this jammed music hub has all the good stuff you can't download yet. Podcasts recorded in-store are available online. Hours can be erratic.

❶ Information

The banks on Main St have ATMs and bureaux de change. The post office is off Lower Main St. Parking is free throughout town, with metered parking at the harbour.

Tourist office (✆066-915 1188; www.dingle-peninsula.ie; The Pier; ⊙9.15am-5pm Mon-Sat) Busy but helpful, this place has maps, guides and plenty of information on the entire peninsula. It books accommodation for a €5 fee.

❶ Getting There & Away

Bus Éireann (www.buseireann.ie) buses stop outside the car park behind the supermarket. Up to six buses a day serve Killarney (€16, 80 minutes) via Tralee (€13, 45 minutes).

❶ Getting Around

Dingle is easily covered on foot. Taxi company **Dingle Co-op Cabs** (✆087 222 5777) can also arrange private tours of the peninsula.

Bike-hire places include **Paddy's Bike Shop** (✆066-915 2311; Dykegate Ln; per day €10; ⊙9am-7pm), as well as **Foxy John's** (✆066-915 1316; Main St; per day €12), where you can abandon your energetic ideas and simply have a pint.

West of Dingle

At the tip of the peninsula is the Slea Head drive along the R559. It has the greatest concentration of ancient sites in Kerry, if not the whole of Ireland.

The landscape is dramatic, especially in shifting mist, although full-on sea fog obliterates everything. For the best views, follow the Slea Head drive in a clockwise direction. Although it's a mere 50km in length, doing this drive justice requires a full day, at least.

Ventry & Around

POP 410
The village of Ventry (Ceann Trá), 6km west of Dingle town, is idyllically set next to a wide sandy bay. It's a departure point for the wild Blasket Islands.

Seafood comes fresh, French-accented and affordable at the marine-coloured Skipper Restaurant (✆085-278 7958; mains €14-22.50; ⊙noon-9pm mid-Mar–Sep); land-based dishes include rabbit stew.

An ideal base for exploring the area is Ceann Trá Heights (✆066-915 9866; www.ceanntraheights.com; s €45-55, d €60-76; ⊙Mar-Oct; ✆), a comfortable, modern five-room guesthouse overlooking Ventry Harbour (rooms 1 and 2 have stunning water views). An open fire warms the cosy sitting room.

Near Ceann Trá Heights is Long's Riding Stables (✆066-915 9723; www.longsriding.com; 1hr/day rides from €30/130), which offers mountain and beach treks, as well as lessons (per hour from €25).

About 3km west of the village, the Celtic & Prehistoric Museum (✆087-770 3280; www.celticmuseum.com; Kilvicadownig, Ventry; admission €5; ⊙10am-5.30pm mid-Mar–Oct) squeezes in an astonishing collection of Celtic and prehistoric artefacts. Among its 500-plus pieces are the largest woolly mammoth skull and tusks in the world, as well as a 40,000-year-old cave bear skeleton, Viking horse-bone ice skates, stone battle-axes, flint daggers and jewellery. It started as the private collection of owner Harry Moore, a US expat musician (ask him to strike up a Celtic tune). The gift shop stocks 'weird stuff', including fossils.

Slea Head & Dunmore Head

Overlooking the mouth of Dingle Bay, Mt Eagle and the Blasket Islands, Slea Head has fine beaches, good walks and some superbly preserved structures from Dingle's ancient past including beehive huts, forts, inscribed stones and church sites. Dunmore Head is the westernmost point on the Irish mainland and the site of the wreckage in 1588 of two Spanish Armada ships.

The Iron Age Dunbeg Fort (www.dunbeg fort.com; admission €3; ⊙9am-7pm) is an example of a promontory fortification, perched atop a sheer sea cliff about 7km southwest of Ventry on the road to Slea Head. The fort has four outer walls of stone. Inside are the remains of a house and a beehive hut and an underground passage. Admission includes a 10-minute audiovisual presentation in the visitor centre. The adjacent Stonehouse Cafe & Restaurant (www.stonehouseventry. com; Dunbeg Fort Visitor Centre; dishes €6-15; ⊙10.30am-8pm Apr-Sep, reduced hours Oct-Mar; ⚐) serves outstanding crab sandwiches and heartier fare such as beef-and-Guinness stew.

Just uphill from the Dunbeg Fort Visitor Centre is the 1845-built **Famine Cottage** (http://famine-cottage.com; admission €3; ⊙10am-6pm daily Apr-Oct, reduced hours winter), with furnishings, cooking utensils and farm animals that evoke the hardship its occupants endured.

The Fahan beehive huts, including two fully intact huts, are 500m west of Dunbeg Fort on the inland side of the road. When the kiosks are open in summer, expect to pay €3 admission.

Dunquin

Yet another pause on a road of scenic pauses, Dunquin is a scattered village beneath Mt Eagle and Croaghmarhin. It's a hub for all things Blasket. The local website (www. dunchaoin.com) notes that it is the next parish to America.

The Blasket Centre (Ionad an Bhlascaoid Mhóir; ☑066-915 6444; www.heritageireland.ie; adult/child €4/2; ⊙10am-6pm Apr–mid-Oct) is a wonderful interpretive centre in a long, white hall ending in a wall-to-ceiling window overlooking the islands. Great Blasket's rich community of storytellers and musicians is profiled along with its literary visitors, including John Millington Synge, writer of *Playboy of the Western World*. The more prosaic practicalities of island life are covered by exhibits on shipbuilding and fishing. There's a cafe and a bookshop.

Europe's westernmost hostel, Dunquin Hostel (☑066-915 6121; www.anoige.ie; dm €15-18.50, tw €42; ⊙Mar-Oct), has a terrific location near the Blasket Centre, with awesome views. Private rooms and smaller dorms have private bathrooms. There's a good self-catering kitchen, but the nearest shop is 8km away – bring supplies.

Blasket Islands

The Blasket Islands (Na Blascaodaí), 5km out into the Atlantic, are the most westerly islands in the country. At 6km by 1.2km, Great Blasket (An Blascaod Mór) is the largest and most visited, and mountainous enough for strenuous walks. All of the Blaskets were inhabited at one time or another; there is evidence of Great Blasket being inhabited during the Iron Age and early Christian times. The last islanders left for the mainland in 1953 after they and the government agreed that it was no longer feasible to live in such isolated and harsh conditions, although today a few people make their home out here for part of the year.

There are no camping facilities on the islands.

Boats trips generally run from Easter to September, but even then weather can cause boat cancellations – call for seasonal sailing times.

Blasket Island Ferries   BOAT TOUR
(☑066-915 1344, 066-915 6422; www.blasketis land.com; adult/child €20/10) Boats depart from Dunquin Harbour and take 20 minutes.

Blasket Islands Eco Marine Tours BOAT TOUR
(☑087 231 6131; www.marinetours.ie; morning/afternoon/day tour €25/40/50) Eco-oriented tours departing from Ventry Harbour.

Dingle Marine & Leisure   BOAT TOUR
(☑066-915 1344, 087 672 6100; www.dinglebay charters.com; ferry adult/child return €30/15, 3hr island tour €40/15) Ferries take 45 minutes from Dingle town's marina. Fishing trips (adult/child from €25/15 for two hours) are also available.

Clogherhead & Ballyferriter

Continuing north from Dunquin, stop at Clogherhead, where a short walk takes you out to the head with views down to a perfect little beach at Clogher. It's a prime resting spot for seals and other mammals with thick layers of insulating blubber not affected by the frigid waters.

Follow the road another 500m around to the crossroads at Clogher. Leave the loop road here and follow a narrow paved track down to the beach. The rugged surf is intoxicating, ceaselessly pounding this perfect crescent of sand.

Back on the loop road, follow the road as it turns inland to reach Ballyferriter (Baile an Fheirtearaigh). It's named after Piaras Ferriter, a poet and soldier who emerged as a local leader in the 1641 rebellion and was the last Kerry commander to submit to Cromwell's army. The entire landscape is a rocky patchwork of varying shades of green, delineated by miles and miles of ancient stone walls.

In the tiny village itself, the Dingle Peninsula Museum (Músaem Chorca Dhuibhne; ☑066-915 6100; www.westkerrymuseum.com; Ballyferriter; admission €3.50; ☉10am-5.30pm May-Sep, by appointment rest of year) is housed in the 19th-century schoolhouse, with displays on the archaeology and ecology of the peninsula. Across the street there's a lonely, lichen-covered church. Next door to the museum, local fare such as oven-roasted rack of Slea Head lamb in plum sauce and hake in lemon cream comes with stunning sea views at Altú Restaurant (☑087 177 7324; Ballyferriter; mains €15.50-21.50; ☉5.30-9pm Thu-Sat).

Louis Mulcahy Pottery (☑066-915 6229; www.louismulcahy.com; Clogher; ☉9am-6pm Mon-Fri, 10am-6pm Sat & Sun) has contemporary clay creations and a workshop where you can see how they're made and have a spin yourself on a pottery wheel (book ahead). Upstairs, its cafe (dishes €5-11; ☉10am-5pm) serves open sandwiches topped with organic smoked salmon and Dingle cheeses.

About 2.5km northeast is Dún an Óir Fort (Fort of Gold), the scene of a hideous massacre during the 1580 Irish rebellion against English rule. The fort was held by Sir James Fitzmaurice, who commanded an international brigade of Italians, Spaniards and Basques. On 7 November English troops under Lord Grey attacked the fort; within three days the defenders surrendered. All that remains of the fort is a network of grassy ridges, but it's a pretty spot overlooking Smerwick Harbour, which has relatively sheltered waters that lack the sense of impending doom of those facing due west. The fort is about 2.5km north of Ballyferriter, near the Beal Bán beach.

The remains of the 5th- or 6th-century Riasc Monastic Settlement are one of the peninsula's more impressive and haunting sites, particularly the pillar with beautiful Celtic designs. Excavations have also revealed the foundations of an oratory first built with wood and later stone, a kiln for drying corn and a cemetery. The ruins are signposted as 'Mainistir Riaisc' along a narrow lane off the R559, about 2km east of Ballyferriter.

A fine base for explorations on foot, An Speíce (☑066-915 6254; www.anspeice.com; Ballyferriter; s €40-45, d €60-70; ☉Feb-Nov; ☎) has four sunny rooms furnished in an attractive modern style that would flummox most Irish B&B owners: where are the garish patterns? The mismatched linen? The colours usually seen these days only on rusting '70s appliances?

Free camping is possible near Ferriter's Cove but there are no facilities; ask locally before pitching.

Gallarus Castle & Oratory

One of the Dingle Peninsula's few surviving castles, Gallarus Castle (www.heritageireland. ie) was built by the FitzGeralds around the 15th century. Although it's closed indefinitely to the public for safety reasons, you can walk around the exterior. There's no parking next to the castle.

The dry-stone Gallarus Oratory (☑066-915 6444; www.heritageireland.ie; ☉10am-6pm May-Aug) FREE is quite a sight, standing in its lonely spot beneath the brown hills as it has done for some 1200 years. It has withstood the elements perfectly, apart from a slight sagging in the roof. Traces of mortar suggest that the interior and exterior walls may have been plastered. Shaped like an upturned boat, it has a doorway on the western side and a round-headed window on the eastern side. Inside the doorway are two projecting stones with holes that once supported the door.

Parking by the oratory is extremely limited and tends to become a mess in summer. There's a nearby private parking area at the visitor centre (☑066-915 5333; adult/child €3/free; ☉9am-9pm Jun-Aug, 10am-6pm Feb-May & Sep-10 Nov) that shows a 15-minute audiovisual display.

The castle and oratory are signposted off the R559, about 2km further on from the Riasc Monastic Settlement turn-off.

Ballydavid

About 2km from Gallarus Castle and Oratory, this little settlement has a fine setting on a sheltered cove and old coastguard

COUNTY KERRY WEST OF DINGLE

breakwater. Europe's westernmost camping ground, **Oratory House Camping** (Campaíl Teach An Aragail; ☑ 066-915 5143; www.dingleac tivities.com; Gallarus; campsites from €18; ☺ Apr–mid-Sep), is nearby. It's a source of much local information on a mass of activities, especially walking.

The pub, **Tigh TP** (☑ 066-915 5300; www. tigh-tp.ie; mains €8-19), is a good place for a waterside pint. Next door to it is the **Coast Guard Lodge** (d €75), which has six rooms with private bathrooms that sleep three to four people each in military comfort, and a self-catering kitchen.

Far and away the best place to eat and/ or sleep in the area is **Gormans Clifftop House** (www.gormans-clifftophouse.com; mains €19.50-28.50; s €95-115, d €130-150; ☺ dinner by reservation; ☎). Book ahead to dine on delicious Kerry mountain lamb stew, Dingle Bay prawns and other exquisite dishes. Rooms are airy, contemporary and immaculate, the welcome is warm and the views superb.

Connor Pass

At 456m, the Connor (or Conor) Pass is Ireland's highest mountain pass. On a foggy day you'll see nothing but the road just in front of you, but in fine weather it offers phenomenal views of Dingle Harbour to the south and Mt Brandon to the north. The road is in good shape, despite being very narrow and *very* steep (large signs portend doom for buses and trucks).

Next to a waterfall, the summit car park yields views down to two lakes in the rockstrewn valley below plus the remains of walls and huts where people once lived impossibly hard lives. When visibility is good, it's well worth the 10-minute climb to the summit to reach hidden **Peddlers Lake** and the kind of vistas that inspire mountainclimbers.

For cyclists, the pass is best approached from the northeast heading southwest, as you'll get the narrowest and steepest section over with early in the ride and can coast down the (relatively) gentler gradient and wider road towards Dingle town.

North Side of the Peninsula

At Kilcummin, a road heads west to the quiet villages of Cloghane and Brandon, and finally to Brandon Point overlooking Brandon Bay.

Cloghane & Around

POP 280

Cloghane (An Clochán) is another little piece of peninsula beauty. The village's friendly pubs and accommodation nestle between Mt Brandon and Brandon Bay, with lovely views across the water to the Stradbally Mountains.

⊙ Sights & Activities

For walkers, the main goal is scaling 951m-high **Mt Brandon** (Cnoc Bhréannain), Ireland's eighth-highest peak. If that sounds too energetic, there are plenty of coastal strolls.

Brandon's Point   VIEWPOINT

The 5km drive out to Brandon's Point from Cloghane follows ever-narrower single-track roads, culminating in cliffs with fantastic views north and east. Sheep wander the constantly eroding rocks, oblivious to their tenuous positions.

St Brendan's Church   CHURCH

This vacuum-silent church has a stained-glass window showing the Gallarus Oratory and Ardfert Cathedral.

✯ Festivals & Events

Lughnasa   HARVEST

(☺ late Jul) On the last weekend in July, Cloghane celebrates the ancient Celtic harvest festival Lughnasa with events – especially bonfires – both in the village and atop Mt Brandon.

Brandon Regatta   BOAT RACE

(☺ late Aug) Traditional *currach* canoe race.

🛏 Sleeping & Eating

Mount Brandon Hostel   HOSTEL €

(☑ 085-136 3454; www.mountbrandonhostel.com; dm/tw €20/45; ☺ Mar-Jan; @ 🐾) A small, simple hostel with scrubbed wooden floors and furniture, and a patio overlooking the bay. Most rooms have private bathrooms. Neighbouring the hostel is the cherry-coloured traditional pub, **O'Donnell's**.

O'Connors   PUB, B&B €€

(☑ 066-713 8113; www.cloghane.com; d €70; @ ☎) Book ahead to bag a room or a table in this welcoming village pub, which serves evening **meals** (mains €14-19; ☺ 7am-8.30pm)

made with local produce, ranging from salmon to steak. Landlord Michael has loads of local info and can also explain why there's an aeroplane engine out the front.

ℹ Information

Pick up tourist information, including local walking and hiking guides, from the shop and post office near the hostel and pub.

Castlegregory & Around

POP 950

Castlegregory (Caislean an Ghriare), which once rivalled Tralee as a busy local centre, is a quiet village, one highlight being the views back to the often snowy hills to the south (a lowlight is the sprawl of unattractive holiday homes).

However, things change when you drive up the sand-strewn road along the Rough Point peninsula, the broad spit of land between Tralee Bay and Brandon Bay. Up here, it's a water-sports playground. A prime windsurfing location, the peninsula also offers adrenaline-inducing wave-sailing and kitesurfing, while divers can glimpse pilot whales, orcas, sunfish and dolphins.

🏃 Activities

Glanteenassig Forest Recreation Area   LAKE, FOREST
(www.coillte.ie; ⊙7am-10pm May-Aug, 9am-6pm Sep-Apr) FREE East of Castlegregory, these 450 hectares of woodland, mountain, lake and bog are a magical, little-visited treasure. There are two lakes; you can drive right up to the higher lake, which is encircled by a plank boardwalk, though it's too narrow for wheelchairs or prams. Make sure you're out before closing (check signs at the entrance), or you'll have to pay a call-out fee to have the gates unlocked. It's signposted 7km south of Castlegregory, and also 7km west of the village of Aughacasla on the northern coast road (the R560), which links up with the N86 to Tralee.

Waterworld   DIVING
(📞066-713 9292; www.waterworld.ie; s-tank dive incl gear €45, intro harbour dive incl gear €80) Professional dive shop based at Harbour House.

Jamie Knox Watersports   WATER SPORTS
(📞066-713 9411; www.jamieknox.com; Maharees, Castlegregory) This place offers surf, windsurf, kitesurf, paddlesurf, canoe and pedalo

hire and lessons. Surf lessons start at €45 for a 'taster'. Look for the garish yellow trailers.

🛏 Sleeping & Eating

★Harbour House   HOTEL €€
(📞066-713 9292; www.maharees.ie; Scraggane Pier; s/d from €55/90; 🕾🖩🖶) In a stunning position overlooking the Maharees Islands, this family-run establishment has the intimate feel of a B&B, with 15 comfortable, contemporary rooms (without TV or wi-fi, but there's both in the comfy communal lounges) and a gorgeous mascot, Lucy the dog. The leisure centre is home to Waterworld dive centre (the pool is also used for diver training). Its **Islands Seafood Restaurant** (mains €11-27; ⊙dinner) is excellent; the family has its own fishing boat, bringing catches 'from tide to table', with vegetables grown in the garden out the back. Harbour House is 5km north of Castlegregory near the end of the peninsula.

Seven Hogs   IRISH €€
(📞066-713 9719; www.sevenhogs.ie; Aughacasla; mains €10-20; s/d €40/50, self-catering cottages per week from €200; ⊙bar food from 6pm Mon-Fri, from 1pm Sat & Sun; 🕾🖶) Set up above the R560 northern coast road, this dark-peach-painted place has an open-plan interior with a stone fireplace and book-filled shelves running the full width of the walls. In-the-know locals head here for its gourmet burgers with handcut chips. There are cosy B&B rooms (with wi-fi) onsite and a cluster of villas (without wi-fi) for self-caterers out the back.

★Spillane's   PUB €€
(📞066-713 9125; www.spillanesbar.com; Fahamore; mains €11.50-22.50; ⊙from 1pm, reduced hours winter; 🖶) 🍴 Outside tables overlook the beach, bay and mountains at this idyllic, laidback pub. Seafood is a speciality (the breaded scampi is a revalation), but it also does fabulous pizzas and house-made burgers with hand-cut chips.

NORTHERN KERRY

The landscape of Northern Kerry is often dull compared with the glories of the Ring of Kerry and the Dingle Peninsula, Killarney and Kenmare. But there are some interesting places that should give you pause on your drive. Tralee has a great museum while

Ballybunion and the blustery beaches south of the Shannon estuary are worth a look.

Tralee

POP 22,800

Although it's the county town, Tralee is often dismissed elsewhere in Kerry as an overflow valve for Limerick and its social problems. While that's unfair – there are some good restaurants and bars, a great museum and excellent new wetlands centre – it's certainly down-to-earth and more engaged with the business of everyday life than the tourist trade.

Founded by the Normans in 1216, Tralee has a long history of rebellion. In the 16th century the last ruling earl of the Desmonds was captured and executed here. His head was sent to Elizabeth I, who spiked it on London Bridge. The Desmond castle once stood at the junction of Denny St and the Mall, but any trace of medieval Tralee that survived the Desmond Wars was razed during the Cromwellian period.

Elegant Denny St and Day Pl are the oldest parts of town, with 18th-century buildings, while the Square, just south of the Mall, is a pleasant open space with a contemporary style.

◉ Sights & Activities

Kerry County Museum   MUSEUM
(☑066-712 7777; Denny St; adult/child €5/free; ◷9.30am-5.30pm Jun-Aug, to 5pm rest of year) An absolute treat, Kerry's county museum has excellent interpretive displays on Irish historical events and trends, with an emphasis on County Kerry. The Medieval Experience re-creates life (smells and all) in Tralee in 1450. Check out the deranged nights, a vision of horror right out of Monty Python. Children will love strolling the medieval streets and there's a commentary in various languages. The Tom Crean Room celebrates the local early-20th-century explorer who accompanied both Scott and Shackleton on epic Antarctic expeditions. It's housed in the neoclassical Ashe Memorial Hall.

Blennerville Windmill &
Visitor Centre   WINDMILL
(☑visitor centre 066-712 1064; adult/child €5/3; ◷9am-6pm Jun-Aug, 9.30am-5.30pm Apr-May & Sep-Oct) Blennerville, just over 1km southwest of central Tralee on the N86 to Dingle, used to be the city's chief port, though the

harbour has long since silted in. A 19th-century flour windmill here has been restored and is the largest working mill in Ireland and Britain. Its modern visitor centre houses an exhibition on grain-milling, and on the thousands of emigrants who boarded 'coffin ships' from what was then Kerry's largest embarkation point. There's also a database of the Irish émigrés who left for America. Admission includes a 30-minute guided tour of the windmill.

Tralee Bay Wetlands Centre   WETLANDS
(☑066-712 6700; www.traleebaywetlands.com; Ballyard Rd; adult/child €6/4; ◷10am-7pm Jul & Aug, 10am-5pm Sep-Jun) ⌘ A 15-minute nature-safari boat ride is the highlight of a visit to Tralee's new wetlands centre. You'll also get a good overview of the reserve's 3000 hectares, encompassing saltwater and freshwater habitats, from the 20m-high viewing tower (accessible by lift/elevator), and spot wildlife from bird hides. The main lake has pedal boats (per 30 minutes €10) and row boats (per 30 minutes €8) for hire, and a light-filled lakeside cafe-bistro; there's also a smaller 'learn to fish' lake.

★ Festivals & Events

Rose of Tralee   BEAUTY PAGEANT
(www.roseoftralee.ie; ◷Aug) In Ireland and beyond, Tralee is synonymous with the Rose of Tralee, a beauty pageant that's open to Irish women and women of Irish descent from around the world (the 'roses'). They're accompanied by unmarried men (known as 'escorts'), who also undergo a selection process. More than just a beauty contest, it's a five-day-long festival bookended by a gala ball and a 'midnight madness' parade led by the newly crowned Rose of Tralee, followed by a fireworks display. Other highlights include a fashion show. If you fancy your chances of becoming a rose or an escort, application forms are available online.

Kerry Film Festival   FILM
(www.kerryfilmfestival.com; ◷Oct) Five-day festival with a short film competition and screenings.

🛏 Sleeping

Denny St has various places to stay in all price ranges.

Finnegan's Holiday Hostel   HOSTEL, B&B €
(☑066-712 7610; www.finneganshostel.com; 17 Denny St; dm/d from €14/50; @�) An elegant

Tralee

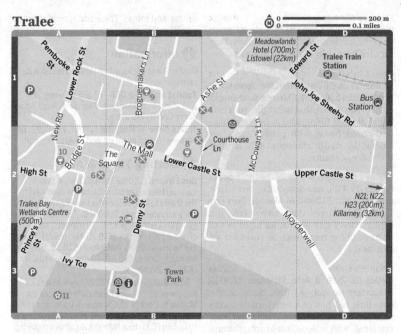

Tralee

◉ Sights
1 Kerry County Museum B3

⬚ Sleeping
2 Finnegan's Holiday Hostel B2

◈ Eating
3 Chez Christophe B2
4 Chopin's Cafe C1
5 Denny Lane Bistro B2

6 Farmers Market A2
7 Quinlan's Fish B2

◔ Drinking & Nightlife
8 Baily's Corner B2
9 Roundy's B1
10 Seán Óg's A2

◉ Entertainment
11 Siamsa Tíre A3

Georgian facade fronts this friendly hostel and B&B. The grandeur has faded, but there is a sizeable kitchen and lounge. The dorms, named after Irish scribblers, have their own bathrooms as do the private rooms. Breakfast is available for €5.

★ **Meadowlands Hotel**　　　　HOTEL €€
(☏066-718 0444; www.meadowlandshotel.com; Oakpark; s €65-95, d €130-160; @🛇🅿) Strolling distance from town but far enough away to be quiet, Meadowlands is an unexpectedly romantic four-star hotel. Rooms are done out in autumnal hues and service is spot-on; ask about discounted rates. Its cavernous, beamed-ceilinged **bar** (bar snacksd €10-22; ⊘11am-9pm), serving top-notch seafood (the owners have their own fishing fleet), is at least as popular with locals as it is with visitors.

◈ Eating

Atmospheric seafood restaurants are a short drive west of Tralee in **Spa** and **Fenit** (p307).

★ **Quinlan's Fish**　　　　SEAFOOD €
(☏066-712 3998; the Mall; fish & chips €8-12; ⊘noon-10pm; 🛇) Quinlan's is Kerry's leading chain of fish shops, with its own fleet, so you know its seafood bar fare is fresh. The fish and chips are great; alternatives include Dingle Bay squid and chips with sweet chilli sauce. The Delft-blue and scrubbed-timber premises have a handful of wine barrel tables, or head to Tralee's Town Park.

Farmers Market MARKET €

(the Square; ⊙10am-4pm Sat) 🍴 Tralee's farmers market sprawls across the main square. Days vary, but it's usually busiest on Saturdays.

Chez Christophe FRENCH €

(🖉066-718 1562; 6 Courthouse Lane; dishes €3.50-10.90; ⊙9am-5.30pm; 🕸) Melt-in-your-mouth quiche, polenta-crusted aubergine with chilli and almond filling, and honey- and mustard-glazed bacon with parsley sauce are among the stylish choices at this scrumptious slice of France.

Denny Lane Bistro CAFE €€

(🖉066-719 4319; www.dennylane.ie; Denny Lane; mains €16-24; ⊙10am-3pm Mon-Sat, from 6pm Thu-Sat; 🍸) Entered via a narrow lane, this contemporary spot is great for tapas as well as more filling meals such as pan-fried sirloin steaks.

Chopin's Cafe CAFE €€

(🖉066-711 7539; 8 Ashe St; mains €8.50-18; ⊙8am-6pm Mon-Sat; 🍸) Irish twists at this cute little red box of a cafe include bacon-wrapped scallops and homemade beef burgers laced with onions, while international options include lasagne.

🍺 Drinking & Entertainment

Castle St is thick with mass-market pubs, many of them offering live entertainment.

★Roundy's BAR

(5 Broguemakers Lane; ⊙from 5pm) Ingeniously converted from a terrace house (with a tree still growing right through the courtyard garden-turned-interior), this funky little bar has hip tunes, regular DJs spinning old school funk and live bands. Very cool.

Baily's Corner PUB

(Lower Castle St; 🕸) Rugby memorabilia-filled pub that's deservedly popular for its regular traditional sessions, with local musicians performing original material.

Seán Óg's PUB

(Bridge St) Fair diddling trad music is on at this rambling and raucous bar from Sunday to Thursday in summer and up to a couple of times a week outside the season.

Siamsa Tíre THEATRE

(🖉066-712 3055; www.siamsatire.com; Town Park; shows per person €15-30; ⊙booking office 9am-6pm Mon-Sat) Siamsa Tíre, the National Folk Theatre of Ireland, re-creates dynamic aspects of Gaelic culture through song, dance,

drama and mime. There are several shows a week year-round.

🛈 Information

Castle St has banks with ATMs and bureaux de change.

Tourist office (🖉066-712 1288; Denny St; ⊙9.15am-5pm Mon-Sat, daily Jul & Aug) Below Kerry County Museum.

Tralee General Hospital (🖉066-712 6222; Boherbee) Has an accident and emergency unit.

🛈 Getting There & Away

Bus Éireann (🖉066-716 4700; www.buseireann.ie) has buses from the bus station next to the train station, east of the town centre. Nine daily services run to Dublin (€27.80, six hours), going via Listowel (€8.50, 30 minutes) and changing in Limerick (€19.70, two hours). There are hourly buses to Waterford (€28.50, 5½ hours), Killarney (€9.80, 40 minutes) and Cork (€20.70, 2½ hours).

Irish Rail (🖉066-712 3522; www.irishrail.ie) has services includes three daily services via Mallow to Cork (€35, 2¼ hours), up to nine to Killarney (€10.80, 45 minutes) and one direct train to Dublin (€33, four hours) with others requiring a change in Mallow.

🛈 Getting Around

There's a taxi rank on the Mall, or try **Jackie Power Tours & Cabs** (🖉066-712 6300; 2 Lower Rock St).

Tralee Gas & Bicycle Supplies (🖉066-712 2018; Strand St; ⊙8.30am-5.45pm Mon-Sat) hires out bikes (€15 per day).

Around Tralee

East of town you'll find one of the country's finest caves. Heading west takes you past the tiny township of Spa to the fishing port of Fenit. Travelling northeast of here takes you to Ardfert's medieval cathedral.

Crag Cave

This **cave** (🖉066-714 1244; www.cragcave.com; Castleisland; adult/child €12/5; ⊙10am-6pm daily Apr-Dec, 10am-6pm Wed-Sun Jan-Mar) was discovered in 1983, when problems with water pollution led to a search for the source of the local river. In 1989 300m of the 4km-long cave were opened to the public. Admission is by 30-minute guided tour; bring a jacket for the 10°C temperature inside. The remarkable rock formations include a stalagmite shaped like a statue of the Madonna (at least to some). There are play areas for kids, as well as a restaurant and, of course, a gift shop.

The cave is 18km east of Tralee. It's signposted from both Castleisland and the Abbeyfeale–Castleisland stretch of the N21. Castleisland is well connected with both Tralee and Killarney by bus.

Spa & Fenit

POP 435

Northwest of Tralee along the coast, it's about 7km to the small settlement of Spa (sometimes referred to on maps as 'The Spa') and another 6km on to Fenit.

Fenit's Irish name, An Fhianait, translates as 'the Wild Place' and, although the remote village itself is tiny, its position on the Atlantic has given rise to a sizeable fishing port and marina, and some sublime seafood restaurants in the area.

✖ Eating

West End Bar & Bistro SEAFOOD €€
(☑066-713 6246; www.westendfenit.ie; Fenit; mains €10-23; ☺restaurant 5-9pm Mon-Sat, 1-8pm Sun; closed Jan-Mar) A local icon, this fifth-generation whitewashed bar has a mouthwatering line-up of seafood, including baguettes filled with Tralee Bay crab, plus plenty of locally sourced meat dishes (their motto is 'fresh or nothing'). Rates for its 10 rooms with private bathrooms (€70) include hearty breakfasts.

Spa Seafoods Restaurant DELI, RESTAURANT €€
(☑066-713 6901; www.spaseafoods.com; Spa; mains €10.50-24; ☺shop 9am-6pm daily, restaurant 12.30-5pm & 6-9pm Fri-Sun) ● Diagonally opposite the Oyster Tavern, a contemporary glass building houses a scrumptious deli selling fresh seafood and condiments that self-caterers will find irresistible, along with a smart restaurant. The short but stellar menu includes home-smokedd-haddock-and-spinach tart and sautéed clams with Spanish sherry and Iberico ham.

Tankard SEAFOOD €€
(☑066-713 6164; Kilfenora, Fenit; mains €15-25; ☺12.30-9.30pm) The menu of this bright-yellow pub-restaurant brims with local catches served in classical styles – pan-fried, deep fried and mornays, including a luscious scallop mornay with piped potato crust.

Oyster Tavern SEAFOOD €€€
(☑066-713 6102; Spa; mains €14-28; ☺from 5pm Mon-Sat, from noon Sun; ❸) Grilled Atlantic

salmon, pan-fried Kerry Head crab claws, Dingle Bay prawn scampi and lobster (in season) star at this classy restaurant, but carnivores and vegetarians aren't forgotten, with plenty of inventive options.

Ardfert

POP 924

Ardfert (Ard Fhearta), about 10km northwest of Tralee on the Ballyheigue road, is most notable for the soaring **Ardfert Cathedral** (☑066-713 4711; www.heritageireland. ie; adult/child €3/1; ☺10am-6pm May-Sep). Most of the building dates back to the 13th century, but it incorporates elements of an 11th-century church. Set into one of the interior walls is an effigy, said to be of St Brendan the Navigator, who was educated in Ardfert and founded a monastery here. The grounds contain the ruins of two other churches, 12th-century Templenahoe and 15th-century Templenagriffin.

Turning right in front of the cathedral and going 500m down the road brings you to the extensive remains of a **Franciscan friary**, dating from the 13th century, but with 15th-century cloisters.

Listowel

POP 4207

The late writer Bryan MacMahon said of Listowel: 'I harbour the absurd notion of motivating a small town in Ireland, a speck on the map, to become a centre of the imagination.' Listowel certainly has more literary credentials than your average provincial town, with connections to such accomplished scribes as John B Keane, Maurice Walsh, George Fitzmaurice and Brendan Kennelly.

Outside these connections and a few venues, however, the town is little more than some tidy Georgian streets. These are arranged around a main square with the St John's Theatre and Arts Centre, formerly St John's Church, and a park running along the edge of the River Feale, which can be reached down a road alongside the castle.

◉ Sights & Activities

Kerry Literary & Cultural Centre CULTURAL CENTRE
(Seanchaí; ☑068-22212; www.kerrywritersmuse um.com; 24 the Square; adult/child €5/3; ☺9.30am-5.30pm daily Jun-Sep, 10-4pm Mon-Fri Oct-May) The audiovisual Writers' Exhibition

at this gem of a cultural centre gives due prominence to Listowel's heritage of literary observers of Irish life. Rooms are devoted to local greats such as John B Keane and Bryan MacMahon, with simple, haunting tableaux narrating their lives and recordings of them reading their work. There's a cafe and a performance space where events are sometimes staged.

Keane is remembered with a statue on the opposite side of the square, in which he seems to be hailing a cab. He wrote with wry humour about subjects ranging from Limerick's beggars to the perils of giving up porter as a New Year's resolution.

On Church St, opposite the police station, a literary mural depicts the local writers and their pronouncements.

Listowel Castle   CASTLE

(☑086 385 7201; www.heritageireland.ie; ⊙10am-5pm Tue-Sat late May-late Aug) FREE Behind the Kerry Literary & Cultural Centre, this 12th-century castle was once the stronghold of the Fitzmaurices, the Anglo-Norman lords of Kerry. It was the last castle in Ireland to succumb to the Elizabethan attacks during the Desmond revolt. What remains of the castle has been thoroughly restored.

St John's Theatre & Arts Centre   ART CENTRE

(☑068-22566; www.stjohnstheatrelistowel.com; the Square) Located in a former church, it now hosts art exhibitions as well as drama, music and dance events.

Lartigue Monorailway   RAILWAY

(☑068-24393; www.lartiguemonorail.com; John B Keane Rd; adult/child €6/3; ⊙1-4.30pm May-Sep) Designed by Frenchman Charles Lartigue, this unique survivor of Victorian railway engineering operated between the town and Ballybunion on the coast. Although it no longer travels as far as Ballybunion, the renovated section of line is short (less than a kilometre) but fascinating, with manual turntables at either end for swinging the train around.

Walking   WALKING

The tourist office has leaflets on walks such as the 3.5km river walk and the 10km Sive walk, which takes in John B Keane Rd, a disused railway track and a bog.

✦ Festivals & Events

Writers' Week   LITERATURE

(www.writersweek.ie; ⊙late May/early Jun) Bibliophiles flock to Listowel for five days of readings, poetry, music, drama, seminars, storytelling and many other events held at various locations around town. The festival attracts an impressive list of writers, which have included Booker Prize–winning Colm Tóibín, John Montague, Jung Chang, Damon Galgut, Rebecca Miller and Terry Jones.

Listowel Races   HORSE RACING

(www.listowelraces.ie; ⊙mid-Sep) Races take place over Whit weekend in June and for a week.

🍴 Sleeping & Eating

Listowel Arms Hotel   HOTEL €€

(☑068-21500; www.listowelarms.com; the Square; s €64-120, d €120-200; @) Listowel's only full-service hotel is a family-run affair housed in a Georgian building that balances touches of grandeur with country charm. Furnished with antiques and marble sinks, the 42 rooms overlook the river and the racecourse. The Writers Bar (🔊) is a good place to find music in the summer; while the Georgian Restaurant (mains €13-22; ⊙from 3pm) specialises in the catch of the day, served battered, grilled or pan-fried.

Farmers Market   MARKET €

(⊙9am-2pm Fri) 🍴 Held on the Square, as markets have been for centuries.

🍷 Drinking

John B Keane   PUB

(37 William St) Once run by the late writer himself, this small, unassuming bar is swathed in Keane memorabilia.

ℹ Information

Tourist office (☑068-22212; www.listowel. ie; ⊙10am-5pm Tue-Sat late May-late Aug) Seasonally opening office housed in the Kerry Literary & Cultural Centre (p307).

ℹ Getting There & Away

Frequent daily buses serve both Tralee (€8.50, 40 minutes) and Limerick (€18.50, 1½ hours).

Around Listowel

Ballybunion

Ballybunion, a one-seahorse beach town 15km northeast of Listowel on the R553, is best known for the Ballybunion Golf Club (☑068-27146; www.ballybuniongolfclub.ie; green fees €65-180; ⊙tee times by reservation), reputed as one of the finest links courses in the world. Beyond the statue of a club-swinging Bill Clinton, commemorating his visit to the course in 1998, there are two expansive beaches; Ballybunion South has a Blue Flag rating.

Overlooking the southern beach are the remains of Ballybunion Castle, the 16th-century seat of the Fitzmaurices. There's an underground passage leading from the castle to the cliff.

The Ballybunion Bachelor Festival (⊙ Aug) sees tuxedo-clad bachelors from Ireland and beyond vying to impress the judges, while the town enjoys a long weekend of street entertainment and celebrations.

Skip the hotels in the town centre and head 2.5km south opposite the golf club to the superb Teach de Broc (http://ballybuniongolf.com; Link Rd; s/d €90/135; ⊙ inn closed Nov-Mar; 🐾). Its 14 rooms are spacious, stylish and thoughtfully appointed (hypoallergenic pillows, free bottled water). Its Strollers Bistro (mains €15-37; ⊙ 6-10pm Mon-Sat, 3-10pm Sun) is something of a misnomer (it's Ballybunion's top gourmet restaurant) and serves dishes such as roast duck with potato rösti and marmalade and ginger sauce and 'mini indulgence' desserts in shot glasses, and the bar is a civilised spot for a craft Icelandic beer or cocktail.

One bus (two in summer) runs from Listowel to Ballybunion Monday to Saturday (€5, 25 minutes).

Tarbert

POP 775

Tarbert is 16km north of Listowel on the N69. Shannon Ferry Limited (☑ 068-905 3124; www.shannonferries.com; one way/return bicycle & foot passengers €5/7, motorcycles €9/14, cars €18/28; ⊙ 7.30am-9.30pm Jun-Aug, to 7.30pm Sep-May, from 9.30am Sun year-round; 🐾) runs a half-hourly ferry between Tarbert and Killimer in County Clare, skipping the traffic congestion around Limerick city. The ferry dock is clearly signposted 2.2km west of Tarbert. If you do go through Limerick city from here, the N69 is the most scenic route.

Before you hop on the ferry, it's worth visiting the historic Tarbert Bridewell Jail & Courthouse (http://tarbertbridewell.com/museum.html; adult/family €3.50/10; ⊙ 10am-5pm Apr-Oct), which has exhibits (including stoic mannequins) on the rough social and political conditions of the 19th century. From the jail, the 6.1km John F Leslie Woodland Walk runs along Tarbert Bay towards the mouth of the Shannon.

If you want to stay overnight, the colourfully renovated 18th-century Ferry House Hostel (☑ 068-36555; www.ferryhousehostel.com; the Square; dm/d €18/48; 🐾), bang in the centre of town, is run by a well-travelled family and has clean, airy dorms and private rooms and a cute onsite cafe. Wi-fi is available in parts of the historic stone building.

In July and August, buses serve Limerick (€15.40, 1¼ hours).

Counties Limerick & Tipperary

POP 350,000 / AREA 6989 SQ KM

Best Places to Eat

➡ Restaurant 1826 Adare (p321)

➡ Mustard Seed at Eco Lodge (p322)

➡ Befani's (p332)

➡ Cafe Hans (p327)

Best Places to Stay

➡ Adare Manor (p321)

➡ The Boutique Hotel (p316)

➡ Aherlow House Hotel (p323)

➡ Dunraven Arms (p321)

Why Go?

From marching ditties to rhyming puns, the names Tipperary and Limerick are part of the lexicon, but both places are relatively unexplored by visitors.

County Limerick is closely tied to its namesake city, which has a history as dramatic as Ireland's. In a nation of hard knocks, it seems to have had more than its fair share. The city's streets have tangible links to the past and a gritty, honest vibrancy, and treasures abound in its lush, green country side.

In contrast, Tipperary town is minor. But amid the county's rolling hills, rich farmland and deep valleys bordered by soaring mountains, it's a peaceful place that's perfect for following a river to its source or climbing a stile to see a lonely ruin.

In both counties, ancient Celtic sites, medieval abbeys and other relics endure in solitude, awaiting discovery. And even Limerick and Tipperary's best-known sights retain a rough, inspiring dignity.

When to Go

➡ As the third-largest city in Ireland, with a sizeable student population, Limerick city bustles year-round, but is at its liveliest during the warmer months, from around April to October. These are also the best months to explore the rural villages, towns and countryside of both counties, when opening hours for attractions are longest (a number close during the rest of the year) and the weather is at its best.

➡ Most of the counties' festivities take place from April to October too, including wonderful walking festivals in the Glen of Aherlow.

COUNTY LIMERICK

Limerick's low-lying farmland is framed on its southern and eastern boundaries by swelling uplands and mountains. Limerick city is boisterously urban in contrast and has enough historic and cultural attractions for a day's diversion. About 15km south of the city are the haunting archaeological sites around Lough Gur, while about the same distance southwest of the city is the cute thatched village of Adare.

Limerick City

POP 56,800

Limerick city straddles the Shannon's broadening tidal stream, where the river swings west to join the Shannon Estuary. Following its tough past as portrayed in Frank McCourt's *Angela's Ashes*, its medieval and Georgian architecture received a glitzy, glossy makeover during the Celtic Tiger era, but the economic downturn has hit the city hard, as evidenced by extensive empty properties and drum-tight security shutters.

The city is rejuvenating again, however. Limerick has been chosen as the country's first-ever Irish City of Culture in 2014 (a designation to be awarded to an Irish city for 12 months every two years), with a packed program of arts, cultural and sporting events. It also has an intriguing, newly renovated castle, a lively art museum and contemporary cafe culture to go with its uncompromised pubs, as well as locals who go out of their way to welcome you.

The city is compact enough to get around on foot or by bike. To walk across town from St Mary's Cathedral to the train station takes about 15 minutes.

History

Viking adventurers established a settlement on an island in the River Shannon in the 9th century. They fought with the native Irish for control of the site until Brian Ború's forces drove them out in AD 968 and established Limerick as the royal seat of the O'Brien kings. Brian Ború finally destroyed Viking power and presence in Ireland at the Battle of Clontarf in 1014. By the late 12th century, invading Normans had supplanted the Irish as the town's rulers. Throughout the Middle Ages the two groups remained divided.

From 1690 to 1691, Limerick acquired heroic status in the saga of Ireland's struggle against occupation by the English. After their defeat in the Battle of the Boyne in 1690, Jacobite forces withdrew west behind the famously strong walls of Limerick town until the Treaty of Limerick guaranteed religious freedom for Catholics. The English later reneged and enforced fierce anti-Catholic legislation, an act of betrayal that came to symbolise the injustice of British rule.

During the 18th century, the old walls of Limerick were demolished and a well-planned and prosperous Georgian town developed. Such prosperity had waned by the early 20th century, as traditional industries fell on hard times. Several high-profile nationalists hailed from here, including Eamon de Valera.

◉ Sights

Limerick's main places of interest are clustered to the north on King's Island (the oldest part of Limerick and once part of Englishtown), to the south around the Crescent and Pery Sq (the city's noteworthy Georgian area), and all along the riverbanks.

★**King John's Castle**　　CASTLE
(www.shannonheritage.com; Nicholas St; adult/child €8/4.50; ⊘9.30am-5.30pm daily Apr-Sep, to 4.30pm Oct-Mar) The massive curtain walls and towers of Limerick's showpiece castle are best viewed from the west bank of the River Shannon. The castle was built by King John of England between 1200 and 1212 on the site of an earlier fortification. It served

TRACING YOUR ANCESTORS

Genealogical centres in counties Limerick and Tipperary can help trace your ancestors; contact the centres in advance to arrange a consultation.

Limerick Genealogy (☑061-496 542; www.limerickgenealogy.com; Dooradoyle Rd, Lissanalta House, Dooradoyle)

Tipperary North Genealogy Centre (☑067-33850; www.tipperarynorth.ie/genealogy; Kickham St, the Governor's House, Nenagh)

Tipperary South Genealogy Centre (☑062-61122; www.comhaltas.ie; Brú Ború Heritage Centre, Cashel)

Tipperary Family History Research (☑062-80555; www.tfhr.org; Mitchell St, Excel Heritage Centre, Tipperary town)

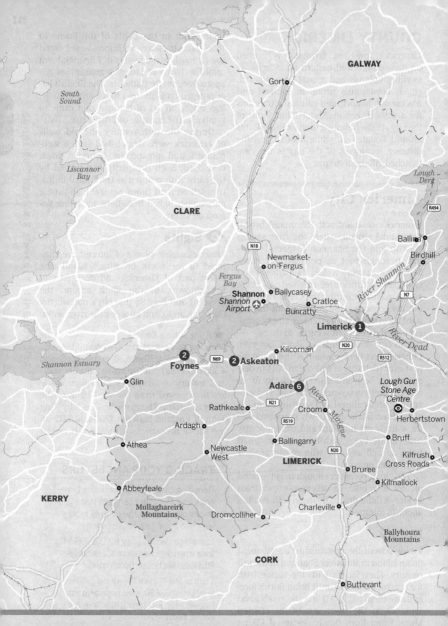

Counties Limerick & Tipperary Highlights

1 Discover Bronze Age, Iron Age and medieval treasures at the **Hunt Museum** (p315) in Limerick city

2 Take in River Shannon vistas along Limerick's back roads via atmospheric ruins at **Askeaton** (p319) and the **flying boat** (p319) museum at Foynes

3 Delve into a dazzling underworld of passages and chambers at the **Mitchelstown Caves** (p329)

4 Walk the walls and keep of Cahir's storybook **castle** (p328)

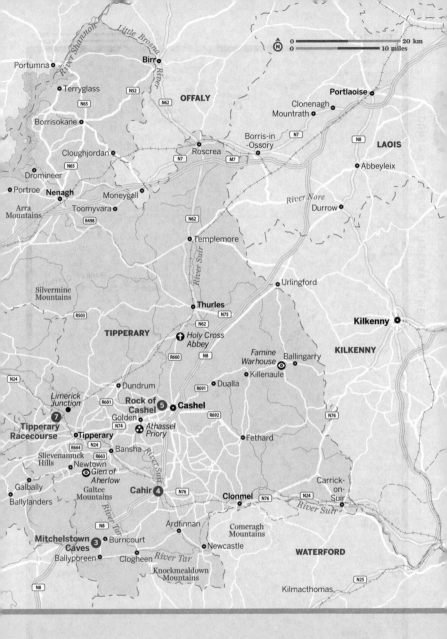

5 Explore the ancient religious buildings crowning the **Rock of Cashel** (p323)

6 Deliberate over mouthwatering menus in the thatched heritage town of **Adare** (p320)

7 Spend a day at the **races** (p322) at Tipperary, one of Ireland's finest tracks

Limerick

COUNTIES LIMERICK & TIPPERARY LIMERICK CITY

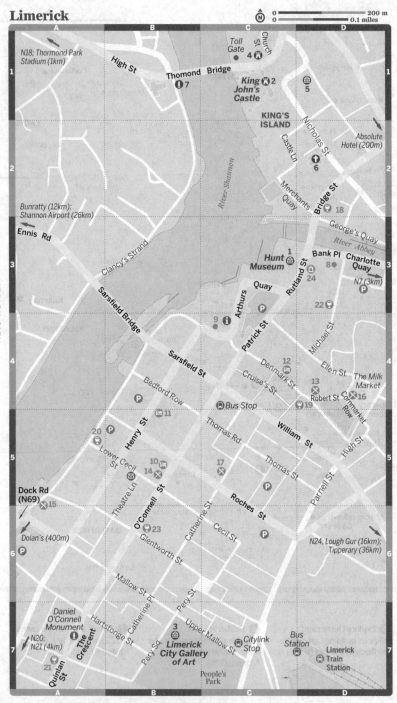

0 — 200 m
0 — 0.1 miles

N18; Thormond Park
Stadium (1km)

High St

Toll
Gate
Church St

Thomond Bridge

7

King
John's
Castle

4

2

5

KING'S
ISLAND

Nicholas St

Castle Ln

6

Absolute
Hotel (200m)

Bunratty (12km);
Shannon Airport (26km)

Ennis Rd

River Shannon

Merchants
Quay

Bridge St

18

George's Quay

River Abbey

Clancy's Strand

Sarsfield Bridge

Hunt
Museum

1

Bank Pl

8

Charlotte
Quay

N7 (3km)

Arthurs
Quay

Rutland St

24

22

Sarsfield St

9

Patrick St

Denmark St

12

Michael St

Ellen St

The Milk
Market

Bedford Row

Cruise's St

13

Robert St

16

Cornmarket
Row

Bus Stop

19

Sarsfield St

Henry St

11

William St

20

Lower Cecil
St

Thomas Rd

High St

Dock Rd
(N69)

15

Theatre Ln

O'Connell St

10

14

17

Roches St

Thomas St

Parnell St

P

Dolan's (400m)

23

Glentworth St

Catherine St

Cecil St

N24; Lough Gur (16km);
Tipperary (36km)

Mallow St

Pery St

Daniel
O'Connell
Monument

N20;
N21 (4km)

The
Crescent

Hartstonge St

Catherine Pl

Pery Sq

Upper Mallow St

3

Limerick
City Gallery
of Art

Citylink
Stop

Bus
Station

Limerick
Train
Station

Quinlan St

21

People's
Park

Limerick

as the military and administrative centre of the rich Shannon region, and reopened after extensive renovations in 2013.

Inside there are recreations of brutal medieval weapons including the trebuchet, as well as excavated Viking sites, reconstructed Norman features and other artefacts. Along with new multimedia displays, kids' exhibits include 'discovery drawers'.

Across medieval Thomond Bridge, on the other side of the river, the Treaty Stone marks the spot on the riverbank where the Treaty of Limerick was signed. Before you cross the bridge, look out for the 18th-century Bishop's Palace (Church St; ⊙10am-1pm & 2-4.30pm Mon-Fri) and the ancient toll gate.

★Hunt Museum   MUSEUM
(www.huntmuseum.com; Custom House, Rutland St; adult/child €5/2.50; ⊙10am-5pm Mon-Sat, 2-5pm Sun; 🛜🚻) Although named for its benefactors, this museum might well be named for a treasure hunt. Visitors are encouraged to open drawers and otherwise poke around the finest collection of Bronze Age, Iron Age and medieval treasures outside Dublin. The 2000-plus items are from the private collection of the late John and Gertrude Hunt, antique dealers and consultants, who championed historic preservation throughout the region. Look out for a tiny but exquisite bronze horse by da Vinci, and a Syracusan coin thought to have been one of the 30 pieces of silver paid to Judas for his betrayal of Christ. Other riches include Cycladic sculptures, a Giacometti drawing

and paintings by Renoir, Picasso and Jack B Yeats. Free one-hour guided tours from the dedicated and colourful volunteers are available. The museum has a good cafe.

★Limerick City Gallery of Art   GALLERY
(www.limerickcitygallery.ie; Carnegie Bldg, Pery Sq; ⊙10am-5.30pm Mon-Wed & Fri, 10am-8.30pm Thu, 10am-5pm Sat, noon-5pm Sun) FREE Limerick's excellent gallery adjoins the peaceful People's Park, at the heart of Georgian Limerick. Among its permanent collection of traditional paintings from the last 300 years are works by Sean Keating and Jack B Yeats. Check out Keating's atmospheric *Kelp Burners* and Sir John Lavery's *Stars in Sunlight;* both infuse their subjects with inner light. The gallery also stages changing exhibitions of often pseudo-scandalous works and is the home of eva International (www.eva.ie), Ireland's contemporary art biennial held across the city in even-numbered years. Check the website for dates.

St Mary's Cathedral   CATHEDRAL
(☑061-310 293; Bridge St; admission €2 donation; ⊙9am-5pm Mon-Fri, 9am-4pm Sat & Sun) Limerick's ancient cathedral was founded in 1168 by Donal Mór O'Brien, king of Munster. Parts of the 12th-century Romanesque western doorway, nave and aisles survive, and the splendid 15th-century black-oak misericords (support ledges for choristers) are unique examples of their kind in Ireland. Call ahead to confirm opening hours and to check if there are any musical events scheduled.

Limerick City Museum MUSEUM

(www.limerickcity.ie; Castle Lane; ⊙10am-1pm & 2.15-5pm Tue-Sat) FREE Also known as the Jim Kemmy Municipal Museum, in honour of the late Irish socialist politician, this small museum is beside King John's Castle. Exhibits include Stone Age and Bronze Age artefacts, the civic sword, Limerick silverwork, and examples of Limerick's lace and kid-glove manufacturing. Tough times in the late 19th century are also covered.

Thomond Park Stadium STADIUM

(✆061-421 109; http://thomondpark.ie; Tours adult/child €10/8, €3/2 on match days) From 1995 until 2007, the Munster rugby team (www.munsterrugby.ie) was undefeated in this legendary stadium, which was massively rebuilt in 2008, the year it won the Heineken European Cup for the second time. Tours of the hallowed ground include its memorabilia-filled museum. It's an easy 1km walk northwest of the centre along High St.

Tours

Walking Tour WALKING

(✆087 235 1339; per person €10) Noel Curtin runs entertaining and informative 90-minute walking tours of the city departing from the tourist office at 2.30pm.

Red Viking BUS

(✆061-334 920; http://redvikingtours.com; Bank Pl; adult/child €10/5; ⊙May-Oct) One-hour open-top bus tours depart from Bank Pl,

adjacent to Charlotte Quay, or beside the tourist office.

Sleeping

Try to find a place to stay near the city centre if you want to enjoy the nightlife. Otherwise you'll be on or near approach roads, in which case you might prefer to opt for something further afield that will be more bucolic.

Alexandra Tce on O'Connell Ave (which runs south from O'Connell St) has several midrange B&Bs. Ennis Rd, leading northwest towards Shannon, also has a selection, although most are at least 1km from the centre.

Courtbrack Accommodation B&B €

(✆061-302 500; www.courtbrackaccom.com; Courtbrack Ave; dm/s/d €23.50/30/52; ⊙May-Aug; @🛜) Student digs during semester, but opens during summertime for visitors. Tourist rates at this spiffy red-hued place include continental breakfast. Spotless facilities include a kitchen, laundry and common area with wi-fi. It's 400m southwest of the city centre, just south of Dock Rd (the N69).

★The Boutique Hotel HOTEL €€

(✆061-315 320; www.theboutique.ie; Denmark St; d from €55; @🛜⛅) Rotating works of original art by Limerick artist Claire De Lacy, a fish tank in the lobby, a glassed-in breakfast room on the 1st-floor balcony and red-and-white-striped decor set this groovy little hotel apart from the pack. Its location near pedestrianised laneways minimises traffic,

---

FRANK McCOURT

No one has been as closely linked to Limerick in recent years as Frank McCourt (1930–2009). His autobiographical novel *Angela's Ashes* was a surprise publishing sensation in 1996, bringing him fame and honours (including the Pulitzer Prize).

Although he was born in New York City, McCourt's immigrant family returned to Limerick four years later, unable to survive in America. His childhood was filled with the kinds of deprivations that were all too common at the time: his father was a drunk who later vanished, three of his six siblings died in childhood and at age 13 he dropped out of school to earn money to help his family survive.

At the age of 19, McCourt returned to New York and later worked for three decades as a high-school teacher. Among the subjects he taught was writing. From the 1970s he dabbled in writing and theatre with his brother Malachy. He started *Angela's Ashes* only after retiring from teaching in 1987. Its early sales success was thanks to a bevy of enthusiastic critics, but in Limerick the reaction was mixed, with many decrying the negative portrait it painted of the city.

Today McCourt's legacy in Limerick is celebrated. Limerick City's tourist office has information about sights related to the book. and you can visit one of the pubs mentioned in the book, South's (p317).

but it can still get noisy on weekends and during events when the city's hopping, with a popular pub downstairs. Still, it's fantastic value for money.

George Boutique Hotel
HOTEL €€

(☑061-460 400; www.thegeorgeboutiquehotel.com; O'Connell St; d from €60; @ 🛜 ⛵) Designed like something out of a Sunday supplement – all warm and luxurious with laminate floors, bold patterned wallpaper and amenities including laptop-size safes – this sleek place has a small terrace above the busy streets of the city centre.

Absolute Hotel
HOTEL €€

(☑061-463 600; www.absolutehotel.com; Sir Harry's Mall; d from €79; @ 🛜) Exposed brick walls, granite bathrooms and a light-filled atrium lobby give this gleaming riverfront hotel a smart, contemporary edge. There's a cocooning inhouse spa, plus a bar and grill. Check in early: secure parking is free but limited.

Savoy
HOTEL €€

(☑061-448 700; www.savoylimerick.com; Henry St; d from €99; @ 🛜 ⛵) This classy five-star hotel does everything right: staff are professional, rooms have super-comfy, king-size beds and a turn-down service, its spa specialises in Thai massages, and there are a couple of top-notch in-house restaurants.

🍴 Eating

Café Noir
CAFE €

(☑061-411 222; www.cafenoir.ie; Robert St; dishes €4.50-11; ◷8am-5.30pm Mon-Wed, 8am-6.30pm Thu-Sat) Gorgeous tarts lead the way at this French-inspired bakery-cafe, which also offers exquisite pastries, salads, pies, quiches and its house speciality, French onion soup. The coffees are just what you need when it rains.

Milk Market
MARKET €

(www.milkmarketlimerick.ie; Cornmarket Row; ◷food market 8am-3pm Sat, shops 10am-4pm Fri, 8am-3pm Sat, 11am-4pm Sun) 🍃 Pick from organic produce and local foods, including cheese, at the traditional food market held in Limerick's old market buildings, or browse its produce and craft shops. Other markets are listed on the website.

Glasshouse Restaurant
IRISH €€

(☑061-469 000; www.glasshouserestaurant.ie; Riverpoint; mains €15-28; ◷5-11.30pm) At the base of a distinctive curved glass building, the Glasshouse has glimmering views over the River Shannon from its minimalist dining room and terrace. The menu is upmarket pub grub, with some creative gourmet burgers, mussels and fries and pies; the wine list is excellent.

Chocolat
INTERNATIONAL €€

(☑061-609 709; www.chocolatrestaurant.ie; 109 O'Connell St; mains €8-25; ◷from noon; ⛵) Make that *very* international. Food spans the globe, from yan pang chicken and Singapore noodles to northern, central and southern American classics, including finger-licking ribs. The inventive, generous cocktails are the best in town, and include a chocolate coffee kiss (Kahlua, Baileys, creme de cacao, Grand Marnier and chocolate syrup).

Sage Cafe
CAFE €€

(☑061-409 458; www.thesagecafe.com; 67-68 Catherine St; dishes €9-14; ◷8.30am-5pm Mon-Sat; ⛵) Breakfast treats and baked goods give way to a line-up of lunch sandwiches, salads such as duck, orange, fennel and sunflower seeds, and hot plates such as lemongrass risotto with chargrilled prawns.

🍷 Drinking & Nightlife

★ Nancy Blake's
PUB

(Upper Denmark St) There's sawdust on the floor and peat on the fire in the cosy front bar of this wonderful old pub. Out the back is a vast covered drinking zone that often features live music or televised matches.

White House Pub
PUB

(www.whitehousebarlimerick.com; 52 O'Connell St) A classic right in the centre, this corner pub has outdoor seating (under a rare tree) and a good beer list. On some nights it has live acoustic music, on others it helps lead a rebirth of local poetry through readings.

Locke Bar
PUB

(George's Quay; 🛜) Picturesque waterside setting, a maze of rooms and bars and great bar food.

South's
PUB

(4 Quinlan St) Frank McCourt's father knocked 'em back here and the *Angela's Ashes* connection is played up – even the toilets are named Frank and Angela.

Peter Clohessy's Bar & Sin Bin Nightclub
BAR, NIGHTCLUB

(www.peterclohessy.ie; Howley's Quay; ◷nightclub 11pm-3am Fri & Sat) Filled with rugby paraphernalia, this sport-obsessed riverfront bar is owned and run by former Munster and Ireland prop Peter Clohessy. Other codes, including American football, also screen. There's live music on Fridays; the downstairs nightclub, called – what else? – the Sin Bin, is class.

Trinity Rooms   NIGHTCLUB
(www.trinityrooms.ie; Michael St, The Granary) Vast club in a 300-year-old waterside building, with hot DJs and a courtyard bar.

☆ Entertainment

Check at the tourist office for events listings. Most clubs have strict door checks.

Dolan's   LIVE MUSIC
(www.dolanspub.com; 3 & 4 Dock Rd) Limerick's best spot for live music promises authentic trad sessions and an unbeatable gig list, as well as cutting-edge stand-ups in two adjoining venues.

University Concert Hall   CONCERT HALL
(UCH; ☎061-322 322; www.uch.ie; University of Limerick) Permanent home of the Irish Chamber Orchestra, with regular concerts from visiting acts, plus opera, drama, comedy and dance.

🛍 Shopping

Celtic Bookshop   BOOKS
(☎061-401 155; 2 Rutland St; ☺11am-5pm Mon & Wed-Fri) Crammed with specialist titles on local and Irish topics.

ℹ Information

DANGERS & ANNOYANCES
Reputation and unfortunate nickname 'Stab City' aside, central Limerick is not any less safe than other urban Irish areas. Keep alert at night and stick to well lit areas.

INTERNET ACCESS
The tourist office website has a map of free wi-fi hotspots throughout the city.
Limerick City Library (www.limerickcity.ie/library; Michael St, The Granary; ☺10am-5.30pm Mon & Tue, to 8pm Wed-Fri, to 1pm Sat)

MEDICAL SERVICES
Midwestern Regional Hospital (☎061-301 111; Dooradoyle) Hospital with an accident and an emergency department.

MONEY
AIB Bank (106/108 O'Connell St) Has a bureau de change.

POST
Main Post Office (Lower Cecil St)

TOURIST INFORMATION
Limerick Tourist Office (☎061-317 522; www.limerick.ie; Arthurs Quay; ☺9am-5.30pm Mon-Sat) A large, impressive facility with helpful staff.

ℹ Getting There & Away

AIR
Shannon Airport (p343) in County Clare handles domestic and international flights.

BUS
Bus Éireann (☎061-313 333; www.buseireann.ie; Parnell St) services operate from the bus and train stations near the city centre. There are regular buses to Cork (€14.25, 1¾ hours), Tralee (€18.75, two hours) and Dublin (€12.35, 3½ hours), as well as to Galway, Killarney, Rosslare, Ennis, Shannon, Derry and most other centres. You can also get off in Limerick at the bus stop on O'Connell St.

Citylink (☎1890 280 808; www.citylink.ie) has up to six buses a day to Galway (€16, 1½ hours) and Cork (€16, two hours). Buses stop on Upper Mallow St.

JJ Kavanagh & Sons (☎081 8333 222; www.jjkavanagh.ie) has seven buses daily to Dublin (€11) and Dublin Airport (€20). Buses stop outside Limerick's tourist office.

TRAIN
Irish Rail (www.irishrail.ie) has regular trains from **Limerick Railway Station** (☎061-315 555; Parnell St) including nine trains daily to Ennis (€10, 40 minutes), hourly services to Dublin Heuston (€51.60, 2½ hours), and nine services to Galway (€21.50, two hours). Other routes, including Cork, Tralee, Tipperary, Cahir and Waterford, involve changing at **Limerick Junction**, 20km southeast of Limerick.

ℹ Getting Around

Regular **Bus Éireann** (€6.75) and **JJ Kavanagh & Sons** (€6) buses connect Limerick's bus and train station with Shannon Airport. A taxi from the city centre to the airport costs around €35 to €45. The airport is 26km northwest of Limerick, about 30 minutes by car.

Taxis can be found outside the tourist office, at the bus and train stations, and in Thomas St, or try **Swift Taxis** (☎061-313 131).

Hire bikes at **Emerald Alpine** (☎061-416 983; www.irelandrentabike.com; Roches St; per day/week €20/80; ☺9.30am-5.30pm). The company will also retrieve or deliver a bike from anywhere in Ireland for €25.

Around Limerick City

Close to the city there's a clutch of outstanding historic sites that reward a day trip by car or a couple of days by bike.

Lough Gur

The area around this horseshoe-shaped lake has dozens of intriguing archaeological sites. Grange Stone Circle, known as the Lios, is a superb 4000-year-old circular enclosure made up of 113 embanked upright stones. It's the largest prehistoric circle of its kind in Ireland. There's roadside parking and access to the site is free (there's a donation box). From Limerick, take the N24 road south towards Waterford and follow the signs onto the R512 for 16km to the stone circle.

Around 1km further south along the R512, at Holycross garage and post office, a left turn takes you towards Lough Gur, past a ruined 15th-century church, and a wedge tomb on the other side of the road.

Another 2km leads to a car park by Lough Gur and the thatched replica of a Neolithic hut containing the Lough Gur Stone Age Centre (☑087 285 2022; www.loughgur.com; adult/child €3/2; ☺10am-5pm Mon-Fri, noon-6pm Sat & Sun) The centre has a good exhibit on prehistoric Irish farms (meaning pre-potato era) and a small museum displaying Neolithic artefacts and a replica of the Lough

Gur shield that's now in the National Museum in Dublin.

Short walks along the lake's edge lead to burial mounds, standing stones, ancient enclosures and other points of interest. Admission to these sites is free. The whole area is ideal for picnics.

Kilmallock

POP 2368

Ireland's third-largest town during the Middle Ages (after Dublin and Kilkenny) still has a smattering of medieval buildings that merit a visit.

Kilmallock developed around a 7th-century abbey and from the 14th to the 17th centuries was the seat of the Earls of Desmond. The village lies beside the River Lubach, 26km south of Limerick and a world away from the city's urban racket.

Coming into Kilmallock from Limerick, the first thing you'll see (to your left) is a medieval stone mansion – one of 30 or so that housed the town's prosperous merchants and landowners. Further along, the street dodges around the four-storey King's Castle, a 15th-century tower house with a ground-floor archway through which the pavement now runs.

Across the road from the castle, a lane leads down to the tiny but fascinating Kilmallock Museum (Sheares St; ☺10am-noon & 1-3pm Mon-Thu, 10am-1.30pm Fri) FREE, which

---

WORTH A TRIP

LIMERICK CITY TO TARBERT VIA THE SCENIC N69

The narrow, peaceful N69 road follows the Shannon Estuary west from Limerick for 58km to Tarbert in northern County Kerry. You'll enjoy some great views of the broadening estuary and seemingly endless rolling green hills laced with stone walls. You'll also discover a number of tiny heritage museums and gardens (most usually only open in the high season, approximately June to September).

Hidden just off the N69, a highlight of the route is the village of Askeaton, with evocative ruins including the mid-1300s Desmond Castle, a 1389-built Franciscan friary, and St Mary's Church of Ireland and Knights Templar Tower, built around 1829, as well as the 1740-built Hellfire Gentlemen's club. Restoration of the ruins started in 2007 and is expected to continue until 2017; progress is impressive. The town's tourist office (☑061-392 149; askeatontouristoffice@gmail.com; The Square; ☺9am-5pm Mon-Fri) has details of ruins that you can freely wander around (depending on restoration works) and can arrange free guided tours lasting about one hour led by passionate local historians (donations welcome).

At Foynes is another of the route's highlights, the fascinating Foynes Flying Boat Museum (www.flyingboatmuseum.com; adult/child €10/5; ☺9am-5pm Apr-Oct). From 1939 to 1945 this was the landing place for the flying boats that linked North America with the British Isles. Big Pan Am clippers – there's a replica here – would set down in the estuary and refuel.

houses a random collection of historical artefacts and a model of the town in 1597 so you can get an idea of what you missed (besides the smells, diseases etc). The museum is the base for the history trail around town.

The excellent Friars' Gate Theatre & Arts Centre (☎063-98727; www.friarsgate.ie; Main St) hosts art exhibitions and has a fine little theatre in which it stages plays and music events, and has tourist information about the village.

Two Bus Éireann buses run Monday to Saturday from Limerick to Kilmallock (€10.90, one hour).

Adare & Around

POP 1100

Often dubbed 'Ireland's prettiest village', Adare centres on its clutch of preserved thatched cottages built by the 19th-century English landlord, the Earl of Dunraven, for workers constructing Adare Manor. Today, the cottages house craft shops and fine restaurants, with prestigious golf courses nearby.

Tourists are drawn to the postcard-perfect village, set 16km southwest of Limerick on the River Maigue, by the busload. This makes the roads even more clogged (the busy N21 is the village's main street). It's also a popular romantic getaway for many Irish visitors at weekends, when it's best to book accommodation and restaurants in advance, but when you'll also find Adare at its most vibrant.

◉ Sights

Adare Heritage Centre   MUSEUM
(☎061-396 666; www.adareheritagecentre.ie; Main St; ◷9am-6pm) FREE In the middle of the village, exhibits at Adare's heritage centre explain the history and the medieval context of the village's buildings in an entertaining way. Try picking up the longbow (have you had your spinach today?). Quality Irish crafts are on sale, there's also a busy cafe.

Adare Castle   CASTLE
(tours adult/family €6/15; ◷tour hourly 10am-5pm Jun-Sep) Dating back to around 1200, this picturesque feudal ruin saw rough usage until it was finally wrecked for good by Cromwell's troops in 1657. By then it had already lost its strategic importance. Restoration work is

ongoing; look for the ruined great hall with its early-13th-century windows.

Book tours through the Heritage Centre. When tours aren't on, you can view the castle from the busy main road, or more peacefully from the riverside footpath or the grounds of the Augustinian priory.

Religious Houses   HISTORIC SITE
Before the Tudor dissolution of the monasteries (1536–39), Adare had three flourishing religious houses, the remains of which can still be seen. In the village itself, next to the heritage centre, the dramatic tower and southern wall of the Church of the Holy Trinity date from the 13th-century Trinitarian priory that was restored by the first Earl of Dunraven. Holy Trinity is now a Catholic church. There's a restored 14th-century dovecote down the side-turning next to the church.

The ruins of a Franciscan friary, founded by the Earl of Kildare in 1464, stand in the middle of Adare Golf Club (☎061-605 200; www.adaremanor.com; 18 holes €95-125) beside the River Maigue. Public access is assured, but let them know at the clubhouse that you intend to visit. A track leads away from the clubhouse car park for about 400m – watch out for flying golf balls. There's a handsome tower and a fine sedilia (row of seats for priests) in the southern wall of the chancel.

North of the village, on the N21 and close to the bridge over the River Maigue, is the Church of Ireland parish church, once the Augustinian priory, founded in 1315. It was also known as the Black Abbey. The interior of the church is agreeably cavernous, but the real joy is the atmospheric little cloister.

A pleasant, signposted riverside path, with wayside seats, starts from just north of the priory gates. Look for a narrow access gap and head off alongside the river. After about 250m, turn left along the road to reach the centre of Adare.

⛌ Sleeping

Adare Village Inn   INN €
(☎087 251 7102; www.adarevillageinn.com; Main St; s/d €45/60; ☜) Excellent-value rooms are cosy, contemporary and extremely comfortable (there's even a choice of pillows). The inn is located near the crossroads bang in the centre of town.

Berkeley Lodge   B&B €€
(☎061-396 857; www.adare.org; Station Rd; d €70; ☜⬛) One of several modern B&Bs on this road, close to the village, this six-room house

has in-room TVs, great breakfasts and welcomes early arrivals from Shannon Airport. It's a three-minute walk to the centre and very kid friendly.

Dunraven Arms INN €€€
(☑061-396 633; www.dunravenhotel.com; Main St; s/d from €100/180; @ 🛜 ⊠ 🚭) This jewel, built in 1792, sits discreetly behind hedged gardens. All 86 rooms have a high standard of traditional luxury, with antiques and high-thread-count linens. Its restaurant (mains €16-26.50; ⊘from 6pm) has an ambitious menu (pan-seared duck with lavender risotto, warm white chocolate cake with caramelised banana), but its bar menu (mains €13-18; ⊘ bar menu 11am-10pm) is a worthy, more affordable option.

⭐ **Adare Manor** HOTEL €€€
(☑061-605 200; www.adaremanor.com; Main St; d from €380; @ 🛜 ⊠ 🚭) The Earl of Dunraven's magnificent estate is now an imposing yet wonderfully intimate castle hotel. Individually decorated rooms have autumnal tones and antique furniture; dining options, also open to nonguests, include its superb Oak Room Restaurant (mains €27-37.50; ⊘6.30-10pm) and high tea (high tea €27.50; ⊘2-5pm) is served on tiered plates in the stately drawing room. Guests get reduced rates at the Adare Golf Club.

🍴 Eating

Good Room Cafe CAFE €
(☑061-396 218; Main St; mains €8-10; ⊘9am-5pm Mon-Sat, 10am-5pm Sun; 🚭) Inventive soups, salads, sandwiches, baked goods and homemade jams at this (very) good room are more contemporary than you'd expect from the cutesy thatched-cottage location. Arrive early before their famous scones sell out.

⭐ **Restaurant 1826 Adare** MODERN IRISH €€
(☑061-396 004; www.1826adare.ie; Main St; mains €19-30; ⊘5.30-9.30pm Wed-Sat, noon-8pm Sun; 🚭) 🍷 Wade Murphy is one of Ireland's most pedigreed chefs (previously heading up the kitchens of The Lodge at Doonbeg and Lisloughrey Lodge, among others), but now he's wowing diners at his own premises. Inside an art-lined 1826-built thatched cottage, Murphy's passion for local seasonal produce shines in dishes such as brown-bread-baked scallops, dry aged sirloin with roasted wild mushrooms, and desserts such as rhubarb and brown-sugar meringue, served in glass preserving jars with chantilly and biscotti.

Wild Geese IRISH €€
(☑061-396 451; www.thewild-geese.com; Main St; 2-/3-course lunch menu €20/25, 2-/3-course dinner menu €29/35; ⊘from 6.30pm Tue-Sat, 1-4pm Sun) The ever-changing menu at this inviting cottage restaurant celebrates the best of southwest Ireland's bounty, from scallops to sumptuous racks of lamb. The service is genial, preparations are imaginative and the bread basket divine.

Blue Door IRISH €€
(☑061-396 481; www.bluedooradare.com; Main St; lunch mains €9-16, dinner mains €19-25; ⊘11am-3pm & 6-10pm Mon-Thu, 11am-10pm Fri, noon-10pm Sat, 1-9pm Sun; 🚭) Gourmet salads, open-faced sandwiches and lasagnes appear at lunch at this cottage restaurant, while dinner ups the ante with creative twists such as confit of duck in Guinness sauce and cod in chardonnay.

🍸 Drinking & Nightlife

Seán Collins PUB
(www.seancollinsbaradare.com; Killarney Rd) Adare's most traditional pub. Live music plays on Monday and Friday.

Bill Chawke Lounge Bar PUB
(www.billchawke.com; Main St) Regular trad music and singalongs.

ℹ Information

The website www.adarevillage.com is a handy source of information.
Tourist Office (☑061-396 255; www.discoverireland.com/shannon; Main St, Adare Heritage Centre; ⊘9am-5pm Mon-Sat)

ℹ Getting There & Around

Hourly Bus Éireann services link Limerick with Adare (€5.50, 25 minutes). Many continue on to Tralee (€19.70, 1¾ hours). Others serve Killarney (€19, 1¾ hours).

Spin around Adare in style in a classic Ferrari, Porsche or Lotus from **Heritage Sports Cars** (☑069-63770; www.heritagesportscars.com; per day from €109), which has free delivery and collection in Adare.

COUNTY TIPPERARY

Landlocked Tipperary boasts the sort of fertile soil that farmers dream of. There's still an upper-crust gloss to traditions here, with fox hunts in full legal cry during the winter season. The centre of the county is low-lying,

WORTH A TRIP

BALLINGARRY

The attractive village of Ballingarry (Baile an Gharraí, meaning 'town of the gardens'), 13km southwest of Adare on the R519, is home to one of County Limerick's hidden dining gems, Mustard Seed at Eco Lodge (☑ 069-68508; www.mustardseed.ie; 4-course menu €60; d from €130; ☺ restaurant 7-9.15pm, restaurant & accommodation closed mid-Jan–mid-Feb; ⊛). Produce picked fresh from this mustard-coloured 19th-century former convent's orchards and kitchen gardens are incorporated in seasonal menus which might include parmesan doughnuts with black olive mousse, blackcurrant and gin sorbet, and wild Irish venison. To avoid having to move too far afterwards, book in to one of the lodge's elegant, country-style rooms (some with four-poster beds).

but rolling hills spill over from adjoining counties.

Walking and cycling opportunities abound, especially in the Glen of Aherlow near Tipperary town. But the real crowd-pleasers are the iconic Rock of Cashel and Cahir Castle. In between, you'll find bucolic charm along pretty much any country road you choose.

Tipperary Town

POP 4320

Tipperary (Tiobrad Árann) has a storied name, largely due to the WWI song. And indeed, you may find it a long way to Tipperary as the N24 and a web of regional roads converge on the centre and traffic often moves at the same speed as the armies at the Somme. 'Tipp town' itself has few pretensions and there's no need to detour here.

Inside the Excel Heritage Centre (Mitchell St), you'll find the tourist information point (☑ 062-80520; ☺ 10am-5pm Mon-Sat, 2-5.30pm Sun). It's reached via St Michael's St, a side street leading 200m off the northern side of Main St. Also here is a small gallery, cafe (dishes €4.50-6.50), cinema, a good genealogy centre and internet access (€1 per 20min).

Midway along Main St, there's a statue of Charles J Kickham (1828-82), a local novelist (author of *Knocknagow,* a novel about rural life) and Young Irelander. He spent four years in London's Pentonville Prison in the 1860s for treason.

Named in honour of the local patriot, traditional pub Kickham House (www.kickhamhouse.com; Main St; mains €8-13; ☺ noon-3pm Mon-Fri) has carvery lunches that include smoked haddock and cod pie.

Tipperary Racecourse (☑ 062-51357; www.tipperaryraces.ie; Limerick Rd) is one of Ireland's leading tracks. It's 3km northwest of town and has regular meetings during the year. The course is within walking distance of Limerick Junction station.

Danny Ryan Music (www.dannyryanmusic.ie; 20 Bank Pl; ☺ 10am-1pm & 2-6pm Mon, Tue & Thu-Sat, 10am-1pm Wed) has a superb selection of traditional musical instruments.

Most buses stop on Abbey St beside the river. Bus Éireann (www.buseireann.ie) runs up to eight buses daily on the Limerick (€9.50, 30 minutes) to Waterford route via Cahir and Clonmel.

To reach the train station, head south along Bridge St. Tipperary is on the Waterford–Limerick Junction line. There are two daily services to Cahir (25 minutes), Clonmel, Carrick-on-Suir, Waterford and Rosslare Harbour. Connect for Cork, Kerry and Dublin at Limerick Junction (☑ 062-51406), barely 3km from Tipperary station along the Limerick road.

Glen of Aherlow & Galtee Mountains

South of Tipperary are the shapely Slievenamuck Hills and Galtee Mountains, separated by the broad, chequered valley of the Glen of Aherlow. A 25km scenic drive through the glen is signposted from Tipperary town. At the eastern end of the Glen, between Tipperary and Cahir, the village of Bansha (An Bháinseach) marks the start of a 20km trip west to Galbally, an easy bike ride or scenic drive along the R663 that takes in the best of the county's landscapes.

Renowned for its walking, the terrain of the region ranges from the lush riverbanks of the Aherlow to pine forests in the hills and windswept, rocky grasslands that seem to stretch on forever. For spectacular views, head 1.6km north of Newtown on the R664 to a lookout adjacent to the statue of Christ.

The R663 from Bansha and the R664 south from Tipperary converge at Newtown at the Coach Road Inn, a fine old pub popular with walkers. Hidden around the back of the pub, the enthusiastically staffed Glen of Aherlow tourist office (062-56331; www.aherlow.com; 9.30am-5pm Mon-Fri year-round plus 10am-4pm Sat Jun-Aug) is an excellent source of information on the area, including walking festivals.

There's a good range of rural accommodation – much of it catering to walkers.

A 1928 hunting lodge has been turned into the luxurious woodland retreat Aherlow House Hotel (062-56153; www.aherlowhouse.ie; Newtown; d/lodge from €69/149; @) with 29 rooms with king-size beds and 15 contemporary countrified self-catering lodges (minimum two-night stay). There's a flowing bar (12.30-9pm) and restaurant (mains €16-30; from 6pm Mon-Sat, from 12.30pm Sun), and glorious mountain views from the terrace. It's signposted up a track from the R663.

Against a great backdrop of the Galtees 10km west from Bansha, excellent facilities at Ballinacourty House Camping Park & B&B (062-56559; www.ballinacourtyhse.com; Glen of Aherlow; campsites €23, s/d €51.50/70;) include a beautiful garden, a much-loved local restaurant (4-course lunch/dinner menu €20/30; 6-9pm Wed-Sat, 12.30-2.30pm & 6-8.30pm Sun), a tennis court and minigolf.

The friendly owners of Homeleigh Farmhouse (062-56228; www.homeleighfarmhouse.com; Newtown; s/d €50/80; dinner €28;), on a working farm just west of Newtown and the Coach Rd Inn, are founts of walking info. The modern house has five comfortable rooms with private bathrooms; book ahead to enjoy a four-course home-cooked meal.

The frequent Bus Éireann link between Tipperary town (€3.80, 10 minutes) and Waterford stops in Bansha. From here it's a walk or bike ride into the hills. A car will enable you to explore far and wide between walks.

Cashel
POP 2276

It's no wonder that Cashel (Caiseal Mumhan) is popular with visitors (the Queen included it in her historic visit in 2011). The iconic Rock of Cashel and historical religious buildings that crown its breezy summit seem like a magical extension of the rocky landscape itself, and Cashel maintains a certain charm as a smallish market town.

◉ Sights

Download a free audioguided tour of the town from the tourist office website.

Rock of Cashel   HISTORIC SITE
(www.heritageireland.com; adult/child €6/2; 9am-5.30pm mid-Mar–mid-Oct, to 7pm mid-Jun–Aug, to 4.30pm mid-Oct–mid-Mar) The Rock of Cashel is one of Ireland's most spectacular archaeological sites. The 'Rock' is a prominent green hill, banded with limestone outcrops. It rises from a grassy plain on the edge of the town and bristles with ancient fortifications – the word 'cashel' is an anglicised version of the Irish word caiseal, meaning 'fortress'. Sturdy walls circle an enclosure that contains a complete round tower, a 13th-century Gothic cathedral and the finest 12th-century Romanesque chapel in Ireland.

In the 4th century the Rock of Cashel was chosen as a base by the Eóghanachta clan from Wales, who went on to conquer much of Munster and become kings of the region. For some 400 years it rivalled

WORTH A TRIP

FAMINE WARHOUSE

A relic of one of Ireland's darkest chapters, the Famine Warhouse (www.heritageireland.ie; 2.30-5.30pm Wed-Sun Apr-Sep, 2-4pm Sat & Sun Oct-Mar) FREE sits seemingly benignly today amid typical farmland near Ballingarry. During the 1848 rebellion, rebels led by William Smith O'Brien besieged police who had barricaded themselves inside and taken children hostage. Things did not go well and this incident marked the effective end of the rebellion. Displays also detail the Famine and the mass exodus of Irish emigrants to America.

The warhouse is 30km northeast of Cashel on the R691 about midway to Kilkenny. Be careful navigating as County Tipperary has two Ballingarrys; the wrong one is over by Roscrea.

Rock of Cashel

For more than 1000 years the Rock of Cashel was a symbol of power and the seat of kings and churchmen who ruled over the region. Exploring this monumental complex offers a fascinating insight into Ireland's past.

Enter via the 15th-century **Hall of the Vicars Choral** 1, built to house the male choristers who sang in the cathedral. Exhibits in its undercroft include rare silverware, stone reliefs and the original St Patrick's Cross. In the courtyard you'll see the replica of **St Patrick's Cross** 2. A small porch leads into the 13th-century Gothic **Cathedral** 3. To the west of the nave are the remains of the **Archbishop's Residence** 4. From the cathedral's north transept on the northeastern corner is the Rock's earliest building, an 11th- or 12th-century **Round Tower** 5. The south transept leads to the compelling **Cormac's Chapel** 6, probably the first Romanesque church in Ireland. It dates from 1127 and the medieval integrity of its trans-European architecture survives. Inside the main door on the left is the sarcophagus said to house King Cormac, dating from between 1125 and 1150. Before leaving, take time for a close-up look at the Rock's **enclosing walls and corner tower** 7.

JOHN ELK/GETTY IMAGES ©

Hall of the Vicars Choral
Head upstairs from the ticket office to see the choristers' restored kitchen and dining hall, complete with period furniture, tapestries and paintings beneath a fine carved-oak roof and gallery.

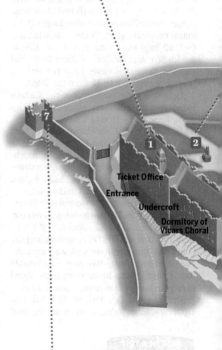

Ticket Office

Entrance

Undercroft

Dormitory of Vicars Choral

TOP TIPS

➤ Good photographic vantage points for framing the mighty Rock are on the road into Cashel from the Dublin Rd roundabout or from the little roads just west of the centre.

➤ The best photo opportunities, however, are from inside the atmospheric ruins of Hore Abbey, 1km to the north.

TRAVEL INK/GETTY IMAGES ©

Enclosing Walls & Corner Tower
Constructed from lime mortar around the 15th century, and originally incorporating five gates, stone walls enclose the entire site. It's thought the surviving corner tower was used as a watchtower.

St Patrick's Cross
In the castle courtyard, this cross replicates the eroded Hall of the Vicars Choral original – an impressive 12th-century crutched cross depicting a crucifixion scene on one face and animals on the other.

Archbishop's Residence
The west side of the cathedral is taken up by the Archbishop's Residence, a 15th-century, four-storey castle, which had its great hall built over the nave, reducing its length. It was last inhabited in the mid-1700s.

Cathedral
A huge square tower with a turret on the southwestern corner soars above the cathedral. Scattered throughout are monuments, a 16th-century altar tomb, coats of arms panels, and stone heads on capitals and corbels.

Turret

4

3

5

6

Choir

Scully Cross

Cormac's Chapel
Look closely at the exquisite doorway arches, the grand chancel arch and ribbed barrel vault, and carved vignettes, including a trefoil-tailed grotesque and a Norman-helmeted centaur firing an arrow at a rampaging lion.

Round Tower
Standing 28m tall, the doorway to this ancient edifice is 3.5m above the ground – perhaps for structural rather than defensive reasons. Its exact age is unknown but may be as early as 1101.

Tara as a centre of power in Ireland. The clan was associated with St Patrick, hence the Rock's alternative name of St Patrick's Rock. In the 10th century, the Eóghanachta lost possession of the rock to the O'Brien (or Dál gCais) tribe under Brian Ború's leadership. In 1101, King Muircheartach O'Brien presented the Rock to the Church to curry favour with the powerful bishops and to end secular rivalry over possession of the Rock with the Eóghanachta, by now known as the MacCarthys.

Numerous buildings must have occupied the Rock over the years, but it is the ecclesiastical relics that have survived even the depredations of the Cromwellian army in 1647. The cathedral was used for worship until the mid-1700s.

Among the graves are a 19th-century high cross and mausoleum for local landowners the Scully family; the top of the Scully Cross was razed by lightning in 1976.

It's a five-minute stroll from the town centre up to the Rock. You can take some pretty paths including the Bishop's Walk from the gardens of the Cashel Palace Hotel. Sheep grudgingly allow you to pass. The scaffolding moves from place to place each year as part of the never-ending struggle to keep the Rock caulked.

Call ahead for details of guided tours.

Hore Abbey HISTORIC SITE
Just under 1km north of the Rock in flat farmland is the formidable ruin of 13th-century Hore Abbey (also known as Hoare Abbey or St Mary's). Originally Benedictine and settled by monks from Glastonbury in England at the end of the 12th century, it later became a Cistercian house. Enjoyably gloomy, it was given to the order by a 13th-century archbishop who expelled the Benedictine monks after dreaming that they planned to murder him.

Brú Ború HERITAGE CENTRE
(☏ 062-61122; www.comhaltas.ie/locations/detail/bru_boru; admission free, exhibitions from €5; ☉ 9am-5pm, hours can vary) The privately run heritage and cultural centre is next to the car park below the Rock of Cashel, and offers an absorbing insight into Irish traditional music, dance and song. The centre's main attraction, the Sounds of History exhibition, relates the story of Ireland and its music through imaginative audio displays; various other musical events take place in summer.

Cashel Folk Village MUSEUM
(☏ 062-62525; www.cashelfolkvillage.ie; Dominic St; adult/child €5/2; ☉ 9am-7.30pm mid-Jun–mid-Sep, reduced hours rest of year) An engaging exhibition of old buildings, shopfronts and memorabilia from around the town. It's a bit slipshod in a heart-warming way.

Cashel Heritage Town Centre Museum MUSEUM
(www.casheltc.ie; Main St, Town Hall; ☉ 9.30am-5.30pm Mon-Sat mid-Mar–mid-Oct, 9.30am-5.30pm Mon-Fri mid-Oct–mid-Mar) FREE Located in the town hall next to the tourist office; displays include a scale model of Cashel in the 1640s with an accompanying soundtrack.

Bolton Library MUSEUM
(John St; admission €2; ☉ by appointment, book at tourist office) A forbidding 1836 stone building houses a splendid 18th-century collection of books, maps and manuscripts from the dawn of printing onwards. There are works by writers from Chaucer to Swift.

🛏 Sleeping

Cashel Holiday Hostel HOSTEL €
(☏ 062-62330; www.cashelhostel.com; 6 John St; dm/s/d from €16/30/45; ☏) A friendly and central budget option in a vividly coloured three-storey Georgian terrace just off Main St. Amenities include a kitchen, laundry, library and bike storage. Musicians can 'perform for their bed' (ie the hostel can set up gigs and source instruments).

Cashel Lodge & Camping Park HOSTEL, CAMPGROUND €
(☏ 062-61003; www.cashel-lodge.com; Dundrum Rd; campsite per person €10, dm/s/d €20/40/65; ☏) In a converted two-century-old stone coach house northwest of town on the R505 (follow the signs for Dundrum), this friendly IHH property has a bare stone and wood interior and terrific views of the Rock and Hore Abbey.

Baileys Hotel BOUTIQUE HOTEL €€
(☏ 062-61937; www.baileyshotelcashel.com; Main St; s/d from €55/70; ☏ 🐾) Clean, contemporary lines and dark woods contrasting with light walls give this restored Georgian townhouse an elegant ambiance. The restaurant (mains €14-25.50; ☉ 6-9.30pm Thu-Sat, noon-2.30pm Sun) and stone-walled, candlelit cellar bar (mains €13-25.50; ☉ noon-9.30pm), are superb, as is the town centre location

with the bonus of lock-up parking. Rates include breakfast.

Cashel Town B&B
B&B €€

(📞 062-62330; www.cashelbandb.com; 5 John St; d from €60; @ 📶 ♿) 🍽 Fresh produce from nearby farmers markets is cooked up for breakfast at this homey B&B, which is part of the Slow Food movement (even the porridge is organic). Within the 1808-built Georgian townhouse are seven comfortable rooms and a cosy guest lounge with a toasty open fire and a piano.

★ Cashel Palace Hotel
HISTORIC HOTEL €€€

(📞 062-62707; www.cashel-palace.ie; Main St; s/d from €95/134; @ 📶) This handsome red-brick, late-Queen Anne archbishop's residence is a local landmark, whose gardens contain the progenies of the original hop plants used to brew the first Guinness. Fully restored, it has 23 antique-furnished rooms in the gracious main building or quaint mews, with direct access through the grounds to the base of the Rock of Cashel. Some rooms have soaking tubs that you'll leave only after you're totally prunified. The bar is the place to talk about your upcoming hunt before dining at the vaulted-ceilinged Bishops Buttery Restaurant (mains €10-21; ⊙ 7.30-9.30pm).

✖ Eating

Apart from the Rock, Cashel is best-known in Ireland and beyond for award-winning Cashel Blue farmhouse cheese, Ireland's first-ever blue cheese. Although it's still handmade locally (and only locally), it's surprisingly hard to find in shops and on restaurant menus in town.

Main St has the greatest concentration of eateries, including the Bishops Buttery Restaurant and Baileys Hotel.

★ Cafe Hans
CAFE €€

(📞 062-63660; Dominic St; mains €13-18; ⊙ noon-5.30pm Tue-Sat; ♿) Competition for the 32 seats is fierce at this gourmet cafe run by the same family as Chez Hans next door. There's a fantastic selection of salads, open sandwiches (including succulent prawns with tangy Marie Rose sauce) and filling fish, shellfish, lamb and vegetarian dishes, with a discerning wine selection and mouthwatering dessertssuch as homemade caramel ice cream with butterscotch sauce. Arrive before or after the lunchtime rush or plan on queuing.

Kearney's Castle Hotel
IRISH €€

(📞 062-61044; Main St; mains €14-25; ⊙ noon-9pm) Although it looks like a grand old castle (part of the building does comprise a medieval fortified tower built in the 15th century), inside it's dungeon-dark and modernised, but there's a good range of meat, fish and poultry dishes.

Chez Hans
IRISH €€€

(📞 062-61177; www.chezhans.net; Dominic St; mains €24-38; ⊙ 6-9.30pm Tue-Sat) Since 1968 this former church has been a place of worship for foodies from all over Ireland and beyond. Still as fresh and inventive as ever, the restaurant gives its blessing to all manner of Irish foods, including lobster, aged beef and quail.

🍷 Drinking & Nightlife

Brian Ború
PUB

(📞 062-63381; http://brianborubar.ie; Main St; bar mains €10-12; 📶) Good-time pub that's become a lynchpin of Cashel's social life with regular live music, DJs and cocktail nights as well as above average pub grub.

Ryan's
PUB

(Ladyswell St) Congenial place with a large beer garden that really is a garden.

ℹ Information

Banks and ATMs are in the centre.

Tourist Office (📞 062-62511; www.cashel.ie; Main St, Town Hall; ⊙ 9.30am-5.30pm Mon-Sat mid-Mar–mid-Oct, 9.30am-5.30pm Mon-Fri mid-Oct–mid-Mar) Helpful office with reams of info on the area.

ℹ Getting There & Away

Bus Éireann (www.buseireann.ie) runs eight buses daily between Cashel and Cork (€14.50, 1½ hours) via Cahir (€5.50, 20 minutes, six to eight daily). The bus stop for Cork is outside the Bake House on Main St. The Dublin stop (€11.70, three hours, six daily) is opposite.

Ring a Link (📞 1890 424 141; www.ringalink. ie), a not-for-profit service for rural residents that's also available to tourists, has a service to Tipperary (€3, 50 minutes).

Around Cashel

The atmospheric – and, at dusk, delightfully creepy – ruins of Athassel Priory sit in the shallow and verdant River Suir Valley, 7km southwest of Cashel. The original buildings date from 1205. Athassel was once one of the richest and most important monasteries in

> ### WALK: TIPPERARY HERITAGE TRAIL
>
> Extending a distance of 56km from the Vee Gap viewpoint near Clogheen in the south to Cashel in the north, the national waymarked Tipperary Heritage Trail takes in some beautiful river valleys and ruins. The 30km north from Cahir to Cashel is the best segment, featuring the verdant lands around the River Suir and passing close to highlights such as Athassel Priory. The best stretches around Golden are off roads. Expect to see a fair amount of wildlife as the paths and very minor roads follow the waters and pass through woodlands. Ordnance Survey Discovery series maps 66 and 74 cover the route.

Ireland. What survives is substantial: the gatehouse and portcullis gateway, the cloister and stretches of walled enclosure, as well as some medieval tomb effigies. To get here, take the N74 to the village of Golden, then head 2km south along the narrow road signed Athassel Abbey. Roadside parking is limited and *very* tight; you're best off leaving your car in Golden. The Priory is reached across often-muddy fields. The welter of back lanes is good for cycling.

Cahir

POP 1150

At the eastern tip of the Galtee Mountains 15km south of Cashel, Cahir (An Cathair; pronounced 'care') is a compact and attractive town that encircles its namesake castle, which does a good job of looking like a castle you ever tried building at the beach, with towers, a moat and battlements. Walking paths follow the banks of the River Suir; you can easily spend a couple of hours wandering about.

◉ Sights

Cahir Castle   HISTORIC SITE
(☑052-744 1011; www.heritageireland.ie; Castle St; adult/child €3/1; ◎9am-6.30pm mid-Jun–Aug, 9.30am-5.30pm mid-Mar–mid-Jun & Sep–mid-Oct, 9.30am-4.30pm mid-Oct–mid-Mar) Cahir's awesome castle is feudal fantasy in a big way: a river-island site with moat, rocky foundations, massive walls, turrets and towers,

defences and dungeons. Founded by Conor O'Brien in 1142, this castle is one of Ireland's largest. It was passed to the Butler family in 1375. In 1599 it lost the arms race of its day when the Earl of Essex used cannons to shatter the walls, an event explained with a huge model.

The castle was surrendered to Cromwell in 1650 without a struggle; its future usefulness may have discouraged the usual Cromwellian 'deconstruction' – it is largely intact and still formidable. It was restored in the 1840s and again in the 1960s when it came under state ownership.

A 15-minute audiovisual presentation puts Cahir in context with other Irish castles. The buildings within the castle are sparsely furnished, although there are good displays. The real rewards come from simply wandering through this remarkable survivor of Ireland's medieval past. There are frequent guided tours.

Swiss Cottage   HISTORIC BUILDING
(☑052-744 1144; www.heritageireland.ie; Cahir Park; adult/child €3/1; ◎10am-6pm Apr–mid-Oct) A pleasant riverside path from behind the town car park meanders 2km south to Cahir Park and the thatched Swiss Cottage, surrounded by roses, lavender and honeysuckle. Built in 1810 as a retreat for Richard Butler, 12th Baron Caher, and his wife, it was designed by London architect John Nash, creator of the Royal Pavilion at Brighton and London's Regent's Park. The cottage-orné style emerged during the late 18th and early 19th centuries in England in response to the prevailing taste for the picturesque. Thatched roofs, natural wood and carved weatherboarding were characteristics and most examples were built as ornamental features on estates.

A lavish example of Regency Picturesque, the cottage is more of a sizeable house and has extensive facilities. The 30-minute (compulsory) guided tours are enjoyable.

🛌 Sleeping & Eating

★ Apple Caravan & Camping Park   CAMPGROUND €
(☑052-744 1459; www.theapplefarm.com; Moorstown, Cahir; campsite per adult/child from €6.50/4.50; ◎campground May-Sep, farm shop 8am-6pm Mon-Fri, 9am-5pm Sat & Sun year-round; 🛜🚲) Ⓟ Set on orchards on the N24 between Cahir (6km) and Clonmel (9km), this peaceful, well-spaced campsite has a free tennis court and racquets, a camp kitchen in a converted apple store and

spring water from its own well. Even if you're not pitching up here, it's worth dropping by its farm shop selling apples, jams and juices as well as fruity ice creams.

Tinsley House   B&B €

(☎052-744 1947; www.tinsleyhouse.com; The Square; d from €55; ⊗Apr-Sep; 🛜) This mannered house has a great location, four period-furnished rooms and a roof garden. The owner, Liam Roche, is an expert on local history and can recommend walks and other activities.

Lazy Bean Cafe   CAFE €

(www.thelazybeancafe.com; The Square; dishes €5-7; ⊗9am-6pm Mon-Sat, 10am-6pm Sun; 🛜) Busy, breezy little cafe dishing out tasty sandwiches, salads, soups and wraps. Its adjacent tearoom, the Coffee Pod, is quieter.

Farmers Market   MARKET €

(Castle car park; ⊗9am-1pm Sat) 🍴 Cahir's farmers market attracts the region's best food vendors.

🛍 Shopping

Cahir Craft Granary   ARTS & CRAFTS

(www.craftgranary.com; Church St; ⊗10am-6pm Mon-Fri, 9am-6pm Sat year-round plus 1-5pm Sun Jul-Aug & Dec) Hundreds of locals toiled away in a notorious linen mill during the 19th century. Almost 200 years later, the once ominous stone building has been reborn as the Cahir Craft Granary, with local artists creating and selling works including pottery, carvings, paintings and jewellery. It's just north of the Square, past the post office.

❶ Information

Post Office (Church St) North of The Square.

Tourist Office (☎052-744 1453; www.discoverireland.ie/tipperary; Cahir Castle car park; ⊗9.30am-5.30pm Mon-Sat Easter-Oct) Has information about the town and region.

❶ Getting There & Away

BUS

Cahir is a hub for several Bus Éireann routes, including Dublin–Cork, Limerick–Waterford, Galway–Waterford, Kilkenny–Cork and Cork–Athlone. There are eight buses per day Monday to Saturday (six buses on Sunday) to Cashel (€5.50, 20 minutes). Buses stop in the car park beside the tourist office.

TRAIN

From Monday to Saturday, the Limerick Junction–Waterford train stops three times daily in each direction.

Mitchelstown Caves

While the Galtee Mountains are mainly sandstone, a narrow band of limestone along their southern side has given rise to the Mitchelstown Caves (☎052-746 7246; www.mitchelstowncave.com; Burncourt; adult/child €9/3; ⊗10am-5.30pm Jun-Aug, shorter hours rest of year). Superior to Kilkenny's Dunmore Cave and yet less developed for tourists, these caves are among the most extensive in the country with nearly 3km of passages and spectacular chambers full of textbook formations with names such as the Pipe Organ, Tower of Babel, House of Commons and Eagle's Wing. Tours take about 30 minutes. Year-round, the cave temperature remains a constant 12°C, making it feel warm in winter and chilly in summer.

The caves are near Burncourt, 16km southwest of Cahir and signposted on the N8 to Mitchelstown (Baile Mhistéala).

Clonmel

POP 17,908

On the wide River Suir, Clonmel (Cluain Meala; 'Meadows of Honey') is Tipperary's largest and busiest town.

WORTH A TRIP

HOLY CROSS ABBEY

Beside the River Suir, 15km north of Cashel and 6km southwest of Thurles, the magnificently restored Holy Cross Abbey (holycrossabbeytours@gmail.com; admission by donation; ⊗9am-8pm) proudly displays two relics of the True Cross. Although the Cistercian abbey was founded in 1168, the large buildings that survive today date from the 15th century. Look for the ornately carved sedilia near the altar and pause to appreciate the early form of 'stadium seating'. Guided tours take place three times a week in spring and summer. A bookshop is open irregular hours.

DESIGN PICS / THE IRISH IMAGE COLLECTION / GETTY IMAGES ©

1. Lough Gur (p319)
Prehistoric Irish farms are one of the attractions in this area.

2. Mountain goat, Tipperary (p321)
The local fauna seem as friendly as the people.

3. Cutting silage, near Mitchelstown (p329)
Farmer working the fields with views of the Galtee Mountains.

4. Rock of Cashel (p323)
One of Ireland's most spectacular archaeological sites.

Laurence Sterne (1713–68), author of *A Sentimental Journey* and *Tristram Shandy*, was a native of the town. However, the commercial cheerleader for Clonmel was Italian-born Charles Bianconi (1786–1875), who, at the precocious age of 16, was sent to Ireland by his father in an attempt to break his liaison with a woman. Bianconi later channelled all his frustrated passion into setting up a coach service between Clonmel and Cahir; his company quickly grew to become a nationwide passenger and mail carrier. For putting Clonmel on the map, Bianconi was twice elected mayor.

Clonmel's centre sits on the northern bank of the river. Set back from the quays and running parallel to the river, the main street runs east–west, starting of as Parnell St and becoming Mitchell St and O'Connell St before passing under West Gate, where it changes to Irishtown and Abbey Rd (there's a handy map on a signboard near St Mary's Church). Running north from this long thoroughfare is Gladstone St, which has a number of hotels and pubs.

The East Munster Way (p334) passes through Clonmel.

Sights

Turning south down Bridge St, crossing the river and following the road around brings you to Lady Blessington's Bath, a picturesque stretch of the river that's perfect for picnicking.

South Tipperary County Museum MUSEUM (www.southtippcoco.ie; Mick Delahunty Sq; ☉10am-5pm Tue-Sat) FREE Informative displays on the history of County Tipperary from Neolithic times to the present are covered at this well-put-together museum, which also hosts changing exhibitions.

Near the museum, look for the life-size Frank Patterson Statue, which portrays the son of Clonmel and Ireland's 'Golden Tenor' in full-throated glory. If only it had sound. Among his long list of accomplishments was performing 'Danny Boy' in the Coen Brothers 1990 film *Miller's Crossing*.

Main Guard HISTORIC BUILDING (☎052-612 7484; www.heritageireland.ie; Sarsfield St; ☉9.30am-6pm Easter-Sep, hours can vary) FREE At the junction of Mitchell and Sarsfield Sts is the beautifully restored Main Guard, a Butler courthouse dating from 1675 and based on a design by Christopher Wren. The columned

porticos are once again open (after renovations) and exhibits include the ubiquitous model of Clonmel as a walled 17th-century town.

County Courthouse HISTORIC BUILDING (Nelson St) South of Parnell St you'll spot the refurbished County Courthouse, designed by Richard Morrison in 1802. It was here that the Young Irelanders of 1848, including Thomas Francis Meagher, were tried and sentenced to transportation to Australia.

Franciscan Friary HISTORIC BUILDING (Mitchell St) West along Mitchell St (past the town hall with its statue commemorating the 1798 Rising) and south down Abbey St is the Franciscan friary. Inside, near the door, is a 1533 Butler tomb depicting a knight and his lady. There's some fine modern stained glass, especially in St Anthony's Chapel to the north.

Sleeping & Eating

Several B&Bs cluster on Marlfield Rd, due west of the centre.

★**Befani's** MEDITERRANEAN, B&B €€ (☎052-617 7893; www.befani.com; 6 Sarsfield St; s/d €40/70; mains €15-26; ☉restaurant 9-11am, 12.30-2.30pm & 5.30-9.30pm; @🙲) Between the Main Guard and the Suir, Befani's brings the Mediterranean to Clonmel. Throughout the day there's a mouthwatering tapas menu (be sure to try the Catalonian spiced mussels); mains include a rich bouillabaisse in lobster broth. Its nine guestrooms, of varying sizes, are attractively fitted out in sunny colours.

Hotel Minella HOTEL €€€ (☎052-612 2388; www.hotelminella.ie; Coleville Rd; d €120-150, ste €180-350; @🙲🙲🙲) Refined yet unpretentious, this family-run luxury hotel sits amid extensive grounds on the south bank of the River Suir, 2km east of the centre. The 90 rooms are divided between an 1863 mansion and a new wing. The latter has almost every kind of convenience, including two suites with their own hot outdoor tubs on private terraces overlooking the river.

Niamh's CAFE, DELI € (1 Mitchell St; mains €10.50-12; ☉8.30am-5.30pm Mon-Sat; 🙲) This smart deli and cafe has a wide range of appealing lunch options (gourmet burgers, pan-fried pork and lasagnes, plus creative sandwiches) to eat here or by the banks of the Suir.

Indian Ocean   INDIAN €€
(✐052-618 4833; www.indianoceanclonmel.com; Sarsfield St; mains €8.50-16; ⊙5-11.30pm) This isn't just Clonmel's best Indian restaurant (and no, it's not the only one), but one of its best restaurants, full stop. The dining room is an elegant affair of timber and white tablecloths and the food is first rate – try the tandoori platter of lamb, steak and chicken.

 Drinking & Entertainment

Sean Tierney   PUB
(13 O'Connell St) Wander the warren of rooms and floors of this narrow old pub until you find a spot that's just right. The ground-level bar is always alive with craic.

Phil Carroll   PUB
(Parnell St) Near Nelson St, this diminutive place is Clonmel's most atmospheric old boozer.

South Tipperary Arts Centre   ARTS CENTRE
(✐052-612 7877; www.southtipparts.com; Nelson St) Has an excellent program of art exhibitions, plays and music.

ℹ **Information**

Post Office (Emmet St)
Tourist Office (✐052-612 2960; Mary St, St Mary's Church; ⊙9.30am-1pm & 2-4.30pm Mon-Fri) Adjoins Main Guard.

ℹ **Getting There & Away**

BUS
Bus Éireann (www.buseireann.ie) has services to Cahir (€6, 30 minutes, eight daily), Cork (€19.70, two hours, three daily), Kilkenny (€10.50, one hour, 12 daily), Waterford (€8.50, one hour, nine daily) and a number of other places. Buses stop at the train station.

TRAIN
The **train station** (✐052-612 1982) is on Prior Park Rd past the Oakville Shopping Centre. From Monday to Saturday, the Limerick Junction–Waterford train stops twice daily in each direction.

Around Clonmel

Directly south of Clonmel, over the border in County Waterford, are the Comeragh Mountains. There's a scenic route south to Ballymacarbry and the Nire Valley.

Fethard

POP 900
Fethard (Fiodh Ard) is a quiet, quaint little village that doesn't have any tourism ambitions, despite the impressive medieval ruins scattered about its compact, linear centre. Located 14km north of Clonmel on the River Clashawley, it has a good slice of its old walls still intact. Driving north on the R689 you cross a small ridge and see Fethard in the emerald valley below, looking much as it would have to travellers centuries ago. Its wide main street testifies to its historic role as an important market town.

◉ **Sights**

Holy Trinity Church   CHURCH
(Main St) Fethard's Holy Trinity Church and churchyard lie within a captivating time warp. The church is right off Main St and is reached through a cast-iron gateway. Get the keys from the XL Stop & Shop (aka Whyte's) on Main St, 50m west of the gate.

The main part of the building dates from the 13th century, but its ancient walls have been blighted with mortar for weatherproofing. The handsome west tower was added later and has had its sturdy stonework uncovered. It looks more like a fortified tower house and has savage-looking finials on its corner turrets. The interior of the church has an aisled nave and a chancel of typical medieval style, but is sparsely furnished. A ruined chapel and sacristy adjoin the south end of the church. Old gravestones descend in ranks to a refurbished stretch of medieval wall complete with a guard tower and a parapet, from where you can look down on the gentle River Clashawley between its horse-trod banks.

Close to the church in Main St is the 17th-century town hall, with coats of arms mounted on the facade.

Other Medieval Sights   HISTORIC SITES
Fethard's main concentration of medieval remains (some of which have been incorporated into later buildings) are just south of the church at the end of Watergate St. Beside Castle Inn are the ruins of several fortified 17th-century tower houses. Just under the archway to the river bank and Watergate Bridge is a fine sheila-na-gig (a sexually explicit medieval depiction of a woman) embedded in the wall to your left. You can stroll along the river

bank, provided the resident geese are feeling friendly.

East along Abbey St is the 14th-century Augustinian friary, now a Catholic church, with medieval stained glass and another in-your-face sheila-na-gig in its east wall.

✗ Eating & Drinking

★ McCarthy's   PUB €€
(http://mccarthyshotel.net; Main St; mains €16-22.50; ⊗noon-3pm daily & from 6pm Wed-Sun) A classic that deserves national acclaim and preservation, McCarthy's proclaims itself as pub, restaurant and undertaker – and not necessarily in that order (making it an efficient set-up for wakes). Closely spaced wooden booths and tables wedge between a thicket of treasures dating back to 1840, and the locals are only too happy to chat.

❶ Getting There & Away

There's no public transport to Fethard but it makes a pleasant cycle from Cashel, 15km to the west.

Carrick-on-Suir

POP 4355

The unassuming market town of Carrick-on-Suir (Carraig na Siúire), 20km east of Clonmel, boasted twice its present population during the late-medieval period, when it was a centre of the brewing and wool industries.

Carrick-on-Suir was once the property of the Butlers, the Earls of Ormond, who built Ormond Castle (www.heritageireland.ie; Castle St; ⊗10am-1.30pm & 2-6pm Mon-Sat Easter-Sep) FREE, also spelt Ormonde Castle, on the banks of the river in the 14th century. The Elizabethan mansion next to the castle was

built by the 10th Earl of Ormond, Black Tom Butler, in long-term anticipation of a visit by his cousin, Queen Elizabeth I, who rather thoughtlessly never turned up. Some rooms in this Dúchas-owned edifice have fine 16th-century stuccowork, especially the Long Gallery with its depictions of Elizabeth and the Butler coat of arms.

From Carrick-on-Suir, the East Munster Way winds west to Clonmel before heading south into Waterford.

Carrick-on-Suir's farmers market (⊗10am-2pm Fri) 🖉 is held next to the tourist office (☑051-640 200; www.carrickonsuir.ie; ⊗10am-4pm Mon-Fri), reached by a narrow laneway off Main St.

Bus Éireann (☑051-879 000; www.buseireann.ie) has numerous services including to Cahir and Clonmel (€7.10, 25 minutes) up to eight times daily. Buses stop at Greenside, the park beside the N24 road.

The train station is north of Greenside, off Cregg Rd. From Monday to Saturday, the Limerick Junction–Waterford train stops twice daily in each direction.

Roscrea

POP 6300

Roscrea owes its beginnings to a 5th-century monk, St Cronan, who set up a waystation for the travelling poor. Most of the historical structures are on or near the main street, Castle St.

Roscrea Castle, a 13th-century stone edifice right in the town centre, was started in 1213 and is remarkably intact. There are two fortified stone towers, surrounded by walls. Look closely and you can see where the original drawbridge was installed. Inside the courtyard stands the early-18th-century

---

WALK: EAST MUNSTER WAY

This 70km walk travels through forest and open moorland, along small country roads and a river towpath. It's clearly laid out with black markers bearing yellow arrows and could be managed in three days, starting at Carrick-on-Suir in County Tipperary and finishing at Clogheen.

The first day takes you to Clonmel following the old towpath on the Suir for significant portions of the route. At Kilsheelan Bridge, you leave the river to Harney's Crossroads, then wander through Gurteen Wood and the Comeraghs to Sir Thomas Bridge where you rejoin the river.

On the second day, the Way first leads south into the hills and then descends to Newcastle and the river once more. The third day sees a lot of very atmospheric walking along the quiet River Tar to Clogheen.

Ordnance Survey Discovery series maps 74 and 75 cover the route.

Damer House, the Queen Anne–style residence of the Damer family.

Inside you'll find the Roscrea Heritage Centre (www.heritageireland.ie; Castle St; adult/concession €4/2; ⊙10am-5.15pm Easter-Sep), which contains some interesting exhibits, including one on the medieval monasteries of the Midlands and another on early 20th-century farming life. There's a peaceful walled garden by the house.

Up to eight Bus Éireann buses stop at Roscrea between Dublin (€11, two hours) and Limerick (€9.50, 1½ hours).

Nenagh & Around

POP 8000

Pretty Nenagh was a garrison town in the 19th century and, before that, the site of a dominant castle. Today it looks like the prototype for the rook in chess and is surrounded by cawing crows. The tower dates from the 13th century and has impossibly thick walls.

Nearby, the civic centre is an imposing complex of dark-stone buildings from the 19th century, including an old gaol.

Next door stands the 1840 Round House, a charming stone building that holds the Nenagh Heritage Centre (☑067-33850; www.tipperarynorth.ie; Kickham St; ⊙9.30am-5pm Mon-Fri) FREE, where you can get tourist information.

It's worth planning your visit around lunchtime to catch Nenagh's excellent delis and cafes, particularly Country Choice (☑067-32596; 25 Kenyon St; dishes €5-11; ⊙9am-5pm Mon-Sat), a lavender-painted place of pilgrimage for lovers of really great Irish artisan foods, with homemade preserves, farmhouse cheeses and myriad other treats.

Nenagh is the gateway to the eastern shore of Lough Derg, a popular swimming, fishing and boating area – enquire at Shannon Sailing (☑067-24499; www.shannonsailing.com). An interesting, scenic lakeside drive from Nenagh is the 24km R494 that winds around to Killaloe and Ballina.

Frequent Bus Éireann services include Limerick city (€8, 50 minutes). Nenagh's train station has four services daily to Limerick city (€12.20, one hour); connect in Ballybrophy for Dublin, Cork and Tralee.

County Clare

POP 117,000 / AREA 3147 SQ KM

Best Places to Eat

➡ Buttermarket Cafe (p352)

➡ Linnane's Lobster Bar (p370)

➡ Naughton's Bar (p353)

➡ Vaughan's Anchor Inn (p358)

Best Places to Sleep

➡ Rowan Tree Hostel (p340)

➡ Old Ground Hotel (p340)

➡ Sheedy's Country House Hotel & Restaurant (p364)

➡ Gregan's Castle Hotel (p369)

Why Go?

Clare combines the stunning natural beauty of its long and meandering coastline with unique windswept landscapes and dollops of Irish culture.

Rugged nature and the timeless ocean meet on the county's coast. The Atlantic relentlessly pounds year-round, eroding the rocks into fantastic landscapes, and forming sheer cliffs like those at the iconic Cliffs of Moher and strange little islands like those near Loop Head. There are even stretches of beach where surfers flock to the (chilly) waves. The Burren, an ancient region of tortured stone and alien vistas, stretches down to the coast and right out to the Aran Islands.

But if the land is hard, Clare's soul is not: traditional Irish culture and music flourish. And it's not just a show for tourists, either. In little villages such as Miltown Malbay, Ennistymon, Doolin and Kilfenora you'll find pubs with year-round sessions of trad music.

When to Go

➡ County Clare's pubs hum to the beats of trad sessions year-round, so even in winter you'll find the craic – often warmed, in the countryside, by a peat fire.

➡ While the unsettled seas of winter have a drama that will fill your days with moody idylls, the county literally shines during the more temperate months when long walks along the spectacular soaring cliffs of the coast and among the desolate rocks of the Burren don't require full foul-weather gear.

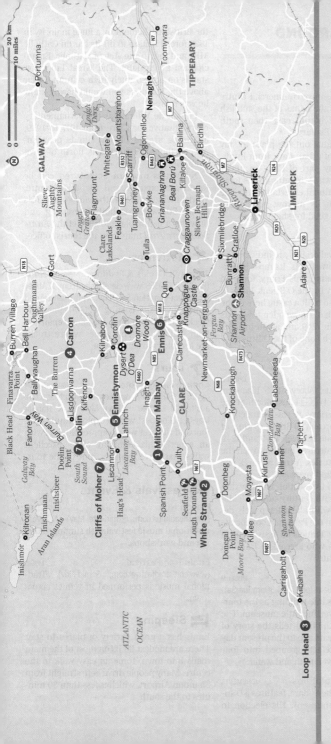

County Clare Highlights

1 Swoon to the music in the traditional pubs of **Miltown Malbay** (p355)

2 Lose yourself on the vast sweep of powdery sandy beach at **White Strand** (p355)

3 Delight in the amazing drives, walks and improbable offshore rocky outcrops of **Loop Head** (p354)

4 Find lost dolmens and abandoned abbeys among the rocky expanse of the Burren at **Carron** (p367)

5 Become part of the scene in the artful, tuneful town of **Ennistymon** (p357)

6 Go pub-hopping in musical **Ennis** (p338), where you can find nightly trad sessions on street after street

7 Catch a late-afternoon boat from **Doolin** (p361) to see the soaring **Cliffs of Moher** (p358) in all their radiant glory

ENNIS & AROUND

Ennis

POP 20,200

Ennis (Inis) is the busy commercial centre of Clare. It lies on the banks of the smallish River Fergus, which runs east, then south into the Shannon Estuary.

It's short on sights but the place to stay if you want a bit of urban flair; from Ennis, you can reach any part of Clare in under two hours. The town's strengths are its food, lodging and traditional entertainment. The town centre, with its narrow, pedestrian-friendly streets, is good for shopping.

History

The town's medieval origins are indicated by its irregular, narrow streets. Its most important historical site is Ennis Friary, founded in the 13th century by the O'Briens, kings of Thomond, who also built a castle here in the 13th century. Much of the wooden town was destroyed by fire in 1249 and again in 1306, when it was razed by one of the O'Briens.

⊙ Sights

★ **Ennis Friary**   CHURCH
(www.heritageireland.ie; Abbey St; ⊘10am-6pm Easter-Sep, to 5pm Oct) FREE Just north of the Square is Ennis Friary. It was founded by Donnchadh Cairbreach O'Brien, a king of Thomond, sometime between 1240 and 1249 and is a mix of structures built between the 13th and 19th centuries. A roof replaces one destroyed a mere 200 years ago.

It has a graceful five-section window dating from the late 13th century, and a McMahon tomb (1460) with alabaster panels depicting scenes from the Passion. Look for the relief carving of St Francis of Assisi, patron of the Franciscans who arrived in Ennis in the early 13th century.

Clare Museum   MUSEUM
(Arthur's Row; ⊘9.30am-1pm & 2-4.30pm Tue-Sat) FREE Sharing the same building as the tourist office is this diverting little museum. The Riches of Clare exhibition tells the story of Clare from 8000 years ago to the present day using original artefacts grouped into four themes: earth, power, faith and water.

Monuments & Sculptures   MONUMENTS
The town centre, the Square, features a Daniel O'Connell monument. His election to the British parliament by a huge majority in 1828 forced Britain to lift its bar on Catholic MPs and led to the Act of Catholic Emancipation a year later. The 'Great Liberator' stands on an extremely high column, so far above the rest of us you would hardly know he was there.

Eamon de Valera was the parliamentary representative for Clare from 1917 to 1959; a bronze statue of him stands near Ennis courthouse, a short walk north of town along Gort Rd.

Numerous modern sculptures can be found scattered around the town centre. Works include the Weathered Woman (Old Barrack St), which is both interesting and provides a handy place to sit. Get the *Ennis Sculpture Trail* map from the tourist office.

Activities

Tierney's Cycles & Fishing   BICYCLE RENTAL
(☑086 803 0369; www.clarebikehire.com; 17 Abbey St; ⊘9am-6pm Mon-Sat) Has well-maintained mountain bikes costing €20/70 per day/week, including helmet, lock and repair kit. Staff will recommend routes where trucks are less likely to squash you.

☞ Tours

Ennis Walking Tours   WALKING TOUR
(☑087 648 3714; www.enniswalkingtours.com; adult/child €8/free; ⊘11am Mon-Tue & Thu-Sat May-Oct) The best way to explore Ennis is on foot and the best way to appreciate it is with an expert. This company offers excellent walks that leave from in front of the tourist office.

✯ Festivals & Events

Fleadh Nua   CULTURE
(www.fleadhnua.com; ⊘mid-late May) A lively traditional music festival with singing, dancing and workshops.

Ennis Trad Festival   MUSIC
(www.ennistradfestival.com; ⊘mid-Nov) Traditional music is performed in venues across town.

⊨ Sleeping

Ennis has a great variety of places to stay. There are modest B&Bs on most of the main roads into town, some an easy walk to the centre. Many people drive here straight from Shannon Airport, which is less than 30 minutes to the south.

Ennis

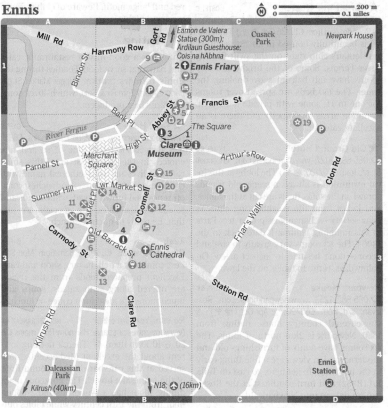

0   200 m
0   0.1 miles

Ennis

⊙ Top Sights
1 Clare Museum	B2
2 Ennis Friary	B1

⊙ Sights
3 Daniel O'Connell Monument	B2
4 Weathered Woman	B3

⊕ Activities, Courses & Tours
5 Tierney's Cycles & Fishing	B1

⊜ Sleeping
6 Banner Lodge	A3
7 Old Ground Hotel	B3
8 Queens Hotel	B1
9 Rowan Tree Hostel	B1

⊗ Eating
Brogan's	(see 15)
10 Ennis Farmers Market	A3

11 Food Heaven	A2
Poet's Corner Bar	(see 7)
Rowan Tree Cafe Bar	(see 9)
12 Town Hall Cafe	B2
13 Tulsi	B3
14 Zest	B2

⊙ Drinking & Nightlife
15 Brogan's	B2
16 Cíaran's Bar	B1
17 Cruise's Pub	B1
18 John O'Dea	B3
Poet's Corner Bar	(see 7)

⊕ Entertainment
19 Glór	D2

⊜ Shopping
20 Custy's Music Shop	B2
21 Ennis Bookshop	B2

★ **Rowan Tree Hostel** HOSTEL €

(☑ 065-686 8687; www.rowantreehostel.ie; Harmony Row; dm/s/d from €19/35/54; @ 🕏) This hostel is beautifully housed in an 18th-century gentleman's club right on the swift-flowing River Fergus. Some of the bright and airy rooms have fab balconies overlooking the water. The 150 beds are spread over rooms for one to 14, some with private bathroom. Common areas are superb and there is an excellent cafe-bar.

★ **Old Ground Hotel** HOTEL €€

(☑ 065-682 8127; www.flynnhotels.com; O'Connell St; s/d from €90/120; @ 🕏) The lobby at this local institution is always a scene: old friends sprawl on the sofas, deals are cut at the tables, and ladies from the neighbouring church's altar society exchange gossip over tea. Parts of this rambling landmark date back to the 1800s. The 83 rooms vary greatly in size and decor – don't hesitate to inspect a few. On balmy days, retire to tables on the lawn.

Newpark House INN €€

(☑ 065-682 1233; www.newparkhouse.com; Roslevan; s/d from €60/90; ⊙Apr-Oct; @ 🕏) A vine-covered country house dating from 1650, Newpark is 2km north of Ennis. The six rooms have a mix of furnishings old and modern; garden views are a fine thing early in the morning. To get here, go east on Tulla Rd (R352) and turn southeast at the Roslevan roudabout into Newpark Rd.

Ardilaun Guesthouse B&B €€

(☑ 065-682 2311; www.ardilaun.com; Gort Rd/R458; s/d from €40/70; 🕏) Drop a line into the River Fergus from the deck out back at this fine B&B, a short walk north from the centre of Ennis. There is a sauna and many of the 10 rooms overlook the water.

Banner Lodge INN €€

(☑ 065-682 4224; www.bannerlodge.com; Market Pl; s/d from €45/70; 🕏) You can't really get more central than this, and at great value. Some of the eight rooms are pretty tight, but given the location it's a fair trade-off. The decor in the 2nd-storey inn is dominated by the bold blue carpet and a scattering of antiques. Service is minimal.

Queens Hotel HOTEL €€

(☑ 065-682 8963; www.irishcourthotels.com; Abbey St; r €65-100; @ 🕏) This corner hotel is perfect for those seeking an anonymous stay right in the centre. The 48 modern rooms are standard-hotel in design, with a timeless red and beige motif. Beware of club noise on weekend nights.

🍴 Eating

Ennis has a good mix of restaurants, cafes and bars that serve food. Foodies throng the **Ennis farmers market** (Upper Market St car park; ⊙8am-2pm Fri & Sat), which lures some of Clare's best producers.

★ **Food Heaven** CAFE €

(www.foodheaven.eu; 21 Market St; mains €6-10; ⊙8.30am-6pm Mon-Sat) One of several fine choices in the Market St area, this small cafe-deli lives up to its ethereal name with creative and fresh fare. Sandwiches come on renowned brown bread, while soups and salads change daily. Hot specials are just that. Be ready to queue at lunch.

Zest CAFE €

(Market Pl; meals €5-10; ⊙8am-6pm Mon-Sat) Zest combines a deli, bakery, shop and cafe. Excellent prepared foods from the region are offered along with salads, soups and much more. It's ideal for a coffee or lunch.

Rowan Tree Cafe Bar MEDITERRANEAN €€

(www.rowantreecafebar.ie; Harmony Row; mains €7-20; ⊙10.30am-11pm) 🌶 There's nothing low-rent about the excellent Med-accented fare served at this cafe-bar on the ground floor of the namesake hostel. The gorgeous main dining room has a wondrous old wooden floor from the 18th century while tables outside have river views. The ingredients are locally and organically sourced.

Poet's Corner Bar IRISH €€

(Old Ground Hotel, O'Connell St; mains €6-15; ⊙12.30-9pm) This famous old bar has a deserved reputation for its traditional dishes, especially the oh-so-fresh fish and chips. Excellent service; many specials.

Town Hall Cafe IRISH €€

(☑ 065-682 8127; O'Connell St; mains €8-25; ⊙10am-4pm & 6-9.30pm; 🕏) Adjacent to, and affiliated with, the Old Ground Hotel, this excellent bistro is in the stylishly resurrected old town hall. High ceilings allow large artwork, while the spare settings don't compete with the food on the ever-changing modern Irish menu. Look for local ingredients, especially seafood, taking front and centre stage.

Tulsi INDIAN €€

(Carmody St; mains €8-18; ⊙5-10pm Mon-Sat, 1-4pm Sun) Indian cuisine is excellent at this most accommodating of restaurants. The staff are gracious and classics such as tandoori chicken are two cuts above the norm.

Brogan's PUB €€
(24 O'Connell St; mains €8-15; ☺10am-10pm) The peas at this popular old pub are always well cooked, and the supply of spuds never-ending. Standards such as roasts get top billing along with steaks and an imposing beer-battered cod. The seafood chowder is loaded with smoked fish.

 Drinking & Nightlife

As the capital of a renowned music county, Ennis bursts with pubs featuring trad music. In fact, that's the best reason to stay here. Where's best changes often; stroll the streets pub-hopping to find what's on any given night.

Brogan's PUB
(24 O'Connell St) On the corner of Cooke's Lane, Brogan's sees a fine bunch of musicians rattling even the stone floors from about 9pm Monday to Thursday, plus even more nights in summer. It's a big pub that rambles from one room to the next.

Cruise's Pub PUB
(Abbey St) This friendly bar has a long side courtyard that's perfect for enjoying a fresh-air pint in the shadow of the old friary. There are trad music sessions most nights from 9.30pm.

Poet's Corner Bar PUB
(Old Ground Hotel, O'Connell St) Old Ground hotel's pub often has massive trad sessions on Fridays.

Cíaran's Bar PUB
(Francis St) Slip into this small place by day and you can become just another geezer pondering a pint. At night there's usually trad music.

John O'Dea PUB
(66 O'Connell St) Unchanged since at least the 1950s, this plain-tile-fronted pub is a hideout for local musicians serious about their trad sessions. Draws some of Clare's best.

☆ **Entertainment**

Cois na hAbhna TRADITIONAL MUSIC
(☎065-682 0996; www.coisnahabhna.ie; Gort Rd; ☺shop 9am-5pm, trad sessions 9pm Tue) This important point for traditional music and culture is 1.5km north of town along the N18. It has performances (plus weekly trad sessions) and a full range of classes in dance and music. The archive covers Irish traditional music, song, dance and folklore relating mainly to County Clare; books and recordings are on sale.

Glór THEATRE
(www.glor.ie; Friar's Walk) Clare's cultural centre is in a striking modern building. Art, traditional music, theatre, dance, photography and film are some of the programs offered.

 Shopping

Ennis has the best shopping in the county. On Saturday morning, there is a market at Market Pl. For the best selection of shops, head to O'Connell and Abbey Sts.

Custy's Music Shop MUSIC
(☎065-682 1727; www.custysmusic.com; Cook's Lane, off O'Connell St; ☺10am-6pm Mon-Sat) A must-stop for Irish music, instruments (including fiddles) other musical items and general info about the local scene.

Ennis Bookshop BOOKS
(13 Abbey St; ☺10am-6pm Mon-Sat) Excellent independent shop for maps and books of local interest.

ℹ **Information**

Tourist Office (☎065-682 8366; www.visitennis.ie; Arthur's Row; ☺9.30am-1pm & 2-5.30pm Tue-Fri) Very helpful and efficient. Can book accommodation for a €4 fee.

ℹ **Getting There & Away**

The M18 bypass east of the city lets traffic between Limerick and Galway whiz right past, although trips to the coast still take you through the centre.

BUS

Bus Éireann (☎065-682 4177; www.buseireann.ie) services operate from the bus station beside the train station.

Buses run from Ennis to Cork (€16, three hours, 11 daily); Doolin (€12, 1½ hours, two daily) via Corofin, Ennistymon, Lahinch and Liscannor; Galway (€10, 1½ hours, hourly) via Gort; Limerick (€9, 40 minutes, hourly) via Bunratty; and Shannon Airport (€8, 50 minutes, hourly).

To reach Dublin (€20), connect through Limerick.

TRAIN

Irish Rail (www.irishrail.ie) trains from **Ennis station** (☎065-684 0444; Station Rd) serve

Limerick (€10, 40 minutes, nine daily), where you can connect to trains to places further afield, including Dublin. The line to Galway (€19, 1¾ hours, five daily) features good Burren scenery.

ℹ Getting Around

Most people get their rental cars at Shannon Airport. Parking is fairly good in Ennis. There's a big car park behind the tourist office in Friar's Walk and one alongside the river just off Abbey St.

Burren Taxis (☑ 065-682 3456) Taxi stands are at the train station and the Square.

Around Ennis

North of Ennis is the early Christian site of Dysert O'Dea. To the southeast are several fine castles. Note that much of the county can be enjoyed as a day trip from Ennis.

Dysert O'Dea

You can feel the past as you navigate the narrow tracks with grass in the middle to Dysert O'Dea (⊙ 24hr), where St Tola founded a monastery in the 8th century. The church and high cross, the White Cross of St Tola, date from the 12th or 13th century. The cross depicts Daniel in the lion's den on one side and a crucified Christ above a bishop carved in relief on the other. Look for carvings of animal and human heads

in a semicircle on the southern doorway of the Romanesque church. There are also 5m-high remains of a round tower.

In 1318 the O'Briens, who were kings of Thomond, and the Norman de Clares of Bunratty fought a pitched battle nearby, which the O'Briens won, thus postponing the Anglo-Norman conquest of Clare for some two centuries. The 15th-century **O'Dea Castle** houses the **Clare Archaeology Centre** (www.dysertcastle.com; Corofin; adult/child €4/2.50; ⊙ 10am-6pm May-Sep). A 3km history trail around the castle passes some two-dozen ancient monuments – from ring forts and high crosses to a prehistoric cooking site. A further 5km walk along a medieval road takes you to another stone fort.

East of Dysert O'Dea, you can wander along a lovely river in **Dromore Wood** (www.heritageireland.ie; Ruan; ⊙ 8am-7.30pm summer, to 6pm winter, visitor centre 10am-5pm Jun-Aug) FREE. This Dúchas nature reserve encompasses some 400 hectares as well as the ruins of the 17th-century O'Brien Castle, two ring forts and the site of Kilakee church.

ℹ Getting There & Away

Dysert O'Dea is 1.7km off the Corofin road (R476), 11km north of Ennis. Dromore Wood is 8km east of Dysert, off R458.

DON'T MISS

FINDING TRADITIONAL MUSIC IN COUNTY CLARE

From atmospheric small pubs in tiny villages where non-instrument-playing patrons are a minority, to rollicking urban boozers in Ennis, Clare is one of Ireland's best counties for traditional music. Eschewing any modern influences from rock or even polkas (as is heard elsewhere), Clare's musicians stick resolutely to the jigs and reels of old, often with little vocal accompaniment.

Although you can find pubs with trad sessions at least one night a week in almost every town and village, the following are our picks for where to start:

➡ **Doolin** A much-hyped collection of pubs with nightly trad music sessions. However, tourist crowds can erase any sense of intimacy or even enjoyment. (p361)

➡ **Ennis** You can bounce from one music-filled pub to another on most nights, especially in the summer. Musicians from around the county come here to show off and there are good venues for serious trad pursuits. (p338)

➡ **Ennistymon** A low-key farming village inland from Doolin with a couple of ancient pubs that attract top local talent. (p357)

➡ **Kilfenora** Small village with a big musical heritage on show at the great local pub Vaughan's. (p364)

➡ **Miltown Malbay** This tiny village hosts the annual Willie Clancy Summer School, one of Ireland's best music festivals. The talented locals can be heard performing throughout the year in several old pubs. (p355)

Bus Éireann generally runs one bus daily from Ennis, which stops along R476.

Quin

POP 930

Quin (Chuinche), a tiny village 10km southeast of Ennis, was the site of the Great Clare Find of 1854 – the most important discovery of prehistoric gold in Ireland. Greed and need beat out any good deeds, and only a few of the several hundred torcs, gorgets and other pieces, discovered by labourers working on the Limerick–Ennis railway, made it to the National Museum in Dublin; most were sold and melted down.

Quin Abbey (⊙24hr) FREE was founded in 1433 using part of the walls of an older de Clare castle built in 1280. Despite many periods of persecution, Franciscan monks lived here until the 19th century. The splendidly named Fireballs MacNamara, a notorious duellist and member of the region's ruling family, is buried here. An elegant belfry rises above the main body of the abbey, and you can climb the narrow spiral staircase to look down on the fine cloister and surrounding countryside.

Beside the friary is the 13th-century Gothic Church of St Finghin. Several cafes and pubs line the quiet streets near the ruins.

Knappogue Castle

About 3km southeast of Quin is Knappogue Castle & Walled Garden (www.shannonheritage.com; R469; adult/child €6/3; ⊙10am-4.30pm May-Aug). It was built in 1467 by the MacNamaras, who held sway over a large part of Clare from the 5th to mid-15th centuries and, like early fast-food franchisers, littered the region with 42 castles. Knappogue's walls are intact, and it has a fine collection of period furniture and fireplaces. The formal gardens have been restored.

When Oliver Cromwell came to Ireland in 1649, he used Knappogue as a base, which is one of the reasons it was spared destruction. The MacNamara family regained the castle after the Restoration in 1660, and since then windows and other features have been added to make it more 'liveable'.

Knappogue also hosts touristy medieval banquets (adult/child €44/22; ⊙6.30pm Apr-Oct).

Craggaunowen

For more ancient Irish heritage tarted up for the masses, visit Craggaunowen (www.shannonheritage.com; off R469; adult/child €8/4.50; ⊙10am-4pm Easter-Sep; 🅟). Around 6km southeast of Quin, the complex includes recreated ancient Celtic farms, dwellings such as a *crannóg* (artificial island) and a 5th-century ring fort, plus real artefacts – including a 2000-year-old oak road. Craggaunowen Castle is a small, well-preserved MacNamara fortified house. With lots of animals such as snot-nosed boars, this is a good place for kids who like dirty critters.

EASTERN & SOUTHEASTERN CLARE

Away from the Atlantic coast and the rugged Burren, Clare rolls gently eastward through low-lying green countryside given emphasis by the occasional range of low hills. The county's eastern boundary is the River Shannon and the long, noodle-like inland waterway of Lough Derg, which stretches 48km from Portumna in County Galway to just south of Killaloe. Lakeside villages such as Mountshannon seem in a different world from the rugged, evocative west of Clare, but this is an intimate countryside of water, woods and panoramic views.

Southeastern Clare, where the Shannon swells into its broad estuary, is a plain landscape dotted with farms and small villages.

Shannon Airport

Ireland's second-largest airport used to be a vital fuelling stop for piston-engine planes lacking the range to make it between the North American and European mainlands. Today Shannon (Sionainn) is a low-stress gateway to the region. It's an ideal entry point for the western counties.

About 3km from the airport, Shannon town, built to serve airport workers, has the feel of one of those old planned Soviet industrial cities – albeit with more reliable hot water. Don't linger.

🛏 Sleeping & Eating

There's B&B accommodation 3km from the airport in Shannon town but it's only

30 minutes to Ennis, Limerick and much prettier spots. The airport terminal has an often-crowded restaurant. Bring food from the cafes of Ennis.

Park Inn Shannon Airport HOTEL **€€**
(☑ 061-471 122; www.parkinns.com; r from €70; @ 🛜) Wake up in one of the 114 generic hotel rooms here and you could be anywhere, which is the idea as the terminal is just across the car park. This is an option if you have an early flight and want to lose the rental car.

ℹ Information

Shannon Airport (SNN; ☑ 061-712 000; www. shannonairport.com; 🛜) Has many facilities, including a free observation area for those stuck waiting. Almost everything, including ATMs and currency exchange, is on one level.

Tourist Office (www.shannonregiontourism.ie; Shannon Airport; ⊙7am-4pm) Near the arrivals area; has regional info.

ℹ Getting There & Around

AIR

There are nonstop services across the Atlantic to the US; travellers can enjoy the great convenience of pre-clearance for US customs and immigration before they leave Ireland, so there's no waiting in queues once you arrive on the other side of the pond.

Airlines with direct flights to/from Shannon:

Aer Lingus (www.aerlingus.ie) Boston, New York JFK and London Heathrow.

Delta (www.delta.com) New York JFK.

Ryanair (www.ryanair.com) London Stansted and Gatwick, Liverpool and numerous secondary and obscure European airports.

United (www.united.com) Chicago and Newark.

BUS

Bus Éireann (☑ 061-474 311; www.buseireann. ie) Buy tickets from a machine or the driver. Destinations served by direct buses include Cork (€17, 2½ hours, hourly), Ennis (€8, 50 minutes, hourly), Galway (€15, 1¾ hours, hourly) and Limerick (€8, 30 to 55 minutes, two per hour). Some frequencies are reduced on Sundays.

CAR

Major car rental firms have desks at the airport.

TAXI

A taxi to the centre of Limerick or Ennis costs about €40 if booked at the taxi desk near arrivals. You may pay more at the outside rank.

Bunratty

Conveniently located beside the N18 motorway and with plenty of bus-sized parking, Bunratty (Bun Raite) – home to government schemes for hawking tourism hard – draws more tourists than any other place in the region. A theme park recreates a clichéd Irish village of old (where's the horseshit, lash and disease, we ask?) and each year more and more shops crowd the access roads – many selling authentic Irish goods just out of the container from China.

Groups lay siege to Bunratty from April to October.

⊙ Sights & Activities

Bunratty Castle & Folk Park CASTLE
(www.shannonheritage.com; adult/child €15/1; ⊙9am-5.30pm, last admission 4.15pm; 🚹) Square and hulking Bunratty Castle is only the latest of several constructions to occupy its location beside the River Ratty. Vikings founded a settlement here in the 10th century, and other occupants included the Norman Thomas de Clare in the 1270s. The present structure was put up in the early 1400s by the energetic MacNamara family, falling shortly thereafter to the O'Briens, in whose possession it remained until the 17th century. Fully restored, the castle is loaded with 14th- to 17th-century furniture, paintings and wall hangings.

Adjoining the castle, the folk park is a reconstructed traditional Irish village with cottages, a forge and working blacksmith, weavers, post office, pub and small cafe.

A few of the buildings were brought here from elsewhere, but most are recreations. In peak season employees in period garb can be found explaining the more family-friendly aspects of the late 19th century (there are no workhouses, trigger-happy English soldiers etc). There's a pervading theme-park artificiality (without the rides).

➡ **Traditional Irish Night**
(☑ 061-360 788; adult/child €40/20; ⊙7-9.30pm Apr-Oct) Traditional Irish nights are held in a corn barn in the folk park. Lots of red-haired (real or fake, it's clearly a big help in securing employment) servers dish up trad chow plus music and dancing. There's nontraditional wine as well, which may put you in the mood for the singalong.

➡ **Medieval Banquet**
(☑ 061-360 788; adult/child €50/25; ⊙5.30pm & 8.45pm Apr-Oct, schedule varies Nov-Mar) If you

skip the highjinks in the corn barn, you may opt for a medieval banquet, replete with harp-playing maidens, court jesters and food with a medieval motif (lots of meaty items, but somehow we think the real stuff would empty the place right out). It's all washed down with mead – a kind of honey wine. The banquets are popular with groups, so book well ahead; you can often find savings online.

The banquets at Knappogue Castle (p343) and Dunguaire Castle (in Galway) are similar but more sedate.

🛏 Sleeping & Eating

Bunratty has a few hotels and dozens of B&Bs, many on Hill Rd north of the castle; a big map by the park entrance shows locations. All are good choices if you have early flights out of Shannon Airport, only 5km west.

⭐ **Cahergal Farmhouse**   B&B **€€**
(☑ 061-368 358; www.cahergal.com; Newmarket-on-Fergus; s/d from €50/80; 🛜) Wake up to the gentle, distant cluck of a chicken at this luxurious B&B on a working farm midway between Bunratty (6km) and the airport (8km). Rooms are posh, with king-size beds and bucolic views. The food is farm-hearty with famous baked treats.

Briar Lodge   B&B **€€**
(☑ 061-363 388; www.briarlodge.com; Hill Rd; s/d from €40/60; ⊘mid-Mar–mid-Oct; 🛜) On a quiet cul-de-sac 1.6km from the castle, this traditionally styled house makes for a good refuge. All five rooms have little extras such as curling irons (for that grand banquet entrance) and some have commodious king-size beds.

Durty Nelly's   PUB **€€**
(www.durtynellys.ie; Bunratty House Mews; mains €6-25; ⊘kitchen noon-10pm) Thronging with tourists all summer long, Nelly's manages to provide some charm amid the hubbub, right across from the castle. Meals are better than you'd expect, although the pub is more enjoyable than the restaurant upstairs. There are trad music sessions many nights.

🛈 Getting There & Away

Bunratty is on the busy **Bus Éireann** (☑ 061-313 333; www.buseireann.ie) Limerick–Shannon Airport route. Service to both is at least hourly and trips (€7) take less than 30 minutes. There are at least five direct buses daily to Ennis (€8, 30 minutes). Buses stop near the castle.

Killaloe & Ballina
POP 4100

Facing each other across a narrow channel, Killaloe and Ballina are really one destination, even if they have different personalities (and counties). A fine 1770 13-arch one-lane bridge spans the river, linking the pair. You can walk it in five minutes or drive it in about 20 (a Byzantine system of lights controls traffic).

Killaloe (Cill Da Lúa) is picturesque Clare at its finest. It lies on the western banks of lower Loch Deirgeirt, the southern extension of Lough Derg, where the lough narrows at one of the principal crossings of the River Shannon. The village lies snugly against the Slieve Bernagh Hills that rise abruptly to the west. The Arra Mountains create a fine balance to the east and all of Lough Derg is at hand.

Not as quaint as Killaloe, Ballina (Béal an Átha) is in County Tipperary and has some of the better pubs and restaurants. It lies at the end of a scenic drive from Nenagh along Lough Derg on the R494.

◉ Sights & Activities

The tiny, charming centre of Killaloe is focused on its tiny, charming (and walkable) waterfront. In Ballina, Main St is the focus; it's up the hill from the water.

Killaloe Cathedral   CHURCH
(St Flannan's Cathedral; Limerick Rd) The present church dates from the early 13th century and was built by the O'Brien family on top of a 6th-century church. Inside, ornate carvings decorate the Romanesque southern doorway, next to which is the shaft of a stone cross, known as Thorgrim's Stone. It dates from the early Christian period and is unusual in that it bears both the old Scandinavian runic and Irish Ogham scripts.

Brian Ború Heritage Centre   MUSEUM
(www.shannonheritage.com; Lock House, Killaloe; adult/child €3.35/1.75; ⊘10am-5pm May–mid-Sep) Named for the local boy who made good as the king who, according to the political spinmeisters of his time, both unified Ireland and freed it from the Viking scourge. The centre does much to celebrate the legends and has good displays about the nautical heritage of this patchwork of lakes and rivers.

TJ's Angling Centre
FISHING

(🖉 061-376 009; www.tjsangling.com; Main St, Ballina; ⏱8am-10pm) You can rent fishing tackle for €15 per day and catch your limit in free advice. The centre also organises fishing trips, although you can hook trout and pike right here in town.

🧭 Tours

Spirit of Killaloe
BOAT TOUR

(🖉086 814 0559; www.killaloerivercruises.com; Lakeside Dr, Ballina; adult/child €12.50/7.50; ⏱May-Sep) Hour-long cruises of the waters.

🛏 Sleeping

B&Bs abound in the area, especially on the roads along Lough Derg. Book ahead in summer.

⭐ Kincora House
B&B €€

(🖉 061-376 149; www.kincorahouse.com; Church St, Killaloe; s/d from €45/76) Set in a town house that's centuries old, this B&B is right in the heart of Killaloe. Four traditional-style rooms have a simple, older feel and could belong to a favoured aunt.

Lakeside Hotel
HOTEL €€

(🖉061-376 122; www.lakesidehotel.ie; Ballina; s/d from €75/100; @🛜🏊) With sweeping views of the bridge and its 13 arches, this gentrified waterfront hotel has several attractive public areas and good grounds for strolling. The 43 rooms vary greatly, and prices work in direct ratio to view. All, however, let you use the way-fun 40m water slide.

Kingfisher Lodge
B&B €€

(🖉061-376 911; www.kingfisherlodge-ireland.com; Lower Ryninch, Ballina; s/d from €45/70; 🛜) Right on Lough Derg, this exquisite three-room B&B has nearly a hectare of gardens, decks and a dock on the water. Rooms are comfy and without pretension. It's about a 1km walk to Ballina.

Arkansas B&B
B&B €€

(🖉061-376 485; Main St, Ballina; s/d from €45/70; 🛜) There are four ground-floor rooms at this well-run B&B only 300m from the bridge. And the name? The lovely owner says she once saw a fishing trawler named *Arkansas* and liked the sound of it.

🍴 Eating & Drinking

The twin towns hold their excellent **farmers market** (⏱9am-4pm Sun) on the islet off the bridge on the Killaloe side.

⭐ Wooden Spoon
CAFE €

(Bridge St, Killaloe; mains €4-10; ⏱noon-6pm Tue-Thu & Sun, noon-9pm Fri & Sat) In a narrow passage just up from the waterfront, this cafe and bakery offers up Med-flavoured fair so flavourful that on balmy days you might think you're near the Riviera. Local chef-done-good Laura Kilkenny also has trad faves such as fresh soda bread, all made with local ingredients and mostly sourced locally.

Tuscany Bistro
ITALIAN €€

(🖉061-376 805; www.tuscany.ie; Main St, Ballina; mains €8-20; ⏱12.30-9pm Tue-Sun; 🍴) Small, smart and stylish, this Italian bistro has delicious and authentic fare. Amid the hearty soups, salads and pasta mains, you can also get pizzas or ponder a daily special. Good, reasonable wine list.

Goosers
SEAFOOD €€

(www.goosers.ie; Main St, Ballina; mains €10-30; ⏱meals noon-10pm) Only the masses of fun-seekers on busy weekends diminish the Goosers experience. This popular thatched pub (with peat fires) is noted for its big selection of fish. Sailors make mirth and plough into the hefty seafood platter in the restaurant or go for pub fare at tables outside.

Liam O'Riains
PUB

(Main St, Ballina) At this grizzled, stone-faced old veteran, you're greeted by a cow-eyed, 12kg pike mounted on a wall near the entrance – he's an ugly mother. Everything else here, however, is lovely. Candles glow softly and windows overlook the river below.

ℹ Information

The AIB bank at the bottom of Church St in Killaloe has an ATM. There are toilets on the Killaloe side in the car park.

Tourist Office (🖉061-376 866; Bridge St, Brian Ború Heritage Centre, Killaloe; ⏱10am-6pm May-Oct) Shares space with the heritage centre on the tiny island. For local info online, try www.discoverkillaloe.com.

ℹ Getting There & Away

There's parking on both sides of the river and that's just what you'll want to do as soon as you arrive. Pretty as it is, the bridge is really a traffic nightmare, so park and walk.

There are four **Bus Éireann** (🖉061-313 333; www.buseireann.ie) services a day Monday to Saturday from Limerick to Killaloe (€8, 45 minutes). The bus stop is outside the cathedral.

Killaloe to Mountshannon

The journey north to Mountshannon along Lough Derg weaves along placid waters shaped like the long dribble left by an over-filled pint of Guinness carried from bar to table. From Killaloe take the R463 to Tua-mgraney, then turn east on the R352. There are good viewpoints of the water and Holy Island plus picnic spots.

About 2km north of Killaloe, Beal Ború is an earthen mound or fort said to have been Kincora, the fabled palace of the famous Irish king Brian Ború, who, besides lending his name to bad Irish bars the world over, took on the Vikings at the Battle of Clontarf in 1014. Traces of Bronze Age settlement have been found. With its commanding view over Lough Derg, this was obviously a site of strategic importance (and if you see a big splash out in the lough it could be a cousin of the record 32.6kg pike that was caught here).

About 4.5km north of Killaloe is Cragliath Hill, which has another fort, Griananlaghna, named after Brian Ború's great-grandfather, King Lachtna.

Tuamgraney, at the junction of the road to Mountshannon (R352), has an interesting old church, St Cronan's, which has parts dating to the 10th century. Inside, a small museum, the East Clare Heritage Centre (www.eastclareheritage.com; R463; adult/child €3/1.50; ⊙10am-3pm Mon-Fri), has a collection of artefacts old and not so old of life in the region. Check out the record salmon caught in 1914. The surrounding moody parish cemetery also offers a fascinating look into Irish genealogy.

Mountshannon

POP 350

More than just a Tidy Town award-winning village, Mountshannon (Baile Uí Bheoláin) is good for an agreeable pause on the southwestern shores of Lough Derg. It was founded in 1742 by an enlightened landlord to house a largely Protestant community of flax workers.

The harbour is host to a fair number of fishing boats, and visiting yachts and cruis-ers in summer. It is the main centre for trips to Holy Island, one of Clare's finest early Christian settlements.

🏃 Activities

There's some great fishing around Mount-shannon, mainly for brown trout, pike, perch and bream. Ask at your lodging about boat hire and equipment. The return of the white-tailed eagle has drawn spotters from afar.

🛏 Sleeping & Eating

Mountshannon Hotel HOTEL €€
(☎061-927 162; www.mountshannon-hotel.ie; Main St; s/d from €42/74, mains €10-18; ⊙Mar-Oct) A low-key inn in the equally low-key centre of town. The 14 rooms are timeless in a nebu-lous place between 1950 and 1980. The pub is perfect for a relaxed pint and fish stories, with food of the chicken Kiev and lasagne school.

DON'T MISS

HOLY ISLAND

Lying 2km offshore from Mountshannon, Holy Island (Inis Cealtra) is the site of a mon-astic settlement thought to have been founded by St Cáimín in the 7th century. On the island you will see a round tower that is more than 27m tall. Even with the top floor missing, it remains a landmark visible from two counties. You'll also find four old chapels, a hermit's cell and some early Christian gravestones dating from the 7th to 13th centuries. One of the chapels has an elegant Romanesque arch and, inside, an Old Irish inscription that translates as 'Pray for Tornog, who made this cross'.

The Vikings treated this monastery roughly in the 9th century, but under the crowd-pleasing protection of Brian Ború and others, it flourished. During the 17th century as many as 15,000 people would make Easter pilgrimages here.

At Mountshannon Harbour in summer, you may find boats willing to take you over to the island or at least sail around it. Gerard Madden (☎086 874 9710; gerardmmadden@ eircom.net; adult/child €10/5; ⊙Apr-Oct) is a noted local historian who leads two-hour tours of the island.

DENNIS K. JOHNSON / GETTY IMAGES ©

DAVID GEE 4 / ALAMY ©

1. Cliffs of Moher (p358)

One of the most popular places in Ireland and the subject of many a song lyric.

2. O'Brien's Tower (p358)

Take in the views and sights along the clifftop on the Doolin Trail.

3. Penny whistle

Also called the tin whistle, this instrument features in much of the traditional music of Ireland.

4. Traditional music, Doolin (p361)

Playing the violin and accordion at a pub in County Clare.

INGOLF POMPE / GETTY IMAGES ©

Sunrise B&B
B&B €€

(☑061-927 343; www.sunrisebandb.com; s/d from €50/70; ☎) The breakfast room at this rural four-room B&B (just 300m from the village) is worthy of an architecture award. Windows literally wrap around the circular room, and a soaring wood ceiling with skylights brings in cheer even on the dullest of days.

Bourke's the Galley
CAFE €

(Main St; mains €4-9; ☉9am-5pm; ☎) The sign at this sparkling cafe across from the church reads: 'Be warm, be welcome, be at home'. Of course, home never had such cupcakes. Attached to a deli, Bourke's offers rich coffees, alluring baked goods and fresh light meals you can enjoy on a small terrace.

★ An Cupán Caifé
MODERN IRISH €€

(☑087 294 3620; www.ancupan.ie; Main St; mains €13-28; ☉6-9.30pm Wed-Sun, plus 1-5pm Sun, May-Oct; ☎) This cottagelike restaurant has a Continental atmosphere and a daily menu of steaks and fish. Presentation is slightly formal and the specials are a draw. A three-course Sunday lunch is €20. The wine list is the best in the area.

❶ Getting There & Away

Your own car or bike (or swimming) are the best ways to reach Mountshannon.

North to Galway

North of Mountshannon, the R352 follows Lough Derg to Portumna in County Galway. It's just one of several not-quite-two-lane country roads that weave through the fertile landscapes under arching trees. Another is the R461 from Scarriff, which heads right to the heart of the Burren.

SOUTHWESTERN & WESTERN CLARE

One look at the map and you can see that Loop Head on Clare's southwestern tip is giving the finger to the Atlantic. OK, it's a stubby finger, but still it's emblematic of the never-ceasing titanic struggle between land and sea along this stretch of Irish coast.

The soaring cliffs south of the beach resort of Kilkee to Loop Head are striking. Long left in the shadow by the hyped charms of the Cliffs of Moher to the north, the Loop Head area is now justifiably popu-

lar and was named by the *Irish Times* as 'best place to holiday in Ireland' in 2013.

Marching in geologic lockstep, the formations are stunning, although in summer you will now be marching in lockstep with hordes of other visitors. Fortunately you can always find a quiet pocket to savour the views.

South of the cliffs to Kilkee are the low-key beach towns of Lahinch, Miltown Malbay and Doonbeg. No part of this coast is remotely tropical, but there's a stark windblown beauty that stretches to the horizon. Many a hapless survivor of the Spanish Armada washed ashore here 400 years ago. Tales of their progeny still spice local gossip.

Your best days here may be spent on the smallest roads you can find. Make your own discoveries, whether it's a stretch of lonely beach or something more settled, like the charming heritage town of Ennistymon.

❶ Getting There & Around

BOAT

Shannon Ferry Limited (☑065-905 3124; www.shannonferries.com; one way/return bicycle & foot passengers €5/7, cars €18/28; ☉at least hourly 9am-9pm Jun-Aug, 9am-7pm Sep-May) runs a ferry that takes 20 minutes between Tarbert in County Kerry and Killimer in County Clare. It's a real time-saver over detouring through Limerick, and puts you close to the Dingle Peninsula. Discounts are available online.

BUS

You can usually count on a **Bus Éireann** (www.buseireann.ie) service or two linking all the main towns in the region each day. From Limerick routes run along the Shannon to Kilrush and Kilkee, as well as up through Corofin, Ennistymon, Lahinch, Liscannor and on to the Cliffs of Moher and Doolin. Buses from Ennis follow the same pattern. On the coast between Lahinch and Kilkee services average twice daily in summer. A few other nondaily routes are geared to schoolkids.

Kilrush

POP 2600

Kilrush (Cill Rois) is a small, atmospheric town that overlooks the Shannon Estuary and the hills of Kerry to the south. It has the western coast's biggest marina (www.kilrushcreekmarina.ie) at Kilrush Creek, and offers various opportunities to experience the bottlenose dolphins living in the Shannon.

⊙ Sights & Activities

The main street, Frances Street, runs directly to the harbour. It is more than 30m wide, reflecting Kilrush's origins as a port and market town in the 19th century when there was much coming and going between land and sea. Look for the Maid of Eireann monument at the top of Frances St, which still shows damage caused by departing English troops in 1921.

St Senan's Church
CHURCH

(Toler St) St Senan's Catholic church contains eight detailed examples of stained glass by well-known early 20th-century artist Harry Clarke.

Vandeleur Walled Garden
GARDEN

(www.vandeleurwalledgarden.ie; Killimer Rd; ⊙10am-4pm Wed-Sun) **FREE** This remarkable 'lost' garden was the private domain of the wealthy Vandeleur family, of merchants and landowners who engaged in harsh evictions and forced emigration of local people in the 19th century (a current resident said of the Vandeleur: 'That lot fled at liberation'). The gardens lie within a large walled forest just east of the centre and feature colourful tropical and rare plants. Woodland trails wind around the area, and there's a cafe.

Shannon Dolphin & Wildlife Centre
NATURE CENTRE

(www.shannondolphins.ie; Merchants Quay; ⊙10am-4pm May-Sep) **FREE** A research facility monitoring the 100-plus bottlenose dolphins swimming out in the Shannon. Look for the mural of the dolphin on the front of the building, which houses exhibits on the playful cetaceans, which are a species unique to the area.

Kilrush Shannon Dolphin Trail
TOURING ROUTE

This 4km route ends 3km south of Kilrush at Aylevarro Point, where signs have dolphin info and where you can often see Flipper's friends frolicking offshore.

⊙ Tours

Dolphin Discovery
BOAT TOUR

(☑065-905 1327; www.discoverdolphins.ie; Kilrush Creek Marina; adult/child €22/10; ⊙Apr-Oct) Two-hour boat rides on the Shannon offer plenty of dolphin-spotting. Trips depart depending on weather and demand.

🛏 Sleeping & Eating

B&Bs are about as common as dolphins in the Shannon. The local farmers market (⊙9am-2pm Thu) is held on the main square.

Katie O'Connor's Holiday Hostel
HOSTEL €

(☑065-905 1133; www.katieshostel.com; Frances St; dm/d from €20/40; ⊙mid-Mar–mid-Oct; 🛜) This fine old main-street house dates from the 18th century, and was one of the town houses of the Vandeleur family. There are 30 beds in two rooms at this delightfully funky IHH-affiliated hostel.

Crotty's
HOTEL €€

(☑065-905 2470; www.crottyspubkilrush.com; Market Sq; s/d from €45/70; ⊙trad music 7pm Tue-Thu Jun-Aug; 🛜) Brimming with character, Crotty's has an old-fashioned high bar, intricately tiled floors and a series of snugs decked out with traditional furnishings. Pub food includes high-end versions of pub fare.

WORTH A TRIP

SCATTERY ISLAND

This uninhabited, windswept, treeless island, 3km southwest of Kilrush in the estuary, was the site of a Christian settlement founded by St Senan in the 6th century. Its 36m-high round tower is one of the tallest and best preserved in Ireland, and the entrance is at ground level instead of the usual position high above the foundation. The remains of five medieval churches include a 9th-century cathedral. This is a moody and evocative place to wander about.

A free exhibition on the history and wildlife of the Heritage Service–administered island is housed in the Scattery Island Visitor Centre (www.heritageireland.ie; ⊙10am-6pm Jun-Aug).

Scattery Island Ferries (☑065-905 1327; www.discoverdolphins.ie; Kilrush Creek Marina; adult/child €12/7; ⊙Jun-Aug) runs boats from Kilrush to the island. There's no strict timetable as the trips are subject to tidal and weather conditions; visits usually last about one hour. You can buy tickets at the small kiosk at the marina.

Upstairs are five small, traditionally decorated rooms.

★ **Buttermarket Cafe** CAFE **€**
(Burton St; mains $4-12; ⊗ 9.30am-5pm Mon-Sat; 🖘) Just off the main square, this little sprite of a cafe has a courtyard where you can enjoy its excellent coffees. There are gourmet sandwiches and hot specials. Baked goods include a house speciality that invariably causes diners to exclaim: 'Ooh! Banoffee pie!'

❶ Information

Tourist ffice (🖉 065-905 1577; Frances St; ⊗ 10am-4pm Mon-Sat mid-Mar–mid-Oct) At Katie O'Connor's Holiday Hostel.

❶ Getting There & Around

Bus Éireann has three to four buses daily to Limerick (1¾ hours), Ennis (one hour) and Kilkee (15 minutes). Fares average €8.

Gleeson's Cycles (🖉 065-905 1127; Henry St; per day/week from €20/80) Hire bikes here.

Kilkee

POP 1100

Kilkee's wide beach has the kind of white, powdery sand that's made the Caribbean, well, the Caribbean. Granted the waters are chilly and the winds often brisk, but in summer the strand is thronged with daytrippers and holidaymakers. The sweeping semicircular bay has high cliffs on the north end and weathered rocks to the south. The waters are very tidal, with wide-open sandy expanses replaced by pounding waves in just a few hours.

Kilkee (Cill Chaoi) first became popular in Victorian times when rich Limerick families built seaside retreats here. Today, it is well supplied with guesthouses, amusement arcades and takeaways, although good taste – mostly – prevails.

⊙ Sights & Activities

Many visitors come for the fine sheltered **beach** and the **Pollock Holes**, natural swimming pools in the Duggerna Rocks. The area offers myriad excellent walks. **St George's Head**, to the north, has good cliff walks and scenery, while south of the bay the **Duggerna Rocks** form an unusual natural amphitheatre. Further south is a huge **sea cave**. These sights can be reached by driving to Kilkee's West End area and following the coastal path.

Kilkee is a well-known **diving** centre as the dramatic rocks of the shore cliffs continue right below the waves. Experience and local knowledge or guidance are strongly advised. Right at the tip of the Duggerna Rocks is the small inlet of Myles Creek, out from which lies excellent underwater scenery.

A 2km vestige of the historic **West Clare Railway** (🖉 065-905 1284; www.westclarerailway.ie; adult/child €8/4; ⊗ 1-4pm Apr-Sep) line survives near Moyasta on the Kilkee Rd (N67) 6km northwest of Kilrush. Run by volunteers, the beautifully restored steam-powered trains shuttle back and forth over the open land.

🛏 Sleeping

Kilkee has plenty of guesthouses and B&Bs, though during the high season rates can soar and you may have a problem finding a vacancy.

Green Acres Caravan & Camping Park CAMPGROUND **€**
(🖉 065-905 7011; Doonaha, Kilkee; campsites €8-24; ⊗ Apr-Sep) Beside the Shannon, 6km south of Kilkee on the R487, this is a small, open and peaceful park with 40 sites. Weekly trailer rentals start at €250.

Lynch's B&B B&B **€**
(🖉 065-905 6420; www.lynchskilkee.com; O'Connell St; s/d from €35/60; 🖘) Everything is shipshape in this perfectly located B&B in the centre. Guest rooms have hardwood floors and bedspreads with designs that will bring a smile to aunties everywhere. It's as quiet as the surf at low tide and the breakfast is vast.

★ **Strand Guest House** INN **€€**
(🖉 065-905 6177; www.thestrandkilkee.com; the Strand; s/d from €50/80; ⊗ Feb-Nov; 🖘) Right across from the water, this six-room guesthouse has been given a bit of a polish, although everything is still as low-key as the town itself. The rooms are simply decorated. Some have great views, as does the inviting **bistro-bar** (mains €10-25; ⊗ Apr-Oct).

Stella Maris Hotel HOTEL **€€**
(🖉 065-905 6455; www.stellamarishotel.com; O'Connell St; s/d from €70/120; @) There are 20 refurbished rooms in the year-round choice for lodging in Kilkee. Some on the top floor have views of the surf, some have high-speed

internet and some have king-size beds. The hotel is right in the centre.

✕ Eating & Drinking

In summer Kilkee's ranks of eateries swell with several that win plaudits with the genteel summer visitors. The small farmers market (◷10am-2pm Sun) is on the large parking area near the bus stop.

★**Diamond Rocks Cafe**   CAFE €

(www.diamondrockscafe.com; West End; mains €5-12; ◷9am-7pm Jun–mid-Sep) The perfect reason to walk out to the point of the bay: this modern cafe (with a huge terrace) serves food far above the norm for the types of places usually found in such a stunning spot. Fresh salads, chowders, sandwiches, breakfasts and a plethora of daily specials delight.

Pantry   CAFE €

(O'Curry St; mains €4-12; ◷8am-6pm Easter-Sep) This bakery/deli/cafe is filled with surprises and fresh treasures. The scones are plainly the best in Clare and the rest of the freshbaked fare is equally good. You can do takeaway or dine in for breakfast, lunch and tea.

★**Naughton's Bar**   SEAFOOD €€

(☑065-905 6597; www.naughtonsbar.com; 46 O'Curry St; mains €10-25; ◷6-9.30pm) The terrace alone is enough to make Naughton's a mandatory stop, but the food is even better. Fresh local produce and seafood combine for some mighty fine pub meals at this very atmospheric family-run pub which dates to the 1870s. Book.

Strand Bistro & Cafe   BISTRO €€

(☑065-905 6177; The Strand; mains €10-25; ◷noon-9pm May-Sep, shorter hours Apr & Oct) Enjoy tables outside for a little salt spray in your stout at this excellent cafe, bar and bis-

tro. It serves amazing seafood and is worth booking for dinner. Good wine list.

Murphy Blacks   IRISH €€

(☑065-905 6854; www.murphyblacks.com; the Square; mains €16-26; ◷5-9.30pm Wed-Sun Easter-Sep) This deservedly popular dinner spot is booked up solid night after night for its carefully crafted seafood and meat dishes. Tables outside are a summer-night treat. Call to confirm opening hours.

Stella Maris   IRISH €€

(☑065-905 6455; www.stellamarishotel.com; O'Connell St; mains €10-25; ◷noon-9.30pm) This popular hotel has a good menu of local seafood and steaks on offer throughout the day. Enjoy quality ocean salmon or shellfish or one of many specials in the bright and simple dining room or in the usually crowded pub.

ⓘ Information

The websites www.loophead.ie and www.kilkee. ie are good sources of local information.

ⓘ Getting There & Away

Bus Éireann has three to four buses daily to Kilkee from Limerick (€19, two hours) and Ennis (€15, 1¼ hours). Both routes pass through Kilrush.

Kilkee to Loop Head

While others are dodging sweater vendors at the Cliffs of Moher, come here for coastal views that in many ways are more dramatic.

The land from Kilkee south to Loop Head has subtle undulations that suddenly end in dramatic cliffs falling off into the Atlantic. It's a windswept place with timeless striations of old stone walls. You can literally

COUNTY CLARE KILKEE TO LOOP HEAD

DON'T MISS

CLARE'S OTHER CLIFFS

For the jaw-dropping moment of your trip, check out the drama of the soaring cliffs west of Kilkee. On the R487, the Loop Head Rd, look for signs that read 'Scenic Loop' (an understatement). A narrow track curves along the coast for 10km until it reaches the west side of Kilkee. Along the way you will be struck by one stunning vista of soaring coastal cliffs after another. Some have holes blasted through by the surf, others have been separated from land and now stand out in the ocean as lonely sentinels. One utterly isolated basalt tower even has old houses perched on top – how in the world did they get there and who built them? Plan on puttering along, stopping for walks and pausing for passing cows.

see for miles and there is a rewarding sense of escape from the mainstream. It's good cycling country and offers coastal walks – which is just as well as there's no public transport.

Carrigaholt

POP 150

On 15 September 1588, seven tattered ships of the Spanish Armada took shelter off Carrigaholt (Carraig an Chabaltaigh), a tiny village near the mouth of the Shannon Estuary. One, probably the *Anunciada,* was torched and abandoned, sinking somewhere out in the estuary. Today, timeless Carrigaholt has one of the simplest and cutest main streets you'll find. The substantial remains of a 15th-century McMahon castle overlook the water.

🏃 Activities

⭐ **Dolphinwatch**   BOAT TOUR
(☏ 065-905 8156; www.dolphinwatch.ie; adult/child €25/12.50; ☉ Apr-Oct) Dolphinwatch runs two-hour trips in the estuary to see the 100-plus resident bottlenose dolphins. Ask about Loop Head sunset cruises. For more on these relatives of Flipper, see the dolphin sites in and around Kilrush.

🍴 Eating & Drinking

The snoozy main street has a couple of uber-atmospheric old pubs.

⭐ **Long Dock**   SEAFOOD €€
(West St; mains €6-25; ☉ kitchen 11am-9pm, Thu-Sun only Nov-Mar) This instant-Foursquare-worthy pub has an excellent kitchen. Stone walls and floors and a welcoming fire are only the start. Fresh fish is the thing here; you'll see the purveyors out working in the estuary or even drinking at the bar. Nab a table outdoors on a summer night.

Kilbaha

POP 50

The land at this minute waterfront village is as barren as the soul of the 19th-century landlord who burned down the local church so his workers wouldn't waste productive hours praying. Even today the scars are felt. Gazing at the ruins of the landlord's house far up the hillside, a local says: 'Yeah, we got rid of him', as if the events of 150 years ago were yesterday.

You can learn more about this story and other aspects of local life from the compelling modern-day scroll, an open-air sculpture that relates the area's history. The road east towards Doonaha follows ancient lava flows on the shoreline.

The Lighthouse Inn (☏ 065-905 8358; www.thelighthouseinn.ie; s/d from €35/50; 🛜) is a mirthful place right on the water, with 11 basic rooms. The gregarious pub serves sandwiches and the like through the year and more complex seafood dinners (from €14) in summer. Trad music sessions some nights are a bonus.

Loop Head

On a clear day, Loop Head (Ceann Léime), Clare's southernmost point, has magnificent views south to the Dingle Peninsula crowned by Mt Brandon (951m), and north to the Aran Islands and Galway Bay. There are bracing walks in the area and a long hiking trail runs along the cliffs to Kilkee.

The working Loop Head Lighthouse (Kilbaha; admission €5; ☉ 10am-5pm May-Sep), complete with Fresnel lens, is the punctuation on the point. Nearby, look for the long crevice in the coastal cliffs where you'll first hear and then see a teeming bird-breeding area. Guillemots, chough and razorbills are among the squawkers nesting in rocky niches.

The often-deserted wilds of the head are perfect for exploration. Bog Road Bike Tours (☏ 086 278 0161; www.bogroadbiketours.com; tours €20-35) cycles laneways denied to cars around Loop Head; bikes and equipment can be rented for a small extra fee. Long Way Round (☏ 086 409 9624; www.thelongwayround.ie) has historical and nature tours led by noted guide Laura Foley.

Kilkee to Ennistymon

North of Kilkee the land flattens, with vistas that sweep across pastures and dunes. The N67 runs inland for some 32km until it reaches Quilty. Take the occasional lane to the west and search out unfrequented places such as White Strand, north of Doonbeg. Ballard Bay is 8km west of Doonbeg, where an old telegraph tower looks over some fine cliffs. Donegal Point has the remains of a promontory fort. There's good fishing all along the coast, and safe beaches at Seafield, Lough Donnell and Quilty. Off the coast of

Quilty, look for Mutton Island, a barren expanse with an ancient tower.

Doonbeg

POP 300

Doonbeg (An Dún Beag) is a tiny seaside village about halfway between Kilkee and Quilty. Another Spanish Armada ship, the *San Esteban,* was wrecked on 20 September 1588 near the mouth of the River Doonbeg. The survivors were later executed at Spanish Point. Note the surviving wee little 16th-century castle tower next to the graceful seven-arch stone bridge over the river.

White Strand (Trá Ban) is a quiet beach, 2km long and backed by dunes. It's north of town and hard to miss, as it's now been surrounded by the Doonbeg Golf Club. From the public car park, you follow a break in the dunes to a perfect sweep of sand.

Doonbeg also has some decent surfing for those who want to get away from the crowds in Lahinch. For golf, the economic collapse means that the Doonbeg Golf Club (065-905 5600; www.doonbeglodge.com; green fees from €170) has lost a load of its previous snoot. The championship course is laid out amid the bare, rolling dunes; the lodge has luxurious rooms (from €200).

Sleeping & Eating

For campers there are often spots on the side roads around Doonbeg that make a good pitch, with glorious sunsets as a bonus. B&Bs also abound, some overlooking the sand.

★ Morrissey's   INN €€
(065-905 5304; www.morrisseysdoonbeg.com; Main St; s/d from €55/90; Mar-Oct; @) Under its fourth-generation owner, this old pub is a stylish coastal haven. The six rooms feature king-size beds and large soaking tubs. The pub's restaurant (mains €12-25) is re-

nowned for its casual but enticing seafood, from fish and chips to succulent local crab claws. Outside there's a terrace overlooking the river.

Miltown Malbay

POP 800

Like Kilkee, Miltown Malbay was a resort favoured by well-to-do Victorians, though the town isn't actually on the sea: the beach is 2km south at Spanish Point. To the north of the point, there are beautiful walks amid the low cliffs, coves and isolated beaches.

A classically friendly place in the chatty Irish way, Miltown Malbay has a thriving music scene. Every year it hosts the Willie Clancy Summer School, one of Ireland's great traditional music events.

Sleeping & Eating

An Gleann B&B   B&B €€
(065-708 4281; www.angleann.net; Ennis Rd; s/d from €30/60;) Possibly the friendliest welcome in town is at this B&B off the R474 about 1km from the centre. The five rooms are basic and comfy and owners Mary and Harry Hughes are a delight. Cyclists are catered for.

Old Bake House   IRISH €
(Main St; mains €5-15; noon-9pm) In a region of great seafood chowder, some of the best is at the Old Bake House, which serves Irish classics in humble surrounds.

Drinking & Nightlife

O'Friel's Bar (Lynch's; The Square) is one of a couple of genuine old-style places with occasional trad music sessions. The other is the dapper Hillery's (Main St).

Information

For local information, drop by the cheery An Ghiolla Finn Gift Shop (Main St; 10.30am-6pm Mon-Sat). The website www.visitmiltown malbay.ie is useful.

CLARE'S BEST MUSIC FESTIVAL

Half the population of Miltown Malbay seems to be part of the annual Willie Clancy Summer School (065-708 4148; www.scoilsamhraidhwillieclancy.com; Jul), a tribute to a native son and one of Ireland's greatest pipers. The nine-day festival usually begins in the first or second week in July, when impromptu sessions occur day and night, the pubs are packed and Guinness is consumed by the barrel.

Workshops and classes underpin the event; don't be surprised to attend a recital with 40 noted fiddlers. Asked how such a huge affair has happened for almost four decades, a local who teaches fiddle said: 'No one knows, it just does.'

ⓘ Getting There & Away

Bus Éireann service is paltry. Expect one or two buses Monday to Saturday north and south along the coast and inland to Ennis.

Lahinch

POP 650

Surf's up, dude! This old holiday town is one of the centres of Ireland's hot surfing scene. Schools and stores dedicated to riding the waves cluster here, like surfers waiting for the perfect set.

For a more methodical water experience, **Clare Kayak Hire** (☑085 148 5856; www.clarekayakhire.com; rental per hr from €15, tours from €35; ⊘rentals Jul & Aug) offers tours on the rivers and lakes in the region and rentals at White Strand Beach near Spanish Point.

Lahinch (Leacht Uí Chonchubhair) has always owed its living to beach-seeking tourists. The town sits on protected Liscannor Bay and has a fine beach. Free-spending mobs descend in summer, many wielding golf clubs for play at the famous traditional-style **Lahinch Golf Club** (☑065-708 1003; www.lahinchgolf.com; green fees from €120). It dates from 1892 when it was laid out amid the dunes by Scottish soldiers.

🛏 Sleeping & Eating

The tourist office has good links to local B&Bs. Waterfront cafes and pubs let you enjoy the action on the waves.

★ **West Coast Lodge** INN €
(☑065-708 2000; www.lahinchaccommodation.com; Station Rd; dm/r from €20/50; @⊛) Flashpackers will cheer this stylish and downright plush hostel and inn in the heart of Lahinch. Power showers, fine cotton sheets and down duvets are just some of the touches found throughout the seven- to 12-bed dorms and private rooms. Check out the surf from the roof deck and rent a bike to go exploring.

Atlantic Hotel HOTEL €€
(☑065-708 1049; www.atlantichotel.ie; Main St; s/d from €50/90; @) There's still a pleasant air of bygone times in the reception rooms and bars at this town-centre classic with 14 well-appointed rooms. The pub is the perfect spot for nursing a pint.

O'Looneys IRISH €
(www.olooneys.ie; the Promenade; mains from €8; ⊘daily Apr-Oct, Sat & Sun Nov-Mar) The best views of the Lahinch surf scene and pounding breaks are from the terrace at this dual-level bar, cafe and club. Pub standards are a cut above average here and weekend parties go late in summer.

Barrtra Seafood Restaurant SEAFOOD €€
(☑065-708 1280; www.barrtra.com; Miltown Malbay Rd; mains €15-28; ⊘1-10pm daily Jul & Aug, fewer days rest of year) The 'Seafood Symphony' menu item says it all at this rural repose 3.5km south of Lahinch. Enjoy views over pastures to the sea from this lovely country

---

SURF'S UP!

Like swells after a storm, Clare's surfing scene keeps getting bigger. On weekends in Lahinch the breaks fill with hundreds of surfers. Thick wetsuits dry on railings and scores of people watch the action from the town's beach and pubs.

Conditions are excellent for much of the year, with the bay's cliffs funnelling regular and reliable sets. And as the waters fill in Lahinch, the action is moving to other spots along the coast, such as Doonbeg and Fanore.

Surf shops are proliferating. You can rent gear and get lessons from about €40 per two-hour session; board and wetsuit rentals are about €15 per day. Local schools set up shop along Lahinch's beach promenade.

Ben's Surf Clinic (☑086 844 8622; www.benssurfclinic.com; Waterfront, Lahinch) Offers lessons plus rents out boards and wetsuits (essential!).

Clare Surf Safari (☑087 634 5469; www.claresurfsafari.com) Lessons are held on various Clare beaches with transport included in the price.

Lahinch Surf School (☑087 960 9667; www.lahinchsurfschool.com; Waterfront, Lahinch) Champion surfer John McCarthy offers lessons and various multiday packages.

Lahinch Surf Shop (☑065-708 1108; www.lahinchsurfshop.com; Old Promenade, Lahinch; ⊘10am-6pm Mon-Sat) Sells gear from a dramatic surfside location.

cottage, surrounded by pretty kitchen gardens. The lavish €35 set meal is great value.

Shopping

Lahinch Bookshop BOOKS
(Main St; ⊙10am-6pm Mon-Sat) The best source for hiking maps outside Ennis.

❶ Information

The *only* reliable ATM in the region is in the town centre on Main St.

❶ Getting There & Away

Bus Éireann runs two to four buses daily through Lahinch on the Doolin–Ennis/Limerick routes and one or two Monday to Saturday south along the coast to Doonbeg in summer.

Ennistymon

POP 1000

Ennistymon (Inis Díomáin) is a timeless country village located just 4km inland from Lahinch, but worlds away in terms of atmosphere. People go about their business (which involves a lot of cheerful chatting) barely noticing the characterful buildings lining Main St. And behind this facade there's a surprise: the roaring Cascades, the stepped falls of the River Inagh. After heavy rain they surge, beer-brown and foaming, and you risk getting drenched on windy days in the flying drizzle. You'll find them through an arch by Byrne's hotel.

◉ Sights

Courthouse Studios & Gallery ARTS CENTRE
(Parliament St; ⊙noon-4pm Tue-Sat) Ennistymon has a healthy arts scene. These studios are in a renovated 1800 building with ever-changing exhibitions by local and international artists.

Ennistymon Horse Market MARKET
Enjoy one of Clare's great spectacles as the horse market takes over the town's streets on the first Monday of each month. People buy and sell donkeys, mares, thoroughbreds and even a few plain old nags.

🛏 Sleeping & Eating

The local farmers market (⊙10am-2pm Sat) spreads its fertile wealth on Market Sq.

Byrne's INN €€
(☑065-707 1080; www.byrnes-ennistymon.ie; Main St; r from €50/70) The Cascades are just out the

❶ **THE ATM HUNT**

It's easy to get caught out cashless in western Clare. Many of the small towns such as Liscannor, Doolin, Lisdoonvarna and Kilfenora have no ATMs. There's an ATM at the Supervalu (Church St) and another at the Bank of Ireland (Parliament St) in Ennistymon, and one in Lahinch. The ATM at the Cliffs of Moher visitor centre is a hassle to reach and may be out of cash.

back of this historic guesthouse and restaurant (mains €15-25; ⊙noon-9pm Jun-Aug, shorter hours other times) and you can enjoy them from the terrace. The short menu features seafood specials. Six large and comfortable rooms await up the creaky heritage stairs.

Falls Hotel HOTEL €€
(☑065-707 1004; www.fallshotel.ie; off N67; s/d from €75/120; @🕸) This handsome and sprawling Georgian house, built on the ruins of an O'Brien castle, has 140 modern rooms and a large, enclosed pool. The view of the Cascades from the entrance steps is breathtaking, and there are walks around the 20 hectares of wooded gardens.

Ungert's Bakery BAKERY €
(Main St; snacks from €2; ⊙8am-5pm Mon-Sat; ✎) Follow your nose right into this tiny but exquisite bakery. Buy a Danish and get a veggie treat for later.

🍷 Drinking & Nightlife

★**Eugene's** PUB
(Main St) Not to be missed, Eugene's is a classic pub that defines craic. It's intimate and cosy and has a trademark collection of visiting cards covering its walls, along with a great whiskey collection.

Cooley's House PUB
(☑065-707 1712; Main St) Another great old pub, but with music most nights in summer and on Wednesday (trad night) in winter.

Nagle's PUB
(Church St) A trad pub and an undertakers in one. Just the spot for wakes or your last earthly pint.

❶ Getting There & Away

Bus Éireann runs two to four buses daily through Ennistymon on the Doolin–Ennis/Limerick routes and one or two Monday to Saturday south along the coast via Lahinch to Doonbeg in summer. Buses stop in front of Aherne's on Church St.

Liscannor & Around

POP 250

This small seaside village overlooks Liscannor Bay, where the road (R478) heads north to the Cliffs of Moher and Doolin. Liscannor (Lios Ceannúir) has given its name to a type of local stone – slatelike and with a rippled surface – that is used for floors, walls and even roofs.

⊨ Sleeping & Eating

Moher Lodge Farmhouse   B&B €€
(☑ 065-708 1269; www.cliffsofmoher-ireland.com; off R478; s/d €50/80; ☺ Apr-Oct; ☎) This big bungalow is in a great position overlooking the owner's open farmlands and the sea. The four rooms are welcoming after a day rambling (there's much to ramble to). It's 3km northwest of Liscannor, 1.6km from the Cliffs of Moher.

★ Vaughan's Anchor Inn   SEAFOOD €€
(☑ 065-708 1548; www.vaughans.ie; Main St; mains €12-25; ☺ kitchen noon-9.30pm) Noted for its excellent seafood (yes to the scallops and halibut), Vaughan's packs 'em in – and out. When it rains, you can settle in the nautical-themed pub by a peat fire, when it shines (sometimes 15 minutes later) you can take in the air at a picnic table. Compact but comfy rooms (s/d from €50/80) offer sleepy refuge.

▼ Drinking & Nightlife

Joseph McHugh's Bar   PUB
(Main St) Lots of courtyard tables and regular trad sessions make this old pub next to Vaughan's a winner.

Hag's Head

Forming the southern end of the Cliffs of Moher, Hag's Head is a dramatic place from which to view the cliffs.

There's a huge sea arch at the tip of Hag's Head and another arch visible to the north. The old signal tower on the head was erected in case Napoleon tried to attack on the western coast of Ireland. A spectacular walking trail links the head with the cliffs and Liscannor.

Cliffs of Moher

Star of a million tourist brochures, the Cliffs of Moher (Aille an Mothair, or Ailltreacha Mothair) are one of the most popular sights in Ireland. But as with many an ageing star, you have to look beyond the famous facade to appreciate its inherent attributes.

The entirely vertical cliffs rise to a height of 203m, their edge falling away abruptly into the constantly churning sea. A series of heads, the dark limestone seems to march in a rigid formation that amazes, no matter how many times you look. On a clear day you'll channel Barbra Streisand as you can see forever; the Aran Islands stand etched on the waters of Galway Bay, and beyond lie the hills of Connemara in western Galway.

Such appeal comes at a price: mobs. This is check-off tourism big time and busloads come and go constantly in summer. A vast visitor centre is set back into the side of a hill; it's impressively unimpressive – it blends right in. As part of the development, however, the main walkways and viewing areas along the cliffs have been surrounded by a 1.5m-high wall that's too high and set too far back from the edge.

But there are good rewards if you're willing to walk for 10 minutes, as you quickly escape the crowds. Past the end of the 'Moher Wall' south, a trail runs along the cliffs to Hag's Head (about 5.5km) – few venture this far, yet the views are uninhibited. From here you can continue on to Liscannor for a total walk of 12km (about 3½ hours). To the north, you can follow the Doolin Trail via O'Brien's Tower right to the village of Doolin (about 7km and 2½ hours). The entire Liscannor-to-Doolin walking path via the cliffs is now signposted, note that there are a lot of ups and downs and narrow, cliff-edge stretches.

With binoculars you can spot some of the more than 30 species of birds – including darling little puffins – that make their homes among the fissure-filled cliff faces.

The roads leading to the cliffs pass through refreshingly undeveloped lands, the rolling hills giving no hint of the dramatic vistas just over the edge.

For awe-inspiring views of the cliffs and wildlife you might consider a cruise. The boat operators in Doolin offer popular tours of the cliffs.

ℹ Information

Visitor centre (www.cliffsofmoher.ie; admission to site adult/child €6/free; ⊙9am-9.30pm Jul & Aug, 9am-7pm May, Jun & Sep, 9am-6pm Mar, Apr & Oct, 9.15am-5pm Nov-Feb) Actually, revealingly, it's called the 'Cliffs of Moher Visitor Experience', and has glitzy exhibitions about the cliffs and the environment called the *Atlantic Edge*.

Vendors of sweaters and other tat have stalls near the large free parking area. The basement cafe seems designed to urge you up to the views at the pricier restaurant.

ℹ Getting There & Away

Bus Éireann runs two to four buses daily past the cliffs on the Doolin–Ennis/Limerick routes. Waits between buses may exceed your ability to enjoy the spectacle, so you might combine a bus with a walk. Numerous private tour operators run tours to the cliffs from Galway and the region.

THE BURREN

The Burren region is rocky and windswept, an apt metaphor for the hardscrabble lives of those who've eked out an existence here. Stretching across northern Clare, from the Atlantic coast to Kinvara in County Galway, it's a unique striated limestone landscape that was shaped beneath ancient seas, then forced high and dry by a great geological cataclysm.

This is not the green Ireland of postcards. But there are wildflowers in spring, giving the 560-sq-km Burren brilliant, if ephemeral, colour amid the arid beauty. There are also intriguing villages to enjoy. These include the music hub of Doolin on the west coast, Kilfenora inland and Ballyvaughan in the north, on the shores of Galway Bay.

History

Despite its apparent harshness, the Burren supported quite large numbers of people in ancient times, and has more than 2500 historic sites. Chief among them is the 5000-year-old Poulnabrone Dolmen, part of a Neolithic/Bronze Age tomb, and one of Ireland's iconic ancient monuments.

Around 70 such tombs are in evidence today. Many are wedge-shaped graves, stone boxes tapering both in height and width, and about the size of a large double bed. The dead were placed inside, and the whole structure covered in earth and stones. Gleninsheen, south of Aillwee Caves, is a good example.

Ring forts dot the Burren in prodigious numbers. There are almost 500, including Iron Age stone forts such as Cahercommaun near Carron.

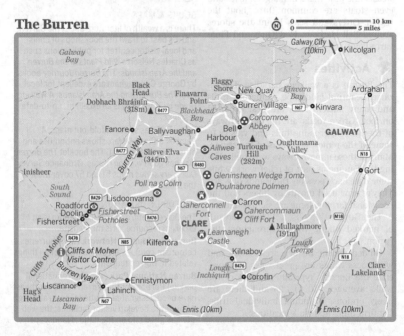

The Burren

ROCK LEGENDS

The geology of the Burren (Boireann is the Irish term for 'rocky country') is the result of immense drama and excitement in ancient times that produced the moonlike landscape we see today. Follow the deep rivulets in the stone and you'll see that the barren Aran Islands just offshore are all part of the same formations.

Massive shifts in the earth's crust some 270 million years ago buckled the edges of Europe and forced the former seabed here above sea level. At the same time the stone sheets were bent and fractured to form the long, deep cracks so characteristic of the Burren today.

During numerous ice ages, glaciers scoured the hills, rounding the edges and sometimes polishing the rock to a shiny finish, and dumping a thin layer of rock and soil in the cracks. Huge boulders were carried by the ice, incongruous aliens on a sea of flat rock.

Flora & Fauna

Soil may be scarce on the Burren, but the small amount that gathers in the cracks is well drained and rich in nutrients. This, together with the mild Atlantic climate, supports an extraordinary mix of Mediterranean, Arctic and alpine plants. Of Ireland's native wildflowers, 75% are found here, including 24 species of beautiful orchids, the creamy-white burnet rose, the little starry flowers of mossy saxifrage and the magenta-coloured bloody cranesbill.

The Burren is a stronghold of Ireland's most elusive mammal, the rather shy and weasel-like pine marten. Badgers, foxes and even stoats are common throughout the region. Otters and seals haunt the shores around Bell Harbour, New Quay and Finavarra Point.

🏃 Activities

The Burren is a walker's paradise. The bizarre, beautiful landscape, numerous trails and many ancient sites are best explored on foot. 'Green roads' are the old highways of the Burren, crossing hills and valleys to some of the remotest corners of the region. Many of these unpaved ways were built during the Famine as part of relief work, while some date back possibly thousands of years. They're now used mostly by hikers and the occasional farmer. Some are signposted.

The **Burren Way** is a 123km network of marked hiking routes throughout the region.

Guided nature, history, archaeology and wilderness **walks** are great ways to appreciate the Burren. Typically the cost of the walks averages €10 to €25 and there are many options, including individual trips. Confirm times and walk locations.

Burren Guided Walks & Hikes WALKING TOUR
(☑ 087 244 6807, 065-707 6100; www.burrenguid edwalks.com) Long-time guide Mary Howard leads groups on a variety of itineraries.

Burren Wild Tours WALKING TOUR
(☑ 087 877 9565; www.burrenwalks.com) John Connolly offers a broad range of walks, from gentle to more strenuous.

Heart of Burren Walks WALKING TOUR
(☑ 065-682 7707; www.heartofburrenwalks.com) Local Burren author Tony Kirby leads walks and archaeology hikes.

ℹ️ Information

BOOKS & MAPS

There is a wealth of literature about the Burren, and it's best to trawl the bookshops of Ennis and local visitor centres for publications such as Charles Nelson's *Wild Plants of the Burren and the Aran Islands*. The *Burren Journey* books by George Cunningham are excellent for local lore. *The Burren and the Aran Islands: A Walking Guide* by Tony Kirby is an excellent, up-to-date resource.

The Tír Eolas series of fold-out maps, *A Rambler's Guide & Map*, shows antiquities and other points of interest. The booklet *The Burren Way* has good walking routes. Ordnance Survey *Discovery series* maps 51 and 57 cover most of the area.

VISITOR INFORMATION

The Burren Centre (p364) in Kilfenora is an excellent resource, as is the website.

Burren Ecotourism Network (www.burrene cotourism.com) A vast compilation of all things related to Burren tourism.

Burren National Park (www.burrennational park.ie) Portions of the Burren in the southeast have been designated a national park, although it has yet to develop visitor facilities; the website has good info on the natural landscape.

Burrenbeo Trust (www.burrenbeo.com) A nonprofit organisation dedicated to promoting the natural beauty of the Burren and increasing awareness. The website is a good source of info.

ⓘ Getting There & Away

A few **Bus Éireann** (www.buseireann.ie) services pass through the Burren. The main routes include one from Limerick and Ennis to Corofin, Ennistymon, Lahinch, Liscannor, the Cliffs of Moher, Doolin and Lisdoonvarna; another connects Galway with Ballyvaughan, Lisdoonvarna and Doolin. Usually there are one to four buses daily, with the most in summer.

ⓘ Getting Around

By car you can cover a fair amount of the Burren in a day and have a chance to explore some of the many unnamed back roads. Bikes are an excellent means of getting off the main roads; ask about rentals at your accommodation. Walking is a superb way to appreciate the area's subtle beauty and dramatic landscapes.

Doolin

POP 250

Doolin gets plenty of press and chatter as a centre of Irish traditional music, owing to a trio of pubs that have sessions throughout the year. It's also known for its setting – 6km north of the Cliffs of Moher and down near the ever-unsettled sea, the land is windblown, with huge rocks exposed by the long-vanished top soil.

Given all its attributes, you might be surprised when you realise that Doolin as it's known barely exists. Rather, you might be forgiven for exclaiming, 'There's no there here!' For Doolin is really three infinitesimally small neighbouring villages. Fisherstreet is right on the water, Doolin itself is about 1km east on the little River Aille, and Roadford is another 1km east. None has more than a handful of buildings, which results in a scattered appearance, without a centre.

Still, the area is hugely popular with music-seeking tourists. There are scores of good-value hostels and B&Bs spread about the rough landscape. It's also a place to get boats to the offshore Aran Islands.

◉ Sights & Activities

Tiny Fisherstreet is a charmer; you can enjoy dramatic surf vistas at the harbour, some 1.5km further along the coast.

Coming from the Cliffs of Moher, take a small, sinuous road off the R478 and follow

it down to Fisherstreet past the stark ruins of a castle. Look for signs banning buses and pointing to the Sea View House B&B at the turn from the R478. Boat tours of the Cliffs of Moher are popular.

One of the most enjoyable ways to pass your time in Doolin is by walking the windswept country. Tracks and paths radiate in all directions; the Cliffs of Moher (p358) are 6km southwest. Doolin Cliff Walk (☏065-707 4170; www.doolincliffwalk.com; adult/child €5/3) offers an entertaining guided walk along this route.

The Doolin area is popular with cavers. The Fisherstreet Potholes are central, and Poll na gColm, 5km northeast of Lisdoonvarna, is Ireland's longest cave, with more than 12km of mapped passageways.

A little over 1km north of Roadford you'll find Doolin Cave (www.doolincave.ie; adult/child €15/8; ⊙10am-5pm Mar-Nov), which boasts an enormous stalactite that looks like a giant squid. The main entrance is at the Fisherstreet Potholes; tour times vary by season.

🎉 Festivals & Events

Micho Russell Festival MUSIC
(www.doolin-tourism.com; ⊙Feb) Held on the last weekend in February, this festival celebrates the work of a legendary Doolin musician and attracts top trad talent.

🛏 Sleeping

During the time of Irish over-optimism, there was a building boom of tourist accommodation in the Doolin area. Many newish B&Bs and inns are inconveniently far from the music pubs. All the places listed here are reasonably central.

Rainbow Hostel HOSTEL €
(☏065-707 4415; www.rainbowhostel.net; Roadford; dm €15-19, d €40-50; 🕱) Many a friendship has started in the cosy lounge here. IHH-affiliated, this hostel has 24 beds and is in an old farmhouse by the road. It rents bikes (€9 per day).

★ **Doolin Hostel** HOSTEL €
(☏087-282 0587; www.doolinhostel.ie; Fisherstreet; dm from €16-20, d €50-55; @🕱♿) Close to the bus stop, this excellent facility has a range of beds in four- and eight-bed rooms plus private rooms (with bathrooms) that range from simple to rather posh. It has a good cafe and nice gardens. The charms of Fisherstreet are steps away.

Aille River Hostel
HOSTEL €

(065-707 4260; www.ailleriverhosteldoolin.ie; Roadford; dm €18-25, d from €55; Mar-Dec; @) In a picturesque spot by the river in the upper village, this converted 17th-century farmhouse is a great choice. There are peat fires and a free laundry. This award-winning hostel has 30 beds, camp-sites from €16 and bike rentals.

Nagles Camping & Caravan Park
CAMPGROUND €

(065-707 4458; www.doolincamping.com; Doolin; campsites €10-19; Apr-Sep;) Let the nearby pounding surf lull you to sleep at this grassy expanse near the harbour. The 60 sites are open to the elements, so pin those pegs down.

★O'Connors Guesthouse
INN €€

(065-707 4498; www.oconnorsdoolin.com; Doolin; s/d from €45/70; Feb-Oct;) On a bend in the Aille, this working farm has 10 largish rooms in a rather plush farmhouse-style inn. It's near the main crossroads and is utterly spotless.

Dounroman House
B&B €€

(065-707 4774; www.doolinbedandbreakfast.com; Doolin; s/d from €45/70;) Near the main Doolin crossroads, this two-storey B&B has views over the rough, grassy countryside. The rooms are large; some are good for families. Breakfast options include locally smoked salmon and potato waffles.

Toomullin House
INN €€

(065-707 4723; www.toomullindoolin.com; Doolin; s/d from €55/70;) This whitewashed old stone cottage has jaunty blue trim and is lo-cated a short walk from the pubs. The four rooms sleep up to three and are furnished with the locally ubiquitous simple pine fur-niture. Good breakfast options.

Daly's House
B&B €€

(065-707 4242; www.dalys-doolin.com; Fisher-street; s/d from €50/80;) Just one field be-hind O'Connor's Pub, this excellent B&B has glimpses of the Cliffs of Moher from its break-fast room. The six rooms are large and comfy, and the hosts are especially welcoming.

Cullinan's Guesthouse
INN €€

(065-707 4183; www.cullinansdoolin.com; Doolin; s/d from €50/80;) The eight rooms here are all of a high standard, with power showers and comfortable fittings. Right on the River Aille (two rooms have balconies), it has a lovely back terrace for enjoying the views.

The owner is well-known local musician James Cullinan.

Sea View House
INN €€

(065-707 4826; www.seaview-doolin.ie; Fisher-street; s/d from €60/90;) On high ground right above Fisherstreet village, this popu-lar large inn and its terrace have sweeping ocean views. The common lounge has a tele-scope for enjoying the vantage point.

Eating

All three of the trad music pubs serve Irish classics such as bacon and cabbage and seafood chowder throughout the day until about 9pm.

★Fabiolas Patisserie
BAKERY €

(Ballyvoe; snacks from €3; 10am-5pm Thu-Mon) A great little pastry shop just up the hill from the Doolin crossroads. The French owner makes the desserts for all the best lo-cal restaurants and when you sample her tarts, you'll see why.

Doolin Cafe
CAFE €€

(www.thedoolincafe.com; Roadford; mains €5-25; 8am-10pm Apr-Oct) The cottage is small, but the flavours are big at this much-loved bistro. Breakfast is the best locally, while salads, soups and sandwiches are the deal at lunch. Dinner features a changing, ambi-tious menu.

Cullinan's
MODERN IRISH €€€

(065-707 4183; www.cullinansdoolin.com; Doolin; mains €20-30; 6-9pm Thu-Sat Apr-Oct, Mon & Tue May-Sep) Attached to the guesthouse of the same name, this excellent and rather posh restaurant offers delicious seafood as well as meat and poultry dishes. The short menu changes depending on what's fresh. There's a long wine list.

Drinking & Nightlife

Doolin's reputation is largely based on mu-sic. A lot of musicians live in the area, and they have a symbiotic relationship with the tourists: each desires the other and each year things grow a little larger. But given the heavy concentration of visitors it's inevita-ble that standards don't always hold up to those in some of the less-trampled villages in Clare. In summer the antics of the tourists (joining in with musicians uninvited, trying to sing, ceaselessly demanding 'When Irish Eyes are Smiling' and 'Danny Boy', sending blurry mobile-phone snaps worldwide etc) can be entertaining or aggravating depending on your mood.

Doolin's three main music pubs (others are recent interlopers) are listed here in order of their importance to the music scene.

⭐ **McGann's**   PUB
(www.mcgannspubdoolin.com; Roadford) McGann's has all the classic touches of a full-on Irish music pub and the action often spills out onto the street. The food here is the best of Doolin's three famous pubs (get the crab claws!). Inside you'll find locals playing darts in its warren of small rooms, some with peat fires. There's a small outside covered area.

O'Connor's   PUB
(www.gusoconnorsdoolin.com; Fisherstreet) Right on the water, this sprawling favourite packs them in and has a rollicking atmosphere when the music is in full swing. It gets the most crowded and has the highest tourist quotient; on some summer nights you won't squeeze inside and trying to eat is like playing the fiddle for the first time.

MacDiarmada's   PUB
(www.mcdermottspubdoolin.com; Roadford) Also known as McDermott's, this simple red-and-white old pub is the rowdy favourite of locals. The inside is pretty basic, as is the menu of sandwiches and roasts. There's an outside area.

ℹ️ Information

There are few services. The closest useful ATMs are 13km away in Ennistymon. The website www.doolin-tourism.com is useful.

Doolin Internet Cafe (Fisherstreet; per 30min €3; ⊗8am-7pm; 🛜) In the Doolin Activity Lodge; also does laundry.

ℹ️ Getting There & Away

BOAT

Doolin is one of two ferry departure points to the Aran Islands from mid-March to October. Two ferry companies offer numerous departures in season. It takes about 45 minutes to cover the 8km to Inisheer, the closest of the three islands and the best choice for a day trip from Doolin. A boat to Inishmór takes at least 1½ hours with an Inisheer stop. Ferries to Inishmaan are infrequent.

Sailings are often cancelled due to high seas or tides which make the small dock inaccessible. Rates vary as prices are very competitive; Inisheer should cost about €15 to €25 return. The companies have offices at the harbour but booking in advance online can net discounts. Confirm times.

The boats also offer Cliffs of Moher tours (about €15 for one hour) which are best done late in the afternoon when the light is from the west.

Doolin 2 Aran Ferries (📞087 245 3239, 065-707 5949; www.doolin2aranferries.com; Doolin Pier; ⊗mid-Mar–Oct) Has a full schedule to the Aran islands plus Cliffs of Moher cruises.

O'Brien Line (📞065-707 5555; www.obrienline.com) Usually has the most sailings to the Arans; also offers cliff cruises and combo tickets.

BUS

Bus Éireann runs one to four buses daily to Doolin from Ennis (€12, 1½ hours) and Limerick (€18, 2½ hours) via Corofin, Lahinch and the Cliffs of Moher. Buses also go to Galway (€16, 1½ hours, one or two daily) via Ballyvaughan.

In summer, various backpacker shuttles often serve Doolin from Galway and other points in Clare. These are amply marketed in hostels.

Lisdoonvarna

POP 750

Lisdoonvarna (Lios Dún Bhearna), often just called 'Lisdoon', is well known for its mineral springs. For centuries people have been visiting the local spa to swallow its waters. Posh in the Victorian era, the town is now a much more plebeian and friendly place. Away from the coast, it's not overrun like Doolin and is a good base for exploring the Burren.

🎯 Sights & Activities

⭐ **Burren Smokehouse**   SMOKE HOUSE
(📞065-707 4432; www.burrensmokehouse.ie; Kincora Rd; ⊗10am-5pm Apr-May, 9am-6pm Jun-Oct, shorter hours in winter) Learn about the ancient Irish art of oak-smoking salmon from a video (available in six languages) at the Burren Smokehouse. Tasty smoked salmon and other fishies in myriad forms are offered for free tasting – perhaps you'll even buy some? Good coffee and tea are sold along with other deli-type foods suitable for picnics. Tourist information is also available. The smoke house is at the edge of Lisdoonvarna on the Kincora road (N67).

Spa Well   LANDMARK
At the southern end of town is a spa well, with a sulphur spring, a Victorian pumphouse and a fine woodland setting. The iron, sulphur, magnesium and iodine in the water are supposed to be good for rheumatic and glandular complaints. Closer to the centre, you can drink the water, even if it's not exactly a vintage wine-tasting

COUNTY CLARE KILFENORA

LISDOONVARNA MATCHMAKING FESTIVAL

Lisdoonvarna was once a centre for *basadóiri* (matchmakers) who, for a fee, would fix up a person with a spouse. Most of the (mainly male) hopefuls would hit town in September, feet shuffling, cap in hand, after the hay was in. Today the tradition continues at the much-hyped and ever-expanding Lisdoonvarna Matchmaking Festival (www.matchmakerireland.com; ☺ Sat & Sun Sep), held in the early fall. Irish and even foreign singles plus those who just enjoy a jolly good time revel in daftness, drinking, merrymaking, music and much, much dancing. Older, more sedate courtships are recalled by the statue on the pub-surrounded Main Sq.

experience. Look for a trail beside the Roadside Tavern that runs 400m down to two wells by the river. One is high in sulphur, the other iron. Mix and match for a cocktail of minerals.

🛏 Sleeping & Eating

Book ahead during September's Matchmaking Festival. Local sleeping, eating and drinking choices are excellent.

Sleepzone HOSTEL €
(☑ 065-707 7168; www.sleepzone.ie; Doolin Rd; dm €16-25, s/d €50/70; @☏) Housed in a formerly posh hotel, this 124-bed hostel has an unusual grace. The grounds reflect its past and there are all the usual facilities.

⭐**Sheedy's Country House Hotel & Restaurant** INN €€
(☑ 065-707 4026; www.sheedys.com; Sulphur Hill; r €80-220; ☺ Apr-Sep; ☏) Take a leek from the kitchen garden – that's just one of the playful bits of fun you can have at this posh yet relaxed 11-room guesthouse just outside of town. A long porch has comfy chairs for pondering the many gardens or just taking a snooze. Food (dinner only) is excellent. The bar has a huge range of whiskey.

Wild Honey Inn INN €€
(☑ 065-707 4300; www.wildhoneyinn.com; Kincora Rd; s/d from €50/80; ☏) In a beautiful old roadside mansion on the edge of town, Wild Honey has 14 stylish rooms which are the perfect weekend getaway (or hideout for that impromptu honeymoon during matchmaking season). The pub (☺1-3.30pm Thu-Sat, 5-9pm Wed-Mon mid-Feb–Dec) has a delectable menu of Irish classics made with local seafood, meats and produce. In summer there's a lovely garden with tables.

⭐**Roadside Tavern** PUB €
(www.roadsidetavern.ie; Kincora Rd; meals €6-12) Down by the river, this pub is pure craic:

third-generation owner Peter Curtin knows every story worth telling. There are trad sessions daily in summer and during the weekends in winter. The trad fun extends to the kitchen, which turns out creamy seafood chowders etc. Anything with smoked fish is good as the same people also run the nearby Burren Smokehouse. The in-house brewery makes beers far above the norm.

ℹ Information

The closest reliable ATM is in Lahinch; worth remembering if you're planning some pricey wooing.

ℹ Getting There & Around

Bus Éireann runs one to four buses daily to Doolin via Lisdoonvarna from Ennis, and to Limerick via Corofin, Lahinch and the Cliffs of Moher. Buses also go to Galway via Ballyvaughan and Black Head.

Kilfenora

POP 250

Kilfenora (Cill Fhionnúrach) lies on the southern fringe of the Burren, 8km (a five-minute drive) southeast of Lisdoonvarna. It's a small place, with low polychromatic buildings surrounding the compact centre.

The town has a strong music tradition that rivals that of Doolin, but without the crowds. The Kilfenora Céili Band (www.kilfenoraceiliband.com) is a celebrated group that's been playing for 100 years. Its traditional music features fiddles, banjos, squeezeboxes and more.

About 6km east of town on the road to Corofin, look for the towering remains of Leamanegh Castle, an old stone manor house.

◉ Sights

Burren Centre MUSEUM
(☑ 065-708 8030; www.theburrencentre.ie; Main St; adult/child €6/4; ☺9am-5pm Mar-Oct) The

centre has a series of entertaining and informative displays on many aspects of the Burren (a video features cute hares). Stone-age mannequins look on the verge of frost-bite. There's a cafe and a very large shop that sells local products.

Cathedral CHURCH
The 11th-century cathedral at Kilfenora was once an important place of pilgrimage. St Fachan (or Fachtna) founded the monastery here in the 6th century, and it later became the seat of Kilfenora diocese, the smallest in the country.

Loop around the more recent protestant church and you can enter the oldest part of the ruins, which have been spiffed up with a glass roof and useful explanatory signs about the carvings. The chancel has two primitive carved figures on top of two tombs and there are three high crosses.

Doorty Cross MONUMENT
About 100m to the west of the cathedral is the 800-year-old Doorty Cross. It lay broken in two until the 1950s, when it was re-erected.

🛌 Sleeping & Eating

Kilfenora has two top-notch pubs.

Kilfenora Hostel HOSTEL €
(☑ 065-708 8908; www.kilfenorahostel.com; Main St; dm €20-24, d €52-60; @ 🛜) 🧺 Affiliated with Vaughan's Pub next door, this guesthouse has 46 beds in nine rooms. There's a laundry and a big kitchen. Weary travellers in the lounge may feel they've fallen into the hand of God.

Ait Aoibhinn B&B B&B €€
(☑ 065-708 8040; aitaoibheann@live.ie; Main St; s/d from €40/60; ⊙ mid-Feb–Nov; 🛜) Right on the main street, Mrs Mary Murphy runs a fine little B&B (the name means Restful Place)

with the kind of simple rooms you could call your own. She has two more houses nearby.

Linnane's PUB €
(☑ 065-708 8157; Main St; mains €5-12; ⊙ kitchen noon-8pm) Irish standards, including smoked salmon and more, are fully honoured here. Peat fires warm the almost bare interior; nary a frill in sight. There's trad music some nights in summer.

★ Vaughan's Pub PUB €€
(www.vaughanspub.ie; Main St; mains €8-15; ⊙ kitchen 10am-8pm) Seafood, traditional foods and local produce feature on the Vaughan's appealing menu. The pub has a big reputation in Irish music circles. Have a pint under the big tree out the front.

There's music in the bar every night during the summer and on many nights the rest of the year. The adjacent barn is the scene of terrific set-dancing sessions on Thursday (10pm) and Sunday (9pm). Don't miss these cultural events that draw talented dancers from across Clare.

❶ Getting There & Away

Kilfenora has a non-daily bus service.

Corofin & Around

POP 700
Corofin (Cora Finne), also spelt Corrofin, is a traditional village on the southern fringes of the Burren. It's low-key and a classic place to sample the rhythms of Clare life. The surrounding area features a number of turloughs (small lakes) and several O'Brien castles, including two on the shores of nearby Lough Inchiquin.

About 4km northwest of Corofin, on the road to Leamanegh Castle and Kilfenora (R476), look for the small town of Kilnaboy. The ruined church here is well worth seeking

---

THE IMMORTAL FATHER TED
······································

Father Ted, the enduring British TV comedy, is set around the high jinks of three Irish priests living on the fictional Craggy Island. Most of the locations used in the show are around Kilfenora and Ennistymon (Eugene's pub was used as a location and the cast drank here). The lonely *Father Ted* house is in Kilnaboy.

Inspired by the great success of Inismór's Tedfest (p386), the good people of Kilfenora and Ennistymon have organised their own Father Ted Festival (www.kilfenora-clare.com; ⊙ May) with costume parties, contests, tours and more. Much is centred on Vaughan's Pub, itself a star of some episodes. Ted Tours (www.tedtours.com; adult/child €25/20) visits the local filming locations.

out for the sheila-na-gig (carved female figure with exaggerated genitalia) over the doorway.

⊙ Sights

Clare Heritage Centre MUSEUM
(www.clareroots.com; Church St; adult/child €4/2; ⊙9.30am-5.30pm Easter-Oct) Housed in an old church, many displays here cover the horrors of the Great Famine. More than 250,000 people lived in Clare before the Famine; today the county's population is almost 60% less. The Clare Genealogical Centre (☑065-683 7955; ⊙9am-5.30pm Mon-Fri), in a separate building nearby, has facilities for people researching their Clare ancestry.

🛏 Sleeping & Eating

Corofin Hostel &
Camping Park HOSTEL, CAMPGROUND €
(☑065-683 7683; www.corofincamping.com; Main St; campsites €20-25, dm/s/d €16/25/40; ⊙Apr-Sep) Campsites out the back have nice open spaces, and inside there are 30 beds. The large common room at this hostel right in town has a pool table.

Lakefield Lodge B&B €€
(☑065-683 7675; www.lakefieldlodgebandb.com; Ennis Rd; s/d from €45/70; ⊙Apr-Oct; 🐕) A well-run place near the southern edge of the village, with four comfy rooms in a pleasant bungalow surrounded by gardens. Conveniently situated for Burren hikes.

Fergus View B&B €€
(☑065-683 7606; www.fergusview.com; R476; s/d from €50/80; ⊙Apr-Oct; @🐕) The name exactly describes the scene: the River Fergus flows right past. A lovely home with six rooms and breakfasts that are famed for being fresh – often organic – and creative. It's 3km north of Corofin.

Inchiquin Inn IRISH €
(☑065-683 7713; Main St; mains €6-12; ⊙kitchen 9am-5pm Mon-Fri; 🐕) Townsfolk follow the horses at this oh-so-local pub with a great kitchen. The seafood chowder and bacon and cabbage are some of the best you'll find. The former is thick, tangy and redolent with smoked fish. An annual stone-throwing championship out the back in June is a huge local party.

ℹ Getting There & Away

Bus Éireann has an infrequent service some weekdays between Corofin and Ennis.

Central Burren

Several roads dotted with sights cross the heart of the Burren. The scenery along the R480 as it passes through the region is harsh but inspiring, highlighting the barren Burren at its best. Remarkable prehistoric stone structures can be found throughout this area.

South from Ballyvaughan the R480 branches off the N67 at the sign for Aillwee Caves, passing Gleninsheen Wedge Tomb and the iconic Poulnabrone Dolmen before reaching the Leamanegh Castle ruins, where it joins the R476, which runs southeast to Corofin. At any point along here, try a small road – especially those to the east – for an escape into otherworldly solitude.

The N67 to Lisdoonvarna is marked by sweeping views of the stark Burren landscape. It was originally a famine relief road built in the 1800s.

Gleninsheen Wedge Tomb

One of Ireland's most famous prehistoric grave sites, Gleninsheen lies beside the R480 just south of Aillwee Caves near Ballyvaughan. It's thought to date from 4000 to 5000 years ago. A magnificent gold torc (a crescent of beaten gold that hung round the neck) found here and dating from around 700 BC is now on display at the National Museum in Dublin. Note: the access gate to the tomb is sometimes locked, and signage is poor.

Caherconnell Fort

For a look at a well-preserved *caher* (walled fort) of the late Iron Age–Early Christian period, stop at Caherconnell Fort (www.burrenforts.ie; R480; adult/child €7/6; ⊙10am-6pm Jul & Aug, 10am-5pm Mar-Jun & Sep-Oct), a privately run heritage attraction that's more serious than sideshow. Exhibits detail how the evolution of these defensive settlements may have reflected territorialism and competition for land among a growing, settling population. The dry stone walling of the fort is in excellent condition. The visitor centre has information on many other monuments in the area. And lest some visitors be bored, there is a fun sheepdog demonstration at various times.

It's about 1km south of Poulnabrone Dolmen.

DON'T MISS

POULNABRONE DOLMEN

What would a Burren brochure designer do without it? Also known as the PortalTomb, Poulnabrone Dolmen is one of Ireland's most photographed ancient monuments. The dolmen (a large slab perched on stone uprights) stands amid a swath of rocky pavements, surprising even the most jaded traveller with its otherworldly appearance; the capstone weighs 5 tonnes. The site is about 8km south of Aillwee and visible from the R480. A large free parking area and excellent displays make it visitor friendly.

Poulnabrone was built more than 5000 years ago. It was excavated in 1986, and the remains of 16 people were found, as well as pieces of pottery and jewellery. Radiocarbon dating suggests that they were buried between 3800 and 3200 BC. When the dead were originally entombed here, the whole structure was partially covered in a mound of earth, which has since worn away. It's your guess as to how they built it.

Carron & Around

The tiny village of Carron (Carran on some maps; An Carn in Gaelic), about 10km east of the R480, is a wonderfully remote spot. Vistas of the rocky Burren stretch in all directions from Carron's elevated position.

Sights

Below Carron lies **Carron Polje**, one of the finest turloughs in Ireland. Polje is a Serbo-Croatian term used universally for these shallow depressions that flood in winter and dry out in summer, when the lush grass that flourishes on the surface is used for grazing. Stretching south from Carron almost to Kilnaboy are some of the Burren's bleakest stretches. Non-native boulders deposited during ice ages litter the stark landscape. Take any narrow track you find, and every so often you'll see an ancient **dolmen**.

★Burren Perfumery & Floral Centre PERFUMERY
(www.burrenperfumery.com; Carron; ⏲9am-7pm Jul-Aug, 10am-5pm Sep-Jun) This sweet-smelling stop is a creative treasure. It uses wildflowers of the Burren to produce subtle and non-cloying scents. There's an audiovisual presentation on the flora of the Burren, which has a surprising diversity. One example: the many fragrant orchids that grow among the rocks. Many items for sale are packaged in handmade paper.

The centre has an organic cafe, and native and herb gardens. Look for perfumery signs at the T-junction near Carron church.

Cahercommaun HISTORIC SITE
About 3km south of Carron and perched on the edge of an inland cliff is the great stone fort of Cahercommaun. It was inhabited in the 8th and 9th centuries AD by people who hunted deer and grew a small amount of grain. The remains of a souterrain (underground passage) lead from the fort to the outer cliff face. To get there, go south from Carron and take a left turn for Kilnaboy. After 1.5km a path on the left leads up to the fort. Look for a good info board at the start of the path.

Sleeping & Eating

★Clare's Rock Hostel HOSTEL €
(☎065-708 9129; www.claresrock.com; Carron; dm/s/d €20/34/48; ⏲May-Sep; @ 📶 👪) This imposing building of grey exposed stone has 30 beds, big spacious rooms and excellent facilities. Guests can hire bikes or cavort with the trolls on the outdoor garden-gnome chessboard.

Cassidy's PUB €€
(www.cassidyspub.com; mains €8-19; ⏲11am-9pm daily May-Sep, Sat & Sun Oct-Apr; 📶) Cassidy's serves up a good range of pub dishes, including famous goat burgers made with locally raised organic meat. The building was once a British Royal Irish Constabulary (RIC) station and then a *garda* (police) barracks. Enjoy trad music and dancing some weekends. The views from the terrace are as intoxicating as the drink.

Fanore

POP 150

The scenic R477 hugs the barren coast of Clare as it curves past the Arran Islands into Galway Bay. Fanore (Fan Óir), 5km south of Black Head, is less a village and more a stretch of coast with a shop, a pub and a few houses scattered along the main road.

◉ Sights & Activities

Surfers flock here throughout the year.

Fanore Beach BEACH
This fine sandy beach off the R477 has an extensive backdrop of dunes. Signs show hiking trails along the water and up in the dramatic hills and Black Head. You'll find good parking and there are showers and toilets open in summer.

Aloha Surf School SURFING
(☑ 087 213 3996; www.surfschool.tv; Fanore Beach; lessons from €35) Offers classes for all ages and abilities. You can rent surfboards, wetsuits and gear, stand-up paddle boards and kayaks (€45 per half-day).

Siopa Fan Óir FISHING
(R477; ☺ 9am-9pm summer, to 7pm winter) There's a well-stocked shop across from O'Donohue's pub where you can buy fishing tackle, walking maps, boogie boards and cheap sand buckets.

⌂ Sleeping & Eating

★**Rocky View Farmhouse** INN €€
(☑ 065-707 6103; www.rockyviewfarmhouse.com; off R477; s/d €40/68; ☎) ✿ One of the Fanore area's few accommodation options, Rocky View Farmhouse is a charming place at the heart of the coastal Burren. Its five open and airy rooms are suited to this especially barren end of the region. Organic food is grown and used in the breakfasts, which are served in a sunny conservatory.

Vasco MEDITERRANEAN €
(www.vasco.ie; mains €8-16; ☺ 9am-9pm daily Jul-Aug, till 8pm May-Jun & Sep, Sat & Sun only Oct-Apr) This stylish outpost is near the beach in Fanore. You can watch the water from the glassed-in terrace or enjoy lounging inside. The food is Med-accented and you can get picnic victuals for the beach.

O'Donohue's PUB €€
(www.odonohuespub.com; R477; meals €8-25; ☺ Apr-Oct) The community centre, 4km south of the beach, offers local seafood, chowders and sandwiches along with its genuine local character. Done up in bright blue, it looks out over the grey sea.

❶ Getting There & Away

Bus Éireann runs one to three buses daily from Galway via Black Head and through Fanore to Lisdoonvarna.

Black Head

Atlantic storms have stripped the land around the unfortunately named Black Head down to bare rock. Grass and the occasional shrub cling to crevices. Standing like sentinels, boulders and the odd cow dot the landscape here, Clare's northwesternmost point. It's a popular spot for hiking.

The main road (R477) curves around the sheer rocks of the head just above the sea.

Ballyvaughan & Around

POP 260
Something of a hub for the otherwise dispersed charms of the Burren, Ballyvaughan (Baile Uí Bheacháin) sits between the hard land of the hills and a quiet leafy corner of Galway Bay. It makes an excellent base for visiting the northern reaches of the Burren.

◉ Sights & Activities

Just west of the junction is the quay, built in 1829 at a time when boats traded with the Aran Islands and Galway, exporting grain and bacon and bringing in peat – a scarce commodity in the windswept rocks of Burren.

A few metres past the harbour, a signposted track leads to a seashore bird shelter offering good views of the tidal shallows.

About 6km south of Ballyvaughan on the Lisdoonvarna road (N67) is a series of severe bends climbing up Corkscrew Hill (180m). The road was built as part of a Great Famine relief scheme in the 1840s. From the top there are spectacular views of the northern Burren and Galway Bay, with Aillwee Mountain and the caves on the right, Cappanawalla Hill on the left, and the partially restored 16th-century Newtown Castle, erstwhile residence of the O'Lochlains, directly below.

Aillwee Caves CAVES
(www.aillweecave.ie; off R480; combined ticket adult/child €17/10; ☺ 10am-5.30pm, to 6.30pm Jul & Aug) Send the kids underground. The main cave here penetrates 600m into the mountain, widening into larger caverns, one with its own waterfall. The caves were carved out by water some two million years ago. Near the entrance are the remains of a brown

bear, a species extinct in Ireland for more than 10,000 years.

Often crowded in summer, the site has a cafe, and a large raptor exhibit has captive hawks, owls and more. A shop sells the excellent locally produced Burren Gold cheese.

Burren By Bike　　　　BICYCLE RENTAL
(info@burrenwine.ie; the Laundrette, off N67; rental per day/week €15/80, tours from €25; ☉9am-5pm Mon-Sat May-Sep) Bikes are a good way to explore the Burren, especially the seashore. These morning tours hit the still-quiet roads followed by a gourmet breakfast.

🛏 Sleeping & Eating

There are several simple B&Bs close to the centre. Ballyvaughan's farmers market (St John's Hall; ☉10am-2pm Sat May-Oct) celebrates the huge range of high-quality local produce.

Oceanville House B&B　　　　B&B €€
(☏065-707 7051; www.clareireland.net/ocean ville; Coast Rd/R477; s/d from €45/68; ☏) Near Monk's and the dock, this oceanfront B&B has views across the bay from the dormer windows in its compact upstairs rooms. It's a good spot for walking the village and sampling its pleasures.

Hyland's Burren Hotel　　　　HOTEL €€
(☏065-707 7037; www.hylandsburren.com; Main St; s/d from €60/90; ☉Apr-Oct; ☏) An appealing place, this central hotel has 30 large rooms (a mix of traditional and more-spacious modern rooms) and manages to retain a local feel alongside modern hotel shtick. There's a bar and a restaurant. Ask for the hotel's *Walks* leaflet.

★ Gregan's Castle Hotel　　　　HOTEL €€€
(☏065-707 7005; www.gregans.ie; N67; r from €200; ☏) This hidden Clare gem is housed in a grand estate dating to the 19th century. The 20 rooms and suites have a plush, stylish feel with just enough modern touches to keep you from feeling you've bedded down in a waxworks. The restaurant specialises in inventive fresh fare sourced locally while the bar is the kind of place to sip something brown and let hours roll away in genteel comfort. The grounds are a fantasy of gardens and, when you're not walking in the Burren, there's croquet. The estate is some 6km south of Ballyvaughan at Corkscrew Hill.

An Fulacht Fia　　　　IRISH €€
(☏065-707 7300; www.anfulachtfia.ie; Coast Rd/ R477; mains €18-24; ☉5.30-9pm daily, from 1pm Sun Jun-Aug, shorter hours other times) A stark, vividly coloured interior stands in contrast to the grey expanse of the sea outside at this excellent restaurant just west of the town centre. The seasonal menu is organic and locally sourced and features a lot of seafood.

🍷 Drinking & Nightlife

★Ólólainn　　　　PUB
(Coast Rd) A tiny family-run place on the left as you head out to the pier, Ólólainn (o-*loch*-lain) is the place for a timeless moment or two in old-fashioned snugs. Look for the old whiskey bottles in the window but save all your energy for the amazing selection of rare whiskeys within.

ℹ Information

Visitor centre (www.ballyvaughantourism.com; ☉9am-5pm daily Mar-Oct, Sat & Sun only Nov-Feb) In a vast gift shop behind a grocery store; has a good section of local guides and maps.

ℹ Getting There & Away

Bus Éireann runs one to three buses daily from Galway through Ballyvaughan and around Black Head to Lisdoonvarna and Doolin.

Northern Burren

Low farmland stretches south from County Galway to the bluff limestone hills of the Burren, which begin west of Kinvara and Doorus in County Galway.

From Oranmore in County Galway to Ballyvaughan, the coastline wriggles along small inlets and peninsulas; some, such as New Quay, are worth a detour. Here, narrow roads traverse low rocky windswept hills dotted with old stone ruins that have yielded to nature.

Inland near Bell Harbour is the largely intact Corcomroe Abbey, while the three ancient churches of Oughtmama lie up a quiet side valley. Galway Bay forms the backdrop to some outstanding scenery: bare stone hills shining in the sun, with small hamlets and rich patches of green wherever there's soil.

Buses to and from Galway pass through the area on the N67. Just over the border in Galway, Kinvara makes a good base for this region.

CORCOMROE ABBEY

Moody and evocative, lonely Corcomroe, a former Cistercian abbey 1.5km inland from Bell Harbour, lies in a quiet green hollow, surrounded by the stark grey Burren hillsides. It is a marvellous building, one of the finest of its kind. The abbey was founded in 1194 by Donal Mór O'Brien. His grandson, Conor na Siudaine O'Brien (died 1267), king of Thomond, is said to occupy the tomb in the northern wall, and there's a crude carving of him below the effigy of a bishop holding a crosier, the pastoral staff that was carried by a bishop or abbot. The surviving vaulting in the presbytery and transepts is very fine and there are some striking Romanesque carvings scattered throughout the abbey, which began a long decline in the 15th century. Often-touching modern graves crowd the ruins.

New Quay & the Flaggy Shore

New Quay (Ceibh Nua), on the Finavarra Peninsula, is a quiet and rather bucolic break from the rocky rigours of the Burren. It's about 1km off the Kinvara–Ballyvaughan road (N67) and is reached by turning off at Ballyvelaghan Lough 3km north of Bell Harbour.

The Flaggy Shore, west of New Quay, is a particularly fine stretch of coastline where limestone terraces step down to the sea. The road hugs the shoreline then curves south past Lough Muirí, where you're likely to see a number of wading birds, as well as swans. There are said to be otters in the area. At a T-junction just past the lough, a right turn leads to a rather dingy-looking Martello tower on Finavarra Point, a relic of the paranoia over the Napoleonic threat.

Walks in this area are excellent and you can ponder the dramatic changes in the ever-tidal inlets.

Sleeping & Eating

Mount Vernon BOUTIQUE HOTEL €€€
(065-707 8126; www.mountvernon.ie; Flaggy Shore; s/d from €125/190; Apr-Oct;) Famed Irish Impressionist Hugh Lane once called Mount Vernon home until he was lost with the *Lusitania*. Today the rural Georgian lodge is a secluded seaside retreat with five luxurious rooms with period furnishings. Expect to spend your days walking the sinuous shore and staring at the grey-clad Burren.

Cafe Linnalla ICE CREAM €
(www.linnallaicecream.ie; New Quay; ice cream from €3; 11am-7pm daily May-Sep, noon-5pm Sat & Sun Oct-Apr) Wander past the curving seaweed-covered shoreline to this isolated cafe for some of the best ice cream you'll have. It's a sweet trip!

★ **Linnane's Lobster Bar** SEAFOOD €€
(New Quay; meals €9-25; 12.30-8pm daily May-Sep, Fri-Sun Oct-Apr) Fresh seafood sourced from the trap-covered docks behind the restaurant are the hallmark of this casual restaurant. It's also famous for oysters and platters of house-smoked fish. The decor is as simple as the plates of goodness.

Shopping

Russell Gallery GALLERY
(065-707 8185; www.russellgallery.net; New Quay; 10am-6pm Mon-Sat, from noon Sun) Specialises in *raku* (Japanese lead-glazed earthenware) work. The airy gallery has a range of other works by Irish artists for sale along with books on the region. You can also find work by local knitting legend Antoinette Hensey. It's about 500m west of Linnane's Lobster Bar, at a crossroads.

Bell Harbour

No more than a crossroads with a growing crop of holiday cottages and a pub, Bell Harbour (Beulaclugga) is about 8km east of Ballyvaughan. There's a pleasant walk along an old green road that begins behind the modern Church of St Patrick, 1km north up the hill from the Y-junction at Bell Harbour, and threads north along Abbey Hill.

Inland from here are the ruins of Corcomroe Abbey, the valley and churches of Oughtmama, and the interior road that takes you through Carron and the the heart of the Burren.

County Galway

POP 251,000 / AREA 3760 SQ KM

Best Places to Eat

➡ Aniar (p383)

➡ Oscar's (p382)

➡ Mitchell's (p404)

➡ Moran's Oyster Cottage (p408)

Best Places to Stay

➡ House Hotel (p381)

➡ Kilmurvey House (p390)

➡ Delphi Lodge (p407)

➡ Quay House (p403)

Why Go?

County Galway is a problem: its namesake city is such a charmer that you might not manage to tear yourself away to the countryside. Conversely, the wild and beautiful Aran Islands and Connemara Peninsula might keep you captive such that you'll never have time for the city. What to do? Both, of course!

Galway city is a swirl of enticing old pubs that hum with trad music sessions throughout the year. More importantly, it has an overlaying vibe of fun and frolic that's addictive.

Offshore, the eroded, sheer swaths of land known as the Aran Islands have a desolate, windswept aura that entrances. Tiny villages cling to the rocks while soft-hearted locals welcome their modern lifeblood: visitors.

In the west, the Connemara Peninsula matches the beauty of other Atlantic outcrops such as Dingle. Tiny roads wander along a coastline studded with islands, surprisingly white beaches and intriguing old villages.

When to Go

➡ Galway City with its excellent restaurants, roaring pubs and student culture is a year-round destination.

➡ Elsewhere in more rural parts of the county, you'll be rewarded for visits during the more moderate months.

➡ Moody in the depths of winter, the Aran Islands may be unreachable during storms.

➡ In scenic Connemara country, many country inns close during December and January and even February.

➡ June is a great month across the county as all the seasonal attractions are open, but crowds are still low.

County Galway Highlights

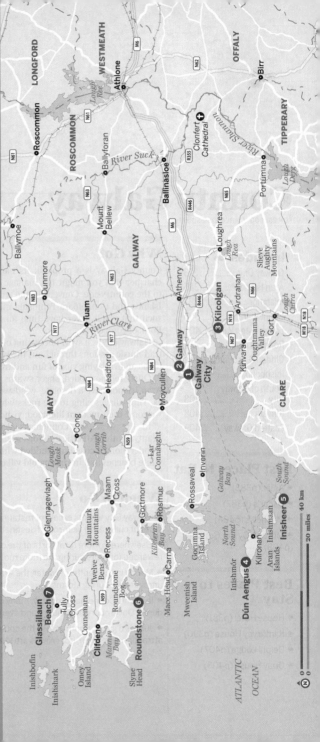

❶ Sample **Galway** city's array of atmospheric pubs and their high-energy trad sessions each week (p383)

❷ Walk the Prom in **Galway**, absorbing the moods of the bay and gazing out at County Clare and the Aran Islands (p377)

❸ Enjoy oysters direct from the bay at an iconic oyster restaurant in **Kilcolgan** (p408)

❹ Ponder the people who built the enigmatic fort **Dún Aengus** (p388) on Inishmór

❺ Visit ancient holy sites and springs, crawl over a famous shipwreck and commune with the rocks on **Inisheer** (p392)

❻ Enjoy the classic bayside village of **Roundstone** (p401)

❼ Frolic on postcard-perfect **Glassillaun Beach** on Connemara's north coast, and consider plunging into the inky depths on a scuba adventure (p406)

GALWAY CITY

POP 75,600

Arty, bohemian Galway (Gaillimh) is renowned for its pleasures. Brightly painted pubs heave with live music, while cafes offer front-row seats for observing street performers, weekend parties run amuck, lovers entwined and more.

Steeped in history, the city nonetheless has a contemporary vibe. Students make up a quarter of its population, and remnants of the medieval town walls lie between shops selling Aran sweaters, handcrafted Claddagh rings and stacks of second-hand and new books. Bridges arch over the salmon-filled River Corrib, and a long promenade leads to the seaside suburb of Salthill, on Galway Bay, the source of the area's famous oysters.

Galway is often referred to as the 'most Irish' of Ireland's cities: it's the only one where you're likely to hear Irish spoken in the streets, shops and pubs. Even as it careens into the modern age, it still respects the fabric of its past.

History

Galway's Irish name, Gaillimh, originates from the Irish word *gaill*, meaning 'outsiders' or 'foreigners', and the term resonates throughout the city's history.

From humble beginnings as the tiny fishing village Claddagh at the mouth of the River Corrib, it grew into an important town when the Anglo-Normans, under Richard de Burgo (also spelled de Burgh or Burke), captured territory from the local O'Flahertys in 1232. Its fortified walls were built from around 1270.

In 1396 Richard II granted a charter transferring power from the de Burgos to 14 merchant families or 'tribes' – hence Galway's enduring nickname: City of the Tribes. (Each of the city's roundabouts is named for one of the tribes.)

Galway maintained its independent status under the ruling merchant families, who were mostly loyal to the English Crown. Its coastal location encouraged a huge trade in wine, spices, fish and salt with Portugal and Spain. Its support of the Crown, however, led to its downfall; the city was besieged by Cromwell in 1651 and fell the following year. Trade with Spain declined and Galway stagnated for centuries.

The early 1900s saw Galway's revival as tourists returned to the city and student numbers grew. In 1934 the cobbled streets and thatched cabins of Claddagh were tarred and flattened to make way for modern, hygienic buildings, and construction has boomed since.

Sights & Activities

★ Spanish Arch   HISTORIC SITE

Framing the river east of Wolfe Tone Bridge, the Spanish Arch is thought to be an extension of Galway's medieval walls. The arch appears to have been designed as a passageway through which ships entered the city to unload goods, such as wine and brandy from Spain.

Today it reverberates to the beat of bongo drums, and the lawns and riverside form a gathering place for locals and visitors on any sunny day. Many watch kayakers manoeuvre over the minor rapids of the River Corrib.

Although a 1651 drawing of Galway clearly shows its extensive fortifications, depredation by Cromwell and William of Orange and subsequent centuries of neglect saw the walls almost completely disappear. Another surviving portion has been cleverly incorporated into the modern shopping mall, Eyre Square Centre (Merchants Rd & Eyre Sq).

Galway City Museum   MUSEUM

(www.galwaycitymuseum.ie; Spanish Pde; ⊙10am-5pm Tue-Sat) FREE Adjacent to the Spanish Arch, the Galway City Museum is in a glossy, glassy building that reflects the old walls. Exhibits trace aspects of daily life through Galway's history; especially good are the areas dealing with life – smelly and otherwise – during medieval times.

Look for the photos of President John F Kennedy's 1963 visit to Galway, including one with dewy-eyed nuns looking on adoringly. Also check out rotating displays of works by local artists. When the roof deck

GALWAY HOOKERS

Obvious jokes aside, Galway hookers are the iconic small sailing boats that were the basis of local seafaring during the 19th century and into the 20th century. Small, tough and highly manoeuvrable, these wooden boats are popular with weekend sailors and hobbyists. The hulls are jet black, due to the pitch used for waterproofing, while the sails flying from the single mast are a distinctive rust colour.

Galway City

Corrib Princess
(120m)

Sports
Ground

Eglinton Canal

Earl's
Island

Corrib
Park

10

46

19

Wood Quay

St Francis St

Corrib River

Salmon Weir
Bridge

Smith St

Eyre St

15

Sports
Ground

5

Gaol Rd

2

Nun's
Island

Bowling Green

Mary St

Market St

39

New Rd

Nun's Island Rd

William
O'Brien
Bridge

22

Mill St

Bridge St

Lombard St

Church Ln

Shop St

8

33

9

3

28

44

36

High St

32

49

27

Middle St

Buttermilk
Ln

St Augustine St

Abbeygate St

Lower

50

29

30

48

Merchant's Rd

Dock Rd

Henry St

Canal
Locks

11

Sea Rd

24

Lower Dominick St

Kirwan's
Ln

13

43

14

31

21

35

7

41

51

47

45

West William
St

38

37

42

WEST
SIDE

34

40

Wolfe Tone
Bridge

Quay St

17

26

Commercial
Dock

Spanish
Arch

1

6

25

Canal
Basin

16

Friar Burke
Park

Father Griffin Rd

Claddagh Quay

Grattan Rd

Salthill (2km)

South Park Prom (180m)

is open, there are bay panoramas. The cafe with its Spanish Arch views is a perfect rest stop.

Hall of the Red Earl ARCHAEOLOGICAL SITE

(www.galwaycivictrust.ie; Druid Lane; ⊗9.30am-4.45pm Mon-Fri, 10am-1pm Sat) **FREE** Back in the 13th century when the de Burgo family ran the show in Galway, Richard – the Red Earl – had a large hall built as a seat of power. Here locals would come looking for favours or to do a little grovelling as a sign of future fealty. After the 14 tribes took over, the hall fell into ruin and was lost. Lost, that is, until 1997 when expansion of the city's Custom House uncovered its foundations. The Custom House was built on stilts overhead, leaving the old foundations open. Artefacts and a plethora of fascinating displays give a sense of Galway life some 900 years ago.

Collegiate Church of
St Nicholas of Myra CHURCH

(Market St; admission by donation; ⊗9am-5.45pm Mon-Sat, 1-5pm Sun Apr-Sep, 10am-4pm Mon-Sat, 1-5pm Sun Oct-Mar) Crowned by a pyramidal spire, the Collegiate Church of St Nicholas of Myra is Ireland's largest medieval parish church still in use. Dating from 1320, it has been rebuilt and enlarged over the centuries, though much of the original form has been retained.

Christopher Columbus reputedly worshipped here in 1477. One theory suggests that the story of Columbus' visit to Galway arose from tales of St Brendan's 6th-century voyage to America. Seafaring has long been associated with the church – St Nicholas, for whom it's named, is the patron saint of sailors.

During the day the church is usually all but empty and makes for a welcome escape from Galway's hubbub.

Eyre Square PARK

Galway's central public square is busy in all but the harshest weather. It's a welcome open green space with sculptures and pathways. Its lawns are formally named Kennedy Park in commemoration of JFK's visit to Galway, though you'll never hear locals refer to it as anything but Eyre Sq.

The street running along the southwestern side of the square is pedestrianised and lined with seating, while the eastern side is taken up almost entirely by the Hotel Meyrick, an elegant grey limestone pile restored to its Victorian glory. Guarding the upper side of the square, **Browne's Doorway**

Galway City

(1627), a classy, if forlorn, fragment from the home of one of the city's merchant rulers, looks like the remains from a carpet-bombing raid (at least the English can't be blamed for this...).

Lynch's Castle HISTORIC BUILDING
(cnr Shop & Upper Abbeygate Sts) Considered the finest town castle in Ireland, the old stone town-house, Lynch's Castle was built in the 14th century, though much of what you see today dates from around 1600. The Lynch family was the most powerful of the 14 ruling Galway 'tribes'.

Stonework on the castle's facade (the real attraction here) includes ghoulish gargoyles and the coats of arms of Henry VII, the Lynches and the Fitzgeralds of Kildare. The castle is now part of AIB Bank and modern-day bankers may wish to shelter behind the thick walls from populist rage.

Salmon Weir LANDMARK
Upstream from Salmon Weir Bridge, which crosses the River Corrib just east of Galway Cathedral, the river cascades down the great weir, one of its final descents before reaching Galway Bay. The weir controls the water levels above it, and when the salmon are running you can often see shoals of them waiting in the clear waters before rushing upriver to spawn.

The salmon and sea-trout seasons usually span February to September, but most fish pass through the weir during May and June.

Galway Cathedral CHURCH
(www.galwaycathedral.org; Gaol Rd; admission by donation; ◎8am-6pm) Lording over the River Corrib, imposing Galway Cathedral was dedicated by the late Cardinal Richard Cushing of Boston in 1965. The cathedral's unwieldy full name is the Catholic Cathedral of Our Lady Assumed into Heaven and St Nicholas.

Its high, curved arches and central dome have a simple, solid elegance even if the greater whole feels rather sterile (although a side chapel with a mosaic of the Resurrection does include a praying JFK in the tableau). The superb acoustics are best appreciated during an organ recital (program dates are posted on the website).

From the Spanish Arch, a riverside path runs upriver and across the Salmon Weir Bridge to the cathedral.

Nora Barnacle House   MUSEUM
(☑ 091-564 743; 8 Bowling Green; adult/child €2.50/2; ☺ phone for hours) James Joyce's wife Nora Barnacle (1884–1951) lived here until shortly before she and Joyce met in Dublin in 1904. It's now a privately owned museum displaying the couple's letters and photographs among period furniture. Looking all of its 100 years and not helped by a grim grey paint job, the house didn't have running water until the 1940s; instead the Barnacle family used a communal pump across the street. Joyce met his future mother-in-law here in 1909; for his part, Joyce's father said after learning Nora's surname: 'She'll stick with him'.

Salthill   NEIGHBOURHOOD
A favourite pastime for Galwegians and visitors alike is walking along the Prom, the seaside promenade running from the edge of the city along Salthill. Local tradition dictates 'kicking the wall' opposite the diving boards (a 2.5km stroll from town, starting at the Wolfe Tone Bridge and following the shoreline path) before turning around.

In and around Salthill there are plenty of cosy pubs from where you can watch storms roll over the bay.

 Tours

If you're short on time, bus tours departing from Galway are a good way to see Connemara, the Burren (p359) and the Cliffs of Moher (p358), while boat tours take you to the heart of Lough Corrib. Tours can be booked directly or at the tourist office.

★ **Burren Wild Tours**   NATURE TOUR
(☑ 087 877 9565; www.burrenwalks.com; departs Galway Coach Station; adult/student €22/18; ☺ 10am-5pm) Seasonal bus tours to the Burren and the Cliffs of Moher incorporating an easy 90-minute guided mountain walk.

COUNTY GALWAY GALWAY CITY

FESTIVALS OF FUN

Galway's packed calendar of festivals turns the city and surrounding communities into what feels like one nonstop party – streets overflow with revellers, and pubs and restaurants often extend their opening hours. Some highlights include:

➡ Galway Food Festival (www.galwayfoodfestival.com; ☺ late Mar) Galway's lively food scene is celebrated.

➡ Cúirt International Festival of Literature (http://www.cuirt.ie; ☺ Apr) Top-name authors converge on Galway for one of Ireland's premier literary festivals, featuring poetry slams, theatrical performances and readings.

➡ Galway Film Fleadh (www.galwayfilmfleadh.com; ☺ early Jul) One of Ireland's biggest film festivals, held right before the arts festival.

➡ Galway Arts Festival (www.galwayartsfestival.ie; ☺ mid-Jul) A two-week extravaganza of theatre, music, art and comedy.

➡ Galway Race Week (www.galwayraces.com; ☺ late Jul or early Aug) Horse races in Ballybrit, 3km east of the city, are the centrepiece of Galway's biggest, most boisterous festival of all. Thursday is a real knees-up: by night the swells have muddy knees on their tuxes and are missing random high heels.

➡ Galway International Oyster Festival (www.galwayoysterfest.com; ☺ late Sep) Oysters are washed down with plenty of pints.

Other regional events of note:

➡ Galway hooker boat races (p408)

➡ Clarenbridge Oyster Festival (p408)

➡ Bodhrán (hand-held goatskin drum) workshops (p396)

➡ The Aran Islands' rollicking *Father Ted* festival, Tedfest (p386)

Galway's Festivals

Galway knows how to party. Major events in its annual calendar draw thousands from across the country, and even the world. Celebrations of culture, food and sport give reasons to visit year-round.

In spring, authors and writers from around the world gather for the Cúirt International Festival of Literature. If this university town already seems literary, wait until you hear readings of prose, verse and poetry streaming out of almost every pub.

As the air warms in summer, the cultural scene heats up for the Galway Arts Festival. The city enjoys performances and exhibits by top drama groups, musicians and bands, comedians, artists and much more. The Galway Film Fleadh, held concurrently, sets screens alight with new and edgy works.

One of the great knees-ups, Galway Race Week, draws tens of thousands of punters for a weekend of partying that's a real race to the finish. Whether wearing fine silks, formal wear or casual gear, the race almost seems secondary to the frolic – unless you have wagers, that is.

One of the great joys of autumn is the Galway International Oyster Festival. The oysters are nurtured throughout the year in the shallow tidal waters of Galway Bay. Good for much of the year, the tasty bivalves seem to reach their peak as the days grow short. At celebrations big and small, oysters star across the region.

1. Galway during the Galway Arts Festival **2.** Horses racing, Galway Races **3.** Race-goers, Galway Races

ℹ NAVIGATING GALWAY

Galway's compact town centre straddles Europe's shortest river, the Corrib, which connects Lough Corrib to the sea. Most shops and services congregate on the river's eastern bank, while some of the city's best music pubs and restaurants cluster to the west. From this area, known logically as the West Side, a 10-minute waterfront walk leads you to the seaside suburb of Salthill.

Galway Tour Company   BUS TOUR
(☎091-566 566; www.galwaytourcompany.com; tours from €18; ⊙Mar-Oct) Offers a variety of tours of County Clare's Burren and Connemara.

Corrib Princess   BOAT TOUR
(☎091-592 447; www.corribprincess.ie; Woodquay; adult/child €15/13; ⊙May-Sep) Two to three 1½-hour cruises per day on the River Corrib and Lough Corrib, departing from Woodquay, just beyond Salmon Weir Bridge.

Historical Walking Tours   WALKING TOUR
(☎086 727 4888; Galway Tourist Office, Forster St; adult/child €8/free; ⊙5pm Mon, Wed, Fri & 2pm Sat Apr-Sep) Enjoyable 80-minute tours unlock some of Galway's hidden secrets.

Lally Tours   BUS TOUR
(☎091-562 905; www.lallytours.com; buses: Galway Coach Station, ticket office: Forster St; tours from adult/child €20/12) Entertaining, informative bus tours of Connemara, the Burren and the Cliffs of Moher.

Old Galway City Tour   BUS TOUR
(☎091-562 905; www.lallytours.com; Galway Tourist Office, Forster St; 24hr ticket adult/child €10/5; ⊙10.30am-3pm Mar-Oct) Hop-on, hop-off open-top bus tours of Galway City and its environs. Buses run every 90 minutes and make 15 stops.

🛏 Sleeping

You'll find B&Bs lining the major approach roads as well as Salthill, but to take full advantage of Galway's tightly packed attractions, try for a room in the city centre. If you're planning an extended stay, the *Galway Advertiser* (www.galwayadvertiser.ie) lists rental properties, or try www.daft.ie.

Galway's festivals and its easy striking distance from Dublin make it *hugely* popular year-round, especially at weekends. Accommodation often fills far in advance – book ahead! And note that ditching the car can be a hassle at places without parking.

🛏 City Centre

★ Kinlay Hostel   HOSTEL €
(☎091-565 244; www.kinlayhouse.ie; Merchants Rd; dm €17-29, d €58-70; @⌐) Easygoing staff, a full range of facilities and a cream-in-the-doughnut location just off Eyre Sq make this a top choice. Spanning two huge, brightly lit floors, amenities include two self-catering kitchens and two cosy TV lounges. Some rooms have bay views.

Salmon Weir Hostel   HOSTEL €
(☎091-561 133; www.salmonweirhostel.com; 3 St Vincent's Ave; dm €14-20, d €48-60; @⌐) Galway's hippie vibe finds its spiritual home in the Salmon Weir's guitar-strewn lounge room, where informal jam sessions take place most nights. The hostel has a share-house feel, including shared bathrooms for all rooms. There's no breakfast, although coffee and tea are free.

Snoozles Tourist Hostel   HOSTEL €
(☎091-530 064; www.snoozleshostelgalway.ie; Forster St; dm €10-25, r €50-70) Dorms and private rooms all have bathrooms at this new hostel. It's ideal for the over-burdened as it sits near the train and bus stations. Extras include a barbecue terrace, pool table and more.

Barnacle's   HOSTEL €
(☎091-568 644; www.barnacles.ie; 10 Quay St; dm €20-30, d €60-70; @⌐) Very central, this well-run hostel is housed in a medieval building with a modern extension. The kitchen is spacious and there's a warm common room with a big gas fireplace and game consoles. Breakfast includes scones and soda bread.

★ Heron's Rest   B&B €€
(☎091-539 574; www.theheronsrest.com; 16A Longwalk; s/d from €70/140; ⌐) Ideally located on the banks of the Corrib, the endlessly thoughtful hosts here will give you deck chairs so you can sit outside and enjoy the scene. Other touches include holiday-friendly breakfast times (8am to 11am), decanters of port etc. Rooms, all with water views, are small and cute.

Spanish Arch Hotel   HOTEL €€
(☎091-569 600; www.spanisharchhotel.ie; Quay St; r €70-160; ⌐) In a sensational spot on the main drag, this 20-room boutique hotel is housed

in a 16th-century former Carmelite convent. Its solid-timber bar has a great line-up of live music, so the rooms at the back, while smaller, are best for a quiet night's sleep.

St Martins B&B
B&B €€

(☑ 091-568 286; www.stmartins.ie; 2 Nun's Island Rd; s/d from €50/80; @ ⓢ) This beautifully kept, renovated older house right on the canal has a flower-filled garden overlooking the William O'Brien Bridge and the River Corrib. The four rooms have all the comforts and the breakfast is a few cuts above the norm (fresh-squeezed OJ!). Owner Mary Sexton wins rave reviews.

7 Cross Street
HOTEL €€

(☑ 091-530 100; www.7crossstreet.com; 7 Cross St; r from €80; ⓢ) The perfect hotel name for finding your way home after a night in Galway's pubs. The 10 rooms here are small but plush, have trendy decor and are named for famous characters. See what magic you can perfrom in the Merlin Room.

Eyre Square Townhouse
INN €€

(☑ 091-568 444; www.eyresquaretownhouse.com; 35 Eyre St; r €60-120; ⓢ) The 11 rooms aren't large but neither is the price at this modest yet well-run walk-up inn just off Eyre Sq. Everything has an Ikea feel, which, combined with the modern bathrooms, makes for a nice stay. The front desk is not continuously staffed.

Western Hotel
HOTEL €€

(☑ 091-562 834; www.thewestern.ie; 33 Prospect Hill; r €60-150; @ ⓢ) Three Georgian buildings have been wedded at this central spot just east of Eyre Sq. The 38 rooms are large, modern and comfortable and there's basement parking. Good-sized desks await the work-encumbered. The full-on breakfasts are above the always-filling average.

★House Hotel
HOTEL €€€

(☑ 091-538 900; www.thehousehotel.ie; Spanish Pde; r €100-220; ⓢ) It's a design odyssey at this boutique hotel. Public spaces contrast modern art with trad details and bold accents. Cat motifs abound. The 40 rooms are plush, with beds having conveniently padded headboards and a range of colour schemes. Bathrooms are commodious and ooze comfort.

🛏 Near the Centre

Among the strips of B&Bs near the centre, College Rd stands out for sheer volume: doz-

ens of choices line the road. You can reach the action after a 10-minute walk along Lough Atalia.

Ballyloughane Caravan & Camping Park
CAMPGROUND €

(☑ 091-755 338; galwcamp@iol.ie; Ballyloughane Beach, Renmore; campsites from €15; ☉ Jun-Aug) This family-run camping ground is clean and secure, and its beachside location affords sweeping views across the bay. It's off the old Dublin Rd (R338), 5km east of the centre.

★Ardawn House
B&B €€

(☑ 091-568 833; www.ardawnhouse.com; College Rd; s/d from €50/80; ⓢ) One of the nicest choices on the B&B-lined College Rd strip, this traditional house has elegant bedrooms. The breakfast room feels regal and the food is royal: all manner of preserves and cheeses plus omelettes and much more.

Four Seasons B&B
B&B €€

(☑ 091-564 078; www.fourseasonsgalway.com; 23 College Rd; s/d from €50/80; ⓢ) 'If the Ritz is full there's always the Four Seasons.' Of course, this Four Seasons only has seven rooms and the nightly rates will leave you with enough loot for many a pint. One of the best choices on this strip; the Fitzgeralds offer a large breakfast menu and free fruit.

Dun Aoibhinn Guest House
INN €€

(☑ 091-583 129; www.dunaoibhinnhouse.com; 12 St Mary's Rd; r €50-100; @ ⓢ) Pronounced doon-*ay*-ven, this restored town house with original leadlight windows and floorboards is less than five minutes' stroll north of West Side's music pubs. Small antique-filled rooms have laptop safes and fridges, which are filled with fixings for making your own continental breakfast.

✕ Eating

Seafood is Galway's speciality, be it fish and chips, ocean-fresh chowder or salmon cooked to perfection. Galway Bay oysters star on many menus. The city's smorgasbord of eating and drinking options ranges from the market – where farmers in gumboots unload

WANT MORE?

Head to Lonely Planet (www.lonely planet.com/galway) for planning advice, author recommendations, traveller reviews and insider tips.

A PERFECT WALK

A fine footpath runs northwest along the Eglinton Canal from the Lower Dominick St Bridge. Passing behind several of Galway's better pubs (nod to the smokers who have ducked out back), the path makes a gentle climb. Look to your right for the spot where two creeks enter the canal, a larger one and a very tiny one. Over the small one is a wee little stone bridge that could be the artefact of some leprechaun fantasy or a leftover from a John Ford film. With the water burbling in all directions – and cascading through the canal locks just upstream – it's a spot where the sounds of Galway are literally washed away, leaving you to your own contemplation.

soil-covered vegetables – to adventurous new restaurants redefining Irish cuisine.

Pedestrianised Quay St is lined with restaurants aimed at the tourist throngs. As one local told us, 'I can remember when all you'd get on Quay St was a hard biscuit, then you'd get run down by a bus.'

Galway's **farmers market** (www.galway market.com; Church Lane; ⊘8am-4pm Sat, noon-5pm Sun) fills the streets around St Nicholas Church. It's the region's best and is the place to see the many briny, earthy and dairy delights of the county. You'll find artisans selling their creations as well.

★**McCambridge's**   CAFE, GROCERY €
(www.mccambridges.com; 38/39 Shop St; snacks from €3, mains €7-15; ⊘cafe noon-5pm Mon-Sat, grocery 9am-6pm Mon-Sat) The long-running food hall here has a superb selection of prepared salads, hot foods and other more exotic treats. Create the perfect picnic or enjoy your selections at the tables out the front. The new cafe above is simply fabulous. Modern Irish fare flavours the ever-changing menu. Creative sandwiches, salads, silky soups and savoury meals are featured.

★**Sheridans Cheesemongers**   DELI €
(14 Churchyard St; snacks from €4; ⊘shop 9.30am-6pm Mon-Fri, 9am-6pm Sat, cafe 5-10pm Tue-Sat) Sheridans Cheesemongers is redolent of the superb local and international cheeses and other deli items within, many with a Med bent. Its real secret, however, is up a narrow flight of stairs. Sample from a huge wine list in an airy room while enjoying many of the best items from below.

Griffin's   CAFE, BAKERY €
(www.griffinsbakery.com; Shop St; mains €4-8; ⊘8am-6pm Mon-Sat) A local institution which, although it's been run by the Griffin family since 1876, remains as fresh as a bun hot out of the oven. The small bakery counter is laden with treats, including great scones. But the real pleasure lies upstairs in the cafe where you can choose from sandwiches, hot specials, luscious desserts and more.

Gourmet Tart Co   DELI, BAKERY €
(Lower Abbeygate St; mains €5-9; ⊘10am-5pm Mon-Sat) Food porn is an apt description for the stunning array of dishes on offer here both in the deli case and at the buffet. Luscious salads, salmon, beautiful sandwiches and, yes, tarts that give pastry a good name. It's all take-out; enjoy your lunch on the grass by the Spanish Arch.

Goya's   CAFE €
(www.goyas.ie; 2 Kirwan's Lane; mains €5-10; ⊘9.30am-6pm Mon-Sat) Cakes in all sizes are supreme at Goya's, a Galway treasure hidden on a small square. Its fine coffee and sweet treats make it a perfect pause. The deli does a booming lunch trade; enjoy a sandwich at a table outside. The desserts may cause spontaneous eruptions of 'oooh!'

Food 4 Thought   VEGETARIAN €
(Lower Abbeygate St; mains €6-9; ⊘8am-6pm Mon-Sat, 11.30am-4pm Sun; ☎🖉) Besides providing organic and vegetarian sandwiches, savoury scones and wholesome dishes such as cashew-nut roast, this New Age place is great for finding out about energy workshops and yoga classes around town. Free refills of coffee!

★**Oscar's**   SEAFOOD €€
(🖉091-582 180; www.oscarsbistro.ie; Upper Dominick St; mains €13-25; ⊘6-9.30pm Mon-Sat) Galway's best seafood restaurant is just west of the tourist bustle. The long and ever-changing menu has a huge range of local specialties, from shellfish to white fish (which make some superb fish and chips). The flavours are bold, not unlike the bright red accents inside and out.

Ard Bia at Nimmo's   MODERN IRISH €€
(www.ardbia.com; Spanish Arch; lunch mains €5-10, dinner mains €19-24; ⊘cafe 10am-3.30pm, restaurant 6-10pm, wine bar 6-11pm; closed Sun) In Irish,

Ard Bia means 'High Food', and that's somewhat apt, given its location in the 18th-century Custom House near the Spanish Arch. Local seafood and organic produce feature on the seasonal menu in a setting that defines funky chic. The cafe is a perfect place for a coffee and a tart.

McDonagh's
SEAFOOD €€

(www.mcdonaghs.net; 22 Quay St; takeaway mains from €6, restaurant mains €15-25; ⊘ cafe & takeaway noon-11pm Mon-Sat, 2-9pm Sun, restaurant 5-10pm Mon-Sat) A trip to Galway isn't complete without stopping at McDonagh's. Divided into two parts, with a takeaway counter and a cafe with long communal wooden tables on one side, and a more upmarket (and creative) restaurant on the other, Galway's best fish-and-chip shop churns out battered cod, plaice, haddock, whiting and salmon nonstop, all accompanied by homemade tartare sauce.

Da Tang Noodle House
ASIAN €€

(☑ 091-561 443; www.datangnoodlehouse.com; 2 Middle St; mains €8-18; ⊘ noon-10pm) The cure for every greasy, gloopy sweet-and-sour yuck you've endured is here at this tidy little noodle house: brilliant fresh fare bursting with flavour. Noodles are the start for soups, stir-fries, sizzling dishes and more. You can get dinner delivered to your hotel room.

Bar No 8
PUB €€

(3 Dock Rd; mains €14-20; ⊘ 6-11pm Tue & Thu-Sun) Bentwood chairs and overstuffed sofas provide comfort in this at once funky and stylish bar overlooking the harbour. Art by patrons is on display. The emphasis on creative pub food places this firmly in the eating category. The menu is short and Med-accented.

Quays
IRISH €€

(Quay St; mains €12-25; ⊘ 11am-10pm) This sprawling pub does a roaring business downstairs in its restaurant, which has hearty carvery lunches and more ambitious mains at night. The cold seafood platter stars the bounty from Galway Bay. Students on dates and out celebrating get rowdier as the pints and hours pass.

★Aniar
MODERN IRISH €€€

(☑ 091-535 947; www.aniarrestaurant.ie; 53 Lower Dominick St; mains from €30; ⊘ 6-10pm Tue-Sat) Deeply committed to the flavours and food producers of Galway and West Ireland, Aniar wears its Michelin star with pride. There's no fuss here, however. The casual spring-green dining area is a relaxed place to taste from the nightly menu. The wine list favours small producers.

🍷 Drinking & Nightlife

Galway's pub selection is second to none, which is why in summer and on weekends they all seem thronged. On Saturday nights, the town fills with party-goers from the hinterlands. The website **Galway City Pub Guide** (www.galwaycitypubguide.com) is a good resource for this heaving scene.

Most of Galway's pubs have live music at least a couple of nights a week, whether in an informal trad session or a headline act.

★Séhán Ua Neáchtain
PUB

(17 Upper Cross St) Painted a bright cornflower blue, this 19th-century pub, known simply as Neáchtain's (*nock*-tans) or Naughtons, has a wraparound string of tables outside, many shaded by a large tree. It's a place where a polyglot mix of locals plop down and let the world pass them by – or stop and join them for a pint. Good lunches.

★Crane Bar
PUB

(www.thecranebar.com; 2 Sea Rd) An atmospheric old pub west of the Corrib, the Crane is the best spot in Galway to catch an informal *céilidh* most nights. Talented bands play its rowdy, good-natured upstairs bar; downstairs at times it seems right out of *The Far Side*.

Tig Cóilí
PUB

(Mainguard St) Two live *céilidh* a day draw the crowds to this authentic fire-engine-red pub, just off High St. It's where musicians go to get drunk or drunks go to become musicians...or something like that. A gem.

Róisín Dubh
PUB

(www.roisindubh.net; Upper Dominick St) From the rooftop terrace you can see sweeping views of Galway; inside, emerging acts play here before they hit the big time. It's *the* place to hear bands.

Monroe's Tavern
PUB

(www.monroes.ie; Upper Dominick St) Often photographed for its classic, world-weary facade, Monroe's delivers traditional music and ballads, plus it remains the only pub in the city with regular Irish dancing.

G Bar
GAY & LESBIAN

(www.gbargalway.com; 1 West William St) The rainbow-hued huge G's out the front are a sign that this Galway bar is proud. Special events and late-night dancing keep it buzzing through the year in the frolicsome West End.

Murphy's   PUB
(9 High St) A complete anomaly among the partying throngs in the centre, Murphy's is a timeless haven where locals still explore the limits of the art of conversation.

Garavan's   PUB
(46 William St) A genteel old boozer in the city centre that is a place of refuge for those in search of a pint *and* a seat on a busy Saturday night.

☆ Entertainment

Most pubs in Galway have live music at least a couple of nights a week. Róisín Dubh is the best place for bands; Tig Cóilí excels at trad sessions.

★ Druid Theatre   THEATRE
(☎091-568 660; www.druid.ie; Druid Lane) This renowned, long-established and award-winning theatre is famed for staging experimental works by young Irish playwrights, as well as new adaptations of classics. Its Galway home is in an old tea warehouse.

Town Hall Theatre   THEATRE
(☎091-569 777; www.tht.ie; Courthouse Sq) The Town Hall Theatre features Broadway and West End shows and visiting singers.

Trad on the Prom   MUSICAL
(☎091-582 860; www.tradontheprom.com; Salthill Hotel; adult/child from €30/10; ☺May-Sep) This long-running summer musical is a festival of Irish dancing and singing. It's led by Máirín Fahy, a local diva of the fiddle. The glossy production is performed several nights per week in a venue right on the Salthill promenade.

Shopping

Galway has an array of speciality shops dotting its narrow streets, stocking cutting-edge fashion, Irish woollens, outdoor clothing and equipment, local jewellery, books, art and, of course, music.

★ Charlie Byrne's Bookstore   BOOKS
(www.charliebyrne.com; Middle St, Cornstore; ☺9am-6pm, to 8pm Thu & Fri, from noon Sun) A civic treasure with a brilliant collection of new, secondhand and discounted books (many €1) in a succession of rambling rooms. Staff can ferret out that obscure Aran Islands title you were seeking.

P Powell & Sons   MUSIC
(William St; ☺10am-5pm Mon-Sat) You can pick up tin whistles, Bodhráns and other instruments here, as well as sheet music. Backpackers note: this shop stocks bongos.

Kiernan Moloney Musical Instruments   MUSIC
(www.moloneymusic.com; 17 High St, Old Malt Centre; ☺10am-5pm Tue-Sat) Fiddles abound at this dealer in fine instruments. If your harp has come unglued, they'll fix it here.

❶ Information

The transport stations are locker-free, but there is a central refuge for your bags while you hunt for a room.
Cara Cabs (☎091-563 939; 17 Eyre Sq; ☺24hr) This taxi office will store your bags for €5 per day.

HOPPY SALVATION

Irish pubs may be atmospheric places to enjoy a pint and, indeed, many folks fly thousands of miles to sit in a little nook happily quaffing a properly poured creamy Guinness. But once past the stout, things go flat in a hurry. In pub after pub the non-Guinness choices amount to a sad array of bland lagers. What did the Irish ever do to America besides send it some of their finest citizens? In return America has sent Budweiser, Miller Genuine Draft (MGD) and, horror of horrors, Coors Light. The Dutch haven't done much better by the Emerald Isle, exporting untold hectolitres of Heineken, a beer that inspired a Dutch friend to ask us, 'Why do you drink our old man's beer?'

But if the beer situation in much of the country is bleak (whatever happened to Harp?), in Galway there's an alternative to the lame lagers: Hooker. Named for the iconic local fishing boats, this fine, hoppy Pale Ale has won plaudits and, more importantly, a local following.

You can get a Hooker (www.galwayhooker.ie) at many Galway pubs including Róisín Dubh, Bar No 8, Tig Cóilí and Monroe's Tavern. Hooker's seasonal brews, including an excellent stout, are available at Séhán Ua Neáchtain.

Tourist information booth (Eyre Sq; ⏱9am-1pm Sun year-round, 9am-6pm Fri-Sun mid-May–Aug) Dispenses free city maps and local info.

Tourist office (www.discoverireland.ie; Forster St; ⏱9am-5.45pm daily Easter-Sep, closed Sun Oct-Easter) Large, efficient regional information centre that can help arrange local accommodation and tours.

❶ Getting There & Away

BUS

Several private bus companies are based at the modern **Galway Coach Station** (New Coach Station; Bothar St), which is located near the tourist office.

Bus Éireann (www.buseireann.ie; Station Rd, Cara Bus Station) Services to all major cities in the Republic and the North from just off Eyre Sq, near the train station. Dublin (€14, three to 3¾ hours) has hourly service. Other services fan out across the region.

Citylink (www.citylink.ie; ticket office Forster St; ⏱office 9am-6pm; ☎) Services depart from Galway Coach Station for Dublin (from €11, 2½ hours, hourly), Dublin Airport (from €17, 2½ hours, hourly), Cork, Limerick and Connemara. Departures are frequent and fares are as low as €10.

gobus.ie (www.gobus.ie; Galway Coach Station; ☎) Frequent services to Dublin (2½ hours) and Dublin Airport (three hours). Fares from €11.

TRAIN

From the **train station** (📞091-564 222; www.irishrail.ie), just off Eyre Sq, there are up to eight fast, comfortable trains daily to/from Dublin's Heuston Station (one way from €34, 2¼ hours). Connections with other train routes can be made at Athlone (one hour). The line to Ennis is scenic (€19, 1¾ hours, five daily).

❶ Getting Around

TO/FROM THE AIRPORTS

Bus Éireann operates daily services to/from **Shannon Airport** (€15, 1¾ hours, hourly). All the major bus companies serve Dublin Airport.

BICYCLE

Europa Bicycles (📞091-588 830; Hunter's Bldg; ⏱9.30am-6pm Mon-Fri) Hires bikes for €8 to €15 for 24 hours. It's on Earl's Island, opposite Galway Cathedral.

BUS

You can walk to almost everything in Galway, including out to Salthill, but you'll also find frequent buses departing from Eyre Sq. For Salthill, take bus 401 (€1.80, 15 minutes).

❶ CLADDAGH RINGS

The fishing village of Claddagh has long been subsumed into Galway's city centre, but its namesake rings survive as both a timeless reminder and a timeless source of profits.

Popular with people of real or imagined Irish descent everywhere, the rings depict a heart (symbolising love) between two outstretched hands (friendship), topped by a crown (loyalty). Rings are handcrafted at jewellers around Galway, and start from about €20 for a simple band to well over €1000 for a blinged-up diamond-covered version.

Jewellers include Ireland's oldest jewellery shop, **Thomas Dillon's Claddagh Gold** (www.claddaghring.ie; 1 Quay St; ⏱10am-6pm), which was established in 1750 and is adorned with Claddagh history placards.

CAR

Parking on Galway's streets is metered. There are several multistorey and pay-and-display car parks around town.

Galway's unprecedented growth and the resulting lack of infrastructure serving its urban sprawl mean that traffic jams can be horrendous. For a stress-free holiday, leave the roads to commuters at peak hours if possible.

TAXI

Taxi ranks are located on Eyre Sq, on Bridge St and next to the bus and train stations.

City Taxis (📞091-525 252; www.citytaxisgalway.com) Charters taxis to the airports. To Shannon Airport, it's €89 for one to four people.

ARAN ISLANDS

Easily visible from large swaths of coastal Galway and Clare Counties, the Aran Islands sing their own siren song to thousands of travellers each year who find their desolate beauty beguiling. Day-trippers shuttle through in a daze of rocky magnificence, while those who stay longer find places that, in many ways, seem further removed from the Irish mainland than a 45-minute ferry ride or 10-minute flight. Hardy travellers find that low season showcases the islands at their wild, windswept best.

An extension of the limestone escarpment that forms the Burren in Clare, the islands have shallow topsoil scattered with wildflowers, grass for grazing and jagged cliffs pounded by surf. Ancient forts such as Dún Aengus on Inishmór and Dún Chonchúir on Inishmaan are some of the oldest archaeological remains in Ireland.

A web of stone walls (1600km in all) runs across all three islands. They also have a smattering of early *clocháns* (drystone beehive huts from the early Christian period), resembling stone igloos.

Although quite close in appearance as well as proximity, the three Arans have distinct personalities.

Inishmór (Árainn in Irish, meaning 'Big Island') is the largest Aran and the most easily accessible from Galway. It is home to one of Ireland's most important and impressive archaeological sites, as well as some lively pubs and restaurants, particularly in the only town, Kilronan. Gets over a thousand day-trippers in summer.

Inishmaan (Inis Meáin, 'Middle Island') is often bypassed by the majority of tourist traffic, preserving its age-old traditions and evoking a sense of timelessness. It is a place of great solitude with isolated B&Bs and stark rocky vistas.

Inisheer (Inis Oírr, 'Eastern Island'), the smallest island, is easily reached from Galway year-round and from Doolin in the summer months. It offers a good combination of ancient sites, interesting walks, trad culture and a bit of life at night.

History

Little is known about the people who built the massive Iron Age stone structures on Inishmór and Inishmaan. Commonly referred to as 'forts', they are believed to have served as pagan religious centres. Folklore holds that they were built by the Firbolgs who invaded Ireland from Europe in prehistoric times.

It is thought that people came to the islands to farm, a major challenge given the rocky terrain. Early islanders augmented their soil by hauling seaweed and sand up from the shore. People also fished the surrounding waters on long *currachs* (rowing boats made of a framework of laths covered with tarred canvas), which remain a symbol of the Aran Islands.

Early Christianity

Christianity reached the islands remarkably early, and some of the oldest monastic settlements were founded by St Enda (Éanna) in the 5th century. Enda appears to have been an Irish chief who converted to Christianity and spent some time studying in Rome before seeking out a suitably remote spot for his monastery.

From the 14th century, control of the islands was disputed by two Gaelic families, the O'Briens and the O'Flahertys. The English took over during the reign of Elizabeth I, and in Cromwell's times a garrison was stationed here.

Modern Isolation

As Galway's importance waned, so did that of the islands, and their isolation meant islanders maintained a traditional lifestyle well into the 20th century. Up to the 1930s, people wore traditional Aran dress: bright red skirts and black shawls for women, baggy woollen trousers and waistcoats with *crios* (colourful belts) for men. The classic heavy cream-coloured Aran sweater, featur-

FATHER TED'S DIVINE INSPIRATION

Devotees of the late 1990s cult British TV series *Father Ted* might recognise Craggy Island – the show's fictional island setting off Ireland's west coast – from its opening sequence showing the *Plassy* shipwreck on Inisheer. However, apart from this single shot, the sitcom was mostly filmed in London studios, with additional location shots in Counties Clare, Wicklow and Dublin. Alas, the Parochial House and Vaughan's Pub are nowhere to be found here (instead you'll find them near Lisdoonvarna and Kilfenora in County Clare).

This hasn't stopped the Aran Islands from embracing the show as their own. Although there has been some grumbling from its smaller neighbours, Inishmór has seized upon *Ted*-mania for itself and each year hosts **Tedfest** (www.tedfest.org; ⊙ late Feb/early Mar), a *Father Ted* festival. Held during the purgatory of tourism in late winter, this three-day carnival of nonsense has been a huge hit.

Meanwhile, County Clare now has a competing Ted festival in Kilfenora (p365). As he might say: 'Oh feck!'

ARTISTIC ARAN

The Aran Islands have sustained a strong creative streak, partly as a means of entertainment during long periods of isolation and partly, in the words of one local composer, to 'make sure the rest of the country doesn't forget we're here'. Artists and writers from the mainland have similarly long been drawn to the elemental nature of island life.

Dramatist JM Synge (1871–1909) spent a lot of time on the islands. His play *Riders to the Sea* (1905) is set on Inishmaan while his renowned *The Playboy of the Western World* (1907) also draws upon his island experiences. Synge's highly readable book *The Aran Islands* (1907) is the classic account of life here and remains in print.

American Robert Flaherty came to the islands in the early 1930s to film *Man of Aran*, a dramatic account of daily life. He was something of a fanatic about the project and got most of the locals involved in its production. One of the cottages built for the film is today a B&B (Man of Aran Cottage, p390)). The film is a classic and is regularly shown in Kilronan on Inishmór.

The noted 1996 play, *The Cripple of Inishmann* by Martin McDonagh, involves tragic characters and a strong desire to leave the island in 1934.

The map-maker Tim Robinson has written a wonderful two-volume account of his explorations on Aran, called *Stones of Aran: Pilgrimage* and *Stones of Aran: Labyrinthe*.

Local literary talent includes Liam O'Flaherty (1896–1984) from Inishmór. He wrote several harrowing novels, including *Famine* (1937).

COUNTY GALWAY INISHMÓR

ing complex patterns, originated and is still hand-knitted on the islands.

Until the last few decades the islands were, if not centuries from civilisation, then at least a perilous all-day journey in unpredictable seas. Air services began in 1970, changing island life forever, and today fast ferries make a quick (if sometimes rough) crossing.

All three islands now have secondary schools, but as recently as a decade ago, students on the two smaller islands had to move to boarding school in Galway to complete their education, which involved an abrupt switch from speaking Irish to English. Farming has all but died out on the islands and tourism is now the primary source of income; while Irish remains the local tongue, most locals speak English with visitors and converse with each other in Irish.

ℹ Information

Although high summer brings throngs of tourists, services on the islands are few. Only Inishmór has a year-round tourist office as well as the only ATM; the majority of places don't accept credit cards (always check ahead). Restaurants, including pubs that serve food, often reduce their opening hours or shut completely during low season.

ℹ Getting There & Away

AIR

All three islands have landing strips. The mainland departure point is Connemara regional airport at Minna, near Inverin (Indreabhán), about 35km west of Galway. **Aer Arann Islands** (☑ 091-593 034; www.aerarannislands.ie) offers return flights to each of the islands several times daily (hourly in summer) for adult/child €45/25; the flights take about 10 minutes, and groups of four or more can get group rates.

If you work out some complex timings, you can visit more than one island in a day. A bus from outside Galway's Kinlay Hostel to the airport costs €3 each way.

BOAT

Island Ferries (www.aranislandferries.com; Merchant's Rd, Galway Ticket Office; adult/child return fare from €25/13; ⊘8am-5pm) serves all three islands and also links Inishmaan and Inisheer. Schedules peak in July and August, with several boats a day. The crossing can take up to one hour and is subject to cancellation in high seas. Boats leave from Rossaveal, 40km west of Galway City on the R336. Buses from Galway (adult/child €7/4) connect with the sailings; ask when you book.

Ferries to the Arans (primarily Inisheer) also operate from Doolin.

Inishmór

POP 830

Most visitors who venture out to the islands don't make it beyond Inishmór (Árainn) and its main attraction, Dún Aengus, the stunning stone fort perched perilously on the island's towering cliffs. The arid landscape west of Kilronan (Cill Rónáin), Inishmór's

Inishmór

main settlement, is dominated by stone walls, boulders, scattered buildings and the odd patch of deep-green grass and potato plants.

Tourism turns the wheels of the island's economy: an armada of tour vans greets each ferry and flight, offering a ride round the sights. As one local said: 'We move 'em through like a conveyor belt.' Happily, you can set your own pace.

Inishmór is 14.5km long and 4km at its widest stretch. All boats arrive and depart from Kilronan, on the southeastern side of the island. One principal road runs the length of the island, intersected by small lanes and paths of packed dirt and stone.

◉ Sights

★**Dún Aengus**   HISTORIC SITE

(Dún Aonghasa; www.heritageireland.ie; adult/child €3/1; ⊙9.45am-6pm Apr-Oct, 9.30am-4pm Nov-Mar, closed Mon & Tue Jan-Feb) Three spectacular forts stand guard over Inishmór,

each believed to be around 2000 years old. Chief among them is Dún Aengus, which has three nonconcentric walls that run right up to sheer drops to the ocean below. It is protected by remarkable *chevaux de frise,* fearsome and densely packed defensive stone spikes that surely helped deter ancient armies from invading the site.

Powerful swells pound the 60m-high cliff face. A complete lack of rails or other modern additions that would spoil this amazing ancient site means that you can not only go right up to the cliff's edge but also potentially fall to your doom below quite easily. When it's uncrowded, you can't help but feel the extraordinary energy that must have been harnessed to build this vast site.

A small visitor centre has displays that put everything in context. A slightly strenuous 900m walkway wanders uphill to the fort, through a rocky landscape lined with hardy plants.

Inishmór

◉ North of Kilronan

Between Kilronan and Dún Aengus you'll find the small, perfectly circular fort **Dún Eochla**. it makes for a good walk from the main road.

The ruins of numerous stone churches trace the island's monastic history. The small **Teampall Chiaráin** (Church of St Kieran), with a high cross in the churchyard, is near Kilronan.

West of Kilmurvey is the perfect **Clochán na Carraige**, an early Christian stone hut that stands 2.5m tall, and various small early Christian ruins known rather inaccurately as the **Na Seacht dTeampaill** (Seven Churches), comprising a couple of ruined churches, monastic houses and some fragments of a high cross from the 8th or 9th century. To the south of the ruins is **Dún Eoghanachta**, another circular fort.

Along the low-lying northern coast, the sheltered little bay of **Port Chorrúch** is home to up to 50 grey seals, who sun themselves and feed in the shallows. Further on, **Kilmurvey Beach** gets an EU Blue Flag for its clean white-sand beach.

◉ South of Kilronan

Most day-trippers focus on Kilronan and Dún Aengus and jam the roads between the sights. If you're spending the night, cycle to sites in the little-visited south in the middle of the day, then you can visit Dún Aengus after the last ferry has left during the long days of summer.

In the southeast, near Cill Éinne Bay, is the early Christian **Teampall Bheanáin** (Church of St Benen). Near the airport are the sunken remains of a church; the spot is said to have been the site of St Enda's Monastery in the 5th century, though what's visible dates from the 8th century onwards.

Dún Dúchathair (the Black Fort) is an ancient fort dramatically perched on a south-facing clifftop promontory. Pause at the long and usually empty **Tranmore Beach** east of the airport.

⚲ Activities

The ride between Kilronan and Dún Aengus takes about 30 to 60 minutes. Bikes also let you explore the myriad sites north and south of town.

Most places to stay have bicycles for use or rent (universally €10 per day).

★**Burke's Bicycle Hire**   BICYCLE RENTAL
(☑ 087 280 8273; www.bikehirearanislands.com; Kilronan; rental per day from €10; ⊗ Apr-Oct) Patrick Burke is an expert on local cycling and can advise on routes that avoid crowds and reach seldom-visited ends of the island.

Aran Cycle Hire   BICYCLE RENTAL
(www.aranislandsbikehire.com; Kilronan; bicycle/ electric bicycle from €10/15; ⊗ Apr-Oct) Hires out hundreds of sturdy bikes, which it'll deliver

> ❶ **ISLAND-HOPPING THE ARANS**
>
> It's possible to bounce between the three Aran Islands, allowing you to start at one and return to the mainland from another. However, schedules are geared to return trips to a single island. In order to find ferries between the islands, you'll need to consult with Island Ferries as well as the boats operating from Doolin. There will be at least one connection a day between any two islands, just be prepared for ad hoc schedules. Fares should run from €5 to €10.

COUNTY GALWAY INISHMÓR

to your accommodation anywhere on the island. It's at the pier.

🛏 Sleeping

After the last day-trippers have left in summer, the island takes on a lovely serenity. Advance bookings are advised, particularly in summer the tourist office can book rooms. Many places offer excellent evening meals; those listed under Eating are open to nonguests.

★ Kilronan Hostel   HOSTEL €
(☑ 099-61255; www.kilronanhostel.com; Kilronan; dm €15-30, tw €42; @ 🛜) You'll see the pistachio-green Kilronan Hostel perched above Tí Joe Mac's pub even before your ferry docks at the pier, a three-minute walk away. Forty beds are spread across spotless four- and six-bed rooms. A terrace has fine harbour views and eggs in the morning come courtesy of the organically fed chickens out the back.

Mainistir House   INN €
(☑ 099-61169; www.aranislandshostel.com; Mainistir; dm/s/d €16/40/50; @ 🛜) 🍴 Quirky and colourful, this 60-bed hostel and guesthouse on the main road north of Kilronan is a fun place for the funky and well-read. A simple breakfast is included in the rates. Dinner is an event.

★ Kilmurvey House   B&B €€
(☑ 099-61218; www.kilmurveyhouse.com; Kilmurvey; s/d from €55/90; ⊘ Apr-Sep) On the path leading to Dún Aengus is this grand 18th-century stone mansion. It's a beautiful setting and the 12 rooms are well maintained. Hearty meals (dinner €30) incorporate vegetables from the garden, and local fish and meats. You can swim at a pretty beach that's a short walk from the house.

Tigh Fitz   INN €€
(☑ 099-61213; www.tighfitz.com; Killeany; s/d from €50/80; 🛜) Near the airport, this well-run guesthouse is a good base if you want to avoid the daytime hubbub of the harbour area. Rooms are simple, the views out to the tidal extremes of the bay sublime.

Man of Aran Cottage   B&B €€
(☑ 099-61301; www.manofarancottage.com; Kilmurvey; s/d from €55/80; ⊘ Mar-Oct) 🍴 Built for the 1930s film of the same name, this thatched B&B doesn't trade on past glories, its authentic stone-and-wood interiors define charming. The owners are avid organic

gardeners (the tomatoes are famous) and their bounty can become your meal (€30).

Ard Mhuiris   B&B €€
(☑ 099-61208; www.ardmhuiris.com; Kilronan; s/d from €60/80) A five-minute stroll from the centre of town, this very tidy B&B hits the sweet spot of Aran Islands accommodation: it is quiet, welcoming and has good sea views – perfect for curling up in your room on a rainy day.

Pier House Guest House   INN €€
(☑ 099-61417; www.pierhousearan.com; Kilronan; s/d from €60/90; ⊘ Mar-Oct; 🛜) You won't have time to lose your sea legs in the 100m walk from the ferry to this two-storey house perched on a small rise. The 10 rooms are bright, extra roomy and comfortable. Breakfast is very good.

🍴 Eating & Drinking

Lunch choices are not overwhelming, although some of the pubs listed offer food. At night, there are more options – some excellent.

★ Mainistir House   VEGETARIAN €€
(☑ 099-61169; Mainistir; buffet €15; ⊘ from 8pm summer, from 7pm winter; 🍴) Mainistir House cooks up renowned organic, largely vegetarian fare featuring dishes redolent with the tastes of summer – pesto is much in evidence. Nonguests are welcome, but be sure to book. Get a ride or make the 20-minute steep walk from Kilronan.

Pier House   IRISH €€€
(Kilronan; mains €20-30; ⊘ noon-9pm, May-Aug) Sitting on the large terrace watching the ferries come and go while grazing your way through a platter of local seafood is one of the island's joys. There's a fireplace inside for when it blows. This is the best place for lunch right in Kilronan.

★ Joe Watty's Bar   PUB
(www.joewattys.com; Kilronan; mains €8-20; ⊘ kitchen 12.30-9pm) The best local pub, with trad sessions most summer nights and weekends other times. Posh pub food ranges from fish and chips to steaks. Peat fires warm the air on the 50 weeks a year when this is needed. Book for dinner in summer.

American Bar   PUB
(Kilronan; mains €8; ⊘ kitchen noon-8pm) Two large rooms fill with happy pint quaffers throughout the year. In low season sloshed

locals anticipate the next year of tourists (especially the namesakes of the bar). The room on the right as you enter, with its windows and access to the terrace, is the best bet. Food is so-so.

Tí Joe Mac's   PUB
(Kilronan) Informal music sessions, peat fires and a broad terrace with harbour views make Tí Joe Mac's a local favourite. Food is limited to a few sandwiches slapped together between pints.

☆ Entertainment

Man of Aran Internet Cafe & Gift Shop   CINEMA
(Kilronan; film: adult/child €5/3; ⊗9am-7.30pm Jul & Aug, 9am-5pm other times; 🛜) This eclectic shop at the main crossroads shows the iconic *Man of Aran* on demand in a tiny 24-seat theatre. It also has w-fi (free with purchase) and a fine little coffee bar.

🔒 Shopping

Glossy shops in Kilronan sell Aran-style sweaters that come with gaudy labels that obfuscate their origins (never the islands, often not Ireland at all).

ℹ Information

The bike rental shops and the tourist office all have useful free maps.

Spar Supermarket (Kilronan; ⊗9am-6pm Mon-Wed, 9am-7pm Thu-Sat year-round, 10am-5pm Sun Jun-Aug) Has the only ATM in the Arans, plus good soda bread.

Tourist office (📞099-61263; Kilronan; ⊗10am-5pm May & Jun, 10am-5.45pm Jul & Aug, 11am-5pm Sep-Apr) Useful office on the waterfront west of the ferry pier in Kilronan.

ℹ Getting Around

The airstrip is 2km southeast of town; a shuttle to Kilronan costs €5 return (be sure to carefully reconfirm return pickups for flights lest you be forgotten).

Year-round, numerous **minibuses** greet each ferry and also prowl the centre of Kilronan. All offer 2½-hour tours of the island (€10) to ad hoc groups. The drive – with commentary – between Kilronan and Dún Aengustakes is about 45 minutes each way. You can also negotiate for private and customised tours.

To see the island at a gentler pace, **pony traps** with a driver are available for trips between Kilronan and Dún Aengus; the return journey costs between €60 and €100 for up to four people.

Inishmaan
POP 150

The least-visited of the islands, with the smallest population, Inishmaan (Inis Meáin) is a rocky respite. Early Christian monks seeking solitude were drawn to Inishmaan, as was the author JM Synge, who spent five summers here over a century ago. The island they knew largely survives today: stoic cows and placid sheep, impressive old forts, and warm-hearted locals, who speak Irish to each other exclusively. Children usually leave the island for college and few return.

Inishmaan's scenery is breathtaking, with a jagged coastline of startling cliffs, empty beaches and fields where the main crop seems to be stone. The island is roughly 5km long by 3km wide. Most of its buildings are spread out along the road that runs east-west across the centre of the island. Inishmaan's down-to-earth islanders are largely unconcerned with the prospect of attracting tourists' euros, so facilities are few.

◎ Sights & Activities

You can easily walk to any place on the island, enjoying the stark, rocky scenery and sweeping views on the way.

Glorious views of Inishmaan's limestone valleys extend from the elliptical stone fort **Dún Chonchúir**, which is thought to have been built sometime between the 1st and 7th centuries AD.

Teach Synge (📞099-73036; admission €3; ⊗by appointment), a thatched cottage on the road just before you head up to the fort, is where the writer JM Synge spent his summers between 1898 and 1902 researching *The Aran Islands*.

Cill Cheannannach is a rough 8th- or 9th-century church south of the pier. The well-preserved stone fort **Dún Fearbhaigh**, a short distance west, dates from the same era. On a hill, **St Mary's Church** has excellent stained-glass windows from 1939.

In the east of the island, about 500m north of the boat-landing stage is **Trá Leitreach**, a safe, sheltered beach.

Synge's Chair   LOOKOUT
At the desolate western edge of the island, Synge's Chair is a lookout at the edge of a sheer limestone cliff with the surf from Gregory's Sound booming below. The cliff ledge is often sheltered from the wind, so do as Synge did and find a comfortable stone

seat to take it all in. The formation is two minutes' walk from the parking area; you can leg it around the bleak west side of the island from here in an hour.

On the walk out to Synge's Chair, a sign points the way to a clochán, hidden behind a house and shed.

🍴 Sleeping & Eating

Most B&Bs serve evening meals, usually using organic local foods. Meals generally cost around €20 to €25.

Ard Alainn   B&B €
(📞 099-73027; s/d without bathroom from €35/55; ☺May-Sep) Signposted just over 2km from the pier, thatched Ard Alainn is a vintage fantasy with fine views out to sea. The five rooms share a bathroom. Breakfasts by hostess Maura Faherty will keep you going all day.

Máire Mulkerrin   B&B €
(📞 099-73016; s/d from €33/55) Now in her 80s, Mrs Mulkerrin is a local legend in her skirts and shawls. She keeps a cosy, spick-and-span home, filled with faded family photos, and her stove warms the kitchen all day. Guests are accepted sporadically.

★ Tig Congaile   B&B €€
(📞 099-73085; www.inismeáinbb.com; s/d from €50/80) Not far from the pier, Guatemalan-born Vilma Conneely serves guests freshly ground coffee from her native land, but it's her use of local foods that really wins plaudits. Her sea-vegetable soup is famous and best enjoyed – if possible – at a table outside. The dining room is open to nonguests (lunch dishes from €5, dinner from €20), but you must book. The seven rooms are spacious and have starkly iconic views.

An Dún   B&B €€
(📞 099-73047; www.inismeainaccommodation.ie; r €50-90; ☺Mar-Oct; 🖥) Opposite the entrance to Dún Chonchúir, modern An Dún has five comfortable rooms. The restaurant is open to nonguests and serves lunch in summer and dinner from March to October, including lauded local cuisine such as pillowy potatoes (fertilised with seaweed), luscious smoked salmon and fresh local fish (mains €8 to €25). There are tables outside.

★ Inis Meáin   INN €€€
(📞 086 826 6026; www.inismeain.com; r 2 nights from €500; ☺Apr-Sep; 🖥) A complete anomaly for the island, where almost everything is as basic as a rock – or is a rock – this posh boutique inn has five lovely units crafted from local materials (rocks). Views seem to go on forever and you can grab a bike and spend your day exploring in blessed isolation. Rates include many extras.

The restaurant serves a changing menu of exquisite dishes made from local foods (dinner mains €15 to €35). Open to nonguests, but book.

Teach Ósta   PUB €€
(mains from €8) The island's perfect pub hums on summer evenings (grab a table outside for the views) and supplies snacks, sandwiches, soups and seafood platters. Though the pub often keeps going until the wee hours, food service generally stops around 7pm and may not be available in the winter months.

🛍 Shopping

Cniotáil Inis Meáin   CLOTHING
(📞 099-73009; www.inismeain.ie) This factory exports fine woollen garments to some of the world's most exclusive shops. You can buy the same sweaters here; call before visiting.

ℹ Information

Not far from the pub, a small shop (☺10am-6pm Mon-Fri, 10am-2pm Sat) sells groceries, offers postal services and dispenses advice.

ℹ Getting Around

Enjoy a fact-filled one- to two-hour car tour of the island with eponymous Brídín Tours (📞 099-73993; tours €15). Bike rentals may be available at the ferry dock, otherwise you can rent one at the shop (€10).

Inisheer

POP 200

Inisheer (Inis Oírr), the smallest of the Aran Islands, has a palpable sense of enchantment, enhanced by the island's deep-rooted mythology, its devotion to traditional culture and ethereal landscapes. With only six surnames among the locals, most given names are highly descriptive.

The wheels of change turn very slowly here. Electricity wasn't fully reliable until 1997. Given that there's at best 15cm of topsoil for farmers to eke out a living, the slow conversion of the economy to tourism has been welcome. Day-trippers from Doolin (as many as 1000 on a balmy summer weekend), 8km across the water, enliven the hiking paths all summer long.

⊙ Sights & Activities

Wandering the lanes with their ivy-covered stone walls and making discoveries here and there is the best way to experience the island. Two marked paths offer routes around the island. Set off from the dock on foot or bicycle, or with a driver. A meander covering the main sites will take about four hours on foot. With more time – or days – you can really savour Inisheer.

★ Tobar Éinne   HISTORIC SITE

Locals still carry out a pilgrimage known as the *Turas*, to the Well of Enda – an ever-burbling spring in a remote rocky expanse in the southwest. The ceremony involves, over the course of three consecutive Sundays, picking up seven stones from the ground nearby and walking around the small well seven times, putting one stone down each time, while saying the rosary until an elusive eel appears from the well's watery depths. If, during this ritual, you're lucky enough to see the eel, it's said your tongue will be bestowed with healing powers, enabling you to literally lick wounds.

O'Brien's Castle   HISTORIC BUILDING

A 100m climb to the island's highest point yields dramatic views over clover-covered fields to the beach and harbour. This 15th-century church (Caisleán Uí Bhriain) was built within the remains of a ring fort called Dún Formna, dating from as early as the 1st century AD. Nearby is an 18th-century signal tower.

Teampall Chaoimháin   HISTORIC BUILDING

Named for Inisheer's patron saint, who is buried close by, the roofless 10th-century Church of St Kevin and its small cemetery perch on a tiny bluff near the Strand. On the eve of St Kevin's 14 June feast day, a Mass is held here in the open air at 9pm. The sick sleep here for a night, hoping to be healed.

Cill Ghobnait   CHURCH

The tiny 8th- or 9th-century church is named after St Gobnait, who fled here from Clare while trying to escape an enemy who was pursuing her.

Plassy   HISTORIC SITE

Dating from 1960, this iconic island sight was a freighter that was thrown up on the rocks in bad weather. Miraculously, all on board were saved; Tigh Ned's pub has a collection of photographs and documents detailing the rescue. An aerial shot of the wreck was used in the opening sequence of the TV series *Father Ted*.

WALKING INISHEER'S SHORE

You can circumnavigate Inisheer's 12km shoreline in about five hours and gain a deep understanding of the island that is impossible on a hurried visit to the top sights.

From the Inisheer ferry pier, walk west along the narrow road parallel to the shore and go straight on to the small fishing pier at the northwest corner of the island. Continue along the road with the shingle shore on one side and a dense patchwork of fields, enclosed by the ubiquitous stone walls, on the other. Look for tide pools and grey seals resting in the sun.

About 1km from the acute junction, turn left at the painted sign; about 100m along the paved lane is the Tobar Éinne.

Continue southwest as it becomes a rough track. After about 600m, head roughly south across the limestone pavement and strips of grass to the shore. Follow the gently sloping rock platform around the southwestern headland (Ceann na Faochnaí) and walk east to the lighthouse near Fardurris Point (two hours from the ferry pier).

Stay with the coast, turning northeast. You'll see the wreck of the *Plassy* in the distance. When necessary, use stiles to cross walls and fences around fields. Note that the grass you see grows on about 5cm of topsoil created by islanders who cleared rocks by hand and then stacked up seaweed over decades.

Head north, following the track, which then becomes a sealed road at the northern end of Lough More. Continue following the road along the northern shore of the island, past the airstrip.

At the airstrip you can diverge for Teampall Chaoimháin and O'Brien's Castle. Otherwise rest on the lovely sands of the curving beach and check out the nearby Cnoc Rathnaí, a Bronze Age burial mound (1500 BC), which is remarkably intact considering it was buried under the sand until the 19th century, when it was rediscovered.

Aran Islands Scenery

Blasted by the wind and washed over by waves, the eroded, striated slivers of rock known as the Aran Islands hold a fascination for travellers. Rocky extensions of the Burren in County Clare, they are home to descendants of unimaginably hardy folk who forged their own culture of survival.

Inishmaan

Escape the crowds on Inishmaan, the least visited of the Arans. You'll see few others on walks across the dramatic countryside, where every path seems to pass the mysterious remains of past lives and end on a beach trod only by you.

Aran Islands

Left to nature, the Arans would be bare rocks in the Atlantic. But generations of islanders have created green – seaweed and sand gathered and spread by hand over the centuries finally rewards with fertile fields.

Inishmór

A thousand day-trippers on a summer weekend come to Inishmór to see one of Ireland's most impressive ancient wonders. Dún Aengus has been guarding a bluff over the Atlantic for 2000 years.

Inisheer

An old castle, ancient churches and a magical spring are just a few of the highlights of Inisheer, the smallest of the Arans. Centuries of history are preserved in rock.

The Plassy Wreck

Star of the opening sequence of the comedy classic *Father Ted*, the *Plassy* was driven ashore on Inisheer by storms in 1963. Its rusting hulk attracts walkers and is the perfect image of the timeless force of the elements.

1. Stone Age fort Dún Aengus, Inishmór **2.** The wreck of the *Plassy* **3.** Ancient stone walls, Inisheer

IIC / AXIOM / GETTY IMAGES ©

Áras Éanna   ARTS CENTRE

(☑099-75150; www.araseanna.ie; ⊙Jun-Sep) In-isheer's large community arts centre sits out on an exposed stretch of the northern side of the island, a 15-minute walk from the village. It has visiting artists programs and various cultural programs and performances.

✴ Festivals & Events

★ Craiceann Inis Oírr International Bodhrán Summer School   CULTURAL

(www.craiceann.com; concerts €15; ⊙late Jun) The island reverberates to the thunder of traditional drums when Bodhrán master-classes, lectures and performances are held. Craiceann takes its name from the Irish word for 'skin', referring to the goat skin used to make these circular drums. The festival features top talent and nightly drumming sessions take place in the pubs.

🛏 Sleeping & Eating

Book well in advance during Craiceann week in June. There is camping (with toilets and showers) at the official site by the main beach. The three pubs are all worth a visit. Confirm opening hours outside Doolin ferry season (March to October).

Brú Radharc Na Mara Hostel   HOSTEL €

(☑099-75024; www.bruhostelaran.com; dm €18-25, r €50; ⊙Mar-Oct; @🖥) Handily located next to a pub and by the pier, this spotless hostel has ocean views, a large kitchen, a warming fireplace and bikes for hire. The owners also run the adjacent B&B, which has basic rooms.

★ Fisherman's Cottage & South Aran House   B&B €€

(☑099-75073; www.southaran.com; Castle Village; s/d €50/80, dinner mains €12 to €20; ⊙Apr-Oct; 🖥) Slow-food enthusiasts run this sprightly B&B and cafe that's a mere five-minute walk from the pier. Lavender grows in profusion at the entrance. Food (nonguests can enjoy cakes by day and dinner at night, but will need to book) celebrates local seafood and organic produce. Rooms are simple yet stylish. Kayaking and fishing are among the activities on offer.

Radharc an Chláir   B&B €€

(☑099-75019; bridpoil@eircom.net; r €45-90) This pleasant, modern B&B near O'Brien's Castle has views of the Cliffs of Moher and Galway Bay. Book several weeks ahead, as hostess Brid Poil's home cooking draws many repeat visitors. Guests can arrange evening meals (€20). Some rooms share bathrooms.

Tigh Ruairí   PUB €€

(Strand House; ☑099-75020; www.tighruairi.com; r €50-90; @) Rory Conneely's atmospheric digs host live music sessions in the cosy pub. There are 20 basic rooms, many with views across the waters.

Tigh Ned   PUB €

(meals €5-10) Here since 1897, Tigh Ned is a welcoming, unpretentious place, with lively traditional music and inexpensive lunch-time fare. Tables in the garden have harbour views.

ℹ Information

In summer a small **kiosk** (⊙10am-6pm Jul-Aug) at the harbour provides tourist information. Like Inishmaan, there's no ATM; bring euros.

Online, www.inisoirr.ie is a handy resource.

ℹ Getting Around

Bicycles can be rented from **Rothair Inis Oírr** (www.rothai-inisoirr.com; per day from €10; ⊙May-Sep), which is near the pier and has a good map. Most places to stay also rent bikes to nonguests.

You can take a tour of the island on a **pony trap** (per person per hr €5-15) in summer. For a great exploration by car, try **Eanna Seoighe** (☑087 284 0767, 099-75040).

CONNEMARA

The filigreed coast of the Connemara Peninsula is endlessly pleasing, with pockets of sheer delight awaiting discovery.

The name Connemara (Conamara) is Irish for 'Inlets of the Sea' and the coastal roads bear this out as they wind around small bays and coves, some with hidden beaches. A succession of seaside hamlets entice.

Connemara's interior is a kaleidoscope of rusty bogs, lonely valleys and shimmering black lakes. At its heart are the Maumturk Mountains and the pewter-tinged quartzite peaks of the Twelve Bens mountain range, with a network of scenic hiking and biking trails. Everywhere the land is laced by stone walls you're glad you didn't have to build. It's dazzling at any time of day but especially when the sky and waters sparkle azure, the hills shine green and bright yellow blooms abound.

❶ Information

Galway's tourist office has lots of information on the area. Online, **Connemara Tourism** (www.connemara.ie) and **Go Connemara** (www.goconnemara.com) have region-wide info and links.

❶ Getting There & Around

BUS

Organised bus tours from Galway are many and offer a good overview of the region, though ideally you'll want more than one day to absorb the area's charms, plus you'll want the freedom to make your own discoveries.

Bus Éireann (✆091-562 000; www.buseireann.ie) Serves most of Connemara. Services can be sporadic, and many buses operate May to September only, or July and August only. Some drivers will stop in between towns.

Citylink (www.citylink.ie) Has several buses a day linking Galway city with Clifden, with stops in Moycullen, Oughterard, Maam Cross and Recess, and on to Cleggan and Letterfrack. If you're going somewhere between towns, you might be able to arrange a drop-off with the driver.

CAR

Your own wheels are the best way to get off this scenic region's beaten track – though watch out for the narrow roads' stone walls.

Keep an eye out, too, for meandering Connemara sheep – characterised by thick creamy fleece and coal-black faces and legs – which frequently wander onto the road. Even Connemara's flattest stretches of road tend to be bumpy due to the uneven bog beneath the tarmac.

Oughterard & Around

POP 1400

The workady village of Oughterard (Uachtar Árd) is one of Ireland's principal angling centres. Immediately west, the countryside opens up to sweeping panoramas of lakes, mountains and bogs, which get more spectacular the further you travel.

◉ Sights

If you see tourists wandering around, talking with a drawl and calling people 'pilgrim', it's probably because they are here to relive the iconic film *The Quiet Man*.

★**Aughnanure Castle**　　　CASTLE
(www.heritageireland.com; off N59; adult/child €3/1; ⊙9.30am-6pm Apr–mid-Oct) Built around 1500, this bleak fortress was home to the 'Fighting O'Flahertys', who controlled the re-

GUIDED WALKS IN CONNEMARA

Maps of the many walking trails in Connemara are sold at bookshops and tourist offices. However, to really appreciate the region's unique geology, natural beauty and ancient history, you may wish to go with a guide.

Connemara Safari (✆095-21071; www.walkingconnemara.com; tours €300-700; ⊙Jun-Sep) runs three- and five-day tours in the region that include meals and accommodation. Tour leaders are experts in fields such as archaeology. Routes include some of the deserted islands off the coast.

gion for hundreds of years after they fought off the Normans. The six-storey tower house stands on a rocky outcrop overlooking Lough Corrib and has been extensively restored. Surrounding the castle are the remains of an unusual double *bawn* (area surrounded by walls outside the main castle, acting as a defence and a place to keep cattle in times of trouble), and underneath the castle the lake washes through a number of natural caverns and caves.

Aughnanure Castle is situated 3km east of Oughterard.

Glengowla Mines　　INDUSTRIAL MUSEUM
(www.glengowlamines.ie; off N59; adult/child €10/4; ⊙10am-6pm mid-Mar–mid-Nov) For such ugly work, it's amazing that beautiful materials were extracted from this mine, a 19th-century hole in the ground that yielded all manner of silver, glistening quartz and much more. Visitors learn about the tough lives led here and see some of the beauty left inside. It is 3km west of Oughterard.

Brigit's Garden　　GARDEN
(www.galwaygarden.com; off N59, Roscahill; adult/child €7/4.50; ⊙10am-5.30pm Feb-Oct) Can you feel the power of the crystal? Halfway between the villages of Moycullen and Oughterard is Brigit's Garden, a New Age place with lots of lovely plants, yoga classes, Celtic festivals, mythology and a vegetarian cafe.

🛏 Sleeping & Eating

Canrawer Holiday Hostel　　HOSTEL €
(✆091-552 388; www.oughterardhostel.com; Station Rd; dm €17-20, d from €46; ⊙Feb-Oct; @)

Connemara

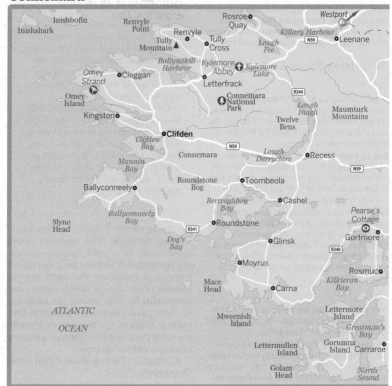

Dorms and family rooms are bright and clean, and there's an outdoor patio where you can chat with other guests while enjoying views of the 1-hectare rural site, 1km from the centre of town. If you want to catch the area's wild brown trout for dinner, the owner will guide you for a fee.

★ **Currarevagh House** HOTEL €€
(☑ 091-552 312; www.currarevagh.com; Glann Rd; r €90-160; ⊘ mid-Mar–Oct; 🛜) Discover romance at this rambling 19th-century mansion, on vast grounds along Lough Corrib. In fact, you might get your romantic vibes from the inn itself: it was given to the ancestors of the present owners as a wedding gift in 1846. Fresh flowers scent the timeless halls and the grounds invite lazy rambles. Meals feature locally caught trout.

Waterfall Lodge B&B €€
(☑ 091-552 168; www.waterfalllodge.net; off N59; s/d from €50/80) Decorated in rose-coloured hues and lit by glowing lamps, this double-fronted traditional-style B&B stands amid wooded gardens beside a brook, a lovely five-minute walk from the village centre. Antiques fill the rooms (try your hand at the old piano).

ℹ Information

The website www.oughterardtourism.com is useful.

ℹ Getting There & Away

Bus Éireann (www.buseireann.ie) and **Citylink** (www.citylink.ie) have regular buses from Galway to Oughterard.

Lough Corrib

The Republic's biggest lake, Lough Corrib, virtually cuts off western Galway from the rest of the country. Over 48km long and cov-

ering some 200 sq km, it encompasses more than 360 islands.

Lough Corrib is world-famous for its salmon, sea trout and brown trout. The highlight of the fishing calendar is the mayfly season, when zillions of the small bugs hatch over a few days (usually in May) and drive the fish – and anglers – into a frenzy. Salmon begin running around June.

In Oughterard, the owner of Canrawer House is a good contact for information and boat hire, as is Thomas Tuck's Fishing Tackle (☑ 091-552 335; Main St, Oughterard; ☺ 9am-6.30pm Mon-Sat), an excellent shop teeming with local knowledge.

The largest island on Lough Corrib, Inchagoill is a lonely place hiding many ancient remains. Most fascinating is an obelisk called Lia Luguaedon Mac Menueh (Stone of Luguaedon, Son of Menueh), which marks a burial site. It stands about 75cm tall, near the Saints' Church, and some people claim

that the Latin writing on the stone is the second-oldest Christian inscription in Europe, after those in the catacombs in Rome. Teampall Phádraig (St Patrick's Church) is a small oratory of a very early design, with some later additions. The prettiest church is the Romanesque Teampall na Naoimh (Saints' Church), probably built in the 9th or 10th century. There are carvings around the arched doorway.

Corrib Cruises (☑ 092-46029; www.corrib cruises.com; adult/child €28/14; ☺ noon Wed-Mon Easter-Oct) has day cruises from Oughterard to Inchagoill and Ashford Castle near Cong.

North of Lough, you can literally go to the dogs near the town of Clonbur. Joyce Country Sheepdogs (☑ 094-954 8853; www. joycecountrysheepdogs.ie; Clonbur; adult/child €7/3; ☺ 3pm Mon-Fri Jun-Sep) offers a chance to see the amazing feats performed by working sheepdogs on an actual farm. Book in advance.

Coastal Drive – Galway City to Mace Head

The slow coastal route between Galway and Connemara takes you past pretty seascapes and villages, although the fun doesn't really begin until after Spiddal.

Opposite the popular Blue Flag beach Silver Strand, 4.8km west of Galway on the R336, are the Barna Woods, a dense, deep green forest preserved for rambling and picnicking. The woods contain the last natural growing oaks in Ireland's west.

Spiddal (An Spidéal) is a refreshingly untouched little village, and the start of the Gaeltacht region. As you approach the village look for the Spiddal Craft & Design Studios (www.ceardlann.com; off R336, Spiddal; ☺ hours vary), where you can watch leatherworkers, sculptors, and weavers plus enjoy a cake at the lauded cafe Builin Blasta.

Experience life in a 17th-century Connemara hill village at Cnoc Suain (☑ 091-555 703; www.cnocsuain.com; Spiddal), a restored and recreated glimpse of pre-Famine life in the countryside. Learn about original dance, language, song and the thatched-roof-cottage lifestyles of the time. It's set amid a large tract of preserved landscape and is 5km north of Spiddal.

Exceptional traditional music sessions take place at the unassuming Tigh Hughes (Spiddal; ☺ Trad sessions 9pm Tue), where it's not uncommon for major musicians to turn

BRIDGING THE QUIET MAN

Whenever an American cable TV station needs a ratings boost with older viewers (and it's already just shown *Gone With the Wind*), it trots out the iconic 1952 film *The Quiet Man*. Starring John Wayne and filmed in lavish colour to capture the crimson locks of his co-star Maureen O'Hara, the film regularly makes the top-10 lists of ageing romantic-comedy lovers for its high-energy portrayal of rural Irish life, replete with drinking and fighting, fighting and drinking etc.

Director John Ford returned to his Irish roots and filmed the movie almost entirely on location in Connemara and the little village of Cong (the beach horse-racing sequences were shot at Lettergesh), just over the border in County Mayo. One of the most photogenic locations in the film, the eponymous Quiet Man Bridge, is just 3km west of Oughterard off the N59. Looking much as it did in the film, the picture-perfect little arched span (whose original name was Leam Bridge) would be a lovely spot even if it hadn't achieved screen immortality. Purists will note, however, that the scene based here had close-ups done on a cheesy set back in Hollywood. That's showbiz.

Hard-core fans will want to buy the excellent book, *The Complete Guide to The Quiet Man* by Des MacHale. It's sold in most tourist offices in the area.

up unannounced and join in the craic. The pub's just adjacent to the main street; turn right at the crossroads next to the bank and it's on your right. Numerous places to stay line the main road.

West of Spiddal the scenery becomes more dramatic, with parched fields crisscrossed by low stone walls rolling to a ragged shore. Carraroe (An Cheathrú Rua) has fine beaches, including the Coral Strand, which is composed entirely of shell and coral fragments. It's worth wandering the small roads on all sides of Greatman's Bay to discover tiny inlets and little coves, often watched over by the genial local donkeys.

Lettermore, Gorumna and Lettermullen islands are low and bleak, with a handful of farmers eking out an existence from minute, rocky fields. Fish farming is big business.

Near Gortmore, along the R340, is Patrick Pearse's Cottage (Teach an Phiarsaigh; www.heritageireland.ie; R340; adult/child €3/1; ☉10am-6pm Easter & Jun-Aug). Pádraig Pearse (1879–1916) led the Easter Rising with James Connolly in 1916; after the revolt he was executed by the British. Pearse wrote some of his short stories and plays in this small thatched cottage with lovely views.

The scenic R340 swings south along Kilkieran Bay, an intricate and interlinked system of tidal marshes, bogs, swift-flowing streams and elaborate tidal basins. This environmentally protected area contains an amazing diversity of life.

Continuing on, Carna is a small fishing village, with pleasant walks out to Mween-

ish Island or north to Moyrus and out to the wild headlands at Mace Head.

🛏 Sleeping

If you aren't planning to make Roundstone or beyond by nightfall, you'll find tidy B&Bs dotting the countryside. Many have water views.

★ Cashel House Hotel   HOTEL €€
(☑095-31001; www.cashel-house-hotel.com; Cashel; s/d from €85/170; ☎) At the head of Cashel Bay, this flowered fantasy of a country mansion has 32 period rooms surrounded by 17 hectares of woodland and gardens. It also has a stable of Connemara ponies (riding lessons available), a superb dining room and even a small private beach.

Cloch na Scíth   B&B €€
(☑091-553 364; www.thatchcottage.com; Kellough, Spiddal; r €45-80) Set in a story-book garden roamed by ducks and chickens, this century-old thatched cottage has a warm, friendly host, Nancy, who cooks bread in an iron pot over the peat fire (as her grandmother taught her and as she'll teach you).

Lough Inagh Valley

This stark brown landscape beguiles by its very simplicity.

The R344 enters the valley from the south, just west of playfully named Recess. The moody waters of Loughs Derryclare and Inagh reflect the colours of the moment. On the western side is the brooding Twelve

Bens mountain range. At the north end of the valley, the R344 meets the N59, which loops around Connemara to Leenane.

Towards the northern end of the valley, a track leads west off the road up a blind valley, which is well worth exploring.

Sleeping & Eating

Ben Lettery Hostel HOSTEL €
(☑085 271 3588; www.anoige.ie; N59, Ballinafad; dm €15-20, d €80; ⊙check-in 5-10pm, Apr-Sep; ☏) About 8km west of where the R344 enters the Lough Inagh Valley (and 13km east of Clifden) stands this renovated YHA hostel. It has a tidy, homey kitchen and living room, and is an excellent base for exploring the valley. Citylink buses will stop here on request.

Lough Inagh Lodge LODGE €€
(☑091-34706; www.loughinaghlodgehotel.ie; off R344; s/d from €100/145; dinner €40; ☏) Steeped in Victorian grandeur, the atmospheric Lough Inagh is midway up the gorgeous Lough Inagh Valley 4.5km north of Recess. Set against a hill, it has a plum position on the water. Peat fires lend the cosy public spaces a scent that says 'country'. You start breathing deeply from the time you enter one of the 13 rooms.

Roundstone

POP 250
Clustered around a boat-filled harbour, Roundstone (Cloch na Rón) is the kind of Irish village you hoped to find. Colourful terrace houses and inviting pubs overlook the shimmering recess of Bertraghboy Bay, which is home to dramatic tidal flows, lobster trawlers and traditional *currachs* with tarred canvas bottoms stretched over wicker frames.

Sights & Activities

Wander the short promenade for views over the water to ribbons of eroded land.

Roundstone Musical Instruments MUSIC
(www.bodhran.com; IDA Craft Park; ⊙9am-7pm Jul-Sep, 9.30am-6pm Mon-Sat Oct-Jun) Just south of the village is Malachy Kearns' music shop, home to Ireland's only full-time maker of traditional Bodhráns. Watch him work, and buy a tin whistle, harp or booklet filled with Irish ballads; there's also a small free folk museum and a cafe. Adjacent craft shops sell everything from fine pottery (don't miss Roundstone Ceramics) to sweaters.

Mt Errisberg WALKING
Looming above the stone pier is Mt Errisberg (298m), the only significant hill along this section of coastline. The pleasant walk from Roundstone to the top takes about two hours. Follow the small road past O'Dowd's pub in the centre of the village. From the summit there are wonderful views across the bay to the distant humps of the Twelve Bens.

Sleeping & Eating

★**Wits End B&B** B&B €
(☑091-35813; www.roundstoneaccommodation.com; Main St; s/d from €30/50; ⊙Mar-Nov; ☏) Right in the centre of town, this pink palace (well, modest pink house) has rooms looking over the road to the water. It's basic but comfortable and is a mere stumble from the fine pubs.

Roundstone House HOTEL €€
(☑091-35864; www.roundstonehousehotel.com; Main St; s/d from €45/90, pub lunch mains €10, dinner mains €20-30; ⊙Apr-Oct) A dignified presence lining Main St, this sprawling inn has 12 restful rooms with tea kettles and other creature comforts, plus views across the bay. The pub, Vaughan's, has trad sessions some nights in summer and you can enjoy pints and local seafood out on the terrace.

Island View B&B B&B €€
(☑095-35701; www.islandview.ie; Main St; s €35-45, d €55-70; ☏) Right in the heart of Roundstone, this ubercomfortable B&B has lots of

COUNTY GALWAY ROUNDSTONE

little plush touches. Rooms have views of the bay.

★ **O'Dowd's** SEAFOOD €€
(☎ 091-35809; www.odowdsseafoodbar.com; Main St; mains €13-22; ⊙ restaurant 10am-9.30pm Jun-Sep, to 9pm Oct-May) This well-worn, comfortable old pub hasn't lost any of its authenticity since it starred in the 1997 Hollywood flick *The Matchmaker*. Specialities at its adjoining restaurant include seafood sourced off the old stone dock right across the street. Produce comes from O'Dowd's own garden. There's a good list of Irish microbrews and you can get breakfast before noon.

Roundstone to Clifden

The R341 shadows the coast from Roundstone to Clifden. Beaches along here have such beautiful white sand and turquoise water that, if you added 10°C to the temperature, you could be in Antigua. About 2.5km from Roundstone, look for the turn to **Gurteen Bay** (sometimes spelt Gorteen Bay). After a further 800m there is a turn for **Dog's Bay**. Together, the pair form the two sides of a dog-bone-shaped peninsula lined with idyllic beaches. Park and enjoy a day strolling the grassy heads and frolicking on the hard-packed sand.

Gurteen Beach Caravan & Camping Park (☎ 091-35882; www.gurteenbay.com; off R341; campsites from €20, caravans from €100; ⊙ Mar-Oct; ⊛) is a peaceful, well-equipped campground in a great spot above the beaches.

At **Ballyconneely** take a detour west off the R341 and visit **Connemara Smokehouse** (www.smokehouse.ie; Bunowen Pier; ⊙ 9am-5pm Mon-Fri). You'll learn about how the region's iconic salmon is smoked and get to try some samples.

Clifden & Around

POP 2100

Connemara's 'capital', Clifden (An Clochán), is an appealing Victorian-era country town with a vaguely harp-shaped oval of streets offering evocative strolls. It presides over the head of the narrow bay where the River Owenglin tumbles into the sea. The surrounding countryside beckons you to walk through woods and above the shoreline.

⊙ Sights & Activities

This is pony country and rides along the beaches are popular. You can see the ponies at their swiftest during the annual **Connemara Pony Show** (www.cpbs.ie; ⊙ mid-Aug). It draws punters from across western Ireland.

Take the 15-minute stroll down Beach Rd to the **harbour** and look back for the view of Clifden's steeples reflected off the tidal waters.

★ **Sky Road** WALKING, CYCLING
This 12km route traces a spectacular loop out to the township of Kingston and back to Clifden, taking in some rugged, stunningly beautiful coastal scenery en route.

The round trip of about 12km can be easily walked or cycled. Head directly west from Clifden's Market Square.

Connemara Heritage & History Centre
MUSEUM

(www.connemaraheritage.com; N59, Lettershea; adult/child €8/4; ⊙ 10am-6pm Apr-Oct; ☎) Farmer Dan O'Hara lived here until his eviction from the farm and subsequent emigration to New York, where he ended up selling matches on the street. Its present owners have restored the property, turning it into a window onto lost traditional ways, with demonstrations of bog cutting, thatching, sheep shearing and so on. It's possible to stay at the farmhouse in more comfort than Dan ever enjoyed. The homestead is 7km east of Clifden.

Station House Museum
MUSEUM

(Clifden Station House; off Hulk St; adult/child €2/1; ⊙ 10am-5pm Mon-Sat, noon-4pm Sun May-Oct) Located in an old train shed in the upscale hotel development, this small museum is devoted to the story of local ponies and various historic events.

Mannion's Bikes
BICYCLE RENTAL

(www.clifdenbikes.com; Bridge St; bike rental from €15 per day; ⊙ 10am-6pm Mon-Sat, 10am-noon Sun) Has a large selection of bikes.

Errislannan Manor
HORSE RIDING

(☑ 095-21134; www.connemaraponyriding.com; Ballyconneely Rd/R341; rides per hour from €30) Guides provide lessons and lead treks along the beach and up into the hills on the iconic local ponies. It's 3.5km south of Clifden.

🛏 Sleeping

Numerous attractive choices in the centre allow you to easily partake of Clifden's many charms.

Acton's Eco Beach
CAMPGROUND €

(☑ 095-44036; www.actonsbeachsidecamping. com; Omey Island/Claddaghduff Rd; campsites from €15) 🖉 With its own white-sand beach, this ecologically aware campground is a fine holiday refuge. It's 7km west of Clifden. Ask about shuttle services.

Clifden Town Hostel
HOSTEL €

(☑ 095-21076; www.clifdentownhostel.com; Market St; dm €17-22, d from €40) Right in the centre of town, this cheery IHH hostel is set in a cream-coloured house framed by big picture windows. Its sunlit rooms hold 34 beds.

WORTH A TRIP

BOGGY DETOUR TO CLIFDEN

Away from the coast, there is an alternative route between Roundstone and Clifden through protected **Roundstone Bog**. The old road is a bumpy ride, passing through eerie, rust-collared desolation. Locals who believe the bog is haunted won't drive this road at night; indeed, the roughness of the road is reason enough to avoid it after dark. In summer, you might see peat being harvested by hand, as blanket bogs cannot be cut mechanically. The road runs west from a junction on the R341 about 4km north of Roundstone. It rejoins the R341 at Ballinaboy.

⭐ Dolphin Beach
B&B €€

(☑ 095-21204; www.dolphinbeachhouse.com; Lower Sky Rd; s/d from €90/130; ☎) It's hard to find the bones of the 19th-century manor house that forms the basis for this posh B&B set amid some of Connemara's best coastal scenery. Clean lines abound in the bright common areas and in the plush yet relaxed rooms. It's 5km west of Clifden.

⭐ Quay House
HOTEL €€

(☑ 095-21369; www.thequayhouse.com; Beach Rd; s/d from €90/150; ⊙ mid-Mar–mid-Nov; ☎) Down by the harbour, a 10-minute walk from town, this rambling 1820 house has 14 rooms filled with antiques but manages an unfussy style that seems contemporary. Run by an offshoot of the Foyle family of hoteliers, it has pleasures unheard of during its past careers as a convent and monastery.

Ben View House
B&B €€

(☑ 095-21256; www.benviewhouse.com; Bridge St; s/d from €45/70; ☎) This central 1848 town house has a vintage charm provided by timber beams, polished floorboards and old-fashioned hospitality. The nine rooms are nutty with antiques. It caters to cyclists, with special storage areas and a tolerance for sweat.

Dun Ri Guesthouse
INN €€

(☑ 095-21625; www.dunri.ie; Hulk St; r €50-100; ☎) Just down the hill from the centre, in a quiet spot near the pony track, this appealing modern inn has 13 spacious rooms. The included breakfast offers many choices; the cheese plate provides an excellent change from the norm.

Foyles Hotel
HOTEL €€

(☑095-21801; www.foyleshotel.com; Main St; s/d from €60/90; ⊙ Apr-Oct; @) A white-trimmed, Wedgwood-blue landmark in the centre of town, Clifden's oldest hotel has been in the same family for decades. Fresh flowers adorn the stately lobby, service is very accommodating, embers glow in the fireplace and the 25 rooms are comfortable.

✖ Eating & Drinking

Pubs and restaurants cluster around Clifden's town centre. As elsewhere in these parts, seafood reigns supreme.

★ Connemara Hamper
DELI €

(Lower Market St; snacks from €3; ⊙ 10am-5.30pm Mon-Sat) The jolly ladies here will gladly package up a chicken-and-leek pie or other savoury treat for your picnic. There's a wide range of prepared foods and fresh breads.

Lowry's Bar
PUB €

(Market St; mains €6-10) A time-worn local, Lowry's has traditional pleasures, ranging from the age-old, unadorned look of the place to its *céilidh* sessions, which take place at least a couple of nights a week. The food is 'unpretentious Irish' (eg bangers and mash). Good whiskey collection.

★ Mitchell's
SEAFOOD €€

(☑095-21867; Market St; lunch mains €8-12, dinner mains €15-25; ⊙ noon-10pm Mar-Oct) Seafood takes centre stage at this elegant spot. From a velvety chowder right through a long list of ever-changing and inventive specials, the produce of the surrounding waters is honoured. The wine list does the food justice. Book for dinner. (Lunch includes sandwiches and casual fare.)

Off the Square
SEAFOOD €€

(www.offthesquarerestaurant.com; Main St; mains €10-20; ⊙ 9am-10pm) Mediterranean flavours accent the fare at this tasty bistro. Casual fare at lunch gives way to superb meals at night. Besides fine seafood, there are locally sourced steaks. Breakfast is tasty.

Mullarky's Pub
PUB

(Main St) This rollicking pub is a riot of local merriment, with live music many nights.

🛍 Shopping

Clifden Bookshop
BOOKS

(Main St; ⊙ 10am-6pm Mon-Sat) Good for local titles and maps.

ⓘ Information

There are banks with ATMs around Market Sq, as well as a large supermarket.

Tourist office (www.clifdenchamber.ie; Galway Rd/N59; ⊙ 10am-5pm Mon-Sat Easter-Jun & Sep, 10am-5pm daily Jul & Aug) In the Clifden Station House complex.

ⓘ Getting There & Around

Bus Éireann (www.buseireann.ie) and **Citylink** (www.citylink.ie) have several services daily to Galway along the N59. Fares start at €13 and the trip takes 90 minutes, passing Oughterard on the way.

Claddaghduff & Omey Island

Following the ragged and rugged coastline north of Clifden brings you to the tiny village of Claddaghduff (An Cladach Dubh), which is signposted off the road to Cleggan. If you turn west down here by the Catholic church, you will come out on Omey Strand, and at low tide you can drive or walk across the sand to Omey Island (population 20), a low islet of rock, grass, sand and a handful of houses. During summer, horse races are held on Omey Strand.

Cleggan

POP 250

Most visitors ignore Cleggan (An Cloiggean), a small fishing village 16km northwest of Clifden, and hop on the Inishbofin ferry. Big mistake! This classic tiny fishing port exudes charm that starts right at its boat-lined docks.

Oliver's (☑095-44640; www.oliversbar.com; mains €20-25; ⊙ kitchen 5-9pm) is a locally loved seafood pub. The classic facade is as black as a pint of Guinness. Specials depend on the catch but you can always get the crab claws fried in garlic. Upstairs are six simple B&B rooms (from €60).

Nearby, the Pier Bar (Dockside) has a more roguish air although the tables out front under the large trees are just fine.

Citylink (www.citylink.ie) buses continue to Cleggan three times daily from Clifden.

West of Cleggan, narrow looping roads follow the spectacular shoreline. The rocks dotting the broad moors look like stepping stones for giants.

Inishbofin

POP 160

By day sleepy Inishbofin is a haven of tranquillity. You can walk or bike its narrow, deserted lanes, green pastures and sandy beaches, with farm animals and seals for company. But with no *gardaí* to enforce closing times at the pub, at night – you guessed it – Inishbofin has mighty fine craic.

Situated 9km offshore, the island is compact – 6km long by 3km wide – and its highest point is a mere 86m above sea level. Just off the northern beach is Lough Bó Finne, from which the island gets its name; *bó finne* means 'white cow'.

◉ Sights & Activities

St Colman exiled himself to Inishbofin in AD 664, after he fell out with the Church over its adoption of a new calendar. He set up a monastery, supposedly northeast of the harbour, where the more recent ruins of a small 13th-century church still stand. Grace O'Malley, the famous pirate queen, used Inishbofin as a base in the 16th century, and Cromwell's forces captured the island in 1652, using it to jail priests and clerics.

Inishbofin's pristine waters offer superb scuba diving. The beaches are pristine.

★ **Walking Trails** WALKING
(www.inishbofin.com) Evocative trails encourage exploring. There are several looped routes, which you can download from the island website.

Heritage Museum MUSEUM
(⊙ hours vary) FREE Just behind the pier, the small but comprehensive museum gives an overview of the island's history.

Kings Bicycle Hire BICYCLE RENTAL
(☑ 095-45833; on the pier; rental from €15 per day; ⊙ ferry arrivals) The island is well-suited for cycling – albeit not for far.

★☆ Festivals & Events

Inishbofin Arts Festival ARTS FESTIVAL
(www.inishbofin.com; ⊙ mid-May) The island well and truly wakes up during this weekend festival, which includes accordion workshops, archaeological walks, art exhibitions and concerts by high-profile Irish bands.

⊨ Sleeping & Eating

The hotels have good restaurants and there's an excellent pub.

Inishbofin Island Hostel HOSTEL €
(☑ 095-45855; www.inishbofin-hostel.ie; campsite per person €10, dm €15-18, d €40-50; ⊙ Easter-Sep) In an old farmhouse, this snug 38-bed hostel has glassed-in common areas with panoramic views and equally scenic campsites. It's 500m up from the ferry dock.

Doonmore Hotel HOTEL €€
(☑ 095-45804; www.doonmorehotel.com; s/d from €50/80; ⊙ Apr-Sep; 🕾) Close to the harbour, Doonmore has comfortable, unpretentious rooms. Lunch (€15) and dinner (€35) in the dining room take advantage of the abundance of local seafood, and the hotel will pack you a lunch to take while exploring the island.

Lapwing House B&B €€
(☑ 095-45996; www.inishbofin.com; per person from €35; 🕾) Named after the local bird species that breeds on the island (let inspiration take flight), this family-run B&B in a vintage-style building has two rooms. It is a 10-minute walk from the port.

ⓘ Information

Inishbofin's small post office has a grocery shop. There are no ATMs and most businesses only accept cash.

Tourism Association (☑ 095-45861; www.inishbofin.com) Has good info, including detailed online walking guides.

ⓘ Getting There & Away

Ferries from Cleggan to Inishbofin take 30 to 45 minutes and are run by **Island Discovery** (☑ 095-45894/19; www.inishbofinislanddiscovery.com; adult/child return €20/10). In low season there is one ferry a day, rising to three in summer. Dolphins often swim alongside the boats. Confirm ahead, as ferries may be cancelled when seas are rough.

Letterfrack & Around

POP 200

Founded by Quakers in the mid-19th century, Letterfrack (Leitir Fraic) is a crossroads with a few pubs and B&Bs. But the forested setting and nearby coast are a magnet for outdoors adventure seekers. A 4km walk to the peak of Tully Mountain takes 40 minutes and affords wonderful ocean views.

◉ Sights

★ **Connemara National Park** NATIONAL PARK
(www.connemaranationalpark.ie; off N59; ⊙ visitor centre 9am-5.30pm Mar-Oct, park 24hr) FREE

COUNTY GALWAY INISHBOFIN

Immediately southeast of Letterfrack, Connemara National Park spans 2000 dramatic hectares of bog, mountain and heath. The visitor centre is in a beautiful setting off a parking area 300m south of the Letterfrack crossroads.

The park encloses a number of the Twelve Bens, including Bencullagh, Benbrack and Benbaun. The heart of the park is Gleann Mór (Big Glen), through which the River Polladirk flows. There's fine walking up the glen and over the surrounding mountains. There are also short, self-guided walks and, if the Bens look too daunting, you can hike up Diamond Hill nearby.

The visitor centre offers an introduction to the park's flora, fauna and geology, and visitors can scrutinise maps and various trails here before heading out into the park. Various types of flora and fauna native to the area are explained, including the Mothra-sized elephant hawkmoth. There is a tearoom.

Guided nature walks (⊙11am Jul & Aug) depart from the visitor centre several days a week. They last two to three hours and cover rough, boggy terrain.

Kylemore Abbey HISTORIC BUILDING
(www.kylemoreabbeytourism.ie; off N59; adult/child €12.50/free; ⊙9am-6.30pm Apr-Sep, 10am-4.30pm Oct-Mar) Magnificently situated on the shores of a lake, this crenulated 19th-century neo-Gothic fantasy was built for a wealthy English businessman Mitchell Henry, who spent his honeymoon in Connemara. His wife died tragically young.

Admission also covers the abbey's Victorian walled gardens. You can stroll around the lake and surrounding woods for free. Improvements are ongoing and a restaurant, shop and various guided hikes are on offer.

Kylemore's tranquillity is shattered in high summer with the arrival of dozens of tour coaches per day, each one followed through the gates by an average of 50 cars (yes, over 2500 cars a day). It's 4.5km east of Letterfrack.

WORTH A TRIP
CONNEMARA'S NORTH COAST

Although Connemara is a pearl necklace of sights, the north coast is diamond encrusted. Gorgeous beaches compete for your attention with stark, raw mountain vistas and views out to the moody sea.

Eschew the N59 for a series of small roads that follow the twists and turns along the coast for about 15km. Start at Letterfrack, where a narrow track leads northwest. Follow various small roads, sticking as close to the water as you can. Watch for sheep. The land here seems to be in the midst of a beautiful dissolution into the sea. You may find yourself on a road that comes to a dead end at a beach. Good! Get out and frolic.

At Renvyle you can pause for the night. Renvyle Beach Caravan & Camping (☎095-43462; www.renvylebeachcaravanpark.com; Renvyle; campsites €10-20; ⊙Easter-Sep) has campsites on a grassy expanse with direct access to a sandy beach.

Renvyle House Hotel (☎095-43511; www.renvyle.com; Renvyle; r €100-250; ☎⊛) is a luxurious 68-room converted country estate set on 80 hectares. It was once owned by the poet Oliver St John Gogarty (among his better lines: 'If anyone thinks that I amn't divine, He gets no free drinks when I'm making the wine').

Continue east, past a couple of fine country pubs at the tiny crossroads of Tully Cross. Stick to the coast and stop often – especially on sunny days to marvel at the rich kaleidoscope of colours: rich cobalt sea, cerulean sky, emerald-green grass, brown hills, slate-grey rocks and white-sand beaches. The beach horse-racing sequences for The Quiet Man were shot at Lettergesh.

Look for a turn to Rosroe Quay, where a truly magnificent crescent of sand awaits at Glassillaun Beach. If you're drawn to the beauty of the water, Scuba Dive West (☎095-43922; www.scubadivewest.com) is here and runs highly recommended courses and dives around the surrounding coastlines and islands. Rates span the gamut.

Continue southeast along the final 5km stretch of road that runs along Lough Fee. In spring when the gorse explodes in yellow bloom, the views here are, again, simply breathtaking.

🛏 Sleeping

Letterfrack Lodge　　　　　　　　HOSTEL €
(📞 095-41222; www.letterfracklodge.com; Letterfrack; campsites from €12, dm €18-22, d €40-60; @🤶) Close to the Letterfrack crossroads, dorms come in a variety of sizes, but all are spacious. Doubles are like a basic B&B. Mike, the owner, is a great source of info on walks of all kinds through the region.

ℹ Getting There & Away

Bus Éireann (www.buseireann.ie) and **Citylink** (www.citylink.ie) buses continue to Letterfrack at least once a day from Clifden, 15km southwest on the N59.

Leenane & Killary Harbour

The small village of Leenane (also spelled Leenaun) drowses on the shore of dramatic Killary Harbour. Dotted with mussel rafts, the long, narrow harbour is Ireland's only fjord – maybe. Slicing 16km inland and more than 45m deep in the centre, it certainly looks like a fjord, although some scientific studies suggest it may not actually have been glaciated. Mt Mweelrea (819m) towers to its north.

Leenane boasts both stage and screen connections. It was the location for *The Field* (1989), a movie with Richard Harris based on John B Keane's poignant play about a tenant farmer's ill-fated plans to pass on a rented piece of land to his son. The village's name made it onto the theatrical map with the success in London and New York of Martin McDonagh's play *The Beauty Queen of Leenane*.

From here the R335 heads north into County Mayo's stunning Doolough Valley.

The local website (www.leenanevillage.com) is a good source of info.

⊙ Sights

★ Sheep & Wool Centre　　　　　MUSEUM
(www.sheepandwoolcentre.com; Main St; adult/child €5/3; ⊙9.30am-6pm Apr-Oct) After surveying the countryside studded with sheep, you can roam among them here. At this surprisingly compelling little museum you can see spinning and weaving demonstrations and learn about the history of dyeing. The centre's shop sells locally made handcrafts as well as topographical walking maps, and there is a cafe.

🏃 Activities

Killary Cruises　　　　　　　　BOAT TOUR
(www.killarycruises.com; N59; adult/child €21/10; ⊙Apr-Oct) From Nancy's Point, about 2km west of Leenane, Killary Cruises offers 1½-hour cruises of Killary Harbour. Dolphins leap around the boat, which passes by a mussel farm and stops at a salmon farm. There are four cruises daily in summer.

Killary Adventure Centre　　ADVENTURE SPORTS
(📞 095-43411; www.killaryadventure.com; off N59; activities adult/child from €46/31; ⊙10am-5pm) Canoeing, sea kayaking, sailing, rock climbing, windsurfing and day hikes are but a few of the activities on offer at this adventure centre about 3km west of Leenane.

Walks　　　　　　　　　　　　WALKING
There are several excellent walks from Leenane, including one to Aasleagh Waterfall (Eas Liath), about 3km away on the northeastern side of Killary Harbour. Also from Leenane, the road runs west for about 2km along the southern shore. Where the highway veers inland, walkers can continue on an old road along the shore to the tiny fishing community of Rosroe Quay.

🛏 Sleeping & Eating

Farmers and other locals come for quiet pints and warming Irish coffees at the gentle sweep of traditional pubs near the bridge. Savour a pint and a meal outside at one of the picnic tables or inside amid the dark wood panelling and enormous open fireplaces.

Sleepzone Connemara　　　　　HOSTEL €
(📞 095-42929; www.sleepzone.ie; off N59; campsites from €12, dm €16-25, r €30-70; ⊙Mar-Oct; @🤶) This renovated 19th-century property has over 100 beds in spotless dorms and private rooms. Popular with walkers, its amenities include a bar, barbecue terrace, tennis court and bike hire. The hostel is 6km west of Leenane; there are transport links to its sister hostel in Galway City.

★ Delphi Lodge　　　　　　　　LODGE €€€
(📞 095-42222; www.delphilodge.ie; off R335; s/d from €125/290; @🤶) You'll wish the dreamy views at this gorgeous country estate could follow you into your dreams. Set among truly stunning mountain and lake vistas, this isolated country house has 12 posh bedrooms and a bevy of common areas including a library and billiards room. The cooking is

modern Irish, sourced locally. Meals (€55) are taken at a vast communal table. Walks, fishing and much more await outside. The lodge is 13km northwest of Leenane.

★ Blackberry Cafe

MODERN IRISH €€

(☑095-42240; www.blackberryrestaurant.ie; Main St; lunch mains €6-17, dinner mains €20-25; ☺10am-4pm & 6-9pm Easter-Sep, closed Tue Apr-May & Sep) Connemara smoked salmon, chunky chowder, hot-smoked trout and rhubarb tarts are some of the treats on offer all day at this gem of a cafe in the centre of Leenane. At night, dinners are more elaborate affairs.

SOUTH OF GALWAY CITY

Take time to smell the oysters on the busy seaside route between Galway City and County Clare. At Kilcolgan, veer east off the N18 and you'll be rewarded with villages such as Kinvara, whose charms may play havoc with your schedule – if you have one.

Clarinbridge & Kilcolgan

POP 1900

Some 16km south of Galway, Clarinbridge (Droichead an Chláirín) and Kilcolgan (Cill Cholgáin) are at their busiest during the post-summer **Clarinbridge Oyster Festival** (www.clarenbridge.com; ☺mid-Sep). However, the oysters are actually at their best from May to August.

Oysters are celebrated year-round at **Paddy Burke's Oyster Inn** (www.paddyburkes galway.com; off N18, Clarinbridge; mains €10-24; ☺10am-10pm Mon-Sat, from noon Sun), a thatched inn by the bridge dishing up heaped servings in a roadside location on the N18.

Moran's Oyster Cottage (www.moransoys tercottage.com; the Weir, Kilcolgan; mains €14-24; ☺food: noon-9.30pm) is a thatched pub and restaurant with a facade as plain as the inside of an oyster shell. Find a seat on the terrace overlooking Dunbulcaun Bay, where the oysters are reared before they arrive on your plate, and you'll think the world's your... It's a well-marked 2km west of the noxious N18, in a quiet cove near Kilcolgan.

Kinvara

POP 650

The small stone harbour of Kinvara (sometimes spelt Kinvarra) sits smugly at the southeastern corner of Galway Bay, which accounts for its Irish name, Cinn Mhara (Head of the Sea). It's a posh little village, the kind of place where all the jeans have creases in them. It makes a good pit stop between Galway and Clare.

Kinvara's website (www.kinvara.com) has info.

⊙ Sights

Dunguaire Castle

HISTORIC BUILDING

(www.shannonheritage.com; off N67; adult/child €6/3; ☺10am-4pm April-early Oct) The chesspiece-style Dunguaire Castle was erected around 1520 by the O'Hynes clan and is in excellent condition following extensive restoration. It is widely believed that the castle occupies the former site of the 6th-century royal palace of Guaire Aidhne, the king of Connaught.

The least authentic way to visit the castle is to attend a **medieval banquet** (☑061-360 788; www.shannonheritage.com; banquet adult/child €44/22; ☺5.30pm & 8.45pm Apr-Oct). Stage shows and shtick provide diversions while you plough through a big group meal.

★☆ Festivals & Events

Fleadh na gCuach

MUSIC

(☺early May) Kinvara's other big date on its annual calendar is the Cuckoo Festival, a traditional music festival that features over 100 musicians performing at upwards of 50 organised sessions. Spin-off events include a parade.

Cruinniú na mBáid

BOAT RACES

(☺2nd weekend in Aug) Traditional Galway hooker sailing boats race here each year in the Cruinniú na mBáid (Gathering of the Boats).

✕ Eating & Drinking

Kinvara has good places to feast on the bounty of its seaside location; a bevy of atmospheric pubs only add to the joy. You won't miss out at the appropriately named **Fahy's Travellers Inn** (☑091-637 116; Main St) and nearby **Connolly's** (☑091-637 131; Main St) on the quay.

★ Keough's

PUB €€

(Main St, Kinvara; mains €7-22; ☺kitchen 9am-9pm; ⏶) This friendly local, where you'll often hear Irish spoken, serves up a fresh battered cod; specials are more ambitious and allow the kitchen to show off its considerable talents. Traditional music sessions take place on Mondays and Thursdays, while Saturday nights swing with old-time dancing.

ℹ Getting There & Away

Bus Éireann (www.buseireann.ie) links Kinvara with Galway city (30 minutes) and towns in County Clare, such as Doolin, up to three times daily.

EASTERN GALWAY

Lough Corrib separates eastern Galway from the dramatic landscape of Connemara and the county's western coast, and this region is markedly different. This is farm country and there's nary a hint of the geologic drama and cultural excitement that exists in the west of the county. Several diversions provide good reason to exit the M6 to Dublin.

Galway East Tourism (www.galwayeast. com) has regional information.

ℹ Getting There & Away

Bus Éireann (www.buseireann.ie) local services connect Galway with Athenry, Ballinasloe and Loughrea.

Athenry

POP 3900

Just 16km east of Galway, Athenry takes its name from a nearby ford (*áth* in Irish) that crosses the River Clare east of the settlement and was the meeting point for three kingdoms, hence Áth an Rí (Ford of the Kings).

The name is synonymous with the stirring song 'The Fields of Athenry', composed by Pete St John in the 1970s, which recounts incarceration resulting from the Famine. Often thought to be adapted from an 1880s ballad (disputed by St John), it's been covered by countless artists and is sung by passionate crowds at sporting matches, including in adapted forms such as Liverpool Football Club's anthem, 'The Fields of Anfield Road'.

The town's old-school website (www. athenry.net) has info.

◉ Sights

Touted as Ireland's most intact collection of medieval architecture, under-visited Athenry boasts the restored Norman-era Athenry

Castle (www.heritageireland.ie; adult/child €3/1; ⊙10am-6pm Easter-Sep), the Medieval Parish Church of St Mary's, a Dominican priory with superb masonry on its occupational gravestones, and an original market cross.

Athenry Arts & Heritage
Activity Centre   MUSEUM
(☑091-844 661; www.athenryheritagecentre.com; The Square; admission €4-7.50; ⊙hours vary) This fascinating heritage centre explores the town's medieval sights and has a fab walking-tour map. It organises recreations of medieval life.

✕ Eating

Old Barracks Pantry   CAFE €
(www.oldbarracks.ie; Main St; mains €6-20; ⊙9am-6pm Mon-Sat, noon-7pm Sun, 6.30-9.30pm Thu-Sat) When you're tired of strolling about and catching surprising ancient views, seek restoration here with upscale cafe fare and baked goods. Evening meals are elaborate affairs.

Loughrea & Around

POP 5000

Named for the little lake at its southern edge, Loughrea (Baile Locha Riach) is a bustling market town 26km southeast of Galway. Loughrea has the shallow remnant of a medieval moat, which runs from the lake at Fair Green near the cathedral to the River Loughrea north of town. Since the opening of the M6, the town is less frenetic with traffic and is good for a stroll.

Not to be confused with St Brendan's Church on Church St, which is now a library, St Brendan's Catholic Cathedral (Barrack St; ⊙11.30am-1pm & 2-5.30pm Mon-Fri), dating from 1902, is renowned for its Celtic-revival stained-glass windows, furnishings and polished granite columns.

Near Bullaun, 7km north of Loughrea on the R350, is the pillar-like Turoe Stone, covered in delicate La Tène–style relief carvings. It dates from between 300 BC and AD 100 and was found at an Iron Age fort a few kilometres away.

East to Ballinasloe, 6.5km from Loughrea, the Dartfield Horse Museum & Park (www. dartfield.com; off R446; adult/child €10/5; ⊙9am-6pm; ♿) allows horse lovers to learn about the horse's role in Irish history. The pony rides thrill kids and you can book longer riding adventures on horseback.

Gort & Around

POP 2700

If you're a fan of WB Yeats, two sights connected to the great poet near the agricultural town of Gort are a worthwhile detour on your way to or from Galway on the M/N18.

◉ Sights

Central to Gort is the Square, with its personable Christ the King statue and shop-filled streets radiating out. But most sights are just outside town.

★ **Thoor Ballylee** HISTORIC BUILDING
(☑091-537 700; www.thoorballylee.com; Peterswell; adult/child €6/1.50; ⊙ 9.30am-5pm Mon-Sat May-Sep) This 16th-century Norman tower was the summer home of WB Yeats from 1921 to 1929 and was the inspiration for one of his best-known works, *The Tower*. In a truly inspired setting by a stream, the tower contains the poet's furnishings. Yeats once wrote 'The sand is running from the upper glass, And when the last grain's through, I shall be lost', a quote which you may well relate to after your last grain falls through while you try to find this place.

From Gort take the Loughrea road (N66) for about 3km northeast and look for the signs, but these are often misaligned, or just missing. Be prepared to ask.

Coole Park PARK
(www.coolepark.ie; off N18; ⊙10am-5pm Wed-Sun Apr & Sep, daily May-Aug) **FREE** Once the home of Lady Augusta Gregory, co-founder of the Abbey Theatre and a patron of WB Yeats, the house here was demolished by bureaucrats in 1941. But displays recall its literary legacy and the present-day nature reserve is a beautiful place to stroll. Look for the autograph tree, on which many of Lady Gregory's literary guests carved their initials. It's about 3km north of Gort.

Kiltartan Gregory Museum MUSEUM
(Kiltartan Cross; adult/child €3/1; ⊙11am-5pm daily Jun-Aug, 1-5pm Sun May & Sep) Housed in an old schoolhouse, this museum traces the life of WB Yeats' literary patron, Lady Augusta Gregory. It's close to Coole Park.

★ **Kilmacduagh** HISTORIC SITE
(off R460) This extensive monastic site beside a small lake includes a well-preserved 34m-high round tower, the remains of a small 14th-century cathedral (Teampall Mór MacDuagh), an oratory dedicated to St John the Baptist, and other little chapels. The original monastery is thought to have been founded by St Colman MacDuagh at the beginning of the 7th century. It's about 5km southwest of Gort.

❶ Getting There & Away

The M18 from Ennis stops at Gort and tosses drivers onto the less fancy N18 (latest date for completion of the M18 to the M6 is 2016). Still, it has extracted traffic from the centre. Most Galway–Ennis buses stop here, as do trains on the Ennis–Galway railway line.

Ballinasloe

POP 6500

Just off the M6, Ballinasloe (Béal Átha na Sluaighe) is famed for its historic horse fair (www.ballinasloeoctoberfair.com; ⊙early Oct), which dates right back to the high kings of Tara. The fair has an old-time carnival atmosphere, created by the 80,000-plus horse traders and merrymakers who roll into town. They include Ireland's Traveller community, who camp nearby in traditional barrel-topped wagons.

Around 6km southwest of town on the R446, Aughrim was the site of the bloodiest battle ever fought on Irish soil, which ended in a crucial victory in 1691 by William of Orange over the Catholic forces of James II. The Battle of Aughrim Interpretive Centre (adult/child €5/2; ⊙10.30am-4pm Tue-Sat, 2-5pm Sun Jun-Aug) helps place it within the context of the War of the Two Kings. Battle sites pepper the surrounding countryside, but thickets of signs often leave visitors going in circles when the centre is closed (it has essential directions).

Heading 21km southeast of Ballinasloe brings you to 12th-century Clonfert Cathedral. It's on the site of a monastery said to have been founded in AD 563 by St Brendan 'the Navigator', who is believed to be buried here. The jury is out on whether St Brendan reached America's shores in a tiny *currach*.

The marvellous six-arch Romanesque doorway, adorned with surreal human heads, is reason enough to visit. The cathedral is off the R356.

Portumna

POP 1600

In the southeast corner of the county, the lakeside town of Portumna is popular for boating and fishing.

Impressive **Portumna Castle & Gardens** (www.heritageireland.ie; Castle Ave; adult/child €3/1; ⊙9.30am-6pm Apr–mid-Sep) was built in the early 1600s by Richard de Burgo and boasts an elaborate, geometrically laid-out organic garden. Don't miss the moody ruins of a 15th-century **friary** down towards the water.

Counties Mayo & Sligo

POP 196,000 / AREA 7234 SQ KM

Best Places to Eat

➡ Source (p435)

➡ Pantry & Corkscrew (p422)

➡ Rua (p432)

➡ Shells (p439)

➡ Cottage Coffee Shop (p426)

Best Places to Stay

➡ Delphi Lodge (p417)

➡ Talbot's (p428)

➡ St Anthony's (p422)

Why Go?

Despite their natural wonders and languid charm, the counties Mayo and Sligo remain a well-kept secret offering all of Ireland's wild, romantic beauty but without the crowds. Mayo is the more rugged of the two with scraggy peaks, sheer cliffs, heather-covered moors and beautiful offshore islands where life is dictated by the elements. Sligo is more pastoral and its lush fields, fish-filled lakes and flat-topped mountains inspired William Butler Yeats to compose some of Ireland's most ardent verse.

Both counties boast grand stretches of golden sands and legendary breaks that lure the surfing cognoscenti from around the globe. Visit and you'll find all this plus an improbable bounty of prehistoric sites, elegant Georgian towns, little fishing villages and good old-fashioned warm-hearted country hospitality.

When to Go

➡ The weather-beaten shores of Mayo and Sligo can be whipped by brutal winds and rain in winter, when only the hardiest tourists and surfers make it here.

➡ If you're interested in catching a swell, spring and autumn are your best shot, with September and October favoured by those in the know.

➡ In summer the region bursts into life with oodles of festivals and in July and August you'll get the pick of the crop with the Yeats festival in Sligo and a variety of small traditional music festivals elsewhere. Plus the weather is often actually balmy.

COUNTY MAYO

Mayo's wild beauty and haunting landscapes are reminiscent of Connemara but you'll find far fewer tourists here, which means there are plenty of untapped opportunities for exploration by car, foot, bicycle or horseback. Life here has never been easy and the Potato Famine (1845–51) ravaged the county and prompted mass emigration. Consequently many people with Irish ancestry around the world can trace their roots to this once-plagued land.

Because of its close proximity to Connemara, this section is arranged going from south to north, starting with the photogenic village of Cong, which is just over the border from County Galway.

Cong

POP 130

Sitting on a sliver-thin isthmus between Lough Corrib and Lough Mask, twee-little Cong complies with romantic notions of a traditional Irish village. Time appears to have stood still ever since the evergreen classic *The Quiet Man* was filmed here in 1951. In fact a lot of effort has been made to preserve Cong as it looked for the filming of the movie – even though that was largely the work of Hollywood set designers.

Cong and the region still attract a lot of tourists hoping for a full helping of *Quiet Man* cliches (there are more film-related sites just over the border in County Galway, see p400). As such, the arrival of the morning's first tour bus instantly doubles the number of people strolling the town's tiny streets, but the wooded trails between the lovely old abbey and stately Ashford Castle offer a respite.

◉ Sights

Cong Abbey   HISTORIC SITE
(admission free; ⊙dawn-dusk) An evocative reminder of ecclesiastical times past, the weathered shell of Cong's 12th-century Augustinian abbey is scored by wisened lines from centuries of exposure to the elements. Nevertheless, several finely sculpted features have survived, including a carved doorway, windows and lovely medieval arches (touched up in the 19th century).

Founded in 1120 by Turlough Mór O'Connor, high king of Ireland and king of Connaught, the abbey occupies the site of an earlier 6th-century church. The community once gathered in the chapter house to confess their sins publicly.

From the abbey, moss-encrusted trees guard a path to the river and the diminutive 16th-century monk's fishing house, built midway over the river so that the monks could haul their catch straight up through a hole in the floor.

Ashford Castle   HISTORIC BUILDING
(☑094-954 6003; www.ashford.ie; grounds adult/child €5/3.50; ⊙9am-dusk) Just beyond Cong Abbey, the village abruptly ends and the woodlands surrounding Ashford Castle begin. First built in 1228 as the seat of the de Burgo family, owners over the years included the Guinness family (of stout fame). Arthur Guinness turned the castle into a regal hunting and fishing lodge, which it remains today.

The only way to peek into its lavishly restored interior is to stay or dine here. But the surrounding estate – 140 hectares of parkland, covered with forests, streams, bridle paths and a golf course – is open to the public. Walking through the Kinlough Woods gets you away from the golfers and out to the shores of Lough Corrib. You can also stroll along the riverbanks to the monk's fishing house.

Quiet Man Museum   MUSEUM
(Circular Rd; admission €5, location tour €15; ⊙10am-4pm Mar-Oct) Modelled on Sean Thornton's White O' Mornin' Cottage from the film, the Quiet Man Museum also squeezes in a fascinating regional archaeological and historical exhibition of items from 7000 BC to the 19th century. Film fanatics (or those with a postmodern fascination for the way reality and fiction blur) can take a 75-minute location tour (time varies), which includes museum entry.

⚓ Activities

Corrib Cruises   BOAT TOUR
(www.corribcruises.com; adult/child €20/10) Cruises on Lough Corrib depart from the Ashford Castle pier. A 75-minute history cruise leaves daily year-round at 10.30am; a two-hour island cruise departs at 2.45pm from June to September and visits Inchagoill, the island at the centre of Lough Corrib with 5th-century monastic ruins. There are also boats to/from Oughterard in County Galway.

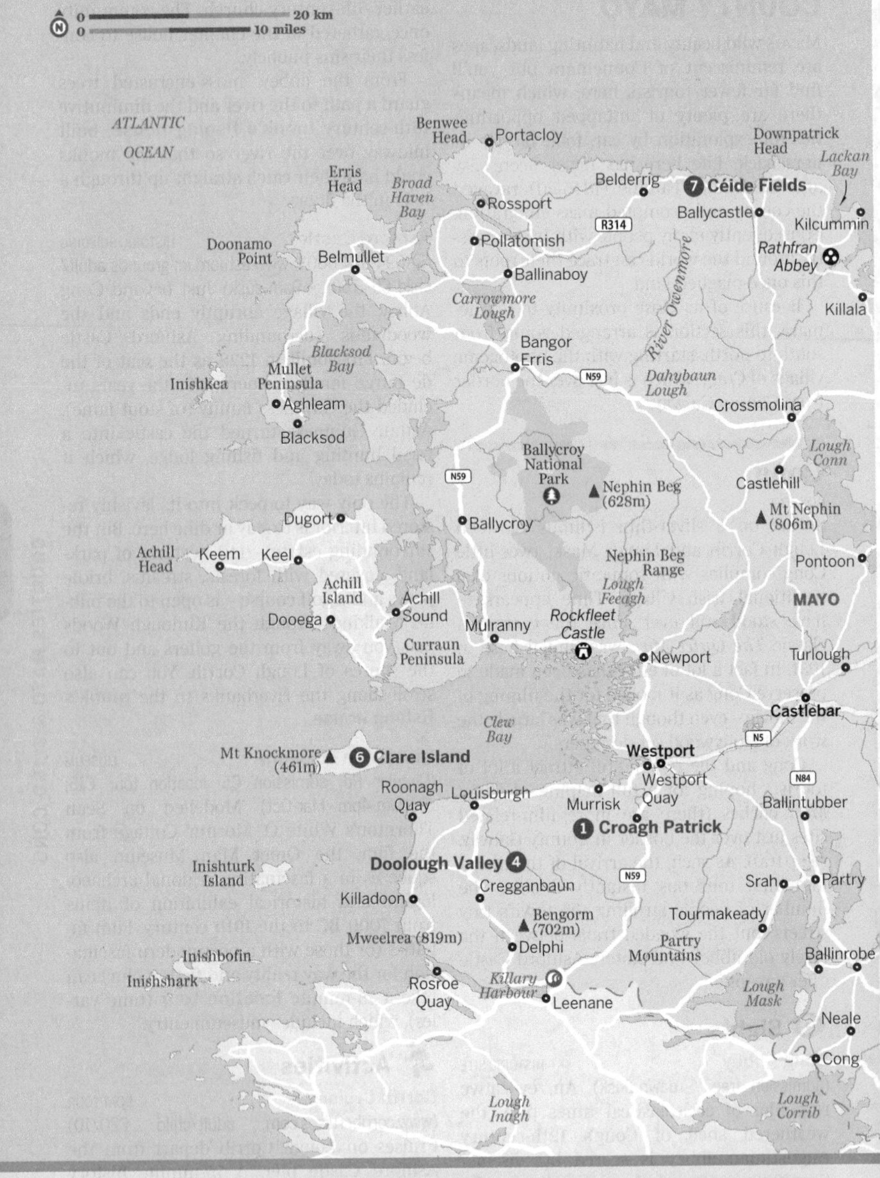

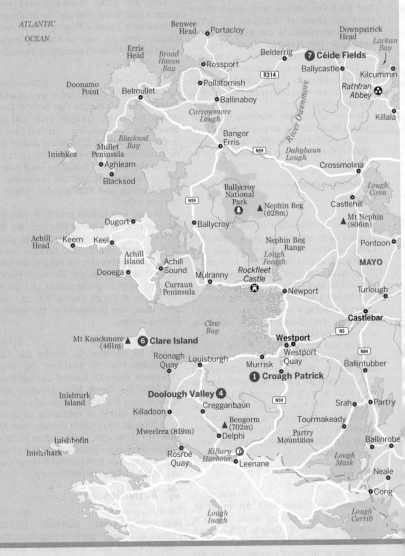

0 20 km
0 10 miles
ATLANTIC
OCEAN
Benwee Head
Portacloy
Downpatrick Head
Lackan Bay
Erris Head
Broad Haven Bay
Belderrig
7 Céide Fields
Rossport
Ballycastle
Kilcummin
R314
Doonamo Point
Pollatomish
Rathfran Abbey
Belmullet
Ballinaboy
River Owenmore
Killala
Carrowmore Lough
Bangor Erris
Blacksod Bay
Mullet Peninsula
N59
Dahybaun Lough
Inishkea
Aghleam
Crossmolina
Blacksod
Ballycroy National Park
Lough Conn
Castlehill
Nephin Beg (628m)
N59
Mt Nephin (806m)
Dugort
Ballycroy
Achill Head
Keem
Keel
Nephin Beg Range
Pontoon
Lough Feeagh
MAYO
Achill Island
Achill Sound
Rockfleet Castle
Dooega
Mulranny
Curraun Peninsula
Newport
Turlough
Castlebar
Clew Bay
N5
Mt Knockmore (461m)
6 Clare Island
Westport
Roonagh Quay
Louisburgh
Westport Quay
N84
Murrisk
Ballintubber
1 Croagh Patrick
Doolough Valley 4
Inishturk Island
N59
Srah
Partry
Cregganbaun
Killadoon
Tourmakeady
Bengorm (702m)
Mweelrea (819m)
Partry Mountains
Delphi
Inishbofin
Ballinrobe
Inishshark
Killary Harbour
Rosroe Quay
Leenane
Lough Mask
Neale
Cong
Lough Inagh
Lough Corrib

Counties Mayo & Sligo Highlights

1 Follow in St Patrick's footsteps up the conical peak of **Croagh Patrick** (p419)

2 Hit the waves year-round at **Easkey** (p442)

3 Feel ancient powers amid mystical ruins at **Carrowmore Megalithic Cemetery** (p437)

4 Walk along the starkly beautiful and poignantly desolate **Doolough Valley** (p417)

5 Make the pilgrimage to the otherworldly **Carrowkeel Megalithic Cemetery** (p439) for panoramic views

6 Go in search of Ireland's pirate queen, Grace O'Malley (Granuaile) on craggy **Clare Island** (p418)

most extensive Stone Age monument at the **Céide Fields** (p429)

7 Marvel at the ancient planning of the world's

Ashford Adventure Company KAYAKING
(☎087 190 3588; www.ashfordadventure.com; Main St; tours from €75, bike rental per day from €15; ⊙times vary) Pedal the shores and then paddle the waters of Lough Corrib on two-hour tours that use bikes and kayaks.

Falconry School FALCONRY
(www.falconry.ie; Ashford Castle; ⊙times vary) The period charm of Ashford Castle is a fitting setting to learn the ancient art of falconry. The falconry school offers a choice of one-hour (€70) or 90-minute (€105) 'hawk walks' where participants learn about and handle the impressive Harris hawks.

🛏 Sleeping

Cong Hostel HOSTEL €
(☎094-954 6089; www.quietman-cong.com; Quay Rd, Lisloughrey; campsites €20, dm/d from €15/70; @ 🛜) Well run and welcoming, this IHH-affiliated hostel has its own *Quiet Man* screening room showing the film *every* night. Between June and mid-September it hires bikes (€15 per day) and boats (€55). There is an adjacent camping ground and you can borrow fishing rods.

Hazel Grove B&B €
(☎094-954 6060; www.hazelgrove.net; Drumshiel; s/d from €48/60; 🛜🖳) Warm and friendly Irish hospitality is in store at this four-room B&B in a modern family home. It's just north (less than 1km) of town.

Ryan's Hotel HOTEL €
(☎094-954 6243; www.ryanshotelcong.ie; Main St; s/d from €45/80; @ 🛜) Right in the centre of Cong, you can stay in one of 12 refurbished rooms at this maroon-fronted guesthouse.

★Michaeleen's Manor B&B €€
(☎094-954 6089; www.congbb.com; Quay Rd, Lisloughrey; s/d from €55/65; 🛜) This large, modern home is something of a shrine to *The Quiet Man*. Each of its 12 sparkling rooms is named after a character in the film and decorated with memorabilia and quotations. There's also a sauna, outdoor hot tub and a large fountain replica of the Quiet Man Bridge.

Lisloughrey Lodge HOTEL €€€
(☎094-954 5400; www.lisloughreylodgehotel.ie; The Quay; r from €140; @ 🛜) The lodge, built in the 1820s by Ashford Castle's owners, has been renovated in bold, contemporary colours. The 50 guest rooms are named for wine regions and champagne houses. Get a room in the original house for the old-world character.

Ashford Castle HOTEL €€€
(☎094-954 6003; www.ashford.ie; r from €380; @ 🛜) Old-world elegance, 83 exquisite rooms and faultless service are on tap at Ashford Castle. It easily the grandest of the grand in Ireland. Even if you're staying elsewhere, you can come for dinner at the George V Dining Room (dinner from €70); be sure to dress up as it's rather posh.

🍴 Eating & Drinking

★Hungry Monk CAFE €
(Abbey St; mains €6-14; ⊙10am-6pm Mon-Sat, 11am-5pm Sun Apr-Aug, 10am-6pm Wed-Mon Sep-Dec & Mar; 🛜) This simple cafe with its bright colours and artfully mismatched furniture is Cong's best lunch spot. Locally sourced ingredients make up the fab sandwiches, soups and salads, the luscious cakes are all homemade and the coffee is excellent.

Fennel Seed IRISH €€
(☎094-954 6004; Ryan's Hotel, Main St; bar food €14-21, mains €15-25; ⊙dinner Mon-Sat, 1-7pm Sun) Michael Crowe and Denis Lenihan used to cook at Ashford Castle and have brought their culinary skills to the village, with great success (don't miss their signature 'smoky bake' pie, filled with trout, salmon, mackerel and haddock. Bar food is served in the adjoining Crowe's Nest Pub until 7pm.

★Wilde's at the Lodge MODERN IRISH €€€
(☎094-954 5400; www.lisloughreylodgehotel.ie; The Quay, Lisloughrey Lodge; mains €19-29; ⊙6-10pm daily, 1-3pm Sun) Chef Jonathan Keane and his team forage the mussels, wild herbs and flowers that adorn the dishes at this exquisite restaurant. Produce and meat come from organic local suppliers and are used in an innovative way to dish up fresh and creative fare. The restaurant takes its name from Sir William Wilde (father of Oscar), who loved the Lough.

Pat Cohan's PUB
(Abbey St) In a bizarre case of life imitating art, this one-time grocery store was disguised in *The Quiet Man* as the fictional Pat Cohan's. But nearly six decades on, *Quiet Man* craziness refuses to die down, and it has now become that pub.

ⓘ Information

Tourist office (☎094-954 6542; www.congtourism.com; Abbey St; ☺10am-1pm & 2-5.45pm daily Mar-Sep, Fri & Sat Oct & Nov) In the old courthouse building opposite Cong Abbey. The closest ATM is 5km west in Clonbur.

ⓘ Getting There & Away

Bus Éireann (www.buseireann.ie; Main St) has three buses to Galway (€12, one hour) Monday to Saturday and four to Westport (€11, one hour).

Around Cong

The Cong area is honeycombed with 10 limestone caves, each with a colourful legend or story to its credit.

One of the best is Pigeon Hole, in a pine forest about 1.5km west of Cong. It can be reached by road or by the walking track from across the river. Steep, slippery stone steps lead down into the cave, where subterranean water flows in winter. Keep an eye out for the white trout of Cong – a mythical woman who turned into a fish to be with her drowned lover.

Just west of the village is the water-filled Captain Webb's Hole. Two centuries ago, a local villain, nicknamed Captain Webb for the deformity of his hands and feet, is said to have lured a succession of 12 women here, stripped them and hurled them into the hole's soggy depths to die. His would-be 13th victim however was a canny lass. She asked Webb to look away as she undressed, then promptly pushed him to his own watery grave.

Weathering the elements since the early Bronze Age, the Cong Stone Circle sticks up from a field about 1.5km northeast of Cong, with a further three stone circles directly behind. About 3.5km east of Cong, north off the Cross road (R346), is the overgrown Ballymacgibbon Cairn, supposedly the site of the legendary Celtic Battle of Moytura between the invading Dananns and the defending Fir Bolgs.

Doolough Valley & Around

The R335 from Leenane in County Galway to Westport is one of Ireland's most beautiful scenic routes. The desolate Doolough Valley is largely untouched by housing, cut turf or even stone walls. The steep sides of the surrounding mountains simply slide into the steely grey waters of Doo Lough as sheep graze quietly on the hills.

It is also one of Ireland's most poignant spots. It was the site of a tragic Famine walk, which took place in 1849. In icy weather, 400 people died along the road as they walked from Louisburgh to Delphi and back. They'd hoped to receive food and aid from a landlord, but were refused.

Choose a dry day to tackle the road as curtains of rain can greatly diminish the views. If you have time, wander down the side roads to the north and west of the valley to reach glorious, often-deserted beaches.

Delphi

Geographically *just* inside County Mayo, this swath of mountainous moorland is miles from any significant population, allowing you to set about the serious business of relaxing.

The southern end of the Doolough Valley was named by its most famous resident, the second marquis of Sligo, who was convinced that it resembled the land around Delphi, Greece. If you can spot the resemblance, you've a better imagination than most. However, the beauty of little creeks babbling over boggish countryside against a backdrop of sun- and cloud-dappled stark hillsides is undeniable.

★Delphi Lodge (☎095-42222; www.delphilodge.ie; off R335; s €125-195, d €190-280; @), a wonderful Georgian mansion built by the marquis of Sligo, is dwarfed by the mountain backdrop. This 12-room country hotel features beautiful interiors, vast grounds, lovely food (dinner €55) and a serious lack of pretension. It's as popular with fishers (half day with fishing tutor €125) as it is with those simply aiming to relax. Other activities include yoga, mountain biking and hillwalking.

Louisburgh
POP 420

The northern gateway to the Doolough Valley, the appealing village of Louisburgh was founded under curious circumstances in 1795. Based on a simple four-street system known as the Cross, the whole town was designed and built as a living memorial to a relative of the first marquis of Sligo, lord Altamont (John Browne): his kinsman was killed at the Battle of Louisburgh in Nova Scotia, 1758.

Sights & Activities

The safe, sandy beach at Carrowmore just east of the village offers good views of Croagh Patrick and has a lifeguard on duty in summer. There are also some excellent surf beaches, like Carrownisky, in the vicinity.

West and south of Louisburgh, you'll find a web of narrow unmarked roads that wander through the scruffy countryside. The rewards come when you hit the water. A good example is tiny Killadoon, from where panoramic ocean views and vast sandy beaches fan out.

Granuaile Visitor Centre   VISITOR CENTRE
(☑ 098-66341; Church St; adult/concession €4/2; ☺ 11am-5pm Mon-Sat Jun-Sep, 10.30am-2pm Mon-Fri Oct-May) Get a quick but illuminating glimpse into the life and times of Grace O'Malley (Gráinne Ní Mháille or Granuaile; 1530–1603) the infamous pirate queen of Connaught (see p420).

Surf Mayo   SURFING
(☑ 087 621 2508; www.surfmayo.com; Bridge St; lessons from €25, surfboard & wetsuit rental per day €15; ☺ hours vary) Offers surfing lessons and camps at Carrownisky Beach and rents out gear, including stand-up paddleboards.

Mweelrea Holidays   HORSE RIDING
(www.mweelreaholidays.com; off R378, Feenone; horse riding from €25; ☺ hours vary) Take a guided horse ride through the dramatic coutryside or along the beach. Guided hikes are also offered.

Sleeping & Eating

Old Head Caravan Park   CAMPGROUND €
(☑ 087 648 6885; www.oldheadcaravanpark.ie; Old Head; campsites €20; ☺ Jul & Aug; ♿) In wood-land, 2km from Louisburgh and a short walk from its namesake beach.

Ponderosa   B&B €
(☑ 098-66440; www.ponderosamayo.com; Tooreen Rd; s/d from €45/60; ☺ Apr-Oct; ☎) Just east of the centre, this prim (and pink) and friendly B&B is set in a modern bungalow.

West View Hotel   HOTEL €€
(☑ 098-66140; www.westviewhotel.ie; Chapel St; s/d from €60/100) Right in town, this small 18-room inn has had a stylish renovation. The bar has trad sessions some nights.

Hudson's Pantry   SEAFOOD €€
(☑ 098-23747; Long St; mains €21-23; ☺ 4.30-9.30pm Mon-Sat) Fresh local seafood stars at this casual bistro that's a local highlight. The outstanding menu changes with what's fresh and you can eat a full meal or graze tapas style. It's a simple-looking place but the menu sees diners coming from miles around. Booking is advisable.

Getting There & Away

Bus Éireann has up to three buses a day to/from Westport (€8).

Clare Island

POP 200

Clew Bay is dotted with some 365 islands, the largest of which is the mountainous Clare Island, 5km offshore but half a world away. Dominated by rocky Mt Knockmore (461m), its varied terrain is terrific for walking and climbing, and swimming can be enjoyed at safe, sandy beaches. The island is also one of the dwindling number of places where you can find choughs (resembling blackbirds but with red beaks).

The website www.clareisland.info has info.

THE FIRST BOYCOTT

It was near the unassuming little village of Neale, near Cong, that the term 'boycott' came into use. In 1880 the Irish Land League, in an effort to press for fair rents and improve the lot of workers, withdrew field hands from the estate of Lord Erne, who owned much of the land in the area. When Lord Erne's land agent, Captain Charles Cunningham Boycott, evicted the striking labourers, the surrounding community began a campaign to ostracise him. Not only did farmers refuse to work his land, people in the town refused to talk to him, provide services or sit next to him in church. The incident attracted attention from the London papers, and soon Boycott's name was synonymous with such organised, nonviolent protests. Within a few months, Boycott fled Ireland.

Sights & Activities

The island has the ruins of the Cistercian Clare Island Abbey (c 1460) and Gran-uaile's Castle, both associated with the piratical Grace O'Malley. The tower castle was her stronghold, although it was altered considerably when the coastguard took it over in 1831. Grace is said to be buried in the small abbey, which contains a stone inscribed with her family motto: 'Invincible on land and sea'.

The island is a great place to retreat from the world. Clare Island Yoga Retreat Centre (www.yogaretreats.ie; three-day retreats from €350) runs yoga retreats. There is a good self-guiding archaeological walk.

Sleeping & Eating

★ Go Explore Hostel   HOSTEL €

(☑ 087 410 8706; www.goexplorehostel.ie; dm €18-22; 🕯) This newish (2012) hostel is a delight. Large windows and a terrace overlook the water and there are vintage areas of the complex that include a large 1840s fireplace. The pub is an islandwide draw and has good food (mains €8 to €15) and frequent live sessions.

O'Grady's   B&B €€

(☑ 098-22991; www.ogradysguesthouse.com; s/d from €60/80) You'll find bright, modern rooms with tasteful, neutral colour schemes at this modern B&B near the pier.

Getting There & Around

Ferries depart from Roonagh Quay, 8km west of Louisburgh, around 10 times daily in July and August, two to four times daily the rest of the year. The trip takes 30 minutes (€15/8 per adult/child return).

You can usually rent bikes (about €10 per day) at the pier and where you stay. There are also taxis.

Clare Island Ferries (☑ 087 241 4653, 098-23737; www.clareislandferry.com)

O'Malley Ferries (☑ 098-25045, 086 887 0814; www.omalleyferries.com)

Inishturk Island

POP 100

Still further off the beaten track is ruggedly beautiful Inishturk, which lies 12km off Mayo's western coast. It's sparsely populated and little visited, despite the two sandy beaches on its eastern side, impressive cliffs, wonderful flora and fauna, and a rugged, hilly landscape that's ideal for walking. In fact, ambling along the island's maze of country roads is a perfect way to adapt to the pace of life here. The island's website (www.inishturkisland.com) has info.

If you want to stay, the scenically positioned Teach Abhainn (☑ 098-45510; s/d from €40/64, dinner €25; ☺ Apr-Oct), a working farm 1.5km west of the harbour, has mesmerising views, hearty home cooking and six comfy rooms.

O'Malley Ferries has services from Roonagh Quay, near Louisburgh; the crossing (€8/5 per adult/child return) takes 45 minutes.

Croagh Patrick

St Patrick couldn't have picked a better spot for a pilgrimage than this conical mountain (also known as 'the Reek'). On a clear day the tough two-hour climb rewards with stunning views over Clew Bay and its sandy islets.

It was on Croagh Patrick that Ireland's patron saint fasted for 40 days and nights, and where he reputedly banished venomous snakes. Climbing the 772m holy mountain is an act of penance for thousands of pilgrims on the last Sunday of July (Reek Sunday). The truly contrite take the original 40km route from Ballintubber Abbey (p431), Tóchar Phádraig (Patrick's Causeway), and ascend the mountain barefoot.

Sights & Activities

The main trail ascends the mountain from the car park in Murrisk. You can rent walking sticks for €1.50 for the steep trail which is rocky in parts. The average return trip takes three to four hours and it gets crowded on sunny weekends. At the summit you'll find a 1905 whitewashed church and a 9th-century oratory fountain. Views are sublime.

Opposite the car park is the National Famine Memorial, a spine-chilling sculpture of a three-masted ghost ship wreathed in swirling skeletons, commemorating the lives lost on so-called 'coffin ships' employed to help people escape the Famine. A path down past the memorial leads to the scant remains of Murrisk Abbey, founded by the O'Malleys in 1547.

COUNTIES MAYO & SLIGO INISHTURK ISLAND

ℹ️ Getting There & Away

Murrisk is 8km southwest of Westport. The best way to get here is along the lovely bayside bike and walking path. Otherwise there are daily buses.

Westport

POP 5600

Bright and vibrant even in the depths of winter, Westport is a photogenic Georgian town with tree-lined streets, a riverside mall and a great vibe. With an excellent choice of accommodation, restaurants and pubs renowned for their music, it's an extremely popular spot yet has never sold its soul to tourism.

Westport is Mayo's nightlife hub, and its central location makes it a convenient and enjoyable base for exploring the county.

👁 Sights

The town's harbour is on Clew Bay, 2km west of the centre. Westport Quay here is a picturesque spot with shops and cafes. In town, the Octogon is a major landmark and is punctuated by a Doric column.

Westport House   HISTORIC BUILDING
(☏ 098-27766; www.westporthouse.ie; Quay Rd; house only adult/child €12/6.50, house & priate adventure park €20/16.50; ⊘ 11am-6pm Jul & Aug, times vary greatly rest of year; 🚻) Built in 1730 on the ruins of Grace O'Malley's 16th-century castle, this charming Georgian mansion retains much of its original contents and has some stunning period-styled rooms. The house is set in glorious gardens but the overall effect is marred by its commercial focus. Children will love it, however, and the Pirate Adventure Park, complete with a swinging pirate ship, a 'pirate's playground' and a roller-coaster-style flume ride through a

---

THE PIRATE QUEEN

The life of Grace O'Malley (Gráinne Ní Mháille or Granuaile, 1530–1603) reads like fantasy adventure fiction. Twice widowed and twice imprisoned for acts of piracy, she was a fearsome presence in the troubled landscape of 16th-century Ireland.

Her unorthodox life was the stuff of legend and mythology; hundreds of stories testify to her unequalled courage, skill and dogged determination to protect her clan against virtually anyone else – from rival chieftains to the English army.

Born into a powerful seafaring family that controlled most of the Mayo coastline and traded internationally, the independent Grace soon decided she should join the family line. Legend has it that while still a child she asked her father if she could join a trip to Spain but was refused on the grounds that seafaring was not for girls. She promptly cut off all her hair, dressed in boys clothing, returned to the ship and announced that she was ready to sail. Her family nicknamed her Gráinne Mhaol (grawn-ya wail; bald Grace), a name which stuck for the rest of her life.

Married & Looting

At 15 she was married off to Donal O'Flaherty, a querulous local chieftain, but using her smarts she soon eclipsed her husband in politics and trade. The O'Flahertys were banned from trading in Galway, one of the largest ports in the British Isles. Grace got around this by waylaying cargo vessels en route to port and demanding payment for safe passage. If they refused, she had them looted.

After her husband's death, Grace settled on Clare Island but continued marauding around the Irish and Scottish coasts. Closer to home, the only part of Clew Bay not under her control was Rockfleet, so in 1566 Grace married Richard an-Iarrain to gain control of his castle (p423). Despite some marital ups and downs (she tried to 'dismiss' him once she controlled his tower), they remained together until his death 17 years later.

By the 1570s Grace's blatant piracy had come to English attention and many attempts were made to capture her. Eventually she was brought to London in 1593, whereupon Queen Elizabeth I granted her a pardon and offered her a title, which Grace declined, saying she was already Queen of Connaught.

Grace O'Malley died in 1603 and is thought to be buried in the family crypt on Clare Island.

Westport

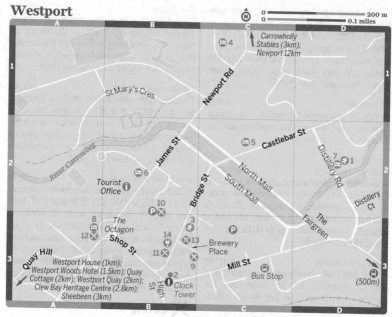

water channel are big hits. It is 3km west of the centre.

Clew Bay Heritage Centre   MUSEUM
(www.westportheritage.com; The Quay; adult/child €3/free; ☉10am-5pm Mon-Fri Jun-Sep, 3-5pm Sun Jul & Aug, 10am-2pm Mon-Fri Apr-May & Oct) Set in a 19th-century stone building, this museum traces the history, customs and traditions of Westport and Clew Bay. It's on The Quay, 2km west of town.

🏃 Activities

The area around Westport is great for cycling with gentle coastal routes or more challenging mountain trails within a few kilometres of town. The popular Great Western Greenway (p424), a 42km cycling route between Westport and Achill, begins 500m from the centre of town off the N59.

   Clew Bay Bike Hire (☎098-24818; www.clewbayoutdoors.ie; Distillery Rd; rentals per day from €15, shuttle price varies; ☉9am-6pm) can offer advice on routes and trails in the area and has depots along the Greenway in Westport, Newport, Mulranny Achill; you can start the trail at any point and be picked up on completion. There's a handy one-way drop-off/collection service.

Westport

◎ Activities, Courses & Tours

⊜ Sleeping

⊗ Eating

⊜ Drinking & Nightlife

★ **Guided Walks of Historic Westport**   WALKING TOUR
(☎098-26852; Clock, Bridge St; adult/child €6/free; ☉11am Wed Jul & Aug) Local historians lead 90-minute walks around Westport.

Carrowholly Stables
HORSE RIDING

(www.carrowholly-stables.com; off N59, Carrowholly; beach rides adult/child from €30/25) Offers guided horse and pony treks on the beach and along trails overlooking Clew Bay. The stables are 3km north of the town centre, next to Westport Golf Club.

Hewetson
FISHING

(Bridge St; ⊙10am-5pm Mon-Sat) For tackle, camping gear, all-weather clothing and information about fishing.

Croagh Patrick
Walking Holidays
WALKING TOUR

(www.walkingguideireland.com; Belclare; tours from €25; ⊙Apr-Oct) Highly customisable walks in the countryside surrounding Westport. You can include St Patrick's holy site and/or a beach. Longer walks up to eight days are regularly scheduled.

Clewbay Cruises
BOAT TOUR

(☑087 606 6146; www.clewbaycruises.com; Quay Harbour; adult/child €15/10; ⊙May-Sep) Enjoy the views from Clew Bay on 90-minute cruises.

🛏 Sleeping

Westport is Mayo's main city and while there's an abundance of B&Bs and hotels, rooms are in short supply during summer and special events. The tourist office can book rooms for a €4 service fee.

Old Mill Holiday Hostel
HOSTEL €

(☑098-27045; www.oldmillhostel.com; James St; dm from €10; 🛜) Inside a converted stone mill, this central hostel has 58 beds spread across four- to 10-bed rooms. Inviting communal areas make for a laid-back social vibe.

Abbeywood Hostel
HOSTEL €

(☑098-25496; www.abbeywoodhouse.com; Newport Rd; dm €10-20, d €60; ⊙May-Sep; @🛜) Originally part of a monastery, this orderly hostel hasn't quite lost its institutional aura with stained-glass windows in places, polished wood floors and high ceilings. Rates include continental breakfast.

★St Anthony's
B&B €€

(☑087 630 1550; www.st-anthonys.com; Distillery Rd; s/d from €50/70; 🛜) This genteel B&B sits under cover of a large hedge and thick, twisted vines inhabited by birds' nests. Rooms have clean lines and restful, light colours. Bathrooms have jacuzzi tubs or power showers. Breakfast is excellent.

Wyatt Hotel
HOTEL €€

(☑098-25027; www.wyatthotel.com; The Octagon; s/d from €75/85; 🛜) Right in the centre of town, this sunflower yellow older hotel is a local landmark. The modern rooms are comfortable but rather corporate in style.

Castlecourt Hotel
HOTEL €€

(☑098-55088; www.castlecourthotel.ie; Castlebar St; r from €120; @🛜🏊) Spacious but cosy rooms that blend contemporary style with classic elegance are on offer at this modern hotel in the town centre. There's a luxurious spa and an outdoor rock pool.

Westport Woods Hotel
HOTEL €€

(☑098-25811; www.westportwoodshotel.com; Quay Rd; s €75-105, d €100-220; @🛜🏊🏄) 🏌 Hidden behind the stone wall of Westport House, this place prides itself on its green credentials. Rooms are large and spacious while service is professional. There's an excellent free children's club, bicycles to borrow, a zip wire, high-rope course, a climbing wall and a beach club.

🍴 Eating

Westport is packed with restaurants and cafes, just wander along Bridge St and the little laneways off it to find many options. The **market** (James St Car Park; ⊙8.30am-2pm Thu Apr-Oct) features prepared and fresh foods from the region.

Book for dinner in summer and on weekends.

★McCormack's at The Andrew Stone Gallery
MODERN IRISH €

(www.katemccormackandsons.ie; Bridge St; mains €6-14; ⊙10.30am-5pm Thu-Sat & Mon-Tue) Excellent food is on offer from this family-run breakfast-and-lunch cafe that has been in business for decades. However, it's far from an antique as it sources its fare from the best local producers. In a hurry? Grab a scone to go.

★Pantry & Corkscrew
MODERN IRISH €€

(☑098-26977; www.thepantryandcorkscrew.com; The Octogon; lunch mains €8-15, dinner mains €12-25; ⊙noon-3.30pm & 5.30-10pm Tue-Sun) The heart of Mayo's slow food movement is found here at this narrow little storefront. The kitchen has huge talent as the changing menu shows, with dishes sourced from local and organic producers.

Sheebeen PUB €€
(☑098-26528; off R335, Rosbeg; mains €8-25; ⊙kitchen noon-9pm Jun-Aug, shorter hours other times) This traditional pub serves a fine selection of sandwiches and fresh seafood in relaxed surroundings on the shores of Clew Bay west of town.

Sol Rio MEDITERRANEAN €€
(☑098-28944; www.solrio.ie; Bridge St; mains lunch €7-14, dinner €13-18; ⊙cafe 9am-6pm, restaurant noon-3pm & 6-10pm; 🖈) The extensive menu here ranges from pizza and pasta to organic meat and fish. Carefully sourced ingredients and attention to detail whether you pause at the simple cafe downstairs or the more stylish restaurant upstairs.

Quay Cottage SEAFOOD €€
(☑098-50692; www.quaycottage.com; Harbour; mains €18-25; ⊙5.30-10pm mid-Feb–mid-Jan) Serving seafood straight off the boats and steeped in salty-dog charm (including lobster pots hanging from the roof beams), this is the pick of places to eat on Westport's lively harbourfront.

An Port Mór MODERN IRISH €€
(☑098-26730; www.anportmor.com; 1 Brewery Pl; mains €20-28; ⊙6-10pm Tue-Sun) Hidden down a lane off Bridge St, this little restaurant packs quite a punch. It's an intimate kind of place with a series of long, narrow rooms and a menu that features excellent meats and seafood. Most everything is sourced locally.

 Drinking & Nightlife
Westport is thronged with pubs, many of them with live music nightly.

★**Matt Molloy's** PUB
(Bridge St) Matt Malloy, the fife player from the Chieftains, opened this old-school pub years ago and the good times haven't let up. Head to the back room around 9pm and you'll catch live *céilidh* (traditional music and dancing). Or perhaps an old man will simply slide into a chair and croon a few classics.

❶ **Information**

Tourist office (☑098-25711; www.westport tourism.com; James St; ⊙9am-5.45pm Jul & Aug, to 5.45pm Mon-Fri, to 4.45pm Sat Mar-Jun & Sep & Oct) Mayo's main tourist office has a lot of walking info.

❶ **Getting There & Away**

BUS
Bus Éireann services include Dublin (€19, 4½ hours, two daily), Galway (€15, two hours, three daily) and Sligo (€20, 2½ hours, one daily). Buses depart from Mill St.

TRAIN
There are five daily trains to Dublin (€35, 3¼ hours).

Newport
POP 620

Newport, a quick 12km drive north of Westport, is a picturesque 18th-century village. The trains on the Westport–Achill Railway stopped in 1936 but a striking seven-arch viaduct built in 1892 remains and is a popular spot with walkers and cyclists.

The Bangor Trail (p427) ends here while the wonderful Great Western Greenway (p424) heads west to Achill, 31km away along the former rail line.

Grab a snack or pause for a true respite in the old-world charms of the Blue Bicycle Tea Rooms (www.bluebicyclearooms.com; Main St; mains from €4; ⊙10.30am-6pm May-Oct), which features sandwiches, salads, soups, baked treats and more, all sourced locally.

Buses between Westport and Achill Island pass through once daily.

Newport to Achill Island

En route look out for signs to Burrishoole Abbey (off N59; admission free; ⊙dawn-dusk), an eerie wind-battered ruin of a Dominican abbey built in 1486 and now surrounded by a cemetery. It's 2km west of Newport.

Another 3.5km further on, look for signs for Rockfleet Castle (Carrigahowley; off N59; ⊙dawn to dusk). This 15th-century tower is associated with 'pirate queen' Grace O'Malley. She married her second husband, Richard an-Iarrain (impressively nicknamed 'Iron Dick' Burke), to gain control of this castle, and famously fought off an English attack here. It's moodily set on a boggy tidal area.

Rising from a narrow isthmus, the hillside village of Mulranny overlooks a wide Blue Flag beach. It's a prime vantage point to try counting the 365 or so seemingly saucer-sized islands that grace Clew Bay.

THE GREAT WESTERN GREENWAY

Following the route of the old Westport–Achill Railway, the Great Western Greenway (www.greenway.ie) is one of the best reasons to pause in this part of Mayo. The 42km trail passes some lovely countryside and waterfront scenery. It consists of three main sections, none of which require more than moderate effort:

➡ **Westport to Newport** This 11km section through pretty, lush countryside starts off the N59 500m north of Westport's centre and ends at the N59 2km before Newport. It's the easiest section.

➡ **Newport to Mulranny** This 18km section is the most popular and passes close to the many sights along Clew Bay. It's off the N59 just north of Newport and ends right in Mulranny.

➡ **Mulranny to Achill** This 13km section starts right in Mulranny and ends as you reach Achill Island. It has some sweeping water views.

You can easily rent bicycles along the Greenway. Clew Bay Bike Hire (www.clewbayout-doors.ie; rentals per day from €15, shuttle price varies; ⏰9am-6pm) has stations at Westport, Newport, Mulranny and Achill. It has an uber-convenient pick-up service (€23) that lets you ride all or part of the Greenway one way and be driven the other way. Book this service in advance at busy times.

Atlantic Way

Instead of following the main road (R319) from Mulranny to Achill Island, take the signposted Atlantic Way, which curves clockwise around the Curraun Peninsula. The narrow road passes the odd fortified tower and as it hugs the isolated southern edge of the Curraun Peninsula the views across Clew Bay and out to sea are simply stunning.

Achill Island

POP 950

Ireland's largest offshore island, Achill (An Caol), is connected to the mainland by a short bridge. Despite its accessibility, it has plenty of that far-flung-island feeling: soaring cliffs, rocky headlands, sheltered sandy beaches, broad expanses of blanket bog and rolling mountains. It also has its share of history, having been a frequent refuge during Ireland's numerous rebellions.

Achill is at its most dramatic during winter, when high winds and lashing seas make the island seem downright inhospitable. The year-round population, though, remains as welcoming as ever. In summer its heather, rhododendrons and wildflowers bloom.

The village of Keel is the island's main centre of activity – which isn't all that much.

⊙ Sights

The signposted Atlantic Drive continues once you cross the bridge, following the island's wild southern shore and passing through the little fishing hamlet of Dooega.

Slievemore Deserted Village   HISTORIC SITE
The remains of this deserted village at the foot of Mt Slievemore are slowly but surely being reduced down to rock piles, and are a poignant reminder of the island's past hardships and a lost way of life. When the Potato Famine took grip, starvation forced the villagers to the sea and its sources of food. The adjacent graveyard compounds the desolation.

Dooagh   HISTORIC SITE
This village is where Don Allum, the first person to row across the Atlantic Ocean in both directions, landed in September 1982 in his 6m-long plywood boat, dubbed the QE3, after 77 days at sea. Opposite the monument, the Pub (that's its name) has memorabilia marking the feat.

Keem Bay   LOOKOUT
The 8km drive west from Keel out to what is literally the end of the road is spectacular: sweeping views across the waters as the road climbs the sheer rock face. But after you spiral down to this perfect cove of a bay, you're rewarded with a gorgeous beach.

☝ Activities

Some of Achill's scalloped bays are tame enough for swimming. Except in the height of the holiday season, the Blue Flag beaches at Dooega, Dugort and Golden Strand (Dugort's other beach) are often deserted. The beaches at Dooagh and Dooniver are just as appealing.

Keel Beach
SURFING

(Keel) The Blue Flag Keel beach is one of Ireland's best surfing spots, but there are dangerous rips from its centre to the eastern end (under the Minaun Cliffs). Heed the signs and stick to the western half of the beach. Several companies offer board hire (per day €15) and lessons (per day €40).

Walking Trails
WALKING

The island is a wonderful place for walking. Mt Slievemore (672m) can be climbed from behind the deserted village for terrific views of Blacksod Bay. A longer climb takes in Mt Croaghaun (668m), Achill Head and a walk atop what locals claim are Europe's highest sea cliffs (though Slieve League in County Donegal is thought to be marginally higher).

Achill Tourism (www.achilltourism.com) produces 14 excellent downloadable guides to walks around the island.

Calvey's Equestrian Centre
HORSE RIDING

(☑ 087 988 1093; www.calveysofachill.com; Slievemore; 2hr beach trek adult/child €60/50) Calvey's arranges riding lessons and one- to four-hour treks on Achill's broad beaches and mountain roads.

Achill Bikes
BICYCLE RENTAL

(☑ 087 245 7686; www.achillbikes.com; Keel; rental per day from €15) Rents bikes, offers advice and arranges for pick-ups and delivery around the island.

☆ Festivals

The island hosts several festivals during the year, including ones devoted to walking, painting, boating and more. The schedule changes annually.

Scoil Acla Festival
CULTURE

(www.scoilacla.com) Traditional Irish music resonates for a week in late July during this festival, which also has Irish dancing, culture and music workshops.

🛏 Sleeping

Achill has B&Bs dotting the main road from the bridge to Keel. You'll also find places to stay along the shores.

★ Valley House Hostel
HOSTEL €

(☑ 098-47204; www.valley-house.com; The Valley; campsites per tent €5, plus per person €5, dm €16-21, d €44-60; @ 🛜) Amid unruly gardens, this remote, 42-bed hostel in a creaking old mansion has atmosphere to spare. JM Synge based his play *The Playboy of the Western World* on misadventures, here and the subsequent film *Love and Rage* (1999) was also partially shot here. Bonuses include scones for breakfast and a pub with patio tables (bar food June to August only).

Keel Sandybanks Caravan & Camping Park
CAMPGROUND €

(☑ 098-43211; www.achillcamping.com; Keel; campsites €15-25, caravan 2 nights €115; ☺ Apr–mid-Sep; 🛜) This campground, an easy stroll from town, overlooks Keel Beach. Non-campers can opt for 'glamping': nights in traditional horse-drawn-style wooden caravans.

Pure Magic Achill
GUESTHOUSE €€

(☑ 085 243 9782; www.puremagic.ie; Slievemore Rd, near Dugort; s/d from €45/70) Not far from the ghost town of Slievemore, this lively spot is anything but ghostly. The bar and cafe hop through the day and night while you can arrange for kitesurfing, snorkelling, cycling and more. The 10 rooms are named for places the owners like worldwide (eg Hawaii).

Lavelles Seaside House
B&B €€

(☑ 098-45116; www.lavellesseasidehouse.com; Dooega; s/d from €45/70) In the quiet fishing village of Dooega, this 14-room whitewashed B&B offers a range of comfortable rooms. Five newer rooms are the nicest and have views down to the water. Next door is the local haunt Mickey's Bar (mains €8-11), which serves decent seafood in the summer season.

Bervie
B&B €€

(☑ 098-43114; www.bervie-guesthouse-achill.com; Keel; s €65-85, d €100-130; 🚲) Once a coastguard station, this delightful B&B is a wonderfully friendly place with views over the ocean and direct access onto the beach from the well-tended garden. The 14 rooms are bright but cosy. There's a playroom with a pool table for wet days. Lauded evening meals are available on request.

COUNTIES MAYO & SLIGO ACHILL ISLAND

Achill Island

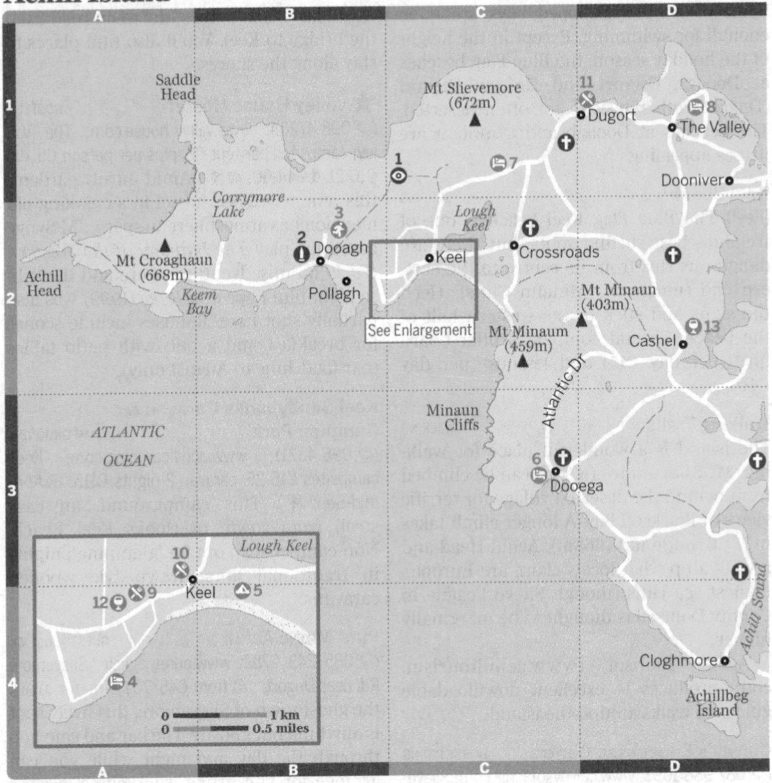

Map labels:
- Saddle Head
- Mt Slievemore (672m)
- 11
- Dugort
- 8
- The Valley
- 7
- Dooniver
- Corrymore Lake
- 3
- 2 Dooagh
- 1
- Lough Keel
- Keel
- Crossroads
- Mt Croaghaun (668m)
- Achill Head
- Keem Bay
- Pollagh
- See Enlargement
- Mt Minaun (403m)
- Cashel
- 13
- Mt Minaun (459m)
- Atlantic Dr
- ATLANTIC OCEAN
- Minaun Cliffs
- 6
- Dooega
- 10
- Lough Keel
- 12 9
- Keel
- 5
- 4
- 0 1 km
- 0 0.5 miles
- Cloghmore
- Achill Sound
- Achillbeg Island

✕ Eating

★ Cottage Coffee Shop CAFE €

(Dugort; mains €4-15; ⊙10am-5pm Jun-Sep) The perfect pause as you soak up the charms of the little seaside village of Dugort, the Cottage has fab baked goods and a variety of sandwiches and slaads. In adition, seafood specials can include a superb crab-claw salad and more.

Beehive CAFE €

(Keel; mains €4-9; ⊙10.30am-6pm Apr-Oct) As much a craft shop as a cafe, the Beehive dishes up healthy homemade soups with brown scones, creative sandwiches and alluring home-baked cakes. It gets crowded at lunch.

Calvey's Restaurant IRISH €€

(☑098-43158; www.calveysofachill.com; Keel; lunch mains €8-15, dinner mains €16-30; ⊙noon-3pm & 5.30-9pm Easter–mid-Sep) As it's attached to its own organic butchery, it's no surprise that this restaurant serves great meat. Don't miss the rack of organic Achill lamb with its distinct island flavour. There's also a good choice of fish and seafood cooked with seasonal local ingredients.

🍸 Drinking & Nightlife

Lynott's PUB

(Cashel; ⊙seasonal opening periods vary) This tiny, traditional stone pub with its flagstone floors and ancient benches is the real deal. There's no TV or radio or even a hint of a ham-and-cheese toastie, just craic.

Annexe Inn PUB

(Keel) This cosy little pub has summer trad sessions almost nightly.

ℹ Information

Most of the villages have post offices. The supermarkets in Keel and Achill Sound have ATMs.

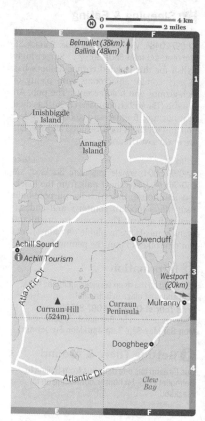

Achill Island

◎ **Sights**
1 Slievemore Deserted Village C1
2 The Pub B2

🎯 **Activities, Courses & Tours**
3 Calvey's Equestrian Centre B2

🛏 **Sleeping**
4 Bervie A4
5 Keel Sandybanks Caravan &
    Camping Park................................. B4
6 Lavelles Seaside House C3
7 Pure Magic Achill C1
8 Valley House Hostel D1

🍴 **Eating**
9 Beehive.. A4
10 Calvey's Restaurant A3
11 Cottage Coffee Shop.......................... D1

🍷 **Drinking & Nightlife**
12 Annexe Inn....................................... A4
13 Lynott's D2

There's one bus daily from Ballina (€12, one hour).

Ballycroy National Park

Covering one of Europe's largest expanses of blanket bog, Ballycroy National Park (www.ballycroynationalpark.ie; off N59, Ballycroy; admission free; ☉ visitor centre 10am-5.30pm mid-Mar–Sep) is in a gorgeously scenic region, where the River Owenduff wends its way through intact bogs.

The park is home to a diverse range of nature including peregrine falcons, corncrakes and whooper swans. A short nature trail with interpretation panels leads from the visitor centre across the bog with great views to the surrounding mountains. The excellent visitor centre can recommend more ambitious hikes and there are displays on whaling and on the ubiquitous purple heather.

Ballycroy is 18km south of Bangor on the N59.

Mullet Peninsula

Dangling some 30km into the Atlantic, this thinly populated Gaeltacht (Irish speaking) peninsula feels more cut off than many islands, and has a similar sense of forsakenness. However, you'll find pristine beaches along its

Achill Tourism (☎ 098-20705; www.achilltourism.com; Davitt Quarter, Achill Sound; ☉ 9am-6pm Mon-Fri Jul & Aug, 10am-4pm Sep-Jun) One of the best sources for information in all Mayo.

ⓘ Getting There & Around

There's one bus daily to Achill from Westport (€14), with stops that include Dooagh, Keel, Dugort, Cashel and Achill Sound.

Bangor Erris

POP 300

This unexceptional little village is the start or end point for the 48km Bangor Trail, which connects Bangor and Newport. It's an extraordinary hike that takes walkers through some of the bleakest and most remote countryside in Ireland. It is very difficult and includes long stretches of bog-walking.

sheltered eastern shore and some holy surprises plus lots of sheep – often fully blocking the road. The main settlement is the busy town of Belmullet (Béal an Mhuirthead).

◉ Sights

The road south (R313) from Belmullet loops round the tip of the peninsula to rejoin itself at Aghleam. Along the way it passes the Blue Flag beach at Elly Bay, a prime spot for birdwatchers and dolphin-watchers, as well as surfers. Further south it passes stunning Mullaghroe Beach.

Near Blacksod (An Fód Dubh) are the remains of an old church. Just up from here is the first of several sites here related to St Dervla. 'Deirbhile's Twist' is a modern-day stone circle that evokes ancient monuments (it's part of the North Mayo Sculpture Trail, p431). Close by, look for signs along the road for Deirbhile's Well, where the miracle of her eyes supposedly occured. Now loop down the short road nearby to the cemetery and beach. Here you'll find St Deirbhile's Church, an intriguing ruin that dates before the 11th century and which is where St Deirbhile is purported to be buried.

In Bellmullet, check the listings for Ára Inis Gluaire (www.arasinisgluaire.ie; Church Rd; ☉schedule varies), a bilingual arts centre. There's usually an interesting selection of exhibitions and performances on offer.

THE LEGEND OF ST DEIRBHILE

Sometime around the year 600, legend has it, a young girl named Deirbhile decided on a pious path in life. However, she was opposed by a military man who was in love with her. Meeting up with him one day on today's Mullet Peninsula, she asked him what he liked best about her. 'Your eyes' he said. Thereupon Deirbhile plucked the eyes out of her head and threw them to the ground. Not surprisingly her suitor fled in horror.

But then a miracle happened: a spring welled up from the earth where Deirbhile's eyes had landed. She washed her face in its waters and her eyes returned. Today the feast day of St Deirbhile is celebrated on August 15 at the sites related to her near Blacksod on the Mullet Peninsula.

🛏 Sleeping & Eating

★ Talbot's   HOTEL €€
(☎097-20484; www.thetalbothotel.ie; Barrack St, Belmullet; s/d from €80/130; 🕿) Surprisingly stylish for this isolated corner, Talbot's has 21 very comfortable rooms with plenty of tech-gizmos and bold accents. The pub, An Chéibh (The Anchor; pub mains €8-25), has dual peat-burning fireplaces, a good beer selection and excellent food. Seafood and specials are always worth noting.

Leim Siar   B&B €€
(☎097-85004; www.leimsiar.com; Blacksod; s/d €50/76) 🚲 Just a short walk from the Blacksod lighthouse, this friendly, purpose-built B&B offers modern comforts and ends-of-the-earth appeal. The rooms are bright and evening meals are available on request. You can rent bikes to tour the peninsula.

ℹ Information

You'll find all the main services including bank, ATM and post office in Belmullet.

Erris Tourist Office (☎097-81500; www. visiterris.ie; Main St, Belmullet; ☉9am-5pm Mon-Sat May-Sep, 9am-4pm Mon-Fri Oct-Apr)

ℹ Getting There & Around

Bus Éireann has one daily bus from Ballina to Belmullet (€15, 1¾ hours), continuing on to Blacksod.

Pollatomish

POP 150

Irresistibly remote and pretty, Pollatomish, also spelled Pullathomas, drowses in a serene bay some 16km east of Belmullet, signposted on the road to Ballycastle (R314).

Those who find their way here often extend their stay to stroll on its sandy beach or continue on up to Benwee Head to take in sensational views.

Kilcommon Lodge Hostel (☎097-84621; www.kilcommonlodge.net; Pollatomish; dm/d from €16/40; dinner €16; @🕿) is run by Ciarán, an outdoors enthusiast who can organise surfing, guided walks and rock climbing. The hostel has a nice garden.

Ballycastle & Around

POP 250

The superbly sited village of Ballycastle consists of a sole sloping street. Its main draw (apart from breathtaking coastal scenery)

PIPELINE PROTEST

The quiet, rural idyll that is Mayo's far-flung northwest has made national headlines over the construction of a high-pressure raw-gas pipeline between Mayo's offshore Corrib gas field and a processing plant at Bellanaboy.

Fearing possible health and safety risks as well as the environmental harm resulting from construction of the massive project, locals and activists have waged a campaign against the project for more than 10 years. There have been arrests and protests but ultimately the pipeline was approved by the Irish government in 2011. Despite additional protests and legal action, construction of the 9km section across north Mayo (landfall is near Pollatomish) was well advanced by 2013.

Yet even as the massive project moves forward and convoys of dump trucks move in conga lines along the narrow roads, local sentiment remains obvious. 'Shell Out!' is just one of many phrases on scores of signs displayed across the region.

For more on the controversy, visit www.shelltosea.com and www.corribgaspipeline.ie.

is its megalithic tombs – one of the greatest concentrations in Europe.

◉ Sights

★**Céide Fields**   ARCHAEOLOGICAL SITE
(☑ 096-43325; www.heritageireland.ie; off R314; adult/child €4/2; ⊙ visitor centre 10am-6pm Jun-Sep, to 5pm Easter-May & Oct, last tour 1hr prior to closing) A famous wit once described archaeology as being all about 'a series of small walls'. But the walls at this barren site, 8km northwest of Ballycastle, have had experts hopping up and down with excitement.

During the 1930s, local man Patrick Caulfield was digging in the bog when he noticed a lot of piled-up stones buried beneath it. Fast forward four decades and his son Seamus began exploration of the area, uncovering what is now considered the world's most extensive Stone Age monument. Stone-walled fields, houses and megalithic tombs – about half a million tonnes of stone – have been found so far, the legacy of a 5000-year-old farming community. The visitor centre, in a glass pyramid overlooking the site, gives a fascinating glimpse into these times. Be sure to take a guided tour of the site itself, or it may seem nothing more than, well, a series of small walls.

Ballinglen Art Foundation   GALLERY
(www.ballinglenartsfoundation.org; R314; ⊙ hours vary) If you see artists out recording their impressions of the sensational scenery around here, they may well be under the patronage of this foundation. Each year scores of artists receive support and their works are shown at the impressive Ballinglen Centre just east of the centre.

🛏 Sleeping & Eating

Stella Maris   HOTEL €€€
(☑ 096-43322; www.stellamarisireland.com; Ballycastle; r €150-240; ⊙ Easter-Oct; 🛜) This salt-spattered building sits on a lonely stretch of coastline 2.5km west of Ballycastle. It was originally a British Coast Guard station, and later a nunnery. Now, upmarket rooms combine antiques and stylish modern furnishings with killer views.

★**Mary's Cottage Kitchen**   CAFE €
(Lower Main St, Ballycastle; treats from €3; ⊙ 10am-3pm Mon-Fri, to 2pm Sat) Cosy stone cottages like this are always appealing, and never more so than when they house a bakery that advertises its wares with the aroma of warm chocolate. During the summer tables are set up out back in a leafy garden. Hours can vary.

Killala & Around

POP 580

The town itself is pretty enough, but Killala is more famous for its namesake bay nearby.

It's claimed that the ever-busy St Patrick founded Killala, and the Church of Ireland cathedral sits on the site of the first Christian church in Ireland. A 25m-high round tower still looms over the town's heart.

◉ Sights

★**Lackan Bay**   BEACH
Lackan Bay beach is a stunning and vast expanse of golden sand. There's good surf here and plenty of places to get lost. Follow the R314 about 4km northwest from Killala, then turn at the signpost for Kilcummin.

WORTH A TRIP

DETOUR TO KILLALA

For a spectacular short looping detour off the main road (R314) to Killala, take the coast road north out of Ballycastle that passes Downpatrick Head. Some of Mayo's most dramatic shoreline here offers no end of excitement. Look for the narrow lane to the head that takes you right up to the surf.

Continue east and south, with Lackan Bay on your left until you rejoin the R314. From Killala, look for the turn to Kilcummin 4km northwest of town and do the route in reverse.

Rathfran Abbey   HISTORIC BUILDING

The silence at the remains of this lonely Dominican friary, dating from 1274, is broken only by the cawing of crows and the whistling wind off the water. In 1590 the friary was burned by the English.

Take the R314 road north out of Killala and, after 5km and crossing the River Cloonaghmore, turn right. After another 2km turn right at the crossroads.

Rosserk Abbey   HISTORIC BUILDING

Dipping its toes into the River Rosserk, a tributary of the Moy, this Franciscan abbey dates from the mid-15th century. There's an eye-catching double piscina (perforated stone basin) in the chancel: look for the exquisite carvings of a round tower and several angels.

The abbey is 4km south of Killala off the R314. Look out for the signposts and then follow narrow farming lanes for another 5km.

❶ Getting There & Away

There are three weekday-only buses between Ballina and Killala (€5, 20 minutes).

Ballina

POP 10,400

Mayo's second-largest town, Ballina, is synonymous with salmon. If you're there during fishing season, you'll see droves of green-garbed waders, poles in hand, heading for the River Moy – which pumps right through the heart of town.

Otherwise, excepting its amazing new musuem, Ballina makes for a quick stop.

◉ Sights

Jackie Clarke Collection   MUSEUM

(www.clarkecollection.ie; Pearse St; ◷10am-5pm Tue-Sat Apr-Sep, tours 11.30am & 2.30pm) FREE Starting at when he was 12 in 1939, the late Jackie Clarke amassed an extraordinary collection of 100,000 items covering 400 years of Irish history. Surprises abound. Opened in 2013, the musem is housed in an 1881 bank building and has a lovely side garden and cafe.

⭐ Activities

A list of fisheries and permit contacts is available at the tourist office. The season is February to September, but the best salmon fishing is June to August. Information, supplies and licences are available at Ridge Pool Tackle Shop (Cathedral Rd; ◷9am-6pm Mon-Sat). Fly-casting lessons can also be arranged.

✲ Festivals & Events

Ballina Salmon Festival   CULTURE

(www.ballinasalmonfestival.ie; ◷Jul) The weeklong festivities include parades, dances, an arts show and more.

🛏 Sleeping

Red River Lodge   B&B €

(☏096-22841; www.redriverlodgebnb.com; The Quay; s/d from €35/60; 🖳) Out of town in a tranquil spot overlooking the Moy estuary, this modern B&B has bright rooms with big windows. Breakfast is served in a large conservatory or on the deck overlooking the well-tended garden. It's 5km north of town off the N59.

Mount Falcon Country
House Hotel   LUXURY HOTEL €€€

(☏096-74472; www.mountfalcon.com; Foxford Rd; r from €140-250; 🖳🏊) Hidden within 40 hectares between Lough Conn and the River Moy, 5km south of Ballina, this gorgeous 1870s mansion is now a lovely lodge. Rooms in the old house ooze old-world grandeur, while those in the modern extension are more contemporary in style. Anglers will be hooked by Mount Falcon's own exclusive fishery.

Eating

★ Clarke's Seafood Delicatessen
SEAFOOD €

(www.clarkes.ie; O'Rahilly St; treats from €5; ⊙9am-6pm Mon-Sat) Can't catch salmon? The wizards at Clarke's will sell you their house-smoked salmon in myriad forms, plus all manner of other fishy creations you can take on a picnic.

Gaughan's
IRISH €

(O'Rahilly St; mains €5-16; ⊙10am-5pm Mon-Sat) Home-cooked staples like old-fashioned roasts and nostalgic desserts are the order of the day at this much-loved Ballina institution. The seafood is top-notch but best of all is the authentic charm of this unpretentious former pub.

ⓘ Information

Tourist office (☑096-70848; Cathedral Rd; ⊙10am-5.30pm Mon-Sat Apr-Oct) Across the River Moy from the centre.

ⓘ Getting There & Away

BUS

The bus station is on Kevin Barry St. Bus Éireann services include Westport (€14, one hour, two to four daily) and Sligo (€16, 1½ hours, one daily).

TRAIN

The train station is on Station Rd at the southern extension of Kevin Barry St. Ballina is on a branch of the main Westport–Dublin line, so you'll have to change at Manulla Junction. There are three connections a day to Dublin (€15, 3½ hours).

Castlebar & Around
POP 10,900

Mayo's county town, Castlebar, is a traffic-choked hub of shops and services; fortunately most places of interest lie outside the town centre.

Castlebar's place in Irish history was cemented in 1798, when General Humbert's outnumbered army of French revolutionary soldiers and Irish peasants pulled off an astonishing victory here. The ignominious British cavalry retreat became known as the Castlebar Races.

◎ Sights

★ National Museum of Country Life
MUSEUM

(www.museum.ie; off N5, Turlough Park; admission free; ⊙10am-5pm Tue-Sat, 2-5pm Sun) A celebration of the pluck of the Irish, this extensive and engrossing museum looks at rural traditions and skills. Set overlooking a lake in the lush grounds of 19th-century Turlough Manor, this purpose-built facility is a branch of the National Museum of Ireland and explores everything from the role of the potato to boat building, and herbal cures to traditional clothing. Exhibits concentrate on the period from 1850 to 1950. There's a good cafe and shop; it's 8km northeast of Castlebar.

Turlough Round Tower
HISTORIC BUILDING

(off N5) With its single lofty window, this impenetrable 9th-century tower calls to mind the fairy tale of Rapunzel. The tower stands on a hilltop by a ruined 18th-century church and cemetery, a short distance northeast of the National Museum of Country Life.

Ballintubber Abbey
HISTORIC BUILDING

(www.ballintubberabbey.ie; Ballintubber; admission free; ⊙9am-midnight) **FREE** Often referred to as 'the abbey that refused to die', this is the only church in Ireland founded by an Irish king that is still in use. It was set up in 1216 next to the site of an earlier church founded by busy St Patrick after he came down from Croagh Patrick.

The abbey was burned by Normans, seized by James I and suppressed by Henry VIII. The nave roof was burned down by

COUNTIES MAYO & SLIGO CASTLEBAR & AROUND

DON'T MISS

NORTH MAYO SCULPTURE TRAIL

Leading artists from eight different countries were commissioned to create this trail of 14 permanent outdoor sculptures reflecting the beauty and wilderness of the northern Mayo countryside. It essentially follows the R314 for 90km from Ballina to Blacksod.

Tourist offices and bookshops sell the 60-page *North Mayo Sculpture Trail* book detailing each sculpture. There are also free maps and simple guides.

FOXFORD WOOLLEN MILL

Founded by the Sisters of Charity in 1892, the Foxford Woollen Mill (www.foxfordwoo-lenmills.ie; Foxford; tours free; ⊗shop 10am-6pm Mon-Sat, noon-6pm Sun, tours 10am-5pm Mon-Thu, to 1pm Fri) was set up to ease post-Famine suffering and provide much-needed work and income for the people of Foxford. The mill was an enormous success and remained open until 1987 by which time its high-quality woven rugs and blankets had an international reputation. Local businesspeople managed to salvage the business and it now employs 15 as opposed to 220 in the 1960s. Today you can tour the mill during working hours and visit the large shop. Besides the sweaters and scarves (under €30) made in the factory there is a huge amount of imported merchandise also for sale (even the vaunted Foxford blazers are assembled in Portugal from the wool tweed made here). Foxford is midway between Ballina and Castlebar at the junction of the N26 and N58.

Cromwell's soldiers in 1653 and not restored until 1965.

Take the N84 south, and after about 13km turn west at the Emo service station; the abbey is 2km along.

🛏 Sleeping & Eating

There are modest B&Bs in the centre of town.

Breaffy House Hotel　　　HOTEL €€
(☑094-902 2033; www.breaffyhousehotel.com; off N60; r from €80; @❄🏠) In a formidable 19th-century country house set on a vast estate, this large hotel retains some of its period charm but has been much modernised. There is a choice of comfortable rooms (the best are in the main house) and plenty of activities for children. The hotel is 3km southeast of Castlebar.

★Rua　　　MODERN IRISH €€
(www.caferua.com; Spencer St, Castlebar; mains €7-14, dinner €40; ⊗9am-6pm Mon-Sat, to 9pm Fri Apr-Oct; 🏠) A gourmet deli downstairs and buzzing cafe upstairs, this place champions artisan, organic produce, Carrowholly cheese, Ballina smoked salmon and luscious prepared foods. The artfully mismatched furniture and bright tablecloths give it an artfully chaotic feel. Load up in the deli for a picnic in the nearby park. Seasonal Friday dinners should not be missed.

ℹ Getting There & Around

BUS

Buses stop on Stephen Garvey Way. Bus Éireann services run to Westport (€6, 20 minutes, seven to 11 daily) and Sligo (€18, 2½ hours, one daily).

TRAIN

Castlebar is on the line between Dublin (€15, three hours) and Westport (€8, 20 minutes). There are three trains each way daily. The station is just out of town on the N84 towards Ballinrobe.

Knock

POP 850

Knock was little more than a downtrodden rural village until 1879, when a divine apparition propelled it to become one of the world's most sacred Catholic shrines. The shrine is now a serious pilgrimage site and dominates the little village. It's large and blandly modern, its appeal spiritual rather than physical.

The tourist office (☑094-938 8193; www.knock-shrine.ie; ⊗9am-6pm) across from the shrine is patiently helpful. There are clusters of souvenir stalls.

◉ Sights

Knock Marian Shrine　　　HISTORIC SITE
(⊗chapel 9am-9pm) The Knock shrine encompasses five churches and a museum in the town centre. The story that led to its development goes thus: on the evening of 21 August 1879, in drenching rain, two young Knock women were startled by a vision of Mary, Joseph, St John the Evangelist and sacrificial lamb upon an altar, freeze-framed in dazzling white light against the southern gable of the parish church. They were soon joined by 13 more villagers, all gazing at the heavenly apparition for around two hours as the daylight faded. A Church investigation confirmed it as a bona fide miracle, and a sudden rush of other Vatican-approved miracles followed as the sick and disabled claimed amazing recoveries upon visiting the spot.

Today, people of all Christian denominations and even other faiths pray at the modern chapel enclosing a scene of the apparition carved from snow white marble. A segment of stone from the original (and long-gone) church mounted on the outside wall (on your right as you're facing the scene of the apparition) has been rubbed smooth by the hands and lips of the faithful. Near the church is the 1970s-built, spiky-topped Basilica of Our Lady, Queen of Ireland, which can accommodate over 10,000 worshippers.

Across a vast plaza from the basilica, the little Knock Museum (adult/child €4/3; ◉10am-6pm) follows the story from the first witnesses, through the miraculous cures, the repeated Church investigations and the visit of Pope John Paul II on the event's centenary in 1979.

❶ Getting There & Away

AIR

Ireland West Airport Knock (NOC; ☎094-936 8100; www.irelandwestairport.com) Located 15 kilometres north of town, this airport has a growing list of flights. Aer Lingus serves London-Gatwick and Birmingham. Ryanair serves UK destinations plus a grab bag of Mediterranean holiday spots. A €10 airport fee is payable on departure. The airport website lists bus services to Westport and Galway.

BUS

Services run to Westport (€10.50, one hour, two daily) and Galway (€17, 4½ hours) twice daily (once on Sunday).

COUNTY SLIGO

County Sligo packs as much poetry, myth and folklore into its countryside's lush splendour as any shamrock lover could hope for. It was Sligo that most inspired the Nobel laureate, poet and dramatist William Butler (WB) Yeats (1865–1939). Ever fascinated by Irish mysticism, he was enchanted by places like prehistoric Carrowmore Megalithic Cemetery and Innisfree Island. But it's no complacent backwater: the county town exudes a worldly vitality, and the coast's surf is internationally renowned.

Sligo Town

POP 17,600

Pedestrian streets lined with inviting shop fronts, stone bridges spanning the River Ga-

ravogue, and *céilidh* sessions spilling from pubs contrast with contemporary art and glass towers rising from prominent corners of compact Sligo. It makes a good and low-key choice for exploring Yeats country.

◉ Sights & Activities

Sligo Abbey HISTORIC BUILDING
(www.heritageireland.ie; Abbey St; adult/child €3/1; ◉10am-6pm Easter–early Oct) This handsome abbey was built around 1252 but then burned down in the 15th century and was later rebuilt. Friends in high places saved the abbey from the worst ravages of the Elizabethan era, and rescued the only sculpted altar to survive the Reformation. The doorways reach only a few feet high at the abbey's rear; the ground around it was swollen by the mass graves from years of famine and war.

Model GALLERY
(www.themodel.ie; The Mall; admission varies; ◉10am-5.30pm Tue-Sat, noon-5pm Sun) The Model houses an impressive collection of contemporary Irish art including works by Jack B Yeats (WB's brother and one of Ireland's most important modern artists) and Louis le Brocquy. There are galleries for temporary exhibitions and a permanent performance space and artists' studios. The centre offers an interesting program of experimental theatre, music and film. The cafe is good.

Sligo County Museum MUSEUM
(Stephen St; admission free; ◉9.30am-12.30pm & 2-4.45pm Tue-Sat May-Sep, 9.30am-12.30pm Tue-Sat Oct-Apr) FREE The major draw of Sligo's county museum is the Yeats room, which features photographs, letters and newspaper cuttings connected with WB Yeats, as well as drawings by Jack B Yeats.

Yeats Memorial Building MUSEUM
(www.yeats-sligo.com; Wine St; adult/child €2/free; ◉10am-5pm Mon-Fri) In a pretty setting in a former 1895 bank, the WB Yeats Exhibition has details of his life and fascinating draft manuscripts. The cafe has outdoor tables overlooking the river.

WB Yeats Statue MONUMENT
(off Hyde Bridge) Erected in 1989, this abstract statue of Yeats in front of the 1863 Ulster Bank (a building he admired) is the source of much local myrth. See if you agree with the popular moniker 'the wank at the bank'.

Sligo Town

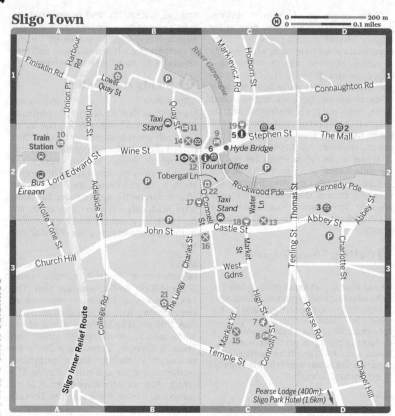

Chain Driven Cycles BICYCLE RENTAL
(☎071-912 9008; www.chaindrivencycles.com; 23 High St; per day from €20; ⊙10am-6pm Mon-Sat) Offers mountain, hybrid and road-bike hire. Rate includes helmet.

✿ Festivals & Events

Sligo manages a festival of some sort almost every weekend throughout the main tourist season.

Tread Softly CULTURAL
(www.yeats-sligo.com) Part of Sligo's 'Season of Yeats', this series of events over two weeks celebrates in late July the iconic man with tours, performances and more.

Sligo Live CULTURAL
(www.sligolive.ie) Sligo's biggest cultural event is this live music festival over five days in late October.

🛏 Sleeping

You'll find lots of B&Bs lining Pearse Rd.

Railway Hostel HOSTEL €
(☎087 690 5539; 1 Union Pl; dm/s/d from €16/25/40; ☎) In a heritage building close to the train station, this cheery hostel has great rates and shared bathrooms. There's a surcharge for arriving after 9pm.

An Crúiscín Lan GUESTHOUSE €€
(☎071-916 2857; www.bandbsligo.ie; Connolly St; s/d from €45/70; ☎) The central location is a good selling point for this simple and convivial place. Some of the 10 rooms share bathrooms.

Sligo City Hotel HOTEL €€
(☎071-914 4000; www.sligocityhotel.com; Quay St; r from €60; ☎) Recently renovated, this four-storey hotel could not be better located. The 60 rooms have a simple corporate col-

Sligo Town

our scheme. The manager wins plaudits for helpfulness.

Pearse Lodge B&B €€
(☑071-916 1090; www.pearselodge.com; Pearse Rd; s/d from €50/74; @🖥) Welcoming owners Mary and Kieron have six stylish guest rooms. The breakfast menu includes smoked salmon, French toast with bananas and homemade muesli. A sunny sitting room opens to a garden. It's 700m southwest of the centre.

Sligo Park Hotel HOTEL €€
(☑071-919 0400; www.sligoparkhotel.com; Pearse Rd/R287; r from €70; 🖥🏊) Set 3km south of the centre in landscaped gardens with mature trees, this modern hotel is large but tranquil. The pretty, tastefully decorated rooms are bright and modern.

Glass House HOTEL €€
(☑071-919 4300; www.theglasshouse.ie; Swan Point; r €70-150; @) You can't miss this contemporary hotel in the centre of town, its sharp glass facade pointing skyward. Inside, the food areas have good river views while rooms come in a choice of psychedelic colours. (Surprisingly, rooms have wired broadband but not wi-fi.)

Eating

Sligo has some creative kitchens that make good use of seasonal fare. Pubs such as Hargadons are great choices as well.

★Fabio's ICE CREAM €
(Wine St; treats from €2; ⊙11am-6pm Mon-Sat) Fabio is a local hero for making Ireland's best Italian gelato and sorbets. He uses mostly local ingredients for his changing line-up of flavours. His coffee is good too.

★Lyons Café CAFE €
(☑071-914 2969; Quay St; mains €7-12; ⊙9am-6pm Mon-Sat) Sligo's flagship department store, Lyons, opened in 1878, and its airy 1st-floor cafe – with original leadlight windows and squeaky timber floors – has been going strong since 1923. Not resting on its laurels, it's fresh and seasonal menu is inventive and many of the dishes are captured in the available cookbook.

Kate's Kitchen CAFE €
(www.kateskitchen.ie; Castle St; mains from €6; ⊙9am-6pm) Only the best local foodstuffs are sold at this lovely, contemporary shop. All the fixings for a prime picnic are combined with prepared foods. It also does a big lunchtime trade.

★Source IRISH €€
(☑071-914 7605; www.sourcesligo.ie; 1 John St; mains €11-23; ⊙restaurant 9.30am-9pm Mon-Sat, wine bar 3pm-late Wed-Sat; 🖥) High-profile Source champions local suppliers and foodstuffs. Arty photos of its favourite fishers, farmers and cheese producers grace the walls of the buzzy ground-floor restaurant with its open kitchen, while upstairs the wine bar serves tipples from the owners' vineyard in France and plates of Irish-style tapas. The top floor is a cookery school.

Montmartre FRENCH €€
(☑071-916 9901; www.montmartrerestaurant.ie; 1 Market Yard; mains €15-25; ⊙5-11pm Tue-Sat) Tucked away on a quiet back road by the market, this excellent French restaurant is unpretentious, simply decorated and good value if you get one of the set-meal specials. The menu offers local seafood

DON'T MISS

MICHAEL QUIRKE: THE WOODCARVER OF WINE ST

The inconspicuous storefront studio of **Michael Quirke** (Wine St, Sligo town; ⊙ hours vary), woodcarver, raconteur and local character, is filled with the scents of locally felled timbers and offcuts of beech stumps. Quirke began cutting and carving wood in 1968.

A modern-day Yeats, Quirke's art is inspired by Irish mythology, a subject about which he is passionate and knowledgable, and as he carves he readily chats with the customers and the curious who enter his shop and end up staying for hours. 'Irish mythology, unlike Greek mythology, is alive and constantly changing', he says. 'It's not set in stone, and that's why it's interesting.'

As he talks and carves, Quirke frequently pulls out a county map, pointing to places (such as his beloved Carrowmore) that spring from the conversation, leading you on your own magical, mystical tour of the county. As one local said: 'he's a treasure'.

but meat lovers and vegetarians are well catered for too. Book ahead.

🍷 Drinking & Nightlife

Sligo enjoys some of the best night-time fun in Ireland's northwest, with many impromptu sessions.

⭐ Hargadons
PUB

(www.hargadons.com; 4/5 O'Connell St; ⊙ food noon-9pm Mon-Sat) A winning blend of old-world fittings and gastropub style, this pub dating from 1864 is the kind of place you just won't want to leave. Its uneven stone floors, peat fire, antique signage, snug corners and bowed shelves laden down with ancient bottles give it a wonderful charm. The great-value food (mains €8 to €12) is renowned, combining local ingredants like oysters with continental flair. There's live music on Saturday nights.

Thomas Connolly
PUB

(Holborn St) Discoloured photos and newspaper clippings, mottled mirrors and ledger books adorn the walls at this old timers' pub. Its down-to-earth atmosphere is perfect for slowly sipping a pint and putting the world to rights.

Shoot the Crows
PUB

(Castle St) Dark and somewhat dishevelled, this old pub oozes bohemian atmosphere. Even when the place is packed to the gills it generally has an easygoing vibe. Singalongs and *céilidh* sessions often start up spontaneously.

☆ Entertainment

Hawk's Well Theatre
THEATRE

(www.hawkswell.com; Temple St) This well-regarded theatre presents concerts, dance and drama.

Factory Performance Space
THEATRE

(www.blueraincoat.com; Lower Quay St) A once-derelict pork abattoir is home to innovative professional theatre company Blue Raincoat, the program of which includes original productions.

🛍 Shopping

⭐ Liber Bookshop
BOOKS

(35 O'Connell St; ⊙ 9am-6pm) Yes you can get Yeats at this fabulous bookshop that has been run by the same family for over 80 years. It's also the place to get recommendatiuons on the best local authors.

ℹ Information

Post office (Wine St)

Tourist office (cnr O'Connell & Wine Sts; ⊙ 10am-5pm Mon-Fri, to 4pm Sat, plus 10am-2pm Sun Jul & Aug) Has info on the whole northwest region. The walking-tour brochure of Sligo is a gem.

ℹ Getting There & Away

BUS

Bus Éireann (📲 071-916 0066; www.buseireann.ie; Lord Edward St) leaves from the bus station situated below the train station. Destinations include Ballina (€16, 1½ hours, one daily), Westport (€20, two hours, one daily) and Donegal town €14, one hour, seven daily). Local buses run to Strandhill and to Rosses Point.

TRAIN

Trains leave the station for Dublin (€22, three hours, seven daily) via Boyle, Carrick-on-Shannon and Mullingar.

ℹ Getting Around

There are taxi stands on Quay St and Grattan St.

Around Sligo Town

Rosses Point

POP 830

Rosses Point is a picturesque seaside town with grassy dunes rolling down to the golden strand. Benbulben (525m), Sligo's most recognisable landmark, looms in the distance. Offshore, the unusual – and jaunty – 1821 Metal Man beacon points the way into harbour. In the distance are ride-free Coney Island (p438) and Oyster Island.

Rosses Point has two wonderful beaches and one of Ireland's most challenging and renowned golf links, County Sligo Golf Course (www.countysligogolfclub.ie; green fees €45-95; ☼ Apr-Oct), which attracts golfers from all over the world. Fringed by the Atlantic and lying in the shadow of Benbulben, this is possibly Ireland's greatest and most picturesque golf links.

Try to nab a terrace table at Waterfront (☎ 071-917 7122; www.waterfrontrestaurant.ie; Main St; lunch mains €4-8, dinner €20-28; ☼ noon-9.30pm Mon-Sat, from 5pm Sun), an old pub that has been transformed into a stylish place for a meal. Lunches are simple but nighttime fare focuses on the best local seafood. There's a good bakery for snacks through the day and music on Friday nights.

Harry's Bar (on your right as you enter town) has a historic well, aquarium and maritime bric-a-brac.

Rosses Point is 8km northwest of Sligo on the R291. There are regular buses from Sligo.

Carrowmore Megalithic Cemetery

One of the largest Stone Age cemeteries in Europe, Carrowmore (www.heritageireland.

WB YEATS & IRISH MYTHS

William Butler Yeats liked to say that by age 24 in 1889 he'd read 'most, if not all, recorded Irish folk tales'. There's certainly no reason to dismiss this claim as hyperbole as his writings, whether poetry, prose or plays, celebrated Celtic legends and myths. It's all the more fitting given his love for County Sligo, a place home to ancient Celtic sites such as the remarkable Carrowmore, which has ancient mysteries and meanings, many still being revealed.

Yeats firmly believed that the Irish could emerge from English domination and create their own purely Irish identity by revelling in the ancient Celtic myths still commonly recounted across the land. In 1888 he collaborated on the landmark *Fairy and Folk Tales of the Irish Peasantry*. Four years later, he wrote the children's book *Irish Fairy Tales*. In these works he codified many of the most common Irish myths, characters and legends that are common today. Among them:

➡ **Fairies** A strong believer in the occult, Yeats had no problems merging his views with the common belief among rural people in fairies. A whole race of little people, fairies had all manner of qualities (with being mischievous near universal) but could be roughly divided into good and bad. In the *Land of Heart's Desire*, Yeats wrote:

Faeries, come take me out of this dull world,

For I would ride with you upon the wind,

Run on the top of the dishevelled tide,

And dance upon the mountains like a flame.

➡ **Leprechauns** Solitary members of the much-larger race of fairies, Yeats called leprechauns 'sluttish, slouching, jeering, mischievous phantoms' and 'great practical jokers'. Contrary to the modern-day green-clad apparitions found in gift shops, Yeats had his leprechauns dressed in red jackets and prone to endless avarice.

➡ **Banshees** Typically a woman of varying age – from cute to crone – who appears wailing before a death. Long feared, Yeats had much more benevolent views, writing: 'You will with the Banshee chat and will find her good at heart'.

Yeats also wrote much about the ancient Irish gods, most derived from Celtic myths, including Aengus, the Irish god of love, and Cuchulain, a great Irish warrior in the spirit of Hercules. In the poem *Cuchulain Comforted*, he combines myth with a classic Irish quality, writing 'Now we shall sing and sing the best we can'.

ie; adult/child €3/1; ⊙10am-6pm Easter-early Oct, final admission 5pm) is slowly getting the fame it deserves and is truly a must-see Sligo attraction.

Some 60 monuments including stone circles, passage tombs and dolmens adorn the rolling hills of this haunting site, which is thought to predate Newgrange in County Meath by 700 years. Although over the centuries many of the stones have been destroyed, ongoing excavations continue to uncover more sites both within the public site and on adjoining private land.

Discoveries about the meaning of Carrowmore are continuing and are dramatic. How the many features of the site relate to the surrounding hills and mountains is rich with meaning. Among the numbered sites, 51 has been found to get direct sunlight at dawn each October 31, or Halloween. Many people claim to feel strong powers here and you'll likely see a few spiritual pilgrims on the site.

The delicately balanced dolmens were originally covered with stones and earth, so it requires some effort to picture what this 2.5km-wide area might once have looked like. A large central cairn has been reconstructed to give visitors some insight into the materials and methods used at this time. The visitor centre has full details and staff are happy to explain much more plus detail the latest discoveries.

To get here, follow the N4 south from Sligo for 5km and follow the signposts.

Knocknarea Cairn

Sligo's ultimate rock pile, 2km northwest of Carrowmore, Knocknarea is popularly believed to be the grave of legendary Queen Maeve (Queen Mab in Welsh and English folk tales). The 40,000 tonnes of stone have never been excavated, despite speculation that a tomb on the scale of the one at Newgrange (p515) lies buried below.

Many think the rocks purposely form a giant nipple, which takes on meaning when the overall horizon is viewed from Carrowmore. Believers in underlying powers at the sites say that you can easily make out the shape of a reclining woman, or a mother god.

The cairn is perched high atop the limestone plateau (328m) and seems to be looking over your shoulder everywhere you dare tread in its ancestral backyard. It's a 45-minute (1.2km) trek to the top, from which a spectacular panoramic view pulls in Benbulben, Rosses Point and the Atlantic Ocean beyond.

The parking area is off the R292. From Carrowmore, continue west along the road, turn right by a church then follow the signposts.

Strandhill

POP 1600

The great Atlantic rollers that sweep the shore front of Strandhill make this long, red-gold beach a surfing mecca.

◉ Sights & Activities

Although it's too rough to swim, there are excellent brisk walks along the beach both north and south. The views of the surf are always spectacular and you can wander up into the dunes.

Coney Island   ISLAND
Up around the coast and back east towards Sligo, you can walk – at low tide only! – to Coney Island. Its New York namesake was supposedly named by a man from Rosses Point. The island's wishing well is reputed to have been dug by St Patrick (who, if all these tales are to be trusted, led a very busy life). Carefully check tide times to avoid getting stranded.

Perfect Day Surf School   SURFING
(☑087 202 9399; www.perfectdaysurfing.com; Shore Rd; lessons from adult/child €30/20; ⊙Apr-Oct) This useful shop offers gear hire and lessons for both surfing and stand-up paddleboarding.

Strandhill Surf School   SURFING
(www.strandhillsurf.eu; Beach Front; lessons from adult/child €30/20; ⊙Apr-Oct) Offers gear hire and lessons. The live surf cams on the website are alluring indeed.

Voya Seaweed Baths   SPA
(☑071-916 8686; www.voyaseaweedbaths.com; Shore Rd, Strandhill; baths from €25; ⊙10am-8pm) Don't just smell seaweed on the beach, immerse yourself in it at this beachfront location. Ask about sharing your bath.

🛏 Sleeping

You can either sleep down by the shore, which puts you close to the action, or up on the hill along the R292, where you *may* have views.

Ocean Wave Lodge
B&B €

(☑ 071-916 8115; www.oceanwavelodge.com; Top Rd/R292; dm/s/d from €20/40/50; ⊙) This large, modern house uphill from the beach has fairly minimalist but comfortable rooms. Breakfast is included and there's a self-catering kitchen and large lounge area for guest use.

Strandhill Lodge & Hostel
LODGE €

(☑ 071-916 8313; www.strandhillaccommodation.com; Shore Rd; dm/s/d from €18/35/50; @⊙) Surfers thaw out by the open fire in the common room of the 34-bed hostel portion of this two-building complex. Rooms in the adjoining house are B&B style and while small are comfy. It's right down near the beach. The owners offer surf-and-stay packages.

Strandhill Lodge & Suites
GUESTHOUSE €€

(☑ 071-912 2122; www.strandhilllodgeandsuites.com; Top Rd/R292; s/d from €60/90; ⊙) This excellent guesthouse offers bright, spacious rooms with king-sized beds, hotel-quality design and trendy neutral styling. Room sizes vary but most have fabulous views down to the ocean and terraces or balconies.

✗ Eating & Drinking

★ Shells
CAFE €

(www.shellscafe.com; Shore Rd; mains from €5; ⊙ 9.30am-6.30pm; 🖪) Thrill to the surf from the terrace at this sprightly little cafe right across from the beach. Flowers on tables and herbs in the food come from the owner's garden. The baked goods are extraordinary. Breakfasts delight and at lunch there are salads, chowders, burgers and splendid fish and chips.

★ Trá Bán
SEAFOOD €€

(☑ 071-912 8402; www.trabansligo.ie; Shore Rd, Strand Bar; mains €16-24; ⊙ 5-9.30pm Tue-Sun; 🖪) This justifiably popular 1st-floor restaurant serves excellent pasta, steaks and seafood. The crab claws starter is a luscious plate of briney joy. Trá Bán has a relaxed atmosphere that is popular with local families with something to celebrate. Book in advance.

Venue
PUB

(Top Rd/R292) Upscale pub fare (mains €10 to €24) line the menu at this whitewashed old boozer. Year-round, you'll catch live music every Thursday, Friday and Saturday in its front bar.

❶ Getting There & Away

Strandhill is 8km due west of Sligo off the R292. Buses run from Sligo regularly.

South of Sligo Town

Riverstown

The endearing **Sligo Folk Park** (☑ 071-916 5001; www.sligofolkpark.com; Millview House; adult/child €6/4; ⊙ 10am-5pm May-Sep) revolves around a restored 19th-century cottage. Humble, thatched structures complement this centrepiece, along with scattered farm tools and other old things. A peacock sounds off as he strolls.

For more heritage charm, albeit with a heavy dose of posh, head for **Coopershill House** (☑ 071-916 5108; www.coopershill.com; Riverstown; s/d from €145/220; ⊙ Apr-Oct; @), an idyllic Georgian retreat in an estate alive with wildflowers, birdsong and deer. Most of the eight bedrooms have original antiques and oil paintings. It's been in the same family since it was built in 1774. Drinking water comes from its own spring.

Riverstown is 2km east of the N4 at Drumfin.

Carrowkeel Megalithic Cemetery

Boasting a bird's-eye view of the county from high in the Bricklieve Mountains, it's little wonder this hilltop site was sacred in prehistoric times. This windswept and lonely location is simultaneously eerie and uplifting. But for a few sheep (you drive though a sheep gate), it's undeveloped and spectacular. Dotted with around 14 cairns, dolmens and the scattered remnants of other graves, the site dates from the late Stone Age (3000 to 2000 BC).

Just the sweeping views down to South Sligo county from the car park make the journey worthwhile. It's a 1km walk to the first ancient site, Cairn G. Above its entrance is a roof-box aligned with the midsummer sunset which illuminates the inner chamber. The only other such roof-box known in Ireland is that at Newgrange (p515) in County Meath. Everywhere you look across the surrounding hills you'll see evidence of early life here, including about 140 stone circles, all that remain of the foundations of a large village thought to have been inhabited by the builders of the tombs.

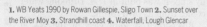

1. WB Yeats 1990 by Rowan Gillespie, Sligo Town **2.** Sunset over the River Moy **3.** Strandhill coast **4.** Waterfall, Lough Glencar

Yeats' Country

County Sligo's lush rolling hills, ancient monuments and simple country life captivated and inspired Nobel laureate, poet and dramatist William Butler Yeats (1865–1939) from an early age. Despite living almost all his life abroad, Yeats returned here frequently, enamoured by the glittering lakes, the looming hulk of Benbulben and the idyllic pastoral setting. On his death Yeats asked to be buried here in what he regarded as 'the country of the heart'.

Sligo is littered with prehistoric monuments and has a rich tradition of myth and folklore, all of which influenced Yeats and his work. You can follow in his footsteps and tour the locations that inspired him, from the waterfall in Glencar referred to in *The Stolen Child*, to picturesque Innisfree Island and rugged Dooney Rock. And keep an eye out for the fairies, regular stars of his writings.

Yeats' great legacy is celebrated with two weeks of Irish poetry, music, literature and festivals during the Season of Yeats held in Sligo each year, while photographs, letters, draft manuscripts and his personal effects can be seen at the Sligo County Museum and Yeats Memorial Building, both in the county town.

Jack B Yeats, William's brother and one of Ireland's most important modern artists, also drew inspiration from Sligo's bucolic countryside, and landscapes remained one of his favoured themes throughout his lifetime.

Carrowkeel is closer to Boyle than Sligo town. It's about 5km from either the R295 in the west or the N4 in the east. Follow the signs.

Ballymote & Around

POP 1600

This pretty little town merits a visit if only to see the immense shell of Ballymote Castle, which could be a model for sandcastle builders everywhere. It was from this early-14th-century castle, fronted by formidable drum towers, that O'Donnell marched to disaster at the Battle of Kinsale in 1601. It's on the Tubbercurry road (R296), opposite the train station in Ballymote.

Eagles soar straight over your head at the volunteer-run research centre Eagles Flying (www.eaglesflying.com; adult/child €10/6; ⊙10.30am-12.30pm & 2.30-4.30pm, demonstrations 11am & 3pm Apr-Oct). Learn about these birds of prey during demonstrations; there's also an on-site minizoo with ducks, donkeys and other cute critters. It's 3.5km northwest of town, near Temple House.

One of Ireland's best places to buy music is in the village of Gurteen (also spelt Gorteen). The Coleman Irish Music Centre (www.colemanirishmusic.com; ⊙10am-5pm Mon-Sat) has multimedia music exhibits and hosts workshops and performances. You can add to your music collection or pick up your own instruments and sheet music at the on-site shop. It's 12km south of Ballymote on the R293.

Temple House (✆071-918 3329; www.templehouse.ie; Ballymote; s/d from €90/140, dinner €45; ⊙Apr-Nov; 🕾), set in 400 hectares of woodlands, overlooks the ruins of a 13th-century Knights Templar castle and a crystalline lake that you can explore by rowboat. The Georgian mansion has been in the same family since the 1600s, and has six shabby-chic period guest rooms (with modern bathrooms), dusty natural-history collections and decapitated hunting trophies. Dinner is communal. It's signposted 500m south of the small village of Ballinacarrow (also spelt Ballynacarrow), close to the N17.

Aughris Head

An invigorating 5km walk traces the cliffs around remote Aughris Head, where dolphins and seals can often be seen swimming into the bay. Birdwatchers should look out for kittiwakes, fulmars, guillemots, shags, storm petrels and curlews along the way.

In a sheltered seaside setting on the lovely beach by the cliff walk, the Beach Bar (www.thebeachbarsligo.com; Aughris Head; mains €10-20; ⊙food served 1-8pm daily summer, weekends only winter) is tucked inside a 17th-century thatched cottage, with cracking traditional music sessions and superb seafood, including creamy chowder and poached salmon. The owners also operate the B&B Aughris House (✆071-917 6465; Aughris Head; tent/van sites from €10/20, s/d from €30/60; 🕾) next door, with seven comfy rooms and adjacent campsites.

Easkey

Easkey is one of Europe's best year-round surfing destinations. However, in pubs with names like Lobster Pot and Fisherman's Weir conversations revolve around hurling and seafood prices; the road to the beach isn't even signposted (turn off next to the day-care centre, just east of town). Facilities are few; most surfers camp (free) around the castle ruins by the sea.

If you're planning on hitting the waves, Easkey Surfing & Information Centre (Irish Surfing Association; ✆096-49428; www.isasurf.ie) is a good resource.

Buses run one to four times daily from Sligo to Ballina via Easkey (€13, one hour).

Enniscrone

Some 14km south at Enniscrone, stunning Hollow Beach stretches for 5km. Surf lessons and board hire are available from Seventh Wave Surf School (✆087 971 6389; www.surfsligo.com; Beach, Enniscrone; lessons adult/child from €30/25; ⊙Apr-Oct). The town is also famous for its traditional seaweed baths which are some of the most atmospheric in the country. Kilcullen's Seaweed Baths (✆091-36238; www.kilcullenseaweedbaths.com; Enniscrone; baths from €25; ⊙10am-8pm daily May-Sep, Thu-Mon Oct-Apr) is the most traditional and has buckets of character.

The coast along here enjoys splendid sunsets and it's worth considering an overnight stay to lap up the view. For accommodation try Seasons Lodge (✆096-37122; www.seasonslodge.ie; Enniscrone; s/d from €65/110; 🕾), a purpose-built guesthouse with bright, spacious rooms. Lots of thoughtful extras make it a wonderful place to stay.

Waterfront House (☎096-37120; www.waterfronthouse.ie; Cliff Rd; s/d from €60/90; @) is perched on the knoll overlooking the broad beach and surf. The rooms are done up in ubiquitous red but the bar and restaurant are where you'll want to be.

Sligo (€14, 1½ hours) buses run one to four times daily.

Lough Gill

The mirrorlike 'Lake of Brightness', Lough Gill was a place of great inspiration for Yeats.

The lake, southeast of Sligo town, is shaded by two magical swaths of woodland – **Hazelwood** and **Slish Wood** – which have loop trails; there are good views of Innisfree Island from the latter.

You can take a **cruise** on the lake from atmospheric Parke's Castle (p507), in nearby County Leitrim.

❶ Getting There & Away

The lake is immediately east of Sligo town. Take the R286 along the north shore for the most interesting views, whether you are driving or riding. The southern route on the R287 is less interesting until you reach Dooney Rock.

Dooney Rock

Immortalised by Yeats in *The Fiddler of Dooney*, this huge fissured limestone knoll bulges awkwardly upward by the lough's southern shore. There's a great lake view from the top.

It's 7km southwest of Sligo town on the R287.

Innisfree Island

This pint-sized island lies tantalisingly close to the lough's southeastern shore, but alas, can't be accessed. Still, it's visible from the shore. Its air of tranquillity so moved Yeats that he famously wrote *The Lake Isle of Innisfree:*

> I will arise and go now, and go to Innisfree,
> And a small cabin build there, of clay and wattles made;
> Nine bean rows will I have there, a hive for the honey bee,
> And live alone in the bee-loud glade.

Access the best vantage point of the island from a small road that starts at the junction of the R287 and the R290. Follow the winding lane for 4.2km to a small parking area by the water.

North of Sligo Town

Evocative coastal drives and lonely mountain paths highlight the heart of Yeats country.

Benbulben

A stolid greenish-grey eminence visible all along Sligo's northern coast, Benbulben (525m), often written Ben Bulben, resembles a table covered by a pleated cloth: its limestone plateau is uncommonly flat, and its near-vertical sides are scored by earthen ribs. Walking here is not for the uninitiated (see below).

COUNTIES MAYO & SLIGO LOUGH GILL

---

❶ WALKING SLIGO

In a country that doesn't hurt for a lack of good walks, County Sligo has more than its share. There are myriad choices, including the **Sligo Way** (www.irishtrails.ie), a 78km waymarked route that includes the Ox Mountains, Lough Easkey and Lough Gill.

Walking resources and organisations are many, and include the following:

➡ **Sligo Walks** (www.sligowalks.ie) An excellent online resource with dozens of walks, maps, ratings and much more.

➡ **Sligo Mountaineering Club** (www.sligomountaineeringclub.org) Good for info on climbing Benbulben, including sensible details on staying safe.

➡ **Muddy Boots Trekking** (☎087 642 9131; franmountainleader@gmail.com) Organises hikes on Benbulben and elsewhere.

➡ **Sea Trails** (☎087 240 5071; www.seatrails.ie) Highly recommended. Runs interesting walks that concentrate on ancient features and natural beauty in and near the coast.

➡ **Sligo Walking Guide** A useful free booklet with scores of walks, available at tourist offices.

Drumcliff

Benbulben's beauty was not lost on WB Yeats. Before the poet died in Menton, France in 1939, he had requested: 'If I die here, bury me up there on the mountain, and then after a year or so, dig me up and bring me privately to Sligo'. His wishes were honoured in 1948, when his body was interred in the churchyard at Drumcliff, where his great-grandfather had been rector.

Yeats' grave (off N15; ☉ dawn-dusk) is next to the doorway of the **Protestant church**, and his youthful bride Georgie Hyde-Lee is buried alongside. Almost three decades her senior, Yeats was 52 when they married. The poet's epitaph is from his poem *Under Ben Bulben*: Cast a cold eye / On life, on death. / Horseman, pass by!

There's a small **cafe and crafts shop** (mains from €4; ☉ 9am-5pm) beside the church. It is popular with locals at lunch and has a good selection of books. Nearby is a fine little **gallery**.

In the 6th century, St Colmcille chose this location for a monastery. You can still see the stumpy remains of a **round tower**, which was struck by lightning in 1396, on the main road nearby. Also in the churchyard is an extraordinary 9th-century **high cross**, etched with intricate biblical scenes that include Adam and Eve as well as Daniel in the Lion's Den.

🛏 Sleeping & Eating

Yeats Lodge   B&B €€
(☎ 071-917 3787; www.yeatslodge.com; Drumcliff; s/d from €50/70; 🖭) Obliging owners, five large, modern rooms and a tranquil atmosphere make this B&B worth seeking out. There's tasteful rustic decor and lovely views of Benbulben. It's 300m off the N15.

Benbulben Farmhouse   LODGE €€
(☎ 071-917 3956; www.benbulbenfarmhouse.com; Barnaribbon; s/d €45/70) Nestled up in the shadow of Benbulben and far from the N15, this farmhouse offers peaceful rural respite. Everything is quite modern and rooms have sitting areas to take in the sylvan views. It's 3km northeast of Drumcliff.

Yeats Tavern   MODERN IRISH €€
(☎ 071-916 3117; www.yeatstavernrestaurant.com; N15, Drumcliff; mains €14-26; ☉ kitchen 9.30am-9.30pm Mon-Sat, noon-9pm Sun) This contemporary pub/restaurant is popular for a pint or Irish coffee, but especially for its seafood, which includes local Drumcliff Bay mussels and Lissadell clams. It's a mere 300m north of Yeats' grave. Lunchtime roast specials are popular.

❶ Getting There & Away

Buses run from Sligo to Drumcliff (€5, 10 minutes, seven to eight daily) and stop at the post office.

Lough Glencar

Straddling counties Sligo and Leitrim, this picturesque lake is famed for fishing as well as its beautiful waterfall, and was referred to by Yeats in *The Stolen Child*. The surrounding countryside is best enjoyed by walking east and taking the steep trail north to the valley.

From Drumcliff it's less than 5km to the lake's western shores.

Raghly

Wide open flats and surf-pounded beaches of battered rocks are the hallmark of this worthwhile drive out to the coast from Drumcliff. Look for the turn just north of Drumcliff.

★**Ardtarmon House** (☎ 071-916 3156; www.ardtarmon.com; Raghly Rd; s/d from €50/80, cottages from €100; ☉ closed late Dec-early Jan), located in an incomparable location 10.5km west of the N15, is a fifth-generation family-run property with four spacious rooms in the manor house, and five self-contained cottages in converted farm buildings. A 450m stroll through wildflower-strewn gardens brings you to a beach. Dinner (€30) featuring home-grown produce can be arranged.

Grange & Streedagh Beach

From the village of Grange, signs point towards Streedagh Beach, a grand crescent of sand that saw some 1100 sailors perish when three ships from the Spanish Armada were wrecked nearby. Views extend from the beach to the cliffs at Slieve League in County Donegal. Locals regularly swim here, even in winter.

You can ride through the grassy countryside or along Trawalua Beach on guided treks with **Island View Riding Stables** (☎ 071-916 6156; www.islandviewridingstables.com; off N15, Moneygold; adult/child per hour €25/18), one of several in the area.

Buses run from Sligo to Grange (€5, 10 minutes, seven to eight daily) and stop at Rooney's newsagent.

Mullaghmore

The sweeping arc of dark-golden sand and the safe shallow waters make the pretty fishing village of Mullaghmore a popular family destination.

◉ Sights & Activities

Take time to cycle or drive the scenic road looping around Mullaghmore Head, where wide shafts of rock slice into the Atlantic surf. En route you'll pass Classiebawn Castle (closed to the public), a neo-Gothic turreted pile built for Lord Palmerston in 1856 and later home to the ill-fated Lord Mountbatten, who was killed near here in 1979 when the IRA rigged his boat with explosives.

Mullaghmore Head is becoming known as one of Ireland's premier big-wave surf spots with swells of up to 17m allowing for Hawaiian-style adventure. Big-wave tow-in surfing competitions are regularly held off Mullaghmore Head. Even if you're not riding these monster waves, you can enjoy their drama from shoreline walks.

Mullaghmore's clear waters, rocky outcrops and coves are also ideal for diving, Offshore Watersports (☑ 087 610 0111, 071-919 4769; www.offshore.ie; The Pier; dive trips with rental gear from €45) offers dive trips and gear rental.

🛏 Sleeping

Pier Head Hotel   HOTEL **€€**
(☑ 071-916 6171; www.pierheadhotel.ie; Mullaghmore; s/d from €50/80; ⊗ closed late Dec; 🛜)
Enjoy magnificent views from this hotel by the harbour. The rooms are clean and crisp (request one with a view), there's a tiny gym, a panoramic rooftop terrace with hot tub, and decent food (mains from €10 to €21) in the bar.

Creevykeel Goort Cairn

Shaped like a lobster's claw, this prehistoric court tomb (off N15; ⊗ dawn-dusk) encloses several burial chambers. The structure was originally built around 2500 BC, with several more chambers added later. Once in the unroofed oval court, smaller visitors can duck under the stone-shielded entrance to reach the site's core.

The tomb is 1.5km north of Cliffony.

Gleniff Horseshoe Valley

From Creevykeel, follow the small road southeast into the broad Gleniff Horseshoe Valley. Set amid the stark, barren drama of the Dartry Mountains, this area begs for exploration. A tiny lane, the Gleniff Horseshoe, makes a 10km loop through the valley, passing wild babbling streams and the

---

WORTH A TRIP

INISHMURRAY ISLAND

It takes some effort to arrange a visit to Inishmurray, an island that was abandoned in 1948, leaving behind early-Christian remains and fascinating pagan relics. There are three well-preserved churches, beehive cells and open-air altars. The old monastery, surrounded by a thickset oval wall, was founded in the early 6th century by St Molaise.

The pagan relics were also assembled by Inishmurray monks. There's a collection of cursing stones: those who wanted to lay a curse did the Stations of the Cross in reverse, turning the stones as they went. There were also separate burial grounds for men and women, and a strong belief that if a body was placed in the wrong ground it would move itself during the night.

Read more at www.inishmurray.com.

Only 6km separates Inishmurray from the mainland, but there's no regular boat service, and the lack of a harbour makes landing subject to the weather. Enthusiastic historian Joe McGowan runs excursions aboard the MV Excalibur (☑ 071-914 2738; www.sligoheritage.com; Mullaghmore; per person from €35; ⊗ Apr-Sep). Inishmurray Island Trips (☑ 087 254 0190; www.inishmurrayislandtrips.com; Mullaghmore; trips per person from €35; ⊗ Apr-Sep) also runs trips.

remains of an old mill. You can imagine Yeats here.

The loop is good by bike or car. You can also walk and branch off into hikes in the hills. Sligo Walks (p443) has online maps.

At the base of the valley, the **Benwiskin Centre** (☑ 071-917 6721; www.benwiskincentre.com; Ballintrillick; dm/s/d €15/30/50; ☎) is a good hostel with dorms and private rooms.

County Donegal

POP 161,150 / AREA 3001 SQ KM

Best Places to Eat

➡ Castle Murray (p456)

➡ Mill Restaurant (p471)

➡ Cove (p471)

➡ Olde Glen Bar &
Restaurant (p475)

Best Places to Stay

➡ Frewin House (p476)

➡ Lough Eske Castle (p453)

➡ Carnaween House (p461)

➡ Corcreggan Mill (p471)

Why Go?

'Up here it's different', the saying goes, and it's true. County Donegal is the wild child of Ireland. Even before the twins of history and politics conspired to isolate it, Donegal was a place like no other on the island. It's a county of extremes: at times bleak and desolate and battered by brutal weather, yet in turn a land of unspoilt splendour where stark peaks and sweeping beaches bask in glorious sunshine. The rugged interior with its remote mountain passes and shimmering lakes is only marginally outdone by the long and labyrinthine coastline with its precipitous cliffs, windswept peninsulas and vast expanses of golden sand. The landscape here easily rivals anything Connemara or Kerry has to offer but Donegal sees only a fraction of their visitors. Proudly different and fiercely independent, one-third of the county is official Gaeltacht territory, where Irish is still the lingua franca.

When to Go

➡ Donegal's character is forged by its impetuous weather. In winter the howling winds and sheeting rain can feel Arctic, and storms arrive unannounced.

➡ In summer the weather isn't much more reliable but the clouds regularly break to allow brilliant sunshine that transforms brooding blues and greys into sparkling green. At this time of year you'll also get the pick of traditional music, storytelling and dance festivals that spring up across the county. The beachside hotels and restaurants come out of hibernation and the surfers hit the waves.

County Donegal Highlights

1 Watch the sun set from the top of Europe's highest sea cliffs, **Slieve League** (p458)

2 Tour flamboyant **Glenveagh Castle** (p474) in beautiful Glenveagh National Park

3 Stroll along the windswept beach at **Tramore** (p459), near Dunfanaghy

4 Sip a quiet pint in **Molly's Bar** (p471), in Dunfanaghy

5 Take in the views at the spectacular **Poisoned Glen** (p467)

6 Learn to surf on the white-sand beach at **Rossnowlagh** (p453)

7 Collect semiprecious stones from the raised beaches at **Malin Head** (p481)

8 Climb to the summit of Donegal's highest peak, **Errigal Mountain** (p467)

9 Explore the stash of international artworks in **Glebe House & Gallery** (p475), on Lough Gartan

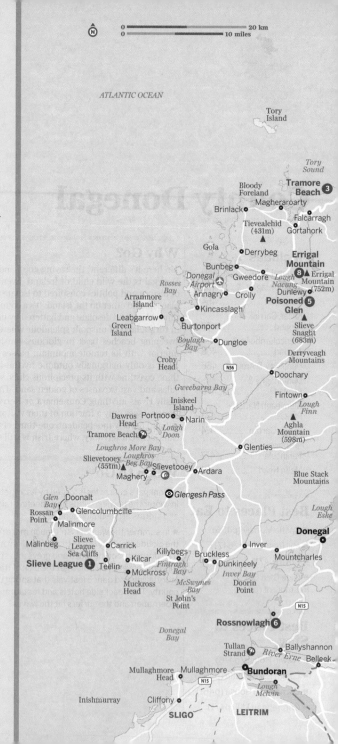

ℹ Getting There & Away

Donegal Airport (www.donegalairport.ie) has flights to/from Dublin (50 minutes, two daily) and to Glasgow Prestwick (50 minutes, four weekly).

It's about 3km northwest of Annagry on the northwestern coast. There's no public transport to the airport, but there are car-rental desks in the terminal.

The **City of Derry Airport** (www.cityofderryairport.com) is just beyond the county's eastern border, in Northern Ireland.

ℹ Getting Around

Donegal is not served by train. Bus is your main transport option if you don't have a car. Timetables change seasonally, so check online for the latest information.

Bus Éireann (☑ in Letterkenny 074-912 1309) Serves mostly the southwestern part of the county. Main routes are 480 (Sligo–Budoran–Donegal town–Letterkenny–Derry), 492 (Donegal town–Killybegs–Ardara–Glenties–Dungloe) and 490 (Killybegs–Kilcar–Glencolumbcille).

Feda O'Donnell (☑ in Annagry 047-954 8114; www.feda.ie) Serves the northwestern part of the county, with a looping route from Galway and Sligo to Bundoran, Donegal town, Letterkenny, Dunfanaghy and Gweedore, terminating in Crolly.

Lough Swilly (☑ in Derry 028-7126 2017, in Letterkenny 074-912 2863; www.loughswillybusco.com) Serves mainly the Inishowen Peninsula, with buses from Derry to Letterkenny, Buncrana and Moville, and on to Carndonagh and Clonmany.

When driving, road signs in the Gaeltacht communities are in Irish only – although we use English transliterations, Irish names are included in brackets.

DONEGAL TOWN

POP 2339

Pretty Donegal town occupies a strategic spot at the mouth of Donegal Bay. With a backdrop of the Blue Stack Mountains, a handsome and well-preserved castle, friendly locals and a good choice of places to eat and sleep, it makes an excellent base for exploring the wild coastline nearby. On the banks of the River Eske, Donegal town was a stamping ground of the O'Donnells, the great chieftains who ruled the northwest from the 15th to 17th centuries. Today, despite being the county's namesake, it's neither its largest town (Letterkenny), nor the county town (the even smaller town of Lifford).

◉ Sights & Activities

★**Donegal Castle**   HISTORIC BUILDING
(www.heritageireland.ie; Castle St; adult/child €4/2; ⊙10am-6pm daily Easter–mid-Sep, 9.30am-4.30pm Thu-Mon mid-Sep–Easter) Guarding a picturesque bend of the River Eske, Donegal Castle remains an imperious monument to both Irish and English might. Built by the O'Donnells in 1474, it served as the seat of their formidable power until 1607, when the English decided to rid themselves of pesky Irish chieftains once and for all. Rory O'Donnell was no pushover though, torching his own castle before fleeing to France in the infamous Flight of the Earls. Their defeat paved the way for the Plantation of Ulster by thousands of newly arrived Scots and English Protestants, sowing the seeds of the divisions that still afflict Ireland to this day.

The castle was rebuilt in 1623 by Sir Basil Brooke, along with the adjacent three-storey Jacobean house. Further restoration in the 1990s has made it a wonderfully atmospheric place to visit, with rooms furnished with French tapestries and Persian rugs. There are guided tours every hour.

TOP FIVE SCENIC DRIVES

Practically any stretch of road qualifies as a scenic drive in this rugged county, but the following are especially captivating. So captivating, in fact, that you'll need to take care to keep your eyes on the road.

➡ Coastal highway from Dunfanaghy to Gweedore.

➡ Hundred-mile loop of the isolated Inishowen Peninsula.

➡ Vertiginous heights of Horn Head.

➡ Lingering arc through stunning Glenveagh National Park.

➡ Snaking switchbacks traversing Glengesh Pass.

Diamond Obelisk

MONUMENT

In 1474 Red Hugh O'Donnell and his wife, Nuala O'Brien, founded Donegal's Franciscan friary by the shore south of town. It was accidentally blown up in 1601 by Rory O'Donnell while laying siege to an English garrison, and little remains. Four of its friars, fearing that the arrival of the English meant the end of Celtic culture, chronicled the whole of known Celtic history and mythology from 40 years before the Flood to AD 1618 in *The Annals of the Four Masters* – still one of the most important sources of early Irish history. The obelisk (1937), in the Diamond, commemorates the work, copies of which are displayed in the National Library in Dublin.

Donegal Bay Waterbus

BOAT TOUR

(www.donegalbaywaterbus.com; Donegal Pier; adult/child €15/5; ⊙ Easter-Oct) The most enjoyable way to explore the highlights of Donegal Bay is on a 1¼-hour boat tour taking in everything from historic sites to seal-inhabited coves, admiring an island manor and a ruined castle along the way. The tour runs up to three times daily.

⊨ Sleeping

Good B&Bs and mediocre hotels are plentiful around Donegal town; for high-end luxury head out to nearby Lough Eske.

Donegal Town Independent Hostel HOSTEL €

(☑074-972 2805; www.donegaltownhostel.com; Killybegs Rd, Doonan; dm/d €17/42; @⊚) Run by an energetic couple, rooms at this IHH hostel 1.2km northwest of town off the Killybegs Rd (N56) have quirky murals – from technicolour landscapes to glow-in-the-dark night skies – and some have water views.

Ard na Breatha

B&B €€

(☑074-972 2288; www.ardnabreatha.com; Drumrooske Middle; d/f €118/139; ⊙ Feb-Oct; ⊚) In an elevated setting 1.5km north of town, this boutique guesthouse on a working farm has tasteful rooms with pine furniture and wrought-iron beds. It's an incredibly warm and welcoming place, with a full bar and restaurant (three-course dinner €39). Food is organic and sourced from the farm or its neighbours where possible. Dinner is available at least Friday to Sunday by reservation.

Cove Lodge

B&B €€

(☑074-972 2302; www.thecovelodgebandb.com; Drumgowan; s/d €50/80; ⊚) You'll find subtle

Donegal

◎ Top Sights
1 Donegal Castle A1

◎ Sights
2 Diamond Obelisk................................A2

⊨ Sleeping
3 Central Hotel A2

⊗ Eating
4 Blueberry Tearoom A1
5 Harbour Restaurant A2
6 La Bella Donna A1
7 Olde Castle Bar A1

◎ Drinking & Nightlife
8 McCafferty's......................................A2
9 Reel Inn... A1

◎ Shopping
10 Magee's B1

floral patterns and rustic charm in the four ground-floor rooms of this tranquil B&B. Located just out of town in a rural setting, it's a taste of Irish country living with all its renowned warmth and friendliness intact. Cove Lodge is 5km south of town on the R267.

Mill Park Hotel

HOTEL €€

(☑074-972 2880; www.millparkhotel.com; The Mullins; s/d from €94/118; @⊚⊠⊞) A modern hotel with corporate styling in the bedrooms and more rustic but contemporary public areas, this is a decent but characterless option in need of a little attention to detail.

Central Hotel HOTEL €€
(☑074-972 1027; www.centralhoteldonegal.com;
The Diamond; s/d from €55/90; 🛜🏊) The Central offers decent but dated rooms, regular
live music in the bar, and a leisure centre
with pool and gym.

✕ Eating

Aroma CAFE €
(www.donegalcraftvillage.com; Ballyshannon Rd,
Donegal Craft Village; dishes €5-13; ⊙9.30am-
5.30pm Mon-Sat) Hidden in the far corner of
Donegal's craft village, this small cafe has
a big reputation for fine food. Along with
the excellent coffee and luscious cakes, the
blackboard specials feature seasonal local produce whipped up into tantalising
soups, salads and wholesome hot dishes.
There's seating outside for extra space on
fine days.

Blueberry Tearoom CAFE €
(Castle St; mains €9-12; ⊙9am-7pm Mon-Sat; 🚻)
A perennial local favourite, this cosy cafe
serves up simple, honest food in hearty portions. Expect soup, toasties, quiche, panini,
sticky cakes of all descriptions and a warm,
friendly atmosphere.

Olde Castle Bar SEAFOOD €€
(☑074-972 1262; www.oldecastlebar.com; Castle
St; mains €9-24; ⊙bar noon-8pm; 🚻) This old-
world boozer just off the Diamond serves
upmarket pub classics such as venison pie,
Donegal Bay oysters, Irish stew, seafood
platters and good old bacon and cabbage.
The restaurant opens at weekends and
has excellent seafood and steaks; the two-
course early-bird menu (6pm to 8pm) costs
€20.

Harbour Restaurant SEAFOOD €€
(☑074-972 1702; www.theharbour.ie; Quay St;
mains €13-26; ⊙5-9.30pm Tue-Sat, 3-9pm Sun)
You'll be surprised by the extensive menu
at this popular local haunt, with its nautical
theme, bare stone walls and plush furnishings. As well known for its pizza as its seafood, you'll find something for everyone at
this friendly, down-to-earth spot.

La Bella Donna ITALIAN €€
(☑074-972 5790; www.labelladonnarestaurant.
com; Bridge St; mains €11-26; ⊙dinner Tue-Sat; 🚻)
Pizza, pasta and sizzling steaks in rich sauces pull in the punters at this lively, modern
restaurant. It gets very busy at weekends so
book in advance.

 ## Drinking & Nightlife

Reel Inn PUB
(Bridge St) The best craic in town is invariably found at this old-school pub. Its owner
plays the button-box accordion, and his pals
join him in traditional music sessions most
nights.

McCafferty's PUB
(The Diamond) Sit by the fire, sip what many
believe to be the best pint of Guinness in
town and just soak up the atmosphere at
this cosy, unassuming pub.

🛍 Shopping

Donegal Craft Village HANDICRAFTS
(www.donegalcraftvillage.com; Ballyshannon Rd;
⊙10am-5pm Mon-Sat Apr-Sep, Tue-Sat Oct)
You won't find any canned leprechauns or
Guinness T-shirts here. Instead, this little
huddle of craft studios showcases pottery,
ironwork, handwoven fabrics, jewellery and
more. It's signposted 1.5km south of town
on the R267.

Magee's CLOTHING
(www.magee1866.com; The Diamond; ⊙10am-6pm
Mon-Sat, 2-6pm Sun) One room of this small
department store is devoted to Donegal
tweed, which has been produced here since
1866.

ℹ Information

Blueberry Cybercafe (Castle St; per hour €4;
⊙9am-7pm Mon-Sat) Internet cafe above the
Blueberry Tearoom. Check in at the counter
downstairs.

Tourist office (☑074-972 1148; donegal@fail-
teireland.ie; Quay St; ⊙9am-5.30pm Mon-Sat,
11am-3pm Sun Jun-Aug, 9am-5pm Mon-Sat
Sep-May) In the 'Discover Ireland' building by
the waterfront.

ℹ Getting There & Away

Bus Éireann (☑074-913 1008; www.buseir
eann.ie) Services connect Donegal with Sligo
(€14.50, one hour, six daily), Galway (€20, four
hours, four daily), Killybegs (€8.50, 35 minutes, three daily), Derry (€17, 1½ hours, seven
Monday to Saturday, six Sunday) and Dublin
(€21, 4½ hours, nine daily). The bus stop is on
the western side of the Diamond.

Feda O'Donnell (☑074-954 8114; www.feda
odonnell.com) Buses run to Galway (€20, four
hours, twice daily, three on Friday and Sunday)
via Bundoran and Sligo (€12). Call to confirm
departure point. Heading north, buses call at
Dungloe, Gweedore and Dunfanaghy (all €10).

DONEGAL'S BEST BEACHES

Donegal's wild and rugged coastline is splashed with broad sweeps of pristine sands and secluded coves. Here are some of our favourites:

➡ **Tramore** (p470) Hike through the dunes west of Dunfanaghy and you'll be rewarded with pristine sands on this secluded stretch of coast.

➡ **Carrick Finn** (p463) A gorgeous sweep of undeveloped sand near Donegal Airport.

➡ **Portnoo** (p461) A wishbone-shaped sheltered cove backed by undulating hills.

➡ **Ballymastocker Bay** (p477) An idyllic stretch of sand lapped by turquoise water.

➡ **Culdaff** (p482) A long stretch of golden sand, popular with families.

➡ **Rossnowlagh** (p453) A sweeping white-sand beach ideal for learning to surf.

❶ Getting Around

Bike Shop (☑ 074-972 2515; Waterloo Pl; per day €10; ⊙ hours vary) Rents bikes and has information on cycling in the area.

AROUND DONEGAL TOWN

Lough Eske

Almost surrounded by the Blue Stack Mountains, tranquil Lough Eske is a scenic spot perfect for walking, cycling or fishing. Lough Eske translates as 'Lake of the Fish' and is a popular angling centre. The season runs from May to September and there's a purpose-built angling centre on the shore where you can buy permits and hire boats.

There is no public transport to the lake.

🛏 Sleeping & Eating

Arches Country House　　　　B&B €€
(☑ 074-972 2029; www.archescountryhse.com; Lough Eske; s/d €50/70; 🛜) A modern dormer bungalow in a tranquil spot overlooking the lake, this welcoming B&B is a bucolic getaway, yet just five minutes' drive from Donegal town. The rooms here are beautifully decorated with a blend of country-house charm and contemporary style, while owner Noreen is a fount of local knowledge and an extremely gracious host.

★ Lough Eske Castle　　　　HOTEL €€€
(☑ 074-972 5100; www.solislougheskecastle.com; Lough Eske; d from €245; ⊙ closed Sun-Wed Nov-Mar; @ 🛜 ⊠) Set in vast grounds, this imposing 19th-century castle was all but razed by fire in 1939 but has been painstakingly re-built and restored and is now the epitome of elegant country living. Most of the complex, including the minimalist rooms, decadent spa and smart restaurant, is spanking new but exudes a sense of classic sophistication mixed with impeccable contemporary style.

Harvey's Point Country Hotel　　HOTEL €€€
(☑ 074-972 2208; www.harveyspoint.com; Harvey's Point; s/d from €149/198; ⊙ closed Sun-Wed Nov-Christmas & early Jan-Mar; @ 🛜) At the water's edge, this elegant retreat is privately owned and run, and it's evident in the pride taken by staff – from the kindly concierge through to the chefs at the excellent French restaurant. Rooms range from large to enormous and are decked out in autumnal colours.

Rossnowlagh

POP 50

Rossnowlagh's spectacular 3km-long Blue Flag beach is a broad, sandy stretch of heaven that attracts families, surfers, kitesurfers and walkers throughout the year. The gentle rollers are great for learning to surf or honing your skills, and Ireland's largest and longest-running surfing competition, the **Rossnowlagh Intercounty Surf Contest**, is held here in late October. It's popularly known as the most sociable event in Ireland's surfing calendar.

◉ Sights & Activities

Franciscan Friary　　　　MONASTERY
(www.franciscans.ie; ⊙ 10am-8pm Mon-Sat) FREE
Hidden deep in a forest at the southern end of the beach, this modern friary is set in beautiful, tranquil gardens which are open to the public. There's also a small museum and a wonderful signed walk, The Way of the Cross, which meanders up a hillside

smothered with rhododendrons for spectacular views.

Fin McCool Surf School
SURFING

(☑071-985 9020; www.finmccoolsurfschool.com; Beach Rd; gear rental per 3hr €29, 2hr lesson incl gear €35; ☺10am-7pm daily Easter-Oct, 10am-7pm Sat & Sun mid-Mar–Easter & Nov-Christmas) Tuition, gear rental and accommodation are available at this friendly surf lodge run by Pro Tour surf judge Neil Britton with the help of his extended family, most of whom have competed on the international circuit. The three- and four-bed dorms cost €20 per night, doubles €50.

🛏 Sleeping & Eating

Smugglers Creek
B&B €€

(☑071-985 2367; www.smugglerscreekinn.com; Cliff Rd; s/d from €45/70, mains €13-25; ☺daily Apr-Sep, Thu-Sun Oct-Mar; 🛜) This combined pub/restaurant/guesthouse perches on the hillside above the bay. It's justifiably popular for its excellent food and sweeping views (room 4 has the best vantage point and a balcony into the bargain). There's live music on summer weekends.

Sandhouse Hotel
HOTEL €€€

(☑071-985 1777; www.sandhouse-hotel.ie; Beach Rd; d from €134; ☺Feb-Nov; @) Once an extravagant 19th-century fishing lodge, this beachside hotel has been modernised and lost much of its character. The views are still spectacular and the rooms are comfortable.

Gaslight Inn
IRISH €€

(☑071-985 1141; www.gaslight-rossnowlagh.com; mains €11-25) Set on the cliff top, the Gaslight Inn offers an extensive menu of well-cooked comfort food and spectacular views over the bay. The owners also run the Ard na Mara (☑071-985 1141; www.ardnamara-rossnow lagh.com; s/d €60/90) guesthouse, which has bright, sunny rooms.

ⓘ Getting There & Away

Rossnowlagh is 17km southwest of Donegal town; there's no public transport.

Bundoran
POP 2140

Blinking amusement arcades, hurdy-gurdy fairground rides and fast-food diners are

---

LOCAL KNOWLEDGE

NEIL BRITTON: SURFER

When local hotelier Mrs Britton bought a surfboard off some visiting surfers in the 1960s, she thought it might make an interesting diversion for her guests. Instead, it became an obsession for her whole family. Her grandson Neil Britton – a pioneer of big-wave tow-in surfing in Ireland and a judge on the International Pro Surfing Tour from 1997 to 2004 – has surfed all over the world and is a bit of a legend on the Irish surf scene.

Neil began surfing 20 years ago on Rossnowlagh Beach in County Donegal and now owns and runs the Fin McCool Surf School and Lodge overlooking the strand where it all started.

'Ireland is a surfer's paradise,' says Neil. 'Its location on the edge of the Atlantic Ocean and the unique geology of large stretches of its coastline mean that there are beaches ideal for beginners, high-performance breaks for the competent surfer and massive big-wave spots for the very brave (or crazy!).'

For Neil, the jewels in Ireland's surfing crown are located in Ireland's northwest: 'One of my favourite places is Mullaghmore in Sligo, one of Ireland's premier big-wave spots. It's an expert's-only wave, breaking over a shallow, left-hand reef and produces huge, heavy tubes.'

Although you can surf year-round in Ireland, Neil advises that conditions are at their best in autumn and spring. 'Surfing in Ireland can be a frustrating experience for a dedicated surfer as although lack of swell is rarely a problem, conditions can lead to weeks of dreaded onshore winds. With a little bit of exploration though, you'll easily find a sheltered bay with better surf.'

Magic Seaweed (www.magicseaweed.com) has a very good forecast and report service for the major breaks in the country and can prove an invaluable tool for the uninitiated travelling surfer. For a full list of approved surf schools, check out the Irish Surfing Association (www.isasurf.ie).

Bundoran's stock-in-trade. But Donegal's best-known seaside resort also has superb surf, and attracts a mixed crowd of young families, pensioners and beach dudes. Outside summer, the carnival atmosphere abates and the town can be quite desolate.

🏃 Activities

Surfing

Bundoran has two main surf spots: the Peak, an imposing reef break directly in front of the town, which should only be attempted by experienced surfers, and the less formidable beach break at Tullan Strand, just north of the town centre. In June, Bundoran hosts the Sea Sessions (www.seasessions.com) festival – three days of surfing, skating, music and partying.

The town has three surf schools, each of which rents gear and has its own basic hostel-style accommodation. A three-hour lesson costs about €35, gear rental €20 per day and accommodation €20 for a dorm room or €50 for a double. All offer deals on surf and accommodation packages.

Bundoran Surf Co SURFING
(☑ 071-984 1968; www.bundoransurfco.com; Main St) Bundoran Surf Co conducts surf lessons, kitesurfing and power-kiting.

Donegal Adventure Centre SURFING
(☑ 071-984 2418; www.donegaladventurecentre.net; Bayview Ave) Youth-oriented place that also offers kayaking and gorge walking.

Turf n Surf SURFING
(☑ 071-984 1091; www.turfnsurf.ie; Bayview Tce) Also runs hill-walking tours and sea-kayaking trips.

Other Water Activities

Waterworld SWIMMING
(www.waterworldbundoran.com; adult/child under 8yr €12/9.50; ⊙10am-7pm daily Jun-Aug, noon-6pm Sat & Sun mid-Apr–May & Sep) Bundoran's Blue Flag beach isn't safe for swimming, so the place to do it is Waterworld on the waterfront, with wave pools and water slides.

Aquamara SPA
(☑ 071-984 1173; baths from €23; ⊙ from 11am daily Jun-Aug, Sat & Sun mid-Apr–May & Sep) On the Waterworld premises, Aquamara provides a decidedly more sedate form of bathing in its seaweed baths.

🛏 Sleeping

Bundoran has a great choice of hostels – nonsurfers are welcome at all the surf school

lodges – and a glut of soulless midrange hotels.

Homefield Rock Hostel HOSTEL €
(☑ 071-982 9357; www.homefieldbackpackers.com; Bayview Ave; dm/d €20/50; ⊙Apr-Nov, bookings only Dec-Mar; @🛜) Once Viscount Enniskillen's holiday pad, this 260-year-old building later served as an altogether more restrained convent. It's now closer to its original purpose, housing a 60-bed rock-music-themed hostel, with vinyl records on the walls and a piano.

Killavil House B&B €€
(☑ 071-984 1556; www.killavilhouse.com; Finner Rd; d/f €76/114; 🛜) A big modern villa at the Ballyshannon end of town, Killavil has smartly appointed bedrooms with polished wooden furniture, mostly multibedded and suitable for families. There's a garden with seating area for those summer evenings, and Tullan Strand is just a five-minute walk away.

🍴 Eating & Drinking

Gastronomy isn't Bundoran's strong suit, but there are a couple of standout places.

Waves CAFE €
(www.surfworld.ie/waves; Main St; mains €4-8; ⊙8am-6pm; 🛜🧒) Popular with local families and bleached-haired beach bums alike, this cool cafe has sofas strewn with surfing magazines and a menu that ranges from big breakfasts to bagels, cakes, smoothies and ice cream.

Maddens Bridge Bar PUB €€
(☑ 071-984 2050; www.maddensbridgebar.com; Main St; mains €10-20) This surfers hang-out, crammed with wave-related bric-a-brac, has a decent menu of classic pub grub that includes excellent homemade burgers. There's a traditional session on Thursdays (more in summer) and fantastic craic.

La Sabbia ITALIAN €€
(☑ 071-984 2253; www.lasabbiarestaurant.com; Bayview Ave; mains €13-25; ⊙dinner nightly Jun-Sep, Thu-Sun Oct-May; 🧒) This colourful cottage decorated with striking contemporary art has tables spilling out onto the front porch and attracts a lively, upbeat crowd. It's run by a Milanese chef, whose home-town specials include delicious risottos as well as crispy pizzas, and pasta dishes like porcini-filled ravioli.

ℹ Information

Bundoran centres on one long main street just back from the beach. You'll find the banks and post office here.

Tourist office (☑071-984 1350; info@discoverbundoran.com; The Bridge, Main St; ⊙9am-3.30pm Mon-Fri, various hours Sat & Sun Apr-Sep) Glass-paned kiosk opposite the Holyrood Hotel.

ℹ Getting There & Around

Bus Éireann buses stop twice on Main St, outside the Phoenix Tavern and the Celtic Bar. A direct service from Sligo (€10.50, 30 minutes) continues on to Donegal (€9.10, 30 minutes) nine times daily Monday to Saturday, seven on Sunday, and there's a service to Galway (€20, 3½ hours, three Monday to Saturday, two Sunday).

You can rent bikes at the **Bike Stop** (☑085 248 8317; East End; per half-day/day/week €10/15/60; ⊙8.30am-6pm Mon-Sat, noon-4pm Sun).

SOUTHWESTERN DONEGAL

Mountcharles

POP 500

Donegal's scenic-o-meter starts to crank up when you reach the coast just west of Donegal town, and steadily intensifies as you head north. Apart from a scattering of pubs and cafes, there are few places to eat (especially in winter), so stock up before leaving Donegal town or Killybegs.

The hillside village of Mountcharles is the first settlement along the coastal road (N56) west of Donegal town. About 2km south of the village is a safe, sandy beach. The shiny,

green pump at the top of this hillside village was once the backdrop for stories of fairies, ghosts, historic battles and mythological encounters. It was at this point that native poet and *seanachaí* (storyteller) Séamus MacManus practised the ancient art in the 1940s and '50s.

Behind century-old stone walls, the contemporary garden design of Salthill Gardens (☑074-973 5387; www.donegalgardens.com; admission €5; ⊙2-6pm Mon-Thu & Sun May-Sep, plus Sat May-Jul) bursts with perennials, roses, lilies and clematis. It's 2km southwest of the village.

The Donegal–Killybegs bus stops in Mountcharles six times daily Monday to Saturday, twice on Sunday.

Killybegs

POP 1280

The stink of fish and the yawp of seagulls waft from the ranks of giant trawlers moored in Ireland's largest fishing port. Though it once exuded the atmosphere of a charming working town, the recession has hit Killybegs hard, with an increasing number of closed shops and empty premises scarring the streets.

◉ Sights & Activities

Killybegs International Carpet Making & Fishing Centre MUSEUM
(www.visitkillybegs.com; Fintra Rd; adult/child €5/4; ⊙9.30am-5.30pm Mon-Fri year-round, plus 12.30-4.30pm Sat & Sun Jul & Aug) This heritage centre provides a good overview of the town's history, and is set in the factory of Donegal Carpets, the rugs of which adorn the White House and Buckingham Palace. You can sometimes see its hand-knotting loom (the world's longest of its kind) at work. The fun wheelhouse simulator lets you 'steer' a fishing trawler into the

---

WORTH A TRIP

CASTLE MURRAY

Overlooking the ruins of the 15th-century McSwyne's Castle, Castle Murray (☑074-973 7022; www.castlemurray.com; St John's Point; s/d €75/140; 🅿) is no castle itself, but a boutique hotel in a sprawling modern beach house. Each of its 10 individually decorated guest rooms is named for townlands (farming communities) contested by 15th-century Scottish clans, but it's best known for its superb French restaurant (four-course dinner €47). Start with the signature prawns and monkfish in garlic butter, move on to mains like seared Donegal scallops with coconut curry, and finish off with a lime soufflé with gin sorbet. Castle Murray is 1.5km south of Dunkineely (on the N56 between Mountcharles and Killybegs), on a minor road leading to St John's Point.

harbour. There's a good cafe and craft shop on-site.

Fintragh Bay
BEACH

The best beach in the area is at secluded Fintragh Bay, about 3km west of town.

Killybegs Angling Charters
FISHING

(🖉087 220 0982; www.killybegsangling.com; Blackrock Pier) If you're interested in taking to the water to catch pollack, ling, brill or turbot, Brian McGilloway has 30 years' experience in charter angling. Boat charter costs €450 for a full day, while gear rental is from €10 per person. Evening mackerel-fishing trips cost €30 per person.

Tour Donegal
GUIDED TOUR

(🖉086 050 0026; www.tourdonegal.com) Archaeologist and guide Derek Vial offers an insight into the region's history with guided trips to Stone Age tombs, Iron Age forts, the Slieve League sea cliffs, secluded beaches and hidden fishing villages. Tours cost €30 per hour for one to two people plus €5 per hour for extra people.

🛏 Sleeping & Eating

Ritz
HOSTEL €

(🖉074-973 1309; www.theritz-killybegs.com; Chapel Brae; dm/d/f €20/50/60; @🖥) The name might be ironic, but this superbly run 38-bed IHO hostel in the town centre has ritzy facilities including an enormous kitchen with an island workbench and dishwasher, colourful rooms with private bathroom and TVs, and a laundry. Continental breakfast is included.

Drumbeagh House
B&B €€

(🖉074-973 1307; www.killybegsbnb.biz.ly; Conlin Rd; d €70; @) Accommodating hosts with plenty of local knowledge and the time to share it make this small B&B a great find. The cosy rooms are tastefully decorated in neutral colours and the locally smoked salmon for breakfast is worth the trip alone.

Tara Hotel
HOTEL €€€

(🖉074-974 1700; www.tarahotel.ie; Main St; s/d from €65/120; 🖥) This friendly, modern hotel overlooking the harbour has comfortable, minimalist rooms, a decent bar and a small gym with jacuzzi, sauna and steam room.

Mrs B's Coffee House
CAFE €

(Upper Main St; mains €4-8; ⊙9am-5pm Mon-Sat; 🖥📶) Mrs B's is a bright and welcoming cafe with comfy sofas, local art on the walls, and a menu of homemade and locally sourced food extending from hearty breakfasts to sandwiches and panini, plus (Thursday to Saturday only) delicious seafood chowder.

Kitty Kelly's
IRISH €€

(🖉074-973 1925; www.kittykellys.com; Kilcar Rd; dinner mains €15-20; ⊙dinner daily, 1-4.30pm Sat & Sun May-Sep) Dining at this restaurant in a 200-year-old farmhouse feels more like attending an intimate dinner party. The menu is a gourmet take on traditional Irish favourites like rich stew and creamy trifle. It's on the coast road, 5km west of Killybegs – you can't miss the lurid pink and green paint job. Opening hours vary annually; bookings are essential.

ℹ Information

There are no banking facilities or ATMs west of Killybegs, so stock up on cash here.

Killybegs Information Centre (🖉074-973 2346; www.killybegs.ie; Quay St; ⊙9.30am-5.30pm Mon-Thu, to 5pm Fri) In a cabin near the harbour.

ℹ Getting There & Away

Bus Éireann buses from Donegal (€8.50, 30 minutes) run six times daily Monday to Saturday, twice on Sunday. Bus 490 heads west to Kilcar (€4.30, 20 minutes) and Glencolumbcille (€8.50, 45 minutes) three times daily Monday to Saturday and once on Sunday.

Kilcar, Carrick & Around

POP 260

Kilcar (Cill Chártha) and its more attractive neighbour Carrick (An Charraig) make good bases for exploring the breathtaking coastline of southwestern Donegal, especially the stunning sea cliffs at Slieve League.

This is fantastic walking country, particularly if you don't mind hoofing up and down a few hills. Kilcar Tourism has some pointers for walking the Kilcar Way; ask at the **Áislann Chill Chartha** (🖉074-973 8376; www.aislann.ie; Main St, Kilcar; ⊙9am-10pm Mon-Fri, 10am-6pm Sat), a community centre that provides information for tourists. Just outside Kilcar is a small, sandy beach.

Local information is available at the excellent **Slieve League Cliffs Centre** (🖉074-973 9077; www.slieveleaguecliffs.ie; Teelin, Carrick; ⊙10.30am-5.30pm daily Easter-Sep, Fri-Tue Feb-Easter & Oct-Nov; 🖥), which also has an artisan cafe and crafts gallery. The centre runs one- and three-day archaeology and hill-walking courses. From Carrick, follow the narrow road towards Teelin Pier, and turn right at the Rusty Bar pub.

Sights & Activities

Slieve League SEA CLIFFS
The Cliffs of Moher get more publicity, but the cliffs of Slieve League are higher. In fact, these spectacular polychrome cliffs are thought to be the highest in Europe, plunging some 600m to the sea (although they're not vertical). Looking down, you'll see two rocks nicknamed the 'school desk and chair' for reasons that are immediately obvious.

The narrow road beyond the Slieve League Cliffs Centre (being widened at the time of writing) leads to the lower car park beside a gate in the road; you can drive another 1.5km beyond the gate (cars only) to the upper car park (often full) right beside the viewpoint. The cliffs are particularly scenic at sunset when the waves crash dramatically far below and the ocean reflects the last rays of the day.

From the upper car park, a rough and eroded footpath leads up and along the top of the near-vertical cliffs to the aptly named **One Man's Pass**, a narrow ridge that leads to the summit of Slieve League (595m; 10km round trip). Be aware that mist and rain can roll in unexpectedly and rapidly, making conditions treacherous.

It's also possible to hike to the summit of Slieve League from Carrick via the **Pilgrim Path** (signposted along the minor road on the right before the Slieve League cliffs road), returning via One Man's Pass and the viewpoint road (12km; allow four to six hours).

Studio Donegal WOOLLEN MILL
(www.studiodonegal.ie; Glebe Mill, Kilcar; ☉9am-5.30pm Mon-Fri, plus 9.30am-5pm Sat May-Oct) **FREE** Though mechanised in the 1960s, there has been a hand-weaving tweed mill here for more than a century. Visitors are often invited upstairs to see spinners and weavers in action, before browsing jackets, hats, throws and other tweed items in the shop.

Nuala Star Teelin BOAT TOUR
(☎074-973 9365; www.sliabhleagueboattrips. com; ☉Apr-Oct) Sightseeing boat trips along the Slieve League cliffs can be arranged by contacting Nuala Star Teelin. Prices are €20 to €25 per person, depending on numbers, with reductions for children. Boats depart from Teelin pier every two hours (weather permitting). Sea angling and diving trips can also be arranged.

Sleeping & Eating

Derrylahan Hostel HOSTEL €
(☎074-973 8079; homepage.eircom.net/~derry lahan; Derrylahan, Kilcar; campsites per person €8, dm/d €18/50; @🖵) Set on a working farm, this rustic, well-run IHH hostel has comfortable rooms with private bathroom as well as a 20-person bunk-house and plenty of scenic spots to pitch a tent. Bike rental (€20) can be organised if you book ahead. It's located 3km west of Kilcar on the coast road. Pick-ups can be arranged.

Inishduff House B&B €€
(☎074-973 8542; www.inishduffhouse.com; Largy, Kilcar; s/d €50/85; 🖵) On the main road about 5km east of Kilcar, this modern B&B has large, comfortable rooms, an incredibly warm welcome and wonderful sea views.

Blue Haven HOTEL €€
(☎074-973 8090; www.bluehaven.ie; Largy, Kilcar; mains €14-25; ☉lunch & dinner) Blue Haven's modern restaurant has giant windows overlooking the bay and an extensive, if predictable, menu of classic dishes. A popular Sunday lunch spot with stunning sea views.

Getting There & Away

Bus Éireann services run from Donegal to Kilcar (€9.80) and from Kilcar to Carrick (€2.90) and Glencolumbcille (€5.50) three times daily Monday to Saturday and once on Sunday.

Glencolumbcille & Around

POP 255

'There's nothing feckin' here!' say the locals, in an endearingly blunt forewarning to visitors. But once you've sampled Glencolumbcille's three-pub village, scalloped beaches, stunning walks and fine little folk museum, chances are you'll disagree.

Approaching Glencolumbcille (Gleann Cholm Cille) via the Glengesh Pass does, however, reinforce just how isolated this starkly beautiful coastal haven is. You drive past miles and miles of hills and bogs before the ocean appears, followed by a narrow, green valley and the small Gaeltacht village within it.

This spot has been inhabited since 3000 BC and you'll find lots of Stone Age remains scattered among the cluster of tiny settlements. It's believed that the 6th-century St Colmcille (Columba) founded a monastery here (hence the name, meaning 'Glen of Columba's Church'), and incorporated Stone Age standing stones into Christian usage by inscribing them with a cross. At midnight on Columba's Feast Day (9 June), penitents perform An Turas Cholm Chille (the Gaelic *turas* meaning a 'pilgrimage' or 'journey'), a walking circuit of the stones and the remains of Cholm Cille's chapel before attending Mass at 3am in the local chapel.

◎ Sights

Father McDyer's Folk Village   MUSEUM
(www.glenfolkvillage.com; Doonalt; adult/child €4.50/2.50; ⊗10am-6pm Mon-Sat, noon-6pm Sun Easter-Sep) A museum with a mission, this folk centre was established by the forward-thinking Father James McDyer in 1967 to freeze-frame traditional folk life for posterity. It's housed in a huddle of thatched cottages re-created in the style of the 18th and 19th centuries, with genuine period fittings. The *shebeen* (illicit drinking place) sells unusual local wines (made from ingredients such as seaweed and fuchsias) alongside marmalade and whiskey truffles. It's 3km west of the village, by the beach.

Beaches   BEACH
There are two sandy beaches with brisk waves in Doonalt, immediately west of the village; access from the car park opposite the folk museum. Continue past the museum for 6km to the road's end at Malinbeg, a sheltered bay bitten out of low cliffs, where 60 steps descend to another gorgeous little beach.

✦ Activities

The 19th-century St Columba's Church is the starting point for several excellent walks. The 5.5km pilgrimage route of An Turas Cholm Cille (www.glencolmcille.ie/turas. htm) visits a series of prehistoric stone slabs, many carved with early Christian symbols, and an ancient ruined chapel attributed to the saint; local landowners grant permission for walkers to visit all the stones on Sundays from June to August (some are accessible year-round).

A couple of waymarked loop walks will lead you into the blustery wilds beyond the town. The Tower Loop (10km; two to three hours) heads north to a signal tower atop stunning coastal cliffs, while the more arduous Drum Loop (13km; three to four hours) heads into the hills northeast of the town.

⌁ Courses

Oideas Gael   LANGUAGE COURSE
(www.oideas-gael.com; ⊗mid-Mar–Oct) The Foras Cultúir Uladh (Ulster Cultural Foundation), 1km west of the village centre, offers a range of 'cultural activity holidays' – adult courses in Irish language and traditional culture, including dancing, painting and musical instruments. The centre also leads hill-walking programs in the Donegal highlands. Three-day courses cost from €100, weeklong courses around €200. Accommodation can be arranged: you'll have a choice of homestay or self-catering, with prices of around €80 for a three-night stay.

⌂ Sleeping & Eating

The area has some excellent budget accommodation but places to eat are limited to a cafe in the Folk Village and another attached to Oideas Gael (up for sale at the time of writing).

Dooey Hostel   HOSTEL €
(☑074-973 0130; Dooey; campsites per person €9, dm/d €15/30) Built into a hillside with a corridor carved out of the plant-strewn rockface and jaw-dropping views of the ocean and hills below, this IHO hostel has character in spades. Facilities are rustic, but clean and comfortable. If you're driving, turn left just after the Glenhead Tavern and continue for 1.5km; walkers can hike up a path behind the Folk Village. No credit cards.

Malinbeg Hostel   HOSTEL €
(☑074-973 0006; www.malinbeghostel.com; Malinbeg; dm/s/d €14/20/30; ⊗closed Dec–mid-Jan) Flung out on a remote stretch of coast, the contemporary Malinbeg Hostel sports spotless rooms (some with private bathroom) and scores big for its proximity to the beach and the grocery store handily situated across the road.

Glencolumbcille Lodge   HOSTEL €
(☑074-973 0302; www.ionadsuil.ie; d €50; ☎) Overlooking sheep-filled paddocks, this place is a wee bit worn around the edges but has decent double and twin rooms with private bathrooms and an enormous self-catering kitchen. The helpful owners live off-site, so call ahead, especially at quiet times.

🛍 Shopping

Glencolmcille Woollen Mill　　CLOTHING
(www.rossanknitwear.ie; Malinmore; ⊙10am-8pm Mar-Oct, to 5.50pm Nov-Feb) This is a great place to shop for Donegal tweed jackets, caps and ties, and lambswool scarves and shawls; you can sometimes see weavers in action. It's about 5km southwest of Glencolumbcille, in Malinmore.

❶ Getting There & Away

Bus Éireann service 490 runs to/from Killybegs (€8.50, 45 minutes) three times daily Monday to Saturday and once on Sunday. There is no public transport direct from Glencolumbcille to Ardara; you need to return to Killybegs to head north.

Maghery & the Glengesh Pass

POP 640

A remote, 25km single-track road leads from Glencolumbcille to Ardara via the Glengesh Pass (Glean Géis; meaning 'Glen of the Swans'), one of Donegal's most scenic driving routes; the cascade of hairpin bends descending into the head of the glen is almost alpine in appearance.

On the northern coast of the Glencolumbcille peninsula, 9km west of Ardara, tiny Maghery has a picturesque waterfront. If you follow the strand westward, you'll get to a rocky promontory full of caves. During Cromwell's 17th-century destruction, 100 villagers sought refuge here but all except one were discovered and massacred. About 1.5km east of Maghery is the enchanting **Assarancagh Waterfall**.

Ardara

POP 570

Gateway to the switchbacks of the Glengesh Pass, the heritage town of Ardara (arda-*rah*) is the heart of Donegal's tweed and knitwear industry. You can visit the weavers at work and see the region's most traditional crafts in action. If you're driving, follow signs to the 'Town Car Park' then walk back along the river to the cramped town centre.

Ardara springs to life in late April or early May for the **Cup of Tae Festival** (www.cupoftaefestival.com), a celebration of traditional music, dance and storytelling, particularly featuring the Donegal style of fiddle playing. The festival takes its name from a local

musician, John 'the tae' Gallagher. Its small scale makes it a very friendly event.

◉ Sights

Ardara Heritage Centre　　MUSEUM
(☑074-954 1704; Main St; adult/child €3/1.20; ⊙10am-6pm Mon-Sat, 2-6pm Sun Easter-Sep) Set in the old town courthouse, this centre traces the story of Donegal tweed from sheep shearing to dye production and weaving. A weaver is usually present to demonstrate how a loom works and explain the stitches used in traditional garments.

🛏 Sleeping & Eating

Gort na Móna　　B&B €€
(☑074-953 7777; www.gortnamonabandb.com; Donegal Rd, Cronkeerin; s/d €50/70; 🐕) Huge but cosy and colourful rooms with orthopaedic mattresses, knotty pine furniture and silky throws make this a real home from home. With excellent home baking and preserves for breakfast, mountain views and a pristine beach just down the road, you won't want to leave. Gort na Móna is 2km southeast of town on the old Donegal road.

Bayview Country House　　B&B €€
(☑074-954 1145; www.bayviewcountryhouse.com; Portnoo Rd; s/d €45/74; ⊙Apr–mid-Oct; 🐕) Just north of town and overlooking the bay, this purpose-built B&B has spacious rooms with pretty floral bedspreads, spotless bathrooms and great views. There's a wood fire, homemade bread and scones, and a genuinely warm welcome for visitors.

Green Gate　　B&B €€
(☑074-954 1546; www.thegreengate.eu; Ardvally; s/d €70/110; ⊙Mar-Nov) The Green Gate is a place you'll either love or hate (no TV, no internet, smokers welcome); the traditional thatched cottages here are rustic in the extreme but the views are breathtaking and the host an eccentric but charming Frenchman. It's 3km southeast of town; take the old Donegal road then fork right almost immediately on a narrow hilly road. Phone bookings essential; no credit cards.

Sheila's Coffee and Cream　　CAFE €
(Main St; mains €4-10; ⊙9am-5.50pm Mon-Sat; 🐕🖶) Attached to the heritage centre, this little cafe is a local favourite and serves a good selection of hot dishes such as quiche and lasagne as well as a luscious selection of desserts. Home-baked loaves to take away.

Nancy's Bar IRISH €
(Front St; mains €7-13) This old-fashioned pub-restaurant, in the same family for seven generations, makes its guests feel as if they're sitting in Nancy's living room. It serves superb seafood and chowder with hearty wheaten bread and is also the best place in town for a sociable pint or two.

 Drinking & Nightlife

Many of the town's pubs host regular traditional music sessions; just stroll down the main drag until you hear the good cheer pouring out the door.

Corner House PUB
(The Diamond) A good spot to listen to an Irish music session (Friday and Saturday year-round; nightly from June to September), it's the type of place where someone will spontaneously break out into song and, if the mood is right, the rest of the pub will join in.

 Shopping

Signs in the town centre point you to the town's knitwear producers.

Eddie Doherty CLOTHING
(www.handwoventweed.com; Front St) Behind Doherty's bar, you can catch Eddie Doherty hand-weaving here on a traditional loom.

John Molloy CLOTHING
(www.johnmolloy.com; Killybegs Rd) Handmade and machine-knitted woollies are available here at the flagship establishment and at the factory outlet in Glencolumbcille.

Kennedy's CLOTHING
(Front St) In business for over a century, Kennedy's helped establish Ardara's reputation as a sweater mecca.

Triona Design CLOTHING
(www.trionadesign.com; Main St) Handwoven Donegal tweed, and quality merino wool knitwear.

ⓘ Information

On the Diamond, the Ulster Bank has an ATM; the post office is nearby on Main St.

Tourist office (074-954 1704; www.ardara. ie; Main St; 10am-6pm Mon-Sat, 2-6pm Sun Easter-Sep)

ⓘ Getting There & Around

Bus Éireann service 492 from Donegal (€9.10, 25 minutes) stops outside the Heritage Centre in Ardara en route to Glenties (€3.90, 10 minutes)

four times daily Monday to Saturday, twice on Sunday.

Don Byrne (074-954 1658; www. donbyrnebikes.com; West End; 10am-6pm Tue-Sat) rents bikes for €15/60 per day/week.

Loughrea Peninsula

The twin settlements of Narin and Portnoo nestle at the western end of a gorgeous wishbone-shaped Blue Flag beach, the sandy tip of which points towards Iniskeel Island, which you can walk out to at low tide. St Connell, a cousin of St Colmcille (Columba), founded a monastery here in the 6th century and the island is studded with early-medieval Christian remains including two ruined churches and some decorated grave slabs. The Dolmen Ecocentre (074-954 5010; www.dolmencentre.com; Kilclooney; 9am-5pm Mon-Fri) can point you towards other archaeological sites.

In the southwest corner of the peninsula, hemmed in by grassy dunes, is the beautiful Tramore Beach. In 1588 part of the Spanish Armada ran aground here. The survivors temporarily occupied O'Boyle's Island in Kiltoorish Lake, but then marched to Killybegs, where they set sail again in the *Girona*. The *Girona* met a similar fate that year in Northern Ireland, with the loss of over a thousand crew members.

★ **Carnaween House** (074-954 5122; www.carnaweenhouse.com; Narin; s/d €60/120; ⓐ) is an unexpected gem of a place with brilliant white bedrooms in luxury beach-house style. Subtle touches of colour and a minimalist eye mean they are crisp and calm yet strangely cosy. The restaurant (mains €12-22; dinner Thu-Tue, noon-9pm Sun Jul & Aug, dinner Fri & Sat Sep-May, lunch Sun Mar-Jun & Sep-Oct) serves an excellent selection of seafood and classic Irish dishes brought bang up to date. Book ahead and arrive early to bag the front window and sunset views.

Glenties

POP 800
At the foot of two valleys with a southern backdrop laid on by the Blue Stack Mountains, the proud Tidy Town of Glenties (Na Gleannta) is a good spot for fishing and has some cracking walks in the surrounding countryside. Glenties is linked with playwright Brian Friel, whose play (and

COUNTY DONEGAL LOUGHREA PENINSULA

THE BLACK PIG

When the first spluttering steam engine arrived in Donegal in 1895, the locals dubbed the monstrous, belching creature the Black Pig. The railways gave Donegal's isolated communities a new lease of life and a much-needed connection to the rest of the country. Over 300km of narrow-gauge tracks crossed the county in the railway's heyday, but after WWII business declined and the railway closed to passengers in June 1947, and to freight in 1952.

Today the county's only operational railway is the Fintown Railway (www.antraen. com; Fintown; adult/child €8/5; ⊙11am-5pm Mon-Sat, 1-5pm Sun Jun-Sep). Lovingly restored to its original condition, the red-and-white 1940s diesel railcar runs along a rebuilt 5km section of the former County Donegal Railway track along picturesque Lough Finn. The return trip, which includes commentary, takes around 40 minutes.

Fintown is on the R250, 20km northeast of Glenties.

subsequent film), *Dancing at Lughnasa,* is set in the town.

Brennan's B&B (☑074-955 1235; www. brennansbnb.com; Main St; s/d €45/70; 🛜) offers a warm welcome and three comfy guest rooms.

Bus Eireann service 492 from Donegal stops in Glenties (€9.10, one hour), and continues to Dungloe (€5.50, 45 minutes) twice daily.

NORTHWESTERN DONEGAL

Few places in Ireland are more savagely beautiful than northwestern Donegal. The rocky Gaeltacht area between Dungloe and Crolly is known as the Rosses (Na Rossa), and is scattered with shimmering lakes, grey-pink granite outcrops and golden-sand beaches pounded by Atlantic surf. Further north, between Bunbeg and Gortahork, the scenery is spoiled a little by the uncontrolled sprawl of holiday homes. Offshore, the islands of Arranmore and Tory are fascinating to those eager for a glimpse of a more traditional way of life.

Dungloe

POP 1100

The hub of the Rosses, Dungloe (An Clochán Liath) is a busy if unprepossessing little town with ample services for anyone passing through this spectacular locale. Immortalised in a hit pop song, 'Mary from Dungloe', in the late 1960s, the town celebrates with the 10-day Mary from Dungloe Festival

(☑074-952 1254; www.maryfromdungloe.com) every summer from late July to early August.

An even more famous musical connection is singer Daniel O'Donnell, who was born in Dungloe and is celebrated in the Daniel O'Donnell Visitor Centre (www.dan ielodonnellvisitorcentre.com; Main St; admisson €5; ⊙10am-6pm Mon-Sat, 11am-6pm Sun).

Fishing for salmon and trout in the River Dungloe and Lough Dungloe is popular; you can get tackle and permits from Bonner's (Main St).

For accommodation, your best bet is Radharc an Oileain (☑074-952 1093; www.dun gloebedandbreakfast.com; Quay Rd; s/d €45/70; ⊙Apr-Nov; @), a beautiful family-run B&B overlooking the bay.

There's a small tourist office (☑074-952 1297; www.dungloe.info; Chapel Rd; ⊙9.30am-5.30pm Jun-Sep) in Ionad Teampall Chróine, a community building housed in an old church.

Bus Éireann service 492 from Donegal runs to Dungloe (€9.80, 1½ hours) via Killybegs, Ardara and Glenties three times daily (twice on Sunday).

Coaches operated by Doherty's Travel (☑074-952 1105; www.dohertyscoaches.com) run once a day (except Sunday) between Letterkenny and the Rosses, stopping at Dungloe, Burtonport, Kincasslagh, Annagry and Crolly (€10, 1¼ hours to Dungloe, 2¼ hours to Crolly).

Burtonport & Kincasslagh

POP 345

Pocket-sized Burtonport (Ailt an Chorráin) is the embarkation point for Arranmore Island, which looks near enough to wade to from here. The village has attracted some famously off-the-wall characters over the years. In the 1970s the Atlantis commune was established here, and practised a primal therapy that earned it the nickname 'the Screamers'. Eventually it relocated to the Colombian jungle. Later, the three Silver Sisters chose Burtonport to live out their Victorian lifestyle, complete with Victorian dress. The village seems perfectly ordinary today.

For fishing and diving trips, contact **Inishfree Charters** (⌨ 074-955 1533; The Pier, Burtonport), which has an office at the cabins by the pier.

Head north of Burtonport on the coast road to reach the picturesque village of Kincasslagh (Cionn Caslach), with ancient cottages perched on top of rocky outcrops, and the stunning Blue Flag beach at **Carrick Finn**. This sweeping stretch of sand with a backdrop of distant mountains is wonderfully undeveloped, despite being right beside Donegal airport.

Cosy **Limekiln House** (⌨ 074-954 8521; www.limekilnhouse.com; Carrick Finn, Kincasslagh; d with/without bathroom €70/60) makes a great overnight stop, with comfortable rooms, tempting home baking and a warm welcome. It's at the far end of the minor road that leads north past Donegal airport.

You can't miss the giant fibreglass lobster clinging to the wall of the **Lobster Pot** (⌨ 074-954 2012; www.lobsterpot.ie; Main St, Burtonport; bar meals €10-22, dinner mains €15-25; ☉ bar meals noon-6pm, dinner from 6pm). Serving up a great selection of seafood, this pub-restaurant is adorned with football jerseys and packed out when big matches are shown on the large-screen TV.

Arranmore Island

POP 520

Ringed by dramatic cliffs, cavernous sea caves and clean sandy beaches, Arranmore (Árainn Mhór) lies just 5km from the mainland. Measuring 9km by 5km, the tiny island has been inhabited since the early Iron Age (800 BC), and a prehistoric promontory fort can be seen near the southeastern corner. The west and north are wild and rugged, with few houses to disturb the sense of isolation. The **Arranmore Way** (Slí Árainn Mhór) walking path circles the island (14km; allow three to four hours). Off the southwestern tip is **Green Island**, a bird sanctuary for corncrakes, snipes and a variety of seabirds;

you can see it from Arranmore (but not visit). Irish is the main language spoken on Arranmore Island, although most inhabitants are bilingual.

The island's pubs put on peat fires and traditional music sessions, and some stay open 24 hours a day to sate thirsty fishers.

Arranmore makes an easy day trip, but there are a couple of hotels, and several homes offer B&B accommodation. Try **Claire's** (⌨ 074-952 0042; www.clairesbandb.wordpress.com; Leabgarrow; s/d €40/60; ☎) by the ferry terminal for simple but pretty rooms.

You can find tourist information, internet access and a cafe at **An Chultúrlann** (Arranmore Holiday Village, Fallagowan; ☉ 9.30am-5pm daily Jun-Aug), 1km south of the ferry pier.

ℹ Getting There & Around

The **Arranmore Ferry** (⌨ 074-952 0532; www.arranmoreferry.com; return adult/child/car & driver €15/7/30) links Burtonport with the main island settlement of Leabgarrow. The journey takes 20 minutes, operates year-round and has up to nine ferries daily in summer.

The same route is covered by the **Arranmore Fast Ferry** (⌨ 087 317 1810; www.arranmorefastferry.com; return per person €15), with a fast, passenger-only crossing (five minutes, two to three daily).

Once on the island, you can save your legs by taking a **taxi** (⌨ 086 331 7885).

Gweedore & Around

POP 4270

The Gaeltacht district of Gweedore (Gaoth Dobhair) is a loose agglomeration of small townships scattered between the N56 road and the coast. It's the most densely populated rural area in Europe, and the largest Gaelic-speaking parish in Ireland, a heartland of traditional Irish music and culture, and birthplace of a number of Celtic bands and musicians such as Altan, Enya and Clannad.

The area is dotted with cosy pubs where the sound of fiddle, flute and penny whistle comes tumbling out of the doors and windows; ask about what's on at your accommodation, or any tourist office. Leo's Tavern (p466) has the most famous pedigree, while the bar at **Teać Hiudái Beag** (⌨ 074-953 1016; www.tradcentre.com/hiudaibeag; Bunbeg) is noted for its Monday- and Friday-night music sessions.

COUNTY DONEGAL ARRANMORE ISLAND

DESIGN PICS / THE IRISH IMAGE COLLECTION / GETTY IMAGES ©

1. Blue Stack Mountains
Straddling the south of County Donegal, these rugged hills are windswept and starkly beautiful.

2. Fanad Head (p476)
The lighthouse on the tip of Fanad Head is a picturesque endpoint to a stunning drive.

3. Horses
Pastoral scenes beckon visitors to hit the county's winding roads.

4. Horn Head (p470)
County Donegal's Muckish Mountain seen from Horn Head.

OLIVER STREWE / GETTY IMAGES ©

LEO'S TAVERN

You never know who'll drop by for one of the legendary singalongs at Leo's Tavern (☎074-954 8143; www.leostavern.com; Meenaleck, Crolly; mains €12-20; ☺food served 5-8.30pm Mon-Fri, 1-9pm Sat & Sun May-Sep, shorter hours Oct-Apr; 🛜). It's owned by Leo and Baba Brennan, parents of Enya and her siblings Moya, Ciaran and Pól (the core of the group Clannad), and now run by younger son Bartley. The pub glitters with gold, silver and platinum discs and various other mementos of the successful kids. There's live music nightly in summer and regular sessions throughout the winter (phone to check). The restaurant is one of the best spots around for honest Irish pub grub. If you're in the area, don't miss it. To get here from Crolly, take the R259 1km towards the airport, and look for the signs for Leo's.

Although the scenery is wild and wind-swept, large parts of the coastal area have been overrun by holiday homes. Consequently, the 'villages' of Derrybeg (Doirí Beaga) and Bunbeg (Bun Beag) virtually blend into each other along the R257, and the sprawl continues north to the spectacular headland of Bloody Foreland (named for the crimson colour of the rocks at sunset).

It's a place best explored by bike, following narrow dead-end roads down to secluded coves and beaches. Away from the coast, dozens of small fishing lakes break up the bleak but beautiful landscape. If you're driving, the N56 heading east out of Gweedore is particularly scenic.

🛏 Sleeping & Eating

Bunbeg Lodge   B&B €€

(☎087 416 7372; www.bunbeglodge.ie; s/d €40/70; 🅿) Excellent B&B accommodation is available at this new guesthouse owned by the Flanagan family. Spacious modern rooms with deep-blue-and-gold feature wallpaper, white linens and sparkling bathrooms make it a top choice. Breakfasts are hearty and the hosts very knowledgable about the local area.

Bunbeg House   B&B €€

(Teach na Céidhe; ☎074-953 1305; www.bunbeg house.com; s/d from €50/80; ☺B&B Easter-Oct, tearoom Jun-Aug) Reminiscent of Italy's Cinque Terre, this converted corn mill has a lovely location overlooking Bunbeg harbour, within earshot of wooden boats knocking against each other. Nonguests can pop in for home-cooked chowder, fishermen's pie or open crab sandwiches at its summertime cafe-bar, or soak up the sun on the bar terrace with a pint.

❶ Information

On the main road in Bunbeg you'll find banks and an ATM, while Derrybeg has a post office.

❶ Getting There & Away

Feda O'Donnell (☎074-954 8114; www.feda. ie) Runs a service twice daily (three Friday and Sunday) from Gweedore to Letterkenny (€7, 1½ hours), Donegal (€10, 2¼ hours), Sligo (€12, 3¼ hours) and Galway (€20, 5½ hours).

Dunlewey & Around

POP 700

Blink and chances are you'll miss the tiny hamlet of Dunlewey (Dún Lúiche). You won't miss the spectacular scenery, however, or quartzite cone of Errigal Mountain, the craggy peak of which dominates the surrounding area. Plan enough time to get out of your car and do some walking here, as it's a magical spot.

🏃 Activities

Dunlewey Lakeside Centre   ACTIVITY CENTRE

(Ionad Cois Locha; ☎074-953 1699; www.dunlewey centre.com; Dunlewey; cottage or boat trip adult/child/family €6/4/14, combined ticket €10/7/15; ☺10.30am-6pm Mon-Sat, 11am-6pm Sun Easter-Oct; 🅿) This place is a strange hotchpotch of craft shop, museum, restaurant, activity centre, theatre and concert venue, but a useful place if you're travelling with the family in tow. Adults will appreciate the 30-minute tour of the thatched cottage that once belonged to local weaver Manus Ferry, who earned world renown for his tweeds (he died in 1975), while kids will adore the petting zoo. But the real highlight, for all ages, is an entertaining boat trip on the lake with a storyteller who vividly brings to life local history, geology and ghoulish folklore. Performances of traditional music (€8) take place on Tuesdays in July and August; you can also catch concerts on some Sunday afternoons.

Poisoned Glen
WALKING

Legend has it that the huge ice-carved hollow of the Poisoned Glen got its sinister name when the ancient one-eyed giant king of Tory, Balor, was killed here by his exiled grandson, Lughaidh, whereupon the poison from his eye split the rock and poisoned the glen. The less interesting truth, however, lies in a cartographic gaffe. Locals were inspired to name it An Gleann Neamhe (The Heavenly Glen), but when an English cartographer mapped the area, he carelessly marked it An Gleann Neimhe – The Poisoned Glen.

Two kilometres east of the Dunlewey Lakeside Centre turn-off, a minor road leads down through the hamlet of Dunlewey, past a ruined church, to limited roadside parking at a hairpin bend. From here, a rough walking path leads into the rocky fastness of the glen (4km round trip). Watch out for the green lady – the resident ghost!

🛏 Sleeping

Errigal Hostel
HOSTEL €

(☑ 074-953 1180; www.anoige.ie; Dunlewey; dm/d €19/50; ⊙ Mar-Oct; 🛜 🚼) At the foot of Errigal Mountain, this gleaming 60-bed An Óige hostel has state-of-the-art facilities including a stainless-steel self-catering kitchen, a large laundry room for your muddy climbing gear, light-filled common areas, and pristine dorms and private rooms. Green initiatives include wood-pellet heating. There's a petrol station that also sells groceries next door.

Glen Heights
B&B €€

(☑ 074-956 0844; www.glenheightsbb.com; Dunlewey; s/d €50/€70; ⊙ Easter-Oct) Your breakfast may well go cold on the plate in front of you at this B&B as you'll find it difficult to take your eyes off the breathtaking views of Dunlewey Lake and the Poisoned Glen from its conservatory. The rooms are simple but cosy, the bathrooms pristine and the Donegal charm in full swing.

Tory Island
POP 150

Swept by sea winds and stung by salt spray, the remote crag of Tory Island (Oileán Thóraí) has taken its fair share of batterings. With nothing to shield it from savage Atlantic storms, it's a tribute to the hardiness of Tory Islanders that the island has been inhabited for more than 4500 years. Although it's only 11km north of the mainland, the rough sea has long consolidated the island's staunch independence.

So it's no surprise that Tory is one of the last places in Ireland to hold onto traditional Irish culture instead of simply paying lip service to it. The island has its own dialect of Irish and even has an elected 'king', who acts as community spokesman and welcomes visitors to the island. Over the decades its inhabitants earned a reputation for distilling and smuggling contraband *poitín* (a peaty whiskey). However, the island is perhaps best known for its 'naive' artists (see p468), many of whom have attracted the attention of international collectors.

In 1974, after an eight-week storm that lashed the island mercilessly, the government made plans to evacuate Tory permanently. Father Diarmuid Ó Peícín came to

COUNTY DONEGAL TORY ISLAND

DON'T MISS

ERRIGAL MOUNTAIN

The pinkish-grey quartzite peak of Errigal Mountain (752m) dominates the landscape of northwestern Donegal, appearing conical from some angles, from others like a ragged shark's fin ripping through the heather bogs. Its name comes from the Gaelic *earagail*, meaning 'oratory', as its shape brings to mind a preacher's pulpit.

Its looming presence seems to dare walkers to attempt the strenuous but satisfying climb to its pyramid-shaped summit. If you're keen to take on the challenge, pay close attention to the weather: it can be a dangerous climb on windy or wet days, when the mountain is shrouded in cloud and visibility is minimal.

The easiest route to the summit, a steep and badly eroded path, begins at a parking area on the R251, about 2km east of Dunlewey hamlet (4.5km round trip; allow three hours). Details are available at the Dunlewey Lakeside Centre (p466).

the rescue, spearheading an international campaign to raise funds, establish a proper ferry service, install an electrical supply and more. The demise of the fishing industry has brought its own share of problems, but the community still doggedly perseveres.

The island has just one pebbly beach and two recognisable villages: West Town (An Baile Thiar), home to most of the island's facilities, and East Town (An Baile Thoir).

◉ Sights & Activities

Cottages mingle with ancient ecclesiastical treasures in West Town. St Colmcille (Columba) is said to have founded a monastery here in the 6th century, and reminders of the early Church are scattered throughout the town. One example is the 12th-century Tau Cross, an odd, T-shaped cruciform that suggests the possibility of seafaring exchanges with early Coptic Christians from Egypt. The cross greets passengers disembarking from the ferry. Also nearby is a 6th- or 7th-century round tower, with a circumference of nearly 16m and a round-headed doorway high above the ground.

An Slí Thoraí (Tory Way) is a waymarked loop walk (map board 50m from the ferry landing) that leads you to the lighthouse at the west end, then back to the eastern end of the island, which is dominated by jagged quartzite cliffs and sea stacks including the spectacular Tor Mór, a 400m-long blade of rock capped with pinnacles.

The island is a wonderful place for birdwatching – over 100 species of seabird inhabit the island, including nesting corncrakes and colonies of puffins (thought to number around 1400).

⌂ Sleeping & Eating

To make the most of your visit, plan an overnight stay and experience the island once the day trippers have left. Book accommodation in advance though, as beds can be hard to find in midsummer.

Tory Island Hostel HOSTEL €
(☎ 087 298 7407; www.toryhostel.com; West Town; per person €25) From the ferry, walk 300m left to find this hostel-cum-B&B with cheery accommodation. Spotless rooms are enlivened with bright splashes of colour, and you'll find the legendary Tory welcome in full force.

Hotel Tory HOTEL €€
(☎ 074-913 5920; West Town; s/d €60/80; ☺ Easter-Oct) The island's only hotel is a fairly rustic place with 14 simple but comfortable bedrooms. The bar here is a hotbed of late-night music, dancing and craic, so be prepared to join in.

Caife an Chreagain IRISH €€
(West Town; mains €10-15; ☺ 10am-10.30pm Easter-Sep) If that sea air has given you an appetite, head for Mary's welcoming cafe-restaurant. Outside the summer months (June to August), opening times can vary depending on the weather (and, by extension, the ferries).

☆ Entertainment

Club Sóisialta Thórai COMMUNITY CENTRE
(Tory Social Club; West Town) The island's social life revolves around this merry spot, which besides the hotel has the island's only other pub. Opening times vary; it usually gets going from around 8pm but don't expect the real craic to start until much, much later.

❶ Information

Information is available from the **Tory Island Co-op** (Comharchumann Thoraí Teo; ☎ 074-913 5502; www.oileanthorai.com; ☺ 9am-5pm Mon-Fri) near the pier, next to the playground. You

---

TORY ISLAND 'NAIVE' ART

Tory Island's distinctive school of painters came about in the 1950s when the English artist Derrick Hill began to spend much of his time on the island. The islanders often watched him as he worked. As the story goes, one of the islanders approached Hill and said, 'I can do that.' He was James Dixon, a self-taught painter who used boat paint and made his own brushes with donkey hairs. Hill was impressed with the 'painterly' quality of Dixon's work and the two formed a lasting friendship. Other islanders were soon inspired to follow suit, forging unique folksy, expressive styles portraying rugged island scenes. Among them were Patsy Dan Rodgers, currently the elected Rí Thoraí (king of Tory). The islanders' work has been exhibited in Chicago, New York, Belfast, London and Paris, and fetches impressive prices at auctions. You can often see it at the island's Dixon Gallery (West Town), and in the Glebe House & Gallery (p475) on the mainland.

can also get information at the craft shop at the top of the pier.

Getting There & Around

Bring waterproofs for the crossing – it can be a wild ride. **Donegal Coastal Cruises** (Turasmara Teo; ☑ 074-953 1320; www.toryislandferry.com) runs passenger ferries to Tory Island (adult/child/student return €26/13/20) from Bunbeg (1½ hours, one daily) and Magheraroarty (35 minutes, two daily). Normal service is April to September, with extra sailings in July and August, and fewer October to March; sailing times vary according to weather and tides, and it's not uncommon for travellers to be stranded on the island in bad weather.

Magheraroarty (Machaire Uí Robhartaigh) is 4km northwest of Gortahork on the R257; the road is signposted Coastal Route/Bloody Foreland. Bunbeg is in the southwest part of Gweedore district.

Bike hire can be arranged with **Rothair ar Cíos** (☑ 074-916 5614; West Town).

Falcarragh & Gortahork

POP 850

You'll find more tourist amenities up the road in Dunfanaghy, but the small towns of Falcarragh (An Fál Carrach) and neighbouring Gortahork (Gort an Choirce) afford an opportunity to experience everyday life in the Gaeltacht region.

Sights & Activities

Get on your bike or don your hiking boots and explore the maze of country lanes and old townlands (farming communities) south of Falcarragh, including the old church and burial ground on the ancient mound of **Ballintemple**.

The grey bulk of **Muckish Mountain** (670m) dominates the view between Gortahork and Dunfanaghy. The easiest route to the top begins southeast of Falcarragh at the highest point of the R256 road through Muckish Gap. Sweeping views to Malin Head and Tory Island unfurl from the summit.

Sleeping & Eating

Óstán Loch Altan HOTEL €€
(☑ 074-913 5267; www.ostanlochaltan.com; Gortahork; s/d €50/100, bar food €10-20, restaurant mains €20-30; ☎) Gortahork's main landmark is this large cream-coloured hotel on the main street. Some of its 39 neutral-toned rooms with satin-quilted fabrics have sea views. It's one of the few places to stay along this stretch of coast that's open all year.

Quality bar food is served from noon to 9pm year-round, while the restaurant opens for lunch and dinner from June to September.

Cuan Na Mara B&B €€
(☑ 074-913 5327; www.cuan-na-mara.com; Ballyness, Falcarragh; s/d €51/66; ☺ Jun-Sep; ☎) Overlooking Ballyness Bay and Tory Island, this dormer bungalow has four cosy guest rooms. It's about 2km from the centre of Falcarragh; take the turn-off signposted Trá.

Maggie Dan's ITALIAN €
(☑ 074-916 5022; An Phanc, Gortahork; pizzas €9-12; ☺ dinner) A little bit of bohemia in the countryside, this excellent pizzeria facing the Market Sq hosts occasional theatre performances.

Drinking & Entertainment

Teach Ruairí PUB
(www.donegalpub.com; Baltoney, Gortahork) Fronted by red wagon wheels and red shutters, this authentic-as-it-gets pub has regular live acoustic music, and decent pub grub served on weekday evenings and all day at weekends. It's tucked away 2km south of Gortahork on a minor road just east of the River Glenna (signposted An Bhealtaine).

Lóistín Na Seamróige PUB
(Shamrock Lodge; Main St, Falcarragh) Owner Margaret grew up on these premises and her pub is the town's living room, especially on Friday mornings when a market sets up outside the front door, and during July and August when there's traditional music.

Information

The Bank of Ireland at the eastern end of Main St has an ATM, and the post office is at Main St's western end in Falcarragh.

Falcarragh Visitors Centre (An tSean Bheairic; ☑ 074-918 0655; www.falcarraghvisitorcentre. com; ☺ 10am-5pm Mon-Fri, 11am-5pm Sat) Has tourist information and a cafe, housed in a 19th-century police barracks.

Getting There & Away

Feda O'Donnell (☑ 074-954 8114; www.feda.ie) Buses from Crolly stop on Main St, Falcarragh (€7, twice daily Monday to Saturday, three daily Friday and Sunday). From Falcarragh, buses continue to Letterkenny (€7, one hour) and Galway (€20, 5¼ hours).

John McGinley (☑ 074-913 5201; www.johnmcginley.com) Buses from Annagry stop at Gortahork and Falcarragh two to four times daily en route to Letterkenny (€6, one hour) and Dublin (€22, five hours).

Dunfanaghy & Around

The attractive little town of Dunfanaghy, clustered along the southern shore of a sandly inlet, lies at the centre of one of the most varied and attractive parts of Donegal. Moors and meadows, sea cliffs and sandy beaches, forest and lake lie scattered below the humpbacked hill of Muckish, all waiting to be explored on foot or by bike.

Dunfanaghy and the neighbouring villages of Port-na-Blagh and Marblehill have a surprisingly wide range of accommodation and some of the finest dining options in northwest Donegal.

◉ Sights

Horn Head   VIEWPOINT
The towering headland of Horn Head has some of Donegal's most spectacular coastal scenery, with dramatic quartzite cliffs, topped with bog and heather, rearing over 180m high. The narrow road from Dunfanaghy ends at a small parking area where you can walk 150m to a WWII lookout point or 1.5km to Horn Head proper.

On a fine day you'll encounter tremendous views of Tory, Inishbofin, Inishdooey and tiny Inishbeg islands to the west; Sheep Haven Bay and the Rosguill Peninsula to the east; Malin Head to the northeast; and the coast of Scotland beyond. Take care in bad weather as the cliff edge can be perilous.

Ards Forest Park   WILDLIFE RESERVE
(www.coillteoutdoors.ie; parking €5; ◉10am-9pm Apr-Sep, to 4.30pm Oct-Mar) Anyone looking to stretch their legs will love this forested park, which is criss-crossed by marked nature trails varying in length from 2km to 13km. It covers the northern shore of the Ards Peninsula and some of the best walks lead to its clean beaches. The woodlands are home to several native species, including ash, birch and sessile oak, and you may encounter foxes, hedgehogs and otters. In 1930 the southern part of the peninsula was taken over by Capuchin monks; the grounds of their friary are open to the public. It's 5km southeast of Dunfanaghy off the N56; daily closing times are posted at the entrance.

Dunfanaghy Workhouse   HISTORIC BUILDING
(www.dunfanaghyworkhouse.ie; Main St, Dunfanaghy; adult/child €4.50/3; ◉9.30am-5.30pm

daily Jul & Aug, 9.30am-4pm Mon-Sat Mar-Jun & Sep) This prominent stone building on the western edge of town was once the local workhouse, built to keep and employ the destitute. Conditions were excessively harsh. Men, women, children and the sick were segregated and their lives were dominated by gruelling work. It was soon inundated with starving people as the Famine took grip. Two years after it opened in 1845, it accommodated some 600 people – double the number originally planned.

The building is now a heritage centre, which tells the powerful true tale of 'Wee Hannah' Herrity (1836–1926) and her passage through the institution, and also hosts various temporary exhibitions and workshops.

Beaches   BEACH
The wide, sandy and virtually empty Killahoey Beach leads right into the heart of Dunfanaghy village. Marble Hill Strand, about 5km east of town in Port-na-Blagh, is backed by static caravans and is often crammed in summer. Reaching Dunfanaghy's loveliest beach, Tramore, requires hiking through the grassy dunes to the west of the village.

🏃 Activities

McSwyne's Gun Coastal Loop   WALKING
At the bridge on the road from Dunfanaghy towards Horn Head (parking), cross the stile by the gate on the left and follow a grassy track for 2.5km through the dunes to the magnificent Tramore Beach. From the north end of the beach a coastal path leads north to Pollaguill Bay past McSwyne's Gun, a natural blowhole in the cliffs (take care in windy weather). At Pollaguill Bay, follow the valley inland to a minor road, where you turn right to return to the starting point (9km; allow three hours; waymarked with blue arrows).

Dunfanaghy Golf Club   GOLF
(☎074-913 6335; www.dunfanaghygolfclub.com; green fees weekdays/weekends €25/30) This stunning waterside 18-hole links course is just outside the village on the Port-na-Blagh road.

Dunfanaghy Stables   HORSE RIDING
(☎074-910 0980; www.dunfanaghystables.com; Main St, Dunfanaghy; adult/child per hour €30/25) Exploring the expansive beaches and surrounding countryside on horseback can be arranged here. Hours vary seasonally.

Richard Bowyer FISHING

(📞086 400 1499; www.hornheadseasafaris.com; 2½hr trip per person €18; ⊙ Easter-Sep) The area around Horn Head is well known for its excellent sea angling. Richard Bowyer organises fishing trips from the small pier in Port-na-Blagh.

Jaws Watersports WATER SPORTS

(📞086 173 5109; www.jawswatersports.ie; The Square, Dunfanaghy) Offers surfing lessons (€40), rents surfing gear (€20 per half-day) and kayaks (from €25 per half-day), and offers guided kayaking trips (€35).

Narosa Life WATER SPORTS

(📞086 883 1090; www.narosalife.com; The Square, Dunfanaghy) Offers two-hour group surf lessons (adult/child €35/25), equipment rental (€25 per half-day) and private one-on-one surf lessons (€90, July and August only), as well as yoga and fitness classes and guided walks on Muckish Mountain and Horn Head.

🛏 Sleeping

⭐**Corcreggan Mill** HOSTEL, CAMPGROUND €

(📞074-913 6409; www.corcreggan.com; Dunfanaghy; tent sites €20, campervans €25, dm/d/tr €20/80/90; @🛜) 🏄 Spotless dorms and private guest rooms (B&B available) are tucked into cosy corners of this lovingly restored former mill house, built and run by the engaging, kilt-wearing Brendan Rohan. An organic vegetable garden provides the ingredients for simple evening meals (Irish stew €8) and continental breakfast is included in the room rates (full Irish breakfast available for €7). The mill is 2.5km southwest of town on the N56.

Whins B&B €€

(📞074-913 6481; www.thewhins.com; Dunfanaghy; s/d €52/74; 🛜) 🏄 The colourful, individually decorated rooms at the Whins have patchwork quilts, quality furniture and a real sense of character. A wide choice of superb breakfasts is served upstairs in a room with a view towards Horn Head. The B&B is about 750m east of the town centre opposite the golf course.

Arnold's Hotel HOTEL €€

(📞074-913 6208; www.arnoldshotel.com; Main St, Dunfanaghy; s/d €80/109; ⊙ Apr-Oct; 🛜) Open since 1922, this family-run hotel has comfortable but rather corporate rooms; the friendly staff with their helpful attitude, warm welcome and suggestions for local activities more than make up for this though.

The hotel's Whiskey Fly bar serves up traditional Irish pub grub (mains €10 to €25).

🍴 Eating

Muck 'n' Muffins CAFE €

(www.mucknmuffins.com; The Square, Dunfanaghy; mains €4-10; ⊙9.30am-5pm Mon-Sat, 10.30am-5pm Sun, to 6pm Jul & Aug; 🛜 👶) A 19th-century stone grain store now houses this waterfront cafe and craft shop. Even on rainy winter days, it's packed with locals tucking into healthy sandwiches, breakfast baps, fajitas, quiches, hot specials, tempting cakes and, of course, muffins.

⭐**Cove** IRISH €€

(📞074-913 6300; Rockhill, Port-na-Blagh; dinner mains €17-25; ⊙lunch Sun, dinner Tue-Sun, closed Jan–mid-Mar) Looks a bit unprepossessing from the outside, but owners Siobhan Sweeney and Peter Byrne are perfectionists who tend to every detail in Cove's art-filled dining room, and on your plate. The seafood-skewed cuisine is inventive and deceptively simple with subtle Asian influences. After dinner, retire to the elegant lounge upstairs. It's on the main road in Port-na-Blagh. Book ahead.

⭐**Mill Restaurant & Guesthouse** IRISH €€€

(📞074-913 6985; www.themillrestaurant.com; Figart, Dunfanaghy; 4-course dinner €41; ⊙dinner Tue-Sun mid-Mar–mid-Dec) An exquisite country setting and perfectly composed meals make dining here a treat. Set in an old flax mill that was for many years the home of renowned watercolour artist Frank Eggington, it also has six high-class guest rooms (singles/doubles €60/96). The mill is just south of town on the N56 road. Book in advance.

🍷 Drinking & Nightlife

⭐**Molly's Bar** PUB

(Main St) Be sure to at least take a peek inside the cherry red Molly's Bar, a wonderfully old-fashioned pub with proper snugs. It hosts regular live music (traditional, jazz, blues and more) and other events, including quiz nights.

ℹ Information

There are no ATMs in town but the **post office** (Main St) has a bureau de change.

ℹ Getting There & Away

Feda O'Donnell (📞074-954 8114; www.feda. ie) Buses between Crolly (€7, 40 minutes) and

Galway (€20, five hours) stop in Dunfanaghy square twice daily Monday to Saturday and three times on Friday and Sunday.

John McGinley (☎074-913 5201; www.john mcginley.com) Buses stop in Dunfanaghy two to four times daily en route to Letterkenny (€5, one hour) and Dublin (€22, five hours).

Lough Swilly (☎028-7126 2017; www. loughswillybusco.com) The bus from Derry to Dungloe (change at Letterkenny) calls at Dunfanaghy once daily Monday to Friday (£10, two to three hours).

CENTRAL DONEGAL

Letterkenny

POP 15,400

Ruined by the excesses of the Celtic Tiger era, Letterkenny is a market town run amok. Mindless development has resulted in numerous faceless retail parks lining the roads, traffic congestion and a complete lack of soul. However, as Donegal's largest town, it's buzzing with students and young professionals, and there's a good choice of restaurants and accommodation. Attractions for visitors are few but if you're using public transport the town is hard to avoid.

⊙ Sights

Main Street   STREET

Letterkenny's long, sloping main street is graced by a cute little market square halfway down. This is the most attractive part of the town, with a terrace of red-brick Georgian houses at the top, one of which was a holiday retreat of Maud Gonne, actress, revolutionary and lover of poet WB Yeats.

Donegal County Museum   MUSEUM

(☎074-912 4613; High Rd; ⊙10am-4.30pm Mon-Fri, 1-4.30pm Sat) FREE Letterkenny's 19th-century workhouse, built to provide Famine relief, now houses the Donegal County Museum. Temporary exhibits feature on the ground floor. Upstairs, the permanent collection is worth a peek for its 8000-plus artefacts from prehistoric times on.

✯ Festivals & Events

Earagail Arts Festival   PERFORMING ARTS

(www.eaf.ie; ⊙Jun-Jul) Theatre performances, concerts and art exhibits lure culture buffs to this diverse monthlong festival, with events staged in Letterkenny, Inishowen and West Donegal.

🛏 Sleeping

Apple Hostel   HOSTEL €

(☎074-911 3291; www.letterkennyhostel.com; Covehill, Port Rd; dm/d from €14/34; 🐾) This brand-new hostel is close to the centre of town, along the road to the right of An Grianán Theatre. It's a smartly painted modern bungalow with accommodation to match, from a dorm with eight bunks to doubles and family rooms with private bathrooms. There's no permanent reception; call ahead to book.

Castle Grove   HOTEL €€

(☎074-915 1118; www.castlegrove.com; s/d from €99/110; 🐾) Set on an enormous estate that rolls down to the estuary, this Georgian manor, filled with fresh flowers, manages to be grand yet warm and personal. Its 15 rooms are well worn but elegantly arranged with antiques, and the restaurant is a local favourite. From Letterkenny, head 5km along the road to Rathmelton and turn right just before the Silver Tassie hotel.

Station House   HOTEL €€

(☎074-912 3100; www.stationhouseletterkenny. com; Lower Main St; s/d €79/99; @🐾🏋) Conveniently located in the centre of town, this large, modern hotel has 81 minimalist rooms with rich red bedspreads, low lighting and glass-panelled bathrooms. Everything is immaculately kept, the staff are incredibly helpful, and the hotel's cafe-bar serves a good choice of classic dishes.

🍴 Eating

Yellow Pepper   IRISH, MEDITERRANEAN €€

(☎074-912 4133; www.yellowpepperrestaurant. com; 36 Lower Main St; mains €11-19; ⊙noon-10pm; 🐾) Set in a 19th-century former shirt factory with stone walls, cast-iron columns and polished wooden floors, this cosy restaurant is a local favourite. The menu is strong on seafood but also offers plenty for meat lovers and vegetarians, including an excellent tapas-style lunch menu (€10 for four portions). Book ahead.

Lemon Tree   IRISH €€

(☎074-912 5788; www.thelemontreerestaurant. com; 39 Lower Main St; mains €15-25; ⊙5-9.30pm daily, plus 1-2.30pm Sun) This place doesn't look too hot from the outside but one taste of the food and you'll be glad you went in. White linen, pale walls and painted wood panelling give it a bright, convivial atmosphere, and the innovative menu offers an excellent choice of fresh seafood, poultry and meat dishes blending French flair with country Irish classics. Early-bird menu €20 (5pm to 6.45pm, except Saturday).

Drinking & Nightlife

McGinley's PUB
(Main St) The best spot in town to catch some live music, this old-style pub with an open fire has trad sessions on Wednesday nights, and live bands Thursday to Saturday. You'll generally find an older crowd downstairs and livelier action upstairs.

Cottage Bar PUB
(49 Upper Main St) Watch your head! All sorts of bric-a-brac hangs precariously from the ceiling of Letterkenny's most atmospheric pub. It's popular with a young student crowd at weekends but is a good spot for a quiet midweek pint.

Entertainment

An Grianán Theatre THEATRE
(☑074-912 0777; www.angrianan.com; Port Rd) An Grianán Theatre is both a community theatre and major arts venue for the northwest, presenting national and international drama, comedy and music. It also has a good cafe and bar.

Regional Cultural Centre THEATRE
(☑074-912 9186; www.regionalculturalcentre.com; Port Rd) In a stunning glass-and-aluminium structure, Letterkenny's cultural centre hosts music and drama performances, fine arts and multimedia exhibits, and film screenings.

Voodoo CLUB, BAR
(www.voodooandink.ie; 21 Lower Main St) This vast lounge and sports bar is the centre of Letterkenny's nightlife, and a popular live-music venue. Check the website or Facebook for events.

Information

You'll find banks and the post office on Letterkenny's elongated Main St. Check out www.letterkenny.ie for useful information on the town and surrounds.

LK Online (Station Roundabout; per 15/60min €1/3; ⊙10.30am-10.30pm Mon-Fri, noon-9pm Sat, noon-6pm Sun) Internet cafe opposite the bus station.

Tourist office (☑074-912 1160; www.discoverireland.ie; Neil Blaney Rd; ⊙9am-5.30pm Mon-Sat Jun-Aug, 9.15am-5pm Mon-Fri Sep-May) Large, efficient office; 1km southeast of town on the road from Derry.

Getting There & Away

Letterkenny is a major bus hub for northwestern Ireland. The bus station is by the roundabout at the junction of Ramelton and Port Rds.

Bus Éireann (☑074-912 1309; www.buseireann.ie) Express bus 32 runs to Dublin (€20.50, four hours) nine times daily via Omagh (€12.40, one hour) and Monaghan (€17.50, 1¾ hours). The Derry–Galway bus 64 stops at Letterkenny four times daily before continuing to Donegal (€10.90, 45 minutes), Bundoran (€15, 1¼ hours), Sligo (€15, two hours) and Galway (€20, five hours).

John McGinley (☑074-913 5201; www.johnmcginley.com) Buses run two to five times daily from Annagry to Dublin (€22, 3¾ hours) through Letterkenny and Monaghan.

Lough Swilly (☑074-912 2863; www.loughswillybusco.com) Has seven buses daily Monday to Friday, and four on Saturday, from Derry to Letterkenny (£7.30, 35 minutes).

Feda O'Donnell (☑074-954 8114; www.feda.ie) Runs a bus from Crolly (€7, 1½ hours) to Galway (€20, four hours) twice daily via Letterkenny, Donegal, Bundoran and Sligo. Buses stop on the road outside the bus station.

Getting Around

Taxis can be ordered from **Letterkenny Taxis** (☑074-912 7400; www.letterkennytaxis.com). There are taxi stands opposite the square on Main St and opposite the bus station.

Glenveagh National Park

Lakes shimmer like dew in the mountainous valley of Glenveagh National Park (Páirc Náisiúnta Ghleann Bheatha; www.glenveaghnationalpark.ie) FREE. Alternating between great knuckles of rock, green-gold swaths of bog and scatterings of oak and birch forest, the 16,500-sq-km protected area is magnificent walking country. Its wealth of wildlife includes the golden eagle, which was hunted to extinction here in the 19th century but reintroduced in 2000.

Such serenity came at a heavy price. The land was once farmed by 244 tenants, who were forcibly evicted by landowner John George Adair in the winter of 1861 following what he called a 'conspiracy', but really because their presence obstructed his vision

COUNTY DONEGAL GLENVEAGH NATIONAL PARK

for the valley. Adair put the final touches on his paradise by building the spectacular lakeside Glenveagh Castle (1870–73), while his wife, Adelia, introduced the park's definitive red deer and rhododendrons.

If anything, things got even more surreal after the Adairs' deaths. The castle was briefly occupied by the Irish Republican Army (IRA) in 1922. Then in 1929 the property was acquired by Kingsley Porter, professor of art at Harvard University, who mysteriously disappeared in 1933 (presumed drowned, but rumoured to have been spotted in Paris afterwards). Six years later the estate was bought by his former student, Henry McIlhenny, once described by Andy Warhol as 'the only person in Philadelphia with glamour'. In 1975, McIlhenny sold the whole kit and caboodle to the Irish government.

The Glenveagh Visitor Centre (☎ 074-913 7090; ⊙ 9am-6pm Mar-Oct, to 5pm Nov-Feb) has a 20-minute audiovisual display on the ecology of the park and the infamous Adair. The cafe (⊙ Easter & Jun-Sep) serves hot food and snacks, and the reception sells the necessary midge repellent, as vital in summer as walking boots and waterproofs are in winter. Camping is not allowed.

◉ Sights & Activities

Glenveagh Castle   CASTLE
(adult/child €5/2) This delightfully showy castle was modelled on Scotland's Balmoral Castle. Henry McIlhenny made it a characterful home with liberal reminders of his passion for deer-stalking. In fact, you'll be hard-pressed to find a single room without a representation – or the taxidermied remains – of a stag.

Access is by guided tour only; tours last 30 minutes and take in a series of flamboyantly decorated rooms that remain as if McIlhenny has just stepped out. The most eye-catching, including the tartan-and-antler-covered music room and the pink candy-striped room demanded by Greta Garbo whenever she stayed here, are in the round tower.

The exotic gardens are similarly spectacular, boasting a host of terraces, an Italian garden, a walled kitchen garden and the Belgian Walk, built by Belgian soldiers who stayed here during WWI. Their cultured charm is in marked contrast to the wildly beautiful landscape that enfolds the area.

The last guided tours of the castle leave about 45 minutes before closing time. Cars are not allowed beyond the Glenveagh Visitor Centre; you can walk or cycle the scenic 3.6km route to the castle or take the shuttle bus (€3 return, every 15 minutes).

Nature Trails   WALKING
The park features nature trails along lakes and through woods and blanket bog, as well as a viewing point that's a short walk behind the castle. You'll get free maps and information on self-guided walks at the visitor centre. Excellent themed ranger-led walks (☎ 076-100 2537; adult/child €10/free) are held fortnightly on Sundays between April and September but must be booked in advance.

Lough Gartan

The patriarch of Irish monasticism, St Colmcille (Columba), was born in the 6th century in a lovely setting near glassy Lough Gartan, where some relics associated with the saint can be seen. The lake is 17km northwest of Letterkenny; it's beautiful driving country, but there's no public transport.

◉ Sights & Activities

Colmcille Heritage Centre   HERITAGE CENTRE
(www.colmcilleheritagecentre.ie; Church Hill; adult/concession €3/2; ⊙ 10.30am-5pm Mon-Sat, 1.30-5pm Sun Easter & May-Sep) Colmcille's Hall of Fame is this comprehensive heritage centre on the shore of Lough Gartan, with a lavish display on the production of illuminated manuscripts. Colmcille's mother, on the run from pagans, supposedly haemorrhaged during childbirth and her blood is believed to have changed the colour of the surrounding Gartan clay to pure white. Ever since, the clay has been regarded as a lucky charm. Ask nicely and the staff may produce some from under the counter.

To reach the heritage centre, leave Letterkenny on the R250 road to Glenties and Ardara. After a few kilometres, turn right on the R251 and then left just after Church Hill village. Alternatively, from Kilmacrennan on the N56, turn west on the R255 and follow the signs.

St Colmcille's Abbey &
Birthplace   HISTORIC SITE
(Lough Gartan; ⊙ 24hr) FREE The 10th-century ruins of Colmcille's abbey lie on a hillside to the north of Lough Gartan, about 3km from the Colmcille Heritage Centre, beside a 16th-century chapel and an O'Donnell clan burial

ground. A kilometre to the south, near the southeastern entrance (hikers and cyclists only) to Glenveagh National Park, is the saint's birthplace, marked by a hefty Celtic cross erected in 1911. Beside it is an intriguing prehistoric cup-marked slab strewn with greening copper coins that's popularly known as the Flagstone of Loneliness, on which Colmcille supposedly slept.

Glebe House & Gallery GALLERY

(www.heritageireland.ie; Church Hill; adult/child €3/1; ⊙ 11am-6.30pm daily Easter & Jul-Aug, Sat-Thu Jun & Sep) The English painter Derrick Hill bought this historic house in 1953, providing him with a mainland base close to his beloved Tory Island. Before Hill arrived, the house served as a rectory and then a hotel. The 1828-built mansion is sumptuously decorated with an evident love of all things exotic, but its real appeal is Hill's astonishing art collection. In addition to paintings by Hill and Tory Island's 'naive' artists (p468) are works by Picasso, Landseer, Hokusai, Jack B Yeats and Kokoschka. The woodland gardens are also wonderful. A guided tour of the house takes about 45 minutes.

NORTHEASTERN DONEGAL

Rosguill Peninsula

The best way to appreciate Rosguill's rugged splendour is by driving, cycling or even walking the 15km Atlantic Drive, a way-marked loop on minor roads signposted to your left as you come into the sprawling village of Carrigart (Carraig Airt) from the south. The sea views are superb, if you can ignore the creeping blight of holiday homes and static caravans.

The pretty, secluded beach at Trá na Rossan in the northern part of the peninsula makes a good objective, rather than the overcrowded holiday strand at Downings (often written as Downies).

⚐ Activities

Rosapenna Golf Resort GOLF

(☎ 074-915 5000; www.rosapenna.ie; Downings; green fees €80) The scenery at this renowned golf club – designed by St Andrew's Old Tom Morris in 1891 and remodelled by Harry Vardon in 1906 – is as spectacular as the layout, which can challenge even the lowest handicapper.

Mevagh Dive Centre DIVING

(☎ 074-915 4708; www.mevaghdiving.com; Carrigart) Donegal's only dive centre offers diving courses, equipment rentals and boat charter, and has excellent accommodation (doubles €70) in its purpose-built B&B. Try-a-dive packages including one nights' B&B and a two-hour introductory pool dive cost €160 for two adults sharing a room.

🛏 Sleeping & Eating

Trá na Rosann Hostel HOSTEL €

(☎ 074-915 5374; www.anoige.ie; Downings; dm €16; ⊙ late May-Aug) Knockout views envelop this heritage-listed former hunting lodge, designed by Sir Edwin Lutyens. It's an atmospheric spot with a colourful history, just 15 minutes' walk from lovely Trá na Rosann beach. The trade-off for its tranquil setting is that it's 8km north of Downings and there's no public transport. Note that reception is generally closed from 10am to 5pm.

★ Olde Glen Bar & Restaurant PUB €€

(☎ 074-915 5130; Glen, Carrigart; mains €15-25; ⊙ dinner Tue-Sat late May–mid-Sep) Authentic down to its original 1700s stone floor, this treasure of a traditional pub serves a sensational pint. Out the back, its small farmhouse-style restaurant serves outstanding blackboard specials. It doesn't take reservations and is popular with locals – turn up by 5.30pm to get a table for the 6pm seating, or by 7pm for a table at the 8pm seating. By the time you leave, you'll feel like a local yourself. Open most weekends out of season, but call to check.

Fanad Peninsula

The second-most northerly point in Donegal, Fanad Head thrusts out into the Atlantic to the east of Rosguill. The peninsula curls around the watery expanses of Mulroy Bay to the west, and Lough Swilly to the east, the latter edged with high cliffs and sandy beaches. Most travellers stick to the peninsula's eastern flank, visiting the beautiful beach and excellent golf course at Portsalon, and the quiet heritage towns of Rathmelton and Rathmullan. Accommodation is relatively limited, so book ahead in summer.

Rathmelton

POP 1100

The first community you come to if you're approaching the peninsula from Derry or Letterkenny is Rathmelton (sometimes called Ramelton), a picture-perfect spot with rows of Georgian houses and rough-walled stone warehouses curving along the River Lennon.

Apart from walking the colourful, picturesque streets there's not much to do here. The ruined **Tullyaughnish Church**, on the hill, is worth a visit because of the Romanesque carvings in the eastern wall, which were taken from a far-older church on nearby Aughnish Island, on the River Lennon. Coming from Letterkenny, turn right at the river and follow it round for about 400m.

🛏 Sleeping & Eating

Ardeen House   B&B €€

(📞 074-915 1243; www.ardeenhouse.com; Aughnish Rd; s/d €55/90) The warm welcome and homemade scones on arrival at Ardeen House, a lovely B&B overlooking the river, make you feel as if you've just arrived home. The bedrooms are beautifully decorated, breakfasts are a feast and like many past guests you'll leave planning a return trip. It's on the east edge of town, on the south side of the river, just beyond the town hall.

★ Frewin House   B&B €€€

(📞 074-915 1246; www.frewinhouse.com; Rectory Rd; d €110-150, cottages per week €550, dinner €45-50; ⊘ closed Christmas) This fine Victorian rectory in secluded grounds would make every weepy heroine's dreams come true. The house combines all the character you would expect from a charming period property – antique furniture, well-thumbed books and open fires – with contemporary style. The bedrooms are pretty but uncluttered, dinner is served communally and by candlelight, and the gardens just beg to be walked with a book and a parasol.

Bridge Bar   IRISH €€€

(📞 074-915 1119; Bridgend; mains €20-26; ⊘ dinner Wed-Sat) The Bridge Bar is one of those lovely old country pubs you came to Ireland for. Its cosy 1st-floor restaurant has classic Irish seafood dishes, such as salmon and cod, and juicy steaks with brandy sauce.

❶ Getting There & Away

Lough Swilly (📞 074-912 2863; www.loughswillybusco.com) buses connect Rathmelton with Letterkenny once daily from Monday to Friday and twice on Saturday (€3, 30 minutes).

Rathmullan

POP 520

The refined little port of Rathmullan has a tranquillity that belies the momentous events that took place here from the 16th to 18th centuries. In 1587 Hugh O'Donnell, the 15-year-old heir to the powerful O'Donnell clan, was tricked into boarding a ship here and taken to Dublin as a prisoner. He escaped four years later on Christmas Eve and, after unsuccessful attempts at revenge, died in Spain, aged only 30. In 1607, despairing of fighting the English, Hugh O'Neill, the earl of Tyrone, and Rory O'Donnell, the earl of Tyrconnell, boarded a ship in Rathmullan harbour and left Ireland for good. This decisive act, known as the Flight of the Earls, marked the effective end of Gaelic Ireland and the rule of Irish chieftains. Large-scale confiscation of their estates took place, preparing for the Plantation of Ulster with settlers from Britain. Also in Rathmullan, Wolfe Tone, leader of the 1798 Rising, was captured.

Sixteenth-century **Rathmullan Castle**, where an English garrison was stationed during the Flight of the Earls, still squats menacingly beside the harbour; it once held a heritage centre but this has been closed for some time, despite the signs at the entrance.

🛏 Sleeping

Glenalla Lodge   B&B

(📞 074-915 8750; www.glenallalodge.com; Ray; s/d €40/70) It's worth heading out of town to find this modern B&B with its four spacious guest rooms. Decked out with tasteful wooden furniture, crisp bedspreads and contemporary rustic style, and with the helpful knowledge of a local historian on tap, it's an excellent spot. Glenalla Lodge is 8km north of Rathmullan on the R247.

❶ Getting There & Away

The **Lough Swilly** (📞 074-912 2863; www.loughswillybusco.com) bus from Letterkenny to Kerrykeel calls at Rathmullan (€4.90, 45 minutes) once daily Monday to Saturday.

In summer a car ferry (p479) operates between Rathmullan and Buncrana.

Portsalon & Fanad Head

A spectacular roller coaster of a road hugs the sea cliffs from Rathmullan to Portsalon, passing the early-19th-century Knockalla Fort, one of six built to defend against a possible French invasion – the history is told at its companion, Fort Dunree (p479) across the lough.

Once named the second-most beautiful beach in the world by British newspaper the *Observer,* the tawny-coloured Blue Flag beach of Ballymastocker Bay, which is safe for swimming, is the principal draw of tiny Portsalon (Port an tSalainn). For golfers, however, the main attraction is the marvellously scenic Portsalon Golf Club (✆074-915 9459; www.portsalongolfclub.com; green fees weekdays/weekends €40/50).

From Portsalon it's another 8km to the lighthouse on the rocky tip of Fanad Head, the best part of which is the scenic drive there.

Inishowen Peninsula

The Inishowen Peninsula reaches just far enough into the Atlantic to grab the title of northernmost point on the island of Ireland: Malin Head. It is remote, rugged, desolate and sparsely populated, making it a special and peaceful sort of place. Ancient sites and ruined castles abound, as do traditional thatched cottages that haven't yet been demoted to storage sheds.

Surrounded by vast sea loughs and open ocean, Inishowen (meaning 'Island of Eoghain', the same chieftain who gave his name to County Tyrone) naturally attracts a lot of bird life. The variety is tremendous, with well over 200 resident and migrant species, including well-travelled avian visitors from Iceland, Greenland and North America. Irregular Atlantic winds mean rare and exotic species also blow in from time to time. Twitchers should check out *Finding Birds in Ireland* by Eric Dempsey and Michael O'Clery, or visit www.birdsireland.com.

For information on everything else, visit www.visitinishowen.com.

Buncrana

POP 3400

On the tame side of the peninsula, Buncrana is a busy but appealing town with its fair share of pubs and a 5km sandy beach on the shores of Lough Swilly. You'll find all the local services you'll need here before heading into the wilds further north.

John Newton, the composer of *Amazing Grace,* was inspired to write his legendary song after his ship the *Greyhound* took refuge in the calm waters of Lough Swilly during a severe storm in 1748. He and his crew were welcomed in Buncrana after their near-death experience, and his spiritual journey from slave trader to antislavery campaigner had its beginnings here. He went on to become a prolific hymn writer and later mentored William Wilberforce in his fight against slavery. For more information on the story, visit www.amazinggrace.ie.

◉ Sights

A waymarked Shore Walk heads north along the coast from the park north of the tourist office, leading to the town's main sights. At the northern end of the seafront, the early-18th-century, six-arched Castle Bridge leads to O'Doherty's Keep, a tower house built by local chieftains in 1430. It was burned by the English and then rebuilt for their own use.

At the side of the keep is the manorlike Buncrana Castle, built in 1718 by John Vaughan, who also constructed the bridge. Wolfe Tone was imprisoned here following the unsuccessful French invasion in 1798. Walking 500m further from the keep (turn left and stick to the shoreline) brings you to Ned's Point Fort (1812), built by the British and now under siege from graffiti artists.

COUNTY DONEGAL INISHOWEN PENINSULA

WASHED-UP TREASURES

Beachcombers will find more than empty shells along the Inishowen coast. The area is renowned for its raised beaches, stranded above the high-water mark by postglacial uplift, and littered with semiprecious stones: cornelian, agate, jasper and more. Good hunting grounds include the beaches along the northern coast of Malin Head, near Banba's Crown and Ballyhillin.

The stones make unique souvenirs, and you can buy these local treasures artfully polished and made into pendants, bracelets, earrings, brooches, candle-holders and other quirky and beautiful items at the workshop of jeweller and craftsperson Petra Watzka at Malin Pebbles (www.malinpebbles.com; Church Brae) in Greencastle.

Inishowen Peninsula

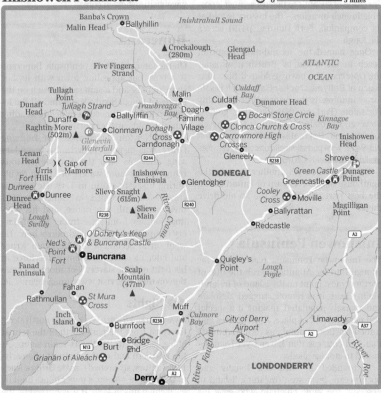

Banba's Crown
Malin Head • Ballyhillin
Inishtrahull Sound

▲ Crockalough
(280m)
Glengad
Head

ATLANTIC
OCEAN

Five Fingers
Strand

*Culdaff
Bay*

Tullagh
Point
Malin • Culdaff Dunmore Head
Dunaff *Tullagh Strand* Doagh
Head •Ballyliffin *Trawbreaga
Bay* Famine
Village •Bocan Stone Circle *Kinnagoe
Bay*
Raghtin More •Clonmany *Donagh
Cross* •Clonca Church & Cross
(502m)▲ *Glenevin
Waterfall* Carndonagh •Carrowmore High
Crosses Inishowen
Head

Lenan
Head
Urris) (Gap of
Fort Hills Mamore
Dunree
Dunree •Dunree
Head

Gleneely
Shrove•

DONEGAL
•Glentogher
Green Castle Dunagree
Greencastle • Point

Inishowen
Peninsula

*Cooley
Cross* •Moville

Slieve Snaght
(615m) ▲
▲ Slieve
Main

R240
•Ballyrattan
Magilligan
Point

*Lough
Swilly*

•Redcastle

A2

O'Doherty's Keep
& Buncrana Castle
Ned's
Point
Fort •Buncrana

Scalp
Mountain
(477m)▲

•Quigley's
Point
*Lough
Foyle*

Fanad
Peninsula

Fahan
Rathmullan *St Mura
Cross*
Inch
Island
Inch •Burnfoot
•Bridge
End
N13 •Burt
Grianán of Aileach

Muff
*Culmore
Bay*
R238
City of Derry
Airport
Limavady A37

River Faughan

LONDONDERRY

River Roe

Derry A2

R238
R244
R238
R238
Glennmakeel
River Crana

🛏 Sleeping & Eating

Tullyarvan Mill
HOSTEL €

(☑ 074-936 1613; www.tullyarvanmill.com; Carndonagh Rd; dm/d/f from €15/40/60; 🛜) This excellent purpose-built hostel is housed in a tasteful modern building attached to the historic Tullyarvan Mill. Set amid riverside gardens, it also hosts regular cultural events and art exhibits. Head north out of town on the R238 and turn left at signs for Dunree.

Westbrook House
B&B €€

(☑ 074-936 1067; www.westbrookhouse.ie; Westbrook Rd; s/d €40/70; 🛜) A handsome Georgian house set in beautiful gardens, Westbrook offers old-world hospitality and charm by the bucketload. Chandeliers, antique furniture and cut glass give it a refined sophistication but the little trinkets and subtle florals make it very much a lived-in and loved home.

Caldra
B&B €€

(☑ 074-936 3703; www.caldrabandb.com; Lisnakelly; s/d €50/80; 🛜🅿) This large, modern B&B has four spacious rooms ideal for families. Expect impressive fireplaces and gilt mirrors in the common areas but more tranquil contemporary style in the guest rooms. The garden and patio overlook Lough Swilly and the mountains.

★ Beach House
SEAFOOD €€

(☑ 074-936 1050; www.thebeachhouse.ie; The Pier, Swilly Rd; lunch mains €11-13, 3-course dinner €30; ⊙ lunch & dinner Jun-Aug, dinner Thu-Sun, lunch Sat & Sun Sep-May; 🅿) With picture windows overlooking the lough, this aptly named cafe-restaurant projects an elegant simplicity. Although the menu is intrinsically simple, the quality and preparation are a cut above: 'surf and turf', for example, comes with fillet steak, crab claws, langoustines and creamy bisque.

Drinking & Nightlife

Atlantic Bar PUB
(Upper Main St) Dating back to 1792, this mustard-and-black-painted watering hole is Buncrana's oldest and most atmospheric pub.

O'Flaherty's PUB
(Main St) A central hub for locals and visitors, this old-world pub is a friendly spot and has live traditional music every Wednesday night.

ℹ Information

Tourist office (☑074-936 2600; www.visitinishowen.com; Railway Rd; ⊙9.30am-5.30pm Mon-Sat Easter-Aug, to 5pm Sep-Easter; 🛜) One kilometre south of the town centre. Free wi-fi.

ℹ Getting There & Away

Lough Foyle Ferry (☑074-938 1901; www.foyleferry.com) From June to September, a car ferry operates between Buncrana and Rathmullan, with eight crossings a day on weekends only in June and September, daily in July and August. One-way fares for a car/adult/child are €15/3.50/2.50.

Lough Swilly (☑028-7126 2017; www.loughswillybusco.com) Buses run from Buncrana eight times daily Monday to Friday, seven on Saturday and four on Sunday to Derry (€6.50, 1½ hours) and once daily Monday to Saturday to Carndonagh (€6, 45 minutes) via Clonmany (€4.90, 25 minutes) and Ballyliffin (€6, 30 minutes).

Buncrana to Clonmany

There are two routes from Buncrana to Clonmany: the scenic coastal road via Dunree Head and the Gap of Mamore, and the speedier inland road (R238). The **Gap of Mamore** (elevation 262m) is a steep and narrow pass through the Urris Hills, with a sacred spring, **St Columba's Well**, on the north side.

The winding fjord of Lough Swilly is one of Ireland's great natural harbours, and has played its part in many historical dramas from Viking invasions and the Flight of the Earls to the 1798 rebellion and WWI.

Fort Dunree (www.dunree.pro.ie; Dunree Head; adult/child €6/4; ⊙10.30am-6pm Mon-Sat, 1-6pm Sun Jun-Sep, 10.30am-4.30pm Mon-Fri, 1-6pm Sat & Sun Oct-May) is the best preserved, and most dramatic, of six forts that were built by the British on the lough following the 1798 uprising of the United Irishmen (which was supported by France), when fears of a French invasion were at fever pitch. Huge naval guns were added in the late 19th century, and during WWI the lough was used as a marshalling area for Atlantic convoys, and as an anchorage for the Royal Navy's Grand Fleet. Unusually, it remained in British hands after the partition of Ireland in 1922, and was only handed over to the Republic of Ireland in 1938.

The original fort, built in 1813, now houses a fascinating military museum, while the surrounding headland is littered with WWI and WWII remains which you can explore at your leisure. There are several waymarked walks, and the sea cliffs are the haunt of choughs, jackdaws and fulmars.

Clonmany & Ballyliffin

POP 700

These two quaint villages and their surrounds have plenty to occupy visitors for a day or two. Clonmany has a working atmosphere and lots of pubs, while Ballyliffin feels more upmarket with more hotels and restaurants. Both have post offices but no banks.

◉ Sights & Activities

Doagh Famine Village MUSEUM
(☑074-938 1901; www.doaghfaminevillage.com; Doagh Island; adult/child €7/5; ⊙10am-5pm Easter-late Sep) A walk along the dunes north of Ballyliffin brings you to Doagh Island (now part of the mainland), capped by the matchbox ruin of 16th-century Carrickabraghey Castle. Also here is the enthusiastically thrown-together Doagh Famine Village, set in a reconstructed village of thatched cottages. A bit of a coach-tour magnet, it's packed with entertaining titbits about a disappearing way of life, and insightful comparisons with famine-stricken countries today. Call ahead to book the guided tour.

Beaches BEACH
About 1km north of Ballyliffin is the lovely, sandy expanse of **Pollan Strand**, but the crashing breakers make it unsafe for swimming. There's another beach at **Tullagh Strand**, 2km northwest of Clonmany. Although swimming's possible, the current can be strong and it isn't recommended when the tide's going out.

GRIANÁN OF AILEÁCH

This amphitheatre-like **stone fort** (admission free; ⊙24hr) encircles the top of Grianán Hill like a halo and offers eye-popping views of the surrounding loughs. On clear days you can see as far as Derry. Its mini-arena can resemble a circus whenever a tour bus rolls up and spills its load inside the 4m-thick walls.

The original fort may have existed at least 2000 years ago, but it's thought that the site itself goes back to pre-Celtic times as a temple to the god Dagda. Between the 5th and 12th centuries it was the seat of the O'Neills, before being demolished by Murtogh O'Brien, king of Munster. Most of what you see today is a reconstruction built between 1874 and 1878.

The fort is 18km south of Buncrana near Burt, signposted off the N13. The circular Burt Church at the foot of the hill was modelled on the fort by Derry architect Liam McCormack and built in 1967.

Ballyliffin Golf Club   GOLF
(☑074-937 6119; www.ballyliffingolfclub.com; green fees €50-90) With two championship courses, Ballyliffin Golf Club is among the best places to play a round of golf in Donegal. The scenery is so beautiful that it can distract even the most focused golfer. Its above-average restaurant, the **Links** (lunch & dinner mains €10-20), overlooks the fairways.

🍴 Sleeping & Eating

⭐ **Glen House**   B&B €€
(☑074-937 6745; www.glenhouse.ie; Straid, Clonmany; s/d from €55/70; ☎📶) Despite the grand surroundings and luxurious rooms, you'll find neither pretension nor high prices at this gem of a guesthouse. The welcome couldn't be friendlier, the rooms are a lesson in restrained sophistication, and the setting is incredibly tranquil. The walking trail to Glenevin Waterfall starts next door to the **Rose Tea Room** (⊙10am-6pm daily Jul-Aug, Sat & Sun Mar-Jun & Sep-Oct), which opens to a timber deck.

Ballyliffin Lodge & Spa   HOTEL €€€
(☑074-937 8200; www.ballyliffinlodge.com; Ballyliffin; s/d from €90/150; ☎🅿️♿) This elegant 40-room hotel has ultraspacious autumn-hued rooms with heavy fabrics and plenty of scatter cushions. Superior rooms have sublime ocean views. You can treat yourself at the state-of-the-art spa, to a round or two of golf, or to a meal at the laid-back **Jack's Bar** (mains €12-24).

❶ Getting There & Away

Lough Swilly (☑074-912 2863; www.loughswillybusco.com) Buses run once daily Monday to Saturday between Clonmany and Carndonagh (€2.80, 20 minutes).

Carndonagh

POP 1900

Carndonagh, surrounded by hills on three sides, is a busy commercial centre serving the local farming community. It's not a choice locale in these parts, but convenient for gathering information and provisions.

👁 Sights

Once an important ecclesiastical centre, Carndonagh has several early-Christian stone monuments. The delightful 7th-century **Donagh Cross** stands under a shelter by an Anglican church at the Ballyliffin end of town. It's carved with a darling short-bodied, big-eyed figure of Jesus, smiling impishly. Flanking the cross are two small pillars, one showing a man, possibly Goliath, with a sword and shield, the other, David and his harp. In the graveyard there's a pillar with a carved marigold on a stem and nearby a crucifixion scene.

❶ Information

There are banks and an ATM on the Diamond; the post office is in the shopping centre halfway down Bridge St towards the Donagh Cross.
Inishowen tourism office (☑074-937 4933; www.visitinishowen.com; Malin Rd; ⊙9.30am-5pm Mon-Fri, plus 11am-3pm Sat Jun-Aug) In the Public Services Centre by the roundabout north of the Diamond; is very helpful.

❶ Getting There & Away

Lough Swilly (☑074-912 2863; www.loughswillybusco.com) A bus leaves Buncrana for Carndonagh (€6, 45 minutes) once daily from Monday to Saturday.

Malin Head

Even if you've already seen Ireland's southernmost and westernmost points, you'll still be impressed when you clap your eyes on Malin Head, the island's northern extreme. It's a name familiar to sailors and weather buffs, as Malin is one of the sea areas, and Malin Head one of the weather stations mentioned in BBC Radio's daily shipping forecast. The weather station is at Bulbinbeg, 2km east of the head, while the nearby array of radio masts and aerials belong to **Malin Head Coastguard Station**, which coordinates marine search-and-rescue operations.

On the northernmost tip, called **Banba's Crown**, stands a cumbersome cliff-top **tower** that was built in 1805 by the British admiralty and later used as a Lloyds signal station. Around it are concrete huts that were used by the Irish army in WWII as lookout posts. To the west from the fortside car park, a path leads to **Hell's Hole**, a chasm where the incoming waters crash against the rocky formations. To the east a longer headland walk leads to the **Wee House of Malin**, a hermit's cave in the cliff face.

The **view** to the west takes in, from left to right, the Inishowen Hills, Dunaff Head, low-lying Fanad Head with its lighthouse, the twin 'horns' of Horn Head and the twin bumps of Tory Island; in the far distance, to the left of Fanad lighthouse, are Muckish and Errigal Mountains. To the east lie raised beach terraces, and offshore you can see the lighthouse on the remote island of Inishtrahull.

The Plantation village of **Malin**, on Trawbreaga Bay, 14km southeast of Malin Head, has a pretty movie-set quality, set around a neat, triangular village green. Bring enough cash with you, as there are no ATMs here.

🛏 Sleeping & Eating

Sandrock Holiday Hostel HOSTEL €
(☑ 074-937 0289; www.sandrockhostel.com; Port Ronan Pier, Malin Head; dm €12, linen €1.50; 🛜) The cinematically changing view from this IHH hostel – at the end of the road, above a rocky bay on the western side of the headland – will take your breath away. Seafood can sometimes be bought straight off the boats out front. Inside you'll find 20 beds in two cosy dorms, musical instruments and laundry facilities. Bike rental (€10 per day) is also available for nonguests, though you'll have to leave a deposit.

Village B&B B&B €€
(☑ 074-937 0763; www.malinvillagebandb.com; The Green; s/d €45/70) Sitting right on the village green, this lovely B&B has a choice of cosy rooms, some traditional with antique furniture and brocade armchairs, others more contemporary with white linen and pretty floral patterns. Although you'll get a hearty breakfast here, guests also have use of a kitchen and utility room.

Malin Hotel HOTEL €€
(☑ 074-937 0606; www.malinhotel.ie; The Green; s/d from €90/100; 🛜) From the village green you'll first spot the old pub, but look beyond it and you'll also see a modern, boxlike hotel behind. Designer wallpapers adorn the lavish rooms, and the pub-restaurant serves up good Irish standards.

🍷 Drinking & Nightlife

McClean's PUB
(Malin) Easily spotted by the petrol pumps out front (it's on the right as you arrive in the village from Carndonagh), this treasure of an old-time pub has the best craic in Malin and often has live music.

OFF THE BEATEN TRACK

WALK: URRIS HILLS

The Urris Hills, a rugged ridge of resistant quartzite (a continuation of the Knockalla Mountains on the Fanad Peninsula to the southwest), provide grandstand views of the Inishowen coast and the distant hills of Muckish, Errigal and Glenveagh. A network of waymarked walking trails has recently been established here, ranging from 2km to 11km in length. Starting points are at Butler's Bridge and the car park at the north end of the Mamore Gap. Ask for the *Urris Walks* leaflet at Buncrana tourist office (p479).

Starting at Glen House, an easy 800m trail leads to the cascading 10m-high **Glenevin Waterfall**, with benches and picnic tables along the way. From Clonmany, follow the road signed to Tullagh Bay, cross the river and bear right at an intersection. Butler's Bridge and the waterfall car park are about 1km further on.

❶ Getting There & Around

The best way to approach Malin Head is by the R238/242 from Carndonagh, rather than up the eastern side from Culdaff.

Lough Swilly (☑074-912 2863; www. loughswillybusco.com) Operates a bus once daily Monday to Saturday between Buncrana and Carndonagh (€8, 50 minutes).

Northwest Busways (☑074-938 2619) Runs a bus from Carndonagh to Malin Head once a day Monday to Saturday.

Culdaff & Around

POP 155

Sheep vastly outnumber people around the secluded resort village of Culdaff on the remote north coast of Inishowen.

Sheep also roam the remains of the Clonca church and cross. Inside is an intricately carved tombstone sporting a sword-and-hurling-stick motif. The carved lintel over the door is thought to come from an earlier church. Outside, the remains of the cross show the miracle of the loaves and fishes on the eastern face. Heading from Culdaff towards Moville on the R238, turn right after 1.2km at Bocan Church. The Clonca church and cross are 1.7km on the left behind some farm buildings.

Culdaff has a Blue Flag beach that's great for swimming and windsurfing. From Bunagee Pier, sea angling and diving are popular.

WALK: INISHOWEN HEAD

The R241 road continues another 4km beyond Greencastle to Shrove, where there's a car park beside a small sandy beach, and the twin towers (one now only a stump) of Shrove Lighthouse, built in 1837. An information board here describes a waymarked walk (8.5km; allow two to three hours) to Inishowen Head, where a WWII lookout point commands a panoramic view east along the Northern Irish coast to the Antrim hills, Rathlin Island and the distant outlines of Islay and the Mull of Kintyre in Scotland. The little bay of Portkille, a short distance to the north, is said to be the final landfall of St Colmcille (Columba) in Ireland before he sailed for Iona in AD 563; a bronze plaque by the path describes the site.

McGrory's of Culdaff (☑074-937 9104; www.mcgrorys.ie; s/d from €60/90, bar meals €10-21, restaurant mains €15-25; ☺bar food 12.30-8pm, dinner Tue-Sun, lunch Sun) is a raspberry red village landmark. It has 17 spiffy rooms decorated with a contemporary eye. Before sleeping, however, head downstairs to catch live music in Mac's Backroom, which books international singer-songwriters and traditional music. McGrory's classic Irish cuisine is the best for miles around.

Greencastle

POP 530

Seals bob their heads hopefully in the busy little fishing port of Greencastle. The 14th-century Northburgh Castle was a supply base for English armies in Scotland, and for this reason was attacked by Robert Bruce in the 1320s. The castle's vine-netted hulk survives – its dark-green stone gives the town its name – but is surrounded by derelict buildings and new-build apartments. Alongside it is a 19th-century Martello tower, companion to the one on Magilligan Point across Lough Foyle.

An eccentric collection of artefacts can be found at the Inishowen Maritime Museum & Planetarium (www.inishowenmaritime.com; adult/child museum €5/3, museum & planetarium €10/6; ☺9.15am-5.30pm Mon-Fri year-round, plus 9.15am-5.30pm Sat & noon-5.30pm Sun Easter-Oct), in a former coastguard station next to the harbour. The most fascinating exhibits are from the sunken wrecks of Lough Foyle, including a pair of perfectly preserved military-issue boxer shorts salvaged by marine archaeologists from a ditched WWII bomber. The demise of the Spanish Armada and the departure from these waters of Irish immigrants are two of the museum's more compelling themes. Take care if visiting on a day when local children are testing their homemade rockets out front.

★ Kealy's Seafood Bar (☑074-938 1010; The Harbour; mains lunch €9-15, dinner €15-50; ☺12.30-9pm Wed-Sun year-round, daily Easter & Jul-Aug) offers catches so fresh you almost have to fight the harbourside seals for it. The unpretentious nautical-style polished timber decor belies the restaurant's numerous culinary awards. It's a splendid spot for a humble bowl of chowder or a lobster extravaganza. Call ahead to check opening times out of season.

ⓘ Getting There & Away

From April to September, Lough Foyle Ferry (p479) operates a car-ferry service from Greencastle to Magilligan, saving a 78km detour via Derry. One-way fares for the 10-minute crossing cost €12/3/1.50 per car/adult/child. It departs hourly on the hour from Greencastle, and at a quarter past the hour from Magilligan. The first ferry is at 9am from Greencastle; the last ferry departs Greencastle at 6pm (8pm in July and August). Timetables are posted online.

Lough Swilly (☑ 074-912 2863; www. loughswillybusco.com) has two buses Monday to Friday (one on Saturday) from Derry, passing through Greencastle (€8.70, one hour).

Moville & Around

POP 1450

Little more than a tight cluster of streets above an industrial-looking jetty, Moville is a neat little town with old, well-kept buildings. It can be sleepy, but on holiday weekends tourists flood in. Moville was a busy port during the 19th and early 20th centuries, when thousands of emigrants set sail for America from here.

◉ Sights & Activities

The coastal walkway from Moville to Greencastle takes in the stretch of coast where the emigrant steamers used to moor, and also affords some rewarding birdwatching opportunities. There's fishing off the pier for mackerel, mullet and coalfish.

✪ Festivals & Events

Summer sees a slew of music-oriented festivals, such the DylanFest on the Lough

(Stuck Inside of Moville) and the Beatles-Fest on the Lough, both held in July or August at various venues in Moville and Greencastle. Check www.craicon.com for details.

🛏 Sleeping & Eating

Moville Holiday Hostel   HOSTEL €
(☑ 074-938 2378; www.movilleholidayhostel.com; Malin Rd; campsites per person €10, dm/d €15/40) A private, unpaved drive leads off the R238 Carndonagh road just north of town to a grove of trees and this secluded 20-bed hostel. It's in a nook-and-cranny-filled 18th-century farmhouse beside a river, with some gorgeous spots to pitch a tent. The owner is a fount of information on the area's rich history and folklore. Cash only.

Washington House   B&B €€
(☑ 074-938 5574; www.washingtonhousebandb.com; Ballyrattan; s/d from €50/80; ⊗ mid-Apr–Sep) The five spacious rooms of this modern villa all have queen- or king-size beds and pristine bathrooms, and there are wonderful views over Lough Foyle from the patio. The house is signposted along a minor road off the R238 5km southwest of Moville.

ⓘ Information

Main St has several banks with ATMs and the post office.

ⓘ Getting There & Away

Lough Swilly (☑ 074-912 2863; www.loughswillybusco.com) Runs two buses Monday to Friday and one on Saturday to Moville (€7.30, 45 minutes) from Derry.

The Midlands

POP 378,106 / AREA 10,782 SQ KM

Best B&Bs

➡ Sandymount House (p486)

➡ Charlotte's Way (p493)

➡ Bastion B&B (p509)

➡ Ardmore House (p493)

➡ Lough Key House (p501)

Best Gardens

➡ Birr Castle Demesne (p490)

➡ Emo Court (p489)

➡ Heywood Gardens (p486)

➡ Belvedere House & Gardens (p511)

Why Go?

Rarely explored by those on their first visit to Ireland and refreshingly free of tour buses and souvenir stalls, the Midlands is brimming with verdant past oral landscapes, stately homes, archaeological remains and sleepy towns where the locals are genuinely glad to see you. Although the region may not have the scenic drama or sophisticated cities of coastal Ireland, getting lost along its twisting back roads is an unhurried pleasure and you're virtually guaranteed to happen upon a local village shop/pub/garage/post office and find it little changed in decades.

The Midlands is dominated by the River Shannon, which meanders through fields and forests, drawing boaters and fishers in shoals. Plush hotels and gourmet restaurants have sprung up along its banks, making it a wonderfully scenic and surprisingly cosmopolitan way to travel. If you're in search of a genuine slice of rural Irish life, this area makes the perfect retreat.

When to Go

➡ Late spring is a great time for appreciating Ireland's famous greener-than-green countryside, reflected in varying brilliant hues in the fields, hedges and trees.

➡ Merrymakers may prefer the summer months when fairs, festivals and special events take place throughout the region.

➡ July through September is also the ideal season for cruising the Shannon, with longer days, better weather and a spirited summertime crowd in the riverside pubs and restaurants.

➡ Eclectic-music lovers should watch out for September's Electric Picnic music festival near Portlaoise.

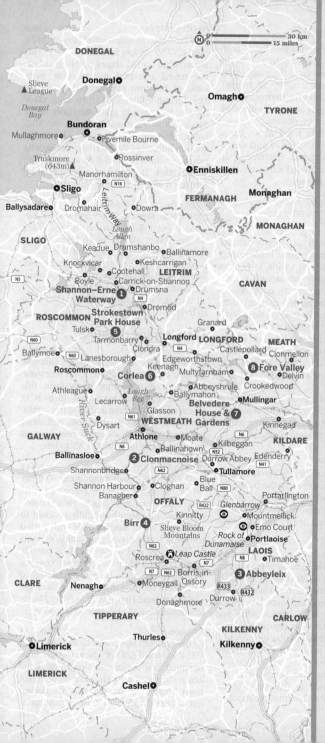

The Midlands Highlights

1 Slow down a gear and discover the rolling landscapes along the **Shannon–Erne Waterway** (p511)

2 Contemplate the lost land of saints and scholars at Ireland's finest monastic site, **Clonmacnoise** (p495)

3 Nurse a quiet pint at Morrissey's in **Abbeyleix** (p486), one of Ireland's most atmospheric pubs

4 Roam the tree-lined streets and explore the castle grounds in elegant **Birr** (p490)

5 Learn about Ireland's greatest disaster at the harrowing Famine museum at **Strokestown Park House** (p498)

6 Explore the Iron Age oak trackway unearthed at **Corlea** (p507)

7 Wander the corridors and gardens of magnificent **Belvedere House & Gardens** (p511) and marvel at its spiteful history

8 Visit the emerald green **Fore Valley** (p512), discovering impressive Christian ruins and suitably other-worldly views

COUNTY LAOIS

Little-visited Laois (pronounced leash) is often overlooked as drivers zoom past to the south and west. Away from the main roads, though, is this hidden corner of Ireland, with historic towns and the dramatic Slieve Bloom Mountains lying against a patchwork backdrop of rivers and walkways.

For all you need to know about Laois, check out www.laoistourism.ie and download the excellent *Laois Heritage Trail* booklet, which does a good job of tying together the county's history.

Abbeyleix

POP 1827

Abbeyleix (abbey-*leeks*) is a pretty heritage town with a Georgian market house, graceful terraced housing and a wide, leafy main street. The town grew up around a 12th-century Cistercian monastery, but problems with frequent flooding led to local 18th-century landowner Viscount de Vesci levelling the village and creating a new, planned estate town in the present location. During the Famine, de Vesci proved a kinder landlord than many, and the fountain obelisk in the square was erected in gratitude from his tenants.

Abbeyleix makes a good base for exploring Laois, with superb food and accommodation options and a chance to sip a pint in one of Ireland's most atmospheric pubs.

◉ Sights

Unfortunately for visitors, de Vesci's magnificent mansion is not open to the public. It's worth taking a look at the elegant Market House in the town centre, however. Built in 1836, it now houses a library and exhibition space.

★ Heywood Gardens   GARDENS
(www.heritageireland.ie; ⊙8.30am-9pm May-Aug, to 7pm Apr & Sep, to 5.30pm Oct-Mar; ⓟ) FREE
Southeast of town, these lavish gardens with lakes and woodland were landscaped by Edwin Lutyens and Gertrude Jekyll and completed in 1912. The centrepiece is a sunken garden, where circular terraces lead down to an oval pool with a magnificent fountain.

The gardens are 7km southeast of Abbeyleix, off the R432 to Ballinakill, in the grounds of Heywood Community School.

Heritage House   MUSEUM
(www.heritagehousemuseum.com; Main St; adult/child €3/2.50; ⊙9am-5pm Mon-Fri; ⓟ) This museum, in an old school building, details the town's colourful history. One room looks at the town's carpet-making legacy. The Turkish-influenced carpets once made here were chosen to grace the floors of the *Titanic*. Another room showcases the Mulhall Collection; a fascinating selection of memorabilia from the Morrissey family who ran the town's renowned shop and pub from 1775 to 2004. The centre also has tourist information and an adjacent playground.

Abbey Sensory Gardens   GARDENS
(Dove House, Main St; ⊙9am-5pm Mon-Fri year-round & 2-6pm Sat & Sun Jun-Sep; ⓟ) FREE
Garden lovers should make their way to this sensory playground set in the walled gardens of a 19th-century Brigidine convent. The vibrant blooms, wind chimes, humming stone and fragrant plants aim to stimulate all the senses and are the first of their kind in Ireland.

🍽 Sleeping & Eating

Farran Farm Hostel   HOSTEL €
(☎057-873 4032; www.farmhostel.com; Ballacolla; dm €20) In a beautifully restored limestone grain loft on a working family farm, this quirky independent hostel has 45 beds in rooms with a bathroom and up to five bunks. When you call, ask for directions and about the possibility of meals, as the hostel is well secluded, about 6km west of Abbeyleix.

★ Sandymount House   B&B €€
(☎057-873 1063; www.abbeyleix.info; Oldtown; s/d €45/80; @�🖘) Once the home of the de Vesci estate manager, this lovely old country house has been beautifully restored to seamlessly blend modern style with period features. A grand sweeping staircase, marble fireplaces and mature gardens provide elegant charm, while the spacious rooms are well equipped with individually designed bathrooms sporting high-pressure showers.

Sandymount House is 2km from Abbeyleix down the R433 towards Rathdowney.

Preston House   GUESTHOUSE €€
(☎057-873 1432; www.prestonhouse.ie; Main St; r €90, d half board €210; 🖘) New owners have breathed new life into this charming hotel and restaurant housed in a classic Georgian town house. The grand rooms are decked out in period style with dark, elegant furni-

ture and large, comfortable beds while the the tearoom (where breakfast is served) is a delight, decorated in muted shades of green with an open fire. The restaurant offers fine dining in an informal atmosphere.

Bramleys CAFE €
(www.bramleys.ie; Main St; dishes €5-9.50; ⏰10am-5pm Tue-Sat; 🅿) 🍴 You'll find a wonderful selection of soups, salads, hot dishes and tempting desserts at this coffee shop in an upmarket interiors store. It's a top-notch offering from the Castle Durrow team with veg coming from the castle gardens, communal tables weighed down with papers and magazines and some lovely outside seating for sunny days.

McEvoy's INTERNATIONAL €€
(www.macsabbeyleix.ie; Main St; mains €10-22; ⏰5-10pm Wed-Sat, 1-9pm Sun; 🌐) Run by the folks from nearby Castle Durrow, this classy place offers international dishes such as Louisiana chicken wings and Thai curries, plus excellent grills. The ingredients are locally sourced, the interior all tasteful neutrals and, as you would expect, the food is cooked to perfection.

🍷 Drinking & Nightlife

★**Morrissey's** PUB
(Main St) This extraordinary pub is one of those increasingly rare places that has withstood the onslaught of modernisation (aside from the obligatory TV). Ancient biscuit tins, jars of sweets, boxes of tea and a hodgepodge of oddities line the shelves above the pew seats and pot-belly stove. Claiming to be the oldest pub in Ireland, dating back to 1775 (when it opened as a grocery store), it's a wonderful place to soak up the atmosphere while you cradle a pint at the sloping counter.

❶ Getting There & Away

You will need your own wheels as buses no longer run to Abbeyleix.

Durrow

POP 843
A pleasant village, Durrow's neat rows of houses, pubs and cafes surround a manicured green. On the western side stands the imposing gateway to the 18th-century **Castle Durrow** (📞057-873 6555; www.castle durrow.com; r from €150, d half board €195; 🌐),

THE MIDLANDS DURROW

❶ GETTING AROUND LAOIS

The county town of Portlaoise is a useful transport hub. **Irish Rail** (www. irishrail.ie) runs direct trains from Portlaoise to Dublin (from €23, one hour, 14 daily); Cork (from €44, two hours, seven daily) and Limerick (from €29.40, 1½ hours, nine daily).

Bus Éireann (www.buseireann. ie) runs frequent buses on three main routes from Portlaoise: to Cork (€13.80, three hours, six daily) via Abbeyleix, Cashel and Cahir; to Dublin (€9, 1½ hours, 12 daily) via Kildare city; and along the N7 to Limerick (€11.85, 2¼ hours, 12 daily) via Mountrath, Borris-in-Ossory and Roscrea.

one of Ireland's top country-house hotels. It is delightfully unstuffy, with a friendly house cat or two and comfortable sitting rooms with open fires and well-aged leather sofas. Rooms here vary from opulent suites with four-poster beds and heavy brocades to more intimate oriental-style decor. Even if you can't stay overnight, enjoy a coffee on the terrace overlooking the sweeping grounds. The excellent **restaurant** (4-course set menus €35; ⏰7pm-9pm Wed-Sun) is supplied by the castle's organic kitchen garden. Half board recommended.

Durrow is signposted 10km south of Abbeyleix.

Slieve Bloom Mountains

One of the best reasons for visiting Laois is to explore the Slieve Bloom Mountains. Although not as spectacular as some Irish ranges, their sudden rise from a great plain and the absence of visitors make them highly attractive. You'll get a real sense of being away from it all as you tread the deserted blanket bogs, moorland, pine forests and isolated valleys.

🏃 Activities

For leisurely walking, **Glenbarrow**, southwest of Rosenallis, has an interesting trail by the cascading **Glendine Park**, near the Glendine Gap and the **Cut Mountain Pass**.

For something more challenging you could stride out on the **Slieve Bloom Way**, an 84km-long signposted trail that does a complete circuit of the mountains, taking

POVERTY'S LAST STOP AT DONAGHMORE

The farm village of Donaghmore is home to a grim survivor of the Famine. The Donaghmore Workhouse (📞086-829 6685; www.donaghmoremuseum.com; adult/child €5/3; ⏱11am-5pm Mon-Fri year-round, plus 2-5pm Sat & Sun Jun-Sep) opened as a last resort for the destitute in 1853. Conditions were intentionally grim, the idea being that if things were especially bad, the poor wouldn't stick around. Overcrowding was rife, families were separated, meals (no more than a bowl of gruel) were taken in silence, toilets were crude and bedding was limited. The loss of dignity that came with entering the workhouse was a tragic reality for many. It was a horrible time, recorded in a chilling fashion at this small museum signposted 20km west of Durrow.

in most major points of interest. The recommended starting point is the car park at Glenbarrow, 5km from Rosenallis, from where the trail follows tracks, forest firebreaks and old roads around the mountains. The trail's highest point is at Glendine Gap (460m).

Slieve Bloom Walking Club WALKING
(📞086 278 9147; www.slievebloom.ie; per person €5; ⏱weekends year-round) You can walk alone or join a guided walk organised by this reputable operator. The website has lots of information on a variety of walks in the mountains and is a good place for initial planning.

🛏 Sleeping

Roundwood House GUESTHOUSE €€
(📞057-873 2120; www.roundwoodhouse.com; Slieve Blooms Rd; main house s/d €85/120, B&B d €140, cottage/forge 3 nights €180/250; ⏱Feb-Dec; 🛜👟) Set in secluded woods, the rooms in this beautiful 17th-century Palladian villa are elegantly decorated, but have a comfortable lived-in feel. Children will love all the outdoor space and the friendly dogs, and the communal five-course dinner (€50 per person) is a chance to meet the amiable owners and enjoy a country treat of local foods. Try to get a room in the main house for the best atmosphere. There is also a cottage and a

forge (where horses were shod; both three nights' minimum stay).

Ballyfin House LUXURY HOTEL €€€
(📞057-875 5866; www.ballyfin.com; d from €950; @🛜🏊) An opulent Regency mansion with lavish interiors, Ballyfin's painstaking eight-year restoration has taken longer than the original build.ith 17th-century Flemish tapestries, a Roman sarcophagus bath, secret doorways, a 'whispering room' and a promise that every need shall be catered for, this is Ireland's most exclusive accommodation option.

❶ Getting There & Away

Although there is no public transport across the Slieve Bloom Mountains, there are occasional buses that stop in the nearby towns of Mountrath and Rosenallis.

Mountmellick

POP 2880

A quiet Georgian town located on the River Owenass, Mountmellick was renowned for its linen production in the 19th century and owes much of its history to its Quaker settlers.

A 4km looped and signed heritage trail, beginning in the square, leads you on a walking tour of the most important landmarks. For an insight into the town's Quaker and industrial heritage, visit Mountmellick Museum (📞057-862 4525; www.mountmellickdevelopment.com; Irishtown; adult/child €5/2; ⏱9am-1pm & 2-5pm Mon-Fri), where you can also see a display of superb Mountmellick embroidery. Various linens and quilts still being made by locals are on sale here.

Mountmellick is on the N80, 10km north of Portlaoise.

Portarlington

POP 7092

Portarlington grew up under the influence of French Huguenot and German settlers and has some fine, if neglected, 18th-century buildings along French and Patrick Sts. The 1851 St Paul's Church (⏱7am-7pm), on the site of the original 17th-century French church, was built for the Huguenots, some of whose tombstones stand in a corner of the churchyard.

About 4km east of town, on the banks of the River Barrow, are the ivy-covered ruins of 13th-century Lea Castle. The castle consists of a fairly intact towered keep with two outer walls and a twin-towered gatehouse. Access is through a farmyard, 500m to the north off the main Monasterevin road (R420).

Emo Court

The unusual, green-domed Emo Court (www.heritageireland.ie; Emo; adult/child €3/1, grounds free; ⊘10am-6pm Easter-Sep, last admission 5pm, grounds open daylight hours year-round) is an impressive house, designed in 1790 by James Gandon, architect of Dublin's Custom House. It was originally the country seat of the first earl of Portarlington. After many years as a Jesuit noviciate, the house, with its elaborate central rotunda, was impressively restored.

The extensive grounds, with their impressive Greek statues, contain over 1000 different trees, including huge sequoias, and shrubs from all over the world. Enjoy refreshments at the cafe or a leisurely picnic, before enjoying a scenic stroll through the woodlands to Emo Lake.

Emo is about 13km northeast of Portlaoise, just off the R422, 2km west of the M7.

Rock of Dunamaise

The Rock of Dunamaise (⊘daylight hours) FREE is an arresting sight: a craggy limestone outcrop rising dramatically out of the flat plains. The rock offered early settlers a superb natural defensive position with sweeping views across the surrounding countryside. It was first fortified in the Bronze Age and was recorded on Ptolemy's map of AD 140.

Over the centuries, successive waves of Viking, Norman, Irish and English invaders fought over its occupation. The ruins you see today are those of a castle built in the 13th century. It was extensively remodelled in the 15th century and finally destroyed by Cromwell's henchmen in 1650.

You'll need some imagination to envisage the site as it once was, but the views from the summit are breathtaking on a clear day. If you're lucky, you'll be able to see Timahoe round tower to the south, the Slieve Blooms to the west and the Wicklow Mountains to the east.

The rock is situated 6km east of Portlaoise along the Stradbally road (N80).

Timahoe

POP 1527

Tiny Timahoe has real charm, even if the village is nothing more than a handful of houses fronting a grassy triangle. Screened by a babbling stream, and seemingly straight out of a fairy tale, is a tilting 30m-tall, 12th-century round tower. The tower, with its unusual carved Romanesque doorway, is part of an ancient site that includes the ruins of a 15th-century church. The entire place has a certain magical quality, enhanced by a dearth of visitors.

Timahoe is 13km southeast of Portlaoise on the R426.

COUNTY OFFALY

Apart from the magnificent ecclesiastical city of Clonmacnoise, the green and watery county of Offaly doesn't feature on many tourists' itineraries, though it deserves far greater attention. Steeped in history with numerous castles to visit and the atmospheric town of Birr to enjoy, Offaly also offers vast swaths of bog recognised internationally for their plant and animal life, and prime fishing and water sports on the River Shannon and the Grand Canal.

Access www.offaly.ie, www.offalytourism.com and www.discoverireland.ie/offaly for more information.

WORTH A TRIP

ELECTRIC PICNIC

Ireland's answer to Glastonbury (though on a much smaller scale) the annual Electric Picnic (www.electricpicnic.ie; 3-day pass €240; ⊘early Sep) is an open-air arts and music festival held over three days. Known for its eclectic line-up, it's attracted the likes of Björk, Bob Geldof, Sinead O'Connor, Massive Attack and the Sex Pistols over the years. Apart from the music, you'll find a Body & Soul arena, comedy and cinema tents and a silent disco. Tickets are usually sold out months in advance. The festival takes place in the grounds of Stradbally Hall, 10km southeast of Portlaoise.

GRAND & ROYAL CANALS

After much debate about linking Dublin to the Shannon by water, work began on the Grand Canal in 1757. The project was beset by problems and encountered huge difficulties and delays. In the meantime, commercial rivals hatched a plan for the competing Royal Canal. The two canals revolutionised transport in Ireland in the early 19th century, but their heyday was short lived, as they were soon superseded by the railway.

Today the canals are popular for cruising and fishing, while their banks are ideal for walking and cycling and they pass through some truly picturesque villages. With the restoration of the final section of the Royal Canal it is now possible to complete a triangular route from Dublin along the Royal Canal or the Grand Canal to the Shannon and back.

Waterways Ireland (www.waterwaysireland.org) and the Inland Waterways Association of Ireland (www.iwai.ie) have a wealth of information on the canals.

Grand Canal

The Grand Canal threads its way from Dublin through Tullamore to join the River Shannon at Shannonbridge, a total of 131km in all. The canal passes through relatively unpopulated countryside, with bogs, pretty villages and 43 finely crafted locks lining the journey. Near the village of Sallins in County Kildare, the graceful seven-arched Leinster Aqueduct carries the canal across the River Liffey. From nearby Robertstown, a 45km spur turns south to join the River Barrow at the pretty town of Athy.

Royal Canal

The 145km Royal Canal follows Kildare's northern border, flowing over a massive aqueduct near Leixlip, before it joins the River Shannon at Clondra in County Longford. The canal has become a popular amenity for thousands of residents along the north Kildare commuter belt and both the canal and the towpaths are open all the way to the Shannon.

Barges & Boats

You can hire narrow boats at several locations along the canals. Two-/six-berth boats cost from around €850/15,955 per week.

Barrowline Cruisers (www.barrowline.ie; Vicarstown, Co Laois)

Canalways (www.canalways.ie; Rathangan, Co Kildare)

Birr

POP 5822

Feel-good Birr is one of the most attractive towns in the Midlands. Elegant Georgian buildings with candy-coloured facades are overlooked by a grande dame of a castle. There is some excellent accommodation, as well as a spirited nightlife with great live music. Despite its appeal, Birr remains off the beaten track and you can enjoy its delights without jostling with the crowds.

◉ Sights

Birr has no shortage of first-class Georgian houses; just stroll down tree-lined Oxmantown Mall or John's Mall to see some of the best examples.

The tourist office hands out a walking map that details the most important landmarks, including the megalithic Seffin Stone (said to be the ancient marker for Umbilicus Hiberniae – the Navel of Ireland – used to mark the centre of the country) and St Brendan's Old Churchyard, reputedly the site of the saint's 6th-century settlement.

★ Birr Castle Demesne   CASTLE
(www.birrcastle.com; gardens adult/child €9/5, gardens & castle adult/child €18/10; ⊙9am-6pm mid-Mar–Oct, noon-4pm Nov–mid-Mar; 🐾) It's easy to spend half a day exploring the attractions and gardens of Birr Castle Demesne. The castle dates from 1620 and is a private home; however, for three months in the summer (May, July and August) visitors can visit the main living quarters of the castle. Most of the present building dates from around 1620, with alterations made in the early 19th century.

The 50-hectare castle grounds are famous for their magnificent gardens set around a large artificial lake with waterfalls, wildflower meadows and a pergola festooned with a 90-year old wisteria. The gardens are home to over 1000 species of plant from all over the world; something always seems to be in bloom. Look for one of the world's tallest box hedges (which has made the *Guinness Book of Records*), planted in the 1780s and now standing 12m high, and the romantic Hornbeam cloister.

The Parsons were a remarkable family of pioneering Irish scientists, and their work is documented in the historic science centre. Exhibits include the massive telescope built by William Parsons in 1845. The 'leviathan of Parsonstown', as it was known, was the largest telescope in the world for 75 years and attracted a wide variety of scientists and astronomers. It was used to make innumerable discoveries, including the spiral galaxies. After the death of William's son, the telescope, unloved and untended, slowly fell to bits. It has recently been completely restored, however, and may be viewed in all its glory in the gardens.

William Parsons' wife, Mary Ross was a keen photographer and her darkroom was reputed to be one of the first of its kind in the world. Unfortunately, it hasn't survived, but an exact replica opened here in 2013. Other new additions are a children's adventure playground, complete with playhouse, hobbit huts and trampolines, and the excellent Castle Courtyard Cafe which showcases local products and produce in its dishes.

🏃 Activities

A beautiful leafy riverside walk runs east along the River Camcor from Oxmantown Bridge to Elmgrove Bridge.

Birr Outdoor Education Centre   ADVENTURE SPORTS
(www.birroec.ie; Roscrea Rd; ⊞) Offers hill walking, rock climbing and abseiling in the nearby Slieve Blooms, as well as sailing and kayaking on local rivers.

Birr Equestrian Centre   HORSE RIDING
(www.birrequestrian.ie; Kingsborough House; horse treks per hour €25; ⊞) This equestrian centre, located 3km outside Birr on the Clareen road, runs hour-long treks in the surrounding farmland and half-day horse treks in the Slieve Bloom Mountains (€70).

Birr Golf Club   GOLF
(☑ 057-912 0082; The Glenns; green fees from €15) A friendly golf club with a course carved out

of natural woodland with plenty of challenging hillocks and hollows.

✬ Festivals & Events

Birr Vintage Week and Arts Festival   ARTS
(www.birrvintageweek.com; ⊙ early Aug) The town celebrates its rich history during this festival, with street parades, theatre, music, exhibitions, workshops, guided walks and a traditional fair.

🛏 Sleeping

Maltings Guesthouse   B&B €€
(☑ 057-912 1345; www.themaltingsbirr.com; Castle St; s/d €35/70; ⊛⊞) Based in an 1810 malt storehouse once used by Guinness, this place has a serene location right by the castle and the River Camcor. The rooms are large with pine furniture and a soothing lilac-and-green colour scheme and, the best news of all, they all overlook the water, as does the delightful breakfast room. Excellent value.

Brendan House   B&B €€
(☑ 057-912 1818; www.tinjugstudio.com; Brendan St; 2-person studio from €15 per person, s/d €50/80; ⊛) Packed to the gills with knick-knacks, books, rugs, art and antiques, this Georgian town house is a bohemian delight. The three rooms share a bathroom, but the four-poster beds, period charm, superb breakfast and artistic style of the place more than make up for this. The owners can arrange guided mountain walks, castle and art tours and holistic treatments. There is a self-catering artist's studio which is a jumble of art materials, but has two (narrow) beds, a small kitchen and a private bathroom. No TVs.

WORTH A TRIP

GHOSTS AT LEAP CASTLE

Ireland's most haunted castle, Leap Castle (☑ 057-913 1115; www.leapcastle. net; admission €6; ⊙ by arrangement) originally kept guard over a crucial route between Munster and Leinster. The castle was the scene of many dreadful deeds and has quaint features like dank dungeons and a 'Bloody Chapel'. It's famous for its eerie apparitions.

Renovations are ongoing, but you can visit. It lies about 12km southeast of Birr between Kinnitty and Roscrea (in Tipperary) off the R421.

Dooley's Hotel
HOTEL €€

(☐ 057-912 0032; www.dooleyshotel.com; Emmet Sq; s/d from €45/70; @ 🛜 🛗) Originally a coaching house, one of the oldest in Ireland, dating from 1740, the hotel has an inviting homey feel with Georgian-style furnishings, friendly, youthful staff, a solidly reliable restaurant, and choice of bars. Rooms are large with contemporary wallpaper and sparkling tan-tiled bathrooms. The only downside is the mildly scuffed state of the carpets.

Emmet House
B&B €€

(☐ 057-916 9885; www.emmethouse.com; Emmet Sq; s/d/tr €50/80/100; 🛜) This handsome historic building stands on the corner of Emmet Sq at the entrance to town. Rooms are simple and elegant with dark wood and cream paintwork; one has a four-poster bed (request when booking).

🍴 Eating

Emma's Cafe & Deli
CAFE, DELI €

(31 Main St; meals €5-8; ⊙ 9am-6pm Mon-Fri, 12.30-6pm Sun; 🛜 🛗) Generally full of families and shoppers, Emma's serves a diverse range of ciabatta, panini, wraps, salads and cakes. There are daily newspapers, plus books and games for children. You can also pick up plenty of tempting deli options for picnics.

Riverbank
MODERN IRISH €€

(☐ 057-912 1528; Riverstown; mains €12-22, Sunday lunch €20; ⊙ 12.30-9.30pm Tue-Sun; 🛜) Look for the ochre facade of this class act of a restaurant set on the banks of the Little Brosna River, beside the bridge. The Sunday lunch attracts locals in droves and is well priced for a choice of six starters and seven mains (including a vegetarian option). The a la carte menu includes traditional favourites, as well as some one offs – like a warm salad of pan-fried kangaroo with a sweet-chilli and pink-peppercorn dressing. Riverbank is 1.5km southwest of Birr on the N52.

Sizzler Tandoori
INDIAN €€

(Market Sq; mains €8-12; ⊙ 5-11.30pm Wed-Sat, noon-4pm Sun; 🛗 🍴) A sound choice for Indian food. All the predictable dishes are here, including biryanis, kormas and madras curries with plenty of vegetarian choice, and (yikes!) chicken nuggets (and similar) for kids. The turmeric-toned paintwork sets the scene nicely.

Thatch
IRISH, INTERNATIONAL €€€

(☐ 057-912 0682; www.thethatchcrinkill.com; Crinkill; mains €22-29; ⊙ 4-10pm Mon-Thu, 10am-late Fri-Sun; 🛗) A traditional thatched pub, 2km southeast of Birr, this 200-year-old inn is a great place to sip a pint or enjoy a meal. The hearty cuisine is a belt notch or two above the norm and has won several awards. As well as traditional roasts, there are Asian-inspired and vegetarian dishes. The interior is a delight with three brick-clad small bars with open fires, plus a more modern light-wood dining room.

🍷 Drinking & Nightlife

Chestnut
PUB

(www.thechestnut.ie; Green St; ⊙ 8pm-late Mon-Thu, from 5pm Fri, from 3pm Sat & Sun) The most appealing pub in the centre, the Chestnut dates from 1823, but has had a pleasing aesthetic update combining dark furniture with a continental-cafe style. Toasted sandwiches are available if you're peckish and there is live music at weekends.

Craughwell's
PUB

(Castle St; ⊙ 7-11.30pm Mon-Sat, 1-11pm Sun) Stop for a pint at Craughwell's, renowned for its rollicking trad session on the first Friday of the month and impromptu sing-along sessions on Saturday. Check out the cap collection over the bar, mainly left by American patrons probably after a pint (or three).

Melba's Nite Club
CLUB

(Emmet Sq; ⊙ 11pm-late Fri-Sun) In the basement of Dooly's Hotel, DJs pump out a selection of chill-out, house and tribal sounds to a spirited local crowd.

⭐ Entertainment

Birr Theatre & Arts Centre
CULTURAL CENTRE

(www.birrtheatre.com; Oxmantown Hall) A vibrant place with a regular line-up of films, theatre and concerts.

ℹ️ Information

Mid-Ireland Tourism (☐ 057-912 0923; www.midirelandtourism.ie; Brendan St; ⊙ 9.30am-1pm & 2-5.30pm Mon-Fri) Useful for when the tourist office is closed.

Tourist office (☐ 057-912 0110; Civic Offices, Wilmer Rd; ⊙ 9.30am-1pm & 2-5.30pm Mon-Sat mid-May–mid-Sep) Good local and regional information.

ℹ️ Getting There & Away

Bus Éireann runs to Dublin (€18, 3½ hours, one daily) via Tullamore, Athlone (€11.40, one hour, four daily Monday to Saturday, two Sunday).

Kinnitty

POP 360

Kinnitty is a quaint village that makes a good base for exploring the Slieve Bloom Mountains to the east. Driving out of the village, the roads across the mountains to Mountrath and Mountmellick, both in County Laois, are particularly scenic.

◉ Sights

Look out for the bizarre 10m-high stone pyramid in the village graveyard behind the Church of Ireland. In the 1830s, Richard Bernard commissioned this scale replica of the Cheops pyramid in Egypt for the family crypt.

The shaft of the 9th-century Kinnitty High Cross was nabbed by Kinnitty Castle in the 19th century and is now displayed on the hotel's terrace. Adam and Eve and the Crucifixion are clearly visible on either face.

⨠ Sleeping

★ Ardmore House   B&B €€
(☏ 057-913 7009; www.kinnitty.com; The Walk; s/d from €55/82; ⊛) This lovely Victorian stone farmhouse oozes old-world charm. The rooms are full of character, with brass beds, subtle floral patterns, antique furniture and views of the nearby mountains. Peat fires and homemade brown bread complete the cosy, rustic atmosphere. The owners can organise walking tours in the nearby Slieve Bloom Mountains. The B&B is set off the R440, about 200m east of Kinnitty.

Kinnitty Castle   LUXURY HOTEL €€
(☏ 057-913 7318; www.kinnittycastlehotel.com; s/d from €50/100; ⊛) One of Ireland's most renowned mansions, 19th-century Kinnitty Castle is built in neo-Gothic style surrounded by a vast estate. A victim of the economic recession, the castle is owned and administered by its bankers but continues to operate as a luxury hotel and wedding venue. Rooms are suitably atmospheric, along with the Dungeon Bar – Kinnitty is supposedly haunted. The castle is 3km southeast of town off the R440.

Banagher & Around

POP 1655

Sleepy Banagher bursts into life in the summer months when the busy marina is awash with boaters. Perhaps Banagher's greatest claim to fame is that it was the location for Charlotte Brontë's honeymoon.

◉ Sights

Situated at a crossing point over the River Shannon, Banagher was a place of enormous strategic importance during turbulent times. The modest fortifications by the bridge include the diminutive Cromwell's Castle, built in the 1650s and modified during the Napoleonic Wars, Fort Eliza (a five-sided gun battery, the guardhouse, moat and retaining walls of which can still be seen), a roofless military barracks and Martello tower.

St Paul's Church, at the far end of Main St, contains a resplendent stained-glass window, originally intended for Westminster Abbey.

⃗ Activities

Boating

Banagher Marina is a good place to rent cruisers for a trip along the Shannon or the Royal Canal. Prices for three-/12-berth boats start at about €878/3376. Try Carrick Craft (www.cruise-ireland.com) or Silverline Cruisers (www.silverlinecruisers.com) for more information.

You can also rent canoes at the marina.

Walking

Head 3km south of Banagher to Lusmagh (just off the R439) to take a tranquil walk down to picturesque Victoria Lock, where the Shannon splits into two channels. Cross the lock and walk north along the west bank of the river for 2km to reach 15th-century Meelick Church, one of the oldest churches still in use in Ireland.

⨠ Sleeping & Eating

★ Charlotte's Way   B&B €€
(☏ 057-915 3864; www.charlottesway.com; The Hill; s/d €40/70; ⊛) This tastefully restored former rectory with its period furniture, old prints and antiques offers five comfy good-value rooms, including a honeymoon room with jacuzzi. A honeymooning Charlotte Brontë was a frequent visitor and, after her death, her husband Arthur lived here as the rector. Breakfast stars eggs fresh from the chickens, and the pretty garden is home to two pint-size Fallabella horses (one of the smallest breeds in the world).

Dún Cromáin   B&B €
(☏ 057-915 3966; www.duncromain.com; Crank Rd; s/d €35/60; ⊛) Surrounded by sweeping lawns, the large rooms are simply decorated

in pastel colours with light wood and white linens. The breakfast-cum-sitting room has a feel-at-home atmosphere and an open fire. Perks include babysitting, fridges and facilities for drying clothes (handy in these parts!).

Flynns Bar & Restaurant IRISH €€
(Main St; mains €9-20; ☺10.30am-11.30pm) Popular with locals for its grills, steak and pasta, this wood-panelled local bar also has a restaurant at the back serving a decent selection of reliable dishes for those with large appetites: portion sizes are huge!

 Drinking & Nightlife

JJ Houghs PUB
(Main St; ☺5pm-late) Rivalling the river as Banagher's most appealing feature, Hough's is a 250-year-old vine-clad pub renowned for its music sessions. You'll find someone playing here most nights in summer and at weekends in winter. If there's no live music, you can entertain yourself by poring over the artefact-covered walls or counting stars in the beer garden.

ⓘ Getting There & Away

Kearns Transport (www.kearnstransport.com) links Banagher to Birr (€3, 15 minutes), Tullamore (€3.75, 45 minutes) and Dublin (€10, 2¾ hours) once daily.

Shannonbridge
POP 650

Perfectly picturesque, Shannonbridge gets its name from a narrow 16-span, 18th-century bridge that crosses the river into County Roscommon. It's a small, sleepy village with just one main street and three pubs.

You can't miss the massive 19th-century fortifications on the western bank, where heavy artillery was installed to bombard Napoleon in case he was cheeky enough to try to invade by river.

 Sleeping & Eating

Rachra House B&B €
(☏090-967 4249; Main St; s/d €45/60) On the main street of town, this place is sparklingly clean with attractive rooms sporting cosy carpets, embroidered bedspreads and private bathrooms with parquetry floors and sky blue tilework.

Old Fort Restaurant MODERN IRISH €€
(☏090-967 4973; www.theoldfortrestaurant.com; mains €21.50-29.50, set menu €20; ☺5-9.30pm Wed-Sat, 12.30-2.30pm Sun) Offers a sophisticated take on traditional cuisine in the suitably grand surroundings of a massive bridgehead.

🍷 Drinking & Nightlife

★Killeens Village Tavern PUB
(Main St) Killeens is an old-world pub and shop that is renowned for its warm welcome and lively traditional music. The ceiling of the bar is plastered with old business cards left by appreciative customers over the years. There's a music session three times a week in summer and at weekends during the rest of the year. Traditional pub grub also available.

WORTH A TRIP

SHANNON HARBOUR & AROUND

Just 1km east of where the Grand Canal joins the River Shannon, sleepy Shannon Harbour is a small, picturesque town that was once a thriving trading centre, constructed to serve the waterways and home to over 1000 people. Along with cargo boats, passenger barges ran from here, many of which took poverty-stricken locals on their first leg of a long journey to North America or Australia.

Today the waterways are again teeming with boats and walking paths stretching in all directions, making Shannon Harbour an enticing stop for walkers, fishers, boaters and birders.

The village is about 10km northeast of Banagher off the R356. Nearby, 16th-century Clonony Castle (☏086 068 1404; www.clononycastle.ie; admission by donation; ☺by appointment May-Dec), a fortified tower house, is enclosed by a castellated wall. Tales that Henry VIII's second wife, Anne Boleyn, was born here are unlikely to be true, but her cousins Elizabeth and Mary Boleyn are buried beside the ruins. Restoration of the first two floors of the castle is complete and the American owner is happy to welcome visitors with advance notice.

Clonmacnoise

Gloriously placed overlooking the River Shannon, Clonmacnoise is one of Ireland's most important ancient monastic cities. The site is enclosed in a walled field and contains several early churches, high crosses, round towers and graves in astonishingly good condition. The surrounding marshy area is known as the Shannon Callows, home to many wild plants and one of the last refuges of the seriously endangered corncrake (a pastel-coloured relative of the coot).

History

When St Ciarán founded a monastery here, in AD 548, it was the most important crossroads in the country, the intersection of the north–south River Shannon, and the east–west Esker Riada (Highway of the Kings).

The giant ecclesiastical city had a humble beginning and Ciarán died just seven months after building his first church. Over the years, however, Clonmacnoise grew to become an unrivalled bastion of Irish religion, literature and art and attracted a large lay population. Between the 7th and 12th centuries, monks from all over Europe came to study and pray here, helping to earn Ireland the title of the 'land of saints and scholars'.

Most of what you can see today dates from the 10th to 12th centuries. The monks would have lived in small huts surrounding the monastery. The site was burned and pillaged on numerous occasions by both the Vikings and the Irish. After the 12th century it fell into decline, and by the 15th century it was home solely to an impoverished bishop. In 1552 the English garrison from Athlone reduced the site to a ruin.

Among the treasures that survived the continued onslaughts are the crosier of the abbots of Clonmacnoise in the National Museum in Dublin, and the 12th-century *Leabhar na hUidhre* (The Book of the Dun Cow), now in the Royal Irish Academy in Dublin.

Sights

Museum   MUSEUM
(www.heritageireland.ie; ☉9am-7pm mid-May–mid-Sep, 10am-5.30pm mid-Sep–mid-May, last admission 45min before closing) Three connected conical huts, echoing the design of early monastic dwellings, house the museum. The centre's 20-minute audiovisual show provides an excellent introduction to the site.

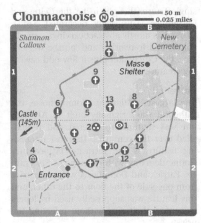

Clonmacnoise   (N)   0 — 50 m / 0 — 0.025 miles

Clonmacnoise

◉ Sights

The exhibition area contains the original high crosses (replicas have been put in their former locations outside), and various artefacts uncovered during excavation, including silver pins, beaded glass and an Ogham stone. It also contains the largest collection of early-Christian grave slabs in Europe, many with inscriptions clearly visible, often starting with *oroit do* or *ar* (a prayer for).

There's a real sense of drama as you descend to the foot of the imposing Cross of the Scriptures (King Flann's Cross), one of Ireland's finest. It's very distinctive, with unique upward-tilting arms and richly decorated panels depicting the Crucifixion, the Last Judgement, the arrest of Jesus, and Christ in the tomb.

Only the shaft of the North Cross, which dates from around AD 800, remains. It is adorned by lions, convoluted spirals and a single figure, thought to be the Celtic god Cernunnos. The richly decorated South Cross has mostly abstract carvings – swirls, spirals and fretwork – and, on the western face, the Crucifixion plus a few odd cavorting creatures.

Cathedral   RUIN
The largest building at Clonmacnoise, the cathedral was originally built in AD 909, but was significantly altered and remodelled over the centuries. Its most interesting feature is the intricate 15th-century Gothic doorway with carvings of Sts Francis, Patrick and Dominic. A whisper carries from one side of the door to the other, and this feature was supposedly used by lepers to confess their sins without infecting the priests.

The last high kings of Tara – Turlough Mór O'Connor (died 1156) and his son Ruairí (Rory; died 1198) – are said to be buried near the altar.

Temples   CHURCH
The small churches are called temples, a derivation of the Irish word *teampall* (church). The little, roofed church is Temple Conner, still used by Church of Ireland parishioners on the last Sunday of the summer months. Walking towards the cathedral, you'll pass the scant foundations of Temple Kelly (1167) before reaching tiny Temple Ciaran, reputed to be the burial place of St Ciarán, the site's founder.

The floor level in Temple Ciaran is lower than outside because local farmers have been taking clay from the church for centuries as a charm to protect their crops and cattle. The floor has been covered in slabs, but handfuls of clay are still removed from outside the church in the early spring.

Near the temple's southwestern corner is a bullaun (ancient grinding stone), supposedly used for making medicines for the monastery's hospital. Today the rainwater that collects in it is said to cure warts.

Continuing round the compound you come to the 12th-century Temple Melaghlin, with its attractive windows, and the twin structures of Temple Hurpan and Temple Doolin.

Round Towers   HISTORIC BUILDING
Overlooking the River Shannon is the 20m-high O'Rourke's Tower. Lightning blasted the top off the tower in 1135, but the remaining structure was used for another 400 years.

Temple Finghin and its round tower are on the northern boundary, also overlooking the Shannon. It dates from around 1160 and has some fine Romanesque carvings. The herringbone-patterned tower roof is the only one in Ireland that has never been altered.

Other Remains   HISTORIC BUILDING
Beyond the site's boundary wall, about 500m east through the modern graveyard, is the secluded Nun's Church with wonderful Romanesque arches and minute carvings; one has been interpreted as Ireland's earliest sheila-na-gig (carved female figure with exaggerated genitalia), in an acrobatic pose with feet tucked behind the ears.

To the west of the site, on the ridge near the car park, is a motte (raised mound) with the oddly shaped ruins of a 13th-century castle, built by John de Grey, bishop of Norwich, to watch over the Shannon.

🍴 Sleeping & Eating

Kajon House   B&B €€
(☑ 090-967 4191; www.kajonhouse.ie; Creevagh; s/d €50/70; ☺ Mar-Oct; ☏) If you want to stay near the ruins, this is your best option, just 1.5km away on the road signposted to Tullamore. It's a very friendly place with cosy rooms, a spacious yard (complete with picnic table) and evening meals on offer. Delicious pancakes available for breakfast.

🛍 Shopping

Core Craft Centre   ARTS & CRAFTS
(www.corecrafteddesign.com; Old School House, Ballinahown; ☺ 10am-6pm Mon-Fri, 11am-6pm Sat) En route to Clonmacnoise, it's worth stopping in Ballinahown, on the N62, to browse the excellent range of contemporary craftwork, bog-oak sculpture and pottery on offer.

ℹ Information

The Clonmacnoise site includes a **tourist office** (☑ 090-967 4134; ☺ 10am-5.45pm mid-Mar–Oct). Allow at least a couple of hours for a visit to the site.

ℹ Getting There & Away

By car Clonmacnoise is 7km northeast of Shannonbridge on the R444.

BOAT
There are river and bus tours to Clonmacnoise from Athlone (p508) in County Westmeath.
Silver Line (www.silverlinecruisers.com; adult/child €12/8; ☺ 2pm Wed & Sun Jul & Aug)

Runs boat trips between Shannonbridge and Clonmacnoise.

TAXI

A taxi from Athlone will cost roughly €50 to €70 round trip, including an hour's wait.

Tullamore

POP 11,575

Tullamore, Offaly's county town, is a bustling place with a pleasant setting on the Grand Canal. The town is most famous for Tullamore Dew whiskey, although production has long since moved to County Tipperary.

Sights

Charleville Castle   CASTLE
(2 057-932 3040; www.charlevillecastle.ie; guided tour per person €24, minimum 3 adults; ⊘tours 1-5pm Jun-Aug, by appointment Sep-Apr) Spires, turrets, clinging ivy and creaking trees combine to give this hulking structure a haunted feel (and, yes, it is reputedly haunted!). Charleville Castle was the family seat of the Burys, who commissioned the design in 1798 from Francis Johnston, one of Ireland's most famous architects. The interior is spectacular, with stunning ceilings, one of the most striking Gothic-revival galleries in Ireland and a kitchen block built to resemble a country church.

Admission is by 35-minute tour only. The entrance is off the N52, south of Tullamore.

Tullamore Dew Heritage Centre   MUSEUM
(www.tullamore-dew.org; Bury Quay; adult/student €8/6; ⊘9am-6pm Mon-Sat, 11.30am-5pm Sun) Located in a 19th-century canalside warehouse, the heritage centre mixes intriguing local history with booze propaganda. Fortunately, the emphasis is on the former and engaging exhibits show the role of the Grand Canal in the town's development. At the end of the tour you'll get to sample three tots what is supposedly the easiest of Irish whiskeys to drink. In the absence of an official tourist office in town, the centre carries a modest selection of general information. Light snacks available.

Sleeping & Eating

Annaharvey Farm   B&B €€
(2 057-934 3544; www.annaharveyfarm.ie; Aharney; s/d from €35/70; ⊞) This tranquil equestrian centre and guesthouse is a great place to enjoy a bit of country life and genuine hospitality. The rooms are tastefully decorated in contemporary neutrals and there's horse riding on your doorstep. The farm is 6km southeast of Tullamore on the R420.

Sea Dew   B&B €€
(2 057-935 2054; www.seadewguesthouse.com; Clonminch Rd; s/d from €45/70; @♠⊞) A purpose-built guesthouse just five minutes' walk from the town centre, this welcoming place has 12 spacious rooms. There's a lovely outdoor deck in the mature gardens, a delightful breakfast room and a play area for children.

Sirocco's   ITALIAN €€
(2 057-935 2839; www.siroccos.net; Patrick St; mains €12-25; ⊘5-11pm Mon-Sat, noon-3pm Thu & Fri, 1-10pm Sun; ⊞) Italian-Irish owned, this popular bistro caters to undecided taste-

MEADHBH LARKIN, GHOST HUNTER

Meadhbh Larkin is a locations manager at Irish Ghost Hunters (www.irishghosthunters.com) involved in paranormal research. Meadhbh sources, contacts and organises investigations at locations throughout Ireland.

Which is the most haunted county in Ireland in your view. And why? It has to be Offaly because it is home to several of Ireland's most haunted castles. I think the landscape also contributes to the creepy feel – Offaly is very flat and marshy, with a lot of bogs which tend to be misty at night.

And the most haunted castles? Both Leap Castle (p491) and Charleville Castle (p497) are considered to be extremely haunted. Leap is home to more than 20 ghosts, ranging from the spirits of two little girls to a terrifying entity known as the elemental which I encountered, in the form of a terrible smell of rotten eggs, during a recent visit to Leap.

And your advice for sceptics? To remain skeptical and keep an open mind but question everything. If you cannot find a logical explanation for what you have experienced, consider that it may well be paranormal.

WORTH A TRIP

LOUGH BOORA

Much of County Offaly's once-extensive bogs were stripped of peat for electricity generation during the 20th century. One area, Lough Boora (www.loughbooraparklands.com), is now the focus of a scheme to restore its environment. Located 5km west of Blue Ball off the R357, there are over 50km of trails across the area, with excellent birdwatching, rare flora, a mesolithic site and a series of impressive environmental sculptures (www.sculptureintheparklands.com) to explore. Bike rental is available (€20 per day).

buds and families with its wide selection of fresh pasta dishes and pizza, as well as meat, chicken and fish dishes. Reservations recommended.

ⓘ Getting There & Away

BUS

Bus Éireann runs a service to Dublin (€16.15, 2½ hours, five weekdays, three Saturday and Sunday) and Waterford (€22, 3¼ hours, two daily) via Portlaoise, Carlow and Kilkenny.

TRAIN

Irish Rail (www.irishrail.ie) trains run east to Dublin (from €15, 1¼ hours, 12 daily) and west to Galway (from €15, 1½ hours, eight daily), as well as Westport and Sligo.

Durrow Abbey

Founded by St Colmcille (also known as St Columba) in the 6th century, Durrow Abbey is most famous for producing the illustrated *Book of Durrow*. The 7th-century text is the earliest of the great manuscripts to have survived, a remarkable feat considering it was recovered from a farm where it was dipped in the cattle's drinking water to cure illnesses. It can be seen at Trinity College, Dublin.

The site contains five early-Christian gravestones and Durrow's splendid 10th-century high cross, the complex, high relief carvings that depict the sacrifice of Isaac, the Last Judgement and the Crucifixion.

The path north past the church leads to St Colmcille's Well, a place of pilgrimage marked by a small cairn.

Durrow Abbey is 7km north of Tullamore down a long lane west off the N52.

COUNTY ROSCOMMON

Studded with over 5000 megalithic tombs, ring forts and mounds, and home to a couple of excellent museums, enigmatic Roscommon is a haven for history buffs and

shrouded in myth. Add to the mix a couple of well-preserved mansions and some wonderful monastic ruins and it's hard to understand why the county sees so few visitors. Beyond the romance of times past, Roscommon has plenty of rolling countryside splashed with lakes and cleaved by the Rivers Shannon and Suck; attributes much appreciated by visiting anglers.

Strokestown & Around

POP 814

Strokestown's main street is a grand tree-lined avenue that remains a testament to the lofty aspirations of one of the local landed gentry who wished it to be Europe's widest. It's a striking feature in what is a now a sleepy town most notable for its historic estate and Famine museum.

Over the May Day Bank Holiday weekend, the town bursts into life during the International Poetry Festival (www.strokestownpoetry.org).

◉ Sights

★ **Strokestown Park House & Famine Museum** HISTORIC BUILDING
(www.strokestownpark.ie; admission house or museum or gardens €9, house, museum & gardens €13; ⊙10.30am-5.30pm, tours noon, 2.30pm & 4.30pm; 🐾) At the end of Strokestown's main avenue, triple Gothic arches lead to Strokestown Park House.

The original 12,000-hectare estate was granted by King Charles II to Nicholas Mahon for his support in the English Civil War. Nicholas' grandson Thomas commissioned Richard Cassels to build him a Palladian mansion in the early 18th century. Over the centuries, the estate decreased in size along with the family's fortunes. When it was eventually sold in 1979, it had been whittled down to 120 hectares. The estate was bought as a complete lot, so virtually all of its remaining contents are intact.

Admission to the house is by a 45-minute guided tour, taking in a galleried kitchen with original ovens dating from 1740, a schoolroom with an exercise book of neatly written dictation dating from 1934 (and, according to her red pen, deemed disgraceful by the governess) and a toy room complete with 19th-century toys and fun-house mirrors.

The walled garden contains the longest herbaceous border in Ireland and Britain, which blooms in a rainbow of colours in summer. There is also a folly, a lily pond and Ireland's oldest glass greenhouse, dating from 1780.

In direct and deliberate contrast to the splendour of the house and its grounds is the harrowing Strokestown Famine Museum, comprising 10 galleries which shed light on the devastating 1840s potato blight. There's a huge amount of information with long panels of text and newer computer consoles where you can delve further into the history. You'll emerge with an unblinking insight into the starvation of the poor, and the ignorance, callousness and cruelty of those who were in a position to help.

Strokestown landlord Major Denis Mahon ruthlessly evicted starving peasants who couldn't pay their rent, chartering boats to transport them away from Ireland. Around half of these 1000 emigrants died on the overcrowded 'coffin ships', a further 200 died while in quarantine in Quebec (the cheapest route). Perhaps unsurprisingly, Mahon was assassinated by three of his tenants in 1847, two of whom were publicly hung in Roscommon.

The museum also focuses attention on present-day famine around the world. There is a cafe serving hot and cold snacks.

Cruachan Aí Visitor Centre HISTORIC SITE
(www.rathcroghan.ie; Tulsk; adult/child €5/3; ☉9am-5pm Mon-Sat; 🖢) Anyone with an interest in Celtic mythology will be enthralled by the area around the village of Tulsk, which contains 60 ancient national monuments including standing stones, barrows, cairns and fortresses, making it the most important Celtic royal site in Europe.

The landscape and its sacred structures have lain largely undisturbed for the past 3000 years. It's hard to grasp just how significant the site is, as archaeological digs are continuing, but it has already been established that the site is bigger and older than Tara in County Meath and was at one time a major seat of Irish power. The site is cur-

rently being considered for Unesco World Heritage status.

The visitor centre has diagrams, photographs, informative panels and maps that explain the significance of the sites, and can let you know the current status of access to the (privately owned) monuments. A 10-minute audiovisual presentation introduced in 2013 includes an introduction to the cave plus an animated story about the legend of the Táin Bó Cúailnge (Cattle Raid of Cooley) which should appeal to all ages.

According to the legend, Queen Maeve (Medbh) had her palace at Cruachan. The Oweynagat Cave (Cave of the Cats), believed to be the entrance to the Celtic otherworld, is also nearby. As it is located on private land, a guide has to accompany any brave souls who wish to enter the cave. This can be arranged at the visitor centre (€20 per person).

Tulsk is 10km west of Strokestown on the N5. Bus Éireann's frequent Dublin to Westport route stops right outside the visitor centre.

Boyle & Around

POP 2588

A quiet town at the foot of the Curlew Mountains, Boyle is a scenic and worthwhile stop, home to beautiful Boyle Abbey, a 4000-year-old dolmen, the hands-on King House Interpretive Centre and a scenic forest park.

If you're here at the end of July, you can catch the lively Boyle Arts Festival (www.boylearts.com), which features music, theatre, storytelling and contemporary Irish art exhibitions.

History

The history of Boyle is the history of the King family. In 1603 Staffordshire-born John King was granted land in Roscommon with the aim of 'reducing the Irish to obedience'. Over the next 150 years, through canny marriages and cold-blooded conquests, his descendants made their name and fortune, becoming one of the largest landowning families in Ireland. The town of Boyle grew around their estate.

King House was built in 1730, and in 1780 the family moved to the grander Rockingham House, built in what is now Lough Key Forest Park. Unfortunately, the house was destroyed by fire in 1957.

◉ Sights

King House Interpretive Centre   HISTORIC BUILDING

(www.kinghouse.ie; Main St; adult/child €5/2; ⊙11am-4pm Tue-Sat Apr-Sep, market 10am-2pm Sat; ⊕) After the King family moved to Lough Key, the imposing Georgian mansion King House became a military barracks for the fearsome Connaught Rangers. The county council bought the property in 1987, and spent several years and €3.8 million turning it into the inspired King House Interpretive Centre.

Sinister-looking dummies from various eras tell the turbulent history of the Connaught kings, the town of Boyle and the King family, including a grim tale of tenant eviction during the Famine. Kids can try on replica ancient Irish cloaks, breeches and leather shoes, write with a quill, play a regimental drum and build a vaulted ceiling from specially designed blocks.

The mansion's sheltered walled courtyard is home to a large souvenir shop selling local crafts and an organic produce market.

Boyle Abbey   HISTORIC BUILDING

(www.heritageireland.ie; admission €3; ⊙10am-6pm Easter-late Sep) Gracing the River Boyle is the finely preserved (and reputedly haunted) Boyle Abbey. Founded in 1161 by monks from Mellifont in County Louth, the abbey captures the transition from Romanesque to Gothic style, best seen in the nave, where a set of arches in each style face each other. Unusually for a Cistercian building, figures and carved animals decorate the capitals to the west as, more bafflingly, do the pagan sheela-na-gigs fertility symbol. After the Dissolution of the Monasteries, the abbey was occupied by the military and became Boyle Castle; the stone chimney on the southern side of the abbey, which was once the refectory, dates from that period.

Guided 40-minute tours of the abbey are available upon request.

Lough Key Forest Park   PARK, HISTORIC SITE

(www.loughkey.ie; forest admission free, parking €4, Lough Key Experience adult/child €7.50/5; Boda Borg €15; Adventure Playground day pass €5; ⊙10am-6pm Apr-Aug, to 5pm Fri-Sun Sep-Mar; ⊕) Sprinkled with small islands, Lough Key Forest Park has long been popular for its picturesque ruins, including a 12th-century abbey on tiny Trinity Island and a 19th-century castle on Castle Island. It's also a time-honoured favourite with families for its wishing chair, bog gardens, fairy bridge and viewing tower. There are plenty of marked walking trails through the park.

The 350-hectare park was once part of the Rockingham estate, owned by the King family from the 17th century until 1957. Rockingham House, designed by John Nash, was destroyed by a fire in the same year; all that remains are some stables, outbuildings and eerie tunnels leading to the lake – built to hide the servants from view.

There is an informative visitor centre, and the Lough Key Experience, incorporating a panoramic, 300m-long treetop canopy walk, which rises 9m above the woodland floor with sweeping lake views. Other attractions include the Boda Borg Challenge, a series of rooms filled with activities and puzzles (great for sudden bursts of rain); and an outdoor adventure playground.

In July and August, Lough Key Boats (www.loughkeyboats.com) provides hourly boat trips (€12/6 per adult/child), rowing-boat hire (€22 per hour, maximum five people) and fishing advice (record-breaking pike have been caught here).

Lough Key is 4km east of Boyle on the N4. The Bus Éireann Sligo to Dublin route has frequent services from Boyle to Lough Key.

Arigna Mining Experience   COAL MINE

(www.arignaminingexperience.ie; adult/child €10/6; ⊙10am-5pm; ⊕) Ireland's first and last coal mine (1600s to 1990) is remembered at the Arigna Mining Experience, set in the hills above Lough Allen. The highlight is the 40-minute underground tour, which takes you 400m down to the coal face and includes a mini-explosion simulation. Tours are led by ex-miners who really bring home the gruelling working conditions and dangers of their job. Wear warm clothing and sturdy shoes as it can be cold and muddy.

Drumanone Dolmen   HISTORIC SITE

FREE This astonishing portal dolmen, one of the largest in Ireland, measures 4.5m by 3.3m and was constructed before 2000 BC. It can be tricky to find: follow Patrick St and then the R294 out of town for 5km, until you pass under a railway arch. A sign indicates the path across the railway line; take care crossing as trains are frequent.

Douglas Hyde Interpretive Centre   MUSEUM

(⊘087 782 3751; dogara@roscommoncoco.ie; Frenchpark; ⊙May-Sep by prior appointment) FREE The life of Roscommon native Dr

Douglas Hyde (1860–1949), poet, writer and first president of Ireland, is celebrated at the Douglas Hyde Interpretive Centre. Outside the political arena, Hyde cofounded the Gaelic League in 1893 and spent a lifetime gathering Gaelic poems and folklore that might otherwise have been lost forever.

The centre is in Frenchpark, 12km southwest of Boyle.

Activities

Covering 118km of north Roscommon, east Sligo and mid-Leitrim, the **Arigna Miners Way & Historical Trail** is a series of well-signposted tracks and hill passes covering the routes taken by miners on their way to work. A guidebook with maps is available from local tourist offices.

Sleeping

Boyle has some great B&Bs.

Lough Key House   B&B €€
(☎071-966 2161; www.loughkeyhouse.com; Rockingham; s/d from €50/85; ☎) This beautifully restored Georgian country house is an atmospheric place to stay with six guest rooms, each individually decorated with stylish period furniture. Two rooms have magnificent four-poster beds, a couple have bathrooms with claw-foot tubs, another a jacuzzi. The downstairs sitting room combines antiques with elegance, comfort and an open fire. Breakfast eggs come from the owner's hens, there are bikes to borrow and, if you arrive by bus, you can be picked up from town.

Lough Key House is 4km east of town on the N4.

Forest Park House   B&B €€
(☎071-966 2227; www.bed-and-breakfast-boyle.com; Rockingham; s/d €45/80; ☎) Just by the entrance to Lough Key Forest Park, this purpose-built guesthouse has light-filled modern rooms with pine woodwork and crisp white linens. Classy cream tiles and ethnic rugs (mainly from Turkey) complete the airy Med-style look.

Cesh Corran   B&B €€
(☎071-966 2265; www.marycooney.com; Abbey Tce; s/d €55/80; ☎) Overlooking the abbey ruins, this immaculately kept place has bright, simple rooms and a very warm welcome. There's a garden, wholesome breakfasts and even a separate bait fridge for anglers.

Eating & Drinking

Boyle has the usual array of Chinese and fast-food restaurants, but, otherwise, is limited. Carrick-on-Shannon (in nearby County Leitrim) has more culinary choice.

Stone House Cafe   CAFE €
(Bridge St; snacks €6-8; ☉10am-6pm Mon-Sat) This delightful stone building on the river was once the gate lodge to a private mansion. The cafe serves a selection of soups, sandwiches, paninis and cakes, which you can enjoy as the water rushes by.

Clarke's   IRISH €€
(St Patrick St; mains €13-24; ☉12.30-3pm & 5.30-9pm Mon-Sat, 5.30-11pm Sun) Dark wood combined with cranberry red walls equal a suitably warm and homely atmosphere for enjoying genuine home cooking. Specialities are the Irish fillet steak and the daily fish special. Live music at weekends.

Wynne's Bar   PUB
(Main St; ☉7pm-late; ☎) This quaint historic bar is in the centre of town. Live music at weekends.

Information

Úna Bhán Tourism Cooperative (☎071-966 3033; www.unabhan.net; Main St; ☉9am-6pm daily May-Aug, to 5pm Mon-Fri Sep-Apr) A local cooperative in the grounds of the King House Interpretive Centre, which supplies general tourist information on the Boyle region.

Getting There & Away

BUS

Bus Éireann (www.buseireann.ie) runs between Dublin (€17.10, 3½ hours) and Sligo (€11.40, 45 minutes), stopping off at Boyle en route. There are six buses daily Monday to Saturday, five on Sunday.

TRAIN

Irish Rail (www.irishrail.ie) trains leave eight times daily to Sligo (from €12.70, half an hour) and Dublin (from €15, 2½ hours) via Mullingar. The station is on Elphin St.

TRAIN FARES

Save money by buying your train tickets across Ireland online (www.irishrail.ie). Internet prices are considerably cheaper than at the ticket office.

Roscommon Town

POP 5020

The county town of Roscommon is very much a place of local business and commerce, but it has a small, stately centre and some significant abbey and castle ruins that make it worth a brief stop.

👁 Sights

Roscommon's central square is dominated by its former courthouse (now the Bank of Ireland). Opposite, the facade of the old jail survives. Ask any local about the grim tale of Lady Betty, its infamous hangwoman.

Roscommon Castle RUIN
(⊙dawn-dusk) The impressive ruins of the town's Norman castle stand alone in a field to the north of town, beautifully framed by the landscaped lawns and small lake of the new town park. Built in 1269, the castle was almost immediately destroyed by Irish forces, and its turbulent history continued until the final surrender to Cromwell in 1652.

Roscommon County Museum MUSEUM
(the Square; admission €2; ⊙10am-3pm Mon-Fri Jun–mid-Sep) Set in a former Presbyterian church, this museum contains some interesting pieces, including an inscribed 9th-century slab from St Coman's monastery and a superb medieval sheila-na-gig. The unusual Star of David window supposedly represents the Trinity.

Dominican Priory HISTORIC BUILDING
(⊙dawn-dusk) At the southern end of town, off Circular Rd, the remains of a 13th-century priory are almost hidden behind a primary school. The priory merits a quick visit for its unusual 15th-century carving of eight *gallógli* ('gallowglasses', who were mercenary soldiers) wielding seven swords and an axe.

🏃 Activities

Pick up a brochure and map at the tourist office detailing the Suck Valley Way, a 75km walking trail along the River Suck, including some pleasant strolls along the river bank.

🛏 Sleeping & Eating

Gleeson's B&B €€
(☑090-662 6954; www.gleesonstownhouse.com; The Square; s/d from €50/70; @ 🛜) There's a wonderfully warm welcome at this listed 19th-century town house, set back from the square in its own courtyard full of fairy lights. The rooms are individually decorated, ranging from sporting extravagant floral wallpaper to pine furniture and buttercup yellow walls. There's a good cafe and restaurant.

Gleeson's Artisan Food & Wine Shop DELI €
(☑090-662 6954; The Square; sandwiches €4.95; ⊙10am-6pm Mon-Sat) It's difficult for the staunchest dieter not to succumb to the tantalising display of deli and baked goodies here, including walnut and treacle bread, potato cakes with bacon and a gourmet create-your-own-sandwich bar. Pick up a slab of creamy organic Mossfield cheddar with garlic and chives for a real tastebud treat.

🍺 Drinking & Nightlife

George's PUB
(The Square; ⊙10.30am-11.30pm Mon-Thu, to 12.30am Fri & Sat; 🛜) The antithesis of ye olde pub, this popular place has a simple uncluttered bar with the novelty of a jukebox where €2 will buy you five songs. Popular with a foot-tapping youthful crowd.

ℹ️ Information

Tourist office (☑090-662 6342; www.visitroscommon.com; The Square; ⊙10am-1pm & 2-5pm Mon-Sat Jun-Aug) Pick up a map of the town and heritage trail here.

ℹ️ Getting There & Away

BUS

Bus Éireann (www.buseireann.ie) runs an express service between Westport (€15.75, 2¼ hours) and Dublin (€19, three hours) via Athlone, stopping in Roscommon three times daily (twice on Sunday).

TRAIN

Roscommon train station is in Abbeytown, just south of the town centre. **Irish Rail** (www.irishrail.ie) runs four trains daily on the line from Dublin (from €22, two hours) to Westport (from €15, 1½ hours).

COUNTY LEITRIM

The delights of the unassuming county of Leitrim are a well-kept secret, and it seems the locals like it that way. The untamed landscape and authentic rural charm are genuinely cherished by those who call it home and there's a reluctance to let anyone or anything spoil it.

Leitrim was ravaged by the Famine in the 19th century and spent subsequent generations struggling with mass emigration and unemployment, but today it has become a beloved hideout for artists, writers and musicians, as well as a huge boating centre.

The county is split virtually in two by Lough Allen, and the mighty River Shannon remains the area's biggest draw. Lively Carrick-on-Shannon, the county town, makes a great base for exploring the region by water or by road.

Carrick-on-Shannon

POP 3980

Carrick-on-Shannon is a charming town with a riverside location and a thriving community. Since the completion of the Shannon–Erne Waterway, the marina here has become incredibly busy. The town is a hugely popular weekend destination with a good choice of accommodation and restaurants and a great music and arts scene.

During the 17th and most of the 18th centuries Carrick was a Protestant enclave, and the local residents' wealth can still be seen in the graceful buildings around the town.

◉ Sights

Carrick has some wonderful examples of early 19th-century architecture on St George's Tce including Hatley Manor, home of the St George family, and the Old Courthouse. Nearby is the refurbished Market Yard, home to several shops and a farmers' market on Thursday from 10am to 2pm.

Costello Chapel   CHURCH
(Bridge St; ⊙ 10am-4.30pm Easter-Sep) This diminutive place measures just 5m by 3.6m, making it Europe's smallest chapel. It was built in 1877 by Edward Costello, distraught at the early death of his wife Mary. Both husband and wife now rest within the grey limestone interior lit by a single stained-glass window. Their embalmed bodies were placed in lead coffins, which sit on either side of the door. If the door is locked, ask at St George's Heritage Centre for the key.

St George's Heritage Centre   MUSEUM
(St Mary's Close; admission €3, tours €5; ⊙ 11am-4pm Wed-Sat) Set in a restored church, this heritage centre looks at the history and landscape of Leitrim from old Gaelic traditions through to Plantation times via an informative video. A Workhouse Attic Tour

visits the old Famine workhouse, which remains a bleak memorial to harder times, as well as the Famine Garden of Remembrance, both a short stroll from the Centre.

☆ Activities

Boat Rental

Carrick is the Shannon–Erne Waterway's boat-hire capital, with several companies based at the marina. The canal's 16 locks are fully automated, you don't need a licence, and you're given full instructions on handling your boat before you set off. High-season prices start at around €1000 per week for a two-berth cruiser. Try Carrick Craft (www.carrickcraft.com) or Emerald Star (www.emeraldstar.ie) for more information.

Cruises

You can take a one-hour cruise on the Shannon on Moon River (www.moonriver. ie; The Quay), a 110-seater vessel. There are one or two sailings per day (€15) between mid-March and October, increasing to four sailings during July and August; check the information board on the quay for details.

Angling

Carrick-on-Shannon Angling Club   FISHING
(☑ 071-962 0313; Ashleigh House, Dublin Rd) The best place for information on fishing.

Regatta

Carrick Rowing Club   BOATING
(www.carrickrowingclub.com) Runs an annual regatta on the first Sunday in August, which draws a big crowd.

🛏 Sleeping

Carrick has a good choice of accommodation, in and around town.

Shannon View House   B&B €€
(☑ 071-962 0594; Shannon View; s/d €35/70; 🐾) One of the winning aspects of this B&B is its position just across the bridge, equalling serene Shannon views from several of the guest rooms (number 3 is the best). Rooms sport pine panelling, pastel shades and tasteful artwork, and the downstairs sitting room has homey appeal with plenty of reading material and an open fire.

Caldra House   B&B €€
(☑ 071-962 3040; www.caldrahouse.ie; Caldragh; s/d €45/78; @) This creeper-clad Georgian house offers four period-style rooms decorated with antiques and subtle floral patterns. Set in mature gardens overlooking the

The Shannon–Erne Waterway

Ireland's two main river systems, the Shannon and the Erne, meander gracefully between the lush green fields, watery meadows and untamed pastures of the Midlands. En route they feed and carve the land and attract families, boaters and fishers all summer long.

The two rivers were linked in the 1800s as part of a much-needed drainage scheme for the poor soil in the area but their connection was short-lived. It was not until 1994, when a far-sighted restoration project created a symbolic link between Northern Ireland and the Republic, that the combined river system became navigable once again.

Running the length of the Shannon and on through northwestern County Cavan to the southern shore of Upper Lough Erne, the Shannon–Erne Waterway creates an amazing 750km network of rivers, lakes and artificial navigations. Plush hotels, gourmet restaurants and lively traditional pubs line its banks, making it a surprisingly cosmopolitan, as well as a wonderfully scenic, way to travel.

1. Cross, Clonmacnoise **2.** Fishing, Shannon–Erne Waterway
3. Athlone Castle on the banks of the Shannon

TOP STOPS

➡ **Carrick-on-Shannon** A charming riverside town with a lively music and arts scene

➡ **Glasson** An estate village best known for its outstanding restaurants

➡ **Athlone** A vibrant town and Midlands hub

➡ **Clonmacnoise** A magnificent ecclesiastical city dating from the 6th century

➡ **Shannonbridge** A sleepy village with a cracking traditional pub

➡ **Banagher** A popular boating centre with formidable riverside fortifications

Arigna Mountains, it's a very tranquil spot, 3km from town. Follow the R280 north out of town, turning left after 2km, then right at the T-junction.

Bush Hotel
HOTEL €€

(☑071-967 1000; www.bushhotel.com; Main St; r from €90; @ 🎧 🛜 👪) 🍴 The first hotel in Ireland to receive the European Ecolabel (www.ecolabel.eu) award for environmental sustainability (mainly via sourcing local ingredients for its culinary fare), this family-run place has a traditional lived-in feel in the public spaces, including bar, bistro and restaurant. The rooms are more contemporary and corporate with slick modern furnishings, plush carpeting and desks. Breakfast included.

Kilronan Castle
LUXURY HOTEL €€€

(☑071-961 8000; www.kilronancastle.ie; Ballyfarnon, Co Roscommon; r from €160; 🛜 👪) About 10km northwest of Carrick, this imposing castle overlooking Lough Meelagh has been transformed into a luxurious spa hotel.

🍴 Eating

★ Lena's Tea Room
CAFE €

(www.lenastearoom.ie; Main St; snacks €4-10; ⊙10am-5pm Tue-Sat; 🛜) The charming cafe has 1920s-vintage-style decor with eclectic furniture, including comfy sofas, muted paintwork and a menu of homebaked cakes, scones and breads, plus soups, savoury tartlets and gourmet sandwiches. Afternoon tea is a specialty with loose leaf teas, china cups and delicious cakes. Music is suitably melodic and relaxing.

★ The Cottage
IRISH €€

(☑071-962 5933; http://cottagerestaurant.ie; Jamestown; mains €16-26; ⊙6-10pm Wed-Sun, plus noon-4pm Sun; 👪) Set in a small whitewashed cottage overlooking a weir, this humble-looking place belies the quality of food on offer within. The menu offers a limited but tantalising choice of dishes created using vegetables from the restaurant's own polytunnel, meats from local suppliers and artisan cheeses. The chef/proprietor's Asian roots are evident in dishes such as grilled rump of lamb with cumin-spiced sweet potato, lamb samosas and coriander yoghurt. It's well worth the trip 5km southeast of Carrick to Jamestown, just off the N4.

Victoria Hall Restaurant
ASIAN €€

(☑071-962 0320; www.victoriahall.ie; Victoria Hall, Quay Rd; lunch mains €10-12, dinner mains €17-24; ⊙12.30-10pm; 🛜) The locals' favourite, this graceful old parochial hall has had a thoroughly modern makeover and now has a stylish minimalist interior, with a lovely 1st-floor dining area. The open kitchen churns out excellent Asian- and European-inspired dishes, with bento boxes (€17) and boxty (a traditional potato pancake) wraps with Thai fillings (€13.50), the speciality at lunch.

Oarsman
INTERNATIONAL €€

(☑071-962 1733; www.theoarsman.com; Bridge St; lunch mains €6-13, dinner mains €19-25; ⊙noon-3pm Tue-Sat, 7-10pm Thu-Sat) 🍴 It may look like a pub from the outside, but the Oarsman is best known for its food. Championing local and organic produce, it serves restaurant-quality food in relaxed, informal surroundings. The menu ranges from traditional Irish with a contemporary twist to Asian-inspired dishes. Snacks and bar food are served between lunch and dinner. Live music Saturday.

Vittos
ITALIAN €€

(www.vittosrestaurant.com; Market Yard; mains €14-25; ⊙5.30-9pm Tue-Fri, 1-10pm Sat; 👪) In a wood-beamed barn, this family-friendly restaurant has an extensive menu of classic Italian dishes, including great pastas and pizzas. The service and atmosphere is friendly and inviting.

🍷 Drinking & Nightlife

★ Anderson's Thatch Pub
PUB

(www.andersonspub.com; Elphin Rd; ⊙6pm-11pm) Dating from 1734, this traditional thatched pub is worth a trip for its live-music sessions (Wednesday, Friday and Saturday), old-world atmosphere and country charm. Take the R368 south from town for about 4km.

Flynn's Corner House
PUB

(cnr Main & Bridge Sts; ⊙5pm-11pm) This authentic stuck-in-a-time-warp pub serves a good pint of Guinness and has live music on Friday nights. Savour it before it's modernised.

Cryan's
PUB

(Bridge St; ⊙6pm-late) A traditional little pub with few frills, this is a good bet for music sessions, including bluegrass and traditional on Thursday, Saturday and Sunday nights.

☆ Entertainment

Dock Arts Centre
THEATRE

(www.thedock.ie; St George's Tce; ⊙10am-6pm Mon-Sat) Set in the grand surroundings of the 19th-century former courthouse, this place hosts performances, exhibitions and workshops. Also here is the Leitrim Design House (www.leitrimdesignhouse.ie; ☺10am-6pm Mon-Fri, to 5pm Sat), which features the work of local artists, designers and craftspeople.

ℹ Information

Tourist office (☎071-962 3274; www.leitrimtourism.com; The Quay, Old Barrel Store; ☺9.30am-5pm Easter-Sep) Has a walking-tour booklet, which takes in Carrick's places of interest.

ℹ Getting There & Away

BUS

Bus Éireann (www.buseireann.ie) runs to Dublin (€17.10, three hours) and to Sligo (€11.40, one hour) coach service stops in Carrick six times in each direction Monday to Saturday (five Sunday).

TRAIN

Irish Rail (www.irishrail.ie) run eight trains daily to Dublin (from €29.50, 2¼ hours) and Sligo (from €16, 55 minutes).

North Leitrim

North of Carrick-on-Shannon, the Leitrim landscape comes into its own, its ruffled hills, steel-grey lakes and isolated cottages exude a genuine rural charm. You'll also find a clutch of attractions in this seemingly forgotten part of the country that are easily accessible on a day trip from Sligo.

◉ Sights & Activities

If you fancy taking to the hills on foot, the Leitrim Way walking trail (48km) begins in Drumshanbo and ends in Manorhamilton.

Parke's Castle   CASTLE
(www.heritageireland.ie; Fivemile Bourne; adult/child €3/1; ☺10am-6pm mid-Apr–Sep; 🅿) The tranquil surrounds of Parke's Castle, with swans drifting by on Lough Gill and neat grass cloaking the old moat, belie the fact that its early Plantation architecture was created out of an unwelcome English landlord's insecurity and fear.

The restored, three-storey castle forms part of one of the five sides of the *bawn* (area surrounded by walls outside the main castle), which also has three rounded turrets at its corners. Join one of the entertaining guided tours after viewing the 20-minute video.

You can take a 1½-hour cruise on Lough Gill from the castle. Trips aboard the Rose

of Innisfree (☎071-916 4266; www.roseofinnisfree.com; adult/child €15/7.50; ☺11am, 12.30pm, 1.30pm, 3.30pm & 4.30pm Easter-Oct) offer live recitals of Yeats' poetry accompanying music. The company runs a bus from Sligo to the castle. Call for departure times and location.

The castle is 11km east of Sligo town on the R286.

Ard Nahoo   HEALTH FARM
(☎071-913 4939; www.ardnahoo.com; Mullagh, Dromahair; 4-bed cabins per weekend/week €300/500) 🍃 Cleanse the mind and spirit and get back to basics at Ard Nahoo, a rustic eco-retreat where you can rent a self-catering ecolodge, join a yoga retreat or detox program, take a course in alternative living or natural healthcare, or simply sign up for some pampering in the spa. Facilities are simple but comfortable.

Rossinver Organic Centre   ORGANIC CENTRE
(www.theorganiccentre.ie; Rossinver; adult/child €5/ free; ☺10am-5pm Feb-Nov; 🅿) 🍃 All things good and wholesome come together at the Rossinver Organic Centre, which aims to promote organic horticulture and sustainable living at its beautiful grounds in north Leitrim. You can simply come and tour the beautiful display gardens, or take a course in anything from organic permaculture to foraging for wild herbs.

COUNTY LONGFORD

A solidly agrarian region, County Longford is a quiet place of low hills and pastoral scenes. It has few tourist sights but is a haven for anglers who come for the superb fishing around Lough Ree and Lanesborough.

Longford suffered massive emigration during the Famine and it has never really recovered. Many Longford emigrants went to Argentina, where one of their descendants, Edel Miro O'Farrell, became president in 1914.

Longford's eponymous county town is a decidedly workaday place, but there are plenty of places to eat and a friendly tourist office (☎043-334 2577; www.longfordtourism.ie; Market Sq; ☺10am-5.30pm Mon-Sat May-Sep).

The county's main attraction is the magnificent Corlea Trackway (www.heritageireland.ie; Keenagh; ☺10am-6pm mid-Apr–Sep) FREE, an Iron Age bog road that was built in 148 BC. An 18m stretch of the historic track has now been preserved in a humidified hall at the site's visitor centre, where you can join a 45-minute tour that details the bog's unique flora and fauna, and fills you in on how the track was discovered, and methods used to preserve it. Wear a windproof jacket as the bog land can be blowy. The centre is 15km south of Longford on the Ballymahon road (R397).

Longford is also home to one of the three biggest portal dolmens in Ireland. The Aughnacliffe dolmen has an improbably balanced top stone and is thought to be around 5000 years old. Aughnacliffe is 18km north of Longford town off the R198.

Bus Éireann (www.buseireann.ie) runs hourly buses from Longford town to Dublin (€13, two hours) and Sligo (€12, 1½ hours, six daily Monday to Saturday, five Sunday).

Irish Rail (www.irishrail.ie) runs trains almost hourly to Dublin (from €22, one hour and 40 minutes).

COUNTY WESTMEATH

Characterised by lakes and pastures grazed by beef cattle, Westmeath has a wealth of attractions, ranging from a wonderful whiskey distillery and the miraculous Fore Valley to the country's oldest pub in the confident county town, Athlone. The rivers and lakes attract a steady stream of visitors and a host of gourmet restaurants and fine accommodation options have sprung up in recent years to cater for the discerning crowds.

Athlone

POP 14,350

Set on the banks of the Shannon, the thriving town of Athlone is a magnet for river traffic and is one of Ireland's most vibrant towns.

The Shannon splits this former garrison town in two, with most businesses and services sitting on its eastern bank. In the shadow of Athlone Castle, the western bank is an enchanting jumble of twisting streets, colourfully painted houses, historic pubs, antique shops and old book binders, as well as some outstanding restaurants.

⊙ Sights & Activities

★ Athlone Castle   CASTLE
(www.athloneartandheritage.ie; adult/child €8/4; ⊙11am-5pm Tue-Sat, noon-5pm Sun; ⊕) The ancient river ford at Athlone was an important crossroads on the Shannon and was

the cause of many squabbles over the centuries. By 1210, the Normans had asserted their power and built a castle here. In 1690 the Jacobite town survived a siege by Protestant forces, but it fell a year later – under a devastating bombardment of 12,000 cannonballs – to William of Orange's troops. The castle was soon remodelled and further major alterations took place over the following centuries.

In February 2013 a superb new visitor centre opened with interactive displays and audiovisual presentations that really do bring to life the tumultuous history of the town. There are eight galleries, each depicting an aspect of life here through the ages. The highlight is the fourth gallery with its Siege Experience which takes place in a circular panoramic gallery with plenty of blood-curdling screams that the kids (in particular) will love.

Dún na Sí Heritage Centre   HISTORIC PARK
(🖉090-648 1183; Knockdomney; adult/child €3.50/1.50; ⊙9.30am-4.30pm Mon-Thu, to 3.30pm Fri; ⊕) This folk park, 16km east of Athlone just off the M6 near Moate, features a re-created ring fort, portal dolmen, lime kiln, mass rock, farmhouse and forge. There's also a genealogy centre to help trace your roots, a *céilidh* (session of traditional music and dancing) on the first Friday of the month year-round and a traditional session with music, song, dance and storytelling at 9pm on Fridays in summer.

Luan Gallery   GALLERY
(wwwathloneartandheritage.ie/luan-gallery; Grace Rd; ⊙11am-5pm Tue-Sat, noon-5pm Sun) FREE Opened in November 2012 across from the castle, this excellent contemporary-art gallery has regular temporary exhibitions of world-class national and international artists.

☞ Tours

Midland Tours   BUS TOUR
(www.midlandtours.com; Ballinahown; tours €20) This company offers a range of half-day tours to Clonmacnoise, the Fore Valley, Birr Castle, Tullamore Heritage Centre and Locke's Distillery, and Strokestown Park House and Famine Museum.

Viking Tours   CRUISE
(🖉086 262 1136; www.vikingtoursireland.ie; 7 St Mary's Pl; adult/child €10/5; ⊙May-Sep; ⊕) Cruise along the Shannon aboard a replica Viking longship, complete with costumed

staff and dress-up clothes, including helmets, swords and shields. Head north to Lough Ree or south to Clonmacnoise. A round trip to Clonmacnoise allows a 90-minute stop at the ruins.

🛌 Sleeping

Athlone has a glut of corporate hotels in the centre of town; the following places have more character.

⭐ Bastion B&B
B&B €€

(☎090-649 4954; www.thebastion.net; 2 Bastion St; s/d from €40/60, studio from €50; 🛜) You can't miss this funky, brightly coloured facade, above a yoga studio. Step within and the white-on-white interiors continue the theme as a canvas for eclectic artwork, cactus collections and Indian wall hangings. The seven rooms (five with private bathrooms) are crisp and clean, with dark wooden floors and neatly folded fluffy towels. Go for the spacious loft if you can. There's an arty lounge-cum-breakfast room, where you can launch your day healthily with cereal, fruit, fresh bread and a cheeseboard.

Coosan Cottage Eco Guesthouse
GUESTHOUSE €€

(☎090-647 3468; www.ecoguesthouse.com; Coosan Point Rd; s/d €50/80) 🌿 This beautiful, ecofriendly 10-bedroom guesthouse was a labour of love for its owners, blending traditional style with modern thinking. Triple-glazed windows, a wood-pellet burner and a heat-recovery system are just some of its green credentials. For visitors, though, it's the tranquil surroundings and great breakfasts that will stick in the mind. The guesthouse is 2.5km from the town centre.

🍴 Eating

Athlone has established itself as the culinary capital of the Midlands. Scout around the western bank's backstreets for some gems.

Planet Life
CAFE €

(www.planetlife.eu; 1 Bastion St; snacks €4-8; ⊙9.30am-5.30pm Mon-Sat; 🧒) 🌿 Grab a stool at this eco-cafe serving snacks such as pitta sandwiches stuffed with tasty fillings including hummus and felafal or feta and sundried tomatoes, as well as homemade soups and baked goodies.

⭐ Left Bank Bistro
INTERNATIONAL €€

(☎090-649 4446; www.leftbankbistro.com; Fry Pl; lunch mains €9-15, dinner mains €18-25; ⊙10.30am-10pm Tue-Sat; 🅿) With an airy, whitewashed interior, shelves of gourmet goods, and a menu combining superior Irish ingredients with Mediterranean and Asian influences, this sophisticated deli-bistro attracts those in the know. Lunch features bowls of steaming pasta, big salads and chunky open sandwiches, while dinner dishes up beautifully grilled meat and fish and some extraordinary desserts.

⭐ Kin Khao
THAI €€

(☎090-649 8805; www.kinkhaothai.ie; Abbey Lane; mains €17-19; ⊙12.30-2.30pm Wed-Fri, 5.30-10.30pm Mon-Sat, 1.30-10.30pm Sun) Possibly the best Thai restaurant in Ireland, renowned for its extensive menu of authentic dishes. All the chefs and staff are Thai (with the exception of one half of the husband-and-wife team who run the place) and you'd be advised to book ahead if you want to join the band of loyal Kin Khao devotees.

Olive Grove
FUSION €€

(☎090-647 6946; www.theolivegrove.ie; Custume Pier; lunch mains €8-12, dinner mains €15-21; ⊙noon-10pm) This slick waterside restaurant gets rave reviews for its stylish design and creative menus. The food is good but at times fussy: think scallops with black-pudding bon bons with crispy bacon and smoked garlic cream. There is outside waterside sitting.

🍷 Drinking & Nightlife

⭐ Sean's Bar
PUB

(13 Main St) Age certainly hasn't wearied Sean's Bar. Dating way back to AD 900, Sean's stakes its claim as Ireland's oldest pub. Its log fires, uneven floors (to help flood waters run back down to the river), sawdust, rickety piano and curios collected over the years attest to the theory. The riverside beer garden has live music most nights in summer; to really see things in full swing, turn up at about 5.30pm on a Saturday.

☆ Entertainment

Dean Crowe Theatre
THEATRE

(www.deancrowetheatre.com; Chapel St) This refurbished theatre has wonderful acoustics and runs a broad program of theatrical and musical events.

ℹ Information

The website www.athlone.ie is a good source of information.

Tourist office (☑090-649 4630; Church St, Civic Centre; ⊙9.30am-1pm & 2-5.15pm Mon-Fri May-Sep) Inside the Athlone Castle's guardhouse.

❶ Getting There & Around

Athlone's bus and train stations are side by side on Southern Station Rd.

BUS

Bus Éireann (www.buseireann.ie) runs half-hourly buses to Dublin (€10.80, two hours) and Galway (€12, 1½ hours) and two daily to Westport (€16, three hours).

TRAIN

Irish Rail (www.irishrail.ie) run hourly trains to Dublin (from €15, 1¾ hours)and four daily to Westport (€15, two hours).

Lough Ree & Around

Many of the 50-plus islands within Lough Ree were once inhabited by monks and their ecclesiastical treasures, drawing Vikings like moths to a flame. These days, the visitors are less bloodthirsty, with sailing, trout fishing and birdwatching the most popular pastimes. Migratory birds that nest here include swans, plovers and curlews.

Poet, playwright and novelist Oliver Goldsmith (1728–74), author of *The Vicar of Wakefield,* is closely associated with the area running alongside the eastern shore of Lough Ree. Known as Goldsmith Country, the region is beautifully captured in his writings.

The Glasson Village Restaurant (☑090-648 5001; www.glassonvillagerestaurant.ie; Glasson, Co Westmeath; mains €20-30; ⊙5.30-9pm Tue-Fri, from 6.30pm Sat, 1-3.30pm Sun; ☎🎮) is a wonderfully informal place serving excellent food, including a reasonable €27 three-course menu. Nearby is the upmarket Wineport Lodge (☑090-643 9010; www.wineport.ie; Glasson, Co Westmeath; mains €24-33; ⊙5.30-10pm Mon-Fri, 2-4pm Sun), which has a reputation for the finest modern Irish cuisine, and also offers fabulous lakeside accommodation. Another popular gastropub, the Fatted Calf (☑090-648 5208; www.thefattedcalf.ie; Pearsonsbrook; mains €14-22; ⊙12.30-4pm & 5-9pm Tue-Sat, to 7.30pm Sun; 🎮), is slightly out of town and known for its ambitious dishes based on seasonal local ingredients.

Golfers may want to head for the Glasson Golf Course (☑090-648 51200; www.glas-soncountryhouse.ie; Glasson; green fees Mon-Fri €35, Sat & Sun €40), part of the Glasson Country House Hotel & Golf Club complex and winner of the 2011 IGTOA Golf Resort of the Year. The course was designed by legendary Irish golfer and Ryder Cup player Christy O'Connor in 1993.

Kilbeggan & Around

Little Kilbeggan has two big claims to fame: a restored distillery-turned-museum and Ireland's only National Hunt racecourse.

◉ Sights & Activities

Kilbeggan Distillery Experience   DISTILLERY
(☑057-933 2134; www.kilbeggandistillery.com; Kilbeggan; admission €8; ⊙9am-6pm Apr-Oct, 10am-4pm Nov-Mar) Whiskey buffs and industrial-technology enthusiasts will get a kick out of the Kilbeggan Distillery Experience. Established in 1757, this whiskey producer is believed to have been the oldest licensed distillery still in the world – and it recently started operations again as a boutique whiskey distillery. Today you can marvel at hulking machinery, visit a cooper's room and warehouse, and listen to the creaks and groans of the working mill wheel. Self-guided tours last 50 minutes, finishing off with a whiskey tasting.

☆ Entertainment

Kilbeggan Races   HORSE RACING
(www.kilbegganraces.com; ⊙approximately fortnightly May-Sep) Punters from all over the country attend the old-time evening meetings at the Kilbeggan Races. The town is transformed on race nights into a buzzing equine centre, where the thrill of the chase is matched by the craic in the pubs.

Mullingar & Around

POP 20,103

A prosperous regional town, Mullingar hums with the activity of locals going about their daily lives. Nearby there are fish-filled lakes and a fantastical mansion with an odious history.

James Joyce visited the town in his youth and it appears in both *Ulysses* and *Finnegans Wake.* Restored sections of the Royal Canal extend in either direction from Mullingar.

THROW AWAY YOUR GUIDEBOOK

Whether you're on the water or travelling by road, there's a string of interesting small towns and villages threaded along and around the Shannon and the Royal and Grand Canals that make enticing and tranquil stops. Most are rarely visited by touring motorists but are brimming with history, picturesque views and fine pubs.

In Leitrim you'll find Ballinamore, a lively spot on the Shannon–Erne Waterway, and Drumshanbo, a pretty traditional town and home to a visitor centre with audiovisual displays and informative exhibits. Nearby Keadue is an attractive village that hosts the O'Carolan Harp Festival (www.ocarolanharpfestival.ie), while just to the south is Keshcarrigan, home to a collapsed dolmen and some unusual St Patrick's Day festivities. Further west, Cootehall, on the River Boyle, has a fine restaurant and a lovely old-world pub. Nearby Knockvicar has a riverfront restaurant at its busy marina. Heading south, Drumsna is a picturesque traditional country village, while nearby Dromod is well known for its excellent fishing. Tarmonbarry is another good stop, with a wide choice of interesting restaurants and pubs, a swish hotel and a lively vibe. Nearby Clondra, where the Shannon meets the Royal Canal, is a stunning little place with lovely walks, and Keenagh, further along the canal, is a sleepy but quaint small town. Finally, stop at Abbeyshrule to find the ruins of a Cistercian abbey and an interesting viaduct.

◉ Sights

★ Belvedere House & Gardens   HISTORIC BUILDING
(www.belvedere-house.ie; adult/child €8.75/4.75; ⊙house & gardens 9.30am-8pm May-Aug, to 4.30pm Sep-Apr; ♿) Don't miss magnificent Belvedere House, an immense 18th-century hunting lodge set in 65 hectares of gardens overlooking Lough Ennell. More than a few skeletons have come out of Belvedere's closets: the first earl, Lord Belfield, accused his wife and younger brother Arthur of adultery. She was placed under house arrest here for 30 years, and Arthur was jailed in London for the rest of his life. Meanwhile, the earl lived a life of decadence and debauchery. On his death, his wife emerged dressed in the fashion of three decades earlier, still protesting her innocence.

Lord Belfield also found time to fall out with his other brother, George, who built a home nearby. Ireland's largest folly, a ready-made 'ruin' called the Jealous Wall, was commissioned by the earl so he wouldn't have to look at George's mansion.

Designed by Richard Cassels, Belvedere House contains some delicate rococo plasterwork in the upper rooms. The gardens, with their Victorian glasshouse, walled garden and lake-shore setting, make for wonderful walking on a sunny day. A airy new annexe houses Catoca, a classy restaurant and cafe and a tasteful souvenir and gift shop There's also a large children's playground.

Belvedere House is 5.5km south of Mullingar on the N52 to Tullamore.

Cathedral of Christ the King   CATHEDRAL
(www.mullingarparish.com; ⊙7.30am-8pm) Mullingar's most obvious landmark is this immense church, built just before WWII. It has large mosaics of St Anne and St Patrick by Russian artist Boris Anrep, as well as a small ecclesiastical museum.

🏃 Activities

Trout fishing is popular in the lakes around Mullingar. The fishing season runs from 1 March or 1 May (depending on the lake) to 12 October. Contact the tourist office or Inland Fisheries Ireland (www.fisheriesireland. ie) for further information.

If you fancy some horse riding, try the Mullingar Equestrian Centre (www.mullin garequestrian.com; Athlone Rd).

You can kayak on Lough Ennell from the Lilliput Adventure Centre (www.lilliputadven ture.com; Jonathan Swift Park; ⊙Mar-Oct). The centre also organises land-based activities, such as gorge walking and abseiling courses.

🛏 Sleeping & Eating

There are few B&Bs in the centre, but you'll find plenty on the approach roads from Dublin and Sligo.

Greville Arms Hotel   HOTEL €€
(📞044 934 8564; www.grevillearmshotel ie; Pearse St; s/d €50/80; 🛜) Dating from 1824,

this grande dame of a hotel is pleasantly dated (as are most of its guests): there are gilt mirrors, statues, dark oil paintings and chandeliers and an overall ambience of a bygone age. The Ulysses bar is named in honour of James Joyce who apparently frequented the place. He is still here, in lifelike waxwork form. Other endearing features include a small museum and a beer garden. Rooms are unremarkable, but comfortable and spacious.

Novara House   B&B €€
(☑044-933 5209; www.novarahouse.com; Dublin Rd; s/d from €50/80; 🛜) This friendly B&B is just five minutes' walk from the town centre. Set in a modern bungalow, the rooms are simple but spotless with pine furniture and neutral colour schemes but it's the amiable hosts and their warm welcome, homemade scones and cups of tea that will make for a most memorable stay.

Oscar's   MEDITERRANEAN €€
(☑044-934 4909; www.oscarsmullingar.com; 21 Oliver Plunkett St; mains €15-25; ⊗6-9.30pm Mon-Sat, 12.30-2.15pm & 6-8.30pm Sun) This perennially popular spot is the place to go for wholesome comfort food in a lively atmosphere. Bright colours, a menu that skirts the Mediterranean (think pastas, pizzas and French-inspired meat and poultry) and a decent wine list make it a good evening option.

 Drinking & Nightlife

You'll find traditional Irish music in many of the town's pubs; ask at the tourist office for details.

Yukon Bar   PUB
(11 Dominick St; ⊗5-11pm) A lively pub with a resident fortune teller, this place has a great atmosphere and regular live music. Depending on the day of the week you'll find a range of soul, blues and rock music on offer.

☆ **Entertainment**

Mullingar Arts Centre   THEATRE
(www.mullingarartscentre.ie; Lower Mount St, County Hall) The centre runs a regular program of music, comedy, drama and art exhibitions. In summer there are family-friendly traditional music sessions every weekend.

ℹ **Information**

Tourist office (☑044-934 8650; Market Sq; ⊗9.30am-1pm & 2-5pm Mon-Sat)

ℹ **Getting There & Away**

BUS
Bus Éireann (www.buseireann.ie) runs to Dublin (€12.90, 1½ hours, six Monday to Friday, five Sunday) and Athlone (€12, one hour, two Monday to Saturday, one Sunday).

TRAIN
Irish Rail (www.irishrail.ie) runs 11 direct services to Dublin (from €15, one hour, 11 Monday to Friday, seven Saturday, five Sunday).

North of Mullingar

The area north of Mullingar is famed for its lakes, the best known is Lough Derravaragh, an 8km-long lake associated with the legend of the children of Lír, who were turned into swans here by their jealous stepmother. Each winter the legend is recalled by thousands of snow white migratory swans that flock here from as far away as Russia and Siberia.

In addition to the lakes and rolling landscapes you'll find plenty of historical interest around the unassuming town of Castlepollard and sleepy Crookedwood.

◉ **Sights**

Fore Valley   HISTORIC SITE
Near the shores of Lough Lene, the emerald green Fore Valley is a superb place to explore by bicycle or on foot. In AD 630, St Fechin founded a monastery just outside the village of Fore. There's nothing left of this early settlement, but three later buildings in the valley are closely associated with 'seven wonders' said to have occurred here. It's a deeply atmospheric place, even in the dead of winter, with sweeping views across a gentle valley.

The oldest of the three buildings is St Fechin's Church, containing an early-13th-century chancel and baptismal font. Over the Cyclopean entrance is a huge lintel stone carved with a Greek cross and thought to weigh about 2.5 tonnes. It's said to have been put into place by St Fechin's devotions – the wonder of the stone raised by prayer.

A path runs from the church to the attractive little anchorite cell – the anchorite in a stone – which dates back to the 15th century and was lived in by a succession of hermits. The Seven Wonders pub in the village holds the key.

On the other side of the road near the car park is St Fechin's Well, filled with water that will not boil. Cynics should beware of testing this claim, as it's said that if you try it, doom will come to your family. Nearby is a branch from the tree that will not burn; the coins pressed into it are a more contemporary superstition.

Further over the plain are the extensive remains of a 13th-century Benedictine priory, the Monastery of the Quaking Scraw, miraculous because it was built on what once was a bog. In the following century it was turned into a fortification, hence the loophole windows and castlelike square towers. The western tower is in a dangerous state – keep clear.

The last two wonders are the mill without a race and the water that flows uphill. The mill site is marked, and legend has it that St Fechin caused water to flow uphill, towards the mill, by throwing his crosier against a rock near Lough Lene, about 1.5km away.

The Fore Abbey Coffee Shop (☑044-966 1780; foreabbeycoffeeshop@gmail.com; ⊙ 10am-6pm daily Jun-Aug, 10am-6pm Sat & Sun Oct-Jun), on the edge of Fore village, acts as a tourist information office, as well as serving delicious home-baked cakes and screening a 20-minute video about the wonders. Guided tours of Fore can be arranged by contacting the coffee shop in advance.

★ Tullynally Castle Gardens   GARDENS
(☑044-966 1159; www.tullynallycastle.com; Castlepollard; gardens adult/child €6/3; ⊙ 11am-6pm Thu-Sun Apr-Sep; ⋒) The imposing Gothic revival Tullynally Castle is the seat of the Pakenham family and although closed to visitors, its 12 hectares of gardens and parkland are a wonderful place to roam. Ornamental lakes, a Chinese and a Tibetan garden, and a wonderful stretch of 200-year-old yews are some of the highlights. There is a tearoom in the castle courtyard. The castle is 2km northwest of Castlepollard.

Multyfarnham Franciscan Friary   CHURCH
(⊙ dawn-dusk) Hidden inside a 19th-century church are the remains of the original 15th-century friary that stood here. Outside, look for the unusual Stations of the Cross set beside a stream. The friary is about 3km west of Crookedwood.

St Munna's Church   CHURCH
Built in a lovely location on the site of a 7th-century church founded by St Munna, this fortified 15th-century church has a barrel-vaulted roof and crenellated battlements. You'll find a weathered sheila-na-gig above a window on the northern side. The church is 2km east of Crookedwood.

🛏 Sleeping & Eating

Mornington House   B&B €€
(☑044-937 2191; www.mornington.ie; Multyfarnham; s/d from €85/130; ⊙ Apr-Oct ; 🛜) For a little bit of old-world luxury, you could stay at this tranquil guesthouse set in a lovely Victorian home surrounded by mature gardens. The whole house is furnished with period charm. Antique furniture, log fires, brass beds and subtle florals give it a pleasingly lived-in atmosphere. Dinner (€45) can be booked in advance and features fruit and veg from the walled garden.

Hotel Castlepollard   HOTEL €€
(☑044-966 1194; www.hotelcastlepollard.ie; Castlepollard; s/d €58/80; 🛜) Overlooking the delightful triangular village green, this cosy country hotel has decent if predictable rooms and a restaurant (mains from €14) serving reliable fare. The hotel bar has live music every weekend.

❶ Getting There & Away

Castlepollard is about 20km north of Mullingar on the R394. Bus Éireann (www.buseireann.ie) runs one service from Mullingar to Crookedwood (20 minutes) and Castlepollard (30 minutes) at 1.30pm on Thursdays – otherwise you're on your own.

Counties Meath, Louth, Cavan & Monaghan

POP 440,700 / AREA 6387 SQ KM

Best Castles

➡ Slane Castle (p522)

➡ Trim Castle (p526)

➡ Dunsany Castle (p526)

➡ Ross Castle (p545)

➡ Castle Leslie (p548)

Best Places to Stay

➡ D Hotel (p536)

➡ McKevitt's Village Hotel (p541)

➡ Newgrange Lodge (p521)

➡ Hilton Park (p549)

➡ Farnham Estate (p543)

Why Go?

The fertile fields of Counties Meath and Louth attracted Ireland's first settlers, making it the birthplace of Irish civilisation. Although the counties are now part of Dublin's commuter belt, their legacies endure at the mystical tombs at Brú na Bóinne and Loughcrew – which both predate the Egyptian pyramids – and at Tara, gateway to the other world and seat of the high kings of Ireland. Following St Patrick's arrival, the faithful built abbeys, high crosses and round towers to protect their treasured manuscripts. Magnificent ruins throughout Meath and Louth still whisper tales of a time when Ireland was known as the Land of Saints and Scholars.

The emerald hills and fish-filled lakes of Counties Cavan and Monaghan are similarly contemplative. Outdoor activities abound in this little-visited corner of Ireland: boats cruise the Shannon–Erne Waterway, while walking trails take in the wild scenery and expansive views of the Cuilcagh Mountains.

When to Go

➡ Sightseers should try and avoid November to March when many of the historic sites have reduced hours or are closed altogether.

➡ April is, unusually, the driest month of the year. The daffodils are in flower, along with a riot of wildflowers, so it's scenic (and less soggy) for walkers.

➡ Summertime is festive time in Drogheda with the annual Arts Festival in May, the Samba Festival in June and the Food Festival in August – the same month as Carlingford's famous Oyster Festival. Foodies take note....

COUNTY MEATH

Meath's rich soil, laid down during the last ice age, attracted settlers as early as 8000 BC. They worked their way up the banks of the River Boyne, transforming the landscape from forest to farmland. One of the five provinces of ancient Ireland, Meath was at the centre of Irish politics for centuries.

Today, Meath's fertile land and plentiful water supply make it an important centre of agriculture. Less happily, its proximity to Dublin brought about unchecked growth during the Celtic Tiger's peak and the larger towns are surrounded with soulless housing estates with heavy traffic at commuter time.

For visitors, though, there are numerous attractions here, including many tangible reminders of Meath's fascinating history. You'll find plenty of information at www.meath.ie/tourism.

Brú na Bóinne

The vast Neolithic necropolis known as Brú na Bóinne (the Boyne Palace) is one of the most extraordinary sites in Europe. A thousand years older than Stonehenge, it's a powerful and evocative testament to the mind-boggling achievements of prehistoric humankind.

The complex was built to house the remains of those who were at the top of the social heap and its tombs were the largest artificial structures in Ireland until the construction of the Anglo-Norman castles 4000 years later. The area consists of many different sites; the three principal ones are Newgrange, Knowth and Dowth.

Over the centuries the tombs decayed, were covered by grass and trees, and were plundered by everybody from Vikings to Victorian treasure hunters, whose carved initials can be seen on the great stones of Newgrange. The countryside around the tombs is home to countless other ancient tumuli (burial mounds) and standing stones.

◉ Sights

★ Newgrange   HISTORIC SITE
(www.newgrange.com; adult/student incl visitor centre €6/3; ◷ 9am-5pm Nov-Jan, 9.30am-5.30pm Feb-Apr, 9am-6.30pm May, 9am-7pm Jun-Sep, 9.30am-5.30pm Oct) Even from afar, you know that Newgrange is something special. Its white round stone walls topped by a grass dome look other-worldly, and just the size is impressive: 80m in diameter and 13m high. But underneath it gets even better. Here lies the finest Stone Age passage tomb in Ireland, and one of the most remarkable prehistoric sites in Europe. It dates from around 3200 BC, pre-dating the pyramids by some six centuries.

No one is quite sure of its original purpose. It could have been a burial place for kings or a centre for ritual, although the tomb's precise alignment with the sun at the time of the winter solstice also suggests it was designed to act as a calendar.

The name derives from 'New Granary' (the tomb did in fact serve as a repository for wheat and grain at one stage), although a more popular belief is that it comes from the Irish for 'Cave of Gráinne', a reference to a popular Celtic myth. *The Pursuit of Diarmuid and Gráinne* that tells of the illicit love between the woman betrothed to Fionn McCumhaill (or Finn McCool), leader of the Fianna, and Diarmuid, one of his most trusted lieutenants. When Diarmuid was fatally wounded, his body was brought to Newgrange by the god Aengus in a vain attempt to save him, and the despairing Gráinne followed him into the cave, where she remained long after he died. This suspiciously Arthurian tale (sub in Lancelot and Guinevere for Diarmuid and Gráinne) is undoubtedly a myth, but it's still a pretty good story. Newgrange also plays another role in Celtic mythology as the site where the hero Cúchulainn was conceived.

Over time, Newgrange, like Dowth and Knowth, deteriorated and at one stage was even used as a quarry. The site was extensively restored in 1962 and again in 1975.

A superbly carved kerbstone with double and triple spirals guards the tomb's main entrance, but the area has been reconstructed so that tourists don't have to clamber in over it. Above the entrance is a slit, or roof-box, which lets light in. Another beautifully decorated kerbstone stands at the exact opposite side of the mound. Some experts say that a ring of standing stones encircled the mound, forming a great circle about 100m in diameter, but only 12 of these stones remain, with traces of others below ground level.

Holding the whole structure together are the 97 boulders of the kerb ring, designed to stop the mound from collapsing outwards. Eleven of these are decorated with motifs similar to those on the main entrance stone, although only three have extensive carvings.

Counties Meath, Louth, Cavan & Monaghan Highlights

1 Explore the prehistoric remains at the ancient burial sites of **Brú na Bóinne** (p515)

2 Soak up the water views, slurping oysters and listening to live music in the medieval village of **Carlingford** (p540)

3 Ramble among the evocative ruins and mighty castle of the unassuming town of **Trim** (p526)

4 Follow in the footsteps of poet and author Patrick Kavanagh on the quiet roads of **Inniskeen** (p550)

5 Shun the crowds and set out for the hilltop tombs of the **Loughcrew Cairns** (p530)

6 Discover the secrets of the massive earthworks, passage graves and 'stone of destiny' at **Tara** (p524)

7 Check out the art, architecture and bustling pubs of **Drogheda** (p531)

8 Reel in fish from the lakes of **County Cavan** (p542)

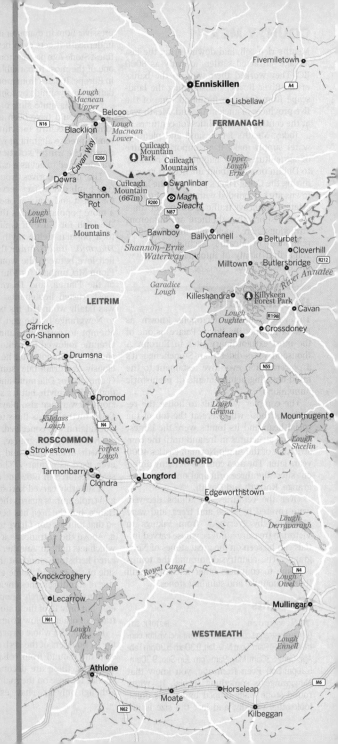

Brú na Bóinne

All visits start at the visitor centre **1**, which has a terrific exhibit that includes a short context-setting film. From here, you board a shuttle bus that takes you to Newgrange **2**, where you'll go past the kerbstone **3** into the main passage **4** and the burial chamber **5**. If you're not a lucky lottery winner for the solstice, fear not – there's an artificial illumination ceremony that replicates it. If you're continuing on to tour Knowth **6**, you'll need to go back to the visitor centre and get on another bus; otherwise, you can drive directly to Dowth **7** and visit, but only from outside (the information panels will tell you what you're looking at).

Newgrange interior passage

The passage is lined with 43 orthostats, or standing stones, averaging 1.5m in height: 22 on the left (western) side, 21 on the right (eastern) side.

Newgrange

Knowth

Roughly one third of all megalithic art in Western Europe is contained within the Knowth complex, including more than 200 decorated stones. Alongside typical motifs like spirals, lozenges and concentric circles are rare crescent shapes.

Top Tip

Best time to visit is early morning midweek during summer, when there are fewer tourists and no school tours.

Newgrange entrance kerbstone

Newgrange is surrounded by 97 kerbstones (24 of which are still buried), numbered sequentially from K1, the beautifully decorated entrance stone.

VISITING BRÚ NA BÓINNE

FACT FILE

The winter solstice event is witnessed by a maximum of 60 people selected by lottery. In 2012, 29,570 people applied.

Dowth

Like Newgrange, Dowth's passage grave is designed to allow for a solar alignment during the winter solstice. The crater at the top was due to a clumsy attempt at excavation in 1847.

ARCHAEO IMAGES / ALAMY ©

.... **7**

Newgrange burial chamber

The corbelled roof of the chamber has remained intact since its construction, and is considered one of the finest of its kind in Europe.

1

Brú na Bóinne Visitor Centre

Opened in 1997, the modern visitor centre was heavily criticised at first as being unsuitable but then gained plaudits for the way it integrated into the landscape.

BRÚ NA BÓINNE VISITOR CENTRE

ℹ️ VISITING BRÚ NA BÓINNE

In an effort to protect the tombs and their mystical surroundings, all visits to Brú na Bóinne start at the Brú na Bóinne Visitor Centre (☑ 041-988 0300; www.heritageire-land.ie; Donore; adult/student visitor centre €3/2; visitor centre & Newgrange €6/3; visitor centre & Knowth €5/3; visitor centre, Newgrange & Knowth €11/6; ☺ 9am-5pm Nov-Jan, 9.30am-5.30 Feb-Apr, 9am-6.30pm May, 9am-7pm Jun-Sep, 9.30am-5.30pm Oct) from where there is a shuttle bus to the tombs. Built in a spiral design echoing Newgrange, the centre houses interactive exhibits on prehistoric Ireland and its passage tombs, and has regional tourism info, an excellent cafeteria, plus a book and souvenir shop. Upstairs, a glassed-in observation mezzanine looks out over Newgrange.

Allow plenty of time: an hour's visit for the visitor centre alone, two hours to include a trip to Newgrange or Knowth, and half a day to see all three (Dowth is closed to tourists).

In summer, particularly at weekends, Brú na Bóinne can be very crowded; on peak days over 2000 people can show up. As there are only 750 tour slots, you may not be guaranteed a visit to either of the passage tombs. Tickets are sold on a first-come, first-served basis (no advance booking) so the best advice is to arrive early in the morning or visit midweek and be prepared to wait.

Importantly, if you turn up at either Newgrange or Knowth first, you'll be sent to the visitor centre from where the official tours depart. Technically you can walk the 4km to either site from the visitor centre, but you're discouraged from doing so as the lanes are narrow and dangerous due to passing tour buses.

The Brú na Bóinne Visitor Centre is well signposted from all directions. Tours are primarily outdoors with no shelter so bring raingear, just in case.

The white quartzite that decorates the tomb was originally obtained from Wicklow, 70km to the south – in an age before horse and wheel, it was transported by sea and then up the River Boyne. Over 200,000 tonnes of earth and stone also went into the mound.

You can walk down the narrow 19m passage, lined with 43 stone uprights (some of them engraved), which leads into the tomb chamber about one-third of the way into the colossal mound. The chamber has three recesses, and in these are large basin stones that held cremated human bones. As well as the remains, the basins would have held funeral offerings of beads and pendants, but these were stolen long before the archaeologists arrived.

Above, the massive stones support a 6m-high corbel-vaulted roof. A complex drainage system means that not a drop of water has penetrated the interior in 40 centuries.

⭐ Knowth   HISTORIC SITE

(adult/student incl visitor centre €5/3; ☺ 9am-5pm Nov-Jan, 9.30am-5.30 Feb-Apr, 9am-6.30pm May, 9am-7pm Jun-Sep, 9.30am-5.30pm Oct) North-west of Newgrange, the burial mound of Knowth was built around the same time and seems set to surpass its better-known neighbour in both its size and the importance of the discoveries made here. It has the greatest collection of passage-grave art ever uncovered in Western Europe, and has been under intermittent excavation since 1962.

The excavations soon cleared a passage leading to the central chamber, which, at 34m, is much longer than the one at Newgrange. In 1968 a 40m passage was unearthed on the opposite side of the mound. Also in the mound are the remains of six early-Christian souterrains (underground chambers) built into the side. Some 300 carved slabs and 17 satellite graves surround the main mound.

Human activity at Knowth continued for thousands of years after its construction, which accounts for the site's complexity. The Beaker folk, so called because they buried their dead with drinking vessels, occupied the site in the early Bronze Age (c 1800 BC), as did the Celts in the Iron Age (c 500 BC). Remnants of bronze and iron workings from these periods have been discovered. Around AD 800 to 900, it was turned into a *ráth* (earthen ring fort), a stronghold of the very powerful O'Neill clan. In 965 it was the seat of Cormac MacMaelmithic, later Ireland's high king for nine years, and in the 12th century the Normans built a motte and bailey (a raised mound with a walled keep) here. The site was finally abandoned around 1400.

Further excavations are likely to continue for the next decade at least, so you may see archaeologists at work when you visit.

Dowth
HISTORIC SITE

The circular mound at Dowth is similar in size to Newgrange – about 63m in diameter – but is slightly taller at 14m high. It has suffered badly at the hands of everyone from road builders and treasure hunters to amateur archaeologists, who scooped out the centre of the tumulus in the 19th century. For a time, Dowth even had a tearoom ignobly perched on its summit. Because it's unsafe, Dowth is closed to visitors, though the mound can be viewed from the road between Newgrange and Drogheda. Serious excavations began in 1998 and will continue for years to come.

Dowth has two entrance passages leading to separate chambers (both sealed), and a 24m early-Christian underground passage at either end, which connect with the western passage. This 8m-long passage leads into a small cruciform chamber, in which a recess acts as an entrance to an additional series of small compartments, a feature unique to Dowth. To the southwest is the entrance to a shorter passage and smaller chamber.

North of the tumulus are the ruins of Dowth Castle and Dowth House.

Tours

Brú na Bóinne is one of the most popular tourist attractions in Ireland, and there are plenty of organised tours. Most depart from Dublin.

Mary Gibbons Tours
GUIDED TOUR

(086 355 1355; www.newgrangetours.com; tours per adult/student €35/30) Tours depart from numerous Dublin hotels, beginning at 9.30am Monday to Friday, 7.50am Saturday and Sunday, and take in the whole of the Boyne Valley including Newgrange and the Hill of Tara. The expert guides offer a fascinating insight into Celtic and pre-Celtic life in Ireland. Pay cash on the bus (no credit cards).

Over the Top Tours
GUIDED TOUR

(01-860 0404; www.overthetoptours.com; tours per adult/student €28/25) Offers a Celtic Experience day tour that concentrates on the Boyne Valley, as well as an intriguing 'Mystery' Tour.

Sleeping & Eating

Newgrange Lodge
HOSTEL, HOTEL €

(041-988 2478; www.newgrangelodge.com; dm/ s/d from €16/45/55; @☎🛜) Located just east of the Brú na Bóinne Visitor Centre, this converted farmhouse has a choice of good-value rooms varying from dorms with four to 10 beds, to hotel-standard doubles with private bathrooms. Reception is open 24 hours, and there's a self-catering kitchen, two outdoor patios and a welcoming dining room-cum-lounge complete with open fire, board games and books. Rates include continental breakfast (with scrumptious homemade scones). Free bikes available.

❶ Getting There & Away

Bus Éireann has a service linking the Brú na Bóinne Visitor Centre with Drogheda's bus station (one way/return €4/7, 20 minutes, two daily Monday to Saturday), with connections to Dublin.

The Battle of Boyne

Battle of Boyne Site
HISTORIC SITE

(www.battleoftheboyne.ie; adult/child €4/2; ⊙10am-6pm May-Sep, 9.30am-5.30pm Mar & Apr, 9am-5pm Oct-Feb; ♿) More than 60,000 soldiers of the armies of King James II and King William III fought in 1690 on this patch of farmland on the border of Counties Meath and Louth. In the end, William prevailed and James sailed off to France.

Today, the battle site is part of the Oldbridge Estate farm. At the visitor centre you can watch a short show about the battle, see original and replica weaponry of the

---

NEWGRANGE WINTER SOLSTICE

At 8.20am on the winter solstice (between 18 and 23 December), the rising sun's rays shine through the roof-box above the entrance, creep slowly down the long passage and illuminate the tomb chamber for 17 minutes. There is little doubt that this is one of the country's most memorable, even mystical, experiences.

There's a simulated winter sunrise for every group taken into the mound. To be in with a chance of witnessing the real thing on one of six mornings around the solstice, enter the free lottery that's drawn in late September or early October. Fill out the form at the Brú na Bóinne Visitor Centre or enter online (www.heritageireland.ie).

time and explore a laser battlefield model. Self-guided walks through the parkland and battle site allow ample time to ponder the events that saw Protestant interests remain in Ireland. Costumed re-enactments take place in summer.

The battle site is 3km north of Donore, signposted off the N51. From Drogheda, it's 3.5km west along Rathmullan Rd (follow the river).

Laytown

Most famous as the site for the only official horse race on the beach in Europe. Laytown is a sleepy seaside village for the rest of the year.

⊙ Sights & Activities

Sonairte ECOLOGY CENTRE
(☑041-982 7572; www.sonairte.ie; the Ninch, Laytown; adult/child €3/1; ☺10.30am-5pm Wed-Sun; ☻) ✐ Just outside Laytown on the road to Julianstown is Sonairte, the National Ecology Centre. Dedicated to promoting ecological awareness, it's a wonderful place to learn about sustainable living and organic horticulture. You can take a guided tour of the walled organic gardens and 200-year-old orchard, follow the nature trail or river walk, or take a course in anything from beekeeping to foraging for wild food and organic gardening. There's a shop and organic cafe on site, and a **farmers market** sets up on Sundays from noon to 4pm. The centre is five minutes walk from Laytown train station.

✿ Festivals & Events

Laytown Races HORSE RACING
(www.laytownstrandraces.ie) In late August or early September, bookies, punters and jockeys descend in force to Laytown for races

❶ HERITAGE CARD

If you are planning to visit several archeological and historic sites, consider investing in a **Heritage Card** (adults €21, students and children €8), valid for one year and available for purchase at the Battle of the Boyne ticket office, as well as other participating sites throughout the country. For more information, check the www.heritageireland.ie website.

that have been held here for over 140 years; for one day, Laytown's 3km of golden sands are transformed into a racecourse, attracting a diverse crowd of locals, celebrities and die-hard racing fans.

❶ Getting There & Away

Irish Rail (Iarnród Éireann; www.irishrail.ie) runs between Dublin and Laytown run every half-hour (€12.50, 50 minutes).

Slane

POP 1349
Blink and you miss it, Slane's 18th-century stone houses and cottages slink down a steep hill to the River Boyne, which glides beneath a narrow bridge. Slane grew up around the enormous castle after which it was named. At the main crossroads four identical houses face each other: local lore has it that they were built for four sisters who had taken an intense dislike to one another and kept a beady-eyed watch from their individual residences.

Slane is just 6km west of Brú na Bóinne.

⊙ Sights

★**Slane Castle** CASTLE
(☑041-982 4080; www.slanecastle.ie; guided tours adult/student €7/5, whiskey-tasting tour incl castle tour €17, minimum 12 people; ☺guided tours noon-5pm Sun-Thu Jun-Aug) Still the private residence of Henry Conyngham, earl of Mountcharles, Slane Castle is best known as the setting for outdoor **concerts** with massive rock-royalty names: Bon Jovi and Eminem were here in 2013, while U2, The Rolling Stones, Madonna and Oasis have all set the stage alive over the years.

Built in the Gothic-revival style by James Wyatt in 1785, the building was later altered by Francis Johnson for George IV's visits to Lady Conyngham, allegedly his mistress. It's said the road between Dublin and Slane was built especially straight and smooth to speed up the randy king's journeys. In 1991 the castle was gutted by a fire, whereupon it was discovered that the earl was underinsured. A major fundraising drive, of which the summer concerts were a part, led to a painstaking restoration.

Guided tours include the neo-Gothic Ballroom, completed in 1821, and the Kings Room, where the monarch stayed while visiting his mistress.

Currently distilled by the nearby Cooley Distillery, Slane Castle Irish Whiskey was specially created for the Conyngham family, and is for sale at the castle. You can taste it and other Irish whiskeys by booking a whiskey-tasting tour. The owners are in the process of building their own Irish whiskey craft distillery at the castle, scheduled for completion in 2014. Check the website for an update.

The castle is signposted 1km west of the town centre.

Hill of Slane   HISTORIC SITE

About 1km north of the village is the Hill of Slane, a fairly plain-looking mound that stands out only for its association with a thick slice of Celto-Christian mythology. According to legend, St Patrick lit a paschal (Easter) fire here in 433 to proclaim Christianity throughout the land. Patrick's fire infuriated Laoghaire, the pagan high king of Ireland, who had expressly ordered that no fire be lit within sight of the Hill of Tara. He was restrained by his far-sighted druids, who warned that 'the man who had kindled the flame would surpass kings and princes'. Laoghaire went to meet Patrick, and all but one of the king's attendants, a man called Erc, greeted Patrick with scorn.

Here the story *really* gets far-fetched. During the meeting, Patrick killed one of the king's guards and summoned an earthquake to subdue the rest. After his Herculean efforts, Patrick calmed down a little and plucked a shamrock from the ground, using its three leaves to explain the paradox of the Holy Trinity: the union of the Father, the Son and the Holy Spirit in one. Laoghaire wasn't convinced, but he agreed to let Patrick continue his missionary work. Patrick's success that day, apart from keeping his own life, starting an earthquake and giving Ireland one of its enduring national symbols, was good old Erc, who was baptised and later became the first bishop of Slane. To this day, the local parish priest lights a fire here on Holy Saturday.

The Hill of Slane originally had a church associated with St Erc and, later, a round tower and monastery, but only an outline of the foundations remains. You can also see the remains of a ruined church and tower that were once part of an early-16th-century Franciscan friary. On a clear day, climb the evocative ancient stone steps of the tower to enjoy magnificent views of the Hill of Tara

and the Boyne Valley, as well as (it's said) seven Irish counties.

Ledwidge Museum   MUSEUM

(☑041-982 4544; www.francisledwidge.com; Janesville; adult/child €3/1; ☺10am-5pm Jul-Sep, to 3.30pm Feb-Jun & Oct-Dec; ♿) Simple yet moving, the Ledwidge Museum is located in a quaint cottage that was the birthplace of poet Francis Ledwidge (1891–1917). He died on the battlefield at Ypres, having survived Gallipoli and Serbia. A keen political activist, Ledwidge was thwarted in his efforts to set up a branch of the Gaelic League in the area, but found an outlet in verse.

The museum provides an insight into Ledwidge's life and works, and the cottage itself is a humbling example of how farm labourers lived in the 19th century. It is about 1.5km east of Slane on the Drogheda road (N51).

🛏 Sleeping & Eating

Slane Farm Hostel   HOSTEL €

(☑041-982 4390; www.slanefarmhostel.ie; Navan Rd, Harlinstown House; campsites per adult/child incl tent €10/free, dm/s/d/self-catering terraced cottages €20/30/55/75; @🛜♿) 🍴 These former stables, built by the Marquis of Conyngham in the 18th century, have been converted into a wonderful hostel that's part of a working dairy farm. Common areas include a games room and kitchen, with free-range eggs and a vegetable plot for guests to use. Free bikes available. Located 2.5km west of Slane.

★ George's Patisserie   BAKERY €

(www.georgespatisserie.com; Chapel St; ☺9am-6pm Tue-Sat) A bakery first, cafe second, producing mouthwatering scones, cakes and specialties like mini apple-crumble tarts and wonderful bread. Soup and light snacks also available. And no need to bring a book, the walls are papered in old newspapers (mainly the *Antique Trade Gazette*).

Old Post Office   BISTRO €€

(☑041-982 4090; Main St; mains €10-28; ☺9am-10pm Mon-Sat, 10am-6.30pm Sun) This former post office is a tastefully restored restaurant with honest homemade food and four small B&B guest rooms (rooms from €70) decorated in earth colours with parquet floors. On the downside (literally), there have been complaints from readers that the beds are too soft.

🍷 Drinking & Nightlife

Boyles   PUB

(www.boylesofslane.com; Main St; 🛜) The owner of this pub with its fire-engine-red facade is musician Andrew Cassidy, who hosts a knockout line-up of live gigs and trad sessions. Check the website for the latest line-up and timings.

ℹ️ Information

Slane info is available at www.slanetourism.com.

ℹ️ Getting There & Away

Bus Éireann has three to seven buses daily to Drogheda (€4.75, 35 minutes), Dublin (€14, one hour) and Navan (€4, 20 minutes).

Navan & Around

POP 28,559

You won't want to waste too much time in the working town of Navan, Meath's main hub. If you do stop here, Trimgate St is lined with restaurants and pubs.

Pleasant walks around Navan include the towpath along the old River Boyne canal towards Slane and Drogheda (otters have been spied here). On the southern bank, you can go as far as Stackallen and the Boyne bridge (about 7km), passing the impressive red-brick Ardmulchan House (closed to the public) and, on the opposite bank, the ruins of 16th-century Dunmoe Castle.

Tara

The Hill of Tara is Ireland's most sacred stretch of turf, occupying a place at the heart of Irish history, legend and folklore. It was the home of the mystical druids, the priest-rulers of ancient Ireland, who practised their particular form of Celtic paganism under the watchful gaze of the all-powerful goddess Maeve (Medbh). Later it was the ceremonial capital of the high kings, all 142 of them, who ruled until the arrival of Christianity in the 5th century. It is also one of the most important ancient sites in Europe, with a Stone Age passage tomb and prehistoric burial mounds that date back up to 5000 years.

Although little remains other than humps and mounds on the hill, its historic and folkloric significance is immense.

History

The Celts believed that Tara was the sacred dwelling place of the gods and the gateway to the other world. The passage grave was thought to be the final resting place of the Tuatha dé Danann, the mythical fairy folk. They were real enough, but instead of pixies and brownies, they were earlier Stone Age arrivals on the island.

As the Celtic political landscape began to evolve, the druids' power was usurped by warlike chieftains who took kingly titles; there was no sense of a united Ireland, so at any given time there were countless *rí tuaithe* (regional kings) controlling many small areas. The king who ruled Tara, though, was generally considered the big shot, the high king, even though his direct rule didn't extend too far beyond the provincial border.

The most important event in Tara's calendar was the three-day harvest *feis* (festival) that took place at Samhain, a precursor to modern Halloween. During the festival, the high king pulled out all the stops: grievances would be heard, laws passed and disputes settled amid an orgy of eating, drinking and partying.

When the early Christians hit town in the 5th century, they targeted Tara straight away. The arrival of Christianity marked the beginning of the end for Celtic pagan civilisation, and the high kings began to desert Tara, though the kings of Leinster continued to be based here until the 11th century.

In August 1843, Tara saw one of the greatest crowds ever to gather in Ireland. Daniel O'Connell, leader of the opposition to union with Great Britain, held one of his monster rallies at Tara, and up to 750,000 people came to hear him speak.

👁️ Sights

Rath of the Synods   HISTORIC SITE

The names applied to Tara's various humps and mounds were adopted from ancient texts, and mythology and religion intertwine with the historical facts. The Protestant church grounds and graveyard spill onto the remains of the Rath of the Synods, a triple-ringed fort where some of St Patrick's early synods (meetings) supposedly took place. Excavations of the enclosure suggest that it was used between AD 200 and 400 for burials, rituals and living quarters. Originally the ring fort would have contained wooden houses surrounded by timber palisades.

Excavations have uncovered Roman glass, shards of pottery and seals, showing links with the Roman Empire even though the Romans never extended their power to Ireland.

Royal Enclosure
HISTORIC SITE

To the south of the church, the Royal Enclosure is a large, oval Iron Age hill fort, 315m in diameter and surrounded by a bank and ditch cut through solid rock under the soil. Inside the Royal Enclosure are several smaller sites.

The Mound of the Hostages, a bump in the northern corner of the enclosure, is the most ancient known part of Tara, but is closed to the public. A treasure trove of artefacts was unearthed, including some ancient Mediterranean beads of amber and faience (glazed pottery). More than 35 Bronze Age burials were found here, as well as extensive cremated remains from the Stone Age.

Although two other earthworks within the enclosure, the Royal Seat and Cormac's House, look similar, the Royal Seat is a ring fort with a house site in the centre, while Cormac's House is a barrow (burial mound) in the side of the circular bank. There are superb views of the surrounding Boyne and Blackwater Valleys from here.

Atop Cormac's House is the phallic Stone of Destiny (originally located near the Mound of the Hostages), which represents the joining of the gods of the earth and the heavens. It's said to be the inauguration stone of the high kings, although alternative sources suggest that the actual coronation stone was the Stone of Scone, which was removed to Edinburgh, Scotland, and used to crown British kings. The would-be king stood on top of the Stone of Destiny and, if the stone let out three roars, he was crowned. The mass grave of 37 men who died in a skirmish on Tara during the 1798 Rising is next to the stone.

Enclosure of King Laoghaire
HISTORIC SITE

South of the Royal Enclosure is this large but worn ring fort where the king, a contemporary of St Patrick, is supposedly buried standing upright and dressed in his armour.

Banquet Hall
HISTORIC SITE

North of the churchyard is Tara's most unusual feature, a rectangular earthwork measuring 230m by 27m along a north–south axis. Tradition holds that it was built to cater for thousands of guests during feasts.

Opinions vary as to the site's real purpose. Its orientation suggests that it was a sunken entrance to Tara, leading directly to the Royal Enclosure. More recent research, however, has uncovered graves within the compound, and it's possible that the banks are in fact the burial sites of some of the kings of Tara.

Gráinne's Fort
HISTORIC SITE

Gráinne was the daughter of King Cormac, the most lauded of all high kings. Betrothed to Fionn McCumhaill (Finn McCool), she eloped with Diarmuid, one of the king's warriors, on her wedding night. This became the subject of the epic *The Pursuit of Diarmuid and Gráinne*. Gráinne's Fort and the northern and southern Sloping Trenches to the northwest are burial mounds.

✕ Eating

McGuires Coffee Shop
CAFE €

(dishes €6-9; ⊙9.30am-5.30pm; 🛜📶) If a walk on the hill has worked up an appetite, this restaurant-cum-cafe and souvenir shop at the base can restore you with tasty dishes like goat's cheese salad and smoked-salmon pasta, plus home-baked sweet treats, including apple and cinnamon pancakes.

🛍 Shopping

Old Tara Book Shop
BOOKS

(⊙10am-5pm Tue, Thu, Sat & Sun) At the base of the hill, this tiny, jumbled secondhand bookshop is run by Michael Slavin, who has authored an informative little book about the site, *The Tara Walk* (€3), as well as a weightier tome, *The Book of Tara* (€29).

ℹ Information

Entrance to Tara is free and the site is always open. There are good explanatory panels by the entrance. Unfortunately, many people let their dogs roam free on the hill – watch your step!

Tara Visitor Centre (☑046-902 5903; www.heritageireland.ie; adult/child €3/1; ⊙10am-6pm end May–mid-Sep) A former Protestant church (with a window by an acclaimed stained-glass artist, the late Evie Hone) is home to Tara's visitor centre and a 20-minute audiovisual presentation about the site.

ℹ Getting There & Away

Tara is 10km southeast of Navan, off the Dublin–Cavan road (R-147). It's well signposted.

Bus Éireann (www.buseireann.ie) services link Dublin to within 1km of the site (€9.10, 40 minutes, hourly Monday to Saturday and four times on Sunday). Ask the driver to drop you off at the Tara Cross, where you take a left turn off the main road. The bus company also organises coach tours to Tara; check the website for info.

Dunsany Castle

See how the other 1% lives at Dunsany Castle (☑ 046-902 5198; www.dunsany.com; Dunsany; adult/child/under 9yr €20/10/free; ⊙ by appointment), the residence of the lords of Dunsany and one of the oldest continually inhabited buildings in Ireland. Construction started on the castle in the 12th century, with major alterations taking place in the 18th and 19th centuries.

Today the castle houses an impressive private art collection and various other treasures related to important figures in Irish history, such as Oliver Plunkett and Patrick Sarsfield, leader of the Irish Jacobite forces at the siege of Limerick in 1691. A guided tour takes almost two hours and offers a fascinating insight into the family history as well as that of the castle. It remains a family home, and maintenance and restoration are ongoing, so opening hours vary and different rooms are open to visitors at different times. Call for details.

You can also buy Dunsany Home Collection homewares here: locally made table linen and accessories, as well as various articles designed by the late 20th Lord Dunsany (Edward Carlos Plunkett), who was an acclaimed international designer and artist, famed for his geometrical abstractions and portraits. He died in May 2011.

The castle is about 5km south of Tara on the Dunshaughlin–Kilmessan road.

Trim

POP 8268

Dominated by its mighty castle and atmospheric ruins, the quiet town of Trim was an important settlement in medieval times. Five city gates surrounded a busy jumble of streets, and as many as seven monasteries were established in the immediate area.

It's hard to imagine nowadays, but a measure of Trim's importance was that Elizabeth I considered building Trinity College here. One student who did study in Trim was Dublin-born Arthur Wellesley, the duke of Wellington, who studied at Talbot Castle and St Mary's Abbey.

Today, Trim's history is everywhere, with various ruins, and streets still lined with tiny workers' cottages.

◉ Sights

★ Trim Castle   CASTLE

(King John's Castle; www.heritageireland.ie; adult/child incl tour €4/2; ⊙ 10am-6pm Easter-Sep, to 5.30pm Oct-Nov, 10am-5pm Sat & Sun Feb-Easter; ⓘ) This remarkably preserved edifice was Ireland's largest Anglo-Norman fortification and is proof of Trim's medieval importance. Hugh de Lacy founded Trim Castle in 1173, but Rory O'Connor, said to have been the last high king of Ireland, destroyed this motte and bailey within a year. The building you see today was begun around 1200 and has hardly been modified since.

Throughout Anglo-Norman times the castle occupied a strategic position on the western edge of the Pale, the area where the Anglo-Normans ruled supreme; beyond Trim was the volatile country where Irish chieftains and lords fought with their Norman rivals and vied for position, power and terrain. By the 16th century, the castle had begun to fall into decline and in 1649, when the town was taken by Cromwellian forces, it was severely damaged.

The castle's grassy 2-hectare enclosure is dominated by a massive stone keep, 25m tall and mounted on a Norman motte. Inside are three levels, the lowest divided by a central wall. Just outside the central keep are the remains of an earlier wall.

The principal outer-curtain wall, 450m long and for the most part still standing, dates from around 1250 and includes eight towers and a gatehouse. It also has a number of sally gates from which defenders could exit to confront the enemy. The finest stretch of the outer wall runs from the River Boyne through Dublin Gate to Castle St.

The entertaining and informative tour includes climbing narrow, steep stairs so is not recommended for very young children or anyone with mobility problems. Self-guided tours also available.

★ St Patrick's Cathedral Church   CATHEDRAL

(Lornan St; ⊙ varies) FREE That huge steeple you see belongs to St Patrick's Cathedral Church, parts of which date to the 15th century, although it wasn't granted cathedral status until 1955. Take a look at the beautiful stained-glass windows, including one showing St Patrick preaching on the Hill of Tara.

Trim

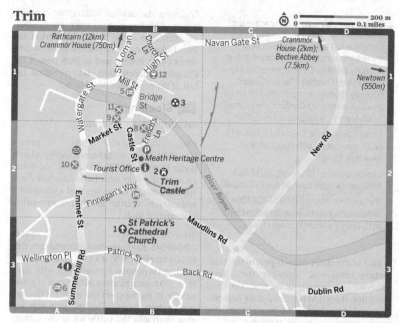

Talbot Castle & St Mary's Abbey   RUINS

Across the River Boyne from the castle are the ruins of the 12th-century Augustinian **St Mary's Abbey**, rebuilt after a fire in 1368 and once home to a wooden statue of Our Lady of Trim, revered by the faithful for its miraculous powers.

In 1415 part of the abbey was converted into a fine manor house by Sir John Talbot, then viceroy of Ireland; it came to be known as **Talbot Castle**. The Talbot coat of arms can be seen on the northern wall. Talbot went to war in France where, in 1429, he was defeated at Orleans by Joan of Arc. He was taken prisoner, released and went on fighting the French until 1453. He became known as 'the scourge of France' and even got a mention in Shakespeare's *Henry VI*: 'Is this the Talbot so much feared abroad/That with his name the mothers still their babes?'

In 1649 Cromwell's soldiers invaded Trim, set fire to the revered statue and destroyed the remaining parts of the abbey. In the early 18th century, Talbot Castle was owned by Esther 'Stella' Johnson, the mistress of Jonathan Swift. He later bought the property from her and lived there for a year. Swift was rector of Laracor, 3km southeast of Trim, from around 1700 until his death in 1745. From 1713 he was also, more signifi-

Trim

◎ Top Sights

◎ Sights

🛏 Sleeping

✖ Eating

🍷 Drinking & Nightlife

cantly, the dean of St Patrick's Cathedral in Dublin.

Just northwest of the abbey building is the 40m **Yellow Steeple**, once the bell tower of the abbey, dating from 1368 but damaged by Cromwell's soldiers. It takes its name from the colour of the stonework at dusk.

TRACING YOUR ANCESTORS

Genealogical centres that can help trace your ancestors are located in Trim (County Meath), Cavan Town (County Cavan) and Dundalk (County Louth). (County Monaghan currently has no genealogical centre.) Contact the centres in advance to arrange a consultation.

Meath Heritage Centre (☑046-943 6633; www.meathroots.com; Castle St, Town Hall, Trim)

Louth County Library (☑042-933 5457; www.louthcoco.ie; Roden Pl, Dundalk)

Cavan Genealogy (☑049-436 1094; www.cavan.rootsireland.ie; Johnston Central Library, Farnham St, Cavan Town)

East of the abbey ruins is part of the 14th-century town wall, including the **Sheep Gate**, the lone survivor of the town's original five gates. It used to be closed daily between 9pm and 4am, and a toll was charged for sheep entering to be sold at market.

Newtown
RUINS

About 1.5km east of town on Lackanash Rd, Newtown has several interesting ruins. The former **Parish Church of Newtown Clonbun** contains the late-16th-century tomb of Sir Luke Dillon, chief baron of the exchequer during the reign of Elizabeth I, and his wife Lady Jane Bathe. The effigies are known locally as the Jealous Man and Woman, perhaps because of the sword lying between them. Rainwater that collects between the two figures is claimed to cure warts.

The other ruins here are the **Cathedral of Sts Peter and Paul** and the 18th-century **Newtown Abbey**. The cathedral was founded in 1206 and burned down two centuries later. Although parts of the cathedral wall were flattened by a storm in 1839, it throws a superb echo back to **Echo Gate** across the river.

Southeast and just over the river is the **Crutched Friary**. There are ruins of a keep, and traces of a watchtower and other buildings from a hospital set up after the Crusades by the Knights of St John of Jerusalem. **St Peter's Bridge**, beside the friary, is said to be the second-oldest bridge in Ireland.

Wellington Column
MONUMENT

(cnr Summerhill Rd & Wellington Pl) The local burghers dedicated this column to Arthur Wellesley, the duke of Wellington, in recognition of his impressive career: after defeating Napoleon at the Battle of Waterloo, the Iron Duke went on to become prime minister of Great Britain and in 1829 passed the Catholic Emancipation Act, repealing the last of the repressive penal laws.

🛏 Sleeping

Accommodation is plentiful.

Bridge House Tourist Hostel HOSTEL €

(☑046-943 1848; bridgehousehostel@gmail.com; Bridge St; dm/d €20/50; 🛜) Quirky old house right on the river with basic four-bed dorm rooms, a couple of doubles and a kitchen for self-caterers. Contact in advance to confirm your arrival time.

Trim Castle Hotel HOTEL €€

(☑046-948 3000; www.trimcastlehotel.com; Castle St; d from €90; @🛜♿) This pleasant, modern hotel is popular for weddings, with more than 150 taking place in 2012. Acres of glossy marble in the foyer set the scene for the stylish modern rooms. The spacious sun terrace overlooks the castle while the carvery restaurant pulls in the punters at weekends. Excellent online deals.

Crannmór House B&B €€

(☑046-943 1635; www.crannmor.com; Dunderry Rd; d €75; 🛜) Rolling farmland and paddocks surround this vine-covered old house about 2km along the road to Dunderry. Bright rooms and traditional hospitality are on offer, and if you're interested in angling, the owner is an experienced *ghillie* (fishing guide).

Castle Arch Hotel HOTEL €€

(☑046-943 1516; www.castlearchhotel.com; Summerhill Rd; d from €80; @🛜♿) The 22 rooms at this modern business-class hotel have an elegant, heavy-drapery design accented with vintage touches. Check the website for golf and half-board packages.

🍴 Eating

Khan Spices INDIAN €

(☑046-943 7696; Emmett St; mains €8-10, set menus €15; ⊙5-11pm Mon-Thu, to midnight Fri & Sat; 🍴) Locals swear by this Indian restaurant and takeaway. The menu has all the standard dishes, ranging from chicken vindaloo to lamb *dhansak* (lamb with curried lentils, pumpkin or gourd, and rice) with plenty of vegetarian choice and some good-value set-menu options.

Harvest Home Bakery BAKERY, CAFE €
(Market St; snacks €3-5; ⊙9am-6pm Mon-Fri) This sweet little place sells delicious breads, cakes, pies and biscuits, as well as lightweight snacks, homemade soups and fit-to-bursting sandwiches. There are outside tables for al fresco dining. Sugar- and gluten-free cakes available.

Franzini O'Brien's INTERNATIONAL €€
(☑046-943 1002; French's Lane; mains €14-25; ⊙5-10pm Mon-Sat, 1-5pm Sun; 🖬) Buzzing local favourite, with a casual atmosphere and an eclectic menu spanning from seafood pasta to teriyaki chicken with noodles.

Wau Asian ASIAN €€
(☑046-948 3873; Bridge St; mains €12-19; ⊙5-11.30pm Mon-Thu, to 12.30am Fri & Sat, 1-11pm Sun; 🖘) Although the portion sizes could be more generous, the Asian cuisine here is solidly authentic and delicately spiced. Includes Chinese, Malaysian, Indonesian and Thai dishes. Afterwards, pop into the Sally Rogers pub below.

🍷 Drinking & Nightlife

James Griffin PUB
(www.jamesgriffinpub.ie; High St; ⊙4pm-late Mon-Fri, from noon Sat & Sun; 🖘) This award-winning historic pub dates from 1904 and offers trad music sessions, live music, live sports plus top DJs at weekends. The interior has retained its traditional Irish pub atmosphere and visitors are made to feel very welcome.

Sally Rogers PUB
(Bridge St; ⊙7pm-late) Pop in here (below Wau Asian) for a drink on the spacious riverfront terrace. Gets packed at weekends.

ℹ️ Information

Post Office (cnr Emmet & Market Sts)
Tourist Office (☑046-943 7227; www.meath tourism.ie; Castle St; ⊙9.30am-5.30pm Mon-Fri, noon-5pm Sat & Sun) Has a handy tourist trail map, a cafe and a genealogical centre.

ℹ️ Getting There & Around

Bus Éireann runs a bus at least hourly between Dublin and Trim (€11.50, 70 minutes).

Around Trim

There are a couple of evocative Anglo-Norman remains in the area around Trim. Bective Abbey was founded in 1147 and was the first Cistercian offspring of magnificent Mellifont Abbey in Louth. The abbey at Bective was much changed in the following years and the remains seen today are 13th- and 15th-century additions, consisting of the chapter house, church, ambulatory and cloister. In 1543, after the Dissolution of the Monasteries, the abbey was used as a fortified house and the tower was built. Bective is 7.5km northeast of Trim on the way to Navan.

Some 12km northwest of Trim, on the road to Athboy, is Rathcairn, the smallest Gaeltacht (Irish-speaking) district in Ireland. Rathcairn's population is descended from a group of Connemara Irish speakers who were settled on an estate here as part of a social experiment in the 1930s.

Kells

POP 5888

Kells is best known for the magnificent illuminated manuscript that bears its name, and which so many visitors queue to see at Trinity College in Dublin. Although the great book wasn't created here, it was kept in Kells, one of the leading monasteries in the country, from the end of the 9th century until 1541, when it was removed by the Church.

The town has been hard hit by the demise of the Celtic Tiger, including the closure of its heritage centre. However, remnants of the once-great monastic site include some interesting high crosses and a thousand-year-old round tower.

⊙ Sights

Market Cross MONUMENT
(Headfort Pl) Until 1996 the Market Cross had stood for centuries in Cross St, at the heart of the town centre. Besides inviting the pious admiration of the faithful, the cross was used as a gallows in the aftermath of the 1798 revolt; the British garrison hanged rebels from the crosspiece, one on each arm so the cross wouldn't fall over.

Round Tower & High Crosses HISTORIC SITE
The Protestant church of St Columba (⊙grounds 10am-1pm & 2-5pm Mon-Sat, church Jun-Aug), west of the town centre, has a 30m-high, 10th-century round tower that dates back at least as far as 1076, when the high king of Tara was murdered here.

Inside the churchyard are four 9th-century high crosses in various states of repair. The

West Cross, at the far end, is the stump of a decorated shaft, which has scenes of the baptism of Jesus, the Fall of Adam and Eve, and the Judgement of Solomon on the eastern face, and Noah's ark on the western face. All that is left of the North Cross is the bowl-shaped base stone.

Near the tower is the best preserved of the crosses, the Cross of Patrick and Columba, with its semilegible inscription, *Patrici et Columbae Crux,* on the eastern face of the base.

The other surviving cross is the unfinished East Cross, with a carving of the Crucifixion and a group of four figures on the right arm.

St Colmcille's House
HISTORIC SITE

(Church Lane; ⊙10am-5pm Sat & Sun Jun-Sep) FREE From the churchyard exit on Church St, St Colmcille's House is left up the hill, among the row of houses on the right side of Church Lane. This squat, solid structure is a survivor from the old monastic settlement. Its name is a misnomer, as it was built in the 10th century and St Colmcille was alive in the 6th century. Experts have suggested that it was used as a scriptorium, a place where monks illuminated books.

The site is usually locked except during the summer months, but ask at the tourist office about the keys or phone Mrs Carpenter (☑046-924 1778; 1 Lower Church View) for access.

🛏 Sleeping & Eating

Headfort Arms Hotel
HOTEL €€

(☑046-924 0063; www.headfortarms.ie; John St; s/d from €69/89; @ ☎) Family-run and right in the town centre, the Headfort Arms has 45 comfortable rooms with classic styling and contemporary facilities, like laptop safes. Rooms in the charming old building have the most character; there's a small spa for indulgent treatments. The hotel's dining options include the independently run Vanilla Pod (mains €17-25; ⊙5.30-10pm daily, noon-3pm Sun) bistro, serving celeb-chef-style dishes like pistachio-and-herb-crusted rack of lamb with wilted greens and a parsnip-and-redcurrant jus.

Teltown House B&B
B&B €€

(☑046-902 3239; www.teltownhouse.webs.com; Teltown; d €90; ☎) This lovingly restored 17th-century farmhouse is full of character and history, with period-style rooms and a very warm welcome. The farm was the location of the Irish equivalent of the Olympic games 2000 years ago, and 2000 years before *that,* rock art was carved on stones that still stand

next to the B&B. Teltown House is midway between Kells and Navan.

ℹ Information

Tourist Office (☑046-924 7840; Headfort Pl; ⊙9.30am-1pm & 2-5pm Mon-Fri) Screens a free 13-minute audiovisual presentation.

ℹ Getting There & Away

Bus Éireann has services from Kells to Dublin (€13.50, 90 minutes, hourly) via Navan. There are also buses to Cavan (€12.50, 45 minutes, hourly).

Loughcrew Cairns

With all the hoopla over Brú na Bóinne, the amazing Stone Age passage graves strewn about the Loughcrew Hills are often overlooked. There are 30-odd tombs here, but they're hard to reach and relatively few people ever bother, which means you can enjoy this moody and evocative place in peace.

Like Brú na Bóinne, the graves were all built around 3000 BC, but unlike their better-known and better-excavated peers, the Loughcrew tombs were used at least until 750 BC.

The cairns are west of Kells, along the R154, near Oldcastle.

👁 Sights

Carnbane East

Carnbane East has a cluster of sites. Cairn T (⊙10am-6pm Jun-Aug) FREE is the biggest at about 35m in diameter, with numerous carved stones. One of its outlying kerbstones is called the Hag's Chair, and is covered in gouged holes, circles and other markings. You need the gate key to enter the passageway and a torch to see anything in detail. It takes about half an hour to climb Carnbane East from the car park.

In summer, access to Cairn T is controlled by Heritage Ireland (www.heritageireland.ie), which provides guides. But locals are passionate about the place and at any time of the year you can arrange for guides who will not only show you Cairn T but take you to some of the other cairns as well. Enquire at Kells' tourist office, or pick up the key from the cafe at Loughcrew Gardens (p531).

Carnbane West

From the car park, it takes about an hour to reach the summit of Carnbane West, where

Cairn D and L, both some 60m in diameter, are located. They're in poor condition, though you can enter the passage and chamber of Cairn L, where there are numerous carved stones and a curved basin stone in which human ashes were placed.

Cairn L is administered by Heritage Ireland (www.heritageireland.ie), which gives out the key only to those with an authentic research interest.

Loughcrew Gardens

A labour of love, Loughcrew Gardens (☑049-854 1060; www.loughcrew.com; adult/child €6/3; adventure centre per half-day €32/27; ⏱12.30-5pm Mar-Oct; 🛜🚻) incorporates 2.5 hectares of lawns, terraces and herbaceous borders along with a lime avenue, yew walk, canal and the so-called 'grotesque grotto' with tortured pillars, frescoes and fantasy sculptures. There is also a medieval moat, tower house and St Oliver Plunkett's family church, plus a cafe with wi-fi in a log-built lodge. The gardens recently added an adventure centre (advance reservations essential), complete with assault course, archery and a climbing wall.

Loughcrew Gardens are northwest of Kells, along the R154, near Oldcastle.

👉 Tours

Beyond the Blarney   GUIDED TOUR
(☑087 151 1511; www.beyondtheblarney.ie) Knowledgeable Oldcastle-based outfit offering day tours and workshops (from €60).

COUNTY LOUTH

The Wee County, as it's dubbed, prospered greatly during the Celtic Tiger era thanks to its proximity to Dublin, leading to a welcome increase in activities, restaurants and nightlife (along with commuter congestion).

In the 5th and 6th centuries, Louth was at the centre of ecclesiastical Ireland, with wealthy religious communities at the monastery at Monasterboice and the Cistercian abbey at Mellifont. The 12th-century Norman invaders were responsible for the development of Dundalk and the two towns on opposite banks of the Boyne that united in 1412 to become what is now Drogheda.

Today Drogheda is Louth's most appealing town, a bustling place steeped in history that makes a good base for visiting nearby Brú na Bóinne. It's a quick trip to the picturesque Cooley Peninsula to enjoy the mountainous landscape and the delightful medieval village of Carlingford.

Louth can easily be covered as a day trip from Dublin, but you'll get more from your visit by spending some time exploring the county.

Drogheda

POP 38,578

Just 48km north of Dublin, Drogheda is a historic fortified town straddling the River Boyne. A clutch of fine old buildings, a handsome cathedral and a riveting museum provide plenty of cultural interest. Drogheda also has atmospheric pubs, fine

---

CROMWELL'S DROGHEDA INVASION

Lauded as England's first democrat and protector of the people, Oliver Cromwell (1599–1658) was an Irish nightmare. Cromwell hated the Irish. To him, they were treacherous infidels, a dirty race of papists who had sided with Charles I during the Civil War. So when 'God's own Englishman' landed his 12,000 troops at Dublin in August 1649, he immediately set out for Drogheda, a strategic fort town and bastion of royalist support.

When Cromwell arrived at the walls of Drogheda, he was met by 2300 men led by Sir Arthur Aston, who boasted that 'he who could take Drogheda could take hell'. After Aston refused to surrender, Cromwell let fly with heavy artillery and after two days the walls were breached. Hell, it seems, was next.

In order to set a terrifying example to any other town that might resist his armies, Cromwell taught the defenders a brutal lesson. Over a period of hours, an estimated 3000 people were massacred, mostly royalist soldiers but also priests, women and children. Aston was bludgeoned to death with his own (wooden) leg. Of the survivors, many were captured and sold into slavery in the Caribbean.

Cromwell defended his action as God's righteous punishment of treacherous Catholics, and was quick to point out that he had never ordered the killing of noncombatants.

Drogheda

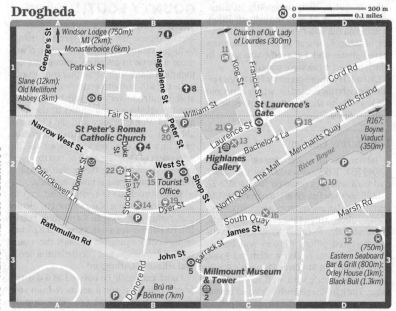

restaurants, numerous sleeping options and good transport links.

This bend in the fertile Boyne Valley has been a desirable location right back to 910, when the Danes built a fortified settlement here. In the 12th century, the Normans added a bridge and expanded the two settlements on either side of the river. By the 15th century, Drogheda was one of Ireland's four largest walled towns.

The 17th century brought devastation, however, when Drogheda was the scene of Cromwell's most notorious Irish slaughter in 1649. Things went from bad to worse in 1690, when the town backed the wrong horse at the Battle of the Boyne and surrendered the day after the defeat of James II.

During the Celtic Tiger years, the city became a cheaper alternative for Dublin commuters, triggering new developments along the riverfront. Today, Drogheda remains a thriving multicultural regional hub.

◉ Sights

★ Millmount Museum & Tower MUSEUM
(☏041-983 3097; www.millmount.net; adult/child museum €3.50/2.50, tower €3/2, museum & tower €5.50/3; ⊙9.30am-5.30pm Mon-Sat, 2-5pm Sun; ⊞) Across the river from town, in a village-like enclave amid a sea of dull suburbia, is Millmount, an artificial hill overlooking the town. The mound may have been a prehistoric burial ground like Newgrange, but has never been excavated.

The Normans constructed a motte-and-bailey fort on top of this convenient command post overlooking the bridge. It was followed by a castle, which in turn was replaced by a Martello tower in 1808. The tower played a dramatic role in the 1922 Civil War, when it was Drogheda's chief defensive feature and suffered heavy shelling from Free State forces. It has been aesthetically restored and offers great views over the town below.

A section of the army barracks is now used as the Millmount Museum. Exhibits include three wonderful late-18th-century guild banners, perhaps the last in the country. There is also a room devoted to Cromwell's brutal siege of Drogheda and the Battle of the Boyne. The pretty cobbled basement is full of gadgets and kitchen utensils from bygone times. Across the courtyard, the Governor's House opens for temporary exhibitions. There is a smart new restaurant, The Tower, here as well.

The 13th-century Butter Gate, just northwest of Millmount, has a distinctive tower and arched passageway.

Drogheda

⭐ **St Peter's Roman Catholic Church**   CHURCH
(West St) Displayed in a glittering brass-and-glass case in the north transept, the shrivelled head of St Oliver Plunkett (1629–81) is this church's main draw (the rest of the martyr was separated at his hanging in 1681). Actually it's two churches in one: the first, a classical style, designed by Francis Johnston in 1791, and the newer late-19th-century neo-Gothic addition.

⭐ **St Laurence's Gate**   HISTORIC SITE
Astride the eastwards extension of the town's main street is St Laurence's Gate, the finest surviving portion of the city walls (which originally extended for 3km) dating from the 13th century.

⭐ **Highlanes Gallery**   GALLERY
(www.highlanes.ie; Laurence St; admission by donation; ⊙10.30am-5pm Mon-Sat) Set in a beautifully converted 19th-century monastery, this gallery has a permanent collection of contemporary art, plus regular temporary exhibitions. Attached is a shop featuring high-quality Louth craftwork, and a chic cafe and food hall.

Other Structures   HISTORIC SITES
Right in the centre of town is the 1770-built Tholsel (cnr West & Shop Sts), an 18th-century limestone town hall, now occupied by the tourist office.

Heading northwest from here is the restored 19th-century former courthouse (Fair St), home to the sword and mace presented to the town council by William of Orange after the Battle of the Boyne.

To the north is St Peter's Church of Ireland (William St), not to be confused with St Peter's Roman Catholic Church. This is the church whose spire was burned by Cromwell's men, resulting in the death of 100 people seeking sanctuary inside. Today's church is the second replacement of the original destroyed by Cromwell.

Head up Magdalene St from the church to see the 14th-century Magdalene Tower, the bell tower of a Dominican friary founded in 1224. It was here that England's King Richard II, accompanied by a great army, accepted the submission of the Gaelic chiefs with suitable ceremony in 1395. Peace lasted only a few months, however, and Richard's return to Ireland led to his overthrow in 1399.

Keep making your way uphill from here to see the charming and more recent Church of Our Lady of Lourdes off Hardmans Gardens.

Finally, admire the 1855 Boyne Viaduct carrying trains over the river east of the centre. Each of the 18 beautiful stone arches has a 20m span; erecting the piers bankrupted one company.

🎉 Festivals & Events

Drogheda Arts Festival   ARTS
(www.droghedaartsfestival.ie) Theatre, music, film, poetry, visual arts and workshops such as silk painting take place over the May Day weekend.

Drogheda Samba Festival   MUSIC
(www.droghedasamba.com) Latin and African beats resonate across Drogheda during the last weekend of June.

Drogheda Food Festival   FOOD
(www.drogheda.ie) A huge farmers market, world beer trail and racing waiters and bar staff are among the highlights of Drogheda's foodie fest, held in late August to September.

1. Coastline of Clogherhead (p539)
A magnet for sea anglers, this area paints a lovely portrait of rural Ireland.

2. Brú na Bóinne (p515)
The Neolithic 'Boyne Palace' contains Ireland's finest Stone Age passage tomb.

3. Muirdach's Cross, Monasterboice (p538)
Now atmospheric ruins, the original monastic settlement here is thought to have been founded in the 5th or 6th century.

4. Trim Castle (p526)
With a 25m-tall keep and a 450m-long outer-curtain wall this massive edifice is remarkably well preserved.

🛏 Sleeping

Drogheda has plenty of high-standard accommodation.

Spoon and the Stars
HOSTEL, HOTEL €

(☑086 405 8465; www.spoonandthestars.com; 13 Dublin Rd; dm/d €18/65; 🛜) Seasoned travellers Rory and Hannah opened up this slickly run budget accommodation in 2013. Rooms range from a double with private bathroom and kitchenette, to eight- to 10- bed dorms, including a female-only option. Facilities include a TV room and a breezy courtyard and garden, complete with barbecue. Free bikes available.

★ D Hotel
HOTEL €€

(☑041-987 7700; www.thedhotel.com; Marsh Rd, Scotch Hall; d from €70; @🛜👪) Slick, hip and unexpected, this is Drogheda's top dog when it comes to accommodation. Minimalist rooms are bathed in light and decked out with designer furniture and cool gadgets. There's a stylish bar and restaurant, a mini gym and fantastic views of the city. The hotel is popular with hen and stag parties, so beware of pounding music on weekends. An adjacent cinema complex opened in late 2013.

Orley House
B&B €€

(☑041-983 6019; www.orleyhouse.com; Dublin Rd, Bryanstown; d €70; @🛜👪) This spick-and-span B&B is about 2km out of town, signposted off the main Dublin Rd. Enjoy large, comfortable rooms, firm mattresses and a warm welcome at this well-run place. A hearty breakfast is served in a sun-dappled conservatory.

Scholars Townhouse Hotel
HOTEL €€

(☑041-983 5410; www.scholarshotel.com; King St; d from €89; 🛜) This former monastery dates from 1867 and has recently been revamped as a family-owned hotel and restaurant. Despite the rooms being on the small side, there is nothing monastic about the facilities, which include power showers, wi-fi and a superb bar and restaurant. The central location is ideal for exploring the town. Breakfast included.

Windsor Lodge
GUESTHOUSE €€

(☑041-984 1966; www.barwindsorlodge.com; The Court, North Rd; s/d €40/70; 🛜👪) This large purpose-built guesthouse has a good choice of modern, spacious rooms with country-style decor and updated bathrooms. There's a lovely conservatory, a large lounge and a relaxing outdoor seating area. Breakfast included.

🍴 Eating

Andersons
CAFE €

(www.andersons.ie; Laurence St, Highlanes Gallery; mains €6-10; ⊙10.30am-5pm Mon-Sat; 🛜👪) Located in the Highlanes Gallery, this split-level cafe serves a stylish range of bruschetta, bagels and gourmet sandwiches, including open prawn or smoked salmon on multigrain. It also offers savoury tarts and daily specials, as well as classic desserts like hot apple crumble and Bakewell tart.

Stockwell Artisan Foods Café
CAFE €

(www.stockwellartisanfoods.ie; 1 Stockwell Lane; mains €7-9; ⊙9am-4pm Mon-Sat) Stripped wooden floors, homely dining rooms, daily newspapers and chunky furniture add to the cosy welcome of this place that serves healthy, wholesome wraps, salads, soups and hot dishes.

Kierans Deli
DELI €

(www.kieransdeli.com; 15 West St; ⊙9am-5.30pm Mon-Sat) Renowned deli with a superb selection of picnic options and a hot-food counter for lunch on the run.

★ Kitchen
MEDITERRANEAN €€

(☑041-983 4630; www.kitchenrestaurant.ie; 2 South Quay; mains €15-20; ⊙11am-10pm Wed-Sat, noon-9pm Sun; 🛜👪) 🍴 Appropriately named after the shiny open-plan kitchen and with a soothing sage-and-cream colour scheme, Kitchen uses organic local produce as far as possible. The chef is a well-travelled Londoner and it shows in such worldly ingredients as fried haloumi from Cyprus and Spanish serrano ham. Breads are made on the premises and there is an excellent choice of wines by the glass.

Black Bull
IRISH €€

(Dublin Rd; mains €8-12; ⊙12.30-10pm; 🛜👪) This popular pub is on the busy Dublin Rd, which doesn't distract the punters from downing their pints in a homey atmosphere of low ceilings, custard-coloured walls and candlelit corners. The modern extension houses a spacious restaurant serving unsophisticated but solidly good grub like fajitas, steaks and pastas, plus a touch of the exotic with Thai curries and similar.

D'vine
MEDITERRANEAN €€

(Dyer St; mains €14-22; ⊙noon-late Wed-Mon) With a cosy interior and sunny courtyard, this wine bar and bistro has a great selection of Mediterranean starting platters, open sandwiches and fish- and meat-based mains like pan-fried sea bass and braised lamb shanks, plus a long wine list. Live music on Sunday at 8pm.

Eastern Seaboard Bar & Grill IRISH €€
(www.easternseaboard.ie; 1 Bryanstown Centre, Dublin Rd; mains €10.50-33; ⊙noon-10pm; 🖹🎦) Despite its unpromising location in a business park near the train station, this stylised, contemporary space is generally packed. Adventurous food like pig's cheek terrine with apple slaw, smoked mackerel pâté, and coffee jelly and vanilla ice cream is served continuously from lunchtime on – along with frothy German beers on tap.

🍸 Drinking & Nightlife

Drogheda has dozens of bars and pubs. Check the event guide at www.drogheda.ie for listings.

C Ní Cairbre PUB
(Carberry's; North Strand; ⊙5-11pm) A national treasure dating from 1880, this tiny pub is under new management but retains its delightful old-fashioned feel. Faded newspaper clippings and artwork cover most surfaces and it's a great place to catch some traditional music, especially on Tuesday nights and Sunday afternoons.

Peter Matthews PUB
(McPhail's; 9 Laurence St; ⊙5pm-late) One of Drogheda's top spots for live music (Thursday to Sunday), McPhail's (as it's always called, no matter what the sign says) is popular with a younger crowd and features everything from heavy-metal cover bands to trad sessions. There's a traditional bar at the front and a beer garden out back.

Clarke & Sons PUB
(Peter St; ⊙2-11.30pm Mon-Thu, to 12.30pm Fri, noon-12.30am Sat & Sun) This wonderful old boozer is right out of a time capsule. Clarke's unrestored wooden interior features snugs and leaded-glass doors that read Open Bar. It attracts an arty crowd and is gay friendly.

Cagney's BAR
(3 Dyer St; ⊙10.30am-11.30 pm Mon-Fri, to 12.30pm Sat & Sun) Opened in early 2013, this bar exudes a mellow sophistication with its charcoal grey deck furnishings, cigar bar and sober lighting. An excellent selection of wines by the glass.

☆ Entertainment

Drogheda Arts Centre PERFORMING ARTS
(☑041-983 3946; www.droichead.com; Narrow West St) Drama, music, comedy, film and visual art take to the stage at Drogheda's lively arts centre, which runs regular workshops such as life drawing.

ℹ Information

Post Office (West St) Near the Westcourt Hotel.

Tourist Office (☑041-987 2843; www.drogheda.ie; 1 West St; ⊙9.30am-5.30pm Mon-Fri, plus 10am-5pm Sat Easter-Sep; 🖹)

ℹ Getting There & Away

BUS
Bus Éireann regularly serves Drogheda from Dublin (€7, one hour, one to four hourly). Drogheda to Dundalk is another busy route (€5.75, 30 minutes, hourly).

Matthews (☑042-937 8188; http://matthews.ie) also runs an hourly or better service to Dublin (€9) and Dundalk (€9).

TRAIN
The **train station** (☑041-983 8749; www.irishrail.ie) is just off Dublin Rd. Drogheda is on the main Belfast–Dublin line (Dublin €13.50, 45 minutes; Belfast €27.50, 1½ hours). There are six express trains (and many slower ones) each way, with five on Sunday.

ℹ Getting Around

Drogheda is excellent for walking, and many of the surrounding sites are within easy cycling distance.

Quay Cycles (☑041-983 4526; www.quaycycles.com; 11A North Quay; per day from €14; ⊙May-Oct) Rents bikes.

Around Drogheda

A number of historic sites and attractions lie close to Drogheda, but you'll still need your own transport.

Beaulieu House, Gardens & Car Museum HISTORIC SITE
(☑041-983 8557; www.beaulieu.ie; admission house €8, garden €6, museum €6; ⊙11am-5pm Mon-Fri May–mid-Sep, plus 1-5pm Sat & Sun Jul & Aug) Before Andrea Palladio and the ubiquitous Georgian style that changed Irish architecture in the early 18th century, there was the Anglo-Dutch style, a simpler, less ornate look that is equally handsome. Beaulieu

House is a particularly good example. It was built between 1660 and 1666 on lands confiscated from Oliver Plunkett's family by Cromwell, and given to the marshal of the army in Ireland, Sir Henry Tichbourne. The red-brick mansion, with its distinctive steep roof and tall chimneys, has been owned by the same family ever since.

The interiors are stunning and house a superb art collection ranging from lesser Dutch masters to 20th-century Irish painters. There's also a beautiful formal garden and a classic racing- and rally-car museum.

Beaulieu is about 5km northeast of Drogheda on the Baltray road.

Old Mellifont Abbey   RUIN

(☎ 041-982 6459; www.heritageireland.ie; Tullyallen; adult/student €3/1; ⊙ visitor centre 10am-6pm Easter-Sep) In its Anglo-Norman prime, this abbey was the Cistercians' first and most magnificent centre in the country. Although the ruins are highly evocative and well worth exploring, they still don't do real justice to the site's former splendour.

In the mid-12th century, Irish monastic orders had grown a little too fond of the good life and were not averse to a bit of corruption. In 1142 an exasperated Malachy, bishop of Down, invited a group of hard-core monks from Clairvaux in France to set up shop in a remote location, where they would act as a sobering influence on the local clergy. Unsurprisingly, the Irish monks didn't get on with their French guests, and the latter soon left for home. Still, the construction of Mellifont continued, and within 10 years, nine more Cistercian monasteries were established. Mellifont was eventually the mother house for 21 lesser monasteries; at one point as many as 400 monks lived here.

Mellifont's most recognisable building, and one of the finest examples of Cistercian architecture in Ireland, is the 13th-century *lavabo*, an octagonal washing room for the monks.

In 1556, after the Dissolution of the Monasteries, a fortified Tudor manor house was built on the site.

The visitor centre describes monastic life in detail. The ruins themselves are always open and there's good picnicking next to the rushing stream. The abbey is about 1.5km off the main Drogheda–Collon road (R168).

Monasterboice   HISTORIC SITE

(⊙ sunrise-sunset) FREE Crowing ravens lend an eerie atmosphere to Monasterboice, an intriguing monastic site containing a cemetery, two ancient church ruins, one of the finest and tallest round towers in Ireland, and two of the best high crosses.

Down a leafy lane in sweeping farmland, the original monastic settlement here is said to have been founded in the 5th or 6th century by St Buithe, a follower of St Patrick, although the site probably had pre-Christian significance. St Buithe's name somehow got converted to Boyne, and the river is named after him. An invading Viking force took over the settlement in 968, only to be comprehensively expelled by Donal, the Irish high king of Tara, who killed at least 300 of the Vikings in the process.

The high crosses of Monasterboice are superb examples of Celtic art. The crosses had an important didactic use, bringing the gospels alive for the uneducated, and they were probably brightly painted originally, although all traces of colour have long disappeared.

The cross near the entrance is known as Muirdach's Cross, named after a 10th-century abbot. The western face relates more to the New Testament, and from the bottom depicts the arrest of Christ, Doubting Thomas, Christ giving a key to St Peter, the Crucifixion, and Moses praying with Aaron and Hur.

The West Cross is near the round tower and stands 6.5m high, making it one of the tallest high crosses in Ireland. It's much more weathered, especially at the base, and only a dozen or so of its 50 panels are still legible. The more distinguishable ones on the eastern face include David killing a lion and a bear.

A third, simpler cross in the northeastern corner of the compound is believed to have been smashed by Cromwell's forces and has only a few straightforward carvings. This cross makes a great evening silhouette photo, with the round tower in the background.

The round tower, minus its cap, is over 30m tall, and stands in a corner of the com-

COUNTIES MEATH, LOUTH, CAVAN & MONAGHAN DUNDALK

plex. Records suggest the tower interior went up in flames in 1097, destroying many valuable manuscripts and other treasures. It's closed to the public.

Come early or late in the day to avoid the crowds. It's just off the M1 motorway, about 8km north of Drogheda.

Dundalk

POP 37,816

An industrial hub, although there's not a lot for visitors here, Dundalk is a pleasant enough place with a couple of interesting sites.

In the Middle Ages the city was at the northern limits of the English-controlled Pale, and with partition in 1921 it once again became a border town, this time providing a quick escape from the 'bandit country' of South Armagh.

Sights

County Museum Dundalk   MUSEUM
(www.dundalkmuseum.ie; Jocelyn St; adult/child €3/1.25; ⊘10am-5pm Tue-Sat; ♿) Different floors in this worthwhile museum are

dedicated to the town's early history and archaeology, and to the Norman period. One floor deals with the growth of industry in the area, from the 1750s up to the 1960s, including the cult classic Heinkel Bubble Car. Other oddities include Oliver Cromwell's shaving mirror.

St Patrick's Cathedral   CATHEDRAL
FREE The richly decorated 19th-century St Patrick's Cathedral was modelled on King's College Chapel in Cambridge, England.

Courthouse   NOTABLE BUILDING
(cnr Crowe & Clanbrassil Sts) The courthouse is a fine neo-Gothic building with large Doric pillars. In the front square is the stone Maid of Éireann, commemorating the 1798 Rising.

Eating

McAteers the
Food House   CAFE, RESTAURANT €€
(www.mcateersthefoodhouse.com; 14 Clanbrassil St; mains €10-17; ⊘9am-6pm Mon-Fri; ♿) Locally sourced organic produce is at the heart of this Aladdin's cave of a deli. If the tantalising goods on display fire up your appetite, its on-site cafe-restaurant prepares pancakes

DROGHEDA TO DUNDALK VIA THE COAST ROAD

Most people just zip north along the M1 motorway but if you want to meander along the coast and see a little of rural Ireland, opt for the R166 coast road from Drogheda.

The picturesque little village of Termonfeckin was, until 1656, the seat and castle of the primate of Armagh. The 15th-century castle (⊘10am-6pm) FREE, or tower house, is tiny and worth a brief stop.

About 2km further north is the busy seaside and fishing centre of Clogherhead, with a good, shallow Blue Flag beach at Lurganboy. Squint to ignore the caravan parks and take in the lovely views of the Cooley and Mourne Mountains instead.

A further 14km north, the teensy village of Annagassan merits a stop for scrumptious picnic goods. At Coastguard Seafoods (☑086 855 8609; Harbour Rd; ⊘by appointment), fisherman Tery Butterly oak-smokes possibly the finest salmon in Ireland and sells it direct to the public, along with seafood, including live lobsters, for astonishingly cheap prices. You can just turn up, but to avoid disappointment, call in advance. For bread to go with the salmon, head to O'Neills Bakery (☑042-937 2253; www.oneillsbakery.ie; ⊘7am-1pm), a cavernous five-generations-old bakery with vast ovens (one over a century old), where you can buy still-warm breads, cakes and buns. It appears closed to the public but knock on the door around the side of the building and one of the bakers will let you in.

The 33km route comes to an end in Castlebellingham. The picturesque village grew up around an 18th-century crenellated mansion (now a luxury hotel). Stop for refreshments at charming Foley's Tea Rooms (Main St, Castlebellingham; ⊘9am-3pm; ☎). Originally two 18th-century thatched cottages, here you can enjoy homemade cakes and tasty snacks before perusing Foley's shop specialising in fascinating curios and collectibles.

From here you can continue 12km north to Dundalk along the suburban R132 or join the M1.

with bacon and free-range eggs, open-faced sandwiches with Annagassan smoked salmon, and heartier meals such as prime Irish sirloin steak.

☆ Entertainment

Spirit Store   LIVE MUSIC
(www.spiritstore.ie; George's Quay; ⊗ Thu-Sun) Downstairs, this is your typical harbour-front bar, full of character and characters. Upstairs is a state-of-the-art live venue, with a terrific sound system that is beloved of both the crowd and the regular streams of touring musicians that play here.

ℹ Information

Tourist Office (www.discoverireland/east coast; Jocelyn St; ⊗ 9.30am-1pm & 2-5.15pm Tue-Fri) The tourist office is located on Market Sq.

ℹ Getting There & Around

Bus Éireann runs an almost hourly service to Dublin (€8.50, 1½ hours). The bus station is near the courthouse.

Clarke Train Station (☑ 042-933 5521; www.irishrail.ie; Carrickmacross Rd) has express trains to Dublin (€20, one hour, seven Monday to Saturday, five Sunday) and Belfast (€15, one hour, eight Monday to Saturday, five Sunday), as well as many slower services.

Cooley Peninsula

Isolated and remote, the Cooley Peninsula has an arresting beauty with forested slopes and sun-dappled, multihued hills rising out of the dark waters of Carlingford Lough. Sweeping views stretch across the water to Northern Ireland's Mourne Mountains, while country lanes wind their scenic way down to deserted stony beaches.

The medieval village of Carlingford is an ideal base. From here, you can continue along the coast road past the picturesque village of Omeath to Newry in Northern Ireland.

Carlingford

POP 1045

Someone apparently forgot to tell Carlingford about the Celtic Tiger's demise. Amid the medieval ruins and whitewashed houses, this vibrant little village buzzes with great pubs, chic restaurants, upmarket boutiques and spirited festivals, and has

gorgeous views of the mountains and across Carlingford Lough to Northern Ireland.

As one of the loveliest spots on the coast, Carlingford can be crowded during the summer, especially at weekends; book accommodation *well* ahead.

◉ Sights

**Holy Trinity
Heritage Centre**   CULTURAL BUILDING
(☑ 042-937 3454; www.carlingfordheritagecentre.com; Churchyard Lane; ⊗ 9.30am-1pm & 2-5pm Mon-Fri) FREE Carlingford's heritage centre is in the former Holy Trinity Church. A mural shows what the village looked like in its heyday, and a short video describes the village history and explains what has been done to give it new life in recent years after villagers got together to revive a dying community.

King John's Castle   RUIN
Carlingford was first settled by the Vikings, and in the Middle Ages became an English stronghold under the protection of the castle, which was built on a pinnacle in the 11th to 12th centuries to control the entrance to the lough. On the western side, the entrance gateway was built to allow only one horse and rider through at a time. King John spent a couple of days here in 1210 en route to battle in Antrim.

Ask at the tourist office about free tours during Heritage Week.

Other Sights   HISTORIC SITES
Near the tourist office is Taafe's Castle, an imposing 16th-century tower house that stood on the waterfront until the land in front was reclaimed to build a short-lived train line. Today it's the storeroom of the attached pub.

Carlingford is the birthplace of Thomas D'Arcy McGee (1825–68), one of Canada's founding fathers. A bust commemorating him stands opposite Taafe's Castle.

The Mint, near the square, is of a similar age and has some interesting Celtic-inspired carvings around the windows. Although Edward IV is thought to have granted a charter to a mint in 1467, no coins were produced here. Near the Mint is the Tholsel, the only surviving gate to the original town.

West of the village centre are the remains of a Dominican friary, built around 1305 and later used as a storehouse by oyster fishermen.

Activities

For information on angling tours, ask at the tourist office or check online at www.carlingford.ie.

Táin Way
WALKING

Carlingford is the starting point for the 40km Táin Way, which makes a circuit of the Cooley Peninsula through the Cooley Mountains. The route is a mixture of surfaced roads, forest tracks and green paths. The tourist office has trail info.

Cooley Birdwatching Trail
BIRDWATCHING

Much of the Cooley Peninsula is protected and is home to various species of birds, including godwits, red-breasted mergansers, buzzards, tits and various finches. Ask at the tourist office for information on the trail.

Carlingford Adventure Centre
ADVENTURE SPORTS

(☑ 042-937 3100; www.carlingfordadventure.com; Tholsel St; 🚲) Runs a wide range of activities including sailing, kayaking, windsurfing, rock climbing, archery and the more unusual body zorbing (if you fancy being strapped into a massive plastic ball and rolled down a hill!). Also offers accommodation.

Festivals & Events

Virtually every weekend during the warmer months, Carlingford goes event crazy: there are summer schools, medieval festivals, food festivals and anything that'll lure folks in off the M1.

Carlingford Oyster Festival
FOOD

(www.carlingford.ie; ⊙ mid-Aug) Celebrates Carlingford's famous oysters with an oyster treasure hunt, fishing competition, music, food markets and a regatta on Carlingford Lough.

Heritage Week
CULTURE

(www.heritageweek.ie; ⊙ late Aug) A weeklong celebration that includes concerts, talks, guided walks and family activities.

Sleeping

★ McKevitt's Village Hotel
HOTEL €€

(☑ 042-937 3116; www.mckevittshotel.com; Market Sq; s/d from €85/120; 🛜) The public areas at this delightful central hotel combine old-style comfort with contemporary artwork by family members. The rooms are spacious and furnished in muted earth colours with the occasional splash of vivid colour. Bathrooms have been updated with walk-in showers and glossy tiles. Breakfast included (including kippers!).

Belvedere House
B&B €€

(☑ 042-938 3828; www.belvederehouse.ie; Newry St; d from €80; 🛜) An excellent deal, rooms at this lovely B&B are modern but cosy with antique pine furniture, subtle lighting and pretty colour schemes. Guests have access to leisure facilities at the local Four Seasons hotel and breakfast is served in the downstairs Bay Tree restaurant.

★ Ghan House
GUESTHOUSE €€€

(☑ 042-937 3682; www.ghanhouse.com; Main Rd; d from €130; @🛜) Set in flower-filled gardens, this 18th-century Georgian house has 12 guest rooms, each exquisitely decorated with period antiques and original artworks. Book one of the four rooms in the main house for the most character and old-world charm. There's a superb restaurant on-site and a cookery school (courses from €75) that attracts top guest chefs and offers an impressive program of events.

COUNTIES MEATH, LOUTH, CAVAN & MONAGHAN COOLEY PENINSULA

LEPRECHAUNS – A PROTECTED SPECIES

The mountains around Carlingford are famed for being the last remaining site of Ireland's leprechauns. And yes, there are plenty of believers in the little people in these parts. Not least, the late PJ O'Hare, a former publican, who found a leprechaun's suit and hat, along with a collection of tiny bones and four gold coins, on Foy mountain back in 1989.

Nineteen years later, after a vigorous lobbying campaign by self-acclaimed 'Leprechaun Whisperer', Kevin Woods (who claims he has seen three leprechauns to date), the EU issued a highly unconventional directive establishing a protective leprechaun zone here. According to Woods, this is apparently the last habitat for Ireland's leprechauns, and every April a celebratory leprechaun hunt takes place, setting off from Carlingford. Even if you don't spot a little fella, this is certainly is a very magical spot. Check www.thelastleprechaunsofireland.com for more information.

✕ Eating & Drinking

Food for Thought   DELI, CAFE €
(Dundalk St; dishes €4.50-12; ⊘9am-6pm Mon-Sat, 10am-7pm Sun) ⊘ A rainbow of jams and chutneys lines the walls of this deli-cafe. Croquettes, quiches and fish cakes are among the tasty treats to eat in or take away, with great daily specials too.

★ PJ O'Hares   PUB €€
(www.pjoharescarlingford.com; Newry St; mains €9.50-19.50) Voted best gastro pub in Louth for three consecutive years by the Restaurant Association of Ireland, main courses here include beef and Guinness pie, but you can easily fill up on sublime tapas-style starters such as pan-fried crab claws in garlic butter, tangy chicken wings and, of course, Carlingford oysters. Live music plays regularly (try to catch rockin' local duo the Nooks). Head for the delightful beer garden or cosy up in front of a roaring fire, depending on the time of year.

Kingfisher Bistro   FUSION €€
(☑042-937 3716; www.kingfisherbistro.com; Dundalk St; mains €17-26; ⊘6.30-9pm Mon-Fri, 6-10pm Sat, 12.30-3pm Sun) Set in a beautifully restored grain store, the Kingfisher serves up a short but sound menu of modern Irish food with international twists. Go for Thai spiced pork with sticky rice and hot and sour onions, roast duck breast or spiced Cajun chicken with sour cream. It's all extremely good.

Bay Tree   MODERN IRISH €€
(☑042-938 3828; www.belvederehouse.ie; Newry St; mains €18-24; ⊘5.30-10pm daily, noon-3pm Sun) Lovely little place at Belvedere House B&B serving simple, stylish food made from seasonal, locally sourced ingredients.

Oystercatcher Bistro   INTERNATIONAL €€
(☑042-937 3989; www.theoystercatcher.com; Market Sq; mains €18-23; ⊘6-10pm) Specialities of these white-tableclothed premises include *cataplana* (North African–spiced seafood and meat) and boar stew.

Ghan House   MODERN IRISH €€€
(☑042-937 3682; www.ghanhouse.com; Main Rd; mains €24-32; ⊘6-9.30pm Mon-Sat, 1-3pm Sun) ⊘ Guests staying at Ghan House receive a discount at its restaurant, which is renowned for its classic food incorporating its own breads, stocks, ice creams and sauces, and herbs and vegetables from its garden. Twice a year, it hosts Georgian banquet nights complete with sword fighting.

ⓘ Information

Tourist Office (☑042-937 3033; www.carlingford.ie; ⊘10am-5pm) In a former train station on the waterfront.

ⓘ Getting There & Around

Bus Éireann (☑042-933 4075; www.buseireann.ie) has services to Drogheda (€14.25) and Dublin (€18).

There's great cycling around the Cooley Peninsula. Rent wheels at **On Your Bike** (☑087 239 7467; per day/week €20/60). Bikes can be delivered to your accommodation or the tourist office.

COUNTY CAVAN

Cavan is paradise for boaters, anglers, walkers, cyclists and artists. Known as the 'Lake Country', there's supposedly a lake for every day of the year, and the county is famed for its coarse fishing. Between the steely grey waters is a gentle landscape of meandering streams, bogs and drumlins (crowded hills formed by retracting glaciers). Cavan has some spectacular walking trails through the wild Cuilcagh Mountains, which are the source of the 300km River Shannon. The county's quiet, rural charm is best appreciated from the water, especially the tranquil Shannon–Erne Waterway.

The area has an intricate history. Magh Sleacht, a plain near the border village of Ballyconnell, was an important Druidic centre in the 5th century when St Patrick

---

WORTH A TRIP

FLAGSTAFF VIEWPOINT

Travelling along the Cooley Peninsula from Carlingford to Newry in Northern Ireland, a quick 3km detour rewards you with sweeping views of Carlingford Lough, framed by rugged, forested mountains, green fields and glittering blue Irish Sea beyond.

Flagstaff Viewpoint lies *just* over the border in County Armagh. Heading northwest along the coast road (the R173), follow the signs to your left onto Ferryhill Rd, then turn right up to the viewpoint's car park. The quickest way to reach Newry from here is to retrace your steps and rejoin the R173.

WALKING THE CAVAN WAY

The highlight for many walkers in the region is the Cavan Way, a 26km trail between the hamlets of Blacklion and Dowra through the Cuilcagh Mountains. Heading south from Blacklion, it takes you through an area known locally as the Burren and its ancient burial site Magh Sleacht, which is dotted with prehistoric monuments – court cairns, ring forts and tombs – and was one of the last strongholds of Druidism. It continues past the Shannon Pot, the source of Ireland's longest river, then by road to Dowra, passing over the Black Pigs Dyke, an ancient fortification that once divided Ireland in two.

From Blacklion it's mainly hill walking; from Shannon Pot to Dowra it's mainly road. The highest point on the walk is Giant's Grave (260m). You'll need Ordinance Survey map No 26 and the *Cavan Way* map guide. Maps are on display in Blacklion and Dowra. Detailed route information (including downloadable PDF maps) is available online at www.cavantourism.com. The route can be boggy, so take spare socks!

At Blacklion you can pick up the Ulster Way and at Dowra you can join the Leitrim Way, which runs between Manorhamilton and Drumshanbo.

was busy converting the pagan Irish to Christianity, and the area is still littered with tombs, standing stones and stone circles dating from this time. The Gaelic O'Reilly clan ruled until the 16th century, when they were defeated by the English. As part of the Ulster Plantation, Cavan was divided among English and Scottish settlers. After the War of Independence in 1922, the Ulster counties of Cavan, Monaghan and Donegal were incorporated into the Republic.

Cavan's lakes create a tangled knot of narrow, twisting roads. Take your time and enjoy the views that appear unexpectedly around each bend.

🏃 Activities

Cavan's exceptional lake fishing reels in anglers, especially to the county's southern and western borders. It's primarily coarse fishing, but there's also some game angling for brown trout in Lough Sheelin. Most lakes are well signposted, and the types of fish available are marked.

For more information, contact the tourist office (p544) in Cavan Town or Inland Fisheries Ireland (☑ 071-985 1435; www.fisheriesireland.ie).

You can also pick up anglers guides from tourist offices.

Cavan Town

POP 10,205

Cavan's county town is a solidly workaday place with some handsome Georgian houses and a famous crystal showroom.

👁 Sights

Cavan Crystal Showroom CRYSTAL SHOWROOM
(www.cavancrystaldesign.com; Dublin Rd; ⊙ 10am-6pm Mon-Sat, noon-5pm Sun) The town's crystal is displayed at this showroom 2km southeast of the town centre on the N3. It also sells a wide variety of local crafts.

Bell Tower HISTORIC SITE
All that remains of the 13th-century Franciscan friary the town grew up around is an ancient bell tower, next to the grave of 17th-century rebel leader Owen Roe O'Neill in Abbey St's cemetery.

🛏 Sleeping & Eating

The tourist office can help with accommodation. If you like your spice, the town has plenty of Asian restaurants.

★ Farnham Estate HOTEL €€€
(☑ 049-437 7700; www.farnhamestate.ie; d from €199; @ 🕸 🏊) Set in misty woodlands, this sprawling 16th-century estate is part of the Radisson group. The luxurious rooms blend contemporary style with period features and character, and there's a garden-view restaurant, a stunning indoor/outdoor infinity swimming pool, a luxurious spa and a world- class golf course (open to nonguests, green fees €40). The estate is 3km west of town on the R198.

Hard Boiled Cafe INTERNATIONAL €
(Dublin Rd; mains €8-12; ⊙ 9am-6pm Mon-Sat, 9.30am-5pm Sun; 🚼) Not the place for a romantic dinner for two, this quaintly named place is based on an American diner with

burgers, steaks, Boston bagels and south-of-the-border favourites like fajitas and burritos. The breakfasts have earned Guinness World Record status with the largest commercially available English-Irish breakfast in the world (a gluttonous cholesterol overdose that includes 10 eggs and five white puddings). If you can down it in 30 minutes you get it free and there's nothing half-baked (or boiled) about that...

McMahons Cafe Bar CAFE €

(79 Main St; dishes €6-12; ⊙10.30am-late Mon-Fri, 11am-late Sat, from 3pm Sun; 🛜) This place has a contemporary big-city vibe. By day McMahons is a funky cafe whipping up squeezed-on-the-spot juices and fresh-filled bagels, baguettes and paninis. At night, its cavernous tiered bar puts on regular live bands, cutting-edge DJs, steaming pizzas and a wicked cocktail list.

Chapter One CAFE €

(www.chapteronecafe.ie; Unit One, Convent Bldg, Main St; dishes €5-8.50; ⊙9am-6pm Mon-Sat; 🛜🖉🖷) Sip a cappuccino while checking your emails at this internet cafe-cum-restaurant. It heaves at lunchtime when locals descend to dine on the huge range of filled bagels, soups, nachos, salads and specials such as quesadillas. Located near Dunnes department store.

Cavan Farmers Market MARKET €

(Town Hall St; ⊙10am-1pm Fri) Held in the Town Hall St public car park.

❶ Information

Tourist Office (☑049-433 1942; www.cavantourism.com; Farnham St; ⊙9.45am-1.30pm & 2-5pm Mon-Fri) Above the library.

❶ Getting There & Around

Buses arrive at and depart from the small **bus station** (☑049-433 1353; www.buseireann.ie; Farnham St). There are 10 services daily to Dublin (€14.25, two hours), and four daily to Donegal (€18.75, two hours). There are also various services to small towns throughout the county.

Around Cavan Town

Lough Oughter & Killykeen Forest Park

Rod-wielding anglers congregate at Lough Oughter, which splatters across the map like spilt steely grey ink. Coarse fishing aside, the wildlife-rich lough is similarly appealing for naturalists, walkers and anyone wanting to vanish into a landscape of shimmering waters and cathedral-like aisles of trees. It's best accessed via Killykeen Forest Park (☑049-433 2541; www.coillteoutdoors.ie; admission free; ⊙9am-9pm), 12km northwest of Cavan, where various nature trails (from 1.5km to 5.8km) lead you through the woods and along the shore. Keep an eye out for stoats, badgers, foxes, grey squirrels and hedgehogs, as well as some impressive bird life.

Many of the low overgrown islands in the lake were *crannógs* (fortified, artificial islands). The most spectacular is home to Clough Oughter Castle, a 13th-century circular tower perched on a tiny speck of land. It was used as a lonely prison, then as a stronghold for rebel leader Owen Roe O'Neill before being destroyed by Cromwell's army in 1653. Although the castle lies out of reach over the water, it's worth walking via the forest trails to enjoy the best view.

Butlersbridge

Heading 7km north from Cavan along the N3 you'll pass the village of Butlersbridge. Set on the banks of the River Annalee, it's ideal for a riverside picnic.

Alternatively, pop into the Derragarra Inn (mains €9; ⊙11.30am-8pm Mon-Wed, 11.30am-9pm Thu-Sat, 12.30-9pm Sun), an ivy-covered pub with a wood-beamed interior and riverside deck overlooking the lovely St Aidan Church across the way. The bar food ranges from toasted sandwiches and homemade soups to more substanial fare like sirloin steak and Irish stew.

Cloverhill

Just 4km north of Butlersbridge on the N54, the lovely little village of Cloverhill is best known for its award-winning restaurant, the Olde Post Inn (☑047-55555; www.theoldepostinn.com; 5-course dinner €55, d €100; ⊙7-10pm Tue-Sat, noon-3pm, 7.30-9.30pm Sun). Overseen by award-winning local chef Gearoid Lynch the contemporary cuisine is based on traditional ingredients such as suckling pig, salmon, pigeon and lamb. In the former post master's residence, the six guest rooms are luxuriously furnished with plush carpets and fabrics, but vary considerably in size.

Belturbet

POP 1407

In a prime position on the Shannon–Erne Waterway, this charming, old-fashioned village, 16km northwest of Cavan, is an anglers' favourite. It's also a busy base for cruise boats, and a good starting point for a cycling trip along the canal and river system.

◉ Sights & Activities

Belturbet Railway Station   HISTORIC BUILDING
(☑049-952 2074; Railway Rd; ☺Apr-Sep) FREE
This beautifully restored railway station houses a visitor centre exploring the history of rail travel in the area, as well as a craft shop that also sells some homemade deli products. Trains used the station from 1885 until 1959, after which it languished for 40 years. Opening times can be sporadic, call ahead if you are planning to visit.

Corleggy   CHEESE
(☑049-952 2930; www.corleggycheeses.com; Corleggy Farmhouse; cheesemaking course €50, incl lunch; ☺May-Sep) Hard pasteurised goat's cheese is something of a rarity, and prize-winning Corleggy Cheese is particularly prized due to its small production runs. Corleggy also produces delicious (and herby) raw-milk artisan cheeses from cow's and sheep's milk. Contact master cheesemaker Silke Cropp about her one-day cheese-making courses.

Emerald Star   CRUISE
(☑049-952 2933; www.emeraldstar.ie; per week from €1352; ☺Apr-Oct) A reliable operator for organising that memorable weeklong river cruise.

🛏 Sleeping & Drinking

Church View Guesthouse   GUESTHOUSE €€
(☑049-952 2358; www.churchviewguesthouse. com; 8 Church St; s/d €35/70; 🛜) The cosiest accommodation option in town is this cherry-coloured guesthouse, but book ahead as it's perennially busy with anglers thanks to its cold storeroom and proximity to the lakes.

🍺 Drinking

Widow's Bar   PUB
(Main St) An earthy local pub in the centre with a warm exposed-stone-and-brick interior, plus a beer garden out back. This pub is best known for its rollicking trad music sessions on Saturday and Sunday nights.

ℹ Getting There & Around

Dublin–Donegal **Bus Éireann** (☑049-433 1353; www.buseireann.ie) services stop outside the post office.

Southern Cavan

Ballyjamesduff & Around

POP 2568

A sleepy market town, Ballyjamesduff was the one-time home of the earl of Fife, James Duff, an early Plantation landlord. His descendant, Sir James Duff, commanded English troops during the suppression of the 1798 Rebellion.

These days the town is best known as the home of the **Cavan County Museum** (☑049-854 4070; www.cavanmuseum.ie; Virginia Rd; adult/child €3/1.50; ☺10am-5pm Tue-Sat, plus 2-6pm Sun Jul-Sep), located inside a superbly preserved former convent. Highlights of the impressive collection include a huge array of 18th-, 19th- and 20th-century costumes and folk items, and relics from the Stone, Bronze, Iron and Middle Ages, including the Celtic Killycluggin stone and the three-faced Corleck Head, as well as a 1000-year-old boat excavated from Lough Errill and an exhibit about the Great Famine.

The area's other main attraction is **Lough Sheelin**, famed for its trout fishing. May and June are the best months for anglers, but it's a scenic place for horse riding, walking or boating year-round.

At Mountnugent, 9km south of Ballyjamesduff, the 1590-built **Ross Castle** (☑086 824 2200; www.ross-castle.com; Mountnugent; d €120) was partially destroyed by Cromwell but rebuilt by the Nugent family. Today it's an atmospheric B&B that's not for the faint-hearted – the steps get steeper and narrow the higher you climb into its tower, one of its guest rooms has no bathroom door (the bathroom is squished into an alcove), and it's haunted (by the castle builder's daughter, who the owners swear leaves lights shimmering and turns taps on and off). But if that doesn't deter you, it's an unforgettable experience. Call ahead to confirm your arrival time.

Bus Éireann runs a Monday to Saturday bus service from Kells.

Eastern Cavan

Many towns in the county's east, such as handsome Virginia, were laid out as 17th-century Plantation estates. While in the area, it's worth stopping at Kingscourt to visit St Mary's Catholic Church, with its superb 1940s stained-glass windows created by famous Dublin stained-glass artist, the late Evie Hone.

Just northeast of Kingscourt is the 225-hectare Dún an Rí Forest Park (042-966 7320; www.coillteoutdoors.ie; cars €5; ⊙ 9am-9pm). There are colour-coded forest walks (all under 4km long), with picnic places and a wishing well. Look out for mink and otters along the river.

Bordering the forest, the 19th-century Cabra Castle (042-966 7030; www.cabracastle.com; s/d/cottages from €95/150/110; ⚡) is now a deluxe hotel decked out in plush period furnishings. Most rooms are in its courtyard area; there are also self-catering cottages. The lobby and some guest rooms have wi-fi. It's 3km out of Kingscourt on the Carrickmacross road.

Northwestern Cavan

Set against the dramatic backdrop of the Cuilcagh Mountains, the remote northwestern edges of Cavan are some of its most scenic. However, local transport is limited so you will need your own wheels to explore the region.

Ballyconnell

POP 1061

The pretty canalside village of Ballyconnell is a popular angling centre and a bustling place in summer with visitors making their way along the Shannon–Erne Waterway, which wends its way through town.

🛏 Sleeping

Sandville House   HOSTEL €
(049-952 6297; http://homepage.eircom.net/~sandville; dm/d from €20/40) You can stay at the simple but cheerful Sandville House, Cavan's only hostel. Set in a converted farmhouse, rooms have two to 10 beds and there's a meditation room as well as a self-catering kitchen. The hostel is 3.5km southeast of the village (signposted off the N87). Check ahead as it's often closed for private retreats. The Dublin to Donegal bus stops on request at the Slieve Russell Hotel, from where you can pre-arrange for a pick-up.

Slieve Russell Hotel   LUXURY HOTEL €€€
(049-952 6444; www.slieverussell.ie; Cranaghan; d from €120; @ 🗐 🐾 🐾) For relaxation of a luxurious kind, the Slieve Russell Hotel, 2km southeast of town, is famed for its marble columns, fountains, restaurants, bars, and an 18- and nine- hole golf course, with golf lessons available from PGA pros (per hour €45). Its 222 rooms are elegantly furnished and spa treatments include flotation tanks, a herbal sauna and a salt grotto. Breakfast included.

Blacklion & Around

POP 174

Traversed by the Cavan Way, the area between Blacklion and Dowra has some extraordinary prehistoric monuments, including the remains of a *cashel* (stone-walled circular fort) and the ruins of several sweathouses, used mostly in the 19th century.

JAMPA LING BUDDHIST CENTRE

On a quest for enlightenment, or just seeking some time out? Jampa Ling Buddhist Centre (049-952 3448; www.jampaling.org; Owendoon House, Bawnboy; dm/s self-catering €18/23, incl meals €32/39), in a beautiful country setting, is peace on earth. Jampa Ling, meaning 'Place of Infinite Loving Kindness', offers courses, retreats and workshops (€25 to €40, per weekend €215) on Tibetan Buddhist teachings, gardening, meditation, tai chi, yoga, and medicinal and culinary herbs. You don't have to take part in a course to stay here, but accommodation may not be available if there is an event taking place. All meals, which are included in the day courses and for overnight guests, are vegetarian (and delicious).

From Ballyconnell, follow the signs to Bawnboy. In the village, turn left at the petrol station and follow the small road for 3km. Continue past the lake and a series of bends; you'll see the centre's stone gates a further 250m ahead on your right.

Dedicated foodies make the pilgrimage here to one of the country's finest restaurants, **MacNean House & Restaurant** (☑ 071-985 3022; www.macneanrestaurant.com; Main St; dinner menus €72-85, with paired wines €125, Sunday lunch €39, d from €140-200; ⊘ 6-11pm Wed-Sat, 12.30-10pm Sun; ☑). Make a reservation before you book your flight to Ireland – the wait for a table at award-winning TV chef Neven Maguire's exceptional restaurant can be several months. Maguire grew up in this gorgeous house and the food here is a celebration of local and seasonal produce. Feast on intricate creations like sea bass with cep tortellini and baby leeks or duck breast with quinoa, kale, cranberries and red peppers. A vegetarian menu is available for €55. Guest rooms (doubles €140 to €200) are beautifully decorated and filled with natural light.

Westport–Belfast buses stop in front of Maguire's pub.

Cuilcagh Mountain Park

The border between the Republic and Northern Ireland runs along the ridge of Cuilcagh Mountain, the distinctive table-top summit of Cuilcagh Mountain Park, the world's first cross-border Geopark. Its lower slopes are important protected peat-land habitats, while the upper slopes have dramatic sweeping cliffs. The visitor centre and the park's biggest attraction, the Marble Arch Caves (p660), lie a short hop over the border from Blacklion, in County Fermanagh.

COUNTY MONAGHAN

Monaghan's quiet, undulating landscape is known for its tiny rounded hills that resemble bubbles in badly pasted wallpaper. Known as drumlins, these bumps are the result of debris left by retreating glaciers during the last ice age. The county's steely grey lakes attract plenty of anglers, but few others make it here, making it a tranquil place to explore.

Unlike much of the province, Monaghan was largely left alone during the Ulster Plantation. After the Cromwellian wars, though, local chieftains were forced to sell their land for a fraction of its true value, or have it seized and redistributed to Cromwell's soldiers.

In the early 19th century, lace making became an important facet of the local economy, providing work and income for women. Clones and Carrickmacross were the two main centres of the industry and you can still see the fine needlework on display in both towns.

Monaghan Town

POP 6221

It may be the county town, but Monaghan's residents live their lives utterly unaffected by tourism. It's a pleasant place to wander the streets admiring the elegant 18th- and 19th-century limestone buildings.

◉ Sights & Activities

Monaghan County Museum MUSEUM
(www.monaghan.ie; 1-2 Hill St; ⊘ 11am-5pm Mon-Fri, noon-5pm Sat) FREE Over 70,000 artefacts from the Stone Age to modern times are housed at this excellent regional museum. Its crowning glory is the 14th-century **Cross of Clogher**, an oaken altar cross encased in decorative bronze panels. Other impressive finds include the Lisdrumturk and Altartate Cauldrons, medieval *crannóg* artefacts, and some frightening knuckledusters and cudgels relating to the border with the North.

Other Sights HISTORIC SITES
In Church Sq, the hefty 1987 obelisk **Dawson Monument** commemorates Colonel Dawson's unfortunate demise in the Crimean War. Overlooking it is the Gothic **St Patrick's Church** and a stately Doric **courthouse** (1829). Heading west you'll find the **Rossmore Memorial** (c 1875), an over-the-top Victorian drinking fountain that dominates the Diamond. The town also has a number of buildings with gently rounded corners, an unusual architectural feature in Ireland.

Just out of the centre of town on the Dublin road is another piece of Victorian whimsy, the mock-14th-century **St Macartan's Catholic Cathedral** (1861), topped by a teetering 77m-high, needle-sharp spire.

Venture Sports FISHING
(☑ 047-81495; venturesports@eircom.net; 71 Glaslough St) Fine fishing abounds in the area; contact Venture Sports for permits, tackle and local knowledge.

✪ Festivals & Events

Féile Oriel Music MUSIC
(www.feileoriel.com) Traditional music festival over May's bank holiday weekend.

WORTH A TRIP

CASTLE LESLIE

The ancestral home of the Leslie family, Castle Leslie (☎ 047-88100; www.castleleslie. com; Glaslough; d from €160; ☎) is a Victorian pile with all the faded grandeur of a well-loved home. The family (who trace their ancestors back to Attila the Hun) acquired the castle in 1665 and its kooky history makes it an entertaining detour for both guests and nonguests.

Each of the 20 guest rooms in the main house has a story: the Red Room, used by WB Yeats, contains the first bath plumbed in Ireland, while in Uncle Norman's Room, guests claim to have been levitated in the Gothic four-poster bed. The Hunting Lodge has a further 30 rooms, with decor ranging from rich traditional drapery to more minimalist contemporary style. Public areas have wi-fi. You can also enjoy pampering treatments at the Victorian spa, or horse riding at the magnificent equestrian centre (from €35 per hour).

Dining options include the open-plan Snaffles Brasserie (mains €21.50-29.50), which serves sophisticated dishes based on locally sourced ingredients, and snug Conor's Bar (mains €13-24.50), specialising in tasty bar-style snacks and more substantial, traditional dishes.

The castle is 11km northeast of Monaghan town at Glaslough, along the R185.

Harvest Blues Festival   MUSIC
(www.harvestblues.com) Fabulous blues festival featuring local and international acts in early September.

🛏 Sleeping & Eating

If you're after something grander than the town's B&Bs and business hotels, Castle Leslie is 11km northeast.

Ashleigh House   B&B €€
(☎ 047-81227; www.ashleighhousemonaghan.com; 37 Dublin St; d €70; ☎) Right in the centre of town, this 10-room B&B offers good-value, albeit mildly scuffed, rooms. All have private bathrooms and are decorated with countrified printed fabrics; there's a small garden area.

Andy's Bar & Restaurant   BISTRO €€
(☎ 047-82277; www.andysmonaghan.com; 12 Market St; restaurant mains €16-26, bar mains €8-12; ⊙ 4-10pm Tue-Fri, from 5pm Sat, from 1.30pm Sun; ☎) A long-standing local favourite, this Victorian bar and old-school restaurant still proudly serves the likes of deep-fried brie, prawn cocktail and pavlova, as well as fillet steak on breaded potato croutons. Vegetarian menu.

Squealing Pig   PUB €€
(www.thesquealingpig.ie; The Diamond; pub mains €8-10, restaurant mains €15-20; ⊙ restaurant 5pm-9.45pm Fri-Sun, 12.30-3pm Sun) This welcoming place sparks on all cylinders. At the downstairs pub you can enjoy inexpensive retro meals like chicken kiev, while upstairs is a beguiling combination of antiques and mod-ern furniture with a menu of classy dishes like chateaubriand and confit leg of duck, as well as tasting boards of cold cuts (and similar) to share.

🍷 Drinking & Nightlife

Sherry's   PUB
(24 Dublin St) Entering Sherry's, one of Monaghan's oldest bars, is like stepping into a family-style parlour from the 1950s. The old tiled floor, beauty board and memorabilia probably haven't been touched in decades.

McKenna's Bar   PUB
(62 Dublin Rd; ⊙ 6pm-late Mon-Sat; ☎) This historic pub is famous throughout the region for its jam sessions – predominantly blues. The upstairs bar is the ideal moody venue with its dark wood, barrel tables and exposed-brick walls.

☆ Entertainment

Market House   CULTURAL CENTRE
(☎ 047-38162; www.monaghan.ie; Market St) This restored 18th-century market hall-turned-arts-venue hosts exhibitions, concerts and drama productions.

ℹ Information

Tourist Office (☎ 047-73718, 047-81122; www. monaghantourism.com; Clones Rd; ⊙ 10am-5pm Mon-Fri)

ℹ Getting There & Around

From the **bus station** (☎ 047-82377; www. buseireann.ie; North Rd), there are numerous daily intercity services, including 10 buses daily to Dublin (€14.25, two hours). There are also frequent daily services to Carrickmacross.

Rossmore Forest Park

Crumbling remains of the Rossmore family's 19th-century castle, including its entrance stairway, buttresses and the family's pet cemetery, can be seen at Rossmore Forest Park (☑047-433 1046; www.coillteoutdoors.ie; cars €5; ☺9am-9pm), where rhododendrons and azaleas blaze with colour in early summer. Along with forest walks and pleasant picnic areas, the park contains several giant redwoods, a fine yew avenue and Iron Age tombs. It's 3km southwest of Monaghan on the Newbliss road (R189).

Clones & Around

POP 1517

Once the site of an important 6th-century monastery that later became an Augustinian abbey, Clones' main sights are ecclesiastical. There's a well-preserved 10th-century high cross on the Diamond, decorated with drama-charged biblical stories such as Daniel in the lion's den.

Along with the remains of the abbey founded by St Tiernach on Abbey St, there's a truncated 22m-high round tower, which dates from the early 9th century, in the cemetery south of town. Nearby is the supposed burial place of Tiernach himself, a chunky 9th-century sarcophagus with worn animal-head carvings.

More recently, Clones found fame as a lace-making centre. To learn about the history of Clones lace, see it on display or purchase samples, visit the Ulster Canal Stores (☑047-52125; www.cloneslace.com; Cara St; ☺9am-5pm Mon-Fri).

★Hilton Park (☑047-56007; www.hiltonpark. ie; d €196-270, gate house per week €495; ☺Apr-Sep) is a country-house retreat that has been in the same family since 1734. It's a magnificent place with stunning views of the 240-hectare estate. Its six spacious guest rooms are bathed in light and decorated with original furniture, free-standing baths and four-poster or half-tester beds. Top-class cuisine, much of it produced in the estate's organic gardens, is served in regal surroundings (dinner €55, by prior arrangement). Rates include breakfast and high tea on arrival. You can also come for literary weekends or cookery courses.

Bus Éireann (☑047-82377; www.buseireann. ie) runs a service from Clones to Monaghan (€5.75, 30 minutes, five buses Monday to Saturday, one Sunday), with connections on to Carrickmacross, Slane and Dublin.

Ulsterbus (☑048-9066 6630; www.translink. co.uk/Ulsterbus) has one direct service per day between Clones and Belfast (€13.20, 2¼ hours, Monday to Friday).

Carrickmacross & Around

POP 1973

Carrickmacross was first settled by early English and Scottish Planters, and its broad main street is dotted with some elegant Georgian houses with gorgeous poster-paint-coloured facades. It's most famous as the home of delicate Carrickmacross lace, an industry revived in 1871 by the St Louis nuns. The town is a peaceful spot to wander and a great base for anglers.

⊙ Sights & Activities

★Carrickmacross Lace Gallery   LACE GALLERY
(☑042-966 2506; www.carrickmacrosslace.ie; Market Sq; ☺10am-4pm Mon-Fri, to 5.30pm Sat) In the town's former cattle yards, a local cooperative runs this tiny but fascinating lace gallery, where you can see lace-making demonstrations and check out exquisite designs. Unlike Clones' crocheted lace, designs here are appliquéd on organza using thick thread and close stitches, then embellished with a variety of point stitches, guipure, pops and the lace's distinctive loop edge. Most famously, Carrickmacross has royal connections: its lace graced the sleeves of Princess Diana's wedding dress and, more recently, the technique was used on the wedding dress for Kate Middleton's wedding to Prince William in April 2011.

Carrickmacross' lace makers can take commissions and you can purchase small exquisite pieces made into fridge magnets, bookmarks and similar for as little as €10. The gallery is planning a move into more spacious premises, but still within the former cattle yards

St Joseph's Catholic Church   CHURCH
(O'Neill St) Craftsmanship shines at St Joseph's Catholic Church, with 10 windows designed by Harry Clarke, Ireland's most renowned stained-glass artist.

Eastern Regional Fisheries · FISHING

Fantastic fishing around Carrickmacross includes Loughs Capragh, Spring, Monalty and Fea. Contact details for guides, boat hire and tackle are listed on www.monaghan tourism.com.

Sleeping & Eating

Carrickmacross has some 20 pubs – around one for every 200 residents! – so you won't go hungry, much less thirsty.

Shirley Arms · HOTEL €€

(☑ 042-967 3100; www.shirleyarmshotel.ie; Main St; d from €110; 🛜) The Shirley Arms has a warm stone exterior, behind which lies a pleasant modern hotel with spacious rooms and decent food right in the centre of town. White linens, walnut floors and modern bathrooms make the rooms contemporary but rather corporate in style while the open-plan bar and lounge create an informal setting for some excellent bar food (mains €12 to €15).

Fiddlers Elbow · BAR, RESTAURANT €

(www.fiddlers.ie; Main St; mains €8-10; ⊙ 11am-10pm Mon-Thu, to late Fri-Sun) One of a row of picturesque colourful facades, Fiddlers Elbow's shamrock green frontage leads to a bar, restaurant and upstairs nightclub (www.vanitynightclub.ie). For diners there's a wide choice and price range with dishes like goat's cheese tartlet, chicken curry coriander and apple and cinnamon crumble. The whole place has a buzzy convivial atmosphere.

ℹ Information

Carrickmacross has no tourist office, but the tourism section of the town's website, www.car rickmacross.ie, has visitor information.

ℹ Getting There & Away

Bus Éireann (☑ 01-836 6111; www.buseireann. ie) services connect with Dublin (€12.15, 1¾ hours, five daily).

Inniskeen

POP 292

Acclaimed poet Patrick Kavanagh (1904–67) was born in the village of Inniskeen, 10km northeast of Carrickmacross.

Kavanagh's long work 'The Great Hunger' (1942) blasted away the earlier clichés of Anglo-Irish verse and revealed Ireland's poor farming communities as half-starved, 'broken-backed' and sexually repressed. His best-known poem, 'On Raglan Road' (1946), was an ode to his unrequited love. It doubled as the lyrics for the traditional Irish air 'The Dawning of the Day', which has been performed by Van Morrison, Mark Knopfler, Billy Bragg, Sinéad O'Connor and countless others.

The **Patrick Kavanagh Centre** (☑ 042-937 8560; www.patrickkavanaghcountry.com; adult/student/child under 12yr €5/3/free; ⊙ 11am-4.30pm Tue-Fri) is housed in the old parish church where Kavanagh was baptised. The staff have a passion for the poet's life and work that is contagious, and the centre hosts annual events including a Writers' Weekend in late July/early August.

Information on guided literary tours around town is posted on the resource centre's website. You can walk or drive around the sites in and around the village and the picturesque surrounding countryside (5.6km in all).

Inniskeen is on the Bus Éireann route between Cavan and Dundalk via Carrickmacross, with four services Monday to Saturday.

Belfast

POP 280,900 / AREA 115 SQ KM

Best Places to Eat

➡ Barking Dog (p576)

➡ Shu (p576)

➡ Mourne Seafood Bar (p575)

➡ Molly's Yard (p576)

➡ Deane's Restaurant (p575)

Best Places to Stay

➡ Tara Lodge (p573)

➡ Old Rectory (p573)

➡ Malmaison Hotel (p572)

➡ Ten Square (p572)

➡ Vagabonds (p573)

Why Go?

Once lumped with Beirut, Baghdad and Bosnia as one the four 'Bs' for travellers to avoid, Belfast has pulled off a remarkable transformation from bombs-and-bullets pariah to a hip-hotels-and-hedonism party town. The opening of Titanic Belfast in 2012, along with the 50th anniversary of the Belfast Festival at Queen's – the UK's second-biggest arts festival – saw visitor numbers soar by more than 40%.

Although the economic recession has slowed development, the old shipyards on the Lagan continue to give way to the luxury waterfront apartments of the Titanic Quarter, while new tourist venues keep popping up – historic Crumlin Road Gaol opened to the public in 2012, SS *Nomadic* in 2013, and there are plans for WWI warship HMS *Caroline* to become a floating museum. They all add to a list of attractions that includes Victorian architecture, a glittering waterfront lined with modern art, and foot-stomping music in packed-out pubs.

When to Go

➡ April can be a great time to visit Belfast, when there are spring brings flowers to the parks and the annual Titanic Belfast Festival is held.

➡ August brings good weather for walking and cycling, along with celebrations of Irish music and dance in West Belfast.

➡ October can start to get chilly, but the Festival at Queen's, the UK's second largest arts festival (after Edinburgh), warms things up.

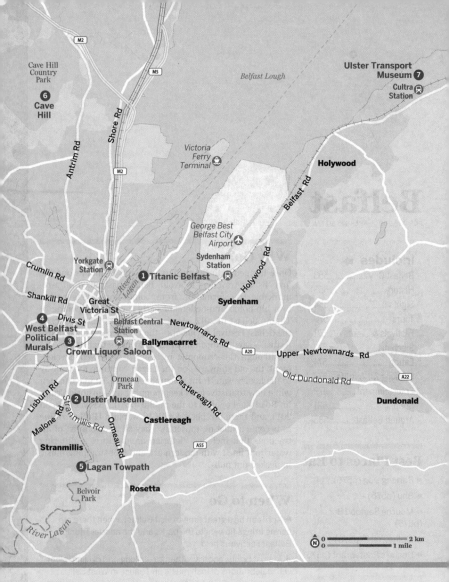

Belfast Highlights

1 Learn all about the world's most famous ocean liner at the new **Titanic Belfast** (p564) attraction

2 Discover prehistoric treasures, an ancient Egyptian mummy and sunken Armada gold at the **Ulster Museum** (p566)

3 Sup on a Guinness or three in some of Belfast's beautiful Victorian pubs, such as the **Crown Liquor Saloon** (p554)

4 Take a taxi tour of the powerful **political murals** in West Belfast

5 Hire a bike and take a spin along the **Lagan Towpath**

to the former linen town of Lisburn

6 Enjoy a panoramic view over the city from the top of **Cave Hill** (p553)

7 Check out the iconic DeLorean DMC at the **Ulster Transport Museum** (p568)

BELFAST CITY

History

Belfast is a relatively young city, with few reminders of its pre-19th-century history. It takes its name from the River Farset (from the Gaelic *feirste*, meaning sandbank, or sandy ford), which flows into the River Lagan at Donegall Quay (it is now channelled through a culvert). The old Gaelic name, Béal Feirste, means 'Mouth of the Farset'.

In 1177, the Norman lord John de Courcy built a castle here, and a small settlement grew up around it. Both were destroyed in battle 20 years later, and the town did not begin to develop in earnest until 1611 when Baron Arthur Chichester built a castle in what is now the city centre (near Castle Pl and Castle St); it was destroyed by fire in 1708.

The early 17th-century Plantation of Ulster brought in the first waves of Scottish and English settlers, followed in the late 17th century by an influx of Huguenots (French Protestants) fleeing persecution in France; they laid the foundations of a thriving linen industry. More Scottish and English settlers arrived, and other industries such as rope-making, tobacco, engineering and shipbuilding developed.

With its textile mills and shipyards, Belfast was the one city in Ireland that truly rode the wave of the Industrial Revolution. Sturdy rows of brick terrace houses were built for the factory and shipyard workers, and a town of around 20,000 people in 1800 grew steadily into a city of 400,000 by the start of WWI, by which time Belfast had nearly overtaken Dublin in size.

The partition of Ireland in 1920 gave Belfast a new role as the capital of Northern Ireland. It also marked the end of the city's industrial growth, although decline didn't really set in until after WWII. With the outbreak of the Troubles in 1969, the city saw more than its fair share of violence and bloodshed, and shocking news images of terrorist bombings, sectarian murders and security forces' brutality made Belfast a household name around the world.

The 1998 Good Friday Agreement, which laid the groundwork for power-sharing among the various political factions in a devolved Northern Ireland Assembly, raised hopes for the future, and a historic milestone was passed on 8 May 2007 when the Reverend Ian Paisley (firebrand Protestant preacher and leader of the Democratic Unionist Party) and Martin McGuinness (Sinn Féin MP and former IRA commander) were sworn in at Stormont as first minister and deputy first minister of a new power-sharing government.

Since 1998 Belfast has seen a huge influx of investment, especially from the EU. Massive swaths of the city centre have been (or are being) redeveloped, and tourism has taken off. But the city was hit hard by the global economic downturn – a meteoric rise in property prices was followed by a devastating tumble as house prices fell by 40% from their 2007 peak. Development projects have been put on hold, and many office and apartment complexes now sit empty.

BELFAST HISTORY

BELFAST IN...

One Day

Start your day with breakfast in one of the many cafes on Botanic Ave – Maggie May's (p576) will do nicely – then stroll north into the city centre and take a free guided tour of City Hall (p554). Take a black taxi tour (p571) of the West Belfast murals, then ask the taxi driver to drop you off at the John Hewitt Bar & Restaurant (p575) for lunch. Then head across the river to spend the rest of the afternoon exploring Titanic Belfast (p564). Round off the day with dinner at Deane's Restaurant (p575) or Ginger (p574).

Two Days

On your second day, take a look at Queen's University (p566), explore the fascinating exhibits in the Ulster Museum (p566) and take a stroll through the Botanic Gardens (p566). In the afternoon either take a guided tour around historic Crumlin Road Gaol (p564), or go for a hike up Cave Hill (p569). Have dinner at Shu (p576) or the Barking Dog (p576), then spend the evening crawling traditional pubs such as the Crown Liquor Saloon (p577), Kelly's Cellars (p577) and the Duke of York (p578).

BELFAST FOR CHILDREN

W5 (p565) is the city's biggest draw for kids – it's hard to drag them away once they get started with the hands-on exhibits. The Odyssey Complex houses other attractions including a video-games arcade, a tenpin bowling alley and an IMAX cinema. Belfast Zoo (p570) is a perennial favourite, and the Ulster Museum (p566) also has plenty of exhibits and special events designed for children of all ages.

For outdoor fun, head for the Botanic Gardens (p566) or the adventure playground in Cave Hill Country Park (p569). Or you can try crazy golf with a difference at Pirates Adventure Golf (Map p568; www.piratesadventuregolf.com; 111A Dundonald Rd, Dundonald Touring Caravan Park; adult/child £6/4; ☺11am-9pm), a landscaped, 36-hole course decked out with waterfalls, fountains and a giant pirate ship.

Sweet treats may not be at the top of parents' shopping lists these days, but you might be prepared to make an exception for Aunt Sandra's Candy Factory (Map p568; www.auntsandras.com; 60 Castlereagh Rd; tours adult/child £4/3; ☺9.30am-5pm Mon-Fri, 10am-4.30pm Sat). This 1950s-style shop sells handmade fudge, candy, chocolates, toffee apples and other traditional sweets, and you can take a tour of the workshop before buying the goods.

Outside of town, but near enough for a day trip, is the Ulster Folk & Transport Museums (p568) and, in County Down, the Ark Open Farm (p594); both are hugely popular with kids.

The free bimonthly *About Belfast* booklet (available from the Belfast Welcome Centre) has a 'Family Fun' section, which lists events and attractions of interest to travellers with children. If you're in town in late March, look out for the Belfast Children's Festival (www.belfastchildrensfestival.com), which is packed with cultural and educational events.

⊙ Sights

⊙ City Centre

★City Hall   HISTORIC BUILDING
(Map p556; www.belfastcity.gov.uk/cityhall; Donegall Sq; ☺guided tours 11am, 2pm & 3pm Mon-Fri, 2pm & 3pm Sat) FREE The Industrial Revolution transformed Belfast in the 19th century, and its rapid rise to muck-and-brass prosperity is manifested in the extravagance of City Hall. Built in classical Renaissance style in fine, white Portland stone, it was completed in 1906 and paid for from the profits of the gas supply company.

The hall is fronted by a statue of a rather dour 'we are not amused' Queen Victoria. The bronze figures on either side of her symbolise the textile and shipbuilding industries, while the child at the back represents education. At the northeastern corner of the grounds is a statue of Sir Edward Harland, the Yorkshire-born marine engineer who founded the Harland & Wolff shipyards and who served as mayor of Belfast from 1885 to 1886. To his south stands a memorial to the victims of the Titanic.

The highlights of the free, 45-minute guided tour of City Hall include the sumptuous wedding-cake Italian marble and colourful stained glass of the entrance hall and rotunda, an opportunity to sit on the mayor's throne in the council chamber and the idiosyncratic portraits of past lord mayors – each lord mayor is allowed to choose his or her own artist and the variations in personal style are intriguing.

The Bobbin Coffee Shop (☺9.30am-4.30pm Mon-Fri, 10am-4pm Sat), in the southeast corner of City Hall, houses an exhibition of photographic portraits of Belfast's most famous citizens, from footballer George Best and musician Van Morrison to broadcaster Gloria Hunniford and president of Ireland Mary McAleese.

★Crown Liquor Saloon   HISTORIC BUILDING
(Map p556; www.nationaltrust.org.uk; 46 Great Victoria St; ☺11.30am-11pm Mon-Wed, 11.30am-midnight Thu-Sat, 12.30-10pm Sun) FREE There are not too many historical monuments that you can enjoy while savouring a pint of beer, but the National Trust's Crown Liquor Saloon is one of them. Belfast's most famous bar was refurbished by Patrick Flanagan in the late 19th century and displays Victorian decorative flamboyance at its best (he was looking to pull in a posh clientele from the

newfangled train station and Grand Opera House across the street).

The exterior (1885) is decorated with ornate and colourful Italian tiles, and boasts a mosaic of a crown on the pavement outside the entrance. Legend has it that Flanagan, a Catholic, argued with his Protestant wife over what the pub's name should be. His wife prevailed and it was named the Crown in honour of the British monarchy. Flanagan took his sneaky revenge by placing the crown mosaic underfoot where customers would tread on it every day.

The interior (1898) sports a mass of stained and cut glass, marble, ceramics, mirrors and mahogany, all atmospherically lit by genuine gas mantles. A long, highly decorated bar dominates one side of the pub, while on the other is a row of ornate wooden snugs. The snugs come equipped with gunmetal plates (from the Crimean War) for striking matches, and bell-pushes that once allowed drinkers to order top-ups without leaving their seats (alas, no longer).

Linen Hall Library   HISTORIC BUILDING
(Map p556; www.linenhall.com; 17 Donegall Sq N; ◷9.30am-5.30pm Mon-Fri, 9.30am-4pm Sat; ☎) FREE Established in 1788 to 'improve the mind and excite a spirit of general inquiry', the Linen Hall Library was moved from its original home in the White Linen Hall (the site is now occupied by City Hall) to the present building a century later. Thomas Russell, the first librarian, was a founding member of the United Irishmen and a close friend of Wolfe Tone – a reminder that this movement for independence from Britain had its origins in Belfast. Russell was hanged in 1803 after Robert Emmet's abortive rebellion.

The library houses some 260,000 books, more than half of which are part of its important Irish- and local-studies collection. The political collection consists of pretty much everything that has been written about Northern Irish politics since 1966. The library also has a small **coffee shop** (◷10am-4pm Mon-Fri, till 3.30pm Sat). The visitors' entrance is on Fountain St, around the corner from the main door.

Grand Opera House   HISTORIC BUILDING
(Map p556; www.goh.co.uk; Great Victoria St) One of Belfast's great Victorian landmarks is the Grand Opera House. Opened in 1895, and completely refurbished in the 1970s, it suffered grievously at the hands of the IRA, having sustained severe bomb damage in 1991 and 1993. It was said that, as the Europa Hotel next door was home to the media during the Troubles, the IRA brought the bombs to them so they wouldn't have to leave the bar.

The interior has been restored to its original, over-the-top Victorian pomp, with swirling wood and plasterwork, fancy giltwork in abundance and carved elephant heads framing the private boxes in the auditorium.

> **ⓘ NORTHERN IRISH ROOTS?**
>
> If you're hoping to track down your Ulster family history, the Public Record Office of Northern Ireland, PRONI (☎028 9053 4800; www.proni.gov.uk; 2 Titanic Blvd; ◷9am-4.45pm Mon-Wed & Fri, 10am-8.45pm Thu), has its headquarters in Belfast's Titanic Quarter. Admission is free, but a charge is made for copies of documents. Check the website for details of how to register and search the records.

BELFAST SIGHTS

RED HAND OF ULSTER

According to legend, the chief of a raiding party – O'Neills or O'Donnells, take your pick – approaching the coast by boat, decided to fire up his troops by decreeing that Ulster would belong to the first man to lay his right hand upon it. As they neared land one particularly competitive chap cut off his own right hand and lobbed it to the shore, thus claiming Ulster as his own. The O'Neill clan later adopted the Red Hand as their emblem and it went on to become the symbol of the Irish province of Ulster.

You'll see the Red Hand of Ulster in many places: on the official Northern Irish flag, in the Ulster coat of arms, above the entrance to the Linen Hall Library on Donegall Sq, and laid out in red flowers in the garden of Mount Stewart House in County Down. It also appears in many political murals in the badges of Loyalist terrorist groups, and as a clenched red fist in the badge of the Ulster Volunteer Force (UVF).

Central Belfast

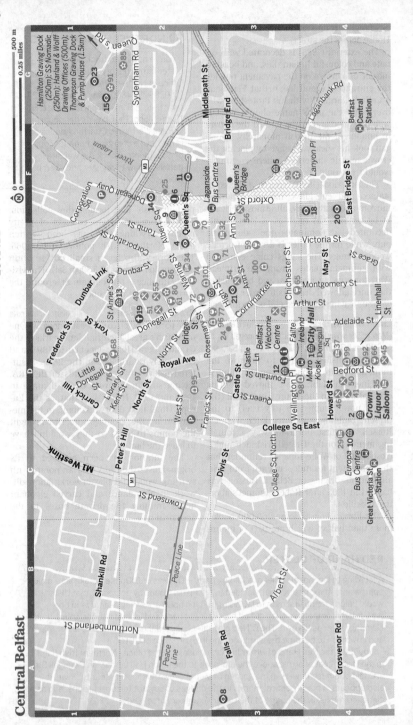

BELFAST

Hamilton Graving Dock (250m); SS Nomadic (250m); Harland & Wolff Drawing Offices (500m); Thompson Graving Dock & Pump House (1.5km)

Queen's Rd

85

23

91

15

Sydenham Rd

River Lagan

M3

Queen's Rd

Middlepath St

Bridge End

Laganbank Rd

Belfast Central Station

Corporation Sq

Donegall Quay

25

9

14

16

11

Tomb St

Albert St

Queen's Sq

70

Corporation St

Laganside Bus Centre

Queen's Bridge

5

93

Oxford St

Lanyon Pl

East Bridge St

Frederick St

York St

Dunbar Link

St Anne's Sq

Dunbar St

13

55

51

19

Waring St

86

80

72

74

34

4

Ann St

56

59

18

20

Victoria St

Grace St

May St

Donegall St

North St

Bridge St

Rosemary St

High St

101

54

21

Cornmarket

100

Ann St

65

Chichester St

Montgomery St

Arthur St

Little Donegall St

64

68

Carrick Hill

Library St

Kent St

76

97

North St

Royal Ave

West St

95

24

9

67

Castle St

Castle Ln

Belfast Welcome Centre

Fáilte Ireland

Metro 1 City Hall

Donegall Sq

Kiosk

98

12

Wellington Pl

Fountain St

Queen St

40

Adelaide St

Linenhall St

37

99

66

92

45

Bedford St

Howard St

46

50

41

2

35

Crown Liquor Saloon

Peter's Hill

Francis St

College Sq East

College Sq North

Divis St

29

Europa Bus Centre

10

Great Victoria St Station

M1 Westlink

Peace Line

Townsend St

Shankill Rd

Peace Line

Northumberland St

Peace Line

Falls Rd

Albert St

Grosvenor Rd

8

500 m
0.25 miles

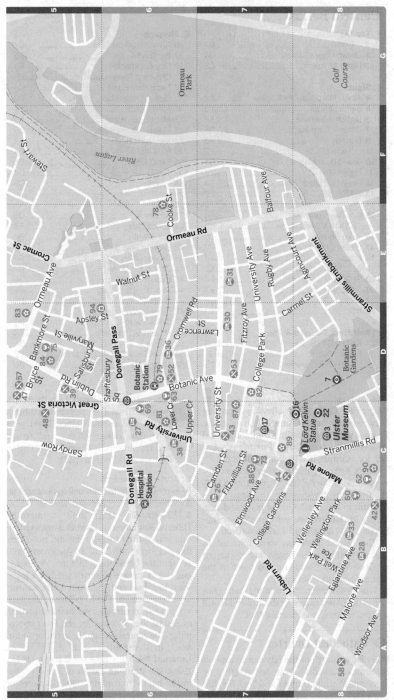

Golf Course

Ormeau Park

River Lagan

Stewart St

Cromac St

Ormeau Ave

Ormeau Rd

Cooke St

78

Walnut St

Balfour Ave

University Ave

Rugby Ave

Agincourt Ave

Stranmillis Embankment

Carmel St

Apsley St

94

Cromwell Rd

31

Fitzroy Ave

Bankmore St

Maryville St

Donegall Pass

Lawrence St

30

83

Ormeau Rd

84

75

Salisbury St

Shaftesbury Sq

Botanic Station

36

79

52

College Park

Bruce St

57

Dublin Rd

39

47

Botanic Ave

53

Botanic Gardens

7

Great Victoria St

48

81

69

University St

82

16

Lord Kelvin Statue

Ulster Museum

Sandy Row

27

Lower Cr

Upper Cr

University Rd

87

43

3 22

17

89

Donegall Rd

Hospital Station

38

Camden St

Stranmillis Rd

Malone Rd

Fitzwilliam St

88

73

44

2

Elmwood Ave

26

College Gardens

Wellesley Ave

Wellington Park

60

62

90

Lisburn Rd

Well Park

42

33

Eglantine Ave

28

Malone Ave

Windsor Ave

58

Central Belfast

The Entries HISTORIC SITE
(Map p556) The narrow alleyways running between High St and Ann St, known as the Entries, were once bustling commercial and residential thoroughfares; **Pottinger's Entry**, for example, had 34 houses in 1822.

Joy's Entry is named after Francis Joy, who founded the *Belfast News Letter* in 1737, the first daily newspaper in the British Isles (it's still in business). One of his grandsons, Henry Joy McCracken, was executed for supporting the 1798 United Irishmen revolt.

The United Irishmen were founded in 1791 by Wolfe Tone in Peggy Barclay's tavern in **Crown Entry**, and used to meet in the historic Kelly's Cellars (p577).

White's Tavern (p577), on **Wine Cellar Entry**, is the oldest tavern in the city and is still a popular lunchtime meeting spot.

◉ Cathedral Quarter

The district north of the city centre around St Anne's Cathedral, bounded roughly by Donegall, Waring, Dunbar and York Sts, has been promoted as Belfast's Left Bank. It's a bohemian district of restored red-brick warehouses and cobbled lanes, lined with artists' studios, design offices, and stylish bars and restaurants. It's home to the Cathedral Quarter Arts Festival (p571).

St Anne's Cathedral CHURCH
(Map p556; www.belfastcathedral.org; Donegall St; donations accepted; ⊙8am-4pm Mon-Sat, 8-11am & 12.30-4pm Sun) **FREE** Built in imposing Hiberno-Romanesque style, St Anne's Cathedral was started in 1899 but did not reach its final form until 1981. As you enter you'll see that the black-and-white marble floor is laid out in a maze pattern – the black route leads to a dead end, the white to the sanctuary and salvation. The 10 pillars of the nave are topped by carvings symbolising aspects of Belfast life; look out for the Freemasons' pillar (the central one on the right, or south, side). In the south aisle is the **tomb of Unionist hero Sir Edward Carson** (1854–1935). The stunning mosaic of *The Creation* in the baptistry contains 150,000 pieces of

BELFAST SIGHTS

coloured glass; it and the mosaic above the west door are the result of seven years' work by sisters Gertrude and Margaret Martin.

MAC GALLERY
(Metropolitan Arts Centre; Map p556; themaclive. com; 10 Exchange St W; ⊙10am-7pm; 🖾) FREE
The MAC is a brand new arts centre with three galleries staging a rolling program of exhibitions that showcase the best of art, photography and sculpture from Ireland and around the world. A beautifully designed venue overlooking the neoclassical St Anne's Sq development, it also includes a writers' room (open to all), a cafe and two theatres (p580).

Oh Yeah Music Centre MUSEUM
(Map p556; www.ohyeahbelfast.com; 15-21 Gordon St; ⊙11am-4pm Mon-Fri, noon-5pm Sat) FREE
A charitable organisation that provides rehearsal space for young musicians in a converted whiskey warehouse, the Oh Yeah Music Centre is also home to a museum of Northern Ireland's musical history from folk music to Snow Patrol, with exhibits that range from shamrock-shaped records and electric guitars to historic gig posters, ticket stubs and stage clothing donated by famous bands.

⊙ Laganside & Lanyon Place

The ambitious Laganside project (www. laganside.com) to redevelop and regenerate the centre of Belfast saw the building of the Waterfront Hall, BT's Riverside Tower and the Belfast Hilton in the 1990s. Projects completed since then include the Lanyon Quay office development next to the Waterfront Hall and the restoration of listed buildings such as McHugh's bar on Queen's Sq, the ornate Victorian warehouses now housing the Malmaison Hotel on Victoria St and the Albert Memorial Clock Tower. There are also 30 public artworks set along the waterfront – ask for a Laganside Art Trail leaflet at the Belfast Welcome Centre.

The latest stage of the project is the 28-storey Obel (Map p556), Belfast's tallest building, which dominates the waterfront

MURALS OF BELFAST

Belfast's tradition of political murals is a century old, dating from 1908 when images of King Billy (William III, Protestant victor over the Catholic James II at the Battle of the Boyne in 1690) were painted by Unionists protesting against home rule for Ireland. The tradition was revived in the late 1970s as the Troubles wore on, with murals used to mark out sectarian territory, make political points, commemorate historical events and glorify terrorist groups. As the 'voice of the community' the murals were rarely permanent, but changed to reflect the issues of the day. Taxi tours (p571) visit many of the more prominent murals, and the driver/guide can provide context and an explanation of the various symbols.

Republican Murals

The first Republican murals appeared in 1981, when the hunger strike by Republican prisoners – demanding recognition as political prisoners – at the Maze Prison saw the emergence of dozens of murals of support. In later years, Republican muralists broadened their scope to cover wider political issues, Irish legends and historical events. After the Good Friday Agreement of 1998, the murals came to demand police reform and the protection of nationalists from sectarian attacks.

Common images seen in Republican murals include the phoenix rising from the flames (symbolising Ireland reborn from the flames of the 1916 Easter Rising), the face of hunger-striker Bobby Sands, and scenes and figures from Irish mythology. Common slogans include 'Free Ireland', the Irish Gaelic '*Éirí Amach na Cásca* 1916' (The Easter Rising of 1916) and '*Tiocfaidh Ár Lá*' (Our Day Will Come).

The main areas for Republican murals are Falls Rd, Beechmount Ave, Donegall Rd, Shaw's Rd and the Ballymurphy district in West Belfast, New Lodge Rd in North Belfast, and Ormeau Rd in South Belfast.

Loyalist Murals

Loyalist murals have traditionally been more militaristic and defiant in tone than the Republican murals, which are often artistic and rich in symbolic imagery. The Loyalist

at Donegall Quay; in a sign of straitened economic times, the company that owns the building went bust in 2012. A few blocks to the south is the new £320-million shopping mall, Victoria Square, whose centrepiece is a soaring atrium topped by a vast glass dome with an airy viewing platform.

Albert Memorial Clock Tower LANDMARK
(Map p556; Queen's Sq) At the east end of High St is Belfast's very own leaning tower. Erected in 1867 in honour of Queen Victoria's dear departed husband, it is not as dramatically out of kilter as the more famously tilted tower in Pisa, but does, nevertheless, lean noticeably to the south – as the locals say, 'Old Albert not only has the time, he also has the inclination.' Restoration work has stabilised its foundations and left its Scrabo sandstone masonry sparkling white.

Lagan Weir LANDMARK
(Map p556) Lagan Weir was the first stage of the Laganside Project, completed in 1994. Years of neglect and industrial decline had turned the River Lagan, the original

lifeblood of the city, into an open sewer flanked by smelly, unsightly mudflats. The weir, along with a program of dredging and aeration, has improved the water quality so much that salmon, eels and sea trout migrate up the river once again. A footbridge over the weir provides access to the Odyssey Complex and Titanic Quarter.

Just to its north is Bigfish (Map p556) (1999), the most prominent of many modern artworks that grace the riverbank between Clarendon Dock and Ormeau Bridge. The giant ceramic salmon – a symbol of the regeneration of the River Lagan – is covered with tiles depicting the history of Belfast.

A five-minute walk south from the Lagan Weir leads to Lanyon Pl, the Laganside Project's flagship site, dominated by the 2235-seat Waterfront Hall (p580). Across Oxford St lie the neoclassical Royal Courts of Justice (Map p556; Lanyon Pl) (1933), bombed by the IRA in 1990 but now freed of the massive security screens that once concealed them.

battle cry of 'No Surrender!' is everywhere, along with red, white and blue painted kerb-stones, paramilitary insignia and images of King Billy, usually shown on a prancing white horse.

You will also see the Red Hand of Ulster, sometimes shown as a clenched fist (the symbol of the Ulster Freedom Fighters, UFF), and references to the WWI Battle of the Somme in 1916 in which many Ulster soldiers died; it is seen as a symbol of Ulster's loyalty to the British Crown, in contrast to the Republican Easter Rising of 1916. Common mottoes include '*Quis Separabit'* (Who Shall Divide Us?), the motto of the Ulster Defence Association (UDA); and the defiant 'We will maintain our faith and our nationality'.

Murals Today

In recent years there has been a lot of debate about what to do with Belfast's murals. Some see them as an ugly and unpleasant reminder of a violent past, while others claim they are a vital part of Northern Ireland's history. There's no doubt they have become an important tourist attraction, but there is now a move to replace the more aggressive and militaristic images with murals dedicated to local heroes and famous figures such as footballer George Best and *Narnia* novelist CS Lewis.

There are also some off-beat and amusing artworks, including one that has been baffling passers-by for years. A gable-end on Balfour Ave, off Ormeau Rd, asks the question 'How can quantum gravity help explain the origin of the universe?' It was part of an art installation in 2001, one of 10 questions selected by scientists as the most important unsolved problems in physics. Perhaps it has survived so long as it reflects the still unsolved – and, to outsiders, equally baffling – problem of Northern Ireland's sectarian divide.

If you want to find out more about Northern Ireland's murals, look out for the books *Drawing Support* (three volumes) by Bill Rolston, *The People's Gallery* by the Bogside Artists and the website of the Mural Directory (www.cain.ulst.ac.uk/murals).

Belfast Barge　　　　　　MUSEUM
(Map p556; www.laganlegacy.com; Lanyon Quay; adult/child £4/3; ⊙10am-4pm) Housed in a barge moored on the River Lagan, this museum tells the story of Belfast's maritime and industrial history, bringing together old photographs, original drawings and documents, ship models and artefacts, and video and audio recordings of interviews with retired engineers, designers and shipyard workers.

St George's Market　　　　　MARKET
(Map p556; cnr Oxford & May Sts; ⊙6am-2pm Fri, 9am-3pm Sat, 10am-4pm Sun) FREE This elegant Victorian covered market, built in 1896 for the sale of fruit, butter, eggs and poultry is the oldest continually operating market in Ireland. Restored in 1999, it now hosts a variety market on Friday, selling fresh flowers, fruit, vegetables, meat and fish, plus general household and secondhand goods, and the City Food and Craft Market on Saturday, which often has live music. The Sunday market combines food, antiques and local arts and crafts. There's also a two-day Christmas Fair and Market in early December.

A free shuttle bus links the market with Donegall Sq and Adelaide St every 20 minutes during opening hours.

Custom House　　　　　HISTORIC BUILDING
(Map p556; Custom House Sq) Opposite the west end of Lagan Weir is the elegant Custom House, built by Charles Lanyon in Italianate style between 1854 and 1857; the writer Anthony Trollope once worked in the post office here. On the waterfront side, the pediment carries sculpted portrayals of Britannia, Neptune and Mercury. The Custom House steps were once Belfast's equivalent of London's Speakers' Corner, a tradition memorialised in a bronze statue preaching to an invisible crowd.

◉ Titanic Quarter

Belfast's former shipbuilding yards – the birthplace of RMS *Titanic* – stretch along the east side of the River Lagan, dominated by the towering yellow cranes known

2

3

1. Belfast Castle (p570)
Built in the Scottish Baronial style, Belfast's eponymous castle lords it over the city below.

2. Palm House (p566)
Set in the Botanic Gardens, this light-filled confection is a masterpiece of cast-iron and curvilinear glass.

3. Crown Liquor Saloon (p554)
Come to see the colourful exterior and gorgeously ornate interior, and stay on for a dram or two.

WORTH A TRIP

CRUMLIN ROAD GAOL

Crumlin Road Gaol (Map p568; ☑ 9074 1500; www.crumlinroadgaol.com; 53-55 Crumlin Rd; adult/child £7.50/5.50; ⊙ 10am-5.30pm) Since it opened in 1846, Belfast's notorious Crumlin Road Gaol has imprisoned a whole range of historic figures, from Éamon de Valera to the Reverend Ian Paisley, and from suffragette Dorothy Evans to the 'Shankill Butcher' murderer Lenny Murphy. Designed by Charles Lanyon (the architect of Queen's University and many other city landmarks), and based on London's Pentonville prison, 'The Crum' was also the scene of 17 executions between 1854 and 1961.

The guided tour takes you from the tunnel beneath Crumlin Rd, built in 1850 to convey prisoners from the courthouse across the street (and allegedly the origin of the judge's phrase 'take him down'), through the echoing halls and cramped cells of C-Wing, to the truly chilling execution chamber – it's hard not to feel that the guide's light-hearted banter is inappropriate here and there's a genuine sense of relief at getting out in the open air again.

It's best to book tours in advance using the website. The jail's pedestrian entrance is on Crumlin Rd; if you're driving, the car park entrance is reached via Cliftonpark Ave on the north side.

as Samson and Goliath (dating from the 1970s). The area is currently undergoing a £1-billion regeneration project known as Titanic Quarter (www.titanicquarter.com), which plans to transform the long-derelict docklands over the next 15 to 20 years.

Queen's Rd strikes northeast from the Odyssey Complex into the heart of the Titanic Quarter, a massive redevelopment area that is part industrial wasteland, part building site and part high-tech business park. Not much remains from the time when the *Titanic* was built, but what does has been restored, and the challenging modern outline of Titanic Belfast now forms the centrepiece of the district. A series of information boards along Queen's Rd describe items and areas of interest.

★Titanic Belfast   EXHIBITION
(Map p568; www.titanicbelfast.com; Queen's Rd; adult/child £14.75/7.25; ⊙ 9am-7pm Apr-Sep, 10am-5pm Oct-Mar) The head of the slipway where the *Titanic* was built is now occupied by the gleaming, angular edifice of Titanic Belfast, an all-singing all-dancing multimedia extravaganza that charts the history of Belfast and the creation of the world's most famous ocean liner. Since opening in April 2012, the centenary of the ship's sinking, it has rapidly become Northern Ireland's most popular tourist attraction, outstripping even the Giant's Causeway.

Cleverly designed exhibits enlivened by historic images, animated projections and soundtracks chart Belfast's rise to turn-of-the-20th-century industrial superpower, fol-

lowed by a high-tech ride through a noisy, smells-and-all re-creation of the city's shipyards. You can then explore every detail of the *Titanic*'s construction, from a computer 'fly-through' from keel to bridge, to replicas of the passenger accommodation. Perhaps most poignant are the few flickering images that constitute the only film footage of the ship in existence.

SS Nomadic   HISTORIC SHIP
(Map p568; www.nomadicbelfast.com; Queen's Rd; adult/child £38.50/5; ⊙ 10am-6pm Apr-Sep, 10am-5pm Oct-Mar) The Hamilton Graving Dock, just northeast of the Odyssey Complex, is now the permanent berth of SS *Nomadic* – the only surviving vessel of the White Star Line (the shipping company that owned the *Titanic*). In 2006 she was rescued from the breaker's yard and brought to Belfast. The little steamship once served as a tender ferrying 1st- and 2nd-class passengers between Cherbourg Harbour and the giant Olympic Class ocean liners (which were too big to dock at the French port); on 10 April 1912 she delivered 142 1st-class passengers to the ill-fated *Titanic*. Now fully restored, she is home to an exhibition on the ship's history and her part in the *Titanic* story.

Harland & Wolff
Drawing Offices   HISTORIC BUILDING
(Map p568; Queen's Rd; ⊙ guided tours only) Just along the road from the *Nomadic* are the original Harland & Wolff drawing offices, where the designs for the *Titanic* were first drawn up; you can see inside only as part of

a guided tour such as Titanic Tours (p570). Behind the building, where the new Titanic Belfast attraction now sits (though best seen from a boat tour on the river), are the two massive slipways where the *Titanic* and her sister ship *Olympic* were built and launched.

Thompson Pump House &
Graving Dock   HISTORIC SITE
(Map p568; www.titanicsdock.com; Queens Rd; 10am-4.30pm Sat-Thu, 9.30am-4.30pm Fri;) **FREE** At the far end of Queens Rd is the most impressive monument to the days of the great liners – the vast Thompson Graving Dock where the *Titanic* was fitted out. Its huge size gives you some idea of the scale of the ship, which could only just fit into it.

Beside the dock is the Thompson Pump House, which has an exhibition on Belfast shipbuilding (there's a cafe, too). Guided tours (adult/child £6/4; hourly 11am-3pm) include a viewing of original film footage from the shipyards, a visit to the inner workings of the pump house and a walk along the floor of the dry dock.

In the dock on the far side of the pump house, naval-history buffs can see HMS Caroline, the UK's last surviving WWI Royal Navy cruiser. Built in 1914, the ship is being converted into a floating museum scheduled to open in 2016.

Odyssey Complex   LANDMARK
(Map p556; Sydenham Rd) The Odyssey Complex is a huge sporting and entertainment centre on the eastern side of the river across from Clarendon Dock. It features a hands-on science centre, W5; a 10,000-seater sports arena (home to the Belfast Giants ice-hockey team); a multiplex cinema with an IMAX screen; a video-games centre; and a dozen restaurants, cafes and bars.

The complex is a five-minute walk across Lagan Weir from the city centre. Metro bus 26 from Wellington Pl to Holywood stops outside the complex (five minutes, hourly Monday to Friday only).

W5   SCIENCE CENTRE
(Map p556; www.w5online.co.uk; Sydenham Rd, Odyssey Complex; adult/child £7.90/5.90, 2 adults & 2 children £23.50; 10am-5pm Mon-Fri, 10am-6pm Sat, noon-6pm Sun, last admission 1hr before closing;) Also known as whowhatwherewhenwhy, W5 is an interactive science centre aimed at children of all ages. Kids can compose their own tunes by biffing the 'air harp' with a foam rubber bat, try to beat a lie detector, create cloud rings and tornadoes, and design and build their own robots and racing cars.

◎ South Belfast (Queen's Quarter)

The Golden Mile – the 1.5km stretch of Great Victoria St and Shaftesbury Sq that links the city centre to Queen's Quarter (the university district) – was once the focus for much of Belfast's nightlife. These days, with the regeneration of the city centre, it's more tarnished brass than gold, but it still has a handful of decent pubs and eateries. Some of the Golden Mile's former glow has moved

BELFAST SIGHTS

WALK: LAGAN TOWPATH

Part of Belfast's Laganside redevelopment project was the restoration of the towpath along the west bank of the River Lagan. You can now walk or cycle for 20km along the winding riverbank from central Belfast to Lisburn. The cafe in Lisburn's Island Arts Centre (www.islandartscentre.com) makes a good target.

A shorter walk along the towpath (10km) starts from Shaw's Bridge on the southern edge of the city and heads back towards the city centre. Take bus 8A or 8B from Donegall Sq E to the stop just before the Malone roundabout (where Malone Rd becomes Upper Malone Rd). Bear left at the roundabout (signposted Outer Ring A55) and you'll reach the River Lagan at Shaw's Bridge.

Turn left and follow the towpath downstream on the left bank of the river (waymarked with red '9' signs), passing a restored lock-keeper's cottage and canalside cafe at lock number 3. The most attractive part of the walk is Lagan Meadows (Map p568), a tree-fringed loop in the river to the right of the path and a good place for a picnic on a summer's day. Further along, Cutters Wharf (p577) is also a great place for a lunch break. From the pub the walk continues to Lagan Weir (p560) in the city centre. Alternatively, make the walk from the city to Shaw's Bridge and catch the bus back.

to Lisburn Rd, which is lined with trendy boutiques, cafes and wine bars.

Metro buses 8A, 8B and 8C run from Donegall Sq E along Bradbury Pl and University Rd to Queen's University.

★ Ulster Museum   MUSEUM
(Map p556; www.nmni.com/um; Stranmillis Rd; ⊘10am-5pm Tue-Sun; ☻) FREE Following a major revamp, the Ulster Museum is now one of the North's don't-miss attractions. You could spend several hours browsing the beautifully designed displays, but if you're pressed for time don't miss the Armada Room, Takabuti (a 2500-year-old Egyptian mummy), the Bann Disc and the Snapshot of an Ancient Sea Floor.

On the ground floor, a potted history of the Troubles leads up to the 1st-floor History Zone where the Armada Room houses a display of artefacts and jewellery recovered from the 1588 wreck of the *Girona* and other Spanish Armada vessels. Among its many treasures is a 16th-century ruby-encrusted golden salamander, bronze cannons, and personal belongings of the officers and crew, including pipes, combs and buttons.

On the same floor is the Early Peoples gallery, a spectacular collection of prehistoric stone and bronze artefacts that help provide a cultural context for Ireland's many archaeological sites. The exhibits are beautifully displayed – the Malone Hoard, a clutch of 16 polished, Neolithic stone axes discovered only a few kilometres from the museum, looks more like a modern sculpture than a museum exhibit, while the Bann Disc is a superb example of Celtic design dating from the Iron Age.

The centrepiece of the Egyptian Room is the mummy of Princess Takabuti. She was unwrapped in Belfast in 1835, the first mummy ever to be displayed outside Egypt; more recently, her bleached hair has led the locals to dub her 'Belfast's oldest bleached blonde'.

The Nature Zone on the 2nd floor covers geological time, evolution and natural history, with interactive exhibits that will keep the children busy for an hour or two. Highlights include the Snapshot of an Ancient Sea Floor – a fossilised portion of 200-million-year-old seabed with jumbled ammonite shells and petrified driftwood – the Sea Around Us gallery, and preserved specimens that include a Mexican red-knee tarantula and the now-extinct Tasmanian tiger.

The top floors are given over to Irish and European art, most notably the works of Belfast-born Sir John Lavery (1856–1941), who became one of the most fashionable and expensive portraitists of Victorian London. More modern paintings include Edward McGuire's 1974 portrait of poet Seamus Heaney.

Queen's University   HISTORIC BUILDING
(Map p556; University Rd; guided tours per person £5) If you think that Charles Lanyon's Queen's College (1849), a Tudor Revival building in red brick and honey-coloured sandstone, has something of an Oxbridge air about it, that may be because he based the design of the central tower on the 15th-century Founder's Tower at Oxford's Magdalen College. Northern Ireland's most prestigious university was founded by Queen Victoria in 1845, one of three Queen's colleges (the others, still around but no longer called Queen's colleges, are in Cork and Galway) created to provide a non-denominational alternative to the Anglican Church's Trinity College in Dublin. In 1908 the college became the Queen's University of Belfast and today its campus spreads across some 250 buildings. Queen's has around 25,000 students and enjoys a strong reputation in medicine, engineering and law.

Just inside the main entrance is the Queen's Welcome Centre (www.queensventus.com; University Rd; ⊘9.30am-4.30pm Mon-Sat, 10am-1pm Sun) FREE with exhibitions and a souvenir shop. Guided tours are available with advance booking, or you can pick up a leaflet that describes a self-guided tour.

Botanic Gardens   GARDENS
(Map p556; Stranmillis Rd; ⊘7.30am-sunset) The green oasis of Belfast's Botanic Gardens is a short stroll from Queen's University. Just inside the Stranmillis Rd gate is a statue of Belfast-born William Thomson, Lord Kelvin, who helped lay the foundation of modern physics and who invented the Kelvin scale, which measures temperatures from absolute zero (-273°C or 0°K).

The gardens' centrepiece is Charles Lanyon's beautiful Palm House (Map p556; ⊘10am-noon & 1-5pm Apr-Sep, to 4pm Oct-Mar) FREE built in 1839 and completed in 1852, with its birdcage dome, a masterpiece in cast-iron and curvilinear glass. Nearby is the Tropical Ravine (Map p556; ⊘10am-noon & 1-4.45pm Apr-Sep, to 3.45pm Oct-Mar) FREE a huge red-brick greenhouse designed by the garden's curator Charles McKimm and completed in 1889. Inside, a raised walkway overlooks a jungle of tropical ferns, orchids, lilies and banana plants growing in a sunken glen.

⊙ West Belfast (Gaeltacht Quarter)

Northwest of Donegall Sq, Divis St leads across the Westlink Motorway to Falls Rd and West Belfast (Gaeltacht Quarter). Though scarred by three decades of civil unrest, the former battleground of West Belfast is one of the most compelling places to visit in Northern Ireland. Recent history hangs heavy in the air, but there is a noticeable spirit of optimism and hope for the future.

The main attractions are the powerful murals that chart the history of the conflict, as well as the political passions of the moment and, for visitors from mainland Britain, there is a grim fascination to be found in wandering through the former 'war zone' in their own backyard.

West Belfast grew up around the linen mills that propelled the city into late-19th-century prosperity. It was an area of low-cost, working-class housing, and even in the Victorian era was divided along religious lines. The advent of the Troubles in 1968 solidified the sectarian divide, and since 1970 the ironically named 'Peace Line' has separated the Loyalist and Protestant Shankill district from the Republican and Catholic Falls district.

Despite its past reputation, the area is safe to visit. The best way to see West Belfast is on a black taxi tour. The cabs visit the more spectacular murals as well as the Peace Line (where you can write a message on the wall) and other significant sites, while the drivers provide a colourful commentary on the history of the area.

There's nothing to stop you visiting under your own steam, either walking or using the shared black taxis that travel along the Falls and Shankill Rds. Alternatively, buses 10A to 10F from Queen St will take you along the Falls Rd; buses 11A to 11D from Wellington Pl go along Shankill Rd.

You can also pick up a range of free leaflets at the Belfast Welcome Centre that describe walking tours around the Falls and Shankill districts.

⊙ Falls Road

Although the signs of past conflict are inescapable, the Falls today is an unexpectedly lively, colourful and optimistic place. Local people are friendly and welcoming, and community ventures such as Conway Mill and the Cultúrlann centre and black taxi tours have seen tourist numbers increase dramatically.

Cultúrlann McAdam Ó Fiaich CULTURAL CENTRE
(Map p568; www.culturlann.ie; 216 Falls Rd; ⊙9am-9pm Mon-Thu, 9am-6pm Fri-Sat, 11am-4pm Sun; ☎) **FREE** This Irish language and cultural centre, housed in a red-brick former Presbyterian church, is the focus for West Belfast's community activity. It's a cosy and welcoming place with a tourist information desk, a shop selling a wide selection of books on Ireland, Irish-language material, crafts and Irish music CDs, and a good cafe-restaurant, Caifé Feirste (p577). The centre also has an art gallery and a theatre that stages music, drama and poetry events.

BELFAST SIGHTS

RMS TITANIC

Perhaps the most famous vessel ever launched, RMS *Titanic* was built in Belfast's Harland & Wolff shipyard for the White Star Line. When her keel was laid in 1909 Belfast was at the height of its fame as a shipbuilding powerhouse, and the *Titanic* was promoted by White Star as the world's biggest and most luxurious ocean liner. Ironically, it was also claimed to be 'unsinkable'.

She was launched from H&W's slipway no 3 on 31 May 1911, and spent almost a year being fitted out in the nearby Thompson Graving Dock before leaving Belfast for her maiden voyage on 2 April 1912. In one of the most notorious nautical disasters of all time, she hit an iceberg in the North Atlantic on 14 April 1912, and sank in the early hours of the following day. Of the 2228 passengers and crew on board, only 705 survived; there were only enough lifeboats for 1178 people.

The **Titanic Stories** (www.the-titanic.com) website contains a wealth of information on the ship and her passengers, and lists all *Titanic*-related museums and memorials throughout Ireland and the rest of the world.

Around Central Belfast

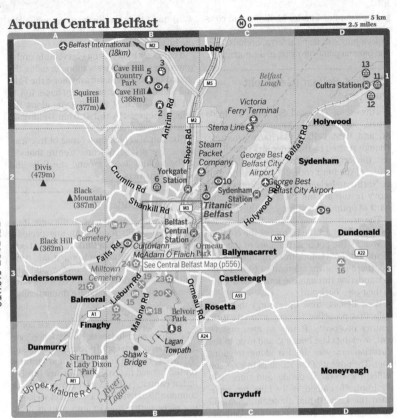

Conway Mill   ARTS CENTRE
(Map p556; www.conwaymill.org; 5-7 Conway St; ⊙10am-5pm Mon-Fri, 10am-2pm Sat) Conway Mill is a restored 19th-century flax mill that now houses around 20 artists' studios, an exhibition on the mill's history, an education centre and work spaces for local enterprises. It also houses the **Irish Republican History Museum** (⊙10am-2pm Tue-Sat), a collection of artefacts, newspaper articles, photos and archives relating to the Republican struggle from 1798 to the Troubles.

◉ Shankill Road

Although the Protestant Shankill district (from the Irish *sean chill,* meaning 'old church') has received less media attention than the Falls, it also contains many interesting murals. The people here are just as friendly, but the Shankill has far fewer tourists than the Falls. Loyalist communities seem to have more difficulty in presenting their side of the story than the Republicans, who have a far more polished approach to public relations.

To reach Shankill Rd on foot, set off north from City Hall along Donegall Pl and Royal Ave, then turn left on North St and continue straight on across the Westlink Motorway.

◉ Outside the Centre

Ulster Folk & Transport Museums   MUSEUM
(Map p568; www.nmni.com/uftm; Cultra, Holywood; adult/child £7.50/4.50, combined ticket to both museums £9/5; ⊙10am-5pm Tue-Sun Mar-Sep, 10am-4pm Tue-Fri & 11am-4pm Sat & Sun Oct-Feb) Really two museums in one, and lying on either side of the A2 road to Bangor, just north of Holywood, the Ulster Folk & Transport Museum is one of Northern Ireland's finest.

Buses to Bangor stop nearby. Cultra Station on the Belfast to Bangor train line is within a 10-minute walk.

Around Central Belfast

➜ Ulster Folk Museum

(Map p568) Farmhouses, forges, churches and mills, and a complete village have been reconstructed here, with human and animal extras combining to give a powerful impression of Irish life over the past few hundred years. From industrial times, there are red-brick terraces from 19th-century Belfast and Dromore. In summer, thatching and ploughing are demonstrated and there are characters dressed in period costume.

➜ Ulster Transport Museum

(Map p568) The Transport Museum is a sort of automotive zoo, with displays of captive steam locomotives, rolling stock, motorcycles, trams, buses and cars. The highlight of the car collection is the stainless-steel-clad prototype of the ill-fated DeLorean DMC, made in Belfast in 1981. The car was a commercial disaster but achieved everlasting fame in the *Back to the Future* films.

Most popular is the new Titanica exhibit, opened in 2012, which includes the original design drawings for the *Titanic* and its sister ship *Olympic,* and photographs of the ships' construction. The story of the tragedy is brought to life with displays of original items including White Star Line brochures, tickets for the ill-fated voyage and objects recovered from the wreck.

Stormont   NOTABLE BUILDING
(Map p568; Parliament Buildings; www.niassembly. gov.uk; Upper Newtonards Rd; ☺grounds 7.30am-dusk) FREE The dazzling white neoclassical facade of the Parliament Buildings at Stormont is one of Belfast's most iconic buildings; in the North, 'Stormont' carries the same connotation as 'Westminster' does in Britain and 'Washington' in the USA – the seat of power. For 40 years, from its completion in 1932 until the introduction of direct rule in 1972, it was the seat of the parliament of Northern Ireland. More recently, on 8 May 2007, it returned to the forefront of Irish politics when Ian Paisley and Martin McGuinness – who had been the best of enemies for decades – laughed and smiled as they were sworn in as first minister and deputy first minister, respectively.

The building occupies a dramatic position at the end of a gently rising, 1.5km avenue and is fronted by a defiant statue of the arch-Unionist Sir Edward Carson. Nearby, 19th-century Stormont Castle is, like Hillsborough in County Down, an official residence of the Secretary of State for Northern Ireland. In July and August only, there are free guided tours of the parliament buildings, departing hourly from 10am to 3pm on weekdays. Otherwise, you are free to walk around the extensive grounds, or you can take a video tour on the website.

Stormont is 8km east of the city centre. Take bus 20A from Donegall Sq W.

Cave Hill Country Park   PARK
(Map p568; Antrim Rd; ☺7.30am-dusk) The best way to get a feel for Belfast's natural setting is to view it from above. The view from the summit of Cave Hill (368m), which looms over the city's northern fringes, takes in the

BELFAST SIGHTS

whole sprawl of the city, the docks and the creeping fingers of urbanisation along the shores of Belfast Lough. The rounded forms of the Mourne Mountains can be seen far away to the south and on a clear day you can even spot Scotland lurking on the horizon.

The hill was originally called Ben Madigan, after the 9th-century Ulster king, Matudhain. Its distinctive, craggy profile, seen from the south, has been known to locals for two centuries as 'Napoleon's Nose' – it supposedly bears some resemblance to Bonaparte's schnoz, but you might take some convincing. On the summit is an Iron Age earthwork known as McArt's Fort where members of the United Irishmen, including Wolfe Tone, looked down over the city in 1795 and pledged to fight for Irish independence. The path leading to the summit from the zoo or castle car park passes beneath the caves that give the hill its name.

Cave Hill Country Park spreads across the hill's eastern slopes, with several waymarked walks and an adventure playground for kids aged three to 14 years. To get here, take any of buses 1A to 1G from Royal Ave to Belfast Castle or Belfast Zoo.

Belfast Castle CASTLE
(Map p568; www.belfastcastle.co.uk; Antrim Rd; ⊙9am-6pm Mon, 9am-10pm Tue-Sat, 9am-5.30pm Sun) FREE Built in 1870 for the third Marquess of Donegall, in the Scottish Baronial style made fashionable by Queen Victoria's then recently built Balmoral, the multi-turreted pomp of Belfast Castle commands the southeastern slopes of Cave Hill. It was presented to the City of Belfast in 1934.

Extensive renovation between 1978 and 1988 has left the interior comfortably modern rather than intriguingly antique, and the castle is now a popular venue for wedding receptions. Upstairs is the Cave Hill Visitor Centre with a few displays on the folklore, history, archaeology and natural history of the park. Downstairs is the Cellar Restaurant and a small antiques shop.

Legend has it that the castle's residents will experience good fortune only as long as a white cat lives there, a tale commemorated in the beautiful formal gardens by nine portrayals of cats in mosaic, painting, sculpture and garden furniture – a good game for the kids is getting them to find all nine.

Belfast Zoo ZOO
(Map p568; www.belfastzoo.co.uk; Antrim Rd; adult/child £10.50/5.25, under 4yrs, seniors & visitors with disabilities free; ⊙10am-6pm Mon-Fri, to 7pm Sat-Sun Apr-Sep, 10am-4pm Oct-Mar) Belfast Zoo is one of the most appealing zoos in Britain and Ireland, with spacious enclosures set on an attractive, sloping site; the sea lion and penguin pool with its underwater viewing is particularly good. Some of the more unusual animals include tamarins, Malaysian sun bears and red pandas, but the biggest attractions are the ultracute meerkats, the colony of ring-tailed lemurs and the herd of Rothschild's giraffe.

Tours

You can find full details of organised tours at the Belfast Welcome Centre. If you want to hire a personal guide, call the Welcome Centre or contact the Northern Ireland Tourist Guide Association (www.bluebadgeireland.com; half-/full-day tours £80/150).

Belfast iTours (belfastitours.com) offers 10 self-guided video tours of the city that you can download to your smartphone or MP4 player; alternatively you can hire a preloaded MP4 player (£9 for 24 hours) from the Belfast Welcome Centre.

Lagan Boat Company BOAT TOUR
(Map p556; ☑9033 0844; www.laganboatcompany.com; adult/child £10/8; ⊙12.30pm, 2pm & 3.30pm daily Apr-Sep, 12.30 & 2pm daily Oct, 12.30 & 2pm Sat & Sun Nov-Mar) The excellent Titanic Tour explores the derelict docklands downstream of Lagan Weir, taking in the slipways where the liners *Titanic* and *Olympic* were launched and the huge dry dock where they could fit with just 23cm to spare; departs from Donegall Quay near the *Bigfish* sculpture.

Titanic Tours GUIDED TOUR
(☑07852 716655; www.titanictours-belfast.co.uk; adult/child £30/15; ⊙on demand) A three-hour luxury tour led by the great-granddaughter of one of the *Titanic*'s crew, visiting various *Titanic*-related sites. For groups of two to five people; includes pick-up and drop-off at your accommodation.

Belfast Bike Tours GUIDED TOUR
(☑07812 114235; www.belfastbiketours.com; per person £15; ⊙10.30am & 2pm Mon, Wed, Fri & Sat Apr-Sep, Sat only Oct-Mar) These 2½-hour guided tours depart from outside Queen's University and take you on a leisurely spin along the Lagan Valley to the Giant's Ring and back again. Bikes provided; book in advance.

Belfast Pub Tours   GUIDED TOUR
(Map p556; ☎028-9268 3665; www.belfastpubtours.
com; per person £8; ☺7pm Thu & 4pm Sat May-Oct)
A two-hour tour (not including drinks) taking in six of the city's historic pubs, departing from the Crown Dining Rooms, above the
Crown Liquor Saloon on Great Victoria St.

Belfast City Sightseeing   BUS TOUR
(Map p556; ☎9032 1321; www.belfastcitysightsee
ing.com; adult/child £12.50/6; ☺every 15-30min
10am-4pm) Runs 1¼-hour open-top bus tours
that take in City Hall, the Albert Clock, the
Titanic Quarter, the Botanic Gardens, and
the Falls Rd and Shankill Rd murals in West
Belfast. Departs from Castle Pl; hop-on hop-
off tickets valid for 48 hours.

Taxi Tours
Black taxi tours of West Belfast's murals –
known locally as the 'bombs and bullets'
or 'doom and gloom' tours – are offered by
a large number of taxi companies and local
cabbies. These can vary in quality and content, but in general they're an intimate and
entertaining way to see the sights and can be
customised to suit your own interests. There
are also historical taxi tours of the city centre.
For a one-hour tour expect to pay around
£30 total for one or two people, and £10 per
person for three to six. Call and they will pick
you up from anywhere in the city centre.
   The following are recommended:

Harpers Taxi Tours (☎07711 757178; www.
harperstaxitours.co.nr)

Official Black Taxi Tours (☎9064 2264;
www.belfasttours.com)

Original Belfast Black Taxi Tours
(☎07751 565359; www.originalbelfasttours.com)

⭐ Festivals & Events

Belfast City Council (www.belfastcity.gov.
uk/events) organises a wide range of events
throughout the year, covering everything
from the St Patrick's Day parade to the Lord
Mayor's Show. It has a useful online events
calendar, as does the **Belfast Welcome
Centre** (visit-belfast.com/whats-on).

Féile an Earraigh   MUSIC
(www.feilebelfast.com; ☺Feb, Mar) This four-day
festival of traditional Irish and Celtic music
attracts artists from all over Ireland, Europe
and America.

St Patrick's Day   CULTURE
(www.belfastcity.gov.uk/events; ☺17 Mar) A celebration of Ireland's patron saint marked by
various community festivals and culminating in a grand city-centre parade.

Belfast Film Festival   FILM
(www.belfastfilmfestival.org; ☺early Apr) Two-
week celebration of Irish and international
film.

Titanic Belfast Festival   CULTURE
(☺late May) Week-long celebration of the
world's most famous ship, and the city that
built her, with special exhibitions, tours,
lectures and film screenings. Check dates at
belfastcity.gov.uk/events.

Festival of Fools   STREET THEATRE
(www.foolsfestival.com; ☺late Apr/early May) This
five-day festival of street entertainment has
events concentrated in the Cathedral Quarter and city centre. The fun continues on
Sunday afternoons in July and August.

Belfast Marathon   SPORT
(www.belfastcitymarathon.com; ☺1st Mon in May)
Avid runners from across the globe come to
compete in the marathon; it's also a people's
event, with a walk and fun run as well.

Cathedral Quarter Arts Festival   ARTS
(www.cqaf.com; ☺early May) Ten days of drama,
music, poetry, street theatre and art exhibitions in and around the Cathedral Quarter.

Belfast Maritime Festival   MARITIME
(visit-belfast.com/whats-on; ☺late May, early Jun)
A three-day festival centred on Queen's Quay
and Clarendon Dock, with sailing ships,
street entertainment, a seafood festival and
live music.

Belfast Book Festival   LITERATURE
(www.belfastbookfestival.com; ☺Jun) A week
of all things book-related, from films and
readings to workshops and meet-the-author
events, at venues throughout the city.

Belfast Pride   GAY & LESBIAN
(www.belfastpride.com; ☺Jul) Ireland's larg-
est celebration of gay, lesbian, bisexual and
transgender culture, culminating in a huge
city-centre parade; takes place over a week.

Féile An Phobail   CULTURE
(www.feilebelfast.com; ☺early Aug) Said to be
the largest community festival in Ireland,
the Féile takes place in West Belfast over
10 days. Events include an opening carnival
parade, street parties, theatre performances,
concerts and historical tours of the City and
Milltown cemeteries.

Belfast Festival at Queen's ARTS
(www.belfastfestival.com; ☺late Oct) The UK's second-largest arts festival held in and around Queen's University over two weeks.

Christmas Festivities CULTURE
(www.belfastcity.gov.uk/events; ☺late Nov-31 Dec) There's a range of events, including a Christmas market, carol singing, lamplight processions and a street carnival.

🛏 Sleeping

From backpacker hostels to boutique hotels, the range of places to stay in Belfast gets wider every year. The traditional accommodation scene – red-brick B&Bs in the leafy suburbs of South Belfast and city-centre business hotels – is lent a splash of colour in the form of stylish hotel–restaurant–nightclub combos or boutique hotels set in refurbished historic buildings.

Most of Belfast's budget and midrange accommodation is south of the centre, in the university district around Botanic Ave, University Rd and Malone Rd. This area is also crammed with good-value restaurants and pubs, and is mostly within a 20-minute walk of City Hall.

Book ahead in summer or during busy festival periods. The Belfast Welcome Centre will make reservations for a fee of £2. You can also book accommodation through the Lonely Planet website (http://hotels.lonely planet.com).

🛏 City Centre

Park Inn HOTEL ££
(Map p556; ☎9067 7710; www.parkinn.co.uk/hotel -belfast; 4 Clarence St W; r from £98; ☎🖳) This modern hotel boasts a bright and breezy at-mosphere, with slick styling and splashes of bold primary colours. It has a top location, too – only five minutes from City Hall and close to loads of good pubs and restaurants – and is excellent value. There are eight wheelchair-accessible rooms, and family rooms can be arranged.

★**Malmaison Hotel** HOTEL £££
(Map p556; ☎0844 693 0650; www.malmaison -belfast.com; 34-38 Victoria St; r from £123, ste from £269; @☎) Housed in a pair of beautifully restored Italianate warehouses (originally built for rival firms in the 1850s), the Malmaison is a luxurious haven of king-size beds, deep leather sofas and roll-top baths big enough for two, all done up in a decadent decor of black, red, dark chocolate and cream. The massive, rock-star Samson suite has a giant bed (almost 3m long), a huge bathtub and, wait for it...a billiard table, with purple baize.

★**Ten Square** HOTEL £££
(Map p556; ☎9024 1001; www.tensquare.co.uk; 10 Donegall Sq S; r from £115; @☎) A former bank building to the south of City Hall that has been given a designer feng-shui makeover, Ten Square is an opulent, Shanghai-inspired boutique hotel with friendly and attentive service. Magazines such as *Cosmopolitan* and *Conde Nast Traveller* drool over the dark lacquered wood, low-slung futon-style beds and sumptuous linen, and the list of former guests includes Bono and Brad Pitt.

Fitzwilliam Hotel HOTEL £££
(Map p556; ☎028-9044 2080; www.fitzwilliam hotelbelfast.com; 1-3 Great Victoria St; r from £115; @☎) Enjoying a truly central location, the Fitzwilliam pushes all the right style buttons

---

THE GLORIOUS TWELFTH

In Northern Ireland the 12 July public holiday marks the anniversary of the Protestant victory at the 1690 Battle of the Boyne. It is celebrated with bonfires, marching bands and street parades staged by the Orange Order, the biggest of which takes place in Belfast.

Although the 12 July parades have regularly been associated with sectarian stand-offs and outbursts of violence, there has been a concerted effort in recent years to promote the Belfast parade as a cultural and family-friendly celebration, even going as far as to rebrand it Orangefest (details from Belfast Welcome Centre).

However, many people still perceive the parades as divisive and confrontational, and with high levels of alcolhol consumption among the crowds there is a potential for dangerous situations. The city centre part of the parade, around Royal Ave and Donegall Sq, is generally safe, but visitors need to be alert for signs of trouble, follow local advice and expect extra security if things escalate in any way.

with its use of designer fabrics, cool colours and mood lighting. Bedrooms have crisp linen sheets, fluffy bathrobes and powerful showers, and the staff are unstintingly helpful. The hotel's restaurant, established by Michelin-starred Dublin chef Kevin Thornton, is excellent too.

Merchant Hotel
HOTEL £££

(Map p556; ☑ 9023 4888; www.themerchanthotel. com; 35-39 Waring St; r/ste from £180/300; @ ☎) Belfast's most flamboyant Victorian building (the old Ulster Bank head office) has been converted into the city's most flamboyant boutique hotel, a fabulous fusion of contemporary styling and old-fashioned elegance.

South Belfast

To get to places on or near Botanic Ave, take bus 7A or 7B from Howard St. For places on or near University and Malone Rds, take bus 8A or 8B, and for places on or near Lisburn Rd, take bus 9A or 9B; buses depart from Donegall Sq E and from the bus stop on Great Victoria St across from the Europa Bus Centre.

★ Vagabonds
HOSTEL £

(Map p556; ☑ 9023 3017; www.vagabondsbelfast. com; 9 University Rd; dm £13-16, tw or d £40; @ ☎) Comfy bunks, lockable luggage baskets, private shower cubicles and a relaxed atmosphere are what you get at one of Belfast's best hostels, run by a couple of experienced travellers. Conveniently located close to both Queen's and the city centre.

City Backpacker
HOSTEL £

(Map p556; ☑ 9066 0030; www.ibackpacker.co.uk; 53-55 Malone Ave; dm/d £14/40; @ ☎) Leafy South Belfast sprouts another top hostel, stylishly decked out with shiny IKEA-style kit. It's squeezed into a three-storey terrace house on a quiet suburban avenue, so can be a bit cramped when busy; off-season, you can often have a room to yourself.

Arnie's Backpackers
HOSTEL £

(Map p556; ☑ 9024 2867; www.arniesbackpack ers.co.uk; 63 Fitzwilliam St; dm £14-16, tw or d £44; @ ☎) This long-established old-school hostel is set in a quiet terraced house in the university area. A bit on the small side, but coal fires and a friendly crowd make it more cosy than cramped.

Global Village Backpackers
HOSTEL £

(Map p556; ☑ 9031 3533; globalvillagebelfast.com; 87 University St; dm £14-16, d £44; @ ☎) This is a relatively new place in a terrace house close to Queen's University, proudly sporting a beer garden, a barbecue and a games room.

★ Tara Lodge
B&B ££

(Map p556; ☑ 9059 0900; www.taralodge.com; 36 Cromwell Rd; s/d from £79/89; @ ☎) This B&B is a cut above the average, feeling more like a boutique hotel with its clean-cut, minimalist decor, friendly and efficient staff, delicious breakfasts (including porridge with Bushmills whiskey) and 24 bright and cheerful rooms. It's in a great location too, on a quiet side street just a few paces from the buzz of Botanic Ave.

★ Old Rectory
B&B ££

(Map p568; ☑ 9066 7882; www.anoldrectory. co.uk; 148 Malone Rd; s/d £55/86; @ ☎) A lovely Victorian villa with lots of original stained glass, this former rectory has five spacious bedrooms, a comfortable drawing room with leather sofa, and fancy breakfasts (wild boar sausages, scrambled eggs with smoked salmon, veggie fry-ups, freshly squeezed OJ). It's a 10-minute bus ride from the centre – the inconspicuous driveway is on the left, just past Deramore Park South. No credit cards.

All Seasons B&B
B&B ££

(Map p568; ☑ 9068 2814; www.allseasonsbelfast. com; 356 Lisburn Rd; s/d/f £35/50/55; ☎) Away from the centre, but right in the heart of trendy Lisburn Rd, All Seasons is a redbrick villa with bright, colourful bedrooms, modern bathrooms, a stylish little breakfast room and a comfortable lounge. Take bus 9A or 9B from the city centre; a taxi will cost around £7. The house is between Cranmore Ave and Cranmore Gardens, 150m past the big police station.

Malone Lodge Hotel
HOTEL ££

(Map p556; ☑ 9038 8060; www.malonelodge hotelbelfast.com; 60 Eglantine Ave; s/d/apt from £79/95/175; ☎) The centrepiece of a tree-lined Victorian terrace, the modern Malone Lodge has pulled in many plaudits for its large, luxurious rooms with elegantly understated decor, good food and pleasant, helpful staff. Some bedrooms are in a separate building; it also offers five-star self-catering apartments (one- and two-bedroom).

Benedicts
HOTEL ££

(Map p556; ☑ 9059 1999; www.benedictshotel. co.uk; 7-21 Bradbury Pl; s/d from £65/75; @ ☎) Set bang in the middle of the Golden Mile,

Benedicts is a modern, style-conscious hotel at the heart of South Belfast's nightlife. The rooms, complete with Egyptian cotton sheets and feather-bedded mattresses, are above a huge Gothic bar and restaurant (where you also have breakfast), so don't expect peace and quiet till after 1am.

Crescent Town House   HOTEL ££

(Map p556; ☑ 9032 3349; www.crescenttown house.com; 13 Lower Cres; s/d from £60/70; @ 🛜) A stylish boutique hotel with a perfect location, the Crescent is an elegant Victorian town house transformed into a den of designer chic, with its finger on the pulse of the city's party zone. Rooms have silky, Ralph Lauren–style decor and luxury bathrooms with Molton Brown toiletries and walk-in rain-head showers.

Kate's B&B   B&B ££

(Map p556; ☑ 9028 2091; katesbb127@hotmail. com; 127 University St; per person £25; 🛏) Kate's is a homey kind of place, from the window boxes bursting with colourful flowers to the cute dining room crammed with bric-a-brac, plus a couple of friendly cats. The bedrooms are basic but comfortable, and the showers are a bit cramped, but at this price – and only a few minutes' walk from Botanic Ave – we're not complaining.

🛏 Outside the Centre

Farset International   HOSTEL £

(Map p568; ☑ 9089 9833; www.farsetinternational. co.uk; 446 Springfield Rd; s/d/f from £30/40/50; 🛜) This community-run complex in West Belfast is best described as a posh hostel, set in grounds overlooking a small lake, offering 38 rooms with private bathroom and TV. Cooked/continental breakfast is £7/4.50 extra, and in the evening you can eat in the restaurant (if arranged in advance) or use the self-catering kitchen.

Dundonald Touring
Caravan Park   CAMPGROUND £

(Map p568; ☑ 9080 9129; www.theicebowl.com; 111 Old Dundonald Rd; campsites per tent/caravan from £15/23; ⊙ Mar-Oct) This small place (22 sites) in a park next to the Dundonald Icebowl is the nearest campground to Belfast, 7km east of the city centre and south of the A20 road to Newtownards.

🍴 Eating

In recent years, Belfast's restaurant scene has been totally transformed by a wave of new restaurants whose standards compare with the best eating places in Europe.

🍴 City Centre

The main shopping area north of Donegall Sq becomes a silent maze of deserted streets and steel shutters after 7pm, but during the day the many pubs, cafes and restaurants do a roaring trade. In the evening, the liveliest part of the city centre stretches south of Donegall Sq to Shaftesbury Sq.

Rhubarb Fresh Food Cafe   CAFE £

(Map p556; www.rhubarb-belfast.co.uk; 2 Little Victoria St; mains lunch £6-9, dinner £13-18; ⊙ 9am-4pm Tue-Wed, 9am-11pm Thu-Sat) Tucked away in a quiet corner, Rhubarb is a great place for tasty, freshly prepared food that's a cut above your usual cafe fare, from breakfast dishes such as French toast, omelettes and Ulster fry, to hot lunches such as fish and chips. The dinner menu takes things up a notch, with dishes such as boeuf bourguignon and slow-roast pork belly. BYO.

Archana   INDIAN £

(Map p556; www.archana.co.uk; 53 Dublin Rd; mains £7-15; ⊙ noon-2pm & 5pm-midnight) Cosy and unpretentious, Archana has a good range of vegetarian dishes. The *thali* – a platter of three curries – is good value at £15/12 for the meat/veggie version.

Morning Star   PUB £

(Map p556; www.themorningstarbar.com; 17 Pottinger's Entry; mains £9-22; ⊙ food 11.45am-9pm Mon-Sat; 🛜) Morning Star is famed for its all-you-can-eat lunch buffet (£6; served noon to 4pm).

★ OX   IRISH ££

(Map p556; ☑ 9031 4121; oxbelfast.com; 1 Oxford St; mains lunch £10, dinner £15-20; ⊙ lunch & dinner Tue-Sat) 🌿 A high-ceilinged space walled with cream-painted brick and furnished with warm golden wood creates a theatre-like ambience for the open kitchen at the back, where Michelin-trained chefs turn out some of Belfast's finest and best-value cuisine. The restaurant works with local suppliers and focuses on fine Irish beef, sustainable seafood and seasonal vegetables and fruit.

★ Ginger   BISTRO ££

(Map p556; ☑ 9024 4421; www.gingerbistro.com; 7-8 Hope St; mains £13-23; ⊙ lunch Tue-Sat, dinner Mon-Sat; 🛏) 🌿 Ginger is one of those places you could walk right past without noticing, but if you do you'll be missing out. It's a cosy and informal little bistro serving food that is anything but ordinary – the flame-haired owner-chef (hence the name) really knows what he's doing, sourcing top-quality Irish produce and turning out exquisite dishes such as scallops with crisp black pudding and chorizo butter. The lunch and pre-theatre (5pm to 6.45pm Monday to Friday) menus offer main courses for £9 to £14.

★Mourne Seafood Bar   SEAFOOD ££
(Map p556; ☑ 9024 8544; www.mourneseafood.com; 34-36 Bank St; mains £8-20; ☺ noon-9.30pm Mon-Thu, noon-4pm & 5-10.30pm Fri & Sat, 1-6pm Sun) ✦ This informal publike place, all red brick and dark wood with old oil lamps dangling from the ceiling, is tucked behind a fishmonger's shop, so the seafood is as fresh as it gets. On the menu are oysters served *au naturel* or Rockefeller, meltingly sweet scallops, lobster, langoustines, gurnard and sea bass. Hugely popular, so best book ahead, especially on Sunday.

★Deane's Restaurant   FRENCH, IRISH ££
(Map p556; ☑ 9033 1134; www.michaeldeane.co.uk; 34-40 Howard St; mains lunch £10, dinner £17-25; ☺ lunch & dinner Mon-Sat) ✦ Despite losing its Michelin star in 2011, the flagship of chef Michael Deane's restaurant fleet is still one of Northern Ireland's top restaurants. A simple, seasonal menu takes the best of Irish and British produce – beef, game, lamb, seafood – and gives it the gourmet treatment. The pre-theatre menu (5.30pm to 7pm) offers two/three courses for £15/20.

James St South   FRENCH, IRISH ££
(Map p556; ☑ 9043 4310; www.jamesstreetsouth.co.uk; 21 James St S; 2-/3-course lunch £16/19, dinner mains £17-22; ☺ lunch & dinner Mon-Sat) Graced by a large, impressionistic landscape by Irish artist Clement McAleer, this starkly beautiful dining room with crisp white table linen creates a perfect stage for the presentation of some of Belfast's finest food – the French-inspired menu offers dishes such as Irish scallops with crab beignet, asparagus and truffle – while the service is relaxed yet highly professional.

Bar & Grill   STEAKHOUSE ££
(Map p556; ☑ 9560 0700; www.belfastbargrill.co.uk; 21 James St S; mains £10-22; ☺ noon-9.30pm) James St South's sister restaurant is less formal, but the quality of the food is just as high. The menu concentrates on steaks,

burgers and lamb chops cooked on a Josper grill (a combined charcoal grill and oven), but also includes pasta, risotto and daily specials that include a fantastic venison pie with champ and red-wine gravy. Good brunch menu served weekends only.

Gingeroot   INDIAN ££
(Map p556; www.gingeroot.com; 73-75 Great Victoria St; mains £8-12; ☺ lunch Mon-Sat, dinner daily) A bright, modern restaurant that serves fresh and flavourful Indian dishes – the *jeera* (cumin) chicken is particularly tasty – Gingeroot offers an exceptionally good-value two-course lunch, available noon to 3pm Monday to Saturday (£6.50).

Deane's Deli Bistro   BISTRO ££
(Map p556; www.michaeldeane.co.uk; 44 Bedford St; mains £11-16; ☺ lunch Mon-Fri, dinner Mon-Sat) Enjoy top-notch nosh at this relaxed and informal bistro, with gourmet burgers and posh fish and chips on the menu.

Avoca Cafe   CAFE ££
(Map p556; 41 Arthur St; mains £9-14; ☺ 9.30am-5pm Mon-Fri, 9am-5pm Sat, 12.30-5pm Sun) You'll find healthy rolls, wraps, salads and sandwiches to eat in or take away here, as well as hot lunch specials such as grilled chicken with Mediterranean vegetables.

Great Room   FRENCH £££
(Map p556; ☑ 9023 4888; www.themerchanthotel.com; 35-39 Waring St, Merchant Hotel; mains £20-29; ☺ 7am-11pm) Set in the former banking hall of the Ulster Bank head office, the Great Room is a jaw-dropping extravaganza of gilded stucco, red plush, white marble cherubs and a vast crystal chandelier glittering beneath a glass dome. The menu matches the decor: decadent but delicious, a French-influenced catalogue of political incorrectness laced with foie gras and truffles. A set three-course dinner menu (£27) is available from 6.30pm to 10pm Monday to Thursday (£23 from 5.30 to 6.30pm).

✖ Cathedral Quarter & Around

John Hewitt Bar & Restaurant   PUB £
(Map p556; www.thejohnhewitt.com; 51 Donegall St; mains £7-9; ☺ food served noon-3pm Mon-Sat) Named for the Belfast poet and socialist, this is a modern pub with a traditional atmosphere and a well-earned reputation for excellent food. The menu changes weekly, but includes inventive dishes such as pork and black-pepper sausages with buttery mash

and red-wine gravy, and butter-bean-and-vegetable fritters. It's also a great place for a drink.

Hill Street Brasserie   FUSION ££
(Map p556; ☑ 9058 6868; www.hillstbrasserie.com; 38 Hill St; mains lunch £6, dinner £11-18; ☺ lunch Tue-Sun, dinner Wed-Sun) In keeping with the design studios and art galleries that throng the nearby streets, this little brasserie is desperately trendy, from the slate-and-wood floor to the aubergine-and-olive colour scheme. The express lunch menu is a bargain, offering a choice of homemade burger, beer-battered fish and chips or veggie dish (Thursday to Saturday).

Nick's Warehouse   BISTRO ££
(Map p556; www.nickswarehouse.co.uk; 35-39 Hill St; mains £11-23; ☺ food noon-3pm & 6-10pm Tue-Sat) ⚑ A Cathedral Quarter pioneer (opened in 1989), Nick's is an enormous red-brick and blond-wood wine bar and restaurant, buzzing with happy drinkers and diners. The seasonal menu is strong on local produce, and the wine list is intriguing.

✕ South Belfast

Maggie May's   CAFE £
(Map p556; 50 Botanic Ave; mains £3-7; ☺ 8am-10.30pm Mon-Sat, 10am-10.30pm Sun) This is a classic little cafe with cosy wooden booths, colourful murals of old Belfast, and a host of hungover students wolfing down huge Ulster fries at lunchtime. The all-day breakfast menu runs from tea and toast to eggy bread and maple syrup, while lunch can be soup and a sarnie or steak-and-Guinness pie; puddings include Dime Bar and sticky toffee. BYOB.

Cafe Fish   FISH & CHIPS £
(Map p568; 340 Lisburn Rd; mains £6-8; ☺ 11.30am-10pm Tue-Sat, 1-10pm Sun; 🖶) Regularly touted as Belfast's best fish-and-chip shop, this no-frills sit-down cafe certainly serves superbly crisp battered haddock along with mushy peas, chunky chips and a slice of buttered bread. If you're in a hurry, there's a takeaway branch just across the street.

★Barking Dog   BISTRO ££
(Map p556; ☑ 9066 1885; www.barkingdogbelfast.com; 33-35 Malone Rd; mains £9-17; ☺ lunch & dinner Mon-Sat, noon-9pm Sun) Chunky hardwood, bare brick, candlelight and quirky design create the atmosphere of a stylishly restored farmhouse, and the menu completes the feeling of cosiness and comfort with simple but sensational dishes such as its signature burger of meltingly tender beef shin wrapped in caramelised onion and horseradish cream. Superb service, too.

★Shu   FRENCH, IRISH ££
(Map p556; ☑ 9038 1655; www.shu-restaurant.com; 253 Lisburn Rd; mains £12-23; ☺ lunch & dinner Mon-Sat) If you want to know who to blame for all those copycat designer restaurants with the dark-wood-and-chocolate-brown-leather decor, then look no further. Lording it over fashionable Lisburn Rd since 2000, Shu is the granddaddy of Belfast chic, and still winning awards for its food. The French-influenced menu includes a two-course lunch for £13.25.

★Molly's Yard   IRISH ££
(Map p556; ☑ 9032 2600; www.mollysyard.co.uk; 1 College Green Mews; bistro mains £8-11, restaurant £14-22; ☺ bistro noon-6pm, restaurant 6-9pm Mon-Sat) ⚑ A restored Victorian stables courtyard is the setting for this quirky restaurant, with a cosy bar-bistro on the ground floor, outdoor tables in the yard and a rustic dining room (open from 6pm) in the airy roof space upstairs. The menu is seasonal and sticks to half a dozen each of starters and mains. Molly's also has its own craft beers, brewed at Lisburn's Hilden Brewery.

Beatrice Kennedy   IRISH ££
(Map p556; ☑ 9020 2290; 44 University Rd; mains £16-20; ☺ dinner Tue-Sat, lunch & dinner Sun; 🍴) ⚑ Organic veg and locally sourced meats are a staple at this perennial Queen's Quarter favourite (it's where students take their visiting parents for dinner). The dining room retains its Victorian elegance, while the menu adds a modern twist to traditional Irish seafood, lamb and beef. There's a separate vegetarian menu (you may have to ask for it), and from 5pm to 7pm you can get a two-course dinner for £15.

Deane's at Queen's   BISTRO ££
(Map p556; www.michaeldeane.co.uk; 1 College Gardens; mains £11-18; ☺ lunch & dinner Mon-Sat, lunch Sun) A chilled-out bar and grill from Belfast's top chef, Michael Deane, this place feels like a Scandinavian design firm's cafeteria (it was once Queen's University's staff club). The menu focuses on what could be described as good-value, gourmet pub grub: salt-and-chilli squid, crisp pork belly with celeriac and horseradish, and smoked haddock-and-leek fishcake with spring-onion velouté.

✕ Outside the Centre

Bia
CAFE **£**

(Map p568; www.culturlann.ie; 216 Falls Rd, Cultúrlann McAdam Ó Fiaich, West Belfast; mains £5-8; ⓧ 9am-6pm Mon, to 8pm Tue-Sat, 10am-6pm Sun; 📶 ♿) If you're exploring West Belfast, drop into Bia (Gaelic for 'food'), the cafe in Cultúrlann McAdam Ó Fiaich, the Irish-language and arts centre, for some good home-cooked food – the menu includes stews, soups, pizzas, cakes, scones and fresh pastries.

Cutters Wharf
GRILL **££**

(Map p568; www.cutterswharf.co.uk; 4 Lockview Rd, Stranmillis; mains £8-22; ⓧ food noon-9pm; 📶) One of the few bar-restaurants in Belfast with a waterside setting, Cutters Wharf has a terrace overlooking the River Lagan where you can enjoy an alfresco drink and a bar meal, and a smart upstairs restaurant serving steaks, burgers and seafood.

🍷 Drinking & Nightlife

Belfast's pub scene is lively and friendly, with the older traditional pubs complemented – and increasingly threatened – by a rising tide of stylish designer bars.

Standard opening hours are from 11am or 11.30am to midnight or 1am Monday to Saturday, and 12.30pm to 11pm or midnight Sunday; some pubs remain closed all day Sunday, or don't open till 4pm or 6pm.

Although the situation is improving, getting past the bouncers on the door can be a problem – there are a huge number of security staff employed in the city and polite, well-trained door staff are a rarity. Some of the flashier bars have a dress code – usually no sneakers, no jeans, no baseball caps (so that the security cameras can get a clear shot of your face) and definitely no football colours. A few even specify 'No political tattoos'.

Club hours are generally 9pm to 3am, with no admittance after 1am; bouncers can be really picky about who they let in, especially if you're under 21.

🍷 City Centre

★ Crown Liquor Saloon
PUB

(Map p556; www.crownbar.com; 46 Great Victoria St) Belfast's most famous bar has a wonderfully ornate Victorian interior. Despite being a tourist attraction (p554), it still fills up with crowds of locals at lunchtime and in the early evening.

TOP FIVE TRADITIONAL PUBS

➜ Bittle's Bar (p578)

➜ Crown Liquor Saloon (p577)

➜ Duke of York (p578)

➜ Kelly's Cellars (p577)

➜ White's Tavern (p577)

★ Harlem Cafe
CAFE-BAR

(Map p556; www.harlembelfast.com; 34-36 Bedford St; 📶) Cool of vibe and quirky of decor, with eclectic art, framed photos of NYC and glass-topped tables full of seashells and starfish, the Harlem is a great place for lounging over coffee with the Sunday papers, or a glass of wine after hitting the shops. Full food menu, from breakfast to brunch and pre-theatre dinner.

Garrick Bar
PUB

(Map p556; www.thegarrickbar.com; 29 Chichester St; 📶) First opened in 1870, the Garrick hangs on to a traditional atmosphere with acres of dark wood panelling, tiled floors, a pillared bar and old brass oil lamps. There are snug booths with buttoned leather benches, and a real coal fire in each room. Traditional music sessions in the front bar at 9.30pm on Wednesday and 5pm Friday.

White's Tavern
PUB

(Map p556; www.whitestavern.co.uk; 1-4 Wine Cellar Entry) Established in 1630 but rebuilt in 1790, White's claims to be Belfast's oldest tavern (unlike a pub, a tavern provided food and lodging). Downstairs is a traditional Irish bar with an open peat fire and live trad music Friday to Sunday; upstairs is like your granny's living room, stuffed with old armchairs and sofas, and hosts DJs and covers bands at the weekends.

Kelly's Cellars
PUB

(Map p556; 1 Bank St) Kelly's is Belfast's oldest pub (1720) – as opposed to tavern – and was a meeting place for Henry Joy McCracken and the United Irishmen when they were planning the 1798 Rising. The story goes that McCracken hid behind the bar when British soldiers came for him. A bit rough around the edges (a description that could apply to some of the regulars), it remains resolutely old-fashioned, but pulls in a broad cross-section of Belfast society and is a good bet for impromptu traditional music sessions.

BELFAST DRINKING & NIGHTLIFE

Bittle's Bar PUB

(Map p556; 103 Victoria St) A cramped and staunchly traditional bar, Bittle's is a 19th-century triangular red-brick building decorated with gilded shamrocks. The wedge-shaped interior is covered in paintings of Ireland's literary heroes by local artist Joe O'Kane. Pride of place on the back wall is a large canvas depicting Yeats, Joyce, Behan and Beckett at the bar with glasses of Guinness, and Wilde pulling the pints on the other side.

Stiff Kitten CLUB

(Map p556; www.thestiffkitten.com; Dublin Rd, Bankmore Sq) If Shine at the student union is too grungy a venue for your tastes, head for the Stiff Kitten, a stylish bar and club under the same management. Same serious attitude to the music, but it's distinctly glitzier, appealing to an over-25 crowd.

Cathedral Quarter & Around

⭐ John Hewitt Bar & Restaurant PUB

(Map p556; www.thejohnhewitt.com; 51 Donegall St) Named for the Belfast poet and socialist, the John Hewitt is one of those treasured bars that has no TV and no gaming machines; the only noise here is the murmur of conversation. As well as Guinness, the bar serves Hilden real ales from nearby Lisburn, plus Hoegaarden and Erdinger wheat beers. There are regular sessions of folk, jazz and bluegrass from 9pm most nights.

⭐ Muriel's Bar BAR

(Map p556; 12-14 Church Lane) Hats meet harlotry (ask who Muriel was) in this delightfully snug and welcoming wee bar with a retro-chic decor of old sofas and armchairs, heavy fabrics in shades of olive and dark red, gilt-framed mirrors and a cast-iron fireplace. Gin is Muriel's favourite tipple, and there's a range of exotic brands to mix with your tonic. The food menu is pretty good, too.

Northern Whig BAR

(Map p556; www.thenorthernwhig.com; 2 Bridge St) A stylish, modern bar set in an elegant Georgian printing works, the Northern Whig's airy interior is dominated by three huge Socialist-Realist statues rescued from Prague in the early 1990s. Its relaxing sofas and armchairs encourage serious afternoon loafing, though the pace hots up considerably after 5pm on Friday and Saturday when the party crowds start knocking back the vodka tonics and alcopops.

Duke of York PUB

(Map p556; 11 Commercial Ct) Hidden away down an alley in the heart of the city's former newspaper district, the snug, traditional Duke was a hangout for print workers and journalists and still pulls in a few hacks. One claim to fame is that the Sinn Féin leader, Gerry Adams, worked behind the bar here during his student days back in 1971.

Spaniard BAR

(Map p556; www.thespaniardbar.com; 3 Skipper St) Forget 'style': this narrow, crowded bar, which looks as if it's been squeezed into someone's apartment, has more atmosphere in one battered sofa than most 'style bars' have in their shiny entirety. Friendly staff, good beer, an eclectic crowd and cool tunes played at a volume that still allows you to talk: bliss.

McHugh's Bar and Restaurant PUB

(Map p556; www.mchughsbar.com; 29-31 Queen's Sq) This restored pub has a traditional feel with its old wooden booths and benches, and pours a superb pint of Guinness. It also boasts a decent restaurant serving steaks, seafood and stir-fries nonstop from noon till 10pm.

South Belfast

Eglantine PUB

(Map p556; www.egbar.co.uk; 32 Malone Rd; 🐾) The 'Eg' is a local institution, and widely reckoned to be the best of Belfast's student pubs. It serves good beer and good food, and there are DJs spinning most nights. Wednesday pulls in the crowds with an electric rodeo bull, bouncy boxing, sumo-wrestler suits and other fun; Tuesday is the big music-and-entertainment quiz night.

Botanic Inn PUB

(Map p556; www.thebotanicinn.com; 23-27 Malone Rd; 🐾) The 'Bot' is the second pillar of Malone Rd's unholy trinity of student pubs, along with the 'Eg' and the 'Welly Park' (Wellington Park). The last has sadly been renovated into airport-departure-lounge anonymity, but the Bot is still a wild place, with dancing in the upstairs Top of the Bot club from Wednesday to Saturday (people queue down the street to get in), live acoustic music in the Back Bar on Monday and Wednesday, and big-screen sport when there's a match on.

Lavery's BAR

(Map p556; www.laverysbelfast.com; 14 Bradbury Pl) Managed by the same family since 1918,

Lavery's is a vast, multilevel, packed-to-the-gills boozing emporium, crammed with drinkers young and old, from students to tourists, businessmen to bikers. The Public Bar has live acoustic music from local musicians on Monday and Tuesday, and a retro disco Wednesday to Saturday, while the bohemian Back Bar boasts a classic jukebox.

QUB Student Union CLUB
(Map p556; www.qubsu-ents.com; Queen's Students Union, University Rd; ☎) The student union has various bars and music venues hosting club nights, live bands and stand-up comedy. The monthly Shine (Map p556; www.shine.net; admission £22; ◷ 1st Sat of month) is one of the city's best club nights with resident and guest DJs pumping out harder and heavier dance music than most of Belfast's other clubs.

Fly CLUB
(Map p556; theflybelfast.co.uk; 5-6 Lower Crescent) Opened in 2012, the crowded club above the Fly Bar, complete with floor-to-ceiling LED screen, is the top place in Belfast to catch local and guest DJs. There are regular club nights on Monday, Friday and Saturday.

☆ Entertainment

The Belfast Welcome Centre issues *About Belfast*, a free bimonthly guide to Belfast events, with pub, club and restaurant listings. The Thursday issue of the *Belfast Telegraph* has an Entertainment section with club, gig and cinema listings, as does the Scene section in Friday's *Irish News*.

Good places to check out the latest in live music and club nights include the Good Vibrations record shop (p582), and the Oh Yeah Music Centre (Map p556; www.belfastmusic.org; 15-21 Gordon St; ◷ noon-3pm Mon-Fri, noon-5pm Sat). The following are also useful:

ArtsListings (www.culturenorthernireland.org) A free monthly that covers the arts scene throughout the whole of Northern Ireland.

Belfast Music (www.belfastmusic.org) Online gig listings.

Big List (www.thebiglist.co.uk) A weekly freesheet, published on Wednesday, that covers pubs, clubs and music events all over Northern Ireland, although the emphasis is heavily on Belfast.

Live Music
Pubs with regular live sessions of traditional Irish music include the Botanic Inn, the Garrick Bar, White's Tavern, the John Hewitt and Kelly's Cellars.

For jazz and blues, head for the John Hewitt, McHugh's, the Crescent Arts Centre or the Black Box (p580).

Belfast Empire LIVE MUSIC
(Map p556; www.thebelfastempire.com; 42 Botanic Ave; admission live bands £5-20) A converted late-Victorian church with three floors of entertainment, the Empire is a legendary live-music venue. The regular Thursday-night Gifted session showcases the best of new talent, both local and UK-wide, while

BELFAST ENTERTAINMENT

GAY & LESBIAN BELFAST

Belfast's gay and lesbian scene is concentrated in the Cathedral Quarter. For information on what's happening, check out www.gaybelfast.net. As well as the listings below, other gay-friendly pubs include Muriel's Bar, the John Hewitt and the Spaniard.

Kremlin (Map p556; www.kremlin-belfast.com; 96 Donegall St; ◷ 10pm-2am Tue & Thu, 9pm-2am Fri-Sat) Gay-owned and operated, the Soviet kitsch–themed Kremlin is the heart and soul of Northern Ireland's gay scene. A statue of Lenin guides you into Tsar, the pre-club bar, from where the Long Bar leads into the main clubbing zone, Red Square. Revolution on Saturdays is the flagship event, with DJs mixing up dance, house, pop and commercial till 2am.

Union Street (Map p556; www.unionstreetpub.com; 8-14 Union St; ☎) A stylish modern bar with retro decor and lots of bare brick and dark wood – check out the Belfast sinks in the loo – Union Street pulls in a mixed gay and straight crowd with nightly cabaret and karaoke, and a tempting food menu.

Fox's Den (Map p556; 108 Donegall St) Upstairs from the Front Page Bar, this is a relaxed and intimate bar that attracts a slightly older crowd, with quiz nights on Thursdays and free karaoke on Fridays.

DON'T MISS

GETTING INTO IRISH CULTURE

An Droichead (Map p556; www.androic head.com; 20 Cooke St, The Bridge; tickets £5-15), based in South Belfast, is a centre dedicated to Irish language, music and culture. It offers courses in Irish Gaelic, stages traditional dance and *céilidh* workshops, hosts art exhibitions and also serves as a live-music venue. It's a great place to hear live Irish folk music, not only big names from around the country but also up-and-coming local talent. Check the website, or pick up a flyer from the Belfast Welcome Centre.

Saturday is either big-name bands or tribute bands.

Limelight   LIVE MUSIC
(Map p556; www.limelightbelfast.com; 17-19 Ormeau Ave) This combined pub and club is one of the city's top venues for live rock and indie music, having hosted bands such as Oasis, Franz Ferdinand, the Manic Street Preachers and the Kaiser Chiefs. It's also home to alternative club night **Helter Skelter** (admission £5; ⊙ from 10pm Sat) and **Tuesdays at the Limelight** (£3; ⊙ from 10pm), Belfast's biggest student night.

Ulster Hall   CONCERT VENUE
(Map p556; www.ulsterhall.co.uk; Bedford St) Ulster Hall (built in 1862) is a popular venue for a range of events including rock concerts, lunchtime organ recitals, boxing bouts and performances by the **Ulster Orchestra** (www.ulsterorchestra.com).

School of Music   CLASSICAL MUSIC
(www.music.qub.ac.uk) Queen's University's School of Music stages free lunchtime recitals on Thursday and regular evening concerts in the beautiful, hammerbeam-roofed **Harty Room** (Map p556; School of Music, University Sq), and at the **Sonic Arts Research Centre** (Map p556; Cloreen Park), with occasional performances in the larger **Sir William Whitla Hall** (Map p556; University Rd). Download a *Current Events* brochure from the website.

Waterfront Hall   CONCERT VENUE
(Map p556; www.waterfront.co.uk; 2 Lanyon Pl) The impressive 2235-seat Waterfront is Belfast's flagship concert venue, hosting local, national and international performers from pop stars to symphony orchestras.

Odyssey Arena   CONCERT VENUE
(Map p556; www.odysseyarena.com; 2 Queen's Quay) The home stadium of the Belfast Giants ice-hockey team is also the venue for big entertainment events such as rock and pop concerts and stage shows.

King's Hall   CONCERT VENUE
(Map p568; www.kingshall.co.uk; Lisburn Rd) Northern Ireland's biggest exhibition and conference centre hosts a range of music shows, trade fairs and sporting events. It's accessible by any bus along Lisburn Rd or by train to Balmoral Station.

Comedy

There's no dedicated comedy club in the city, but there are regular comedy nights at various venues including the Belfast Empire (p579), Black Box and QUB Student Union (p579).

Opera & Theatre

Lyric Theatre   THEATRE
(Map p568; www.lyrictheatre.co.uk; 55 Ridgeway St) This stunning modern theatre opened to great dramatic and architectural acclaim in 2011; it is built on the site of the old Lyric Theatre, where Hollywood star Liam Neeson first trod the boards (he is now a patron).

MAC   ARTS CENTRE
(Metropolitan Arts Centre; Map p556; themaclive.com; St Anne's Sq) The Cathedral Quarter's beautiful new designer arts centre houses two theatres and stages regular drama performances, including shows for children.

Black Box   ARTS CENTRE
(Map p556; www.blackboxbelfast.com; 18-22 Hill St) Describing itself as a 'home for live music, theatre, literature, comedy, film, visual art, live art, circus, cabaret and all points in between', Black Box is an intimate venue in the heart of the Cathedral Quarter.

Crescent Arts Centre   ARTS CENTRE
(Map p556; www.crescentarts.org; 2-4 University Rd) The Crescent hosts a range of concerts, plays, workshops, readings and dance classes. The Crescent is also the headquarters of the Belfast Book Festival (p571), and a dance festival, **CityDance** (www.citydancebelfast.com; ⊙Nov).

Grand Opera House
OPERA

(Map p556; www.goh.co.uk; 2-4 Great Victoria St; ⊙box office 8.30am-9pm Mon-Fri, to 6pm Sat) This grand old venue plays host to opera, popular musicals and comedy shows. The box office is across the street on the corner of Howard St.

Cinemas

Queen's Film Theatre
CINEMA

(Map p556; www.queensfilmtheatre.com; 20 University Sq) A two-screen art-house cinema close to the university and a major venue for the Belfast Film Festival.

Movie House
CINEMA

(Map p556; www.moviehouse.co.uk; 14 Dublin Rd) A convenient city-centre 10-screen multiplex.

Storm Cinemas
CINEMA

(Map p556; www.odysseycinemas.co.uk; Odyssey Pavilion) Belfast's biggest multiplex, with 12 screens and stadium seats throughout. It's part of the Odyssey Complex.

Sport

Rugby, football (soccer), Gaelic football and hockey are played through the winter; cricket and hurling through the summer.

Windsor Park
FOOTBALL

(Map p568; off Lisburn Rd) International soccer matches take place here, south of the centre; the ageing stadium is slated for a £29-million makeover in 2014. For details of matches held here, see www.irishfa.com.

Casement Park
GAELIC FOOTBALL

(Map p568; www.antrimgaa.net; Andersonstown Rd) In West Belfast; you can see Gaelic football and hurling here.

Odyssey Arena
ICE HOCKEY

(Map p556; www.belfastgiants.com; 2 Queen's Quay) The Belfast Giants ice-hockey team draws big crowds to the arena at the Odyssey Complex; the season is September to March. The arena also hosts indoor sporting events including tennis and athletics.

🔒 Shopping

For general shopping you'll find all the usual high-street chains and department stores in the compact central shopping area north of City Hall, centred on Royal Ave. The main shopping malls are Victoria Square (Map p556; www.victoriasquare.com; btwn Ann & Chichester St; ⊙9.30am-6pm Mon-Tue, to 9pm Wed-Fri, 9am-6pm Sat, 1-6pm Sun) and the Castle Court Centre (Map p556; www.castlecourt-uk.com; Royal Ave; ⊙9am-6pm Mon-Wed & Fri-Sat, 9am-9pm Thu, 1-6pm Sun). There's late-night shopping on Thursdays till 8pm or 9pm.

Other shopping districts include Lisburn Rd and the unexpected concentration of designer fashion shops (about a dozen of them) on Bloomfield Ave off Newtonards Rd in East Belfast.

Items particular to Northern Ireland that you may like to look out for include fine Belleek china and Irish linen (antique and new). A good place to shop for Irish crafts and traditional Irish music is Cultúrlann McAdam Ó Fiaich (p567).

Wicker Man
JEWELLERY, SOUVENIRS

(Map p556; www.thewickerman.co.uk; 44-46 High St; ⊙9am-5.30pm Mon-Wed & Fri, to 9pm Thu, to 5.30pm Sat, 1-5.30pm Sun) This shop sells a wide range of contemporary Irish crafts and gifts, including silver jewellery, glassware and knitwear.

Fresh Garbage
CLOTHING, JEWELLERY

(Map p556; 24 Rosemary St; ⊙10.30am-5.30pm Mon-Wed, Fri & Sat, to 8pm Thu) Easily recognised by the glumfest of Goths hovering outside the door, this place has been around for more than 20 years but remains a cult favourite for hippie and Goth clothes, band T-shirts and Celtic jewellery.

Steensons
JEWELLERY

(Map p556; www.thesteensons.com; Bedford St, Bedford House; ⊙10am-5.30pm Mon-Sat, to 8pm Thu) Showroom selling a range of stylish, contemporary, handmade jewellery in silver,

WORTH A TRIP

LISBURN ROAD

Belfast's chicest shopping district is the ultrahip Lisburn Rd (www.thelisburnroad.com), which runs southwest for 3km or more from Shaftesbury Sq. From Eglantine Ave out to Balmoral Ave it's a straggling strip of red-brick and mock-Tudor facades lined with fashion boutiques, interior-design studios, art galleries, antique shops, delicatessens, coffee houses, wine bars and top restaurants, nestled among the wealthy, tree-lined suburbs of South Belfast.

BELFAST SHOPPING

gold and platinum, from a workshop in Glenarm, County Antrim.

Archives Antique Centre ANTIQUES
(Map p556; www.archivesantiquecentre.co.uk; 88 Donegall Pass; ⏰10.30am-5.30pm Mon-Sat) This is a warren of curios and collectables spread over three floors, with Irish silver, brass, pub memorabilia, militaria, books and light fittings.

Matchetts Music MUSIC
(Map p556; www.matchettsmusic.com; 6 Wellington Pl; ⏰9am-5.30pm Mon-Sat) Stocks a range of acoustic instruments, from guitars and mandolins to penny whistles and bodhráns (hand-held goatskin drums), as well as books of lyrics and guitar chords for traditional Irish songs.

Good Vibrations MUSIC
(Map p556; 89-93 North St, Bigg Life Arts Centre) Owned by music producer Terry Hooley (who released 'Teenage Kicks' by the Undertones on his Good Vibrations label back in 1978), this is Belfast's best alternative record shop, and a source of tickets for and info on the latest gigs.

ℹ Information

DANGERS & ANNOYANCES

Even at the height of the Troubles Belfast wasn't a particularly dangerous city for tourists, and today you're less at risk from crime here than you are in London. It's best, however, to avoid the so-called interface areas – near the peace lines in West Belfast, Crumlin Rd and the Short Strand (just east of Queen's Bridge) – after dark; if in doubt about any area, ask at your hotel or hostel.

Dissident Republican groups continue a campaign of violent attacks aimed at police and military targets, but have very little public support. Security alerts usually have no effect on visiting tourists (other than roads being closed), but be aware of the potential danger. You can follow the Police Service of Northern Ireland (PSNI) on Twitter (@policeserviceni) and receive immediate notification of any alerts.

One irritating legacy of the Troubles is the absence of left-luggage facilities at bus and train stations. You will also notice a more obvious security presence than elsewhere in the UK and Ireland, in the form of armoured police Land Rovers, fortified police stations and security doors on some shops (mostly outside the city centre), where you have to press the buzzer to be allowed in. There are doormen on many city-centre pubs.

If you want to take photos of fortified police stations, army posts or other military or quasi-military paraphernalia, get permission first,

just to be on the safe side. In the Protestant and Catholic strongholds of West Belfast it's best not to photograph people without permission; always ask first and be prepared to accept a refusal. Taking pictures of the murals is not a problem.

EMERGENCY

The national emergency phone number for police, fire and ambulance is ☎999.

Rape Crisis & Sexual Abuse Centre (☎9032 9002; ⏰10am-midnight Mon-Fri)

Victim Support (☎9024 3133; www.victim supportni.co.uk) Victim Support is the independent charity that helps people cope with the effects of crime.

INTERNET ACCESS

Belfast Computer Repairs (5 Great Northern Mall, Great Victoria St; per 15min £1; ⏰8.30am-8pm Mon-Fri, from 10am Sat, from 11am Sun) Convenient internet cafe.

Belfast Welcome Centre (visit-belfast.com; 8-9 Donegall Sq N; per 20min £1; ⏰9am-5.30pm Mon-Sat, 11am-4pm Sun year-round, to 7pm Mon-Sat Jun-Sep)

Ground@Waterstones (44-46 Fountain St; per 20min £1; ⏰9am-6pm Mon-Wed, Fri & Sat, to 9pm Thu, 1-5.30pm Sun) Three computers in the bookshop cafe; free wi-fi – ask at the counter for password.

Linen Hall Library (cnr Fountain St & Donegall Sq; per 30min £1.50; ⏰9.30am-5.30pm Mon-Fri, to 4.30pm Sat; 🛜) One computer on each floor; ask at desk before using. Wi-fi £3 for up to three hours (ask for log-in details).

LEFT LUGGAGE

Because of security concerns, there are no left-luggage facilities at Belfast's airports, train stations and bus stations. However, most hotels and hostels allow guests to leave their bags for the day, and the Belfast Welcome Centre also offers a daytime left-luggage service (£4.50 per item).

MEDICAL SERVICES

Accident and emergency services are available at these hospitals:

City Hospital (☎9032 9241; 51 Lisburn Rd)

Mater Hospital (☎9074 1211; 45-51 Crumlin Rd) Near the junction of Antrim Rd and Clifton St.

Royal Victoria Hospital (☎9024 0503; 274 Grosvenor Rd) West of the city centre.

Ulster Hospital (☎9048 4511; Upper Newtownards Rd, Dundonald) Near Stormont.

POST

Post office Main post office (Map p556; 12-16 Bridge St; ⏰9am-5.30pm Mon-Sat); Bedford St (Map p556; 16-22 Bedford St; ⏰8am-5.30pm Mon-Fri, 8am-1pm Sat); Botanic Gardens (Map p556; cnr University Rd & College Gardens; ⊙8am-9pm Mon-Sat, 10am-6pm Sun); Shaftesbury Sq (Map p556; 1-5 Botanic Ave; ⊙9am-5.30pm Mon-Fri, 9am-1pm Sat)

TOURIST INFORMATION

Belfast Welcome Centre (Map p556; ☑9024 6609; visit-belfast.com; 8-9 Donegall Sq N; ⊙9am-5.30pm Mon-Sat & 11am-4pm Sun year-round, to 7pm Mon-Sat Jun-Sep; ☎) Provides information about the whole of Northern Ireland, and can book accommodation anywhere in Ireland and Britain. Services include left luggage (not overnight), currency exchange and internet access.

Cultúrlann McAdam Ó Fiaich (Map p568; ☑9096 4188; 216 Falls Rd; ⊙9.30am-5.30pm Mon-Fri) This cultural centre in West Belfast has a tourist information desk.

Fáilte Ireland (Irish Tourist Board; Map p556; ☑9031 2345; 8-9 Donegall Sq N) In the Belfast Welcome Centre, can book accommodation in the Republic of Ireland.

Tourist Information Desks George Best Belfast City Airport (☑9093 5372; ⊙8am-7pm Mon-Sat, to 5pm Sun) Belfast International Airport (☑9448 4677; ⊙7.30am-7pm Mon-Sat, 8am-5pm Sun)

ⓘ Getting There & Away

AIR

Belfast International Airport (BFS; www.belfastairport.com) Located 30km northwest of the city; flights from Galway, UK, Europe and New York.

George Best Belfast City Airport (BHD; Map p568; www.belfastcityairport.com; Airport Rd) Located 6km northeast of the city centre; flights from the UK and Paris.

BOAT

Steam Packet Company (Map p568; ☑08722 992 992; www.steam-packet.com) Car ferries between Belfast and Douglas on the Isle of Man (two or three a week, April to September only) dock at Albert Quay, 2km north of the city centre.

Stena Line (Map p568; ☑08447 707070; www.stenaline.co.uk) Car ferries to Belfast from Liverpool (England) and Cairnryan (Scotland) dock at Victoria Terminal 5km north of the city centre; take the M2 motorway north and turn right at junction no 1.

Other car ferries to and from Scotland and England dock at Larne, 37km north of Belfast.

BUS

There are **information desks** (⊙7.45am-6.30pm Mon-Fri, 8am-6pm Sat) at both of Belfast's bus stations, where you can pick up regional bus timetables. Contact **Translink**

(☑9066 6630; www.translink.co.uk) for timetable and fare information.

National Express (☑08717 818 178; www.nationalexpress.com) Runs a daily coach service between Belfast and London (one way £47, 15 hours) via the Cairnryan ferry, Dumfries, Carlisle, Preston, Manchester and Birmingham. The ticket office is in the Europa Bus Centre.

Scottish Citylink (☑0871 266 3333; www.citylink.co.uk) Runs four buses a day from Glasgow to Belfast (£32, six hours), via the same ferry.

Europa Bus Centre (Map p556; ☑9066 6630; Great Victoria St, Great Northern Mall) Belfast's main bus station is behind the Europa Hotel and next door to Great Victoria St train station; This is reached via the Great Northern Mall beside the hotel. It's the main terminus for buses to Derry, Dublin and destinations in the west and south of Northern Ireland.

Laganside Bus Centre (Map p556; ☑9066 6630; Oxford St) The smaller of Belfast's two bus stations, Laganside is near the river and is mainly for buses to County Antrim, eastern County Down and eastern County Tyrone.

TRAIN

For information on train fares and timetables, contact Translink. The **NIR Travel Shop** (☑9023 0671; Great Victoria St Station; ⊙9am-5pm Mon-Fri, to 12.30pm Sat) books train tickets, ferries and holiday packages.

Belfast Central Station (East Bridge St) East of the city centre; trains run to Dublin and all destinations in Northern Ireland. If you arrive by train at Central Station, your rail ticket entitles you to a free bus ride into the city centre.

Great Victoria St Station (Great Victoria St, Great Northern Mall) Next to the Europa Bus Centre; has trains for Portadown, Lisburn, Bangor, Larne Harbour and Derry.

ⓘ Getting Around

Belfast possesses that rare but wonderful thing – an integrated public-transport system, with buses linking both airports to the central train and bus stations.

TO/FROM THE AIRPORTS

Belfast International Airport Airport Express bus 300 runs to the Europa Bus Centre (one way/return £7.50/10.50, 30 minutes) every 10 or 15 minutes between 7am and 8pm, every 30 minutes from 8pm to 11pm, and hourly through the night; a return ticket is valid for one month. A taxi costs about £30.

George Best Belfast City Airport Airport Express bus 600 runs to the Europa Bus Centre (one way/return £2.40/3.60, 15 minutes) every 15 or 20 minutes between 6am and 10pm. A return ticket is valid for one month. The taxi fare to the city centre is about £10.

BELFAST GETTING THERE & AWAY

TO/FROM THE FERRY TERMINALS

There is no public transport to the Stena Line and Steam Packet Company ferry terminals. Trains to the ferry terminal at Larne Harbour depart from Great Victoria St Station.

BICYCLE

National Cycle Network route 9 runs through central Belfast, mostly following the western bank of the River Lagan and the north shore of Belfast Lough.

BUS

Metro (☎ 9066 6630; www.translink.co.uk) operates the bus network in Belfast. Most city bus services depart from various stops on and around Donegall Sq, at City Hall and along Queen St. You can pick up a free bus map (and buy tickets) from the **Metro kiosk** (Map p556; ⏰ 8am-5.30pm Mon-Fri) at the northwest corner of the square.

Buy your ticket from the driver (change given); fares range from £1.40 to £2.20 depending on distance. The driver can also sell you a **Metro Day Ticket** (£3.70), giving you unlimited bus travel within the City Zone all day Monday to Saturday. Cheaper versions allow travel any time after 10am Monday to Saturday or all day Sunday (£3.20).

An increasing number of buses are low-floor, 'kneeling' buses with space for one wheelchair.

CAR & MOTORCYCLE

A car can be more of a hindrance than a help in Belfast, as parking is restricted in the city centre. For on-street parking between 8am and 6pm Monday to Saturday, you'll need to buy a ticket from a machine. For longer periods, head for one of the many multistorey car parks that are dotted around the city centre.

The major car-hire agencies in Belfast:

Avis (www.avis.co.uk); City (☎ 0844 544 6036; 69-71 Great Victoria St); Belfast International Airport (☎ 0844 544 6012); George Best Belfast City Airport (☎ 0844 544 6028)

Budget (www.budget-ireland.co.uk) City (☎ 9023 0700; 96-102 Great Victoria St); Belfast International Airport (☎ 9442 3332); George Best Belfast City Airport (☎ 9045 1111)

Dooley Car Rentals (☎ Republic of Ireland 062 53103, UK 0800 282189; www.dooleycar rentals.com; Airport Rd, Belfast International Airport, Aldergrove) This Ireland-wide agency is reliable and offers good rates – around £200 a week for a compact car, with no extra charge for driving cross-border to the Republic. You pay up front for a full tank of petrol, but if you return the car with an almost empty tank Dooley is cheaper than the big names.

TRANSPORT FROM BELFAST

Buses

DESTINATION	PRICE	DURATION (HR)	FREQUENCY
Armagh	£9	1¼	hourly Mon-Fri, 6 Sat, 4 Sun
Ballycastle	£11.50	2	3 daily Mon-Fri, 2 Sat
Bangor	£3.70	¾	half-hourly Mon-Sat, 8 Sun
Derry	£11.50	1¾	half-hourly Mon-Sat, 11 Sun
Downpatrick	£5.80	1	at least hourly Mon-Sat, 6 Sun
Dublin	£14.15	3	hourly
Enniskillen	£11.50	2¼	hourly Mon-Sat, 2 Sun
Newcastle	£7.80	1¼	hourly Mon-Sat, 8 Sun

Trains

DESTINATION	PRICE	DURATION (HR)	FREQUENCY
Bangor	£5.40	½	half-hourly Mon-Sat, hourly Sun
Dublin	£30	8	8 Mon-Sat, 5 Sun
Larne Harbour	£6.90	1	hourly
Newry	£11	¾	8 Mon-Sat, 5 Sun
Portrush	£11.50	1¾	7 or 8 Mon-Sat, four Sun

TRANSPORT PASSES

Smartlink Travel Card

If you plan on using city buses a lot, it's worth buying a Smartlink Travel Card (available from the Metro kiosk, the Belfast Welcome Centre and the Europa and Laganside Bus Centres). The card costs an initial fee of £1.50, plus £10.50 per 10 journeys – you can get it topped up as you want. Or you can get seven days' unlimited travel for £16. When you board the bus, you simply place the card on top of the ticket machine and it automatically issues a ticket.

Visitor Pass

The Belfast Visitor Pass (per one/two/three days £6.30/10.50/14) allows unlimited travel on bus and train services in Belfast and around; it can be purchased at airports, main train and bus stations, the Metro kiosk on Donegall Sq and the Belfast Welcome Centre.

Europcar (www.europcar.co.uk) City (☑ 0871 384 3428; 90-92 Grosvenor Rd) Belfast International Airport (p585) George Best Belfast City Airport (☑ 0871 384 3425)

Hertz (www.hertz.co.uk) Belfast International Airport (☑ 9442 2533); George Best Belfast City Airport (☑ 9073 2451)

TAXI

Fona Cab (☑ 9033 3333; www.fonacab.com)
Value Cabs (☑ 9080 9080; www.valuecabs.co.uk)

AROUND BELFAST

The southwestern fringes of Belfast extend as far as Lisburn (Lios na gCearrbhach), 12km southwest of the city centre. Like Belfast, Lisburn grew rich on the proceeds of the linen industry in the 18th and 19th centuries. This history is celebrated in the excellent Irish Linen Centre & Lisburn Museum (Market Sq; ☉ 9.30am-5pm Mon-Sat) FREE, housed in the fine 17th-century Market House.

The museum on the ground floor has displays on the cultural and historic heritage of the region, while upstairs the award-winning 'Flax to Fabric' exhibition details the fascinating history of the linen industry in Northern Ireland – on the eve of WWI, Ulster was the largest linen-producing region in the world, employing some 75,000 people.

There are plenty of audiovisual and hands-on exhibits – you can watch weavers working on Jacquard looms and even try your hand at spinning flax.

Lisburn Tourist Information Centre (☑ 9266 0038; Lisburn Sq; ☉ 9.30am-5pm Mon-Sat) is on the town's main square. Buses 523, 530 and 532 from Belfast's Upper Queen St go to Lisburn (£2.60, 40 minutes, half-hourly Monday to Friday, hourly Saturday and Sunday), or catch the train (£3.60, 30 minutes, at least half-hourly Monday to Saturday, hourly Sunday) from either Belfast Central or Great Victoria St Stations.

Counties Down & Armagh

POP 652,000 / AREA 3702 SQ KM

Best Places to Eat

➡ Vanilla (p600)

➡ Niki's Kitchen Café (p600)

➡ Restaurant 23 (p605)

➡ Uluru Bistro (p611)

➡ Mourne Seafood Bar (p601)

Best Places to Stay

➡ Anna's House B&B (p595)

➡ Fortwilliam Country House (p590)

➡ Dufferin Coaching Inn (p596)

➡ Briers Country House (p599)

➡ River Mill (p597)

Why Go?

From the hilltop viewpoint of Scrabo Tower, near New-townards, the treasures of County Down lie scattered all around you. The sparkling, island-fringed waters of Strangford Lough stretch to the south, with the bird-haunted mudflats of Castle Espie and Nendrum's ancient monastery on one shore, and the picturesque Ards Peninsula on the other. On a clear day you can see the Mourne Mountains in the distance, their velvet curves sweeping down to the sea. Nearby are Downpatrick and Lecale, the old stamping grounds of Ireland's patron saint.

Down's neighbour County Armagh is largely rural, from the low, rugged hills of the south to the lush apple orchards and strawberry fields of the north, with Ireland's ecclesiastical capital, the neat little city of Armagh, in the middle. South Armagh is a peaceful backwater, where you can wander back and forth across the border with the Republic without even noticing.

When to Go

➡ May brings white clouds of apple blossom to County Armagh's orchards, a season celebrated by the Apple Blossom Fair in the early part of the month.

➡ Summertime generally has the best weather for hiking and cycling, and August sees the International Walking Festival in the Mourne Mountains.

➡ Spring and autumn are both good for birdwatching, but keen birders have a big X on their calendars in October, when tens of thousands of overwintering brent geese begin to arrive at Castle Espie on Strangford Lough.

Counties Down & Armagh Highlights

1 Hike along ancient smugglers' trails among the granite peaks of the **Mourne Mountains**

2 Test the menus at top-notch restaurants in **Hillsborough, Warrenpoint** and **Bangor**

3 Explore the stately halls and exquisite gardens of **Mount Stewart House** (p593)

4 Watch vast flocks of geese, ducks and waders at **Castle Espie** (p594)

5 Get off the beaten track on the back roads of **South Armagh**

6 Follow in the footsteps of Ireland's patron saint in and around **Downpatrick**

7 Learn the rules of the esoteric Irish sport of road bowling in **Armagh City**

Bangor

POP 55,000

Bangor is to Belfast what Brighton is to London – a Victorian seaside resort that has enjoyed a renaissance as an out-of-town base for city commuters. The Belfast–Bangor train line was built in the late-19th century to connect the capital with the then flourishing resort. The opening of a huge marina and the redevelopment of the seafront have boosted Bangor's fortunes – it's widely regarded as the most desirable address in Northern Ireland – though the kitsch tradition of British seaside towns survives in the Pickie Family Fun Park.

Until spring 2015, a previously derelict stretch of waterfront real estate is home to Project 24 (www.project24ni.com). This collection of artists' studios housed in brightly coloured shipping containers set amid a community garden provides an attractive public space where visitors can watch artists at work.

The bus and train stations are together on Abbey St, at the uphill end of Main St. At the bottom of Main St is the marina, with B&Bs clustered to the east and west on Queen's Pde and Seacliff Rd. Bangor has both a Main St and a High St, which converge on Bridge St at the marina.

◎ Sights & Activities

North Down Museum MUSEUM
(www.northdownmuseum.com; Castle Park Ave; ◎10am-4.30pm Tue-Sat, 2-4.30pm Sun, plus 10am-4.30pm Mon Jul & Aug) FREE Housed in the converted laundry, stables and stores of Bangor Castle, this museum displays, among other historical curiosities, a facsimile of *The Antiphonary of Bangor,* a small 7th-century prayer book and the oldest surviving Irish manuscript (the original

> **TOP FIVE ROMANTIC HIDEAWAYS IN NORTHERN IRELAND**
> ●
> ➡ Bushmills Inn Hotel (p634)
> ➡ Galgorm Resort & Spa (p645)
> ➡ Malmaison Hotel (p572)
> ➡ Westville Hotel (p650)
> ➡ Old Inn (p590)

is housed in Milan's Ambrosian Library). There's also an interesting section on the life of William Percy French (1854–1920), the famous entertainer and songwriter (Bangor is also home to the Percy French Society; www.percyfrench.org). The museum is in Castle Park, west of the train and bus stations.

Pickie Family Fun Park AMUSEMENT PARK
(www.pickiefunpark.com; Marine Gardens; per ride £1.50-4.50; ◎9am-7.30pm Easter-Sep, to 9pm Jul & Aug, to 4pm Sat & Sun Oct-Easter; ☏) Apart from strolling along the seafront, Bangor's main attraction is this old-fashioned seaside entertainment complex that's famous for its swan-shaped pedal boats. It comes complete with a kids' adventure playground, karts and miniature steam train.

Blue Aquarius CRUISE
(☏07510 006000; www.bangorboat.com; adult/child from £6/3, fishing trips per adult/child incl tackle & bait £17/12; ◎departures from 2pm daily Jul & Aug, Sat & Sun only Apr-Jun & Sep) *Blue Aquarius* offers pleasure cruises around Bangor Bay, departing from the marina pontoon next to the Pickie Family Fun Park. In July and August, there are family-friendly fishing trips departing at 9.30am and 7pm daily from the Eisenhower Pier (on the right-hand side of the harbour, looking out to sea).

⌻ Sleeping

Cairn Bay Lodge B&B ££
(☏9146 7636; www.cairnbaylodge.com; 278 Seacliff Rd; s/d from £45/80; ☏) This lovely seaside villa overlooking Ballyholme Bay, 1km east of the town centre, oozes Edwardian elegance with its oak-panelled lounge and dining room. There are three bedrooms with private bathrooms that blend antique charm with contemporary style, plus beautiful gardens, gourmet breakfasts and sea views.

Clandeboye Lodge Hotel HOTEL ££
(☏9185 2500; www.clandeboyelodge.com; 10 Estate Rd, Clandeboye; s/d from £70/90; @☏) Looking a little like a modern red-brick church set amid landscaped gardens on the southwest edge of town, the Clandeboye offers informal luxury – big bedrooms, polished-granite bathrooms, fluffy bathrobes, champagne and chocolates – plus a log fire in winter and a drinks terrace in summer.

Ennislare House B&B ££
(☏9127 0858; www.ennislarehouse.com; 7-9 Princetown Rd; s/d £35/65; ☏) Set in a lovely Victo-

rian town house just 300m north of the train station, the Ennislare has big, bright rooms, stylish decor and a friendly owner who can't do enough to make you feel welcome.

Eating & Drinking

Red Berry Coffee House CAFE £
(2-4 Main St; mains £3-6; 9am-10pm Mon-Sat, 1-9pm Sun;) A chilled-out fairtrade coffee shop that serves big breakfasts (including a stack of pancakes with bacon and maple syrup) till 11.30am, and deli sandwiches and salads thereafter.

★ **Boat House** FRENCH, IRISH ££
(9146 9253; www.theboathouseni.co.uk; 1a Seacliff Rd; 2-/3-course lunch £20/25, dinner mains £16-23; lunch & dinner Wed-Sat, 1-8pm Sun) The Boat House is a cosy little nook of stone, brick and designer decor, tucked into the former Harbour Master's office across the street from the tourist office. The menu features local seafood, lamb and game, deftly prepared with a light Gallic touch.

Ava Grill STEAKHOUSE ££
(9146 5490; www.theava.co.uk; 132 Main St; mains £8-18; lunch & dinner;) A big local favourite, the family-run Ava has a relaxing, loungelike atmosphere decorated with bare brick walls and vast wine racks, and scattered with sofas, armchairs and snug booths. The menu is crammed with full-fat, crowd-pleasing favourites, such as garlic mushrooms, rib-eye steak, southern fried chicken and Caesar salad.

Coyle's Bistro BISTRO ££
(9127 0362; 44 High St; mains £15-20; 5-9pm Tue-Sat, to 8pm Sun) Despite being upstairs from a busy bar, this place is surprisingly intimate and inviting, with wood panelling, mirrored walls and subdued lighting, and a varied menu that ranges from ox cheeks braised in red wine to Moroccan lamb stew. The two-course set menu for two (available 5pm to 7pm) includes a bottle of wine and costs £30.

Jenny Watts PUB
(41 High St) A traditional pub with a beer garden out back, Jenny's pulls in a mixed-age crowd, offering live music three nights a week, cool tunes (in the upstairs lounge) on Friday and Saturday, and jazz and blues Sunday lunchtime and evening. It also serves good pub grub, and kids are welcome at meal times.

THE GOLD COAST

The coastal region stretching east from Belfast to Bangor and beyond is commuter territory for the capital, and home to many of the North's wealthiest citizens – it's known locally as the 'Gold Coast'. The attractive **North Down Coastal Path** follows the shore from Holywood train station to Bangor Marina (15km), and continues east to Orlock Point.

Information

Tourist Office (9127 0069; www.northdowntourism.com; 34 Quay St; 9am-5pm Mon, Tue, Thu & Fri, 10am-5pm Wed & Sat, 1-5pm Sun May-Aug, shorter hours & closed Sun Sep-Apr) Housed in a tower built in 1637 as a fortified customs post.

Getting There & Away

BUS

Ulsterbus services 1 and 2 run from Belfast's Laganside BusCentre to Bangor (£3.70, 50 minutes, half-hourly Monday to Saturday, eight Sunday). From Bangor, bus 3 goes to Donaghadee (£2.90, 25 minutes, hourly Monday to Saturday, four Sunday).

TRAIN

A regular train service runs from Belfast's Great Victoria St and Central stations to Bangor (£5.40, 30 minutes, half-hourly Monday to Saturday, hourly Sunday).

Central County Down

Rich farmland spreads to the south of Belfast, with only the rough moorland of Slieve Croob, southwest of Ballynahinch, breaking the flatness of the terrain. The attractive town of Hillsborough lies on the main A1 road from Belfast to Newry.

Hillsborough

POP 3400

Hillsborough is a name familiar to British ears, as it is the official residence of the Secretary of State for Northern Ireland. Hillsborough Castle is also used to entertain visiting heads of state (US presidents George W Bush and Bill Clinton have both enjoyed its hospitality). This is the Queen's official residence when she is in Northern Ireland.

WORTH A TRIP

CRAWFORDSBURN

The pretty little conservation village of Crawfordsburn lies just over 3km west of Bangor on the B20. The picturesque Old Inn (☑ 9185 1300; www.theoldinn.com; 15 Main St; r from £115; @ ☎) here was once a resting place on the coach route between Belfast and Donaghadee (formerly the main ferry port for mainland Britain). As a result, it has been patronised by many famous names, including the young Peter the Great (tsar of Russia), Dick Turpin (highwayman), former US president George HW Bush, and a veritable roll call of literary figures, including Swift, Tennyson, Thackeray, Dickens, Trollope and CS Lewis.

Established in 1614, the Old Inn claims to be Ireland's oldest hotel, with the original thatched cottage (now the bar) flanked by 18th-century additions. The atmosphere is cosy and welcoming, with log fires, low ceilings and wood panelling, and there's a lovely garden terrace at the back. The rooms, dressed up with Arts and Crafts–style wallpaper and mahogany woodwork, have bags of character, and the inn's lavishly decorated Lewis Restaurant (☑ 9185 1300; mains £17-25, 4-course lunch Sun £23; ⊙ dinner daily, lunch Sun) is one of Northern Ireland's best.

The elegant little town was founded in the 1640s by Colonel Arthur Hill, who built a fort here to quell Irish insurgents. Fine Georgian architecture rings the square and lines Main St.

⊙ Sights

Hillsborough Castle HISTORIC BUILDING
(www.gov.uk/hillsborough-castle; Main St; guided tours adult/child/family £7/4/18, grounds only £3.50; ⊙ 10.30am-4pm Sat, noon-4pm Sun Apr-Sep) The town's main attraction is this rambling, two-storey late-Georgian mansion built in 1797 for Wills Hill, the first marquess of Downshire, and extensively remodelled in the 1830s and '40s. The guided tour takes in the state drawing room and dining rooms, and the Lady Grey Room where Tony Blair and George W Bush had talks on Iraq in 2003.

Hillsborough Courthouse HISTORIC BUILDING
(The Square; ⊙ 9.30am-5.30pm Mon-Sat) FREE A fine old Georgian building, the courthouse exhibits various displays describing the working of the courts in the 18th and 19th centuries.

St Malachy's Parish Church CHURCH
(Main St; ⊙ 9am-5.30pm Mon-Sat) FREE St Malachy's is one of Ireland's most splendid 18th-century churches, with twin towers at the ends of the transepts and a graceful spire at the western end. A tree-lined avenue leads to the church from a statue of Arthur Hill, fourth marquess of Downshire, at the bottom of Main St.

Hillsborough Fort HISTORIC BUILDING
(Main St; ⊙ 10am-7pm Tue-Sat, 2-7pm Sun Apr-Sep, to 4pm Oct-Mar) FREE Close to St Malachy's church, Hillsborough Fort was built as an artillery fort by Colonel Hill in 1650 and remodelled as a Gothic-style tower house in 1758.

✯ Festivals & Events

Oyster Festival FOOD
(www.hillsboroughoysterfestival.com) Each year in late August/early September, around 10,000 people – plus 6000 oysters from Dundrum Bay – converge on Hillsborough for the three-day Oyster Festival. This celebration of local food, drink and general good fun includes an international oyster-eating competition.

⛌ Sleeping & Eating

Hillsborough is a bit of a culinary hot spot, with several excellent restaurants. These are popular places, so book a table at weekends to avoid disappointment.

★ Fortwilliam Country House B&B ££
(☑ 9268 2255; www.fortwilliamcountryhouse.com; 210 Ballynahinch Rd; s/d £50/70; @ ☎) The Fortwilliam offers B&B in four luxurious rooms stuffed with period furniture – our favourite is the Victorian room, with its rose wallpaper, huge antique mahogany wardrobe and view over the garden. Your host's hospitality knows no bounds, and breakfast includes fresh eggs from the chickens in the yard, and the smell of home-baked wheaten bread wafting from the Aga. Book well in advance.

★ **Plough Inn**   BISTRO ££
(☑9268 2985; www.theploughhillsborough.co.uk;
3 The Square; mains lunch £9-11, dinner £10-20;
☺lunch & dinner Mon-Sat, noon-8pm Sun) This
fine old pub, with its maze of dark, wood-
panelled nooks and crannies, has been offering 'beer and banter' since 1758. It serves
gourmet bar lunches and also offers fine
dining in the restaurant around the back,
where stone walls, low ceilings and a roaring fireplace make a cosy setting for a menu
ranging from wood pigeon to rack of lamb.

Hillside Bar & Restaurant   FRENCH, IRISH ££
(☑9268 2765; www.hillsidehillsborough.co.uk; 21
Main St; mains lunch £9-14, dinner £14-23; ☺lunch
& dinner) This is a homely pub serving real
ale (and mulled wine beside the fireplace in
winter), with live jazz Sunday evenings and
a dinky wee beer garden in a cobbled courtyard out the back. The kitchen serves gastropub cuisine, and there's a two-course set
menu for £12.50 between 5pm and 6.30pm.

ⓘ Information

Tourist Office (☑9268 9717; www.visitlisburn.
com; The Square; ☺9am-5pm Mon-Sat) In
the Georgian courthouse in the centre of the
village.

ⓘ Getting There & Away

Goldline Express bus 238 from Belfast's Europa
BusCentre to Newry stops at Hillsborough
(£3.70, 25 minutes, at least hourly Monday to
Saturday, eight Sunday).

Ards Peninsula

The low-lying Ards Peninsula (An Aird) is
the finger of land that encloses Strangford
Lough, pinching against the thumb of the
Lecale Peninsula at the Portaferry Narrows.
The northern half of the peninsula has some
of Ireland's most fertile farmland, with large
expanses of wheat and barley, while the
south is a landscape of neat fields, white cottages and narrow, winding roads. The eastern coast has some good sandy beaches.

Donaghadee

POP 6500
Donaghadee (Domhnach Daoi) was the main
ferry port for Scotland until 1874, when the
34km sea crossing to Portpatrick was superseded by the Stranraer–Larne route. Now it's
a pleasant harbour town that's fast becoming part of Belfast's commuter belt.

The town is home to Grace Neill's, which
dates from 1611 and claims to be Ireland's
oldest pub. Among its 17th-century guests
was Peter the Great, tsar of Russia, who
stopped in for lunch in 1697 on his grand
tour of Europe. In the early 19th century,
John Keats found the place 'charming and
clean' but was 'treated to ridicule, scorn
and violent abuse by the local people who
objected to my mode of dress and thought I
was some strange foreigner'.

In July and August, **MV The Brothers**
(☑9188 3403; www.nelsonsboats.co.uk; adult/child
£5/3; ☺departs 2pm daily, weather permitting)
runs boat trips to Copeland Island, which
was abandoned to the seabirds at the turn
of the 20th century. There are also **sea-
angling trips** (£10 per person, departures
at 10am and 7pm), with all tackle and bait
provided.

🍴 Sleeping & Eating

Pier 36   B&B ££
(☑9188 4466; www.pier36.co.uk; 36 The Parade; s/d
from £50/70, restaurant mains £11-19; ☺restaurant
noon-9pm) An excellent pub with comfortable
B&B rooms upstairs and a red-brick and
terracotta-tiled restaurant at the back, dominated by a yellow Rayburn stove that turns
out home-baked bread and the daily roast.
The hearty menu includes soups, stews, sausage and champ (a Northern Irish dish of potatoes mashed with spring onions), mussels
and other seafood, steaks and a good range
of veggie dishes.

★ **Grace Neill's**   IRISH ££
(☑9188 4595; www.graceneills.com; 33 High St;
2-course lunch £11, dinner mains £10-19; ☺lunch
& dinner Mon-Fri, noon-9.30pm Sat, 12.30-8pm
Sun) At the back of Ireland's oldest pub is
one of the North's best modern bistros, its
sea-green, khaki and red-brick walls decked
with arty photos of old Donaghadee. The
menu could be described as upmarket comfort food, from haddock and chips to steak-
and-Guinness pie to braised shoulder of
lamb with buttery mashed potatoes.

Portaferry

POP 3300
Portaferry (Port an Pheire), a neat huddle
of streets around a medieval tower house,
enjoys an attractive setting looking across
the turbulent Narrows to a matching tower
house in Strangford. A renowned marine-
biology station on the waterfront uses the

lough as an outdoor laboratory, and you can investigate the local marine life yourself at the Exploris aquarium.

◉ Sights & Activities

Exploris   AQUARIUM
(www.exploris.org.uk; Castle St; adult/child £7.50/5; ⊙ 10am-6pm Mon-Fri, 11am-6pm Sat, noon-6pm Sun Apr-Aug, shorter hours Sep-Mar) This outstanding state-of-the-art aquarium, with displays of marine life from Strangford Lough and the Irish Sea, has touch tanks that allow visitors to stroke and hold rays, starfish, sea anemones and other sea creatures. Exploris also has a seal sanctuary where orphaned, sick and injured seals are nursed back to health before being released into the wild.

Portaferry Castle   CASTLE
(Castle St; ⊙ 10am-5pm Mon-Sat, 2-6pm Sun Easter-Aug) FREE Portaferry's castle is a small 16th-century tower house beside the tourist information centre, which, together with the tower house in Strangford, used to control sea traffic through the Narrows.

Local Walks   WALKING
Walk up to Windmill Hill, topped by an old windmill tower, for a good view over the Narrows to Strangford. The Vikings named this stretch of water Strangfjörthr, meaning 'powerful fjord', because when the tide turns, as it does four times a day, 400,000 tonnes of water per minute churn through the gap at speeds of up to 8 knots. You get some idea of the tide's remarkable strength when you see the ferry being whipped sideways by the current.

Portaferry hit the headlines in 2008 when SeaGen – the world's first commercial-scale tidal energy turbine, built at Belfast's Harland & Wolff shipyard – was installed in the Narrows. The generator is clearly visible, squatting in the channel just south of town like a stumpy red-and-black lighthouse. The business end is underwater, where two giant turbine blades spin in the tidal currents, generating around 1.2 megawatts of electricity for 18 to 20 hours a day.

There are pleasant walks on the minor roads along the coast, north for 2.5km to Ballyhenry Island (accessible at low tide), and south for 6km to the National Trust nature reserve at Ballyquintin Point, both good for birdwatching, seal spotting or just admiring the views of the Mourne Mountains.

Des Rogers   BOAT TOUR
(☑ 4272 8297; desmondrogers@netscapeonline. co.uk; per half-/full day around £75/150) Fishing and birdwatching trips from May to October, as well as pleasure cruises on the lough. Book in advance.

John Murray   BOAT TOUR
(☑ 4272 8414; per half-/full day around £75/150) Also organises fishing and birdwatching trips from Easter to October, along with pleasure cruises. Book in advance.

🍴 Sleeping & Eating

Adair's B&B   B&B £
(☑ 4272 8412; 22 The Square; s/tw £24/46; 🐾) Mrs Adair's friendly and good-value B&B is an anonymous-looking house right on the main square (there's no sign outside; look for No 22). It has three spacious rooms – a single (shared bathroom), a twin (with private bathroom) and a family room (with private bathroom; for up to four people).

Barholm   HOSTEL, B&B £
(☑ 4272 9967; www.barholmportaferry.co.uk; 11 The Strand; dm/s/d from £16/21/50) Barholm offers year-round B&B and hostel-style accommodation in a Victorian villa with a superb seafront location opposite the ferry slipway. There's a spacious kitchen, laundry facilities and a big, sunny conservatory that doubles as a tearoom. It's popular with groups, so be sure to book ahead.

Portaferry Hotel   HOTEL ££
(☑ 4272 8231; www.portaferryhotel.com; 10 The Strand; s/d from £75/85, 3-course dinner £26; @ 🐾) Converted from a row of 18th-century terrace houses, this charming seafront hotel has an elegant, Georgian look to its rooms – ask for one with a sea view (£10 extra). There's also a good, family friendly restaurant with a French-influenced menu.

❶ Information

Tourist Office (☑ 4272 9882; tourism.portaferry@ards-council.gov.uk; Castle St; ⊙ 10am-5pm Mon-Sat, 2-6pm Sun Easter-Aug) In a restored stable near the tower house.

❶ Getting There & Away

A car ferry (one-way car & driver £6.50, motorcyclists £4, car passengers & pedestrians £1.10) between Portaferry and Strangford sails every half-hour between 7.30am and 10.30pm Monday to Friday, 8am to 11pm Saturday and 9.30am to

10.30pm on Sunday. Journey time is about 10 minutes.

Ulsterbus services 9 and 10 travel from Belfast to Portaferry (£6.50, 1½ hours, six daily Monday to Saturday, two Sunday) via Newtownards, Mount Stewart and Greyabbey. More frequent services begin from Newtownards (some buses go via Carrowdore and don't stop at Mount Stewart and Greyabbey; check first).

Greyabbey

POP 1000

The village of Greyabbey is home to the splendid ruins of Grey Abbey (Church Rd; admission free; ☉10am-5pm Easter-Sep, noon-4pm Sun only Oct-Easter). The Cistercian abbey was founded in 1193 by Affreca, wife of the Norman aristocrat John de Courcy (the builder of Carrickfergus Castle), in thanks for surviving a stormy sea crossing from the Isle of Man. The small visitor centre explains Cistercian life with paintings and panels.

The abbey church, which remained in use as late as the 18th century, was the first in Ireland to be built in the Gothic style. At the east end is a carved tomb, possibly depicting Affreca; the effigy in the north transept may be her husband. The grounds, overlooked by 18th-century Rosemount House, are awash with trees and flowers on spreading lawns, making this an ideal picnic spot.

Hoops Courtyard, off Main St in the village centre, has a cluster of 18 little shops selling antiques and collectables; opening times vary, but all are open on Wednesday, Friday and Saturday afternoons.

Hoops Coffee Shop (Main St, Hoops Courtyard; mains £4-6; ☉10am-5pm daily Jul & Aug, Tue-Sat Sep-Jun) is a traditional tearoom serving good lunches and wicked cream teas. There are outdoor tables in the courtyard in fine weather.

Mount Stewart

The magnificent 18th-century Mount Stewart House & Gardens (www.nationaltrust.org.uk; adult/child £7.30/3.65; ☉house noon-5pm mid-Mar–Oct, gardens 10am-6pm mid-Mar–Oct) is one of Northern Ireland's grandest stately homes. It was built for the marquess of Londonderry and is decorated with lavish plasterwork, marble nudes and priceless artworks. (Note that the house will be undergoing a major renovation project until 2015, but remains open to the public.)

Lady Mairi Vane-Tempest-Stewart (1920-2009) – daughter of the seventh marquess – gifted Mount Stewart to the National Trust in 1977, but continued to live and entertain guests in part of the house until her death in November 2009. The family is related by marriage to the Goldsmiths via Annabel (born 1934), daughter of the eighth marquess, after whom the famous London nightclub was named. The house's treasures include the chairs used at the Congress of Vienna in 1815 (embroidery added in 1918–22), and a painting of the racehorse

COUNTIES DOWN & ARMAGH ARDS PENINSULA

LORD CASTLEREAGH

As you wander around Mount Stewart, spare a thought for Robert Stewart, Lord Castlereagh (1769–1822), who spent his childhood here. Despite going down in history as one of Britain's most accomplished foreign secretaries, during his lifetime he was enormously unpopular with the public, who saw him as the spokesman for a violently repressive government. He was savagely attacked in print by liberal reformers, including Daniel O'Connell – who denounced him as 'the assassin of his country' – and the poets Percy Bysshe Shelley and Lord Byron. The latter's notorious *Epitaph for Lord Castlereagh* could hardly be bettered for withering contempt:

Posterity will ne'er survey
A nobler scene than this:
Here lie the bones of Castlereagh;
Stop, traveller, and piss!

As Chief Secretary for Ireland in the government of William Pitt, Castlereagh was responsible for quelling the 1798 Rising and for passing the 1801 Act of Union. Later he served as foreign secretary during the Napoleonic Wars, and represented Britain at the Congress of Vienna in 1815. Political success did not bring happiness, however; while still in office, Castlereagh succumbed to paranoia and depression and committed suicide by slitting his own throat with a letter knife.

Hambletonian by George Stubbs, one of the most important paintings in Ireland.

Much of the landscaping of the beautiful gardens was supervised in the early 20th century by Lady Edith, wife of the seventh marquess, for the benefit of her children – the Dodo Terrace at the front of the house is populated with unusual creatures from history (dinosaurs and dodos) and myth (griffins and mermaids), accompanied by giant frogs and duck-billed platypuses. The 18th-century Temple of the Winds (⊙ 2-5pm Sun mid-Mar–Oct) is a folly in the classical Greek style built on a high point above the lough.

Mount Stewart is on the A20, 3km northwest of Greyabbey and 8km southeast of Newtownards. Buses from Belfast and Newtownards to Portaferry stop at the gate. The ground floor of the house and most of the gardens are wheelchair accessible. Last admission is one hour before closing time.

Newtownards & Around

POP 27,800

Founded in the 17th century on the site of the 6th-century Movilla monastery, Newtownards (Baile Nua na hArda) today is a busy but unexceptional commercial centre.

The tourist office (☑ 9182 6846; www.visit strangfordlough.co.uk; 31 Regent St; ⊙ 9.15am-5pm Mon-Fri, 9.30am-5pm Sat) is next to the bus station.

◉ Sights

Scrabo Country Park   PARK

Newtownards is overlooked by the prominent landmark of Scrabo Hill, located 2km southwest of town. It was once the site of extensive prehistoric earthworks, which were largely removed during construction of the 41m 1857 Memorial Tower (⊙ 10am-5pm Jun–mid-Sep, noon-4pm Sat & Sun Mar-May, late Sep & Oct, Sun only Nov-Feb) FREE, built in honour of the third marquess of Londonderry. Inside there's an audiovisual display on the tower's history and a 122-step climb to the superb viewpoint at the top – on a clear day you can see Scotland, the Isle of Man and even Snowdon in Wales. The disused sandstone quarries nearby provided material for many famous buildings, including Belfast's Albert Memorial Clock Tower.

Somme Heritage Centre   HERITAGE CENTRE

(www.irishsoldier.org; 233 Bangor Rd; adult/child £5/4; ⊙ 10am-5pm Mon-Fri, 11am-5pm Sat

& Sun Jul & Aug, 10am-4pm Mon-Thu, noon-4pm Sat Apr-Jun & Sep, shorter hours Oct-Mar) This grimly fascinating centre vividly illustrates the horrors of the WWI Somme campaign of 1916 from the perspective of men of the 10th (Irish), 16th (Irish) and 36th (Ulster) divisions. It's a high-tech show with short films and reconstructions of the trenches, but there's nothing celebratory about the exhibits, which are intended as a memorial to the men and women who died. A photographic display commemorates the suffragette movement and the part that women played in WWI.

The centre is 3km north of Newtownards on the A21 towards Bangor. Bus 6 from Bangor to Newtownards passes the entrance every half-hour or so.

Ark Open Farm   FARM

(www.thearkopenfarm.co.uk; 296 Bangor Rd; adult/child/family £5.20/4.40/19; ⊙ 10am-6pm Mon-Sat, 2-5pm Sun Apr-Oct, to 5pm daily Nov-Mar) The Ark Open Farm is hugely popular with families, with displays of rare breeds of sheep, cattle, poultry, llamas and donkeys. Kids get to stroke and handfeed the lambs, piglets and ducklings.

Strangford Lough

Almost landlocked, Strangford Lough (Loch Cuan; www.strangfordlough.org) is connected to the open sea by a 700m-wide strait (The Narrows) at Portaferry. Its western shore is fringed by humpbacked islands – half-drowned mounds of boulder clay (called drumlins) left behind by ice sheets at the end of the last ice age. On the eastern shore, the drumlins have been broken down by the waves into heaps of boulders that form shallow tidal reefs (known locally as 'pladdies').

Large colonies of grey seals frequent the lough, especially at the southern tip of the Ards Peninsula where the exit channel opens out into the sea. Birds abound on the shores and tidal mudflats, including brent geese wintering from Arctic Canada, eider ducks and many species of wader. Strangford Lough oysters are a local delicacy.

◉ Sights

Castle Espie Wildfowl & Wetlands

Centre   WILDLIFE RESERVE

(www.wwt.org.uk; Ballydrain Rd, Comber; adult/child £7.30/3.60; ⊙ 10am-5pm Mar-Oct, to 4.30pm Nov-Feb) ◢ The Castle Espie reserve is a haven for huge flocks of geese, ducks and swans – around 30,000 light-bellied brent geese (75% of the world's population) spend the winter here – and is a paradise for fledgling naturalists, with family bird-feeding and pond-dipping sessions.

The **visitor centre** is a showcase for sustainable development, and the landscaped grounds are dotted with hides for observing waders and waterfowl, as well as the centre's important collection of duck and goose species from all over the world. The best times to visit are in May and June, when the grounds are overrun with goslings, ducklings and cygnets, and October, when the vast flocks of brent geese begin to arrive from Arctic Canada.

The centre is about 2km southeast of Comber, off the Downpatrick road (A22).

Nendrum Monastic Site HISTORIC SITE
(Lisbane; ☉ site 24hr, visitor centre 10am-5pm Jun-Sep, 10am-5pm Tue-Sun Apr-May, noon-4pm Sun only Oct-Mar) FREE The Celtic monastic community of Nendrum was built in the 5th century under the guidance of St Mochaoi (St Mahee). It is much older than the Norman monastery at Greyabbey on the opposite shore and couldn't be more different. The scant remains provide a clear outline of its early plan, with the foundations of a number of churches, a **round tower**, beehive cells and other buildings, as well as three concentric stone ramparts and a monks' cemetery, all in a wonderful island setting. A particularly interesting relic is the **stone sundial** that has been reconstructed using some of the original pieces. The minor road to Mahee Island from the lough's western shore crosses a causeway to Reagh Island and then a bridge guarded by the ruined tower of 15th-century Mahee Castle.

The small **visitor centre** screens an excellent video comparing Nendrum with Grey Abbey, and there's some interesting material about the concept of time and how we measure it, presented in a child-friendly fashion.

The site is signposted from Lisbane on the A20, 5km south of Comber.

🛏 Sleeping & Eating

⭐ **Anna's House B&B** B&B ££
(☑ 9754 1566; www.annashouse.com; 35 Lisbarnett Rd, Tullynagee, Lisbane; s/d from £60/90; 🛜) Just west of Lisbane, Anna's is a spacious, ecofriendly country house set in a superb garden with views over a lake from a stunning glass-walled extension. The hospitality is second to none, the food is almost all organic and the bread is home baked, with a breakfast menu that ranges from an Ulster fry or smoked-salmon omelette to fresh fruit salad (special diets catered for).

Old Schoolhouse Inn B&B ££
(☑ 9754 1182; www.theoldschoolhouseinn.com; Ballydrain Rd, Comber; s/d £55/80; 🛜) Just south of Castle Espie on the road to Nendrum, the characterful Old Schoolhouse has seven luxurious, modern rooms, each named for a former US president. The former classroom, now swathed in shades of deep claret and decorated with old musical instruments, houses an award-winning **restaurant** (mains £16-23; ☉ lunch & dinner Mon-Sat, 12.30-9.30pm Sun) serving local produce cooked in French-country-kitchen style.

Old Post Office Tearoom CAFE £
(191 Killinchy Rd, Lisbane; mains £4-7; ☉ 9.30am-5pm Mon-Sat) The thatched cottage that once housed the village post office has been lovingly converted into a tearoom and art gallery, with walls of cream plaster and bare stone, pine furniture and a wood-burning stove. It serves great coffee and home-baked scones, plus lunch specials such as lasagne and lovely fresh salads.

Killyleagh
POP 2200
Killyleagh (Cill O Laoch) is a former fishing village dominated by the impressive **castle** (closed to the public) of the Hamilton family. Built originally by John de Courcy in the 12th century, the Scottish-baronial-style reconstruction of 1850 sits on the original Norman motte and bailey. Outside the gatehouse, a plaque commemorates Sir Hans Sloane, the naturalist, born in Killyleagh in 1660, whose collection was the basis for the founding of the British Museum (London's Sloane Sq is named after him). The parish **church** houses the tombs of members of the Blackwood family (marquesses of Dufferin), who married into the Hamiltons in the 18th century.

In September the **Magnus Barelegs Viking Festival** (www.magnusvikings.com) features processions, craft fairs, live music and a Viking boat race on nearby Strangford Lough.

🛏 Sleeping & Eating

★ Dufferin Coaching Inn B&B ££
(☑ 4482 1134; www.dufferincoachinginn.com; 35 High St; s/d £65/90; 🖻) The comfortable lounge in this lovely Georgian house, complete with coal-fired stove and free Sunday papers, was once the village bank – the manager's office in the corner now houses a little library. The seven plush rooms have crisp linen and fluffy towels, and some have four-poster beds; unusually, the smallest double has the bath *in* the bedroom, charmingly hidden behind a curtain. The excellent breakfasts include freshly squeezed orange juice, good coffee and scrambled eggs with smoked salmon.

★ Dufferin Arms PUB ££
(www.dufferinarms.co.uk; 35 High St; mains £8-15; ⊙ lunch & dinner Mon-Wed, noon-8.30pm Thu, noon-10pm Fri & Sat, noon-7.30pm Sun) This comfortably old-fashioned pub serves decent pub grub, while the cosy, candlelit Kitchen Restaurant offers a more intimate atmosphere. Bands play on Friday and Saturday nights from 9pm, with folk and bluegrass sessions on Saturday afternoons from 4pm.

❶ Getting There & Away

Ulsterbus service 11 runs from Belfast to Kil-lyleagh (£5, one hour, 10 daily Monday to Friday, five Saturday, two Sunday) via Comber. Bus 14 continues from Killyleagh to Downpatrick (£2.90, 20 minutes, 10 daily Monday to Friday, five Saturday).

Downpatrick

POP 10,300

St Patrick's mission to spread Christianity to Ireland began and ended in Downpatrick. Ireland's patron saint is associated with numerous places in this corner of Down – he made his first convert at nearby Saul, and is buried at Down Cathedral – and, on St Patrick's Day (17 March), the town is crammed with crowds of pilgrims and revellers.

Downpatrick – now County Down's administrative centre – was settled long before the saint's arrival. His first church here was constructed inside the earthwork *dún* (fort) of Rath Celtchair, still visible to the southwest of the cathedral. The place later became known as Dún Pádraig (Patrick's Fort), anglicised to Downpatrick in the 17th century.

In 1176 the Norman John de Courcy is said to have brought the relics of St Colm-cille and St Brigid to Downpatrick to rest with the remains of St Patrick, hence the local saying, 'In Down, three saints one grave do fill, Patrick, Brigid and Colmcille'. Later the town declined along with the cathedral until the 17th and 18th centuries, when the Southwell family developed the old town centre you see today. The best of its Georgian architecture is centred on English St and the Mall, which lead up to the cathedral, but the rest of the town is a bit bedraggled and looking a little down at heel. Be warned that the town centre is also a major traffic bottleneck.

⊙ Sights

The Mall is the most attractive street in Downpatrick, with some lovely 18th-century architecture, including Soundwell School, built in 1733, and a courthouse with a finely decorated pediment.

Saint Patrick Centre HERITAGE CENTRE
(www.saintpatrickcentre.com; 53a Market St; adult/child £5.50/3; ⊙ 9am-5pm Mon-Sat, plus 1-5pm Sun Jul & Aug, 9am-7pm St Patrick's Day) This heritage centre houses a multimedia exhibition called Ego Patricius, charting the life and legacy of Ireland's patron saint. Occasionally filled with parties of school kids, the exhibition uses audio and video presentations to tell St Patrick's story, often in his own words (taken from his *Confession*, written in Latin around the year 450, which begins with the words *'Ego Patricius'*, meaning 'I am Patrick'). At the end is a spectacular widescreen film that takes the audience on a swooping, low-level helicopter ride over the landscapes of Ireland.

Down Cathedral CATHEDRAL
(www.downcathedral.org; The Mall; ⊙ 9.30am-4pm Mon-Sat) 🆓 According to legend, St Patrick died in Saul, where angels told his followers to place his body on a cart drawn by two untamed oxen, and that wherever the oxen halted was where the saint should be buried. They supposedly stopped at the church on the hill of Down, now the site of the Church of Ireland's Down Cathedral.

The cathedral is testimony to 1600 years of building and rebuilding. Viking attacks wiped away all trace of the earliest churches, and the subsequent Norman cathedral and monasteries were destroyed by Scottish raiders in 1316. The rubble was used in a

15th-century church finished in 1512, but after the Dissolution of the Monasteries it was razed to the ground in 1541. Today's building dates largely from the 18th and 19th centuries, with a completely new interior installed in the 1980s.

In the churchyard immediately south of the cathedral is a slab of Mourne granite with the inscription 'Patric', placed there by the Belfast Naturalists' Field Club in 1900, marking the traditional site of St Patrick's grave.

To reach the cathedral from the Saint Patrick Centre, take the path to its left, uphill through the landscaped grounds.

Down County Museum   MUSEUM
(www.downcountymuseum.com; The Mall; ⊙10am-5pm Mon-Fri, noon-5pm Sat & Sun) FREE Down County Museum is housed in the town's restored 18th-century jail. In a former cell block at the back are models of some of the prisoners once incarcerated there, and details of their sad stories. Displays cover the story of the Norman conquest of Down, but the biggest exhibit of all is outside – a short signposted trail leads to the Mound of Down, a good example of a Norman motte and bailey.

🛏 Sleeping & Eating

★ River Mill   B&B ££
(☑4484 1988; www.river-mill.com; 43 Ballyclander Rd; d £70; ☏) ✔ This beautifully restored 18th-century mill house is hidden away in the countryside 6km southeast of Downpatrick, off the road to Ardglass. The traditional stone exterior hides a gorgeous, minimalist, modern interior, with split-level lounge and two good-sized, en suite guest rooms with wooden floor, white walls and plain timber furniture. The helpful hosts can arrange massage and reiki treatments at the alternative-therapy centre next door.

Denvir's Hotel & Pub   B&B ££
(☑4461 2012; www.denvirshotel.com; 14 English St; s/d £40/70; ☏) Recently given a stylish makeover, Denvir's is an old coaching inn dating back to 1642. It offers B&B in six idiosyncratic rooms with polished floorboards, Georgian windows and period fireplaces. Good food is served in the snug bar and rustic restaurant (mains £7-11; ⊙noon-8pm), which has an enormous, 17th-century stone fireplace.

ℹ Information

Downpatrick Tourist Office (☑4461 2233; www.visitdownpatrick.com; 53a Market St; ⊙9.30am-6pm Mon-Sat, 2-6pm Sun Jul & Aug, 10am-5pm Mon-Sat Sep-Jun) In the Saint Patrick Centre, just north of the bus station.

ℹ Getting There & Away

Downpatrick is 32km southeast of Belfast. Buses 15, 15A and 515 depart from the Europa BusCentre in Belfast for Downpatrick (£5.80, one hour, at least hourly Monday to Saturday, six Sunday). There's also the Goldline Express bus 215 (50 minutes, hourly Monday to Saturday).

Goldline Express bus 240 runs from Downpatrick to Newry (£9, 1¼ hours, six daily Monday to Saturday, two Sunday) via Dundrum, Newcastle, Castlewellan and Hilltown.

Around Downpatrick

According to popular tradition, the young St Patrick was kidnapped from Britain by Irish pirates and spent six years as a slave tending sheep (possibly on Slemish). His faith grew in captivity and he prayed daily, eventually escaping back home to his family.

After religious training, St Patrick returned to Ireland to spread the faith and is said to have landed on the shores of Strangford Lough near Saul, northeast of Downpatrick. He preached his first sermon in a nearby barn, and eventually retired to Saul after some 30 years of evangelising.

Saul

On landing near this spot in 432, St Patrick made his first convert: Díchú, the local chieftain, gave the holy man a sheep barn (*sabhal* in Gaelic, pronounced 'sawl') in which to preach. West of Saul village is the supposed site of the *sabhal*, with a replica 10th-century church and round tower built in 1932 to mark the 1500th anniversary of his arrival.

East of the village is the small hill of Slieve Patrick (120m), with stations of the cross along the path to the top and a massive 10m-high statue of St Patrick, also dating from 1932, on the summit. The hill is the object of a popular pilgrimage on St Patrick's Day.

Saul is 3km northeast of Downpatrick off the A2 Strangford road.

Struell Wells

These supposedly curative spring waters are traditionally associated with St Patrick – it is said he scourged himself here, spending 'a great part of the night, stark naked and singing psalms' immersed in what is now the Drinking Well.

He must have been a hardy soul – the well-preserved but chilly 17th-century bathhouses here look more likely to induce ill health than cure it! The site has been venerated for centuries, although the buildings are all post-1600.

Between the bathhouses and the ruined chapel stands the Eye Well, the waters of which are said to cure eye ailments.

The wells are in a scenic, secluded glen 2km east of Downpatrick. Take the B1 road towards Ardglass, and turn left after passing the hospital.

Lecale Peninsula

The low-lying Lecale Peninsula is situated east of Downpatrick, isolated by the sea and Strangford Lough to the north, south and east, and the marshes of the Quoile and Blackstaff Rivers to the west. In Irish it's called Leath Chathail (lay-ca-*hal*), meaning 'the territory of Cathal' (an 8th-century prince), and is a region of fertile farmland that is fringed by fishing harbours, rocky bluffs and sandy beaches.

Lecale is a place of pilgrimage for Van Morrison fans – Coney Island, immortalised in his song of the same name, is between Ardglass and Killough in the south of the peninsula.

Strangford

POP 550

The picturesque fishing village of Strangford (Baile Loch Cuan) is dominated by Strangford Castle (Castle St), a 16th-century tower house that faces its counterpart across the Narrows in Portaferry; it's not open to the public. At the end of Castle St is a footpath called the Squeeze Gut, which leads over the hill behind the village, with a fine view of the lough, before looping back to Strangford via tree-lined Dufferin Ave (1.5km), or continuing around the shoreline to Castle Ward Estate (4.5km).

Strangford Sea Safari (☑4372 3933; www.strangford-seasafari.com; Strangford Harbour;

adult/child from £18/15) offers a range of exciting speedboat tours into the swirling tidal streams of The Narrows, including visits to the SeaGen tidal generator, Angus Rock lighthouse and local seal colonies.

Strangford is 16km northeast of Downpatrick.

🛏 Sleeping & Eating

★Cuan   B&B ££

(☑4488 1222; www.thecuan.com; The Square; s/d £65/95; 🕸) You can't miss the Cuan's green facade, just around the corner from the ferry slip, or the warm welcome from Peter and Caroline, the husband-and-wife team that runs the place. The atmospheric, wood-panelled restaurant (mains £11-16; ⊘noon-9pm Mon-Thu, to 9.30pm Fri & Sat, to 8.30pm Sun) here is the main attraction, serving giant portions of local seafood, lamb and beef, but there are also nine neat, comfortable and well-equipped rooms if you want to stay the night.

Castle Ward Estate

Castle Ward enjoys a superb setting overlooking the bay to the west of Strangford, but it has something of a split personality. Castle Ward House was built in the 1760s for Lord and Lady Bangor – Bernard Ward and his wife, Anne – who were a bit of an odd couple. Their widely differing tastes in architecture resulted in an eccentric country residence – and a subsequent divorce. Bernard favoured the neoclassical style seen in the front facade and the main staircase, while Anne leant towards the Strawberry Hill Gothic of the rear facade, which reaches a peak in the incredible fan vaulting of her Gothic boudoir. Guided tours (included in the admission price to the estate) depart hourly from noon to 4pm.

The house is part of the National Trust's Castle Ward Estate (www.nationaltrust.org.uk; Park Rd; adult/child £7.30/3.65; ⊘house noon-5pm Easter-Oct, grounds 10am-8pm Apr-Sep, to 4pm Oct-Mar). While in the grounds you can visit a Victorian laundry museum, the Strangford Lough Wildlife Centre, Old Castle Ward (a fine 16th-century plantation tower) and Castle Audley (a 15th-century tower house), and explore a range of walking and cycling trails.

Newcastle

POP 7500

The Victorian seaside resort of Newcastle (An Caisleán Nua) has been given a multimillion-pound makeover and sports a snazzy modern promenade, stretching for more than a kilometre along the seafront, complete with modern sculptures and an elegant footbridge over the River Shimna. The facelift makes the most of Newcastle's superb setting on a 5km strand of golden sand at the foot of the Mourne Mountains, and there are hopes that it will transform the town's fortunes from fading bucket-and-spade resort to outdoor activities capital.

The town is the traditional base for exploring the Mourne Mountains – accessible from here on foot, by car or by public transport. Golfers from around the globe flock to the Royal County Down Golf Course, voted the 'best in the world outside the US' by the magazine *Planet Golf*.

If you're driving, be aware that the town can be snarled up with traffic on summer weekends.

Sights & Activities

The little harbour at the south end of town once served the 'stone boats' that exported Mourne granite from the quarries of Slieve Donard. Newcastle's main attraction is the beach, which stretches 5km northeast to the nature reserve.

Murlough National Nature Reserve   WILDLIFE RESERVE
(car park May-Sep £3.50; ⊙24hr) FREE Footpaths and boardwalks meander among the grassy dunes, with great views back towards the Mournes.

Royal County Down Golf Course   GOLF
(www.royalcountydown.org; green fees £165-180 May-Oct, lower rates Nov-Apr) Stretching north of town is the Royal County Down Golf Course; its challenging Championship Links – venue for the 2007 Walker Cup and 2012 Palmer Cup – is full of blind tee shots and monster rough, and is regularly voted one of the world's top 10 golf courses. It's open to visitors on Monday, Tuesday, Thursday, Friday and Sunday.

Granite Trail   WALKING
(www.walkni.com/walks/333/granite-trail) Beginning across the road from the harbour, the 5km Granite Trail is a waymarked footpath that leads up a disused funicular railway line that once carried granite blocks to the harbour. The view from the top is worth the steep 200m climb.

Rock Pool   SWIMMING
(South Promenade; adult/child £2/1.50; ⊙10am-5pm Mon-Fri, 11am-5.30pm Sat, 2-5pm Sun Jul & Aug) At the south end of the seafront, this outdoor seawater swimming pool dates from the 1930s.

Soak   SPA
(www.soakseaweedbaths.co.uk; 5a South Promenade; 1hr session £25; ⊙11.30am-8pm Thu-Mon Sep-Jun) If it's too cold for outdoor bathing, you can simmer away in a hot seaweed bath at Soak.

Sleeping

Tollymore Forest Park   CAMPGROUND £
(☑4372 2428; 176 Tullybranigan Rd; tent & caravan sites £16.50-19) Many of Newcastle's 'camping sites' are for caravans only; the nearest place you can pitch a tent is amid the attractive scenery of Tollymore Forest Park, in the foothills of the Mourne Mountains, 3km northwest of the town centre. You can hike here (along Bryansford Ave and Bryansford Rd) in 45 minutes.

★ Briers Country House   B&B £
(☑4372 4347; www.thebriers.co.uk; 39 Middle Tollymore Rd; s/d from £43/65) A peaceful farmhouse B&B with a country setting and views of the Mournes, Briers is just 1.5km northwest of the town centre (signposted off the road between Newcastle and Bryansford). Huge breakfasts – vegetarian if you like – are served with a view over the garden, and evening meals are available by prior arrangement.

Beach House   B&B ££
(☑4372 2345; beachhouse22@tiscali.co.uk; 22 Downs Rd; s/d £50/90; ☎) Enjoy a sea view with your breakfast at the Beach House, an elegant Victorian B&B with three rooms (all with private bathroom) and a balcony (open to all guests) overlooking the beach.

Harbour House Inn   B&B ££
(☑4372 3445; www.harbourhouseinn.co.uk; 4 South Promenade; s/d from £50/70; 🖳) The Harbour House is a family-friendly pub and restaurant with four plain but serviceable rooms upstairs that are clean and comfortable. It's next to the old harbour, almost 2km south of the bus station, a perfect base for climbing Slieve Donard (p600).

Slieve Donard Resort & Spa   HOTEL £££
(☑4372 1066; www.hastingshotels.com; Downs Rd; s/d from £100/140; ☎▨) Established in 1897,

WALK: SLIEVE DONARD

You can hike to the summit of Slieve Donard (853m; the highest hill in Northern Ireland) from various starting points in and around Newcastle, but it's a stiff climb and you shouldn't attempt it without proper walking boots, waterproofs and a map and compass.

On a good day the view from the top extends to the hills of Donegal, the Wicklow Mountains, the coast of Scotland, the Isle of Man and even the hills of Snowdonia in Wales. Two cairns near the summit were long believed to have been cells of St Donard, who retreated here to pray in early Christian times.

The shortest route to the top is via the River Glen from Newcastle. Begin at Donard Park car park, at the edge of town, 1km south of the bus station. At the far end of the car park, turn right through the gate and head into the woods, with the river on your left. A gravel path leads up the River Glen valley to the saddle between Slieve Donard and Slieve Commedagh. From here, turn left and follow the Mourne Wall to the summit. Return by the same route (round trip 9km, allow at least three hours).

the Slieve Donard is a magnificent Victorian red-brick pile overlooking the beach, equipped with several restaurants and a luxurious spa. This is where golf legends Tom Watson, Tiger Woods and Rory McIlroy stay when they're in town.

 Eating

★ **Niki's Kitchen Café** CAFE £
(📞4372 6777; www.nikiskitchencafe.co.uk; 107 Central Promenade; mains £5-10; ⊙8am-5pm daily, 5-9pm Wed-Sun; 🛜 🚼) The crowds queuing at the counter testify to the success of this attractive new eatery, where the menu focuses on quality versions of classic cafe cuisine, including seafood chowder, fish cakes, beef burgers and vegetarian quiche, with chunky chips on the side in a wee wire basket. There are high chairs, a kids' menu and sofas for chilling out with a cappuccino.

Maud's CAFE £
(106 Main St; mains £5-7; ⊙9am-9.30pm; 🚼) Maud's is a bright, modern cafe with picture windows framing a stunning view across the river to the Mournes. It serves breakfast, good coffee, a range of tempting scones and sticky buns, plus salads, crêpes, pizzas and pastas; there's a kids' menu, too.

Sea Salt BISTRO, DELI £
(51 Central Promenade; mains £5-8; ⊙10am-5pm Mon-Fri, 9am-5pm Sat & Sun, 7-9pm Fri & Sat) Both delicatessen and bistro, Sea Salt serves everything from a morning cappuccino to a lunchtime seafood chowder with wheaten bread, with an evening menu that ranges from Spanish tapas to themed menus from around the world.

★ **Vanilla** IRISH ££
(📞4372 2268; www.vanillarestaurant.co.uk; 67 Main St; mains lunch £7-11, dinner £15-25; ⊙noon-3.30pm daily, 5-8.30pm Sun-Thu, 6-9.30pm Fri & Sat; 🚼) 🌱 Newcastle-born chef Darren Ireland has introduced a dash of verve and enthusiasm to the local dining scene with this sharply styled bistro, and a menu that shamelessly promotes Irish produce in dishes such as rump of lamb with creamed savoy cabbage and celeriac, and puy lentils. Two-/three-course early-bird menu for £15/19 from 5pm to 8pm Sunday to Thursday.

ℹ️ **Information**

There is free public wi-fi all along the promenade.

Tourist Office (📞4372 2222; newcastle.tic@downdc.gov.uk; 10-14 Central Promenade; ⊙9.30am-7pm Mon-Sat, 1-7pm Sun Jul & Aug, 10am-5pm Mon-Sat, 2-6pm Sun Sep-Jun; 🛜) Sells local-interest books and maps, and a range of traditional and contemporary crafts.

ℹ️ **Getting There & Around**

Ulsterbus 20 runs to Newcastle from Belfast's Europa BusCentre (£7.80, 1¼ hours, at least hourly Monday to Saturday, eight Sunday) via Dundrum. Bus 37 continues along the coast road from Newcastle to Annalong and Kilkeel (£4.20, 35 minutes, hourly Monday to Saturday, eight Sunday).

Goldline Express bus 240 takes the inland route from Newry to Newcastle (£6.50, 50 minutes, six daily Monday to Saturday, two Sunday) via Hilltown, and continues on to Downpatrick. You can also get to Newry along the coast road, changing buses at Kilkeel.

Around Newcastle

Tollymore Forest Park

This scenic forest park (Bryansford; car/pedestrian £4.50/2; ⊙10am-dusk), 3km west of Newcastle, offers lovely walks and bike rides along the River Shimna and across the northern slopes of the Mournes. The park is littered with Victorian follies, including Clanbrassil Barn, which looks more like a church, as well as grottoes, caves, bridges and stepping stones. An electronic kiosk at the car park provides information on the flora, fauna and history of the park.

Castlewellan

A less rugged outdoor experience is offered by Castlewellan Forest Park (Main St, Castlewellan; car/pedestrian £4.50/2; ⊙10am-dusk), with gentle walks around the castle grounds, a maze to get lost in and trout fishing (3-day permit £9) in its lovely lake. A recent addition is a network of exciting mountain bike trails – see www.mountainbikeni.com for details. You can hire bikes from Ross Cycles (☑4377 8029; 44 Clarkhill Rd, Castlewellan; ⊙9.30am-6pm Mon-Sat, 2-5pm Sun) for around £15/80 per day/week.

In late June or early July Castlewellan village is the focus of the Celtic Fusion Festival (www.celticfusion.co.uk), a celebration of Celtic music, art, drama and dance at venues around County Down, including Castlewellan, Newcastle and Downpatrick.

Dundrum

Second only to Carrickfergus as Northern Ireland's finest Norman fortress, Dundrum Castle (⊙10am-5pm daily Easter-Oct, noon-4pm Sun only Nov-Easter) **FREE** was founded in 1177 by John de Courcy of Carrickfergus. The castle overlooks the sheltered waters of Dundrum Bay, famous for its oysters and mussels.

You can sample the oysters at the Mourne Seafood Bar (☑4375 1377; www.mournesea food.com; 10 Main St; mains £11-17; ⊙5-9.30pm Thu, 12.30-9.30pm Fri-Sun) 🖉, a friendly and informal fishmonger-cum-restaurant set in a wood-panelled Victorian house with local art brightening the walls. As well as a choice of local oysters served five different ways, the menu includes seafood chowder, crab, langoustines and daily fish specials, all sourced locally.

Dundrum is 5km north of Newcastle. Bus 17 from Newcastle to Downpatrick stops in Dundrum (£2.70, 12 minutes, eight daily Monday to Friday, four Saturday, two Sunday).

Mourne Mountains

The humpbacked granite hills of the Mourne Mountains dominate the horizon as you head south from Belfast towards Newcastle. This is one of the most beautiful corners of Northern Ireland, with a distinctive landscape of grey granite, yellow gorse and whitewashed cottages, the lower slopes of the hills latticed with a neat patchwork of drystone walls cobbled together from huge, rounded granite boulders.

The hills were made famous in a popular song penned by Irish songwriter William Percy French in 1896, whose chorus, 'Where the Mountains of Mourne sweep down to the sea', captures perfectly their scenic blend of ocean, sky and hillside.

History

The crescent of low-lying land on the southern side of the mountains is known as the Kingdom of Mourne. Cut off for centuries by its difficult approaches (the main overland route passed north of the hills), it developed a distinctive landscape and culture. Until the coast road was built in the early 19th century, the only access was on foot or by sea.

Smuggling provided a source of income in the 18th century. Boats carrying French spirits would land at night and packhorses would carry the casks through the hills to the inland road, avoiding the excise men at Newcastle. The Brandy Pad, a former smugglers' path from Bloody Bridge to Tollymore, is a popular walking route today.

⊙ Sights

Silent Valley Reservoir   LAKE
(car/motorcycle £4.50/2, plus per adult/child £1.60/60p; ⊙10am-6.30pm Apr-Oct, to 4pm Nov-Mar) At the heart of the Mournes is the beautiful Silent Valley Reservoir, where the River Kilkeel was dammed in 1933. There are scenic, waymarked walks around the grounds, a coffee shop and an interesting exhibition on the building of the dam. From the car park, a shuttle bus will take you another

COUNTIES DOWN & ARMAGH AROUND NEWCASTLE

Counties Down & Armagh: Walking & Wildlife

Strangford Lough and the Mourne Mountains have long served as a weekend escape for the people of Belfast, with tranquil coastlines and rugged uplands offering superb wildlife-watching opportunities, challenging hiking routes and glorious scenery.

Mountains of Mourne

Celebrated in song and story, the Mountains of Mourne sweep down to the sea near the holiday resort of Newcastle. These shapely granite hills provide some of the finest hill walking and rock climbing in the North.

Castle Espie Wildfowl & Wetlands Centre

Castle Espie Wildfowl & Wetlands Centre not only protects the wetlands environment that the geese and other migratory birds depend on, but also has its own colourful collection of duck and goose species from around the world.

Mourne Wall

Built between 1904 and 1922, the 35km-long Mourne Wall is one of the most impressive features of the Mourne Mountains. Traversing no fewer than 15 of the Mournes' highest summits, it delineates the catchment area of the Silent Valley reservoirs.

Strangford Lough

One of the great birdwatching spectacles of Ireland is the autumn arrival of vast flocks of light-bellied brent geese (75% of the world population) at Strangford Lough. Around 30,000 geese overwinter here.

1. Mountains of Mourne 2. Birdlife at Castle Espie 3. Hiking along Mourne Wall

COUNTIES DOWN & ARMAGH MOURNE MOUNTAINS

4km up the valley to the Crom Dam. It runs daily in July and August, weekends only in May, June and September.

Mourne Wall
LANDMARK

The dry-stone Mourne Wall was built between 1904 and 1922 to keep livestock out of the catchment area of the Kilkeel and Annalong Rivers, which were to be dammed to provide a water supply for Belfast. (Poor geological conditions meant the Annalong could not be dammed, and its waters were diverted to the Silent Valley Reservoir via a 3.6km-long tunnel beneath Slieve Binnian.) The spectacular wall, 2m high, 1m thick and over 35km long, marches across the summits of 15 of the surrounding peaks including the highest, Slieve Donard (853m). You can walk the entire length of the wall, or just a short section (as on the ascent of Slieve Donard).

Activities

The Mournes offer some of the best hill walking and rock climbing in the North. Specialist guidebooks include *The Mournes: Walks* by Paddy Dillon and *A Rock-Climbing Guide to the Mourne Mountains* by Robert Bankhead. You'll also need an Ordnance Survey map, either the 1:50,000 Discoverer Series (Sheet No 29: *The Mournes*), or the 1:25,000 Activity Series *(The Mournes)*. You can buy maps at the tourist office in Newcastle.

Life Adventure Centre
OUTDOORS

(4377 0714; www.onegreatadventure.com; Grange Courtyard, Castlewellan Forest Park) If you fancy a shot at hill walking, rock climbing, canoeing or a range of other outdoor activities, this centre offers one-day, have-a-go sessions for individuals, couples and families (around £60 to £100 per person), as well as Sunday-afternoon taster sessions. It also rents canoes for £30/45 per half-/full day.

Hotrock
ROCK CLIMBING

(4372 5354; www.tollymore.com; Tollymore National Outdoor Centre; adult/child £5/2.50; ☺10am-10pm Tue-Thu, to 5pm Fri-Mon) If the weather is wet, you can still go rock climbing at this indoor climbing wall; you can hire rock boots and harness for £3.50. The entrance is on the B180, 2km west of the Tollymore Forest Park exit gate.

Gasp Action Sports
ADVENTURE SPORTS

(07739 210119; www.gaspactionsports.com; Tullyree Rd, Bryansford; ☺10am-6pm Tue-Sun Jul & Aug, 11am-6pm Sat & Sun Apr-Jun & Sep-Nov) A three-hour beginner's session, including board, safety gear and instruction, at this mountain-boarding centre costs £20. It's off the B180, 3km west of Bryansford village.

Mount Pleasant
HORSE RIDING

(4377 8651; www.mountpleasantcentre.com; Bannonstown Rd, Castlewellan; per hour £12-15) More sedate outdoor activities are offered by this horse-riding and pony-trekking centre, which caters for both experienced riders and beginners, and offers various guided treks into the park. Short rides, beach rides and pony trekking can also be arranged.

Festivals & Events

The Mournes are the venue for various hiking festivals, including the Mourne International Walking Festival (www.mournewalking. co.uk) in late June, and the Down District Walking Festival in early August.

Sleeping & Eating

Meelmore Lodge
HOSTEL £

(4372 6657; www.meelmorelodge.com; 52 Trassey Rd, Bryansford; tent sites per adult/child £6/3, dm/tw/f £15/40/70) Meelmore is the best hostel in the Mourne Mountains, with a cosy lounge and kitchen, two four-bunk dorms, a couple of private rooms, a tents-only campsite and a good coffee shop. It's set on the northern slopes of the Mournes, 5km west of Bryansford village, so you can hike into the hills from the hostel's front door.

Mourne Lodge
HOSTEL £

(4176 5859; www.themournelodge.com; Bog Rd, Atticall; dm/tw from £18/45; @ ☎) This recently refurbished, purpose-built hostel offers bright and appealing budget accommodation, complete with outdoor barbecue patio. As well as a self-catering kitchen, there's a restaurant that serves breakfast, lunch and dinner. It's in the village of Atticall, 6km north of Kilkeel, off the B27 Hilltown road, and 3km west of the entrance to Silent Valley.

Getting There & Away

In July and August only, the Ulsterbus 405 Mourne Rambler service runs a circular route from Newcastle, calling at a dozen stops around the Mournes, including Bryansford (8 minutes), Meelmore (17 minutes), Silent Valley (40 minutes), Carrick Little (45 minutes) and Bloody Bridge (one hour). There are six buses daily: the first leaves at 9.30am, the last at 5pm; the maximum single fare is £4.20.

Bus 34A (July and August only) runs from Newcastle to the Silent Valley car park (45 minutes, two daily), calling at Donard Park (five minutes) and Bloody Bridge (10 minutes).

Mournes Coast Road

The scenic drive south along the A2 coast road from Newcastle to Newry is the most memorable journey in Down. Annalong, Kilkeel and Rostrevor offer convenient stopping points from which you can detour into the mountains.

Rostrevor

Rostrevor (Caislean Ruairi) is a pretty Victorian seaside resort famed for its lively pubs. Each year in late July, folk musicians converge on the village for the Fiddler's Green International Festival (www.fiddlersgreenfestival.co.uk).

The town is noted for its many pubs, most of which have regular live music. There are Tuesday-night sessions from 10pm in the Corner House (1 Bridge St), and regular impromptu sessions at the Old Killowen Inn (10 Bridge St), which also has an appealing beer garden. For food, try the Kilbroney (31 Church St).

To the east is Kilbroney Forest Park (Shore Rd; ⊙9am-10pm Jun-Aug, to 5pm Sep-May) FREE. From the car park at the top of the forest drive, a 10-minute hike leads up to a superb view over the lough to Carlingford Mountain, as well as to the Cloughmore Stone, a 30-tonne granite boulder inscribed with Victorian-era graffiti. The park is also home to Northern Ireland's best downhill mountain-biking trails; bike hire and uplift from East Coast Adventure (✆4175 3535; eastcoastadventure.com), at the trailhead.

Warrenpoint

POP 7000

Warrenpoint (An Pointe) is a Victorian resort at the head of Carlingford Lough, its seaside appeal somewhat diminished by the large industrial harbour at the west end of town. Its broad streets, main square and renovated prom are pleasant enough though, and it has better sleeping and eating options than either Newry or Rostrevor, including a couple of excellent restaurants.

About 2km northwest of the town centre is Narrow Water Castle (⊙10am-6pm Fri Jul & Aug) FREE, a fine Elizabethan tower house

built in 1568 to command the entrance to the River Newry.

🛏 Sleeping & Eating

Whistledown Hotel BOUTIQUE HOTEL ££
(✆4175 4174; www.thewhistledownhotel.com; 6 Seaview; s/d from £70/100; ⊛⊕) A small boutique hotel with a superb waterfront setting, the Whistledown has 20 bedrooms with scarlet and pistachio crushed-velvet trimmings, large flat-screen TVs, and bathrooms with triple shower heads and colourful designer tiling. It's a popular venue for weddings, so if you're looking for peace and quiet, check there isn't one on!

★Restaurant 23 IRISH ££
(✆4175 3222; www.restaurant23warrenpoint.com; 13 Seaview; mains £12-19; ⊙lunch & dinner Mon-Sat, 12.30-9pm Sun; ✐) ✒ Set in the Balmoral Hotel on Warrenpoint's waterfront, this innovative restaurant garnered a Michelin Bib Gourmand for TV chef Raymond McArdle, whose fresh and fun approach to fine Irish produce has helped turn this corner of County Down into a foodie destination. From Monday to Friday there's a three-course set-dinner menu for £15.

Bennett's SEAFOOD ££
(✆4175 2314; www.bennettsseafood.com; 21 Church St; mains £11-18; ⊙lunch & dinner) ✒ A stalwart of Warrenpoint's fine-dining scene, Bennett's combines relaxed and friendly service with seafood sourced from various Irish ports, spiced up with Mediterranean and Asian flavours. There's a special midweek menu that offers three courses for £14.

ⓘ Information

Tourist Office (✆4175 2256; www.visitnewryandmourne.com; Church St; ⊙9am-1pm & 2-5pm Mon-Fri, plus Sat & Sun Jun-Sep) In the town hall.

ⓘ Getting There & Away

Bus 39 runs between Newry and Warrenpoint (£2.90, 20 minutes, at least hourly Monday to Saturday, 10 on Sunday), with some services continuing on to Kilkeel (one hour).

Newry

POP 22,975

Newry has long been a frontier town, guarding the land route from Dublin to Ulster through the 'Gap of the North', the pass between Slieve Gullion and the Carlingford hills, still followed by the main Dublin–Belfast road and railway. Its name derives from a yew tree (An tIúr) supposedly planted here by St Patrick.

The opening of the Newry Canal in 1742, linking the town with the River Bann at Portadown, made Newry a busy trading port, exporting coal from Coalisland on Lough Neagh, as well as linen and butter from the surrounding area.

Newry today is a major shopping centre, with a busy market on Thursday and Saturday. It's invaded at weekends by shoppers from the South taking advantage of the euro exchange rate and the relative bargains available across the border.

◉ Sights

Newry & Mourne Museum MUSEUM
(www.bagenalscastle.com; Castle St, Bagenal's Castle; ⊙10am-4.30pm Mon-Sat, 1.30-5pm Sun) FREE This museum is housed in Bagenal's Castle, the town's oldest surviving building, with exhibits on the Newry Canal and local archaeology, culture and folklore. Recently rediscovered (having been incorporated into more recent buildings), the 16th-century castle was built for Nicholas Bagenal, grand marshal of the English army in Ireland. The building also houses the tourist office.

🛌 Sleeping

Marymount B&B ££
(☑3026 1099; www.marymount.freeservers.com; 15 Windsor Ave; s/d £35/60; 🅿🐾) A modern bungalow in a quiet location up a hill off the A1 Belfast road, Marymount is only a 10-minute walk from the town centre. There are three country-style bedrooms and a lovely breakfast room opening onto the garden, and the owners are welcoming and helpful to a fault.

Canal Court Hotel HOTEL £££
(☑3025 1234; www.canalcourthotel.com; Merchants Quay; s/d from £80/125; @🐾) You can't miss this huge yellow building opposite the bus station. Although it's a modern hotel, it affects a deliberately old-fashioned atmosphere, with leather sofas dotted around the vast wood-panelled lobby and a restaurant that veers dangerously close to chintzy.

✕ Eating & Drinking

Grounded CAFE £
(2a Monaghan St; mains £3-8; ⊙7am-midnight Mon-Fri, 8am-11pm Sat & Sun; 🐾) A great little neighbourhood cafe, always packed with locals, Grounded not only has the best coffee in town but also serves good breakfasts, snacks (including pastrami bagels), light meals (including Caesar salad) and huge scones and cakes. The only downside is trying to find a seat!

Brass Monkey PUB ££
(☑3026 3176; 1-4 Sandy St; mains £9-16; ⊙food served noon-8.30pm Mon-Thu, noon-9pm Fri & Sat, 5-9pm Sun) Newry's most popular pub, with Victorian brass, brick and timber decor, serves good bar meals ranging from lasagne and burgers to seafood and steaks. At weekends you can get a full Irish fried breakfast for £5 (9am till noon).

ℹ Information

Tourist Office (☑3031 3170; www.visitnewry andmourne.com; Castle St, Bagenal's Castle; ⊙9am-5pm Mon-Fri, plus 10am-4pm Sat Apr-Sep, closed 1-2pm Oct-Mar)

ℹ Getting There & Away

BUS
Newry BusCentre is on the Mall, opposite the Canal Court Hotel. Goldline Express bus 238 runs regularly to Newry from Belfast's Europa BusCentre (£9, 1¼ hours, at least hourly Monday to Saturday, eight Sunday) via Hillsborough and Banbridge.

Bus 44 runs from Newry to Armagh (£5.80, 1¼ hours, twice daily Monday to Saturday), and bus 39 departs for Warrenpoint (£2.90, 20 minutes, at least hourly Monday to Saturday, 10 on Sunday) and Rostrevor (30 minutes).

TRAIN
The train station is 2.5km northwest of the centre, on the A25; bus 341 (free for train passengers) links train arrivals and departures to the bus station. Newry is a stop on the Enterprise rail service between Dublin (£20, 1¼ hours, eight daily) and Belfast (£11, 50 minutes, eight daily).

COUNTY ARMAGH

South Armagh

Rural and staunchly Republican, South Armagh is known to its inhabitants as 'God's Country'. But to the British soldiers stationed there in the 1970s it had another, more sinister nickname – 'Bandit Country'. With the Republic only a few miles away,

South Armagh was a favourite area for IRA cross-border attacks and bombings. For more than 30 years, British soldiers on foot patrol in village streets and the constant clatter of army helicopters were a part of everyday life.

The peace process has probably had more visible effect here than anywhere else in Northern Ireland. As part of the UK government's 'normalisation process', the army pulled out in 2007 – the hilltop watchtowers have been removed (their former location marked here and there by a defiant Irish tricolour) and the huge barracks at Bessbrook Mill and Crossmaglen have been closed down.

Today, South Armagh (www.south-armagh.com) is a peaceful backwater, known for its historic sites, enchanting scenery and traditional music. Its network of narrow rural roads is ideal for exploring by bike, while the rolling hills of the Ring of Gullion make for ideal walking country.

Bessbrook

POP 3150

Bessbrook (An Sruthán) was founded in the mid-19th century by Quaker linen manufacturer John Grubb Richardson as a 'model village' to house the workers at his flax mill. Rows of pretty terraced houses line the two main squares, Charlemont and College, each with a green in the middle, and are complemented by a town hall, school, bathhouse and dispensary. It is said that Bessbrook was the inspiration for Bournville (near Birmingham in England), the model village built by the Cadbury family for their chocolate factory.

At the centre of the village is the massive Bessbrook Mill. Requisitioned by the British Army in 1970, it served as a military base for more than 30 years – the helipad here was reputedly the busiest in Europe – until the troops moved out in 2007. In 2013 developers were given the go-ahead to convert the mill building into a residential complex.

Just south of Bessbrook is Derrymore House (www.nationaltrust.org.uk; gardens free, house adult/child £2/1; ☺ gardens dawn-dusk), an elegant thatched cottage built in 1776 for Isaac Corry, the Irish MP for Newry for 30 years; the Act of Union was drafted in the drawing room here in 1800. The house is only open on a handful of days each year – call or check the website – but the surrounding parkland, laid out by John Sutherland (1745–1826), one of the most celebrated disciples of English landscape gardener Capability Brown, offers scenic trails with views to the Ring of Gullion.

Bessbrook is 5km northwest of Newry. Bus 41 runs from Newry to Bessbrook (15 minutes, hourly Monday to Saturday), while buses 42 (to Crossmaglen) and 44 (to Armagh) pass the entrance to Derrymore House on the A25 Camlough road.

Ring of Gullion

The Ring of Gullion (www.ringofgullion.org) is a magical region steeped in Celtic legend, centred on Slieve Gullion (Sliabh gCuilinn), where the Celtic warrior Cúchulainn is said to have taken his name after killing the dog (cú) belonging to the smith Culainn. The 'ring' is a necklace of rugged hills strung between Newry and Forkhill, 15km to the southwest, encircling the central whaleback ridge of Slieve Gullion. This unusual concentric formation is a geological structure known as a ring dyke.

◉ Sights

Slieve Gullion Forest Park   FOREST
(☺8am-dusk) FREE A 13km scenic drive through this forest park provides picturesque views over the surrounding hills. From the parking and picnic area at the top of the drive, you can hike to the summit of Slieve Gullion (576m), the highest point in County Armagh, topped by two early Bronze Age cairns and a tiny lake (1.5km round trip). The park entrance is 10km southwest of Newry on the B113 road to Forkhill.

Killevy Churches   HISTORIC SITE
(☺24hr) FREE Surrounded by beech trees, these ruined, conjoined churches were constructed on the site of a 5th-century nunnery that was founded by St Moninna. The eastern church dates from the 15th century, and shares a gable wall with the 12th-century western one. The west door, with a massive lintel and granite jambs, may be 200 years older still. At the side of the churchyard, a footpath leads uphill to a white cross that marks St Moninna's holy well.

The churches are 6km south of Camlough, on a minor road to Meigh. Look out for a crossroads with a sign pointing west to the churches and east to Bernish Rock Viewpoint.

Armagh City

POP 14,600

The little cathedral city of Armagh (Ard Macha) has been an important religious centre since the 5th century, and remains the ecclesiastical capital of Ireland, the seat of both the Anglican and Roman Catholic archbishops of Armagh, and Primates of All Ireland. Their two cathedrals, both named for St Patrick, stare each other out from their respective hilltops.

Despite having a number of attractive Georgian buildings, the town has a bit of a dreary, rundown feel to it, with gap sites, wasteland and boarded-up windows spoiling the streetscape, but it's still worth a visit for the fascinating Armagh Public Library and nearby Navan Fort.

History

When St Patrick began his mission to spread Christianity throughout Ireland, he chose a site close to Emain Macha (Navan Fort), the nerve centre of pagan Ulster, for his power base. In 445 he built Ireland's first stone church on a hill nearby (now home to the Church of Ireland cathedral), and later decreed that Armagh should have pre-eminence over all the churches in Ireland.

By the 8th century Armagh was one of Europe's best-known centres of religion, learning and craftwork. The city was divided into three districts (called *trians*), centred around English, Scottish and Irish streets. Armagh's fame was its undoing, however, as the Vikings plundered the city 10 times between 831 and 1013.

The city gained a new prosperity from the linen trade in the 18th century, a period whose legacy includes a Royal School, an astronomical observatory, a renowned public library and a fine crop of Georgian architecture.

Armagh is associated with some prominent historical figures. James Ussher (1580–1655), archbishop of Armagh, was an avid scholar who is best known for pinning down the day of the Creation to Sunday 23 October 4004 BC by adding up the generations quoted in the Bible, a date that was accepted as fact until the late 19th century. His extensive library became the nucleus of the great library at Trinity College, Dublin. Jonathan Swift (1667–1745), dean of St Patrick's Cathedral in Dublin, and author of *Gulliver's Travels,* was a frequent visitor to Armagh, while the architect Francis Johnston (1760–1829), responsible for many of Dublin's finest Georgian streetscapes, was born in the city.

◉ Sights

Armagh Public Library　　　　MUSEUM
(http://armaghpubliclibrary.arm.ac.uk; 43 Abbey St; ⊙10am-1pm & 2-4pm Mon-Fri) FREE The Greek inscription above the main entrance to Armagh Public Library, founded in 1771 by Archbishop Robinson, means 'the medicine shop of the soul'. Step inside and you'd swear that the archbishop had just swept out of the door, leaving you to browse among his personal collection of 17th- and 18th-century books, maps and engravings.

The library's most prized possession is a first edition of *Gulliver's Travels,* published in 1726 and annotated by none other than Swift himself. It was stolen in an armed robbery in 1999, but was recovered, undamaged, in Dublin 20 months later.

Other treasures of the library include Sir Walter Raleigh's 1614 *History of the World,* the *Claims of the Innocents* (pleas to Oliver Cromwell) and a large collection of engravings by Hogarth and others.

The collection spills over into the nearby **Registry** (5 Vicar's Hill; adult/child £2/1; ⊙10am-1pm & 2-4pm Tue-Sat), a depository for Church of Ireland records, where you can see ancient coins, early Christian artefacts and other curiosities from the library's archives.

The Mall　　　　PARK
The Mall, a long lozenge of neatly barbered grass to the east of the town centre, was a venue for horse racing, cock fighting and bull baiting until the 18th century, when Archbishop Robinson decided that it was all a tad vulgar for a city of learning, and transformed it into an elegant Georgian park. It remains the most attractive part of Armagh.

At its northern end stands **Armagh Courthouse**, rebuilt after being destroyed by a huge IRA bomb blast in 1993. It originally dates from 1809, designed by local man Francis Johnston, who later became one of Ireland's most famous architects. Directly opposite the courthouse is the forbidding **Armagh Gaol**. Built in 1780 to the design of Thomas Cooley, it remained in use until 1988; it is currently being redeveloped to create a hotel, shopping mall and apartments.

The east side of the park is lined with handsome Georgian terraces including

Charlemont Place, another creation of Francis Johnston.

Armagh County Museum MUSEUM
(www.nmni.com/acm; The Mall East; ⏲10am-5pm Mon-Fri, 10am-1pm & 2-5pm Sat) FREE The city museum displays prehistoric axe heads, items found in bogs, corn dollies and straw-boy outfits, and military costumes and equipment. Don't miss the gruesome cast-iron skull that once graced the top of the Armagh gallows.

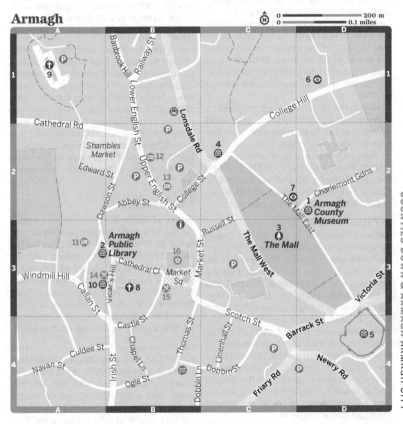

Armagh

◉ **Top Sights**
1 Armagh County Museum D2
2 Armagh Public Library A3
3 The Mall C3

◉ **Sights**
4 Armagh Courthouse C2
5 Armagh Gaol D4
6 Armagh Planetarium D1
7 Charlemont Place C2
8 St Patrick's Church of Ireland
    Cathedral B3
9 St Patrick's Roman Catholic
    Cathedral A1

10 The Registry A3

🛌 **Sleeping**
11 Armagh City Hostel A3
12 Charlemont Arms Hotel B2
13 De Averell House B2

🍴 **Eating**
14 One Eighty Two A3
15 Uluru Bistro B3

🎭 **Entertainment**
16 Market Place Theatre & Arts
    Centre B3

St Patrick's Church of Ireland Cathedral
CATHEDRAL

(☑3752 3142; www.stpatricks-cathedral.org; Cathedral Close; admission by donation; ☺9am-5pm Apr-Oct, to 4pm Nov-Mar) The city's Anglican cathedral occupies the site of St Patrick's original stone church. The present cathedral's ground plan is 13th century but the building itself is a Gothic restoration dating from 1834 to 1840. A stone slab on the exterior wall of the north transept marks the burial place of Brian Ború, the high king of Ireland, who died near Dublin during the last great battle against the Vikings in 1014.

Within the church are the remains of an 11th-century Celtic Cross that once stood nearby, and the Tandragee Idol, a curious granite figure dating back to the Iron Age. In the south aisle is a memorial to Archbishop Richard Robinson (1709–94), who founded Armagh's observatory and public library. Guided tours, which should be arranged in advance, cost £3 per person.

St Patrick's Roman Catholic Cathedral
CATHEDRAL

(www.armagharchdiocese.org; Cathedral Rd; admission by donation; ☺9am-6pm Mon-Fri, to 8pm Sat, 8am-6.30pm Sun) The city's Roman Catholic Cathedral was built between 1838 and 1873 in Gothic Revival style, with huge twin towers dominating the approach up flight after flight of steps. Inside it seems almost Byzantine, with every piece of wall and ceiling covered in brilliantly coloured mosaics. The sanctuary was modernised in 1981 and has a very distinctive tabernacle holder and crucifix that seem out of place among the mosaics and statues of the rest of the church. Mass is said at 10am Monday to Friday, and at 9am, 11am and 5.30pm on Sunday.

Armagh Planetarium
PLANETARIUM

(☑3752 3689; www.armaghplanet.com; College Hill; admission to exhibition area per person £2, shows adult/child £6/5; ☺10am-5pm Mon-Sat year-round, plus 10am-5pm Sun Jul & Aug) The Armagh Observatory was founded by Archbishop Robinson in 1790 and is still Ireland's leading astronomical research institute. Aimed mainly at educating young people, the nearby Armagh Planetarium has an interactive exhibition on space exploration, and a digital theatre that screens a range of spectacular half-hour shows on its domed ceiling (check the website for show times).

⚔ Festivals & Events

Apple Blossom Fair
FOOD

(www.armagh.co.uk) Held on the first Saturday in May at Loughgall Manor Estate (10km northeast of Armagh) in the heart of orchard country. Includes orchard tours, a farmers market, cookery demonstrations and stalls selling all kinds of apple-based products.

Road Bowling
SPORT

(www.irishroadbowling.ie) You may be lucky enough to catch a road bowling match, a traditional Irish game now played mostly in Armagh and Cork. Contestants hurl small metal bowls weighing approximately 800g along quiet country lanes to see who can make it to the finishing line with the least number of throws. Games usually take place on Sunday afternoons in summer, with the Ulster Finals held at Armagh in late June. Ask for details at the tourist information centre.

🛏 Sleeping

Armagh City Hostel
HOSTEL £

(☑3751 1800; www.hini.org.uk; 39 Abbey St; dm/tw £18/38; ☺daily Mar-Oct, Fri & Sat only Nov-Feb, closed 23 Dec-2 Jan; 🕸) This modern, purpose-built hostel near the Church of Ireland Cathedral is more like a small hotel. There are six comfortable twin rooms with private bathrooms, TV and tea-and-coffee facilities, as well as 12 small dorms, a well-equipped kitchen, laundry, lounge and reading room.

De Averell House
B&B ££

(☑3751 1213; www.deaverellhouse.co.uk; 47 Upper English St; s/d/f £45/75/100; 🕸) A converted Georgian town house with five spacious rooms and a self-catering apartment, the De Averell is run by a friendly landlord who can't do enough to help. Rooms at the front can be noisy; the twin at the back is the quietest.

Charlemont Arms Hotel
HOTEL ££

(☑3752 2028; www.charlemontarmshotel.com; 57-65 Lower English St; s/d from £49/79; 🕸) This hotel dates from the 19th century and has been renovated in charming period decor – oak-panelled dining room, Victorian fireplaces and flagstone-floored cellar restaurant. The bedrooms, in contrast, are modern and stylish.

Hillview Lodge
B&B ££

(☑3752 2000; www.hillviewlodge.com; 33 Newtownhamilton Rd; s/d £39/58; 🕸) Hillview,

1.5km south of Armagh, is a welcoming, family-run guesthouse. Its self-contained block holds six appealing rooms with great countryside views, and there's a driving range next door if you feel like improving your golf swing.

Eating

One Eighty Two CAFE £
(☑ 3752 5523; www.oneeightyrestaurant.co.uk; 4 Vicar's Hill; mains £5-7; ⊙ 10am-4pm Tue-Sat) Established to provide employment training for young people with special needs, this chintzy but charming Georgian tearoom has rapidly won a reputation as a great place to eat, offering soups, salads and hot lunch specials, plus a full breakfast menu. Best to book a table for lunch.

★ Uluru Bistro FUSION ££
(☑ 3751 8051; www.ulurubistro.co.uk; 16-18 Market St; mains lunch £7-8, dinner £15-24; ⊙ noon-3pm Tue-Sat, 5-10.30pm Tue-Sun) The Aussie chef at Uluru brings a bit of antipodean flair to Armagh, with a fusion menu that ranges from salt 'n' chilli tempura prawns to chargrilled medallions of marinated kangaroo with sweet-potato chips, plus Irish steak, seafood and venison dishes.

☆ Entertainment

Market Place Theatre & Arts Centre THEATRE
(www.marketplacearmagh.com; Market St; ⊙ box office 9.30am-4.30pm Mon-Sat) Armagh's main cultural venue hosts a 400-seat theatre, exhibition galleries and the Footlights Bar & Bistro, which has live bands on Saturday nights.

ⓘ Information

Tourist Office (☑ 3752 1800; www.armagh.co.uk; 40 Upper English St; ⊙ 9am-5pm Mon-Sat, 2-5pm Sun, from noon Sun Jul & Aug)

ⓘ Getting There & Away

Goldline Express bus 251 runs from Belfast's Europa BusCentre (£9, one to 1½ hours, hourly Monday to Friday, six Saturday, four Sunday) to Armagh. Bus 44 runs from Armagh to Newry (£5.80, 1¼ hours, twice daily Monday to Saturday).

Bus Éireann service 36 runs from Dublin to Armagh (€17, three hours, hourly Monday to Friday, five Saturday, four Sunday).

Around Armagh City

Navan Fort

Perched atop a drumlin a little over 3km west of Armagh is Navan Fort (Emain Macha), the most important archaeological site in Ulster. It was probably a prehistoric provincial capital and ritual site, on a par with Tara in County Meath. The site is linked in legend with the tales of Cúchulainn and named as capital of Ulster and the seat of the legendary Knights of the Red Branch.

It was an important centre from around 1150 BC until the coming of Christianity; the discovery of the skull of a Barbary ape on the site indicates trading links with North Africa. The main circular **earthwork enclosure** is no less than 240m in diameter, and encloses a smaller circular structure and an Iron Age **burial mound**. The circular structure has intrigued archaeologists – it ap-

---

WORTH A TRIP

OXFORD ISLAND

Oxford Island National Nature Reserve protects a range of habitats – woodland, wildflower meadows, reedy shoreline and shallow lake margins – on the southern edge of Lough Neagh. It's criss-crossed with walking and cycling trails, information boards and birdwatching hides.

The **Lough Neagh Discovery Centre** (www.oxfordisland.com; Oxford Island, Lurgan; ⊙ 10am-1pm & 2-4pm Mon-Sat, plus 2-5pm Sun Apr-Sep) FREE, set in the middle of a reed-fringed pond inhabited by waterfowl, has a tourist-information desk, a museum and a great little cafe with lake-shore views.

One-hour **boat trips** (☑ 3832 7573; adult/child £5/3; ⊙ 1.30-5pm Sat & Sun Apr-Oct) on the lough depart from nearby Kinnego Marina, aboard the 12-seater cabin cruiser *Master McGra*.

Oxford Island is just north of Lurgan, signposted from Junction 10 on the M1 motorway.

pears to be some sort of temple, the roof of which was supported by concentric rows of wooden posts, and the interior of which was filled with a vast pile of stones. Stranger still, the whole thing was set on fire soon after its construction around 95 BC, possibly for ritual purposes.

The nearby **Navan Centre** (www.navan.com; 81 Killylea Rd, Armagh; adult/child £6/4; ⊙10am-6.30pm Apr-Sep, to 4pm Oct-Mar, last admission 90min before closing, or 1hr before in winter) has exhibitions placing the fort in its historical context, and a re-creation of an Iron Age settlement.

You can walk to the site from Armagh (45 minutes), or take bus 73 to Navan village (10 minutes, 10 daily Monday to Friday).

Lough Neagh

Lough Neagh (pronounced 'nay') is the largest freshwater lake in all of Britain and Ireland, big enough to swallow the city of Birmingham (West Midlands, UK, or Ala-bama, USA – either one would fit). Though vast (around 32km long and 16km wide), the lough is relatively shallow – never more than 9m deep – and is an important habitat for waterfowl. Its waters are home to the pollan, a freshwater herring found only in Ireland, and the dollaghan, a subspecies of trout unique to Lough Neagh. Connected to the sea by the River Bann, the lough has been an important waterway and food source since prehistoric times, and still has an eel fishery that employs around 200 people.

The main points of access to the lough include Antrim town on the eastern shore, Oxford Island in the south and Ardboe in the west.

The **Loughshore Trail** (www.loughshoretrail.com) is a 180km cycle route that encircles the lough. For most of its length it follows quiet country roads set back from the shore; the best sections for actually seeing the lough itself are west of Oxford Island and south from Antrim town.

Counties Londonderry & Antrim

POP 532,000 / AREA 4918 SQ KM

Best Places to Eat

➡ Lime Tree (p628)

➡ 55 Degrees North (p632)

➡ Brown's Restaurant (p623)

➡ Burger Club (p630)

➡ Bushmills Inn (p634)

Best Places to Stay

➡ Merchant's House (p622)

➡ Downhill Hostel (p629)

➡ Galgorm Resort & Spa (p645)

➡ Whitepark House (p636)

➡ Villa Farmhouse (p642)

Why Go?

The north coast of Northern Ireland, from Carrickfergus to Coleraine, is like a giant geology classroom. Here the patient workmanship of the ocean has laid bare the black basalt and white chalk that underlie much of County Antrim, and dissected the rocks into a scenic extravaganza of sea stacks, pinnacles, cliffs and caves. Tourists flock to the surreal geological centrepiece of the Giant's Causeway, its popularity challenged only by the nearby test-your-nerve tightrope of the Carrick-a-Rede rope bridge.

To the west, County Londonderry's chief attraction is the historic city of Derry, nestled in a broad sweep of the River Foyle. It is the only surviving walled city in Ireland, and a walk around the city walls is one of the highlights of a visit to Northern Ireland. Derry's other drawcards include the powerful political murals in the Bogside district and the lively music scene in the city's many pubs.

When to Go

➡ May is the best month for walking the Causeway Coast, as you'll avoid the summer crowds at the Giant's Causeway and enjoy a colourful sprinkling of spring flowers to boot.

➡ June and July see the peak of the seabird nesting season – an ideal time to visit the Kebble National Nature Reserve on Rathlin Island – and also bring the best weather for lounging on the local beaches.

➡ The traditional festivities of the Ould Lammas Fair at Ballycastle take place on the last Monday and Tuesday of August.

Counties Londonderry & Antrim Highlights

① Enjoy a hike along the spectacular Causeway Coast from Carrick-a-Rede to the **Giant's Causeway** (p634)

② Discover ancient walls, modern murals and foot-stomping music in the historic city of **Derry** (p616)

③ Test your nerve as you wobble across the slender, swaying **Carrick-a-Rede Rope Bridge** (p635)

④ Surf or body-board among the Atlantic breakers at beaches around **Portrush** (p632)

⑤ Spot seabirds and seals at the remote western end of **Rathlin Island** (p638)

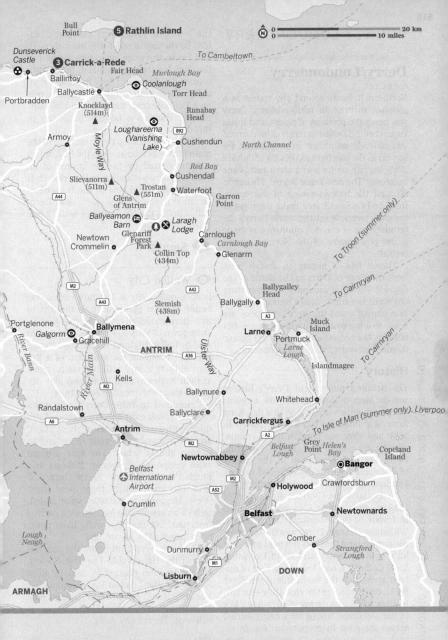

6 Learn the secrets of Irish whiskey-making on a tour of the **Old Bushmills Distillery** (p633)

7 Soak up the spectacular coastal views from the

photogenic **Mussenden Temple** (p629) at Downhill

COUNTY LONDONDERRY

Derry/Londonderry

POP 83,700

Northern Ireland's second city comes as a pleasant surprise to many visitors. Derry was never the prettiest of places, and it has lagged behind Belfast in terms of investment and redevelopment but, in preparation for its year in the limelight as UK City of Culture 2013, the city centre was given a handsome makeover. The new Peace Bridge, Ebrington Sq, and the redevelopment of the waterfront and Guildhall area make the most of the city's riverside setting, while Derry's determined air of can-do optimism has made it the powerhouse of the North's cultural revival.

There's lots of history to absorb here, from the Siege of Derry to the Battle of the Bogside – a stroll around the 17th-century city walls is a must, as is a tour of the Bogside murals – and the city's lively pubs are home to a burgeoning live-music scene. But perhaps the biggest attraction is the people themselves: warm, witty and welcoming.

History

The defining moment of Derry's history was the Siege of Derry in 1688–89, an event whose echoes reverberate to this day. King James I granted the city a royal charter in 1613, and gave the London livery companies (trade guilds) the task of fortifying Derry and the Plantation of the county of Coleraine (soon to be renamed County Londonderry) with Protestant settlers.

In England the Glorious Revolution of 1688 saw the Catholic King James II ousted in favour of the Protestant Dutch prince, William of Orange. Derry was the only garrison in Ireland that was not held by forces loyal to King James, and so, in December 1688, Catholic forces led by the Earl of Antrim arrived on the east bank of the River Foyle, ready to seize the city. They sent emissaries to discuss terms of surrender, but in the meantime troops were being ferried across the river in preparation for an assault. On seeing this, 13 apprentice boys barred the city gates with a cry of 'There'll be no surrender!'

And so, on 7 December 1688, the Siege of Derry began. For 105 days the Protestant citizens of Derry withstood bombardment, disease and starvation (the condition of the besieging forces was not much better). By the time a relief ship burst through and broke the siege, an estimated half of the city's inhabitants had died. In the 20th century the Siege of Derry became a symbol of Ulster Protestants' resistance to rule by a Catholic Irish Republic, and 'No surrender!' remains a Loyalist battle cry to this day.

In the 19th century Derry was one of the main ports of emigration to the USA, a fact commemorated by the sculptures of an emigrant family standing in Waterloo Pl. It also played a vital role in the transatlantic trade in linen shirts. Even now, Derry still supplies the US president with 12 free shirts every year.

◉ Sights

◉ Walled City

Derry's walled city is Ireland's earliest example of town planning. It is thought to have been modelled on the French Renaissance town of Vitry-le-François, designed in 1545 by Italian engineer Hieronimo Marino; both are based on the grid plan of a Roman military camp, with two main streets at right angles to each other, and four city gates, one at either end of each street.

Completed in 1619, Derry's city walls (www.derryswalls.com) are 8m high and 9m thick, with a circumference of about 1.5km, and are the only city walls in Ireland to survive almost intact. The four original gates (Shipquay, Ferryquay, Bishop's and Butcher's) were rebuilt in the 18th and 19th centuries, when three new gates (New, Magazine and Castle) were added. Derry's nickname, the Maiden City, derives from the fact that the walls have never been breached by an invader.

The walls were built under the supervision of the Honourable The Irish Society, an organisation created in 1613 by King James and the London livery companies. The society still exists today (though now its activities are mainly charitable) and it still owns Derry's city walls.

★ **Tower Museum**   MUSEUM
(www.derrycity.gov.uk/Museums; Union Hall Pl; adult/child £4.20/2.65; ⊙10am-5pm Tue-Sat year-round, plus 11am-3pm Sun Jul-Sep) Inside the Magazine Gate is this award-winning museum, housed in a replica 16th-century tower house. Head straight to the 5th floor

COUNTIES LONDONDERRY & ANTRIM DERRY/LONDONDERRY

for a view from the top of the tower, then work your way down through the excellent Armada Shipwreck exhibition, which tells the story of *La Trinidad Valenciera* – a ship of the Spanish Armada that was wrecked at Kinnagoe Bay in Donegal in 1588. It was discovered by the City of Derry Sub-Aqua Club in 1971 and excavated by marine archaeologists. On display are bronze guns, pewter tableware and personal items – a wooden comb, an olive jar, a shoe sole – recovered from the site, including a 2.5-tonne siege gun bearing the arms of Phillip II of Spain showing him as king of England.

The museum's other exhibition is the Story of Derry, where well-thought-out exhibits and audiovisuals lead you through the city's history from the founding of the monastery of St Colmcille (Columba) in the 6th century to the Battle of the Bogside in the late 1960s. Allow a good two hours to do the museum justice.

⭐ **St Columb's Cathedral**   CATHEDRAL
(www.stcolumbscathedral.org; London St; admission free, donation appreciated; ⊘ 9am-5pm Mon-Sat year-round) Built between 1628 and 1633 from the same grey-green schist as the city walls, this was the first post-Reformation church to be erected in Britain and Ireland, and is Derry's oldest surviving building. In the porch (under the spire, by the St Columb's Court entrance) you can see the original foundation stone of 1633 that records the cathedral's completion, inscribed:

If stones could speake
Then London's prayse
Should sounde who
Built this church and
Cittie from the grounde.

The smaller stone inset, inscribed '*In Templo Verus Deus Est Vereo Colendus*' (The True God is in His Temple and is to be truly worshipped), comes from the original church built here in 1164 and dedicated to the city's patron saint, Colmcille.

Also in the porch is a hollow mortar shell fired into the churchyard during the Great Siege of 1688–89; inside the shell were the terms of surrender. The neighbouring chapter house contains more historical artefacts, including paintings, old photos and the four huge padlocks used to secure the city gates in the 17th century.

The nave, built in a squat, solid style known as Planter's Gothic, shares the austerity of many Church of Ireland cathedrals, with thick walls, small windows and an open-timbered roof (from 1823) resting on corbels depicting the heads of past bishops and deans. The bishop's throne, at the far end of the nave, is an 18th-century mahogany chair in ornate, Chinese Chippendale style.

The chancel and the stained-glass east window depicting the Ascension date from 1887. The flags on either side of the window were captured from the French during the Great Siege; although the yellow silk has been renewed several times since, the poles and gold wirework are original.

Centre for Contemporary Art   GALLERY
(cca-derry-londonderry.org; 10-12 Artillery St; ⊘ noon-6pm Tue-Sat) FREE Opened in late 2012, the CCA was founded to provide a showcase for emerging artists in Northern Ireland and to stage changing exhibitions of the best of contemporary art from around the world.

⦿ Outside the Walls

⭐ **Guildhall**   NOTABLE BUILDING
(www.derrycity.gov.uk/Guildhall; Guildhall Sq; ⊘ 10am-5.30pm daily) FREE Standing just outside the city walls, the neo-Gothic Guildhall was originally built in 1890, then rebuilt after a fire in 1908. As the seat of the old Londonderry Corporation, which institutionalised the policy of discriminating against Catholics over housing and jobs, it incurred the wrath of Nationalists and was bombed twice by the Irish Republican Army (IRA) in 1972. From 2000 to 2005 it was the seat of the Bloody Sunday Inquiry.

The Guildhall is noted for its fine stained-glass windows, presented by the London Livery companies, and its clock tower which is modelled on the one that houses London's Big Ben. Following a major restoration in 2012-13, the Guildhall now hosts a historical exhibition on the Plantation of Ulster, and a tourist information point.

Peace Bridge   BRIDGE
The most visible legacy of Derry's pre-2013 City of Culture facelift is the magnificent Peace Bridge, a sinuously elegant pedestrian bridge spanning the River Foyle, linking the Walled City on the west bank to Ebrington Sq on the east in a symbolic handshake. It provides a useful walking or cycling shortcut from the train station to the Guildhall area.

Derry

N

0   500 m
0   0.25 miles

Rock Rd

26

30

Strand Rd

River Foyle

Northland Rd

Lawrence Hill

Strand Rd

14

Asylum Rd

18   19

Clarendon St

Strand Rd

Queen St

17   20

28

Great James St

22

Harbour Sq

William St

16

BOGSIDE

Queen's Quay

Waterloo Pl

Harbour Museum

Tower Museum

Guildhall

Rossville St

13

11   5

27

Bank Pl

4

1

2

12

7

Lough Swilly Bus Company

Fahan St

10

Magazine St

Waterloo St

31

24

Shipquay St

39

37   35

Foyle Embankment

Waterside Theatre (350m)

8

Fahan St

33

38   40

32

East Wall

Foyle St

Waterside Link

Bond's Hill

The Diamond

36

25

Society St

London St

Pump St

Linenhall St

41

Foyle St

Palace St

34

Orchard St

6

7

Artillery St

St Columb's Cathedral

3

42

15

Bridge St

Derry Tourist Information Centre

23

WATERSIDE

Mall Wall

Church Wall

THE FOUNTAIN

Hawkin St

Long Tower St

Bishop St Without

9

Carlisle Rd

21

Bishop St

Abercorn Rd

Foyle Rd

Craigavon Bridge

Duke St

Spencer Rd

Chapel Rd

Derry

Ebrington Square PLAZA
Orignally a 19th-century fort, and later a British Army base, Ebrington Barracks was demilitarised in 2003, and reinvented as a public area during the city's recent renovations. The former parade ground now serves as a public square, performance venue and exhibition space, famously hosting the 2013 Turner Prize.

★**Harbour Museum** MUSEUM
(Harbour Sq; ⊙10am-1pm & 2-5pm Mon-Fri) FREE
The small, old-fashioned Harbour Museum, with models of ships, a replica of a *currach* (an early sailing boat of the type that carried St Colmcille to Iona) and the bosomy figurehead of the *Minnehaha,* is housed in the old Harbour Commissioner's Building next to the Guildhall.

Hands Across the Divide MONUMENT
As you enter the city across Craigavon Bridge, the first thing you see is the Hands Across the Divide monument. This striking bronze sculpture of two men reaching out to each other symbolises the spirit of reconciliation and hope for the future; it was unveiled in 1992, 20 years after Bloody Sunday.

⊙ **Bogside**

The Bogside district, to the west of the walled city, developed in the 19th and early 20th centuries as a working-class, predominantly Catholic, residential area. By the 1960s its serried ranks of small, terrace houses had become an overcrowded ghetto of poverty and unemployment, a focus for the emerging civil rights movement and a hotbed of Nationalist discontent.

In August 1969 the three-day 'Battle of the Bogside' – a running street battle between local youths and the Royal Ulster Constabulary (RUC) – prompted the UK government to send British troops into Northern Ireland. The residents of the Bogside and neighbouring Brandywell districts – 33,000 of them – declared themselves independent of the civil authorities and barricaded the streets to keep the security forces out. 'Free Derry', as it was known, was a no-go area for the police and army, its streets patrolled by IRA volunteers. In January of 1972 the area around Rossville St witnessed the horrific events of Bloody Sunday. 'Free Derry' ended with Operation Motorman on 31 July 1972, when thousands of British troops and armoured cars moved in to occupy the Bogside.

Since then the area has been extensively redeveloped, the old houses and flats demolished and replaced with modern housing, and the population is now down to 8000. All that remains of the old Bogside is **Free Derry Corner** (intersection of Fahan & Rossville Sts), where the gable end of a house painted with the famous slogan 'You are Now Entering Free Derry' still stands. Nearby is the H-shaped **Hunger Strikers' Memorial** (Rossville St) and, a little further north along Rossville St, the **Bloody Sunday Memorial**, a simple granite obelisk that commemorates the 14 civilians who were shot dead by the British Army on 30 January 1972.

People's Gallery Murals   MURALS
(Rossville St) The 12 murals that decorate the gable ends of houses along Rossville St, near Free Derry Corner, are popularly referred to as the People's Gallery. They are the work of Tom Kelly, Will Kelly and Kevin Hasson, known as 'the Bogside Artists', who have spent most of their lives in the Bogside, and lived through the worst of the Troubles.

Their murals, mostly painted between 1997 and 2001, commemorate key events in the Troubles, including the Battle of the Bogside, Bloody Sunday, Operation Motorman (the British Army's operation to retake IRA-controlled no-go areas in Derry and Belfast in July 1972) and the 1981 hunger strike. The most powerful images are those painted largely in monochrome, consciously evoking journalistic imagery – *Operation Motorman,* showing a British soldier breaking down a door with a sledgehammer; *Bloody Sunday,* with a group of men led by local priest Father Daly carrying the body of Jackie Duddy (the first fatality on that day); and *The Petrol Bomber,* a young boy wearing a gas mask and holding a petrol bomb.

The most moving image is *The Death of Innocence,* which shows the radiant figure of 14-year-old schoolgirl Annette McGavigan, killed in crossfire between the IRA and the British Army on 6 September 1971, the 100th victim of the Troubles. Representing

all the children who died in the conflict, she stands against the brooding chaos of a bombed-out building, the roof beams forming a crucifix in the top right-hand corner. At the left, a downward-pointing rifle, broken in the middle, stands for the failure of violence, while the butterfly symbolises resurrection and the hope embodied in the peace process.

The final mural in the sequence, completed in 2004, is the *Peace Mural,* a swirling image of a dove (symbol of peace and of Derry's patron saint, Columba) rising out of the blood and sadness of the past towards the sunny yellow hope of a peaceful future.

The murals can be seen online at www.cain.ulst.ac.uk/bogsideartists, and in the book *The People's Gallery,* which is available from the artists' website.

Museum of Free Derry   MUSEUM
(www.museumoffreederry.org; 55-61 Glenfada Park; adult/child £3/2; ⊙9.30am-4.30pm Mon-Fri, plus 1-4pm Sat Apr-Sep, 1-4pm Sun Jul-Sep) Just off Rossville St, this museum chronicles the history of the Bogside, the civil rights movement and the events of Bloody Sunday through photographs, film clips, newspaper reports, and the accounts of first-hand witnesses, including some of the original photographs that inspired the murals of the People's Gallery.

☞ Tours

Bogside Artists Tours   WALKING TOUR
(☑07514 052481; www.bogsideartists.com; per person £6) These guided walking tours of the famous People's Gallery murals are led by the artists themselves. Book in advance by phone or on the website.

City Tours   GUIDED TOUR
(☑7127 1996; www.irishtourguides.com; Carlisle Stores, 11 Carlisle Rd; adult/child £4/2) Runs one-hour Historic Derry walking tours starting from Carlisle Stores at 10am, noon and 2pm year-round. There are also tours of the Bogside and of Derry's murals.

Tours'n'Trails   WALKING TOUR
(☑7136 7000; www.toursntrails.co.uk; adult/child £6/4) Offers 1½-hour guided walking tours of the walled city, starting from the tourist office at 11am and 3pm Monday to Saturday from April to October. The price includes admission to St Columb's Cathedral.

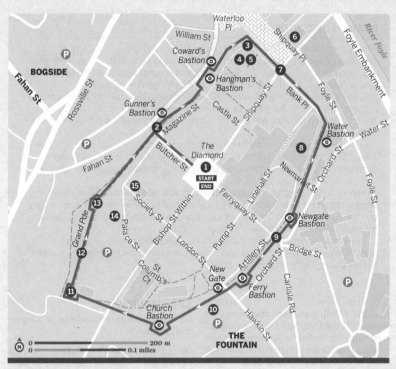

🏃 Walking Tour
Derry's Walled City

START THE DIAMOND
FINISH THE DIAMOND
DISTANCE 2KM
DURATION 30 TO 40 MINUTES

This walk starts from the Diamond, Derry's central square, dominated by the **1** **war memorial**. Head along Butcher St to **2** **Butcher's Gate** and climb the steps to the top of the city walls.

Stroll to **3** **Magazine Gate**, named for the powder magazine that used to be close by. Inside the walls is the modern **4** **O'Doherty's Tower**, housing the excellent **5** **Tower Museum** (p616); outside the walls stands the red-brick, neo-gothic **6** **Guildhall**. (p617)

The River Foyle used to come up to the northeastern wall. In the middle is the **7** **Shipquay Gate**. The walls turn southwest and climb beside the **8** **Millennium Forum** (p625) to the **9** **Ferryquay Gate**, where the apprentice boys barred the gate at the start of the Great Siege of 1688–89.

The stretch of wall beyond overlooks the **10** **Fountain housing estate**, the last significant Protestant community on the western bank of the Foyle.

Continue around the southern stretch of wall to the **11** **Double Bastion** at the southwestern corner, home to Roaring Meg, the most famous of the cannons used during the Siege of Derry. The next section of wall is known as the **12** **Grand Parade**, and offers an excellent view of the murals painted by the Bogside Artists.

An empty plinth on **13** **Royal Bastion** marks the former site of a monument to the Reverend George Walker, joint governor of the city during the Great Siege; it was blown up by the IRA in 1973. Behind the Royal Bastion is the 1872 Church of Ireland **14** **Chapel of St Augustine**, built on the site of St Colmcille's 6th-century monastery. A little further along is the **15** **Apprentice Boys' Memorial Hall**, with a high mesh fence to protect it from paint bombs hurled from below.

DERRY/LONDONDERRY

Derry/Londonderry is a town with two names. Nationalists always use Derry, and vandals often deface the 'London' part of the name on road signs. Staunch Unionists insist on Londonderry, which is still the city's (and county's) official name. All the same, many people, regardless of political persuasion, call it Derry in everyday speech.

The settlement was originally named Doíre Calgaigh (Oak Grove of Calgach), after a pagan warrior-hero; in the 10th century it was renamed Doíre Colmcille (Oak Grove of Columba), in honour of the 6th-century saint who established the first monastic settlement here.

In the following centuries the name was shortened and anglicised to Derrie or Derry. Then in 1613, in recognition of the Corporation of London's role in the 'plantation' of northwest Ulster with Protestant settlers, Derry was granted a royal charter and the city was renamed Londonderry.

A new County Londonderry was created from what was originally County Coleraine, along with parts of Tyrone and Antrim; unlike the city, there has never been an officially sanctioned county called Derry. Nevertheless, those with nationalist leanings, including the county's Gaelic football team, prefer to use County Derry.

Today, road signs in Northern Ireland point to Londonderry, those in the Republic point to Derry (Doíre in Irish), and some tourism industry promotional material covers all bases, using Derry-Londonderry-Doíre.

Blue Boat Tours BOAT TOUR
(☑ 07882 233911; www.blueboattours.com; Foyle Marina; ☺ Mon-Sat May-Sep) Offers a range of boat trips, including a 45-minute 'Three Bridges Tour'. Departs from the pontoon just north of Queen's Quay roundabout.

✪ Festivals & Events

City of Derry Jazz Festival MUSIC
(www.cityofderryjazzfestival.com; ☺ early May) Four days of jazz at various venues.

Gasyard Wall Féile IRISH CULTURE
(www.facebook.com/gasyardwallfeile; ☺ Aug) A major cultural festival that features live music, street performers, carnival, theatre and Irish-language events.

City of Derry Guitar Festival MUSIC
(www.cityofderryguitarfestival.com; ☺ late Aug) The grounds of Magee College (University of Ulster) host performances and master classes from guitar greats around the world, including classical, acoustic, electric, flamenco and bass.

Halloween Carnival CARNIVAL
(www.derrycity.gov.uk/halloween; ☺ 27-31 Oct) Ireland's biggest street party has the entire city dressing up and dancing in the streets.

Foyle Film Festival CINEMA
(www.foylefilmfestival.org; ☺ Nov) This week-long event is the North's biggest film festival.

🛏 Sleeping

It's best to book accommodation in advance during festivals.

Derry City Independent Hostel HOSTEL £
(☑ 7128 0542; www.derry-hostel.co.uk; 44 Great James St; dm/d/q from £13/40/60; @ �) Run by experienced backpackers and decorated with souvenirs from their travels around the world, this small, friendly hostel is set in a Georgian town house, just a short walk northwest of the bus station. It has a second property around the corner called Dolce Vita, with stylishly decorated double, twin and quad rooms (all with shared bathroom).

Derry Palace Hostel HOSTEL £
(☑ 7130 9051; www.paddyspalace.com; 1 Woodleigh Tce, Asylum Rd; dm/tw from £13/45; @ ☎) Part of the Ireland-wide Paddy's Palace chain, this hostel is central, comfortable and as friendly as they come. There's a sunny garden and a good party atmosphere, and the staff regularly organise nights out at local pubs with traditional music.

★ Merchant's House B&B ££
(☑ 7126 9691; www.thesaddlershouse.com; 16 Queen St; s/d £55/80; @ ☎) This historic, Georgian-style town house is a gem of a B&B. It has an elegant lounge and dining room with marble fireplaces and antique furniture, TV, coffee-making facilities and even bathrobes in the bedrooms (only one

has a private bathroom), and homemade marmalade at breakfast. Call at Saddler's House first to pick up a key.

Saddler's House B&B **££**
(☎7126 9691; www.thesaddlershouse.com; 36 Great James St; s/d £55/75; @⊕) Centrally located within a five-minute walk of the walled city, this friendly B&B is set in a lovely Victorian town house. All seven rooms have private bathrooms, and you get to enjoy a huge breakfast in the family kitchen.

Laburnum Lodge B&B **££**
(☎7135 4221; www.laburnumlodge.com; 9 Rockfield, Madam's Bank Rd; s/d £40/55; @⊕) Readers have been impressed by the friendly welcome, spacious bedrooms and hearty breakfasts and recommend this suburban villa on a quiet street on the northern edge of town. From the big roundabout just west of the Foyle Bridge, take the Buncrana road – Rockfield is the first turning on the right. If you don't have your own transport, the owner can pick you up from the train or bus station.

Sunbeam House B&B **££**
(☎7126 3606; sunbeamhouse@hotmail.com; 147 Sunbeam Tce, Bishop St; s/d £44/65; ⊕⛾) This attractive red-brick terrace house is a five-minute walk southwest of the walled city. The four cheerfully decorated rooms are a bit on the small side, but there's nothing cramped about the hospitality – or the size of the breakfasts!

Abbey B&B B&B **££**
(☎7127 9000; www.abbeyaccommodation.com; 4 Abbey St; s/d/f £60/70/105; @⊕) There's a warm welcome waiting at this family-run B&B just a short walk from the walled city, on the edge of the Bogside. The six rooms are stylishly decorated and include family rooms able to sleep four.

Arkle House B&B **££**
(☎7127 1157; www.derryhotel.co.uk; 2 Coshquin Rd; s/d £55/65; @⊕) Located 2km northwest of the city centre, this grand Victorian house is set in private gardens and offers five large, lush bedrooms and a private kitchen for guests to use.

Da Vinci's Hotel HOTEL **£££**
(☎7127 9111; www.davincishotel.com; 15 Culmore Rd; r/ste from £90/150; @⊕) This sleek boutique hotel on the west bank of the Foyle is the accommodation of choice for visiting celebrities, businesspeople and politicians,

offering spacious, stylish rooms and a hip cocktail bar and restaurant. It's 1.5km north of the city centre.

Eating

Primrose Cafe CAFE **£**
(15 Carlisle Rd; mains £4-6; ⊙8am-5pm Mon-Sat; ⛾) The latest addition to Derry's cafe culture, the Primrose has prospered by sticking to the classics and doing them really well, from pancakes with maple syrup to Irish stew, and a Sunday brunch that ranges from eggs Benedict to the full Ulster fry. Even with the outdoor terrace at the back, it can be hard to find a seat.

★Brown's Restaurant IRISH **££**
(☎7134 5180; brownsrestaurant.com; 1 Bond's Hill, Waterside; 3-course lunch £16.50, dinner mains £17-23; ⊙noon-3pm Tue-Fri, 5-9.30pm Tue-Sat; ⛾) *
From the outside Brown's may not have the most promising appearance, but step inside and you're in an elegant little enclave of brandy-coloured banquettes and ornate metal light fittings, with vintage monochrome prints adorning the walls. The everchanging menu is a gastronome's delight, making creative use of fresh local produce.

Brown's in Town IRISH **££**
(☎7136 2889; brownsrestaurant.com; 21-23 Strand Rd; ⊙noon-2.30pm Tue-Fri, 5.30-8pm Tue-Sat) There's a definite art deco feel to the decor in Brown's new restaurant, bringing a much-needed touch of glamour and sophistication to Derry's city-centre restaurant scene. The early-bird three-course dinner menu (£20; till 7.30pm Tuesday to Thursday, till 7pm Friday and Saturday) is terrific value.

Café del Mondo CAFE, IRISH **££**
(☎7136 6877; www.cafedelmondo.org; Craft Village, Shipquay St; mains cafe £6-7, dinner £13-22; ⊙cafe 9am-6pm Mon-Sat, noon-5pm Sun, restaurant 6-11.30pm Tue-Sat; ⊕⛾) * A bohemian cafe that serves excellent fairtrade coffee as well as hearty homemade soups, artisan breads and hot lunch specials that use locally sourced produce. A restaurant menu is served in the evening (best to book), offering steak, venison, seafood and a couple of vegetarian dishes.

Encore Brasserie INTERNATIONAL **££**
(☎7137 2492; Millennium Forum, Newmarket St; mains lunch £6-10, dinner £18; ⊙noon-6pm Mon-Sat, dinner Tue-Sat; ⛾) Set in the lobby of the city's main cultural venue, this is a stylish little place with friendly, efficient service and a crowd-pleasing menu of perennial

THE BOGSIDE ARTISTS

The Bogside Artists – brothers Will and Tom Kelly, and friend Kevin Hasson – are famous as the creators of the murals that make up the People's Gallery. Tom and Kevin were 10 and 11 years old when the Troubles broke out in 1969, Will in his early 20s.

What was it like growing up in Derry during the Troubles?

Kevin: 'One minute nobody knows about us or Derry or even Northern Ireland; the next thing, we are all over the international news. You could watch the daily riot later on TV in your own front room. As kids, you must understand, we were still on fantasy island, as most kids are. Soldiers were, to us, aliens from another planet. We painted the soldier as such on our Bloody Sunday mural depicting the death of Jackie Duddy for that reason. That was our perception at the time and kids tend to see things bereft of all historical or other considerations. All in all, our growing up in Derry at that time could be described as very intense and very bitter-sweet.'

Will: 'We felt that our destiny had come. We were well clued-up on Marxist doctrine and, what with the riots in Paris and the struggle of the black population in America for democratic rights, we truly believed we were part of a global working-class revolution. A new world order was coming into being and we were in the front line. As a young man, the unfolding events faced one with questions of ultimate concern at a time when, in other circumstances, we would likely have been thinking of finding a secure job and starting a family. Individualistic pursuits had to be shelved in the face of imminent threats to oneself and one's family. In retrospect, the whole experience was very hyper-real. During the Hunger Strikes of 1980–81 it became surreal.'

Whose art do you admire?

Will: 'Those old masters like Raphael, Mantegna, the Tiepolos and Michelangelo cannot be equalled when it comes to mural art. Diego Rivera was summoned from Paris 20 years or

favourites, from chicken Caesar salad to herb-crusted salmon.

 Drinking & Nightlife

Whatever you do in Derry, don't miss an evening in the city's lively pubs – for the craic rather than the beer, which is nothing to write home about. They're friendly and atmospheric, mostly open until 1am, and are within easy walking distance of each other. There are six within dancing distance along Waterloo St.

 Peadar O'Donnell's PUB
(www.peadars.com; 63 Waterloo St) A backpackers' favourite, Peadar's has traditional music sessions every night and often on weekend afternoons as well. It's done up as a typical Irish pub-cum-grocer, down to the shelves of grocery items, shopkeepers scales on the counter and a museum's-worth of old bric-a-brac.

Badgers Bar PUB
(16-18 Orchard St) A fine polished-brass and stained-glass Victorian pub crammed with wood-panelled nooks and crannies, Badgers overflows at lunchtime with shoppers enjoying quality pub grub, and offers a quiet

haven in the evenings when it attracts a crowd of more mature drinkers.

Earth Nite Club NIGHTCLUB
(125-135 Strand Rd; ☺ Tue, Thu & Sat) Derry's main nightclub and bar complex, close to the university, has student nights on Tuesdays, local DJs on Thursdays and dress-smart parties on Saturdays; search for 'Earth Nite Club Derry' on Facebook.

 Entertainment
Live Music
Sandino's Cafe LIVE MUSIC
(www.sandinos.com; 1 Water St; ☺ 11.30am-1am Mon-Sat, 1pm-midnight Sun) From the posters of Che to the Free Palestine flag to the fairtrade coffee, this relaxed cafe-bar exudes a liberal, left-wing vibe. There are live bands on Friday nights and DJ sessions on Saturdays. On Sundays there's a traditional Irish music session at 5pm, and live jazz/soul or DJs from 9pm, plus regular theme nights and events.

Mason's Bar LIVE MUSIC
(www.facebook.com/masonsbarderry; 10 Magazine St) The city that spawned the Undertones

so *after* the revolution, so we are not as impressed by his work as those who have bought into the myth of Rivera as a contemporary freedom fighter. Incidentally, he did not portray Mexico's history as it was. What he did was offer a Marxist *interpretation* of that history. Not that we compare ourselves to Rivera. His body of work far exceeds our own. But we do recall one lady who came to our studio and told us that she had just returned from Mexico and considered our murals to be better than his! Go figure, as they say.'

Tom: '*The Death of Innocence*, for me, is the one that stands out, both the pictorial content of it and the fact that it is a peace and antiwar mural painted long before any of us in Derry thought peace was even possible.'

Kevin: 'Our *Peace Mural* means most to me, as we decided to do that 10 years before we were actually able to get around to realising it. Also, it had a strong community input where both Catholic and Protestant kids worked together to help design it. The dove, in fact, is not just a cliché – it refers to our city's patron saint, St Columba, whose Latin name Columbanus means "dove".'

Will: 'They're like our children – it's unfair to single any one out at the expense of the others. That said, it would be dishonest to admit that our first-born, *The Petrol Bomber*, is a wee bit special.'

What does Derry being the UK City of Culture 2013 mean for you?

'Where do the Bogside Artists fit in? We don't. We are outside "the loop", not that we were not asked to join. But we figured that we cannot barter our creative freedom for money or anything else. On the contrary, we will be moving into satirical murals – we will be able then to make our views seen. The best is yet to come from the Bogside Artists.'

is still turning out raw, rumbustious music; Mason's Friday night sessions are the place to catch the latest offerings from local talent. There are student night on Tuesdays, live music or DJs on Thursdays and Fridays, and cover bands on Saturdays.

Gweedore Bar LIVE MUSIC
(www.peadars.com; 59-61 Waterloo St) The Gweedore Bar hosts live rock bands most nights, while the DJ bar upstairs is home to a regular Saturday-night disco.

Nerve Centre ARTS CENTRE
(www.nerve-centre.org.uk; 7-8 Magazine St) The Nerve Centre was set up in 1990 as a multimedia arts centre to encourage young, local talent in the fields of music and film. The centre has a performance area (live music at weekends), a theatre, a cinema (with an art-house program), a bar and a cafe.

Concerts & Theatre

Playhouse THEATRE
(www.derryplayhouse.co.uk; 5-7 Artillery St; ☺ box office 10am-5pm Mon-Fri, Context Gallery 11am-5.30pm Tue-Sat) Housed in beautifully restored former school buildings with an award-winning modern extension at the rear, this community arts centre stages music, dance and theatre by local and international performers.

Cultúrlann Uí Chanáin CULTURAL CENTRE
(www.culturlann-doire.ie; 37 Great James St) This cultural centre devoted to the Irish language stages performances of traditional Irish music, poetry and dance.

Waterside Theatre THEATRE
(www.watersidetheatre.com; Glendermott Rd) Housed in a former factory 500m east of the River Foyle. Stages drama, dance, comedy, children's theatre and live music.

Millennium Forum THEATRE
(www.millenniumforum.co.uk; Newmarket St) Ireland's biggest theatre auditorium is a major venue for dance, drama, concerts, opera and musicals.

Magee College THEATRE
(www.culture.ulster.ac.uk; Northland Rd, Magee College, University of Ulster) The college hosts a variety of arts, theatre and classical-concert performances throughout the year.

SUNDAY, BLOODY SUNDAY

Tragically echoing Dublin's Bloody Sunday of November 1920, when British security forces shot dead 14 spectators at a Gaelic football match in Croke Park, Derry's Bloody Sunday was a turning point in the history of the Troubles.

On Sunday 30 January 1972, the Northern Ireland Civil Rights Association organised a peaceful march through Derry in protest against internment without trial, which had been introduced by the British government the previous year. Some 15,000 people marched from Creggan through the Bogside towards the Guildhall, but they were stopped by British Army barricades at the junction of William and Rossville Sts. The main march was diverted along Rossville St to Free Derry Corner, but a small number of youths began hurling stones and insults at the British soldiers.

The exact sequence of events was disputed, but it now seems clear that soldiers of the 1st Battalion the Parachute Regiment opened fire on unarmed civilians. Fourteen people were shot dead, some of them shot in the back; six were aged just 17. Another 14 people were injured, 12 by gunshots and two from being knocked down by armoured personnel carriers. The Catholic population of Derry, who had originally welcomed the British troops as a neutral force protecting them from Protestant violence and persecution, now saw the army as enemy and occupier. The ranks of the Provisional Irish Republican Army (IRA) swelled with a fresh surge of volunteers.

The Widgery Commission, set up in 1972 to investigate the affair, failed to find anyone responsible. None of the soldiers who fired at civilians, nor the officers in charge, were brought to trial or even disciplined; records disappeared and weapons were destroyed.

Long-standing public dissatisfaction with the Widgery investigation led to the massive Bloody Sunday Inquiry, headed by Lord Saville, which sat from March 2000 till December 2004. The inquiry heard from 900 witnesses, received 2500 witness statements and allegedly cost British taxpayers £400 million; its report (available on www.official-documents.gov.uk) was finally published in June 2010.

Lord Saville found that 'The firing by soldiers of 1 PARA on Bloody Sunday caused the deaths of 13 people and injury to a similar number, none of whom was posing a threat of causing death or serious injury. What happened on Bloody Sunday strengthened the Provisional IRA, increased nationalist resentment and hostility towards the Army and exacerbated the violent conflict of the years that followed. Bloody Sunday was a tragedy for the bereaved and the wounded, and a catastrophe for the people of Northern Ireland.'

Following publication of the report, Prime Minister David Cameron publicly apologised on behalf of the UK government, describing the killings as 'unjustified and unjustifiable'. In July 2010, the Police Service of Northern Ireland (PSNI) said it would launch a murder inquiry into the deaths, which could last up to four years.

The events of Bloody Sunday inspired rock band U2's most overtly political song, 'Sunday Bloody Sunday' (1983), and are commemorated in the Museum of Free Derry (p620), the People's Gallery (p620) and the Bloody Sunday Memorial (p620), all in the Bogside.

Shopping

An Cló Ceart
BOOKS, CRAFTS

(37 Great James St) Housed in the Cultúrlann Uí Chanáin cultural centre, this shop stocks a good range of Irish-language books, traditional music CDs, glasswork, woodwork and jewellery.

Donegal Shop
CRAFTS

(8 Shipquay St) A long-established craft shop, the Donegal is crammed with Irish knitwear, Celtic jewellery, Donegal tweeds, Irish linen and souvenirs.

Cowley Cooper Fine Art
ART

(6 Shipquay St) A commercial gallery that provides a showcase for the best of contemporary Irish art, selling work by local artists and staging around half a dozen exhibitions each year.

Craft Village
CRAFTS

(www.derrycraftvillage.com; off Shipquay St) This renovated courtyard is home to a handful of craft shops selling Derry crystal, hand-woven cloth, ceramics, jewellery and other local craft items. Enter from Shipquay St, Magazine St or Tower Museum.

Whatnot
ANTIQUES

(22 Bishop St Within) The Whatnot is an interesting little antique shop crammed with jewellery, militaria, bric-a-brac and collectables.

Cool Discs Music
MUSIC

(www.cooldiscsmusic.com; Foyle St, 6/7 Lesley House) One of Northern Ireland's best independent record shops, Cool Discs has a wide selection of music by Irish artists old and new.

Austins
DEPARTMENT STORE

(2 The Diamond) The world's oldest independent department store (established 1830), Austins is a good place to shop for Irish linen (it can ship your purchases overseas).

Foyleside Shopping Centre
MALL

(Orchard St; ⊙9am-6pm Mon & Tue, to 9pm Wed-Fri, to 7pm Sat, 1-6pm Sun) This huge, four-level mall just outside the eastern city walls contains a Marks & Spencer, Eason bookshop and other high-street chain stores.

ⓘ Information

Derry Tourist Information Centre (⌨7126 7284; www.derryvisitor.com; 44 Foyle St; ⊙9am-6pm Mon-Sat, 11am-6pm Sun; 🕾) Covers all of Northern Ireland and the Republic as well as Derry. Sells books and maps, can book accommodation throughout Ireland and has a bureau de change and free wi-fi.

ⓘ Getting There & Away

AIR

City of Derry Airport (⌨7181 0784; www.cityofderryairport.com) About 13km east of Derry along the A2 towards Limavady. Direct flights daily to London Stansted, Liverpool, Birmingham and Glasgow Prestwick (Ryanair).

BUS

The **bus station** (⌨7126 2261; Foyle St) is just northeast of the walled city.

Maiden City Flyer (bus 212) A fast and frequent service between Derry and Belfast (£11.50, 1¾ hours, every 30 minutes Monday to Saturday, 11 services on Sunday), calling at Dungiven.

Ulsterbus Goldline Express 274 goes from Derry to Dublin (£18.35, four hours, every two hours daily). Other useful Ulsterbus services include the 273 to Omagh (£7.80, 1¼ hours, hourly Monday to Saturday, six Sunday) and the 234 to Limavady and Coleraine (£7.80, one

hour, five daily Monday to Saturday, two Sunday), continuing to Portstewart and Portrush on weekday evenings.

Airporter (⌨7126 9996; www.airporter.co.uk; 1 Bay Rd, Culmore Rd) Runs direct from Derry to Belfast International (one way/return £18.50/29.50, 1½ hours) and George Best Belfast City (£18.50/29.50, two hours) airports every 90 minutes Monday to Friday, every two hours Saturday and Sunday; and to City of Derry (£5/8, 20 minutes, two to four a day, to connect with flights). Buses depart from the Airporter office, 1.5km north of the city centre next to Da Vinci's Hotel.

Bus Éireann (⌨in Donegal 353-74 912 1309) Bus 64 runs from Derry to Galway (£20, 5¼ hours, three daily, two on Sunday) via Letterkenny, Donegal and Sligo; another four a day terminate at Sligo.

Lough Swilly Bus Company (⌨7126 2017; bus station, Foyle St) Buses to Buncrana, Carndonagh, Dungloe, Letterkenny (£5, 30 to 45 minutes, eight daily Monday to Friday, five on Saturday) and Greencastle (one hour, two daily Monday to Friday, one on Saturday) in County Donegal. There's also a bus from Derry to Malin Head (£6, 1¼ hours) via Carndonagh on Saturdays only.

TRAIN

Derry's train station (always referred to as Londonderry in Northern Ireland timetables) is on the eastern side of the River Foyle; a free Rail Link bus connects with the bus station. There are trains to Belfast (£11.50, 2¼ hours, seven or eight daily Monday to Saturday, four on Sunday) and Coleraine (£9, 45 minutes, seven daily), with connections to Portrush (£11.50, 1¼ hours).

ⓘ Getting Around

Bus 143A to Limavady stops at City of Derry Airport (£3.40, 30 minutes, seven daily Monday to Friday, three Saturday, one Sunday); a taxi costs about £15. The **Derry Taxi Association** (⌨7126 0247) and **Foyle Delta Cabs** (⌨7127 9999) operate from the city centre to all areas.

Local buses leave from Foyle St, outside the bus station, leading to the suburbs and surrounding villages; a day ticket giving unlimited travel on these buses costs £1.90.

TOP FIVE VIEWPOINTS IN NORTHERN IRELAND

➜ Binevenagh Lake

➜ Fair Head

➜ Cuilcagh Mountain

➜ Scrabo Hill

➜ Slieve Donard

You can hire bikes from the Derry Tourist Information Centre. The **Foyle Valley cycle route** runs through Derry, along the west bank of the river.

Limavady & Around

POP 12,000

Enchanted by a folk tune played by a blind fiddler outside her window in 1851, Limavady resident Jane Ross (1810–79) jotted down the melody – then known as 'O'Cahan's Lament', and later as the 'Londonderry Air'. The tune came to be known around the world as 'Danny Boy' – probably the most famous Irish song of all time.

Limavady was granted to Sir Thomas Phillips, the organiser of the Plantation of County Londonderry, by James I in 1612, after the last ruling chief, Sir Donnell Ballagh O'Cahan, was found guilty of rebellion. The town's original Gaelic name is Léim an Mhadaidh, which means 'the Dog's Leap', commemorating one of the O'Cahans' dogs that jumped across a gorge on the River Roe to bring warning of an unexpected enemy attack.

Sights & Activities

Today Limavady is a peaceful and prosperous small town. There's not much to see except the blue plaque on the wall at 51 Main St, opposite the Alexander Arms, commemorating the home of Jane Ross. The town hosts a jazz and blues festival (www.limavadyjazzandblues.com; ☺Jun).

Roe Valley Country Park PARK
This lovely country park, about 3km south of Limavady, has riverside walks stretching for 5km either side of the River Roe. The area is associated with the O'Cahans, who ruled the valley until the Plantation. The 17th-century settlers saw the flax-growing potential of the damp river valley and the area became an important linen-manufacturing centre.

The Dogleap Centre (41 Dogleap Rd, Roe Valley Country Park; ☺10am-5pm Jun-Aug, noon-5pm Sat & Sun Easter-May & Sep) FREE houses a visitor centre and tearoom. Next door is Ulster's first domestic hydroelectric power station, opened in 1896; it opens by request at the visitor centre. The nearby Green Lane Museum (☺1-5pm Sat & Sun Jun-Aug) FREE contains old photographs and relics of the valley's flax industry. The scutch mill, where the flax was pounded, is a 20-minute walk away, along the river, past two watch-towers built to guard the linen when it was spread out in the fields for bleaching.

The River Roe is famous for its sea trout and salmon fishing (www.roeangling.com). Day tickets cost £20, and are available from SJ Mitchell & Co (☑7772 2128; Central Car Park, Limavady) and the Alexander Arms Hotel (p628). The season runs from the third week in May until 20 October.

The park is signposted off the B192 road between Limavady and Dungiven. Bus 146 from Limavady to Dungiven will drop you at the turn-off; the park is about a 3km walk from the main road.

Sleeping & Eating

Alexander Arms Hotel B&B ££
(☑7776 2660; 34 Main St; s/d from £30/50) A long-established hotel and pub dating from 1875, the centrally located Alexander Arms is a friendly, family-run place that offers B&B (only one room has its own private bathroom) and serves pub grub and restaurant meals.

Hunter's Bakery & Oven Door Café CAFE £
(5 Market St; mains £4-7; ☺9am-5.30pm Mon-Sat) If you fancy a quick snack, this homely bakery has a comfy cafeteria at the back, serving good coffee, cakes and light meals. It's a local institution, patronised by a broad cross-section of the community, with a pleasantly old-fashioned feel.

★ **Lime Tree** IRISH ££
(☑7776 4300; www.limetreerest.com; 60 Catherine St; mains £15-24; ☺lunch Thu-Fri, dinner Tue-Sat; ☻) Unfussy decor in shades of burgundy and beige softened by flickering tea-lights makes for a relaxing atmosphere in Limavady's top eatery. The menu promotes local produce – from seafood thermidor made with Donegal fish to fillet steak from award-winning butcher Hunter's of Limavady – and includes vegetarian dishes that are a cut above the usual. There's also an early-bird menu (two/three courses £16/19) available before 7pm.

Information

Tourist Office (☑7776 0650; 24 Main St; ☺9.30am-5pm Mon-Fri, 10am-2pm Sat) In the Roe Valley Arts Centre.

Getting There & Away

Bus 143A runs between Derry and Limavady hourly (£5, four daily on Sunday). There's no direct bus to Belfast from Limavady but connections can be made at Coleraine.

Coastal County Londonderry

Magilligan Point

The huge triangular spit of land that almost closes off the mouth of Lough Foyle is mostly taken up by a military firing range, and is home to a once-notorious prison. Still, it's worth a visit for its vast sandy beaches – Magilligan Strand to the west, and the 9km sweep of Benone Strand to the northeast, the latter providing a superb venue for kite buggies and mini land yachts. On the point itself, watching over the entrance to Lough Foyle, stands a Martello tower, built during the Napoleonic Wars in 1812 to guard against French invasion.

The Benone Tourist Complex (☑7775 0555; limavady.campstead.com; 59 Benone Ave; campsites per tent £18.50; ☉9am-9pm Jul & Aug, to dusk Apr-Jun & Sep, to 4pm Oct-Mar; ☒), adjacent to Benone Strand, is a campsite with outdoor heated pool, a children's pool, tennis courts and a putting green (all open to nonresidents). Note that dogs are not allowed on the beach from May to September.

The Lough Foyle Ferry (www.foyleferry. com; one way car/adult/child £10/2.50/1.25) runs between Magilligan Point and Greencastle in County Donegal year-round. The trip takes 10 minutes and runs hourly, departing on the hour from Greencastle, 15 minutes past from Magilligan. The last ferry is at 9.15pm June to August, 8.15pm May, 7.15pm April and September, and 6.15pm October to March.

Downhill

In 1774 the eccentric Bishop of Derry and fourth Earl of Bristol, Frederick Augustus Hervey, built himself a palatial home, Downhill, on the coast west of Castlerock. It burnt down in 1851, was rebuilt in 1876, and was finally abandoned after WWII. The ruins of the house now stand forlornly on a cliff top.

The original demesne covered some 160 hectares, which is now part of the National Trust's Downhill Estate (www.nationaltrust. org.uk; adult/child £4.70/2.35; ☉temple & facilities 10am-5pm Apr-Sep, grounds dawn-dusk year-round). The beautiful landscaped gardens below the ruins of the house are the work of celebrated gardener Jan Eccles, who became custodian of Downhill at the age of 60 and created the garden over a period of 30 years. She died in 1997 aged 94.

The main attraction here is the little Mussenden Temple, built by the bishop to house either his library or his mistress – opinions differ! The clergyman continued an affair with the mistress of Frederick William II of Prussia well into old age. The main access is from the car parks at the Lion's Gate and Bishop's Gate on the coast road.

On the main road 1km west of the temple, opposite the Downhill Hostel, the scenic Bishop's Road climbs steeply up through a ravine and heads over the hills to Limavady. There are spectacular views over Lough Foyle, Donegal and the Sperrin Mountains from the Gortmore picnic area, and from the cliff top at Binevenagh Lake.

★ Downhill Hostel (☑7084 9077; www. downhillhostel.com; 12 Mussenden Rd; dm/d £14/55, f from £45 plus per child £5; @☎⌨) is a beautifully restored late-19th-century house, tucked beneath the sea cliffs and overlooking the beach, offering very comfortable accommodation in seven-bed dorms, doubles and family rooms. There's a big lounge with an open fire and a view of the sea, and you can hire wetsuits and body boards when the surf's up. You can even paint your own mugs, plates and bowls in the neighbouring pottery. There are no shops in Downhill so bring supplies with you.

Bus 134 between Limavady and Coleraine (20 minutes, nine daily Monday to Friday, six Saturday) stops at Downhill, as does bus 234 between Derry and Coleraine.

Portstewart

POP 7800

Ever since Victorian times, when English novelist William Thackeray described it as having an 'air of comfort and neatness', the seaside and golfing resort of Portstewart has cultivated a sedate, upmarket atmosphere that distinguishes it from populist Portrush, 6km further east. There's also a sizeable student community from the University of Ulster in Coleraine.

The fantastic beach is the main attraction, along with a couple of world-class golf courses – a combination that created the North's highest property prices and a large demand for holiday homes. However, concerns about overdevelopment were realised when the economic downturn of 2008 hit the North – you'll see no shortage of half-built houses and 'For Sale' signs.

◉ Sights & Activities

The central promenade is dominated by the castellated facade of a Dominican college, looming over the seaside fun and games like a Catholic conscience.

The broad, 2.5km beach of Portstewart Strand is a 20-minute walk south of the centre along a coastal path, or a short bus ride along Strand Rd. Parking is allowed on the firm sand, which can accommodate over 1000 cars (open year-round, £4.50 per car from Easter to October).

Heading in the opposite direction, the Port Path is a 10.5km coastal footpath (part of the Causeway Coast Way) that stretches from Portstewart Strand to White Rocks, 3km east of Portrush.

Portstewart is within a few kilometres of three of Northern Ireland's top golf courses:

Royal Portrush Golf Club　　GOLF
(www.royalportrushgolfclub.com; green fees weekday/weekend £145/165) The only golf club in Ireland to host the Open Championship. On the eastern edge of Portrush, 8km northeast of Portstewart.

Portstewart Golf Club　　GOLF
(www.portstewartgc.co.uk; green fees weekday/weekend £90/110) Championship links course that has hosted many professional competitions. To the west of Portstewart, on the road to Portstewart Strand.

Castlerock Golf Club　　GOLF
(www.castlerockgc.co.uk; green fees weekday/weekend £75/90) Classic links course amid huge sand dunes. At Castlerock village, 17km west of Portstewart.

⚝ Festivals & Events

North West 200 Motorcycle Race　　SPORT
(www.northwest200.org; ⊘ mid-May) The North West 200 motorcycle race is run on a road circuit taking in Portrush, Portstewart and Coleraine – you can see the starting grid painted on the main road on the eastern edge of town. This classic race – Ireland's biggest outdoor sporting event – is one of the last to be run on closed public roads anywhere in Europe, and attracts up to 150,000 spectators; if you're not one of them, it's best to avoid the area on the race weekend.

🛏 Sleeping

Don't even think about turning up without a booking during the North West 200 weekend in May.

Causeway Coast Independent Hostel　　HOSTEL £
(📞7083 3789; rick@causewaycoasthostel.fsnet.co.uk; 4 Victoria Tce; dm/s/tw from £14/26/36; @🌐) This neat terrace house just northeast of the harbour has spacious four-, six- and eight-bed dorms plus a double room, and good power showers. It has its own kitchen, laundry and welcoming open fire in winter.

York　　HOTEL ££
(📞7083 3594; www.theyorkportstewart.co.uk; 2 Station Rd; s/d £79/115; 🌐) The York brings a bit of boutique chic to Portstewart's mostly staid accommodation scene, with designer rooms in shades of chocolate, cream and cappuccino, red leather chairs, spacious bathrooms with rain-head showers, and big breakfasts served in a glass-lined dining room with stunning views along the coast.

Cromore Halt Inn　　INN ££
(📞7083 6888; www.cromorehalt.co.uk; 158 Station Rd; s/d £89/99; 🌐) Located about 1km east of the harbour, on the corner of Station and Mill Rds, the motel-style Cromore has a dozen modern, businesslike rooms, along with friendly, helpful staff and a good restaurant.

Cul-Erg B&B　　B&B ££
(📞7083 6610; www.culerg.co.uk; 9 Hillside, Atlantic Circle; s/d £55/80; 🌐) This family-run B&B is in a modern, flower-bedecked terrace house just a couple of minutes' walk from the promenade. Warm and welcoming, it's set in a quiet cul-de-sac; the rooms at the back have a view of the sea.

🍴 Eating & Drinking

★ **Burger Club**　　BURGERS £
(📞7083 2302; www.burgerclubni.com; 81 the Promenade; mains £5-9; ⊘ noon-10pm; 🌐🚸) Yes, it's a fast food joint, but fast food with a difference: locally sourced, freshly cooked and prettily presented. As well as classic beef burgers, the menu includes lamb burgers, fish burgers, barbecue pulled pork, and felafel wraps, with a choice of chunky or skinny fries and exceedingly crunchy onion rings.

Morelli's　　CAFE £
(www.morellisofportstewart.co.uk; 53 the Promenade; mains £4-9; ⊘ 9am-11pm, food to 8pm,

shorter hours in winter; 🛜 ♿) Morelli's is a local institution, founded by Italian immigrants and famous for its mouth-watering ice cream since 1911. The menu includes breakfast fry-ups, pizza, sandwiches, omelettes, and fish and chips, as well as good coffee and cakes, and there's a great view across the bay to Mussenden Temple, Benone Strand and Donegal.

Anchor Bar & Skippers Restaurant   PUB
(www.theanchorbar.co.uk; 87-89 the Promenade) The liveliest of Portstewart's traditional pubs, famed for its Guinness and hugely popular with students from the University of Ulster, the Anchor serves decent pub grub is open till 1am and has live bands on Friday and Saturday. There's also Skippers Restaurant (food served noon to 9pm), which serves pub grub (mains £8 to £15), such as seafood chowder, piri piri chicken and vegetable stir-fry.

❶ Getting There & Away

Bus 140 plies between Coleraine and Portstewart (£2.60, 20 to 30 minutes) roughly every half-hour (fewer on Sunday).

COUNTY ANTRIM

❶ Getting There & Around

Translink (📞 9066 6630; www.translink.co.uk) operates several bus services specially designed for tourists visiting the popular Antrim coast

---

WALK: CAUSEWAY COAST WAY

The official Causeway Coast Way (www.walkni.com) stretches for 53km from Portstewart to Ballycastle, but the most scenic section – the 16.5km between Carrick-a-Rede and the Giant's Causeway – can be done in a day and offers one of the finest coastal walks in Ireland.

There are cafes and public toilets at Larrybane, Ballintoy Harbour and the Giant's Causeway, and bus stops at Larrybane, Ballintoy village, Whitepark Bay Hostel, Dunseverick Castle and the Giant's Causeway. Note that parts of the walk follow a narrow, muddy path along the top of unfenced cliffs, and can be dangerous in wet and windy weather. Also, high tides can temporarily block the way at either end of White Park Bay; check tide times at any tourist office.

Begin at Larrybane, the car park for Carrick-a-Rede. The path starts off along a cliff top with views of Sheep Island, then cuts inland straight towards Ballintoy church. At the church, turn right and follow the road down to the harbour. Continue along the shoreline past a series of conical sea stacks and arches, and scramble around the foot of a limestone crag to reach the 2km-long sandy sweep of White Park Bay.

The going here is easiest at low tide, when you can walk on the firm sand. At the far end of the bay (the building with the yellow gable above the dunes is Whitepark Bay Hostel), scramble over rocks and boulders at the bottom of a high limestone cliff for 250m (slippery in places) to Portbradden. If you've timed it badly and the way is blocked by high tide, you can detour up to the hostel and reach Portbradden by walking along the road.

Beyond Portbradden white limestone gives way to black basalt, and the path threads through a natural tunnel in the rocks before weaving around several rocky coves with the high cliffs of Benbane Head visible in the distance. At tiny Dunseverick Harbour you follow a minor road for 200m before descending steps on the right at a waymark. The path then wanders along the grassy foreshore, rounds a headland and crosses a footbridge above a waterfall before reaching the car park at Dunseverick Castle.

From here the cliff-top path, narrow in places, climbs steadily, passing an old salmon fishery (the little rusty-roofed cottage on the shore far below). Near Benbane Head, the highest and most northerly point on the walk, a wooden bench marks the viewpoint known as Hamilton's Seat (William Hamilton was an 18th-century clergyman and amateur geologist from Derry, who wrote one of the earliest descriptions of the Causeway Coast's geology). Soak up the spectacular panorama of 100m-high sea cliffs, stacks and pinnacles stretching away to the west, before you set off on the final stretch. If you want to visit the causeway itself, descend the Shepherd's Steps (signposted), about 1km before the visitor centre and the end of the walk. (Total: 16.5km. Allow five to six hours.)

and Giant's Causeway areas. In July and August only, Translink's **Bus Rambler** ticket (adult/child £9/4.50) allows one day's unlimited bus travel (after 9.30am) anywhere in Northern Ireland.

From April to September the **Antrim Coaster** (bus 252/256) links Coleraine with Belfast (£11.50, four hours, two daily Monday to Saturday) via Portstewart, Portrush, Bushmills, the Giant's Causeway, Ballycastle, the Glens of Antrim and Larne, departing Belfast at 9.05am and 3pm. South-bound buses leave Coleraine at 9.35am and 3.50pm. A Sunday service operates from July to September only.

From June to mid-September the **Causeway Rambler** (bus 402) links Bushmills Distillery and Carrick-a-Rede (£6, 25 minutes, seven daily) via the Giant's Causeway, White Park Bay and Ballintoy. The ticket allows unlimited travel in both directions for one day, and is also valid on the **Open Topper** service from Coleraine to the Giant's Causeway.

Portrush

POP 6300

The bustling seaside resort of Portrush (Port Rois) bursts at the seams with holiday-makers in high season and, not surprisingly, many of its attractions are focused unashamedly on good old-fashioned family fun. However, it is also one of Ireland's top surfing centres and home to the North's hottest nightclub.

◉ Sights & Activities

Curran Strand   BEACH
Portrush's main attraction is the beautiful sandy beach of Curran Strand that stretches for 3km to the east of the town, ending at the scenic chalk cliffs of White Rocks. In summer, boats depart regularly for cruises or fishing trips.

Coastal Zone   AQUARIUM
(8 Bath Rd; ⊙10am-5pm daily Easter week & Jun-Aug, Sat & Sun only May & Sep; 🖽) FREE You'll find activities for kids at the Coastal Zone, including marine-life exhibits, a touch pool, rock-pool rambles and fossil hunts.

Troggs Surf Shop   SURFING
(www.troggssurfshop.co.uk; 88 Main St; ⊙10am-6pm) Portrush is the centre of Northern Ireland's surfing scene – the Portrush Open in March is a regular feature on the Irish Surfing Association competition calendar, and the UK Pro Surf Tour held a contest here for the first time in 2007. From April to November the friendly Troggs Surf Shop

offers bodyboard/surfboard hire (per day £5/10) and wetsuit hire (per day £7), surf reports and general advice. A two-hour lesson including equipment hire costs £25 per person.

⌕ Sleeping

Places fill up quickly during summer, so it's advisable to book in advance.

Portrush Holiday Hostel   HOSTEL £
(☎7082 1288; www.portrushholidayhostel.co.uk; 24 Princess St; dm/d from £15/34; @🏵) Just a few minutes' walk from both beach and harbour, this popular hostel is set in a Victorian terrace house, but feels cosy rather than cramped. Staff are friendly and helpful, and facilities include a washing machine, barbecue area and secure storage for bikes.

★Clarmont   B&B ££
(☎7082 2397; www.clarmontguesthouse.com; 10 Landsdowne Cres; d £80; 🖽) Our favourite among several guesthouses on Landsdowne Cres, the recently refurbished Clarmont has great views and, from polished pine floors to period fireplaces, has a decor that tastefully mixes Victorian and modern styles. Ask for one of the bay-window bedrooms with sea views and spa.

Albany Lodge Guest House   B&B ££
(☎7082 3492; www.albanylodgeni.co.uk; 2 Eglinton St; s/d from £50/80; @🏵) This elegant, four-storey Victorian villa has a great location close to the beach, with spectacular views along the coast. The rooms are spacious and welcoming, and the owners are friendly without being in your face. It's worth shelling out a few extra quid for the four-poster suite on the top floor, where you can soak up the view while reclining on your chaise longue.

✕ Eating

Café 55   CAFE £
(1 Causeway St; lunch mains £5, dinner mains £10-13; ⊙9am-4pm Mon-Thu, 9am-3.30pm & 5pm-late Fri & Sat) Tucked beneath 55 Degrees North, this licensed cafe serves good coffee plus breakfast rolls and pancakes (10am to 11.30am) on an outdoor terrace; it also has daily lunch specials such as fish pie, and an evening menu in summer.

★55 Degrees North   INTERNATIONAL ££
(☎7082 2811; www.55-north.com; 1 Causeway St; mains £10-20; ⊙12.30-2.30pm & 5-9pm; 🖽🖽)

One of the north coast's most stylish restaurants, 55 Degrees North boasts a wall of floor-to-ceiling windows allowing diners to soak up a spectacular panorama of sand and sea. The food is excellent, concentrating on clean, simple flavours and unfussy presentation. There's an early-bird menu (three courses £10 to £12) available 5pm to 6.45pm.

☆ Entertainment

Kelly's Complex   CLUB
(www.kellysportrush.co.uk; 1 Bushmills Rd; ⊗ Wed & Sat) The North's top clubbing venue is still going strong, and attracts clubbers from as far afield as Belfast and Dublin – it came 48th in DJ Magazine's list of the Top 100 Clubs in the world. Plain and small-looking from the outside, the TARDIS effect takes over as you enter a wonderland of five bars and three dance floors. It's been around since 1996, but Lush! is still one of the best club nights in Ireland.

The complex is on the A2 just east of Portrush, beside the Golf Links Holiday Park.

❶ Getting There & Around

The bus terminal is near the Dunluce Centre. Bus 140 links Portrush with Coleraine (20 minutes) and Portstewart (£2.60, 20 to 30 minutes) every 30 minutes or so.

The train station is just south of the harbour. Portrush is served by trains from Coleraine (£2.20, 12 minutes, hourly Monday to Saturday, 10 on Sunday), where there are connections to Belfast or Derry.

For taxis, try **Andy Brown's** (⌨ 7082 2223) or **North West Taxis** (⌨ 7082 4446). A taxi to Kelly's Complex is around £8, and it's £15 to the Giant's Causeway.

Dunluce Castle

Views along the Causeway Coast between Portrush and Portballintrae are dominated by the ruins of Dunluce Castle (87 Dunluce Rd; adult/child £5/3; ⊗ 10am-6pm Apr-Sep, shorter hours winter, last admission 30min before closing), perched atop a dramatic basalt crag. In the 16th and 17th centuries it was the seat of the MacDonnell family (the Earls of Antrim from 1620), who built a Renaissance-style manor house within the walls. Part of the castle, including the kitchen, collapsed into the sea in 1639, taking seven servants and that night's dinner with it.

A narrow bridge leads from the mainland courtyard across a dizzying gap to the main part of the fortress. Below, a path leads down from the gatehouse to the Mermaid's Cave beneath the castle crag.

Dunluce is 5km east of Portrush, a one-hour walk away along the coastal path. All the buses that run along the coast stop at Dunluce Castle.

Bushmills

POP 1350

The small town of Bushmills has long been a place of pilgrimage for connoisseurs of Irish whiskey. A good youth hostel and a restored rail link with the Giant's Causeway have also made it an attractive stop for hikers exploring the Causeway Coast.

◉ Sights & Activities

Giant's Causeway & Bushmills Railway   HERITAGE RAILWAY
(www.freewebs.com/giantscausewayrailway; adult/child return £7.50/5.50) Brought from a private line on the shores of Lough Neagh, the narrow-gauge line and locomotives (two steam and one diesel) follow the route of a 19th-century tourist tramway for 3km from Bushmills to below the Giant's Causeway visitor centre. Trains run hourly between 11am and 5.30pm, departing on the hour from the Causeway, on the half-hour from Bushmills, daily in July and August, weekends only from Easter to June and September and October.

Old Bushmills Distillery   DISTILLERY
(www.bushmills.com; Distillery Rd; tour adult/child £7/3.50; ⊗ 9.15am-5pm Mon-Sat Jul-Oct, 10am-5pm Mon-Sat Nov-Jun, noon-5pm Sun year-round) Bushmills is the world's oldest legal distillery, having been granted a licence by King James I in 1608. Bushmills whiskey is made with Irish barley and water from St Columb's Rill, a tributary of the River Bush, and matured in oak barrels. During ageing, the alcohol content drops from around 60% to 40%; the spirit lost through evaporation is known, rather sweetly, as 'the angels' share'. After a tour of the distillery you're rewarded with a free sample (or a soft drink), and four lucky volunteers get a whiskey-tasting session to compare Bushmills with other brands.

🛏 Sleeping & Eating

Mill Rest Youth Hostel   HOSTEL £
(⌨ 2073 1222; www.hini.org.uk; 49 Main St; dm/tw £18.50/41; ⊗ closed 11am-2pm Jul & Aug, to 5pm

Mar–Jun, Sep & Oct; @ ⊞) This modern, purpose-built hostel is just off the Diamond in the centre of town. Accommodation is mostly in four- to six-bed dorms with one twin room with private bathroom. There's also a kitchen, restaurant, laundry and bike shed. The hostel is open daily March to October, Friday and Saturday nights only November to February (but still closed 11am to 5pm on Saturday).

Ballyness Caravan Park & B&B B&B ££
(☑ 2073 2393; www.ballynesscaravanpark.com; 40 Castlecatt Rd; campervan sites £24; ☺ mid-Mar–Oct; @ �) This ecofriendly caravan park (no tents) is about 1km south of Bushmills town centre on the B66.

Bushmills Inn Hotel HOTEL £££
(☑ 2073 3000; www.bushmillsinn.com; 9 Dunluce Rd; s/d from £158/178, ste £298; @ �) One of Northern Ireland's most atmospheric hotels, the Bushmills is an old coaching inn complete with peat fires, gas lamps and a round tower with a secret library. There are no longer any bedrooms in the old part of the hotel – the luxurious accommodation is in the neighbouring, modern Mill House complex.

Copper Kettle CAFE £
(61 Main St; mains £3-6; ☺ 8.30am-5pm Mon-Sat, from 10am Sun) This rustic tearoom serves breakfast fry-ups till 11.30am, and has daily lunch specials as well as good tea, coffee, cakes and scones.

★ **Bushmills Inn** IRISH ££
(9 Dunluce Rd; lunch mains £11-15, dinner mains £16-24; ☺ noon-9.30pm Mon-Sat, 12.30-9pm Sun; �) The inn's excellent restaurant, with intimate wooden booths set in the old 17th-century stables, specialises in fresh Ulster produce and serves everything from sandwiches to full à-la-carte dinners.

Giant's Causeway

When you first see it you'll understand why the ancients believed the causeway was not a natural feature. The vast expanse of regular, closely packed, hexagonal stone columns dipping gently beneath the waves looks for all the world like the handiwork of giants.

This spectacular rock formation – a national nature reserve and Northern Ireland's only Unesco World Heritage site – is one of Ireland's most impressive and atmospheric landscape features, but it is all too often swamped by visitors – around 750,000 each year. If you can, try to visit midweek or out of season to experience it at its most evocative. Sunset in spring and autumn is the best time for photographs.

Visiting the Giant's Causeway itself is free of charge but you pay to use the car park and the impressive new **Giant's Causeway Visitor Experience** (☑ 2073 1855; www.giantscausewaycentre.com; adult/child £8.50/4.25; ☺ 9am-9pm Jul & Aug, to 7pm Apr-Jun & Sep, to 6pm Feb-Mar & Oct, to 7pm Nov-Jan; �)). Admission fee is reduced by £1.50 if you arrive by bus, bike or on foot. This ecofriendly visitor centre, built into the hillside and walled in tall black basalt slabs that mimic the basalt columns of the Causeway, houses an exhibition explaining the geology of the region, as well as a tourist information desk, restaurant and shop.

From the visitor centre it's an easy 1km walk from the car park down to the Causeway; minibuses with wheelchair access ply the route every 15 minutes (adult/child £2/1 return). Guided tours of the site (June to August only) cost £3.50/2.25 per adult/child.

◉ Sights & Activities

From the car park, it's an easy 10- to 15-minute walk downhill on a tarmac road (wheelchair accessible) to the Giant's Causeway itself. However, a much more interesting approach is to follow the cliff-top path northeast for 2km to the **Chimney Tops** headland, which has an excellent view of the Causeway and the coastline to the west, including Inishowen and Malin Heads.

This pinnacled promontory was bombarded by ships of the Spanish Armada in 1588, who thought it was Dunluce Castle, and the wreck of the Spanish galleon *Girona* lies just off the tip of the headland. Return towards the car park and about halfway back descend the **Shepherd's Steps** (signposted) to a lower-level footpath that leads down to the Causeway. Allow 1½ hours for the round trip.

Alternatively, you can visit the Causeway first, then follow the lower coastal path as far as the **Amphitheatre** viewpoint at Port Reostan, passing impressive rock formations such as the **Organ** (a stack of vertical basalt columns resembling organ pipes), and return by climbing the Shepherd's Steps.

You can also follow the cliff-top path east as far as Dunseverick or beyond.

THE MAKING OF THE CAUSEWAY

The story goes that the Irish giant, Finn McCool, built the Causeway so he could cross the sea to fight the Scottish giant Benandonner. Benandonner pursued Finn back across the Causeway, but in turn took fright and fled back to Scotland, ripping up the causeway as he went. All that remains are its ends – the Giant's Causeway in Ireland, and the island of Staffa in Scotland (which has similar rock formations).

The more prosaic scientific explanation is that the causeway rocks were formed 60 million years ago, when a thick layer of molten basaltic lava flowed along a valley in the existing chalk beds. As the lava flow cooled and hardened – from the top and bottom surfaces inward – it contracted, creating a pattern of hexagonal cracks at right angles to the cooling surfaces (think of mud contracting and cracking in a hexagonal pattern as a lake bed dries out). As solidification progressed towards the centre of the flow, the cracks spread down from the top and up from the bottom, until the lava was completely solid. Erosion has cut into the lava flow, and the basalt has split along the contraction cracks, creating the hexagonal columns.

🛏 Sleeping

Causeway Hotel   HOTEL **££**
(☑ 2073 1226; www.giants-causeway-hotel.com; 40 Causeway Rd; s/d £79/99; 🕾) You can't beat it for location – this National Trust–owned hotel is within a stone's throw of the Causeway, a useful base to explore the coast early or late in the day without the crowds. Ask for one of the rooms at the west end, with terraces that enjoy sunset views over the Atlantic.

❶ Getting There & Away

As well as the **Antrim Coaster** and **Causeway Rambler** services, bus 172 from Ballycastle (£4.20, 30 minutes, seven daily weekdays, four at weekends) to Coleraine and Bushmills stops here year-round.

From mid-May to August, Goldline Express bus 221 runs from Belfast's Europa BusCentre direct to the Giant's Causeway via Ballymena and Bushmills (£11.50, 1½ hours, one daily).

In July and August, the **Open Topper** bus 177 runs between Coleraine and the Giant's Causeway (£6, 1¼ hours, four daily) stopping at Portstewart, Portrush and Bushmills. The ticket allows hop-on hop-off travel, and is also valid on the Causeway Rambler service.

From Coleraine you can continue by train to Belfast (£11, two hours, seven or eight daily Monday to Saturday, four on Sunday) or Derry (£9, 45 minutes, seven or eight daily Monday to Saturday, four on Sunday).

Giant's Causeway to Ballycastle

Between the Giant's Causeway and Ballycastle lies the most scenic stretch of the Causeway Coast, with sea cliffs of contrasting black basalt and white chalk, rocky islands, picturesque little harbours and broad sweeps of sandy beach. It's best enjoyed on foot, following the 16.5km of waymarked Causeway Coast Way between the Carrick-a-Rede car park and the Giant's Causeway, although the main attractions can also be reached by car or bus.

About 8km east of the Giant's Causeway is the meagre ruin of 16th-century Dunseverick Castle, spectacularly sited on a grassy bluff. Another 1.5km on is the tiny seaside hamlet of Portbradden, with half a dozen harbourside houses and the tiny, blue-and-white St Gobban's Church, said to be the smallest in Ireland. Visible from Portbradden and accessible via the next junction off the A2 is the spectacular White Park Bay, with its wide, sweeping sandy beach.

A few kilometres further on is Ballintoy (Baile an Tuaighe), another pretty village tumbling down the hillside to a picture-postcard harbour. The restored limekiln on the quayside once made quicklime using stone from the chalk cliffs and coal from Ballymoney.

Carrick-a-Rede Rope Bridge   BRIDGE
(www.nationaltrust.org.uk; Ballintoy; adult/child £5.60/2.90; ⊙ 10am-7pm Jun-Aug, to 6pm Mar-May, Sep & Oct) The main attraction on the stretch of coast between Ballycastle and the Giant's Causeway is the famous (or notorious, depending on your head for heights) Carrick-a-Rede Rope Bridge. The 20m-long, 1m-wide bridge of wire rope spans the chasm between the sea cliffs and the little

Causeway Walks

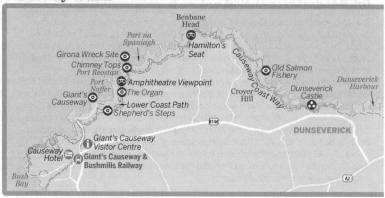

island of Carrick-a-Rede, swaying gently 30m above the rock-strewn water.

The island has sustained a salmon fishery for centuries; fishermen stretch their nets out from the tip of the island to intercept the passage of salmon migrating along the coast to their home rivers. The fishermen put the bridge up every spring as they have done for the last 200 years – though it's not, of course, the original bridge.

Crossing the bridge is perfectly safe, but it can be frightening if you don't have a head for heights, especially if it's breezy (in high winds the bridge is closed). Once on the island there are good views of Rathlin Island and Fair Head to the east. There's a small National Trust information centre and cafe at the car park.

🛏 Sleeping & Eating

Whitepark Bay Hostel   HOSTEL £
(☑ 2073 1745; www.hini.org.uk; 157 White Park Rd, Ballintoy; dm/tw £18/42; ☺ Apr-Oct; @) This modern, purpose-built hostel near the west end of White Park Bay has mostly four-bed dorms, plus twin rooms with TV, all with private bathroom. There is a common room positioned to soak up the view, and the beach is just a few minutes' walk through the dunes.

Sheep Island View Hostel   HOSTEL ££
(☑ 2076 9391; www.sheepislandview.com; 42A Main St; campsites/dm/d £6/15/40; @☎) This excellent independent hostel offers dorm beds, basic shared accommodation in the camping barn, or a place to pitch a tent. There's a kitchen and laundry, a village store nearby

and a free pick-up service from the Giant's Causeway, Bushmills and Ballycastle. It's on the main coast road near the turn-off to Ballintoy harbour, and makes an ideal overnight stop if you're hiking between Bushmills and Ballycastle.

★**Whitepark House**   B&B £££
(☑ 2073 1482; www.whiteparkhouse.com; 150 White Park Rd, Ballintoy; s/d £80/120; ☎) A beautifully restored 18th-century house overlooking White Park Bay, this B&B has traditional features such as antique furniture and a peat fire complemented by Asian artefacts gathered during the welcoming owners' oriental travels. There are three rooms – ask for one with a sea view.

Roark's Kitchen   CAFE £
(Ballintoy Harbour; mains £4-6; ☺ 11am-7pm Jun-Aug, Sat & Sun only May & Sep) This cute little chalk-built tearoom on the quayside at Ballintoy serves teas, coffees, ice cream, home-baked apple tart and lunch dishes, such as Irish stew or chicken-and-ham pie.

❶ Getting There & Away

Bus 172 between Ballycastle, Bushmills and Coleraine (seven daily Monday to Friday, four on Saturday and Sunday) is the main, year-round service along this coast, stopping at the Giant's Causeway, Ballintoy and Carrick-a-Rede.

Ballycastle

POP 4000

The harbour town and holiday resort of Ballycastle (Baile an Chaisil) marks the eastern end of the Causeway Coast. It's a pretty town

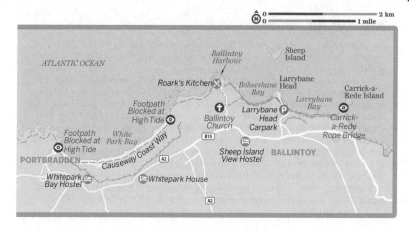

with a good bucket-and-spade beach, but apart from that there's not a lot to see. It's also the port for ferries to Rathlin Island.

Sights & Activities

The town has a family-friendly promenade, with a giant sandpit for kids overlooking the marina. A footbridge leads east across the mouth of the River Glenshesk to a good sandy beach.

Marconi Memorial　　　　　　MONUMENT
In the harbour car park, a plaque at the foot of a rock pinnacle commemorates the day in 1898 when Guglielmo Marconi's assistants contacted Rathlin Island by radio from Ballycastle to prove to Lloyds of London that wireless communication was a viable proposition. The idea was to send notice to London or Liverpool of ships arriving safely after a transatlantic crossing – most vessels on this route would have to pass through the channel north of Rathlin.

Aquasports　　　　　　　　BOAT TOURS
(www.aquasports.biz) Offers a range of high-speed boat trips out of Ballycastle harbour, including wildlife tours, cruises along the coast to the Giant's Causeway and tours around Rathlin Island from £25 per person.

Festivals & Events

Ould Lammas Fair　　　　　　CULTURAL
(☉last Mon & Tue in Aug) Ballycastle's Ould Lammas Fair dates back to 1606. Thousands of people descend on the town for the market stalls and fairground rides, and to sample 'yellowman' (a hard chewy toffee) and dulse (dried edible seaweed).

Sleeping

Ballycastle Backpackers　　　　HOSTEL £
(☎2076 3612; www.ballycastlebackpackers.net; 4 North St; dm/tw from £15/40; @🛜) This is a small and homely hostel set in a terrace house overlooking the harbour, with one six-bed dorm, a family room and a couple of twin and double rooms. There's also a cosy self-catering cottage in the backyard, with two twin rooms with private bathroom (£25 per person per night, also available for rental by the week).

Watertop Open Farm　　　　CAMPGROUND £
(☎2076 2576; www.watertopfarm.co.uk; 188 Cushendall Rd; campsites per person £5, caravan sites from £22; ☉Easter-Oct) About 10km east of Ballycastle on the road to Cushendun, child-friendly Watertop is based in a working farm and activity centre, offering pony trekking, sheep-shearing and farm tours.

An Caislean Guesthouse　　　　B&B ££
(☎2076 2845; www.ancaislean.co.uk; 42 Quay Rd; s/d/f £40/80/110; 🛜🖫) Originally two guesthouses now joined together, An Caislean is our favourite among several B&Bs on Quay Rd. It has a luxurious lounge, its own tea shop, and a warm and welcoming family atmosphere. Rooms are spacious and comfortable, if a bit creaky in the floorboard department, and the house is only a few minutes' walk from the beach. It also offers hostel accommodation in a neighbouring building from £15 per person.

Crockatinney Guest House　　　　B&B ££
(☎2076 8801; www.crockatinneyguesthouse.com; 80 Whitepark Rd; s/d/f £50/60/90; 🖫) This

WRECK OF THE GIRONA

The little bay 1km to the northeast of the Giant's Causeway is called Port na Spaniagh – Bay of the Spaniards. It was here, in October 1588, that the *Girona* – a ship of the Spanish Armada – was driven onto the rocks by a storm.

The *Girona* had escaped the famous confrontation with Sir Walter Raleigh's fleet in the English Channel but, along with many other fleeing Spanish ships, had been driven north around Scotland and Ireland by bad weather. Though designed for a crew of 500, when she struck the rocks she was loaded with 1300 people – mostly survivors gathered from other shipwrecks – including the cream of the Spanish aristocracy. Barely a dozen survived.

Somhairle Buidhe (Sorley Boy) MacDonnell (1505–90), the constable of nearby Dunluce Castle, salvaged gold and cannons from the wreck, and used the money to extend and modernise his fortress – cannons from the ship can still be seen on the castle's landward wall. But it was not until 1968 that the wreck site was excavated by a team of archaeological divers. They recovered magnificent treasure of gold, silver and precious stones, as well as everyday sailors' possessions, which are now on display in Belfast's Ulster Museum (p566).

large, purpose-built guesthouse enjoys a superb location on the coast road 3km west of Ballycastle, with a panoramic view of Rathlin Island, Fair Head and the Scottish coast. All six stylishly decorated rooms have private bathrooms – upstairs rooms have the best views, while the ground-floor room is equipped for guests with limited mobility.

✕ Eating

Thyme & Co   CAFE £
(www.thymeandco.co.uk; 5 Quay Rd; mains £6; ⊙8am-4.30pm Tue-Fri, 9.30am-4.30pm Sat, 10.30am-3.30pm Sun; 🐾) 🍴 Thyme is a welcoming cafe with the distinction of a menu that is chock-a-block with homemade dishes prepared using local produce as much as possible – lush salads, shepherd's pie, salmon-and-egg crumble. Great home-baked scones and excellent coffee, too.

★ Cellar Restaurant   IRISH ££
(📞2076 3037; www.cellarballycastle.com; 11 The Diamond; mains £12-24; ⊙noon-10pm Mon-Sat, 5-10pm Sun Jun-Aug, 5-10pm Sep-May) This cosy little basement restaurant with intimate wooden booths and a big fireplace is the place to sample Ulster produce – locally caught crab claws grilled with garlic butter, and Carrick-a-Rede salmon are both on the menu, along with Irish beef and lamb, and lobster from Rathlin Island. Early-bird menu offers two courses for £10 (5pm to 7pm weekdays).

ℹ Information

There are a couple of banks with ATMs on Ann St, near the Diamond.

Ballycastle Visitor Centre (📞2076 2024; tourism@moyle-council.org; 14 Bayview Rd; ⊙9.30am-5.30pm Mon-Fri, 10am-4pm Sat, plus 1-4pm Sun Jun-Aug) On the road leading to the Rathlin Island ferry.

ℹ Getting There & Away

The bus station is on Station Rd, just east of the Diamond. Ulsterbus Express 217 links Ballycastle with Ballymena, where you change to Goldline Express 218 or 219 for Belfast (£10, two hours, three daily Monday to Friday, two Saturday).

Bus 172 goes along the coast to Coleraine (£6.50, one hour, seven daily Monday to Friday, four on Saturday and Sunday) via Ballintoy, the Giant's Causeway and Bushmills.

Kintyre Express (📞01586-555895; kintyreexpress.com; one way/return £35/60) High-speed passenger ferry linking Ballycastle with Campbeltown in Scotland; 1½-hour crossing departs once daily May to August, Friday to Monday in April and September, and Friday and Monday only October to March.

Rathlin Island

POP 110

In spring and summer, rugged Rathlin Island (Reachlainn; www.rathlincommunity.org), 6km offshore from Ballycastle, is home to hundreds of seals and thousands of nesting seabirds. An L-shaped island just 6.5km long and 4km wide, Rathlin is famous for the coastal scenery and bird life at Kebble Nature Reserve at its western end.

The island's most illustrious visitor was Scottish hero Robert the Bruce, who spent some time here in 1306 while hiding out after being defeated by the English king.

Watching a spider's resoluteness in repeatedly trying to spin a web gave him the courage to have another go at the English, whom he subsequently defeated at Bannockburn. The cave where he is said to have stayed is beneath the East Lighthouse, at the northeastern tip of the island.

The RSPB's Rathlin Seabird Centre (www.rspb.org.uk; ⊙10am-4pm Apr-Aug) FREE at Rathlin West lighthouse provides stunning views of the neighbouring sea stacks, thick with guillemots, kittiwakes, razorbills and puffins from mid-April to August. During the summer a minibus service runs there from the harbour; public toilets and binocular hire are available.

If you don't have time to visit the Kebble Nature Reserve, the best short walk on the island is through the National Trust's Ballyconagan Nature Reserve to the Old Coastguard Lookout on the north coast, with great views along the sea cliffs and across to the Scottish islands of Islay and Jura.

The Boathouse Visitor Centre (⊙9.30am-5pm Apr-Sep) FREE, south of the harbour, details the history, culture and ecology of the island, and can give advice on walks and wildlife. Paul Quinn (☑07745 566924, 7032 7960; www.rathlinwalkingtours.com; per person £4-12) offers guided walking tours of the island.

🍴 Sleeping & Eating

The island has a pub, a restaurant and a handful of accommodation options; it is essential to book accommodation in advance. You can camp for free in the field beside McCuaig's Bar (☑2076 3974), just east of the harbour; ask at the bar first. There's a chip shop, a cafe by the harbour.

Kinramer Camping Barn HOSTEL £
(☑2076 3948; Kinramer; dm £10) This is a basic bunkhouse located on an organic farm, 5km (a one-hour walk) west from the harbour, where you bring your own food and bedding; it must be booked in advance (groups only April to August). You might be able to get a lift there on one of the island minibuses.

Soerneog View Hostel HOSTEL £
(☑2076 3954; www.rathlin-island.co.uk; Ouig; per person from £15; ⊙Apr-Sep) A private house, a 10-minute walk south of the harbour, Soerneog offers basic hostel-style accommodation in one double and two twin rooms.

Manor House B&B ££
(☑2076 3964; www.rathlinmanorhouse.co.uk; Church Quarter; s/d £35/70) Restored and run by the National Trust, the 18th-century Manor House, on the north side of the harbour, is the island's biggest (12 rooms) and most pleasant place to stay. All rooms have sea views, and a light supper is available by arrangement. The Manor House restaurant was closed at the time of research (it may open again once a manager has been found); however, there is a grocery shop here.

Coolnagrock B&B B&B ££
(☑2076 3983; Coolnagrock; s/d from £35/60; ⊙closed Dec; 🐾) This well-appointed guesthouse is in the eastern part of the island, with great views across the sea to Kintyre. It's a 15-minute walk from the ferry, but you can arrange for the owner to pick you up.

❶ Getting There & Around

A **ferry** (☑2076 9299; www.rathlinballycastle ferry.com; adult/child/bicycle return £12/6/3) operates daily from Ballycastle; advance booking is recommended in spring and summer. From April to September there are eight or nine crossings a day, half of which are fast catamaran services (20 minutes), the rest via a slower car ferry (45 minutes); in winter the service is reduced.

Only residents can take their car to Rathlin (except for disabled drivers), but nowhere on the island is more than 6km (about 1½ hours' walk) from the ferry pier. You can hire a bicycle (£10 per day) from Soerneog View Hostel, or take a minibus tour with **McGinn's** (☑2076 3451; per person £5), which also shuttles visitors between the ferry and Kebble Nature Reserve (£5 return) from April to August.

Glens of Antrim

The northeastern corner of Antrim is a high plateau of black basalt lava overlying beds of white chalk. Along the coast, between Cushendun and Glenarm, the plateau has been dissected by a series of scenic, glacier-gouged valleys known as the Glens of Antrim.

Two waymarked footpaths traverse the region: the Ulster Way sticks close to the sea, passing through all the coastal villages, while the 32km Moyle Way runs inland across the high plateau from Glenariff Forest Park to Ballycastle.

Counties Londonderry & Antrim: The Causeway Coast

The north coast of County Antrim from Ballycastle west to Portrush is known as the Causeway Coast, one of the most impressively scenic stretches of coastline in all of Ireland. Whether you drive, cycle or walk its length, it's not to be missed.

Giant's Causeway

The grand geological centrepiece of the Antrim Coast is the Giant's Causeway, a spectacular rock formation composed of countless hexagonal basalt columns. A Unesco World Heritage site, it is the north coast's most popular tourist attraction.

Causeway Coast

The Causeway Coast isn't just about the scenery. There are picturesque villages at Ballintoy and Portbradden, historic ruined fortresses at Dunluce and Dunseverick castles, and the chance to savour a dram of Irish whiskey at Bushmills Distillery.

Carrick-a-Rede Rope Bridge

Originally rigged and used by local salmon fishermen, the famous Carrick-a-Rede Rope Bridge is now a popular test of nerve for Causeway Coast visitors, swaying gently 30m above the rocks and the sea.

Antrim Coast

Although famous for its dramatic sea-cliff scenery, the Antrim coast also has some excellent sandy beaches. As well as the family-friendly strand at Ballycastle, there's the harder-to-reach but twice-as-beautiful White Park Bay.

1. Rope bridge, Carrick-a-Rede **2.** Ballintoy beach, Causeway Coast **3.** Stepping stones, Antrim Coast

Torr Head Scenic Road

A few kilometres east of Ballycastle, a minor road signposted 'Scenic Route' branches north off the A2. This alternative route to Cushendun is not for the faint-hearted driver, as it clings, precarious and narrow, to steep slopes high above the sea. Side roads lead off to the main points of interest – Fair Head, Murlough Bay and Torr Head. On a clear day, there are superb views across the sea to Scotland, from the Mull of Kintyre to the peaks of Arran.

The first turn-off ends at the National Trust car park at Coolanlough, the starting point for a hike to Fair Head. The second turn-off leads steeply down to Murlough Bay. From the parking area at the end of this road, you can walk north along the shoreline to some ruined miners' cottages (10 minutes); coal and chalk were once mined in the cliffs above, and burned in a limekiln (south of the car park) to make quicklime.

The third turn-off leads you past some ruined coastguard houses to the rocky headland of Torr Head, crowned with a 19th-century coastguard station (abandoned in the 1920s). This is Ireland's closest point to Scotland – the Mull of Kintyre is a mere 19km away across the North Channel. In late spring and summer, a salmon fishery like the one at Carrick-a-Rede operates here, with a net strung out from the headland. The ancient ice house beside the approach road was once used to store the catch.

Cushendun

POP 350

The pretty seaside village of Cushendun is famous for its distinctive Cornish-style cottages, now owned by the National Trust.

Built between 1912 and 1925 at the behest of the local landowner, Lord Cushendun, they were designed by Clough Williams-Ellis, the architect of Portmeirion in north Wales. There's a nice sandy beach, various short coastal walks (outlined on an information board beside the car park), and some impressive caves cut into the overhanging conglomerate sea cliffs south of the village (follow the trail around the far end of the holiday apartments south of the river mouth).

Another natural curiosity lies 6km north of the village on the A2 road to Ballycastle – Loughareema, also known as the Vanishing Lake. Three streams flow in but none flow out. The lough fills up to a respectable size (400m long and 6m deep) after heavy rain, but then the water gradually drains away through fissures in the underlying limestone, leaving a dry lake bed.

🛏 Sleeping & Eating

There's a pub in Cushendun, Mary McBride's, but the kitchen keeps unreliable hours. Cushendall is the nearest place where you can be sure of finding an evening meal.

⭐ **Villa Farmhouse**   B&B ££
(☎2176 1252; www.thevillafarmhouse.com; 185 Torr Rd; s/d from £35/60; @) This lovely old whitewashed farmhouse is set on a hillside, 1km north of Cushendun, with great views over the bay and the warm atmosphere of a family home, decorated with photos of children and grandchildren. The owner is an expert chef and breakfast will be a highlight of your stay – best scrambled eggs in Northern Ireland?

Cloneymore House   B&B ££
(☎2176 1443; ann.cloneymore@btinternet.com; 103 Knocknacarry Rd; s/d £40/50; 🛜🖶) A tra-

---

WALK: FAIR HEAD

From the National Trust's Fair Head car park, a waymarked path leads north past a small lake dotted with tiny islands, one of which is a *crannóg* (artificial island). After 1.5km you arrive at the top of the impressive 180m-high basalt cliffs that mark Fair Head. The panorama of sea and islands extends from Rathlin Island in the west (to your left), with the Scottish island of Islay to its right, followed by the three pointed hills of Jura, to the dark mass of the Mull of Kintyre and the tiny island of Sanda. To the east is the squat cone of Ailsa Craig with the coast of Ayrshire far beyond.

Turn right and follow the faint trail south along the cliff tops for 1.5km, passing a spectacular gully bridged by a fallen rock, known as the Grey Man's Path, until you reach the upper car park on the Murlough Bay road. From here, another faint path, marked by yellow paint marks, strikes west for 1km back to the car park (total 5km; allow two hours).

ditional family B&B on the B92 road 500m southwest of Cushendun, Cloneymore has three spacious and spotless rooms named after Irish and Scottish islands – Aran is the biggest. There are wheelchair ramps and a stairlift, and all rooms are equipped for visitors with limited mobility.

❶ Getting There & Away

Bus 150 runs from Ballymena to Cushendun (£6.50, one hour, six daily Monday to Friday, four Saturday) via Glenariff Forest Park and Cushendall; Ballymena can be reached by train from Belfast and Derry.

From April to September the **Antrim Coaster** bus 252/256 links Belfast and Larne with Cushendun (£10, 2¼ hours, twice daily).

Cushendall

POP 1250

Cushendall is a holiday centre (and traffic bottleneck) at the foot of Glenballyeamon, overlooked by the prominent flat-topped hill of Lurigethan. The beach is small and shingly, though; there are better ones at Waterfoot and Cushendun.

◉ Sights

Curfew Tower   HISTORIC BUILDING
The unusual red sandstone Curfew Tower at the central crossroads was built in 1817, based on a building the landowner had seen in China. It was originally a prison 'for the confinement of idlers and rioters'.

Layd Old Church   CHURCH
From the car park beside the beach (follow signs to golf club), a coastal path leads 1km north to the picturesque ruins of Layd Old Church, with views across to Ailsa Craig (a prominent conical island also known as Paddy's Milestone) and the Scottish coast. Founded by the Franciscans, it was used as a parish church from the early 14th century until 1790. The graveyard contains several grand MacDonnell memorials. Near the gate stands an ancient, weathered ring-cross (with the arms missing), much older than the 19th-century inscription on its shaft.

🛏 Sleeping & Eating

Village B&B   B&B ££
(☎2177 2366; www.thevillagebandb.com; 18 Mill St; s/d/f £35/60/90; ⊙Apr-Sep; ☜☍) Bang in the middle of town, the Village offers three spotless rooms with private bathrooms and huge hearty breakfasts, and is just across the road

from McCollams, the best pub in Cushendall for traditional music.

Cullentra House   B&B ££
(☎2177 1762; www.cullentrahouseireland.com; 16 Cloughs Rd; s/d from £35/50; ☜) This modern bungalow sits high above the village at the end of Cloughs Rd, offering good views of the craggy Antrim coast. The three rooms are spacious and comfy, and the breakfasts (accompanied by home-baked wheaten bread) are as big as the owners' hospitality.

Harry's Restaurant   BISTRO ££
(☎2177 2022; harryscushendall.com; 10 Mill St; mains day menu £8-13, evening £10-19; ⊙noon-9pm; ☜) With its cosy lounge-bar atmosphere and friendly welcome, Harry's is a local institution, serving pub grub from noon to 6pm – battered cod with mushy peas, burger or Caesar salad, for example – plus an à-la-carte dinner menu in the evenings that ranges from steak to lobster.

❶ Information

Tourist Office (☎2177 1180; 24 Mill St; ⊙10am-1pm & 2-5pm Mon-Fri, 10am-2pm Sat Jun-Sep, 10am-1pm Tue-Sat Oct-May) Run by the Glens of Antrim Historical Society; also offers internet access.

❶ Getting There & Away

Bus 162 travels from Larne to Cushendall (£6.50, one hour, three daily Monday to Friday), stopping at Glenarm; there are frequent trains and buses from Belfast to Larne. Bus 150 goes to Cushendun and Glenariff Forest Park.

Glenariff

About 2km south of Cushendall is the village of Waterfoot, with a 2km-long sandy beach, the best on Antrim's east coast. From here the A43 Ballymena road runs inland along Glenariff, the loveliest of Antrim's glens. Views of the valley led the writer Thackeray to exclaim that it was a 'Switzerland in miniature', a claim that makes you wonder if he'd ever been to Switzerland!

At the head of the valley is Glenariff Forest Park (car/motorcycle/pedestrian £4.50/2.30/1.50; ⊙10am-dusk), where the main attraction is Ess-na-Larach Waterfall, an 800m walk from the visitor centre. You can also walk to the waterfall from Laragh Lodge, 600m downstream. There are various good walks in the park; the longest is a 10km circular trail.

There's hostel accommodation for hikers at Ballyeamon Barn (☑ 2175 8451; www. ballyeamonbarn.com; 127 Ballyeamon Rd; dm £14; @ ⬤), 8km southwest of Cushendall on the B14 (1km north of its junction with the A43), close to the Moyle Way and about a 1.5km walk from the main entrance to the forest park. Run by Liz Weir, a professional storyteller, the barn hosts regular sessions of traditional Irish music, poetry, dance and storytelling.

Laragh Lodge (☑ 2175 8221; 120 Glen Rd; mains £10-16, 4-course Sun lunch £16; ◷ 11am-9pm daily Mar-Oct, Fri-Sun only Nov-Feb) is a restaurant and bar on a side road off the A43, 3km northeast of the main park entrance. A renovated Victorian tourist lodge with assorted bric-a-brac dangling from the rafters, the Laragh dates from 1890 and serves hearty pub-grub-style meals – beef and Guinness pie, fish and chips, sausage and mash (with a couple of vegetarian options) – and offers a traditional roast lunch on Sunday.

You can reach Glenariff Forest Park on Ulsterbus 150 from Cushendun (£4, 30 minutes, six daily Monday to Friday, four Saturday) and Ballymena (£4, 30 minutes).

Glenarm

POP 600

Glenarm (Gleann Arma), the oldest village in the glens, has been the family seat of the MacDonnell family since 1750; the present 14th Earl of Antrim lives in Glenarm Castle (www.glenarmcastle.com), on a private estate hidden behind the impressive wall that runs along the main road north of the bridge. The castle itself is closed to the public, except for two days in July when a Highland Games competition is held, but you can visit the lovely walled garden (adult/child £5/2.50; ◷ 10am-5pm Mon-Sat, 11am-5pm Sun May-Sep), which opens in May with its annual Tulip Festival.

The tourist office (☑ 2884 1087; www. glenarmtourism.org; 2 The Bridge; ◷ 9.30am-5pm Mon-Fri, 2-6pm Sun; @) is beside the bridge on the main road. It has internet access for £2 per 30 minutes.

Take a stroll into the old village of neat Georgian houses (off the main road, immediately south of the river). Where the street opens into the broad expanse of Altmore St, look right to see the Barbican Gate (1682), the entrance to Glenarm Castle grounds. On the left is Steensons (www.thesteensons.com; Toberwine St; ◷ 9am-5pm Mon-Sat), a designer jewellery workshop and visitor centre where you can watch craftspeople at work.

Turn left here and climb steeply up Vennel St, then left again immediately after the last house along the Layde Path to the viewpoint, which has a grand view of the village and the coast.

Larne

POP 17,600

As a major port for ferries from Scotland, Larne (Lutharna) is one of Northern Ireland's main points of arrival. However, with its concrete overpasses and the huge chimneys of Ballylumford power station opposite the harbour, poor old Larne is a little lacking in the charm department. After a visit to the excellent tourist information centre, there's no real reason to linger.

Larne Harbour train station is in the ferry terminal. It's a short bus ride or a 15-minute walk from here to the town centre – turn right on Fleet St and right again on Curran Rd, then left on Circular Rd. At the big roundabout, Larne Town train station is to your left, the tourist office is to the right, and the bus station is ahead (beneath the road bridge).

ⓘ Information

Tourist Office (☑ 2826 0088; larnetourism@ btconnect.com; Narrow Gauge Rd; ◷ 9am-5pm Mon-Sat Easter-Sep, Mon-Fri Oct-Easter) Offers friendly service, extensive information on all of Northern Ireland, and an exhibition on local history and wildlife.

ⓘ Getting There & Away

Bus 256 provides a direct service between the town centre and Belfast (£4.90, one hour, hourly Monday to Friday, six Saturday, plus two on Sunday July to September only).

Heading north to the Glens of Antrim, take bus 162 or the **Antrim Coaster**.

P&O Irish Sea (www.poirishsea.com) ferries run from Larne to Scotland and England.

Larne has two train stations, **Larne Town** and **Larne Harbour**. Trains from Larne Town to Belfast Central (£6.90, one hour) depart at least hourly; those from the harbour are timed to connect with ferries.

Carrickfergus

POP 28,000

Northern Ireland's most impressive medieval fortress commands the entrance to

GALGORM

About 6km west of Ballymena is the Galgorm Resort & Spa (☑ 2588 1001; www.galgorm.com; 136 Fenaghy Rd, Galgorm; d/f from £110/140; @ 🐾 📶), a 19th-century manor house in a lovely setting on the bank of the River Main. Refurbished by the owners of Belfast's boutique hotel Ten Square, the Galgorm has been redeveloped and extended to create one of Ireland's top country-house hotels.

The rustic atmosphere of the original Gillie's Bar (mains lunch £10-15, dinner £11-27; ⊙kitchen noon-10pm), set in the former stables, has been retained, with bare stone walls, huge timber beams, a log fire and cosy sofas, but it has been extended into a spectacular, high-roofed barn with a huge, central free-standing chimney and a monumental staircase framed by crouching sphinxes – all in all, a pretty jaw-dropping setting for some of the fanciest pub grub in Ireland.

Belfast Lough from the rocky promontory of Carrickfergus (Carraig Fhearghais). The old town centre opposite the castle has some attractive 18th-century houses and you can still trace a good part of the 17th-century city walls.

◉ Sights

Carrickfergus Castle CASTLE
(Marine Hwy; adult/child £5/3; ⊙ 10am-6pm during Easter-Sep, to 4pm Oct-Easter) The central keep of Ireland's first and finest Norman fortress was built by John de Courcy soon after his 1177 invasion of Ulster. The massive walls of the outer ward were completed in 1242, while the red-brick gun ports were added in the 16th century. The keep houses a museum and the site is dotted with life-size figures illustrating the castle's history.

The castle overlooks the harbour where William of Orange landed on 14 June 1690, on his way to the Battle of the Boyne; a blue plaque on the old harbour wall marks the place where he stepped ashore, and a bronze statue of 'King Billy' himself stands on the shore nearby.

Carrickfergus Museum MUSEUM
(11 Antrim St; ⊙ 10am-5pm Mon-Fri & 10am-4pm Sat, to 5pm Mon-Fri Oct-Mar) FREE The glass-fronted Heritage Plaza on Antrim St houses the local museum, which has a small collection of artefacts that relate to the town's history, and a pleasant coffee shop.

Andrew Jackson Centre HISTORIC SITE
(Boneybefore) FREE The parents of the seventh US president left Carrickfergus in the second half of the 18th century. His ancestral home was demolished in 1860, but a replica thatched cottage complete with fireside crane and earthen floor now houses this

memorial on the coast, 2km north of Carrickfergus Castle. It has displays on the life of Jackson, the Jackson family in Ulster, and Ulster's connection with the USA.

Next door is the US Rangers Centre, with a small exhibition on the first US rangers, who were trained during WWII in Carrickfergus before heading for Europe.

The centre is open by appointment only; contact the tourist office in advance.

🍴 Sleeping & Eating

Keep Guesthouse B&B ££
(☑ 9336 7007; www.thekeepguesthousecarrickfergus.co.uk; 93 Irish Quarter S; s/d from £35/50; 🐾 📶) Just across the main road from the marina, and close to the town centre, the Keep has four rooms with attractive, modern decor and original art on the walls; go for the spacious double/family room on the 1st floor if possible.

Dobbin's Inn Hotel HOTEL ££
(☑ 9335 1905; www.dobbinsinnhotel.co.uk; 6-8 High St; s/d/f from £45/55/80; @ 🐾 📶) In the centre of the old town, Dobbin's is a friendly and informal place with 15 small and creaky-floored but comfortable rooms, one of them supposedly haunted! The building has been around for over three centuries, and has a priest's hole and an original 16th-century fireplace to prove it.

Sozo CAFE £
(☑ 9332 6060; 2 North St; mains £4-10; ⊙ 8am-5pm Mon-Thu, to 9pm Fri & Sat; 🐾 📶) Hugely popular with the locals, Sozo is an unpretentious little place with friendly service and a menu of plain, freshly made comfort food, from sandwiches and salads to lasagne and garlic bread, plus steaks and Asian dishes. It's tiny, so best to book if you want a table for dinner.

WALK: SLEMISH

The skyline to the east of Ballymena is dominated by the distinctive craggy peak of Slemish (438m). The hill is one of many sites in the North associated with Ireland's patron saint – the young St Patrick is said to have tended goats on its slopes. On St Patrick's Day, thousands of people make a pilgrimage to its summit; the rest of the year it's a pleasant climb, though steep and slippery in wet weather, rewarded with a fine view (allow one hour return from the parking area).

Windrose INTERNATIONAL **££**
(☑9335 1164; www.thewindrose.co.uk; Rodgers Quay; mains £8-15; ⊘kitchen noon-9pm) This stylish, modern bar-bistro, with a more formal restaurant upstairs (mains £12 to £19, dinner only), serves a range of dishes, from fisherman's pie and mussels to steaks and stir-fries. The outdoor terrace overlooking the forest of yacht masts in the marina is a real sun-trap on a summer afternoon.

ⓘ Information

Tourist Office (☑9335 8049; www.carrickfergus.org/tourism; 11 Antrim St, Heritage Plaza; ⊘10am-5pm Mon-Fri & 10am-4pm Sat year-round, to 6pm Mon-Fri Apr-Sep; ☜)

ⓘ Getting There & Away

There's an hourly train service between Carrickfergus and Belfast (£4.10, 30 minutes).

Inland County Antrim

To the west of the high moorland plateau above the Glens of Antrim, the hills slope down to the agricultural lowlands of Lough Neagh and the broad valley of the River Bann. This region is rarely visited by tourists, who either take the coast road or speed through on the way from Belfast to Derry, but it is worth seeking out if you have time to spare.

Antrim Town

POP 19,800

The town of Antrim (Aontroim) straddles the River Sixmilewater, close to an attractive bay on the shores of Lough Neagh. During the 1798 Rising, the United Irishmen fought a pitched battle along the length of the town's High St.

The tourist office (☑9442 8331; www.antrim.gov.uk; Market Sq; ⊘9am-5pm Mon-Fri, plus 10am-1pm Sat May-Sep, Mon-Fri only Oct-Apr) is housed in the beautifully restored Old Courthouse (1762), a gem of Georgian architecture. Pick up a free, self-guided heritage trail booklet.

Beyond the courthouse is the Barbican Gate (1818) and a portion of the old castle walls. Pass through the gate and the underpass beyond to reach Antrim Castle Gardens (⊘9.30am-7pm, or dusk if earlier) FREE. The castle burned down many years ago, but the grounds remain as one of the few surviving examples of a 17th-century ornamental garden.

Antrim's 10th-century Round Tower (Steeple Rd), on the northeast edge of town, is 28m tall, and one of the finest examples of these monastic towers in all of Ireland. You can explore the site freely, but the tower itself is closed to the public.

A walking and cycling trail leads west along the river from the castle gardens to Antrim Lough Shore Park, where the vast size of Lough Neagh is apparent. There are picnic tables and lakeside walking trails.

The vintage launch Maid of Antrim (☑2582 2159; www.loughneaghcruises.co.uk; adult/child £8/5), built on Scotland's River Clyde in 1963, offers cruises on the lough, departing from Antrim Marina (next to Lough Shore Park) on Sunday afternoons from Easter to October. Booking is essential.

Goldline Express 219 from Belfast to Ballymena stops in Antrim (£6.50, 40 minutes, hourly Monday to Friday, seven on Saturday). There are also frequent trains from Belfast to Antrim (£5.50, 25 minutes, 10 daily Monday to Saturday, five on Sunday) continuing to Derry.

Counties Fermanagh & Tyrone

POP 230,000 / AREA 4846 SQ KM

Best Places to Eat

➡ Dollakis (p651)

➡ Deli on the Green (p663)

➡ Terrace Restaurant (p651)

➡ Cedars Bistro (p657)

➡ Philly's Phinest (p661)

Best Places to Stay

➡ Westville Hotel (p650)

➡ Cedars Guesthouse (p657)

➡ Tullylagan Country House (p663)

➡ Kilmore Quay Club (p656)

➡ Mullaghmore House (p661)

Why Go?

The ancient landscape of Fermanagh is shaped by ice and water, with rugged hills rising above quilted plains of half-drowned drumlins (rounded hills formed by retreating glaciers) and shimmering, reed-fringed lakes. A glance at the map shows the county is around one-third water – as the locals will tell you, the lakes are in Fermanagh for six months of the year; for the other six, Fermanagh is in the lakes. This watery maze is a natural playground for anglers and canoeists.

County Tyrone – from Tír Eoghain (Land of Owen, a legendary chieftain) – is the homeland of the O'Neill clan, and is dominated by the tweed-tinted moorlands of the Sperrin Mountains, whose southern flanks are dotted with prehistoric sites. Apart from the hiking opportunities offered by these heather-clad hills, the county's main attraction is the Ulster American Folk Park, a fascinating outdoor museum celebrating Ulster's historic links with the USA.

When to Go

➡ May marks the start of the mayfly season, the most exciting time for trout fishing on Lough Erne, while June is the ideal month for cruising the lakes.

➡ If hiking is more to your taste, July is ideal for hill walking in the Sperrins. You can join a mass pilgrimage to the summit of Mullaghcarn, above Gortin, on Cairn Sunday, the last Sunday in the month.

➡ The tail end of summer is enlivened by the Ulster American Folk Park's annual Appalachian and Bluegrass Music Festival.

Counties Fermanagh & Tyrone Highlights

1 Hike over rare blanket bog to the remote summit of **Cuilcagh Mountain** (p660)

2 Ponder the meaning of the strange stone figures on **White Island** (p657) and **Boa Island** (p657)

3 Follow the course of an underground river through the **Marble Arch Caves** (p660)

4 Hire a canoe and explore the reed-fringed backwaters of **Lough Erne** (p653)

5 Learn about the historical links between Ireland and the USA at the **Ulster American Folk Park** (p661)

6 See how the Irish aristocracy enjoyed the high life in the elegant country house of **Florence Court** (p659)

7 Explore the Celtic monastic settlement on **Devenish Island** (p656), and climb to the top of its ancient round tower

COUNTY FERMANAGH

Enniskillen

POP 13,600

Though neither was born here, both Oscar Wilde and Samuel Beckett were pupils at Enniskillen's Portora Royal School (Wilde from 1864 to 1871, Beckett from 1919 to 1923); it was here that Beckett first studied French, a language he would later write in. The town's name is also prominent in the history of the Troubles – on Poppy Day (11 November) in 1987 an IRA bomb killed 11 people during a service at Enniskillen's war memorial.

Perched amid the web of waterways that link Upper and Lower Lough Erne, Enniskillen (Inis Ceithleann, meaning Ceithleann's Island, after a legendary woman warrior) is an appealing town with a mile-long main street that rides the roller-coaster spine of an island drumlin. Its attractive waterside setting, bustling with boats in summer, plus a range of lively pubs and restaurants, make Enniskillen a good base for exploring Upper and Lower Lough Erne, Florence Court and the Marble Arch Caves.

The main street changes name half a dozen times between the bridges at either end; the prominent clock tower marks the town centre. The other principal street is Wellington Rd, south of and parallel to the main street, where you'll find the bus station, tourist office and car parking. If you're driving, try to avoid rush hour – the bridge at the west end is a traffic bottleneck.

◉ Sights & Activities

Enniskillen Castle   MUSEUM
(www.enniskillencastle.co.uk; Castle Barracks; adult/child £4/3; ⊙2-5pm Mon, 10am-5pm Tue-Fri year-round, also 2-5pm Sat May-Sep & 2-5pm Sun Jul & Aug) Enniskillen Castle, a former stronghold of the 16th-century Maguire chieftains, guards the western end of the town's central island, its twin-turreted Watergate looming over passing fleets of cabin cruisers. Within the walls you'll find the Fermanagh County Museum, which has displays on the county's history, archaeology, landscape and wildlife. The 15th-century keep contains the Royal Inniskilling Fusiliers Regimental Museum, full of guns, uniforms and medals, including eight Victoria Crosses awarded in WWI; it's dedicated to the regiment that was raised at the castle in 1689 to support the army of William I.

Kingfisher Trail   CYCLING
(www.cycleni.com) The Kingfisher Trail is a waymarked, long-distance cycling trail that starts in Enniskillen and wends its way through the back roads of Counties Fermanagh, Leitrim, Cavan and Monaghan. The full route is around 370km long, but a shorter loop, starting and finishing in Enniskillen, and travelling via Kesh, Belleek, Garrison, Belcoo and the village of Florencecourt, is only 115km – easily done in two days with an overnight stay at Belleek. You can get a trail map from the Enniskillen Tourist Information Centre. There's no bicycle hire available in Enniskillen, though; the nearest is in Castle Archdale Country Park.

⌲ Tours

Erne Tours   BOAT TOUR
(✆6632 2882; www.ernetoursltd.com; The Brook, Round 'O' Quay; adult/child £10/6, dinner cruises £25/15; ⊙4 daily Jul & Aug, 2 daily Jun, 2 on Tue, Sat & Sun May, Sep & Oct) Operates 1¾-hour cruises on Lower Lough Erne aboard the 56-seat waterbus MV *Kestrel*, calling at Devenish Island (April to September) along the way. It departs from the Round 'O' Quay, just west of the town centre on the A46 to Belleek. There are also Saturday evening cruises (May to September) that include a three-course dinner at the Killyhevlin Hotel, departing from the hotel jetty.

⌕ Sleeping

★ Westville Hotel   HOTEL ££
(✆6632 0333; www.westvillehotel.co.uk; 14-20 Tempo Rd; s/d from £75/90; @ 🛜 🐾 ⭐) The Westville adds a dash of style to Enniskillen's rather staid accommodation scene with designer fabrics, cool colour combinations, good food and welcoming staff. The family suite (from £155) offers great value, sleeping four in two adjoining rooms.

Greenwood Lodge   B&B ££
(✆6632 5636; www.greenwoodlodge.co.uk; 17 Killyvilly Ct, Tempo Rd; s/d £40/55) The owners of this spacious and modern villa, set on a quiet side street 3km northeast of town off the B80, go out of their way to make you feel welcome. The three homey bedrooms all have private bathrooms, the breakfasts are freshly prepared, and secure storage is available for bikes.

Belmore Court & Motel   HOTEL ££
(✆6632 6633; www.motel.co.uk; Tempo Rd; s/d from £80/95, apt from £100; 🛜 ⭐) Set in an

original row of terrace houses linked to a large modern extension, the friendly Belmore offers stylish and spacious 'superior' rooms in the new building and, in the old, family 'mini-apartments' with self-catering facilities.

Rossole Guesthouse B&B **££**
(📞 6632 3462; rossoleguesthouse.com; 85 Sligo Rd; s/d from £35/55; 🐾) A modern Georgian-style house with a sunny conservatory overlooking a small lake, the five-room Rossole is an angler's delight – you can fish in the lake, and there's a rowing boat for guests at the bottom of the garden. It's 1km southwest of the town centre on the A4 Sligo road.

Mountview Guesthouse B&B **££**
(📞 6632 3147; www.mountviewguests.com; 61 Irvinestown Rd; s/d from £50/75; 🐾) Indulge in a spot of country-house comfort in this large, ivy-clad Victorian villa set in wooded grounds. There are three bedrooms with private bathrooms, a luxurious lounge and a view over Race Course Lough. It's just a 10-minute (800m) walk north from the town centre.

Killyhevlin Hotel HOTEL **£££**
(📞 6632 3481; www.killyhevlin.com; Killyhevlin; s/d £110/160; @🐾) Enniskillen's top hotel is 1.5km south of town on the A4 Maguiresbridge road, in an idyllic setting overlooking Upper Lough Erne. Many of its 43 effortlessly elegant rooms enjoy stunning views over landscaped gardens to the lough.

🍴 Eating

⭐ **Dollakis** MEDITERRANEAN **££**
(📞 6634 2616; www.dollakis.co.uk; 2 Cross St; mains lunch £7-9, dinner £14-20; ⏰ 10am-10pm Tue-Sat) As well as serving lunch (from noon to 4pm), cakes and snacks through the day, this chic little cafe transforms into a Greek-Mediterranean restaurant in the evening (from 6pm). The dinner menu includes things such as grilled sea bream stuffed with lemon and herbs, chicken souvlaki and vegetarian moussaka.

⭐ **Terrace Restaurant** IRISH **££**
(📞 6632 0333; Westville Hotel, 14-20 Tempo Rd; mains £16-20; ⏰ dinner) The restaurant at the Westville Hotel combines understated elegance in the dining room with a deft touch in the kitchen. Candlelight creates a romantic atmosphere, while delightful, perfectly presented dishes make for a memorable meal.

Uno Restaurant & Cocktail Bar IRISH **££**
(📞 6634 2622; 17 Belmore St; mains £12-19; ⏰ 4.30pm-late Mon-Sat, 4.30-9pm Sun) This revamped restaurant has a retro vibe with chunky timber tables and painted wood panelling, and a menu of locally sourced beef, lamb and seafood. There's a set dinner menu offering two/three courses for £22/25. (Give the cocktail bar a miss – it has no atmosphere.)

🍸 Drinking & Nightlife

⭐ **Blake's of the Hollow** PUB
(William Blake; 6 Church St) Ulster's best pint of Guinness awaits you in this traditional Victorian pub, almost unchanged since 1887, complete with marble-topped bar, four huge sherry casks, antique silver lamp holders, open fire, and ancient wood panelling kippered by a century of cigarette smoke. There's traditional music from 9pm on Fridays.

Crowe's Nest BAR
(12 High St) A lively bar with a conservatory and patio out the back for those sunny summer afternoons, the Nest has live music most nights from 9pm in the back bar and traditional music sessions downstairs on Saturday afternoons.

☆ Entertainment

Ardhowen Theatre THEATRE
(www.ardhowentheatre.com; Dublin Rd; ⏰ box office 9.30am-4.30pm Mon-Fri, to 7pm before performances, 11am-1pm, 2-5pm & 6-7pm Sat) The program here includes concerts, local amateur and professional drama and musical productions, pantomimes and films. The theatre is about 2km southeast of the town centre on the A4, in an impressive glass-fronted building overlooking a lake.

ℹ Information

Tourist Office (📞 6632 3110; www.fermanagh. gov.uk; Wellington Rd; ⏰ 9am-5.30pm Mon-Fri

---

TOP FIVE TRADITIONAL PUBS IN NORTHERN IRELAND
....
➡ Bittle's Bar (p578)
➡ Blake's of the Hollow (p651)
➡ Grace Neill's (p591)
➡ Dufferin Arms (p596)
➡ Peadar O'Donnell's (p624)

Enniskillen

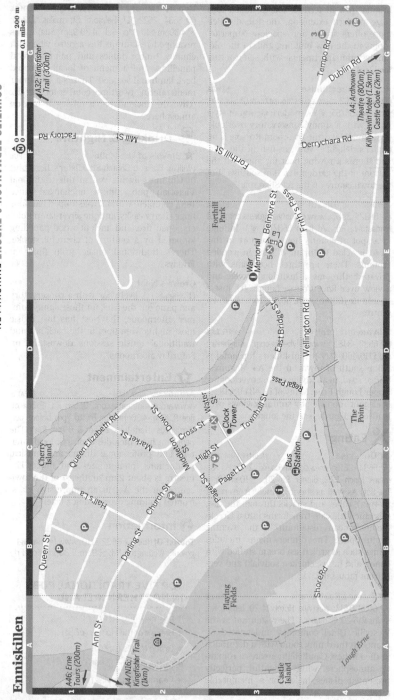

200 m
0.1 miles
N

A32; Kingfisher Trail (300m)

Factory Rd

Mill St

Forthill St

Forthill Park

Belmore St

Quay La

Frith's Pass

Derrychara Rd

Tempo Rd

Dublin Rd

A4; Ardhowen Theatre (800m); Killyhevlin Hotel (1.5km); Castle Coole (2km)

War Memorial

East Bridge St

Wellington Rd

Regal Pass

The Point

Cherry Island

Queen Elizabeth Rd

Market St

Middleton Down St

Cross St

Water St

Clock Tower

Townhall St

High St

Paget Ln

Church St

Paget Sq

Darling St

Hall's La

Queen St

Ann St

A46; Erne Tours (200m)

A4/N16; Kingfisher Trail (1km)

Bus Station

Shore Rd

Playing Fields

Castle Island

Lough Erne

Enniskillen

year-round, plus 10am-6pm Sat, 11am-5pm Sun Easter-Sep, 10am-2pm Sat & Sun Oct; @) About 100m south of the town centre; has internet access (£1 per 20 minutes).

ⓘ Getting There & Away

Ulsterbus and Bus Éireann services run to/from Belfast (£11.50, 2¼ hours, hourly Monday to Saturday, two on Sunday), Omagh (£8, one hour, one daily Monday to Saturday, Dublin (£19, 2½ hours, seven daily Monday to Saturday, four Sunday), Sligo (£13, 1½ hours, five daily Monday to Saturday, two on Sunday) and Donegal (£11.50, one hour, five daily Monday to Saturday, two on Sunday).

In July and August only, bus 99 goes from Enniskillen to Bundoran (£6.50, 1¼ hours, four daily Monday to Friday, three Saturday, one on Sunday) via Belleek (45 minutes). Bus 64 goes to Bundoran year-round, twice on Thursday and once on Sunday.

Around Enniskillen

◎ Sights

Castle Coole   HISTORIC BUILDING
(www.nationaltrust.org.uk; Dublin Rd; house adult/child £5/2, grounds £2.50/1.25; ⊙house 11am-5pm daily Jul & Aug, Fri-Wed Jun, Sat, Sun & public hols mid-Mar–May & Sep, grounds 10am-7pm Mar-Oct, 10am-4pm Nov-Feb) When King George IV visited Ireland in 1821, the second Earl of Belmore had a state bedroom specially prepared at Castle Coole in anticipation of the monarch's visit. The king, however, was more interested in dallying with his mistress at Slane Castle and never turned up. The bedroom, draped in red silk and decorated with paintings depicting *The Rake's Progress* (the earl's sniffy riposte to the king's extramarital shenanigans), is one of the highlights of the one-hour guided tour.

Designed by James Wyatt, this Palladian mansion was built between 1789 and 1795 for Armar Lowry-Corry, the first Earl of Belmore, and is probably the purest expression of late-18th-century neoclassical architecture in Ireland. It is built of silvery-white Portland stone, which was brought in at great expense from southern England – first sent by ship to Ballyshannon, then overland to Lough Erne, by boat again to Enniskillen, and finally by bullock cart for the last 3km.

The 600 hectares of landscaped grounds contain a lake that is home to the UK's only nonmigratory colony of greylag geese. It is said that, if the geese ever leave, the Earls of Belmore will lose Castle Coole.

Castle Coole is on the A4 Dublin road, 2.5km southeast of Enniskillen. You can easily walk there from Enniskillen town centre in 30 minutes – beyond Dunnes Stores, fork left on Tempo Rd and keep going straight on along Castlecoole Rd.

Sheelin Irish Lace Museum   MUSEUM
(www.irishlacemuseum.com; Bellanaleck; adult/child £2.50/free; ⊙10am-6pm Mon-Sat Apr-Oct) This museum houses a collection of beautiful Irish lace dating from 1850 to 1900. Lacemaking was an important cottage industry in the region both before and after the Famine – prior to WWI there were at least 10 lace schools in County Fermanagh. The museum is just over 6km southwest of Enniskillen.

Upper Lough Erne

About 80km long, Lough Erne is made up of two sections: the Upper Lough to the south of Enniskillen, and the Lower Lough to the north. The two are connected by the River Erne, which begins its journey in County Cavan and meets the sea at Donegal Bay west of Ballyshannon.

Upper Lough Erne is not so much a lake as a watery maze of islands (more than 150 of them), inlets, reedy bays and meandering backwaters. Bird life is abundant, with flocks of whooper swan and goldeneye overwintering here, great crested grebes nesting in the spring, and Ireland's biggest heronry in a 400-year-old oak grove on the island of Inishfendra, just south of Crom Estate.

Lisnaskea is the main town, with shops, pubs, ATMs and a post office.

DESIGN PICS / PETER ZOELLER / GETTY IMAGES ©

GARETH MCCORMACK / GETTY IMAGES ©

HOLGER LEUE / GETTY IMAGES ©

3

1. Caldragh graveyard (p657)
The bilateral stone 'Janus' figure stares out enigmatically over the early Christian graveyard.

2. Lower Lough Erne (p656)
The evening panorama from atop the Cliffs of Magho is spectacular.

3. Boating on Lough Erne (p658)
Become your own captain on a self-drive cabin cruiser.

4. Boa Island (p657)
Bucolic Boa is just one of the 90-odd islands in Lower Lough Erne.

ULSTER WAY

The Ulster Way long-distance walking trail makes a circuit around the six counties of Northern Ireland and Donegal. In total the route covers just over 900km, so walking all of it might take four to five weeks. However, much of the way is on minor roads rather than footpaths, a criticism that has been taken on board by the Northern Ireland Tourist Board (NITB), which has 'relaunched' the Ulster Way and divided it into 'Quality Sections' – good, scenic, off-road walking – separated by 'Link Sections', which can be covered by public transport. Check the website of WalkNI (www.walkni.com) for details.

Short sections of the Ulster Way that make good day walks include Cuilcagh Mountain (www.cuilcaghmountainpark.com) and the Causeway Coast Way (www.causewaycoastway.com).

❶ Getting Around

From Enniskillen, Ulsterbus service 95 runs along the east side of the lough to Lisnaskea (£3.70, 30 minutes, five daily Monday to Friday, three on Saturday, plus one on Sunday in July and August only). Bus 58 goes down the west side to Derrylin (£3.70, 40 minutes, five daily Monday to Friday, two on Saturday), and continues to Belturbet in County Cavan.

◉ Sights & Activities

Crom Estate   WILDLIFE RESERVE
(Newtownbutler; adult/child £3.50/1.50; ⊙ grounds 10am-7pm Jun-Aug, to 6pm mid-Mar–May, Sep & Oct, visitor centre 11am-5pm daily Easter-Sep, Sat & Sun only Oct) Home to the largest area of natural woodland in Northern Ireland, the National Trust's beautiful Crom Estate is a haven for pine martens, rare bats and many species of bird.

You can walk from the visitor centre to the ruins of old Crom Castle, with its ancient walled garden, abandoned bowling green and gnarled yew trees, and views over the reed-fringed lough to an island folly. There are rowing boats for hire (£6 per hour).

Check the website of the National Trust (www.ntni.org.uk) for details of bat-watching and other wildlife events.

The estate is on the eastern shore of the Upper Lough, 5km west of Newtownbutler.

Inishcruiser   BOAT TOUR
(www.sharevillage.org/inishcruiser; adult/child/family £10/6/28; ⊙ 2.30pm Sun & public holidays Easter-Sep) The *Inishcruiser* offers 1½- to two-hour cruises on the lough leaving from the Share Holiday Village, 5km southwest of Lisnaskea.

⌂ Sleeping & Eating

★ **Kilmore Quay Club**   B&B **££**
(☑ 6772 4369; www.kilmorequayclub.com; Kilmore Quay, Lisnaskea; s/d from £59/79) A secluded lakeside setting makes for a peaceful night's rest in one of the seven luxurious guest rooms here. The rooms are next to the plush, thatch-roofed Watermill Restaurant (3-course dinner from £25; ⊙ lunch & dinner), where a French-influenced menu leans towards the gourmet end of the spectrum.

Kissin Crust   CAFE **£**
(125 Main St, Lisnaskea; mains £3-6; ⊙ 8.30am-5pm Mon-Sat) Very popular with the locals, this friendly coffee shop is stacked with home-baked apple pie, lemon meringue pie, quiches and scones, and serves up a lunch menu of homemade soup, freshly made sandwiches and a hot dish of the day.

Lower Lough Erne

Lower Lough Erne is a more open expanse of water than the Upper Lough, with its 90-odd islands clustered mainly in the southern reaches. In early Christian times, when overland travel was difficult, Lough Erne was an important highway between the Donegal coast and inland Leitrim, and there are many ancient religious sites and other antiquities dotted around its shores. In medieval times the lough was part of an important pilgrimage route to Station Island in Lough Derg.

❶ Getting Around

On the eastern side of the lough, Ulsterbus service 194 from Enniskillen to Pettigo via Irvinestown (three to five daily Monday to Saturday) stops near Castle Archdale Country Park (35 minutes) and Kesh (one hour). Bus Eireann's Dublin to Donegal service 30 links Enniskillen and Belleek (£6.50, 35 minutes, seven daily).

Devenish Island

Devenish Island (from Daimh Inis, meaning Ox Island) is the biggest of several 'holy islands' in Lough Erne. The remains of an Augustinian monastery, founded here in the 6th century by St Molaise, include a superb 12th-century round tower in near-perfect condition, the ruins of St Molaise's Church and St Mary's Abbey, an unusual 15th-century high cross, and many fascinating old gravestones. Four ladders allow you to climb to the top of the round tower for a cramped view out of the five tiny windows.

A speedboat ferry (07702 052873; adult/child return £3/2; 10am, 1pm, 3pm & 5pm daily Jul & Aug, Thu-Mon Sep) crosses to Devenish Island from Trory Point landing. From Enniskillen, take the A32 towards Irvinestown and after 5km look for the sign on the left, just after a service station and immediately before the junction where the B82 and A32 part company. At the foot of the hill by the lough, turn left for the jetty.

You can also visit as part of a cruise with Erne Tours (p650) in Enniskillen.

Castle Archdale Country Park

This park (Lisnarick; 9am-7pm Easter-Sep, to 9pm Jul & Aug) FREE has pleasant woodland and lakeshore walks and cycle tracks in the former estate of 18th-century Archdale Manor. The island-filled bay was used in WWII as a base for Catalina flying boats, a history explained in the visitor centre.

You can hire bikes for £4/8/12 per hour/half-/full day, or swap two wheels for four legs – the park offers pony trekking (£15 per hour), as well as short rides (£5 per 15 minutes) for beginners. There are also boats for hire (£60/85 per half-/full day), and you can rent fishing rods (£5 per day including bait).

The park is 16km northwest of Enniskillen on the B82, near Lisnarick.

🛏 Sleeping & Eating

Castle Archdale Caravan Park CAMPGROUND £ (6862 1333; www.castlearchdale.com; Castle Archdale Country Park; campsites per tent £20-30, caravan sites £25-30; Easter-Oct;) This attractive, tree-sheltered site is dominated by on-site caravans, but has good facilities, including a shop, launderette, playground and restaurant.

★**Cedars Guesthouse** B&B ££ (6862 1493; www.cedarsguesthouse.com; Drummal, Castle Archdale; s/d from £45/70;) Set in a former rectory just south of the park entrance, this peaceful 10-room guesthouse goes for a Victorian country-house feel, with rose-patterned bedspreads and antique-style furniture.

★**Cedars Bistro** IRISH ££ (6862 1493; mains £11-18; 6-9pm Wed-Sat, 12.30-3pm & 5-9pm Sun) Adjoining the Cedars Guesthouse, this bistro has a welcoming open fireplace, lots of golden pine lit by chunky candles and a sprinkling of Gothic motifs. The hearty menu ranges from a fresh seafood linguine to beef-and-Guinness pie with peas and champ.

White Island

White Island, in the bay to the north of Castle Archdale Country Park, is the most haunting of Lough Erne's monastic sites. At the eastern tip of the island are the ruins of a small 12th-century church with a beautiful Romanesque door on its southern side. Inside are six extraordinary Celtic stone figures, thought to date from the 9th century, lined up along the wall like miniature Easter Island statues.

This line-up is a modern arrangement; most of the figures were discovered buried in the walls of the church in the 19th century, where the medieval masons had used them as ordinary building stones. The six main figures, all created by the same hand, are flanked on the left by a sheila-na-gig (carved female figure with exaggerated genitalia), which is probably contemporary with the church, and flanked on the right by a scowling stone face. The age and interpretation of these figures has been the subject of much debate; it has been suggested that the two central pairs, of equal height, were pillars that once supported a pulpit, and that they represent either saints or aspects of the life of Christ.

A ferry (per person £4; 11am-6pm daily Jul & Aug, to 5pm Sat & Sun Apr-Jun & Sep) crosses to the island hourly, on the hour (except for 1pm), from the marina in Castle Archdale Country Park; buy your ticket from the Castle Archdale Boat Hire office. The crossing takes 15 minutes, and allows you around half an hour on the island.

Boa Island

Boa Island, at the northern end of Lower Lough Erne, is connected to the mainland at both ends – the main A47 road runs along its length. A spooky moss-grown Caldragh graveyard towards the western end of the island, contains the famous Janus Stone.

Perhaps 2000 years old, this pagan figure is carved with two grotesque human heads, back to back. Nearby is a smaller figure called the Lusty Man, brought here from Lusty More island. Their origin and meaning have been lost to the mists of time.

There's a small sign indicating the graveyard about 1.5km from the bridge at the western tip of the island.

Sleeping & Eating

Lusty Beg Island
B&B £££

(6863 3300; www.lustybegisland.com; Boa Island, Kesh; s/d from £80/120;) This private island retreat, reached by ferry (on demand from 8.30am to 11pm) from a jetty halfway along Boa Island, has self-catering chalets that sleep four to six people (£560 to £855 per week in July and August), but also offers B&B in its rustic 40-room Courtyard Motel. There's a tennis court, a nature trail and canoeing on the lough for guests.

Lusty Beg's informal Island Restaurant (6863 1342; 3-course dinner £26; 1-9pm Jul & Aug) is open to all, and serves everything from burgers and lasagne to beef Wellington and salmon en croute. Booking is necessary; you can summon the ferry from a telephone in the blockhouse on the slipway.

Belleek

POP 550

Belleek's (Beal Leice) village street of colourful, flower-bedecked houses slopes up

from a bridge across the River Erne where it flows out of the Lower Lough towards Ballyshannon and the sea. The village is right on the border – the road south across the bridge passes through a finger of the Republic's territory for about 200m before leaving again – and shops accept both pounds sterling and euros.

The imposing Georgian-style building beside the bridge houses the world-famous Belleek Pottery (www.belleek.ie; Main St; tours adult/child £4/free; 9am-6pm Mon-Fri, 10am-6pm Sat, noon-5.30pm Sun Jul-Sep, shorter hours Oct-Jun, closed Sat & Sun Jan-Feb), founded in 1857 to provide local employment in the wake of the Potato Famine. It has been producing fine Parian china ever since, and is especially noted for its delicate basketware. The visitor centre houses a small museum, showroom and restaurant, and there are guided tours of the pottery every half-hour from 9.30am to 12.15pm and 1.45pm to 4pm (till 3pm on Friday) weekdays year-round.

Eating & Drinking

Thatch Coffee Shop
CAFE £

(20 Main St; mains £3-7; 9am-5pm Mon-Sat) This cute little thatched cottage may be Belleek's oldest building (late 18th century), but it serves a thoroughly modern cup of coffee, a delicious smoked-salmon toastie, and excellent homemade cakes and scones.

Black Cat Cove
PUB

(28 Main St; noon-9pm) This friendly, family run pub with antique furniture and an open fire serves good bar meals (mains £7 to £10). It also has live music most nights in summer, and at weekends in winter.

Lough Navar Forest Park

This forest park (10am-dusk) FREE lies at the western end of Lower Lough Erne, where the Cliffs of Magho (a 250m-high and 9km-long limestone escarpment) rise above a fringe of native woodland on the south shore. An 11km scenic drive through the park leads to the Magho Viewpoint – the panorama from the clifftop here is one of the finest in Ireland, especially before sunset. The view looks out over the shimmering expanse of lough and river to the Blue Stack Mountains, the sparkling waters of Donegal Bay and the sea cliffs of Slieve League.

It's also possible to hike up to the viewpoint via a steep trail leading from the

Lough Navar Forest car park on the A46 road, 13km east of Belleek.

The entrance to Lough Navar Forest Park is on the minor Glennasheevar road between Garrison and Derrygonnelly, 20km southeast of Belleek (take the B52 towards Garrison, and fork left after 2.5km).

🏃 Activities

Fishing

The lakes of Fermanagh are renowned for both coarse and game fishing. The Lough Erne trout-fishing season runs from the beginning of March to the end of September. Salmon fishing begins in June and also continues to the end of September. The mayfly season usually lasts a month from the second week in May. There's no closed season for coarse fish.

You'll need both a licence (issued by the Department of Culture, Arts and Leisure) and a permit (from the owner of the fishery); see www.nidirect.gov.uk/angling for details. Licences and permits can be purchased from the tourist information centre and Home, Field & Stream (☑6632 2114; hfs-online.com; 18 Church St), both in Enniskillen, and from the marina in Castle Archdale Country Park, which also hires out fishing rods. A combined licence and permit for game fishing on Lough Erne costs £9/25.50 for three/14 days.

The Belleek Angling Centre in the Thatch Coffee Shop in Belleek sells fishing tackle and can arrange boat hire for anglers, and you can get expert instruction in fly-casting from Colin Chartres (☑07884 472121; www.erneangling.com).

Enniskillen's tourist information centre provides a free guide to angling in Fermanagh and South Tyrone, which has full details of lakes and rivers, fish species, seasons and permit requirements.

Boat Hire

A number of companies hire out day boats at Enniskillen, Killadeas and Castle Archdale Country Park. Rates range from about £10 to £15 per hour for an open rowing boat with outboard motor to £60/90 per half-/full day for a six-seater with cabin and engine. The tourist information centre in Enniskillen has a full list of companies and costs.

Canoeing

The Lough Erne Canoe Trail (www.canoeni.com) highlights the attractions along the 50km of lough and river between Belleek

and Belturbet. The wide open expanses of the Lower Lough can build up big waves in a strong breeze and are best left to experts, but the sheltered backwaters of the Upper Lough are ideal for beginners and families.

You can pick up a map and guide (£1.50) showing public access points, camping sites and other facilities along the trail from the tourist office in Enniskillen, which also has a list of places where you can hire a canoe.

Watersports

Ultimate Watersports   WATER SPORTS
(www.ultimatewatersports.co.uk) Based at Castle Archdale marina and Lusty Beg island; offers equipment hire and instruction in water-skiing, wakeboarding, jet-skiing, canoeing, dinghy sailing and power-boating.

West of Lough Erne

◉ Sights

Florence Court   HISTORIC BUILDING
(www.nationaltrust.org.uk; Swanlinbar Rd; house adult/child £4.50/2, grounds £4.50/2; ⊙house 11am-5pm daily Jul & Aug, Wed-Mon May & Jun, Sat-Thu Sep, Sat & Sun Apr & Oct, grounds 10am-7pm Mar-Oct, 10am-4pm Nov-Feb) Part of the first Earl of Belmore's motivation for building Castle Coole (near Enniskillen) was keeping up with the Joneses – in the 1770s his aristocratic neighbour William Willoughby Cole, the first Earl of Enniskillen, had overseen the addition of grand Palladian wings to a beautiful, baroque country house called Florence Court, named after his Cornish grandmother Florence Wrey.

Set in lovely wooded grounds in the shadow of Cuilcagh Mountain, and not to be confused with the nearby, single-worded village of Florencecourt, Florence Court is famous for its rococo plasterwork and antique Irish furniture. The house was badly damaged by a fire in 1955 and much of what you see on the one-hour guided tour is the result of meticulous restoration, but the magnificent plaster work on the ceiling of the dining room is original.

In the grounds you can explore the walled garden and, on the edge of Cottage Wood, southeast of the house, admire an ancient Irish yew tree. It's said that every Irish yew around the world is descended from this one.

The house is 12km southwest of Enniskillen. Take the A4 Sligo road and fork left onto the A32 to Swanlinbar. Ulsterbus service 192 from Enniskillen to Swanlinbar (twice daily Monday to Saturday) can drop you at Creamery Cross, a 2km walk from the house.

Marble Arch Caves   CAVE
(☑ 6634 8855; www.marblearchcaves.net; Marlbank Scenic Loop; adult/child £8.75/5.75; ☺ 10am-5pm Jul & Aug, to 4.30pm Easter-Jun & Sep) To the south of Lower Lough Erne lies a limestone plateau, where Fermanagh's abundant rainwater has carved out a network of subterranean caverns. The largest of these are the Marble Arch Caves, first explored by the French caving pioneer Edouard Martel in 1895, but not opened to the public until 1985.

The 1¼-hour tour of the caves begins with a short boat trip along the peaty, foam-flecked waters of the underground River Cladagh to Junction Jetty, where three subterranean streams meet up. You then continue on foot past the Grand Gallery and Pool Chamber, regaled all the time with food-related jokes from your guide. An artificial tunnel leads into the New Chamber, from which the route follows the underground River Owenbrean through the Moses Walk (a walled pathway sunk waist-deep into the river) to the Calcite Cradle, where the most picturesque formations are to be found. The caves are very popular, so it's wise to phone ahead and book a tour, especially if you're in a group of four or more. (The listed closing time is the starting time of the last tour.)

The caves take their name from a natural limestone arch that spans the River Cla-

---

OFF THE BEATEN TRACK

WALK: CUILCAGH MOUNTAIN VIA THE LEGNABROCKY TRAIL

Rising above Marble Arch and Florence Court, Cuilcagh (*cull*-kay) Mountain (666m) is the highest point in Counties Fermanagh and Cavan, its summit right on the border between Northern Ireland and the Republic.

The mountain is a geological layer cake, with a cave-riddled limestone base, shale and sandstone flanks draped with a shaggy tweed skirt of blanket bog, and a high gritstone plateau ringed by steep, craggy slopes, all part of the Marble Arch Caves European Geopark (www.europeangeoparks.org).

Hidden among the sphagnum moss, bog cotton and heather of the blanket bog, you can find the sticky-fingered sundew, an insect-eating plant, while the crags echo to the 'krok-krok-krok' of ravens and the mewing of peregrine falcons. The otherworldly summit plateau is a breeding ground for golden plover and is rich in rare plants such as alpine clubmoss.

The hike to the summit is a 15km round trip (allow five or six hours); the first part is on an easy gravel track, but you'll need good boots to negotiate the boggy ground and steep slopes further on. Start at the Cuilcagh Mountain Park car park, 300m west of the entrance to Marble Arch Caves visitor centre (grid reference 121335; you'll need the Ordnance Survey 1:50,000 *Discovery series map*, sheet 26). Right next to the car park is the Monastir sink hole, a deep depression ringed by limestone cliffs where the River Aghinrawn disappears underground for its journey through the Marble Arch Caves system. (Note that the OS map has wrongly labelled this river the Owenbrean.)

Climb the stile beside the gate and set out along the Legnabrocky Trail, a 4WD track that winds through rich green limestone meadows before climbing across the blanket bog on a 'floating' bed of gravel and geotextiles – boardwalks off to one side offer a closer look at bog regeneration areas. The gravel track comes to an end at a gate about 4.5km from the start. From here you follow a line of waymarked wooden posts, squelching your way across spongy bog (don't stray from the route – there are deep bog holes where you can get stuck) before climbing steeply up to the summit ridge, with great views west to the crags above little Lough Atona. The waymarkers come to an end here, so you're on your own for the final kilometre across the plateau, aiming for the prominent cairn on the summit (a map and compass are essential in poor visibility).

The summit cairn is actually a Neolithic burial chamber; about 100m south of the summit you will find two rings of boulders, the foundations of prehistoric huts. On a clear day the view extends from the Blue Stack Mountains of Donegal to Croagh Patrick, and from the Atlantic Ocean to the Irish Sea. Return the way you came.

dagh where it emerges from the caves; you can reach it via a short walk along a signposted footpath from the visitor centre.

Unexpected serious flooding of the caves in the 1990s was found to have been caused by mechanised peat-cutting in the blanket bog on the slopes of Cuilcagh Mountain, whose rivers feed the caves. Cuilcagh Mountain Park (www.cuilcaghmountainpark.com) was established to restore and preserve the bog environment, and in 2001 the entire area was designated a Unesco Geopark. The park's geology and ecology are explained in the caves' visitor centre.

The Marble Arch Caves are 16km southwest of Enniskillen, and some 4km from Florence Court (an hour's walk), reached via the A4 Sligo road and the A32.

Loughs Melvin & McNean

Lough Melvin and Lough Macnean are situated along the border with the Republic, on the B52 road from Belcoo to Belleek. Lough Melvin is famous for its salmon and trout fishing, and is home to two unusual trout species that are unique to the lough – the sonaghan, with its distinctive black spots, and the crimson-spotted gillaroo – as well as brown trout, ferox trout and char.

COUNTY TYRONE

Omagh

POP 20,000

Situated at the confluence of the Rivers Camowen and Drumragh, which join to form the River Strule, Omagh is a busy market town with a handful of historic Georgian buildings. Pick up a *Town Trail* leaflet from the tourist office.

Sadly, for a long time to come, Omagh (An Óghmhagh) will be remembered for the devastating 1998 car bomb that killed 29 people and injured 200. Planted by the breakaway group Real IRA, the bomb was the worst single atrocity in the 30-year history of the Troubles. A memorial garden on Drumragh Ave, 200m east of the bus station, remembers the dead.

🛏 Sleeping & Eating

★ **Mullaghmore House**   B&B **££**
(☎ 8224 2314; www.mullaghmorehouse.com; Old Mountfield Rd; s/d £42/78; @ 🛜) Offering af-

fordable country-house luxury, this beautifully restored Georgian villa boasts a gleaming mahogany-panelled library, billiards room and marble-lined steam room. The bedrooms have period cast-iron fireplaces and antique furniture, and the owners run courses on antique restoration and traditional crafts. It's 1.5km northeast of the town centre.

★ **Philly's Phinest**   FAST FOOD **£**
(Bridge St; mains £3-5; 🛜) This tiny fast-food joint, a popular hangout for local students, serves up some of the tastiest food in town, inspired by the street food of Philadelphia. The Philly cheese-steak (fried steak, onion and cheese in a soft bun) will fill you up for under a fiver.

Weir Cafe   CAFE **£**
(Strule Arts Centre, Bridge St; 🛜 ♿) A pleasant spot for coffee and cake, with comfy sofas, plenty of books to read and huge picture windows overlooking the river and bridge.

ℹ Information

The **tourist office** (☎ 8224 7831; info@omagh.gov.uk; Strule Arts Centre, Bridge St; ⊙ 10am-5.30pm Mon-Sat) is in the arts centre, just across the river from the bus station.

ℹ Getting There & Away

The bus station is on Mountjoy Rd, just north of the town centre along Bridge St.

Goldline Express bus 273 goes from Belfast to Omagh (£11.50, 1¾ hours, hourly Monday to Saturday, six on Sunday) via Dungannon and on to Derry (£7.80, 1¼ hours). Bus 94 goes to Enniskillen (£7.80, one hour, six or seven daily Monday to Friday, three on Saturday, one on Sunday), where you can change for Donegal, Bundoran or Sligo. Goldline Express bus 274 runs from Derry to Omagh (£7.80, one hour, every two hours), and continues to Dublin (£18.35, three hours) via Monaghan.

Around Omagh

◉ Sights

★ **Ulster American Folk Park**   HERITAGE CENTRE
(www.nmni.com/uafp; Mellon Rd; adult/child £7.50/4.50; ⊙ 10am-5pm Tue-Sun Mar-Sep, 10am-4pm Tue-Fri, 11am-4pm Sat & Sun Oct-Feb) In the 18th and 19th centuries thousands of Ulster people left their homes to forge a new life across the Atlantic; 200,000 emigrated in

OFF THE BEATEN TRACK

DAVAGH FOREST PARK MTB TRAILS

Newly opened in 2013, remote Davagh Forest Park provides some of the best mountain biking in all of Ireland, ranging from family friendly green and blue trails along a wooded stream to 16km of red trails leading to the top of Beleevenamore Mountain, with several challenging rock slabs and drop-offs on the descents.

The trailhead is on a minor road, 10km northwest of Cookstown, signposted from the A505 Cookstown-to-Omagh road at Dunnamore. For details see www.mountainbikeni.com.

the 18th century alone. Their story is told here at one of Ireland's best museums.

The Exhibition Hall explains the close connections between Ulster and the USA – the American Declaration of Independence was signed by several Ulstermen – and includes a genuine Calistoga wagon. But the real appeal of the folk park is the outdoor museum, where the 'living history' exhibits are split into Old World and New World areas, cleverly linked by passing through a mock-up of an emigrant ship. Original buildings from various parts of Ulster have been dismantled and re-erected here, including a blacksmith's forge, a weaver's thatched cottage, a Presbyterian meeting house and a schoolhouse. In the 'American' section of the park you can visit a genuine 18th-century settler's stone cottage and a log house, both shipped across the Atlantic from Pennsylvania.

Costumed guides and artisans are on hand to explain the arts of spinning, weaving, candle-making and so on, and various events are held throughout the year, including re-enactments of American Civil War battles, a festival of traditional Irish music in May, American Independence Day celebrations in July, and the Appalachian and Bluegrass Music Festival in late August/September. At least half a day is needed to do the place justice.

The park is 8km northwest of Omagh on the A5. Goldline bus 273 from Belfast to Derry (hourly Monday to Saturday, six on Sunday) stops in Omagh, and will stop on request at the park gates. Last admission is 1½ hours before closing.

Sperrin Mountains

When representatives of the London guilds visited Ulster in 1609, the Lord Deputy of Ireland made sure they were kept well away from the Sperrin Mountains (www.sperrins tourism.com), fearing that the sight of these bleak, moorland hills would put them off the idea of sending settlers here. And when it rains there's no denying that the Sperrins can be dismal, but on a sunny spring day, when the russet bogs and yellow gorse stand out against a clear blue sky, they can offer some grand walking. The area is also dotted with thousands of standing stones and prehistoric tombs.

ℹ Getting Around

Ulsterbus service 403, the *Sperrin Rambler*, runs twice daily Monday to Saturday between Omagh and Magherafelt, stopping at Gortin, Plumbridge, Cranagh and Draperstown (in County Derry).

Gortin

The village of Gortin, about 15km north of Omagh, lies at the foot of Mullaghcarn (542m), the southernmost of the Sperrin summits (unfortunately capped by two prominent radio masts). Hundreds of hikers converge for a mass ascent of the hill on Cairn Sunday (the last Sunday in July), a revival of an ancient pilgrimage. There are several good walks around the village, and a scenic drive to Gortin Lakes, with views north to the main Sperrin ridge.

Creggan

About halfway along the A505 between Omagh and Cookstown (20km east of Omagh) is An Creagán Visitor Centre (www.an-creagan.com; Creggan; ⊙11am-6.30pm Apr-Sep, to 4.30pm Oct-Mar) FREE with an exhibition covering the ecology of the surrounding bogs and the archaeology of the region. Informative nature trails start near the visitor centre. There are 44 prehistoric monuments within 8km of the centre, including the Beaghmore Stone Circles. What this site lacks in stature – the stones are all less than 1m tall – it makes up for in complexity, with seven stone circles (one filled with smaller stones, nicknamed 'dragon's teeth') and a dozen or so alignments and cairns. The stones are signposted about 8km east of Creggan, and 4km north of the A505.

East Tyrone

The market towns of Cookstown and Dungannon are the main settlements in the eastern part of County Tyrone, but the main sights here are in the surrounding countryside.

◉ Sights

Ardboe High Cross   CHRISTIAN SITE

A 6th-century monastic site overlooking Lough Neagh is home to one of Ireland's best-preserved and most elaborately decorated Celtic stone crosses. The 10th-century Ardboe high cross is 5.5m tall, with 22 carved panels depicting biblical scenes. The western side (facing the road) has New Testament scenes, including the Adoration of the Magi and Christ's entry into Jerusalem; the more weathered eastern face (towards the lough) shows Old Testament scenes.

Ardboe is 16km east of Cookstown. Take the B73 through Coagh and ignore the first (white) road sign for Ardboe. Keep straight on until you find the brown sign (on the right) for Ardboe High Cross.

Wellbrook Beetling Mill   HISTORIC BUILDING

(www.nationaltrust.org.uk; 20 Wellbrook Rd, Corkhill; adult/child £4/2; ⊙2-5pm Thu-Sat Jul & Aug, 2-5pm Sat, Sun & public holidays mid-Mar–Jun & Sep) Beetling, the final stage of linen making, involves pounding the cloth with wooden hammers, or beetles, to give it a smooth sheen. The 18th-century Wellbrook Beetling Mill still has its original machinery, and stages demonstrations of the linen-making process led by guides in period costume. The mill is on a pretty stretch of the River Ballinderry, 7km west of Cookstown, just off the A505 Omagh road.

Grant Ancestral Homestead   HISTORIC SITE

(Dergina, Ballygawley; ⊙9am-5pm daily) FREE Ulysses Simpson Grant (1822–85) led the Union forces to victory in the American Civil War and later served as the USA's 18th president for two terms, from 1869 to 1877. His maternal grandfather, John Simpson, emigrated from County Tyrone to Pennsylvania in 1760. The farm he left behind at Dergina has now been restored in the style of a typical Ulster smallholding, as it would have been during the time of Grant's presidency.

The furnishings in the cottage are not authentic, but the original field plan of the farm survives, together with various old farming implements. There's also an exhibition on the American Civil War, a picnic area and children's playground.

The site is 20km west of Dungannon, signposted south of the A4 road. You can wander around the farm and visit the cottage for free; to arrange a guided tour, call the Ranfurly House Visitor Centre (p664), in Dungannon.

⊨ Sleeping & Eating

★ Tullylagan Country House   HOTEL ££

(☑8676 5100; www.tullylaganhotel.com; 40b Tullylagan Rd, Cookstown; s/d from £69/99; ⊛⊞) Set amid beautiful riverside gardens 4km south of Cookstown (just off the A29), the ivy-clad Tullylagan goes for the Victorian country-manor feel, with shabby-chic sofas, gilt-framed mirrors, polished wooden floors, and marble-effect bathrooms with period taps. The hotel's Kitchen Restaurant (40b Tullylagan Rd, Cookstown; mains £13-23; ⊙lunch daily, dinner Mon-Sat) specialises in locally produced seafood, game and beef with a Mediterranean twist.

Grange Lodge   B&B ££

(☑8778 4212; www.grangelodgecountryhouse.com; 7 Grange Rd, Dungannon; s/d from £65/84; ⊛) The five-room Grange is a period gem set in its own 8-hectare grounds. Parts of the house, which is packed with antiques, date from 1698, though most are Georgian with Victorian additions. The proprietor is an award-winning chef, and the Grange runs cookery courses. A four-course dinner (£40) is available (except on Sunday) if booked at least 48 hours in advance. It's 5km southeast of Dungannon, signposted off the A29 Moy road.

★ Deli on the Green   CAFE, BISTRO ££

(☑8775 1775; www.delionthegreen.com; 2 Linen Green, Moygashel; mains lunch £8-10, dinner £13-22; ⊙cafe 8.30-5pm Mon-Sat, bistro lunch Mon-Sat, dinner Thu-Sat) Take a break from browsing the Linen Green shops to relax over a meal in this stylish little cafe-bistro. As well as the sandwiches and salads on offer at the deli counter, there are succulent homemade steak burgers and chicken caesar salad, while the breakfast menu includes pancakes with bacon and maple syrup. The evening menu ranges from roast fillet of hake with fennel purée to rib-eye steak with chunky garlic chips.

🛍 Shopping

Linen Green Designer Village FASHION, GIFTS
(www.thelinengreen.co.uk; Moygashel; ⊙9.30am-
5.30pm Mon-Sat) Housed in the former Moygashel Linen Mills, the Linen Green complex
includes a range of designer shops and factory outlets, plus a visitor centre with an
exhibition covering the history of the local
linen industry. It's a good place to shop for
men's and women's fashion, shoes, accessories and linen goods, or to stop for lunch at
the Deli on the Green.

❶ Information

Ranfurly House Visitor Centre (☎8772 8600;
www.dungannon.info; 26 Market Sq, Dungannon; ⊙9am-5pm daily Apr-Dec, closed Sun
Jan-Mar; ☎) Tourist information for County
Tyrone, and a cafe with free wi-fi.

Understand Ireland

Ireland Today

Times are tough, and austerity – a catch-all term for the unforgiving program of forced cuts and revenue increases that Ireland has been dealing with of late – is neither an abstract concept nor a temporary inconvenience. The Irish are used to tough times and have gone to great lengths to adjust accordingly, but the struggle is profound and ongoing.

Top Fiction

Dubliners (James Joyce, 1914) A collection of short stories still as poignant and relevant today as when they were written.

The Speckled People (Hugo Hamilton, 2003) Superb memoir of growing up with mixed parentage, told as a novel.

Paddy Clarke Ha Ha Ha (Roddy Doyle, 1993) Wonderful portrait of a 10-year-old boy's trials that was made into a popular film.

The Gathering (Anne Enright, 2007) Powerful account of alcoholism and domestic abuse in an Irish family.

Top Films

Bloody Sunday (Paul Greengrass, 2002) Unmissable account of events in Derry in 1972.

The Dead (John Huston, 1987) Huston brings James Joyce's story to life in his last film, with powerful performances by Donal McCann and Anjelica Huston.

The Magdalene Sisters (Peter Mullan, 2002) The tough story of the brutal treatment of young girls sent to infamous industrial schools.

Garage (Lenny Abrahamson, 2007) A tragicomic story of a hapless and lonely garage attendant and his search for friendship and love.

The Cost of a Bailout

Ever since the infamous bank guarantee of October 2008 – when the six Irish pillar banks were given a blanket guarantee of *all* their liabilities (totalling €440 billion) by a panicked government – Ireland has been in profound economic crisis. The guarantee expired in 2010 and the government was forced to turn to the EU, the European Financial Stability Fund (EFSF) and the International Monetary Fund (IMF) – referred to as the 'troika' – for a bailout, totalling about €85 billion. All of it has to be repaid, and the terms set by the troika – who show up every three months for a progress report – have resulted in one draconian budget after another.

Political Rhetoric

The year 2011 saw a change of government – out went Fianna Fáil and the Green Party (blamed for the economic crisis), in came a new coalition of centre-right Fine Gael and left-leaning Labour. It was initially greeted with cautious hope, but that hope turned to despair when the pre-election rhetoric about creating jobs and making 'Ireland the best small country in the world to do business in' was revealed to be just that – rhetoric. The unemployment rate hovers stubbornly around 14%, while any downward adjustment is ascribed to skyrocketing emigration: in the year up to April 2013, 56,000 people left Ireland (a 6% increase on the previous year); 57% of whom were Irish nationals.

Tightening Irish Belts

The harsh reality for the majority of the Irish is a rising unemployment rate – in 2013 it was just shy of 14%, the highest in 20 years – and emigration, which is bleeding Ireland of 3000 people a month, the highest rate since the Famine. Ordinary people find themselves facing acute mortgage distress, unable to make payments on properties that in some cases have lost more than half their value – in 2013, one in five mortgages were reckoned to be delinquent.

'Doing more with less' is the dispiriting buzz phrase of the moment – whether it's feeding the family, paying off debts or running a business in the face of a dwindling client base. Most Irish are working harder than ever for less money: salary cuts are the price they pay for the privilege of still having a job.

Not Silent but Stoic?

A question that puzzles observers inside and outside the country is why the Irish haven't taken to the streets to protest an injustice they believe has been perpetrated on them by greedy bankers and spineless politicians. The Irish are angry, but with few exceptions have not followed their bedraggled brethren in Greece, Spain or Cyprus onto the streets. They may sympathise with them and even admire their defiance, but the Irish psyche is permeated by a kind of stoic pragmatism that inevitably concludes that protesting doesn't really change anything. But for many, stoicism is but a public front: anecdotal evidence suggests that mental health issues have increased dramatically among the hard-pressed – anxiety, depression and suicide are a growing problem in Irish society.

Hope for the Future

Some Irish console themselves by declaring that the country has a long history of hard times and that nothing much has changed. But something has changed, especially in the perception of that generation of Irish that has never known difficult times or recession: it grew up with the unfettered ambitions of the Celtic Tiger, inured to the belief that everything was possible so long as you were willing to chase it. Rather than surrender their ambitions, many have opted to emigrate – and they seem to do so with confidence rather than cap in hand – while those staying must endeavour to find new opportunities amid the mayhem. Whereas previous generations may have treated tough times as an unavoidable birthright, this generation continues to struggle in the knowledge that it deserves better.

AREA: **70,273/13,843 SQ KM (R/NI)**

POPULATION: **4.72/1.81 MILLION (R/NI)**

GDP: **€191.5/£29.1 BILLION (R/NI)**

UNEMPLOYMENT: **13.7%/7.5% (R/NI)**

INFLATION: **0.72%/2.8% (R/NI)**

if Ireland were 100 people

34 would be aged 24 years old or younger
32 would be between 25 and 44
23 would be between 45 and 64
11 would be 65 or older

belief systems
(% of population)

84 — Roman Catholic
2.8 — Church of Ireland
1 — Muslim
1 — Other Christian
1 — Other religion
8.2 — No religion/not stated

population per sq km

REPUBLIC OF IRELAND   NORTHERN IRELAND   DUBLIN

≈ 65 people

History

From pre-Celts to Celtic cubs, Ireland's history has been a search for identity, which would have been a little more straightforward if this small island hadn't been of such interest to a host of foreign parties – Celtic tribes, Viking marauders, Norman invaders and the English. Indeed, it is Ireland's fractious relationship with its nearest neighbour that has occupied much of the last thousand years, and it is through the prism of that relationship that a huge part of the Irish identity is reflected – but what emerges isn't nearly as clear-cut as you might expect.

Who are the Irish?

For a concise, 10-minute read on who the Celts were, see www.ibiblio.org/gaelic/celts.html.

It took the various Celtic tribes roughly 500 years to settle in Ireland, beginning in the 8th century BC. The last of the tribes, commonly known as the Gaels (which in the local language came to mean 'foreigner'), came ashore in the 3rd century BC and proceeded to divide the island into five provinces – Leinster, Meath, Connaught, Ulster and Munster (Meath later merged with Leinster) – that were subdivided into territories controlled by as many as one hundred minor kings and chieftains, all of whom nominally paid allegiance to a high king who sat at Tara, in County Meath.

The Celts set about creating the basics of what we now term 'Irish' culture: they devised a sophisticated code of law called the Brehon Law, which remained in use until the early 17th century; and their swirling, mazelike design style, evident on artefacts nearly 2000 years old, is considered the epitome of Irish design. Some excellent ancient Celtic designs survive in the Broighter Hoard in the National Museum in Dublin. The Turoe Stone in County Galway is another fine representative of Celtic artwork.

Getting into the Habit

Although St Patrick gets all the credit, between the 3rd and 5th centuries Ireland was Christianised by a host of missionaries, who converted pagan tribes by fusing their local druidic rituals with the new Christian teaching, thereby creating a hybrid known as Celtic or Insular Christianity.

TIMELINE	10,000–8000 BC	4500 BC	700–300 BC
	After the last ice age ends, humans arrive in Ireland during the Mesolithic era, originally crossing a land bridge between Scotland and Ireland. Few archaeological traces remain of this group.	The first Neolithic farmers arrive in Ireland by boat from as far afield as the Iberian peninsula, bringing cattle, sheep and crops, marking the beginnings of a settled agricultural economy.	Iron technology gradually replaces bronze. The Celtic culture and language arrive, ushering in a thousand years of cultural and political dominance and leaving a legacy still visible today.

Irish Christian scholars excelled in the study of Latin and Greek philosophy and Christian theology in the monasteries that flourished at, among other places, Clonmacnoise in County Offaly, Glendalough in County Wicklow and Lismore in County Waterford. It was the Golden Age, and the arts of manuscript illumination, metalworking and sculpture flourished, producing such treasures as the *Book of Kells,* ornate jewellery and the many carved stone crosses that dot the 'island of saints and scholars'.

The Course of Irish History by TW Moody and FX Martin is a hefty volume by two Trinity College professors who trace much of Ireland's history back to its land and its proximity to England.

Rape, Pillage & Plunder: A Viking's Day Out

The next group to try their luck were the Vikings, who first showed up in AD 795 and began plundering the prosperous monasteries. In self-defence, the monks built round towers, which served as lookout posts and places of refuge during attacks; you can see surviving examples of these at the likes of Glendalough.

Despite the monks' best efforts, the Vikings had their way, mostly due to superior weaponry but also thanks to elements of the local population, who sided with the marauders for profit or protection. By the 10th century, the Norsemen were well established in Ireland, having founded

ST PATRICK

Ireland's patron saint is remembered all around the world on 17 March, when people of all ethnicities drink Guinness and wear green clothing. But behind the hoopla was a real man with a serious mission. For it was Patrick (389–461) who introduced Christianity to Ireland.

The plain truth of it is that he wasn't Irish. This symbol of Irish pride hailed from what is now Wales, which at the time of his birth was under Roman rule.

Patrick's arrival in Ireland was made possible by Irish raiders who kidnapped him when he was 16, and took him across the channel to work as a slave. He found religion, escaped from captivity and returned to Britain. But he vowed to make it his life's work to make Christians out of the Irish. He was ordained, then appointed Bishop of Ireland. Back he went over the channel.

He based himself in Armagh, where St Patrick's Church of Ireland Cathedral stands on the site of his old church. Patrick quickly converted peasants and noblemen in great numbers. Within 30 years, much of Ireland had been baptised and the country was divided into Catholic dioceses and parishes. He also established monasteries throughout Ireland, which would be the foundations of Irish scholarship for many centuries.

So next St Paddy's Day, as you're swilling Guinness and champing down corned beef and cabbage, think of who the man really was.

AD 431–2	550–800	795–841	1014
Pope Celestine I sends Bishop Palladius to Ireland to minister to those 'already believing in Christ'; St Patrick arrives the following year to continue the mission.	The flowering of early monasticism in Ireland. The great monastic teachers begin exporting their knowledge across Europe, ushering in Ireland's 'Golden Age'.	Vikings plunder Irish monasteries; their raping and pillaging urges sated, they establish settlements throughout the country, including Dublin, and soon turn it into a centre of economic power.	The Battle of Clontarf takes place on Good Friday between the forces of the high king, Brian Ború, and the forces led by the king of Leinster, Máelmorda mac Murchada.

towns such as Wicklow, Waterford, Wexford and their capital Dyfflin, which later became Dublin. The Vikings were defeated at the Battle of Clontarf in 1014 by Brian Ború, king of Munster, but Ború was killed and the Vikings, much like the Celts before them, eventually settled, giving up the rape-rob-and-run policy in favour of integration and assimilation: by intermarrying with the Celtic tribes, they introduced red hair and freckles to the Irish gene pool.

Top Monastic Sites

Cashel *County Tipperary*

Clonmacnoise *County Offaly*

Glendalough *County Wicklow*

The English are Coming!

The '800 years' of English rule in Ireland nominally began with the Norman invasion of 1169, which was really more of an invitation as the barons, led by Richard Fitz Gilbert de Clare, earl of Pembroke (1130–76; aka Strongbow), had been asked to assist the king of Leinster in a territorial squabble. Two years later, King Henry II of England came ashore with a substantial army and a request from Pope Adrian IV to bring the rebel Christian missionaries to heel.

Despite the king's overall authority, the Anglo-Norman barons carved Ireland up between them and over the next 300 years set about consolidating their feudal power. Once again the effects of assimilation were in play, as the Anglo-Normans and their hirelings became, in the oft-quoted phrase, *Hiberniores Hibernis ipsis* ('more Irish than the Irish themselves'). They dotted the country with castles, but their real legacy is in the cities they built, such as magnificent Kilkenny, which today retains much of its medieval character. The Anglo-Normans may have pledged allegiance to the English king, but in truth they were loyal only to themselves: by the turn of the 16th century, the Crown's direct rule didn't extend any further than a cordon surrounding Dublin known as the Pale. But you can only ignore an English king for so long...

The expression 'beyond the Pale' came into use when the Pale was the Anglo-Norman-controlled part of Ireland. To them, the rest of Ireland was an uncivilised territory populated by barbarians.

Divorce, Dissolution & Destruction

When Henry VIII declared himself head of the church in England in 1534, following his split with the papacy over his divorce from Catherine of Aragon, the Anglo-Normans cried foul and some took arms against the crown. Worried that an Irish rising would be of help to Spain or France, Henry responded firmly, quashing the rebellion, confiscating the rebels' lands and (as in England) dissolving all Irish monasteries. He then had himself declared King of Ireland.

Elizabeth I (1533–1603) came to the throne in 1558 with the same uncompromising attitude to Ireland as her father. Ulster was the most hostile to her, with the Irish fighting doggedly under the command of Hugh O'Neill, earl of Tyrone, but they too were finally defeated in 1603. O'Neill, though, achieved something of a Pyrrhic victory when he refused to surrender until after he heard of Elizabeth's death. He and his fellow earls

1169	1171	1350–1530
Henry II's Welsh and Norman barons land in Wexford and capture Waterford and Wexford with MacMurrough's help. It is the beginning of an 800-year occupation by Britain.	King Henry II invades Ireland, forcing the Cambro-Norman warlords and some of the Gaelic Irish kings to accept him as their overlord.	The Anglo-Norman barons establish power bases independent of the English Crown. Over the following two centuries, English control gradually recedes to an area around Dublin known as 'the Pale'.

GEORGE MUNDAY / GETTY IMAGES ©

→ *Fuascailt*, Eamonn O'Doherty

then fled the country in what become known as the Flight of the Earls. It left Ulster open to English rule and to the policy of Plantation, which involved confiscating the lands of the flown earls and redistributing them to subjects loyal to the crown. Although the confiscations happened all over the country, they were most thorough in Ulster.

Bloody Religion

At the outset of the English Civil War in 1642, the Irish threw their support behind Charles I against the very Protestant parliamentarians in the hope that victory for the king would lead to the restoration of Catholic power in Ireland. When Oliver Cromwell and his Roundheads defeated the Royalists and took Charles' head off in 1649, Cromwell turned his attention to the disloyal Irish. His nine-month campaign was effective and brutal (Drogheda was particularly mistreated); yet more lands were confiscated – Cromwell's famous utterance that the Irish could 'go to hell or to Connaught' seems odd given the province's beauty, but there wasn't much arable land out there – and Catholic rights restricted even more.

The Boyne & Penal Laws

Catholic Ireland's next major setback came in 1690. Yet again the Irish had backed the wrong horse, this time supporting James II after his deposition in the Glorious Revolution by the Dutch Protestant King William of Orange (who was married to James' daughter Mary!). After James had unsuccessfully laid siege to Derry for 105 days (the Loyalist cry of 'No surrender!', in use to this day, dates from the siege), in July he fought William's armies by the banks of the Boyne in County Louth and was roundly defeated.

The final ignominy for Catholics came in 1695 with the passing of the Penal Laws, which prohibited them from owning land or entering any higher profession. Irish culture, music and education were banned in the hope that Catholicism would be eradicated. Most Catholics continued to worship at secret locations, but some prosperous Irish converted to Protestantism to preserve their careers and wealth. Land was steadily transferred to Protestant owners, and a significant majority of the Catholic population became tenants living in wretched conditions. By the late 18th century, Catholics owned barely 5% of the land.

If at First You Don't Succeed...

Beginning towards the end of the 18th century, the main thrust of opposition to Irish inequalities resulting from the Penal Laws came from an unlikely source. A handful of liberal Protestants, versed in the ideologies of the Enlightenment and inspired by the revolutions in France and the

A History of Ulster by Jonathan Bardon is a serious and far-reaching attempt to come to grips with Northern Ireland's saga.

Cromwell: An Honourable Enemy by Tom Reilly advances the unpopular view that perhaps the destruction of Cromwell's campaign is grossly exaggerated. You're no doubt familiar with the common view; here's the contrary position. (Yes, Reilly is Irish.)

1366	1536–41	1594	1601
The English Crown enacts the Statutes of Kilkenny, outlawing intermarriage, the Irish language and other Irish customs to stop the Anglo-Normans from assimilating too much with the Irish. It doesn't work.	Henry VIII orders the dissolution of the monasteries and confiscation of church property. In 1541 he arranges for the Irish Parliament to declare him King of Ireland.	Hugh O'Neill, earl of Tyrone, orders lead from England to reroof his castle, but instead uses it for bullets – instigating the start of the Nine Years' War.	The Battle of Kinsale is fought between Elizabeth's armies and the combined rebel forces led by Hugh O'Neill. O'Neill surrenders and the back of the Irish rebellion against the Crown is broken.

newly established United States of America, began organising direct opposition to British rule.

The best known was Theobald Wolfe Tone (1763–98), a young Dublin lawyer who led a group called the United Irishmen in their attempts to reform and reduce British power in Ireland (Loyalist Protestants prepared for the possibility of conflict by forming the Protestant Orange Society, later known as the Orange Order). Wolfe Tone attempted to enlist French help in his uprising, but the French failure to land an army of succour in 1796 left the organisation exposed to retribution and the men met their bloody end in the Battle of Vinegar Hill in 1798. Three years later, the British sought to put an end to Irish agitation with the Act of Union, but the Nationalist genie was already out of the bottle.

Hunger & Heroic Leadership

The 19th century was marked by repeated efforts to wrest some kind of control from Britain. There were the radical Republicans, who advocated use of force to found a secular, egalitarian republic that tried – and failed – in 1848 and 1867. And there were the moderates, who advocated non-violent and legal action to force the government into concession.

The Great Liberator

Dominating the moderate landscape for nearly three decades was Kerry-born Daniel O'Connell (1775–1847), who tirelessly devoted himself to the cause of Catholic Emancipation. In 1828 he was elected to the British Parliament but, being a Catholic, he couldn't actually take his seat: to avoid the possibility of an uprising, the government was forced to pass the 1829 Act of Catholic Emancipation, allowing some well-off Catholics voting rights and the right to be elected as MPs.

O'Connell continued to fight for Irish self-determination and became known as a powerful speaker, not only on behalf of Ireland but against all kinds of injustice, including slavery: the abolitionist leader Frederick Douglass was one of his greatest admirers (their relationship was specifically referred to by President Obama during his 2011 visit). O'Connell, known as 'the Liberator', was adored by the Irish, who turned out in their tens of thousands to hear him speak, but his unwillingness to step outside the law was to prove his undoing: when the government banned one of his rallies from going ahead, O'Connell stood down – ostensibly to avoid the prospect of violence and bloodshed. But Ireland was in the midst of the Potato Famine, and his failure to defy the British was seen as capitulation; he was imprisoned for a time and died a broken man in 1847.

For the Cause of Liberty: A Thousand Years of Ireland's Heroes by Terry Golway vividly describes the struggles of Irish nationalism.

Ireland Since the Famine by FSL Lyons is a standard text for all students of modern Irish history.

1607	1649–53	1688–90	1695
O'Neill and 90 other Ulster chiefs sail to Europe, leaving Ireland forever. Known as the Flight of the Earls, it leaves Ulster open to English rule and the policy of Plantation.	Cromwell lays waste to Ireland after the Irish support Charles I in the English Civil War; this includes the mass slaughter of Catholic Irish and the confiscation of two million hectares of land.	Following the deposition of King James II, James' Catholic army fights William's Protestant forces, resulting in William's victory at the Battle of the Boyne, 12 July 1690.	The Penal Laws (aka the 'popery code') prohibit Catholics from owning a horse, marrying outside their religion, building churches out of anything but wood, and from buying or inheriting property.

The Uncrowned King of Ireland

Charles Stewart Parnell (1846–91) was the other great 19th-century statesman. Like O'Connell, he too was a powerful orator, but the primary focus of his artful attentions was land reform, particularly the reduction of rents and the improvement of working conditions (conveniently referred to as the 'Three Fs': fair rent, free sale and fixity of tenure). Parnell championed the activities of the Land League, which instigated the strategy of 'boycotting' (named after one particularly unpleasant agent called Charles Boycott) tenants, agents and landlords who didn't adhere to the Land League's aims: these people were treated like lepers by the local population. In 1881 they won an important victory with the passing of the Land Act, which granted most of the League's demands.

Parnell's other great struggle was for a limited form of autonomy for Ireland. Despite the nominal support of the Liberal leader William Gladstone, Home Rule bills introduced in 1886 and 1892 were uniformly rejected by Parliament. Like O'Connell before him, Parnell's star plummeted dramatically: in 1890 he was embroiled in a divorce proceeding that scandalised puritanical Ireland. The 'uncrowned king of Ireland' was forced to resign and died less than a year later.

The Great Hunger by Cecil Woodham-Smith is the classic study of the Great Famine of 1845–51.

Rebellion Once Again

Ireland's struggle for some kind of autonomy picked up pace in the second decade of the 20th century. The radicalism that had always been at the fringes of Irish Nationalist aspirations was once again beginning to assert itself, partly in response to a hardening of attitudes in Ulster. Mass opposition to any kind of Irish independence had resulted in the formation of the Ulster Volunteer Force (UVF), a Loyalist vigilante group whose 100,000-plus members swore to resist any attempt to impose home rule on Ireland. Nationalists responded by creating the Irish Volunteer Force (IVF) and a showdown seemed inevitable.

Home Rule was finally passed in 1914, but the outbreak of WWI meant that its enactment was shelved for the duration. For most Irish, the suspension was disappointing but hardly unreasonable, and the majority of the volunteers enlisted to help fight the Germans.

For articles exploring the Irish struggle, check out http://larkspirit.com.

The Easter Rising

A few, however, did not heed the call. Two small groups – a section of the Irish Volunteers under Pádraig Pearse and the Irish Citizens' Army led by James Connolly – conspired in a rebellion that took the country by surprise. A depleted Volunteer group marched into Dublin on Easter Monday 1916 and took over a number of key positions in the city, claiming the General Post Office on O'Connell St as its headquarters. From its

The Irish in America by Michael Coffey takes up the history of the Famine where many histories leave off: the turbulent experiences of Irish immigrants in the USA.

1795	1798	1801	1828–29
Concerned at the attempts of the Society of United Irishmen to secure equal rights for non-establishment Protestants and Catholics, a group of Protestants create the Orange Order.	The flogging and killing of potential rebels sparks a rising led by the United Irishmen and their leader, Wolfe Tone. Wolfe Tone is captured and taken to Dublin, where he commits suicide.	The Act of Union comes into effect, uniting Ireland with Britain. The Irish Parliament votes itself out of existence following a campaign of bribery. Around 100 Members move to the House of Commons in London.	Daniel O'Connell exploits a loophole in the law to win a seat in Parliament but is unable to take it because he is Catholic. The prime minister passes the Catholic Emancipation Act, giving limited rights to Catholics.

THE GREAT FAMINE

As a result of the Great Famine of 1845–51, a staggering three million people died or were forced to emigrate from Ireland. This great tragedy is all the more inconceivable given that the scale of suffering was attributable to selfishness as much as to natural causes. Potatoes were the staple food of a rapidly growing, desperately poor population and, when a blight hit the crops, prices soared. The repressive Penal Laws ensured that farmers, already crippled with high rents, could ill afford the few subsistence potatoes provided. Inevitably, most tenants fell into arrears with little or no concession given by the mostly indifferent landlords and were evicted or sent to the dire conditions of the workhouses.

Shamefully, during this time there were abundant harvests of wheat and dairy produce – the country was producing more than enough grain to feed the entire population and it's said that more cattle were sold abroad than there were people on the island. But while millions of its citizens were starving, Ireland was forced to export its food to Britain and overseas.

The Poor Laws, in place at the height of the Famine, deemed landlords responsible for the maintenance of their poor and encouraged many to 'remove' tenants from their estates by paying their way to America. Many Irish were sent unwittingly to their deaths on board the notoriously scourged 'coffin ships'. British prime minister Sir Robert Peel made well-intentioned but inadequate gestures at famine relief, and some – but far too few – landlords did their best for their tenants.

Mass emigration continued to reduce the population during the next one hundred years and huge numbers of Irish emigrants who found their way abroad, particularly to the USA, carried with them a lasting bitterness.

steps, Pearse read out to passers-by a declaration that Ireland was now a republic and that his band was the provisional government. Less than a week of fighting ensued before the rebels surrendered to the superior British forces. The rebels weren't popular and had to be protected from angry Dubliners as they were marched to jail.

The Easter Rising would probably have had little impact on the Irish situation had the British not made martyrs of the rebel leaders. Of the 77 given death sentences, 15 were executed, including the injured Connolly, who was shot while strapped to a chair. This brought about a sea change in public attitudes, and support for the Republicans rose dramatically.

War with Britain

By the end of WWI, Home Rule was far too little, far too late. In the 1918 general election, the Republicans stood under the banner of Sinn Féin and won a large majority of the Irish seats. Ignoring London's Par-

1845–51

A mould ravages the potato harvest. The British government adopts a laissez-faire attitude, resulting in the deaths of between 500,000 and one million, and the emigration of up to two million others.

1879–82

The Land War, led by the Land League, sees tenant farmers defying their landlords en masse to force the passing of the Land Act in 1881, which allows for fair rent, fixity of tenure and free sale.

OLIVER STREWE / GETTY IMAGES ©

→ Potatoes, County Cork

liament, where technically they were supposed to sit, the newly elected Sinn Féin deputies – many of them veterans of the 1916 Easter Rising – declared Ireland independent and formed the first Dáil Éireann (Irish assembly or lower house), which sat in Dublin's Mansion House under the leadership of Éamon de Valera (1882–1975). The Irish Volunteers became the Irish Republican Army (IRA) and the Dáil authorised it to wage war on British troops in Ireland.

As wars go, the War of Independence was pretty small fry. It lasted two and a half years and cost around 1200 casualties. But it was a pretty nasty affair, as the IRA fought a guerrilla-style, hit-and-run campaign against the British, whose numbers were swelled by returning veterans of WWI known as Black and Tans (on account of their uniforms, a mix of army khaki and police black), most of whom were so traumatised by their wartime experiences that they were prone to all kinds of brutality.

A Kind of Freedom

A truce in July 1921 led to intense negotiations between the two sides. The resulting treaty, signed on 6 December 1921, created the Irish Free State, made up of 26 of 32 Irish counties. The remaining six – all in Ulster – remained part of the UK. The treaty was an imperfect document: not only did it cement the geographic divisions on the island that 50 years later would explode into the Troubles, it also caused a split among Nationalists – between those who believed the treaty to be a necessary stepping stone towards full independence, and those who saw it as capitulation to the British and a betrayal of Republican ideals. This division was to determine the course of Irish political affairs for virtually the remainder of the century.

Neil Jordan's movie *Michael Collins*, starring Liam Neeson as the revolutionary, depicts the Easter Rising, the founding of the Free State and Collins' violent demise.

Civil War

The treaty was ratified after a bitter debate and the June 1922 elections resulted in a victory for the pro-treaty side. But the anti-treaty forces rallied behind de Valera, who, though president of the Dáil, had not been a member of the treaty negotiating team (affording him, in the eyes of his critics and opponents, maximum deniability should the negotiations go pear-shaped) and objected to some of the treaty's provisions, most notably the oath of allegiance to the British monarch.

Within two weeks of the elections, civil war broke out between comrades who, a year previously, had fought alongside each other. The most prominent casualty of this particularly bitter conflict was Michael Collins (1890–1922), mastermind of the IRA's campaign during the War of Independence and a chief negotiator of the Anglo-Irish Treaty – shot in an ambush in his native Cork. Collins himself had presaged the bitterness that would result from the treaty: upon signing it, he is said to have declared 'I tell you, I have signed my own death warrant.'

1884	1890s	1916	1919–21
The Gaelic Athletic Association (GAA) is founded in Hayes Hotel, Thurles, County Tipperary. Its aim is to promote Gaelic games and culture; today hurling and Gaelic football are immensely popular.	The Gaelic Revival, championed by poet WB Yeats, sees a focused interest in the Irish language and Irish culture, including folklore, sport, music and the arts.	The Easter Rising: a group of Republicans take Dublin's General Post Office and announce the formation of an Irish republic. After less than a week of fighting, the rebels surrender to the superior British forces.	Irish War of Independence, aka the Black and Tan War on account of British irregulars wearing mixed police (black) and army (khaki) uniforms, begins in January 1919.

The Making of a Republic

The Civil War ground to an exhausted halt in 1923 with the victory of the pro-treaty side, who governed the new state until 1932. Defeated but unbowed, de Valera founded a new party in 1926 called Fianna Fáil (Soldiers of Ireland) and won a majority in the 1932 elections – they would remain in charge until 1948. In the meantime, de Valera created a new constitution in 1937 that did away with the hated oath of allegiance, reaffirmed the special position of the Catholic Church and once again laid claim to the six counties of Northern Ireland. In 1948 Ireland officially left the Commonwealth and became a republic but, as historical irony would have it, it was Fine Gael, as the old pro-treaty party was now known, that declared it – Fianna Fáil had surprisingly lost the election that year. After 800 years, Ireland – or at least a substantial chunk of it – was independent.

Brendan O'Brien's popular *Pocket History of the IRA* summarises a lot of complex history in a mere 150 pages; it's a good introduction.

Growing Pains & Roaring Tigers

Unquestionably the most significant figure since independence, Éamon de Valera made an immense contribution to an independent Ireland but, as the 1950s stretched into the 1960s, his vision for the country was mired in a conservative and traditional orthodoxy that was at odds with the reality of a country in desperate economic straits, where chronic unemployment and emigration were but the more visible effects of inadequate policy. De Valera's successor as Taoiseach (Republic of Ireland prime minister) was Sean Lemass, whose tenure began in 1959 with the dictum 'a rising tide lifts all boats'. By the mid-1960s his economic policies had halved emigration and ushered in a new prosperity that was to be mirrored 30 years later by the Celtic Tiger.

Partners in Europe

In 1972 the Republic (along with Northern Ireland) became a member of the European Economic Community (EEC). This brought an increased measure of prosperity thanks to the benefits of the Common Agricultural Policy, which set fixed prices and guaranteed quotas for Irish farming produce. Nevertheless, the broader global depression, provoked by the oil crisis of 1973, forced the country into yet another slump and emigration figures rose again, reaching a peak in the mid-1980s.

The events leading up to the Anglo-Irish War and their effect on ordinary people are movingly and powerfully related in JG Farrell's novel *Troubles*, first published in 1970.

From Celtic Tiger...

In the early 1990s, European funds helped kick-start economic growth. Huge sums of money were invested in education and physical infrastructure, while the policy of low corporate tax rates coupled with attractive incentives made Ireland very attractive to high-tech businesses looking for a door into EU markets. In less than a decade, Ireland went from

1921	1921–22	1922–23
Two years and 1200 casualties later, the war ends in a truce on 11 July 1921 that leads to peace talks. After negotiations in London, the Irish delegation signs the Anglo-Irish Treaty on 6 December.	The treaty gives 26 counties of Ireland independence and allows six largely Protestant Ulster counties the choice of opting out. The Irish Free State is founded in 1922.	Unwilling to accept the terms of the treaty, forces led by Éamon de Valera take up arms against their former comrades, led by Michael Collins. A brief but bloody civil war ensues, resulting in the death of Collins.

→ Éamon de Valera's grave

LONELY PLANET / GETTY IMAGES ©

being one of the poorest countries in Europe to one of the wealthiest: unemployment fell from 18% to 3.5%, the average industrial wage somersaulted to the top of the European league, and the dramatic rise in GDP meant that the country laid claim to an economic model of success that was the envy of the entire world. Ireland became synonymous with the term 'Celtic Tiger'.

...to Rescue Cat

From 2002 the Irish economy was kept buoyant by a gigantic construction boom that was completely out of step with any measure of responsible growth forecasting. The out-of-control international derivatives market flooded Irish banks with cheap money, and they lent it freely.

Then Lehman Bros and the credit crunch happened. The Irish banks nearly went to the wall, but were bailed out at the last minute, and before Ireland could draw breath, the International Monetary Fund (IMF) and the EU held the chits of the country's mid-term economic future. Ireland found itself yet again confronting the demons of its past: high unemployment, limited opportunity and massive emigration.

It's (Not So) Grim Up North

Since 8 May 2007, Northern Ireland has been governed in relative harmony by a constituent assembly, currently led by First Minister Peter

1932	1948	1969	1972
After 10 years in the political wilderness, de Valera leads his Fianna Fáil party into government and goes about weakening the ties between the Free State and Britain.	Fianna Fáil loses the 1948 general election to Fine Gael in coalition with the new Republican Clann an Poblachta. The new government declares the Free State to be a republic at last.	Marches by the Northern Ireland Civil Rights Association are disrupted by Loyalist attacks and police action, resulting in rioting and culminating in the Battle of the Bogside. The Troubles begin.	The Republic (and Northern Ireland) become members of the EEC. On Bloody Sunday, 13 civilians are killed by British troops; Westminster suspends the Stormont government and introduces direct rule.

Robinson of the Democratic Unionist Party (DUP) and Deputy First Minister Martin McGuinness of Sinn Féin (SF). Even if you'd only kept a lazy eye on Irish affairs these last four decades, you'd know that the presence of a one-time Loyalist firebrand like Robinson – who made his career on his vocal enmity towards all forms of Irish nationalism – and an ex-IRA commander like McGuinness in the same cabinet is a minor political miracle.

But it isn't really. It's the painstaking result of a process of dialogue and negotiation that has sought to untie a Gordian knot of historical resentment, mistrust, violence and engrained prejudice that began with the Plantations of Ireland in the 16th century.

Ireland Divided

Following the Anglo-Irish Treaty, a new Northern Ireland Parliament was constituted on 22 June 1922, with James Craig as the first prime minister. His Ulster Unionist Party (UUP) was to rule the new state until 1972, with the minority Catholic population (roughly 40%) stripped of any real power or representative strength by a Parliament that favoured the Unionists through economic subsidy, bias in housing allocations and gerrymandering: Derry's electoral boundaries were redrawn so as to guarantee a Protestant council, even though the city was two-thirds Catholic. The overwhelmingly Protestant Royal Ulster Constabulary (RUC) and their paramilitary force, the B-Specials, made little effort to mask their sectarian bias. To all intents and purposes, Northern Ireland was an apartheid state.

In 1870, after the Great Famine and ongoing emigration, more than a third of all native-born Irish lived outside Ireland.

We Shall Overcome

The first challenge to the Unionist hegemony came with the long-dormant IRA's border campaign in the 1950s, but it was quickly quashed and its leaders imprisoned. A decade later, however, the authorities met with a far more defiant foe in the shape of the Civil Rights Association, founded in 1967 and heavily influenced by its US counterpart as it sought to redress the blatant sectarianism in Derry. In October 1968 a mainly Catholic march in Derry was violently broken up by the RUC amid rumours that the IRA had provided 'security' for the marchers. Nobody knew it at the time, but the Troubles had begun.

In January 1969 another civil rights movement, called People's Democracy, organised a march from Belfast to Derry. As the marchers neared their destination, they were attacked by a group of Protestants. The police first stood to one side and then swept through the predominantly Catholic Bogside district. Further marches, protests and violence followed, with many Republicans arguing that the police only added to the problem. In August British troops went to Derry and then Belfast

1973–74	1981	1993	Mid-1990s
The Sunningdale Agreement results in a new Northern Ireland Assembly. Unionists oppose the agreement and the Ulster Workers' Council calls a strike that paralyses the province and brings an end to the Assembly.	Ten Republican prisoners die from a hunger strike. The first to die, Bobby Sands, had three weeks earlier been elected to Parliament on an Anti-H-Block ticket. Over 100,000 people attend Sands' funeral.	Downing Street Declaration is signed by British prime minister, John Major, and Irish prime minister, Albert Reynolds. It states that Britain has no 'selfish, strategic or economic interest in Northern Ireland'.	Low corporate tax, restraint in government spending, transfer payments from the EU and a low-cost labour market result in the 'Celtic Tiger' boom, transforming Ireland into one of Europe's wealthiest countries.

to maintain law and order. The British army was initially welcomed in some Catholic quarters, but soon it too came to be seen as a tool of the Protestant majority. Overreaction by the army actually fuelled recruitment into the long-dormant IRA, whose numbers especially increased after Bloody Sunday (30 January 1972), when British troops killed 13 civilians in Derry.

The Troubles

Following Bloody Sunday, the IRA more or less declared war on Britain. While continuing to target people in Northern Ireland, it moved its campaign of bombing to the British mainland, targeting innocents and earning the condemnation of citizens and parties from both sides of the sectarian divide. Meanwhile, Loyalist paramilitaries began a sectarian campaign against Catholics. Passions reached fever pitch in 1981 when Republican prisoners in the North went on a hunger strike, demanding the right to be recognised as political prisoners. Ten of them fasted to death, the best known being an elected MP, Bobby Sands.

The waters were further muddied by an incredible variety of parties splintering into subgroups with different agendas. The IRA had split into 'official' and 'provisional' wings, from which sprang more extreme Republican organisations such as the Irish National Liberation Army (INLA). Myriad Protestant, Loyalist paramilitary organisations sprang up in opposition to the IRA, and violence was typically met with violence.

Overtures of Peace

By the early 1990s, it was clear to Republicans that armed struggle was a bankrupted policy. Northern Ireland was a transformed society – most of the injustices that had sparked the conflict in the late 1960s had long since been rectified and most ordinary citizens were desperate for an end to hostilities. A series of negotiated statements between the Unionists, Nationalists and the British and Irish governments – brokered in part by George Mitchell, Bill Clinton's special envoy to Northern Ireland – eventually resulted in the historic Good Friday Agreement of 1998.

The agreement called for the devolution of legislative power from Westminster (where it had been since 1972) to a new Northern Ireland Assembly, but posturing, disagreement, sectarianism and downright obstinance on both sides made slow work of progress, and the assembly was suspended four times – the last from October 2002 until May 2007.

During this period, the politics of Northern Ireland polarised dramatically, resulting in the falling away of the more moderate UUP and the emergence of the hardline Democratic Unionist Party (DUP), led by Ian Paisley; and, on the Nationalist side, the emergence of the IRA's political

Many films depict events related to the Troubles, including *Bloody Sunday* (2002), *The Boxer* (1997; starring Daniel Day-Lewis) and *In the Name of the Father* (1994; also starring Day-Lewis).

HISTORY IT'S (NOT SO) GRIM UP NORTH

1994	1998	1998	2005
Sinn Féin leader Gerry Adams announces a 'cessation of violence' on behalf of the IRA on 31 August. In October the Combined Loyalist Military Command also announces a ceasefire.	On 10 April negotiations culminate in the Good Friday Agreement, under which the new Northern Ireland Assembly is given full legislative and executive authority.	The 'Real IRA' detonates a bomb in Omagh, killing 29 people and injuring 200. It is the worst single atrocity in the history of the Troubles, but public outrage and swift action by politicians prevent a Loyalist backlash.	The IRA orders its units not to engage in 'any other activities' apart from assisting 'the development of purely political and democratic programmes through exclusively peaceful means'.

A History of Ireland by Mike Cronin summarises all of Ireland's history in less than 300 pages. It's an easy read, but doesn't offer much in the way of analysis.

wing, Sinn Féin, as the main torch-bearer of Nationalist aspirations, under the leadership of Gerry Adams and Martin McGuinness.

A New Northern Ireland

Eager to avoid being seen to surrender any ground, the DUP and Sinn Féin dug their heels in on key issues, with the main sticking points being decommissioning of IRA weapons and the identity and composition of the new police force ushered in to replace the RUC. Paisley and the Unionists made increasing demands of the decommissioning bodies (photographic evidence, Unionist witnesses etc) as they refused to accept anything less than an open and complete surrender of the IRA. Sinn Féin refused to join the police board that monitored the affairs of the Police Service of Northern Ireland (PSNI), effectively making no change to their policy of total noncooperation with the security forces.

But the IRA did finally decommission all of its weapons, and Sinn Féin eventually agreed to join the police board. The DUP abandoned its intransigence towards its former Republican enemies and the two sides got down to the business of governing a province whose pressing needs had long since been shunted aside by sectarianism. Proof that Northern Ireland had finally achieved some kind of normality came with the 2011 Assembly elections, which returned the DUP and Sinn Féin as the two largest parties, mandating them to keep going.

But old enmities die hard. The murder of a young PSNI officer called Ronan Kerr in April 2011 was a bitter reminder of the province's violent history, but even in tragedy there was a sense that something fundamental had shifted: Kerr was a Catholic member of a police force that has gone to great lengths to disavow its traditionally pro-Protestant bias and his murder was condemned with equal strength by both sides of the divide. Perhaps most tellingly, First Minister Peter Robinson's presence at the funeral was the first time Robinson had ever been to a Catholic requiem mass.

2007	2008	2010	2011
The Northern Ireland Assembly resumes after a five-year break when talks between Unionists and Republicans remain in stalemate. They resolve their primary issues.	The Irish banking system is declared virtually bankrupt following the collapse of Lehman Bros; Ireland is on the brink of economic disaster as the extent of the crisis is revealed.	Ireland receives €85 billion bailout package from the IMF and the EU, which alleviates the banking crisis but leaves the country in strict financial shackles.	Queen Elizabeth II is the first British monarch to visit the Republic of Ireland; the visit is heralded as a resounding affirmation of the close ties between the two nations.

The Irish Way of Life

The Irish reputation for being affable is largely well deserved, but it only hints at a more profound character, one that is more complex and contradictory than the image of the silver-tongued master of blarney might suggest. This dichotomy is best summarised by a quote usually ascribed to the poet William Butler Yeats: *Being Irish, he had an abiding sense of tragedy, which sustained him through temporary periods of joy.*

The Irish Pulse

The Irish are famous for being warm and friendly, which is just another way of saying that the Irish love a bit of a chat, whether it be with friends or strangers. They will entertain you with their humour, alarm you with their willingness to get stuck into a good debate and cut you down with their razor-sharp wit. Slagging – the Irish version of teasing – is an art form, which may seem caustic to unfamiliar ears, but is quickly revealed as an intrinsic element of how the Irish relate to one another. It is commonly assumed that the mettle of friendship is proven by how well you can take a joke rather than by the payment of a cheap compliment.

Yet beneath all of the garrulous sociability and self-deprecating twaddle lurks a dark secret: at heart the Irish are low on self-esteem. They're therefore very suspicious of praise and tend not to believe anything nice that's said about them. The Irish play at false modesty like a sport.

Nevertheless, the prosperity of the last two decades and the radical lifestyle shifts it entailed have imbued the Irish with a renewed sense of confidence and a conviction that the world is theirs for the taking. For the first time, the Irish, particularly the under-30s, have no problem relaying their achievements and successes, in contrast to the older generation who were brought up in the belief that telling anyone they were doing well was unseemly and boastful.

As Ireland adjusts to the new, post-crash economic realities, an interesting gap in perspective has emerged: despite their material struggles, older people have found a measure of comfort in the familiarity of it all, having been raised at a time when unemployment, emigration and a cap on ambition were basic facts of life. Members of the younger generation, raised on boundless possibility, view austerity as a tough-but-temporary measure rather than a fulfillment of their destiny: they are the legacy of the Celtic Tiger and its transformative effect on traditional attitudes and social mores.

> According to the 2011 census, the average number of children per family has fallen to 1.38, the lowest in Irish history.

Nurse & Curse of the People

Ireland has a fractious relationship with alcohol. The Republic regularly tops the list of the world's biggest binge drinkers, and while there is an increasing awareness of, and alarm at, the devastation caused by alcohol to Irish society (especially to young people), drinking remains the country's most popular social pastime, with no sign of letting up; spend a weekend night walking around any town in the country and you'll get a firsthand feel of the influence and effect of the booze.

Some experts put Ireland's binge-drinking antics down to the dramatic rise in the country's economic fortunes, but statistics have long revealed that Ireland has had an unhealthy fondness for 'taking the cure', although the acceptability of public drunkenness is a far more recent phenomenon: the older generation are never done reminding the youngsters that they would *never* have been seen staggering in public.

Lifestyle

The Irish may like to grumble – about work, the weather, the government and those *feckin' eejits* on reality TV shows – but, if pressed, will tell you that they live in the best country on earth. There's loads *wrong* with the place, but isn't it the same way everywhere else?

Traditional Ireland – of the large family, closely linked to church and community – is quickly disappearing, as the increased urbanisation of the country continues to break up the social fabric of community interdependence that was a necessary element of relative poverty. Contemporary Ireland is therefore not altogether different from any other European country, and you have to travel further to the margins of the country – the islands and the isolated rural communities – to find an older version of society.

Gay-Friendly Ireland

Same-sex sexual activity was decriminalised in 1993 following a long campaign led by Joycean scholar and gay-rights activist David Norris. The 20 ensuing years have seen a dramatic shift in Irish attitudes to homosexuality, particularly in urban centres: where once upon a time the merest hint of homosexual activity was treated with open contempt, the LGBT community is now out and proud – there are gay bars and clubs in all the big cities and Dublin Pride is one of the biggest and most boisterous festivals on the calendar. Rural communities remain far more conservative, and the old trope of young gay men and women needing to move to larger urban centres in order to find greater acceptance of their sexuality is still very much true.

In 2010 the government passed the Civil Partnership Act, which gave same-sex couples rights and responsibilities comparable with civil marriage. Although welcomed by many, the law has its critics, especially as it stops well short of granting gay couples equal status as married couples, particularly in regard to the adoption of children and tax law.

Multiculturalism

Ireland has long been a pretty homogenous country, but the arrival of thousands of immigrants from all over the world – 17% of the population is foreign-born – has challenged the mores of racial tolerance and integration. To a large extent it has been successful, although if you scratch beneath the surface racial tensions can be exposed.

The tanking of the economy has exacerbated these tensions and the 'Irish jobs for Irish people' opinion is being stated with greater vehemence and authority – even though its supporters remain very much a minority for now. Irrespectively, the flow of emigrants from Eastern Europe has slowed up dramatically as many believe their prospects to be better at home.

Religion

About 3.8 million residents in the Republic (or 84.2%) call themselves Roman Catholic, followed by 2.8% Protestant, 0.5% Muslim and the rest an assortment of other beliefs including none at all. In the North, the breakdown is about 53% Protestant and 44% Catholic (with about 3%

In 2011 there were 98.1 men for every 100 women living in Ireland, down from 100.1 in 2006.

Polish people have overtaken UK nationals as the largest non-Irish group living in Ireland.

other or no religion). Most Irish Protestants are members of the Church of Ireland, an offshoot of the Church of England, and the Presbyterian and Methodist churches.

But while Catholicism remains a powerful cultural identifier, many Irish (especially the younger generation) have distanced themselves from the Church, whose teachings appear out of step with the major social issues of the day, including divorce, contraception, abortion, homosexuality and cohabitation. The Church has also been roundly condemned for its role in the clerical abuse scandal and its untidy efforts to avoid responsibility, provoking an acute sense of betrayal in many older believers that has made them question a lifetime's devotion to their local parishes.

According to a poll, 70% of Irish citizens believe in God and 22% believe in some kind of spirit or life-force. Only 4% declared themselves non-believers.

TV & Radio

There are four terrestrial TV channels in Ireland, three operated by the national broadcaster, Raidió Teilifís Éireann (RTE), the other a privately owned commercial station. RTE's strengths are its widespread sports coverage and news and current affairs programming. TV3 has a lightweight programming philosophy, with second-string US fluff to complement its diet of reality TV shows and celebrity profiles. The Irish-language station TG4 shows movies and dramas, mostly *as gaeilge* (in Irish with English subtitles). The main British TV stations – BBC, ITV and Channel 4 – are also available in most Irish homes, through satellite or cable; in Northern Ireland they're the main players.

The Irish are avid radio listeners – up to 85% of the population tunes in on any given day. The majority tend to stick with RTE, the dominant player with three stations: Radio 1 (88.2-90FM; mostly news and discussion), Radio 2 (90.4-92.2FM; lifestyle and music) and Lyric FM (96-99FM; classical music). Telecommunications impresario Denis O'Brien owns a number of radio stations including talk radio Newstalk (106-108FM; news, current affairs and lifestyle) and Today FM (100-102FM; music, chat and news). The rest of the radio landscape is filled out by the 25 or so local radio stations that represent local issues and tastes: the northwest's Highland Radio – heard in Donegal, Sligo, Tyrone and Fermanagh – is Europe's most successful local radio station, with an 84% market share. In Northern Ireland, the BBC rules supreme, with BBC Radio Ulster flying the local flag in addition to the four main BBC stations.

Top of the list for most popular baby names in 2012 were Jack and Emily.

THE IRISH WAY OF LIFE TV & RADIO

Music

Ireland's literary tradition may have the critics nodding sagely, but it's the country's ability to render music to the ear that will remain with you long after your Irish day is done. There's music for every occasion and every mood, from celebration to sorrow. The Irish do popular music as well as anyone, but it is with its traditional forms that make Ireland a special place to hear live music.

Traditional & Folk

US *Late Show* host David Letterman once described the uillean pipes as 'a sofa hooked up to a stick'.

Irish music (traditional music, or just trad) has retained a vibrancy not found in other traditional European forms, which have lost out to the overbearing influence of pop music. Although Irish music has kept many of its traditional aspects, it has itself influenced many forms of music, most notably US country and western – a fusion of Mississippi Delta blues and Irish traditional tunes that, combined with other influences such as gospel, is at the root of rock and roll. Other reasons for trad music's current success include the willingness of its exponents to update the way it's played (in ensembles rather than the customary *céilidh* – traditional music and dance – bands), the habit of pub sessions (introduced by returning migrants) and the economic good times that encouraged the Irish to celebrate their culture rather than trying to replicate international trends. And then, of course, there's *Riverdance,* which became a worldwide phenomenon, despite the fact that most aficionados of traditional music are seriously underwhelmed by its musical worth. Good stage show, crap music.

Traditionally, music was performed as a background to dancing and, while this has been true ever since Celtic times, the many thousands of tunes that fill up the repertoire aren't nearly as ancient as that; most aren't much older than a couple of hundred years. Because much Irish music is handed down aurally, there are myriad variations in the way a single tune is played, depending on time and place. The blind itinerant harpist Turlough O'Carolan (1680–1738) wrote more than 200 tunes – it's difficult to know how many versions their repeated learning has spawned.

More folksy than traditional, the Dubliners, fronted by the distinctive gravel voice and grey beard of Ronnie Drew (1934–2008), made a career

THE NUTS & BOLTS OF TRADITIONAL MUSIC

Despite popular perception, the harp isn't widely used in traditional music (it *is* the national emblem, but that probably has more to do with the country traditionally being run by people pulling strings). The bodhrán (*bow*-rawn) goat-skin drum is much more prevalent, although it makes for a lousy symbol. The uillean pipes, played by squeezing bellows under the elbow, provide another distinctive sound, although you're not likely to see them in a pub. The fiddle isn't unique to Ireland but it is one of the main instruments in the country's indigenous music, along with the flute, tin whistle, accordion and bouzouki (a version of the mandolin). Music fits into five main categories (jigs, reels, hornpipes, polkas and slow airs), while the old style of singing unaccompanied versions of traditional ballads and airs is called *sean-nós*.

> **TOP U2 MOMENT**
>
> Need proof that Bono can still belt them out? Just listen to the live version of 'Miss Sarajevo', recorded in Milan in 2005 and available on the 'All Because of You' single. Luciano Pavarotti wasn't around to sing his bit as he did on the studio version (on U2 and Brian Eno's *Original Soundtracks 1* album from 1995), so Bono does the honours – in Italian, and with a power and intensity that has reduced us to tears. *Grazie, maestro.*

out of bawdy drinking songs that got *everybody* singing along. Other popular bands include the Fureys, comprising four brothers originally from the travelling community (no, not like the Wilburys) along with guitarist Davey Arthur. And if it's rousing renditions of Irish rebel songs you're after, you can't go past the Wolfe Tones.

Since the 1970s, various bands have tried to blend traditional with more progressive genres, with mixed success. The first band to pull it off was Moving Hearts, led by Christy Moore, who went on to become the greatest Irish folk musician ever.

Popular Music

From the 1960s onward, Ireland produced its fair share of great rock musicians, including Van Morrison, Thin Lizzy, Celtic rockers Horslips, punk poppers the Undertones and Belfast's own Stiff Little Fingers (SLF), Ireland's answer to the Clash. And then there was Bob Geldof's Boomtown Rats, who didn't like Mondays or much else either.

Ireland has created its fair share of global superstars, beginning with Sinead O'Connor, whose 1987 debut *The Lion and the Cobra* won her a Grammy nomination. Her follow-up record, *I Do Not Want What I Haven't Got* (1990) featured a version of Prince's 'Nothing Compares 2 U', still one of the high points of pop history. She was a big deal in the US until her memorable appearance on *Saturday Night Live* in 1992 when she tore up a picture of Pope John Paul II, for which she was roundly criticised.

Far less controversial – and way more successful – were The Cranberries, formed in Limerick in 1989 and fronted by Dolores O'Riordan. After getting to No 1 on the UK charts with their first record *Everybody Else is Doing It, So Why Can't We* (1993), they became huge on the back of their second album, the triple-platinum-selling *No Need to Argue* (1994), whose big hit 'Zombie' made it to the top of the US charts.

But these all pale in comparison to the supernova that is U2, formed in 1976 in North Dublin. What else can we say about them that hasn't already been said? After 13 studio albums, 22 Grammy awards and 150 million album sales they have nothing to prove to anyone, but it's a reflection of Ireland's peculiar relationship with success that their biggest critics are homegrown, with Bono receiving most of the vitriol. Lay off the preaching and stick to the music is the basic jist of it. The criticism became harsher when the band moved the publishing part of its empire to Holland for tax reasons. Still, U2's 2009–11 360° Tour was the best-attended and most successful rock tour in history, so they must be doing something right.

The Contemporary Scene

The contemporary scene is perhaps richer and more varied than ever, as every new band and performer looks to negotiate the vicissitudes of the new-look music industry: lucrative record deals are as rare as hen's teeth, which leaves most acts reliant on gigging, word of mouth and online media to spread their respective musical gospels.

There are far more bands on the scene than we have room to mention here, but the good news is that there are gigs all the time.

Traditional Playlist

The Quiet Glen (Tommy Peoples)

Paddy Keenan (Paddy Keenan)

Compendium: The Best of Patrick Street (Various)

The Chieftains 6: Bonaparte's Retreat (The Chieftains)

Old Hag You Have Killed Me (The Bothy Band)

BEST IRISH ROCK ALBUMS

→ *The Joshua Street* (U2)

→ *The End of History* (Fionn Regan)

→ *Loveless* (My Bloody Valentine)

→ *Live & Dangerous* (Thin Lizzy)

→ *I Do Not Want What I Haven't Got* (Sinead O'Connor)

→ *St Dominic's Preview* (Van Morrison)

→ *Keep on Keepin' On* (The Riptide Movement)

→ *Inflammable Material* (Stiff Little Fingers)

→ *The Book of Invasion* (Horslips)

→ *Becoming a Jackal* (Villagers)

One of the most anticipated releases of 2013 was *Absolute Zero*, the debut album of Little Green Cars, a band with incredibly catchy melodies rooted in rock, folk, roots and Americana. Stevie Appleby's quivering vocals lead the way, but the rest of the band back it up with some gorgeous harmonies – it's not a million miles away from Bon Iver. Wexford-born folk singer Wallis Bird released her third album, *Wallis Bird*, in 2012; on it you'll hear exactly why she's labelled the Irish Fiona Apple or, if you like, a young Janis Joplin (and that's ignoring the fact that she's older than Joplin was when she died). Fusing electronica with alt rock is Richie Egan, whose band Jape released *Oceans of Frequency* in 2011 and picked up its second Choice Music prize, Ireland's highest rock accolade, following on from 2008's *Ritual*. There's something hypnotic about Egan's songs, whether it's his brilliant basslines or the Brian Eno–influenced melodies on songs like 'You Make the Love'.

Another electro-pop act to look out for is Two-Door Cinema Club, a three-piece from Bangor, Northern Ireland. Their debut album, *Tourist History* (2010), was a wonderful combination of slightly left-of-centre tunes that still managed to be eminently danceable. Their follow-up, *Beacon*, came out in 2012: the tunes were crisper, more polished and a little too poppy for our taste.

For straight-up rock (think the Doors meets AC/DC with a touch of Lynyrd Skynyrd), the Riptide Movement's 2012 release *Keep On Keepin' On* is popular, none catchier than 'Hot Tramp', one of our favourite songs from the last few years. If you're looking for some stadium rock, the Script is Ireland's answer to Keane, but not quite as edgy: they're melodic and their sound is huge if a little…dull. But they've sold four million records (including bucketloads of their latest release, 2012's *#3*), so what do we know?

But if we had to pick one Irish act to take home, it would be Villagers, an indie folk group fronted by Conor O'Brien, who writes all the songs and plays most of the instruments (in studio). O'Brien bears enviable comparisons with the likes of Conor Oberst's Bright Eyes and Nick Cave – surgical lyrics carried across stunningly beautiful melodies infused with the melancholy of lost love and missed opportunities. His debut *Becoming a Jackal* (2010) was the album of that particular year, and and *Awayland* (2013) proved he has plenty more in the tank.

The live music scene is especially vibrant, with performances in virtually every kind of venue, from an impromptu stage at the back of a pub to a mega-gig in an 80,000-capacity stadium, regularly filling the pages of the 'what's on' guides. But what makes live music so special is the Irish crowds themselves, who engage fully with the performers, lending the whole experience an added quality that has been remarked upon by musicians as diverse as the Rolling Stones and Barbra Streisand.

Hot Press (www. hotpress.com) is a fortnightly magazine featuring local and international music interviews and listings.

Literary Ireland

Of all their national traits, characteristics and cultural expressions, it's perhaps the way the Irish speak and write that best distinguishes them. Their love of language and their great oral tradition have contributed to Ireland's legacy of world-renowned writers and storytellers. And all this in a language imposed on them by a foreign invader. The Irish responded to this act of cultural piracy by mastering a magnificent hybrid – English in every respect but flavoured and enriched by the rhythms, pronunciation patterns and grammatical peculiarities of Irish.

The Mythic Cycle

Before there was anything like modern literature there was the Ulaid (Ulster) Cycle – Ireland's version of the Homeric epic – written down from oral tradition between the 8th and 12th centuries. The chief story is the Táin Bó Cúailnge (Cattle Raid of Cooley), about a battle between Queen Maeve of Connaught and Cúchulainn, the principal hero of Irish mythology. Cúchulainn appears in the work of Irish writers right up to the present day, from Samuel Beckett to Frank McCourt.

One of the most successful Irish authors is Eoin Colfer, creator of the *Artemis Fowl* series, eight fantasy novels following the adventures of Artemis Fowl II as he grows from criminal antihero to saviour of the fairies.

Modern Literature

From the mythic cycle, zip forward 1000 years, past the genius of Jonathan Swift (1667–1745) and his *Gulliver's Travels*, stopping to acknowledge acclaimed dramatist Oscar Wilde (1854–1900), *Dracula* creator Bram Stoker (1847–1912) – some say that the name of the count may have come from the Irish *droch fhola* (bad blood) – and the literary giant that was James Joyce (1882–1941), whose name and books elicit enormous pride in Ireland.

The majority of Joyce's literary output came when he had left Ireland for the artistic hotbed that was Paris, which was also true for another great experimenter in language and style, Samuel Beckett (1906–89). Beckett's work centres on fundamental existential questions about the human condition and the nature of self. He is probably best known for his play *Waiting for Godot*.

Of the dozens of 20th-century Irish authors to have achieved published renown, some names to look out for include playwright and novelist Brendan Behan (1923–64), who wove tragedy, wit and a turbulent life into his best works including *Borstal Boy*, *The Quare Fellow* and *The Hostage*. Inevitably, Behan died young of alcoholism.

THE GAELIC REVIVAL

While Home Rule was being debated and shunted, something of a revolution was taking place in Irish arts, literature and identity. The poet William Butler Yeats (1865–1939) and his coterie of literary friends (including Lady Gregory, Douglas Hyde, John Millington Synge and George Russell) championed the Anglo-Irish literary revival, unearthing old Celtic tales and writing with fresh enthusiasm about a romantic Ireland of epic battles and warrior queens. For a country that had suffered centuries of invasion and deprivation, these images presented a much more attractive version of history.

Belfast-born CS Lewis (1898–1963) died a year earlier, but he left us *The Chronicles of Narnia,* a series of allegorical children's stories, three of which have been made into films. Other Northern writers have, not surprisingly, featured the Troubles in their work: Bernard McLaverty's *Cal* (also made into a film) and his more recent *The Anatomy School* are both wonderful.

Contemporary Scene

'I love James Joyce. Never read him, but he's a true genius.' Yes, the stalwarts are great, but ask your average Irish person who their favourite writer is and they'll most likely mention someone who's still alive.

They might mention Roddy Doyle (1958–), whose mega-successful Barrytown quartet – *The Commitments, The Snapper, The Van* and *Paddy Clarke, Ha Ha Ha* – have all been made into films; his latest book, *The Guts* (2013), was eagerly anticipated by his fans as it marked the return of Jimmy Rabbitte, the memorable protagonist of *The Commitments*: older, wiser and battling illness.

Sebastian Barry (1955–) started his career as a poet with *The Water Colorist* (1983), became famous as a playwright, but achieved his greatest success as a novelist. He was shortlisted for the Man Booker Prize twice: in 2005 for his WWI drama *A Long Way Down* and the for absolutely compelling *The Secret Scripture* (2008), about a 100-year-old inmate of a mental hospital who decides to write an autobiography. His novel, *On Canaan's Side* (2011), is a compelling story of tragedy and loss as told by Lily Bere, who escapes Ireland in the 1920s and makes a life for herself in the Hamptons.

Anne Enright (1962–) did nab the Booker for *The Gathering* (2007), a zeitgeist tale of alcoholism and abuse – she described it as 'the intellectual equivalent of a Hollywood weepie'. Another Booker Prize winner is heavyweight John Banville (1945–), who won it for *The Sea* (2009); we also recommend either *The Book of Evidence* (1989) or the masterful roman-à-clef *The Untouchable* (1998), based loosely on the secret-agent life of art historian Anthony Blunt. Banville's precise and often cold prose divides critics, who consider him either the English language's greatest living stylist or an unreadable intellectual; if you're of the latter inclination then you should check out his immensely enjoyable (and highly readable) crime novels, written under the pseudonym of Benjamin Black: the most recent ones include *A Death in Summer* (2011), *Vengeance* (2012) and *Holy Orders* (2013).

TOP IRISH READS

➡ **Angela's Ashes** (1996) The Pulitzer Prize–winning novel by Frank McCourt tells the relentlessly bleak autobiographical story of the author's poverty-stricken Limerick childhood in the Depression of the 1930s.

➡ **Amongst Women** (1990) John McGahern's simple, economical piece centres on a west-of-Ireland family in the social aftermath of the War of Independence.

➡ **Reading in the Dark** (1996) Seamus Deane (the Guardian Fiction Prize winner) recounts a young boy's struggles to unravel the truth of his own history growing up during the Troubles of Belfast.

➡ **The Sea** (2005) The Booker Prize–winning novel by John Banville is a meditation on mortality, grief, death, childhood and memory; it was made into a film in 2013.

➡ **Strumpet City** (1969) James Plunkett brings Dublin to life around the time of the 1913 Lockout in what is considered to be a masterpiece of 20th-century Irish literature.

➡ **The Butcher Boy** (1992) Patrick McCabe's novel is a brilliant, gruesome, tragicomedy about an orphaned Monaghan boy's descent into madness. It was later made into a successful film by Neil Jordan.

LIVING POET'S SOCIETY

Ireland's greatest modern bard was Derry-born Nobel laureate Seamus Heaney (1939–2013), whose enormous personal warmth and wry humour flows through each of his evocative works. He was, unquestionably, the successor to Yeats and one of the most important contemporary poets of the English language. After winning the Nobel Prize in 1995 he compared the ensuing attention to someone mentioning sex in front of their mammy. *Opened Ground – Poems 1966–1996* (1998) is our favourite of his books.

Dubliner Paul Durcan (1944–) is one of the most reliable chroniclers of changing Dublin. He won the prestigious Whitbread Prize for Poetry in 1990 for 'Daddy, Daddy' and is a funny, engaging, tender and savage writer. Poet, playwright and Kerryman Brendan Kennelly (1936–) is an immensely popular character around town. He lectures at Trinity College and writes a unique brand of poetry that is marked by its playfulness, as well as historical and intellectual impact. Eavan Boland (1944–) is a prolific and much-admired writer, best known for her poetry, who combines Irish politics with outspoken feminism; *In a Time of Violence* (1995) and *The Lost Land* (1998) are two of her most celebrated collections.

To find out more about poetry in Ireland in general, visit the website of the excellent **Poetry Ireland** (www.poetryireland.ie), which showcases the work of new and established poets. For a taste of modern Irish poetry in print, try *Contemporary Irish Poetry*, edited by Fallon and Mahon. *A Rage for Order,* edited by Frank Ormsby, is a vibrant collection of the poetry of the North.

Another big hitter is Wexford-born Colm Tóibín (1955–), author of nine novels including *Brooklyn* (2009) and the novella *The Testament of Mary* (2012), which deals with the life of Mary, mother of Jesus, in her old age.

Besides these established authors, the contemporary scene is benefiting from the arrival of a slew of new writers with a Generation Y perspective on life, love and growing up in Ireland. New themes are being explored to wonderful effect, including the experience of the migrant communities, the atomising effect of the Celtic Tiger and the struggle for sexual equality, which have all found their way onto the pages of books by new voices eager to tell the story of contemporary Ireland. Outstanding talents include Ciarán Collins, whose debut novel *The Gamal* (2013) is a wonderfully poignant and funny look at the pains of adolescence in a small Irish community. Gavin Corbett's *This is the Way* (2013) tells of the travails of a Traveller (a member of Ireland's indigenous itinerant community) in 21st-century Dublin. Niamh Boyce won the Hennessy XO New Writer of the Year Award in 2012 and has followed it with her first novel, *The Herbalist* (2013), about an exotic stranger in a small Irish town whose presence uncovers the town's worst secrets. And in one of the most successful examples of self-publishing, debut novelist Helen Seymour's *Beautiful Noise* (2013) – about a fictional group of friends in 1980s Dublin – had its movie rights bought by Irish director John Moore.

Modern Fiction

The Empty Family
(Colm Tóibín)

Ghost Light
(Joseph O'Connor)

Ancient Light
(John Banville)

Room (Emma
Donoghue)

The Gamal (Ciarán
Collins)

Chick Lit

Authors hate the label and publishers profess to disregard it, but chick lit is big business, and few have mastered it as well as the Irish. Doyenne of them all is Maeve Binchy (1940–2012), whose mastery of the style saw her outsell most of the literary greats – her last novel before she died was *A Week in Winter* (2012). Marian Keyes (1963–) is another author with a long line of best-sellers, including her latest, *The Mystery of Mercy Close* (2012). She's a terrific storyteller with a rare ability to tackle sensitive issues such as alcoholism and depression, issues that she herself has suffered from and is admiringly honest about. Former agony aunt Cathy Kelly turns out novels at the rate of one a year: a recent book is *The Honey Queen* (2013), about all not being well in the fictional town of Redstone.

Irish Landscapes

Irish literature, song and painting makes it pretty clear that the landscape - spread across 486km north to south and only 275km from east to west - exerts a powerful sway on the people who have lived in it. This is especially true for those who have left, for whom the aul' sod is still a land worth pining for, and for many visitors the vibrant greenness of gentle hills and the fearsome violence of jagged coasts are an integral part of experiencing Ireland.

Cliffs & Stones

In 1821 the body of an Iron Age man was found in a bog in Galway with his cape, shoes and beard still intact.

Massive rocky outcrops, such as the Burren in County Clare, are for the most part inhospitable to grass, and although even there the green stuff does sprout up in enough patches for sheep and goats to graze on, these vast, otherworldly landscapes are mostly grey and bleak. Nearby, the dramatic Cliffs of Moher are a sheer drop into the thundering surf below. Similarly, there is no preparing for the extraordinary hexagonal stone columns of the Giant's Causeway in County Antrim or the rugged drop of County Donegal's Slieve League, Europe's highest sea cliffs. Sand dunes buffer many of the more gentle stretches of coast. Smaller islands dot the shores of Ireland, many of them barren rock piles supporting unique eco-systems – Skellig Michael is a breathtakingly jagged example just off the Kerry coast.

The rural farms of the west coast have a rugged, hard-earned look to them, due mostly to the rock that lies so close to the surface. Much of this rock has been dug up to create tillable soil and converted into stone walls that divide tiny paddocks. The Aran Islands stand out for their spectacular networks of stone walls.

Mountains & Forests

The west of Ireland is a bulwark of cliffs, hills and mountains and is the country's most mountainous area. The highest mountains are in the southwest; the tallest mountain in Ireland is Carrantuohil (1039m) in County Kerry's Macgillycuddy's Reeks.

Look for *Reading the Irish Landscape* by Frank Mitchell and Michael Ryan for info on Ireland's geology, archaeology, urban growth, agriculture and afforestation.

The Irish frequently lament the loss of their woodlands, much of which were cleared by the British (during the reign of Elizabeth I) to build ships for the Royal Navy. Little of the island's once plentiful oak forests survive today, and much of what you'll see is the result of relatively recent planting. Instead, the countryside largely comprises green fields divided by hedgerows and stone walls. Use of this land is divided between cultivated fields and pasture for cattle and sheep.

Plants

Although Ireland is sparsely wooded, the range of surviving plant species is larger here than in many other European countries, thanks in part to the comparatively late arrival of agriculture.

There are remnants of the original oak forest in Killarney National Park and in southern Wicklow near Shillelagh. Far more common are pine plantations, which are growing steadily. Hedgerows, planted to divide fields and delineate land boundaries throughout Ireland, actually host many of the native plant species that once thrived in the oak forests – it's an intriguing example of nature adapting and reasserting itself. The Burren in County Clare is home to a remarkable mixture of Mediterranean, alpine and arctic species.

The bogs of Ireland are home to a unique flora adapted to wet, acidic, nutrient-poor conditions, whose survival is threatened by the depletion of bogs for energy use. Sphagnum moss is the key bog plant and is joined by other species such as bog rosemary, bog cotton, black-beaked sedge (whose spindly stem grows up to 30cm in height) and various types of heather and lichen. Carnivorous plants also thrive, such as the sundew, whose sticky tentacles trap insects, and bladderwort, whose tiny explosive bladders trap aquatic animals in bog pools.

Mammals

Apart from the fox and badger, which tend to shy away from humans and are rarely seen, the wild mammals of Ireland are mostly of the ankle-high 'critter' category, such as rabbits, hedgehogs and shrews. Hikers often spot the Irish hare, or at least glimpse the blazing-fast blur of one running away. Red deer roam the hillsides in many of the wilder parts of the country, particularly the Wicklow Mountains and in Killarney National Park, which holds the country's largest herd.

For most visitors, the most commonly sighted mammals are those inhabiting the sea and waterways. The otter, rarely seen elsewhere in Europe, is thriving in Ireland. Seals are a common sight in rivers and along the shore, as are dolphins, which follow the warm waters of the Gulf Stream towards Ireland. Some colonise the coast of Ireland year-round, frequently swimming into the bays and inlets off the western coast.

For information on parks, gardens, monuments and inland waterways see www.heritageire land.ie.

Birdlife

Many travellers visit Ireland specifically for the birding. Ireland's westerly location on the fringe of Europe makes it an ideal stopover point for birds migrating from North America and the Arctic. In autumn, the southern counties become a temporary home to the American waders (mainly sandpipers and plovers) and warblers. Migrants from Africa, such as shearwaters, petrels and auks, begin to arrive in spring in the southwestern counties.

The reasonably rare corncrake, which migrates from Africa, can be found in the western counties, in Donegal and around the Shannon Callows, and on islands such as Inishbofin in Galway. In late spring and early summer, the rugged coastlines, particularly cliff areas and islands, become a haven for breeding seabirds, mainly gannet, kittiwake, Manx shearwater, fulmar, cormorant and heron. Puffins, resembling penguins with their tuxedo colour scheme, nest in large colonies on coastal cliffs.

The lakes and low-lying wetlands attract large numbers of Arctic and northern European waterfowl and waders such as whooper swans, lapwing, barnacle geese, white-fronted geese and golden plovers. The important Wexford Wildfowl Reserve holds half the world's population of

The illustrated pocket guide *Animals of Ireland* by Gordon D'Arcy is a handy, inexpensive introduction to Ireland's varied fauna.

THE BOG

The boglands, which once covered one-fifth of the island, are more of a whiskey hue than green – that's the brown of heather and sphagnum moss, which cover uncut bogs. Visitors will likely encounter a bog in County Kildare's Bog of Allen or while driving through the western counties – much of the Mayo coast is covered by bog, and huge swaths also cover Donegal.

Greenland white-fronted geese, and little tern breed on the beach there, protected by the dunes. Also found during the winter are teal, redshank and curlew. The main migration periods are April to May and September to October.

The magnificent peregrine falcon has been making something of a recovery and can be found nesting on cliffs in Wicklow and elsewhere. In 2001, 46 golden eagle chicks from Scotland were released into Glenveagh National Park in Donegal in an effort to reintroduce the species. The project has been afflicted by adverse weather and, sadly, by unknowns poisoning and shooting the birds, but as of 2013 it has managed to survive courtesy of two separate nests that have produced a handful of surviving chicks between them. More recent reintroductions include the white-tailed sea eagle, with the first breeding attempts expected in 2013.

For more information, check out www.goldeneagle.ie.

Irish Birds by David Cabot is a pocket guide describing birds and their habitats, which outlines the best places for serious birdwatching.

Environmental Issues

Ireland does not rate among the world's biggest offenders when it comes to polluting the environment, but the country's recent economic growth has led to an increase in industry and consumerism, which in turn generate more pollution and waste. While the population density is among Europe's lowest, the population is rising. The last 10 years have seen the untrammelled expansion of suburban developments around all of Ireland's major towns and cities; the biggest by far is, inevitably, around Dublin, especially in the broadening commuter belt of Counties Meath and Kildare. The collapse of the construction bubble in 2008 has put an end to much of this development, but the rows of semi-detached houses still remain. As more people drive cars and fly in planes, Ireland grows more dependent on nonrenewable sources of energy. The amount of waste has risen substantially since the early 1990s.

Needless to say, concern for the environment is growing and the government has taken some measures to offset the damage that thriving economy can cause. In 2007 the Irish Energy Centre was renamed **Sustainable Energy Authority of Ireland** (SEAI; www.seai.ie) and charged with promoting and assisting the development of renewable energy resources, including solar, wind, hydropower, geothermal and biomass resources. As it stands, the country is only tapping a fraction of these: in 2013 less than 5% of the country's energy requirements (heat, electricity and transport) were being met by renewables.

The European Renewables Directive set Ireland a target of sourcing 16% of all energy requirements by 2020, which – given the economic constraints put upon the country – now seems overly optimistic: Ireland just doesn't have the funds to make major infrastructural investments in renewable technology such as wind farms or the manufacture of solar panels.

On a more practical level, a number of recycling programs have been very successful, especially the 'plastax' – a €0.24 levy on all plastic bags

NATIONAL NATURE RESERVES

There are 66 state-owned and 10 privately owned National Nature Reserves (NNRs) in the Republic, represented by Dúchas (the government department in charge of parks, monuments and gardens), which are defined as areas of importance for their special flora, fauna or geology. Northern Ireland has more than 45 NNRs which are leased or owned by the Department of the Environment. These include the Giant's Causeway and Glenariff in Antrim, and North Strangford Lough in County Down. More information is available from the **Northern Ireland Environment Agency** (www.ni-environment.gov.uk).

used within the retail sector, which has seen their use reduced by a whopping 90%.

While this is a positive sign, it doesn't really put Ireland at the vanguard of the environmental movement. Polls seem to indicate the Irish are slightly less concerned about the environment than are the citizens of most other European countries, and the country is a long way from meeting its Kyoto Protocol requirement for reduced emissions. The government isn't pushing the environmental agenda much beyond ratifying EU agreements, although it must be said that these have established fairly ambitious goals for reduced air pollution and tighter management of water quality.

The annual number of tourists in Ireland far exceeds the number of residents (by a ratio of about 1.5 to one), so visitors can have a huge impact on the local environment. Tourism is frequently cited as potentially beneficial to the environment – that is, responsible visitor spending can help stimulate ecofriendly sectors of the economy. Ecotourism is not really burgeoning in a formalised way, although an organisation called the **Greenbox** (www.greenbox.ie) has established standards for ecotourism on the island and promotes tour companies that comply with these standards. The rising popularity of outdoor activities such as diving, surfing and fishing creates economic incentives for maintaining the cleanliness of Ireland's coasts and inland waters, but increased activity in these environments can be harmful if not managed carefully.

Ireland's comprehensive and efficient bus network makes it easy to avoid the use of a car, and the country is well suited to cycling and walking holidays. Many hotels, guesthouses and hostels tout green credentials, and organic ingredients are frequently promoted on restaurant menus. It's not difficult for visitors to minimise their environmental footprint while in Ireland.

Ireland's National Parks

Burren

Connemara

Glenveagh

Killarney

Wicklow Mountains

Ballycroy

IRISH LANDSCAPES ENVIRONMENTAL ISSUES

Sporting Ireland

For many Irish, sport is akin to religion. For some it's all about faith through good works such as jogging, cycling and organised team sports. For everybody else, observance is enough, especially from the living room couch or the pub stool, where the mixed fortunes of their favourite teams are followed with elevated hope and vocalised despair.

Gaelic Football & Hurling

Most counties are good at one Gaelic sport and not the other. Kilkenny, Waterford, Clare and Tipperary are traditionally hurling counties; Kerry, Meath, Mayo and all nine Ulster counties are better at football. Cork, Galway, Offaly, Wexford and Dublin have the privilege of being good at both sports.

Gaelic games are at the core of Irishness; they are enmeshed in the fabric of Irish life and hold a unique place in the heart of its culture. Their resurgence towards the end of the 19th century was entwined with the whole Gaelic revival and the march towards Irish independence. The beating heart of Gaelic sports is the **Gaelic Athletic Association** (GAA; www.gaa.ie), set up in 1884 'for the preservation and cultivation of National pastimes'. The GAA is still responsible for fostering these amateur games. It warms our hearts to see that after all this time – and amid the onslaught of globalisation and the general commercialisation of sport – they are still far and away the most popular sports in Ireland.

Gaelic games are fast, furious and not for the faint-hearted. Challenges are fierce, and contact between players is extremely aggressive. Both sports are county-based games. The dream of every club player is to represent his county, with the hope of perhaps playing in an All-Ireland final in September at Croke Park in Dublin, the climax of a knockout championship that is played first at a provincial and then interprovincial level.

Football

There is huge support in Ireland for the 'world game', although fans are much more enthusiastic about the likes of Manchester United, Liverpool and the two Glasgow clubs (Rangers and Celtic) than the struggling pros and part-timers who make up the **National League** (www.fai.ie) in the Republic and the **Irish League** (www.irishfa.com) in Northern Ireland. It's just too difficult for domestic teams to compete with the multimillionaire

RULES OF THE GAMES

Both Gaelic football and hurling are played by two teams of 15 players whose aim is to get the ball through what resembles a rugby goal: two long vertical posts joined by a horizontal bar, below which is a soccer-style goal, protected by a goalkeeper. Goals (below the crossbar) are worth three points, whereas a ball placed over the bar between the posts is worth one point. Scores are shown thus: 1-12, meaning one goal and 12 points, giving a total of 15 points.

Gaelic football is played with a round, soccer-size ball, and players are allowed to kick it or hand-pass it, like Australian Rules. Hurling, which is considered by far the more beautiful game, is played with a flat stick or bat known as a hurley or *camán*. The small leather ball, called a *slíothar*, is hit or carried on the hurley; handpassing is also allowed. Both games are played over 70 action-filled minutes.

YOU SAY SOCCER, I SAY FOOTBALL

To distinguish it from Gaelic football, you'll often hear football referred to as 'soccer' – especially in Gaelic strongholds whereby doing so implies scorn on so-called 'garrison sports' – which will allay American confusion but only irritate the Brits. But Irish fans of Association Football (the official name of the sport) will always call it football and the other Gaelic football or, in Dublin, 'gah' – which is just the pronunciation of the letters GAA (Gaelic Athletic Association).

glitz and glamour of the English Premiership, which has always drawn off the cream of Irish talent.

At an international level, the Republic and Northern Ireland field separate teams; in 2009 both were performing adequately, but it was all a far cry from their respective moments of glory – the 1980s for Northern Ireland and 1988 to 2002 for the Republic.

In order to avoid competing (and losing) with the more popular English Premier League, whose season runs from mid-August to mid-May, the League of Ireland runs its season from April to November, the only European league to do so. Northern Ireland's Irish League still follows the British winter timetable.

Rugby

Although traditionally the preserve of Ireland's middle classes, rugby captures the mood of the whole island in February and March during the annual Six Nations Championships, because the Irish team is drawn from both sides of the border and is supported by both Nationalists and Unionists. In recognition of this, the Irish national anthem is no longer played at internationals, and is replaced by the slightly dodgy but thoroughly inoffensive *Ireland's Call*, a song written especially for the purpose – although nobody seemed to mind it in 2009 when Ireland won its first Grand Slam (a clean sweep of victories in one campaign) since 1948.

Rugby is arguably more exciting at a provincial level, where Leinster and Munster have an ongoing rivalry (both have won the Heineken Cup, Europe's premier competition, twice; Leinster most recently in 2009 and 2011) and Ulster are just a step behind them. Rugby isn't big in the west so Connaught aren't very good.

Golf

Scotland may be the home of golf, but Ireland is where golf goes on holiday. The Scots have some fine courses, it's true – but Ireland has its own names that can hold their own with the very best in the world.

With over 400 courses to choose from, there's no shortage of choice when it comes to teeing it up. These include a host of parkland (or inland) courses – worth checking out are the wonderful, American-style resort courses built over the last couple of decades, with immaculate, lawn-like fairways, white sand bunkers and strategically placed water features ready to swallow the chunkily hit ball.

But the essence of Irish golf is to be found on seaside links, dotted in a spectacular string of scenery along virtually the entire coastline. Here, nature provides the perfect raw material, and the very best of them are not quite built into the landscape as found within it, much like Michelangelo 'found' his figures hiding in the blocks of marble.

Finally, a word about the Irish golfer. Clubhouse snobs and high-handicap etiquette junkies aside, the real Irish golfer is the man or woman who puts their shoes on in the car park and can't wait to tee it up on the first; they know all the safe spots to land the ball and see it as their duty to share local knowledge. If you land up in the club on your own and they're doing a little putting practice before heading out, they're the ones that will offer a twosome because it's just not right to play on your own. The Irish golfer is friendly, easygoing and always recognises that you will never win at golf, and that today's bad round is just for today and tomorrow will turn up something different. And they know that golf is played over 19 holes – sure what's the point of playing unless you can laugh about it all over a drink when the round is done?

Horse Racing & Greyhound Racing

A passion for horse racing is deeply entrenched in Irish life and comes without the snobbery of its English counterpart. If you fancy a flutter on the gee-gees you can watch racing from around Ireland and England on the TV in bookmakers shops every day. No money ever seems to change hands in the betting, however, and every Irish punter will tell you they 'broke even'.

Ireland has a reputation for producing world-class horses for racing and other equestrian events such as showjumping, also very popular albeit in a much less egalitarian kind of way. Major annual races include the Irish Grand National (Fairyhouse, April), Irish Derby (the Curragh, June) and Irish Leger (the Curragh, September). For more information on events contact **Horse Racing Ireland** (www.hri.ie).

Traditionally the poor-man's punt, greyhound racing ('the dogs'), has been smartened up in recent years and partly turned into a corporate outing. It offers a cheaper, more accessible and more local alternative to horse racing. There are 20 tracks across the country, administered by the **Irish Greyhound Board** (www.igb.ie).

Irish academic Dr Fintan Lane's book Long Bullets: A History of Road Bowling in Ireland traces the sport to the 17th century.

Road Bowling

The object of this sport is to throw a cast-iron ball weighing approximately 800g along a public road (normally one with little traffic) for a designated distance, usually 1km or 2km, with speed, control and accuracy. The person who does it in the least number of throws is the winner. Participants traditionally bet during the game.

The ball is known as a bowl or bullet. A shot is a throw and a kitter-paw is a left-handed thrower. If you hear someone talking about their butt, they are referring to the throwing mark on the road. Breaking butt means someone has stepped over the mark before releasing the ball. Faugh an Bheallach is a traditional Irish battle cry and means you should get out of the way. A sop is a tuft of grass placed where the bowl should first strike the road and a score is a match.

The main centre for road bowling is Cork, which has 200 clubs, and, to a lesser extent, Armagh. Competitions take place throughout the year, attracting considerable crowds. The sport has been taken up in various countries around the world, including the US, UK, Germany and the Netherlands, and a world championship competition has been set up (see www.irishroadbowling.ie). In Ireland the sport is governed by the Irish Road Bowling Association.

Survival Guide

Directory A–Z

Accommodation

Accommodation options range from bare and basic to pricey and palatial. The spine of the Irish hospitality business is the ubiquitous B&B, but in recent years they have been challenged by a plethora of midrange hotels and guesthouses. Online resources for accommodation include the following:

➤ **www.daft.ie** Online classified paper for short- and long-term rentals.

➤ **www.elegant.ie** Specialises in self-catering castles, period houses and unique properties.

➤ **www.familyhomes.ie** Lists (you guessed it) family-run guesthouses and self-catering properties.

➤ **www.gulliver.ie** Fáilte Ireland and the Northern Ireland Tourist Board's web-based accommodation reservation system.

➤ **www.irishlandmark.com** Not-for-profit conservation group that rents self-catering properties of historical and cultural significance, such as castles, gate lodges and lighthouses.

➤ **www.imagineireland. com** Modern cottage rentals throughout the whole island, including Northern Ireland.

➤ **www.stayinireland.com** Lists guesthouses and self-catering options.

B&Bs & Guesthouses

Bed and breakfasts are small, family-run houses, farmhouses and period country houses with fewer than five bedrooms. Standards vary enormously, but most have some bedrooms with private bathroom at a cost of roughly €35 to €40 (£20 to £25) per person per night. In luxurious B&Bs, expect to pay €55 (£38) or more per person. Off-season rates – usually October through to March – are usually lower, as are midweek prices.

Guesthouses are like upmarket B&Bs, but bigger – the Irish equivalent of a boutique hotel. Facilities are usually better and sometimes include a restaurant.

Other tips:

➤ Facilities in B&Bs range from basic (bed, bathroom, kettle) to beatific (whirlpool baths, LCD TVs, wi-fi) the more you are prepared to pay.

➤ Most B&Bs take credit cards, but the occasional rural one might not have facilities; check when you book.

➤ Advance reservations are strongly recommended, especially in peak season (June to September).

➤ If full, B&B owners may recommend another house in the area (possibly a private house taking occasional guests, not in tourist listings).

Camping, Caravan Parks & Canals

Camping and caravan parks aren't as common in Ireland as they are elsewhere in Europe. Some hostels have camping space for tents and also offer house facilities, which makes them better value than the main camping grounds. At commercial parks the cost is typically somewhere between €12 and €20 (£7 to £12) for a tent and two people. Prices for campsites in this book are for two people unless stated otherwise. Caravan sites cost around €15 to €25 (£11 to £15). Most parks are open only from Easter to the end of September or October.

An alternative to normal caravanning is to hire a horse-drawn caravan with which to wander the countryside. In high season you can hire one for around €800 a week. Search Fáilte Ireland's www.discoverireland.ie for a

---

BOOK YOUR STAY ONLINE

For more accommodation reviews by Lonely Planet authors, check out http://lonelyplanet.com/hotels/ireland. You'll find independent reviews, as well as recommendations on the best places to stay. Best of all, you can book online.

list of operators, or see www.irishhorsedrawncaravans.com.

Another unhurried and pleasurable way to see the countryside (with slightly less maintenance) is by barge on one of the country's canal systems. Contact Fáilte Ireland for a list of rental companies.

Another option is to hire a boat, which you can live aboard while cruising Ireland's inland waterways. One company offering boats for hire on the Shannon-Erne Waterway is **Emerald Star** (📞071-962 0234; www.emeraldstar.ie).

Hostels

The prices quoted in this book for hostel accommodation are for those aged over 18. A dorm bed in high season generally costs €10 to €25 (£8 to £14). Many hostels now have family and smaller rooms.

The following is a list of the relevant hostel associations:

An Óige (www.anoige.ie) Hostelling International (HI)–associated national organisation with 26 hostels scattered around the Republic.

HINI (www.hini.org.uk) HI-associated organisation with six hostels in Northern Ireland.

Independent Holiday Hostels of Ireland (IHH; www.hostels-ireland.com) Eighty tourist-board approved hostels throughout all of Ireland.

Independent Hostel Owners of Ireland (IHO; www.independenthostelsireland.com) Independent hostelling association.

Hotels

Hotels range from the local pub to medieval castles. In most cases, you'll get a better rate than the one published if you go online or negotiate directly with the hotel, especially out of season. The explosion of bland midrange chain hotels (many Irish-owned) has proven to

A 'STANDARD' HOTEL RATE?

There is no such thing. Prices vary according to demand – or have different rates for online, phone or walk-in bookings. B&B rates are more consistent, but virtually every other accommodation will charge wildly different rates depending on the time of year, day, festival schedule and even your ability to do a little negotiating. The following price ranges have been used in our reviews of places to stay. Prices are all based on a double room with private bathroom in high season.

BUDGET	REPUBLIC	NORTHERN IRELAND
Budget (€/£)	<€60	<£50
Midrange (€€/££)	€60-150	£50-120
Top end (€€€/£££)	>€150	>£120

be a major challenge to the traditional B&Bs and guesthouses: they might not have the same personalised service, but their rooms are clean and their facilities generally quite good.

House Swapping

House swapping has become a popular and affordable way to visit a country and enjoy a real home away from home. There are several agencies in Ireland that, for an annual fee, facilitate international swaps. The fee pays for access to a website and a book giving house descriptions, photographs and the owner's details. After that, it's up to you to make arrangements. Use of the family car is sometimes included.

Homelink International House Exchange (www.homelink.ie)

Intervac International Holiday Service (www.intervac-homeexchange.com)

Rental Accommodation

Self-catering accommodation is often rented on a weekly basis and usually means an apartment or house where you look after yourself. The rates vary from one region and season to another. **Fáilte Ireland**

(📞Republic 1850 230 330, the UK 0800 039 7000; www.discoverireland.ie) publishes a guide for registered self-catering accommodation; you can check listings at their website.

Children

➡ Children are not allowed in pubs after 9pm (10pm May to September).

➡ Car seats (around €50/£30 per week) are mandatory in rental cars for children aged nine months to four years.

➡ Baby-changing facilities can be found only in larger cities, and then only in large shopping centres.

For further general information see Lonely Planet's *Travel with Children*. Also check out the following:

www.eumom.ie For pregnant women and parents with young children.

www.babygoes2.com Travel site with family-friendly accommodation worldwide.

Customs Regulations

Both the Republic of Ireland and Northern Ireland have a two-tier customs system: one for goods bought duty-

Climate

Belfast

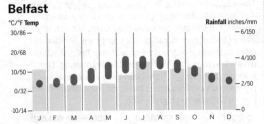

Dublin

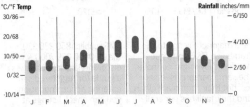

Galway

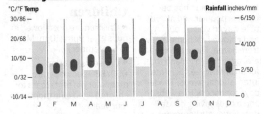

Electricity

230V/50Hz

free outside the European Union (EU), the other for goods bought in another EU country where tax and duty is paid. There is technically no limit to the amount of goods transportable within the EU, but customs will use certain guidelines to distinguish personal use from commercial purpose. Allowances are as follows:

Duty free For duty-free goods from outside the EU, limits include 200 cigarettes, 1L of spirits or 2L of wine, 60ml of perfume and 250ml of eau de toilette.

Tax and duty paid Amounts that officially constitute personal use include 3200 cigarettes (or 400 cigarillos, 200 cigars or 3kg of tobacco) and either 10L of spirits, 20L of fortified wine, 60L of sparkling wine, 90L of still wine or 110L of beer.

Cats & Dogs

Cats and dogs from anywhere outside Ireland and the UK are subject to strict quarantine laws. The EU Pet Travel Scheme, whereby animals are fitted with a micro chip, vaccinated against rabies and blood-tested six months *prior* to entry, is in force in the UK and the Republic of Ireland. No preparation or documentation is necessary for the movement of pets directly between the UK and the Republic. Contact the **Department of Agriculture, Food & Rural Development** (☑01-607 2000; www.agriculture.gov.ie) in Dublin for further details.

Embassies & Consulates

This is a selection of embassies in Dublin and consular offices in Belfast. For a complete list of embassies, see the website of the **Department of Foreign Affairs** (www.dfa.ie), which also lists Ireland's diplomatic missions overseas.

Australian Embassy (☑01-664 5300; www.ireland.embassy.gov.au; Fitzwilton House, 7th fl, Wilton Tce, Dublin 2)

Canadian Embassy (☑01-234 4000; www.canada.ie; 7-8 Wilton Tce, Dublin 2)

Dutch embassy (☑269 3444; www.netherlandsembassy.ie; 160 Merrion Rd, Ballsbridge, Dublin 4); consulate (☑028-9077 9088; 14-16 West Bank Rd, c/o All-Route Shipping Ltd, Belfast).

French Embassy (☑277 5000; www.ambafrance.ie; 36 Ailesbury Rd, Dublin 4)

German embassy (☑269 3011; www.dublin.diplo.de; 31 Trimleston Ave, Booterstown, Blackrock, County Dublin); consulate (☑028-9024 4113;

22 Great Victoria St, Chamber of Commerce House, Belfast).

Italian Embassy (☏660 1744; www.ambdublin.esteri. it; 63-65 Northumberland Rd, Ballsbridge, Dublin 4)

UK (☏205 3700; www.brit ishembassy.ie; 29 Merrion Rd, Ballsbridge, Dublin 4)

USA (☏01-630 6200; dublin. usembassy.gov/; 42 Elgin Rd, Ballsbridge, Dublin) embassy (☏01-630 6200; dublin. usembassy.gov/; 42 Elgin Rd, Ballsbridge, Dublin); consulate (☏028-9038 6100; Danesfort House, 223 Stranmillis Rd, Belfast).

Food

Our cafe and restaurant listings appear in budget order, with the cheapest budget range first. Within the ranges, listings are given in preference order. Please note that our hierarchies of favourite places aren't written in stone (as authors, we can crave caviar on a Monday and cod and chips on a Friday).

Gay & Lesbian Travellers

Ireland is a pretty tolerant place for gays and lesbians. Bigger cities such as Dublin, Galway and Cork have a well-established gay scene, as does Belfast and Derry in Northern Ireland. That said, you'll still find pockets of homophobia throughout the island, particularly in smaller towns and rural areas. Resources include the following:

Gaire (www.gaire.com) Message board and info for a host of gay-related issues.

Gay & Lesbian Youth Northern Ireland (www. glyni.org.uk)

Gay Men's Health Project (☏01-660 2189; www.hse.ie) Practical advice on men's health issues.

National Lesbian & Gay Federation (NLGF; ☏01-671 9076; www.nlgf.ie) Publishes the monthly *Gay Community News* (www.gcn.ie).

Northern Ireland Gay Rights Association (Nigra; ☏9066 5257)

Outhouse (☏01-873 4932; www.outhouse.ie; 105 Capel St) Gay, lesbian and bisexual resource centre.

Health

No jabs are required to travel to Ireland. Excellent health care is readily available. For minor, self-limiting illnesses, pharmacists can give valuable advice and sell over-the-counter medication. They can also advise when more specialised help is required and point you in the right direction.

EU citizens equipped with a European Health Insurance Card (EHIC), available from health centres or, in the UK, post offices, will be covered for most medical care – but not non-emergencies or emergency repatriation. While other countries, such as Australia, also have reciprocal agreements with Ireland and Britain, many do not.

In Northern Ireland, everyone receives free emergency treatment at accident and emergency (A&E) departments of state-run NHS hospitals, irrespective of nationality.

Insurance

Insurance is important: it covers you for everything from medical expenses and luggage loss to cancellations or delays in your travel arrangements, depending on your policy.

While EU citizens have most medical care covered with an EHIC card, an additional insurance policy for all other issues is recommended.

Worldwide travel insurance is available at www.lonely planet.com/travel_services. You can buy, extend and claim

EATING PRICES RANGES

BUDGET	REPUBLIC	NORTHERN IRELAND
Budget (€/£)	<€12	<£12
Midrange (€€/££)	€12-25	£12-20
Top end (€€€/£££)	>€25	>£20

online at any time – even if you're already on the road.

All cars on public roads need to be insured. If you are bringing your own vehicle, be sure to check that your insurance will cover you in Ireland.

Internet Access

With the advent of 3G and wi-fi networks, internet cafes are increasingly disappearing from a number of Irish towns. The ones that are left generally charge up to €6/£5 per hour.

If you'll be using your laptop or mobile device to get online, most hotels and an increasing number of B&Bs, hostels, bars and restaurants offer wi-fi access, charging anything from nothing to €5/£5 per hour.

Otherwise, most hotels and hostels in larger towns and cities have internet access via a desktop for customer use.

Legal Matters

Illegal drugs are widely available, especially in clubs. The possession of small quantities of marijuana attracts a fine or warning, but harder drugs are treated more seriously. Public drunkenness is illegal but commonplace – the police will usually ignore it unless you're causing trouble.

Contact the following for assistance:

Legal Aid Board (☑066-947 1000; www.legalaidboard.ie) Has a network of local law centres.

Northern Ireland Legal Services Commission (www.nilsc.org.uk)

Maps

Michelin's 1:400,000-scale Ireland map (No 923) is a decent single sheet map, with clear cartography and most of the island's scenic roads marked. The four maps – North, South, East and West – that make up the Ordnance Survey Holiday map series at 1:250,000 scale are useful if you want more detail.

The Ordnance Survey Discovery series covers the whole island in 89 maps at a scale of 1:50,000.

Collins also publishes a range of maps covering Ireland.

These are all available at the **National Map Centre** (☑476 0471; www.mapcentre.ie; 34 Aungier St, Dublin; ☺10am-6pm Mon-Sat), through www.osi.ie and many bookshops around Ireland.

Money

The currency in the Republic of Ireland is the euro (€). The island's peculiar political history means that the six Ulster counties that make up Northern Ireland – Antrim, Armagh, Down, Fermanagh, Londonderry and Tyrone – use the pound sterling (£). Although notes issued by Northern Irish banks are legal tender throughout the UK, many businesses outside of Northern Ireland refuse to accept them and you'll have to swap them in British banks.

ATMs

Usually called 'cash machines', ATMs are easy to find in cities and all but the smallest of towns. Watch out for ATMs that have been tampered with; card-reader scams ('skimming') have become a real problem.

Credit & Debit Cards

Visa and MasterCard credit and debit cards are widely accepted in Ireland. American Express is only accepted by the major chains, and very few places accept Diners or JCB. Smaller businesses, such as pubs and some B&Bs, prefer debit cards (and will charge a fee for credit cards). Nearly all credit and debit cards use the chip-and-PIN system and an increasing number of places will not accept your card if you don't.

Taxes & Refunds

Non-EU residents can claim Value Added Tax (VAT, a sales tax of 21% added to the purchase price of luxury goods – excluding books, children's clothing and educational items) back on their purchases, so long as the store operates either the Cashback or Taxback refund program (they should display a sticker). You'll get a voucher with your purchase that must be stamped at the *last point of exit* from the EU. If you're travelling on to Britain or mainland Europe from Ireland, hold on to your voucher until you pass through your final customs stop in the EU; it can then be stamped and you can post it back for a refund of duty paid.

VAT in Northern Ireland is 20%; shops participating in the Tax-Free Shopping refund scheme will give you a form or invoice on request to be presented to customs when you leave. After customs have certified the form, it will be returned to the shop for a refund and the cheque sent to you at home.

Tipping

You're not obliged to tip if the service or food was unsatisfactory (even if it's been automatically added to your bill as a 'service charge').

Hotels Only for bellhops who carry luggage, then €1/£1 per bag

Pubs Not expected unless table service is provided, then €1/£1 for a round of drinks

Restaurants 10% for decent service, up to 15% in more expensive places

Taxis 10% or rounded up to the nearest euro/pound

Toilet attendants €0.50/50p

Opening Hours

Hours in both the Republic and Northern Ireland are roughly the same.

Banks 10am to 4pm Monday to Friday (to 5pm Thursday)

Offices 9am to 5pm Monday to Friday

Post offices Northern Ireland 9am to 5.30pm Monday to Friday, 9am to 12.30pm Saturday; Republic 9am to 6pm Monday to Friday, 9am to 1pm Saturday. Smaller post offices may close at lunch and one day per week.

Pubs Northern Ireland 11.30am to 11pm Monday to Saturday, 12.30pm to 10pm Sunday. Pubs with late licences open until 1am Monday to Saturday and midnight Sunday; Republic 10.30am to 11.30pm Monday to Thursday, 10.30am to 12.30am Friday and Saturday, noon to 11pm Sunday (30 minutes 'drinking up' time allowed). Pubs with bar extensions open to 2.30am Thursday to Saturday. All pubs close Christmas Day and Good Friday.

Restaurants Noon to 10.30pm; many close one day of the week.

Shops 9am to 5.30pm or 6pm Monday to Saturday (until 8pm on Thursday & sometimes Friday), noon to 6pm Sunday (in bigger towns only). Shops in rural towns may close at lunch and one day per week.

Tourist offices 9am to 5pm Monday to Friday, 9am to 1pm Saturday. Many extend their hours in summer and open fewer hours/days or close from October to April.

Photography

➜ Natural light can be very dull, so use higher ISO speeds than usual, such as 400 for daylight shots.

➜ In Northern Ireland, get permission before taking photos of fortified police stations, army posts or other military or quasi-military paraphernalia.

➜ Don't take photos of people in Protestant or Catholic strongholds of West Belfast without permission; always ask and be prepared to accept a refusal.

Public Holidays

Public holidays can cause road chaos as everyone tries to get somewhere else for the break. It's wise to book accommodation in advance around these times.

The following are public holidays in both the Republic and Northern Ireland:

New Year's Day 1 January

St Patrick's Day 17 March

Easter (Good Friday to Easter Monday inclusive) March/April

May Holiday 1st Monday in May

Christmas Day 25 December

St Stephen's Day (Boxing Day) 26 December

St Patrick's Day and St Stephen's Day holidays are taken on the following Monday when they fall on a weekend. In the Republic, nearly everywhere closes on Good Friday even though it isn't an official public holiday. In the North, most shops open on Good Friday, but close the following Tuesday.

Northern Ireland

Spring Bank Holiday Last Monday in May

Orangeman's Day 12 July

August Holiday Last Monday in August

Republic

June Holiday 1st Monday in June

August Holiday 1st Monday in August

October Holiday Last Monday in October

Safe Travel

Ireland is safer than most countries in Europe, but normal precautions should be observed.

Northern Ireland is as safe as anywhere else, but there are areas where the sectarian divide is bitterly pronounced, most notably in parts of Belfast. It's probably best to ensure your visit to Northern Ireland doesn't coincide with the climax of the Orange marching season on 12 July; sectarian passions are usually inflamed and even many Northerners leave the province at this time.

Telephone

Area codes in the Republic have three digits and begin with a 0, eg ☎021 for Cork, ☎091 for Galway and ☎061 for Limerick. The only exception is Dublin, which has a two-digit code (☎01). Always use the area code if calling from a mobile phone, but you don't need it if calling from a fixed-line number within the area code.

In Northern Ireland, the area code for all fixed-line numbers is ☎028, but you only need to use it if calling from a mobile phone or from outside Northern Ireland. To call Northern Ireland from the Republic, use ☎048 instead of ☎028, without the international dialling code.

Other codes:

➜ ☎1550 or ☎1580 – premium rate

➜ ☎1890 or ☎1850 – local or shared rate

➜ ☎0818 – calls at local rate, wherever you're dialling from within the Republic

➜ ☎1800 – free calls Free-call and low-call numbers are not accessible from outside the Republic. Other tips:

➜ Prices are lower during evenings after 6pm and weekends.

➜ If you can find a public phone that works, local calls in the Republic cost €0.30 for around three minutes (around €0.60 to a mobile), regardless of when you call. From Northern Ireland local calls cost about 40p, or 60p to a mobile, although this varies somewhat.

→ Pre-paid phonecards can be purchased at both news agencies and post offices, and work from all payphones for both domestic and international calls.

Directory Enquiries

For directory enquiries, a number of agencies compete for your business.

→ In the Republic, dial 📞11811 or 📞11850; for international enquiries it's 📞11818.

→ In the North, call 📞118 118, 📞118 192, 📞118 500 or 📞118 811.

→ Expect to pay at least €1/£1 from a land line and up to €2/£2 from a mobile phone.

International Calls

To call out from Ireland dial 00, then the country code (1 for USA, 61 Australia etc), the area code (you usually drop the initial zero) then the number. Ireland's international dialling code is 353, Northern Ireland's is 44.

Mobile Phone

→ Ireland uses the GSM 900/1800 cellular phone system, which is compatible with European and Australian, but not North American or Japanese, phones.

→ Pay-as-you-go mobile phone packages with any of the main providers start at around €40 and usually include a basic handset and credit of around €10.

→ SIM-only packages are also available, but make sure your phone is compatible with the local provider.

Time

In winter, Ireland is on Greenwich Mean Time (GMT), also known as Universal Time Coordinated (UTC), the same as Britain. In summer, the clock shifts to GMT plus one hour, so when it's noon in Dublin and London, it's 4am in Los Angeles and Vancouver, 7am in New York and Toronto, 1pm in Paris, 7pm in Singapore, and 9pm in Sydney.

Tourist Information

In both the Republic and the North there's a tourist office or information point in almost every big town; most can offer a variety of services, including accommodation and attraction reservations, currency-changing services, map and guidebook sales, and free publications.

In the Republic, the tourism purview falls to **Fáilte Ireland** (www.discoverireland. ie); in Northern Ireland, it's the **Northern Irish Tourist Board** (NITB; 📞head office 028-9023 1221; www.discover northernireland.com). Outside Ireland, Fáilte Ireland and the NITB unite under the banner **Tourism Ireland** (www.tour ismireland.com).

The main branches of Fáilte Ireland in the Republic:

Cork Discover Ireland Centre (📞021-425 5100; Grand Pde, Cork) For Counties Cork and Kerry.

Discover Ireland Dublin Tourism Centre (📞01-605 7700; www.visitdublin.com; St Andrew's Church, 2 Suffolk St, Dublin)

Donegal Discover Ireland Centre (The Quay, Donegal Town)

Galway Discover Ireland Centre (📞091-537 700; Forster St) For Galway, Roscommon and Mayo.

Mullingar Discover Ireland Centre (📞044-934 8761; Market Sq, Mullingar) For Kildare, Laois, Longford, Louth, Meath, North Offaly, Westmeath and Wicklow.

Sligo Discover Ireland Centre (📞071-916 1201; Old Bank Building, O'Connell St) For Cavan, Donegal, Leitrim, Monaghan and Sligo.

Waterford Discover Ireland Centre (📞051-875 823; The Granary, 41 The Quay) For Carlow, Kilkenny, South Tipperary, Waterford and Wexford.

Travellers with Disabilities

All new buildings have wheelchair access, and many hotels have installed lifts, ramps and other facilities. Others, especially B&Bs, have not adapted as successfully so you'll have far less choice. Fáilte Ireland and NITB's accommodation guides indicate which places are wheelchair accessible.

In big cities, most buses have low-floor access and priority space on board, but the number of kneeling buses on regional routes is still relatively small.

Trains are accessible with help. In theory, if you call ahead, an employee of Irish Rail (Iarnród Éireann) will arrange to accompany you to the train. Newer trains have audio and visual information systems for visually impaired and hearing-impaired passengers.

The **Citizens' Information Board** (📞01-605 9000; www.citizensinformationboard. ie) in the Republic and **Disability Action** (📞028-9066 1252; www.disabilityaction.org) in Northern Ireland can give some advice to travellers with disabilities. Travellers to Northern Ireland can also check out the website www. allgohere.com.

Visas

If you're a European Economic Area (EEA) national, you don't need a visa to visit (or work in) either the Republic or Northern Ireland. Citizens of Australia, Canada, New Zealand, South Africa and the US can visit the Republic for up to three months, and Northern Ireland for up to six months. They are not allowed to work unless sponsored by an employer.

Full visa requirements for visiting the Republic are available online at www.dfa.ie; for Northern Ireland's visa requirements see www.ukvisas.gov.uk.

To stay longer in the Republic, contact the local *garda* (police) station or the **Garda National Immigration Bureau** (☏01-666 9100; www.garda.ie; 13-14 Burgh Quay). To stay longer in Northern Ireland, contact the **Home Office** (UK Border Agency; ☏0870-606 7766; www.ukba.homeoffice.gov.uk).

Volunteering

Volunteering opportunities are limited, but there are projects where you can lend a helping hand. Check out www.volunteeringireland.ie for all relevant information, including how to sign up and where to go.

Women Travellers

Ireland should pose no problems for women travellers. Finding contraception is not the problem it once was, although anyone on the pill should bring adequate supplies.

Rape Crisis Network Ireland (☏1800-77 88 88; www.rcni.ie) In the Republic. Runs a 24-hour helpline.

Rape Crisis & Sexual Abuse Centre (☏028-9032 9002; www.rapecrisisni.com) In Northern Ireland. Operates a 24-hour helpline.

Work

EEA citizens are entitled to work legally in the Republic of Ireland and Northern Ireland. Non-EEA citizens with an Irish parent or grandparent are eligible for dual citizenship (and the right to work), although this procedure can be quite lengthy – enquire at an Irish embassy or consulate in your own country.

Full-time US students aged 18 and over can get a four-month work permit for Ireland, plus insurance and support information, through **Work & Travel Ireland** (☏01-602 1788; www.workandtravelireland.org).

Most Commonwealth citizens with a UK-born parent are entitled to work in the North (and the rest of the UK) through the 'Right of Abode'. Most Commonwealth citizens under 31 are eligible for a Working Holidaymaker Visa – valid for two years, allows you to work for a total of 12 months and must be obtained in advance. Check with the **UK Border Agency** (UK Border Agency; ☏0870-606 7766; www.ukba.homeoffice.gov.uk) for more info.

Transport

GETTING THERE & AWAY

Entering the Country

Dublin is the main point of entry for most visitors. In recent years, the growth of no-frills airlines means more routes and cheaper prices between Ireland and other European countries. If arriving in the Republic of Ireland:

➡ The overwhelming majority of airlines serving Ireland fly into the capital.

➡ Dublin is home to two seaports that serve as the main points of sea transport with Britain; ferries from France arrive in the southern port of Rosslare.

➡ Dublin is also the nation's premier rail hub.
Flights, tours and rail tickets can be booked online at www.lonelyplanet.com/bookings.

Air

Airports

Ireland's main airports:

Cork Airport (ORK;☏021-431 3131; www.corkairport.com)

Dublin Airport (DUB;☏01-814 1111; www.dublinairport.com)

Shannon Airport (SNN; ☏061-712 000; www.shannonairport.com; ☎)

Other airports in the Republic with scheduled services from Britain:

Donegal Airport (CFN; ☏074-954 8284; www.donegalairport.ie)

Ireland West Airport Knock (NOC;☏094-936 8100; www.irelandwestairport.com; off N17) Fifteen kilometres north of Knock just off the N17, Ireland West Airport Knock has daily flights to seven cities in the UK and less frequent services to Portugal, Spain, Germany, Italy and the Canaries.

Kerry Airport (KIR;☏066-976 4644; www.kerryairport.ie; Farranfore)

Waterford Airport (WAT; ☏051-875 589; www.flywaterford.com)

Northern Ireland's airports:

Belfast International Airport (BFS;☏028-9448 4848; www.belfastairport.com) Flights from Britain, Continental Europe and the USA.

City of Derry Airport (LDY; ☏028-7181 0784; www.cityofderryairport.com)

George Best Belfast City Airport (BHD;☏028-9093 9093; www.belfastcityairport.com)

Land

Eurolines (www.eurolines.com) has a thrice-daily coach and ferry service from London's Victoria Station to Dublin Busáras.

CLIMATE CHANGE & TRAVEL

Every form of transport that relies on carbon-based fuel generates CO_2, the main cause of human-induced climate change. Modern travel is dependent on aeroplanes, which might use less fuel per kilometre per person than most cars but travel much greater distances. The altitude at which aircraft emit gases (including CO_2) and particles also contributes to their climate change impact. Many websites offer 'carbon calculators' that allow people to estimate the carbon emissions generated by their journey and, for those who wish to do so, to offset the impact of the greenhouse gases emitted with contributions to portfolios of climate-friendly initiatives throughout the world. Lonely Planet offsets the carbon footprint of all staff and author travel.

Ferry Fast Boat Routes

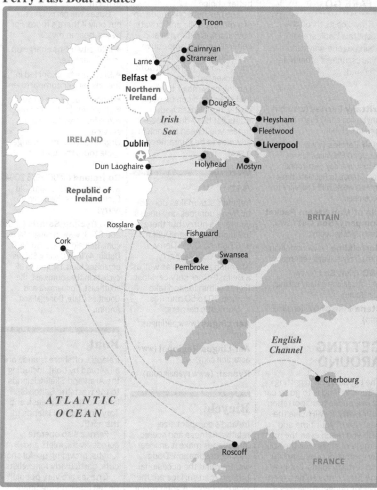

Sea

The main ferry routes between Ireland and the UK and mainland Europe:

➡ Belfast to Liverpool (England; 8½ hours)

➡ Belfast to Stranraer (Scotland; 1¾ hours)

➡ Cork to Roscoff (France; 14 hours)

➡ Dublin to Liverpool (England; fast/slow four/8½ hours)

➡ Dublin & Dun Laoghaire to Holyhead (Wales; fast/slow 1½/three hours)

➡ Larne to Cairnryan (Scotland; 1½ hours)

➡ Larne to Fleetwood (England; six hours)

➡ Rosslare to Cherbourg & Roscoff (France; 20½ hours)

➡ Rosslare to Fishguard & Pembroke (Wales; 3½ hours) Competition from budget airlines has forced ferry operators to discount heavily and offer flexible fares, meaning

great bargains at quiet times of the day or year. For example, the popular route across the Irish Sea between Dublin and Holyhead can be had for as little as €15 for a foot passenger and €90 for a car plus up to four passengers.

A very useful online tool is www.ferrybooker.com, a single site covering all sea-ferry routes and operators out of the UK (the mainstay of sea travel to Ireland).

Main operators include the following:

Brittany Ferries (www.brittanyferries.com) Every Saturday April to October.

Irish Ferries (www.irishferries.com) Holyhead ferries up to four a day year-round; from France to Rosslare three times a week, mid-February to December.

Isle of Man Steam Packet Company/Sea Cat (www.steam-packet.com)

Norfolkline (www.norfolkline.com) Daily sailings year-round.

P&O Irish Sea (www.poirishsea.com) Daily sailings year-round.

Stena Line (www.stenaline.com)

GETTING AROUND

The big decision in getting around Ireland is to go by car or use public transportation. Your own car will make the best use of your time and help you reach even the most remote of places via the spidery network of secondary and tertiary roads, but hire and fuel costs can be expensive for budget travellers – while parking hassles and traffic jams in most urban centres affect everyone – so public transport is often the better choice.

The bus network, made up of a mix of public and private operators, is extensive and generally quite competitive – although journey times can be slow. The rail network is quicker but more limited, serving only major towns and cities, and can be quite costly. Both buses and trains get busy during peak times; you'll need to book in advance to be guaranteed a seat.

Air

Ireland's size makes domestic flying unnecessary unless you're in a hurry, but there are flights between Dublin and Belfast, Cork, Derry, Donegal, Galway, Kerry, Shannon and Sligo, as well as a Belfast–Cork service. Most flights within Ireland take around 30 to 50 minutes.

Domestic carriers:

Aer Lingus (www.aerlingus.com)

Aer Lingus Regional (www.aerarann.com)

Ryanair (www.ryanair.com)

Bicycle

Ireland's compact size, relative flatness and scenic landscapes make it an ideal cycling destination. Dodgy weather and the occasional uneven road surface are the only concerns. A good tip for cyclists in the west is that the prevailing winds make it easier to cycle from south to north.

Buses will carry bikes, but only if there's room. For trains, bear in mind:

➧ Intercity trains charge up to €10 per bike.

➧ Bikes are transported in the passenger compartment.

➧ Book in advance (www.irishrail.ie), as there's only room for three bikes per service.

Organisations that arrange cycle tours throughout Ireland:

Go Ireland (☎066-976 2094; www.govisitireland.com; Old Orchard House, Killorglin, Co Kerry)

Irish Cycling Safaris (☎01-260 0749; www.cyclingsafaris.com; Belfield Bike Shop, UCD, Dublin 4) Irish Cycling Safaris organises tours for groups of cyclists in the southwest, the southeast, Connemara and Counties Clare, Donegal and Antrim.

Boat

Ireland's offshore islands are all served by boat, including the Aran and Skellig Islands to the west, the Saltee Islands to the southeast, and Tory and Rathlin Islands to the north.

Ferries also operate across rivers, inlets and loughs, providing useful short cuts, particularly for cyclists.

Cruises are very popular on the 258km-long Shannon–Erne Waterway and on a variety of other lakes and loughs. The tourist offices only recommend operators that are registered with them. Details of non-tourist-board-affiliated boat trips are given under the relevant sections throughout this book.

Border Crossings

Security has been progressively scaled down in Northern Ireland in recent years and all border crossings with the Republic are now open and generally unstaffed. Permanent checkpoints have been removed and ramps levelled. On major routes your only indication that you have crossed the border will be a change in road signs and the colour of number plates and postboxes.

Bus

Private buses compete – often very favourably – with Bus Éireann in the Republic and also run where the national buses are irregular or absent.

Distances are not especially long: no bus journey will last longer than five hours. A typical fare on a popular route like Dublin to Cork is about €12 one way; distance and competitiveness will reflect pricing, but you can also find higher fares on routes that are shorter but less frequented.

Bus Éireann bookings can be made online, but you can't reserve a seat for a particular service.

The main bus services in Ireland:

Bus Éireann (☎01-836 6111; www.buseireann.ie) The Republic's bus line.

Dublin Bus (www.dublinbus. ie) Dublin's bus service.

Metro (☎028-9066 6630; www.translink.co.uk) Belfast's bus service.

Ulsterbus (☎028-9066 6600; www.ulsterbus.co.uk) Northern Ireland's bus service.

Car & Motorcycle

Travelling by car or motorbike means greater flexibility and independence. The road system is extensive, and the constantly growing network of motorways has cut driving times considerably. Downsides include traffic jams, problems with parking in urban centres and the high cost of petrol.

Hire

Compared with many countries (especially the USA), hire rates are expensive in Ireland; you should expect to pay around €250 a week for a small car (unlimited mileage) but rates go up at busy times and drop off in quieter seasons.

The major car-hire companies have different web pages on their websites for different countries, so the price of a car on the Irish page can differ from the same car's price on the USA or Australia page. You have to surf a lot of sites to get the best deals. **Nova Car Hire** (www.novacarhire. com) acts as an agent for Alamo, Budget, European and National, and offers greatly discounted rates.

Other tips:

➡ Most cars are manual; automatic cars are available, but they're more expensive to hire.

➡ If you're travelling from the Republic into Northern Ireland, it's important to be sure that your insurance covers journeys to the North.

➡ The majority of hire companies won't rent you a car if you're under 23 and haven't had a valid driving licence for at least a year.

➡ Some companies in the Republic won't rent to you if you're aged 74 or over; there's no upper age limit in the North.

BUS & RAIL PASSES

There are a number of bus- or train-only and bus-and-rail passes worth considering if you plan on doing a lot of travel using public transport. All of the following passes are issued by **Bus Éireann** (☎01-836 6111; www.buseireann.ie).

Emerald Card (Bus & Rail) Eight days' travel out of 15 consecutive days (€218) to 15 days out of 30 (€375) on all national and local services within the Republic and Northern Ireland.

Irish Rambler (Bus) Three days' travel out of eight consecutive days (€53) to 15 days out of 30 (€168) on all Bus Éireann services.

Irish Rover (Bus) Three days' travel out of eight consecutive days (€68) to 15 days out of 30 on all Bus Éireann and Ulster Bus services, as well as local services in Cork, Galway, Limerick, Waterford and Belfast.

Irish Explorer (Bus & Rail) Eight days' travel out of 15 consecutive days (€194) on trains and buses within the Republic.

Irish Explorer (Rail) Five days' travel out of 15 consecutive days (€115.50) on trains in the Republic.

Children aged under 16 pay half-price for all these passes and for all normal tickets. Children aged under three travel for free on public transport. You can buy the above passes at most major train and bus stations in Ireland.

➤ Motorbikes and mopeds are not available for rent in Ireland.
The main car-hire companies:

Avis (www.avis.ie)

Budget (www.budget.ie)

Europcar (www.europcar.ie)

Hertz (www.hertz.ie)

Sixt (www.sixt.ie)

Thrifty Car Rental (☎1800 515 800; www.thrifty.ie)

Parking

All big towns and cities have covered short-stay car parks that are conveniently signposted.

➤ On-street parking is usually by 'pay and display' tickets available from on-street machines or disc parking (discs, which rotate to display the time you park your car, are available from newsagencies). Costs range from €1.50 to €4.50 per hour; all-day parking in a car park will cost around €24.

➤ Yellow lines (single or double) along the edge of the road indicate restrictions. Usually you can park on single yellow lines between 7pm and 8am while double yellow lines means no parking at any time. Always look for the nearby sign that spells out when you can and cannot park.

➤ In Dublin, Cork and Galway, clamping is rigorously enforced: it'll cost you €85 to have the yellow beast removed. In Northern Ireland, the fee is £100 for removal.

Roads & Rules

Motorways (marked by M+number on a blue background) and primary roads (N+number on a green background) are the fastest way to get around and will deliver you quickly from one end of the country to another. Secondary and tertiary roads (marked as R+number) are much more scenic and fun, but they can be very winding and exceedingly narrow – perfect for going slowly and enjoying the views.

➤ EU licences are treated like Irish licences.

➤ Non-EU licences are valid in Ireland for up to 12 months.

➤ You must carry your driving licence at all times.

➤ If you plan to bring a car from Europe, it's illegal to drive without at least third-party insurance.
The basic rules of the road:

➤ Drive on the left; overtake to the right.

➤ Safety belts must be worn by the driver and all passengers.

➤ Children aged under 12 aren't allowed to sit in the front passenger seat.

➤ Motorcyclists and their passengers must wear helmets.

➤ When entering a roundabout, give way to the right.

➤ In the Republic, speed-limit and distance signs are in kilometres (although the occasional older white sign shows distances in miles); in the North, speed-limit and distance signs are in miles.
Speed limits:

Republic 120km/h on motorways, 100km/h on national roads, 80km/h on regional and local roads, and 50km/h or as signposted in towns.

Northern Ireland 70mph on motorways, 60mph on main roads, 30mph in built-up areas.

Drinking and driving is taken very seriously; in both the Republic and Northern Ireland you're allowed a maximum blood-alcohol level of 80mg/100mL (0.08%) – and campaigners want it reduced to 50mg/100mL.

Hitching

Hitching is becoming increasingly less popular in Ireland, even though it's still pretty easy compared to other European countries. Travellers who decide to hitch should understand that they are taking a small but potentially serious risk, and we don't recommend it. If you do plan to travel by thumb, remember it's illegal to hitch on motorways.

Local Transport

Dublin and Belfast have comprehensive local bus networks, as do some other larger towns.

➤ The Dublin Area Rapid Transport (DART) rail line runs roughly the length of Dublin's coastline, while the Luas tram system has two popular lines.

➤ Taxis tend to be expensive. For daytime rates, flagfall is €4.10 and fares start at €1.03 per km after that (night-time rates are a bit higher).

Tours

Organised tours are a convenient way of exploring the

MOTORING ORGANISATIONS

The two main motoring organisations:

Automobile Association (AA; www.aaireland.ie) Republic (☎breakdown assistance 1800 667 788, in Cork 021-425 2444, in Dublin 01-617 9999; www.aaireland.ie); Northern Ireland (☎0870-950 0600, breakdown assistance 0800 667 788; www.aaireland.ie)

Royal Automobile Club (RAC; www.rac.ie) Republic (☎1890 483 483; www.rac.ie); Northern Ireland (☎0800 029 029, breakdown assistance 0800 828 282; www.rac.ie)

country's main highlights if your time is limited. Tours can be booked through travel agencies, tourist offices in the major cities, or directly through the tour companies

themselves. Some of the most reputable operators:

Bus Éireann (www.buseir eann.ie) Runs day tours to various parts of the Republic and the North.

CIE Tours International (www.cietours.ie) Runs four- to 11-day coach tours of the Republic and the North, including accommodation and meals.

Grayline Tours (www. irishcitytours.com) Dublin-

Train Routes

based company offering half- and full-day tours of attractions around Dublin as well as the Ring of Kerry.

Paddywagon Tours (www. paddywagontours.com) Activity-filled three- and six-day tours all over Ireland with friendly tour guides. Accommodation is in IHH hostels.

Railtours Ireland (☑01-856 0045; www.railtoursireland. com) For train enthusiasts. Organises a series of one- and two-day train trips in association with Iarnród Éireann.

Ulsterbus Tours (www. ulsterbus.co.uk) Runs a large number of day trips throughout the North and the Republic.

Train

Given Ireland's relatively small size, train travel is an expensive luxury. All of the Republic's major towns and cities are on the limited rail network, which is operated by **Irish Rail** (Iarnród Éireann; ☑1850 366 222; www.irishrail. ie) and fans out from Dublin in such a way that connections between destinations not on the same line usually involve an out-of-the-way trip to the capital. There's no north–south route along the western coast, no network in Donegal and no direct connections from Waterford to Cork or Killarney.

Fares are high. A mid-week one-way ticket from Dublin to Cork will cost around €65. The return fare is only marginally more expensive – a feature designed to offer an incentive for rail travel but making for poor-value one-way fares. The cheapest fares are always online.

Northern Ireland Railways (NIR; ☑028-9089 9411; www.nirailways.co.uk; Belfast Central Station) runs four routes from Belfast: one links with the system in the Republic via Newry to Dublin; the other three go east to Bangor, northeast to Larne and northwest to Derry via Coleraine.

Language

Irish (Gaeilge) is the country's official language. In 2003 the government introduced the Official Languages Act, whereby all official documents, street signs and official titles must be either in Irish or in both Irish and English. Despite its official status, Irish is really only spoken in pockets of rural Ireland known as the Gaeltacht, the main ones being Cork (Corcaigh), Donegal (Dún na nGall), Galway (Gaillimh), Kerry (Ciarraí) and Mayo (Maigh Eo).

Ask people outside the Gaeltacht if they can speak Irish and nine out of 10 of them will probably reply, 'ah, cupla focal' (a couple of words), and they generally mean it. Irish is a compulsory subject in schools for those aged six to 15, but Irish classes have traditionally been rather academic and unimaginative, leading many students to resent it as a waste of time. As a result, many adults regret not having a greater grasp of it. In recent times, at long last, a new Irish curriculum has been introduced cutting the hours devoted to the subject but making the lessons more fun, practical and celebratory.

PRONUNCIATION

Irish divides vowels into long (those with an accent) and short (those without) and also distinguishes between broad (**a**, **á**, **o**, **ó**, **u**) and slender (**e**, **é**, **i** and **í**), which can affect the pronunciation of preceding consonants. Other than a few odd-looking clusters, like

WANT MORE?

For in-depth language information and handy phrases, check out Lonely Planet's *Irish Language & Culture*. You'll find it at **shop.lonelyplanet.com**, or you can buy Lonely Planet's iPhone phrasebooks at the Apple App Store.

mh and **bhf** (pronounced both as w), consonants are generally pronounced as they are in English.

Irish has three main dialects: Connaught Irish (in Galway and northern Mayo), Munster Irish (in Cork, Kerry and Waterford) and Ulster Irish (in Donegal). The blue pronunciation guidelines given here are an anglicised version of modern standard Irish, which is essentially an amalgam of the three – if you read them as if they were English, you'll be able to get your point across in Gaeilge without even having to think about the specifics of Irish pronunciation or spelling.

BASICS

Hello.	*Dia duit.*	deea gwit
Hello. (reply)	*Dia is Muire duit.*	deeas moyra gwit
Good morning.	*Maidin mhaith.*	mawjin wah
Good night.	*Oíche mhaith.*	eekheh wah
Goodbye.		
(when leaving)	*Slán leat.*	slawn lyat
(when staying)	*Slán agat.*	slawn agut
Yes.	*Tá.*	taw
It is.	*Sea.*	sheh
No.	*Níl.*	neel
It isn't.	*Ní hea.*	nee heh

Thank you (very) much.
Go raibh (míle) maith agat. — goh rev (meela) mah agut

Excuse me.
Gabh mo leithscéal. — gamoh lesh scale

I'm sorry.
Tá brón orm. — taw brohn oruhm

I don't understand.
Ní thuigim. — nee higgim

Do you speak Irish?
An bhfuil Gaeilge agat? — on wil gaylge oguht

What is this?
Cad é seo? — kod ay shoh

What is that?
Cad é sin? — kod ay shin

I'd like to go to ...
Ba mhaith liom — baw wah lohm
dul go dtí ... — dull go dee ...

I'd like to buy ...
Ba mhaith liom ... — bah wah lohm ...
a cheannach. — a kyanukh

another/ one more	ceann eile	kyawn ella
nice	go deas	goh dyass

MAKING CONVERSATION

Welcome.
Ceád míle fáilte. — kade meela fawlcha
(lit: 100,000 welcomes)

How are you?
Conas a tá tú? — kunas aw taw too

..., (if you) please.
...más é do thoil é. — ... maws ay do hall ay

What's your name?
Cad is ainm duit? — kod is anim dwit

My name is (Sean Frayne).
(Sean Frayne) is — (shawn frain) is
ainm dom. — anim dohm

DATES OF THE WEEK

Monday	Dé Luaín	day loon
Tuesday	Dé Máirt	day maart
Wednesday	Dé Ceádaoin	day kaydeen
Thursday	Déardaoin	daredeen
Friday	Dé hAoine	day heeneh
Saturday	Dé Sathairn	day sahern
Sunday	Dé Domhnaigh	day downick

Signs			
Fir	fear	Men	
Gardaí	gardee	Police	
Leithreas	lehrass	Toilet	
Mna	mnaw	Women	
Oifig	iffig	Post	
An Phoist	ohn fwisht	Office	

CUPLA FOCAL

Here are a few phrases *os Gaeilge* (in Irish) to help you impress the locals:

Tóg é gobogé.
Take it easy.
tohg ay gobogay

Ní féidir é!
Impossible!
nee faydir ay

Ráiméis!
Nonsense!
rawmaysh

Go huafásach!
That's terrible!
guh hoofawsokh

Ní ólfaidh mé go brách arís!
I'm never ever drinking again!
knee ohlhee mey gu brawkh ureeshch

Slainte!
Your health!/Cheers!
slawncha

Táim go maith.
I'm fine.
thawm go mah

Nollaig shona!
Happy Christmas!
nuhlig hona

Cáisc shona!
Happy Easter!
kawshk hona

Go n-éirí an bóthar leat!
Bon voyage!
go nairee on bohhar lat

NUMBERS

1	haon	hayin
2	dó	doe
3	trí	tree
4	ceathaír	kahirr
5	cúig	kooig
6	sé	shay
7	seacht	shocked
8	hocht	hukt
9	naoi	nay
10	deich	jeh
11	haon déag	hayin jague
12	dó dhéag	doe yague
20	fiche	feekhe

GLOSSARY

12 July – the day the *Orange Order* marches to celebrate Protestant King William III's victory over the Catholic King James II at the Battle of the Boyne in 1690

An Óige – literally 'the Youth'; Republic of Ireland Youth Hostel Association

An Taisce – National Trust for the Republic of Ireland

Anglo-Norman – Norman, English and Welsh peoples who invaded Ireland in the 12th century

Apprentice Boys – *Loyalist* organisation founded in 1814 to commemorate the Great Siege of Derry in August every year

ard – literally 'high'; Irish place name

Ascendancy – refers to the Protestant aristocracy descended from the Anglo- Normans and those who were installed here during the *Plantation*

bailey – outer wall of a castle

bawn – area surrounded by walls outside the main castle, acting as a defence and as a place to keep cattle in times of trouble

beehive hut – see *clochán*

Black & Tans – British recruits to the Royal Irish Constabulary shortly after WWI, noted for their brutality

Blarney Stone – sacred stone perched on top of Blarney Castle; bending over backwards to kiss the stone is said to bestow the gift of gab

bodhrán – hand-held goatskin drum

Bronze Age – earliest metalusing period, around 2500 BC to 300 BC in Ireland; after the Stone Age and before the *Iron Age*

B-Specials – Northern Irish auxiliary police force, disbanded in 1971

bullaun – stone with a depression, probably used as a mortar for grinding medicine or food, often found at monastic sites

caher – circular area enclosed by stone walls

cairn – mound of stones over a prehistoric grave

cashel – stone-walled *ring fort*; see also *ráth*

céilidh – session of traditional music and dancing; also called 'ceili'

Celtic Tiger – nickname of the Irish economy during the growth years from 1990 to about 2002

Celts – *Iron Age* warrior tribes that arrived in Ireland around 300 BC and controlled the country for 1000 years

ceol – music

chancel – eastern end of a church, where the altar is situated, reserved for the clergy and choir

chipper – slang term for fish 'n' chips fast-food restaurant

cill – literally 'church'; Irish place name; also 'kill'

cillín – literally 'little cell'; a hermitage, or sometimes a small, isolated burial ground for unbaptised children and other 'undesirables'

Claddagh ring – ring worn in much of *Connaught* since the mid-18th century, with a crowned heart nestling between two hands; if the heart points towards the hand then the wearer is partnered or married, if towards the fingertip he or she is looking for a mate

clochán – circular stone building, shaped like an oldfashioned beehive, from the early Christian period

Connaught – one of the four ancient provinces of Ireland, made up of Counties Galway, Leitrim, Mayo, Roscommon and Sligo; sometimes spelled 'Connacht'; see also *Leinster, Munster* and *Ulster*

craic – conversation, gossip, fun, good times; also known as 'crack'

crannóg – artificial island made in a lake to provide habitation in a good defensive position

currach – rowing boat made of a framework of laths covered with tarred canvas; also known as 'cúrach'

Dáil – lower house of the parliament of the Republic of Ireland; see also *Oireachtas* and *Seanad*

DART – Dublin Area Rapid Transport train line

demesne – landed property close to a house or castle

diamond – town square

dolmen – tomb chamber or portal tomb made of vertical stones topped by a huge capstone; from around 2000 BC

drumlin – rounded hill formed by retreating glaciers

Dúchas – government department in charge of parks, monuments and gardens in the Republic; formerly known as the Office of Public Works

dún – fort, usually constructed of stone

DUP – Democratic Unionist Party; founded principally by Ian Paisley in 1971 in hardline opposition to Unionist policies held by the *UUP*

Éire – Irish name for the Republic of Ireland

esker – raised ridge formed by glaciers

Fáilte Ireland – 'Welcome Board'; Irish Tourist Board

Fianna – mythical band of warriors who feature in many tales of ancient Ireland

Fianna Fáil – literally 'Warriors of Ireland'; a major political party in the Republic, originating from the *Sinn Féin* faction opposed to the 1921 treaty with Britain

Fine Gael – literally 'Tribe of the Gael'; a major political party in the Republic, originating from the *Sinn Féin* faction that favoured the 1921 treaty with Britain; formed the first government of independent Ireland

fir – men (singular 'fear'); sign on men's toilets; see also *leithreas* and *mná*

fleadh – festival

GAA – Gaelic Athletic Association; promotes Gaelic football and hurling, among other Irish games

Gaeltacht – Irish-speaking

gallóglí – mercenary soldiers of the 14th to 15th century; anglicised to 'gallowglasses'

garda – Irish Republic police; plural 'gardaí'

ghillie – fishing or hunting guide; also known as 'ghilly'

gort – literally 'field'; Irish place name

hill fort – a hilltop fortified with ramparts and ditches, usually dating from the *Iron Age*

HINI – Hostelling International of Northern Ireland

Hunger, the – colloquial name for the Great Famine of 1845-51

hurling – Irish sport similar to hockey

Iarnród Éireann – Republic of Ireland Railways

INLA – Irish National Liberation Association; formed in 1975 as an *IRA* splinter group; it has maintained a ceasefire since 1998

IRA – Irish Republican Army; the largest Republican paramilitary organisation, founded 80 years ago with the aim to fight for a united Ireland; in 1969 the IRA split into the Official IRA and the Provisional IRA; the Official IRA is no longer active and the PIRA has become the IRA

Iron Age – metal-using period that lasted from the end of the *Bronze Age*, around 300 BC (the arrival of the Celts), to the arrival of Christianity, around the 5th century AD

jarvey – driver of a *jaunting car*

jaunting car – Killarney's traditional horse-drawn transport; see also *jarvey*

knackered – slang for tired or worn out

Leinster – one of the four ancient provinces of Ireland, made up of Counties Carlow, Dublin, Kildare, Kilkenny, Laois, Long-

ford, Louth, Meath, Offaly, West Meath, Wexford and Wicklow; see also *Connaught, Munster* and *Ulster*

leithreas – toilets; see also *mná* and *fir*

leprechaun – mischievous elf or sprite from Irish folklore

lough – lake, or long narrow bay or arm of the sea

Loyalist – person, usually a Northern Irish Protestant, insisting on the continuation of Northern Ireland's links with Britain

Luas – light-rail transit system in Dublin; Irish for 'speed'

marching season – *Orange Order* parades, which take place from Easter and throughout summer to celebrate the victory by Protestant King William III of Orange over Catholic James II in the Battle of the Boyne on 12 July 1690, and the union with Britain

Mesolithic – also known as the Middle Stone Age; time of the first human settlers in Ireland, about 8000 BC to 4000 BC; see also *Neolithic*

midden – refuse heap left by a prehistoric settlement

mná – women; sign on women's toilets; see also *fir* and *leithreas*

motte – early Norman fortification consisting of a raised, flattened mound with a keep on top; when attached to a *bailey* it is known as a motte-and-*bailey* fort, many of which were built in Ireland until the early 13th century

Munster – one of the four ancient provinces of Ireland, made up of Counties Clare, Cork, Kerry, Limerick, Tipperary and Waterford; see also *Connaught, Leinster* and *Ulster*

nationalism – belief in a reunited Ireland

Nationalist – proponent of a united Ireland

Neolithic – also known as the New Stone Age; a period characterised by settled agriculture lasting from around 4000 BC to 2500 BC in Ireland; followed

by the *Bronze Age;* see also *Mesolithic*

NIR – Northern Ireland Railways

NITB – Northern Ireland Tourist Board

NNR – National Nature Reserves

North, the – political entity of Northern Ireland, not the northernmost geographic part of Ireland

NUI – National University of Ireland; made up of branches in Dublin, Cork, Galway and Limerick

Ogham stone – a stone etched with Ogham characters, the earliest form of writing in Ireland, with a variety of notched strokes

Oireachtas – Parliament of the Republic of Ireland, consisting of the *Dáil,* the lower house, and the *Seanad,* the upper house

Orange Order – the largest Protestant organisation in Northern Ireland, founded in 1795, with a membership of up to 100,000; name commemorates the victory of King William of Orange in the Battle of the Boyne

óstán – hotel

Palladian – style of architecture developed by Andrea Palladio (1508-80), based on ancient Roman architecture

paramilitaries – armed illegal organisations, either *Loyalist* or *Republican,* usually associated with the use of violence and crime for political and economic gain

partition – division of Ireland in 1921

passage grave – Celtic tomb with a chamber reached by a narrow passage, typically buried in a mound

penal laws – laws passed in the 18th century forbidding Catholics from buying land and holding public office

Plantation – settlement of Protestant immigrants (known as Planters) in Ireland in the 17th century

poitín – illegally brewed whiskey, also spelled 'poteen'

Prod – slang for Northern Irish Protestant

provisionals – Provisional IRA, formed after a break with the official *IRA* (who are now largely inconsequential); named after the provisional government declared in 1916, they have been the main force combating the British army in *the North;* also known as 'provos'

PSNI – Police Service of Northern Ireland

ráth – *ring fort* with earthen banks around a timber wall; see also *cashel*

Real IRA – splinter movement of the *IRA*; opposed to *Sinn Féin's* support of the Good Friday Agreement; responsible for the Omagh bombing in 1998 in which 29 people died; subsequently called a ceasefire but has been responsible for bombs in Britain and other acts of violence

Republic of Ireland – the 26 counties of the South

Republican – supporter of a united Ireland

republicanism – belief in a united Ireland, sometimes referred to as militant nationalism

ring fort – circular habitation area surrounded by banks and ditches, used from the *Bronze Age* right through to the Middle Ages, particularly in the early Christian period

RTE – Radio Telifís Éireann; the national broadcasting service of the Republic of Ireland, with two TV and four radio stations

RUC – Royal Ulster Constabulary, the former name for the armed Police Service of Northern Ireland *(PSNI)*

SDLP – Social Democratic and Labour Party; the largest nationalist party in the Northern Ireland Assembly, instrumental in achieving the Good Friday Agreement; its goal is a united Ireland through nonviolent means; mostly Catholic

Seanad – upper house of the parliament of the Republic of Ireland; see also *Oireachtas* and *Dáil*

shamrock – three-leafed plant said to have been used by St Patrick to illustrate the Holy Trinity

shebeen – from the Irish 'síbín'; illicit drinking place or speakeasy

sheila-na-gig – literally 'Sheila of the teats'; female figure with exaggerated genitalia, carved in stone on the exteriors of some churches and castles; explanations include male clerics warning against the perils of sex to the idea that they represent Celtic war goddesses

Sinn Féin – literally 'We Ourselves'; a *Republican* party with the aim of a united Ireland; seen as the political wing of the *IRA* but it maintains that both organisations are completely separate

slí – hiking trail or way

snug – partitioned-off drinking area in a pub

souterrain – underground chamber usually associated with *ring* and *hill forts;* probably provided a hiding place or escape route in times of trouble and/or storage space for goods

South, the – Republic of Ireland

standing stone – upright stone set in the ground, common across Ireland and dating from a variety of periods; some are burial markers

Taoiseach – Republic of Ireland prime minister

teampall – church

TD – *teachta Dála;* member of the lower house *(Dáil)* of the parliament of the Republic of Ireland

Tinkers – derogatory term used to describe Irish itinerant communities; see also *Travellers*

trá – beach or strand

Travellers – the term used today to describe Ireland's itinerant communities

Treaty – Anglo-Irish Treaty of 1921, which divided Ireland and gave relative independence to the South; cause of the 1922-23 Civil War

tricolour – green, white and orange Irish flag symbolising the hoped-for union of the 'green' Catholic Southern Irish with the 'orange' Protestant Northern Irish

turlough – a small lake that often disappears in dry summers; from the Irish 'turlach'

UDA – Ulster Defence Association; the largest *Loyalist* paramilitary group; it has observed a ceasefire since 1994

uillean pipes – Irish bagpipes with a bellow strapped to the arm; 'uillean' is Irish for 'elbow'

Ulster – one of the four ancient provinces of Ireland; sometimes used to describe the six counties of *the North,* despite the fact that Ulster also includes Counties Cavan, Monaghan and Donegal (all in the Republic); see also *Connaught, Leinster* and *Munster*

Unionist – person who wants to retain Northern Ireland's links with Britain

United Irishmen – organisation founded in 1791 aiming to reduce British power in Ireland; it led a series of unsuccessful risings and invasions

UUP – Ulster Unionist Party; the largest *Unionist* party in Northern Ireland and the majority party in the Assembly; founded in 1905 and led by Unionist hero Edward Carson from 1910 to 1921; from 1921 to 1972 the sole Unionist organisation but is now under threat from the *DUP*

UVF – Ulster Volunteer Force; an illegal *Loyalist* Northern Irish paramilitary organisation

Volunteers – offshoot of the IRB that came to be known as the *IRA*

Behind the Scenes

SEND US YOUR FEEDBACK

We love to hear from travellers – your comments keep us on our toes and help make our books better. Our well-travelled team reads every word on what you loved or loathed about this book. Although we cannot reply individually to postal submissions, we always guarantee that your feedback goes straight to the appropriate authors, in time for the next edition. Each person who sends us information is thanked in the next edition – the most useful submissions are rewarded with a selection of digital PDF chapters.

Visit **lonelyplanet.com/contact** to submit your updates and suggestions or to ask for help. Our award-winning website also features inspirational travel stories, news and discussions.

Note: We may edit, reproduce and incorporate your comments in Lonely Planet products such as guidebooks, websites and digital products, so let us know if you don't want your comments reproduced or your name acknowledged. For a copy of our privacy policy visit lonelyplanet.com/privacy.

OUR READERS

Many thanks to the travellers who used the last edition and wrote to us with helpful hints, useful advice and interesting anecdotes:

Janet Armstrong, David Bellamy, Sonja Bergin, Darryl Bourke, Karsten Brauckmann, Brian Callahan, Nora Casey, Kate Cooke, Marie Coyne, William Dalrymple, Doug Eager, Tony Eklof, Anna Ellis, Kinga Eysturland, Kennet Fischer, Patrick Foley, Bryan Gray, Mechthild Hißler, Fiona Holdsworth, Kelly Hoskin, Aoife Kelly, Robert Keyes, Francis Lu, Melanie Luangsay, Tim McGowan, Jane O'Brien, Maitiú Ó Coimín, Arie van Oosterwijk, J-Me Peaker, Stuart Routledge, Rudy Trullemans, M Van De Merwe

AUTHOR THANKS

Fionn Davenport

Thanks to Cliff, Gina and all the format boffins at LP who answered my every query – no matter what time of day or night – in a timely and helpful fashion. Thanks to my fellow authors Catherine, Ryan, Neil and Josephine, whose sterling work has improved the book even more. Cheers also to everyone in Dublin and Ireland for all of their suggestions, critiques and helpful hints: your advice wasn't always sought, but it was always appreciated!

Catherine Le Nevez

Sláinte first and foremost to Julian, and to all of the locals, fellow travellers and tourism professionals in the southwest for insights, information and great craic. Thanks in particular to Michael in Tipperary, Denise and Dave in Clonakilty, Pat Joe in Bantry, Daniel in Dingle, and Anne and all in Killarney. Thanks, too, to Cliff Wilkinson, Angela Tinson, Fionn and the *Ireland* team and all at Lonely Planet. As ever, merci encore to my parents, brother, *belle-soeur* and *neveu*.

Josephine Quintero

Thanks to the staff at the tourist information offices that were unfailingly helpful throughout the regions I covered. Thanks, too, to Rosalind Fanning for her invaluable insight and advice, and to Robin Chapman for his brilliant company and map-reading skills. Finally thanks go to Clifton Wilkinson at Lonely Planet for his consistent support throughout this project.

Ryan Ver Berkmoes

Like a conversation over nothing in particular in an Irish pub, thanks to those who helped me on this book threaten to go on and on and on... But a few: in Galway, Charley Adley was a friend and muse as always. Anna Farrell was irreverent as always and Eva Dearie was super-helpful. And amidst uncommonly golden skies, I picked me a plum with Alexis.

Neil Wilson

Thanks to the Belfast Welcome Centre, to friendly and helpful tourist office and Translink staff all over Northern Ireland, to Carol Downie, and to Tom and Will Kelly and Kevin Hasson (the Bogside Artists).

ACKNOWLEDGMENTS

Climate map data adapted from Peel MC, Finlayson BL & McMahon TA (2007) 'Updated World Map of the Köppen-Geiger Climate Classification', Hydrology and Earth System Sciences, 11, 1633¬44

Illustrations pp64-5 and pp144-5 by Javier Zarracina. Illustrations pp324-5 and pp518-19 by Michael Weldon.

Cover photograph: Cyclist on rural road, Inishmore, Aran Islands, Ireland/Douglas Pearson, Corbis ©.

THIS BOOK

This 11th edition of Lonely Planet's *Ireland* guidebook was researched and written by Fionn Davenport, Catherine Le Nevez, Josephine Quintero, Ryan Ver Berkmoes and Neil Wilson. This guidebook was commissioned in Lonely Planet's London office, and produced by the following:

Commissioning Editor Clifton Wilkinson

Coordinating Editors Gina Tsarouhas, Tasmin Waby

Senior Cartographer Jennifer Johnston

Coordinating Layout Designer Wibowo Rusli

Managing Editors Bruce Evans, Annelies Mertens, Martine Power

Managing Layout Designer Jane Hart

Assisting Editors Judith Bamber, Michelle Bennett, Elin Berglund, Janice Bird, Penny Cordner, Elizabeth Jones, Alan Murphy, Charlotte Orr, Gabrielle Stefanos, Fionnuala Twomey

Assisting Cartographers Julie Dodkins, Rachel Imeson, Jackson James, Drishya Liji, Anoop Shetty

Assisting Layout Designer Nicholas Colicchia

Cover Research Naomi Parker

Internal Image Research Kylie McLaughlin

Language Content Branislava Vladisavljevic

Thanks to Anita Banh, Sasha Baskett, Laura Crawford, Brendan Dempsey, Ryan Evans, Larissa Frost, Chris Girdler, Genesys India, Jouve India, Carol Jackson, Annelies Mertens, Wayne Murphy, Trent Paton, Dianne Schallmeiner, Rebecca Skinner, Angela Tinson

Index

NOTES

Map Legend

Sights

- Beach
- Bird Sanctuary
- Buddhist
- Castle/Palace
- Christian
- Confucian
- Hindu
- Islamic
- Jain
- Jewish
- Monument
- Museum/Gallery/Historic Building
- Ruin
- Sento Hot Baths/Onsen
- Shinto
- Sikh
- Taoist
- Winery/Vineyard
- Zoo/Wildlife Sanctuary
- Other Sight

Activities, Courses & Tours

- Bodysurfing
- Diving
- Canoeing/Kayaking
- Course/Tour
- Skiing
- Snorkelling
- Surfing
- Swimming/Pool
- Walking
- Windsurfing
- Other Activity

Sleeping

- Sleeping
- Camping

Eating

- Eating

Drinking & Nightlife

- Drinking & Nightlife
- Cafe

Entertainment

- Entertainment

Shopping

- Shopping

Information

- Bank
- Embassy/Consulate
- Hospital/Medical
- Internet
- Police
- Post Office
- Telephone
- Toilet
- Tourist Information
- Other Information

Geographic

- Beach
- Hut/Shelter
- Lighthouse
- Lookout
- Mountain/Volcano
- Oasis
- Park
- Pass
- Picnic Area
- Waterfall

Population

- Capital (National)
- Capital (State/Province)
- City/Large Town
- Town/Village

Transport

- Airport
- Border crossing
- Bus
- Cable car/Funicular
- Cycling
- Ferry
- Metro station
- Monorail
- Parking
- Petrol station
- S-Bahn/Subway station
- Taxi
- T-bane/Tunnelbana station
- Train station/Railway
- Tram
- Tube station
- U-Bahn/Underground station
- Other Transport

Note: Not all symbols displayed above appear on the maps in this book

Routes

- Tollway
- Freeway
- Primary
- Secondary
- Tertiary
- Lane
- Unsealed road
- Road under construction
- Plaza/Mall
- Steps
- Tunnel
- Pedestrian overpass
- Walking Tour
- Walking Tour detour
- Path/Walking Trail

Boundaries

- International
- State/Province
- Disputed
- Regional/Suburb
- Marine Park
- Cliff
- Wall

Hydrography

- River, Creek
- Intermittent River
- Canal
- Water
- Dry/Salt/Intermittent Lake
- Reef

Areas

- Airport/Runway
- Beach/Desert
- Cemetery (Christian)
- Cemetery (Other)
- Glacier
- Mudflat
- Park/Forest
- Sight (Building)
- Sportsground
- Swamp/Mangrove

Neil Wilson
County Donegal; Belfast; Counties Down & Armagh; Counties Londonderry & Antrim; Counties Fermanagh & Tyrone Neil's first visit to Northern Ireland was in 1994, during the first flush of post-ceasefire optimism, and his interest in the history and politics of the place intensified when he found out that most of his mum's ancestors were from Ulster. Working on the *Ireland* guidebook has allowed him to witness first-hand the progress being made towards a lasting peace. Neil is a full-time travel writer based in Scotland, and has written more than 50 guidebooks for half a dozen publishers.

OUR STORY

A beat-up old car, a few dollars in the pocket and a sense of adventure. In 1972 that's all Tony and Maureen Wheeler needed for the trip of a lifetime – across Europe and Asia overland to Australia. It took several months, and at the end – broke but inspired – they sat at their kitchen table writing and stapling together their first travel guide, *Across Asia on the Cheap*. Within a week they'd sold 1500 copies. Lonely Planet was born.

Today, Lonely Planet has offices in Melbourne, London and Oakland, with more than 600 staff and writers. We share Tony's belief that 'a great guidebook should do three things: inform, educate and amuse'.

OUR WRITERS

Fionn Davenport
Coordinating Author; Dublin; Counties Wicklow & Kildare A Dubliner by birth and by persuasion, Fionn has worked on at least seven editions of this guide, and more and more is reminded of Tancredi's aphorism in *The Leopard*: 'everything needs to change, so everything can stay the same.' Everything has changed in Ireland, but it has managed to hold on to its traditional strengths – beautiful landscapes, a friendly people and a general conviviality that makes a repeat trip unavoidable. Fionn also wrote the Plan Your Trip section, the Understand Ireland section and Survival Guide chapters.

Catherine Le Nevez
County Cork; County Kerry; Counties Limerick & Tipperary Catherine's wanderlust kicked in when she road-tripped across Europe aged four and she's been hitting the road at every opportunity since, completing her Doctorate of Creative Arts in Writing, Masters in Professional Writing, and post-grad qualifications in Editing and Publishing along the way. Catherine's Celtic connections include Irish and Breton heritage (and a love of Guinness!). She's travelled throughout every county in the emerald isle, and covered the majority of them for Lonely Planet, including several editions of this book.

Josephine Quintero
Counties Wexford, Waterford, Carlow & Kilkenny; The Midlands; Counties Meath, Louth, Cavan & Monaghan Exploring some of the lesser visited counties Josephine discovered such delights as mystical caves, a belief in the little people and restaurant food so retro it included jelly and cream. Throughout these counties, history reverberated in the castles, landscape and evocative ruins, while a spell in the wonderfully vibrant cities of Waterford and Kilkenny was the ideal antidote to those more rural terrains. Josephine has contributed to more than 35 guides for Lonely Planet and her delight in Ireland increases with every trip.

Read more about Josephine at:
lonelyplanet.com/members/JosephineQuintero

Ryan Ver Berkmoes
County Clare; County Galway; Counties Mayo & Sligo From Loop Head to Sligo, with plenty of pleasures in between, Ryan has delighted in the great swath of Ireland. He first visited Galway in 1985 when he remembers a grey place where the locals wandered the muddy tidal flats for fun and frolic. Times have changed! From lost rural pubs to lost memory, he's revelled in a place where his first name brings a smile and his surname brings a 'huh?'. Follow him at ryanverberkmoes. com; and on Twitter @ryanvb.

OVER PAGE | MORE WRITERS

Published by Lonely Planet Publications Pty Ltd
ABN 36 005 607 983
11th edition – Mar 2014
ISBN 978 1 74220 749 0
© Lonely Planet 2014   Photographs © as indicated 2014
10 9 8 7 6 5 4 3 2 1
Printed in China